T0332495

Computational Complexity

A Conceptual Perspective

Complexity Theory is a central field of the theoretical foundations of computer science. It is concerned with the general study of the intrinsic complexity of computational tasks; that is, it addresses the question of what can be achieved within limited time (and/or with other limited natural computational resources).

This book offers a conceptual perspective on Complexity Theory. It is intended to serve as an introduction for advanced undergraduate and graduate students, either as a textbook or for self-study. The book will also be useful to experts, since it provides expositions of the various sub-areas of Complexity Theory such as hardness amplification, pseudorandomness, and probabilistic proof systems.

In each case, the author starts by posing the intuitive questions that are addressed by the sub-area and then discusses the choices made in the actual formulation of these questions, the approaches that lead to the answers, and the ideas that are embedded in these answers.

Oded Goldreich is a Professor of Computer Science at the Weizmann Institute of Science and an Incumbent of the Meyer W. Weisgal Professorial Chair. He is an editor for the *SIAM Journal on Computing*, the *Journal of Cryptology*, and *Computational Complexity* and previously authored the books *Modern Cryptography, Probabilistic Proofs and Pseudorandomness*, and the two-volume work *Foundations of Cryptography*.

Computational Complexity

A Conceptual Perspective

Oded Goldreich

Weizmann Institute of Science

CAMBRIDGE
UNIVERSITY PRESS

CAMBRIDGE
UNIVERSITY PRESS

32 Avenue of the Americas, New York NY 10013-2473, USA

Cambridge University Press is part of the University of Cambridge.

It furthers the University's mission by disseminating knowledge in the pursuit of education, learning and research at the highest international levels of excellence.

www.cambridge.org
Information on this title: www.cambridge.org/9780521884730

First published 2008

A catalogue record for this publication is available from the British Library

Library of Congress Cataloguing in Publication data

Goldreich, Oded.
Computational complexity : a conceptual perspective / Oded Goldreich.
p.   cm.
Includes bibliographical references and index.
ISBN 978-0-521-88473-0 (hardback)
1. Computational complexity.   2. Turing machines.   I. Title.

QA267.7.G65   2008
511.3′52–dc22   2008006750

ISBN 978-0-521-88473-0 Hardback

to Dana

Contents

List of Figures

Preface

The quest for efficiency is ancient and universal, as time and other resources are always in shortage. Thus, the question of which tasks can be performed efficiently is central to the human experience.

A key step toward the systematic study of the aforementioned question is a rigorous definition of the notion of a task and of procedures for solving tasks. These definitions were provided by computability theory, which emerged in the 1930s. This theory focuses on computational tasks, and considers automated procedures (i.e., computing devices and algorithms) that may solve such tasks.

In focusing attention on computational tasks and algorithms, computability theory has set the stage for the study of the computational resources (like time) that are required by such algorithms. When this study focuses on the resources that are necessary for *any* algorithm that solves a particular task (or a task of a particular type), the study becomes part of the theory of Computational Complexity (also known as Complexity Theory).[1]

Complexity Theory is a central field of the theoretical foundations of computer science. It is concerned with the study of the *intrinsic complexity of computational tasks*. That is, a typical complexity theoretic study refers to the computational resources required to solve a computational task (or a class of such tasks), rather than referring to a specific algorithm or an algorithmic schema. Actually, research in Complexity Theory tends to *start with and focus on the computational resources themselves*, and addresses the effect of limiting these resources on the class of tasks that can be solved. Thus, Computational Complexity is the general study of what can be achieved within limited time (and/or other limited natural computational resources).

The (half-century) history of Complexity Theory has witnessed two main research efforts (or directions). The first direction is aimed toward actually establishing concrete lower bounds on the complexity of computational problems, via an analysis of the evolution of the process of computation. Thus, in a sense, the heart of this direction is a "low-level" analysis of computation. Most research in circuit complexity and in proof complexity falls within this category. In contrast, a second research effort is aimed at exploring the connections among computational problems and notions, without being able to provide absolute statements regarding the individual problems or notions. This effort may be

---

[1]In contrast, when the focus is on the design and analysis of specific algorithms (rather than on the intrinsic complexity of the task), the study becomes part of a related subfield that may be called Algorithmic Design and Analysis. Furthermore, Algorithmic Design and Analysis tends to be sub-divided according to the domain of mathematics, science, and engineering in which the computational tasks arise. In contrast, Complexity Theory typically maintains a unity of the study of tasks solvable within certain resources (regardless of the origins of these tasks).

viewed as a "high-level" study of computation. The theory of NP-completeness as well as the studies of approximation, probabilistic proof systems, pseudorandomness, and cryptography all fall within this category.

The current book focuses on the latter effort (or direction). The main reason for our decision to focus on the "high-level" direction is the clear *conceptual significance* of the known results. That is, many known results in this direction have an extremely appealing conceptual message, which can be appreciated also by non-experts. Furthermore, these conceptual aspects can be explained without entering excessive technical detail. Consequently, the "high-level" direction is more suitable for an exposition in a book of the current nature.[2]

The last paragraph brings us to a discussion of the nature of the current book, which is captured by the subtitle (i.e., "a conceptual perspective"). Our main thesis is that *Complexity Theory is extremely rich in conceptual content*, and that *this content should be explicitly communicated in expositions and courses on the subject*. The desire to provide a corresponding textbook is indeed the motivation for writing the current book and its main governing principle.

This book offers a conceptual perspective on Complexity Theory, and the presentation is designed to highlight this perspective. It is intended to serve as an introduction to the field, and can be used either as a textbook or for self-study. Indeed, the book's primary target audience consists of students who wish to learn Complexity Theory and educators who intend to teach a course on Complexity Theory. Still, we hope that the book will be useful also to experts, especially to experts in one sub-area of Complexity Theory who seek an introduction to and/or an overview of some other sub-area.

It is also hoped that the book may help promote general interest in Complexity Theory and make this field acccessible to general readers with adequate background (which consists mainly of being comfortable with abstract discussions, definitions, and proofs). However, we do expect most readers to have a basic knowledge of algorithms, or at least be fairly comfortable with the notion of an algorithm.

The book focuses on several sub-areas of Complexity Theory (see the following organization and chapter summaries). In each case, the exposition starts from the intuitive questions addressed by the sub-area, as embodied in the concepts that it studies. The exposition discusses the fundamental *importance* of these questions, the *choices* made in the actual formulation of these questions and notions, the *approaches* that underlie the answers, and the *ideas* that are embedded in these answers. Our view is that these ("non-technical") aspects are the core of the field, and the presentation attempts to reflect this view.

We note that being guided by the conceptual contents of the material leads, in some cases, to technical simplifications. Indeed, for many of the results presented in this book, the presentation of the proof is different (and arguably easier to understand) than the standard presentations.

Web site for notices regarding this book. We intend to maintain a Web site listing corrections of various types. The location of the site is

    http://www.wisdom.weizmann.ac.il/~oded/cc-book.html

---

[2]In addition, we mention a subjective reason for our decision: The "high-level" direction is within our own expertise, while this cannot be said about the "low-level" direction.

Organization and Chapter Summaries

This book consists of ten chapters and seven appendices. The chapters constitute the core of this book and are written in a style adequate for a textbook, whereas the appendices provide either relevant background or additional perspective and are written in the style of a survey article. The relative length and ordering of the chapters (and appendices) do not reflect their relative importance, but rather an attempt at the best logical order (i.e., minimizing the number of forward pointers).

Following are brief summaries of the book's chapters and appendices. These summaries are more novice-friendly than those provided in Section 1.1.3 but less detailed than the summaries provided at the beginning of each chapter.

Chapter 1: Introduction and Preliminaries. The introduction provides a high-level overview of some of the content of Complexity Theory as well as a discussion of some of the characteristic features of this field. In addition, the introduction contains several important comments regarding the approach and conventions of the current book. The preliminaries provide the relevant background on *computability theory*, which is the setting in which complexity theoretic questions are being studied. Most importantly, central notions such as search and decision problems, algorithms that solve such problems, and their complexity are defined. In addition, this part presents the basic notions underlying non-uniform models of computation (like Boolean circuits).

Chapter 2: P, NP, and NP-Completeness. The P versus NP Question can be phrased as asking whether or not finding solutions is harder than checking the correctness of solutions. An alternative formulation asks whether or not discovering proofs is harder than verifying their correctness, that is, is proving harder than verifying. It is widely believed that the answer to the two equivalent formulations is that finding (resp., proving) is harder than checking (resp., verifying); that is, it is believed that P is different from NP. At present, when faced with a hard problem in NP, we can only hope to prove that it is not in P assuming that NP is different from P. This is where the theory of NP-completeness, which is based on the notion of a reduction, comes into the picture. In general, one computational problem is reducible to another problem if it is possible to efficiently solve the former when provided with an (efficient) algorithm for solving the latter. A problem (in NP) is NP-complete if any problem in NP is reducible to it. Amazingly enough, NP-complete problems exist, and furthermore, hundreds of natural computational problems arising in many different areas of mathematics and science are NP-complete.

Chapter 3: Variations on P and NP. Non-uniform polynomial time (P/poly) captures efficient computations that are carried out by devices that handle specific input lengths. The basic formalism ignores the complexity of constructing such devices (i.e., a uniformity condition), but a finer formalism (based on "machines that take advice") allows us to quantify the amount of non-uniformity. This provides a generalization of P. In contrast, the Polynomial-time Hierarchy (PH) generalizes NP by considering statements expressed by a quantified Boolean formula with a fixed number of alternations of existential and universal quantifiers. It is widely believed that each quantifier alternation adds expressive power to the class of such formulae. The two different classes are related by showing that if NP is contained in P/poly then the Polynomial-time Hierarchy collapses to its second level (i.e., Σ_2).

Chapter 4: More Resources, More Power? When using "nice" functions to determine an algorithm's resources, it is indeed the case that more resources allow for more tasks to be performed. However, when "ugly" functions are used for the same purpose, increasing the resources may have no effect. By nice functions we mean functions that can be computed without exceeding the amount of resources that they specify. Thus, we get results asserting, for example, that there are problems that are solvable in cubic time but not in quadratic time. In the case of non-uniform models of computation, the issue of "nicety" does not arise, and it is easy to establish separation results.

Chapter 5: Space Complexity. This chapter is devoted to the study of the space complexity of computations, while focusing on two rather extreme cases. The first case is that of algorithms having logarithmic space complexity, which seem a proper and natural subset of the set of polynomial-time algorithms. The second case is that of algorithms having polynomial space complexity, which in turn can solve almost all computational problems considered in this book. Among the many results presented in this chapter are a log-space algorithm for exploring (undirected) graphs, and a log-space reduction of the set of directed graphs that are *not* strongly connected to the set of directed graphs that are strongly connected. These results capture fundamental properties of space complexity, which seems to differentiate it from time complexity.

Chapter 6: Randomness and Counting. Probabilistic polynomial-time algorithms with various types of failure give rise to complexity classes such as $\mathcal{BPP}$, $\mathcal{RP}$, and $\mathcal{ZPP}$. The results presented include the emulation of probabilistic choices by non-uniform advice (i.e., $\mathcal{BPP} \subset \mathcal{P}/\text{poly}$) and the emulation of two-sided probabilistic error by an $\exists\forall$-sequence of quantifiers (i.e., $\mathcal{BPP} \subseteq \Sigma_2$). Turning to counting problems (i.e., counting the number of solutions for NP-type problems), we distinguish between exact counting and approximate counting (in the sense of relative approximation). While any problem in $\mathcal{PH}$ is reducible to the exact counting class $\#\mathcal{P}$, approximate counting (for $\#\mathcal{P}$) is (probabilistically) reducible to $\mathcal{NP}$. Additional related topics include $\#\mathcal{P}$-completeness, the complexity of searching for unique solutions, and the relation between approximate counting and generating almost uniformly distributed solutions.

Chapter 7: The Bright Side of Hardness. It turns out that hard problems can be "put to work" to our benefit, most notably in cryptography. One key issue that arises in this context is bridging the gap between "occasional" hardness (e.g., worst-case hardness or mild average-case hardness) and "typical" hardness (i.e., strong average-case hardness).

We consider two conjectures that are related to $\mathcal{P} \neq \mathcal{NP}$. The first conjecture is that there are problems that are solvable in exponential time but are not solvable by (non-uniform) families of small (say, polynomial-size) circuits. We show that these types of worst-case conjectures can be transformed into average-case hardness results that yield non-trivial derandomizations of $\mathcal{BPP}$ (and even $\mathcal{BPP} = \mathcal{P}$). The second conjecture is that there are problems in NP for which it is easy to generate (solved) instances that are hard to solve for other people. This conjecture is captured in the notion of *one-way functions*, which are functions that are easy to evaluate but hard to invert (in an average-case sense). We show that functions that are hard to invert in a relatively mild average-case sense yield functions that are hard to invert almost everywhere, and that the latter yield predicates that are very hard to approximate (called *hard-core predicates*). The latter are useful for the construction of general-purpose pseudorandom generators, as well as for a host of cryptographic applications.

Chapter 8: Pseudorandom Generators. A fresh view of the *question of randomness* was taken in the theory of computing: It has been postulated that a distribution is pseudorandom if it cannot be told apart from the uniform distribution by any efficient procedure. The paradigm, originally associating efficient procedures with polynomial-time algorithms, has been applied also with respect to a variety of limited classes of such distinguishing procedures. The archetypical case of pseudorandom generators refers to efficient generators that fool any feasible procedure; that is, the potential distinguisher is any probabilistic polynomial-time algorithm, which may be more complex than the generator itself. These generators are called general-purpose, because their output can be safely used in any efficient application. In contrast, for purposes of derandomization, one may use pseudorandom generators that are somewhat more complex than the potential distinguisher (which represents the algorithm to be derandomized). Following this approach and using various hardness assumptions, one may obtain corresponding derandomizations of $\mathcal{BPP}$ (including a full derandomization; i.e., $\mathcal{BPP} = \mathcal{P}$). Other forms of pseudorandom generators include ones that fool space-bounded distinguishers, and even weaker ones that only exhibit some limited random behavior (e.g., outputting a pairwise independent sequence).

Chapter 9: Probabilistic Proof Systems. Randomized and interactive verification procedures, giving rise to *interactive proof systems*, seem much more powerful than their deterministic counterparts. In particular, interactive proof systems exist for any set in $\mathcal{PSPACE} \supseteq \mathrm{co}\mathcal{NP}$ (e.g., for the set of unsatisfied propositional formulae), whereas it is widely believed that some sets in $\mathrm{co}\mathcal{NP}$ do *not* have NP-proof systems. Interactive proofs allow the meaningful conceptualization of *zero-knowledge proofs*, which are interactive proofs that yield nothing (to the verifier) beyond the fact that the assertion is indeed valid. Under reasonable complexity assumptions, every set in $\mathcal{NP}$ has a zero-knowledge proof system. (This result has many applications in cryptography.) A third type of probabilistic proof system underlies the model of PCPs, which stands for *probabilistically checkable proofs*. These are (redundant) NP-proofs that offer a trade-off between the number of locations (randomly) examined in the proof and the confidence in its validity. In particular, a small constant error probability can be obtained by reading a constant number of bits in the redundant NP-proof. The PCP Theorem asserts that NP-proofs can be efficiently transformed into PCPs. The study of PCPs is closely related to the study of the complexity of approximation problems.

Chapter 10: Relaxing the Requirements. In light of the apparent infeasibility of solving numerous useful computational problems, it is natural to seek relaxations of those problems that remain useful for the original applications and yet allow for feasible solving procedures. Two such types of relaxation are provided by adequate notions of approximation and a theory of average-case complexity. The notions of approximation refer to the computational problems themselves; that is, for each problem instance we extend the set of admissible solutions. In the context of search problems this means settling for solutions that have a value that is "sufficiently close" to the value of the optimal solution, whereas in the context of decision problems this means settling for procedures that distinguish yes-instances from instances that are "far" from any yes-instance. Turning to average-case complexity, we note that a systematic study of this notion requires the development of a non-trivial conceptual framework. One major aspect of this framework is limiting the class of distributions in a way that, on the one hand, allows for various types of natural distributions and, on the other hand, prevents the collapse of average-case hardness to worst-case hardness.

Appendix A: Glossary of Complexity Classes. The glossary provides self-contained definitions of most complexity classes mentioned in the book. The glossary is partitioned into two parts, dealing separately with complexity classes that are defined in terms of algorithms and their resources (i.e., time and space complexity of Turing machines) and complexity classes defined in terms of non-uniform circuits (and referring to their size and depth). In particular, the following classes are defined: $\mathcal{P}$, $\mathcal{NP}$, co$\mathcal{NP}$, $\mathcal{BPP}$, $\mathcal{RP}$, co$\mathcal{RP}$, $\mathcal{ZPP}$, #$\mathcal{P}$, $\mathcal{PH}$, $\mathcal{E}$, $\mathcal{EXP}$, $\mathcal{NEXP}$, $\mathcal{L}$, $\mathcal{NL}$, $\mathcal{RL}$, $\mathcal{PSPACE}$, $\mathcal{P}$/poly, $\mathcal{NC}^k$, and $\mathcal{AC}^k$.

Appendix B: On the Quest for Lower Bounds. This brief survey describes the most famous attempts at proving lower bounds on the complexity of natural computational problems. The first part, devoted to Circuit Complexity, reviews lower bounds for the *size* of (restricted) circuits that solve natural computational problems. This represents a program whose long-term goal is proving that $\mathcal{P} \neq \mathcal{NP}$. The second part, devoted to Proof Complexity, reviews lower bounds on the length of (restricted) propositional proofs of natural tautologies. This represents a program whose long-term goal is proving that $\mathcal{NP} \neq$ co$\mathcal{NP}$.

Appendix C: On the Foundations of Modern Cryptography. This survey of the foundations of cryptography focuses on the paradigms, approaches, and techniques that are used to conceptualize, define, and provide solutions to natural security concerns. It presents some of these conceptual tools as well as some of the fundamental results obtained using them. The appendix augments the partial treatment of one-way functions, pseudorandom generators, and zero-knowledge proofs (included in Chapters 7–9). Using these basic tools, the appendix provides a treatment of basic cryptographic applications such as encryption, signatures, and general cryptographic protocols.

Appendix D: Probabilistic Preliminaries and Advanced Topics in Randomization. The probabilistic preliminaries include conventions regarding random variables as well as three useful inequalities (i.e., Markov's Inequality, Chebyshev's Inequality, and Chernoff Bound). The advanced topics include constructions and lemmas regarding families of hashing functions, a study of the sample and randomness complexities of estimating the average value of an arbitrary function, and the problem of randomness extraction (i.e., procedures for extracting almost perfect randomness from sources of weak or defected randomness).

Appendix E: Explicit Constructions. Complexity Theory provides a clear perspective on the intuitive notion of an explicit construction. This perspective is demonstrated with respect to error-correcting codes and expander graphs. Starting with codes, the appendix focuses on various computational aspects, and offers a review of several popular constructions as well as a construction of a binary code of constant rate and constant relative distance. Also included are a brief review of the notions of locally testable and locally decodable codes, and a useful upper bound on the number of codewords that are close to any single sequence. Turning to expander graphs, the appendix contains a review of two standard definitions of expanders, two levels of explicitness, two properties of expanders that are related to (single-step and multi-step) random walks on them, and two explicit constructions of expander graphs.

Appendix F: Some Omitted Proofs. This appendix contains some proofs that were not included in the main text (for a variety of reasons) and still are beneficial as alternatives to the original and/or standard presentations. Included are a proof that $\mathcal{PH}$ is reducible to $\#\mathcal{P}$ via randomized Karp-reductions, and the presentation of two useful transformations regarding interactive proof systems.

Appendix G: Some Computational Problems. This appendix includes definitions of most of the specific computational problems that are referred to in the main text. In particular, it contains a brief introduction to graph algorithms, Boolean formulae, and finite fields.

Acknowledgments

My perspective on Complexity Theory was most influenced by Shimon Even and Leonid Levin. In fact, it was hard not to be influenced by these two remarkable and highly opinionated researchers (especially for somebody like me who was fortunate to spend a lot of time with them).[1]

Shimon Even viewed Complexity Theory as the study of the limitations of algorithms, a study concerned with natural computational resources and natural computational tasks. Complexity Theory was there to guide the engineer and to address the deepest questions that bother an intellectually curious computer scientist. I believe that this book shares Shimon's perspective of Complexity Theory as evolving around such questions.

Leonid Levin emphasized the general principles that underlie Complexity Theory, rejecting any "model-dependent effects" as well as the common coupling of Complexity Theory with the theory of automata and formal languages. In my opinion, this book is greatly influenced by these perspectives of Leonid.

I wish to acknowledge the influence of numerous other colleagues on my professional perspectives and attitudes. These include Shafi Goldwasser, Dick Karp, Silvio Micali, and Avi Wigderson. Needless to say, this is but a partial list that reflects influences of which I am most aware.

The year I spent at Radcliffe Institute for Advanced Study (of Harvard University) was instrumental in my decision to undertake the writing of this book. I am grateful to Radcliffe for creating such an empowering atmosphere. I also wish to thank many colleagues for their comments and advice (or help) regarding earlier versions of this text. A partial list includes Noga Alon, Noam Livne, Dieter van Melkebeek, Omer Reingold, Dana Ron, Ronen Shaltiel, Amir Shpilka, Madhu Sudan, Salil Vadhan, and Avi Wigderson.

Lastly, I am grateful to Mohammad Mahmoody Ghidary and Or Meir for their careful reading of drafts of this manuscript and for the numerous corrections and suggestions that they have provided.

Relation to previous texts. Some of the text of this book has been adapted from previous texts of mine. In particular, Chapters 8 and 9 were written based on my surveys [90, Chap. 3] and [90, Chap. 2], respectively; but the exposition has been extensively revised

---

[1]Shimon Even was my graduate studies adviser (at the Technion, 1980–83), whereas I had a lot of meetings with Leonid Levin during my postdoctoral period (at MIT, 1983–86).

to fit the significantly different aims of the current book. Similarly, Section 7.1 and Appendix C were written based on my survey [90, Chap. 1] and books [91, 92]; but, again, the previous texts are very different in many ways. In contrast, Appendix B was adapted with relatively little modifications from an early draft of a section in an article by Avi Wigderson and myself [107].

CHAPTER ONE

Introduction and Preliminaries

When you set out on your journey to Ithaca,
pray that the road is long,
full of adventure, full of knowledge.

K. P. Cavafy, "Ithaca"

The current chapter consists of two parts. The first part provides a high-level introduction to (computational) Complexity Theory. This introduction is much more detailed than the laconic statements made in the preface, but is quite sparse when compared to the richness of the field. In addition, the introduction contains several important comments regarding the contents, approach, and conventions of the current book.

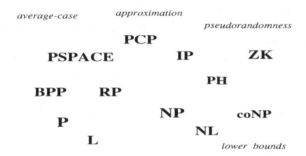

The second part of this chapter provides the necessary preliminaries to the rest of the book. It includes a discussion of computational tasks and computational models, as well as natural complexity measures associated with the latter. More specifically, this part recalls the basic notions and results of computability theory (including the definition of Turing machines, some undecidability results, the notion of universal machines, and the definition of oracle machines). In addition, this part presents the basic notions underlying non-uniform models of computation (like Boolean circuits).

1.1. Introduction

This introduction consists of two parts: The first part refers to the area itself, whereas the second part refers to the current book. The first part provides a brief overview of Complexity Theory (Section 1.1.1) as well as some reflections about its characteristics (Section 1.1.2). The second part describes the contents of this book (Section 1.1.3), the considerations underlying the choice of topics as well as the way they are presented (Section 1.1.4), and various notations and conventions (Section 1.1.5).

1.1.1. A Brief Overview of Complexity Theory

Out of the tough came forth sweetness[1]

Judges, 14:14

The following brief overview is intended to give a flavor of the questions addressed by Complexity Theory. This overview is quite vague, and is merely meant as a teaser. Most of the topics mentioned in it will be discussed at length in the various chapters of this book.

Complexity Theory is concerned with the study of the *intrinsic complexity* of computational tasks. Its "final" goals include the determination of the complexity of any well-defined task. Additional goals include obtaining an understanding of the relations between various computational phenomena (e.g., relating one fact regarding computational complexity to another). Indeed, we may say that the former type of goal is concerned with *absolute* answers regarding specific computational phenomena, whereas the latter type is concerned with questions regarding the *relation* between computational phenomena.

Interestingly, so far Complexity Theory has been more successful in coping with goals of the latter ("relative") type. In fact, the failure to resolve questions of the "absolute" type led to the flourishing of methods for coping with questions of the "relative" type. Musing for a moment, let us say that, in general, the difficulty of obtaining absolute answers may naturally lead to seeking conditional answers, which may in turn reveal interesting relations between phenomena. Furthermore, the lack of absolute understanding of individual phenomena seems to facilitate the development of methods for relating different phenomena. Anyhow, this is what happened in Complexity Theory.

Putting aside for a moment the frustration caused by the failure of obtaining absolute answers, we must admit that there is something fascinating in the success of relating different phenomena: In some sense, relations between phenomena are more revealing than absolute statements about individual phenomena. Indeed, the first example that comes to mind is the theory of NP-completeness. Let us consider this theory, for a moment, from the perspective of these two types of goals.

Complexity Theory has failed to determine the intrinsic complexity of tasks such as finding a satisfying assignment to a given (satisfiable) propositional formula or finding a 3-coloring of a given (3-colorable) graph. But it has succeeded in establishing that these two seemingly different computational tasks are in some sense the same (or, more precisely, are computationally equivalent). We find this success amazing and exciting, and hope that the reader shares these feelings. The same feeling of wonder and excitement is generated by many of the other discoveries of Complexity Theory. Indeed, the reader is invited to join a fast tour of some of the other questions and answers that make up the field of Complexity Theory.

We will indeed start with the *P versus NP Question*. Our daily experience is that it is harder to solve a problem than it is to check the correctness of a solution (e.g., think of either a puzzle or a research problem). Is this experience merely a coincidence or does it represent a fundamental fact of life (i.e., a property of the world)? Could you imagine a

---

[1]The quote is commonly interpreted as meaning that benefit arose out of misfortune.

world in which solving any problem is not significantly harder than checking a solution to it? Would the term "solving a problem" not lose its meaning in such a hypothetical (and impossible, in our opinion) world? The denial of the plausibility of such a hypothetical world (in which "solving" is not harder than "checking") is what "P different from NP" actually means, where P represents tasks that are efficiently solvable and NP represents tasks for which solutions can be efficiently checked.

The mathematically (or theoretically) inclined reader may also consider the task of proving theorems versus the task of verifying the validity of proofs. Indeed, finding proofs is a special type of the aforementioned task of "solving a problem" (and verifying the validity of proofs is a corresponding case of checking correctness). Again, "P different from NP" means that there are theorems that are harder to prove than to be convinced of their correctness when presented with a proof. This means that the notion of a "proof" is meaningful; that is, proofs do help when one is seeking to be convinced of the correctness of assertions. Here NP represents sets of assertions that can be efficiently verified with the help of adequate proofs, and P represents sets of assertions that can be efficiently verified from scratch (i.e., without proofs).

In light of the foregoing discussion it is clear that the P versus NP Question is a fundamental scientific question of far-reaching consequences. The fact that this question seems beyond our current reach led to the development of the theory of *NP-completeness*. Loosely speaking, this theory identifies a set of computational problems that are as hard as NP. That is, the fate of the P versus NP Question lies with each of these problems: If any of these problems is easy to solve then so are all problems in NP. Thus, showing that a problem is NP-complete provides evidence of its intractability (assuming, of course, "P different than NP"). Indeed, demonstrating the NP-completeness of computational tasks is a central tool in indicating hardness of natural computational problems, and it has been used extensively both in computer science and in other disciplines. We note that NP-completeness indicates not only the conjectured intractability of a problem but also its "richness" in the sense that the problem is rich enough to "encode" any other problem in NP. The use of the term "encoding" is justified by the exact meaning of NP-completeness, which in turn establishes relations between different computational problems (without referring to their "absolute" complexity).

The foregoing discussion of NP-completeness hints at *the importance of representation*, since it referred to different problems that encode one another. Indeed, the importance of representation is a central aspect of Complexity Theory. In general, Complexity Theory is concerned with problems for which the solutions are implicit in the problem's statement (or rather in the instance). That is, the problem (or rather its instance) contains all necessary information, and one merely needs to process this information in order to supply the answer.[2] Thus, Complexity Theory is concerned with manipulation of information, and its transformation from one representation (in which the information is given) to another representation (which is the one desired). Indeed, a solution to a computational problem is merely a different representation of the information given, that is, a representation in which the answer is explicit rather than implicit. For example, the answer to the question of whether or not a given Boolean formula is satisfiable is implicit in the formula itself (but the task is to make the answer explicit). Thus, Complexity Theory clarifies a central

---

[2]In contrast, in other disciplines, solving a problem may require gathering information that is not available in the problem's statement. This information may either be available from auxiliary (past) records or be obtained by conducting new experiments.

3

issue regarding representation, that is, the distinction between what is explicit and what is implicit in a representation. Furthermore, it even suggests a quantification of the level of non-explicitness.

In general, Complexity Theory provides new viewpoints on various phenomena that were considered also by past thinkers. Examples include the aforementioned concepts of solutions, proofs, and representation as well as concepts like randomness, knowledge, interaction, secrecy, and learning. We next discuss the latter concepts and the perspective offered by Complexity Theory.

The concept of *randomness* has puzzled thinkers for ages. Their perspective can be described as ontological: They asked "what is randomness" and wondered whether it exists, at all (or is the world deterministic). The perspective of Complexity Theory is behavioristic: It is based on defining objects as equivalent if they cannot be told apart by any efficient procedure. That is, a coin toss is (defined to be) "random" (even if one believes that the universe is deterministic) if it is infeasible to predict the coin's outcome. Likewise, a string (or a distribution of strings) is "random" if it is infeasible to distinguish it from the uniform distribution (regardless of whether or not one can generate the latter). Interestingly, randomness (or rather pseudorandomness) defined this way is efficiently expandable; that is, under a reasonable complexity assumption (to be discussed next), short pseudorandom strings can be deterministically expanded into long pseudorandom strings. Indeed, it turns out that randomness is intimately related to intractability. Firstly, note that the very definition of pseudorandomness refers to intractability (i.e., the infeasibility of distinguishing a pseudorandomness object from a uniformly distributed object). Secondly, as stated, a complexity assumption, which refers to the existence of functions that are easy to evaluate but hard to invert (called *one-way functions*), implies the existence of deterministic programs (called *pseudorandom generators*) that stretch short random seeds into long pseudorandom sequences. In fact, it turns out that the existence of pseudorandom generators is equivalent to the existence of one-way functions.

Complexity Theory offers its own perspective on the concept of *knowledge* (and distinguishes it from information). Specifically, Complexity Theory views knowledge as the result of a hard computation. Thus, whatever can be efficiently done by anyone is not considered knowledge. In particular, the result of an easy computation applied to publicly available information is not considered knowledge. In contrast, the value of a hard-to-compute function applied to publicly available information is knowledge, and if somebody provides you with such a value then it has provided you with knowledge. This discussion is related to the notion of *zero-knowledge* interactions, which are interactions in which no knowledge is gained. Such interactions may still be useful, because they may convince a party of the *correctness* of specific data that was provided beforehand. For example, a zero-knowledge interactive proof may convince a party that a given graph is 3-colorable without yielding any 3-coloring.

The foregoing paragraph has explicitly referred to *interaction*, viewing it as a vehicle for gaining knowledge and/or gaining confidence. Let us highlight the latter application by noting that it may be easier to verify an assertion when allowed to interact with a prover rather than when reading a proof. Put differently, interaction with a good teacher may be more beneficial than reading any book. We comment that the added power of such *interactive proofs* is rooted in their being randomized (i.e., the verification procedure is randomized), because if the verifier's questions can be determined beforehand then the prover may just provide the transcript of the interaction as a traditional written proof.

Another concept related to knowledge is that of *secrecy*: Knowledge is something that one party may have while another party does not have (and cannot feasibly obtain by itself) – thus, in some sense knowledge is a secret. In general, Complexity Theory is related to *cryptography*, where the latter is broadly defined as the study of systems that are easy to use but hard to abuse. Typically, such systems involve secrets, randomness, and interaction as well as a complexity gap between the ease of proper usage and the infeasibility of causing the system to deviate from its prescribed behavior. Thus, much of cryptography is based on complexity theoretic assumptions and its results are typically transformations of relatively simple computational primitives (e.g., one-way functions) into more complex cryptographic applications (e.g., secure encryption schemes).

We have already mentioned the concept of *learning* when referring to learning from a teacher versus learning from a book. Recall that Complexity Theory provides evidence to the advantage of the former. This is in the context of gaining knowledge about publicly available information. In contrast, computational learning theory is concerned with learning objects that are only partially available to the learner (i.e., reconstructing a function based on its value at a few random locations or even at locations chosen by the learner). Complexity Theory sheds light on the intrinsic limitations of learning (in this sense).

Complexity Theory deals with a variety of computational tasks. We have already mentioned two fundamental types of tasks: *searching for solutions* (or rather "finding solutions") and *making decisions* (e.g., regarding the validity of assertions). We have also hinted that in some cases these two types of tasks can be related. Now we consider two additional types of tasks: *counting the number of solutions* and *generating random solutions*. Clearly, both the latter tasks are at least as hard as finding arbitrary solutions to the corresponding problem, but it turns out that for some natural problems they are not significantly harder. Specifically, under some natural conditions on the problem, approximately counting the number of solutions and generating an approximately random solution is not significantly harder than finding an arbitrary solution.

Having mentioned the notion of *approximation*, we note that the study of the complexity of finding "approximate solutions" is also of natural importance. One type of approximation problems refers to an objective function defined on the set of potential solutions: Rather than finding a solution that attains the optimal value, the approximation task consists of finding a solution that attains an "almost optimal" value, where the notion of "almost optimal" may be understood in different ways giving rise to different levels of approximation. Interestingly, in many cases, even a very relaxed level of approximation is as difficult to obtain as solving the original (exact) search problem (i.e., finding an approximate solution is as hard as finding an optimal solution). Surprisingly, these hardness-of-approximation results are related to the study of *probabilistically checkable proofs*, which are proofs that allow for ultra-fast probabilistic verification. Amazingly, every proof can be efficiently transformed into one that allows for probabilistic verification based on probing a *constant* number of bits (in the alleged proof). Turning back to approximation problems, we note that in other cases a reasonable level of approximation is easier to achieve than solving the original (exact) search problem.

Approximation is a natural relaxation of various computational problems. Another natural relaxation is the study of *average-case complexity*, where the "average" is taken over some "simple" distributions (representing a model of the problem's instances that may occur in practice). We stress that, although it was not stated explicitly, the entire discussion so far has referred to "worst-case" analysis of algorithms. We mention that worst-case complexity is a more robust notion than average-case complexity. For starters, one avoids the controversial question of which instances are "important in practice" and correspondingly the selection of the class of distributions for which average-case analysis is to be conducted. Nevertheless, a relatively robust theory of average-case complexity has been suggested, albeit it is less developed than the theory of worst-case complexity.

In view of the central role of randomness in Complexity Theory (as evident, say, in the study of pseudorandomness, probabilistic proof systems, and cryptography), one may wonder as to whether the randomness needed for the various applications can be obtained in real life. One specific question, which received a lot of attention, is the possibility of "purifying" randomness (or "extracting good randomness from bad sources"). That is, can we use "defected" sources of randomness in order to implement almost perfect sources of randomness? The answer depends, of course, on the model of such defected sources. This study turned out to be related to Complexity Theory, where the most tight connection is between some type of *randomness extractors* and some type of pseudorandom generators.

So far we have focused on the time complexity of computational tasks, while relying on the natural association of efficiency with time. However, time is not the only resource one should care about. Another important resource is *space*: the amount of (temporary) memory consumed by the computation. The study of space complexity has uncovered several fascinating phenomena, which seem to indicate a fundamental difference between space complexity and time complexity. For example, in the context of space complexity, verifying proofs of validity of assertions (of any specific type) has the same complexity as verifying proofs of invalidity for the same type of assertions.

In case the reader feels dizzy, it is no wonder. We took an ultra-fast air tour of some mountain tops, and dizziness is to be expected. Needless to say, the rest of the book offers a totally different touring experience. We will climb some of these mountains by foot, step by step, and will often stop to look around and reflect.

Absolute Results (aka. Lower Bounds). As stated up-front, absolute results are not known for many of the "big questions" of Complexity Theory (most notably the P versus NP Question). However, several highly non-trivial absolute results have been proved. For example, it was shown that using negation can speed up the computation of monotone functions (which do not require negation for their mere computation). In addition, many promising techniques were introduced and employed with the aim of providing a low-level analysis of the progress of computation. However, as stated in the preface, the focus of this book is elsewhere.

1.1.2. Characteristics of Complexity Theory

We are successful because we use the right level of abstraction.
Avi Wigderson (1996)

Using the "right level of abstraction" seems to be a main characteristic of the theory of computation at large. The right level of abstraction means abstracting away second-order details, which tend to be context dependent, while using definitions that reflect the main issues (rather than abstracting them away, too). Indeed, using the right level of abstraction calls for an extensive exercising of good judgment, and one indication for having chosen the right abstractions is the result of their study.

One major choice, taken by the theory of computation at large, is the *choice of a model of computation and corresponding complexity measures and classes*. The choice, which is currently taken for granted, was to use a simple model that avoids both the extreme of being too realistic (and thus too detailed) as well as the extreme of being too abstract (and vague). On the one hand, the main model of computation (which is used in Complexity Theory) does not try to mimic (or mirror) the actual operation of real-life computers used at a specific historical time. Such a choice would have made it very hard to develop Complexity Theory as we know it and to uncover the fundamental relations discussed in this book: The mass of details would have obscured the view. On the other hand, avoiding any reference to any concrete model (like in the case of recursive function theory) does not encourage the introduction and study of natural measures of complexity. Indeed, as we shall see in Section 1.2.3, the choice was (and is) to use a simple model of computation (which does not mirror real-life computers), while avoiding any effects that are specific to that model (by keeping an eye on a host of variants and alternative models). The freedom from the specifics of the basic model is obtained by considering complexity classes that are invariant under a change of model (as long as the alternative model is "reasonable").

Another major choice is the use of *asymptotic analysis*. Specifically, we consider the complexity of an algorithm as a function of its input length, and study the asymptotic behavior of this function. It turns out that structure that is hidden by concrete quantities appears at the limit. Furthermore, depending on the case, we classify functions according to different criteria. For example, in the case of time complexity we consider classes of functions that are closed under multiplication, whereas in case of space complexity we consider closure under addition. In each case, the choice is governed by the nature of the complexity measure being considered. Indeed, one could have developed a theory without using these conventions, but this would have resulted in a far more cumbersome theory. For example, rather than saying that finding a satisfying assignment for a given formula is polynomial-time reducible to deciding the satisfiability of some other formulae, one could have stated the exact functional dependence of the complexity of the search problem on the complexity of the decision problem.

Both the aforementioned choices are common to other branches of the theory of computation. One aspect that makes Complexity Theory unique is its perspective on the most basic question of the theory of computation, that is, the way it studies the question of *what can be efficiently computed*. The perspective of Complexity Theory is general in nature. This is reflected in its primary focus on the relevant *notion of efficiency* (captured by corresponding resource bounds) rather than on specific computational problems. In most cases, complexity theoretic studies do not refer to any specific computational problems or refer to such problems merely as an illustration. Furthermore, even when specific computational problems are studied, this study is (explicitly or at least implicitly) aimed at understanding the computational limitations of certain resource bounds.

The aforementioned general perspective seems linked to the significant role of *conceptual considerations* in the field: The rigorous study of an intuitive notion of efficiency must be initiated with an adequate choice of definitions. Since this study refers to any possible (relevant) computation, the definitions cannot be derived by abstracting some concrete reality (e.g., a specific algorithmic schema). Indeed, the definitions attempt to capture any possible reality, which means that the choice of definitions is governed by conceptual principles and not merely by empirical observations.

1.1.3. Contents of This Book

This book is intended to serve as an introduction to Computational Complexity Theory. It consists of ten chapters and seven appendices, and can be used either as a textbook or for self-study. The chapters constitute the core of this book and are written in a style adequate for a textbook, whereas the appendices provide either relevant background or additional perspective and are written in the style of a survey article.

1.1.3.1. Overall Organization of the Book

Section 1.2 and Chapter 2 are a prerequisite for the rest of the book. Technically speaking, the notions and results that appear in these parts are extensively used in the rest of the book. More importantly, the former parts are the conceptual framework that shapes the field and provides a good perspective on the field's questions and answers. Indeed, Section 1.2 and Chapter 2 provide the very basic material that must be understood by anybody having an interest in Complexity Theory.

In contrast, the rest of the book covers more advanced material, which means that none of it can be claimed to be absolutely necessary for a basic understanding of Complexity Theory. In particular, although some advanced chapters refer to material in other advanced chapters, the relation between these chapters is not a fundamental one. Thus, one may choose to read and/or teach an arbitrary subset of the advanced chapters and do so in an arbitrary order, provided one is willing to follow the relevant references to some parts of other chapters (see Figure 1.1). Needless to say, we recommend reading and/or teaching all the advanced chapters, and doing so by following the order presented in this book.

As illustrated by Figure 1.1, some chapters (i.e., Chapters 3, 6, and 10) lump together topics that are usually presented separately. These decisions are related to our perspective on the corresponding topics.

Turning to the appendices, we note that some of them (e.g., Appendix G and parts of Appendices D and E) provide background information that is required in some of the advanced chapters. In contrast, other appendices (e.g., Appendices B and C and other parts of Appendices D and E) provide additional perspective that augments the advanced chapters. (The function of Appendices A and F will be clarified in §1.1.3.2.)

1.1.3.2. Contents of the Specific Parts

The rest of this section provides a brief summary of the contents of the various chapters and appendices. This summary is intended for the teacher and/or the expert, whereas the student is referred to the more novice-friendly summaries that appear in the book's preface.

Section 1.2: Preliminaries. This section provides the relevant background on computability theory, which is the basis for the rest of this book (as well as for Complexity Theory at large). Most importantly, it contains a discussion of central notions such as search and decision problems, algorithms that solve such problems, and their complexity. In addition, this section presents non-uniform models of computation (e.g., Boolean circuits).

Chapter 2: P, NP, and NP-completeness. This chapter presents the P-vs-NP Question both in terms of search problems and in terms of decision problems. The second main

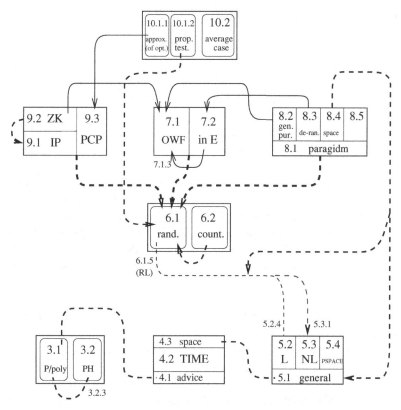

Figure 1.1: Dependencies among the advanced chapters. Solid arrows indicate the use of specific results that are stated in the section to which the arrow points. Dashed lines (and arrows) indicate an important conceptual connection; the wider the line, the tighter the connection. When relations are only between subsections, their index is indicated.

topic of this chapter is the theory of NP-completeness. The chapter also provides a treatment of the general notion of a (polynomial time) reduction, with special emphasis on self-reducibility. Additional topics include the existence of problems in NP that are neither NP-complete nor in P, optimal search algorithms, the class coNP, and promise problems.

Chapter 3: Variations on P and NP. This chapter provides a treatment of non-uniform polynomial time (P/poly) and of the Polynomial-time Hierarchy (PH). Each of the two classes is defined in two equivalent ways (e.g., P/poly is defined both in terms of circuits and in terms of "machines that take advice"). In addition, it is shown that if NP is contained in P/poly then PH collapses to its second level (i.e., Σ_2).

Chapter 4: More Resources, More Power? The focus of this chapter is on hierarchy theorems, which assert that typically more resources allow for solving more problems. These results depend on using bounding functions that can be computed without exceeding the amount of resources that they specify, and otherwise gap theorems may apply.

Chapter 5: Space Complexity. Among the results presented in this chapter are a log-space algorithm for testing connectivity of (undirected) graphs, a proof that $\mathcal{NL} = \text{co}\mathcal{NL}$, and complete problems for $\mathcal{NL}$ and $\mathcal{PSPACE}$ (under log-space and poly-time reductions, respectively).

Chapter 6: Randomness and Counting. This chapter focuses on various randomized complexity classes (i.e., $\mathcal{BPP}$, $\mathcal{RP}$, and $\mathcal{ZPP}$) and the counting class #$\mathcal{P}$. The results presented in this chapter include $\mathcal{BPP} \subset \mathcal{P}/\text{poly}$ and $\mathcal{BPP} \subseteq \Sigma_2$, the #$\mathcal{P}$-completeness of the Permanent, the connection between approximate counting and uniform generation of solutions, and the randomized reductions of approximate counting to $\mathcal{NP}$ and of $\mathcal{NP}$ to solving problems with unique solutions.

Chapter 7: The Bright Side of Hardness. This chapter deals with two conjectures that are related to $\mathcal{P} \neq \mathcal{NP}$. The first conjecture is that there are problems in $\mathcal{E}$ that are not solvable by (non-uniform) families of small (say, polynomial-size) circuits, whereas the second conjecture is equivalent to the notion of *one-way functions*. Most of this chapter is devoted to "hardness amplification" results that convert these conjectures into tools that can be used for non-trivial derandomizations of $\mathcal{BPP}$ (resp., for a host of cryptographic applications).

Chapter 8: Pseudorandom Generators. The pivot of this chapter is the notion of *computational indistinguishability* and corresponding notions of pseudorandomness. The definition of general-purpose pseudorandom generators (running in polynomial time and withstanding any polynomial-time distinguisher) is presented as a special case of a general paradigm. The chapter also contains a presentation of other instantiations of the latter paradigm, including generators aimed at derandomizing complexity classes such as $\mathcal{BPP}$, generators withstanding space-bounded distinguishers, and some special-purpose generators.

Chapter 9: Probabilistic Proof Systems. This chapter provides a treatment of three types of probabilistic proof systems: *interactive proofs*, *zero-knowledge proofs*, and *probabilistic checkable proofs*. The results presented include $\mathcal{IP} = \mathcal{PSPACE}$, zero-knowledge proofs for any NP-set, and the PCP Theorem. For the latter, only overviews of the two different known proofs are provided.

Chapter 10: Relaxing the Requirements. This chapter provides a treatment of two types of approximation problems and a theory of average-case (or rather typical-case) complexity. The traditional type of approximation problem refers to search problems and consists of a relaxation of standard optimization problems. The second type is known as "property testing" and consists of a relaxation of standard decision problems. The theory of average-case complexity involves several non-trivial definitional choices (e.g., an adequate choice of the class of distributions).

Appendix A: Glossary of Complexity Classes. The glossary provides self-contained definitions of most complexity classes mentioned in the book.

Appendix B: On the Quest for Lower Bounds. The first part, devoted to Circuit Complexity, reviews lower bounds for the *size* of (restricted) circuits that solve natural computational problems. The second part, devoted to Proof Complexity, reviews lower bounds on the length of (restricted) propositional proofs of natural tautologies.

Appendix C: On the Foundations of Modern Cryptography. The first part of this appendix augments the partial treatment of one-way functions, pseudorandom generators, and zero-knowledge proofs (included in Chapters 7–9). Using these basic tools, the second part provides a treatment of basic cryptographic applications such as encryption, signatures, and general cryptographic protocols.

Appendix D: Probabilistic Preliminaries and Advanced Topics in Randomization. The probabilistic preliminaries include conventions regarding random variables and overviews of three useful inequalities (i.e., Markov's Inequality, Chebyshev's Inequality, and Chernoff Bound). The advanced topics include constructions of *hashing* functions and variants of the Leftover Hashing Lemma, and overviews of *samplers* and *extractors* (i.e., the problem of randomness extraction).

Appendix E: Explicit Constructions. This appendix focuses on various computational aspects of error-correcting codes and expander graphs. On the topic of codes, the appendix contains a review of the Hadamard code, Reed-Solomon codes, Reed-Muller codes, and a construction of a binary code of constant rate and constant relative distance. Also included are a brief review of the notions of locally testable and locally decodable codes, and a list-decoding bound. On the topic of expander graphs, the appendix contains a review of the standard definitions and properties as well as a presentation of the Margulis-Gabber-Galil and the Zig-Zag constructions.

Appendix F: Some Omitted Proofs. This appendix contains some proofs that are beneficial as alternatives to the original and/or standard presentations. Included are proofs that $\mathcal{PH}$ is reducible to $\#\mathcal{P}$ via randomized Karp-reductions, and that $\mathcal{IP}(f) \subseteq \mathcal{AM}(O(f)) \subseteq \mathcal{AM}(f)$.

Appendix G: Some Computational Problems. This appendix contains a brief introduction to graph algorithms, Boolean formulae, and finite fields.

Bibliography. As stated in §1.1.4.4, we tried to keep the bibliographic list as short as possible (and still reached over a couple of hundred entries). As a result, many relevant references were omitted. In general, our choice of references was biased in favor of textbooks and survey articles. We tried, however, not to omit references to key papers in an area.

Absent from this book. As stated in the preface, the current book does not provide a uniform cover of the various areas of Complexity Theory. Notable omissions include the areas of *Circuit Complexity* (cf. [46, 236]) and *Proof Complexity* (cf. [27]), which are briefly reviewed in Appendix B. Additional topics that are commonly covered in Complexity Theory courses but are omitted here include the study of *branching programs* and *decision trees* (cf. [237]), *parallel computation* [141], and *communication complexity* [148]. We mention that the forthcoming textbook of Arora and Barak [14] contains a treatment of all these topics. Finally, we mention two areas that we consider related to Complexity Theory, although this view is not very common. These areas are *distributed computing* [17] and *computational learning theory* [142].

1.1.4. Approach and Style of This Book

According to a common opinion, the most important aspect of a scientific work is the technical result that it achieves, whereas explanations and motivations are merely redundancy introduced for the sake of "error correction" and/or comfort. It is further believed that, like in a work of art, the interpretation of the work should be left with the reader.

The author strongly disagrees with the aforementioned opinions, and argues that there is a fundamental difference between art and science, and that this difference refers exactly to the meaning of a piece of work. Science is concerned with meaning (and not with form), and in its quest for truth and/or understanding, science follows philosophy (and not art). The author holds the opinion that the most important aspects of a scientific work are the intuitive question that it addresses, the reason that it addresses this question, the way it phrases the question, the approach that underlies its answer, and the ideas that are embedded in the answer. Following this view, it is important to communicate these aspects of the work.

The foregoing issues are even more acute when it comes to Complexity Theory, firstly because conceptual considerations seem to play an even more central role in Complexity Theory than in other fields (cf. Section 1.1.2). Secondly (and even more importantly), Complexity Theory is extremely rich in conceptual content. Thus, communicating this content is of primary importance, and failing to do so misses the most important aspects of this theory.

Unfortunately, the conceptual content of Complexity Theory is rarely communicated (explicitly) in books and/or surveys of the area.[3] The annoying (and quite amazing) consequences are students who have only a vague understanding of the *meaning* and general relevance of the fundamental notions and results that they were taught. The author's view is that these consequences are easy to avoid by taking the time to explicitly discuss the *meaning* of definitions and results. A closely related issue is using the "right" definitions (i.e., those that reflect better the fundamental nature of the notion being defined) and emphasizing the (conceptually) "right" results. The current book is written accordingly.

1.1.4.1. The General Principle

In accordance with the foregoing, the focus of this book is on the conceptual aspects of the technical material. Whenever presenting a subject, the starting point is the intuitive questions being addressed. The presentation explains the *importance* of these questions, the specific ways that they are phrased (i.e., the *choices* made in the actual formulation), the *approaches* that underlie the answers, and the *ideas* that are embedded in these answers. Thus, a significant portion of the text is devoted to motivating discussions that refer to the concepts and ideas that underlie the actual definitions and results.

The material is organized around conceptual themes, which reflect fundamental notions and/or general questions. Specific computational problems are rarely referred to, with exceptions that are used either for the sake of clarity or because the specific

---

[3]It is tempting to speculate on the reasons for this phenomenon. One speculation is that communicating the conceptual content of Complexity Theory involves making bold philosophical assertions that are technically straightforward, whereas this combination does not fit the personality of most researchers in Complexity Theory.

problem happens to capture a general conceptual phenomenon. For example, in this book, "complete problems" (e.g., NP-complete problems) are always secondary to the class for which they are complete.[4]

1.1.4.2. On a Few Specific Choices

Our technical presentation often differs from the standard one. In many cases this is due to conceptual considerations. At times, this leads to some technical simplifications. In this subsection we only discuss general themes and/or choices that have a global impact on much of the presentation. This discussion is intended mainly for the teacher and/or the expert.

Avoiding non-deterministic machines. We try to avoid non-deterministic machines as much as possible. As argued in several places (e.g., Section 2.1.5), we believe that these fictitious "machines" have a negative effect both from a conceptual and technical point of view. The conceptual damage caused by using non-deterministic machines is that it is unclear why one should care about what such machines can do. Needless to say, the reason to care is clear when noting that these fictitious "machines" offer a (convenient but rather slothful) way of phrasing fundamental issues. The technical damage caused by using non-deterministic machines is that they tend to confuse the students. Furthermore, they do not offer the best way to handle more advanced issues (e.g., counting classes).

In contrast, we use search problems as the basis for much of the presentation. Specifically, the class $\mathcal{PC}$ (see Definition 2.3), which consists of search problems having efficiently checkable solutions, plays a central role in our presentation. Indeed, defining this class is slightly more complicated than the standard definition of $\mathcal{NP}$ (which is based on non-deterministic machines), but the technical benefits start accumulating as we proceed. Needless to say, the class $\mathcal{PC}$ is a fundamental class of computational problems and this fact is the main motivation for its presentation. (Indeed, the most conceptually appealing phrasing of the P-vs-NP Question consists of asking whether every search problem in $\mathcal{PC}$ can be solved efficiently.)

Avoiding model-dependent effects. Complexity Theory evolves around the notion of efficient computation. Indeed, a rigorous study of this notion seems to require reference to some concrete model of computation; however, *all questions and answers considered in this book are invariant under the choice of such a concrete model*, provided of course that the model is "reasonable" (which, needless to say, is a matter of intuition). The foregoing text reflects the tension between the need to make rigorous definitions and the desire to be independent of technical choices, which are unavoidable when making rigorous definitions. It also reflects the fact that, by their fundamental nature, the questions that we address are quite model-independent (i.e., are independent of various technical choices). Note that we do not deny the existence of model-dependent

---

[4]We admit that a very natural computational problem can give rise to a class of problems that are computationally equivalent to it, and that in such a case the class may be less interesting than the original problem. This is not the case for any of the complexity classes presented in this book. Still, in some cases (e.g., $\mathcal{NP}$ and $\#\mathcal{P}$), the historical evolution actually went from a specific computational problem to a class of problems that are computationally equivalent to it. However, in all cases presented in this book, a retrospective evaluation of the material suggests that the class is actually more important than the original problem.

questions, but rather avoid addressing such questions and view them as less fundamental in nature. In contrast to common beliefs, the foregoing comments refer not only to time complexity but also to space complexity. However, in both cases, the claim of invariance may not hold for marginally small resources (e.g., linear time or sub-logarithmic space).

In contrast to the foregoing paragraph, in some cases we choose to be specific. The most notorious case is the association of efficiency with polynomial-time complexity (see §1.2.3.5). Indeed, all the questions and answers regarding efficient computation can be phrased without referring to polynomial-time complexity (i.e., by stating explicit functional relations between the complexities of the problems involved), but such a generalized treatment will be painful to follow.

1.1.4.3. On the Presentation of Technical Details

In general, the more complex the technical material is, the more levels of expositions we employ (starting from the most high-level exposition, and when necessary providing more than one level of details). In particular, whenever a proof is not very simple, we try to present the key ideas first, and postpone implementation details to later. We also try to clearly indicate the passage from a high-level presentation to its implementation details (e.g., by using phrases such as "details follow"). In some cases, especially in the case of advanced results, only proof sketches are provided and the implication is that the reader should be able to fill up the missing details.

Few results are stated without a proof. In some of these cases the proof idea or a proof overview is provided, but the reader is *not* expected to be able to fill up the highly nontrivial details. (In these cases, the text clearly indicates this state of affairs.) One notable example is the proof of the PCP Theorem (9.16).

We tried to avoid the presentation of material that, in our opinion, neither is the "last word" on the subject nor represents the "right" way of approaching the subject. Thus, we do not always present the "best" known result.

1.1.4.4. Organizational Principles

Each of the main chapters starts with a high-level summary and ends with chapter notes and exercises. The latter are not aimed at testing or inspiring creativity, but are rather designed to help verify the basic understanding of the main text. In some cases, exercises (augmented by adequate guidelines) are used for presenting additional related material.

The book contains material that ranges from topics currently taught in undergraduate courses (on computability and basic Complexity Theory) to topics currently taught mostly in advanced graduate courses. Although this situation may (and hopefully will) change in the future so that undergraduates will enjoy greater exposure to Complexity Theory, we believe that it will continue to be the case that typical readers of the advanced chapters will be more sophisticated than typical readers of the basic chapters (i.e., Section 1.2 and Chapter 2). Accordingly, the style of presentation becomes more sophisticated as one progresses from Chapter 2 to later chapters.

As stated in the preface, this book focuses on the high-level approach to Complexity Theory, whereas the low-level approach (i.e., lower bounds) is only briefly reviewed in Appendix B. Other appendices contain material that is closely related to Complexity Theory but is not an integral part of it (e.g., the foundations of cryptography).[5] Further details on the contents of the various chapters and appendices are provided in Section 1.1.3.

In an attempt to keep the bibliographic list from becoming longer than an average chapter, we omitted many relevant references. One trick used toward this end is referring to lists of references in other texts, especially when the latter are cited anyhow. Indeed, our choices of references were biased in favor of textbooks and survey articles, because we believe that they provide the best way to further learn about a research direction and/or approach. We tried, however, not to omit references to key papers in an area. In some cases, when we needed a reference for a result of interest and could not resort to the aforementioned trick, we also cited less central papers.

As a matter of policy, we tried to avoid references and credits in the main text. The few exceptions are either pointers to texts that provide details that we chose to omit or usage of terms (bearing researchers' names) that are too popular to avoid. In general, in each chapter, references and credits are provided in the chapter's notes.

> **Teaching note:** The text also includes some teaching notes, which are typeset as this one. Some of these notes express quite opinionated recommendations and/or justify various expositional choices made in the text.

1.1.4.5. A Call for Tolerance

This book attempts to accommodate a wide variety of readers, ranging from readers with no prior knowledge of Complexity Theory to experts in the field. This attempt is reflected in tailoring the presentation, in each part of the book, for the readers with the least background who are expected to read this part. However, in a few cases, advanced comments that are mostly directed at more advanced readers could not be avoided. Thus, readers with more background may skip some details, while readers with less background may ignore some advanced comments. An attempt was made to facilitate such selective reading by an adequate labeling of the text, but in many places the readers are expected to exercise their own judgment (and tolerate the fact that they are asked to invest some extra effort in order to accommodate the interests of other types of readers).

We stress that the different parts of the book do envision different ranges of possible readers. Specifically, while Section 1.2 and Chapter 2 are intended mainly for readers with no background in Complexity Theory (and even no background in computability), the subsequent chapters do assume such basic background. In addition to familiarity with the basic material, the more advanced parts of the book also assume a higher level of technical sophistication.

1.1.4.6. Additional Comments Regarding Motivation

The author's guess is that the text will be criticized for lengthy discussions of technically trivial issues. Indeed, most researchers dismiss various conceptual clarifications as being

---

[5]As further articulated in Section 7.1, we recommend not including a basic treatment of cryptography within a course on Complexity Theory. Indeed, cryptography may be claimed to be the most appealing application of Complexity Theory, but a superficial treatment of cryptography (from this perspective) is likely to be misleading and cause more harm than good.

trivial and devote all their attention to the technically challenging parts of the material. The consequence is students who master the technical material but are confused about its meaning. In contrast, the author recommends not being embarrassed at devoting time to conceptual clarifications, even if some students may view them as obvious.

The motivational discussions presented in the text do not necessarily represent the original motivation of the researchers who pioneered a specific study and/or contributed greatly to it. Instead, these discussions provide what the author considers to be a good motivation and/or a good perspective on the corresponding concepts.

1.1.5. Standard Notations and Other Conventions

Following are some notations and conventions that are freely used in this book.

Standard asymptotic notation: When referring to integral functions, we use the standard asymptotic notation; that is, for $f, g : \mathbb{N} \to \mathbb{N}$, we write $f = O(g)$ (resp., $f = \Omega(g)$) if there exists a constant $c > 0$ such that $f(n) \leq c \cdot g(n)$ (resp., $f(n) \geq c \cdot g(n)$) holds for all $n \in \mathbb{N}$. We usually denote by "poly" an unspecified polynomial, and write $f(n) = \text{poly}(n)$ instead of "there exists a polynomial p such that $f(n) \leq p(n)$ for all $n \in \mathbb{N}$." We also use the notation $f = \widetilde{O}(g)$ that means $f(n) = \text{poly}(\log n) \cdot g(n)$, and $f = o(g)$ (resp., $f = \omega(g)$) that means $f(n) < c \cdot g(n)$ (resp., $f(n) > c \cdot g(n)$) for every constant $c > 0$ and all sufficiently large n.

Integrality issues: Typically, we ignore integrality issues. This means that we may assume that $\log_2 n$ is an integer rather than using a more cumbersome form as $\lfloor \log_2 n \rfloor$. Likewise, we may assume that various equalities are satisfied by integers (e.g., $2^n = m^m$), even when this cannot possibly be the case (e.g., $2^n = 3^m$). In all these cases, one should consider integers that approximately satisfy the relevant equations (and deal with the problems that emerge by such approximations, which will be ignored in the current text).

Standard combinatorial and graph theory terms and notation: For any set S, we denote by 2^S the set of all subsets of S (i.e., $2^S = \{S' : S' \subseteq S\}$). For a natural number $n \in \mathbb{N}$, we denote $[n] \stackrel{\text{def}}{=} \{1, \ldots, n\}$. Many of the computational problems that we mention refer to finite (undirected) graphs. Such a graph, denoted $G = (V, E)$, consists of a set of vertices, denoted V, and a set of edges, denoted E, which are unordered pairs of vertices. By default, graphs are undirected, whereas directed graphs consist of vertices and directed edges, where a directed edge is an order pair of vertices. We also refer to other graph-theoretic terms such as connectivity, being acyclic (i.e., having no simple cycles), being a tree (i.e., being connected and acyclic), k-colorability, etc. For further background on graphs and computational problems regarding graphs, the reader is referred to Appendix G.1.

Typographic conventions: We denote formally defined complexity classes by calligraphic letters (e.g., $\mathcal{NP}$), but we do so only after defining these classes. Furthermore, when we wish to maintain some ambiguity regarding the specific formulation of a class of problems we use Roman font (e.g., NP may denote either a class of search problems or a class of decision problems). Likewise, we denote formally defined computational problems by typewriter font (e.g., SAT). In contrast, generic problems and algorithms will be denoted by *italic* font.

1.2. Computational Tasks and Models

> *But, you may say, we asked you to speak about women and fiction –*
> *what, has that got to do with a room of one's own? I will try to explain.*
>
> Virginia Woolf, *A Room of One's Own*

This section provides the necessary preliminaries for the rest of the book; that is, we discuss the notion of a computational task and present computational models (for describing methods) for solving such tasks. We start by introducing the general framework for our discussion of computational tasks (or problems): This framework refers to the *representation of instances* (as binary sequences) and focuses on *two types of tasks* (i.e., searching for solutions and making decisions). In order to facilitate a study of methods for solving such tasks, the latter are defined with respect to infinitely many possible instances (each being a finite object).[6]

Once computational tasks are defined, we turn to methods for solving such tasks, which are described in terms of some *model of computation*. The description of such models is the main contents of this section. Specifically, we consider two types of models of computation: uniform models and non-uniform models. The *uniform models correspond to the intuitive notion of an algorithm*, and will provide the stage for the rest of the book (which focuses on efficient algorithms). In contrast, non-uniform models (e.g., Boolean circuits) facilitate a closer look at the way a computation progresses, and will be used only sporadically in this book.

Organization of Section 1.2. Sections 1.2.1–1.2.3 correspond to the contents of a traditional *computability course*, except that our presentation emphasizes some aspects and deemphasizes others. In particular, the presentation highlights the notion of a universal machine (see §1.2.3.4), justifies the association of efficient computation with polynomial-time algorithms (§1.2.3.5), and provides a definition of oracle machines (§1.2.3.6). This material (with the exception of Kolmogorov Complexity) is taken for granted in the rest of the current book. In contrast, Section 1.2.4 presents basic preliminaries regarding non-uniform models of computation (i.e., various types of Boolean circuits), and these are only used lightly in the rest of the book. (We also call the reader's attention to the discussion of generic complexity classes in Section 1.2.5.) Thus, whereas Sections 1.2.1–1.2.3 (and 1.2.5) are absolute prerequisites for the rest of this book, Section 1.2.4 is not.

Teaching note: The author believes that there is no real need for a semester-long course in computability (i.e., a course that focuses on what can be computed rather than on what can be computed efficiently). Instead, undergraduates should take a course in Computational Complexity, which should contain the computability aspects that serve as a basis for the rest of the course. Specifically, the former aspects should occupy at most 25% of the course, and the focus should be on basic complexity issues (captured by P, NP, and NP-completeness) augmented by a selection of some more advanced material. Indeed, such a course can be based on Chapters 1 and 2 of the current book (augmented by a selection of some topics from other chapters).

---

[6]The comparison of different methods seems to require the consideration of infinitely many possible instances; otherwise, the choice of the language in which the methods are described may totally dominate and even distort the discussion (cf. the discussion of Kolmogorov Complexity in §1.2.3.4).

1.2.1. Representation

In mathematics and related sciences, it is customary to discuss objects without specifying their representation. This is not possible in the theory of computation, where the representation of objects plays a central role. In a sense, a computation merely transforms one representation of an object to another representation of the same object. In particular, a computation designed to solve some problem merely transforms the problem instance to its solution, where the latter can be thought of as a (possibly partial) representation of the instance. Indeed, the answer to any fully specified question is implicit in the question itself, and computation is employed to make this answer explicit.

Computational tasks refers to objects that are represented in some canonical way, where such canonical representation provides an "explicit" and "full" (but not "overly redundant") description of the corresponding object. We will consider only *finite* objects like numbers, sets, graphs, and functions (and keep distinguishing these types of objects although, actually, they are all equivalent). While the representation of numbers, sets, and functions is quite straightforward, we refer the reader to Appendix G.1 for a discussion of the representation of graphs.

Strings. We consider finite objects, each represented by a finite binary sequence, called a string. For a natural number n, we denote by $\{0, 1\}^n$ the set of all strings of length n, hereafter referred to as n-bit (long) strings. The set of all strings is denoted $\{0, 1\}^*$; that is, $\{0, 1\}^* = \cup_{n \in \mathbb{N}} \{0, 1\}^n$. For $x \in \{0, 1\}^*$, we denote by $|x|$ the length of x (i.e., $x \in \{0, 1\}^{|x|}$), and often denote by x_i the ith bit of x (i.e., $x = x_1 x_2 \cdots x_{|x|}$). For $x, y \in \{0, 1\}^*$, we denote by xy the string resulting from concatenation of the strings x and y.

At times, we associate $\{0, 1\}^* \times \{0, 1\}^*$ with $\{0, 1\}^*$; the reader should merely consider an adequate encoding (e.g., the pair $(x_1 \cdots x_m, y_1 \cdots y_n) \in \{0, 1\}^* \times \{0, 1\}^*$ may be encoded by the string $x_1 x_1 \cdots x_m x_m 01 y_1 \cdots y_n \in \{0, 1\}^*$). Likewise, we may represent sequences of strings (of fixed or varying length) as single strings. When we wish to emphasize that such a sequence (or some other object) is to be considered as a single object we use the notation $\langle \cdot \rangle$ (e.g., "the pair (x, y) is encoded as the string $\langle x, y \rangle$").

Numbers. Unless stated differently, natural numbers will be encoded by their binary expansion; that is, the string $b_{n-1} \cdots b_1 b_0 \in \{0, 1\}^n$ encodes the number $\sum_{i=0}^{n-1} b_i \cdot 2^i$, where typically we assume that this representation has no leading zeros (i.e., $b_{n-1} = 1$). Rational numbers will be represented as pairs of natural numbers. In the rare cases in which one considers real numbers as part of the input to a computational problem, one actually means rational approximations of these real numbers.

Special symbols. We denote the empty string by λ (i.e., $\lambda \in \{0, 1\}^*$ and $|\lambda| = 0$), and the empty set by $\emptyset$. It will be convenient to use some special symbols that are not in $\{0, 1\}^*$. One such symbol is $\perp$, which typically denotes an indication (e.g., produced by some algorithm) that something is wrong.

1.2.2. Computational Tasks

Two fundamental types of computational tasks are the so-called search problems and decision problems. In both cases, the key notions are the problem's *instances* and the problem's specification.

1.2.2.1. Search Problems

A search problem consists of a specification of a set of valid solutions (possibly an empty one) for each possible instance. That is, given an instance, one is required to find a corresponding solution (or to determine that no such solution exists). For example, consider the problem in which one is given a system of equations and is asked to find a valid solution. Needless to say, much of computer science is concerned with solving various search problems (e.g., finding shortest paths in a graph, sorting a list of numbers, finding an occurrence of a given pattern in a given string, etc). Furthermore, search problems correspond to the daily notion of "solving a problem" (e.g., finding one's way between two locations), and thus a discussion of the possibility and complexity of solving search problems corresponds to the natural concerns of most people.

In the following definition of solving search problems, the potential solver is a function (which may be thought of as a solving strategy), and the sets of possible solutions associated with each of the various instances are "packed" into a single binary relation.

Definition 1.1 (solving a search problem): *Let $R \subseteq \{0, 1\}^* \times \{0, 1\}^*$ and $R(x) \stackrel{\text{def}}{=} \{y : (x, y) \in R\}$ denote the set of solutions for the instance x. A function $f : \{0, 1\}^* \to \{0, 1\}^* \cup \{\bot\}$ solves the search problem of R if for every x the following holds: if $R(x) \neq \emptyset$ then $f(x) \in R(x)$ and otherwise $f(x) = \bot$.*

Indeed, $R = \{(x, y) \in \{0, 1\}^* \times \{0, 1\}^* : y \in R(x)\}$, and the solver f is required to find a solution (i.e., given x output $y \in R(x)$) whenever one exists (i.e., the set $R(x)$ is not empty). It is also required that the solver f never outputs a wrong solution (i.e., if $R(x) \neq \emptyset$ then $f(x) \in R(x)$ and if $R(x) = \emptyset$ then $f(x) = \bot$), which in turn means that f indicates whether x has any solution.

A special case of interest is the case of search problems having a unique solution (for each possible instance); that is, the case that $|R(x)| = 1$ for every x. In this case, R is essentially a (total) function, and solving the search problem of R means computing (or evaluating) the function R (or rather the function R' defined by $R'(x) \stackrel{\text{def}}{=} y$ if and only if $R(x) = \{y\}$). Popular examples include sorting a sequence of numbers, multiplying integers, finding the prime factorization of a composite number, etc.

1.2.2.2. Decision Problems

A decision problem consists of a specification of a subset of the possible instances. Given an instance, one is required to determine whether the instance is in the specified set (e.g., the set of prime numbers, the set of connected graphs, or the set of sorted sequences). For example, consider the problem where one is given a natural number, and is asked to determine whether or not the number is a prime. One important case, which corresponds to the aforementioned search problems, is the case of the set of instances having a solution; that is, for any binary relation $R \subseteq \{0, 1\}^* \times \{0, 1\}^*$ we consider the set $\{x : R(x) \neq \emptyset\}$. Indeed, being able to determine whether or not a solution exists is a prerequisite to being able to solve the corresponding search problem (as per Definition 1.1). In general, decision problems refer to the natural task of making a binary decision, a task that is not uncommon in daily life (e.g., determining whether a traffic light is red). In any case, in the following definition of solving decision problems, the potential solver is again a function; that is, in this case the solver is a Boolean function, which is supposed to indicate membership in a predetermined set.

Definition 1.2 (solving a decision problem): *Let $S \subseteq \{0, 1\}^*$. A function f :* $\{0, 1\}^* \to \{0, 1\}$ solves the decision problem of S (or decides membership in S) *if for every x it holds that $f(x) = 1$ if and only if $x \in S$.*

We often identify the decision problem of S with S itself, and identify S with its characteristic function (i.e., with the function $\chi_S : \{0, 1\}^* \to \{0, 1\}$ defined such that $\chi_S(x) = 1$ if and only if $x \in S$). Note that if f solves the search problem of R then the Boolean function $f' : \{0, 1\}^* \to \{0, 1\}$ defined by $f'(x) \overset{\text{def}}{=} 1$ if and only if $f(x) \neq \perp$ solves the decision problem of $\{x : R(x) \neq \emptyset\}$.

Reflection. Most people would consider search problems to be more natural than decision problems: Typically, people seek solutions more than they stop to wonder whether or not solutions exist. Definitely, search problems are not less important than decision problems; it is merely that their study tends to require more cumbersome formulations. This is the main reason that most expositions choose to focus on decision problems. The current book attempts to devote at least a significant amount of attention also to search problems.

1.2.2.3. Promise Problems (an Advanced Comment)

Many natural search and decision problems are captured more naturally by the terminology of promise problems, in which the domain of possible instances is a subset of $\{0, 1\}^*$ rather than $\{0, 1\}^*$ itself. In particular, note that the natural formulation of many search and decision problems refers to instances of a certain type (e.g., a system of equations, a pair of numbers, a graph), whereas the natural representation of these objects uses only a strict subset of $\{0, 1\}^*$. For the time being, we ignore this issue, but we shall revisit it in Section 2.4.1. Here we just note that, in typical cases, the issue can be ignored by postulating that every string represents some legitimate object (e.g., each string that is not used in the natural representation of these objects is postulated as a representation of some fixed object).

1.2.3. Uniform Models (Algorithms)

Science is One.
Laci Lovász (according to Silvio Micali, ca. 1990)

We finally reach the heart of the current section (Section 1.2), which is the definition of uniform models of computation. We are all familiar with computers and with the ability of computer programs to manipulate data. This familiarity seems to be rooted in the positive side of computing; that is, we have some experience regarding some things that computers can do. In contrast, Complexity Theory is focused at what computers cannot do, or rather with drawing the line between what can be done and what cannot be done. Drawing such a line requires a precise formulation of *all* possible computational processes; that is, we should have a clear model of *all* possible computational processes (rather than some familiarity with some computational processes).

1.2.3.1. Overview and General Principles

Before being formal, let we offer a general and abstract description, which is aimed at capturing any artificial as well as natural process. Indeed, artificial processes will be associated with computers, whereas by natural processes we mean (attempts to model) the "mechanical" aspects of the natural reality (be it physical, biological, or even social).

A computation is a process that modifies an environment via repeated applications of a predetermined rule. The key restriction is that this rule is *simple*: In each application it depends on and affects only a (small) portion of the environment, called the active zone. We contrast the *a priori bounded* size of the active zone (and of the modification rule) with the *a priori unbounded* size of the entire environment. We note that, although each application of the rule has a very limited effect, the effect of many applications of the rule may be very complex. Put in other words, a computation may modify the relevant environment in a very complex way, although it is merely a process of repeatedly applying a simple rule.

As hinted, the notion of computation can be used to model the "mechanical" aspects of the natural reality, that is, the rules that determine the evolution of the reality (rather than the specific state of the reality at a specific time). In this case, the starting point of the study is the actual evolution process that takes place in the natural reality, and the goal of the study is finding the (computation) rule that underlies this natural process. In a sense, the goal of science at large can be phrased as finding (simple) rules that govern various aspects of reality (or rather one's abstraction of these aspects of reality).

Our focus, however, is on artificial computation rules designed by humans in order to achieve specific desired effects on a corresponding artificial environment. Thus, our starting point is a desired functionality, and our aim is to design computation rules that effect it. Such a computation rule is referred to as an algorithm. Loosely speaking, an algorithm corresponds to a computer program written in a high-level (abstract) programming language. Let us elaborate.

We are interested in the transformation of the environment as affected by the computational process (or the algorithm). Throughout (most of) this book, we will assume that, *when invoked on any finite initial environment, the computation halts after a finite number of steps*. Typically, the initial environment to which the computation is applied encodes an input string, and the end environment (i.e., at the termination of the computation) encodes an output string. We consider the mapping from inputs to outputs induced by the computation; that is, for each possible input x, we consider the output y obtained at the end of a computation initiated with input x, and say that the computation maps input x to output y. Thus, a computation rule (or an algorithm) determines a function (computed by it): This function is exactly the aforementioned mapping of inputs to outputs.

In the rest of this book (i.e., outside the current chapter), we will also consider the number of steps (i.e., applications of the rule) taken by the computation on each possible input. The latter function is called the time complexity of the computational process (or algorithm). While time complexity is defined per input, we will often consider it per input length, taking the maximum over all inputs of the same length.

In order to define computation (and computation time) rigorously, one needs to specify some model of computation, that is, provide a concrete definition of environments and a class of rules that may be applied to them. Such a model corresponds to an abstraction of a real computer (be it a PC, mainframe, or network of computers). One simple abstract model that is commonly used is that of *Turing machines* (see, §1.2.3.2). Thus, specific algorithms are typically formalized by corresponding Turing machines (and their time complexity is represented by the time complexity of the corresponding Turing machines). We stress, however, that most results in the theory of computation hold regardless of the specific computational model used, as long as it is "reasonable" (i.e., satisfies the aforementioned simplicity condition and can perform some apparently simple computations).

What is being computed? The foregoing discussion has implicitly referred to algorithms (i.e., computational processes) as means of computing functions. Specifically, an algorithm A computes the function $f_A : \{0, 1\}^* \to \{0, 1\}^*$ defined by $f_A(x) = y$ if, when invoked on input x, algorithm A halts with output y. However, algorithms can also serve as means of "solving search problems" or "making decisions" (as in Definitions 1.1 and 1.2). Specifically, we will say that algorithm A solves the search problem of R (resp., decides membership in S) if f_A solves the search problem of R (resp., decides membership in S). In the rest of this exposition we associate the algorithm A with the function f_A computed by it; that is, we write $A(x)$ instead of $f_A(x)$. For the sake of future reference, we summarize the foregoing discussion.

> **Definition 1.3** (algorithms as problem solvers): *We denote by $A(x)$ the output of algorithm A on input x. Algorithm A* solves the search problem R (resp., the decision problem S) *if A, viewed as a function, solves R (resp., S).*

Organization of the rest of Section 1.2.3. In §1.2.3.2 we provide a rough description of the model of Turing machines. This is done merely for the sake of providing a concrete model that supports the study of computation and its complexity, whereas most of the material in this book will not depend on the specifics of this model. In §1.2.3.3 and §1.2.3.4 we discuss two fundamental properties of any reasonable model of computation: the existence of uncomputable functions and the existence of universal computations. The time (and space) complexity of computation is defined in §1.2.3.5. We also discuss oracle machines and restricted models of computation (in §1.2.3.6 and §1.2.3.7, respectively).

1.2.3.2. A Concrete Model: Turing Machines

The model of Turing machines offers a relatively simple formulation of the notion of an algorithm. The fact that the model is very simple complicates the design of machines that solve problems of interest, but makes the analysis of such machines simpler. Since the focus of Complexity Theory is on the analysis of machines and not on their design, the trade-off offered by this model is suitable for our purposes. We stress again that the model is merely used as a concrete formulation of the intuitive notion of an algorithm, whereas we actually care about the intuitive notion and not about its formulation. In particular, all results mentioned in this book hold for any other "reasonable" formulation of the notion of an algorithm.

The model of Turing machines is not meant to provide an accurate (or "tight") model of real-life computers, but rather to capture their inherent limitations and abilities (i.e., a computational task can be solved by a real-life computer if and only if it can be solved by a Turing machine). In comparison to real-life computers, the model of Turing machines is extremely oversimplified and abstracts away many issues that are of great concern to computer practice. However, these issues are irrelevant to the higher-level questions addressed by Complexity Theory. Indeed, as usual, good practice requires more refined understanding than the one provided by a good theory, but one should first provide the latter.

Historically, the model of Turing machines was invented before modern computers were even built, and was meant to provide a concrete model of computation and a definition

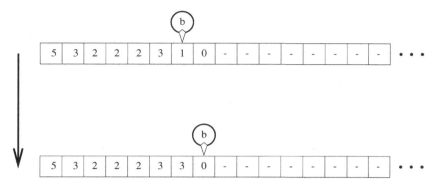

Figure 1.2: A single step by a Turing machine.

of computable functions.[7] Indeed, this concrete model clarified fundamental properties of computable functions and plays a key role in defining the complexity of computable functions.

The model of Turing machines was envisioned as an abstraction of the process of an algebraic computation carried out by a human using a sheet of paper. In such a process, at each time, the human looks at some location on the paper, and depending on what he/she sees and what he/she has in mind (which is little . . .), he/she modifies the contents of this location and shifts his/her look to an adjacent location.

The Actual Model. Following is a high-level description of the model of Turing machines; the interested reader is referred to standard textbooks (e.g., [208]) for further details. Recall that we need to specify the set of possible environments, the set of machines (or computation rules), and the effect of applying such a rule on an environment.

- The main component in the *environment* of a Turing machine is an infinite sequence of cells, each capable of holding a single symbol (i.e., member of a finite set $\Sigma \supset \{0, 1\}$). This sequence is envisioned as starting at a leftmost cell, and extending infinitely to the right (cf. Figure 1.2). In addition, the environment contains the current location of the machine on this sequence, and the internal state of the machine (which is a member of a finite set Q). The aforementioned sequence of cells is called the tape, and its contents combined with the machine's location and its internal state is called the instantaneous configuration of the machine.

- The main component in the *Turing machine itself* is a finite rule (i.e., a finite function), called the transition function, which is defined over the set of all possible symbol-state pairs. Specifically, the transition function is a mapping from $\Sigma \times Q$ to $\Sigma \times Q \times \{-1, 0, +1\}$, where $\{-1, +1, 0\}$ correspond to a movement instruction (which is either "left" or "right" or "stay," respectively). In addition, the machine's description specifies an initial state and a halting state, and the computation of the machine halts when the machine enters its halting state.[8]

---

[7]In contrast, the abstract definition of "recursive functions" yields a class of "computable" functions without referring to any model of computation (but rather based on the intuition that any such model should support recursive functional composition).

[8]Envisioning the tape as in Figure 1.2, we also use the convention that if the machine tries to move left of the end of the tape then it is considered to have halted.

We stress that, in contrast to the finite description of the machine, the tape has an a priori unbounded length (and is considered, for simplicity, as being infinite).

* A single *computation step* of such a Turing machine depends on its current location on the tape, on the contents of the corresponding cell, and on the internal state of the machine. Based on the latter two elements, the transition function determines a new symbol-state pair as well as a movement instruction (i.e., "left" or "right" or "stay"). The machine modifies the contents of the said cell and its internal state accordingly, and moves as directed. That is, suppose that the machine is in state q and resides in a cell containing the symbol σ, and suppose that the transition function maps (σ, q) to (σ', q', D). Then, the machine modifies the contents of the said cell to σ', modifies its internal state to q', and moves one cell in direction D. Figure 1.2 shows a single step of a Turing machine that, when in state 'b' and seeing a binary symbol σ, replaces σ with the symbol $\sigma + 2$, maintains its internal state, and moves one position to the right.[9]

  Formally, we define the successive configuration function that maps each instantaneous configuration to the one resulting by letting the machine take a single step. This function modifies its argument in a very minor manner, as described in the foregoing; that is, the contents of at most one cell (i.e., at which the machine currently resides) is changed, and in addition the internal state of the machine and its location may change, too.

The initial environment (or configuration) of a Turing machine consists of the machine residing in the first (i.e., leftmost) cell and being in its initial state. Typically, one also mandates that, in the initial configuration, a prefix of the tape's cells hold bit values, which concatenated together are considered the input, and the rest of the tape's cells hold a special symbol (which in Figure 1.2 is denoted by '-'). Once the machine halts, the output is defined as the contents of the cells that are to the left of its location (at termination time).[10] Thus, each machine defines a function mapping inputs to outputs, called the function computed by the machine.

Multi-tape Turing machines. We comment that in most expositions, one refers to the location of the "head of the machine" on the tape (rather than to the "location of the machine on the tape"). The standard terminology is more intuitive when extending the basic model, which refers to a single tape, to a model that supports a constant number of tapes. In the corresponding model of so-called multi-tape machines, the machine maintains a single head on each such tape, and each step of the machine depends on and affects the cells that are at the machine's head location on each tape. As we shall see in Chapter 5 (and in §1.2.3.5), the extension of the model to multi-tape Turing machines is crucial to the definition of space complexity. A less fundamental advantage of the model of multi-tape Turing machines is that it facilitates the design of machines that compute functions of interest.

---

[9]Figure 1.2 corresponds to a machine that, when in the initial state (i.e., 'a'), replaces the symbol σ by $\sigma + 4$, modifies its internal state to 'b', and moves one position to the right. Indeed, "marking" the leftmost cell (in order to allow for recognizing it in the future) is a common practice in the design of Turing machines.

[10]By an alternative convention, the machine halts while residing in the leftmost cell, and the output is defined as the maximal prefix of the tape contents that contains only bit values.

> **Teaching note:** We strongly recommend avoiding the standard practice of teaching the student to program with Turing machines. These exercises seem very painful and pointless. Instead, one should prove that the Turing machine model is exactly as powerful as a model that is closer to a real-life computer (see the following "sanity check"); that is, a function can be computed by a Turing machine if and only if it is computable by a machine of the latter model. For starters, one may prove that a function can be computed by a single-tape Turing machine if and only if it is computable by a multi-tape (e.g., two-tape) Turing machine.

The Church-Turing Thesis. The entire point of the model of Turing machines is its simplicity. That is, in comparison to more "realistic" models of computation, it is simpler to formulate the model of Turing machines and to analyze machines in this model. The Church-Turing Thesis asserts that nothing is lost by considering the Turing machine model: *A function can be computed by some Turing machine if and only if it can be computed by some machine of any other* "reasonable and general" *model of computation.*

This is a thesis, rather than a theorem, because it refers to an intuitive notion (i.e., the notion of a *reasonable and general model of computation*) that is left undefined on purpose. The model should be reasonable in the sense that it should allow only computation rules that are "simple" in some intuitive sense. For example, we should be able to envision a mechanical implementation of these computation rules. On the other hand, the model should allow for computation of "simple" functions that are definitely computable according to our intuition. At the very least the model should allow for emulation of Turing machines (i.e., computation of the function that, given a description of a Turing machine and an instantaneous configuration, returns the successive configuration).

A philosophical comment. The fact that a thesis is used to link an intuitive concept to a formal definition is common practice in any science (or, more broadly, in any attempt to reason rigorously about intuitive concepts). Any attempt to rigorously define an intuitive concept yields a formal definition that necessarily differs from the original intuition, and the question of correspondence between these two objects arises. This question can never be rigorously treated, because one of the objects that it relates to is undefined. That is, the question of correspondence between the intuition and the definition always transcends a rigorous treatment (i.e., it always belongs to the domain of the intuition).

A sanity check: Turing machines can emulate an abstract RAM. To gain confidence in the Church-Turing Thesis, one may attempt to define an abstract random-access machine (RAM), and verify that it can be emulated by a Turing machine. An abstract RAM consists of an infinite number of memory cells, each capable of holding an integer, a finite number of similar registers, one designated as program counter, and a program consisting of instructions selected from a finite set. The set of possible instructions includes the following instructions:

- reset(r), where r is an index of a register, results in setting the value of register r to zero;
- inc(r), where r is an index of a register, results in incrementing the content of register r. Similarly dec(r) causes a decrement;

- load(r_1, r_2), where r_1 and r_2 are indices of registers, results in loading to register r_1 the contents of the memory location m, where m is the current contents of register r_2;
- store(r_1, r_2), stores the contents of register r_1 in the memory, analogously to load;
- cond-goto(r, ℓ), where r is an index of a register and ℓ does not exceed the program length, results in setting the program counter to $\ell - 1$ if the content of register r is non-negative.

The program counter is incremented after the execution of each instruction, and the next instruction to be executed by the machine is the one to which the program counter points (and the machine halts if the program counter exceeds the program's length). The input to the machine may be defined as the contents of the first n memory cells, where n is placed in a special input register.

We note that, as stated, the abstract RAM model is as powerful as the Turing machine model (see the following details). However, in order to make the RAM model closer to real-life computers, we may augment it with additional instructions that are available on real-life computers like the instruction add(r_1, r_2) (resp., mult(r_1, r_2)) that results in adding (resp., multiplying) the contents of registers r_1 and r_2 (and placing the result in register r_1). We suggest proving that *this abstract RAM can be emulated by a Turing machine*.[11] (Hint: note that during the emulation, we only need to hold the input, the contents of all registers, and the contents of the memory cells that were accessed during the computation.)[12]

Reflections: Observe that the abstract RAM model is significantly more cumbersome than the Turing machine model. Furthermore, seeking a sound choice of the instruction set (i.e., the instructions to be allowed in the model) creates a vicious cycle (because the sound guideline for such a choice should have been allowing only instructions that correspond to "simple" operations, whereas the latter correspond to easily computable functions . . .). This vicious cycle was avoided in the foregoing paragraph by trusting the reader to include only instructions that are available in some real-life computer. (We comment that this empirical consideration is justifiable in the current context, because our current goal is merely linking the Turing machine model with the reader's experience of real-life computers.)

1.2.3.3. Uncomputable Functions

Strictly speaking, the current subsection is not necessary for the rest of this book, but we feel that it provides a useful perspective.

In contrast to what every layman would think, we know that not all functions are computable. Indeed, an important message to be communicated to the world is that *not every well-defined task can be solved* by applying a "reasonable" automated procedure (i.e., a procedure that has a simple description that can be applied to any instance of the problem at hand). Furthermore, not only is it the case that there exist uncomputable

---

[11]We emphasize this direction of the equivalence of the two models, because the RAM model is introduced in order to convince the reader that Turing machines are not too weak (as a model of general computation). The fact that they are not too strong seems self-evident. Thus, it seems pointless to prove that the RAM model can emulate Turing machines. Still, note that this is indeed the case, by using the RAM's memory cells to store the contents of the cells of the Turing machine's tape.

[12]Thus, at each time, the Turning machine's tape contains a list of the RAM's memory cells that were accessed so far as well as their current contents. When we emulate a RAM instruction, we first check whether the relevant RAM cell appears on this list, and augment the list by a corresponding entry or modify this entry as needed.

functions, but it is also the case that most functions are uncomputable. In fact, only relatively few functions are computable.

Theorem 1.4 (on the scarcity of computable functions): *The set of computable functions is countable, whereas the set of all functions* (from strings to string) *has cardinality* $\aleph$.

We stress that the theorem holds for any reasonable model of computation. In fact, it only relies on the postulate that each machine in the model has a finite description (i.e., can be described by a string).

Proof: Since each computable function is computable by a machine that has a finite description, there is a 1–1 correspondence between the set of computable functions and the set of strings (which in turn is in 1–1 correspondence to the natural numbers). On the other hand, there is a 1–1 correspondence between the set of Boolean functions (i.e., functions from strings to a single bit) and the set of real number in $[0, 1)$. This correspondence associates each real $r \in [0, 1)$ to the function $f : \mathbb{N} \to \{0, 1\}$ such that $f(i)$ is the ith bit in the infinite binary expansion of r. ∎

The Halting Problem: In contrast to the discussion in §1.2.3.1, at this point we also consider machines that may not halt on some inputs. (The functions computed by such machines are partial functions that are defined only on inputs on which the machine halts.) Again, we rely on the postulate that each machine in the model has a finite description, and denote the description of machine M by $\langle M \rangle \in \{0, 1\}^*$. The halting function, $\mathrm{h} : \{0, 1\}^* \times \{0, 1\}^* \to \{0, 1\}$, is defined such that $\mathrm{h}(\langle M \rangle, x) \overset{\text{def}}{=} 1$ if and only if M halts on input x. The following result goes beyond Theorem 1.4 by pointing to an explicit function (of natural interest) that is not computable.

Theorem 1.5 (undecidability of the halting problem): *The halting function is not computable.*

The term undecidability means that the corresponding decision problem cannot be solved by an algorithm. That is, Theorem 1.5 asserts that the decision problem associated with the set $\mathrm{h}^{-1}(1) = \{(\langle M \rangle, x) : \mathrm{h}(\langle M \rangle, x) = 1\}$ is not solvable by an algorithm (i.e., there exists no algorithm that, given a pair $(\langle M \rangle, x)$, decides whether or not M halts on input x). Actually, the following proof shows that there exists no algorithm that, given $\langle M \rangle$, decides whether or not M halts on input $\langle M \rangle$.

Proof: We will show that even the restriction of h to its "diagonal" (i.e., the function $\mathrm{d}(\langle M \rangle) \overset{\text{def}}{=} \mathrm{h}(\langle M \rangle, \langle M \rangle)$) is not computable. Note that the value of $\mathrm{d}(\langle M \rangle)$ refers to the question of what happens when we feed M with its own description, which is indeed a "nasty" (but legitimate) thing to do. We will actually do something "worse": toward the contradiction, we will consider the value of d when evaluated at a (machine that is related to a) hypothetical machine that supposedly computes d.

We start by considering a related function, d', and showing that this function is uncomputable. The function d' is defined on purpose so as to foil any attempt to compute it; that is, for every machine M, the value $d'(\langle M \rangle)$ is defined to differ from $M(\langle M \rangle)$. Specifically, the function $d' : \{0, 1\}^* \to \{0, 1\}$ is defined such that $d'(\langle M \rangle) \stackrel{\text{def}}{=} 1$ *if and only if M halts on input $\langle M \rangle$ with output 0.* (That is, $d'(\langle M \rangle) = 0$ if either M does not halt on input $\langle M \rangle$ or its output does not equal the value 0.) Now, suppose, toward the contradiction, that d' is computable by some machine, denoted $M_{d'}$. Note that machine $M_{d'}$ is supposed to halt on every input, and so $M_{d'}$ halts on input $\langle M_{d'} \rangle$. But, by definition of d', it holds that $d'(\langle M_{d'} \rangle) = 1$ if and only if $M_{d'}$ halts on input $\langle M_{d'} \rangle$ with output 0 (i.e., if and only if $M_{d'}(\langle M_{d'} \rangle) = 0$). Thus, $M_{d'}(\langle M_{d'} \rangle) \neq d'(\langle M_{d'} \rangle)$ in contradiction to the hypothesis that $M_{d'}$ computes d'.

We next prove that d is uncomputable, and thus h is uncomputable (because $d(z) = h(z, z)$ for every z). To prove that d is uncomputable, we show that if d is computable then so is d' (which we already know not to be the case). Indeed, suppose toward the contradiction that A is an algorithm for computing d (i.e., $A(\langle M \rangle) = d(\langle M \rangle)$ for every machine M). Then we construct an algorithm for computing d', which given $\langle M' \rangle$, invokes A on $\langle M'' \rangle$, where M'' is defined to operate as follows:

1. On input x, machine M'' emulates M' on input x.
2. If M' halts on input x with output 0 then M'' halts.
3. If M' halts on input x with an output different from 0 then M'' enters an infinite loop (and thus does not halt).
4. Otherwise (i.e., M' does not halt on input x), then machine M'' does not halt (because it just stays stuck in Step 1 forever).

Note that the mapping from $\langle M' \rangle$ to $\langle M'' \rangle$ is easily computable (by augmenting M' with instructions to test its output and enter an infinite loop if necessary), and that $d(\langle M'' \rangle) = d'(\langle M' \rangle)$, because M'' halts on x if and only if M'' halts on x with output 0. We thus derived an algorithm for computing d' (i.e., transform the input $\langle M' \rangle$ into $\langle M'' \rangle$ and output $A(\langle M'' \rangle)$), which contradicts the already established fact by which d' is uncomputable. ∎

Turing-reductions. The core of the second part of the proof of Theorem 1.5 is an algorithm that solves one problem (i.e., computes d') by using as a subroutine an algorithm that solves another problem (i.e., computes d (or h)). In fact, the first algorithm is actually an algorithmic scheme that refers to a "functionally specified" subroutine rather than to an actual (implementation of such a) subroutine, which may not exist. Such an algorithmic scheme is called a Turing-reduction (see formulation in §1.2.3.6). Hence, we have Turing-reduced the computation of d' to the computation of d, which in turn Turing-reduces to h. The "natural" ("positive") meaning of a Turing-reduction of f' to f is that, when given an algorithm for computing f, we obtain an algorithm for computing f'. In contrast, the proof of Theorem 1.5 uses the "unnatural" ("negative") counter-positive: If (as we know) there exists no algorithm for computing $f' = d'$ then there exists no algorithm for computing $f = d$ (which is what we wanted to prove). Jumping ahead, we mention that resource-bounded Turing-reductions (e.g., polynomial-time reductions) play a central role in Complexity Theory itself, and again they are used mostly in a "negative" way. We will define such reductions and extensively use them in subsequent chapters.

Rice's Theorem. The undecidability of the halting problem (or rather the fact that the function d is uncomputable) is a special case of a more general phenomenon: Every non-trivial decision problem *regarding the function computed by a given Turing machine* has no algorithmic solution. We state this fact next, clarifying the definition of the aforementioned class of problems. (Again, we refer to Turing machines that may not halt on all inputs.)

Theorem 1.6 (Rice's Theorem): *Let $\mathcal{F}$ be any non-trivial subset[13] of the set of all computable partial functions, and let $S_{\mathcal{F}}$ be the set of strings that describe machines that compute functions in $\mathcal{F}$. Then deciding membership in $S_{\mathcal{F}}$ cannot be solved by an algorithm.*

Theorem 1.6 can be proved by a Turing-reduction from d. We do not provide a proof because this is too remote from the main subject matter of the book. We stress that Theorems 1.5 and 1.6 hold for any reasonable model of computation (referring both to the potential solvers and to the machines the description of which is given as input to these solvers). Thus, Theorem 1.6 means that *no algorithm can determine any non-trivial property of the function computed by a given computer program* (written in any programming language). For example, *no algorithm can determine whether or not a given computer program halts on each possible input.* The relevance of this assertion to the project of program verification is obvious.

The Post Correspondence Problem. We mention that undecidability arises also outside of the domain of questions regarding computing devices (given as input). Specifically, we consider the Post Correspondence Problem in which the input consists of two sequences of strings, $(\alpha_1, \ldots, \alpha_k)$ and $(\beta_1, \ldots, \beta_k)$, and the question is whether or not there exists a sequence of indices $i_1, \ldots, i_\ell \in \{1, \ldots, k\}$ such that $\alpha_{i_1} \cdots \alpha_{i_\ell} = \beta_{i_1} \cdots \beta_{i_\ell}$. (We stress that the length of this sequence is *not a priori bounded*.)[14]

Theorem 1.7: *The Post Correspondence Problem is undecidable.*

Again, the omitted proof is by a Turing-reduction from d (or h).[15]

1.2.3.4. Universal Algorithms

So far we have used the postulate that, in any reasonable model of computation, each machine (or computation rule) has a finite description. Furthermore, we also used the fact that such model should allow for the easy modification of such descriptions such that the resulting machine computes an easily related function (see the proof of Theorem 1.5). Here we go one step further and postulate that the description of machines (in this model) is "effective" in the following natural sense: There exists an algorithm that, given a description of a machine (resp., computation rule) and a corresponding environment, determines the environment that results from performing a single step of this machine on

---

[13]The set S is called a non-trivial subset of U if both S and $U \setminus S$ are non-empty. Clearly, if $\mathcal{F}$ is a trivial set of computable functions then the corresponding decision problem can be solved by a "trivial" algorithm that outputs the corresponding constant bit.

[14]In contrast, the existence of an adequate sequence of a specified length can be determined in time that is exponential in this length.

[15]We mention that the reduction maps an instance $(\langle M \rangle, x)$ of h to a pair of sequences $((\alpha_1, \ldots, \alpha_k), (\beta_1, \ldots, \beta_k))$ such that only α_1 and β_1 depend on x, whereas k as well as the other strings depend only on M.

this environment (resp., the effect of a single application of the computation rule). This algorithm can, in turn, be implemented in the said model of computation (assuming this model is general; see the Church-Turing Thesis). Successive applications of this algorithm leads to the notion of a universal machine, which (for concreteness) is formulated next in terms of Turing machines.

Definition 1.8 (universal machines): *A universal Turing machine is a Turing machine that on input a description of a machine M and an input x returns the value of M(x) if M halts on x and otherwise does not halt.*

That is, a universal Turing machine computes the partial function u on pairs $(\langle M \rangle, x)$ such that M halts on input x, in which case it holds that $u(\langle M \rangle, x) = M(x)$. That is, $u(\langle M \rangle, x) = M(x)$ if M halts on input x and u is undefined on $(\langle M \rangle, x)$ otherwise. We note that if M halts on all possible inputs then $u(\langle M \rangle, x)$ is defined for every x.

We stress that the mere fact that we have defined something (i.e., a universal Turing machine) does not mean that it exists. Yet, as hinted in the foregoing discussion and obvious to anyone who has written a computer program (and thought about what he/she was doing), universal Turing machines do exist.

Theorem 1.9: *There exists a universal Turing machine.*

Theorem 1.9 asserts that the partial function u is computable. In contrast, it can be shown that any extension of u to a total function is uncomputable. That is, for any total function $\hat{u}$ that agrees with the partial function u on all the inputs on which the latter is defined, it holds that $\hat{u}$ is uncomputable.[16]

Proof: Given a pair $(\langle M \rangle, x)$, we just emulate the computation of machine M on input x. This emulation is straightforward, because (by the effectiveness of the description of M) we can iteratively determine the next instantaneous configuration of the computation of M on input x. If the said computation halts then we will obtain its output and can output it (and so, on input $(\langle M \rangle, x)$, our algorithm returns $M(x)$). Otherwise, we turn out emulating an infinite computation, which means that our algorithm does not halt on input $(\langle M \rangle, x)$. Thus, the foregoing emulation procedure constitutes a universal machine (i.e., yields an algorithm for computing u). ∎

As hinted already, the existence of universal machines is the fundamental fact underlying the paradigm of general-purpose computers. Indeed, a specific Turing machine (or algorithm) is a device that solves a specific problem. A priori, solving each problem would have required building a new physical device, that allows for this problem to be solved in the physical world (rather than as a thought experiment). The existence of a universal machine asserts that it is enough to build one physical device, that is, a general purpose computer. Any specific problem can then be solved by writing a corresponding program

---

[16]The claim is easy to prove for the total function $\hat{u}$ that extends u and assigns the special symbol $\perp$ to inputs on which u is undefined (i.e., $\hat{u}(\langle M \rangle, x) \stackrel{\text{def}}{=} \perp$ if u is not defined on $(\langle M \rangle, x)$ and $\hat{u}(\langle M \rangle, x) \stackrel{\text{def}}{=} u(\langle M \rangle, x)$ otherwise). In this case $h(\langle M \rangle, x) = 1$ if and only if $\hat{u}(\langle M \rangle, x) \neq \perp$, and so the halting function h is Turing-reducible to $\hat{u}$. In the general case, we may adapt the proof of Theorem 1.5 by using the fact that, for a machine M that halts on every input, it holds that $\hat{u}(\langle M \rangle, x) = u(\langle M \rangle, x)$ for every x (and in particular for $x = \langle M \rangle$).

to be executed (or emulated) by the general-purpose computer. Thus, universal machines correspond to general-purpose computers, and provide the basis for separating hardware from software. In other words, the existence of universal machines says that software can be viewed as (part of the) input.

In addition to their practical importance, the existence of universal machines (and their variants) has important consequences in the theories of computability and Computational Complexity. To demonstrate the point, we note that Theorem 1.6 implies that many questions about the behavior of a fixed universal machine on certain input types are undecidable. For example, it follows that, for some fixed machines (i.e., universal ones), there is no algorithm that determines whether or not the (fixed) machine halts on a given input. Revisiting the proof of Theorem 1.7 (see footnote 15), it follows that the Post Correspondence Problem remains undecidable even if the input sequences are restricted to have a specific length (i.e., k is fixed). A more important application of universal machines to the theory of computability follows.

A detour: Kolmogorov Complexity. The existence of universal machines, which may be viewed as universal languages for writing effective and succinct descriptions of objects, plays a central role in Kolmogorov Complexity. Loosely speaking, the latter theory is concerned with the length of (effective) descriptions of objects, and views the minimum such length as the inherent "complexity" of the object; that is, "simple" objects (or phenomena) are those having short description (resp., short explanation), whereas "complex" objects have no short description. Needless to say, these (effective) descriptions have to refer to some fixed "language" (i.e., to a fixed machine that, given a succinct description of an object, produces its explicit description). Fixing any machine M, a string x is called a description of s with respect to M if $M(x) = s$. The complexity of s with respect to M, denoted $K_M(s)$, is the length of the shortest description of s with respect to M. Certainly, we want to fix M such that every string has a description with respect to M, and furthermore such that this description is not "significantly" longer than the description with respect to a different machine M'. The following theorem makes it natural to use a universal machine as the "point of reference" (i.e., as the aforementioned M).

Theorem 1.10 (complexity wrt a universal machine): *Let U be a universal machine. Then, for every machine M', there exists a constant c such that $K_U(s) \leq K_{M'}(s) + c$ for every string s.*

The theorem follows by (setting $c = O(|\langle M' \rangle|)$ and) observing that if x is a description of s with respect to M' then $(\langle M' \rangle, x)$ is a description of s with respect to U. Here it is important to use an adequate encoding of pairs of strings (e.g., the pair $(\sigma_1 \cdots \sigma_k, \tau_1 \cdots \tau_\ell)$ is encoded by the string $\sigma_1 \sigma_1 \cdots \sigma_k \sigma_k 01 \tau_1 \cdots \tau_\ell$). Fixing any universal machine U, we define the Kolmogorov Complexity of a string s as $K(s) \overset{\text{def}}{=} K_U(s)$. The reader may easily verify the following facts:

1. $K(s) \leq |s| + O(1)$, for every s.

    (Hint: Apply Theorem 1.10 to a machine that computes the identity mapping.)

2. There exist infinitely many strings s such that $K(s) \ll |s|$.

    (Hint: Consider $s = 1^n$. Alternatively, consider any machine M such that $|M(x)| \gg |x|$ for every x.)

3. Some strings of length n have complexity at least n. Furthermore, for every n and i,

$$|\{s \in \{0, 1\}^n : K(s) \leq n - i\}| < 2^{n-i+1}$$

(Hint: Different strings must have different descriptions with respect to U.)

It can be shown that *the function K is uncomputable*. The proof is related to the paradox captured by the following "description" of a natural number: the largest natural number that can be described by an English sentence of up to a thousand letters. (The paradox amounts to observing that if the above number is well defined then so is the integer successor of the largest natural number that can be described by an English sentence of up to a thousand letters.) Needless to say, the foregoing sentences presuppose that any English sentence is a legitimate description in some adequate sense (e.g., in the sense captured by Kolmogorov Complexity). Specifically, the foregoing sentences presuppose that we can determine the Kolmogorov Complexity of each natural number, and furthermore that we can effectively produce the largest number that has Kolmogorov Complexity not exceeding some threshold. Indeed, the paradox suggests a proof of the fact that the latter task cannot be performed; that is, *there exists no algorithm that given t produces the lexicographically last string s such that $K(s) \leq t$*, because if such an algorithm A would have existed then $K(s) \leq O(|\langle A \rangle|) + \log t$ and $K(s0) < K(s) + O(1) < t$ in contradiction to the definition of s.

1.2.3.5. Time and Space Complexity

Fixing a model of computation (e.g., Turing machines) and *focusing on algorithms that halt on each input*, we consider the number of steps (i.e., applications of the computation rule) taken by the algorithm on each possible input. The latter function is called the time complexity of the algorithm (or machine); that is, $t_A : \{0, 1\}^* \to \mathbb{N}$ is called the time complexity of algorithm A if, for every x, on input x algorithm A halts after exactly $t_A(x)$ steps.

We will be mostly interested in the dependence of the time complexity on the input length, when taking the maximum over all inputs of the relevant length. That is, for t_A as in the foregoing, we will consider $T_A : \mathbb{N} \to \mathbb{N}$ defined by $T_A(n) \overset{\text{def}}{=} \max_{x \in \{0,1\}^n}\{t_A(x)\}$. Abusing terminology, we sometimes refer to T_A as the time complexity of A.

The time complexity of a problem. As stated in the preface and in the introduction, typically Complexity Theory is not concerned with the (time) complexity of a specific algorithm. It is rather concerned with the (time) complexity of a problem, assuming that this problem is solvable at all (by some algorithm). Intuitively, the time complexity of such a problem is defined as the time complexity of the fastest algorithm that solves this problem (assuming that the latter term is well defined).[17] Actually, we shall be interested in upper and lower bounds on the (time) complexity of algorithms that solve the problem. Thus, when we say that a certain problem Π has complexity T, we actually mean that Π has complexity at most T. Likewise, when we say that Π requires time T, we actually mean that Π has time complexity at least T.

---

[17]**Advanced comment:** As we shall see in Section 4.2.2 (cf. Theorem 4.8), the naive assumption that a "fastest algorithm" for solving a problem exists is not always justified. On the other hand, the assumption is essentially justified in some important cases (see, e.g., Theorem 2.33). But even in these cases the said algorithm is "fastest" (or "optimal") only up to a constant factor.

Recall that the foregoing discussion refers to some fixed model of computation. Indeed, the complexity of a problem Π may depend on the specific model of computation in which algorithms that solve Π are implemented. The following Cobham-Edmonds Thesis asserts that the variation (in the time complexity) is not too big, and in particular is irrelevant to much of the current focus of Complexity Theory (e.g., for the P-vs-NP Question).

The Cobham-Edmonds Thesis. As just stated, the time complexity of a problem may depend on the model of computation. For example, deciding membership in the set $\{xx : x \in \{0, 1\}^*\}$ can be done in linear time on a two-tape Turing machine, but requires quadratic time on a single-tape Turing machine.[18] On the other hand, any problem that has time complexity t in the model of multi-tape Turing machines has complexity $O(t^2)$ in the model of single-tape Turing machines. The Cobham-Edmonds Thesis asserts that the time complexities in any two "reasonable and general" models of computation are polynomially related. That is, *a problem has time complexity t in some* "reasonable and general" *model of computation if and only if it has time complexity* $\text{poly}(t)$ *in the model of* (single-tape) *Turing machines*.

Indeed, the Cobham-Edmonds Thesis strengthens the Church-Turing Thesis. It asserts not only that the class of solvable problems is invariant as far as "reasonable and general" models of computation are concerned, but also that the time complexity (of the solvable problems) in such models is polynomially related.

Efficient algorithms. As hinted in the foregoing discussions, much of Complexity Theory is concerned with efficient algorithms. The latter are defined as polynomial-time algorithms (i.e., algorithms that have time complexity that is upper-bounded by a polynomial in the length of the input). By the Cobham-Edmonds Thesis, the definition of this class is invariant under the choice of a "reasonable and general" model of computation. The association of efficient algorithms with polynomial-time computation is grounded in the following two considerations:

- *Philosophical consideration*: Intuitively, efficient algorithms are those that can be implemented within a number of steps that is a moderately growing function of the input length. To allow for reading the entire input, at least linear time should be allowed. On the other hand, apparently slow algorithms and in particular "exhaustive search" algorithms, which take exponential time, must be avoided. Furthermore, a good definition of the class of efficient algorithms should be closed under natural compositions of algorithms (as well as be robust with respect to reasonable models of computation and with respect to simple changes in the encoding of problems' instances).

  Choosing polynomials as the set of time bounds for efficient algorithms satisfies all the foregoing requirements: Polynomials constitute a "closed" set of moderately growing functions, where "closure" means closure under addition, multiplication, and functional composition. These closure properties guarantee the closure of the class of efficient

---

[18]Proving the latter fact is quite non-trivial. One proof is by a "reduction" from a communication complexity problem [148, Sec. 12.2]. Intuitively, a single-tape Turing machine that decides membership in the aforementioned set can be viewed as a channel of communication between the two parts of the input. Focusing our attention on inputs of the form $y0^n z0^n$, for $y, z \in \{0, 1\}^n$, each time the machine passes from the first part to the second part it carries $O(1)$ bits of information (in its internal state) while making at least n steps. The proof is completed by invoking the linear lower bound on the communication complexity of the (two-argument) identity function (i.e., $\text{id}(y, z) = 1$ if $y = z$ and $\text{id}(y, z) = 0$ otherwise, cf. [148, Chap. 1]).

algorithms under natural compositions of algorithms (as well as its robustness with respect to any reasonable and general model of computation). Furthermore, polynomial-time algorithms can conduct computations that are apparently simple (although not necessarily trivial), and on the other hand they do not include algorithms that are apparently inefficient (like exhaustive search).

- *Empirical consideration*: It is clear that algorithms that are considered efficient in practice have a running time that is bounded by a small polynomial (at least on the inputs that occur in practice). The question is whether any polynomial time algorithm can be considered efficient in an intuitive sense. The belief, which is supported by past experience, is that every *natural* problem that can be solved in polynomial time also has a "reasonably efficient" algorithm.

We stress that the association of efficient algorithms with polynomial-time computation is not essential to most of the notions, results, and questions of Complexity Theory. Any other class of algorithms that supports the aforementioned closure properties and allows for conducting some simple computations but not overly complex ones gives rise to a similar theory, albeit the formulation of such a theory may be more complicated. Specifically, all results and questions treated in this book are concerned with the relation among the complexities of different computational tasks (rather than with providing absolute assertions about the complexity of some computational tasks). These relations can be stated explicitly, by stating how any upper bound on the time complexity of one task gets translated to an upper bound on the time complexity of another task.[19] Such cumbersome statements will maintain the contents of the standard statements; they will merely be much more complicated. Thus, we follow the tradition of focusing on polynomial-time computations, while stressing that this focus both is natural and provides the simplest way of addressing the fundamental issues underlying the nature of efficient computation.

Universal machines, revisited. The notion of time complexity gives rise to a time-bounded version of the universal function u (presented in §1.2.3.4). Specifically, we define $u'(\langle M \rangle, x, t) \stackrel{\text{def}}{=} y$ if on input x machine M halts within t steps and outputs the string y, and $u'(\langle M \rangle, x, t) \stackrel{\text{def}}{=} \bot$ if on input x machine M makes more than t steps. Unlike u, the function u' is a total function. Furthermore, unlike any extension of u to a total function, the function u' is computable. Moreover, u' is computable by a machine U' that, on input $X = (\langle M \rangle, x, t)$, halts after $\text{poly}(|X|)$ steps. Indeed, machine U' is a variant of a universal machine (i.e., on input X, machine U' merely emulates M for t steps rather than emulating M till it halts (and potentially indefinitely)). Note that the number of steps taken by U' depends on the specific model of computation (and that some overhead is unavoidable because emulating each step of M requires reading the relevant portion of the description of M).

Space complexity. Another natural measure of the "complexity" of an algorithm (or a task) is the amount of memory consumed by the computation. We refer to the memory

---

[19]For example, the NP-completeness of SAT (cf. Theorem 2.22) implies that any algorithm solving SAT in time T yields an algorithm that factors composite numbers in time T' such that $T'(n) = \text{poly}(n) \cdot (1 + T(\text{poly}(n)))$. (More generally, if the correctness of solutions for n-bit instances of some search problem R can be verified in time $t(n)$ then the hypothesis regarding SAT implies that solutions (for n-bit instances of R) can be found in time T' such that $T'(n) = t(n) \cdot (1 + T(O(t(n))^2))$.)

---

used for storing some intermediate results of the computation. Since much of our focus will be on using memory that is sub-linear in the input length, it is important to use a model in which one can differentiate memory used for computation from memory used for storing the initial input or the final output. In the context of Turing machines, this is done by considering multi-tape Turing machines such that the input is presented on a special read-only tape (called the input tape), the output is written on a special write-only tape (called the output tape), and intermediate results are stored on a work-tape. Thus, the input and output tapes cannot be used for storing intermediate results. The space complexity of such a machine M is defined as a function s_M such that $s_M(x)$ is the number of cells of the work-tape that are scanned by M on input x. As in the case of time complexity, we will usually refer to $S_A(n) \overset{\text{def}}{=} \max_{x \in \{0,1\}^n} \{s_A(x)\}$.

1.2.3.6. Oracle Machines

The notion of Turing-reductions, which was discussed in §1.2.3.3, is captured by the following definition of so-called *oracle machines*. Loosely speaking, an oracle machine is a machine that is augmented such that it may pose questions to the outside. We consider the case in which these questions, called queries, are answered consistently by some function $f : \{0,1\}^* \to \{0,1\}^*$, called the oracle. That is, if the machine makes a query q then the answer it obtains is $f(q)$. In such a case, we say that the oracle machine is given access to the oracle f. For an oracle machine M, a string x and a function f, we denote by $M^f(x)$ the output of M on input x when given access to the oracle f. (Reexamining the second part of the proof of Theorem 1.5, observe that we have actually described an oracle machine that computes d' when given access to the oracle d.)

The notion of an oracle machine extends the notion of a standard computing device (machine), and thus a rigorous formulation of the former extends a formal model of the latter. Specifically, extending the model of Turing machines, we derive the following model of oracle Turing machines.

Definition 1.11 (using an oracle):

- *An* oracle machine *is a Turing machine with a special additional tape, called the* oracle tape, *and two special states, called* oracle invocation *and* oracle spoke.
- *The* computation of the oracle machine M on input x and access to the oracle $f: \{0,1\}^* \to \{0,1\}^*$ *is defined based on the successive configuration function. For configurations with a state different from* oracle invocation *the next configuration is defined as usual. Let γ be a configuration in which the machine's state is* oracle invocation *and suppose that the actual contents of the oracle tape is q (i.e., q is the contents of the maximal prefix of the tape that holds bit values).*[20] *Then, the configuration following γ is identical to γ, except that the state is* oracle spoke, *and the actual contents of the oracle tape is $f(q)$. The string q is called M's* query *and $f(q)$ is called the* oracle's reply.
- *The output of the oracle machine M on input x when given oracle access to f is denoted $M^f(x)$.*

---

[20]This fits the definition of the *actual initial contents of a tape of a Turing machine* (cf. §1.2.3.2). A common convention is that the oracle can be invoked only when the machine's head resides at the leftmost cell of the oracle tape. We comment that, in the context of space complexity, one uses two oracle tapes: a write-only tape for the query and a read-only tape for the answer.

We stress that the running time of an oracle machine is the number of steps made during its (own) computation, and that the oracle's reply on each query is obtained in a single step.

1.2.3.7. Restricted Models

We mention that restricted models of computation are often mentioned in the context of a course on computability, but they will play no role in the current book. One such model is the model of finite automata, which in some variant coincides with Turing machines that have space-complexity zero (equiv., constant).

In our opinion, the most important motivation for the study of these restricted models of computation is that they provide simple models for some natural (or artificial) phenomena. This motivation, however, seems only remotely related to the study of the complexity of various computational tasks, which calls for the consideration of general models of computation and the evaluation of the complexity of computation with respect to such models.

Teaching note: Indeed, we reject the common coupling of computability theory with the theory of automata and formal languages. Although the historical links between these two theories (at least in the West) cannot be denied, this fact cannot justify coupling two fundamentally different theories (especially when such a coupling promotes a wrong perspective on computability theory). Thus, in our opinion, the study of any of the lower levels of Chomsky's Hierarchy [123, Chap. 9] should be decoupled from the study of computability theory (let alone the study of Complexity Theory).

1.2.4. Non-uniform Models (Circuits and Advice)

> Camille: Like Thelma and Louise. But . . . without the guns.
> Petra: Oh, well, no guns, I don't know . . .
> Patricia Rozema, *When Night Is Falling*, 1995

The main use of non-uniform models of computation, in this book, will be as a source of some natural computational problems (cf. §2.3.3.1 and Theorem 5.4). In addition, these models will be briefly studied in Sections 3.1 and 4.1.

By a non-uniform model of computation we mean a model in which for each possible input length a different computing device is considered, while there is no "uniformity" requirement relating devices that correspond to different input lengths. Furthermore, this collection of devices is infinite by nature, and (in the absence of a uniformity requirement) this collection may not even have a finite description. Nevertheless, each device in the collection has a finite description. In fact, the relationship between the size of the device (resp., the length of its description) and the length of the input that it handles will be of major concern.

Non-uniform models of computation are studied either toward the development of lower-bound techniques or as simplified limits on the ability of efficient algorithms.[21]

---

[21] The second case refers mainly to efficient algorithms that are given a pair of inputs (of (polynomially) related length) such that these algorithms are analyzed with respect to fixing one input (arbitrarily) and varying the other input (typically, at random). Typical examples include the context of derandomization (cf. Section 8.3) and the setting of zero-knowledge (cf. Section 9.2).

In both cases, the uniformity condition is eliminated in the interest of simplicity and with the hope (and belief) that nothing substantial is lost as far as the issues at hand are concerned. In the context of developing lower bounds, the hope is that the finiteness of all parameters (i.e., the input length and the device's description) will allow for the application of combinatorial techniques to analyze the limitations of certain settings of parameters.

We will focus on two related models of non-uniform computing devices: Boolean circuits (§1.2.4.1) and "machines that take advice" (§1.2.4.2). The former model is more adequate for the study of the evolution of computation (i.e., development of lower-bound techniques), whereas the latter is more adequate for modeling purposes (e.g., limiting the ability of efficient algorithms).

1.2.4.1. Boolean Circuits

The most popular model of non-uniform computation is the one of Boolean circuits. Historically, this model was introduced for the purpose of describing the "logic operation" of real-life electronic circuits. Ironically, nowadays this model provides the stage for some of the most practically removed studies in Complexity Theory (which aim at developing methods that may eventually lead to an understanding of the inherent limitations of efficient algorithms).

A Boolean circuit is a directed acyclic graph[22] *with labels on the vertices*, to be discussed shortly. For the sake of simplicity, we disallow isolated vertices (i.e., vertices with no incoming or outgoing edges), and thus the graph's vertices are of three types: *sources*, *sinks*, and *internal vertices*.

1. Internal vertices are vertices having incoming and outgoing edges (i.e., they have in-degree and out-degree at least 1). In the context of Boolean circuits, internal vertices are called gates. Each gate is labeled by a Boolean operation, where the operations that are typically considered are $\wedge$, $\vee$, and $\neg$ (corresponding to and, or, and neg). In addition, we require that gates labeled $\neg$ have in-degree 1. The in-degree of $\wedge$-gates and $\vee$-gates may be any number greater than zero, and the same holds for the out-degree of any gate.

2. The graph sources (i.e., vertices with no incoming edges) are called input terminals. Each input terminal is labeled by a natural number (which is to be thought of as the index of an input variable). (For the sake of defining formulae (see §1.2.4.3), we allow different input terminals to be labeled by the same number.)[23]

3. The graph sinks (i.e., vertices with no outgoing edges) are called output terminals, and we require that they have in-degree 1. Each output terminal is labeled by a natural number such that if the circuit has m output terminals then they are labeled $1, 2, \ldots, m$. That is, we disallow different output terminals to be labeled by the same number, and insist that the labels of the output terminals be consecutive numbers. (Indeed, the labels of the output terminals will correspond to the indices of locations in the circuit's output.)

---

[22]See Appendix G.1.

[23]This is not needed in the case of general circuits, because we can just feed outgoing edges of the same input terminal to many gates. Note, however, that this is not allowed in the case of formulae, where all non-sinks are required to have out-degree exactly 1.

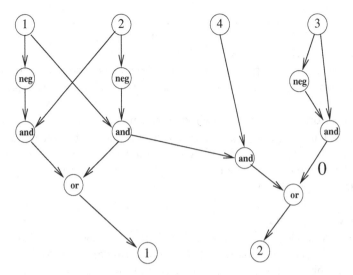

Figure 1.3: A circuit computing $f(x_1, x_2, x_3, x_4) = (x_1 \oplus x_2, x_1 \wedge \neg x_2 \wedge x_4)$.

For the sake of simplicity, we also mandate that the labels of the input terminals be consecutive numbers.[24]

A Boolean circuit with n different input labels and m output terminals induces (and indeed computes) a function from $\{0, 1\}^n$ to $\{0, 1\}^m$ defined as follows. For any fixed string $x \in \{0, 1\}^n$, we iteratively define the value of vertices in the circuit such that the input terminals are assigned the corresponding bits in $x = x_1 \cdots x_n$ and the values of other vertices are determined in the natural manner. That is:

- An input terminal with label $i \in \{1, \ldots, n\}$ is assigned the ith bit of x (i.e., the value x_i).
- If the children of a gate (of in-degree d) that is labeled $\wedge$ have values $v_1, v_2, \ldots, v_d$, then the gate is assigned the value $\wedge_{i=1}^{d} v_i$. The value of a gate labeled $\vee$ (or $\neg$) is determined analogously.

Indeed, the hypothesis that the circuit is acyclic implies that the following natural process of determining values for the circuit's vertices is well defined: As long as the value of some vertex is undetermined, there exists a vertex such that its value is undetermined but the values of all its children are determined. Thus, the process can make progress, and terminates when the values of all vertices (including the output terminals) are determined.

The value of the circuit on input x (i.e., the output computed by the circuit on input x) is $y = y_1 \cdots y_m$, where y_i is the value assigned by the foregoing process to the output terminal labeled i. We note that *there exists a polynomial-time algorithm that, given a circuit C and a corresponding input x, outputs the value of C on input x*. This algorithm determines the values of the circuit's vertices, going from the circuit's input terminals to its output terminals.

---

[24]This convention slightly complicates the construction of circuits that ignore some of the input values. Specifically, we use artificial gadgets that have incoming edges from the corresponding input terminals, and compute an adequate constant. To avoid having this constant as an output terminal, we feed it into an auxiliary gate such that the value of the latter is determined by the other incoming edge (e.g., a constant 0 fed into an $\vee$-gate). See an example of dealing with x_3 in Figure 1.3.

We say that a family of circuits $(C_n)_{n \in \mathbb{N}}$ computes a function $f : \{0, 1\}^* \to \{0, 1\}^*$ if for every n the circuit C_n computes the restriction of f to strings of length n. In other words, for every $x \in \{0, 1\}^*$, it must hold that $C_{|x|}(x) = f(x)$.

Bounded and unbounded fan-in. We will be most interested in circuits in which each gate has at most two incoming edges. In this case, the types of (two-argument) Boolean operations that we allow is immaterial (as long as we consider a "full basis" of such operations, i.e., a set of operations that can implement any other two-argument Boolean operation). Such circuits are called circuits of bounded fan-in. In contrast, other studies are concerned with circuits of unbounded fan-in, where each gate may have an arbitrary number of incoming edges. Needless to say, in the case of circuits of unbounded fan-in, the choice of allowed Boolean operations is important and one focuses on operations that are "uniform" (across the number of operants, e.g., $\wedge$ and $\vee$).

Circuit size as a complexity measure. The size of a circuit is the number of its edges. When considering a family of circuits $(C_n)_{n \in \mathbb{N}}$ that computes a function $f : \{0, 1\}^* \to \{0, 1\}^*$, we are interested in the size of C_n as a function of n. Specifically, we say that this family has size complexity $s : \mathbb{N} \to \mathbb{N}$ if for every n the size of C_n is $s(n)$. The circuit complexity of a function f, denoted s_f, is the infimum of the size complexity of all families of circuits that compute f. Alternatively, for each n we may consider the size of the smallest circuit that computes the restriction of f to n-bit strings (denoted f_n), and set $s_f(n)$ accordingly. We stress that non-uniformity is implicit in this definition, because no conditions are made regarding the relation between the various circuits used to compute the function on different input lengths.[25]

On the circuit complexity of functions. We highlight some simple facts about the circuit complexity of functions. (These facts are in clear correspondence to facts regarding Kolmogorov Complexity mentioned in §1.2.3.4.)

1. Most importantly, any Boolean function can be computed by some family of circuits, and thus the circuit complexity of any function is well defined. Furthermore, each function has at most exponential circuit complexity.

    (Hint: The function $f_n : \{0, 1\}^n \to \{0, 1\}$ can be computed by a circuit of size $O(n2^n)$ that implements a look-up table.)

2. Some functions have polynomial circuit complexity. In particular, any function that has time complexity t (i.e., is computed by an algorithm of time complexity t) has circuit complexity $\mathrm{poly}(t)$. Furthermore, the corresponding circuit family is uniform (in a natural sense to be discussed in the next paragraph).

    (Hint: Consider a Turing machine that computes the function, and consider its computation on a generic n-bit long input. The corresponding computation can be emulated by a circuit that consists of $t(n)$ layers such that each layer represents an instantaneous configuration of the machine, and the relation between consecutive configurations is captured by ("uniform") local gadgets in the circuit. For further details see the proof of Theorem 2.21, which presents a similar emulation.)

---

[25]**Advanced comment:** We also note that, in contrast to footnote 17, the circuit model and the (circuit size) complexity measure support the notion of an optimal computing device: Each function f has a unique size complexity s_f (and not merely upper and lower bounds on its complexity).

3. Almost all Boolean functions have exponential circuit complexity. Specifically, the number of functions mapping $\{0, 1\}^n$ to $\{0, 1\}$ that can be computed by some circuit of size s is smaller than s^{2s}.

   (Hint: The number of circuits having v vertices and s edges is at most $\left(2 \cdot \binom{v}{2} + v\right)^s$.)

Note that the first fact implies that families of circuits can compute functions that are uncomputable by algorithms. Furthermore, this phenomenon also occurs when restricting attention to families of polynomial size circuits. See further discussion in §1.2.4.2.

Uniform families. A family of polynomial-size circuits $(C_n)_{n \in \mathbb{N}}$ is called uniform if given n one can construct the circuit C_n in poly(n)-time. Note that *if a function is computable by a uniform family of polynomial-size circuits then it is computable by a polynomial-time algorithm*. This algorithm first constructs the adequate circuit (which can be done in polynomial time by the uniformity hypothesis), and then evaluates this circuit on the given input (which can be done in time that is polynomial in the size of the circuit).

Note that limitations on the computing power of arbitrary families of polynomial-size circuits certainly hold for uniform families (of polynomial size), which in turn yield limitations on the computing power of polynomial-time algorithms. Thus, lower bounds on the circuit complexity of functions yield analogous lower bounds on their time complexity. Furthermore, as is often the case in mathematics and science, disposing of an auxiliary condition that is not well understood (i.e., uniformity) may turn out fruitful. Indeed, this has occured in the study of classes of restricted circuits, which is reviewed in §1.2.4.3 (and Appendix B.2).

1.2.4.2. Machines That Take Advice

General (non-uniform) circuit families and uniform circuit families are two extremes with respect to the "amounts of non-uniformity" in the computing device. Intuitively, in the former, non-uniformity is only bounded by the size of the device, whereas in the latter the amounts of non-uniformity is zero. Here we consider a model that allows the decoupling of the size of the computing device from the amount of non-uniformity, which may range from zero to the device's size. Specifically, we consider algorithms that "take a non-uniform advice" that depends only on the input length. The amount of non-uniformity will be defined as equaling the length of the corresponding advice (as a function of the input length).

> **Definition 1.12** (taking advice): *We say that* algorithm A computes the function f using advice of length $\ell : \mathbb{N} \to \mathbb{N}$ *if there exists an infinite sequence* $(a_n)_{n \in \mathbb{N}}$ *such that*
>
> 1. *for every $x \in \{0, 1\}^*$, it holds that $A(a_{|x|}, x) = f(x)$.*
> 2. *for every $n \in \mathbb{N}$, it holds that $|a_n| = \ell(n)$.*
>
> *The sequence $(a_n)_{n \in \mathbb{N}}$ is called the* advice sequence.

Note that any function having circuit complexity s can be computed using advice of length $O(s \log s)$, where the log factor is due to the fact that a graph with v vertices and e edges can be described by a string of length $2e \log_2 v$. Note that the model of machines that use advice allows for some sharper bounds than the ones stated in §1.2.4.1: Every function can be computed using advice of length ℓ such that $\ell(n) = 2^n$, and some uncomputable functions can be computed using advice of length 1.

Theorem 1.13 (the power of advice): *There exist functions that can be computed using one-bit advice but cannot be computed without advice.*

Proof: Starting with any uncomputable Boolean function $f : \mathbb{N} \to \{0, 1\}$, consider the function f' defined as $f'(x) = f(|x|)$. Note that f is Turing-reducible to f' (e.g., on input n make any n-bit query to f', and return the answer).[26] Thus, f' cannot be computed without advice. On the other hand, f' can be easily computed by using the advice sequence $(a_n)_{n\in\mathbb{N}}$ such that $a_n = f(n)$; that is, the algorithm merely outputs the advice bit (and indeed $a_{|x|} = f(|x|) = f'(x)$, for every $x \in \{0, 1\}^*$). ∎

1.2.4.3. Restricted Models

The model of Boolean circuits (cf. §1.2.4.1) allows for the introduction of many natural subclasses of computing devices. Following is a laconic review of a few of these subclasses. For further detail regarding the study of these subclasses, the interested reader is referred to Appendix B.2. *Since we shall refer to various types of Boolean formulae in the rest of this book, we suggest not skiping the following two paragraphs.*

Boolean formulae. In (general) Boolean circuits the non-sink vertices are allowed arbitrary out-degree. This means that the same intermediate value can be reused without being recomputed (and while increasing the size complexity by only one unit). Such "free" reusage of intermediate values is disallowed in Boolean formula, which are formally defined as Boolean circuits in which all non-sink vertices have out-degree 1. This means that the underlying graph of a Boolean formula is a tree (see §G.2), and it can be written as a Boolean expression over Boolean variables by traversing this tree (and registering the vertices' labels in the order traversed). Indeed, we have allowed different input terminals to be assigned the same label in order to allow formulae in which the same variable occurs multiple times. As in the case of general circuits, one is interested in the size of these restricted circuits (i.e., the size of families of formulae computing various functions). We mention that quadratic lower bounds are known for the formula size of simple functions (e.g., `parity`), whereas these functions have linear circuit complexity. This discrepancy is depicted in Figure 1.4.

Formulae in CNF and DNF. A restricted type of Boolean formula consists of formulae that are in conjunctive normal form (CNF). Such a formula consists of a conjunction of clauses, where each clause is a disjunction of literals each being either a variable or its negation. That is, such formulae are represented by layered circuits of unbounded fan-in in which the first layer consists of `neg`-gates that compute the negation of input variables, the second layer consists of `or`-gates that compute the logical-or of subsets of inputs and negated inputs, and the third layer consists of a single `and`-gate that computes the logical-and of the values computed in the second layer. Note that each Boolean function can be computed by a family of CNF formula of exponential size, and that the size of

---

[26]Indeed, this Turing-reduction is not efficient (i.e., it runs in exponential time in $|n| = \log_2 n$), but this is immaterial in the current context.

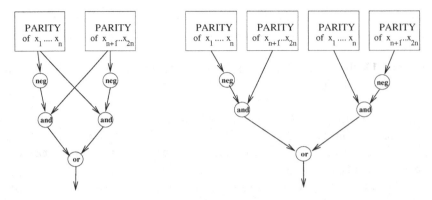

Figure 1.4: Recursive construction of parity circuits and formulae.

CNF formulae may be exponentially larger than the size of ordinary formulae computing the same function (e.g., `parity`). For a constant k, a formula is said to be in k-CNF if its CNF has disjunctions of size at most k. An analogous restricted type of Boolean formula refers to formulae that are in disjunctive normal form (DNF). Such a formula consists of a disjunction of conjunctions of literals, and when each conjunction has at most k literals we say that the formula is in k-DNF.

Constant-depth circuits. Circuits have a "natural structure" (i.e., their structure as graphs). One natural parameter regarding this structure is the depth of a circuit, which is defined as the longest directed path from any source to any sink. Of special interest are constant-depth circuits of unbounded fan-in. We mention that sub-exponential lower bounds are known for the size of such circuits that compute a simple function (e.g., `parity`).

Monotone circuits. The circuit model also allows for the consideration of monotone computing devices: A monotone circuit is one having only monotone gates (e.g., gates computing $\wedge$ and $\vee$, but no negation gates (i.e., $\neg$-gates)). Needless to say, monotone circuits can only compute monotone functions, where a function $f : \{0,1\}^n \to \{0,1\}$ is called monotone if for any $x \preceq y$ it holds that $f(x) \leq f(y)$ (where $x_1 \cdots x_n \preceq y_1 \cdots y_n$ if and only if for every bit position i it holds that $x_i \leq y_i$). One natural question is whether, as far as monotone functions are concerned, there is a substantial loss in using only monotone circuits. The answer is *yes*: There exist monotone functions that have polynomial circuit complexity but require sub-exponential size monotone circuits.

1.2.5. Complexity Classes

Complexity classes are sets of computational problems. Typically, such classes are defined by fixing three parameters:

1. A *type of computational problems* (see Section 1.2.2). Indeed, most classes refer to decision problems, but classes of search problems, promise problems, and other types of problems will also be considered.
2. A *model of computation*, which may be either uniform (see Section 1.2.3) or non-uniform (see Section 1.2.4).

3. A *complexity measure* and a *limiting function* (or a set of functions), which put together limit the class of computations of the previous item; that is, we refer to the class of computations that have complexity not exceeding the specified function (or set of functions). For example, in §1.2.3.5, we mentioned time complexity and space complexity, which apply to any uniform model of computation. We also mentioned polynomial-time computations, which are computations in which the time complexity (as a function) does not exceed some polynomial (i.e., a member of the set of polynomial functions).

The most common complexity classes refer to decision problems, and are sometimes defined as classes of sets rather than classes of the corresponding decision problems. That is, one often says that a set $S \subseteq \{0, 1\}^*$ is in the class $\mathcal{C}$ rather than saying that *the problem of deciding membership in S* is in the class $\mathcal{C}$. Likewise, one talks of classes of relations rather than classes of the corresponding search problems (i.e., saying that $R \subseteq \{0, 1\}^* \times \{0, 1\}^*$ is in the class $\mathcal{C}$ means that *the search problem of R* is in the class $\mathcal{C}$).

Chapter Notes

It is quite remarkable that the theories of uniform and non-uniform computational devices have emerged in two single papers. We refer to Turing's paper [225], which introduced the model of Turing machines, and to Shannon's paper [203], which introduced Boolean circuits.

In addition to introducing the Turing machine model and arguing that it corresponds to the intuitive notion of computability, Turing's paper [225] introduces universal machines and contains proofs of undecidability (e.g., of the Halting Problem).

The Church-Turing Thesis is attributed to the works of Church [55] and Turing [225]. In both works, this thesis is invoked for claiming that the fact that Turing machines cannot solve some problem implies that this problem cannot be solved in any "reasonable" model of computation. The RAM model is attributed to von Neumann's report [234].

The association of efficient computation with polynomial-time algorithms is attributed to the papers of Cobham [57] and Edmonds [70]. It is interesting to note that Cobham's starting point was his desire to present a philosophically sound concept of efficient algorithms, whereas Edmonds's starting point was his desire to articulate why certain algorithms are "good" in practice.

Rice's Theorem is proven in [192], and the undecidability of the Post Correspondence Problem is proven in [181]. The formulation of machines that take advice (as well as the equivalence to the circuit model) originates in [139].

CHAPTER TWO

P, NP, and NP-Completeness

*For as much as many have taken in hand to set forth in order a declaration
of those things which are most surely believed among us; Even as they
delivered them unto us, who from the beginning were eyewitnesses, and
ministers of the word; It seems good to me also, having had perfect
understanding of all things from the very first, to write unto thee in
order, most excellent Theophilus; That thou mightest know the certainty
of those things, wherein thou hast been instructed.*

Luke, 1:1–4

The main focus of this chapter is the P-vs-NP Question and the theory of NP-completeness.
Additional topics covered in this chapter include the general notion of a polynomial-time
reduction (with a special emphasis on self-reducibility), the existence of problems in NP
that are neither NP-complete nor in P, the class coNP, optimal search algorithms, and
promise problems.

Summary: Loosely speaking, the P-vs-NP Question refers to search
problems for which the correctness of solutions can be efficiently
checked (i.e., if there is an efficient algorithm that given a solution to a
given instance determines whether or not the solution is correct). Such
search problems correspond to the class NP, and the question is whether
or not all these search problems can be solved efficiently (i.e., if there
is an efficient algorithm that given an instance finds a correct solution).
Thus, the P-vs-NP Question can be phrased as asking *whether or not
finding solutions is harder than checking the correctness of solutions.*

An alternative formulation, in terms of decision problems, refers to assertions that have efficiently verifiable proofs (of relatively short length).
Such sets of assertions correspond to the class NP, and the question is
whether or not proofs for such assertions can be found efficiently (i.e.,
if there is an efficient algorithm that given an assertion determines its
validity and/or finds a proof for its validity). Thus, the P-vs-NP Question
can be phrased as asking *whether or not discovering proofs is harder than
verifying their correctness*, that is, if proving is harder than verifying (or
if proofs are valuable at all).

Indeed, it is widely believed that the answer to the two equivalent formulations is that finding (resp., discovering) is harder than checking (resp.,

verifying), that is, that *P is different than NP.* The fact that this natural conjecture is unsettled seems to be one of the big sources of frustration of Complexity Theory. The author's opinion, however, is that this feeling of frustration is out of place. In any case, at present, when faced with a hard problem in NP, we cannot expect to prove that the problem is not in P (unconditionally). The best we can expect is a conditional proof that the said problem is not in P, based on the assumption that NP is different from P. The contrapositive is proving that if the said problem is in P, then so is any problem in NP (i.e., NP equals P). This is where the theory of NP-completeness comes into the picture.

The theory of NP-completeness is based on the notion of a reduction, which is a relation between computational problems. Loosely speaking, one computational problem is reducible to another problem if it is possible to efficiently solve the former when provided with an (efficient) algorithm for solving the latter. Thus, the first problem is not harder to solve than the second one. A problem (in NP) is NP-complete if any problem in NP is reducible to it. Thus, the fate of the entire class NP (with respect to inclusion in P) rests with each individual NP-complete problem. In particular, showing that a problem is NP-complete implies that this problem is not in P unless NP equals P. Amazingly enough, NP-complete problems exist, and furthermore, hundreds of natural computational problems arising in many different areas of mathematics and science are NP-complete.

We stress that NP-complete problems are not the only hard problems in NP (i.e., if P is different than NP then NP contains problems that are neither NP-complete nor in P). We also note that the P-vs-NP Question is not about inventing sophisticated algorithms or ruling out their existence, but rather boils down to the analysis of a single known algorithm; that is, we will present an optimal search algorithm for any problem in NP, while having no clue about its time complexity.

Teaching note: Indeed, we suggest presenting the P-vs-NP Question both in terms of search problems and in terms of decision problems. Furthermore, in the latter case, we suggest introducing NP by explicitly referring to the terminology of proof systems. As for the theory of NP-completeness, we suggest emphasizing the mere existence of NP-complete problems.

Prerequisites. We assume familiarity with the notions of search and decision problems (see Section 1.2.2), algorithms (see Section 1.2.3), and their time complexity (see §1.2.3.5). We will also refer to the notion of an oracle machine (see §1.2.3.6).

Organization. In Section 2.1 we present the two formulations of the P-vs-NP Question. The general notion of a reduction is presented in Section 2.2, where we highlight its applicability outside the domain of NP-completeness. Section 2.3 is devoted to the theory of NP-completeness, whereas Section 2.4 treats three relatively advanced topics (i.e., the framework of promise problems, the existence of optimal search algorithms for NP, and the class coNP).

> **Teaching note:** This chapter has more teaching notes than any other chapter in the book. This reflects the author's concern regarding the way in which this fundamental material is often taught. Specifically, it is the author's impression that the material covered in this chapter is often taught in wrong ways, which fail to communicate its fundamental nature.

2.1. The P Versus NP Question

Our daily experience is that it is harder to solve a problem than it is to check the correctness of a solution. Is this experience merely a coincidence or does it represent a fundamental fact of life (or a property of the world)? This is the essence of the P versus NP Question, where *P represents search problems that are efficiently solvable and NP represents search problems for which solutions can be efficiently checked*.

Another natural question captured by the P versus NP Question is whether proving theorems is harder that verifying the validity of these proofs. In other words, the question is whether deciding membership in a set is harder than being convinced of this membership by an adequate proof. In this case, *P represents decision problems that are efficiently solvable, whereas NP represents sets that have efficiently checkable proofs of membership*.

These two meanings of the P versus NP Question are rigorously presented and discussed in Sections 2.1.1 and 2.1.2, respectively. The equivalence of the two formulations is shown in Section 2.1.3, and the common belief that P is different from NP is further discussed in Section 2.1.6. We start by recalling the notion of efficient computation.

> **Teaching note:** Most students have heard of P and NP before, but we suspect that many of them have not obtained a good explanation of what the P-vs-NP Question actually represents. This unfortunate situation is due to using the standard technical definition of NP (which refers to the fictitious and confusing device called a non-deterministic polynomial-time machine). Instead, we advocate the use of the more cumbersome definitions, sketched in the foregoing paragraphs (and elaborated in Sections 2.1.1 and 2.1.2), which clearly capture the fundamental nature of NP.

The notion of efficient computation. Recall that we associate efficient computation with polynomial-time algorithms.[1] This association is justified by the fact that polynomials are a class of moderately growing functions that is closed under operations that correspond to natural composition of algorithms. Furthermore, the class of polynomial-time algorithms is independent of the specific model of computation, as long as the latter is "reasonable" (cf. the Cobham-Edmonds Thesis). Both issues are discussed in §1.2.3.5.

Advanced note on the representation of problem instances. As noted in §1.2.2.3, many natural (search and decision) problems are captured more naturally by the terminology of promise problems (cf. Section 2.4.1), where the domain of possible instances is a subset of $\{0, 1\}^*$ rather than $\{0, 1\}^*$ itself. For example, computational problems in graph theory presume some simple encoding of graphs as strings, but this encoding is typically not

---

[1] **Advanced comment:** In this chapter, we consider *deterministic* (polynomial-time) algorithms as the basic model of efficient computation. A more liberal view, which also includes *probabilistic* (polynomial-time) algorithms, is presented in Chapter 6. We stress that the most important facts and questions that are addressed in the current chapter hold also with respect to probabilistic polynomial-time algorithms.

onto (i.e., not all strings encode graphs), and thus not all strings are legitimate instances. However, in these cases, the set of legitimate instances (e.g., encodings of graphs) is efficiently recognizable (i.e., membership in it can be decided in polynomial time). Thus, artificially extending the set of instances to the set of all possible strings (and allowing trivial solutions for the corresponding dummy instances) does not change the complexity of the original problem. We further discuss this issue in Section 2.4.1.

2.1.1. The Search Version: Finding Versus Checking

Teaching note: Complexity theorists are so accustomed to focusing on decision problems that they seem to forget that search problems are at least as natural as decision problems. Furthermore, to many non-experts, search problems may seem even more natural than decision problems: Typically, people seek solutions more than they pause to wonder whether or not solutions exist. Thus, we recommend starting with a formulation of the P-vs-NP Question in terms of search problems. Admittedly, the cost is more cumbersome formulations, but it is more than worthwhile.

Teaching note: In order to reflect the importance of the search version as well as allow less cumbersome formulations, we chose to introduce notations for the two search classes corresponding to P and NP: These classes are denoted PF and PC (standing for Polynomial-time Find and Polynomial-time Check, respectively). The teacher may prefer using notations and terms that are more evocative of P and NP (such as P-search and NP-search), and actually we also do so in some motivational discussions (especially in advanced chapters of this book). (Still, in our opinion, in the long run, the students and the field may be served better by using standard-looking notations.)

Much of computer science is concerned with solving various search problems (as in Definition 1.1). Examples of such problems include finding a solution to a system of linear (or polynomial) equations, finding a prime factor of a given integer, finding a spanning tree in a graph, finding a short traveling salesman tour in a metric space, and finding a scheduling of jobs to machines such that various constraints are satisfied. Furthermore, search problems correspond to the daily notion of "solving problems" and thus are of natural general interest. In the current section, we will consider the question of *which search problems can be solved efficiently*.

One type of search problems that cannot be solved efficiently consists of search problems for which the solutions are too long in terms of the problem's instances. In such a case, merely typing the solution amounts to an activity that is deemed inefficient. Thus, we focus our attention on search problems that are not in this class. That is, we consider only search problems in which the length of the solution is bounded by a polynomial in the length of the instance. Recalling that search problems are associated with binary relations (see Definition 1.1), we focus our attention on polynomially bounded relations.

Definition 2.1 (polynomially bounded relations): *We say that $R \subseteq \{0, 1\}^* \times \{0, 1\}^*$ is* polynomially bounded *if there exists a polynomial p such that for every $(x, y) \in R$ it holds that $|y| \leq p(|x|)$.*

Recall that $(x, y) \in R$ means that y is a solution to the problem instance x, where R represents the problem itself. For example, in the case of finding a prime factor of a given integer, we refer to a relation R such that $(x, y) \in R$ if the integer y is a prime factor of the integer x.

For a polynomially bounded relation R it makes sense to ask whether or not, given a problem instance x, one can efficiently find an adequate solution y (i.e., find y such that $(x, y) \in R$). The polynomial bound on the length of the solution (i.e., y) guarantees that a negative answer is not merely due to the length of the required solution.

2.1.1.1. The Class P as a Natural Class of Search Problems

Recall that we are interested in the class of search problems that can be solved efficiently, that is, problems for which solutions (whenever they exist) can be found efficiently. Restricting our attention to polynomially bounded relations, we identify the corresponding fundamental class of search problem (or binary relation), denoted $\mathcal{PF}$ (standing for "Polynomial-time Find"). (The relationship between $\mathcal{PF}$ and the standard definition of P will be discussed in Sections 2.1.3 and 2.2.3.) The following definition refers to the formulation of solving search problems provided in Definition 1.1.

Definition 2.2 (efficiently solvable search problems):

- *The search problem of a polynomially bounded relation $R \subseteq \{0, 1\}^* \times \{0, 1\}^*$ is efficiently solvable if there exists a polynomial time algorithm A such that, for every x, it holds that $A(x) \in R(x) \stackrel{\text{def}}{=} \{y : (x, y) \in R\}$ if and only if $R(x)$ is not empty. Furthermore, if $R(x) = \emptyset$ then $A(x) = \bot$, indicating that x has no solution.*
- *We denote by $\mathcal{PF}$ the class of search problems that are efficiently solvable (and correspond to polynomially bounded relations). That is, $R \in \mathcal{PF}$ if R is polynomially bounded and there exists a polynomial-time algorithm that given x finds y such that $(x, y) \in R$ (or asserts that no such y exists).*

Note that $R(x)$ denotes the set of valid solutions for the problem instance x. Thus, the solver A is required to find a valid solution (i.e., satisfy $A(x) \in R(x)$) whenever such a solution exists (i.e., $R(x)$ is not empty). On the other hand, if the instance x has no solution (i.e., $R(x) = \emptyset$) then clearly $A(x) \notin R(x)$. The extra condition (also made in Definition 1.1) requires that in this case $A(x) = \bot$. Thus, algorithm A always outputs a correct answer, which is a valid solution in the case that such a solution exists and otherwise provides an indication that no solution exists.

We have defined a fundamental class of problems, and we do know of many natural problems in this class (e.g., solving linear equations over the rationals, finding a perfect matching in a graph, etc). However, we must admit that we do not have a good understanding regarding the actual contents of this class (i.e., we are unable to characterize many natural problems with respect to membership in this class). This situation is quite common in Complexity Theory, and seems to be a consequence of the fact that complexity classes are defined in terms of the "external behavior" (of potential algorithms) rather than in terms of the "internal structure" (of the problem). Turning back to $\mathcal{PF}$, we note that, while it contains many natural search problems, there are also many natural search problems that are not known to be in $\mathcal{PF}$. A natural class containing a host of such problems is presented next.

2.1.1.2. The Class NP as Another Natural Class of Search Problems

Natural search problems have the property that valid solutions can be efficiently recognized. That is, given an instance x of the problem R and a candidate solution y, one can efficiently determine whether or not y is a valid solution for x (with respect to the problem R, i.e., whether or not $y \in R(x)$). The class of all such search problems is a natural class *per se*, because it is not clear why one should care about a solution unless one can recognize a valid solution once given. Furthermore, this class is a natural domain of candidates for $\mathcal{PF}$, because the ability to efficiently recognize a valid solution seems to be a natural (albeit not absolute) prerequisite for a discussion regarding the complexity of finding such solutions.

We restrict our attention again to polynomially bounded relations, and consider the class of relations for which membership of pairs in the relation can be decided efficiently. We stress that we consider deciding membership of given pairs of the form (x, y) in a fixed relation R, and not deciding membership of x in the set $S_R \stackrel{\text{def}}{=} \{x : R(x) \neq \emptyset\}$. (The relationship between the following definition and the standard definition of NP will be discussed in Sections 2.1.3–2.1.5 and 2.2.3.)

Definition 2.3 (search problems with efficiently checkable solutions):

- *The search problem of a polynomially bounded relation $R \subseteq \{0, 1\}^* \times \{0, 1\}^*$ has* efficiently checkable solutions *if there exists a polynomial-time algorithm A such that, for every x and y, it holds that $A(x, y) = 1$ if and only if $(x, y) \in R$.*
- *We denote by $\mathcal{PC}$ (standing for "Polynomial-time Check") the class of search problems that correspond to polynomially bounded binary relations that have efficiently checkable solutions. That is, $R \in \mathcal{PC}$ if the following two conditions hold:*
  1. *For some polynomial p, if $(x, y) \in R$ then $|y| \leq p(|x|)$.*
  2. *There exists a polynomial-time algorithm that given (x, y) determines whether or not $(x, y) \in R$.*

The class $\mathcal{PC}$ contains thousands of natural problems (e.g., finding a traveling salesman tour of length that does not exceed a given threshold, finding the prime factorization of a given composite, etc). In each of these natural problems, the correctness of solutions can be checked efficiently (e.g., given a traveling salesman tour it is easy to compute its length and check whether or not it exceeds the given threshold).[2]

The class $\mathcal{PC}$ is the natural domain for the study of which problems are in $\mathcal{PF}$, because the ability to efficiently recognize a valid solution is a *natural* prerequisite for a discussion regarding the complexity of finding such solutions. We warn, however, that $\mathcal{PF}$ contains (unnatural) problems that are not in $\mathcal{PC}$ (see Exercise 2.1).

2.1.1.3. The P Versus NP Question in Terms of Search Problems

Is it the case that every search problem in $\mathcal{PC}$ is in $\mathcal{PF}$? That is, if one can efficiently check the correctness of solutions with respect to some (polynomially bounded) relation R, then is it necessarily the case that the search problem of R can be solved efficiently? In other words, if it is *easy to check* whether or not a given solution for a given instance is correct, then is it also *easy to find* a solution to a given instance?

---

[2] In the traveling salesman problem (TSP), the instance is a matrix of distances between cities and a threshold, and the task is to find a tour that passes all cities and covers a total distance that does not exceed the threshold.

If $\mathcal{PC} \subseteq \mathcal{PF}$ then this would mean that whenever solutions to given instances can be efficiently checked (for correctness) it is also the case that such solutions can be efficiently found (when given only the instance). This would mean that all reasonable search problems (i.e., all problems in $\mathcal{PC}$) are easy to solve. Needless to say, such a situation would contradict the intuitive feeling (and the daily experience) that some reasonable search problems are hard to solve. Furthermore, in such a case, the notion of "solving a problem" would lose its meaning (because finding a solution will not be significantly more difficult than checking its validity).

On the other hand, if $\mathcal{PC} \setminus \mathcal{PF} \neq \emptyset$ then there exist reasonable search problems (i.e., some problems in $\mathcal{PC}$) that are hard to solve. This conforms with our basic intuition by which some reasonable problems are easy to solve whereas others are hard to solve. Furthermore, it reconfirms the intuitive gap between the notions of solving and checking (asserting that in some cases "solving" is significantly harder than "checking").

2.1.2. The Decision Version: Proving Versus Verifying

As we shall see in the sequel, the study of search problems (e.g., the $\mathcal{PC}$-vs-$\mathcal{PF}$ Question) can be "reduced" to the study of decision problems. Since the latter problems have a less cumbersome terminology, Complexity Theory tends to focus on them (and maintains its relevance to the study of search problems via the aforementioned reduction). Thus, the study of decision problems provides a convenient way for studying search problems. For example, the study of the complexity of deciding the satisfiability of Boolean formulae provides a convenient way for studying the complexity of finding satisfying assignments for such formulae.

We wish to stress, however, that decision problems are interesting and natural *per se* (i.e., beyond their role in the study of search problems). After all, some people do care about the truth, and so determining whether certain claims are true is a natural computational problem. Specifically, determining whether a given object (e.g., a Boolean formula) has some predetermined property (e.g., is satisfiable) constitutes an appealing computational problem. The P-vs-NP Question refers to the complexity of solving such problems for a wide and natural class of properties associated with the class NP. The latter class refers to properties that have "efficient proof systems" allowing for the verification of the claim that a given object has a predetermined property (i.e., is a member of a predetermined set). Jumping ahead, we mention that the P-vs-NP Question refers to the question of whether properties that have efficient proof systems can also be decided efficiently (without proofs). Let us clarify all these notions.

Properties of objects are modeled as subsets of the set of all possible objects (i.e., a property is associated with the set of objects having this property). For example, the property of being a prime is associated with the set of prime numbers, and the property of being connected (resp., having a Hamiltonian path) is associated with the set of connected (resp., Hamiltonian) graphs. Thus, we focus on deciding membership in sets (as in Definition 1.2). The standard formulation of the P-vs-NP Question refers to the questionable equality of two natural classes of decision problems, denoted P and NP (and defined in §2.1.2.1 and §2.1.2.2, respectively).

2.1.2.1. The Class P as a Natural Class of Decision Problems

Needless to say, we are interested in the class of decision problems that are efficiently solvable. This class is traditionally denoted $\mathcal{P}$ (standing for "Polynomial time"). The following definition refers to the formulation of solving decision problems (provided in Definition 1.2).

Definition 2.4 (efficiently solvable decision problems)**:**

- *A decision problem $S \subseteq \{0, 1\}^*$ is* efficiently solvable *if there exists a polynomial-time algorithm A such that, for every x, it holds that $A(x) = 1$ if and only if $x \in S$.*
- *We denote by $\mathcal{P}$ the class of decision problems that are efficiently solvable.*

As in Definition 2.2, we have defined a fundamental class of problems, which contains many natural problems (e.g., determining whether or not a given graph is connected), but we do not have a good understanding regarding its actual contents (i.e., we are unable to characterize many natural problems with respect to membership in this class). In fact, there are many natural decision problems that are not known to reside in $\mathcal{P}$, and a natural class containing a host of such problems is presented next. This class of decision problems is denoted NP (for reasons that will become evident in Section 2.1.5).

2.1.2.2. The Class NP and NP-proof Systems

We view NP as the class of decision problems that have efficiently verifiable proof systems. Loosely speaking, we say that a set S has a proof system if instances in S have valid proofs of membership (i.e., proofs accepted as valid by the system), whereas instances not in S have no valid proofs. Indeed, proofs are defined as strings that (when accompanying the instance) are accepted by the (efficient) verification procedure. We say that V is a verification procedure for membership in S if it satisfies the following two conditions:

1. Completeness: True assertions have valid proofs; that is, proofs accepted as valid by V. Bearing in mind that assertions refer to membership in S, this means that for every $x \in S$ there exists a string y such that $V(x, y) = 1$ (i.e., V accepts y as a valid proof for the membership of x in S).

2. Soundness: False assertions have no valid proofs. That is, for every $x \notin S$ and every string y it holds that $V(x, y) = 0$, which means that V rejects y as a proof for the membership of x in S.

We note that the soundness condition captures the "security" of the verification procedure, that is, its ability not to be fooled (by anything) into proclaiming a wrong assertion. The completeness condition captures the "viability" of the verification procedure, that is, its ability to be convinced of any valid assertion, when presented with an adequate proof. (We stress that, in general, proof systems are defined in terms of their verification procedures, which must satisfy adequate completeness and soundness conditions.) Our focus here is on efficient verification procedures that utilize relatively short proofs (i.e., proofs that are of length that is polynomially bounded by the length of the corresponding assertion).[3]

---

[3]**Advanced comment:** In a continuation of footnote 1, we note that in this chapter we consider *deterministic* (polynomial-time) verification procedures, and consequently, the completeness and soundness conditions that we state here are errorless. In contrast, in Chapter 9, we will consider various types of probabilistic (polynomial-time) verification procedures as well as probabilistic completeness and soundness conditions. A common theme that underlies both treatments is that efficient verification is interpreted as meaning verification by a process that runs in time that is polynomial in the length of the assertion. In the current chapter, we use the equivalent formulation that

Let us consider a couple of examples before turning to the actual definition. Starting with the set of Hamiltonian graphs, we note that this set has a verification procedure that, given a pair (G, π), accepts if and only if π is a Hamiltonian path in the graph G. In this case π serves as a proof that G is Hamiltonian. Note that such proofs are relatively short (i.e., the path is actually shorter than the description of the graph) and are easy to verify. Needless to say, this proof system satisfies the aforementioned completeness and soundness conditions. Turning to the case of satisfiable Boolean formulae, given a formula ϕ and a truth assignment τ, the verification procedure instantiates ϕ (according to τ), and accepts if and only if simplifying the resulting Boolean expression yields the value `true`. In this case τ serves as a proof that ϕ is satisfiable, and the alleged proofs are indeed relatively short and easy to verify.

Definition 2.5 (efficiently verifiable proof systems):

- *A decision problem $S \subseteq \{0, 1\}^*$ has an* efficiently verifiable proof system *if there exists a polynomial p and a polynomial-time* (verification) *algorithm V such that the following two conditions hold:*
    1. Completeness: *For every $x \in S$, there exists y of length at most $p(|x|)$ such that $V(x, y) = 1$.*

       (Such a string y is called an NP-witness for $x \in S$.)
    2. Soundness: *For every $x \notin S$ and every y, it holds that $V(x, y) = 0$.*

    Thus, $x \in S$ if and only if there exists y of length at most $p(|x|)$ such that $V(x, y) = 1$.

    In such a case, we say that S has an NP-proof system, *and refer to V as its* verification procedure *(or as the proof system itself).*
- *We denote by $\mathcal{NP}$ the class of decision problems that have efficiently verifiable proof systems.*

We note that the term *NP-witness* is commonly used.[4] In some cases, V (or the set of pairs accepted by V) is called a witness relation of S. We stress that the same set S may have many different NP-proof systems (see Exercise 2.2), and that in some cases the difference is not artificial (see Exercise 2.3).

Teaching note: Using Definition 2.5, it is typically easy to show that natural decision problems are in $\mathcal{NP}$. All that is needed is designing adequate NP-proofs of membership, which is typically quite straightforward and natural, because natural decision problems are typically phrased as asking about the existence of a structure (or object) that can be easily verified as valid. For example, SAT is defined as the set of satisfiable Boolean formulae, which means asking about the existence of satisfying assignments. Indeed, we can efficiently check whether a given assignment satisfies a given formula, which means that we have (a verification procedure for) an NP-proof system for SAT.

---

considers the running time as a function of the total length of the assertion and the proof, but require that the latter has length that is polynomially bounded by the length of the assertion.

[4]In most cases this is done without explicitly defining V, which is understood from the context and/or by common practice. In many texts, V is not called a proof system (nor a verification procedure of such a system), although this term is most adequate.

Note that for any search problem R in $\mathcal{PC}$, the set of instances that have a solution with respect to R (i.e., the set $S_R \overset{\text{def}}{=} \{x : R(x) \neq \emptyset\}$) is in $\mathcal{NP}$. Specifically, for any $R \in \mathcal{PC}$, consider the verification procedure V such that $V(x, y) \overset{\text{def}}{=} 1$ if and only if $(x, y) \in R$, and note that the latter condition can be decided in poly($|x|$)-time. Thus, *any search problem in $\mathcal{PC}$ can be viewed as a problem of searching for* (efficiently verifiable) *proofs* (i.e., NP-witnesses for membership in the set of instances having solutions). On the other hand, any NP-proof system gives rise to a natural search problem in $\mathcal{PC}$; that is, the problem of searching for a valid proof (i.e., an NP-witness) for the given instance (i.e, the verification procedure V yields the search problem that corresponds to $R = \{(x, y) : V(x, y) = 1\}$). Thus, *$S \in \mathcal{NP}$ if and only if there exists $R \in \mathcal{PC}$ such that $S = \{x : R(x) \neq \emptyset\}$.*

> **Teaching note:** The last paragraph suggests another easy way of showing that natural decision problems are in $\mathcal{NP}$: just thinking of the corresponding natural search problem. The point is that natural decision problems (in $\mathcal{NP}$) are phrased as referring to whether a solution exists for the corresponding natural search problem. For example, in the case of SAT, the question is whether there exists a satisfying assignment to a given Boolean formula, and the corresponding search problem is finding such an assignment. But in all these cases, it is easy to check the correctness of solutions; that is, the corresponding search problem is in $\mathcal{PC}$, which implies that the decision problem is in $\mathcal{NP}$.

Observe that $\mathcal{P} \subseteq \mathcal{NP}$ holds: A verification procedure for claims of membership in a set $S \in \mathcal{P}$ may just ignore the alleged NP-witness and run the decision procedure that is guaranteed by the hypothesis $S \in \mathcal{P}$; that is, $V(x, y) = A(x)$, where A is the aforementioned decision procedure. Indeed, the latter verification procedure is quite an abuse of the term (because it makes no use of the proof); however, it is a legitimate one. As we shall shortly see, the P-vs-NP Question refers to the question of whether such proof-oblivious verification procedures can be used for every set that has some efficiently verifiable proof system. (Indeed, given that $\mathcal{P} \subseteq \mathcal{NP}$, the P-vs-NP Question is whether $\mathcal{NP} \subseteq \mathcal{P}$.)

2.1.2.3. The P Versus NP Question in Terms of Decision Problems

Is it the case that NP-proofs are useless? That is, is it the case that for every efficiently verifiable proof system one can easily determine the validity of assertions without looking at the proof? If that were the case, then proofs would be meaningless, because they would offer no fundamental advantage over directly determining the validity of the assertion. The conjecture $\mathcal{P} \neq \mathcal{NP}$ asserts that proofs are useful: There exists sets in $\mathcal{NP}$ that cannot be decided by a polynomial-time algorithm, and so for these sets obtaining a proof of membership (for some instances) is useful (because we cannot efficiently determine membership by ourselves).

In the foregoing paragraph we viewed $\mathcal{P} \neq \mathcal{NP}$ as asserting the advantage of obtaining proofs over deciding the truth by ourselves. That is, $\mathcal{P} \neq \mathcal{NP}$ asserts that (in some cases) verifying is easier than deciding. A slightly different perspective is that $\mathcal{P} \neq \mathcal{NP}$ asserts that finding proofs is harder than verifying their validity. This is the case because, for any set S that has an NP-proof system, the ability to efficiently find proofs of membership with respect to this system (i.e., finding an NP-witness of membership in S for any given $x \in S$), yields the ability to decide membership in S. Thus, for $S \in \mathcal{NP} \setminus \mathcal{P}$, it must be harder to find proofs of membership in S than to verify the validity of such proofs (which can be done in polynomial time).

2.1.3. Equivalence of the Two Formulations

As hinted several times, *the two formulations of the P-vs-NP Questions are equivalent*. That is, every search problem having efficiently checkable solutions is solvable in polynomial-time (i.e., $\mathcal{PC} \subseteq \mathcal{PF}$) if and only if membership in any set that has an NP-proof system can be decided in polynomial-time (i.e., $\mathcal{NP} \subseteq \mathcal{P}$). Recalling that $\mathcal{P} \subseteq \mathcal{NP}$ (whereas $\mathcal{PF}$ is not contained in $\mathcal{PC}$ (Exercise 2.1)), we prove the following.

Theorem 2.6: $\mathcal{PC} \subseteq \mathcal{PF}$ *if and only if* $\mathcal{P} = \mathcal{NP}$.

Proof: Suppose, on the one hand, that the inclusion holds for the search version (i.e., $\mathcal{PC} \subseteq \mathcal{PF}$). We will show that this implies the existence of an efficient algorithm for finding NP-witnesses for any set in $\mathcal{NP}$, which in turn implies that this set is in $\mathcal{P}$. Specifically, let S be an arbitrary set in $\mathcal{NP}$, and V be the corresponding verification procedure (i.e., satisfying the conditions in Definition 2.5). Then $R \stackrel{\text{def}}{=} \{(x, y) : V(x, y) = 1\}$ is a polynomially bounded relation in $\mathcal{PC}$, and by the hypothesis its search problem is solvable in polynomial-time (i.e., $R \in \mathcal{PC} \subseteq \mathcal{PF}$). Denoting by A the polynomial-time algorithm solving the search problem of R, we decide membership in S in the obvious way. That is, on input x, we output 1 if and only if $A(x) \neq \bot$, where the latter event holds if and only if $A(x) \in R(x)$, which in turn occurs if and only if $R(x) \neq \emptyset$ (equiv., $x \in S$). Thus, $\mathcal{NP} \subseteq \mathcal{P}$ (and $\mathcal{NP} = \mathcal{P}$) follows.

Suppose, on the other hand, that $\mathcal{NP} = \mathcal{P}$. We will show that this implies an efficient algorithm for determining whether a given string y' is a prefix of some solution to a given instance x of a search problem in $\mathcal{PC}$, which in turn yields an efficient algorithm for finding solutions. Specifically, let R be an arbitrary search problem in $\mathcal{PC}$. Then the set $S'_R \stackrel{\text{def}}{=} \{\langle x, y' \rangle : \exists y'' \text{ s.t. } (x, y'y'') \in R\}$ is in $\mathcal{NP}$ (because $R \in \mathcal{PC}$), and hence S'_R is in $\mathcal{P}$ (by the hypothesis $\mathcal{NP} = \mathcal{P}$). This yields a polynomial-time algorithm for solving the search problem of R, by extending a prefix of a potential solution bit by bit (while using the decision procedure to determine whether or not the current prefix is valid). That is, on input x, we first check whether or not $(x, \lambda) \in S'_R$ and output $\bot$ (indicating $R(x) = \emptyset$) in case $(x, \lambda) \notin S'_R$. Next, we proceed in iterations, maintaining the invariant that $(x, y') \in S'_R$. In each iteration, we set $y' \leftarrow y'0$ if $(x, y'0) \in S'_R$ and $y' \leftarrow y'1$ if $(x, y'1) \in S'_R$. If none of these conditions hold (which happens after at most polynomially many iterations) then the current y' satisfies $(x, y') \in R$. Thus, for an arbitrary $R \in \mathcal{PC}$ we obtain that $R \in \mathcal{PF}$, and $\mathcal{PC} \subseteq \mathcal{PF}$ follows. ∎

Reflection. The first part of the proof of Theorem 2.6 associates with each set S in $\mathcal{NP}$ a natural relation R (in $\mathcal{PC}$). Specifically, R consists of all pairs (x, y) such that y is an NP-witness for membership of x in S. Thus, the search problem of R consists of finding such an NP-witness, when given x as input. Indeed, R is called the witness relation of S, and solving the search problem of R allows for deciding membership in S. Thus, $R \in \mathcal{PC} \subseteq \mathcal{PF}$ implies $S \in \mathcal{P}$. In the second part of the proof, we associate with each $R \in \mathcal{PC}$ a set S'_R

(in $\mathcal{NP}$), but S_R' is more "expressive" than the set $S_R \stackrel{\text{def}}{=} \{x : \exists y \text{ s.t. } (x, y) \in R\}$ (which gives rise to R as its witness relation). Specifically, S_R' consists of strings that encode pairs (x, y') such that y' is a prefix of some string in $R(x) = \{y : (x, y) \in R\}$. The key observation is that deciding membership in S_R' allows for solving the search problem of R; that is, $S_R' \in \mathcal{P}$ implies $R \in \mathcal{PF}$.

Conclusion. Theorem 2.6 justifies the traditional focus on the decision version of the P-vs-NP Question. Indeed, given that both formulations of the question are equivalent, we may just study the less cumbersome one.

2.1.4. Two Technical Comments Regarding NP

Recall that when defining $\mathcal{PC}$ (resp., $\mathcal{NP}$) we have explicitly confined our attention to search problems of polynomially bounded relations (resp., NP-witnesses of polynomial length). An alternative formulation may allow a binary relation R to be in $\mathcal{PC}$ (resp., $S \in \mathcal{NP}$) if membership of (x, y) in R can be decided in time that is polynomial in the length of x (resp., the verification of a candidate NP-witness y for membership of x in S is required to be performed in poly($|x|$)-time). Indeed, this means that the validity of y can be determined without reading all of it (which means that some substring of y can be used as the effective y in the original definitions).

We comment that problems in $\mathcal{PC}$ (resp., $\mathcal{NP}$) can be solved in exponential time (i.e., time exp(poly($|x|$)) for input x). This can be done by an exhaustive search among all possible candidate solutions (resp., all possible candidate NP-witnesses). Thus, $\mathcal{NP} \subseteq \mathcal{EXP}$, where $\mathcal{EXP}$ denote the class of decision problems that can be solved in exponential time (i.e., time exp(poly($|x|$)) for input x).

2.1.5. The Traditional Definition of NP

Unfortunately, Definition 2.5 is not the commonly used definition of $\mathcal{NP}$. Instead, traditionally, $\mathcal{NP}$ is defined as the class of sets that can be decided by a *fictitious* device called a non-deterministic polynomial-time machine (which explains the source of the notation NP). The reason that this class of fictitious devices is interesting is due to the fact that it captures (indirectly) the definition of NP-proofs. Since the reader may come across the traditional definition of $\mathcal{NP}$ when studying different works, the author feels obliged to provide the traditional definition as well as a proof of its equivalence to Definition 2.5.

Definition 2.7 (non-deterministic polynomial-time Turing machines):

- *A non-deterministic Turing machine is defined as in §1.2.3.2, except that the transition function maps symbol-state pairs to subsets of triples* (rather than to a single triple) *in $\Sigma \times Q \times \{-1, 0, +1\}$. Accordingly, the configuration following a specific instantaneous configuration may be one of several possibilities, each determined by a different possible triple. Thus, the* computations of a non-deterministic machine *on a* fixed *input may result in different outputs.*

  In the context of decision problems, one typically considers the question of whether or not there exists a computation that starting with a fixed input halts with output 1. We say that the non-deterministic machine M accept x *if there exists a computation of M, on input x, that halts with output 1. The* set accepted by a non-deterministic machine *is the set of inputs that are accepted by the machine.*

- *A* non-deterministic polynomial-time Turing machine *is defined as one that makes a number of steps that is polynomial in the length of the input. Traditionally, $\mathcal{NP}$ is defined as the class of sets that are each accepted by some non-deterministic polynomial-time Turing machine.*

We stress that Definition 2.7 refers to a fictitious model of computation. Specifically, Definition 2.7 makes no reference to the number (or fraction) of possible computations of the machine (on a specific input) that yield a specific output.[5] Definition 2.7 only refers to whether or not computations leading to a certain output exist (for a specific input). The question of what the mere existence of such possible computations means (in terms of real life) is not addressed, because the model of a non-deterministic machine is not meant to provide a reasonable model of a (real-life) computer. The model is meant to capture something completely different (i.e., it is meant to provide an elegant definition of the class $\mathcal{NP}$, while relying on the fact that Definition 2.7 is equivalent to Definition 2.5).

Teaching note: Whether or not Definition 2.7 is elegant is a matter of taste. For sure, many students find Definition 2.7 quite confusing, possibly because they assume that it represents some natural model of computation and consequently they allow themselves to be fooled by their intuition regarding such models. (Needless to say, the students' intuition regarding computation is irrelevant when applied to a fictitious model.)

Note that, unlike other definitions in this chapter, Definition 2.7 makes explicit reference to a specific model of computation. Still, a similar extension can be applied to other models of computation by considering adequate non-deterministic computation rules. Also note that, without loss of generality, we may assume that the transition function maps each possible symbol-state pair to exactly two triples (cf. Exercise 2.4).

Theorem 2.8: *Definition 2.5 is equivalent to Definition 2.7. That is, a set S has an NP-proof system if and only if there exists a non-deterministic polynomial-time machine that accepts S.*

Proof Sketch: Suppose, on the one hand, that the set S has an NP-proof system, and let us denote the corresponding verification procedure by V. Consider the following non-deterministic polynomial-time machine, denoted M. On input x, machine M makes an adequate $m = \text{poly}(|x|)$ number of non-deterministic steps, producing (non-deterministically) a string $y \in \{0, 1\}^m$, and then emulates $V(x, y)$. We stress that these non-deterministic steps may result in producing any m-bit string y. Recall that $x \in S$ if and only if there exists y of length at most $\text{poly}(|x|)$ such that $V(x, y) = 1$. This implies that the set accepted by M equals S.

---

[5]**Advanced comment:** In contrast, the definition of a probabilistic machine refers to this number (or, equivalently, to the probability that the machine produces a specific output, when the probability is essentially taken uniformly over all possible computations). Thus, a probabilistic machine refers to a natural model of computation that can be realized provided we can equip the machine with a source of randomness. For details, see Section 6.1.1.

Suppose, on the other hand, that there exists a non-deterministic polynomial-time machine M that accepts the set S. Consider a deterministic machine M' that on input (x, y), where y has adequate length, emulates a computation of M on input x while using y to determine the non-deterministic steps of M. That is, the ith step of M on input x is determined by the ith bit of y (which indicates which of the two possible moves to make at the current step). Note that $x \in S$ if and only if there exists y of length at most $\text{poly}(|x|)$ such that $M'(x, y) = 1$. Thus, M' gives rise to an NP-proof system for S. $\qquad\square$

2.1.6. In Support of P Different from NP

Intuition and concepts constitute . . . the elements of all our knowledge, so that neither concepts without an intuition in some way corresponding to them, nor intuition without concepts, can yield knowledge.

Immanuel Kant (1724–1804)

Kant speaks of the importance of *both* philosophical considerations (referred to as "concepts") and empirical considerations (referred to as "intuition") to science (referred to as (sound) "knowledge").

It is widely believed that P is different than NP; that is, that $\mathcal{PC}$ contains search problems that are not efficiently solvable, and that there are NP-proof systems for sets that cannot be decided efficiently. This belief is supported by both philosophical and empirical considerations.

- *Philosophical considerations*: Both formulations of the P-vs-NP Question refer to natural questions about which we have strong conceptions. The notion of solving a (search) problem seems to presume that, at least in some cases (if not in general), finding a solution is significantly harder than checking whether a presented solution is correct. This translates to $\mathcal{PC} \setminus \mathcal{PF} \neq \emptyset$. Likewise, the notion of a proof seems to presume that, at least in some cases (if not in general), the proof is useful in determining the validity of the assertion, that is, that verifying the validity of an assertion may be made significantly easier when provided with a proof. This translates to $\mathcal{P} \neq \mathcal{NP}$, which also implies that it is significantly harder to find proofs than to verify their correctness, which again coincides with the daily experience of researchers and students.
- *Empirical considerations*: The class NP (or rather $\mathcal{PC}$) contains thousands of different problems for which no efficient solving procedure is known. Many of these problems have arisen in vastly different disciplines, and were the subject of extensive research by numerous different communities of scientists and engineers. These essentially independent studies have all failed to provide efficient algorithms for solving these problems, a failure that is extremely hard to attribute to sheer coincidence or a stroke of bad luck.

Throughout the rest of this book, we will adopt the common belief that P is different from NP. At some places, we will explicitly use this conjecture (or even stronger assumptions), whereas in other places we will present results that are interesting (if and) only if $\mathcal{P} \neq \mathcal{NP}$ (e.g., the entire theory of NP-completeness becomes uninteresting if $\mathcal{P} = \mathcal{NP}$).

The $\mathcal{P} \neq \mathcal{NP}$ conjecture is indeed very appealing and intuitive. The fact that this natural conjecture is unsettled seems to be one of the sources of frustration of many complexity theorists. The author's opinion, however, is that this feeling of frustration is not justified. In contrast, the fact that Complexity Theory evolves around natural and simply stated questions that are so difficult to resolve makes its study very exciting.

2.1.7. Philosophical Meditations

Whoever does not value preoccupation with thoughts, can skip this chapter.
Robert Musil, *The Man Without Qualities*, Chap. 28

The inherent limitations of our scientific knowledgewe were articulated by Kant, who argued that our knowledge cannot transcend our way of understanding. The "ways of understanding" are predetermined; they precede any knowledge acquisition and are the precondition to such acquisition. In a sense, Wittgenstein refined the analysis, arguing that knowledge must be formulated in a language, and the latter must be subject to a (sound) mechanism of assigning meaning. Thus, the inherent limitations of any possible "meaning-assigning mechanism" impose limitations on what can be (meaningfully) said.

Both philosophers spoke of the relation between the world and our thoughts. They took for granted (or rather assumed) that, in the domain of well-formulated thoughts (e.g., logic), every valid conclusion can be effectively reached (i.e., every valid assertion can be effectively proved). Indeed, this naive assumption was refuted by Gödel. In a similar vain, Turing's work asserts that *there exist well-defined problems that cannot be solved by well-defined methods.*

The latter assertion transcends the philosophical considerations of the first paragraph: It asserts that the limitations of our ability are not due only to the gap between the "world as is" and our model of it. Indeed, this assertion refers to inherent limitations on any rational process even when this process is applied to well-formulated information and is aimed at a well-formulated goal. Indeed, in contrast to naive presumptions, not every well-formulated problem can be (effectively) solved.

The $\mathcal{P} \neq \mathcal{NP}$ conjecture goes even beyond the foregoing. It limits the domain of the discussion to "fair" problems, that is, to problems for which valid solutions can be efficiently recognized as such. Indeed, there is something feigned in problems for which one cannot efficiently recognize valid solutions. Avoiding such feigned and/or unfair problems, $\mathcal{P} \neq \mathcal{NP}$ means that (even with this limitation) there exist problems that are inherently unsolvable in the sense that they cannot be solved *efficiently*. That is, in contrast to naive presumptions, *not every problem that refers to efficiently recognizable solutions can be solved efficiently*. In fact, the gap between the complexity of recognizing solutions and the complexity of finding them vouches for the meaningfulness of the notion of a problem.

2.2. Polynomial-Time Reductions

We present a general notion of (polynomial-time) reductions among computational problems, and view the notion of a "Karp-reduction" as an important special case that suffices (and is more convenient) in many cases. Reductions play a key role in the theory of NP-completeness, which is the topic of Section 2.3. In the current section, we stress the fundamental nature of the notion of a reduction *per se* and highlight two specific applications (i.e., reducing search and optimization problems to decision problems). Furthermore, in the latter applications, it will be important to use the general notion of a reduction (i.e., "Cook-reduction" rather than "Karp-reduction").

Teaching note: We assume that many students have heard of reductions, but we fear that most have obtained a conceptually poor view of their fundamental nature. In particular, we fear that reductions are identified with the theory of NP-completeness, while reductions have numerous other important applications that have little to do with NP-completeness (or completeness with respect to some other class). Furthermore, we believe that it is important to show that natural search and optimization problems can be reduced to decision problems.

2.2.1. The General Notion of a Reduction

Reductions are procedures that use "functionally specified" subroutines. That is, the functionality of the subroutine is specified, but its operation remains unspecified and its running time is counted at unit cost. Analogously to algorithms, which are modeled by Turing machines, reductions can be modeled as *oracle* (Turing) machines. A reduction solves one computational problem (which may be either a search or a decision problem) by using oracle (or subroutine) calls to another computational problem (which again may be either a search or a decision problem).

2.2.1.1. The Actual Formulation

The notion of a general algorithmic reduction was discussed in §1.2.3.3 and §1.2.3.6. These reductions, called Turing-reductions (cf. §1.2.3.3) and modeled by oracle machines (cf. §1.2.3.6), made no reference to the time complexity of the main algorithm (i.e., the oracle machine). Here, we focus on efficient (i.e., polynomial-time) reductions, which are often called *Cook-reductions*. That is, we consider oracle machines (as in Definition 1.11) that run in time polynomial in the length of their input. We stress that the running time of an oracle machine is the number of steps made during its (own) computation, and that the oracle's reply on each query is obtained in a single step.

The key property of efficient reductions is that they allow for the transformation of efficient implementations of the subroutine into efficient implementations of the task reduced to it. That is, as we shall see, if one problem is Cook-reducible to another problem and the latter is polynomial-time solvable then so is the former.

The most popular case is that of reducing decision problems to decision problems, but we will also consider reducing search problems to search problems and reducing search problems to decision problems. Note that when reducing to a decision problem, the oracle is determined as the single valid solver of the decision problem (i.e., the function $f : \{0, 1\}^* \to \{0, 1\}$ solves the decision problem of membership in S if, for every x, it holds that $f(x) = 1$ if $x \in S$ and $f(x) = 0$ otherwise). In contrast, when reducing to a search problem the oracle is not uniquely determined because there may be many different valid solvers (i.e., the function $f : \{0, 1\}^* \to \{0, 1\}^* \cup \{\bot\}$ solves the search problem of R if, for every x, it holds that $f(x) \in R(x)$ if $x \in S_R$ and $f(x) = \bot$ otherwise). We capture both cases in the following definition.

Definition 2.9 (Cook-reduction): *A problem Π is* Cook-reducible *to a problem Π' if there exists a polynomial-time oracle machine M such that for every function f that solves Π' it holds that M^f solves Π, where $M^f(x)$ denotes the output of machine M on input x when given oracle access to f.*

Note that Π (resp., Π') may be either a search problem or a decision problem (or even a yet undefined type of a problem). At this point the reader should verify that if Π is Cook-reducible to Π' and Π' is solvable in polynomial time then so is Π. (See Exercise 2.5 for other properties of Cook-reductions.)

Observe that the second part of the proof of Theorem 2.6 is actually a Cook-reduction of the search problem of any R in $\mathcal{PC}$ to a decision problem regarding a related set $S'_R = \{(x, y') : \exists y'' \text{ s.t. } (x, y'y'') \in R\}$, which in $\mathcal{NP}$. Thus, that proof establishes the following result.

Theorem 2.10: *Every search problem in $\mathcal{PC}$ is Cook-reducible to some decision problem in $\mathcal{NP}$.*

We shall see a tighter relation between search and decision problems in Section 2.2.3; that is, in some cases, R will be reduced to $S_R = \{x : \exists y \text{ s.t. } (x, y) \in R\}$ rather than to S'_R.

2.2.1.2. Special Cases

A Karp-reduction is a special case of a reduction (from a decision problem to a decision problem). Specifically, for decision problems S and S', we say that S is Karp-reducible to S' if there is a reduction of S to S' *that operates as follows*: On input x (an instance for S), the reduction computes x', makes query x' to the oracle S' (i.e., invokes the subroutine for S' on input x'), and answers whatever the latter returns. This reduction is often represented by the polynomial-time computable mapping of x to x'; that is, the standard definition of a Karp-reduction is actually as follows.

Definition 2.11 (Karp-reduction): *A polynomial-time computable function f is called a Karp-reduction of S to S' if, for every x, it holds that $x \in S$ if and only if $f(x) \in S'$.*

Thus, syntactically speaking, a Karp-reduction is not a Cook-reduction, but it trivially gives rise to one (i.e., on input x, the oracle machine makes query $f(x)$, and returns the oracle answer). Being slightly inaccurate but essentially correct, we shall say that Karp-reductions are special cases of Cook-reductions. Needless to say, Karp-reductions constitute a very restricted case of Cook-reductions. Still, this restricted case suffices for many applications (e.g., most importantly for the theory of NP-completeness (when developed for decision problems)), but not for reducing a search problem to a decision problem. Furthermore, whereas each decision problem is Cook-reducible to its complement, some decision problems are *not* Karp-reducible to their complement (see Exercises 2.7 and 2.33).

We comment that Karp-reductions may (and should) be augmented in order to handle reductions of search problems to search problems. Such an augmented Karp-reduction of the search problem of R to the search problem of R' operates as follows: On input x (an instance for R), the reduction computes x', makes query x' to the oracle R' (i.e., invokes the subroutine for searching R' on input x') obtaining y' such that $(x', y') \in R'$, and uses y' to compute a solution y to x (i.e., $y \in R(x)$). Thus, such a reduction can be represented by two polynomial-time computable mappings, f and g, such that $(x, g(x, y')) \in R$ for any y' that is a solution of $f(x)$ (i.e., for y' that satisfies $(f(x), y') \in R'$). (Indeed, in general, unlike in the case of decision problems, the reduction cannot just return y' as an answer to x.) This augmentation is called a Levin-reduction and, analogously to the case of a Karp-reduction, it is often represented by the two aforementioned polynomial-time computable mappings (i.e., of x to x', and of (x, y') to y).

Definition 2.12 (Levin-reduction): *A pair of polynomial-time computable functions, f and g, is called a* Levin-reduction *of R to R' if f is a Karp-reduction of $S_R = \{x : \exists y \text{ s.t. } (x, y) \in R\}$ to $S_{R'} = \{x' : \exists y' \text{ s.t. } (x', y') \in R'\}$ and for every $x \in S_R$ and $y' \in R'(f(x))$ it holds that $(x, g(x, y')) \in R$, where $R'(x') = \{y' : (x', y') \in R'\}$.*

Indeed, the function f preserves the existence of solutions; that is, for any x, it holds that $R(x) \neq \emptyset$ if and only if $R'(f(x)) \neq \emptyset$. As for the second function (i.e., g), it maps any solution y' for the reduced instance $f(x)$ to a solution for the original instance x (where this mapping may also depend on x). We note that it is also natural to consider a third function that maps solutions for R to solutions for R' (see Exercise 2.28).

2.2.1.3. Terminology and a Brief Discussion

In the sequel, whenever we neglect to mention the type of a reduction, we refer to a Cook-reduction. Two additional terms, which will be particularly useful in the advanced chapters, are presented next.

- We say that two problems are computationally equivalent if they are reducible to one another. This means that the two problems are essentially as hard (or as easy). Note that computationally equivalent problems need not reside in the same complexity class.

  For example, as we shall see in Section 2.2.3, there exist many natural $R \in \mathcal{PC}$ such that the search problem of R and the decision problem of $S_R = \{x : \exists y \text{ s.t. } (x, y) \in R\}$ are computationally equivalent, although (even syntactically) the two problems do not belong to the same class (i.e., $R \in \mathcal{PC}$ whereas $S_R \in \mathcal{NP}$). Also, each decision problem is computationally equivalent to its complement, although the two problems may not belong to the same class (see, e.g., Section 2.4.3).

- We say that a *class of problems, $\mathcal{C}$, is reducible to a problem Π' if every problem in $\mathcal{C}$ is reducible to Π'. We say that the class $\mathcal{C}$ is reducible to the class $\mathcal{C}'$ if for every $\Pi \in \mathcal{C}$ there exists $\Pi' \in \mathcal{C}'$ such that Π is reducible to Π'.*

  For example, Theorem 2.10 asserts that $\mathcal{PC}$ *is reducible to $\mathcal{NP}$.*

The fact that we allow Cook-reductions is essential to various important connections between decision problems and other computational problems. For example, as will be shown in Section 2.2.2, a natural class of optimization problems is reducible to $\mathcal{NP}$. Also recall that $\mathcal{PC}$ is reducible to $\mathcal{NP}$ (cf. Theorem 2.10). Furthermore, as will be shown in Section 2.2.3, many natural search problems in $\mathcal{PC}$ are reducible to a corresponding *natural* decision problem in $\mathcal{NP}$ (rather than merely to some problem in $\mathcal{NP}$). In all of these results, the reductions in use are (and must be) Cook-reductions.

2.2.2. Reducing Optimization Problems to Search Problems

Many search problems refer to a set of potential solutions, associated with each problem instance, such that different solutions are assigned different "values" (resp., "costs"). In such a case, one may be interested in finding a solution that has value exceeding some threshold (resp., cost below some threshold). Alternatively, one may seek a solution of maximum value (resp., minimum cost). For simplicity, let us focus on the case of a value that we wish to maximize. Still, there are two different objectives (i.e., exceeding a threshold and optimizing), giving rise to two different (auxiliary) search problems related to the same relation R. Specifically, for a binary relation R and a *value function* $f : \{0, 1\}^* \times \{0, 1\}^* \to \mathbb{R}$, we consider two search problems.

1. *Exceeding a threshold*: Given a pair (x, v) the task is to find $y \in R(x)$ such that $f(x, y) \geq v$, where $R(x) = \{y : (x, y) \in R\}$. That is, we are actually referring to the search problem of the relation

$$R_f \overset{\text{def}}{=} \{(\langle x, v \rangle, y) : (x, y) \in R \wedge f(x, y) \geq v\}, \tag{2.1}$$

   where $\langle x, v \rangle$ denotes a string that encodes the pair (x, v).

2. *Maximization*: Given x the task is to find $y \in R(x)$ such that $f(x, y) = v_x$, where v_x is the maximum value of $f(x, y')$ over all $y' \in R(x)$. That is, we are actually referring to the search problem of the relation

$$R'_f \overset{\text{def}}{=} \{(x, y) \in R : f(x, y) = \max_{y' \in R(x)} \{f(x, y')\}\}. \tag{2.2}$$

Examples of value functions include the size of a clique in a graph, the amount of flow in a network (with link capacities), etc. The task may be to find a clique of size exceeding a given threshold in a given graph or to find a maximum-size clique in a given graph. Note that, in these examples, the "base" search problem (i.e., the relation R) is quite easy to solve, and the difficulty arises from the auxiliary condition on the value of a solution (presented in R_f and R'_f). Indeed, one may trivialize R (i.e., let $R(x) = \{0, 1\}^{\text{poly}(|x|)}$ for every x), and impose all necessary structure by the function f (see Exercise 2.8).

We confine ourselves to the case that f is polynomial-time computable, which in particular means that $f(x, y)$ can be represented by a rational number of length polynomial in $|x| + |y|$. We will show next that, in this case, the two aforementioned search problems (i.e., of R_f and R'_f) are computationally equivalent.

Theorem 2.13: *For any polynomial-time computable $f : \{0, 1\}^* \times \{0, 1\}^* \to \mathbb{R}$ and a polynomially bounded binary relation R, let R_f and R'_f be as in Eq. (2.1) and Eq. (2.2), respectively. Then the search problems of R_f and R'_f are computationally equivalent.*

Note that, *for $R \in \mathcal{PC}$ and polynomial-time computable f, it holds that $R_f \in \mathcal{PC}$.* Combining Theorems 2.10 and 2.13, it follows that *in this case both R_f and R'_f are reducible to $\mathcal{NP}$.* We note, however, that even in this case it does not necessarily hold that $R'_f \in \mathcal{PC}$. See further discussion following the proof.

Proof: The search problem of R_f is reduced to the search problem of R'_f by finding an optimal solution (for the given instance) and comparing its value to the given threshold value. That is, we construct an oracle machine that solves R_f by making a single query to R'_f. Specifically, on input (x, v), the machine issues the query x (to a solver for R'_f), obtaining the optimal solution y (or an indication $\perp$ that $R(x) = \emptyset$), computes $f(x, y)$, and returns y if $f(x, y) \geq v$. Otherwise (i.e., either $y = \perp$ or $f(x, y) < v$), the machine returns an indication that $R_f(x, v) = \emptyset$.

Turning to the opposite direction, we reduce the search problem of R'_f to the search problem of R_f by first finding the optimal value $v_x = \max_{y \in R(x)}\{f(x, y)\}$

(by binary search on its possible values), and next finding a solution of value v_x. In both steps, we use oracle calls to R_f. For simplicity, we assume that f assigns *positive* integer values, and let $\ell = \text{poly}(|x|)$ be such that $f(x, y) \leq 2^\ell - 1$ for every $y \in R(x)$. Then, on input x, we first find $v_x = \max\{f(x, y) : y \in R(x)\}$, by making oracle calls of the form $\langle x, v \rangle$. The point is that $v_x < v$ if and only if $R_f(\langle x, v \rangle) = \emptyset$, which in turn is indicated by the oracle answer $\perp$ (to the query $\langle x, v \rangle$). Making ℓ queries, we determine v_x (see Exercise 2.9). Note that in case $R(x) = \emptyset$, all answers will indicate that $R_f(\langle x, v \rangle) = \emptyset$, which we treat as if $v_x = 0$. Finally, we make the query (x, v_x), and halt returning the oracle's answer (which is $y \in R(x)$ such that $f(x, y) = v_x$ if $v_x > 0$ and an indication that $R(x) = \emptyset$ otherwise). ∎

Proof's Digest: Note that the first direction uses the hypothesis that f is polynomial-time computable, whereas the opposite direction only used the fact that the optimal value lies in a finite space of exponential size that can be "efficiently searched." While the first direction can be proved using a Levin-reduction, this seems impossible for the opposite direction (in general).

On the complexity of R_f and R'_f. We focus on the natural case in which $R \in \mathcal{PC}$ and f is polynomial-time computable. In this case, Theorem 2.13 asserts that R_f and R'_f are computationally equivalent. A closer look reveals, however, that $R_f \in \mathcal{PC}$ always holds, whereas $R'_f \in \mathcal{PC}$ does *not* necessarily hold. That is, the problem of finding a solution (for a given instance) that exceeds a given threshold is in the class $\mathcal{PC}$, whereas the problem of finding an optimal solution is not necessarily in the class $\mathcal{PC}$. For example, the problem of finding a clique of a given size K in a given graph G is in $\mathcal{PC}$, whereas the problem of finding a maximum size clique in a given graph G is not known (and is quite unlikely) to be in $\mathcal{PC}$ (although it is Cook-reducible to $\mathcal{PC}$). Indeed, the class of problems that are reducible to $\mathcal{PC}$ is a natural and interesting class (see further discussion at the end of Section 3.2.1). Needless to say, for every $R \in \mathcal{PC}$ and polynomial-time computable f, the former class contains R'_f.

2.2.3. Self-Reducibility of Search Problems

The results to be presented in this section further justify the focus on decision problems. Loosely speaking, these results show that for many natural relations R, the question of whether or not the search problem of R is efficiently solvable (i.e., is in $\mathcal{PF}$) is equivalent to the question of whether or not the "decision problem implicit in R" (i.e., $S_R = \{x : \exists y \text{ s.t. } (x, y) \in R\}$) is efficiently solvable (i.e., is in $\mathcal{P}$). In fact, we will show that these two computational problems (i.e., R and S_R) are computationally equivalent. Note that the decision problem of S_R is easily reducible to the search problem of R, and so our focus is on the other direction. That is, we are interested in relations R for which the search problem of R is reducible to the decision problem of S_R. In such a case, we say that R is self-reducible.

Teaching note: Our usage of the term self-reducibility differs from the traditional one. Traditionally, a decision problem is called (downward) self-reducible if it is Cook-reducible to itself via a reduction that on input x only makes queries that are smaller than x (according to some appropriate measure on the size of strings). Under some natural restrictions

---

(i.e., the reduction takes the disjunction of the oracle answers) such reductions yield reductions of search to decision (as discussed in the main text). For further details, see Exercise 2.13.

Definition 2.14 (the decision implicit in a search and self-reducibility): *The deci-*sion problem implicit in the search problem of R is *deciding membership in the set* $S_R = \{x : R(x) \neq \emptyset\}$, *where* $R(x) = \{y : (x, y) \in R\}$. *The search problem of R is* called **self-reducible** *if it can be reduced to the decision problem of S_R.*

Note that the search problem of R and the problem of deciding membership in S_R refer to the same instances: The search problem requires finding an adequate solution (i.e., given x find $y \in R(x)$), whereas the decision problem refers to the question of whether such solutions exist (i.e., given x determine whether or not $R(x)$ is non-empty). Thus, S_R is really the "decision problem implicit in R," because it is a decision problem that one implicitly solves when solving the search problem of R. Indeed, for any R, *the decision problem of S_R is easily reducible to the search problem for R* (and if R is in $\mathcal{PC}$ then S_R is in $\mathcal{NP}$).[6] It follows that *if a search problem R is self-reducible then it is computationally equivalent to the decision problem S_R.*

Note that the general notion of a reduction (i.e., Cook-reduction) seems inherent to the notion of self-reducibility. This is the case not only due to syntactic considerations, but also due to the following inherent reason. An oracle to any decision problem returns a single bit per invocation, while the intractability of a search problem in $\mathcal{PC}$ must be due to lacking more than a "single bit of information" (see Exercise 2.10).

We shall see that self-reducibility is a property of many natural search problems (including all NP-complete search problems). This justifies the relevance of decision problems to search problems in a stronger sense than established in Section 2.1.3: Recall that in Section 2.1.3 we showed that the fate of the search problem class $\mathcal{PC}$ (wrt $\mathcal{PF}$) is determined by the fate of the decision problem class $\mathcal{NP}$ (wrt $\mathcal{P}$). Here we show that, for many natural search problems in $\mathcal{PC}$ (i.e., self-reducible ones), the fate of such a problem R (wrt $\mathcal{PF}$) is determined by the fate of the decision problem S_R (wrt $\mathcal{P}$), where S_R is the decision problem implicit in R.

2.2.3.1. Examples

We now present a few search problems that are self-reducible. We start with SAT (see Appendix G.2), the set of satisfiable Boolean formulae (in CNF), and consider the search problem in which given a formula one should provide a truth assignment that satisfies it. The corresponding relation is denoted R_{SAT}; that is, $(\phi, \tau) \in R_{\text{SAT}}$ if τ is a satisfying assignment to the formula ϕ. The decision problem implicit in R_{SAT} is indeed SAT. Note that R_{SAT} is in $\mathcal{PC}$ (i.e., it is polynomially bounded and membership of (ϕ, τ) in R_{SAT} is easy to decide (by evaluating a Boolean expression)).

Proposition 2.15 (R_{SAT} is self-reducible): *The search problem of R_{SAT} is reducible to SAT.*

Thus, the search problem of R_{SAT} is computationally equivalent to deciding membership in SAT. Hence, in studying the complexity of SAT, we also address the complexity of the search problem of R_{SAT}.

---

[6]For example, the reduction invokes the search oracle and answer 1 if and only if the oracle returns some string (rather than the "no solution" symbol).

Proof: We present an oracle machine that solves the search problem of R_{SAT} by making oracle calls to SAT. Given a formula ϕ, we find a satisfying assignment to ϕ (in case such an assignment exists) as follows. First, we query SAT on ϕ itself, and return an indication that there is no solution if the oracle answer is 0 (indicating $\phi \notin \text{SAT}$). Otherwise, we let τ, initiated to the empty string, denote a prefix of a satisfying assignment of ϕ. We proceed in iterations, where in each iteration we extend τ by one bit. This is done as follows: First we derive a formula, denoted ϕ', by setting the first $|\tau| + 1$ variables of ϕ according to the values $\tau 0$. We then query SAT on ϕ' (which means that we ask whether or not $\tau 0$ is a prefix of a satisfying assignment of ϕ). If the answer is positive then we set $\tau \leftarrow \tau 0$; otherwise we set $\tau \leftarrow \tau 1$. This procedure relies on the fact that if τ is a prefix of a satisfying assignment of ϕ and $\tau 0$ is not a prefix of a satisfying assignment of ϕ then $\tau 1$ must be a prefix of a satisfying assignment of ϕ.

We wish to highlight a key point that has been blurred in the foregoing description. Recall that the formula ϕ' is obtained by replacing some variables by constants, which means that ϕ' *per se* contains Boolean variables as well as Boolean constants. However, the standard definition of SAT disallows Boolean constants in its instances.[7] Nevertheless, ϕ' can be simplified such that the resulting formula contains no Boolean constants. This simplification is performed according to the straightforward Boolean rules: That is, the constant `false` can be omitted from any clause, but if a clause contains only occurrences of the constant `false` then the entire formula simplifies to `false`. Likewise, if the constant `true` appears in a clause then the entire clause can be omitted, and if all clauses are omitted then the entire formula simplifies to `true`. Needless to say, if the simplification process yields a Boolean constant then we may skip the query, and otherwise we just use the simplified form of ϕ' as our query. ∎

Other examples. Reductions analogous to the one used in the proof of Proposition 2.15 can also be presented for other search problems (and not only for NP-complete ones). Two such examples are searching for a 3-coloring of a given graph and searching for an isomorphism between a given pair of graphs (where the first problem is known to be NP-complete and the second problem is believed not to be NP-complete). In both cases, the reduction of the search problem to the corresponding decision problem consists of iteratively extending a prefix of a valid solution, by making suitable queries in order to decide which extension to use. Note, however, that in these two cases the process of getting rid of constants (representing partial solutions) is more involved. Specifically, in the case of Graph 3-Colorability (resp., Graph Isomorphism) we need to enforce a partial coloring of a given graph (resp., a partial isomorphism between a given pair of graphs); see Exercises 2.11 and 2.12, respectively.

Reflection. The proof of Proposition 2.15 (as well as the proofs of similar results) consists of two observations.

1. For every relation R in $\mathcal{PC}$, it holds that the search problem of R is reducible to the decision problem of $S'_R = \{(x, y') : \exists y'' \text{ s.t. } (x, y'y'') \in R\}$. Such a

---

[7]While the problem seems rather technical at the current setting (as it merely amounts to whether or not the definition of SAT allows Boolean constants in its instances), it is far from being so technical in other cases (see Exercises 2.11 and 2.12).

reduction is explicit in the proof of Theorem 2.6 and is implicit in the proof of Proposition 2.15.

2. For specific $R \in \mathcal{PC}$ (e.g., S_{SAT}), deciding membership in S'_R is reducible to deciding membership in $S_R = \{x : \exists y \text{ s.t. } (x, y) \in R\}$. This is where the specific structure of SAT was used, allowing for a direct and natural transformation of instances of S'_R to instances of S_R.

   (We comment that if S_R is NP-complete then S'_R, which is always in $\mathcal{NP}$, is reducible to S_R by the mere fact that S_R is NP-complete; this comment is related to the following advanced comment.)

For an arbitrary $R \in \mathcal{PC}$, deciding membership in S'_R is not necessarily reducible to deciding membership in S_R. Furthermore, deciding membership in S'_R is not necessarily reducible to the search problem of R. (See Exercises 2.14, 2.15, and 2.16.)

In general, self-reducibility is a property of the search problem and not of the decision problem implicit in it. Furthermore, under plausible assumptions (e.g., the intractability of factoring), there exist relations $R_1, R_2 \in \mathcal{PC}$ having the same implicit-decision problem (i.e., $\{x : R_1(x) \neq \emptyset\} = \{x : R_2(x) \neq \emptyset\}$) such that R_1 is self-reducible but R_2 is not (see Exercise 2.17). However, for many natural decision problems this phenomenon does not arise; that is, *for many natural NP-decision problems S, any NP-witness relation associated with S* (i.e., $R \in \mathcal{PC}$ such that $\{x : R(x) \neq \emptyset\} = S$) *is self-reducible*. Indeed, see the other examples following the proof of Proposition 2.15 as well as the advanced discussion in §2.2.3.2.

2.2.3.2. Self-Reducibility of NP-Complete Problems

> **Teaching note:** In this advanced subsection, we assume that the students have heard of NP-completeness. Actually, we only need the students to know the definition of NP-completeness (i.e., a set S is $\mathcal{NP}$-complete if $S \in \mathcal{NP}$ and every set in $\mathcal{NP}$ is reducible to S). Yet, the teacher may prefer postponing the presentation of the following advanced discussion to Section 2.3.1 (or even to a later stage).

Recall that, in general, self-reducibility is a property of the search problem R and not of the decision problem implicit in it (i.e., $S_R = \{x : R(x) \neq \emptyset\}$). In contrast, in the special case of NP-complete problems, self-reducibility holds for any witness relation associated with the (NP-complete) decision problem. That is, *all search problems that refer to finding NP-witnesses for any NP-complete decision problem are self-reducible.*

   Theorem 2.16: *For every R in $\mathcal{PC}$ such that S_R is $\mathcal{NP}$-complete, the search problem of R is reducible to deciding membership in S_R.*

In many cases, as in the proof of Proposition 2.15, the reduction of the search problem to the corresponding decision problem is quite natural. The following proof presents a generic reduction (which may be "unnatural" in some cases).

   Proof: In order to reduce the search problem of R to deciding S_R, we compose the following two reductions:

   1. A reduction of the search problem of R to deciding membership in $S'_R = \{(x, y') : \exists y'' \text{ s.t. } (x, y'y'') \in R\}$.

——— **66** ———

As stated in the foregoing paragraph (titled "Reflection"), such a reduction is implicit in the proof of Proposition 2.15 (as well as being explicit in the proof of Theorem 2.6).

2. A reduction of S'_R to S_R.

This reduction exists by the hypothesis that S_R is $\mathcal{NP}$-complete and the fact that $S'_R \in \mathcal{NP}$. (Note that we do not assume that this reduction is a Karp-reduction, and furthermore it may be an "unnatural" reduction).

The theorem follows. ∎

2.2.4. Digest and General Perspective

Recall that we presented (polynomial-time) reductions as (efficient) algorithms that use functionally specified subroutines. That is, an efficient reduction of problem Π to problem Π' is an efficient algorithm that solves Π while making subroutine calls to any procedure that solves Π'. This presentation fits the "natural" ("positive") application of such a reduction; that is, combining such a reduction with an efficient implementation of the subroutine (solving Π'), we obtain an efficient algorithm for solving Π. We note that the existence of a polynomial-time reduction of Π to Π' actually means more than the latter implication. For example, even applying such a reduction to an inefficient algorithm for solving Π' yields something for Π; that is, if Π' is solvable in time t' then Π is solvable in time t such that $t(n) = \mathrm{poly}(n) \cdot t'(\mathrm{poly}(n))$ (e.g., if $t'(n) = n^{\log_2 n}$ then $t(n) = n^{O(\log n)}$). Thus, the existence of a polynomial-time reduction of Π to Π' yields an upper bound on the time complexity of Π in terms of the time complexity of Π'.

We note that tighter relations between the complexity of Π and Π' can be established whenever the reduction satisfies additional properties. For example, suppose that Π is polynomial-time reducible to Π' by a reduction that makes queries of linear length (i.e., on input x each query has length $O(|x|)$). Then, if Π' is solvable in time t' then Π is solvable in time t such that $t(n) = \mathrm{poly}(n) \cdot t'(O(n))$ (e.g., if $t'(n) = 2^{\sqrt{n}}$ then $t(n) = 2^{O(\sqrt{n})}$). We further note that bounding other complexity measures of the reduction (e.g., its space complexity) allows for relating the corresponding complexities of the problems; see Section 5.2.2.

In contrast to the foregoing "positive" applications of polynomial-time reductions, the theory of NP-completeness (presented in Section 2.3) is famous for its "negative" application of such reductions. Let us elaborate. The fact that Π is polynomial-time reducible to Π' means that *if solving Π' is feasible then solving Π is feasible*. The direct "positive" application starts with the hypothesis that Π' is feasibly solvable and infers that so is Π. In contrast, the "negative" application uses the counter-positive: it starts with the hypothesis that solving Π is infeasible and infers that the same holds for Π'.

2.3. NP-Completeness

In light of the difficulty of settling the P-vs-NP Question, when faced with a hard problem H in NP, we cannot expect to prove that H is not in P (unconditionally). The best we can expect is a conditional proof that H is not in P, based on the assumption that NP is different from P. The contrapositive is proving that if H is in P, then so is any problem in NP (i.e., NP equals P). One possible way of proving such an assertion is showing that any problem in NP is polynomial-time reducible to H. This is the essence of the theory of NP-completeness.

> **Teaching note:** Some students have heard of NP-completeness before, but we suspect that many have missed important conceptual points. Specifically, we fear that they missed the point that the mere existence of NP-complete problems is amazing (let alone that these problems include natural ones such as SAT). We believe that this situation is a consequence of presenting the detailed proof of Cook's Theorem as the very first thing right after defining NP-completeness.

2.3.1. Definitions

The standard definition of NP-completeness refers to decision problems. In the following we will also present a definition of NP-complete (or rather $\mathcal{PC}$-complete) search problems. In both cases, NP-completeness of a problem Π combines two conditions:

1. Π is in the class (i.e., Π being in $\mathcal{NP}$ or $\mathcal{PC}$, depending on whether Π is a decision or a search problem).
2. Each problem in the class is reducible to Π. This condition is called NP-hardness.

Although a perfectly good definition of NP-hardness could have allowed arbitrary Cook-reductions, it turns out that Karp-reductions (resp., Levin-reductions) suffice for establishing the NP-hardness of all natural NP-complete decision (resp., search) problems. Consequently, NP-completeness is usually defined using this restricted notion of a polynomial-time reduction.

> **Definition 2.17** (NP-completeness of decision problems, restricted notion): *A set S is $\mathcal{NP}$-complete if it is in $\mathcal{NP}$ and every set in $\mathcal{NP}$ is Karp-reducible to S.*

A set is $\mathcal{NP}$-hard if every set in $\mathcal{NP}$ is Karp-reducible to it. Indeed, there is no reason to insist on Karp-reductions (rather than using arbitrary Cook-reductions), except that the restricted notion suffices for all known demonstrations of NP-completeness and is easier to work with. An analogous definition applies to search problems.

> **Definition 2.18** (NP-completeness of search problems, restricted notion): *A binary relation R is $\mathcal{PC}$-complete if it is in $\mathcal{PC}$ and every relation in $\mathcal{PC}$ is Levin-reducible to R.*

In the sequel, we will sometimes abuse the terminology and refer to search problems as NP-complete (rather than $\mathcal{PC}$-complete). Likewise, we will say that a search problem is NP-hard (rather than $\mathcal{PC}$-hard) if every relation in $\mathcal{PC}$ is Levin-reducible to it.

We stress that the mere fact that we have defined a property (i.e., NP-completeness) does not mean that there exist objects that satisfy this property. *It is indeed remarkable that NP-complete problems do exist.* Such problems are "universal" in the sense that solving them allows for solving any other (reasonable) problem (i.e., problems in NP).

2.3.2. The Existence of NP-Complete Problems

We suggest not to confuse the mere existence of NP-complete problems, which is remarkable by itself, with the even more remarkable existence of "natural" NP-complete problems. The following proof delivers the first message as well as focuses on the essence of NP-completeness, rather than on more complicated technical details. The essence of NP-completeness is that a single computational problem may "effectively encode" a wide class of seemingly unrelated problems.

Theorem 2.19: *There exist NP-complete relations and sets.*

Proof: The proof (as well as any other NP-completeness proofs) is based on the observation that some decision problems in $\mathcal{NP}$ (resp., search problems in $\mathcal{PC}$) are "rich enough" to encode all decision problems in $\mathcal{NP}$ (resp., all search problems in $\mathcal{PC}$). This fact is most obvious for the "generic" decision and search problems, denoted S_u and R_u (and defined next), which are used to derive the simplest proof of the current theorem.

We consider the following relation R_u and the decision problem S_u implicit in R_u (i.e., $S_u = \{\overline{x} : \exists y \text{ s.t. } (\overline{x}, y) \in R_u\}$). Both problems refer to the same type of instances, which in turn have the form $\overline{x} = \langle M, x, 1^t \rangle$, where M is a description of a (deterministic) Turing machine, x is a string, and t is a natural number. The number t is given in unary (rather than in binary) in order to allow various complexity measures, which depend on the instance length, to be polynomial in t (rather than poly-logarithmic in t).

Definition. *The relation R_u consists of pairs $(\langle M, x, 1^t \rangle, y)$ such that M accepts the input pair (x, y) within t steps, where $|y| \leq t$.[8] The corresponding set $S_u \stackrel{\text{def}}{=} \{\overline{x} : \exists y \text{ s.t. } (\overline{x}, y) \in R_u\}$ consists of triples $\langle M, x, 1^t \rangle$ such that machine M accepts some input of the form $(x, \cdot)$ within t steps.*

It is easy to see that R_u is in $\mathcal{PC}$ and that S_u is in $\mathcal{NP}$. Indeed, R_u is recognizable by a universal Turing machine, which on input $(\langle M, x, 1^t \rangle, y)$ emulates (t steps of) the computation of M on (x, y). (The fact that $S_u \in \mathcal{NP}$ follows similarly.) We comment that u indeed stands for *universal* (i.e., universal machine), and the proof extends to any reasonable model of computation (which has adequate universal machines).

We now turn to show that R_u and S_u are NP-hard in the adequate sense (i.e., R_u is $\mathcal{PC}$-hard and S_u is $\mathcal{NP}$-hard). We first show that any set in $\mathcal{NP}$ is Karp-reducible to S_u. Let S be a set in $\mathcal{NP}$ and let us denote its witness relation by R; that is, R is in $\mathcal{PC}$ and $x \in S$ if and only if there exists y such that $(x, y) \in R$. Let p_R be a polynomial bounding the length of solutions in R (i.e., $|y| \leq p_R(|x|)$ for every $(x, y) \in R$), let M_R be a polynomial-time machine deciding membership (of alleged (x, y) pairs) in R, and let t_R be a polynomial bounding its running time. Then, the desired Karp-reduction maps an instance x (for S) to the instance $\langle M_R, x, 1^{t_R(|x|+p_R(|x|))} \rangle$ (for S_u); that is,

$$x \mapsto f(x) \stackrel{\text{def}}{=} \langle M_R, x, 1^{t_R(|x|+p_R(|x|))} \rangle. \tag{2.3}$$

---

[8]Instead of requiring that $|y| \leq t$, one may require that M is "canonical" in the sense that it reads its entire input before halting.

Note that this mapping can be computed in polynomial time, and that $x \in S$ if and only if $f(x) = \langle M_R, x, 1^{t_R(|x|+p_R(|x|))} \rangle \in S_u$. Details follow.

First, note that the mapping f does depend (of course) on S, and so it may depend on the fixed objects M_R, p_R, and T_R (which depend on S). Thus, computing f on input x calls for printing the fixed string M_R, copying x, and printing a number of 1's that is a fixed polynomial in the length of x. Hence, f is polynomial-time computable. Second, recall that $x \in S$ if and only if there exists y such that $|y| \leq p_R(|x|)$ and $(x, y) \in R$. Since M_R accepts $(x, y) \in R$ within $t_R(|x| + |y|)$ steps, it follows that $x \in S$ if and only if there exists y such that $|y| \leq p_R(|x|)$ and M_R accepts (x, y) within $t_R(|x| + |y|)$ steps. It follows that $x \in S$ if and only if $f(x) \in S_u$.

We now turn to the search version. For reducing the search problem of any $R \in \mathcal{PC}$ to the search problem of R_u, we use essentially the same reduction. On input an instance x (for R), we make the query $\langle M_R, x, 1^{t_R(|x|+p_R(|x|))} \rangle$ to the search problem of R_u and return whatever the latter returns. Note that if $x \notin S$ then the answer will be "no solution," whereas for every x and y it holds that $(x, y) \in R$ if and only if $(\langle M_R, x, 1^{t_R(|x|+p_R(|x|))} \rangle, y) \in R_u$. Thus, a Levin-reduction of R to R_u consists of the pair of functions (f, g), where f is the foregoing Karp-reduction and $g(x, y) = y$. Note that indeed, for every $(f(x), y) \in R_u$, it holds that $(x, g(x, y)) = (x, y) \in R$. ∎

Advanced comment. Note that the role of 1^t in the definition of R_u is to allow placing R_u in $\mathcal{PC}$. In contrast, consider the relation R'_u that consists of pairs $(\langle M, x, t \rangle, y)$ such that M accepts xy within t steps. Indeed, the difference is that in R_u the time bound t appears in unary notation, whereas in R'_u it appears in binary. Then, as will become obvious in §4.2.1.2, membership in R'_u cannot be decided in polynomial-time. Going even further, we note that omitting t altogether from the problem instance yields a search problem that is not solvable at all. That is, consider the relation $R_H \overset{\text{def}}{=} \{(\langle M, x \rangle, y) : M(xy) = 1\}$ (which is related to the halting problem). Indeed, the search problem of any relation (and in particular of any relation in $\mathcal{PC}$) is Karp-reducible to the search problem of R_H, but the latter is not solvable at all (i.e., there exists no algorithm that halts on every input and on input $\bar{x} = \langle M, x \rangle$ outputs y such that $(\bar{x}, y) \in R_H$ if and only if such a y exists).

Bounded Halting and Non-halting

We note that the problem shown to be NP-complete in the proof of Theorem 2.19 is related to the following two problems, called Bounded Halting and Bounded Non-halting. Fixing any programming language, the instance to each of these problems consists of a program π and a time bound t (presented in unary). The decision version of Bounded Halting (resp., Bounded Non-halting) consists of determining whether or not *there exists an input* (of length at most t) *on which the program π halts in t steps* (resp., does *not* halt in t steps), whereas the search problem consists of finding such an input.

The decision version of Bounded Non-halting refers to a fundamental computational problem in the area of program verification; specifically, the problem of *determining whether a given program halts within a given time bound on all inputs of a given length*.[9]

---

[9]The length parameter need not equal the time bound. Indeed, a more general version of the problem refers to two bounds, ℓ and t, and to whether the given program halts within t steps on each possible ℓ-bit input. It is easy to prove

We have mentioned `Bounded Halting` because it is often referred to in the literature, but we believe that `Bounded Non-halting` is much more relevant to the project of program verification (because one seeks programs that halt on all inputs rather than programs that halt on some input).

It is easy to prove that both problems are NP-complete (see Exercise 2.19). Note that the two (decision) problems are not complementary (i.e., $(M, 1^t)$ may be a yes-instance of both decision problems).[10]

The fact that `Bounded Non-halting` is probably intractable (i.e., is intractable provided that $\mathcal{P} \neq \mathcal{NP}$) is even more relevant to the project of program verification than the fact that the Halting Problem is undecidable. The reason being that the latter problem (as well as other related undecidable problems) refers to arbitrarily long computations, whereas the former problem refers to an explicitly bounded number of computational steps. Specifically, `Bounded Non-halting` is concerned with the *existence of an input that causes the program to violate a certain condition* (i.e., halting) *within a given time-bound*.

In light of the foregoing, the common practice of bashing Bounded (Non-)halting as an "unnatural" problem seems very odd at an age in which computer programs play such a central role. (Nevertheless, we will use the term "natural" in this traditionally and odd sense in the next title, which refers to natural computational problems that seem unrelated to computation.)

2.3.3. Some Natural NP-Complete Problems

Having established the mere existence of NP-complete problems, we now turn to prove the existence of NP-complete problems that do not (explicitly) refer to computation in the problem's definition. We stress that thousands of such problems are known (and a list of several hundreds can be found in [85]).

We will prove that deciding the satisfiability of propositional formulae is NP-complete (i.e., Cook's Theorem), and also present some combinatorial problems that are NP-complete. This presentation is aimed at providing a (small) sample of natural NP-completeness results as well as some tools toward proving NP-completeness of new problems of interest. We start by making a comment regarding the latter issue.

The reduction presented in the proof of Theorem 2.19 is called "generic" because it (explicitly) refers to any (generic) NP-problem. That is, we actually presented a scheme for the design of reductions from any desired NP-problem to the single problem proved to be NP-complete. Indeed, in doing so, we have followed the definition of NP-completeness. However, once we know some NP-complete problems, a different route is open to us. We may establish the NP-completeness of a new problem by reducing a known NP-complete problem to the new problem. This alternative route is indeed a common practice, and it is based on the following simple proposition.

---

that the problem remains NP-complete also in the case that the instances are restricted to having parameters ℓ and t such that $t = p(\ell)$, for any fixed polynomial p (e.g., $p(n) = n^2$, rather than $p(n) = n$ as used in the main text).

[10]Indeed, $(M, 1^t)$ can not be a no-instance of both decision problems, but this does not make the problems complementary. In fact, the two decision problems yield a three-way partition of the instances $(M, 1^t)$: (1) pairs $(M, 1^t)$ such that for *every input x* (of length at most t) the computation of $M(x)$ halts within t steps, (2) pairs $(M, 1^t)$ for which such halting occurs on *some inputs but not on all inputs*, and (3) pairs $(M, 1^t)$ such that there *exists no input* (of length at most t) on which M halts in t steps. Note that instances of type (1) are exactly the no-instances of `Bounded Non-halting`, whereas instances of type (3) are exactly the no-instances of `Bounded Halting`.

Proposition 2.20: *If an NP-complete problem Π is reducible to some problem Π' in NP then Π' is NP-complete. Furthermore, reducibility via Karp-reductions* (resp., Levin-reductions) *is preserved.*

Proof: The proof boils down to asserting the transitivity of reductions. Specifically, the NP-hardness of Π means that every problem in NP is reducible to Π, which in turn is reducible to Π'. Thus, by transitivity of reduction (see Exercise 2.6), every problem in NP is reducible to Π', which means that Π' is NP-hard and the proposition follows. ∎

2.3.3.1. Circuit and Formula Satisfiability: CSAT and SAT

We consider two related computational problems, CSAT and SAT, which refer (in the decision version) to the satisfiability of Boolean circuits and formulae, respectively. (We refer the reader to the definitions of Boolean circuits, formulae, and CNF formulae that appear in §1.2.4.1.)

> **Teaching note:** We suggest establishing the NP-completeness of SAT by a reduction from the circuit satisfaction problem (CSAT), after establishing the NP-completeness of the latter. Doing so allows for decoupling two important parts of the proof of the NP-completeness of SAT: the emulation of Turing machines by circuits, and the emulation of circuits by formulae with auxiliary variables.

CSAT. Recall that Boolean circuits are directed acyclic graphs with internal vertices, called gates, labeled by Boolean operations (of arity either 2 or 1), and external vertices called terminals that are associated with either inputs or outputs. When setting the inputs of such a circuit, all internal nodes are assigned values in the natural way, and this yields a value to the output(s), called an evaluation of the circuit on the given input. The evaluation of circuit C on input z is denoted $C(z)$. We focus on circuits with a single output, and let CSAT denote the set of satisfiable Boolean circuits (i.e., a circuit C is in CSAT if there exists an input z such that $C(z) = 1$). We also consider the related relation $R_{\text{CSAT}} = \{(C, z) : C(z) = 1\}$.

Theorem 2.21 (NP-completeness of CSAT): *The set* (resp., *relation*) CSAT (resp., R_{CSAT}) *is $\mathcal{NP}$-complete* (resp., $\mathcal{PC}$-complete).

Proof: It is easy to see that CSAT $\in \mathcal{NP}$ (resp., $R_{\text{CSAT}} \in \mathcal{PC}$). Thus, we turn to showing that these problems are NP-hard. We will focus on the decision version (but also discuss the search version).

We will present (again, but for the last time in this book) a generic reduction, this time of any NP-problem to CSAT. The reduction is based on the observation, mentioned in §1.2.4.1, that the computation of polynomial-time algorithms can be emulated by polynomial-size circuits. In the current context, we wish to emulate the computation of a fixed machine M on input (x, y), *where x is fixed and y varies* (but $|y| = \text{poly}(|x|)$ and the total number of steps of $M(x, y)$ is polynomial in $|x| + |y|$). Thus, x will be "hard-wired" into the circuit, whereas y will serve as the input to the circuit. The circuit itself, denoted C_x, will consists of "layers" such that each layer will represent an instantaneous configuration of the machine M, and the relation between consecutive configurations in a computation of this machine will be captured by ("uniform") local gadgets in the circuit. The number of layers will depend on (x and on) the polynomial that upper-bounds the running time of M, and an additional gadget will be used to detect whether the last configuration is accepting. Thus, only the first layer of the circuit C_x (which will represent an initial configuration with input prefixed by x) will depend on x. The punch line is that determining whether, for a given x, there exists a y ($|y| = \text{poly}(|x|)$) such that $M(x, y) = 1$ (in a given number of steps) will be reduced to whether there exists a y such that $C_x(y) = 1$. Performing this reduction for any machine M_R that corresponds to any $R \in \mathcal{PC}$ (as in the proof of Theorem 2.19), we establish the fact that CSAT is NP-complete. Details follow.

Recall that we wish to reduce an arbitrary set $S \in \mathcal{NP}$ to CSAT. Let R, p_R, M_R, and t_R be as in the proof of Theorem 2.19 (i.e., R is the witness relation of S, whereas p_R bounds the length of the NP-witnesses, M_R is the machine deciding membership in R, and t_R is its polynomial time bound). Without loss of generality (and for simplicity), suppose that M_R is a one-tape Turing machine. We will construct a Karp-reduction that maps an instance x (for S) to a circuit, denoted $f(x) \overset{\text{def}}{=} C_x$, such that $C_x(y) = 1$ if and only if M_R accepts the input (x, y) within $t_R(|x| + p_R(|x|))$ steps. Thus, it will follow that $x \in S$ if and only if there exists $y \in \{0, 1\}^{p_R(|x|)}$ such that $C_x(y) = 1$ (i.e., if and only if $C_x \in \text{CSAT}$). The circuit C_x will depend on x as well as on M_R, p_R, and t_R. (We stress that M_R, p_R, and t_R are fixed, whereas x varies and is thus explicit in our notation.)

Before describing the circuit C_x, let us consider a possible computation of M_R on input (x, y), where x is fixed and y represents a generic string of length at most $p_R(|x|)$. Such a computation proceeds for $t = t_R(|x| + p_R(|x|))$ steps, and corresponds to a sequence of $t + 1$ instantaneous configurations, each of length t. Each such configuration can be encoded by t pairs of symbols, where the first symbol in each pair indicates the contents of a cell and the second symbol indicates either a state of the machine or the fact that the machine is not located in this cell. Thus, each pair is a member of $\Sigma \times (Q \cup \{\bot\})$, where Σ is the finite "work alphabet" of M_R, Q is its finite set of internal states, and $\bot$ is an indication that the machine is not present at a cell. The initial configuration includes xy as input, and the decision of $M_R(x, y)$ can be read from (the leftmost cell of) the last configuration.[11] With the exception of the first row, the values of the entries in each row are determined by the entries of the row just above it, where this determination reflects the transition function of M_R. Furthermore, the value of each entry in the said array is determined by the values of (up to) three entries that reside in the row above it (see Exercise 2.20). Thus, the aforementioned computation is represented by a $(t + 1) \times t$ array, where each entry encodes one out of a constant number of possibilities, which in turn can be encoded by a constant-length bit string. See Figure 2.1.

The circuit C_x has a structure that corresponds to the aforementioned array. Each entry in the array is represented by a *constant* number of gates such that when C_x is evaluated at y these gates will be assigned values that encode the contents of the said entry (in the computation of $M_R(x, y)$). In particular, the entries of the first row of

---

[11]We refer to the output convention presented in §1.2.3.2, by which the output is written in the leftmost cells and the machine halts at the cell to its right.

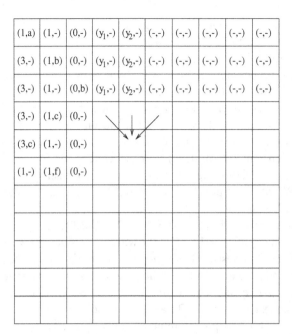

(1,a)	(1,-)	(0,-)	$(y_1,-)$	$(y_2,-)$	(-,-)	(-,-)	(-,-)	(-,-)	(-,-)
(3,-)	(1,b)	(0,-)	$(y_1,-)$	$(y_2,-)$	(-,-)	(-,-)	(-,-)	(-,-)	(-,-)
(3,-)	(1,-)	(0,b)	$(y_1,-)$	$(y_2,-)$	(-,-)	(-,-)	(-,-)	(-,-)	(-,-)
(3,-)	(1,c)	(0,-)							
(3,c)	(1,-)	(0,-)							
(1,-)	(1,f)	(0,-)							

initial configuration
(with input $110y_1y_2$)

last configuration

Figure 2.1: An array representing ten consecutive computation steps on input $110y_1y_2$. Blank characters as well as the indication that the machine is not present in the cell are marked by a hyphen (-). The three arrows represent the determination of an entry by the three entries that reside above it. The machine underlying this example accepts the input if and only if the input contains a zero.

the array are "encoded" by hard-wiring the reduction's input (i.e., x), and feeding the circuit's input (i.e., y) to the adequate input terminals. That is, the circuit has $p_R(|x|)$ ("real") input terminals (corresponding to y), and the hard-wiring of constants to the other $O(t - p_R(|x|))$ gates that represent the first row is done by simple gadgets (as in Figure 1.3). Indeed, the additional hard-wiring in the first row corresponds to the other fixed elements of the initial configuration (i.e., the blank symbols, and the encoding of the initial state and of the initial location; cf. Figure 2.1). The entries of subsequent rows will be "encoded" (or rather computed at evaluation time) by using *constant-size* circuits that determine the value of an entry based on the three relevant entries in the row above it. Recall that each entry is encoded by a constant number of gates, and thus these constant-size circuits merely compute the constant-size function described in Exercise 2.20. In addition, the circuit C_x has a few extra gates that check the values of the entries of the last row in order to determine whether or not it encodes an accepting configuration.[12] Note that the circuit C_x can be constructed in polynomial-time from the string x, because we just need to encode x in an appropriate manner as well as generate a "highly uniform" gridlike circuit of size $O(t_R(|x| + p_R(|x|))^2)$.[13]

Although the foregoing construction of C_x capitalizes on various specific details of the (one-tape) Turing machine model, it can be easily adapted to other natural

---

[12]In continuation of footnote 11, we note that it suffices to check the values of the two leftmost entries of the last row. We assumed here that the circuit propagates a halting configuration to the last row. Alternatively, we may check for the existence of an accepting/halting configuration in the entire array, since this condition is quite simple.

[13]**Advanced comment:** A more efficient construction, which generates almost-linear sized circuits (i.e., circuits of size $\widetilde{O}(t_R(|x| + p_R(|x|)))$) is known; see [180].

models of efficient computation (by showing that in such models the transformation from one configuration to the subsequent one can be emulated by a (polynomial-time constructible) circuit).[14] Alternatively, we recall the Cobham-Edmonds Thesis asserting that any problem that is solvable in polynomial time (on some "reasonable" model) can be solved in polynomial time by a (one-tape) Turing machine.

Turning back to the circuit C_x, we observe that indeed $C_x(y) = 1$ if and only if M_R accepts the input (x, y) while making at most $t = t_R(|x| + p_R(|x|))$ steps. Recalling that $S = \{x : \exists y \text{ s.t. } |y| \leq p_R(|x|) \land (x, y) \in R\}$ and that M_R decides membership in R in time t_R, we infer that $x \in S$ if and only if $f(x) = C_x \in$ CSAT. Furthermore, $(x, y) \in R$ if and only if $(f(x), y) \in R_{\text{CSAT}}$. It follows that f is a Karp-reduction of S to CSAT, and, for $g(x, y) \overset{\text{def}}{=} y$, it holds that (f, g) is a Levin-reduction of R to R_{CSAT}. The theorem follows. ∎

SAT. Recall that Boolean formulae are special types of Boolean circuits (i.e., circuits having a tree structure).[15] We further restrict our attention to formulae given in conjunctive normal form (CNF). We denote by SAT the set of satisfiable CNF formulae (i.e., a CNF formula ϕ is in SAT if there exists a truth assignment τ such that $\phi(\tau) = 1$). We also consider the related relation $R_{\text{SAT}} = \{(\phi, \tau) : \phi(\tau) = 1\}$.

Theorem 2.22 (NP-completeness of SAT): *The set* (resp., relation) SAT (resp., R_{SAT}) *is* $\mathcal{NP}$*-complete* (resp., $\mathcal{PC}$*-complete*).

Proof: Since the set of possible instances of SAT is a subset of the set of instances of CSAT, it is clear that SAT $\in \mathcal{NP}$ (resp., $R_{\text{SAT}} \in \mathcal{PC}$). To prove that SAT is NP-hard, we reduce CSAT to SAT (and use Proposition 2.20). The reduction boils down to introducing auxiliary variables in order to "cut" the computation of an arbitrary ("deep") circuit into a conjunction of related computations of "shallow" circuits (i.e., depth-2 circuits) of unbounded fan-in, which in turn may be presented as a CNF formula. The aforementioned auxiliary variables hold the *possible* values of the internal gates of the original circuit, and the clauses of the CNF formula enforce the consistency of these values with the corresponding gate operation. For example, if gate_i and gate_j feed into gate_k, which is a $\land$-gate, then the corresponding auxiliary variables g_i, g_j, g_k should satisfy the Boolean condition $g_k \equiv (g_i \land g_j)$, which can be written as a 3CNF with four clauses. Details follow.

We start by Karp-reducing CSAT to SAT. Given a Boolean circuit C, with n input terminals and m gates, we first construct m *constant-size* formulae on $n + m$ variables, where the first n variables correspond to the input terminals of the circuit, and the other m variables correspond to its gates. The ith formula will depend on the variable that correspond to the ith gate and the 1-2 variables that correspond to the vertices that feed into this gate (i.e., 2 vertices in case of $\land$-gate or $\lor$-gate and a single vertex in case of a $\neg$-gate, where these vertices may be either input terminals or other gates). This (constant-size) formula will be satisfied by a truth assignment if and only if this assignment matches the gate's functionality (i.e., feeding this gate

---

[14]**Advanced comment:** Indeed, presenting such circuits is very easy in the case of all natural models (e.g., the RAM model), where each bit in the next configuration can be expressed by a simple Boolean formula in the bits of the previous configuration.

[15]For an alternative definition, see Appendix G.2.

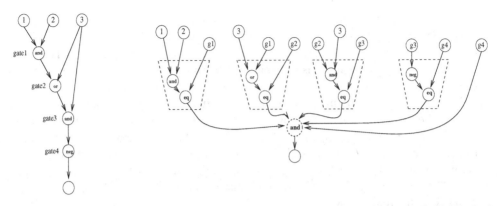

Figure 2.2: Using auxiliary variables (i.e., the g_i's) to "cut" a depth-5 circuit (into a CNF). The dashed regions will be replaced by equivalent CNF formulae. The dashed cycle representing an unbounded fan-in and-gate is the conjunction of all constant-size circuits (which enforce the functionalities of the original gates) and the variable that represents the gate that feeds the output terminal in the original circuit.

with the corresponding values result in the corresponding output value). Note that these *constant-size* formulae can be written as constant-size CNF formulae (in fact, as 3CNF formulae).[16] Taking the conjunction of these m formulae and the variable associated with the gate that feeds into the output terminal, we obtain a formula ϕ in CNF (see Figure 2.2, where $n = 3$ and $m = 4$).

Note that ϕ can be constructed in polynomial time from the circuit C; that is, the mapping of C to $\phi = f(C)$ is polynomial-time computable. We claim that C is in CSAT if and only if ϕ is in SAT.

1. Suppose that for some string s it holds that $C(s) = 1$. Then, assigning to the ith auxiliary variable the value that is assigned to the ith gate of C when evaluated on s, we obtain (together with s) a truth assignment that satisfies ϕ. This is the case because such an assignment satisfies all m constant-size CNFs as well as the variable associated with the output of C.

2. On the other hand, if τ satisfies ϕ then the first n bits in τ correspond to an input on which C evaluates to 1. This is the case because the m constant-size CNFs guarantee that the variables of ϕ are assigned values that correspond to the evaluation of C on the first n bits of τ, while the fact that the variable associated with the output of C has value true guarantees that this evaluation of C yields the value 1.

Note that the latter mapping (of τ to its n-bit prefix) is the second mapping required by the definition of a Levin-reduction.

Thus, we have established that f is a Karp-reduction of CSAT to SAT, and that augmenting f with the aforementioned second mapping yields a Levin-reduction of R_{CSAT} to R_{SAT}. ∎

[16]Recall that any Boolean function can be written as a CNF formula having size that is exponential in the length of its input, which in this case is a constant (i.e., either 2 or 3). Indeed, note that the Boolean functions that we refer to here depend on 2-3 Boolean variables (since they indicate whether or not the corresponding values respect the gate's functionality).

Comment. The fact that the second mapping required by the definition of a Levin-reduction is explicit in the proof of the validity of the corresponding Karp-reduction is a fairly common phenomenon. Actually (see Exercise 2.28), typical presentations of Karp-reductions provide two auxiliary polynomial-time computable mappings (in addition to the main mapping of instances from one problem (e.g., CSAT) to instances of another problem (e.g., SAT)): The first auxiliary mapping is of solutions for the preimage instance (e.g., of CSAT) to solutions for the image instance of the reduction (e.g., of SAT), whereas the second mapping goes the other way around. (Note that only the main mapping and the second auxiliary mapping are required in the definition of a Levin-reduction.) For example, the proof of the validity of the Karp-reduction of CSAT to SAT, denoted f, specified two additional mappings h and g such that $(C, s) \in R_{\text{CSAT}}$ implies $(f(C), h(C, s)) \in R_{\text{SAT}}$ and $(f(C), \tau) \in R_{\text{SAT}}$ implies $(C, g(C, \tau)) \in R_{\text{CSAT}}$. Specifically, in the proof of Theorem 2.22, we used $h(C, s) = (s, a_1, \ldots, a_m)$ where a_i is the value assigned to the ith gate in the evaluation of $C(s)$, and $g(C, \tau)$ being the n-bit prefix of τ.

3SAT. Note that the formulae resulting from the Karp-reduction presented in the proof of Theorem 2.22 are in conjunctive normal form (CNF) with each clause referring to at most three variables. Thus, the above reduction actually establishes the NP-completeness of 3SAT (i.e., SAT restricted to CNF formula with up to three variables per clause). Alternatively, one may Karp-reduce SAT (i.e., satisfiability of CNF formula) to 3SAT (i.e., satisfiability of 3CNF formula), by replacing long clauses with conjunctions of three-variable clauses (using auxiliary variables; see Exercise 2.21). Either way, we get the following result, where the furthermore part is proved by an additional reduction.

> **Proposition 2.23:** *3SAT is NP-complete. Furthermore, the problem remains NP-complete also if we restrict the instances such that each variable appears in at most three clauses.*
>
> **Proof Sketch:** The furthermore part is proved by reduction from 3SAT. We just replace each occurrence of each Boolean variable by a new copy of this variable, and add clauses to enforce that all these copies are assigned the same value. Specifically, replacing the variable z by copies $z^{(1)}, \ldots, z^{(m)}$, we add the clauses $z^{(i+1)} \vee \neg z^{(i)}$ for $i = 1 \ldots, m$ (where $m + 1$ is understood as 1). $\qquad\square$

Related problems. Note that instances of SAT can be viewed as systems of Boolean conditions over Boolean variables. Such systems can be emulated by various types of systems of arithmetic conditions, implying the NP-hardness of solving the latter types of systems. Examples include systems of *integer* linear inequalities (see Exercise 2.23), and systems of quadratic equalities (see Exercise 2.25).

2.3.3.2. Combinatorics and Graph Theory

> **Teaching note:** The purpose of this subsection is to expose the students to a sample of NP-completeness results and proof techniques (i.e., the design of reductions among computational problems). The author believes that this traditional material is insightful, but one may skip it in the context of a complexity class.

We present just a few of the many appealing combinatorial problems that are known to be NP-complete. Throughout this section, we focus on the decision versions of the various problems, and adopt a more informal style. Specifically, we will present a typical decision problem as a problem of deciding whether a given instance, which belongs to a set of relevant instances, is a "yes-instance" or a "no-instance" (rather than referring to deciding membership of arbitrary strings in a set of yes-instances). For further discussion of this style and its rigorous formulation, see Section 2.4.1. We will also neglect showing that these decision problems are in NP; indeed, for natural problems in NP, showing membership in NP is typically straightforward.

Set Cover. We start with the Set Cover problem, in which an instance consists of a collection of finite sets $S_1, \ldots, S_m$ and an integer K and the question (for decision) is whether or not there exist (at most)[17] K sets that cover $\bigcup_{i=1}^{m} S_i$ (i.e., indices $i_1, \ldots, i_K$ such that $\bigcup_{j=1}^{K} S_{i_j} = \bigcup_{i=1}^{m} S_i$).

Proposition 2.24: Set Cover *is NP-complete.*

Proof Sketch: We sketch a reduction of SAT to Set Cover. For a CNF formula ϕ with m clauses and n variables, we consider the sets $S_{1,\texttt{t}}, S_{1,\texttt{f}}, \ldots, S_{n,\texttt{t}}, S_{n,\texttt{f}} \subseteq \{1, \ldots, m\}$ such that $S_{i,\texttt{t}}$ (resp., $S_{i,\texttt{f}}$) is the set of the indices of the clauses (of ϕ) that are satisfied by setting the ith variable to $\texttt{true}$ (resp., $\texttt{false}$). That is, if the ith variable appears unnegated (resp., negated) in the jth clause then $j \in S_{i,\texttt{t}}$ (resp., $j \in S_{i,\texttt{f}}$). Note that the union of these $2n$ sets equals $\{1, \ldots, m\}$. Now, on input ϕ, the reduction outputs the Set Cover instance $f(\phi) \stackrel{\text{def}}{=} ((S_1, \ldots, S_{2n}), n)$, where $S_{2i-1} = S_{i,\texttt{t}} \cup \{m + i\}$ and $S_{2i} = S_{i,\texttt{f}} \cup \{m + i\}$ for $i = 1, \ldots, n$.

Note that f is computable in polynomial time, and that if ϕ is satisfied by $\tau_1 \cdots \tau_n$ then the collection $\{S_{2i-\tau_i} : i = 1, \ldots, n\}$ covers $\{1, \ldots, m + n\}$. Thus, $\phi \in SAT$ implies that $f(\phi)$ is a yes-instance of Set Cover. On the other hand, each cover of $\{m + 1, \ldots, m + n\} \subset \{1, \ldots, m + n\}$ must include either S_{2i-1} or S_{2i} for each i. Thus, a cover of $\{1, \ldots, m + n\}$ using n of the S_j's must contain, for every i, either S_{2i-1} or S_{2i} but not both. Setting τ_i accordingly (i.e., $\tau_i = 1$ if and only if S_{2i-1} is in the cover) implies that $\{S_{2i-\tau_i} : i = 1, \ldots, n\}$ covers $\{1, \ldots, m\}$, which in turn implies that $\tau_1 \cdots \tau_n$ satisfies ϕ. Thus, if $f(\phi)$ is a yes-instance of Set Cover then $\phi \in$ SAT. $\square$

Exact Cover and 3XC. The Exact Cover problem is similar to the set cover problem, except that here the sets that are used in the cover are not allowed to intersect. That is, each element in the universe should be covered by *exactly* one set in the cover. Restricting the set of instances to sequences of subsets each having exactly three elements, we get the restricted problem called 3-Exact Cover (3XC), where it is unnecessary to specify the number of sets to be used in the cover. The problem 3XC is rather technical, but it is quite useful for demonstrating the NP-completeness of other problems (by reducing 3XC to them).

Proposition 2.25: 3-Exact Cover *is NP-complete.*

---

[17] Clearly, in the case of Set Cover, the two formulations (i.e., asking for exactly K sets or at most K sets) are computationally equivalent.

Indeed, it follows that the Exact Cover (in which sets of arbitrary size are allowed) is NP-complete. This follows both for the case that the number of sets in the desired cover is unspecified and for the various cases in which this number is bounded (i.e., upper-bounded or lower-bounded or both).

> **Proof Sketch:** The reduction is obtained by composing three reductions. We first reduce a *restricted case* of 3SAT to a restricted version of Set Cover, denoted 3SC, in which each set has at most three elements (and an instance consists, as in the general case, of a sequence of finite sets as well as an integer K). Specifically, we refer to 3SAT instances that are restricted such that each *variable* appears in at most three clauses, and recall that this restricted problem is NP-complete (see Proposition 2.23). Actually, we further reduce this special case of 3SAT to one in which each *literal* appears in at most two clauses.[18] Now, we reduce the new version of 3SAT to 3SC by using the (very same) reduction presented in the proof of Proposition 2.24, and observing that the size of each set in the reduced instance is at most three (i.e., one more than the number of occurrences of the corresponding literal).
>
> Next, we reduce 3SC to the following restricted case of Exact Cover, denoted 3XC', in which each set has *at most* three elements, an instance consists of a sequence of finite sets as well as an integer K, and the question is whether there exists an exact cover with at most K sets. The reduction maps an instance $((S_1, \ldots, S_m), K)$ of 3SC to the instance (C', K) such that C' is a collection of all subsets of each of the sets $S_1, \ldots, S_m$. Since each S_i has size at most 3, we introduce at most 7 non-empty subsets per each such set, and the reduction can be computed in polynomial time. The reader may easily verify the validity of this reduction.
>
> Finally, we reduce 3XC' to 3XC. Consider an instance $((S_1, \ldots, S_m), K)$ of 3XC', and suppose that $\bigcup_{i=1}^{m} S_i = [n]$. If $n > 3K$ then this is definitely a no-instance, which can be mapped to a dummy no-instance of 3XC, and so we assume that $x \stackrel{\text{def}}{=} 3K - n \geq 0$. Note that x represents the "excess" covering ability of an exact cover having K sets, each having three elements. Thus, we augment the set system with x new elements, denoted $n + 1, \ldots, 3K$, and replace each S_i such that $|S_i| < 3$ by a sub-collection of 3-sets that cover S_i as well as arbitrary elements from $\{n + 1, \ldots, 3K\}$. That is, in case $|S_i| = 2$, the set S_i is replaced by the sub-collection $(S_i \cup \{n + 1\}, \ldots, S_i \cup \{3K\})$, whereas a singleton S_i is replaced by the sets $S_i \cup \{j_1, j_2\}$ for every $j_1 < j_2$ in $\{n + 1, \ldots, 3K\}$. In addition, we add all possible 3-subsets of $\{n + 1, \ldots, 3K\}$. This completes the description of the third reduction, the validity of which is left as an exercise. $\qquad\square$

Vertex Cover, Independent Set, and Clique. Turning to graph theoretic problems (see Appendix G.1), we start with the Vertex Cover problem, which is a special case of the Set Cover problem. The instances consist of pairs (G, K), where $G = (V, E)$ is a simple graph and K is an integer, and the problem is whether or not there exists a set

---

[18]This can be done by observing that if all three occurrences of a variable are of the same type (i.e., they are all negated or all non-negated) then this variable can be assigned a value that satisfies all clauses in which it appears, and so the variable and the clauses in which it appears can be omitted from the instance. This yields a reduction of 3SAT instances in which each variable appears in at most three clauses to 3SAT instances in which each literal appears in at most two clauses. Actually, a closer look at the proof of Proposition 2.23 reveals the fact that the reduced instances satisfy the latter property anyhow.

of (at most) K vertices that is incident to all graph edges (i.e., each edge in G has at least one endpoint in this set). Indeed, this instance of Vertex Cover can be viewed as an instance of Set Cover by considering the collection of sets $(S_v)_{v \in V}$, where S_v denotes the set of edges incident at vertex v (i.e., $S_v = \{e \in E : v \in e\}$). Thus, the NP-hardness of Set Cover follows from the NP-hardness of Vertex Cover (but this implication is unhelpful for us here: We already know that Set Cover is NP-hard and we wish to prove that Vertex Cover is NP-hard). We also note that the Vertex Cover problem is computationally equivalent to the Independent Set and Clique problems (see Exercise 2.26), and thus it suffices to establish the NP-hardness of one of these problems.

Proposition 2.26: *The problems* Vertex Cover, Independent Set *and* Clique *are NP-complete.*

Teaching note: The following reduction is not the "standard" one (see Exercise 2.27). It is rather adapted from the FGLSS-reduction (see Exercise 9.18), and is used here in anticipation of the latter. Furthermore, although the following reduction tends to create a larger graph, the author finds it clearer than the "standard" reduction.

Proof Sketch: We show a reduction from 3SAT to Independent Set. On input a 3CNF formula ϕ with m clauses and n variables, we construct a graph with $7m$ vertices, denoted G_ϕ. The vertices are grouped in m cliques, each corresponding to one of the clauses and containing 7 vertices that correspond to the 7 truth assignments (to the 3 variables in the clause) that *satisfy the clause*. In addition to the internal edges of these m cliques, we add an edge between each pair of vertices that correspond to partial assignments that are *mutually inconsistent*. That is, if a specific (satisfying) assignment to the variables of the ith clause is inconsistent with some (satisfying) assignment to the variables of the jth clause then we connect the corresponding vertices by an edge. (Note that the internal edges of the m cliques may be viewed as a special case of the edges connecting mutually inconsistent partial assignments.) Thus, on input ϕ, the reduction outputs the pair (G_ϕ, m).

Note that if ϕ is satisfiable by a truth assignment τ then there are no edges between the m vertices that correspond to the partial satisfying assignment derived from τ. (We stress that any truth assignment to ϕ yields an independent set, but only a satisfying assignment guarantees that this independent set contains a vertex from each of the m cliques.) Thus, $\phi \in$ SAT implies that G_ϕ has an independent set of size m. On the other hand, an independent set of size m in G_ϕ must contain exactly one vertex in each of the m cliques, and thus induces a truth assignment that satisfies ϕ. (We stress that each independent set induces a consistent truth assignment to ϕ, because the partial assignments selected in the various cliques must be consistent, and that an independent set containing a vertex from a specific clique induces an assignment that satisfies the corresponding clause.) Thus, if G_ϕ has an independent set of size m then $\phi \in$ SAT. $\square$

Graph 3-Colorability (G3C). In this problem the instances are graphs and the question is whether or not the graph can be colored using three colors such that neighboring vertices are not assigned the same color.

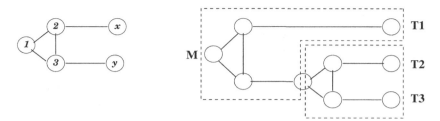

Figure 2.3: The clause gadget and its sub-gadget. In a generic 3-coloring of the sub-gadget it must hold that if $x = y$ then $x = y = 1$. Thus, if the three terminals of the gadget are assigned the same color, χ, then M is also assigned the color χ.

Proposition 2.27: Graph 3-Colorability *is NP-complete.*

Proof Sketch: We reduce 3SAT to G3C by mapping a 3CNF formula ϕ to the graph G_ϕ, which consists of two special ("designated") vertices, a gadget per each variable of ϕ, a gadget per each clause of ϕ, and edges connecting some of these components.

- The two designated vertices are called ground and false, and are connected by an edge that ensures that they must be given different colors in any 3-coloring of G_ϕ. We will refer to the color assigned to the vertex ground (resp., false) by the name ground (resp., false). The third color will be called true.
- The gadget associated with variable x is a pair of vertices, associated with the two literals of x (i.e., x and $\neg x$). These vertices are connected by an edge, and each of them is also connected to the vertex ground. Thus, in a 3-coloring of G_ϕ one of the vertices associated with the variable is colored true and the other is colored false.
- The gadget associated with a clause C is depicted in Figure 2.3. It contains a master vertex, denoted **M**, and three terminal vertices, denoted **T1**, **T2**, and **T3**. The master vertex is connected by edges to the vertices ground and false, and thus in a 3-coloring of G_ϕ the master vertex must be colored true. The gadget has the property that it is possible to color the terminals with any combination of the colors true and false, except for coloring all terminals with false. The terminals of the gadget associated with clause C will be *identified* with the vertices that are associated with the corresponding literals appearing in C. This means that the various clause gadgets are not vertex-disjoint but may rather share some terminals (with the variable gadgets as well as among themselves).[19] See Figure 2.4.

Verifying the validity of the reduction is left as an exercise. □

2.3.4. NP Sets That Are Neither in P nor NP-Complete

As stated in Section 2.3.3, thousands of problems have been shown to be NP-complete (cf., [85, Apdx.], which contains a list of more than three hundreds main entries). Things have reached a situation in which people seem to expect any NP-set to be either NP-complete or in $\mathcal{P}$. This naive view is wrong: *Assuming $\mathcal{NP} \neq \mathcal{P}$, there exist, sets*

---

[19]Alternatively, we may use disjoint gadgets and "connect" each terminal with the corresponding literal (in the corresponding vertex gadget). Such a connection (i.e., an auxiliary gadget) should force the two endpoints to have the same color in any 3-coloring of the graph.

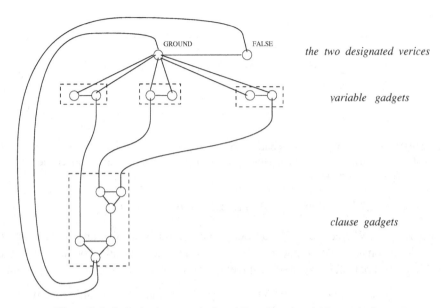

the two designated verices

variable gadgets

clause gadgets

Figure 2.4: A single clause gadget and the relevant variables gadgets.

in $\mathcal{NP}$ that are neither NP-complete nor in $\mathcal{P}$, where here NP-hardness allows also Cook-reductions.

Theorem 2.28: *Assuming $\mathcal{NP} \neq \mathcal{P}$, there exists a set T in $\mathcal{NP} \setminus \mathcal{P}$ such that some sets in $\mathcal{NP}$ are not Cook-reducible to T.*

Theorem 2.28 asserts that if $\mathcal{NP} \neq \mathcal{P}$ then $\mathcal{NP}$ is partitioned into three non-empty classes: the class $\mathcal{P}$, the class of problems to which $\mathcal{NP}$ is Cook-reducible, and the rest, denoted $\mathcal{NPI}$. We already know that the first two classes are not empty, and Theorem 2.28 establishes the non-emptiness of $\mathcal{NPI}$ under the condition that $\mathcal{NP} \neq \mathcal{P}$, which is actually a necessary condition (because if $\mathcal{NP} = \mathcal{P}$ then every set in $\mathcal{NP}$ is Cook-reducible to any other set in $\mathcal{NP}$).

The following proof of Theorem 2.28 presents an unnatural decision problem in $\mathcal{NPI}$. We mention that some natural decision problems (e.g., some that are computationally equivalent to factoring) are conjectured to be in $\mathcal{NPI}$. We also mention that if $\mathcal{NP} \neq \text{co}\mathcal{NP}$, where $\text{co}\mathcal{NP} = \{\{0, 1\}^* \setminus S : S \in \mathcal{NP}\}$, then $\Delta \overset{\text{def}}{=} \mathcal{NP} \cap \text{co}\mathcal{NP} \subseteq \mathcal{P} \cup \mathcal{NPI}$ holds (as a corollary to Theorem 2.35). Thus, if $\mathcal{NP} \neq \text{co}\mathcal{NP}$ then $\Delta \setminus \mathcal{P}$ is a (natural) subset of $\mathcal{NPI}$, and the non-emptiness of $\mathcal{NPI}$ follows provided that $\Delta \neq \mathcal{P}$. Recall that Theorem 2.28 establishes the non-emptiness of $\mathcal{NPI}$ under the seemingly weaker assumption that $\mathcal{NP} \neq \mathcal{P}$.

> **Teaching note:** We recommend either stating Theorem 2.28 without a proof or merely presenting the proof idea.

Proof Sketch: The basic idea is modifying an arbitrary set in $\mathcal{NP} \setminus \mathcal{P}$ so as to fail all possible reductions (from $\mathcal{NP}$ to the modified set) as well as all possible polynomial-time decision procedures (for the modified set). Specifically, starting with $S \in \mathcal{NP} \setminus \mathcal{P}$, we derive $S' \subset S$ such that on the one hand there is no polynomial-time reduction of S to S' while on the other hand $S' \in \mathcal{NP} \setminus \mathcal{P}$. The process of modifying S into S' proceeds in iterations, alternatively failing a potential reduction (by dropping sufficiently many strings from the rest of S) and failing a potential decision procedure (by including sufficiently many strings from the rest of S). Specifically, each potential reduction of S to S' can be failed by dropping finitely many elements from the current S', whereas each potential decision procedure can be failed by keeping finitely many elements of the current S'. These two assertions are based on the following two corresponding facts:

1. Any polynomial-time reduction (of any set not in $\mathcal{P}$) to any finite set (e.g., a finite subset of S) must fail, because only sets in $\mathcal{P}$ are Cook-reducible to a finite set. Thus, for any finite set F_1 and any potential reduction (i.e., a polynomial-time oracle machine), there exists an input x on which this reduction to F_1 fails.

   We stress that the aforementioned reduction fails while the only queries that are answered positively are those residing in F_1. Furthermore, the aforementioned failure is due to a finite set of queries (i.e., the set of all queries made by the reduction when invoked on an input that is smaller or equal to x). Thus, for every finite set $F_1 \subset S' \subseteq S$, any reduction of S to S' can be failed by dropping a finite number of elements from S' and without dropping elements of F_1.

2. For every finite set F_2, any polynomial-time decision procedure for $S \setminus F_2$ must fail, because S is Cook-reducible to $S \setminus F_2$. Thus, for any potential decision procedure (i.e., a polynomial-time algorithm), there exists an input x on which this procedure fails.

   We stress that this failure is due to a finite "prefix" of $S \setminus F_2$ (i.e., the set $\{z \in S \setminus F_2 : z \leq x\}$). Thus, for every finite set F_2, any polynomial-time decision procedure for $S \setminus F_2$ can be failed by keeping a finite subset of $S \setminus F_2$.

As stated, the process of modifying S into S' proceeds in iterations, alternatively failing a potential reduction (by dropping finitely many strings from the rest of S) and failing a potential decision procedure (by including finitely many strings from the rest of S). This can be done efficiently because *it is inessential to determine the first possible points of alternation* (in which sufficiently many strings were dropped (resp., included) to fail the next potential reduction (resp., decision procedure)). It suffices to guarantee that adequate points of alternation (albeit highly non-optimal ones) can be efficiently determined. Thus, S' is the intersection of S and some set in $\mathcal{P}$, which implies that $S' \in \mathcal{NP}$. Following are some comments regarding the implementation of the foregoing idea.

The first issue is that the foregoing plan calls for an ("effective") enumeration of all polynomial-time oracle machines (resp., polynomial-time algorithms). However, none of these sets can be enumerated (by an algorithm). Instead, we enumerate all corresponding machines along with all possible polynomials, and for each pair (M, p) we consider executions of machine M with time bound specified by the polynomial p. That is, we use the machine M_p obtained from the pair (M, p) by suspending the execution of M on input x after $p(|x|)$ steps. We stress that we do not know whether machine M runs in polynomial time, but the computations of any polynomial-time machine is "covered" by some pair (M, p).

Next, let us clarify the process in which reductions and decision procedures are ruled out. We present a construction of a "filter" set F in $\mathcal{P}$ such that the final set S'

will equal $S \cap F$. Recall that we need to select F such that each polynomial-time reduction of S to $S \cap F$ fails, and each polynomial-time procedure for deciding $S \cap F$ fails. The key observation is that for every finite F' each polynomial-time reduction of S to $S \cap F'$ fails, whereas for every co-finite F' (i.e., finite $\{0, 1\}^* \setminus F'$) each polynomial-time procedure for deciding $S \cap F'$ fails. Furthermore, each of these failures occurs on some input, and such an input can be determined by finite portions of S and F. Thus, we alternate between failing possible reductions and decision procedures on some inputs, while not trying to determine the "optimal" points of alternation but rather determining points of alternation in an efficient manner (which in turn allows for efficiently deciding membership in F). Specifically, we let $F = \{x : f(|x|) \equiv 1 \bmod 2\}$, where $f : \mathbb{N} \to \{0\} \cup \mathbb{N}$ will be defined such that (i) each of the first $f(n) - 1$ machines is failed by some input of length at most n, and (ii) the value $f(n)$ can be computed in time poly(n).

The value of $f(n)$ is defined by the following process that performs exactly n^3 computation steps (where cubic time is a rather arbitrary choice). The process proceeds in (an *a priori* unknown number of) iterations, where in the $i + 1^{st}$ iteration we try to find an input on which the $i + 1^{st}$ (modified) machine fails. Specifically, in the $i + 1^{st}$ iteration we scan all inputs, in lexicographic order, until we find an input on which the $i + 1^{st}$ (modified) machine fails, where this machine is an oracle machine if $i + 1$ is odd and a standard machine otherwise. If we detect a failure of the $i + 1^{st}$ machine, then we increment i and proceed to the next iteration. When we reach the allowed number of steps (i.e., n^3 steps), we halt outputting the current value of i (i.e., the current i is output as the value of $f(n)$). Needless to say, this description is heavily based on determining whether or not the $i + 1^{st}$ machine fails on specific inputs. Intuitively, these inputs will be much shorter than n, and so performing these decisions in time n^3 (or so) is not out of the question – see next paragraph.

In order to determine whether or not a failure (of the $i + 1^{st}$ machine) occurs on a particular input x, we need to emulate the computation of this machine on input x as well as determine whether x is in the relevant set (which is either S or $S' = S \cap F$). Recall that if $i + 1$ is even then we need to fail a standard machine (which attempts to decide S') and otherwise we need to fail an oracle machine (which attempts to reduce S to S'). Thus, for even $i + 1$ we need to determine whether x is in $S' = S \cap F$, whereas for odd $i + 1$ we need to determine whether x is in S as well as whether some other strings (which appear as queries) are in S'. Deciding membership in $S \in \mathcal{NP}$ can be done in exponential time (by using the exhaustive search algorithm that tries all possible NP-witnesses). Indeed, this means that when computing $f(n)$ we may only complete the treatment of inputs that are of logarithmic (in n) length, but anyhow in n^3 steps we cannot hope to reach (in our lexicographic scanning) strings of length greater than $3 \log_2 n$. As for deciding membership in F, this requires the ability to compute f on adequate integers. That is, we may need to compute the value of $f(n')$ for various integers n', but as noted n' will be much smaller than n (since $n' \leq \text{poly}(|x|) \leq \text{poly}(\log n)$). Thus, the value of $f(n')$ is just computed recursively (while counting the recursive steps in our total number of steps).[20] The point is that, when considering an input x, we may need the

---

[20]We do not bother to present a more efficient implementation of this process. That is, we may afford to recompute $f(n')$ every time we need it (rather than store it for later use).

values of f only on $\{1, \ldots, p_{i+1}(|x|)\}$, where p_{i+1} is the polynomial bounding the running time of the $i+1^{\text{st}}$ (modified) machine, and obtaining such a value takes at most $p_{i+1}(|x|)^3$ steps. We conclude that the number of steps performed toward determining whether or not a failure (of the $i+1^{\text{st}}$ machine) occurs on the input x is upper-bounded by an (exponential) function of $|x|$.

As hinted in the foregoing, the procedure will complete n^3 steps long before examining inputs of length greater than $3 \log_2 n$, but this does not matter. What matters is that f *is unbounded* (see Exercise 2.34). Furthermore, by construction, $f(n)$ is computed in poly(n) time. ☐

Comment. The proof of Theorem 2.28 actually establishes that *for every $S \notin \mathcal{P}$ there exists $S' \notin \mathcal{P}$ such that S' is Karp-reducible to S but S is not Cook-reducible to S'.*[21] Thus, if $\mathcal{P} \neq \mathcal{NP}$ then there exists an infinite sequence of sets $S_1, S_2, \ldots$ in $\mathcal{NP} \setminus \mathcal{P}$ such that S_{i+1} is Karp-reducible to S_i but S_i is not Cook-reducible to S_{i+1}. That is, there exists an infinite hierarchy of problems (albeit unnatural ones), all in $\mathcal{NP}$, such that each problem is "easier" than the previous ones (in the sense that it can be reduced to the previous problems while these problems cannot be reduced to it).

2.3.5. Reflections on Complete Problems

This book will perhaps only be understood by those who have themselves already thought the thoughts which are expressed in it – or similar thoughts. It is therefore not a text-book. Its object would be attained if it afforded pleasure to one who read it with understanding.

Ludwig Wittgenstein, *Tractatus Logico-Philosophicus*

Indeed, this section should be viewed as an invitation to meditate together on questions of the type *what enables the existence of complete problems?* Accordingly, the style is intentionally naive and imprecise; this entire section may be viewed as an open-ended exercise, asking the reader to consider substantiations of the vague text.

We know that NP-complete problems exist. The question we ask here is what aspects in our modeling of problems enables the existence of complete problems. We should, of course, bear in mind that completeness refers to a class of problems; the complete problem should "encode" each problem in the class and be itself in the class. Since the first aspect, hereafter referred to as encodability of a class, is amazing enough (at least to a layman), we start by asking what enables it. We identify two fundamental paradigms, regarding the modeling of problems, that seem essential to the encodability of any (infinite) class of problems:

1. Each problem refers to an infinite set of possible instances.
2. The specification of each problem uses a finite description (e.g., an algorithm that enumerates all the possible solutions for any given instance).[22]

These two paradigms seem somewhat conflicting, yet put together they suggest the definition of a universal problem, that is, a problem that refers to instances of the form (D, x),

---

[21]The said Karp-reduction (of S' to S) maps x to itself if $x \in F$ and otherwise maps x to a fixed no-instance of S.

[22]This seems the most naive notion of a description of a problem. An alternative notion of a description refers to an algorithm that recognizes all valid instance-solution pairs (as in the definition of NP). However, at this point, we allow also "non-effective" descriptions (as giving rise to the Halting Problem).

where D is a description of a problem and x is an instance to that problem (and we seek a solution to x with respect to D). Intuitively, this universal problem can encode any other problem (provided that problems are modeled in a way that conforms with the foregoing paradigms): Solving the universal problem allows solving any other problem.[23]

Note that the foregoing universal problem is actually complete with respect to the class of all problems, but it is not complete with respect to any class that contains only (algorithmically) solvable problems (because this universal problem is not solvable). Turning our attention to classes of solvable problems, we seek versions of the universal problem that are complete for these classes. One archetypical difficulty that arises is that, given a description D (as part of the instance to the universal problem), we cannot tell whether or not D is a description of a problem in a predetermined class $\mathcal{C}$ (because this decision problem is unsolvable). This fact is relevant because[24] if the universal problem requires solving instances that refer to a problem not in $\mathcal{C}$ then intuitively it cannot be itself in $\mathcal{C}$.

Before turning to the resolution of the foregoing difficulty, we note that the aforementioned modeling paradigms are pivotal to the theory of computation at large. In particular, so far we made no reference to any complexity consideration. Indeed, a complexity consideration is the key to resolving the foregoing difficulty: The idea is modifying any description D into a description D' such that D' is always in $\mathcal{C}$, and D' agrees with D in the case that D is in $\mathcal{C}$ (i.e., in this case they described exactly the same problem). We stress that in the case that D is not in $\mathcal{C}$, the corresponding problem D' may be arbitrary (as long as it is in $\mathcal{C}$). Such a modification is possible with respect to many complexity theoretic classes. We consider two different types of classes, where in both cases the class is defined in terms of the time complexity of algorithms that do something related to the problem (e.g., recognize valid solutions, as in the definition of NP).

1. *Classes defined by a single time-bound function t* (e.g., $t(n) = n^3$). In this case, any algorithm D is modified to the algorithm D' that, on input x, emulates (up to) $t(|x|)$ steps of the execution of $D(x)$. The modified version of the universal problem treats the instance (D, x) as (D', x). This version can encode any problem in the said class $\mathcal{C}$.

   But will this (version of the universal) problem be itself in $\mathcal{C}$? The answer depends both on the efficiency of emulation in the corresponding computational model and on the growth rate of t. For example, for triple-exponential t, the answer will be definitely yes, because $t(|x|)$ steps can be emulated in $\mathrm{poly}(t(|x|))$ time (in any reasonable model) while $t(|(D, x)|) > t(|x| + 1) > \mathrm{poly}(t(|x|))$. On the other hand, in most reasonable models, the emulation of $t(|x|)$ steps requires $\omega(t(|x|))$ time while for any polynomial t it holds that $t(n + O(1)) < 2t(n)$.

2. *Classes defined by a family of infinitely many functions of different growth rate* (e.g., polynomials). We can, of course, select a function t that grows faster than any function in the family and proceed as in the prior case, but then the resulting universal problem will definitely not be in the class.

---

[23] Recall, however, that the universal problem is not (algorithmically) solvable. Thus, both clauses of the implication are false. Indeed, the notion of a problem is rather vague at this stage; it certainly extends beyond the set of all solvable problems.

[24] Here we ignore the possibility of using promise problems, which do enable avoiding such instances without requiring anybody to recognize them. Indeed, using promise problems resolves this difficulty, but the issues discussed following the next paragraph remain valid.

Note that in the current case, a complete problem will indeed be striking because, in particular, it will be associated with one function t_0 that grows more moderately than some other functions in the family (e.g., a fixed polynomial grows more moderately than other polynomials). Seemingly this means that the algorithm describing the universal machine should be faster than some algorithms that describe some other problems in the class. This impression presumes that the instances of both problems are (approximately) of the same length, and so we intensionally violate this presumption by artificially increasing the length of the description of the instances to the universal problem. For example, if D is associated with the time bound t_D, then the instance (D, x) to the universal problem is presented as, say, $(D, x, 1^{t_0^{-1}(t_D(|x|)^2)})$, where in the case of NP we used $t_0(n) = n$.

We believe that the last item explains the existence of NP-complete problems. But *what about the NP-completeness of SAT?*

We first note that the NP-hardness of CSAT is an immediate consequence of the fact that Boolean circuits can emulate algorithms.[25] This fundamental fact is rooted in the notion of an algorithm (which postulates the simplicity of a single computational step) and holds for any reasonable model of computation. Thus, for every D and x, the problem of finding a string y such that $D(x, y) = 1$ is "encoded" as finding a string y such that $C_{D,x}(y) = 1$, where $C_{D,x}$ is a Boolean circuit that is easily derived from (D, x). In contrast to the fundamental fact underlying the NP-hardness of CSAT, the NP-hardness of SAT relies on a clever trick that allows for encoding instances of CSAT as instances of SAT.

As stated, the NP-completeness of SAT is proved by encoding instances of CSAT as instances of SAT. Similarly, the NP-completeness of other new problems is proved by encoding instances of problems that are already known to be NP-complete. Typically, these encodings operate in a local manner, mapping small components of the original instance to local gadgets in the produced instance. Indeed, these problem-specific gadgets are the core of the encoding phenomenon. Presented with such a gadget, it is typically easy to verify that it works. Thus, *one cannot be surprised by most of these gadgets, but the fact that they exist for thousands of natural problem is definitely amazing.*

2.4. Three Relatively Advanced Topics

In this section we discuss three relatively advanced topics. The first topic, which was eluded to in previous sections, is the notion of promise problems (Section 2.4.1). Next we present an optimal search algorithm for NP (Section 2.4.2), and discuss the class (coNP) of sets that are complements of sets in NP.

Teaching note: These topics are typically not mentioned in a basic course on complexity. Still, depending on time constraints, we suggest discussing them at least at a high level.

2.4.1. Promise Problems

Promise problems are a natural generalization of search and decision problems, where one explicitly considers a set of legitimate instances (rather than considering any string as

---

[25]The fact that CSAT is in NP is a consequence of the fact that the circuit evaluation problem is solvable in polynomial time.

a legitimate instance). As noted previously, this generalization provides a more adequate formulation of natural computational problems (and indeed this formulation is used in all informal discussions). For example, in §2.3.3.2 we presented such problems using phrases like "given a graph and an integer . . ." (or "given a collection of sets . . ."). In other words, we assumed that the input instance has a certain format (or rather we "promised the solver" that this is the case). Indeed, we claimed that in these cases the assumption can be removed without affecting the complexity of the problem, but we avoided providing a formal treatment of this issue, which is done next.

Teaching note: The notion of promise problems was originally introduced in the context of decision problems, and is typically used only in that context. However, we believe that promise problems are as natural in the context of search problems.

2.4.1.1. Definitions

In the context of search problems, a promise problem is a relaxation in which one is only required to find solutions to instances in a predetermined set, called the promise. The requirement regarding efficient checkability of solutions is adapted in an analogous manner.

Definition 2.29 (search problems with a promise): *A* search problem with a promise *consists of a binary relation $R \subseteq \{0, 1\}^* \times \{0, 1\}^*$ and a* promise *set P. Such a problem is also referred to as the* search problem R with promise P.

- *The search problem R with promise P is* solved by algorithm A *if for every $x \in P$ it holds that $(x, A(x)) \in R$ if $x \in S_R = \{x : R(x) \neq \emptyset\}$ and $A(x) = \bot$ otherwise, where $R(x) = \{y : (x, y) \in R\}$.*
  The time complexity *of A on inputs in P is defined as $T_{A|P}(n) \stackrel{\text{def}}{=} \max_{x \in P \cap \{0,1\}^n}\{t_A(x)\}$, where $t_A(x)$ is the running time of $A(x)$ and $T_{A|P}(n) = 0$ if $P \cap \{0, 1\}^n = \emptyset$.*
- *The search problem R with promise P is in the* promise problem extension of $\mathcal{PF}$ *if there exists a polynomial-time algorithm that solves this problem.*[26]
- *The search problem R with promise P is in the* promise problem extension of $\mathcal{PC}$ *if there exists a polynomial T and an algorithm A such that, for every $x \in P$ and $y \in \{0, 1\}^*$, algorithm A makes at most $T(|x|)$ steps and it holds that $A(x, y) = 1$ if and only if $(x, y) \in R$.*

We stress that nothing is required of the solver in the case that the input violates the promise (i.e., $x \notin P$); in particular, in such a case the algorithm may halt with a wrong output. (Indeed, the standard formulation of search problems is obtained by considering the trivial promise $P = \{0, 1\}^*$.)[27] In addition to the foregoing motivation for promise problems, we mention one natural class of search problems with a promise. These are search problem in which the promise is that the instance has a solution (i.e., in terms of

---

[26]In this case it does not matter whether the time complexity of A is defined on inputs in P or on all possible strings. Suppose that A has (polynomial) time complexity T on inputs in P; then we can modify A to halt on any input x after at most $T(|x|)$ steps. This modification may only effects the output of A on inputs not in P (which is OK by us). The modification can be implemented in polynomial time by computing $t = T(|x|)$ and emulating the execution of $A(x)$ for t steps. A similar comment applies to the definition of $\mathcal{PC}$, $\mathcal{P}$, and $\mathcal{NP}$.

[27]Here we refer to the formulation presented in Section 2.1.4.

the foregoing notation $P = S_R$, where $S_R \stackrel{\text{def}}{=} \{x : \exists y \text{ s.t. } (x, y) \in R\}$). We refer to such search problems by the name *candid search problems*.

Definition 2.30 (candid search problems): *An algorithm A solves the* candid search problem *of the binary relation R if for every $x \in S_R$ (i.e., for every $(x, y) \in R$) it holds that $(x, A(x)) \in R$. The time complexity of such an algorithm is defined as $T_{A|S_R}(n) \stackrel{\text{def}}{=} \max_{x \in P \cap \{0,1\}^n} \{t_A(x)\}$, where $t_A(x)$ is the running time of $A(x)$ and $T_{A|S_R}(n) = 0$ if $P \cap \{0, 1\}^n = \emptyset$.*

Note that nothing is required when $x \notin S_R$: In particular, algorithm A may either output a wrong solution (although no solutions exist) or run for more than $T_{A|S_R}(|x|)$ steps. The first case can be essentially eliminated whenever $R \in \mathcal{PC}$. Furthermore, for $R \in \mathcal{PC}$, *if we "know" the time complexity of algorithm A* (e.g., if we can compute $T_{A|S_R}(n)$ in poly(n)-time), then we may modify A into an algorithm A' that solves the (general) search problem of R (i.e., halts with a correct output on each input) in time $T_{A'}(n) = T_{A|S_R}(n) + \text{poly}(n)$. However, we do not necessarily know the running time of an algorithm that we consider. Furthermore, as we shall see in Section 2.4.2, the naive assumption by which we always know the running time of an algorithm that we design is not valid either.

Decision problems with a promise. In the context of decision problems, a promise problem is a relaxation in which one is only required to determine the status of instances that belong to a predetermined set, called the promise. The requirement of efficient verification is adapted in an analogous manner. In view of the standard usage of the term, we refer to *decision problems with a promise* by the name *promise problems*. Formally, promise problems refer to a three-way partition of the set of all strings into yes-instances, no-instances, and instances that violate the promise. Standard decision problems are obtained as a special case by insisting that all inputs are allowed (i.e., the promise is trivial).

Definition 2.31 (promise problems): *A* promise problem *consists of a pair of non-intersecting sets of strings, denoted $(S_{\text{yes}}, S_{\text{no}})$, and $S_{\text{yes}} \cup S_{\text{no}}$ is called the* promise.

- *The promise problem $(S_{\text{yes}}, S_{\text{no}})$ is* solved by algorithm A *if for every $x \in S_{\text{yes}}$ it holds that $A(x) = 1$ and for every $x \in S_{\text{no}}$ it holds that $A(x) = 0$. The promise problem is in the* promise problem extension *of $\mathcal{P}$ if there exists a polynomial-time algorithm that solves it.*
- *The promise problem $(S_{\text{yes}}, S_{\text{no}})$ is in the* promise problem extension *of $\mathcal{NP}$ if there exists a polynomial p and a polynomial-time algorithm V such that the following two conditions hold:*
  1. Completeness: *For every $x \in S_{\text{yes}}$, there exists y of length at most $p(|x|)$ such that $V(x, y) = 1$.*
  2. Soundness: *For every $x \in S_{\text{no}}$ and every y, it holds that $V(x, y) = 0$.*

We stress that for algorithms of polynomial-time complexity, it does not matter whether the time complexity is defined only on inputs that satisfy the promise or on all strings (see footnote 26). Thus, the extended classes $\mathcal{P}$ and $\mathcal{NP}$ (like $\mathcal{PF}$ and $\mathcal{PC}$) are invariant under this choice.

Reducibility among promise problems. The notion of a Cook-reduction extend naturally to promise problems, when postulating that a query that violates the promise (of the problem at the target of the reduction) may be answered arbitrarily.[28] That is, the oracle machine should solve the original problem no matter how queries that violate the promise are answered. The latter requirement is consistent with the conceptual meaning of reductions and promise problems. Recall that reductions capture procedures that make subroutine calls to an arbitrary procedure that solves the reduced problem. But, in the case of promise problems, such a solver may behave arbitrarily on instances that violate the promise. We stress that the main property of a reduction is preserved (see Exercise 2.35): *If the promise problem Π is Cook-reducible to a promise problem that is solvable in polynomial time, then Π is solvable in polynomial time.*

We warn that the extension of a complexity class to promise problems does not necessarily inherit the "structural" properties of the standard class. For example, in contrast to Theorem 2.35, there exists promise problems in $\mathcal{NP} \cap \mathrm{co}\mathcal{NP}$ such that every set in $\mathcal{NP}$ can be Cook-reduced to them: see Exercise 2.36. Needless to say, $\mathcal{NP} = \mathrm{co}\mathcal{NP}$ does not seem to follow from Exercise 2.36. See further discussion at the end of §2.4.1.2.

2.4.1.2. Applications

The following discussion refers both to the decision and search versions of promise problems. Recall that *promise problems offer the most direct way of formulating natural computational problems* (e.g., when referring to computational problems regarding graphs, the promise mandates that the input is a graph). In addition to the foregoing application of promise problems, we mention their use in formulating the natural notion of a *restriction of a computational problem to a subset of the instances*. Specifically, such a restriction means that the promise set of the restricted problem is a subset of the promise set of the unrestricted problem.

Definition 2.32 (restriction of computational problems):

- *For any $P' \subseteq P$ and binary relation R, we say that the search problem R with promise P' is a restriction of the search problem R with promise P.*
- *We say that the promise problem $(S'_{\text{yes}}, S'_{\text{no}})$ is a restriction of the promise problem $(S_{\text{yes}}, S_{\text{no}})$ if both $S'_{\text{yes}} \subseteq S_{\text{yes}}$ and $S'_{\text{no}} \subseteq S_{\text{no}}$ hold.*

For example, when we say that 3SAT is a restriction of SAT, we refer to the fact that the set of allowed instances is now restricted to 3CNF formulae (rather than to arbitrary CNF formulae). In both cases, the computational problem is to determine satisfiability (or to find a satisfying assignment), but the set of instances (i.e., the promise set) is further restricted in the case of 3SAT. The fact that a restricted problem is never harder than the original problem is captured by the fact that the restricted problem is reducible to the original one (via the identity mapping).

Other uses and some reservations. In addition to the two aforementioned generic uses of the notion of a promise problem, we mention that this notion provides adequate

---

[28]It follows that Karp-reductions among promise problems are not allowed to make queries that violate the promise. Specifically, we say that the promise problem $\Pi = (\Pi_{\text{yes}}, \Pi_{\text{no}})$ is Karp-reducible to the promise problem $\Pi' = (\Pi'_{\text{yes}}, \Pi'_{\text{no}})$ if there exists a polynomial-time mapping f such that for every $x \in \Pi_{\text{yes}}$ (resp., $x \in \Pi_{\text{no}}$) it holds that $f(x) \in \Pi'_{\text{yes}}$ (resp., $f(x) \in \Pi'_{\text{no}}$).

formulations for a variety of specific computational complexity notions and results. Examples include the notion of "unique solutions" (see Section 6.2.3) and the formulation of "gap problems" as capturing various approximation tasks (see Section 10.1). In all these cases, promise problems allow for discussing natural computational problems and making statements about their inherent complexity. Thus, the complexity of promise problems (and classes of such problems) addresses natural questions and concerns. Consequently, demonstrating the intractability of a promise problem that belongs to some class (e.g., saying that some promise problem in $\mathcal{NP}$ cannot be solved by a polynomial-time algorithm) carries the same conceptual message as demonstrating the intractability of a standard problem in the corresponding class. In contrast, as indicated at the end of §2.4.1.1, structural properties of promise problems may not hold for the corresponding classes of standard problems (e.g., see Exercise 2.36). Indeed, we do distinguish here between the inherent (or absolute) properties such as intractability and structural (or relative) properties such as reducibility.

2.4.1.3. The Standard Convention of Avoiding Promise Problems

Recall that, although promise problems provide a good framework for presenting natural computational problems, we managed to avoid this framework in previous sections. This was done by relying on the fact that, for all the (natural) problems considered in the previous sections, it is easy to decide whether or not a given instance satisfies the promise. For example, given a formula it is easy to decide whether or not it is in CNF (or 3CNF). Actually, the issue arises already when talking about formulae: What we are actually given is a string that is supposed to encode a formula (under some predetermined encoding scheme), and so the promise (which is easy to decide for natural encoding schemes) is that the input string is a valid encoding of some formula. In any case, if the promise is efficiently recognizable (i.e., membership in it can be decided in polynomial time), then we may avoid mentioning the promise by using one of the following two "nasty" conventions:

1. *Extending the set of instances to the set of all possible strings* (and allowing trivial solutions for the corresponding dummy instances). For example, in the case of a search problem, we may either define all instances that violate the promise to have no solution or define them to have a trivial solution (e.g., be a solution for themselves); that is, for a search problem R with promise P, we may consider the (standard) search problem of R where R is modified such that $R(x) = \emptyset$ for every $x \notin P$ (or, say, $R(x) = \{x\}$ for every $x \notin P$). In the case of a promise (decision) problem (S_{yes}, S_{no}), we may consider the problem of deciding membership in S_{yes}, which means that instances that violate the promise are considered as no-instances.

2. *Considering every string as a valid encoding of an object that satisfies the promise.* That is, fixing any string x_0 that satisfies the promise, we consider every string that violates the promise as if it were x_0. In the case of a search problem R with promise P, this means considering the (standard) search problem of R where R is modified such that $R(x) = R(x_0)$ for every $x \notin P$. Similarly, in the case of a promise (decision) problem (S_{yes}, S_{no}), we consider the problem of deciding membership in S_{yes} (provided $x_0 \in S_{no}$ and otherwise we consider the problem of deciding membership in $\{0, 1\}^* \setminus S_{no}$).

We stress that *in the case that the promise is efficiently recognizable* the aforementioned conventions (or modifications) do not effect the complexity of the relevant (search or decision) problem. That is, rather than considering the original promise problem, we consider a (search or decision) problem (without a promise) that is computationally equivalent to the original one. Thus, in some sense we lose nothing by studying the latter problem rather than the original one. On the other hand, even in the case that these two problems are computationally equivalent, it is useful to have a formulation that allows for distinguishing between them (as we do distinguish between the different NP-complete problems although they are all computationally equivalent). This conceptual concern becomes of crucial importance in the case (to be discussed next) that the promise is *not* efficiently recognizable.

The foregoing transformations of promise problems into computationally equivalent standard (decision and search) problems do not necessarily preserve the complexity of the problem in the case that the promise is not efficiently recognizable. In this case, the terminology of promise problems is unavoidable. Consider, for example, the problem of deciding whether a Hamiltonian graph is 3-colorable. On the face of it, such a problem may have fundamentally different complexity than the problem of deciding whether a given graph is both Hamiltonian and 3-colorable.

In spite of the foregoing opinions, we adopt the convention of focusing on standard decision and search problems. That is, by default, all complexity classes discussed in this book refer to standard decision and search problems, and the exceptions in which we refer to promise problems are explicitly stated as such. Such exceptions appear in Sections 2.4.2, 6.1.3, 6.2.3, and 10.1.

2.4.2. Optimal Search Algorithms for NP

We actually refer to solving the candid search problem of any relation in $\mathcal{PC}$. Recall that $\mathcal{PC}$ is the class of search problems that allow for efficient checking of the correctness of candidate solutions (see Definition 2.3), and that the candid search problem is a search problem in which the solver is promised that the given instance has a solution (see Definition 2.30).

We claim the existence of an *optimal algorithm for solving the candid search problem of any relation in $\mathcal{PC}$*. Furthermore, we will explicitly present such an algorithm, and prove that it is optimal in a very strong sense: For any algorithm solving the candid search problem of $R \in \mathcal{PC}$, our algorithm solves the same problem in time that is at most a constant factor slower (ignoring a fixed additive polynomial term, which may be disregarded in the case that the problem is not solvable in polynomial time). Needless to say, we do not know the time complexity of the aforementioned optimal algorithm (indeed if we knew it then we would have resolved the P-vs-NP Question). In fact, the P-vs-NP Question boils down to determining the time complexity of a single explicitly presented algorithm (i.e., the optimal algorithm claimed in Theorem 2.33).

Theorem 2.33: *For every binary relation $R \in \mathcal{PC}$ there exists an algorithm A that satisfies the following:*

1. *A solves the candid search problem of R.*
2. *There exists a polynomial p such that for every algorithm A' that solves the candid search problem of R and for every $x \in S_R$ (i.e., for every $(x, y) \in R$) it holds that $t_A(x) = O(t_{A'}(x) + p(|x|))$, where $t_A(x)$ (resp., $t_{A'}(x)$) denotes the number of steps taken by A (resp., A') on input x.*

Interestingly, we establish the optimality of A without knowing what its (optimal) running time is. Furthermore, the optimality claim is "pointwise" (i.e., it refers to any input) rather than "global" (i.e., referring to the (worst-case) time complexity as a function of the input length).

We stress that the hidden constant in the O-notation depends only on A', but in the following proof this dependence is exponential in the length of the description of algorithm A' (and it is not known whether a better dependence can be achieved). Indeed, this dependence as well as the idea underlying it constitute one negative aspect of this otherwise amazing result. Another negative aspect is that the optimality of algorithm A refers only to inputs that have a solution (i.e., inputs in S_R). Finally, we note that the theorem as stated refers only to models of computation that have machines that can emulate a given number of steps of other machines with a constant overhead. We mention that in most natural models the overhead of such emulation is at most poly-logarithmic in the number of steps, in which case it holds that $t_A(x) = \widetilde{O}(t_{A'}(x) + p(|x|))$.

Proof Sketch: Fixing R, we let M be a polynomial-time algorithm that decides membership in R, and let p be a polynomial bounding the running time of M (as a function of the length of the first element in the input pair). Using M, we present an algorithm A that solves the candid search problem of R as follows. On input x, algorithm A emulates all possible search algorithms "in parallel" (on input x), checks the result provided by each of them (using M), and halts whenever it recognizes a correct solution. Indeed, most of the emulated algorithms are totally irrelevant to the search, but using M we can screen the bad solutions offered by them and output a good solution once obtained.

Since there are infinitely many possible algorithms, it may not be clear what we mean by the expression "emulating all possible algorithms in parallel." What we mean is emulating them at different "rates" such that the infinite sum of these rates converges to 1 (or to any other constant). Specifically, we will emulate the ith possible algorithm at rate $1/(i + 1)^2$, which means emulating a single step of this algorithm per $(i + 1)^2$ emulation steps (performed for all algorithms). Note that a straightforward implementation of this idea may create a significant overhead, involved in switching frequently from the emulation of one machine to the emulation of another. Instead, we present an alternative implementation that proceeds in iterations.

In the jth iteration, for $i = 1, \ldots, 2^{j/2} - 1$, algorithm A emulates $2^j/(i + 1)^2$ steps of the ith machine (where the machines are ordered according to the lexicographic order of their descriptions). Each of these emulations is conducted in one chunk, and thus the overhead of switching between the various emulations is insignificant (in comparison to the total number of steps being emulated). In the case that one or more of these emulations (on input x) halt with output y, algorithm A invokes M on input (x, y) and output y if and only if $M(x, y) = 1$. Furthermore, the verification of a solution provided by a candidate algorithm is also emulated at the expense of its step count. (Put in other words, we augment each algorithm with a canonical procedure (i.e., M) that checks the validity of the solution offered by the algorithm.)

By its construction, whenever $A(x)$ outputs a string y (i.e., $y \neq \bot$) it must hold that $(x, y) \in R$. To show the optimality of A, we consider an arbitrary algorithm A' that solves the candid search problem of R. Our aim is to show that A is not much slower than A'. Intuitively, this is the case because the overhead of A results from emulating other algorithms (in addition to A'), but the total number of emulation steps wasted (due to these algorithms) is inversely proportional to the rate of algorithm A', which in turn is exponentially related to the length of the description of A'. The punch line is that since A' is fixed, the length of its description is a constant. Details follow.

For every x, let us denote by $t'(x)$ the number of steps taken by A' on input x, where $t'(x)$ also accounts for the running time of $M(x, \cdot)$; that is, $t'(x) = t_{A'}(x) + p(|x|)$, where $t_{A'}(x)$ is the number of steps taken by $A'(x)$ itself. Then, the emulation of $t'(x)$ steps of A' on input x is "covered" by the jth iteration of A, provided that $2^j/(2^{|A'|+1})^2 \geq t'(x)$ where $|A'|$ denotes the length of the description of A'. (Indeed, we use the fact that the algorithms are emulated in lexicographic order, and note that there are at most $2^{|A'|+1} - 2$ algorithms that precede A' in lexicographic order.) Thus, on input x, algorithm A halts after at most $j_{A'}(x)$ iterations, where $j_{A'}(x) = 2(|A'| + 1) + \log_2(t_{A'}(x) + p(|x|))$, after emulating a total number of steps that is at most

$$t(x) \overset{\text{def}}{=} \sum_{j=1}^{j_{A'}(x)} \sum_{i=1}^{2^{j/2}-1} \frac{2^j}{(i+1)^2} < 2^{j_{A'}(x)+1} = 2^{2|A'|+3} \cdot (t_{A'}(x) + p(|x|)).$$

The question of how much time is required for emulating these many steps depends on the specific model of computation. In many models of computation, the emulation of t steps of one machine by another machine requires $\widetilde{O}(t)$ steps of the emulating machines, and in some models this emulation can even be performed with constant overhead. The theorem follows. $\qquad\qquad\qquad\qquad\qquad\qquad\qquad\qquad\quad\square$

Comment. By construction, the foregoing algorithm A does not halt on input $x \notin S_R$. This can be easily rectified by letting A emulate a straightforward exhaustive search for a solution, and halt with output $\bot$ if and only if this exhaustive search indicates that there is no solution to the current input. This extra emulation can be performed in parallel to all other emulations (e.g., at a rate of one step for the extra emulation per each step of everything else).

2.4.3. The Class coNP and Its Intersection with NP

By prepending the name of a complexity class (of decision problems) with the prefix "co" we mean the class of complement sets; that is,

$$\text{co}\mathcal{C} \overset{\text{def}}{=} \{\{0, 1\}^* \setminus S : S \in \mathcal{C}\}. \qquad (2.4)$$

Specifically, $\text{co}\mathcal{NP} = \{\{0, 1\}^* \setminus S : S \in \mathcal{NP}\}$ is the class of sets that are complements of sets in $\mathcal{NP}$.

Recalling that sets in $\mathcal{NP}$ are characterized by their witness relations such that $x \in S$ if and only if there exists an adequate NP-witness, it follows that their complement sets consist of all instances for which there are no NP-witnesses (i.e., $x \in \{0, 1\}^* \setminus S$ if there is no NP-witness for x being in S). For example, SAT $\in \mathcal{NP}$ implies that the set of unsatisfiable CNF formulae is in $\text{co}\mathcal{NP}$. Likewise, the set of graphs that are not 3-colorable is in $\text{co}\mathcal{NP}$. (Jumping ahead, we mention that it is widely believed that these sets are not in $\mathcal{NP}$.)

Another perspective on $\text{co}\mathcal{NP}$ is obtained by considering the search problems in $\mathcal{PC}$. Recall that for such $R \in \mathcal{PC}$, the set of instances having a solution (i.e., $S_R = \{x : \exists y \text{ s.t. } (x, y) \in R\}$) is in $\mathcal{NP}$. It follows that the set of instances having no solution (i.e., $\{0, 1\}^* \setminus S_R = \{x : \forall y \ (x, y) \notin R\}$) is in $\text{co}\mathcal{NP}$.

It is widely believed that $\mathcal{NP} \neq \text{co}\mathcal{NP}$ (which means that $\mathcal{NP}$ is not closed under complementation). Indeed, this conjecture implies $\mathcal{P} \neq \mathcal{NP}$ (because $\mathcal{P}$ is closed under complementation). The conjecture $\mathcal{NP} \neq \text{co}\mathcal{NP}$ means that some sets in $\text{co}\mathcal{NP}$ do not have NP-proof systems (because $\mathcal{NP}$ is the class of sets having NP-proof systems). As we will show next, under this conjecture, the complements of NP-complete sets do not have NP-proof systems; for example, there exists no NP-proof system for proving that a given CNF formula is not satisfiable. We first establish this fact for NP-completeness in the standard sense (i.e., under Karp-reductions, as in Definition 2.17).

Proposition 2.34: *Suppose that $\mathcal{NP} \neq \text{co}\mathcal{NP}$ and let $S \in \mathcal{NP}$ such that every set in $\mathcal{NP}$ is Karp-reducible to S. Then $\overline{S} \overset{\text{def}}{=} \{0, 1\}^* \setminus S$ is not in $\mathcal{NP}$.*

Proof Sketch: We first observe that the fact that every set in $\mathcal{NP}$ is Karp-reducible to S implies that every set in $\text{co}\mathcal{NP}$ is Karp-reducible to $\overline{S}$. We next claim that *if S' is in $\mathcal{NP}$ then every set that is Karp-reducible to S' is also in $\mathcal{NP}$*. Applying the claim to $S' = \overline{S}$, we conclude that $\overline{S} \in \mathcal{NP}$ implies $\text{co}\mathcal{NP} \subseteq \mathcal{NP}$, which in turn implies $\mathcal{NP} = \text{co}\mathcal{NP}$ in contradiction to the main hypothesis.

We now turn to prove the foregoing claim; that is, we prove that if S' has an NP-proof system and S'' is Karp-reducible to S' then S'' has an NP-proof system. Let V' be the verification procedure associated with S', and let f be a Karp-reduction of S'' to S'. Then, we define the verification procedure V'' (for membership in S'') by $V''(x, y) = V'(f(x), y)$. That is, any NP-witness that $f(x) \in S'$ serves as an NP-witness for $x \in S''$ (and these are the only NP-witnesses for $x \in S''$). This may not be a "natural" proof system (for S''), but it is definitely an NP-proof system for S''. $\qquad\square$

Assuming that $\mathcal{NP} \neq \text{co}\mathcal{NP}$, Proposition 2.34 implies that sets in $\mathcal{NP} \cap \text{co}\mathcal{NP}$ cannot be NP-complete with respect to Karp-reductions. In light of other limitations of Karp-reductions (see, e.g., Exercise 2.7), one may wonder whether or not the exclusion of NP-complete sets from the class $\mathcal{NP} \cap \text{co}\mathcal{NP}$ is due to the use of a restricted notion of reductions (i.e., Karp-reductions). The following theorem asserts that this is not the case: *Some sets in $\mathcal{NP}$ cannot be reduced to sets in the intersection $\mathcal{NP} \cap \text{co}\mathcal{NP}$ even under general reductions* (i.e., Cook-reductions).

Theorem 2.35: *If every set in $\mathcal{NP}$ can be Cook-reduced to some set in $\mathcal{NP} \cap \text{co}\mathcal{NP}$ then $\mathcal{NP} = \text{co}\mathcal{NP}$.*

In particular, assuming $\mathcal{NP} \neq \text{co}\mathcal{NP}$, no set in $\mathcal{NP} \cap \text{co}\mathcal{NP}$ can be NP-complete, even when NP-completeness is defined with respect to Cook-reductions. Since $\mathcal{NP} \cap \text{co}\mathcal{NP}$ is conjectured to be a proper superset of $\mathcal{P}$, it follows (assuming $\mathcal{NP} \neq \text{co}\mathcal{NP}$) that there are decision problems in $\mathcal{NP}$ that are neither in $\mathcal{P}$ nor NP-hard (i.e., specifically, the decision problems in $(\mathcal{NP} \cap \text{co}\mathcal{NP}) \setminus \mathcal{P}$). We stress that Theorem 2.35 refers to standard decision problems and not to promise problems (see Section 2.4.1 and Exercise 2.36).

Proof: Analogously to the proof of Proposition 2.34 , the current proof boils down to proving that *if S is Cook-reducible to a set in $\mathcal{NP} \cap \mathrm{co}\mathcal{NP}$ then $S \in \mathcal{NP} \cap \mathrm{co}\mathcal{NP}$.* Using this claim, the theorem's hypothesis implies that $\mathcal{NP} \subseteq \mathcal{NP} \cap \mathrm{co}\mathcal{NP}$, which in turn implies $\mathcal{NP} \subseteq \mathrm{co}\mathcal{NP}$ and $\mathcal{NP} = \mathrm{co}\mathcal{NP}$ (see Exercise 2.37).

Fixing any S and $S' \in \mathcal{NP} \cap \mathrm{co}\mathcal{NP}$ such that S is Cook-reducible to S', we prove that $S \in \mathcal{NP}$ (and the proof that $S \in \mathrm{co}\mathcal{NP}$ is similar).[29] Let us denote by M the oracle machine reducing S to S'. That is, on input x, machine M makes queries and decides whether or not to accept x, and its decision is correct provided that all queries are answered according to S'. To show that $S \in \mathcal{NP}$, we will present an NP-proof system for S. This proof system (or rather its verification procedure), denoted V, accepts a pair of the form $(x, ((z_1, \sigma_1, w_1), \ldots, (z_t, \sigma_t, w_t)))$ if the following two conditions hold:

1. On input x, machine M accepts after making the queries $z_1, \ldots, z_t$, and obtaining the corresponding answers $\sigma_1, \ldots, \sigma_t$.

   That is, V checks that, on input x, after obtaining the answers $\sigma_1, \ldots, \sigma_{i-1}$ to the first $i-1$ queries, the ith query made by M equals z_i. In addition, V checks that, on input x and after receiving the answers $\sigma_1, \ldots, \sigma_t$, machine M halts with output 1 (indicating acceptance).

   Note that V does not have oracle access to S'. The procedure V rather emulates the computation of $M(x)$ by answering, for each i, the ith query of $M(x)$ by using the bit σ_i (provided to V as part of its input). The correctness of these answers will be verified (by V) separately (i.e., see the next item).

2. For every i, it holds that if $\sigma_i = 1$ then w_i is an NP-witness for $z_i \in S'$, whereas if $\sigma_i = 0$ then w_i is an NP-witness for $z_i \in \{0, 1\}^* \setminus S'$.

   Thus, if this condition holds then it is the case that each σ_i indicates the correct status of z_i with respect to S' (i.e., $\sigma_i = 1$ if and only if $z_i \in S'$).

We stress that we use the fact that both S' and $\overline{S}' \stackrel{\text{def}}{=} \{0, 1\}^* \setminus S$ have NP-proof systems, and refer to the corresponding NP-witnesses.

Note that V is indeed an NP-proof system for S. Firstly, the length of the corresponding witnesses is bounded by the running time of the reduction (and the length of the NP-witnesses supplied for the various queries). Next note that V runs in polynomial-time (i.e., verifying the first condition requires an emulation of the polynomial-time execution of M on input x when using the σ_i's to emulate the oracle, whereas verifying the second condition is done by invoking the relevant NP-proof systems). Finally, observe that $x \in S$ if and only if there exists a sequence $y \stackrel{\text{def}}{=} ((z_1, \sigma_1, w_1), \ldots, (z_t, \sigma_t, w_t))$ such that $V(x, y) = 1$. In particular, $V(x, y) = 1$ holds only if y contains a valid sequence of queries and answers as made in a computation of M on input x and oracle access to S', and M accepts based on that sequence. ∎

The world view – a digest. Recall that on top of the $\mathcal{P} \neq \mathcal{NP}$ conjecture, we mentioned two other conjectures (which clearly imply $\mathcal{P} \neq \mathcal{NP}$):

---

[29]Alternatively, we show that $S \in \mathrm{co}\mathcal{NP}$ by applying the following argument to $\overline{S} \stackrel{\text{def}}{=} \{0, 1\}^* \setminus S$ and noting that $\overline{S}$ is Cook-reducible to S' (via S, or alternatively that $\overline{S}$ is Cook-reducible to $\{0, 1\}^* \setminus S' \in \mathcal{NP} \cap \mathrm{co}\mathcal{NP}$).

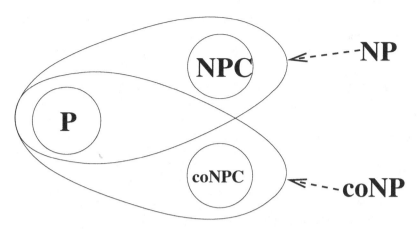

Figure 2.5: The world view under $\mathcal{P} \neq \text{co}\mathcal{NP} \cap \mathcal{NP} \neq \mathcal{NP}$.

1. The conjecture that $\mathcal{NP} \neq \text{co}\mathcal{NP}$ (equivalently, $\mathcal{NP} \cap \text{co}\mathcal{NP} \neq \mathcal{NP}$).

   This conjecture is equivalent to the conjecture that CNF formulae have no short proofs of unsatisfiability (i.e., the set $\{0, 1\}^* \setminus \text{SAT}$ has no NP-proof system).

2. The conjecture that $\mathcal{NP} \cap \text{co}\mathcal{NP} \neq \mathcal{P}$.

   Notable candidates for the class $\mathcal{NP} \cap \text{co}\mathcal{NP} \neq \mathcal{P}$ include decision problems that are computationally equivalent to the integer factorization problem (i.e., the search problem (in $\mathcal{PC}$) in which, given a composite number, the task is to find its prime factors).

Combining these conjectures, we get the world view depicted in Figure 2.5, which also shows the class of $\text{co}\mathcal{NP}$-complete sets (defined next).

> **Definition 2.36:** *A set S is called* $\text{co}\mathcal{NP}$-hard *if every set in* $\text{co}\mathcal{NP}$ *is Karp-reducible to S. A set is called* $\text{co}\mathcal{NP}$-complete *if it is both in* $\text{co}\mathcal{NP}$ *and* $\text{co}\mathcal{NP}$-hard.

Indeed, insisting on Karp-reductions is essential for a distinction between $\mathcal{NP}$-hardness and $\text{co}\mathcal{NP}$-hardness.

Chapter Notes

Many sources provide historical accounts of the developments that led to the formulation of the *P-vs-NP Problem* and to the discovery of the theory of NP-completeness (see, e.g., [85, Sec. 1.5] and [221]). Still, we feel that we should not refrain from offering our own impressions, which are *based on the texts of the original papers*.

Nowadays, the theory of NP-completeness is commonly attributed to Cook [58], Karp [138], and Levin [152]. It seems that Cook's starting point was his interest in theorem-proving procedures for propositional calculus [58, p. 151]. Trying to provide evidence of the difficulty of deciding whether or not a given formula is a tautology, he identified $\mathcal{NP}$ as a class containing "many apparently difficult problems" (cf, e.g., [58, p. 151]), and showed that any problem in $\mathcal{NP}$ is reducible to deciding membership in the set of 3DNF tautologies. In particular, Cook emphasized the importance of the concept of polynomial-time reductions and the complexity class $\mathcal{NP}$ (both explicitly defined for the first time in his paper). He also showed that CLIQUE is computationally equivalent to SAT, and envisioned a class of problems of the same nature.

Karp's paper [138] can be viewed as fulfilling Cook's prophecy: Stimulated by Cook's work, Karp demonstrated that a "large number of classic difficult computational problems, arising in fields such as mathematical programming, graph theory, combinatorics, computational logic and switching theory, are [NP-]complete (and thus equivalent)" [138, p. 86]. Specifically, his list of twenty-one NP-complete problems includes Integer Linear Programming, Hamilton Circuit, Chromatic Number, Exact Set Cover, Steiner Tree, Knapsack, Job Scheduling, and Max Cut. Interestingly, Karp defined $\mathcal{NP}$ in terms of verification procedures (i.e., Definition 2.5), pointed to its relation to "backtrack search of polynomial bounded depth" [138, p. 86], and viewed $\mathcal{NP}$ as the residence of a "wide range of important computational problems" (which are not in $\mathcal{P}$).

Independently of these developments, while being in the USSR, Levin proved the existence of "universal search problems" (where universality meant NP-completeness). The starting point of Levin's work [152] was his interest in the "*perebor*" conjecture asserting the inherent need for brute force in some search problems that have efficiently checkable solutions (i.e., problems in $\mathcal{PC}$). Levin emphasized the implication of polynomial-time reductions on the relation between the time complexity of the related problems (for any growth rate of the time complexity), asserted the NP-completeness of six "classical search problems," and claimed that the underlying method "provides a mean for readily obtaining" similar results for "many other important search problems."

It is interesting to note that although the works of Cook [58], Karp [138], and Levin [152] were received with different levels of enthusiasm, none of the contemporaries realized the depth of the discovery and the difficulty of the question posed (i.e., the P-vs-NP Question). This fact is evident in every account from the early 1970s, and may explain the frustration of the corresponding generation of researchers, which expected the P-vs-NP Question to be resolved in their lifetime (if not in a matter of years). Needless to say, the author's opinion is that there was absolutely no justification for these expectations, and that one should have actually expected quite the opposite.

We mention that the three "founding papers" of the theory of NP-completeness (i.e., Cook [58], Karp [138], and Levin [152]) use the three different types of reductions used in this chapter. Specifically, Cook uses the general notion of polynomial-time reduction [58], often referred to as Cook-reductions (Definition 2.9). The notion of Karp-reductions (Definition 2.11) originates from Karp's paper [138], whereas its augmentation to search problems (i.e., Definition 2.12) originates from Levin's paper [152]. It is worth stressing that Levin's work is stated in terms of search problems, unlike Cook's and Karp's works, which treat decision problems.

The reductions presented in §2.3.3.2 are not necessarily the original ones. Most notably, the reduction establishing the NP-hardness of the Independent Set problem (i.e., Proposition 2.26) is adapted from [74] (see also Exercise 9.18). In contrast, the reductions presented in §2.3.3.1 are merely a reinterpretation of the original reduction as presented in [58]. The equivalence of the two definitions of $\mathcal{NP}$ (i.e., Theorem 2.8) was proved in [138].

The existence of NP-sets that are neither in P nor NP-complete (i.e., Theorem 2.28) was proven by Ladner [149], Theorem 2.35 was proven by Selman [198], and the existence of optimal search algorithms for NP-relations (i.e., Theorem 2.33) was proven by Levin [152]. (Interestingly, the latter result was proven in the same paper in which Levin presented the discovery of NP-completeness, independently of Cook and Karp.) Promise problems were explicitly introduced by Even, Selman, and Yacobi [72]; see [94] for a survey of their numerous applications.

We mention that the standard reductions used to establish natural NP-completeness results have several additional properties or can be modified to have such properties. These properties include an efficient transformation of solutions in the direction of the reduction (see Exercise 2.28), the preservation of the number of solutions (see Exercise 2.29), the computability by a log-space algorithm (see Section 5.2.2), and the invertibility in polynomial-time (see Exercise 2.30). We also mention the fact that all known NP-complete sets are (effectively) isomorphic (see Exercise 2.31).

Exercises

Exercise 2.1 ($\mathcal{PF}$ **contains problems that are not in** $\mathcal{PC}$): Show that $\mathcal{PF}$ contains some (unnatural) problems that are not in $\mathcal{PC}$.

> **Guideline:** Consider the relation $R = \{(x, 1) : x \in \{0, 1\}^*\} \cup \{(x, 0) : x \in S\}$, where S is some undecidable set. Note that R is the disjoint union of two binary relations, denoted R_1 and R_2, where R_1 is in $\mathcal{PF}$ whereas R_2 is not in $\mathcal{PC}$. Furthermore, for every x it holds that $R_1(x) \neq \emptyset$.

Exercise 2.2: Show that any $S \in \mathcal{NP}$ has many different NP-proof systems (i.e., verification procedures $V_1, V_2, \ldots$ such that $V_i(x, y) = 1$ does not imply $V_j(x, y) = 1$ for $i \neq j$).

> **Guideline:** For V and p as in Definition 2.5, define $V_i(x, y) = 1$ if $|y| = p(|x|) + i$ and there exists a prefix y' of y such that $V(x, y') = 1$.

Exercise 2.3: Relying on the fact that primality is decidable in polynomial time and assuming that there is no polynomial-time factorization algorithm, present two "natural but fundamentally different" NP-proof systems for the set of composite numbers.

> **Guideline:** Consider the following verification procedures V_1 and V_2 for the set of composite numbers. Let $V_1(n, y) = 1$ if and only if $y = n$ and n is not a prime, and $V_2(n, m) = 1$ if and only if m is a non-trivial divisor of n. Show that valid proofs with respect to V_1 are easy to find, whereas valid proofs with respect to V_2 are hard to find.

Exercise 2.4: Regarding Definition 2.7, show that if S is accepted by some non-deterministic machine of time complexity t then it is accepted by a non-deterministic machine of time complexity $O(t)$ that has a transition function that maps each possible symbol-state pair to exactly two triples.

Exercise 2.5: Verify the following properties of Cook-reductions:

1. If Π is Cook-reducible to Π' and Π' is solvable in polynomial time then so is Π.
2. Cook-reductions are transitive (i.e., if Π is Cook-reducible to Π' and Π' is Cook-reducible to Π'' then Π is Cook-reducible to Π'').
3. If Π is solvable in polynomial time then it is Cook-reducible to any problem Π'.

In continuation of the last item, show that a problem Π is solvable in polynomial time if and only if it is Cook-reducible to a trivial problem (e.g., deciding membership in the empty set).

Exercise 2.6: Show that Karp-reductions (and Levin-reductions) are transitive.

Exercise 2.7: Show that some decision problems are not Karp-reducible to their complement (e.g., the empty set is not Karp-reducible to $\{0, 1\}^*$).

A popular exercise of dubious nature is showing that any decision problem in $\mathcal{P}$ is Karp-reducible to any *non-trivial* decision problem, where the decision problem regarding a set S is called non-trivial if $S \neq \emptyset$ and $S \neq \{0, 1\}^*$. It follows that every non-trivial set in $\mathcal{P}$ is Karp-reducible to its complement.

Exercise 2.8 (reducing search problems to optimization problems): For every polynomially bounded relation R (resp., $R \in \mathcal{PC}$), present a function f (resp., a polynomial-time computable function f) such that the search problem of R is computationally equivalent to the search problem in which given (x, v) one has to find a $y \in \{0, 1\}^{\text{poly}(|x|)}$ such that $f(x, y) \geq v$.

(Hint: Use a Boolean function.)

Exercise 2.9 (binary search): Show that using ℓ binary queries of the form "is $z < v$" it is possible to determine the value of an integer z that is a priori known to reside in the interval $[0, 2^\ell - 1]$.

> **Guideline:** Consider a process that iteratively halves the interval in which z is known to reside.

Exercise 2.10: Show that if $R \in \mathcal{PC} \setminus \mathcal{PF}$ is self-reducible then the relevant Cook-reduction makes more than a logarithmic number of queries to S_R. More generally, show that if $R \in \mathcal{PC} \setminus \mathcal{PF}$ is Cook-reducible to any decision problem, then this reduction makes more than a logarithmic number of queries.

> **Guideline:** Note that the oracle answers can be emulated by trying all possibilities, and that the correctness of the output of the oracle machine can be efficiently tested.

Exercise 2.11: Show that the standard search problem of Graph 3-Colorability is self-reducible, where this search problem consists of finding a 3-coloring for a given input graph.

> **Guideline:** Iteratively extend the current prefix of a 3-coloring of the graph by making adequate oracle calls to the decision problem of Graph 3-Colorability. (Specifically, encode the question of whether or not $(\chi_1, \ldots, \chi_t) \in \{1, 2, 3\}^t$ is a prefix of a 3-coloring of the graph G as a query regarding the 3-colorability of an auxiliary graph G'.)[30]

Exercise 2.12: Show that the standard search problem of Graph Isomorphism is self-reducible, where this search problem consists of finding an isomorphism between a given pair of graphs.

> **Guideline:** Iteratively extend the current prefix of an isomorphism between the two N-vertex graphs by making adequate oracle calls to the decision problem of Graph Isomorphism. (Specifically, encode the question of whether or not $(\pi_1, \ldots, \pi_t) \in [N]^t$

---

[30]Note that we merely need to check whether G has a 3-coloring in which the equalities and inequalities induced by $(\chi_1, \ldots, \chi_t)$ hold. This can be done by adequate gadgets (e.g., inequality is enforced by an edge between the corresponding vertices, whereas equality is enforced by an adequate subgraph that includes the relevant vertices as well as auxiliary vertices). For Part 1 of Exercise 2.13, equality is better enforced by combining the two vertices.

is a prefix of an isomorphism between $G_1 = ([N], E_1)$ and $G_2 = ([N], E_2)$ as a query regarding isomorphism between two auxiliary graphs G'_1 and G'_2.)[31]

Exercise 2.13 (downward self-reducibility): We say that a set S is downward self-reducible if there exists a Cook-reduction of S to itself that only makes queries that are each shorter than the reduction's input (i.e., if on input x the reduction makes the query q then $|q| < |x|$).[32]

1. Show that SAT is downward self-reducible with respect to a natural encoding of CNF formulae. Note that this encoding should have the property that instantiating a variable in a formula results in a shorter formula.

   A harder exercise consists of showing that Graph 3-Colorability is downward self-reducible with respect to some reasonable encoding of graphs. Note that this encoding has to be selected carefully (if it is to work for a process analogous to the one used in Exercise 2.11).

2. Suppose that S is downward self-reducible *by a reduction that outputs the disjunction of the oracle answers*. (Note that this is the case for SAT.) Show that in this case, S is characterized by a witness relation $R \in \mathcal{PC}$ (i.e., $S = \{x : R(x) \neq \emptyset\}$) that is self-reducible (i.e., the search problem of R is Cook-reducible to S). Needless to say, it follows that $S \in \mathcal{NP}$.

   Guideline: Include $(x_0, \langle x_1, \ldots, x_t \rangle)$ in R if $x_t \in S \cap \{0, 1\}^{O(1)}$ and, for every $i \in \{0, 1, \ldots, t-1\}$, on input x_i the self-reduction makes a set of queries that contains x_{i+1}. Prove that, indeed, $R \in \mathcal{PC}$ and $S = \{x : R(x) \neq \emptyset\}$.

Note that the notion of downward self-reducibility may be generalized in some natural ways. For example, we may say that S is downward self-reducible also in case it is computationally equivalent via Karp-reductions to some set that is downward self-reducible (in the foregoing strict sense). Note that Part 2 still holds.

Exercise 2.14 (NP problems that are not self-reducible):

1. Assuming that $\mathcal{P} \neq \mathcal{NP} \cap \text{co}\mathcal{NP}$, show that there exists a search problem that is in $\mathcal{PC}$ but is not self-reducible.

   Guideline: Given $S \in \mathcal{NP} \cap \text{co}\mathcal{NP} \setminus \mathcal{P}$, present relations $R_1, R_2 \in \mathcal{PC}$ such that $S = \{x : R_1(x) \neq \emptyset\} = \{x : R_2(x) = \emptyset\}$. Then, consider the relation $R = \{(x, 1y) : (x, y) \in R_1\} \cup \{(x, 0y) : (x, y) \in R_2\}$, and prove that $R \notin \mathcal{PF}$ but $S_R = \{0, 1\}^*$.

2. Prove that if a search problem R is not self-reducible then (1) $R \notin \mathcal{PF}$ and (2) the set $S'_R = \{(x, y') : \exists y'' \text{ s.t. } (x, y'y'') \in R\}$ is not Cook-reducible to $S_R = \{x : \exists y \text{ s.t. } (x, y) \in R\}$.

Exercise 2.15 (extending any prefix of any solution versus $\mathcal{PC}$ and $\mathcal{PF}$): Assuming that $\mathcal{P} \neq \mathcal{NP}$, present a search problem R in $\mathcal{PC} \cap \mathcal{PF}$ such that deciding S'_R is not reducible to the search problem of R.

---

[31]This can be done by attaching adequate gadgets to pairs of vertices that we wish to be mapped to one another (by the isomorphism). For example, we may connect the vertices in the ith pair to an auxiliary star consisting of $(N + i)$ vertices.

[32]Note that on some instances the reduction may make no queries at all. (This prevents a possible non-viability of the definition due to very short instances.)

Guideline: Consider the relation $R = \{(x, 0x) : x \in \{0, 1\}^*\} \cup \{(x, 1y) : (x, y) \in R'\}$, where R' is an arbitrary relation in $\mathcal{PC} \setminus \mathcal{PF}$, and prove that $R \in \mathcal{PF}$ but $S'_R \notin \mathcal{P}$.

Exercise 2.16: In continuation of Exercise 2.14, present a natural search problem R in $\mathcal{PC}$ such that if factoring integers is intractable then the search problem R (and so also S'_R) is not reducible to S_R.

> **Guideline:** Consider the relation R such that $(N, Q) \in R$ if the integer Q is a non-trivial divisor of the integer N. Use the fact that the set of prime numbers is in $\mathcal{P}$.

Exercise 2.17: In continuation of Exercises 2.14 and 2.16, show that under suitable assumptions, there exist relations $R_1, R_2 \in \mathcal{PC}$ having the same implicit decision problem (i.e., $\{x : R_1(x) \neq \emptyset\} = \{x : R_2(x) \neq \emptyset\}$) such that R_1 is self-reducible but R_2 is not.

Exercise 2.18: Provide an alternative proof of Theorem 2.16 without referring to the set $S'_R = \{(x, y') : \exists y'' \text{ s.t. } (x, y'y'') \in R\}$.

(Hint: Use Proposition 2.15.)

> **Guideline:** Reduce the search problem of R to the search problem of R_{SAT}, next reduce R_{SAT} to SAT, and finally reduce SAT to S_R. Justify the existence of each of these three reductions.

Exercise 2.19: Prove that Bounded Halting and Bounded Non-halting are NP-complete, where the problems are defined as follows. The instance consists of a pair $(M, 1^t)$, where M is a Turing machine and t is an integer. The decision version of Bounded Halting (resp., Bounded Non-halting) consists of determining whether or not there exists an input (of length at most t) on which M halts (resp., does *not* halt) in t steps, whereas the search problem consists of finding such an input.

> **Guideline:** Either modify the proof of Theorem 2.19 or present a reduction of (say) the search problem of R_u to the search problem of Bounded (Non-)Halting. (Indeed, the exercise is more straightforward in the case of Bounded Halting.)

Exercise 2.20: In the proof of Theorem 2.21, we claimed that the value of each entry in the "array of configurations" of a machine M is determined by the values of the three entries that reside in the row above it (as in Figure 2.1). Present a function $f_M : \Gamma^3 \to \Gamma$, where $\Gamma = \Sigma \times (Q \cup \{\perp\})$, that substantiates this claim.

> **Guideline:** For example, for every $\sigma_1, \sigma_2, \sigma_3 \in \Sigma$, it holds that $f_M((\sigma_1, \perp), (\sigma_2, \perp), (\sigma_3, \perp)) = (\sigma_2, \perp)$. More interestingly, if the transition function of M maps (σ, q) to $(\tau, p, +1)$ then, for every $\sigma_1, \sigma_2, \sigma_3 \in Q$, it holds that $f_M((\sigma, q), (\sigma_2, \perp), (\sigma_3, \perp)) = (\sigma_2, p)$ and $f_M((\sigma_1, \perp), (\sigma, q), (\sigma_3, \perp)) = (\tau, \perp)$.

Exercise 2.21: Present and analyze a reduction of SAT to 3SAT.

> **Guideline:** For a clause C, consider auxiliary variables such that the ith variable indicates whether one of the first i literals is satisfied, and replace C by a 3CNF that uses the original variables of C as well as the auxiliary variables. For example, the clause $\vee_{i=1}^t x_i$ is replaced by the conjunction of 3CNFs that are logically equivalent to the formulae $(y_2 \equiv (x_1 \vee x_2)), (y_i \equiv (y_{i-1} \vee x_i))$ for $i = 3, \ldots, t$, and y_t. We comment that this is not the standard reduction, but we find it conceptually more appealing.[33]

---

[33] The standard reduction replaces the clause $\vee_{i=1}^t x_i$ by the conjunction of the 3CNFs $(x_1 \vee x_2 \vee z_2), ((\neg z_{i-1}) \vee x_i \vee z_i)$ for $i = 3, \ldots, t$, and $\neg z_t$.

Exercise 2.22 (efficient solvability of 2SAT): In contrast to Exercise 2.21, prove that 2SAT (i.e., the satisfiability of 2CNF formulae) is in $\mathcal{P}$.

> **Guideline:** Consider the following "forcing process" for CNF formulae. If the formula contains a singleton clause (i.e., a clause having a single literal), then the corresponding variable is assigned the only value that satisfies the clause, and the formula is simplified accordingly (possibly yielding a constant formula, which is either true or false). The process is repeated until the formula is either a constant or contains only non-singleton clauses. Note that a formula ϕ is satisfiable if and only if the formula obtained from ϕ by the forcing process is satisfiable. Consider the following algorithm for solving the search problem associated with 2SAT.
>
> 1. Choose an arbitrary variable in ϕ. For each $\sigma \in \{0, 1\}$, denote by ϕ_σ the formula obtained from ϕ by assigning this variable the value σ.
> 2. If, for some $\sigma \in \{0, 1\}$, applying the forcing process to ϕ_σ yields a (non-constant) 2CNF formula ϕ', then set $\phi \leftarrow \phi'$ and goto Step 1. (The case that this happens for both $\sigma \in \{0, 1\}$ is treated as the case that this happens for a single σ; that is, in such a case we proceed with an arbitrary choice of σ.)
> 3. If one of these assignments yields (via the application of the forcing process) the constant true then we halt with a satisfying assignment for the original formula. Otherwise (i.e., both assignments yield the constant false), we halt asserting that the original formula is unsatisfiable.
>
> Proving the correctness of this algorithm boils down to observing that the arbitrary choice made in Step 2 is immaterial. Indeed, this observation relies on the fact that we refer to 2CNF formulae.

Exercise 2.23 (Integer Linear Programming): Prove that the following problem is NP-complete. An instance of the problem is a systems of linear inequalities (say with integer constants), and the problem is to determine whether the system has an integer solution. A typical instance of this decision problem follows.

$$x + 2y - z \geq 3$$
$$-3x - z \geq -5$$
$$x \geq 0$$
$$-x \geq -1$$

> **Guideline:** Reduce from SAT. Specifically, consider an arithmetization of the input CNF by replacing $\vee$ with addition and $\neg x$ by $1 - x$. Thus, each clause gives rise to an inequality (e.g., the clause $x \vee \neg y$ is replaced by the inequality $x + (1 - y) \geq 1$, which simplifies to $x - y \geq 2$). Enforce a 0-1 solution by introducing inequalities of the form $x \geq 0$ and $-x \geq -1$, for every variable x.

Exercise 2.24 (Maximum Satisfiability of Linear Systems over GF(2)**):** Prove that the following problem is NP-complete. An instance of the problem consists of a systems of linear equations over GF(2) and an integer k, and the problem is to determine whether there exists an assignment that satisfies at least k equations. (Note that the problem of determining whether there exists an assignment that satisfies all the equations is in $\mathcal{P}$.)

> **Guideline:** Reduce from 3SAT, using the following arithmetization. Replace each clause that contains $t \leq 3$ literals by $2^t - 1$ linear GF(2) equations that correspond to

the different non-empty subsets of these literals, and assert that their sum (modulo 2) equals one; for example, the clause $x \lor \neg y$ is replaced by the equations $x + (1 - y) = 1$, $x = 1$, and $1 - y = 1$. Identifying {false, true} with {0, 1}, prove that if the original clause is satisfied by a Boolean assignment $\bar{v}$ then exactly 2^{t-1} of the corresponding equations are satisfied by $\bar{v}$, whereas if the original clause is unsatisfied by $\bar{v}$ then none of the corresponding equations is satisfied by $\bar{v}$.

Exercise 2.25 (Satisfiability of Quadratic Systems over GF(2)**):** Prove that the following problem is NP-complete. An instance of the problem consists of a system of quadratic equations over GF(2), and the problem is to determine whether there exists an assignment that satisfies all the equations. Note that the result holds also for systems of quadratic equations over the reals (by adding conditions that enforce a value in {0, 1}).

> **Guideline:** Start by showing that the corresponding problem for cubic equations is NP-complete, by a reduction from 3SAT that maps the clause $x \lor \neg y \lor z$ to the equation $(1 - x) \cdot y \cdot (1 - z) = 0$. Reduce the problem for cubic equations to the problem for quadratic equations by introducing auxiliary variables; that is, given an instance with variables $x_1, \ldots, x_n$, introduce the auxiliary variables $x_{i,j}$'s and add equations of the form $x_{i,j} = x_i \cdot x_j$.

Exercise 2.26 (Clique and Independent Set): An instance of the Independent Set problem consists of a pair (G, K), where G is a graph and K is an integer, and the question is whether or not the graph G contains an independent set (i.e., a set with no edges between its members) of size (at least) K. The Clique problem is analogous. Prove that both problems are computationally equivalent via Karp-reductions to the Vertex Cover problem.

Exercise 2.27 (an alternative proof of Proposition 2.26): Consider the following sketch of a reduction of 3SAT to Independent Set. On input a 3CNF formula ϕ with m clauses and n variables, we construct a graph G_ϕ consisting of m triangles (corresponding to the m clauses) augmented with edges that link conflicting literals. That is, if x appears as the i_1^{th} literal of the j_1^{th} clause and $\neg x$ appears as the i_2^{th} literal of the j_2^{th} clause, then we draw an edge between the i_1^{th} vertex of the j_1^{th} triangle and the i_2^{th} vertex of the j_2^{th} triangle. Prove that $\phi \in$ 3SAT if and only if G_ϕ has an independent set of size m.

Exercise 2.28 (additional properties of standard reductions): In continuation of the discussion in the main text, consider the following augmented form of Karp-reductions. Such a reduction of R to R' consists of three polynomial-time mappings (f, h, g) such that f is a Karp-reduction of S_R to $S_{R'}$ and the following two conditions hold:

1. For every $(x, y) \in R$ it holds that $(f(x), h(x, y)) \in R'$.
2. For every $(f(x), y') \in R'$ it holds that $(x, g(x, y')) \in R$.

(We note that this definition is actually the one used by Levin in [152], except that he restricted h and g to depend only on their second argument.)

Prove that such a reduction implies both a Karp-reduction and a Levin-reduction, and show that all reductions presented in this chapter satisfy this augmented requirement. Furthermore, prove that in all *these cases* the main mapping (i.e., f) is 1-1 and polynomial-time invertible.

Exercise 2.29 (parsimonious reductions): Let $R, R' \in \mathcal{PC}$ and let f be a Karp-reduction of $S_R = \{x : R(x) \neq \emptyset\}$ to $S_{R'} = \{x : R'(x) \neq \emptyset\}$. We say that f is parsimonious (with respect to R and R') if for every x it holds that $|R(x)| = |R'(f(x))|$. For each of the reductions presented in this chapter, check whether or not it is parsimonious. For the reductions that are not parsimonious, find alternative reductions that are parsimonious (cf. [85, Sec. 7.3]).

Exercise 2.30 (on polynomial-time invertible reductions (following [37])): We say that a set S is markable if there exists a polynomial-time (marking) algorithm M such that

1. For every $x, \alpha \in \{0, 1\}^*$ it holds that
   (a) $M(x, \alpha) \in S$ if and only if $x \in S$.
   (b) $|M(x, \alpha)| > |x|$.
2. There exists a polynomial-time (de-marking) algorithm D such that, for every $x, \alpha \in \{0, 1\}^*$, it holds that $D(M(x, \alpha)) = \alpha$.

Note that all natural NP-sets (e.g., those considered in this chapter) are markable (e.g., for SAT, one may mark a formula by augmenting it with additional satisfiable clauses that use specially designated auxiliary variables). Prove that *if S' is Karp-reducible to S and S is markable then S' is Karp-reducible to S by a length-increasing, one-to-one, and polynomial-time invertible mapping.*[34] Infer that for any natural NP-complete problem S, any set in $\mathcal{NP}$ is Karp-reducible to S by a length-increasing, one-to-one, and polynomial-time invertible mapping.

> **Guideline:** Let f be a Karp-reduction of S' to S, and let M be the guaranteed marking algorithm. Consider the reduction that maps x to $M(f(x), x)$.

Exercise 2.31 (on the isomorphism of NP-complete sets (following [37])): Suppose that S and T are Karp-reducible to one another by length-increasing, one-to-one, and polynomial-time invertible mappings, denoted f and g, respectively. Using the following guidelines, prove that S and T are "effectively" *isomorphic*; that is, present a polynomial-time computable and invertible one-to-one mapping ϕ such that $T = \phi(S) \overset{\text{def}}{=} \{\phi(x) : x \in S\}$.

1. Let $F \overset{\text{def}}{=} \{f(x) : x \in \{0, 1\}^*\}$ and $G \overset{\text{def}}{=} \{g(x) : x \in \{0, 1\}^*\}$. Using the length-preserving condition of f (resp., g), prove that F (resp., G) is a proper subset of $\{0, 1\}^*$. Prove that for every $y \in \{0, 1\}^*$ there exists a unique triple $(j, x, i) \in \{1, 2\} \times \{0, 1\}^* \times (\{0\} \cup \mathbb{N})$ that satisfies one of the following two conditions:
   (a) $j = 1$, $x \in \overline{G} \overset{\text{def}}{=} \{0, 1\}^* \setminus G$, and $y = (g \circ f)^i(x)$;
   (b) $j = 2$, $x \in \overline{F} \overset{\text{def}}{=} \{0, 1\}^* \setminus F$, and $y = (g \circ f)^i(g(x))$.
   (In both cases $h^0(z) = z$, $h^i(z) = h(h^{i-1}(z))$, and $(g \circ f)(z) = g(f(z))$. Hint: consider the maximal sequence of inverse operations $g^{-1}, f^{-1}, g^{-1}, \ldots$ that can be applied to y, and note that each inverse shrinks the current string.)
2. Let $U_1 \overset{\text{def}}{=} \{(g \circ f)^i(x) : x \in \overline{G} \wedge i \geq 0\}$ and $U_2 \overset{\text{def}}{=} \{(g \circ f)^i(g(x)) : x \in \overline{F} \wedge i \geq 0\}$. Prove that (U_1, U_2) is a partition of $\{0, 1\}^*$. Using the fact that f and g are length-increasing and polynomial-time invertible, present a polynomial-time procedure for deciding membership in the set U_1.

---

[34]When given a string that is not in the image of the mapping, the inverting algorithm returns a special symbol.

Prove the same for the sets $V_1 = \{(f \circ g)^i(x) : x \in \overline{F} \land i \geq 0\}$ and $V_2 = \{(f \circ g)^i(f(x)) : x \in \overline{G} \land i \geq 0\}$.

3. Note that $U_2 \subseteq G$, and define $\phi(x) \overset{\text{def}}{=} f(x)$ if $x \in U_1$ and $\phi(x) \overset{\text{def}}{=} g^{-1}(x)$ otherwise.
   (a) Prove that ϕ is a Karp-reduction of S to T.
   (b) Note that ϕ maps U_1 to $f(U_1) = \{f(x) : x \in U_1\} = V_2$ and U_2 to $g^{-1}(U_2) = \{g^{-1}(x) : x \in U_2\} = V_1$. Prove that ϕ is one-to-one and onto.

   Observe that $\phi^{-1}(x) = f^{-1}(x)$ if $x \in f(U_1)$ and $\phi^{-1}(x) = g(x)$ otherwise. Prove that ϕ^{-1} is a Karp-reduction of T to S. Infer that $\phi(S) = T$.

Using Exercise 2.30, infer that all natural NP-complete sets are isomorphic.

Exercise 2.32: Prove that a set S is Karp-reducible to some set in $\mathcal{NP}$ if and only if S is in $\mathcal{NP}$.

> **Guideline:** For the non-trivial direction, see the proof of Proposition 2.34.

Exercise 2.33: Recall that the empty set is not Karp-reducible to $\{0, 1\}^*$, whereas any set is Cook-reducible to its complement. Thus, our focus here is on the *Karp-reducibility of non-trivial sets to their complements*, where a set is non-trivial if it is neither empty nor contains all strings. Furthermore, since any non-trivial set in $\mathcal{P}$ is Karp-reducible to its complement (see Exercise 2.7), we assume that $\mathcal{P} \neq \mathcal{NP}$ and focus on sets in $\mathcal{NP} \setminus \mathcal{P}$.

1. Prove that $\mathcal{NP} = \text{co}\mathcal{NP}$ implies that some sets in $\mathcal{NP} \setminus \mathcal{P}$ are Karp-reducible to their complements.
2. Prove that $\mathcal{NP} \neq \text{co}\mathcal{NP}$ implies that some sets in $\mathcal{NP} \setminus \mathcal{P}$ are not Karp-reducible to their complements.

> **Guideline:** Use NP-complete sets in both parts, and Exercise 2.32 in the second part.

Exercise 2.34: Referring to the proof of Theorem 2.28, prove that the function f is unbounded (i.e., for every i there exists an n such that n^3 steps of the process defined in the proof allow for failing the $i + 1^{\text{st}}$ machine).

> **Guideline:** Note that f is monotonically non-decreasing (because more steps allow for failing at least as many machines). Assume toward the contradiction that f is bounded. Let $i = \sup_{n \in \mathbb{N}}\{f(n)\}$ and n' be the smallest integer such that $f(n') = i$. If i is odd then the set F determined by f is co-finite (because $F = \{x : f(|x|) \equiv 1 \pmod{2}\} \supseteq \{x : |x| \geq n'\}$). In this case, the $i + 1^{\text{st}}$ machine tries to decide $S \cap F$ (which differs from S on finitely many strings), and must fail on some x. Derive a contradiction by showing that the number of steps taken till reaching and considering this x is at most $\exp(\text{poly}(|x|))$, which is smaller than n^3 for some sufficiently large n. A similar argument applies to the case that i is even, where we use the fact that $F \subseteq \{x : |x| < n'\}$ is finite and so the relevant reduction of S to $S \cap F$ must fail on some input x.

Exercise 2.35: Prove that if the promise problem Π is Cook-reducible to a promise problem that is solvable in polynomial time, then Π is solvable in polynomial time. Note that the solver may not halt on inputs that violate the promise.

> **Guideline:** Any polynomial-time algorithm solving any promise problem can be modified such that it halts on all inputs.

Exercise 2.36 (NP-complete promise problems in coNP (following [72])): Consider the promise problem xSAT having instances that are pairs of CNF formulae. The yes-instances consists of pairs (ϕ_1, ϕ_2) such that ϕ_1 is satisfiable and ϕ_2 is unsatisfiable, whereas the no-instances consists of pairs such that ϕ_1 is unsatisfiable and ϕ_2 is satisfiable.

1. Show that xSAT is in the intersection of (the promise problem classes that are analogous to) $\mathcal{NP}$ and co$\mathcal{NP}$.

2. Prove that any promise problem in $\mathcal{NP}$ is Cook-reducible to xSAT. In designing the reduction, recall that queries that violate the promise may be answered arbitrarily.

   Guideline: Note that the promise problem version of $\mathcal{NP}$ is reducible to SAT, and show a reduction of SAT to xSAT. Specifically, show that the search problem associated with SAT is Cook-reducible to xSAT, by adapting the ideas of the proof of Proposition 2.15. That is, suppose that we know (or assume) that τ is a prefix of a satisfying assignment to ϕ, and we wish to extend τ by one bit. Then, for each $\sigma \in \{0, 1\}$, we construct a formula, denoted ϕ'_σ, by setting the first $|\tau| + 1$ variables of ϕ according to the values $\tau\sigma$. We query the oracle about the pair (ϕ'_1, ϕ'_0), and extend τ accordingly (i.e., we extend τ by the value 1 if and only if the answer is positive). Note that if both ϕ'_1 and ϕ'_0 are satisfiable then it does not matter which bit we use in the extension, whereas if exactly one formula is satisfiable then the oracle answer is reliable.

3. Pinpoint the source of failure of the proof of Theorem 2.35 when applied to the reduction provided in the previous item.

Exercise 2.37: For any class $\mathcal{C}$, prove that $\mathcal{C} \subseteq \text{co}\mathcal{C}$ if and only if $\mathcal{C} = \text{co}\mathcal{C}$.

CHAPTER THREE

Variations on P and NP

> *Cast a cold eye*
> *On life, on death.*
> *Horseman, pass by!*
> W. B. Yeats, "Under Ben Bulben"

In this chapter we consider variations on the complexity classes P and NP. We refer specifically to the non-uniform version of P, and to the Polynomial-time Hierarchy (which extends NP). These variations are motivated by relatively technical considerations; still, the resulting classes are referred to quite frequently in the literature.

Summary: Non-uniform polynomial-time (P/poly) captures efficient computations that are carried out by devices that can each handle only inputs of a specific length. The basic formalism ignores the complexity of constructing such devices (i.e., a uniformity condition). A finer formalism that allows for quantifying the amount of non-uniformity refers to so-called "machines that take advice."

The Polynomial-time Hierarchy (PH) generalizes NP by considering statements expressed by quantified Boolean formulae with a fixed number of alternations of existential and universal quantifiers. It is widely believed that each quantifier alternation adds expressive power to the class of such formulae.

An interesting result that refers to both classes asserts that if NP is contained in P/poly then the Polynomial-time Hierarchy collapses to its second level. This result is commonly interpreted as supporting the common belief that non-uniformity is irrelevant to the P-vs-NP Question; that is, although P/poly extends beyond the class P, it is believed that P/poly does not contain NP.

Except for the latter result, which is presented in Section 3.2.3, the treatments of P/poly (in Section 3.1) and of the Polynomial-time Hierarchy (in Section 3.2) are independent of one another.

3.1. Non-uniform Polynomial Time (P/poly)

In this section we consider two formulations of the notion of non-uniform polynomial time, based on the two models of non-uniform computing devices that were presented in Section 1.2.4. That is, we specialize the treatment of non-uniform computing devices, provided in Section 1.2.4, to the case of polynomially bounded complexities. It turns out that both (polynomially bounded) formulations allow for solving the same class of computational problems, which is a strict superset of the class of problems solvable by polynomial-time algorithms.

The two models of non-uniform computing devices are Boolean circuits and "machines that take advice" (cf. §1.2.4.1 and §1.2.4.2, respectively). We will focus on the restriction of both models to the case of polynomial complexities, considering (non-uniform) polynomial-size circuits and polynomial-time algorithms that take (non-uniform) advice of polynomially bounded length.

The main motivation for considering non-uniform polynomial-size circuits is that their computational limitations imply analogous limitations on polynomial-time algorithms. The hope is that, as is often the case in mathematics and science, disposing of an auxiliary condition (i.e., uniformity) that seems secondary[1] and is not well understood may turn out to be fruitful. In particular, the (non-uniform) circuit model facilitates a low-level analysis of the evolution of a computation, and allows for the application of combinatorial techniques. The benefit of this approach has been demonstrated in the study of restricted classes of circuits (see Appendix B.2.2 and B.2.3).

The main motivation for considering polynomial-time algorithms that take polynomially bounded advice is that such devices are useful in modeling auxiliary information that is available to possible efficient strategies that are of interest to us. We mention two such settings. In cryptography (see Appendix C), the advice is used for accounting for auxiliary information that is available to an adversary. In the context of derandomization (see Section 8.3), the advice is used for accounting for the main input to the randomized algorithm. In addition, the model of polynomial-time algorithms that take advice allows for a quantitative study of the amount of non-uniformity, ranging from zero to polynomial.

3.1.1. Boolean Circuits

We refer the reader to §1.2.4.1 for a definition of (families of) Boolean circuits and the functions computed by them. For concreteness and simplicity, we assume throughout this section that all circuits have bounded fan-in. We highlight the following result stated in §1.2.4.1:

> **Theorem 3.1** (circuit evaluation): *There exists a polynomial-time algorithm that, given a circuit $C : \{0, 1\}^n \to \{0, 1\}^m$ and an n-bit long string x, returns $C(x)$.*

Recall that the algorithm works by performing the "value-determination" process that underlies the definition of the computation of the circuit on a given input. This process assigns values to each of the circuit vertices based on the values of its children (or the values of the corresponding bit of the input, in the case of an input-terminal vertex).

Circuit size as a complexity measure. We recall the definitions of circuit complexity presented in §1.2.4.1: The size of a circuit is defined as the number of edges, and the length of its description is almost linear in the latter; that is, a circuit of size s is

---

[1]The common belief is that the issue of non-uniformity is irrelevant to the P-vs-NP Question, that is, that resolving the latter question by proving that $\mathcal{P} \neq \mathcal{NP}$ is not easier than proving that NP does not have polynomial-size circuits. For further discussion see Appendix B.2 and Section 3.2.3.

commonly described by the list of its edges and the labels of its vertices, which means that its description length is $O(s \log s)$. We are interested in families of circuits that solve computational problems, and thus we say that the circuit family $(C_n)_{n \in \mathbb{N}}$ computes the function $f : \{0, 1\}^* \to \{0, 1\}^*$ if for every $x \in \{0, 1\}^*$ it holds that $C_{|x|}(x) = f(x)$. The size complexity of this family is the function $s : \mathbb{N} \to \mathbb{N}$ such that $s(n)$ is the size of C_n. The circuit complexity of a function f, denoted s_f, is the size complexity of the smallest family of circuits that computes f. An equivalent formulation follows.

> **Definition 3.2** (circuit complexity): *The circuit complexity of $f : \{0, 1\}^* \to \{0, 1\}^*$ is the function $s_f : \mathbb{N} \to \mathbb{N}$ such that $s_f(n)$ is the size of the smallest circuit that computes the restriction of f to n-bit strings.*

We stress that non-uniformity is implicit in this definition, because no conditions are made regarding the relation between the various circuits that are used to compute the function value on different input lengths.

An interesting feature of Definition 3.2 is that, unlike in the case of uniform model of computations, it allows for considering the actual complexity of the function rather than an upper bound on its complexity (cf. §1.2.3.5 and Section 4.2.1). This is a consequence of the fact that the circuit model has no "free parameters" (such as various parameters of the possible algorithm that are used in the uniform model).[2]

We will be interested in the class of problems that are solvable by families of polynomial-size circuits. That is, a problem is solvable by polynomial-size circuits if it can be solved by a function f that has polynomial circuit complexity (i.e., there exists a polynomial p such that $s_f(n) \leq p(n)$, for every $n \in \mathbb{N}$).

A detour: Uniform families. A family of *polynomial-size* circuits $(C_n)_{n \in \mathbb{N}}$ is called uniform if given n one can construct the circuit C_n in poly(n)-time. More generally:

> **Definition 3.3** (uniformity): *A family of circuits $(C_n)_{n \in \mathbb{N}}$ is called uniform if there exists an algorithm that on input n outputs C_n within a number of steps that is polynomial in the size of C_n.*

We note that stronger notions of uniformity have been considered. For example, one may require the existence of a polynomial-time algorithm that on input n and v, returns the label of vertex v as well as the list of its children (or an indication that v is not a vertex in C_n). For further discussion see Section 5.2.3. Turning back to Definition 3.3, we note that indeed the computation of a uniform family of circuits can be emulated by a uniform computing device.

> **Proposition 3.4:** *If a problem is solvable by a uniform family of polynomial-size circuits then it is solvable by a polynomial-time algorithm.*

As was hinted in §1.2.4.1, the converse holds as well. The latter fact follows easily from the proof of Theorem 2.21 (see also the proof of Theorem 3.6).

---

[2]**Advanced comment:** The "free parameters" in the uniform model include the length of the description of the finite algorithm and its alphabet size. Note that these "free parameters" underlie linear speed-up results such as Exercise 4.4, which in turn prevent the specification of the exact (uniform) complexities of functions.

Proof: On input x, the algorithm operates in two stages. In the first stage, it invokes the algorithm guaranteed by the uniformity condition, on input $n \overset{\text{def}}{=} |x|$, and obtains the circuit C_n. Next, it invokes the circuit evaluation algorithm (asserted in Theorem 3.1) on input C_n and x, and obtains $C_n(x)$. Since the size of C_n (as well as its description length) is polynomial in n, it follows that each stage of our algorithm runs in polynomial time (i.e., polynomial in $n = |x|$). Thus, the algorithm emulates the computation of $C_{|x|}(x)$, and does so in time polynomial in the length of its own input (i.e., x). ∎

3.1.2. Machines That Take Advice

General (i.e., possibly non-uniform) families of polynomial-size circuits and uniform families of polynomial-size circuits are two extremes with respect to the "amounts of non-uniformity" in the computing device. Intuitively, in the former, non-uniformity is only bounded by the size of the device, whereas in the latter the amounts of non-uniformity is zero. Here we consider a model that allows for decoupling the size of the computing device from the amount of non-uniformity, which may indeed range from zero to the device's size. Specifically, we consider algorithms that "take a non-uniform advice" that depends only on the input length. The amount of non-uniformity will be defined to equal the length of the corresponding advice (as a function of the input length). Thus, we specialize Definition 1.12 to the case of polynomial-time algorithms.

Definition 3.5 (non-uniform polynomial-time and $\mathcal{P}/\text{poly}$): *We say that a function f is computed in polynomial time with advice of length $\ell : \mathbb{N} \to \mathbb{N}$ if these exists a polynomial-time algorithm A and an infinite advice sequence $(a_n)_{n \in \mathbb{N}}$ such that*

1. *For every $x \in \{0, 1\}^*$, it holds that $A(a_{|x|}, x) = f(x)$.*
2. *For every $n \in \mathbb{N}$, it holds that $|a_n| = \ell(n)$.*

We say that a computational problem can be solved in polynomial time with advice of length ℓ if a function solving this problem can be computed within these resources. We denote by $\mathcal{P}/\ell$ the class of decision problems that can be solved in polynomial time with advice of length ℓ, and by $\mathcal{P}/\text{poly}$ the union of $\mathcal{P}/p$ taken over all polynomials p.

Clearly, $\mathcal{P}/0 = \mathcal{P}$. But allowing some (non-empty) advice increases the power of the class (see Theorem 3.7), and allowing advice of length comparable to the time complexity yields a formulation equivalent to circuit complexity (see Theorem 3.6). We highlight the greater flexibility available by the formalism of machines that take advice, which allows for separate specification of time complexity and advice length. (Indeed, this comes at the expense of a more cumbersome formulation; thus, we shall prefer the circuit formulation whenever we consider the case that both complexity measures are polynomial.)

Relation to families of polynomial-size circuits. As hinted before, the class of problems solvable by polynomial-time algorithms with polynomially bounded advice equals the class of problems solvable by families of polynomial-size circuits. For concreteness, we state this fact for decision problems.

Theorem 3.6: *A decision problem is in $\mathcal{P}/\text{poly}$ if and only if it can be solved by a family of polynomial-size circuits.*

More generally, for any function t, the following proof establishes the equivalence of the power of polynomial-time machines that take advice of length t and families of circuits of size polynomially related to t.

> **Proof Sketch:** Suppose that a problem can be solved by a polynomial-time algorithm A using the polynomially bounded advice sequence $(a_n)_{n\in\mathbb{N}}$. We obtain a family of polynomial-size circuits that solves the same problem by adapting the proof of Theorem 2.21. Specifically, we observe that the computation of $A(a_{|x|}, x)$ can be emulated by a circuit of $\text{poly}(|x|)$-size, *which incorporates $a_{|x|}$ and is given x as input.* That is, we construct a circuit C_n such that $C_n(x) = A(a_n, x)$ holds for every $x \in \{0, 1\}^n$ (analogously to the way C_x was constructed in the proof of Theorem 2.21, where it holds that $C_x(y) = M_R(x, y)$ for every y of adequate length).[3]
>
> On the other hand, given a family of polynomial-size circuits, we obtain a polynomial-time advice-taking machine that emulates this family when *using advice that provides the description of the relevant circuits.* Specifically, we transform the evaluation algorithm asserted in Theorem 3.1 into a machine that, given advice α and input x, treats α as a description of a circuit C and evaluates $C(x)$. Indeed, we use the fact that a circuit of size s can be described by a string of length $O(s \log s)$, where the log factor is due to the fact that a graph with v vertices and e edges can be described by a string of length $2e \log_2 v$. $\square$

Another perspective. A set S is called sparse if there exists a polynomial p such that for every n it holds that $|S \cap \{0, 1\}^n| \leq p(n)$. We note that $\mathcal{P}/\text{poly}$ equals the class of sets that are Cook-reducible to a sparse set (see Exercise 3.2). Thus, SAT is Cook-reducible to a sparse set if and only if $\mathcal{NP} \subset \mathcal{P}/\text{poly}$. In contrast, SAT is Karp-reducible to a sparse set if and only if $\mathcal{NP} = \mathcal{P}$ (see Exercise 3.12).

The power of $\mathcal{P}/\text{poly}$. In continuation of Theorem 1.13 (which focuses on advice and ignores the time complexity of the machine that takes this advice), we prove the following (stronger) result.

Theorem 3.7 (the power of advice, revisited): *The class $\mathcal{P}/1 \subseteq \mathcal{P}/\text{poly}$ contains $\mathcal{P}$ as well as some undecidable problems.*

Actually, $\mathcal{P}/1 \subset \mathcal{P}/\text{poly}$. Furthermore, by using a counting argument, one can show that for any two polynomially bounded functions $\ell_1, \ell_2 : \mathbb{N} \to \mathbb{N}$ such that $\ell_2 - \ell_1 > 0$ is unbounded, it holds that $\mathcal{P}/\ell_1$ is strictly contained in $\mathcal{P}/\ell_2$; see Exercise 3.3.

> **Proof:** Clearly, $\mathcal{P} = \mathcal{P}/0 \subseteq \mathcal{P}/1 \subseteq \mathcal{P}/\text{poly}$. To prove that $\mathcal{P}/1$ contains some undecidable problems, we review the proof of Theorem 1.13. The latter proof established the existence of an uncomputable Boolean function that only depends on its input length. That is, there exists an undecidable set $S \subset \{0, 1\}^*$ such that for every pair

---

[3]**Advanced comment:** Note that a_n is the only "non-uniform" part in the circuit C_n. Thus, if algorithm A takes no advice (i.e., $a_n = \lambda$ for every n) then we obtain a uniform family of circuits.

(x, y) of equal length strings it holds that $x \in S$ if and only if $y \in S$. In other words, for every $x \in \{0, 1\}^*$ it holds that $x \in S$ if and only if $1^{|x|} \in S$. But such a set is easily decidable in polynomial time by a machine that takes one bit of advice; that is, consider the algorithm A that satisfies $A(a, x) = a$ (for $a \in \{0, 1\}$ and $x \in \{0, 1\}^*$) and the advice sequence $(a_n)_{n \in \mathbb{N}}$ such that $a_n = 1$ if and only if $1^n \in S$. Note that, indeed, $A(a_{|x|}, x) = 1$ if and only if $x \in S$. ∎

3.2. The Polynomial-Time Hierarchy (PH)

The Polynomial-time Hierarchy is a rather natural generalization of $\mathcal{NP}$. Interestingly, this generalization collapses to $\mathcal{P}$ if and only if $\mathcal{NP} = \mathcal{P}$, and furthermore it is the largest natural generalization of $\mathcal{NP}$ that is known to have this feature. We start with an informal motivating discussion, which will be made formal in Section 3.2.1.

Sets in $\mathcal{NP}$ can be viewed as sets of valid assertions that can be expressed as quantified Boolean formulae using only existential quantifiers. That is, a set S is in $\mathcal{NP}$ if there is a Karp-reduction of S to the problem of deciding whether or not an existentially quantified Boolean formula is valid (i.e., an instance x is mapped by this reduction to a formula of the form $\exists y_1 \cdots \exists y_{m(x)} \phi_x(y_1, \ldots, y_{m(x)})$).

The conjectured intractability of $\mathcal{NP}$ seems due to the long sequence of existential quantifiers. Of course, if somebody else (i.e., a "prover") were to provide us with an adequate assignment (to the y_i's) whenever such an assignment exists then we would be in good shape. That is, we can efficiently verify proofs of validity of existentially quantified Boolean formulae.

But what if we want to verify the validity of universally quantified Boolean formulae (i.e., formulae of the form $\forall y_1 \cdots \forall y_m \phi(y_1, \ldots, y_m)$). Here we seem to need the help of a totally different entity: We need a "refuter" that is guaranteed to provide us with a refutation whenever such exists, and we need to believe that if we were not presented with such a refutation then it is the case that no refutation exists (and hence the universally quantified formula is valid). Indeed, this new setting (of a "refutation system") is fundamentally different from the setting of a proof system: In a proof system we are only convinced by proofs (to assertions) that we have verified by ourselves, whereas in the "refutation system" we trust the "refuter" to provide evidence against false assertions.[4] Furthermore, there seems to be no way of converting one setting (e.g., the proof system) into another (resp., the refutation system).

Taking an additional step, we may consider a more complicated system in which we use two agents: a "supporter" that tries to provide evidence in favor of an assertion and an "objector" that tries to refute it. These two agents conduct a debate (or an argument) in our presence, exchanging messages with the goal of making us (the referee) rule their way. The assertions that can be proven in this system take the form of general quantified formulae with alternating sequences of quantifiers, where the number of alternating sequences equals the number of rounds of interaction in the said system. We stress that the exact length of each sequence of quantifiers of the same type does not matter; what matters is the number of alternating sequences, denoted k.

---

[4]More formally, in proof systems the soundness condition relies only on the actions of the verifier, whereas completeness also relies on the prover's action (i.e., its using an adequate strategy). In contrast, in a "refutation system" the soundness condition relies on the proper actions of the refuter, whereas completeness does not depend on the refuter's actions.

The aforementioned system of alternations can be viewed as a two-party game, and we may ask ourselves which of the two parties has a k-move winning strategy. In general, we may consider any (0-1 zero-sum) two-party game, in which the game's position can be efficiently updated (by any given move) and efficiently evaluated. For such a fixed game, given an initial position, we may ask whether the first party has a (k-move) winning strategy. It seems that answering this type of question for some fixed k does not necessarily allow answering it for $k + 1$. We now turn to formalizing the foregoing discussion.

3.2.1. Alternation of Quantifiers

In the following definition, the aforementioned propositional formula ϕ_x is replaced by the input x itself. (Correspondingly, the combination of the Karp-reduction and a formula-evaluation algorithm is replaced by the verification algorithm V (see Exercise 3.7).) This is done in order to make the comparison to the definition of $\mathcal{NP}$ more transparent (as well as to fit the standard presentations). We also replace a sequence of Boolean quantifiers of the same type by a single corresponding quantifier that quantifies over all strings of the corresponding length.

Definition 3.8 (the class Σ_k): *For a natural number k, a decision problem $S \subseteq \{0, 1\}^*$ is in Σ_k if there exists a polynomial p and a polynomial-time algorithm V such that $x \in S$ if and only if*

$$\exists y_1 \in \{0, 1\}^{p(|x|)} \forall y_2 \in \{0, 1\}^{p(|x|)} \exists y_3 \in \{0, 1\}^{p(|x|)} \cdots Q_k y_k \in \{0, 1\}^{p(|x|)}$$

$$\text{s.t. } V(x, y_1, \ldots, y_k) = 1$$

where Q_k is an existential quantifier if k is odd and is a universal quantifier otherwise.

Note that $\Sigma_1 = \mathcal{NP}$ and $\Sigma_0 = \mathcal{P}$. The Polynomial-time Hierarchy, denoted $\mathcal{PH}$, is the union of all the aforementioned classes (i.e., $\mathcal{PH} = \cup_k \Sigma_k$), and Σ_k is often referred to as the kth level of $\mathcal{PH}$. The levels of the Polynomial-time Hierarchy can also be defined inductively, by defining Σ_{k+1} based on $\Pi_k \overset{\text{def}}{=} \text{co}\Sigma_k$, where $\text{co}\Sigma_k \overset{\text{def}}{=} \{\{0, 1\}^* \setminus S : S \in \Sigma_k\}$ (cf. Eq. (2.4)).

Proposition 3.9: *For every $k \geq 0$, a set S is in Σ_{k+1} if and only if there exists a polynomial p and a set $S' \in \Pi_k$ such that $S = \{x : \exists y \in \{0, 1\}^{p(|x|)} \text{ s.t. } (x, y) \in S'\}$.*

Proof: Suppose that S is in Σ_{k+1} and let p and V be as in Definition 3.8. Then define S' as the set of pairs (x, y) such that $|y| = p(|x|)$ and

$$\forall z_1 \in \{0, 1\}^{p(|x|)} \exists z_2 \in \{0, 1\}^{p(|x|)} \cdots Q_k z_k \in \{0, 1\}^{p(|x|)} \text{ s.t. } V(x, y, z_1, \ldots, z_k) = 1.$$

Note that $x \in S$ if and only if there exists $y \in \{0, 1\}^{p(|x|)}$ such that $(x, y) \in S'$, and that $S' \in \Pi_k$ (see Exercise 3.6).

On the other hand, suppose that for some polynomial p and a set $S' \in \Pi_k$ it holds that $S = \{x : \exists y \in \{0, 1\}^{p(|x|)} \text{ s.t. } (x, y) \in S'\}$. Then, for some p' and V', it holds that $(x, y) \in S'$ if and only if $|y| = p(|x|)$ and

$$\forall z_1 \in \{0, 1\}^{p'(|x|)} \exists z_2 \in \{0, 1\}^{p'(|x|)} \cdots Q_k z_k \in \{0, 1\}^{p'(|x|)} \text{ s.t. } V'((x, y), z_1, \ldots, z_k) = 1$$

(see Exercise 3.6 again). By using a suitable encoding of y and the z_i's (as strings of length $\max(p(|x|), p'(|x|))$) and a trivial modification of V', we conclude that $S \in \Sigma_{k+1}$. ∎

Determining the winner in k-move games. Definition 3.8 can be interpreted as capturing the complexity of determining the winner in certain *efficient two-party games*. Specifically, we refer to two-party games that satisfy the following three conditions:

1. The parties alternate in taking moves that affect the game's (global) position, where each move has a description length that is bounded by a polynomial in the length of the current position.
2. The current position can be updated in polynomial time based on the previous position and the current party's move.[5]
3. The winner in each position can be determined in polynomial time.

Note that the set of initial positions for which the first party has a k-move winning strategy with respect to the foregoing game is in Σ_k. Specifically, denoting this set by G, note that an initial position x is in G if there exists a move y_1 for the first party, such that for every response move y_2 of the second party, there exists a move y_3 for the first party, etc., such that after k moves the parties reach a position in which the first party wins, where the final position is determined according to the foregoing Item 2 and the winner in it is determined according to Item 3.[6] Thus, $G \in \Sigma_k$. On the other hand, note that any set $S \in \Sigma_k$ can be viewed as the set of initial positions (in a suitable game) for which the first party has a k-move winning strategy. Specifically, $x \in S$ if starting at the initial position x, there exists a move y_1 for the first party, such that for every response move y_2 of the second party, there exists a move y_3 for the first party, etc., such that after k moves the parties reach a position in which the first party wins, where the final position is defined as $(x, y_1, \ldots, y_k)$ and the winner is determined by the predicate V (as in Definition 3.8).

PH and the P Versus NP Question. We highlight the fact that $\mathcal{PH} = \mathcal{P}$ if and only if $\mathcal{P} = \mathcal{NP}$. Indeed, the fact that $\mathcal{PH} = \mathcal{P}$ implies $\mathcal{P} = \mathcal{NP}$ is purely syntactic, whereas the opposite implication follows from Proposition 3.9 (see also the second part of the proof of Proposition 3.10).[7] The fact that $\mathcal{P} = \mathcal{NP}$ implies $\mathcal{PH} = \mathcal{P}$ suggests that $\mathcal{P} \neq \mathcal{NP}$ can be proved by proving that $\mathcal{PH} \neq \mathcal{P}$. Thus, a separation between two classes (i.e., $\mathcal{P} \neq \mathcal{NP}$) can be shown by separating the smaller class (i.e., $\mathcal{P}$) from a class (i.e., $\mathcal{PH}$) that is believed to be a superset of the other class (i.e., $\mathcal{NP}$).

---

[5]Note that, since we consider a constant number of moves, the length of all possible final positions is bounded by a polynomial in the length of the initial position, and thus all items have an equivalent form in which one refers to the complexity as a function of the length of the initial position. The latter form allows for a smooth generalization to games with a polynomial number of moves (as in Section 5.4), where it is essential to state all complexities in terms of the length of the initial position.

[6]Let U be the update algorithm of Item 2 and W be the algorithm that decides the winner as in Item 3. Then the final position is given by computing $x_i \leftarrow U(x_{i-1}, y_i)$, for $i = 1, \ldots, k$ (where $x_0 = x$), and the winner is $W(x_k)$. Note that, by Item 1, there exists a polynomial p such that $|y_i| \leq p(|x_i|)$, for every $i \in [k]$, and it follows that $|y_i| \leq \text{poly}(|x|)$. Using a suitable encoding, we obtain a polynomial-time algorithm V such that $V(x, y_1, \ldots, y_k) = W(x_k)$, where $x_k = U(\cdots U(U(U(x, y_1), y_2), y_3) \ldots, y_k)$.

[7]**Advanced comment:** We stress that the latter implication is *not* due to a Cook-reduction of $\mathcal{PH}$ to $\mathcal{NP}$; in fact, such Cook-reductions exist only for a subclass of $\mathcal{PH}$ (which is contained in $\Sigma_2 \cap \Pi_2$).

The collapsing effect of other equalities. Extending the intuition that underlies the $\mathcal{NP} \neq \text{co}\mathcal{NP}$ conjecture, it is commonly conjectured that $\Sigma_k \neq \Pi_k$ for every $k \in \mathbb{N}$. The failure of this conjecture causes the collapse of the Polynomial-time Hierarchy to the corresponding level.

> **Proposition 3.10:** *For every $k \geq 1$, if $\Sigma_k = \Pi_k$ then $\Sigma_{k+1} = \Sigma_k$, which in turn implies $\mathcal{PH} = \Sigma_k$.*

The converse also holds (i.e., $\mathcal{PH} = \Sigma_k$ implies $\Sigma_{k+1} = \Sigma_k$ and $\Sigma_k = \Pi_k$). Needless to say, the first part of Proposition 3.10 (i.e., $\Sigma_k = \Pi_k$ implies $\Sigma_{k+1} = \Sigma_k$) does not seem to hold for $k = 0$, but indeed the second part holds also for $k = 0$ (i.e., $\Sigma_1 = \Sigma_0$ implies $\mathcal{PH} = \Sigma_0$).

> **Proof:** Assuming that $\Sigma_k = \Pi_k$, we first show that $\Sigma_{k+1} = \Sigma_k$. For any set S in Σ_{k+1}, by Proposition 3.9, there exists a polynomial p and a set $S' \in \Pi_k$ such that $S = \{x : \exists y \in \{0, 1\}^{p(|x|)} \text{ s.t. } (x, y) \in S'\}$. Using the hypothesis, we infer that $S' \in \Sigma_k$, and so (using Proposition 3.9 and $k \geq 1$) there exists a polynomial p' and a set $S'' \in \Pi_{k-1}$ such that $S' = \{x' : \exists y' \in \{0, 1\}^{p'(|x'|)} \text{ s.t. } (x', y') \in S''\}$. It follows that
>
> $$S = \{x : \exists y \in \{0, 1\}^{p(|x|)} \exists z \in \{0, 1\}^{p'(|(x,y)|)} \text{ s.t. } ((x, y), z) \in S''\}.$$
>
> By collapsing the two adjacent existential quantifiers (and using Proposition 3.9 yet again), we conclude that $S \in \Sigma_k$. This proves the first part of the proposition.
>
> Turning to the second part, we note that $\Sigma_{k+1} = \Sigma_k$ (or, equivalently, $\Pi_{k+1} = \Pi_k$) implies $\Sigma_{k+2} = \Sigma_{k+1}$ (again by using Proposition 3.9), and similarly $\Sigma_{j+2} = \Sigma_{j+1}$ for any $j \geq k$. Thus, $\Sigma_{k+1} = \Sigma_k$ implies $\mathcal{PH} = \Sigma_k$. ∎

Decision problems that are Cook-reductions to NP. The Polynomial-time Hierarchy contains all decision problems that are Cook-reductions to $\mathcal{NP}$ (see Exercise 3.4). As shown next, the latter class contains many natural problems. Recall that in Section 2.2.2 we defined two types of optimization problems and showed that under some natural conditions these two types are computationally equivalent (under Cook-reductions). Specifically, one type of problems referred to finding solutions that have a value *exceeding some given threshold*, whereas the second type called for finding *optimal solutions*. In Section 2.3 we presented several problems of the first type, and proved that they are NP-complete. We note that corresponding versions of the second type are believed not to be in NP. For example, we discussed the problem of deciding whether or not a given graph G has a clique of a given size K, and showed that it is NP-complete. In contract, the problem of deciding whether or not K is the maximum clique size of the graph G is not known (and quite unlikely) to be in $\mathcal{NP}$, although it is Cook-reducible to $\mathcal{NP}$. Thus, the class of decision problems that are Cook-reducible to $\mathcal{NP}$ contains many natural problems that are unlikely to be in $\mathcal{NP}$. The Polynomial-time Hierarchy contains all these problems.

Complete problems and a relation to AC0. We note that quantified Boolean formulae with a bounded number of quantifier alternations provide complete problems for the various levels of the Polynomial-time Hierarchy (see Exercise 3.7). We also note the correspondence between these formulae and (highly uniform) constant-depth circuits of unbounded fan-in that get as input the truth table of the underlying (quantifier-free) formula (see Exercise 3.8).

3.2.2. Non-deterministic Oracle Machines

The Polynomial-time Hierarchy is commonly defined in terms of non-deterministic polynomial-time (oracle) machines that are given oracle access to a set in the lower level of the same hierarchy. Such machines are defined by combining the definitions of non-deterministic (polynomial-time) machines (cf. Definition 2.7) and oracle machines (cf. Definition 1.11). Specifically, for an oracle $f : \{0, 1\}^* \to \{0, 1\}^*$, a non-deterministic oracle machine M, and a string x, one considers the question of whether or not there exists an accepting (non-deterministic) computation of M on input x and access to the oracle f. The class of sets that can be accepted by non-deterministic polynomial-time (oracle) machines with access to f is denoted $\mathcal{NP}^f$. (We note that this notation makes sense because we can associate the class $\mathcal{NP}$ with a collection of machines that lends itself to being extended to oracle machines.) For any class of decision problems $\mathcal{C}$, we denote by $\mathcal{NP}^{\mathcal{C}}$ the union of $\mathcal{NP}^f$ taken over all decision problems f in $\mathcal{C}$. The following result provides an alternative definition of the Polynomial-time Hierarchy.

Proposition 3.11: *For every $k \geq 1$, it holds that $\Sigma_{k+1} = \mathcal{NP}^{\Sigma_k}$.*

Needless to say, $\Sigma_1 = \mathcal{NP}^{\Sigma_0}$, but this fact is due to simple considerations (i.e., $\Sigma_1 = \mathcal{NP} = \mathcal{NP}^{\mathcal{P}} = \mathcal{NP}^{\Sigma_0}$, where only $\mathcal{NP} = \mathcal{NP}^{\mathcal{P}}$ is non-syntactic).

Proof: Containment in one direction (i.e., $\Sigma_{k+1} \subseteq \mathcal{NP}^{\Sigma_k}$) is almost straightforward: For any $S \in \Sigma_{k+1}$, let $S' \in \Pi_k$ and p be as in Proposition 3.9; that is, $S = \{x : \exists y \in \{0, 1\}^{p(|x|)} \text{ s.t. } (x, y) \in S'\}$. Consider the non-deterministic oracle machine that, on input x, non-deterministically generates $y \in \{0, 1\}^{p(|x|)}$ and accepts if and only if (the oracle indicates that) $(x, y) \in S'$. This machine demonstrates that $S \in \mathcal{NP}^{\Pi_k} = \mathcal{NP}^{\Sigma_k}$, where the equality holds by letting the oracle machine flip each (binary) answer that is provided by the oracle.[8]

For the opposite containment (i.e., $\mathcal{NP}^{\Sigma_k} \subseteq \Sigma_{k+1}$), we generalize the main idea underlying the proof of Theorem 2.35 (which referred to $\mathcal{P}^{\mathcal{NP} \cap \text{co}\mathcal{NP}}$). Specifically, consider any $S \in \mathcal{NP}^{\Sigma_k}$, and let M be a non-deterministic polynomial-time oracle machine that accepts S when given oracle access to $S' \in \Sigma_k$. Note that machine M may issue several queries to S', and these queries may be determined based on previous oracle answers.[9] To simplify the argument, we assume, without loss of generality, that at the very beginning of its execution machine M guesses (non-deterministically) all oracle answers and accepts only if the actual answers match its guesses. Thus, M's queries to the oracle are determined by its input, denoted x, and its non-deterministic choices, denoted y. We denote by $q^{(i)}(x, y)$ the ith query made by M (on input x and non-deterministic choices y), and by $a^{(i)}(x, y)$

---

[8]Do not get confused by the fact that the class of oracles may *not* be closed under complementation. From the point of view of the oracle machine, the oracle is merely a function, and the machine may do with its answer whatever it pleases (and in particular negate it).

[9]Indeed, this is unlike the specific machine used toward proving that $\Sigma_{k+1} \subseteq \mathcal{NP}^{\Sigma_k}$.

the corresponding (a priori) guessed answer (which is a bit in y). Thus, $x \in S$ if and only if there exists $y \in \{0, 1\}^{\text{poly}(|x|)}$ such that the following two conditions hold:

1. Machine M accepts when it is invoked on input x, makes non-deterministic choices y, and is given $a^{(i)}(x, y)$ as the answer to its ith oracle query. We denote the corresponding ("acceptance") predicate, which is polynomial-time computable, by $A(x, y)$.

We stress that we do not assume here that the $a^{(i)}(x, y)$'s are consistent with answers that would have been given by the oracle S'; this will be the subject of the next condition. The current condition refers only to the decision of M on a specific input, when M makes a specific sequence of non-deterministic choices, and is provided with specific answers.

2. Each bit $a^{(i)}(x, y)$ is consistent with S'; that is, for every i, it holds that $a^{(i)}(x, y) = 1$ if and only if $q^{(i)}(x, y) \in S'$.

Denoting the number of queries made by M (on input x and non-deterministic choices y) by $q(x, y) \leq \text{poly}(|x|)$, it follows that $x \in S$ if and only if

$$\exists y \left(A(x, y) \wedge \bigwedge_{i=1}^{q(x,y)} \left((a^{(i)}(x, y) = 1) \Leftrightarrow (q^{(i)}(x, y) \in S') \right) \right) \tag{3.1}$$

Denoting the verification algorithm of S' by V', Eq. (3.1) equals

$$\exists y \left(A(x, y) \wedge \bigwedge_{i=1}^{q(x,y)} \left((a^{(i)}(x, y) = 1) \right.\right.$$

$$\left.\left. \Leftrightarrow \exists y_1^{(i)} \forall y_2^{(i)} \cdots Q_k y_k^{(i)} \, V'(q^{(i)}(x, y), y_1^{(i)}, \ldots, y_k^{(i)}) = 1) \right) \right)$$

The proof is completed by observing that the foregoing expression can be rearranged to fit the definition of Σ_{k+1}. Details follow.

Starting with the foregoing expression, we first replace the sub-expression $E_1 \Leftrightarrow E_2$ by $(E_1 \wedge E_2) \vee (\neg E_1 \wedge \neg E_2)$, and then pull all quantifiers outside.[10] This way we obtain a quantified expression with $k + 1$ alternating quantifiers, starting with an existential quantifier. (Note that we get $k + 1$ alternating quantifiers rather than k, because the case of $\neg a^{(i)}(x, y) = 1$ introduces an expression of the form $\neg \exists y_1^{(i)} \forall y_2^{(i)} \cdots Q_k y_k^{(i)} \, V'(q^{(i)}(x, y), y_1^{(i)}, \ldots, y_k^{(i)}) = 1$, which in turn is equivalent to the expression $\forall y_1^{(i)} \exists y_2^{(i)} \cdots \overline{Q}_k y_k^{(i)} \, \neg V'(q^{(i)}(x, y), y_1^{(i)}, \ldots, y_k^{(i)}) = 1$.) Once this is done, we may incorporate the computation of all the $q^{(i)}(x, y)$'s (and $a^{(i)}(x, y)$'s) as well as the polynomial number of invocations of V' (and other logical operations) into the new verification algorithm V. It follows that $S \in \Sigma_{k+1}$. ∎

A general perspective – what does $\mathcal{C}_1^{\mathcal{C}_2}$ mean? By the foregoing discussion it should be clear that the class $\mathcal{C}_1^{\mathcal{C}_2}$ can be defined for two complexity classes $\mathcal{C}_1$ and $\mathcal{C}_2$, *provided that*

---

[10] For example, note that for predicates P_1 and P_2, the expression $\exists y \, (P_1(y) \Leftrightarrow \exists z \, P_2(y, z))$ is equivalent to the expression $\exists y \, ((P_1(y) \wedge \exists z \, P_2(y, z)) \vee (\neg P_1(y) \wedge \neg \exists z \, P_2(y, z)))$, which in turn is equivalent to the expression $\exists y \exists z' \forall z'' \, ((P_1(y) \wedge P_2(y, z')) \vee (\neg P_1(y) \wedge \neg P_2(y, z'')))$. Note that pulling the quantifiers outside in $\wedge_{i=1}^t \exists y^{(i)} \forall z^{(i)} \, P(y^{(i)}, z^{(i)})$ yields an expression of the type $\exists y^{(1)}, \ldots, y^{(t)} \forall z^{(1)}, \ldots, z^{(t)} \wedge_{i=1}^t P(y^{(i)}, z^{(i)})$.

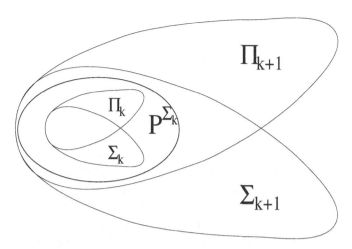

Figure 3.1: Two levels of the Polynomial-time Hierarchy.

$\mathcal{C}_1$ *is associated with a class of standard machines that generalizes naturally to a class of oracle machines.* Actually, the class $\mathcal{C}_1^{\mathcal{C}_2}$ *is not defined based on the class $\mathcal{C}_1$ but rather by analogy to it.* Specifically, suppose that $\mathcal{C}_1$ is the class of sets that are recognizable (or rather accepted) by machines of a certain type (e.g., deterministic or non-deterministic) with certain resource bounds (e.g., time and/or space bounds). Then, we consider analogous oracle machines (i.e., of the same type and with the same resource bounds), and say that $S \in \mathcal{C}_1^{\mathcal{C}_2}$ if there exists an adequate oracle machine M_1 (i.e., of this type and resource bounds) and a set $S_2 \in \mathcal{C}_2$ such that $M_1^{S_2}$ accepts the set S.

Decision problems that are Cook-reductions to NP, revisited. Using the foregoing notation, the class of decision problems that are Cook-reductions to $\mathcal{NP}$ is denoted $\mathcal{P}^{\mathcal{NP}}$, and thus is a subset of $\mathcal{NP}^{\mathcal{NP}} = \Sigma_2$ (see Exercise 3.9). In contrast, recall that the class of decision problems that are Karp-reductions to $\mathcal{NP}$ equals $\mathcal{NP}$.

The world view. Using the foregoing notation and relying on Exercise 3.9, we note that for every $k \geq 1$ it holds that $\Sigma_k \cup \Pi_k \subseteq \mathcal{P}^{\Sigma_k} \subseteq \Sigma_{k+1} \cap \Pi_{k+1}$. See Figure 3.1 that depicts the situation, assuming that all the containments are strict.

3.2.3. The P/poly Versus NP Question and PH

As stated in Section 3.1, a main motivation for the definition of $\mathcal{P}/\text{poly}$ is the hope that it can serve to separate $\mathcal{P}$ from $\mathcal{NP}$ (by showing that $\mathcal{NP}$ is not even contained in $\mathcal{P}/\text{poly}$, which is a (strict) superset of $\mathcal{P}$). In light of the fact that $\mathcal{P}/\text{poly}$ extends far beyond $\mathcal{P}$ (and in particular contains undecidable problems), one may wonder if this approach does not run the risk of asking too much (because it may be that $\mathcal{NP}$ is in $\mathcal{P}/\text{poly}$ even if $\mathcal{P} \neq \mathcal{NP}$). The common feeling is that the added power of non-uniformity is irrelevant with respect to the P-vs-NP Question. Ideally, we would like to know that $\mathcal{NP} \subset \mathcal{P}/\text{poly}$ may occur only if $\mathcal{P} = \mathcal{NP}$, which may be phrased as saying that the Polynomial-time Hierarchy collapses to its zero level. The following result seems to get close to such an implication, showing that $\mathcal{NP} \subset \mathcal{P}/\text{poly}$ may occur only if the Polynomial-time Hierarchy collapses to its second level.

Theorem 3.12: *If* $\mathcal{NP} \subset \mathcal{P}/\text{poly}$ *then* $\Sigma_2 = \Pi_2$.

Recall that $\Sigma_2 = \Pi_2$ implies $\mathcal{PH} = \Sigma_2$ (see Proposition 3.10). Thus, an unexpected behavior of the non-uniform complexity class $\mathcal{P}/\text{poly}$ implies an unexpected behavior in the world of uniform complexity (which is the habitat of $\mathcal{PH}$).

Proof: Using the hypothesis (i.e., $\mathcal{NP} \subset \mathcal{P}/\text{poly}$) and starting with an arbitrary set $S \in \Pi_2$, we shall show that $S \in \Sigma_2$. Let us describe, first, our high-level approach.

Loosely speaking, $S \in \Pi_2$ means that $x \in S$ if and only if for all y there exists a z such that some (fixed) polynomial-time verifiable condition regarding (x, y, z) holds. Note that the residual condition regarding (x, y) is of the NP-type, and thus (by the hypothesis) it can be verified by a polynomial-size circuit. This suggests saying that $x \in S$ if and only if there exists an *adequate* circuit C such that for all y it holds that $C(x, y) = 1$. Thus, we managed to switch the order of the universal and existential quantifiers. Specifically, the resulting assertion is of the desired Σ_2-type provided that we can either verify the *adequacy condition* in $\text{co}\mathcal{NP}$ (or even in Σ_2) or keep out of trouble even in the case that $x \notin S$ and C is inadequate. In the following proof we implement the latter option by observing that the hypothesis yields small circuits for NP-search problems (and not only for NP-decision problems). Specifically, we obtain (small) circuits that, given (x, y), find an NP-witness for (x, y) (whenever such a witness exists), and rely on the fact that we can efficiently verify the correctness of NP-witnesses. (The alternative approach of providing a coNP-type procedure for verifying the adequacy of the circuit is pursued in Exercise 3.11.)

We now turn to a detailed implementation of the foregoing approach. Let S be an arbitrary set in Π_2. Then, by Proposition 3.9, there exists a polynomial p and a set $S' \in \mathcal{NP}$ such that $S = \{x : \forall y \in \{0, 1\}^{p(|x|)} \ (x, y) \in S'\}$. Let $R' \in \mathcal{PC}$ be the witness relation corresponding to S'; that is, there exists a polynomial p', such that $x' = \langle x, y \rangle \in S'$ if and only if there exists $z \in \{0, 1\}^{p'(|x'|)}$ such that $(x', z) \in R'$. It follows that

$$S = \{x : \forall y \in \{0, 1\}^{p(|x|)} \exists z \in \{0, 1\}^{p'(|\langle x, y \rangle|)} \ (\langle x, y \rangle, z) \in R'\}. \tag{3.2}$$

Our argument proceeds essentially as follows. By the reduction of $\mathcal{PC}$ to $\mathcal{NP}$ (see Theorem 2.10), the theorem's hypothesis (i.e., $\mathcal{NP} \subseteq \mathcal{P}/\text{poly}$) implies the existence of polynomial-size circuits for solving the search problem of R'. Using the existence of these circuits, it follows that for any $x \in S$ there exists a small circuit C' such that for every y it holds that $C'(x, y) \in R'(x, y)$ (because $\langle x, y \rangle \in S'$ and hence $R'(x, y) \neq \emptyset$). On the other hand, for any $x \notin S$ there exists a y such that $\langle x, y \rangle \notin S'$, and hence for any circuit C' it holds that $C'(x, y) \notin R'(x, y)$ (for the trivial reason that $R'(x, y) = \emptyset$). Thus, $x \in S$ if and only if there exists a $\text{poly}(|x| + p(|x|))$-size circuit C' such that for all $y \in \{0, 1\}^{p(|x|)}$ it holds that $(\langle x, y \rangle, C'(x, y)) \in R'$. Letting $V(x, C', y) = 1$ if and only if $(\langle x, y \rangle, C'(x, y)) \in R'$, we infer that $S \in \Sigma_2$. Details follow.

Let us first spell out what we mean by polynomial-size circuits for solving a search problem and further justify their existence for the search problem of R'. In Section 3.1, we have focused on polynomial-size circuits that solve decision problems. However, the definition sketched in Section 3.1.1 also applies to solving search problems, provided that an appropriate convention is used for encoding solutions of possibly varying lengths (for instances of fixed length) as strings of fixed length. Next, observe that combining the Cook-reduction of $\mathcal{PC}$ to $\mathcal{NP}$ with the hypothesis $\mathcal{NP} \subseteq \mathcal{P}/\text{poly}$ implies that $\mathcal{PC}$ is Cook-reducible to $\mathcal{P}/\text{poly}$. In particular, this implies that any search problem in $\mathcal{PC}$ can be solved by a family of polynomial-size circuits. Note that the resulting circuit that solves n-bit long instances of such a problem may incorporate polynomially (in n) many circuits, each solving a decision problem for m-bit long instances, where $m \in [\text{poly}(n)]$. Needless to say, the size of the resulting circuit that solves the search problem of the aforementioned $R' \in \mathcal{PC}$ (for instances of length n) is upper-bounded by $\text{poly}(n) \cdot \sum_{m=1}^{\text{poly}(n)} \text{poly}(m)$.

We next (revisit and) establish the claim that $x \in S$ if and only if *there exists a $\text{poly}(|x| + p(|x|))$-size circuit C' such that for all $y \in \{0,1\}^{p(|x|)}$ it holds that* $(\langle x, y \rangle, C'(x, y)) \in R'$. Recall that $x \in S$ if and only if for every $y \in \{0,1\}^{p(|x|)}$ it holds that $(x, y) \in S'$, which means that there exists $z \in \{0,1\}^{p'(|x|)}$ such that $(\langle x, y \rangle, z) \in R'$. Also recall that (by the foregoing discussion) there exist polynomial-size circuits for solving the search problem of R'. Thus, in the case that $x \in S$, we just use the corresponding circuit C' that solves the search problem of R' on inputs of length $|x| + p(|x|)$. Indeed, this circuit C' only depends on $n' = |x| + p(|x|)$, which in turn is determined by $|x|$, and for every $x' \in \{0,1\}^{n'}$ it holds that $(x', C'(x')) \in R'$ if and only if $x' \in S'$. Thus, for $x \in S$, there exists a $\text{poly}(|x| + p(|x|))$-size circuit C' such that for every $y \in \{0,1\}^{p(|x|)}$ it holds that $(\langle x, y \rangle, C'(x, y)) \in R'$. On the other hand, if $x \notin S$ then there exists a y such that for all z it holds that $(\langle x, y \rangle, z) \notin R'$. It follows that, in this case, for every C' there exists a y such that $(\langle x, y \rangle, C'(x, y)) \notin R'$. We conclude that $x \in S$ if and only if

$$\exists C' \in \{0,1\}^{\text{poly}(|x|+p(|x|))} \forall y \in \{0,1\}^{p(|x|)} \ (\langle x, y \rangle, C'(x, y)) \in R'. \tag{3.3}$$

The key observation regarding the condition stated in Equation (3.3) is that it is of the desired form (of a Σ_2 statement). Specifically, consider the polynomial-time verification procedure V that given x, y and the description of the circuit C', first computes $z \leftarrow C'(x, y)$ and accepts if and only if $(\langle x, y \rangle, z) \in R'$, where the latter condition can be verified in polynomial time (because $R' \in \mathcal{PC}$). Denoting the description of a potential circuit by $\langle C' \rangle$, the aforementioned (polynomial-time) computation of V is denoted $V(x, \langle C' \rangle, y)$, and indeed $x \in S$ if and only if

$$\exists \langle C' \rangle \in \{0,1\}^{\text{poly}(|x|+p(|x|))} \forall y \in \{0,1\}^{p(|x|)} \ V(x, \langle C' \rangle, y) = 1.$$

Having established that $S \in \Sigma_2$ for an arbitrary $S \in \Pi_2$, we conclude that $\Pi_2 \subseteq \Sigma_2$. The theorem follows (by applying Exercise 3.9.4). ∎

Chapter Notes

The class $\mathcal{P}/\text{poly}$ was defined by Karp and Lipton [139] as part of a general formulation of "machines that take advice" [139]. They also noted the equivalence to the traditional formulation of polynomial-size circuits as well as the effect of uniformity (Proposition 3.4).

The Polynomial-Time Hierarchy ($\mathcal{PH}$) was introduced by Stockmeyer [213]. A third equivalent formulation of $\mathcal{PH}$ (via so-called alternating machines) can be found in [52].

The implication of the failure of the conjecture that $\mathcal{NP}$ is not contained in $\mathcal{P}/\text{poly}$ on the Polynomial-time Hierarchy (i.e., Theorem 3.12) was discovered by Karp and Lipton [139]. This interesting connection between non-uniform and uniform complexity provides the main motivation for presenting $\mathcal{P}/\text{poly}$ and $\mathcal{PH}$ in the same chapter.

Exercises

Exercise 3.1 (a small variation on the definitions of $\mathcal{P}/\text{poly}$): Using an adequate encoding of strings of length smaller than n as n-bit strings (e.g., $x \in \cup_{i<n}\{0,1\}^i$ is encoded as $x01^{n-|x|-1}$), define circuits (resp., machines that take advice) as devices that can handle inputs of various lengths up to a given bound (rather than as devices that can handle inputs of a fixed length). Show that the class $\mathcal{P}/\text{poly}$ remains invariant under this change (and Theorem 3.6 remains valid).

Exercise 3.2 (sparse sets): A set $S \subset \{0,1\}^*$ is called sparse if there exists a polynomial p such that $|S \cap \{0,1\}^n| \leq p(n)$ for every n.

1. Prove that any sparse set is in $\mathcal{P}/\text{poly}$. Note that a sparse set may be undecidable.
2. Prove that a set is in $\mathcal{P}/\text{poly}$ if and only if it is Cook-reducible to some sparse set.

> **Guideline:** For the forward direction of Part 2, encode the advice sequence $(a_n)_{n\in\mathbb{N}}$ as a sparse set $\{(1^n, i, \sigma_{n,i}) : n \in \mathbb{N}, i \leq |a_n|\}$, where $\sigma_{n,i}$ is the ith bit of a_n. For the opposite direction, note that the emulation of a Cook-reduction to a set S, on input x, only requires knowledge of $S \cap \cup_{i=1}^{\text{poly}(|x|)}\{0,1\}^i$.

Exercise 3.3 (advice hierarchy): Prove that for any two functions $\ell, \delta : \mathbb{N} \to \mathbb{N}$ such that $\ell(n) < 2^{n-1}$ and δ is unbounded, it holds that $\mathcal{P}/\ell$ is strictly contained in $\mathcal{P}/(\ell + \delta)$.

> **Guideline:** For every sequence $\bar{a} = (a_n)_{n\in\mathbb{N}}$ such that $|a_n| = \ell(n) + \delta(n) \leq 2^n$, consider the set $S_{\bar{a}}$ that encodes $\bar{a}$ such that $x \in S_{\bar{a}} \cap \{0,1\}^n$ if and only if the $\text{idx}(x)^{\text{th}}$ bit in a_n equals 1 (and $\text{idx}(x) \leq |a_n|$), where $\text{idx}(x)$ denotes the index of x in $\{0,1\}^n$. For more details see Section 4.1.

Exercise 3.4: Prove that Σ_2 contains all sets that are Cook-reducible to $\mathcal{NP}$.

> **Guideline:** This is quite obvious when using the definition of Σ_2 as presented in Section 3.2.2; see Exercise 3.9. Alternatively, the fact can be proved by using *some* of the ideas that underlie the proof of Theorem 2.35, while noting that a conjunction of NP and coNP assertions forms an assertion of type Σ_2 (see also the second part of the proof of Proposition 3.11).

Exercise 3.5: Let $\Delta = \mathcal{NP} \cap \text{co}\mathcal{NP}$. Prove that Δ equals the class of decision problems that are Cook-reducible to Δ (i.e., $\Delta = \mathcal{P}^{\Delta}$).

> **Guideline:** See proof of Theorem 2.35.

Exercise 3.6 (the class Π_k): Recall that Π_k is defined to equal $\text{co}\Sigma_k$, which in turn is defined to equal $\{\{0,1\}^* \setminus S : S \in \Sigma_k\}$. Prove that for any natural number k, a decision problem $S \subseteq \{0,1\}^*$ is in Π_k if there exists a polynomial p and a polynomial-time algorithm V such that $x \in S$ if and only if

$$\forall y_1 \in \{0,1\}^{p(|x|)} \exists y_2 \in \{0,1\}^{p(|x|)} \forall y_3 \in \{0,1\}^{p(|x|)} \cdots Q_k y_k \in \{0,1\}^{p(|x|)}$$

$$\text{s.t. } V(x, y_1, \ldots, y_k) = 1$$

where Q_k is a universal quantifier if k is odd and is an existential quantifier otherwise.

Exercise 3.7 (complete problems for the various levels of $\mathcal{PH}$): A k-alternating quantified Boolean formula is a quantified Boolean formula with up to k alternating sequences of existential and universal quantifiers, starting with an existential quantifier. For example, $\exists z_1 \exists z_2 \forall z_3 \phi(z_1, z_2, z_3)$ (where the z_i's are Boolean variables) is a 2-alternating quantified Boolean formula. Prove that, for every $k \geq 1$, the problem of *deciding whether or not a k-alternating quantified Boolean formula is valid* is Σ_k-complete under Karp-reductions. That is, denoting the aforementioned problem by kQBF, prove that kQBF is in Σ_k and that every problem in Σ_k is Karp-reducible to kQBF.

> **Guideline:** Start with the case of odd k. This allows for incorporating the existential quantification of the auxiliary variables (introduced by the reduction) in the last sequence of quantifiers. For even $k > 1$, consider first an analogous complete problem for Π_k, and then consider its complement.

Exercise 3.8 (on the relation between $\mathcal{PH}$ and $\mathcal{AC}^0$): Note that there is an obvious analogy between $\mathcal{PH}$ and constant-depth circuits of unbounded fan-in, where existential (resp., universal) quantifiers are represented by "large" $\bigvee$ (resp., $\bigwedge$) gates. To articulate this relationship, consider the following definitions.

- A family of circuits $\{C_N\}$ is called highly uniform if there exists a polynomial-time algorithm that answers local queries regarding the structure of the relevant circuit. Specifically, on input (N, u, v), the algorithm determines the type of gates represented by the vertices u and v in C_N as well as whether there exists a directed edge from u to v. If the vertex represents a terminal then the algorithm also indicates the index of the corresponding input-bit (or output-bit). Note that this algorithm operates in time that is polylogarithmic in the size of C_N.

  We focus on the family of polynomial-size circuits, meaning that the size of C_N is polynomial in N, which in turn represents the number of inputs to C_N.

- Fixing a polynomial p, a p-succinctly represented input $Z \in \{0, 1\}^N$ is a circuit c_Z of size at most $p(\log_2 N)$ such that for every $i \in [N]$ it holds that $c_Z(i)$ equals the ith bit of Z.

- For a fixed family of highly uniform circuits $\{C_N\}$ and a fixed polynomial p, the problem of evaluating a succinctly represented input is defined as follows. *Given p-succinct representation of an input $Z \in \{0, 1\}^N$, determine whether or not $C_N(Z) = 1$.*

Prove the following relationship between $\mathcal{PH}$ and the problem of evaluating a succinctly represented input with respect to some families of highly uniform circuits of bounded depth.

1. For every k and every $S \in \Sigma_k$, show that there exists a family of highly uniform unbounded fan-in circuits of depth k and polynomial size such that S is Karp-reducible to evaluating a succinctly represented input (with respect to that family of circuits). That is, the reduction should map an instance $x \in \{0, 1\}^n$ to a p-succinct representation of some $Z \in \{0, 1\}^N$ such that $x \in S$ if and only if $C_N(Z) = 1$. (Note

that Z is represented by a circuit c_Z such that $\log_2 N \leq |c_Z| \leq \text{poly}(n)$, and thus $N \leq \exp(\text{poly}(n))$.)[11]

Guideline: Let $S \in \Sigma_k$ and let V be the corresponding verification algorithm as in Definition 3.8. That is, $x \in S$ if and only if $\exists y_1 \forall y_2 \cdots Q_k y_k$, where each $y_i \in \{0, 1\}^{\text{poly}(|x|)}$ such that $V(x, y_1, \ldots, y_k) = 1$. Then, for $m = \text{poly}(|x|)$ and $N = 2^{k \cdot m}$, consider the fixed circuit $C_N(Z) = \bigvee_{i_1 \in [2^m]} \bigwedge_{i_2 \in [2^m]} \cdots Q'_{i_k \in [2^m]} Z_{i_1, i_2, \ldots, i_k}$, and the problem of evaluating C_N at an input consisting of the truth table of $V(x, \cdots)$ (i.e., when setting $Z_{i_1, i_2, \ldots, i_k} = V(x, i_1, \ldots, i_k)$, where $[2^m] \equiv \{0, 1\}^m$, which means that Z is essentially represented by x).[12] Note that the size of C_N is $O(N)$.

2. For every k and every fixed family of highly uniform unbounded fan-in circuits of depth k and polynomial size, show that the corresponding problem of evaluating a succinctly represented input is either in Σ_k or in Π_k.

Guideline: Given a succinct representation of Z, the value of $C_N(Z)$ can be captured by a quantified Boolean formula with k alternating quantifier sequences. This formula quantifies on certain paths from the output of C_N to its input terminals; for example, an $\vee$-gate (resp., $\wedge$-gate) evaluates to 1 if and only if one (resp., all) of its children evaluates to 1. The children of a vertex as well as the corresponding input-bits can be efficiently recognized based on the uniformity condition regarding C_N. The value of the input-bit itself can be efficiently computed from the succinct representation of Z.

Exercise 3.9: Verify the following facts:

1. For every $k \geq 0$, it holds that $\Sigma_k \subseteq \mathcal{P}^{\Sigma_k} \subseteq \Sigma_{k+1}$.

   (Recall that, for any complexity class $\mathcal{C}$, the class $\mathcal{P}^{\mathcal{C}}$ denotes the class of sets that are Cook-reducible to some set in $\mathcal{C}$. In particular, $\mathcal{P}^{\mathcal{P}} = \mathcal{P}$.)

2. For every $k \geq 0$, $\Pi_k \subseteq \mathcal{P}^{\Pi_k} \subseteq \Pi_{k+1}$.

   (Hint: For any complexity class $\mathcal{C}$, it holds that $\mathcal{P}^{\mathcal{C}} = \mathcal{P}^{\text{co}\mathcal{C}}$ and $\mathcal{P}^{\mathcal{C}} = \text{co}\mathcal{P}^{\mathcal{C}}$.)

3. For every $k \geq 0$, it holds that $\Sigma_k \subseteq \Pi_{k+1}$ and $\Pi_k \subseteq \Sigma_{k+1}$. Thus, $\mathcal{PH} = \cup_k \Pi_k$.

4. For every $k \geq 0$, if $\Sigma_k \subseteq \Pi_k$ (resp., $\Pi_k \subseteq \Sigma_k$) then $\Sigma_k = \Pi_k$.

   (Hint: See Exercise 2.37.)

Exercise 3.10: In continuation of Exercise 3.7, prove the following claims:

1. SAT is computationally equivalent (under Karp-reductions) to 1QBF.
2. For every $k \geq 1$, it holds that $\mathcal{P}^{\Sigma_k} = \mathcal{P}^{\text{kQBF}}$ and $\Sigma_{k+1} = \mathcal{NP}^{\text{kQBF}}$.

   Guideline: Prove that if S is $\mathcal{C}$-complete then $\mathcal{P}^{\mathcal{C}} = \mathcal{P}^S$. Note that $\mathcal{P}^{\mathcal{C}} \subseteq \mathcal{P}^S$ uses the polynomial-time reductions of $\mathcal{C}$ to S, whereas $\mathcal{P}^S \subseteq \mathcal{P}^{\mathcal{C}}$ uses $S \in \mathcal{C}$.

---

[11]Assuming $\mathcal{P} \neq \mathcal{NP}$, it cannot be that $N \leq \text{poly}(n)$ (because circuit evaluation can be performed in time polynomial in the size of the circuit).

[12]**Advanced comment:** Note that the computational limitations of $\mathcal{AC}^0$ circuits (see, e.g., [83, 115]) imply limitations on the functions of a *generic* input Z that the aforementioned circuits C_N can compute. More importantly, these limitations apply also to $Z = h(Z')$, where $Z' \in \{0, 1\}^{N^{\Omega(1)}}$ is generic and each bit of Z equals either some fixed bit in Z' or its negation. Unfortunately, these computational limitations do not seem to provide useful information on the limitations of functions of inputs Z that have succinct representation (as obtained by setting $Z_{i_1, i_2, \ldots, i_k} = V(x, i_1, \ldots, i_k)$, where V is a fixed polynomial-time algorithm and only $x \in \{0, 1\}^{\text{poly}(\log N)}$ varies). This fundamental problem is "resolved" in the context of "relativization" by providing V with oracle access to an arbitrary input of length $N^{\Omega(1)}$ (or so); cf. [83].

Exercise 3.11 (an alternative proof of Theorem 3.12): In continuation of the discussion in the proof of Theorem 3.12, use the following guidelines to provide an alternative proof of Theorem 3.12.

1. First, prove that *if T is downward self-reducible* (as defined in Exercise 2.13) *then the correctness of circuits deciding T can be decided in* $\text{co}\mathcal{NP}$. Specifically, denoting by χ the characteristic function of T, show that the set

$$\text{ckt}_\chi \stackrel{\text{def}}{=} \{(1^n, \langle C \rangle) : \forall w \in \{0, 1\}^n \ C(w) = \chi(w)\}$$

is in $\text{co}\mathcal{NP}$. Note that you may assume nothing about T, except for the hypothesis that T is downward self-reducible.

   Guideline: Using the more flexible formulation suggested in Exercise 3.1, it suffices to verify that, for every $i < n$ and every i-bit string w, the value $C(w)$ equals the output of the downward self-reduction on input w when obtaining answers according to C. Thus, for every $i < n$, the correctness of C on inputs of length i follows from its correctness on inputs of length less than i. Needless to say, the correctness of C on the empty string (or on all inputs of some constant length) can be verified by comparison to the fixed value of χ on the empty string (resp., the values of χ on a constant number of strings).

2. Recalling that SAT is downward self-reducible and that $\mathcal{NP}$ is Karp-reducible to SAT, derive Theorem 3.12 as a corollary of Part 1.

   Guideline: Let $S \in \Pi_2$ and $S' \in \mathcal{NP}$ be as in the proof of Theorem 3.12. Letting f denote a Karp-reduction of S' to SAT, note that $S = \{x : \forall y \in \{0, 1\}^{p(|x|)} \ f(x, y) \in \text{SAT}\}$. Using the hypothesis that SAT has polynomial-size circuits, note that $x \in S$ if and only if there exists a $\text{poly}(|x|)$-size circuit C such that (1) C decides SAT correctly on every input of length at most $\text{poly}(|x|)$, and (2) for every $y \in \{0, 1\}^{p(|x|)}$ it holds that $C(f(x, y)) = 1$. Infer that $S \in \Sigma_2$.

Exercise 3.12: In continuation of Part 2 of Exercise 3.2, we consider the class of sets that are Karp-reducible to a sparse set. It can be proven that this class contains SAT if and only if $\mathcal{P} = \mathcal{NP}$ (see [81]). Here, we consider only the special case in which the sparse set is contained in a polynomial-time decidable set that is itself sparse (e.g., the latter set may be $\{1\}^*$, in which case the former set may be an arbitrary unary set). Actually, prove the following seemingly stronger claim:

   If SAT is Karp-reducible to a set $S \subseteq G$ such that $G \in \mathcal{P}$ and $G \setminus S$ is sparse then SAT $\in \mathcal{P}$.

Using the hypothesis, we outline a polynomial-time procedure for solving the search problem of SAT, and leave the task of providing the details as an exercise. The procedure conducts a DFS on the tree of all possible partial truth assignments to the input formula,[13] while truncating the search at nodes that correspond to partial truth assignments that were already demonstrated to be useless.

   Guideline: The key observation is that each internal node (which yields a formula derived from the initial formulae by instantiating the corresponding partial truth assignment) is mapped by the Karp-reduction either to a string not in G (in which case we conclude that the sub-tree contains no satisfying assignments and backtrack from

---

[13] For an n-variable formulae, the leaves of the tree correspond to all possible n-bit long strings, and an internal node corresponding to τ is the parent of the nodes corresponding to $\tau 0$ and $\tau 1$.

this node) or to a string in G. In the latter case, unless we already know that this string is not in S, we *start a scan of the sub-tree rooted at this node*. However, once we backtrack from this internal node, we know that the corresponding element of G is not in S, and we will never scan again a sub-tree rooted at a node that is mapped to this element. Also note that once we reach a leaf, we can check by ourselves whether or not it corresponds to a satisfying assignment to the initial formula.

(Hint: When analyzing the foregoing procedure, note that on input an n-variable formulae ϕ the number of times we start to scan a sub-tree is at most $n \cdot |\bigcup_{i=1}^{\text{poly}(|\phi|)} \{0, 1\}^i \cap (G \setminus S)|$.)

CHAPTER FOUR

More Resources, More Power?

More electricity, less toil.
The Israeli Electricity Company, 1960s

Is it indeed the case that the more resources one has, the more one can achieve? The answer may seem obvious, but the obvious answer (of yes) actually presumes that the worker knows what resources are at his/her disposal. In this case, when allocated more resources, the worker (or computation) can indeed achieve more. But otherwise, nothing may be gained by adding resources.

In the context of Computational Complexity, an algorithm knows the amount of resources that it is allocated if it can determine this amount without exceeding the corresponding resources. This condition is satisfied in all "reasonable" cases, but it may not hold in general. The latter fact should not be that surprising: We already know that some functions are not computable, and if these functions are used to determine resources then the algorithm may be in trouble. Needless to say, this discussion requires some formalization, which is provided in the current chapter.

Summary: When using "nice" functions to determine an algorithm's resources, it is indeed the case that more resources allow for more tasks to be performed. However, when "ugly" functions are used for the same purpose, increasing the resources may have no effect. By nice functions we mean functions that can be computed without exceeding the amount of resources that they specify (e.g., $t(n) = n^2$ or $t(n) = 2^n$). Naturally, "ugly" functions do not allow for presenting themselves in such nice forms.

The foregoing discussion refers to uniform models of computation and to (natural) resources such as time and space complexities. Thus, we get results asserting, for example, that there are problems that are solvable in cubic time but not in quadratic time. In case of non-uniform models of computation, the issue of "nicety" does not arise, and it is easy to establish separations between levels of circuit complexity that differ by any unbounded amount.

Results that *separate* the class of problems solvable within one resource bound from the class of problems solvable within a larger resource bound are called hierarchy theorems. Results that indicate the nonexistence of such separations, hence indicating a "gap" in the growth of computing power (or a "gap" in the existence of algorithms that utilize the added resources), are called gap theorems. A somewhat related phenomenon, called speed-up theorems, refers to the inability to define the complexity of some problems.

Caveat. Uniform complexity classes based on specific resource bounds (e.g., cubic time) are model dependent. Furthermore, the tightness of separation results (i.e., how much "more time" is required for solving some additional computational problems) is also model dependent. Still, the existence of such separations is a phenomenon common to all reasonable and general models of computation (as referred to in the Cobham-Edmonds Thesis). In the following presentation, we will explicitly differentiate model-specific effects from generic ones.

Organization. We will first demonstrate the "more resources yield more power" phenomenon in the context of non-uniform complexity. In this case, the issue of "knowing" the amount of resources allocated to the computing device does not arise, because each device is tailored to the amount of resources allowed for the input length that it handles (see Section 4.1). We then turn to the time complexity of uniform algorithms; indeed, hierarchy and gap theorems for time complexity, presented in Section 4.2, constitute the main part of the current chapter. We end by mentioning analogous results for space complexity (see Section 4.3, which may also be read after Section 5.1).

4.1. Non-uniform Complexity Hierarchies

The model of machines that use advice (cf. §1.2.4.2 and Section 3.1.2) offers a very convenient setting for separation results. We refer specifically to classes of the form $\mathcal{P}/\ell$, where $\ell : \mathbb{N} \to \mathbb{N}$ is an arbitrary function (see Definition 3.5). Recall that every Boolean function is in $\mathcal{P}/2^n$, by virtue of a trivial algorithm that is given, as advice, the truth table of the function (restricted to the relevant input length). An analogous algorithm underlies the following separation result.

Theorem 4.1: *For any two functions $\ell', \delta : \mathbb{N} \to \mathbb{N}$ such that $\ell'(n) + \delta(n) \leq 2^n$ and δ is unbounded, it holds that $\mathcal{P}/\ell'$ is strictly contained in $\mathcal{P}/(\ell' + \delta)$.*

Proof: Let $\ell \stackrel{\text{def}}{=} \ell' + \delta$, and consider the following advice-taking algorithm A: Given advice $a_n \in \{0, 1\}^{\ell(n)}$ and input $i \in \{1, \ldots, 2^n\}$ (viewed as an n-bit long string), algorithm A outputs the ith bit of a_n if $i \leq |a_n|$ and zero otherwise. Clearly, for any $\bar{a} = (a_n)_{n \in \mathbb{N}}$ such that $|a_n| = \ell(n)$, it holds that the function $f_{\bar{a}}(x) \stackrel{\text{def}}{=} A(a_{|x|}, x)$ is in $\mathcal{P}/\ell$. Furthermore, different sequences $\bar{a}$ yield different functions $f_{\bar{a}}$. We claim that some of these functions $f_{\bar{a}}$ are not in $\mathcal{P}/\ell'$, thus obtaining a separation.

The claim is proved by considering all possible (polynomial-time) algorithms A' and all possible sequences $\bar{a}' = (a'_n)_{n \in \mathbb{N}}$ such that $|a'_n| = \ell'(n)$. Fixing any algorithm A', we consider the number of n-bit long functions that are correctly computed by $A'(a'_n, \cdot)$. Clearly, the number of these functions is at most $2^{\ell'(n)}$, and thus A' may account for at most $2^{-\delta(n)}$ fraction of the functions $f_{\bar{a}}$ (even when restricted to n-bit strings). Essentially, this consideration holds for every n and every possible A', and thus the measure of the set of functions that are computable by algorithms that take advice of length ℓ' is zero.

Formally, for every n, we consider all advice-taking algorithms that have a description of length shorter than $\delta(n) - 2$. (This guarantees that every advice-taking algorithm will be considered.) Coupled with all possible advice sequences of length ℓ', these algorithms can compute at most $2^{(\delta(n)-2)+\ell'(n)}$ different functions of n-bit long inputs. The latter number falls short of the $2^{\ell(n)}$ corresponding functions (of n-bit long inputs) that are computable by A with advice of length $\ell(n)$. ∎

A somewhat less tight bound can be obtained by using the model of Boolean circuits. In this case, some slackness is needed in order to account for the gap between the upper and lower bounds regarding the number of Boolean functions over $\{0, 1\}^n$ that are computed by Boolean circuits of size $s < 2^n$. Specifically (see Exercise 4.1), an obvious lower bound on this number is $2^{s/O(\log s)}$ whereas an obvious upper bound is $s^{2s} = 2^{2s \log_2 s}$. Compare these bounds to the lower-bound $2^{\ell(n)}$ and the upper-bound $2^{\ell'(n)+(\delta(n)/2)}$ (on the number of functions computable with advice of length $\ell'(n)$), which were used in the proof of Theorem 4.1.

4.2. Time Hierarchies and Gaps

In this section we show that in "reasonable cases," increasing the time complexity allows for more problems to be solved, whereas in "pathological cases," it may happen that even a dramatic increase in the time complexity provides no additional computing power. As hinted in the introductory comments to the current chapter, the "reasonable cases" correspond to time bounds that can be determined by the algorithm itself within the specified time complexity.

We stress that also in the aforementioned "reasonable cases," the added power does not necessarily refer to natural computational problems. That is, like in the case of non-uniform complexity (i.e., Theorem 4.1), the hierarchy theorems are proven by introducing artificial computational problems. Needless to say, we do not know of natural problems in $\mathcal{P}$ that are unsolvable in cubic (or some other fixed polynomial) time (on, say, a two-tape Turing machine). Thus, although $\mathcal{P}$ contains an infinite hierarchy of computational problems, with each level requiring significantly more time than the previous level, we know of no such hierarchy of natural computational problems. In contrast, so far it has been the case that any natural problem that was shown to be solvable in polynomial time was eventually followed by algorithms having running time that is bounded by a moderate polynomial.

4.2.1. Time Hierarchies

Note that the non-uniform computing devices, considered in Section 4.1, were explicitly given the relevant resource bounds (e.g., the length of advice). Actually, they were given the resources themselves (e.g., the advice itself) and did not need to monitor their usage of these resources. In contrast, when designing algorithms of arbitrary time complexity $t : \mathbb{N} \to \mathbb{N}$, we need to make sure that the algorithm does not exceed the time bound. Furthermore, when invoked on input x, the algorithm is not given the time bound $t(|x|)$ explicitly, and a reasonable design methodology is to have the algorithm compute this bound (i.e., $t(|x|)$) before doing anything else. This, in turn, requires the algorithm to read the entire input (see Exercise 4.3) as well as to compute $t(n)$ in $O(t(n))$ steps (as otherwise this preliminary stage already consumes too much time). The latter requirement motivates the following definition (which is related to the standard definition of "fully time constructibility" (cf. [123, Sec. 12.3])).

> **Definition 4.2** (time constructible functions): *A function $t : \mathbb{N} \to \mathbb{N}$ is called* time constructible *if there exists an algorithm that on input n outputs $t(n)$ using at most $t(n)$ steps.*

Equivalently, we may require that the mapping $1^n \mapsto t(n)$ be computable within time complexity t. We warn that the foregoing definition is model dependent; however, typically nice functions are computable even faster (e.g., in poly$(\log t(n))$ steps), in which case the model dependency is irrelevant (for reasonable and general models of computation, as referred to in the Cobham-Edmonds Thesis). For example, in any reasonable and general model, functions like $t_1(n) = n^2$, $t_2(n) = 2^n$, and $t_3(n) = 2^{2^n}$ are computable in poly$(\log t_i(n))$ steps.

Likewise, for a fixed model of computation (to be understood from the context) and for any function $t : \mathbb{N} \to \mathbb{N}$, we *denote by* DTIME$(t)$ *the class of decision problems that are solvable in time complexity t*. We call the reader's attention to Exercise 4.4 that asserts that in many cases DTIME$(t) =$ DTIME$(t/2)$.

4.2.1.1. The Time Hierarchy Theorem

In the following theorem (which separates DTIME(t_1) from DTIME(t_2)), we refer to the model of two-tape Turing machines. In this case we obtain quite a tight hierarchy in terms of the relation between t_1 and t_2. We stress that, using the Cobham-Edmonds Thesis, this result yields (possibly less tight) hierarchy theorems for any reasonable and general model of computation.

> **Teaching note:** The standard statement of Theorem 4.3 asserts that *for any time-constructible function t_2 and every function t_1 such that $t_2 = \omega(t_1 \log t_1)$ and $t_1(n) > n$ it holds that* DTIME(t_1) *is strictly contained in* DTIME(t_2). The current version is only slightly weaker, but it allows a somewhat simpler and more intuitive proof. We comment on the proof of the standard version of Theorem 4.3 in a teaching note following the proof of the current version.

> **Theorem 4.3** (time hierarchy for two-tape Turing machines): *For any time-constructible function t_1 and every function t_2 such that $t_2(n) \geq (\log t_1(n))^2 \cdot t_1(n)$ and $t_1(n) > n$ it holds that* DTIME(t_1) *is strictly contained in* DTIME(t_2).

As will become clear from the proof, an analogous result holds for any model in which a universal machine can emulate t steps of another machine in $O(t \log t)$ time, where the constant in the O-notation depends on the emulated machine. Before proving Theorem 4.3, we derive the following corollary.

> **Corollary 4.4** (time hierarchy for any reasonable and general model): *For any reasonable and general model of computation there exists a positive polynomial p such that for any time-computable function t_1 and every function t_2 such that $t_2 > p(t_1)$ and $t_1(n) > n$ it holds that* DTIME(t_1) *is strictly contained in* DTIME(t_2).

It follows that, for every such model and every polynomial t (such that $t(n) > n$), there exist problems in $\mathcal{P}$ that are not in DTIME(t). It also follows that $\mathcal{P}$ is a strict subset of $\mathcal{E}$ and even of "quasi-polynomial time" (i.e., DTIME(q), where $q(n) = \exp(\text{poly}(\log n))$); moreover, $\mathcal{P}$ is a strict subset of DTIME(q), for any super-polynomial function q (i.e., $q(n) = n^{\omega(1)}$).

We comment that Corollary 4.4 can be proven directly (rather than by invoking Theorem 4.3). This can be done by implementing the ideas that underlie the proof of Theorem 4.3 directly to the model of computation at hand (see Exercise 4.5). In fact, such a direct implementation, which is allowed "polynomial slackness" (i.e., $t_2 > p(t_1)$), is less cumbersome than the implementation presented in the proof of Theorem 4.3 where only a polylogarithmic factor is allowed in the slackness (i.e., $t_2 \geq \tilde{O}(t_1)$). We also note that the separation result in Corollary 4.4 can be tightened – for details see Exercise 4.6.

Proof of Corollary 4.4: The underlying fact is that separation results regarding any reasonable and general model of computation can be "translated" to analogous results regarding any other such model. Such a translation may affect the time bounds as demonstrated next. Letting DTIME$_2$ denote the classes that correspond to two-tape Turing machines (and recalling that DTIME denotes the classes that correspond to the alternative model), we note that DTIME(t_1) $\subseteq$ DTIME$_2$(t_1') and DTIME$_2$(t_2') $\subseteq$ DTIME(t_2), where $t_1' = \text{poly}(t_1)$ and t_2' is defined such that $t_2(n) = \text{poly}(t_2'(n))$. The latter unspecified polynomials, hereafter denoted p_1 and p_2, respectively, are the ones guaranteed by the Cobham-Edmonds Thesis. Also, the hypothesis that t_1 is time-constructible implies that $t_1' = p_1(t_1)$ is time-constructible with respect to the two-tape Turing machine model. Thus, for a suitable choice of the polynomial p (i.e., $p(p_1^{-1}(m)) \geq p_2(m^2)$), it holds that

$$t_2'(n) = p_2^{-1}(t_2(n)) > p_2^{-1}(p(t_1(n))) = p_2^{-1}\left(p\left(p_1^{-1}(t_1'(n))\right)\right) \geq t_1'(n)^2 \,,$$

where the first inequality holds by the corollary's hypothesis (i.e., $t_2 > p(t_1)$) and the last inequality holds by the choice of p. Invoking Theorem 4.3 (while noting that $t_2'(n) > t_1'(n)^2$), we obtain the strict inclusion DTIME$_2$(t_1') $\subset$ DTIME$_2$(t_2'). Combining the latter with DTIME(t_1) $\subseteq$ DTIME$_2$(t_1') and DTIME$_2$(t_2') $\subseteq$ DTIME(t_2), the corollary follows. ∎

Proof of Theorem 4.3: The idea is constructing a Boolean function f such that all machines having time complexity t_1 fail to compute f. This is done by associating with each possible machine M a different input x_M (e.g., $x_M = \langle M \rangle$) and making sure that $f(x_M) \neq M'(x_M)$, where $M'(x)$ denotes an emulation of $M(x)$ that is suspended after $t_1(|x|)$ steps. For example, we may define $f(x_M) = 1 - M'(x_M)$. We note that M' is used instead of M in order to allow for computing f in time that is related to t_1. The point is that M may be an arbitrary machine that is associated with the input x_M, and so M does not necessarily run in time t_1 (but, by construction, the corresponding M' does run in time t_1).

Implementing the foregoing idea calls for an efficient association of machines to inputs as well as for a relatively efficient emulation of t_1 steps of an arbitrary machine. As shown next, both requirements can be met easily. Actually, we are going to use a mapping μ of inputs to machines (i.e., μ will map the aforementioned x_M to M) such that each machine is in the range of μ and μ is very easy to compute (e.g., indeed, for starters, assume that μ is the identity mapping). Thus, by construction, $f \notin \text{DTIME}(t_1)$. The issue is presenting a relatively efficient algorithm for computing f, that is, showing that $f \in \text{DTIME}(t_2)$.

The algorithm for computing f as well as the definition of f (sketched in the first paragraph) are straightforward: On input x, the algorithm computes $t = t_1(|x|)$, determines the machine $M = \mu(x)$ that corresponds to x (outputting a default value if no such machine exists), emulates $M(x)$ *for t steps*, and returns the value $1 - M'(x)$. Recall that $M'(x)$ denotes the time-truncated emulation of $M(x)$ (i.e., the emulation of $M(x)$ suspended after t steps); that is, if $M(x)$ halts within t steps then $M'(x) = M(x)$, and otherwise $M'(x)$ may be defined arbitrarily. Thus, $f(x) = 1 - M'(x)$ if $M = \mu(x)$ and (say) $f(x) = 0$ otherwise.

In order to show that $f \notin \text{DTIME}(t_1)$, we show that each machine of time complexity t_1 fails to compute f. Fixing any such machine, M, we consider an input x_M such that $M = \mu(x_M)$, where such an input exists because μ is onto. Now, on the one hand, $M'(x_M) = M(x_M)$ (because M has time complexity t_1), while on the other hand, $f(x_M) = 1 - M'(x_M)$ (by the definition of f). It follows that $M(x) \neq f(x)$.

We now turn to upper-bounding the time complexity of f by analyzing the time complexity of the foregoing algorithm that computes f. Using the time constructibility of t_1 and ignoring the easy computation of μ, we focus on the question of how much time is required for emulating t steps of machine M (on input x). We should bear in mind that the time complexity of our algorithm needs to be analyzed in the two-tape Turing machine model, whereas M itself is a two-tape Turing machine. We start by implementing our algorithm on a three-tape Turing machine, and next emulate this machine on a two-tape Turing machine.

The obvious implementation of our algorithm on a three-tape Turing machine uses two tapes for the emulation itself and designates the third tape for the actions of the emulation procedure (e.g., storing the code of the emulated machine and maintaining a step-counter). Thus, each step of the two-tape machine M is emulated using $O(|\langle M \rangle|)$ steps on the three-tape machine.[1] This also includes the amortized complexity of maintaining a step counter for the emulation (see Exercise 4.7).

Next, we need to emulate the foregoing three-tape machine on a two-tape machine. This is done by using the fact (cf., e.g., [123, Thm. 12.6]) that t' steps of a three-tape machine can be emulated on a two-tape machine in $O(t' \log t')$ steps. Thus, the complexity of computing f on input x is upper-bounded by $O(T_{\mu(x)}(|x|) \log T_{\mu(x)}(|x|))$, where $T_M(n) = O(|\langle M \rangle| \cdot t_1(n))$ represents the cost of emulating $t_1(n)$ steps of the two-tape machine M on a three-tape machine (as in the foregoing discussion).

It turns out that the quality of the separation result that we obtain depends on the choice of the mapping μ (of inputs to machines). Using the naive (identity) mapping (i.e., $\mu(x) = x$) we can only establish the theorem for $t_2(n) = \widetilde{O}(n \cdot t_1(n))$ rather than $t_2(n) = \widetilde{O}(t_1(n))$, because in this case $T_{\mu(x)}(|x|) = O(|x| \cdot t_1(|x|))$. (Note that, in this case, $x_M = \langle M \rangle$ is a description of $\mu(x_M) = M$.) The theorem follows by associating the machine M with the input $x_M = \langle M \rangle 01^m$, where $m = 2^{|\langle M \rangle|}$; that is, we may use the mapping μ such that $\mu(x) = M$ if $x = \langle M \rangle 01^{2^{|\langle M \rangle|}}$ and $\mu(x)$ equals some fixed machine otherwise. In this case $|\mu(x)| < \log_2 |x| < \log t_1(|x|)$ and so $T_{\mu(x)}(|x|) = O((\log t_1(|x|)) \cdot t_1(|x|))$. The theorem follows. ∎

---

[1] This overhead accounts both for searching the code of M for the adequate action and for the effecting of this action (which may refer to a larger alphabet than the one used by the emulator).

> **Teaching note:** Proving the standard version of Theorem 4.3 cannot be done by associating a sufficiently long input x_M with each machine M, because this does not allow for geting rid of the additional unbounded factor in $T_{\mu(x)}(|x|)$ (i.e., the $|\mu(x)|$ factor that multiplies $t_1(|x|)$). Note that the latter factor needs to be computable (at the very least) and thus cannot be accounted for by the generic ω-notation that appears in the standard version (cf. [123, Thm. 12.9]). Instead, a different approach is taken (see footnote 2).

Technical comments. The proof of Theorem 4.3 associates with each potential machine M some input x_M and defines the computational problem such that machine M errs on input x_M. The association of machines with inputs is rather flexible: We can use any onto mapping of inputs to machines that is efficiently computable and sufficiently shrinking. Specifically, in the proof, we used the mapping μ such that $\mu(x) = M$ if $x = \langle M \rangle 01^{2^{|\langle M \rangle|}}$ and $\mu(x)$ equals some fixed machine otherwise. We comment that each machine can be made to err on infinitely many inputs by redefining μ such that $\mu(x) = M$ if $\langle M \rangle 01^{2^{|\langle M \rangle|}}$ is a suffix of x (and $\mu(x)$ equals some fixed machine otherwise). We also comment that, in contrast to the proof of Theorem 4.3, the proof of Theorem 1.5 utilizes a rigid mapping of inputs to machines (i.e., there $\mu(x) = M$ if $x = \langle M \rangle$).

Digest: Diagonalization. The last comment highlights the fact that the proof of Theorem 4.3 is merely a sophisticated version of the proof of Theorem 1.5. Both proofs refer to versions of the universal function, which in the case of the proof of Theorem 4.3 is (implicitly) defined such that its value at $(\langle M \rangle, x)$ equals $M'(x)$, where $M'(x)$ denotes an emulation of $M(x)$ that is suspended after $t_1(|x|)$ steps.[3] Actually, both proofs refers to the "diagonal" of the aforementioned function, which in the case of the proof of Theorem 4.3 is only defined implicitly. That is, the value of the diagonal function at x, denoted $d(x)$, equals the value of the universal function at $(\langle \mu(x) \rangle, x)$. This is actually a definitional schema, as the choice of the function μ remains unspecified. Indeed, setting $\mu(x) = x$ corresponds to a "real" diagonal in the matrix depicting the universal function, but any other choice of a 1-1 mappings μ also yields a "kind of diagonal" of the universal function. Either way, the function f is defined such that for every x it holds that $f(x) \neq d(x)$. This guarantees that no machine of time complexity t_1 can compute f, and the focus is on presenting an algorithm that computes f (which, needless to say, has time complexity greater than t_1). Part of the proof of Theorem 4.3 is devoted to selecting μ in a way that minimizes the time complexity of computing f, whereas in the proof of Theorem 1.5 we merely need to guarantee that f is computable.

4.2.1.2. Impossibility of Speedup for Universal Computation

The time hierarchy theorem (Theorem 4.3) implies that the computation of a universal machine cannot be significantly sped up. That is, consider the function $u'(\langle M \rangle, x, t) \overset{\text{def}}{=} y$ if

---

[2]In the standard proof the function f is not defined with reference to $t_1(|x_M|)$ steps of $M(x_M)$, but rather with reference to the result of emulating $M(x_M)$ while using a total of $t_2(|x_M|)$ steps in the emulation process (i.e., in the algorithm used to compute f). This guarantees that f is in DTIME(t_2), and "pushes the problem" to showing that f is not in DTIME(t_1). It also explains why t_2 (rather than t_1) is assumed to be time-constructible. As for the foregoing problem, it is resolved by observing that for each relevant machine (i.e., having time complexity t_1) the executions on any sufficiently long input will be fully emulated. Thus, we merely need to associate with each M a disjoint set of infinitely many inputs and make sure that M errs on each of these inputs.

[3]Needless to say, in the proof of Theorem 1.5, $M' = M$.

on input x machine M halts within t steps and outputs the string y, and $\mathrm{u}'(\langle M \rangle, x, t) \overset{\text{def}}{=} \perp$ if on input x machine M makes more than t steps. Recall that the value of $\mathrm{u}'(\langle M \rangle, x, t)$ can be computed in $\widetilde{O}(|x| + |\langle M \rangle| \cdot t)$ steps. As shown next, Theorem 4.3 implies that this value (i.e., $\mathrm{u}'(\langle M \rangle, x, t)$) cannot be computed within significantly fewer steps.

> **Theorem 4.5:** *There exists no two-tape Turing machine that, on input $\langle M \rangle$, x and t, computes $\mathrm{u}'(\langle M \rangle, x, t)$ in $o((t + |x|) \cdot f(M) / \log^2(t + |x|))$ steps, where f is an arbitrary function.*

A similar result holds for any reasonable and general model of computation (cf., Corollary 4.4). In particular, it follows that u' is not computable in polynomial time (because the input t is presented in binary). In fact, one can show that there exists no polynomial-time algorithm for *deciding whether or not M halts on input x in t steps* (i.e., the set $\{(\langle M \rangle, x, t) : \mathrm{u}'(\langle M \rangle, x, t) \neq \perp\}$ is not in $\mathcal{P}$); see Exercise 4.8.

Proof: Suppose (toward the contradiction) that, for every fixed M, given x and $t > |x|$, the value of $\mathrm{u}'(\langle M \rangle, x, t)$ can be computed in $o(t / \log^2 t)$ steps, where the o-notation hides a constant that may depend on M. We shall show that this hypothesis implies that *for any time-constructible t_1 and $t_2(n) = t_1(n) \cdot \log^2 t_1(n)$ it holds that* $\mathrm{DTIME}(t_2) = \mathrm{DTIME}(t_1)$, which (strongly) contradicts Theorem 4.3.

Consider an arbitrary time-constructible t_1 (s.t. $t_1(n) > n$) and an arbitrary set $S \in \mathrm{DTIME}(t_2)$, where $t_2(n) = t_1(n) \cdot \log^2 t_1(n)$. Let M be a machine of time complexity t_2 that decides membership in S, and consider the following algorithm: On input x, the algorithm first computes $t = t_1(|x|)$, and then computes (and outputs) the value $\mathrm{u}'(\langle M \rangle, x, t \log^2 t)$. By the time constructibility of t_1, the first computation can be implemented in t steps, and by the contradiction hypothesis the same holds for the second computation. Thus, S can be decided in $\mathrm{DTIME}(2t_1) = \mathrm{DTIME}(t_1)$, implying that $\mathrm{DTIME}(t_2) = \mathrm{DTIME}(t_1)$, which in turn contradicts Theorem 4.3. We conclude that the contradiction hypothesis is wrong, and the theorem follows. ∎

4.2.1.3. Hierarchy Theorem for Non-deterministic Time

Analogously to DTIME, for a fixed model of computation (to be understood from the context) and for any function $t : \mathbb{N} \to \mathbb{N}$, we *denote by $\mathrm{NTIME}(t)$ the class of sets that are accepted by some non-deterministic machine of time complexity t.* Indeed, this definition extends the traditional formulation of $\mathcal{NP}$ (as presented in Definition 2.7). Alternatively, analogously to our preferred definition of $\mathcal{NP}$ (i.e., Definition 2.5), a set $S \subseteq \{0, 1\}^*$ is in $\mathrm{NTIME}(t)$ if there exists a *linear-time* algorithm V such that the two conditions hold:

1. For every $x \in S$ there exists $y \in \{0, 1\}^{t(|x|)}$ such that $V(x, y) = 1$.
2. For every $x \notin S$ and every $y \in \{0, 1\}^*$ it holds that $V(x, y) = 0$.

We warn that the two formulations are not identical, but in sufficiently strong models (e.g., two-tape Turing machines) they are related up to logarithmic factors (see Exercise 4.10). The hierarchy theorem itself is similar to the one for deterministic time, except that here we require that $t_2(n) \geq (\log t_1(n + 1))^2 \cdot t_1(n + 1)$ (rather than $t_2(n) \geq (\log t_1(n))^2 \cdot t_1(n)$). That is:

Theorem 4.6 (non-deterministic time hierarchy for two-tape Turing machines): *For any time-constructible and monotonically non-decreasing function t_1 and every function t_2 such that $t_2(n) \geq (\log t_1(n+1))^2 \cdot t_1(n+1)$ and $t_1(n) > n$ it holds that $\mathrm{NTIME}(t_1)$ is strictly contained in $\mathrm{NTIME}(t_2)$.*

Proof**:** We cannot just apply the proof of Theorem 4.3, because the Boolean function f defined there requires the ability to determine whether there exists a computation of M that accepts the input x_M in $t_1(|x_M|)$ steps. In the current context, M is a non-deterministic machine and so the only way we know how to determine this question (both for a "yes" and "no" answers) is to try all the $(2^{t_1(|x_M|)})$ relevant executions.[4] But this would put f in $\mathrm{DTIME}(2^{t_1})$, rather than in $\mathrm{NTIME}(\widetilde{O}(t_1))$, and so a different approach is needed.

We associate with each (non-deterministic) machine M a large interval of strings (viewed as integers), denoted $I_M = [\alpha_M, \beta_M]$, such that the various intervals do not intersect and such that it is easy to determine for each string x in which interval it resides. For each $x \in [\alpha_M, \beta_M - 1]$, we define $f(x) = 1$ if and only if there exists a non-deterministic computation of M that accepts the input $x' \stackrel{\text{def}}{=} x + 1$ in $t_1(|x'|) \leq t_1(|x| + 1)$ steps. Thus, if M has time complexity t_1 and (non-deterministically) accepts $\{x : f(x)=1\}$, then either M (non-deterministically) accepts each string in the interval I_M or M (non-deterministically) accepts no string in I_M, because M must non-deterministically accept x if and only if it non-deterministically accepts $x' = x + 1$. So, it is left to deal with the case that M is invariant on I_M, which is where the definition of the value of $f(\beta_M)$ comes into play: We define $f(\beta_M)$ to equal *zero* if and only if there exists a non-deterministic computation of M that accepts the input α_M in $t_1(|\alpha_M|)$ steps. We shall select β_M to be large enough relative to α_M such that we can afford to try all possible computations of M on input α_M. Details follow.

Let us first recapitulate the definition of $f : \{0, 1\}^* \to \{0, 1\}$, focusing on the case that the input is in some interval I_M. We define a Boolean function A_M such that $A_M(z) = 1$ if and only if there exists a non-deterministic computation of M that accepts the input z in $t_1(|z|)$ steps. Then, for $x \in I_M$ we have

$$f(x) = \begin{cases} A_M(x+1) & \text{if } x \in [\alpha_M, \beta_M - 1] \\ 1 - A_M(\alpha_M) & \text{if } x = \beta_M \end{cases}$$

Next, we present the following non-deterministic machine for accepting the set $\{x : f(x) = 1\}$. We assume that, on input x, it is easy to determine the machine M that corresponds to the interval $[\alpha_M, \beta_M]$ in which x resides.[5] We distinguish two cases:

1. On input $x \in [\alpha_M, \beta_M - 1]$, our non-deterministic machine emulates $t_1(|x'|)$ steps of a (single) non-deterministic computation of M on input $x' = x + 1$, and decides accordingly (i.e., our machine accepts if and only if the said emulation has accepted). Indeed (as in the proof of Theorem 4.3), this emulation can be performed in time $(\log t_1(|x + 1|))^2 \cdot t_1(|x + 1|) \leq t_2(|x|)$.

---

[4]Indeed, we can non-deterministically recognize "yes" answers in $\widetilde{O}(t_1(|x_M|))$ steps, but we cannot do so for "no" answers.

[5]For example, we may partition the strings to consecutive intervals such that the ith interval, denoted $[\alpha_i, \beta_i]$, corresponds to the ith machine and for $T_1(m) = 2^{2t_1(m)}$ it holds that $\beta_i = 1^{T_1(|\alpha_i|)}$ and $\alpha_{i+1} = 0^{T_1(|\alpha_i|)+1}$. Note that $|\beta_i| = T_1(|\alpha_i|)$, and thus $t_1(|\beta_i|) > t_1(|\alpha_i|) \cdot 2^{t_1(|\alpha_i|)}$.

2. On input $x = \beta_M$, our machine just tries all $2^{t_1(|\alpha_M|)}$ executions of M on input α_M and decides in a suitable manner; that is, our machine emulates $t_1(|\alpha_M|)$ steps in each of the $2^{t_1(|\alpha_M|)}$ possible executions of $M(\alpha_M)$ and accepts β_M if and only if none of the emulated executions ended accepting α_M. Note that this part of our machine is deterministic, and it amounts to emulating $T_M \stackrel{\text{def}}{=} 2^{t_1(|\alpha_M|)} \cdot t_1(|\alpha_M|)$ steps of M. By a suitable choice of the interval $[\alpha_M, \beta_M]$ (e.g., $|\beta_M| > T_M$), this number of steps (i.e., T_M) is smaller than $|\beta_M| \leq t_1(|\beta_M|)$, and it follows that these T_M steps of M can be emulated in time $(\log_2 t_1(|\beta_M|))^2 \cdot t_1(|\beta_M|) \leq t_2(|\beta_M|)$.

Thus, our non-deterministic machine has time complexity t_2, and it follows that f is in $\text{NTIME}(t_2)$. It remains to show that f is not in $\text{NTIME}(t_1)$.

Suppose, on the contrary, that some non-deterministic machine M of time complexity t_1 accepts the set $\{x : f(x) = 1\}$; that is, for every x it holds that $A_M(x) = f(x)$, where A_M is as defined in the foregoing (i.e., $A_M(x) = 1$ if and only if there exists a non-deterministic computation of M that accepts the input x in $t_1(|x|)$ steps). Focusing on the interval $[\alpha_M, \beta_M]$, we have $A_M(x) = f(x)$ for every $x \in [\alpha_M, \beta_M]$, which (combined with the definition of f) implies that $A_M(x) = f(x) = A_M(x + 1)$ for every $x \in [\alpha_M, \beta_M - 1]$ and $A_M(\beta_M) = f(\beta_M) = 1 - A_M(\alpha_M)$. Thus, we reached a contraction (because we got $A_M(\alpha_M) = \cdots = A_M(\beta_M) = 1 - A_M(\alpha_M)$). ∎

4.2.2. Time Gaps and Speedup

In contrast to Theorem 4.3, there exists functions $t : \mathbb{N} \to \mathbb{N}$ such that $\text{DTIME}(t) = \text{DTIME}(t^2)$ (or even $\text{DTIME}(t) = \text{DTIME}(2^t)$). Needless to say, these functions are not time-constructible (and thus the aforementioned fact does not contradict Theorem 4.3). The reason for this phenomenon is that, for such functions t, there exist no algorithms that have time complexity above t but below t^2 (resp., 2^t).

Theorem 4.7 (the time gap theorem): *For every non-decreasing computable function $g : \mathbb{N} \to \mathbb{N}$ there exists a non-decreasing computable function $t : \mathbb{N} \to \mathbb{N}$ such that $\text{DTIME}(t) = \text{DTIME}(g(t))$.*

The foregoing examples referred to $g(m) = m^2$ and $g(m) = 2^m$. Since we are mainly interested in dramatic gaps (i.e., super-polynomial functions g), the model of computation does not matter here (as long as it is reasonable and general).

Proof: Consider an enumeration of all possible algorithms (or machines), which also includes machines that do not halt on some inputs. (Recall that we cannot enumerate the set of all machines that halt on every input.) Let t_i denote the time complexity of the ith algorithm; that is, $t_i(n) = \infty$ if the ith machine does not halt on some n-bit long input and otherwise $t_i(n) = \max_{x \in \{0,1\}^n} \{T_i(x)\}$, where $T_i(x)$ denotes the number of steps taken by the ith machine on input x.

The basic idea is to define t such that no t_i is "sandwiched" between t and $g(t)$, and thus no algorithm will have time complexity between t and $g(t)$. Intuitively, if $t_i(n)$ is finite, then we may define t such that $t(n) > t_i(n)$ and thus guarantee that $t_i(n) \notin [t(n), g(t(n))]$, whereas if $t_i(n) = \infty$ then any finite value of $t(n)$ will do

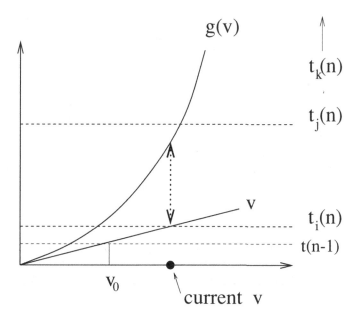

Figure 4.1: The Gap Theorem – determining the value of $t(n)$.

(because then $t_i(n) > g(t(n))$). Thus, for every m and n, we can define $t(n)$ such that $t_i(n) \notin [t(n), g(t(n))]$ for every $i \in [m]$ (e.g., $t(n) = \max_{i \in [m]:t_i(n) \neq \infty}\{t_i(n)\} + 1$).[6] This yields a weaker version of the theorem in which the function t is neither computable nor non-decreasing. It is easy to modify t such that it is non-decreasing (e.g., $t(n) = \max(t(n-1), \max_{i \in [m]:t_i(n) \neq \infty}\{t_i(n)\}) + 1$) and so the real challenge is to make t computable.

The problem is that we want t to be computable, whereas given n we cannot tell whether or not $t_i(n)$ is finite. However, we do not really need to make the latter decision: For each candidate value v of $t(n)$, we should just determine whether or not $t_i(n) \in [v, g(v)]$, which can be decided by running the ith machine for at most $g(v) + 1$ steps (on each n-bit long string). That is, as far as the ith machine is concerned, we should just find a value v such that either $v > t_i(n)$ or $g(v) < t_i(n)$ (which includes the case $t_i(n) = \infty$). This can be done by starting with $v = v_0$ (where, say, $v_0 = t(n-1) + 1$), and increasing v until either $v > t_i(n)$ or $g(v) < t_i(n)$. The point is that if $t_i(n)$ is infinite then we may output $v = v_0$ after emulating $2^n \cdot (g(v_0) + 1)$ steps, and otherwise we reach a safe value $v > t_i(n)$ after performing at most $\sum_{j=v_0}^{t_i(n)} 2^n \cdot j$ emulation steps. Bearing in mind that we should deal with all possible machines, we obtain the following procedure for setting $t(n)$.

Let $\mu : \mathbb{N} \to \mathbb{N}$ be any unbounded and computable function (e.g., $\mu(n) = n$ will do). Starting with $v = t(n-1) + 1$, we keep incrementing v until v satisfies, for every $i \in \{1, \ldots, \mu(n)\}$, either $t_i(n) < v$ or $t_i(n) > g(v)$. This condition can be verified by computing $\mu(n)$ and $g(v)$, and emulating the execution of each of the first $\mu(n)$ machines on each of the n-bit long strings for $g(v) + 1$ steps. The procedure sets $t(n)$ to equal the first value v satisfying the aforementioned condition, and halts. (Figure 4.1 depicts the search for a good value v for $t(n)$.)

---

[6]We may assume, without loss of generality, that $t_1(n) = 1$ for every n, e.g., by letting the machine that always halts after a single step be the first machine in our enumeration.

To show that the foregoing procedure halts on every n, consider the set $H_n \subseteq \{1, \ldots, \mu(n)\}$ of the indices of the (relevant) machines that halt on all inputs of length n. Then, the procedure definitely halts before reaching the value $v = \max(T_n, t(n - 1)) + 2$, where $T_n = \max_{i \in H_n}\{t_i(n)\}$. (Indeed, the procedure may halt with a value $v \leq T_n$, but this will happen only if $g(v) < T_n$.)

Finally, for the foregoing function t, we prove that $\mathrm{DTIME}(t) = \mathrm{DTIME}(g(t))$ holds. Indeed, consider an arbitrary $S \in \mathrm{DTIME}(g(t))$, and suppose that the ith algorithm decides S in time at most $g(t)$; that is, for every n, it holds that $t_i(n) \leq g(t(n))$. Then (by the construction of t), for every n satisfying $\mu(n) \geq i$, it holds that $t_i(n) < t(n)$. It follows that the ith algorithm decides S in time at most t on all but finitely many inputs. Combining this algorithm with a "look-up table" machine that handles the exceptional inputs, we conclude that $S \in \mathrm{DTIME}(t)$. The theorem follows. ■

Comment. The function t defined by the foregoing proof is computable in time that exceeds $g(t)$. Specifically, the presented procedure computes $t(n)$ (as well as $g(f(n))$) in time $\tilde{O}(2^n \cdot g(t(n)) + T_g(t(n)))$, where $T_g(m)$ denotes the number of steps required to compute $g(m)$ on input m.

Speedup theorems. Theorem 4.7 can be viewed as asserting that some time complexity classes (i.e., $\mathrm{DTIME}(g(t))$ in the theorem) collapse to lower classes (i.e., to $\mathrm{DTIME}(t)$). A conceptually related phenomenon is of problems that have no optimal algorithm (not even in a very mild sense); that is, every algorithm for these ("pathological") problems can be drastically sped up. It follows that the complexity of these problems cannot be defined (i.e., as the complexity of the best algorithm solving this problem). The following drastic speed-up theorem should not be confused with the linear speed-up that is an artifact of the definition of a Turing machine (see Exercise 4.4).[7]

> **Theorem 4.8** (the time speed-up theorem): *For every computable* (and super-linear) *function g there exists a decidable set S such that if $S \in \mathrm{DTIME}(t)$ then $S \in \mathrm{DTIME}(t')$ for t' satisfying $g(t'(n)) < t(n)$.*

Taking $g(n) = n^2$ (or $g(n) = 2^n$), the theorem asserts that, for every t, if $S \in \mathrm{DTIME}(t)$ then $S \in \mathrm{DTIME}(\sqrt{t})$ (resp., $S \in \mathrm{DTIME}(\log t)$). Note that Theorem 4.8 can be applied any (constant) number of times, which means that we cannot give a reasonable estimate to the complexity of deciding membership in S. In contrast, recall that in some important cases, optimal algorithms for solving computational problems do exist. Specifically, algorithms solving (candid) search problems in NP cannot be sped up (see Theorem 2.33), nor can the computation of a universal machine (see Theorem 4.5).

We refrain from presenting a proof of Theorem 4.8, but comment on the complexity of the sets involved in this proof. The proof (presented in [123, Sec. 12.6]) provides a construction of a set S in $\mathrm{DTIME}(t') \setminus \mathrm{DTIME}(t'')$ for $t'(n) = h(n - O(1))$ and $t''(n) = h(n - \omega(1))$, where $h(n)$ denoted g iterated n times on 2 (i.e., $h(n) = g^{(n)}(2)$, where $g^{(i+1)}(m) = g(g^{(i)}(m))$ and $g^{(1)} = g$). The set S is constructed such that for every $i > 0$

---

[7]**Advanced comment:** We note that the linear speed-up phenomenon was implicitly addressed in the proof of Theorem 4.3, by allowing an emulation overhead that depends on the length of the description of the emulated machine.

there exists a $j > i$ and an algorithm that decides S in time t_i but not in time t_j, where $t_k(n) = h(n - k)$.

4.3. Space Hierarchies and Gaps

Hierarchy and gap theorems analogous to Theorem 4.3 and Theorem 4.7, respectively, are known for space complexity. In fact, since space-efficient emulation of space-bounded machines is simpler than time-efficient emulations of time-bounded machines, the results tend to be sharper (and their proofs tend to be simpler). This is most conspicuous in the case of the separation result (stated next), which is optimal (in light of the corresponding linear speed-up result; see Exercise 4.12).

Before stating the separation result, we need a few preliminaries. We refer the reader to §1.2.3.5 for a definition of space complexity (and to Chapter 5 for further discussion). As in the case of time complexity, we consider a specific model of computation, but the results hold for any other reasonable and general model. Specifically, we consider three-tape Turing machines, because we designate two special tapes for input and output. For any function $s : \mathbb{N} \to \mathbb{N}$, we *denote by* DSPACE($s$) *the class of decision problems that are solvable in space complexity s.* Analogously to Definition 4.2, we call a function $s : \mathbb{N} \to \mathbb{N}$ space-constructible if there exists an algorithm that on input n outputs $s(n)$ while using at most $s(n)$ cells of the work-tape. Actually, functions like $s_1(n) = \log n$, $s_2(n) = (\log n)^2$, and $s_3(n) = 2^n$ are computable using $O(\log s_i(n))$ space.

Theorem 4.9 (space hierarchy for three-tape Turing machines): *For any space-constructible function s_2 and every function s_1 such that $s_2 = \omega(s_1)$ and $s_1(n) > \log n$ it holds that* DSPACE(s_1) *is strictly contained in* DSPACE(s_2).

Theorem 4.9 is analogous to the traditional version of Theorem 4.3 (rather than to the one we presented), and is proven using the alternative approach sketched in footnote 2. The details are left as an exercise (see Exercise 4.13).

Chapter Notes

The material presented in this chapter predates the theory of NP-completeness and the dominant stature of the P-vs-NP Question. In these early days, the field (to be known as Complexity Theory) had not yet developed an independent identity and its perspectives were dominated by two classical theories: the theory of computability (and recursive function) and the theory of formal languages. Nevertheless, we believe that the results presented in this chapter are interesting for two reasons. Firstly, as stated up front, these results address the natural question of under what conditions it is the case that more computational resources help. Secondly, these results demonstrate the type of results that one can get with respect to "generic" questions regarding Computational Complexity; that is, questions that refer to arbitrary resource bounds (e.g., the relation between DTIME(t_1) and DTIME(t_2) for arbitrary t_1 and t_2).

We note that, in contrast to the "generic" questions considered in this chapter, the P-vs-NP Question as well as the related questions that will be addressed in the rest of this book are not "generic" since they refer to specific classes (which capture natural computational issues). Furthermore, whereas time and space complexity behave in similar manner with respect to hierarchies and gaps, they behave quite differently with respect to other questions. The interested reader is referred to Sections 5.1 and 5.3.

Getting back to the concrete contents of the current chapter, let us briefly mention the most relevant credits. The hierarchy theorems (e.g., Theorem 4.3) were proven by Hartmanis and Stearns [114]. Gap theorems (e.g., Theorem 4.7) were proven by Borodin [47] (and are often referred to as Borodin's Gap Theorem). An axiomatic treatment of complexity measures was developed by Blum [38], who also proved corresponding speed-up theorems (e.g., Theorem 4.8, which is often referred to as Blum's Speed-up Theorem). A traditional presentation of all the aforementioned topics is provided in [123, Chap. 12], which also presents related techniques (e.g., "translation lemmas").

Exercises

Exercise 4.1: Let $F_n(s)$ denote the number of different Boolean functions over $\{0, 1\}^n$ that are computed by Boolean circuits of size s. Prove that, for any $s < 2^n$, it holds that $F_n(s) \geq 2^{s/O(\log s)}$ and $F_n(s) \leq s^{2s}$.

> **Guideline:** Any Boolean function $f : \{0, 1\}^\ell \to \{0, 1\}$ can be computed by a circuit of size $s_\ell = O(\ell \cdot 2^\ell)$. Thus, for every $\ell \leq n$, it holds that $F_n(s_\ell) \geq 2^{2^\ell} > 2^{s_\ell/O(\log s_\ell)}$. On the other hand, the number of circuits of size s is less than $2^s \cdot \binom{s^2}{s}$, where the second factor represents the number of possible choices of pairs of gates that feed any gate in the circuit.

Exercise 4.2 (advice can speed up computation): For every time-constructible function t, show that there exists a set S in $\mathrm{DTIME}(t^2) \setminus \mathrm{DTIME}(t)$ that can be decided in linear time using an advice of linear length (i.e., $S \in \mathrm{DTIME}(\ell)/\ell$ where $\ell(n) = O(n)$).

> **Guideline:** Starting with a set $S' \in \mathrm{DTIME}(T^2) \setminus \mathrm{DTIME}(T)$, where $T(m) = t(2^m)$, consider the set $S = \{x0^{2^{|x|}-|x|} : x \in S'\}$.

Exercise 4.3: Referring to any reasonable model of computation (and assuming that the input length is not given explicitly (unlike as in, e.g., Definition 10.10)), prove that any algorithm that has sub-linear time complexity actually has constant time complexity.

> **Guideline:** Consider the question of whether or not there exists an infinite set of strings S such that when invoked on any input $x \in S$ the algorithm reads all of x. Note that if S is infinite then the algorithm cannot have sub-linear time complexity, and prove that if S is finite then the algorithm has constant time complexity.

Exercise 4.4 (linear speed-up of Turing machine): Prove that any problem that can be solved by a two-tape Turing machine that has time complexity t can be solved by another two-tape Turing machine having time complexity t', where $t'(n) = O(n) + (t(n)/2)$.

> **Guideline:** Consider a machine that uses a larger alphabet, capable of encoding a constant (denoted c) number of symbols of the original machine, and thus capable of emulating c steps of the original machine in $O(1)$ steps, where the constant in the O-notation is a universal constant (independent of c). Note that the $O(n)$ term accounts for a preprocessing that converts the binary input to the work alphabet of the new machine (which encodes c input bits in one alphabet symbol). Thus, a similar result for a one-tape Turing machine seems to require an additive $O(n^2)$ term.

Exercise 4.5 (a direct proof of Corollary 4.4): Present a direct proof of Corollary 4.4 by using the ideas that underlie the proof of Theorem 4.3. Furthermore, prove that *if t steps of machine M* (in the model at hand) *can be emulated by $g(|M|, t)$ steps of a corresponding universal machine, then Corollary 4.4 holds for any $t_2(n) \geq g(\log n, t_1(n))$.*

> **Guideline:** The function $f \notin \text{DTIME}(t_1)$ is defined exactly as in the proof of Theorem 4.3, where here DTIME denotes the time-complexity classes of the model at hand. When upper-bounding the time complexity of f in this model, let $T_M(n)$ denote the number of steps used in emulating $t_1(n)$ steps of machine M, and note that $T_M(n) = g(|M|, t_1(n))$ and that $f \in \text{DTIME}(T')$, where $T'(n) = \max_{x \in \{0,1\}^n} \{T_{\mu(x)}(n)\}$.

Exercise 4.6 (tightening Corollary 4.4): Prove that, *for any reasonable and general model of computation, any constant $\varepsilon > 0$ and any "nice" function t* (e.g., either $t(n) = n^c$ for any constant $c \geq 1$ or $t(n) = 2^{c'n}$ for any constant $c' > 0$), *it holds that* $\text{DTIME}(t)$ *is strictly contained in* $\text{DTIME}(t^{1+\varepsilon})$.

> **Guideline:** Assuming toward the contradiction that $\text{DTIME}(t) = \text{DTIME}(f \circ t)$, for $f(k) = k^{1+\varepsilon}$, derive a contradiction to Corollary 4.4 by proving that for every constant i it holds that $\text{DTIME}(t) = \text{DTIME}(f^i \circ t)$, where f^i denotes i iterative applications of f. Note that proving that $\text{DTIME}(t) = \text{DTIME}(f \circ t)$ implies that $\text{DTIME}(f^{i-1} \circ t) = \text{DTIME}(f^i \circ t)$ (for every constant i) requires a "padding argument" (i.e., n-bit long inputs are encoded as m-bit long inputs such that $t(m) = (f^{i-1} \circ t)(n)$, and indeed $n \mapsto m = (t^{-1} \circ f^{i-1} \circ t)(n)$ should be computable in time $t(m)$).

Exercise 4.7 (constant amortized-time step-counter): A step-counter is an algorithm that runs for a number of steps that is specified in its input. Actually, such an algorithm may run for a somewhat larger number of steps but halt after issuing a number of "signals" as specified in its input, where these signals are defined as entering (and leaving) a designated state (of the algorithm). A step-counter may be run in parallel to another procedure in order to suspend the execution after a predetermined number of steps (of the other procedure) have elapsed. Show that there exists a simple deterministic machine that, on input n, halts after issuing n signals while making $O(n)$ steps.

> **Guideline:** A slightly careful implementation of the straightforward algorithm will do, when coupled with an "amortized" time-complexity analysis.

Exercise 4.8 (a natural set in $\mathcal{E} \setminus \mathcal{P}$): In continuation of the proof of Theorem 4.5, prove that the set $\{(\langle M \rangle, x, t) : u'(\langle M \rangle, x, t) \neq \bot\}$ is in $\mathcal{E} \setminus \mathcal{P}$, where $\mathcal{E} \stackrel{\text{def}}{=} \cup_c \text{DTIME}(e_c)$ and $e_c(n) = 2^{cn}$.

Exercise 4.9 (EXP-completeness): In continuation of Exercise 4.8, prove that every set in $\mathcal{EXP}$ is Karp-reducible to the set $\{(\langle M \rangle, x, t) : u'(\langle M \rangle, x, t) \neq \bot\}$.

Exercise 4.10: Prove that the two definitions of NTIME, presented in §4.2.1.3, are related up to logarithmic factors. Note the importance of the condition that V has linear (rather than polynomial) time complexity.

> **Guideline:** When emulating a non-deterministic machine by the verification procedure V, encode the non-deterministic choices in a "witness" string y such that $|y|$ is slightly larger than the number of steps taken by the original machine. Specifically, having $|y| = O(t \log t)$, where t denotes the number of steps taken by the original machine, allows for emulating the latter computation in linear time (i.e., linear in $|y|$).

Exercise 4.11: In continuation of Theorem 4.7, prove that *for every computable function* $t' : \mathbb{N} \to \mathbb{N}$ *and every non-decreasing computable function* $g : \mathbb{N} \to \mathbb{N}$ *there exists a non-decreasing computable function* $t : \mathbb{N} \to \mathbb{N}$ *such that* $t > t'$ *and* $\mathrm{DTIME}(t) = \mathrm{DTIME}(g(t))$.

Exercise 4.12: In continuation of Exercise 4.4, state and prove a linear speed-up result for space complexity, when using the standard definition of space as recalled in Section 4.3. (Note that this result does not hold with respect to "binary space complexity" as defined in Section 5.1.1.)

Exercise 4.13: Prove Theorem 4.9. As a warm-up, prove first a space-complexity version of Theorem 4.3.

> **Guideline:** Note that providing a space-efficient emulation of one machine by another machine is easier than providing an analogous time-efficient emulation.

Exercise 4.14 (space gap theorem): In continuation of Theorem 4.7, state and prove a gap theorem for space complexity.

CHAPTER FIVE

Space Complexity

Open are the double doors of the horizon; unlocked are its bolts.
Philip Glass, *Akhnaten,* Prelude

Whereas the number of steps taken during a computation is the primary measure of its efficiency, the amount of temporary storage used by the computation is also a major concern. Furthermore, in some settings, space is even more scarce than time.

In addition to the intrinsic interest in space complexity, its study provides an interesting perspective on the study of time complexity. For example, in contrast to the common conjecture by which $\mathcal{NP} \neq \text{co}\mathcal{NP}$, we shall see that analogous space-complexity classes (e.g., $\mathcal{NL}$) are closed under complementation (e.g., $\mathcal{NL} = \text{co}\mathcal{NL}$).

Summary: This chapter is devoted to the study of the space complexity of computations, while focusing on two rather extreme cases. The first case is that of algorithms having logarithmic space complexity. We view such algorithms as utilizing the naturally minimal amount of temporary storage, where the term "minimal" is used here in an intuitive (but somewhat inaccurate) sense, and note that logarithmic space complexity seems a more stringent requirement than polynomial time. The second case is that of algorithms having polynomial space complexity, which seems a strictly more liberal restriction than polynomial time complexity. Indeed, algorithms utilizing polynomial space can perform almost all the computational tasks considered in this book (e.g., the class $\mathcal{PSPACE}$ contains almost all complexity classes considered in this book).

We first consider algorithms of logarithmic space complexity. Such algorithms may be used for solving various natural search and decision problems, for providing reductions among such problems, and for yielding a strong notion of uniformity for Boolean circuits. The climax of this part is a log-space algorithm for exploring (undirected) graphs.

We then turn to non-deterministic computations, focusing on the complexity class $\mathcal{NL}$ that is captured by the problem of deciding directed connectivity of (directed) graphs. The climax of this part is a proof that $\mathcal{NL} = \text{co}\mathcal{NL}$, which may be paraphrased as a log-space reduction of directed unconnectivity to directed connectivity.

We conclude with a short discussion of the class $\mathcal{PSPACE}$, proving that the set of satisfiable quantified Boolean formulae is $\mathcal{PSPACE}$-complete (under polynomial-time reductions). We mention the similarity between this proof and the proof that $\text{NSPACE}(s) \subseteq \text{DSPACE}(O(s^2))$.

We stress that, as in the case of time complexity, the main results presented in this chapter hold for any reasonable model of computation.[1] In fact, when properly defined, space complexity is even more robust than time complexity. Still, for the sake of clarity, we often refer to the specific model of Turing machines.

Organization. Space complexity seems to behave quite differently from time complexity, and seems to require a different mind-set as well as auxiliary conventions. Some of the relevant issues are discussed in Section 5.1. We then turn to the study of logarithmic space complexity (see Section 5.2) and the corresponding non-deterministic version (see Section 5.3). Finally, we consider polynomial space complexity (see Section 5.4).

5.1. General Preliminaries and Issues

We start by discussing several very important conventions regarding space complexity (see Section 5.1.1). Needless to say, reading Section 5.1.1 is essential for the understanding of the rest of this chapter. (In contrast, the rather parenthetical Section 5.1.2 can be skipped with no significant loss.) We then discuss a variety of issues, highlighting the differences between space complexity and time complexity (see Section 5.1.3). In particular, we call the reader's attention to the composition lemmas (§5.1.3.1) and related reductions (§5.1.3.3) as well as to the obvious simulation result presented in §5.1.3.2 (i.e., $\text{DSPACE}(s) \subseteq \text{DTIME}(2^{O(s)})$). Lastly, in Section 5.1.4 we relate circuit size to space complexity by considering the space complexity of circuit evaluation.

5.1.1. Important Conventions

Space complexity is meant to measure the amount of *temporary storage* (i.e., computer's memory) used when performing a computational task. Since much of our focus will be on using an amount of memory that is sub-linear in the input length, it is important to use a model in which one can differentiate memory used for computation from memory used for storing the initial input and/or the final output. That is, we do not want to count the input and output themselves within the space of computation, and thus formulate that they are delivered on special devices that are not considered memory. On the other hand, we have to make sure that the input and output devices cannot be abused for providing work space (which is unaccounted for). This leads to the convention by which the input device (e.g., a designated input-tape of a multi-tape Turing machine) is read-only, whereas the output device (e.g., a designated output-tape of a such machine) is write-only. With this convention in place, we define space complexity as accounting only for the use of space on the other (storage) devices (e.g., the work-tapes of a multi-tape Turing machine).

Fixing a concrete model of computation (e.g., multi-tape Turing machines), we *denote by* $\text{DSPACE}(s)$ *the class of decision problems that are solvable in space complexity s. The*

---

[1]The only exceptions appear in Exercises 5.4 and 5.18, which refer to the notion of a *crossing sequence*. The use of this notion in these proofs presumes that the machine scans its storage devices in a serial manner. In contrast, we stress that the various notions of an instantaneous configuration do not assume such a machine model.

space complexity of search problems is defined analogously. Specifically, the standard definition *of space complexity* (see §1.2.3.5) *refers to the number of cells of the work-tape scanned by the machine on each input.* We prefer, however, an alternative definition, which provides a more accurate account of the actual storage. Specifically, the binary space complexity of a computation *refers to the number of bits that can be stored in these cells*, thus multiplying the number of cells by the logarithm of the finite set of work-tape symbols of the machine.[2]

The difference between the two aforementioned definitions is mostly immaterial because it amounts to a constant factor and we will usually discard such factors. Nevertheless, aside from being conceptually right, using the definition of *binary space complexity* facilitates some technical details (because the number of possible "instantaneous configurations" is explicitly upper-bounded in terms of binary space complexity, whereas its relation to the standard definition depends on the machine in question). Toward such applications, *we also count the finite state of the machine in its space complexity.* Furthermore, for the sake of simplicity, we also assume that the machine does not scan the input tape beyond the boundaries of the input, which are indicated by special symbols.[3]

We stress that individual locations of the (read-only) input-tape (or device) may be read several times. This is essential for many algorithms that use a sub-linear amount of space (because such algorithms may need to scan their input more than once while they cannot afford copying their input to their storage device). In contrast, rewriting on (the same location of) the write-only output-tape is inessential, and in fact can be eliminated at a relatively small cost (see Exercise 5.2).

Summary. Let us compile a list of the foregoing conventions. As stated, the first two items on the list are of crucial importance, while the rest are of technical nature (but do facilitate our exposition).

1. Space complexity discards the use of the input and output devices.
2. The input device is read-only and the output device is write-only.
3. We will usually refer to the binary space complexity of algorithms, where the binary space complexity of a machine M that uses the alphabet Σ, finite state set Q, and has standard space complexity S_M is defined as $(\log_2 |Q|) + (\log_2 |\Sigma|) \cdot S_M$. (Recall that S_M measures the number of cells of the temporary storage device that are used by M during the computation.)
4. We will assume that the machine does not scan the input device beyond the boundaries of the input.
5. We will assume that the machine does not rewrite to locations of its output device (i.e., it writes to each cell of the output device at most once).

5.1.2. On the Minimal Amount of Useful Computation Space

Bearing in mind that one of our main objectives is identifying natural subclasses of $\mathcal{P}$, we consider the question of what is the minimal amount of space that allows for meaningful computations. We note that regular sets [123, Chap. 2] are decidable by constant-space

---

[2]We note that, unlike in the context of time complexity, linear speedup (as in Exercise 4.12) does not seem to represent an actual saving in space resources. Indeed, time can be sped up by using stronger hardware (i.e., a Turing machine with a bigger work alphabet), but the actual space is not really affected by partitioning it into bigger chunks (i.e., using bigger cells). This fact is demonstrated when considering the *binary* space complexity of the two machines.

[3]As indicated by Exercise 5.1, little is lost by this natural assumption.

Turing machines and that this is all that the latter can decide (see, e.g., [123, Sec. 2.6]). It is tempting to say that sub-logarithmic space machines are not more useful than constant-space machines, because it *seems* impossible to allocate a sub-logarithmic amount of space. This wrong intuition is based on the presumption that the allocation of a non-constant amount of space requires explicitly computing the length of the input, which in turn requires logarithmic space. However, this presumption is wrong: The input itself (in case it is of a proper form) can be used to determine its length (and/or the allowed amount of space).[4] In fact, *for $\ell(n) = \log\log n$, the class* DSPACE($O(\ell)$) *is a proper superset of* DSPACE($O(1)$); see Exercise 5.3. On the other hand, it turns out that double-logarithmic space is indeed the smallest amount of space that is more useful than constant space (see Exercise 5.4); that is, *for $\ell(n) = \log\log n$, it holds that* DSPACE($o(\ell)$) = DSPACE($O(1)$).

In spite of the fact that some non-trivial things can be done in sub-logarithmic space complexity, the lowest space-complexity class that we shall study in depth is logarithmic space (see Section 5.2). As we shall see, this class is the natural habitat of several fundamental computational phenomena.

A parenthetical comment (or a side lesson). Before proceeding, let us highlight the fact that a naive presumption about arbitrary algorithms (i.e., that the use of a non-constant amount of space requires explicitly computing the length of the input) could have led us to a wrong conclusion. This demonstrates the danger in making "reasonable looking" (but unjustified) presumptions about *arbitrary* algorithms. We need to be fully aware of this danger whenever we seek impossibility results and/or complexity lower bounds.

5.1.3. Time Versus Space

Space complexity behaves very different from time complexity and indeed different paradigms are used in studying it. One notable example is provided by the context of algorithmic composition, discussed next.

5.1.3.1. Two Composition Lemmas
Unlike time, space can be reused; but, on the other hand, intermediate results of a computation cannot be recorded for free. These two conflicting aspects are captured in the following composition lemma.

Lemma 5.1 (naive composition): *Let $f_1 : \{0, 1\}^* \to \{0, 1\}^*$ and $f_2 : \{0, 1\}^* \times \{0, 1\}^* \to \{0, 1\}^*$ be computable in space s_1 and s_2, respectively.[5] Then f defined by $f(x) \overset{\text{def}}{=} f_2(x, f_1(x))$ is computable in space s such that*

$$s(n) = \max(s_1(n), s_2(n + \ell(n))) + \ell(n) + \delta(n),$$

---

[4]Indeed, for this approach to work, we should be able to detect the case that the input is not of the proper form (and do so within sub-logarithmic space).

[5]Here (and throughout the chapter) we assume, for simplicity, that all complexity bounds are monotonically non-decreasing. Another minor inaccuracy (in the text) is that we stated the complexity of the algorithm that computes f_2 in a somewhat non-standard way. Recall that by the standard convention, the complexity of an algorithm should be stated in terms of the length of its input, which in this case is a pair (x, y) that may be encoded as a string of length $|x| + |y| + 2\log_2 |x|$ (but not as a string of length $|x| + |y|$). An alternative convention is to state the complexity of such computations in terms of the length of both parts of the input (i.e., have $s : \mathbb{N} \times \mathbb{N} \to \mathbb{N}$ rather than $s : \mathbb{N} \to \mathbb{N}$), but we did not do this either.

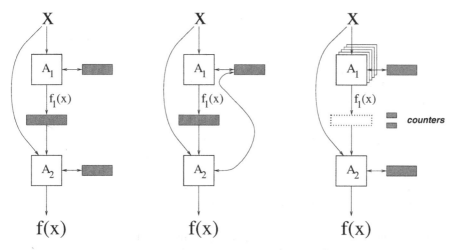

Figure 5.1: Three composition methods for space-bounded computation. The leftmost figure shows the trivial composition (which just invokes A_1 and A_2 without attempting to economize storage), the middle figure shows the naive composition (of Lemma 5.1), and the rightmost figure shows the emulative composition (of Lemma 5.2). In all figures the filled rectangles represent designated storage spaces. The dotted rectangle represents a virtual storage device.

where $\ell(n) = \max_{x \in \{0,1\}^n}\{|f_1(x)|\}$ and $\delta(n) = O(\log(\ell(n) + s_2(n + \ell(n)))) = o(s(n))$.

Lemma 5.1 is useful when ℓ is relatively small, but in many cases $\ell \gg \max(s_1, s_2)$. In these cases, the following composition lemma is more useful.

Proof: Indeed, $f(x)$ is computed by first computing and storing $f_1(x)$, and then reusing the space (used in the first computation) when computing $f_2(x, f_1(x))$. This explains the dominant terms in $s(n)$; that is, the term $\max(s_1(n), s_2(n + \ell(n)))$ accounts for the computations themselves (which reuse the same space), whereas the term $\ell(n)$ accounts for storing the intermediate result (i.e., $f_1(x)$). The extra term is due to implementation details. Specifically, the same storage device is used both for storing $f_1(x)$ and for providing work-space for the computation of f_2, which means that we need to maintain our location on each of these two parts (i.e., the location of the algorithm (that computes f_2) on $f_1(x)$ and its location on its own work space). (See further discussion at end of the proof of Lemma 5.2.) The extra $O(1)$ term accounts for the overhead involved in emulating two algorithms. ∎

Lemma 5.2 (emulative composition): *Let f_1, f_2, s_1, s_2, ℓ and f be as in Lemma 5.1. Then f is computable in space s such that*

$$s(n) = s_1(n) + s_2(n + \ell(n)) + O(\log(n + \ell(n))) + \delta(n),$$

where $\delta(n) = O(\log(s_1(n) + s_2(n + \ell(n)))) = o(s(n))$.

The alternative compositions are depicted in Figure 5.1 (which also shows the most straightforward composition that makes no attempt to economize space).

Proof: The idea is avoiding the storage of the temporary value of $f_1(x)$ by computing each of its bits ("on the fly") whenever this bit is needed for the computation of

f_2. That is, we do not start by computing $f_1(x)$, but rather start by computing $f_2(x, f_1(x))$ although we do not have some of the bits of the relevant input (i.e., the bits of $f_1(x)$). The missing bits will be computed (and recomputed) whenever we need them in the computation of $f_2(x, f_1(x))$. Details follow.

Let A_1 and A_2 be the algorithms (for computing f_1 and f_2, respectively) guaranteed in the hypothesis.[6] Then, on input $x \in \{0, 1\}^n$, we invoke algorithm A_2 (for computing f_2). Algorithm A_2 is invoked on a virtual input, and so when emulating each of its steps we should provide it with the relevant bit. Thus, we should also keep track of the location of A_2 on the imaginary (virtual) input-tape. Whenever A_2 seeks to read the ith bit of its input, where $i \in [n + \ell(n)]$, we provide A_2 with this bit by reading it from x if $i \leq n$ and invoke $A_1(x)$ otherwise. When invoking $A_1(x)$ we provide it with a virtual output-tape, which means that we get the bits of its output one by one and do not record them anywhere. Instead, we count until reaching the $(i - n)^{\text{th}}$ output-bit, which we then pass to A_2 (as the ith bit of $\langle x, f_1(x) \rangle$).

Note that while invoking $A_1(x)$, we suspend the execution of A_2 but keep its current configuration such that we can resume the execution (of A_2) once we get the desired bit. Thus, we need to allocate separate space for the computation of A_2 and for the computation of A_1. In addition, we need to allocate separate storage for maintaining the aforementioned counters (i.e., we use $\log_2(n + \ell(n))$ bits to hold the location of the input-bit currently read by A_2, and $\log_2 \ell(n)$ bits to hold the index of the output-bit currently produced in the current invocation of A_1).

A final (and tedious) issue is that our description of the composed algorithm refers to two storage devices, one for emulating the computation of A_1 and the other for emulating the computation of A_2. The issue is not the fact that the storage (of the composed algorithm) is partitioned between two devices, but rather that our algorithm uses two pointers (one per each of the two storage devices). In contrast, a ("fair") composition result should yield an algorithm (like A_1 and A_2) that uses a single storage device with a single pointer to locations on this device. Indeed, such an algorithm can be obtained by holding the two original pointers in memory; the additional $\delta(n)$ term accounts for this additional storage. ∎

Reflection. The algorithm presented in the proof of Lemma 5.2 is wasteful in terms of time: it recomputes $f_1(x)$ again and again (i.e., once per each access of A_2 to the second part of its input). Indeed, our aim was economizing on space and not on time (and the two goals may be conflicting (see, e.g., [59, Sec. 4.3])).

5.1.3.2. An Obvious Bound

The time complexity of an algorithm is essentially upper bounded by an exponential function in its space complexity. This is due to an upper bound on the number of possible instantaneous "configurations" of the algorithm (as formulated in the proof of Theorem 5.3), and to the fact that if the computation passes through the same configuration twice then it must loop forever.

Theorem 5.3: *If an algorithm A has* binary *space complexity s and halts on every input then it has time complexity t such that $t(n) \leq n \cdot 2^{s(n) + \log_2 s(n)}$.*

---

[6]We assume, for simplicity, that algorithm A_1 never rewrites on (the same location of) its write-only output-tape. As shown in Exercise 5.2, this assumption can be justified at an additive cost of $O(\log \ell(n))$. Alternatively, the idea presented in Exercise 5.2 can be incorporated directly in the current proof.

Note that for $s(n) = \Omega(\log n)$, the factor of n can be absorbed by $2^{O(s(n))}$, and so we may just write $t(n) = 2^{O(s(n))}$. Indeed, throughout this chapter (as in most of this book), we will consider only algorithms that halt on every input (see Exercise 5.5 for further discussion).

Proof: The proof refers to the notion of an *instantaneous configuration* (in a computation). Before starting, we warn the reader that this notion may be given different definitions, each tailored to the application at hand. All these definitions share the desire to specify *variable information* that together with some *fixed information* determines the next step of the computation being analyzed. In the current proof, we fix an algorithm A and an input x, and consider as variable the contents of the storage device (e.g., work-tape of a Turing machine as well as its finite state) and the machine's location on the input device and on the storage device. Thus, an instantaneous configuration of $A(x)$ consists of the latter three objects (i.e., the contents of the storage device and a pair of locations), and can be encoded by a binary string of length $\ell(|x|) = s(|x|) + \log_2 |x| + \log_2 s(|x|)$.[7]

The key observation is that the computation $A(x)$ cannot pass through the same instantaneous configuration twice, because otherwise the computation $A(x)$ passes through this configuration infinitely many times, which means that this computation does not halt. This observation is justified by noting that the instantaneous configuration, together with the fixed information (i.e., A and x), determines the next step of the computation. Thus, whatever happens (i steps) after the first time that the computation $A(x)$ passes through configuration γ will also happen (i steps) after the second time that the computation $A(x)$ passes through γ.

By the foregoing observation, we infer that the number of steps taken by A on input x is at most $2^{\ell(|x|)}$, because otherwise the same configuration will appear twice in the computation (which contradicts the halting hypothesis). The theorem follows. ∎

5.1.3.3. Subtleties Regarding Space-Bounded Reductions

Lemmas 5.1 and 5.2 suffice for the analysis of the effect of many-to-one reductions in the context of space-bounded computations. (By a many-to-one reduction of the function f to the function g, we mean a mapping π such that for every x it holds that $f(x) = g(\pi(x))$.)[8]

1. (In the spirit of Lemma 5.1:) If f is reducible to g via a many-to-one reduction that can be computed in space s_1, and g is computable in space s_2, then f is computable in space s such that $s(n) = \max(s_1(n), s_2(\ell(n))) + \ell(n) + \delta(n)$, where $\ell(n)$ denotes the maximum length of the image of the reduction when applied to some n-bit string and $\delta(n) = O(\log(\ell(n) + s_2(\ell(n)))) = o(s(n))$.

2. (In the spirit of Lemma 5.2:) For f and g as in Item 1, it follows that f is computable in space s such that $s(n) = s_1(n) + s_2(\ell(n)) + O(\log \ell(n)) + \delta(n)$, where $\delta(n) = O(\log(s_1(n) + s_2(\ell(n)))) = o(s(n))$.

---

[7]Here we rely on the fact that s is the binary space complexity (and not the standard space complexity); see summary item 3 in Section 5.1.1.

[8]This is indeed a special case of the setting of Lemmas 5.1 and 5.2 (obtained by letting $f_1 = \pi$ and $f_2(x, y) = g(y)$). However, the results claimed for this special case are better than those obtained by invoking the corresponding lemma (i.e., s_2 is applied to $\ell(n)$ rather than to $n + \ell(n)$).

Note that by Theorem 5.3, it holds that $\ell(n) \leq 2^{s_1(n)+\log_2 s_1(n)} \cdot n$. We stress the fact that ℓ is not upper-bounded by s_1 itself (as in the analogous case of time-bounded computation), but rather by $\exp(s_1)$.

Things get much more complicated when we turn to general (space-bounded) reductions, especially when referring to general reductions that make a non-constant number of queries. A preliminary issue is defining the space complexity of general reductions (i.e., of oracle machines). In the standard definition, the length of the queries and answers is not counted in the space complexity, but the queries of the reduction (resp., answers given to it) are written on (resp., read from) a special device that is write-only (resp., read-only) for the reduction (and read-only (resp., write-only) for the invoked oracle). Note that these convention are analogous to the conventions regarding input and output (as well as fit the definitions of space-bounded many-to-one reductions that were outlined in the foregoing items).

The foregoing conventions suffice for defining general space-bounded reductions. They also suffice for obtaining appealing composition results in some cases (e.g., for reductions that make a single query or, more generally, for the case of non-adaptive queries). But more difficulties arise when seeking composition results for general reductions, which may make several adaptive queries (i.e., queries that depend on the answers to prior queries). As we shall show next, in this case it is essential to *upper-bound the length of every query and/or every answer in terms of the length of the initial input*.

> **Teaching note:** The rest of the discussion is quite advanced and laconic (but is inessential to the rest of the chapter).

Recall that the complexity of the algorithm resulting from the composition of an oracle machine and an actual algorithm (which implements the oracle) depends on the length of the queries made by the oracle machine. For example, the space complexity of the foregoing compositions, which referred to single-query reductions, had an $s_2(\ell(n))$ term (where $\ell(n)$ represents the length of the query). In general, the length of the first query is upper-bounded by an exponential function in the space complexity of the oracle machine, but the same does not necessarily hold for subsequent queries, *unless some conventions are added to enforce it*. For example, consider a reduction that, on input x and access to an oracle f such that $|f(z)| = 2|z|$, invokes the oracle $|x|$ times, where each time it uses as a query the answer obtained to the previous query. This reduction uses constant space, but produces queries that are exponentially longer than the input, whereas the first query of any constant-space reduction has length that is linear in its input. This problem can be resolved by placing explicit bounds on the length of the queries that space-bounded reductions are allowed to make; for example, we may bound the length of all queries by the obvious bound that holds for the length of the first query (i.e., a reduction of space complexity s is allowed to make queries of length at most $2^{s(n)+\log_2 s(n)} \cdot n$).

With the aforementioned convention (or restriction) in place, let us consider the composition of *general* space-bounded reductions with a space-bounded implementation of the oracle. Specifically, we say that a reduction is (ℓ, ℓ')-restricted if, on input x, all oracle queries are of length at most $\ell(|x|)$ and the corresponding oracle answers are of length at most $\ell'(|x|)$. It turns out that naive composition (in the spirit of Lemma 5.1) remains useful, whereas the emulative composition of Lemma 5.2 breaks down (in the sense that it yields very weak results).

1. Following Lemma 5.1, we claim that *if Π can be solved in space s_1 when given (ℓ, ℓ')-restricted oracle access to Π' and Π' is solvable is space s_2, then Π is solvable in space s such that $s(n) = s_1(n) + s_2(\ell(n)) + \ell(n) + \ell'(n) + \delta(n)$, where $\delta(n) = O(\log(\ell(n) + \ell'(n) + s_1(n) + s_2(\ell(n)))) = o(s(n))$.* This claim is proved by using a naive emulation that allocates separate space for the reduction (i.e., oracle machine) itself, for the emulation of its query and answer devices, and for the algorithm solving Π'. Note, however, that here we cannot reuse the space of the reduction when running the algorithm that solves Π', because the reduction's computation continues after the oracle answer is obtained. The additional $\delta(n)$ term accounts for the various pointers of the oracle machine, which need to be stored when the algorithm that solves Π' is invoked (cf. last paragraph in the proof of Lemma 5.2).

   A related composition result is presented in Exercise 5.7. This composition refrains from storing the current oracle query (but does store the corresponding answer). It yields $s(n) = O(s_1(n) + s_2(\ell(n)) + \ell'(n) + \log \ell(n))$, which for $\ell(n) < 2^{O(s_1(n))}$ means $s(n) = O(s_1(n) + s_2(\ell(n)) + \ell'(n))$.

2. Turning to the approach underlying the proof of Lemma 5.2, we get into more serious trouble. Specifically, note that recomputing the answer to the ith query requires recomputing the query itself, which unlike in Lemma 5.2 is not the input to the reduction but rather depends on the answers to prior queries, which need to be recomputed as well. Thus, the space required for such an emulation is at least linear in the number of queries.

We note that one should not expect a general composition result (i.e., in the spirit of the foregoing Item 1) in which $s(n) = F(s_1(n), s_2(\ell(n))) + o(\min(\ell(n), \ell'(n)))$, where F is any function. One demonstration of this fact is implied by the observation that *any computation of space complexity s can be emulated by a constant-space $(2s, 2s)$-restricted reduction to a problem that is solvable in constant space* (see Exercise 5.9).

Non-adaptive reductions. Composition is much easier in the special case of non-adaptive reductions. Loosely speaking, the queries made by such reductions do not depend on the answers obtained to previous queries. Formulating this notion is not straightforward in the context of space-bounded computation. In the context of time-bounded computations, non-adaptive reductions are viewed as consisting of two algorithms: a query-generating algorithm, which generates a sequence of queries, and an evaluation algorithm, which given the input and a sequence of answers (obtained from the oracle) produces the actual output. The reduction is then viewed as invoking the query-generating algorithm (and recording the sequence of generated queries), making the designated queries (and recording the answers obtained), and finally invoking the evaluation algorithm on the sequence of answers. Using such a formulation raises the question of how to describe non-adaptive reductions of small space complexity. This question is resolved by designated special storage devices for the aforementioned sequences (of queries and answers) and postulating that these devices can be used only as described. For details, see Exercise 5.8. Note that non-adaptivity resolves most of the difficulties discussed in the foregoing. In particular, the length of each query made by a non-adaptive reduction is upper-bounded by an exponential in the space complexity of the reduction (just as in the case of single-query reductions). Furthermore, composing such reductions with an algorithm that implements the oracle is not more involved than doing the same for single-query reductions. Thus, as shown in Exercise 5.8, *if Π is reducible to Π' via a non-adaptive reduction of space* *complexity s_1 that makes queries of length at most ℓ and Π' is solvable is space s_2, then Π is solvable in space s such that $s(n) = O(s_1(n) + s_2(\ell(n)))$. (Indeed $\ell(n) < 2^{O(s_1(n))} \cdot n$ always hold.)*

Reductions to decision problems. Composition in the case of reductions to decision problems is also easier, because also in this case the length of each query made by the reduction is upper-bounded by an exponential in the space complexity of the reduction (see Exercise 5.10). Thus, applying the semi-naive composition result of Exercise 5.7 (mentioned in the foregoing Item 1) is very appealing. It follows that *if Π can be solved in space s_1 when given oracle access to a decision problem that is solvable is space s_2, then Π is solvable in space s such that $s(n) = O(s_1(n) + s_2(2^{s_1(n)+\log(n \cdot s_1(n))}))$.* Indeed, if the length of each query in such a reduction is upper-bounded by ℓ, then we may use $s(n) = O(s_1(n) + s_2(\ell(n)))$. These results, however, are of limited interest, because it seems difficult to construct *small-space* reductions of search problems to decision problems (see §5.1.3.4).

We mention that an alternative notion of space-bounded reductions is discussed in §5.2.4.2. This notion is more cumbersome and more restricted, but in some cases it allows recursive composition with a smaller overhead than offered by the aforementioned composition results.

5.1.3.4. Search Versus Decision

Recall that in the setting of time complexity we allowed ourselves to focus on decision problems, since search problems could be efficiently reduced to decision problems. Unfortunately, these reductions (e.g., the ones underlying Theorem 2.10 and Proposition 2.15) are not adequate for the study of (small) space complexity. Recall that these reductions extend the currently *stored prefix of a solution* by making a query to an adequate decision problem. Thus, these reductions have space complexity that is lower-bounded by the length of the solution, which makes them irrelevant for the study of small-space complexity.

In light of the foregoing, the study of the space complexity of search problems cannot be "reduced" to the study of the space complexity of decision problems. Thus, while much of our exposition will focus on decision problems, we will keep an eye on the corresponding search problems. Indeed, in many cases, the ideas developed in the study of the decision problems can be adapted to the study of the corresponding search problems (see, e.g., Exercise 5.17).

5.1.3.5. Complexity Hierarchies and Gaps

Recall that more space allows for more computation (see Theorem 4.9), provided that the space-bounding function is "nice" in an adequate sense. Actually, the proofs of space-complexity hierarchies and gaps are simpler than the analogous proofs for time complexity, because emulations are easier in the context of space-bounded algorithms (cf. Section 4.3).

5.1.3.6. Simultaneous Time-Space Complexity

Recall that, for space complexity that is at least logarithmic, the time of a computation is always upper-bounded by an exponential function in the space complexity (see Theorem 5.3). Thus, polylogarithmic space complexity may extend beyond polynomial time, and it make sense to define a class that consists of all decision problems that may be solved by a polynomial-time algorithm of polylogarithmic space complexity. This class, denoted $\mathcal{SC}$, is indeed a natural subclass of $\mathcal{P}$ (and contains the class $\mathcal{L}$, which is defined in Section 5.2.1).[9]

In general, one may define $\text{DTISP}(t, s)$ as the class of decision problems solvable by an algorithm that has time complexity t and space complexity s. Note that $\text{DTISP}(t, s) \subseteq \text{DTIME}(t) \cap \text{DSPACE}(s)$ and that a strict containment may hold. We mention that $\text{DTISP}(\cdot, \cdot)$ provides the arena for the only known absolute (and highly non-trivial) lower bound regarding $\mathcal{NP}$; see [79]. We also note that lower bounds on time-space trade-offs (see, e.g., [59, Sec. 4.3]) may be stated as referring to the classes $\text{DTISP}(\cdot, \cdot)$.

5.1.4. Circuit Evaluation

Recall that Theorem 3.1 asserts the existence of a polynomial-time algorithm that, given a circuit $C : \{0, 1\}^n \to \{0, 1\}^m$ and an n-bit long string x, returns $C(x)$. For circuits of bounded fan-in, the space complexity of such an algorithm can be made linear in the depth of the circuit (which may be logarithmic in its size). This is obtained by the following DFS-type algorithm.

The algorithm (recursively) determines the value of a gate in the circuit by first determining the value of its first incoming edge and next determining the value of the second incoming edge. Thus, the recursive procedure, started at each output terminal of the circuit, needs only store the path that leads to the currently processed vertex as well as the temporary values computed for each ancestor. Note that this path is determined by indicating, for each vertex on the path, whether we currently process its first or second incoming edge. In the case that we currently process the vertex's second incoming edge, we need also store the value computed for its first incoming edge.

The temporary storage used by the foregoing algorithm, on input (C, x), is thus $2d_C + O(\log |x| + \log |C(x)|)$, where d_C denotes the depth of C. The first term in the space bound accounts for the core activity of the algorithm (i.e., the recursion), whereas the other terms account for the overhead involved in manipulating the initial input and final output (i.e., assigning the bits of x to the corresponding input terminals of C and scanning all output terminals of C).

Note. Further connections between circuit complexity and space complexity are mentioned in Section 5.2.3 and §5.3.2.2.

5.2. Logarithmic Space

Although Exercise 5.3 asserts that "there is life below log-space," logarithmic space seems to be the smallest amount of space that supports interesting computational phenomena. In particular, logarithmic space is required for merely maintaining an auxiliary counter that holds a position in the input, which seems required in many computations. On the other hand, logarithmic space suffices for solving many natural computational problems, for establishing reductions among many natural computational problems, and for a stringent notion of uniformity (of families of Boolean circuits). Indeed, an important feature of logarithmic space computations is that they are a natural subclass of the polynomial-time computations (see Theorem 5.3).

---

[9]We also mention that $\mathcal{BPL} \subseteq \mathcal{SC}$, where $\mathcal{BPL}$ is defined in §6.1.5.1 and the result is proved in Section 8.4 (see Theorem 8.23).

5.2.1. The Class L

Focusing on decision problems, we denote by $\mathcal{L}$ the class of decision problems that are solvable by algorithms of logarithmic space complexity; that is, $\mathcal{L} = \cup_c \mathrm{DSPACE}(\ell_c)$, where $\ell_c(n) \stackrel{\text{def}}{=} c \log_2 n$. Note that, by Theorem 5.3, $\mathcal{L} \subseteq \mathcal{P}$. As hinted, many natural computational problems are in $\mathcal{L}$ (see Exercises 5.6 and 5.12 as well as Section 5.2.4). On the other hand, *it is widely believed that $\mathcal{L} \neq \mathcal{P}$.*

5.2.2. Log-Space Reductions

Another class of important log-space computations is the class of *logarithmic space reductions*. In light of the subtleties discussed in §5.1.3.3, we focus on the case of many-to-one reductions. Analogously to the definition of Karp-reductions (Definition 2.11), we say that f is a log-space (many-to-one) reduction of S to S' if f is log-space computable and, for every x, it holds that $x \in S$ if and only if $f(x) \in S'$. By Lemma 5.2 (and Theorem 5.3), *if S is log-space reducible to some set in $\mathcal{L}$ then $S \in \mathcal{L}$.* Similarly, one can define a log-space variant of Levin-reductions (Definition 2.12). Both types of reductions are transitive (see Exercise 5.11). Note that Theorem 5.3 applies in this context and implies that these reductions run in polynomial time. Thus, the notion of a log-space many-to-one reduction is a special case of a Karp-reduction.

We observe that all known Karp-reductions establishing NP-completeness results are actually log-space reductions. This is easily verifiable in the case of the reductions presented in Section 2.3.3 (as well as in Section 2.3.2). For example, consider the generic reduction to CSAT presented in the proof of Theorem 2.21: The constructed circuit is "highly uniform" and can be easily constructed in logarithmic space (see also Section 5.2.3). A degeneration of this reduction suffices for proving that every problem in $\mathcal{P}$ is log-space reducible to the problem of evaluating a given circuit on a given input. Recall that the latter problem is in $\mathcal{P}$, and thus we may say that it is *P-complete under log-space reductions*.

Theorem 5.4 (The complexity of Circuit Evaluation): *Let CEVL denote the set of pairs (C, α) such that C is a Boolean circuit and $C(\alpha) = 1$. Then CEVL is in $\mathcal{P}$ and every problem in $\mathcal{P}$ is log-space Karp-reducible to CEVL.*

Proof Sketch: Recall that the observation underlying the proof of Theorem 2.21 (as well as the proof of Theorem 3.6) is that the computation of a Turing machine can be emulated by a ("highly uniform") family of circuits. In the proof of Theorem 2.21, we hard-wired the input to the reduction (denoted x) into the circuit (denoted C_x) and introduced input terminals corresponding to the bits of the NP-witness (denoted y). In the current context we leave x as an input to the circuit, while noting that the auxiliary NP-witness does not exist (or has length zero). Thus, the reduction from $S \in \mathcal{P}$ to CEVL maps the instance x (for S) to the pair $(C_{|x|}, x)$, where $C_{|x|}$ is a circuit that emulates the computation of the machine that decides membership in S (on any $|x|$-bit long input). For the sake of future use (in Section 5.2.3), we highlight the fact that $C_{|x|}$ can be constructed by a log-space machine that is given the input $1^{|x|}$. $\qquad\square$

The impact of P-completeness under log-space reductions. Indeed, Theorem 5.4 implies that $\mathcal{L} \neq \mathcal{P}$ if and only if CEVL $\notin \mathcal{L}$. Other natural problems were proved to have the same property (i.e., being P-complete under log-space reductions; cf. [60]).

Log-space reductions are used to define completeness with respect to other classes that are assumed to extend beyond $\mathcal{L}$. This restriction of the power of the reduction is definitely needed when the class of interest is contained in $\mathcal{P}$ (e.g., $\mathcal{NL}$; see Section 5.3.2). In general, we say that a problem Π is $\mathcal{C}$-complete under log-space reductions if Π is in $\mathcal{C}$ and every problem in $\mathcal{C}$ is log-space (many-to-one) reducible to Π. In such a case, if $\Pi \in \mathcal{L}$ then $\mathcal{C} \subseteq \mathcal{L}$.

As in the case of polynomial-time reductions, we wish to stress that the relevance of log-space reductions extends beyond being a tool for defining complete problems.

5.2.3. Log-Space Uniformity and Stronger Notions

Recall that a basic notion of uniformity of a family of circuits $(C_n)_{n \in \mathbb{N}}$, introduced in Definition 3.3, requires the existence of an algorithm that on input n outputs the description of C_n, while using time that is polynomial in the size of C_n. Strengthening Definition 3.3, we say that a family of circuits $(C_n)_{n \in \mathbb{N}}$ is log-space uniform if there exists an algorithm that on input n outputs C_n while using space that is logarithmic in the size of C_n. As implied by the following Theorem 5.5 (and implicitly proved in the foregoing Theorem 5.4), *the computation of any polynomial-time algorithm can be emulated by a log-space uniform family of* (bounded fan-in) *polynomial-size circuits*. On the other hand, in continuation of Section 5.1.4, we note that *log-space uniform circuits of bounded fan-in and logarithmic depth can be emulated by an algorithm of logarithmic space complexity* (i.e., "log-space uniform $\mathcal{NC}^1$" is in $\mathcal{L}$; see Exercise 5.12).

As mentioned in Section 3.1.1, stronger notions of uniformity have also been considered. Specifically, in an analogy to the discussion in §E.2.1.2, we say that $(C_n)_{n \in \mathbb{N}}$ has a strongly explicit construction if there exists an algorithm that runs in polynomial time and linear space such that, on input n and v, the algorithm returns the label of vertex v in C_n as well as the list of its children (or an indication that v is not a vertex in C_n). Note that if $(C_n)_{n \in \mathbb{N}}$ has a strongly explicit construction then it is log-space uniform, because the length of the description of a vertex in C_n is logarithmic in the size of C_n. The proof of Theorem 5.4 actually establishes the following.

Theorem 5.5 (strongly uniform circuits emulating $\mathcal{P}$): *For every polynomial-time algorithm A there exists a strongly explicit construction of a family of polynomial-size circuits $(C_n)_{n \in \mathbb{N}}$ such that for every x it holds that $C_{|x|}(x) = A(x)$.*

Proof Sketch: As noted already, the circuits $(C_{|x|})_{|x|}$ (considered in the proof of Theorem 5.4) are highly uniform. In particular, the underlying (directed) graph consists of constant-size gadgets that are arranged in an array and are only connected to adjacent gadgets (see the proof of Theorem 2.21). $\qquad \square$

5.2.4. Undirected Connectivity

Exploring a graph (e.g., toward determining its connectivity) is one of the most basic and ubiquitous computational tasks regarding graphs. The standard graph-exploration algorithms (e.g., BFS and DFS) require temporary storage that is linear in the number of vertices. In contrast, the algorithm presented in this section uses temporary storage that is only logarithmic in the number of vertices. In addition to demonstrating the power of log-space computation, this algorithm (or rather its actual implementation) provides a taste of the type of issues arising in the design of sophisticated log-space algorithms.

The intuitive task of "exploring a graph" is captured by the task of *deciding whether a given graph is connected*.[10] In addition to the intrinsic interest in this natural computational problem, we mention that it is computationally equivalent (under log-space reductions) to numerous other computational problems (see, e.g., Exercise 5.16). We note that some related computational problems seem actually harder; for example, determining directed connectivity (in directed graphs) captures the essence of the class $\mathcal{NL}$ (see Section 5.3.2). In view of this state of affairs, we emphasize the fact that the computational problem considered here refers to undirected graphs by calling it undirected connectivity.

Theorem 5.6: *Deciding undirected connectivity* (UCONN) *is in* $\mathcal{L}$

The algorithm is based on the fact that UCONN is easy in the special case that the graph consists of a collection of constant degree expanders.[11] In particular, if the graph has constant degree and logarithmic diameter then it can be explored using a logarithmic amount of space (which is used for determining a generic path from a fixed starting vertex).[12]

Needless to say, the input graph does not necessarily consist of a collection of constant degree expanders. The main idea is then to transform the input graph into one that does satisfy the aforementioned condition, while preserving the number of connected components of the graph. Furthermore, the key point is performing such a transformation in logarithmic space. The rest of this section is devoted to the description of such a transformation. We first present the basic approach and next turn to the highly non-trivial implementation details.

Teaching note: We recommend leaving the actual proof of Theorem 5.6 (i.e., the rest of this section) for advanced reading. The main reason is its heavy dependence on technical material that is beyond the scope of a course in Complexity Theory.

Getting started. We first note that it is easy to transform the input graph $G_0 = (V_0, E_0)$ into a constant-degree graph G_1 that preserves the number of connected components in G_0. Specifically, each vertex $v \in V$ having degree $d(v)$ (in G_0) is represented by a cycle C_v of $d(v)$ vertices (in G_1), and each edge $\{u, v\} \in E_0$ is replaced by an edge having one end-point on the cycle C_v and the other end-point on the cycle C_u such that each vertex in G_1 has degree three (i.e., has two cycle edges and a single intra-cycle edge). This transformation can be performed using logarithmic space, and thus (relying on Lemma 5.2) we assume that the input graph has degree three.

---

[10]See Appendix G.1 for basic terminology.

[11]At this point, the reader may think that expanders are merely graphs of logarithmic diameter. At a later stage, we will rely on a basic familiarity with a specific definition of expanders as well as with a specific technique for constructing them. The relevant material is contained in Appendix E.2.

[12]Indeed, this is analogous to the circuit-evaluation algorithm of Section 5.1.4, where the circuit depth corresponds to the diameter and the bounded fan-in corresponds to the constant degree. For further details, see Exercise 5.13.

Our goal is to transform this graph into a collection of expanders, while maintaining the number of connected components. In fact, *we shall describe the transformation while pretending that the graph is connected, while noting that otherwise the transformation acts separately on each connected component.*

A couple of technicalities. For a constant integer $d > 2$ determined so as to satisfy some additional condition, we may assume that the input graph is actually d^2-regular (albeit is not necessarily simple). Furthermore, we shall assume that this graph is not bipartite. Both assumptions can be justified by augmenting the aforementioned construction of a 3-regular graph by adding $d^2 - 3$ self-loops to each vertex.

Prerequisites. Evidently, the notion of an expander graph plays a key role in the afore-mentioned transformation. For a brief review of this notion, the reader is referred to Appendix E.2. In particular, we assume familiarity with the algebraic definition of ex-panders (as presented in §E.2.1.1). Furthermore, the transformation relies heavily on the *Zig-Zag product*, defined in §E.2.2.2, and the following exposition assumes familiarity with this definition.

5.2.4.1. The Basic Approach

Recall that our goal is to transform G_1 into an expander. The transformation is grad-ual and consists of logarithmically many iterations, where in each iteration an adequate expansion parameter doubles while the graph becomes a constant factor larger and main-tains the degree bound. The (expansion) parameter of interest is the relative eigenvalue gap (see §E.2.1.1).[13] A constant value of this parameter indicates that the graph is an expander. Initially, this parameter is lower-bounded by $\Omega(n^{-2})$, where n is the size of the graph. Since this parameter doubles in each iteration, after logarithmically many itera-tions this parameter is lower-bounded by a constant (and hence the current graph is an expander).

The crux of the aforementioned gradual transformation is the transformation that takes place in each single iteration. This transformation is supposed to double the expansion parameter while maintaining the graph's degree and increasing the number of vertices by a constant factor. The transformation combines the (standard) graph-powering oper-ation and the *Zig-Zag product* presented in §E.2.2.2. Specifically, for adequate positive integers d and c, we start with the d^2-regular graph $G_1 = (V_1, E_1)$, and go through a logarithmic number of iterations letting $G_{i+1} = G_i^c \textcircled{z} G$ for $i = 1, \ldots, t - 1$, where G is a fixed d-regular graph with d^{2c} vertices. That is, in each iteration, we raise the cur-rent graph (i.e., G_i) to the power c and combine the resulting graph (d^{2c}-regular) with the fixed (d^{2c}-vertex) graph G using the Zig-Zag product. Thus, G_{i+1} is a d^2-regular graph with $d^{i \cdot 2c} \cdot |V_1|$ vertices, where this invariant is preserved by definition of the Zig-Zag product (i.e., the Zig-Zag product of a d^{2c}-regular graph $G' = (V', E')$ with the d-regular graph G (which has d^{2c} vertices) yields a d^2-regular graph with $d^{2c} \cdot |V'|$ vertices).

The analysis of the improvement in the expansion parameter (i.e., the relative eigen-value gap), denoted $\delta(\cdot) \overset{\text{def}}{=} 1 - \bar{\lambda}(\cdot)$, relies on Eq. (E.11). Recall that Eq. (E.11) implies

---

[13]Recall that the eigenvalue gap of a regular graph is the difference between the graph's degree (i.e., the graph's largest eigenvalue) and the absolute value of each of the other eigenvalues. The relative eigenvalue bound, denoted $\bar{\lambda}$, is the eigenvalue bound divided by the graph's degree.

that if $\bar{\lambda}(G) < 1/2$ then $1 - \bar{\lambda}(G' \textcircled{z} G) > (1 - \bar{\lambda}(G'))/3$. Thus, the fixed graph G is selected such that $\bar{\lambda}(G) < 1/2$, which requires a sufficiently large constant d. Thus, we have

$$\delta(G_{i+1}) = 1 - \bar{\lambda}(G_i^c \textcircled{z} G) > \frac{1 - \bar{\lambda}(G_i^c)}{3} = \frac{1 - \bar{\lambda}(G_i)^c}{3}$$

whereas, for a sufficiently large constant integer $c > 0$, it holds that $1 - \bar{\lambda}(G_i)^c >$ $\min(6 \cdot (1 - \bar{\lambda}(G_i)), 1/2)$.[14] It follows that $\delta(G_{i+1}) > \min(2\delta(G_i), 1/6)$. Thus, setting $t = O(\log|V_1|)$ and using $\delta(G_1) = 1 - \bar{\lambda}(G_1) = \Omega(|V_1|^{-2})$, we obtain $\delta(G_t) > 1/6$ as desired.

Needless to say, a "detail" of crucial importance is the ability to transform G_1 into G_t via a log-space computation. Indeed, the transformation of G_i to G_{i+1} can be performed in logarithmic space (see Exercise 5.14), but we need to compose a logarithmic number of such transformations. Unfortunately, the standard composition lemmas for space-bounded algorithms involve overhead that we cannot afford.[15] Still, taking a closer look at the transformation of G_i to G_{i+1}, one may note that it is highly structured, and in some sense it can be implemented in constant space and supports a stronger composition result that incurs only a constant amount of storage per iteration. The resulting implementation (of the iterative transformation of G_1 to G_t) and the underlying formalism will be the subject of §5.2.4.2. (An alternative implementation, provided in [190], can be obtained by unraveling the composition.)

5.2.4.2. The Actual Implementation

The space-efficient implementation of the iterative transformation outlined in §5.2.4.1 is based on the observation that we do not need to explicitly construct the various graphs but merely provide "oracle access" to them. This observation is crucial when applied to the intermediate graphs; that is, rather than constructing G_{i+1}, when given G_i as input, we show how to provide oracle access to G_{i+1} (i.e., answer "neighborhood queries" regarding G_{i+1}) when given oracle access to G_i (i.e., an oracle that answers neighborhood queries regarding G_i). This means that we view G_i and G_{i+1} (or rather their incidence lists) as functions (to be evaluated) rather than as strings (to be printed), and show how to reduce the task of finding neighbors in G_{i+1} (i.e., evaluating the "incidence function" at a given vertex) to the task of finding neighbors in G_i.

A clarifying discussion. Note that here we are referring to oracle machines that access a finite oracle, which represents a *finite variable object* (which, in turn, is an instance of some computational problem). Such a machine provides access to a complex object by using its access to a more basic object, which is represented by the oracle. Specifically, such a machine gets an input, which is a "query" regarding the complex object (i.e, the object that the machine tries to emulate), and produces an output (which is the answer to the query). Analogously, these machines make queries, which are queries

---

[14]Consider the following two cases: In the case that $\bar{\lambda}(G_i) < (1 - (1/c))$, show that $1 - \bar{\lambda}(G_i)^c > 1/2$. Otherwise, let $\varepsilon \stackrel{\text{def}}{=} 1 - \bar{\lambda}(G_i)$, and using $\varepsilon \leq 1/c$ show that $1 - \bar{\lambda}(G_i)^c > c\varepsilon/2$.

[15]We cannot afford the naive composition (of Lemma 5.1), because it causes an overhead linear in the size of the intermediate result. As for the emulative composition (of Lemma 5.2), it sums up the space complexities of the composed algorithms (not to mention adding another logarithmic term), which would result in a log-squared bound on the space complexity.

regarding another object (i.e., the one represented in the oracle), and obtain corresponding answers.[16]

Like in §5.1.3.3, queries are made via a special write-only device and the answers are read from a corresponding read-only device, where the use of these devices is not charged in the space complexity. With these conventions in place, we claim that neighborhoods in the d^2-regular graph G_{i+1} can be computed by a constant-space oracle machine that is given oracle access to the d^2-regular graph G_i. That is, letting $g_i : V_i \times [d^2] \to V_i \times [d^2]$ (resp., $g_{i+1} : V_{i+1} \times [d^2] \to V_{i+1} \times [d^2]$) denote the edge-rotation function[17] of G_i (resp., G_{i+1}), we have:

Claim 5.7: *There exists a constant-space oracle machine that evaluates g_{i+1} when given oracle access to g_i, where the state of the machine is counted in the space complexity.*

Proof Sketch: We first show that the two basic operations that underlie the definition of G_{i+1} (i.e., powering and Zig-Zag product with a constant graph) can be performed in constant space.

The edge-rotation function of G_i^2 (i.e., the square of the graph G_i) can be evaluated at any desired pair, by evaluating the edge-rotation function of G_i twice, and using a constant amount of space. Specifically, given $v \in V_i$ and $j_1, j_2 \in [d^2]$, we compute $g_i(g_i(v, j_1), j_2)$, which is the edge rotation of $(v, \langle j_1, j_2 \rangle)$ in G_i^2, as follows. First, making the query (v, j_1), we obtain the edge rotation of (v, j_1), denoted (u, k_1). Next, making the query (u, j_2), we obtain (w, k_2), and finally we output $(w, \langle k_2, k_1 \rangle)$. We stress that we only use the temporary storage to record k_1, *whereas u is directly copied from the oracle answer device to the oracle query device.* Accounting also for a constant number of states needed for the various stages of the foregoing activity, we conclude that graph squaring can be performed in constant space. The argument extends to the task of raising the graph to any constant power.

Turning to the Zig-Zag product (of an arbitrary regular graph G' with a fixed graph G), we note that the corresponding edge-rotation function can be evaluated in constant space (given oracle access to the edge-rotation function of G'). This follows directly from Eq. (E.9), noting that the latter calls for a single evaluation of the edge-rotation function of G' and two simple modifications that only depend on the constant-size graph G (and affect a constant number of bits of the relevant strings). Again, using the fact that it suffices to copy vertex names from the input to the oracle query device (or from the oracle answer device to the output), we conclude that the aforementioned activity can be performed using constant space.

The argument extends to a sequential composition of a constant number of operations of the aforementioned type (i.e., graph squaring and Zig-Zag product with a constant graph). ☐

---

[16]Indeed, the current setting (in which the oracle represents a *finite variable object*, which in turn is an instance of some computational problem) is different from the standard setting, where the oracle represents a *fixed computational problem*. Still the mechanism (and/or operations) of these two types of oracle machines is the same: They both get an input (which here is a "query" regarding a variable object rather than an instance of a fixed computational problem) and produce an output (which here is the answer to the query rather than a "solution" for the given instance). Analogously, these machines make queries (which here are queries regarding another variable object rather than queries regarding another fixed computational problem) and obtain corresponding answers.

[17]Recall that the edge-rotation function of a graph maps the pair (v, j) to the pair (u, k) if vertex u is the jth neighbor of vertex v and v is the kth neighbor of u (see §E.2.2.2).

Recursive composition. Using Claim 5.7, we wish to obtain a $O(t)$-space oracle machine that evaluates g_t by making oracle calls to g_1, where $t = O(\log |V_1|)$. Such an oracle machine will yield a log-space transformation of G_1 to G_t (by evaluating g_t at all possible values). It is tempting to hope that an adequate composition lemma, when applied to Claim 5.7, will yield the desired $O(t)$-space oracle machine (reducing the evaluation of g_t to g_1). This is indeed the case, except that the adequate composition lemma is still to be developed (as we do next).

We first note that applying a naive composition (as in Lemma 5.1) amounts to an additive overhead of $O(\log |V_1|)$ *per each composition*. But we cannot afford more than an amortized constant additive overhead per composition. Applying the emulative composition (as in Lemma 5.2) causes a multiplicative overhead per each composition, which is certainly unaffordable. The composition developed next is a variant of the naive composition, which is beneficial in the context of recursive calls. The basic idea is deviating from the paradigm that allocates *separate* input/output and query devices to *each level in the recursion*, and combining all these devices in a single ("global") device that will be used by all levels of the recursion. That is, rather than following the "structured programming" methodology of using locally designated space for passing information to the subroutine, we use the "bad programming" methodology of passing information through global variables. (As usual, this notion is formulated by referring to the model of multi-tape Turing machine, but it can be formulated in any other reasonable model of computation.)

Definition 5.8 (global-tape oracle machines): *A* global-tape oracle machine *is defined as an oracle machine* (cf. Definition 1.11)*, except that the input-, output-, and oracle tapes are replaced by a single* global-tape. *In addition, the machine has a constant number of work-tapes, called the* local-tapes. *The machine obtains its input from the global-tape, writes each query on this very tape, obtains the corresponding answer from this tape, and writes its final output on this tape.* (We stress that, as a result of invoking the oracle f, the contents of the global-tape changes from q to $f(q)$.)[18] *The space complexity of such a machine is stated when referring separately to its use of the global-tape and to its use of the local-tapes.*

Clearly, any ordinary oracle machine can be converted into an equivalent global-tape oracle machine. The resulting machine uses a global-tape of length at most $n + \ell + m$, where n denotes the length of the input, ℓ denote the length of the longest query or oracle answer, and m denotes the length of the output. However, combining these three different tapes into one global-tape seems to require holding separate pointers for each of the original tapes, which means that the local-tape has to store three corresponding counters (in addition to storing the original work-tape). Thus, the resulting machine uses a local-tape of length $w + \log_2 n + \log_2 \ell + \log_2 m$, where w denotes the space complexity of the original machine and the additional logarithmic terms (which are logarithmic in the length of the global-tape) account for the aforementioned counters.

Fortunately, the aforementioned counters can be avoided in the case that the original oracle machine can be described as an iterative sequence of transformations (i.e., the input is transformed to the first query, and the ith answer is transformed to the $i + 1^{\text{st}}$ query or

---

[18]This means that the prior contents of the global-tape (i.e., the query q) is lost (i.e., it is replaced by the answer $f(q)$). Thus, if we wish to keep such prior contents then we need to copy it to a local-tape. We also stress that, according to the standard oracle invocation conventions, the head location after the oracle responds is at the leftmost cell of the global-tape.

to the output, all while maintaining auxiliary information on the work-tape). Indeed, the machine presented in the proof of Claim 5.7 has this form, and thus it can be implemented by a global-tape oracle machine that uses a global-tape not longer than its input and a local-tape of constant length (rather than a local-tape of length that is logarithmic in the length of the global-tape).

Claim 5.9 (Claim 5.7, revisited): *There exists a global-tape oracle machine that evaluates g_{i+1} when given oracle access to g_i, while using global-tape of length $\log_2(d^2 \cdot |V_{i+1}|)$ and a local-tape of constant length.*

Proof Sketch: Following the proof of Claim 5.7, we merely indicate the exact use of the two tapes. For example, recall that the edge-rotation function of the square of G_i is evaluated at $(v, \langle j_1, j_2 \rangle)$ by evaluating the edge-rotation function of the original graph first at (v, j_1) and then at (u, j_2), where $(u, k_1) = g_i(v, j_1)$. This means the global-tape machine first reads $(v, \langle j_1, j_2 \rangle)$ from the global-tape and replaces it by the query (v, j_1), while storing j_2 on the local-tape. Thus, the machine merely deletes a constant number of bits from the global-tape (and leaves its prefix intact). After invoking the oracle, the machine copies k_1 from the global-tape (which currently holds (u, k_1)) to its local-tape, and copies j_2 from its local-tape to the global-tape (such that it contains (u, j_2)). After invoking the oracle for the second time, the global-tape contains $(w, k_2) = g_i(u, j_2)$, and the machine merely modifies it to $(w, \langle k_2, k_1 \rangle)$, which is the desired output.

Similarly, note that the edge-rotation function of the Zig-Zag product of the variable graph G' with the fixed graph G is evaluated at $(\langle u, i \rangle, \langle \alpha, \beta \rangle)$ by querying G' at $(u, E_\alpha(i))$ and outputting $(\langle v, E_\beta(j') \rangle, \langle \beta, \alpha \rangle)$, where (v, j') denotes the oracle answer (see Eq. (E.9)). This means that the global-tape oracle machine first copies α, β from the global-tape to the local-tape, transforms the contents of the global-tape from $(\langle u, i \rangle, \langle \alpha, \beta \rangle)$ to $(u, E_\alpha(i))$, and makes an analogous transformation after the oracle is invoked. □

Composing global-tape oracle machines. In the proof of Claim 5.9, we implicitly used sequential composition of computations conducted by global-tape oracle machines.[19] In general, when sequentially composing such computations the length of the global-tape (resp., local-tape) is the maximum among all composed computations; that is, the current formalism offers a tight bound on naive *sequential composition* (as opposed to Lemma 5.1). Furthermore, global-tape oracle machines are beneficial in the context of *recursive composition*, as indicated by Lemma 5.10 (which relies on this model in a crucial way). The key observation is that all levels in the recursive composition may reuse the same global storage, and only the local storage gets added. Consequently, we have the following composition lemma.

Lemma 5.10 (recursive composition in the global-tape model): *Suppose that there exists a global-tape oracle machine that, for every $i = 1, \ldots, t - 1$, computes f_{i+1} by making oracle calls to f_i while using a global-tape of length L and a local-tape of length l_i, which also accounts for the machine's state. Then f_t can be*

---

[19] A similar composition took place in the proof of Claim 5.7, but in Claim 5.9 we asserted a stronger feature of this specific computation.

computed by a standard oracle machine *that makes calls to* f_1 *and uses space*
$L + \sum_{i=1}^{t-1}(l_i + \log_2 l_i)$.

We shall apply this lemma with $f_i = g_i$ and $t = O(\log|V_1|) = O(\log|V_t|)$, using the bounds $L = \log_2(d^2 \cdot |V_t|)$ and $l_i = O(1)$ (as guaranteed by Claim 5.9). Indeed, in this application L equals the length of the input to $f_t = g_t$.

Proof Sketch: We compute f_t by allocating space for the emulation of the global-tape and the local-tapes of each level in the recursion. We emulate the recursive computation by capitalizing on the fact that all recursive levels use the same global-tape (for making queries and receiving answers). Recall that in the actual recursion, each level may use the global-tape arbitrarily so long as when it returns control to the invoking machine the global-tape contains the right answer. Thus, the emulation may do the same, and emulate each recursive call by using the space allocated for the global-tape as well as the space designated for the local-tape of this level. The emulation should also store the locations of the other levels of the recursion on the corresponding local-tapes, but the space needed for this (i.e., $\sum_{i=1}^{t-1} \log_2 l_i$) is clearly smaller than the length of the various local-tapes (i.e., $\sum_{i=1}^{t-1} l_i$). □

Conclusion. Combining Claim 5.9 and Lemma 5.10, we conclude that the evaluation of $g_{O(\log|V_1|)}$ can be reduced to the evaluation of g_1 in space $O(\log|V_1|)$; that is, $g_{O(\log|V_1|)}$ can be computed by a standard oracle machine that makes calls to g_1 and uses space $O(\log|V_1|)$. Recalling that G_1 can be constructed in log-space (based on the input graph G_0), we infer that $G' = G_{O(\log|V_1|)}$ can be constructed in log-space. Theorem 5.6 follows by recalling that G' (which has constant degree and logarithmic diameter) can be tested for connectivity in log-space (see Exercise 5.13). Using a similar argument, we can test whether a given pair of vertices are connected in the input graph (see Exercise 5.15). Furthermore, a corresponding path can be found within the same complexity (see Exercise 5.17).

5.3. Non-deterministic Space Complexity

The difference between space complexity and time complexity is quite striking in the context of non-deterministic computations. One phenomenon is the huge gap between the power of two formulation of non-deterministic space complexity (see Section 5.3.1), which stands in contrast to the fact that the analogous formulations are equivalent in the context of time complexity. We also highlight the contrast between various results regarding (the standard model of) non-deterministic space-bounded computation (see Section 5.3.2) and the analogous questions in the context of time complexity; one good example is the "question of complementation" (cf. §5.3.2.3).

5.3.1. Two Models

Recall that non-deterministic time-bounded computations were defined via two equivalent models. In the off-line model (underlying the definition of NP as a proof system (see Definition 2.5)), non-determinism is captured by reference to the existential choice of an *auxiliary* ("non-deterministic") *input*. Thus, in this model, non-determinism refers to choices that are transcendental to the machine itself (i.e., choices that are performed "off-line"). In contrast, in the on-line model (underlying the traditional definition of NP (see Definition 2.7)) non-determinism is captured by reference to the non-deterministic *choices of the machine itself.* In the context of time complexity, these models are equivalent because the latter on-line choices can be recorded (almost) for free (see the proof of Theorem 2.8). However, such a recording is not free of charge in the context of space complexity.

Let us take a closer look at the relation between the off-line and on-line models. The issue at hand is the cost of emulating off-line choices by on-line choices and vice versa. We stress the fact that in the off-line model the non-deterministic choices are recorded "for free" on an adequate auxiliary input device, whereas such a free record is not available in the on-line model. The fact that the on-line model can be efficiently emulated by the off-line model is almost generic; that is, it holds for any natural notion of complexity, because on-line non-deterministic choices can be emulated by using consecutive bits of the (off-line) non-deterministic input (and without significantly affecting any natural complexity measure). In contrast, the efficient emulation of the off-line model by the on-line model relies on the ability to efficiently maintain (in the on-line model) a record of non-deterministic choices, which eliminates the advantage of the off-line non-deterministic input (which is recorded for free in the off-line model). This efficient emulation is possible *in the context of time complexity*, because in that context a machine may store a sequence of non-deterministic choices (performed on-line) and retrieve bits of it without significantly affecting the running-time (i.e., almost "free of charge"). This naive emulation of the off-line choices by on-line choices is not free of charge in the context of space-bounded computation, because (in the on-line model) each on-line choice that we record (i.e., store) is charged in the space complexity. Furthermore, typically the number of non-deterministic choices is much larger than the space bound, and thus the naive emulation is not possible *in the context of space complexity* (because it is prohibitively expensive in terms of space complexity).

Let us recapitulate the two models and consider the relation between them in the context of space complexity. In the standard model, called the on-line model, the machine makes non-deterministic choices "on the fly" (as in Definition 2.7).[20] Thus, if the machine may need to refer to such a non-deterministic choice at a latter stage in its computation, then it must store this choice on its storage device (and be charged for it). In contrast, in the so-called off-line model the non-deterministic choices are provided from the outside as the bits of a special non-deterministic input. This non-deterministic input is presented on a special read-only device (or tape) *that can be scanned in both directions like the main input.*

We denote by $\text{NSPACE}_{\text{on-line}}(s)$ (resp., $\text{NSPACE}_{\text{off-line}}(s)$) the class of sets that are acceptable by an on-line (resp., off-line) non-deterministic machine having space complexity s. We stress that, as in Definition 2.7, the set accepted by a non-deterministic machine M is the set of strings x such that there exists a computation of M on input x that is accepting. (In the case of an on-line model this existential statement refers to possible non-deterministic choices of the machine itself, whereas in the case of an off-line model we refer to a possible choice of a corresponding non-deterministic input.)

---

[20] An alternative but equivalent definition is obtained by considering machines that read a non-deterministic input from a special read-only tape *that can be read only in one direction*. This stands in contrast to the off-line model, where the non-deterministic input is presented on a read-only tape *that can be scanned freely*.

The relationship between these two types of classes is not obvious. Indeed, $\text{NSPACE}_{\text{on-line}}(s) \subseteq \text{NSPACE}_{\text{off-line}}(s)$, but (in general) containment does not hold in the opposite direction. In fact, for s that is at least logarithmic, not only that $\text{NSPACE}_{\text{on-line}}(s) \neq \text{NSPACE}_{\text{off-line}}(s)$ but rather $\text{NSPACE}_{\text{on-line}}(s) \subseteq \text{NSPACE}_{\text{off-line}}(s')$, where $s'(n) = O(\log s(n)) = o(s(n))$. Furthermore, for s that is at least linear, it holds that $\text{NSPACE}_{\text{on-line}}(s) = \text{NSPACE}_{\text{off-line}}(\Theta(\log s))$; see Exercise 5.18.

Before proceeding any further, let us justify the focus on the on-line model in the rest of this section. Indeed, the off-line model fits better the motivations to $\mathcal{NP}$ (as presented in Section 2.1.2), but the on-line model seems more adequate for the study of non-determinism in the context of space complexity. One reason is that an off-line non-deterministic input can be used to code computations (see Exercise 5.18), and in a sense allows for "cheating" with respect to the "actual" space complexity of the computation. This is reflected in the fact that the off-line model can emulate the on-line model while using space that is logarithmic in the space used by the on-line model. A related phenomenon is that $\text{NSPACE}_{\text{off-line}}(s)$ is only known to be contained in $\text{DTIME}(2^{2^s})$, whereas $\text{NSPACE}_{\text{on-line}}(s) \subseteq \text{DTIME}(2^s)$. This fact motivates the study of $\mathcal{NL} = \text{NSPACE}_{\text{on-line}}(\log)$, as a study of a (natural) subclass of $\mathcal{P}$. Indeed, the various results regarding $\mathcal{NL}$ justify its study in retrospect.

In light of the foregoing, we adopt the standard conventions and let $\text{NSPACE}(s) = \text{NSPACE}_{\text{on-line}}(s)$. Our main focus will be the study of $\mathcal{NL} = \text{NSPACE}(\log)$. After studying this class in Section 5.3.2, we shall return to the "question of modeling" in Section 5.3.3.

5.3.2. NL and Directed Connectivity

This section is devoted to the study of $\mathcal{NL}$, which we view as the non-deterministic analogue of $\mathcal{L}$. Specifically, $\mathcal{NL} = \cup_c \text{NSPACE}(\ell_c)$, where $\ell_c(n) = c \log_2 n$. (We refer the reader to the definitional issues pertaining to $\text{NSPACE} = \text{NSPACE}_{\text{on-line}}$, which are discussed in Section 5.3.1.)

We first note that the proof of Theorem 5.3 can be easily extended to the (on-line) non-deterministic context. The reason is that moving from the deterministic model to the current model does not affect the number of instantaneous configurations (as defined in the proof of Theorem 5.3), whereas this number bounds the time complexity. Thus, $\mathcal{NL} \subseteq \mathcal{P}$.

The following problem, called **directed connectivity** (st-CONN), captures the essence of non-deterministic log-space computations (and, in particular, is complete for $\mathcal{NL}$ under log-space reductions). The input to st-CONN consists of a directed graph $G = (V, E)$ and a pair of vertices (s, t), and the task is to determine whether there exists a directed path from s to t (in G).[21] Indeed, the study of $\mathcal{NL}$ is often conducted via st-CONN. For example, note that $\mathcal{NL} \subseteq \mathcal{P}$ follows easily from the fact that st-CONN is in $\mathcal{P}$ (and the fact that $\mathcal{NL}$ is log-space reducible to st-CONN).

5.3.2.1. Completeness and Beyond

Clearly, st-CONN is in $\mathcal{NL}$ (see Exercise 5.19). As shown next, the $\mathcal{NL}$-completeness of st-CONN under log-space reductions follows by noting that the computation of any non-deterministic space-bounded machine yields a directed graph in which vertices

---

[21] See Appendix G.1 for basic graph theoretic terminology. We note that, here (and in the sequel), s stands for *start* and t stands for *terminate*.

correspond to possible configurations and edges represent the "successive" relation of the computation. In particular, for log-space computations the graph has polynomial size, but in general the relevant graph is strongly explicit (in a natural sense; see Exercise 5.21).

Theorem 5.11: *Every problem in $\mathcal{NL}$ is log-space reducible to* st-CONN *(via a many-to-one reduction).*

Proof Sketch: Fixing a non-deterministic machine M and an input x, we consider the following directed graph $G_x = (V_x, E_x)$. The vertices of V_x are possible instantaneous configurations of $M(x)$, where each configuration consists of the contents of the work-tape (and the machine's finite state), the machine's location on it, and the machine's location on the input. The directed edges represent single possible moves in such a computation. We stress that such a move depends on the machine M as well as on the (single) bit of x that resides in the location specified by the first configuration (i.e., the configuration corresponding to the start point of the potential edge).[22] Note that (for a fixed machine M), given x, the graph G_x can be constructed in log-space (by scanning all pairs of vertices and outputting only the pairs that are valid edges (which, in turn, can be tested in constant space)).

By definition, the graph G_x represents the possible computations of M on input x. In particular, there exists an accepting computation of M on input x if and only if there exists a directed path, in G_x, starting at the vertex s that corresponds to the initial configuration and ending at the vertex t that corresponds to a canonical accepting configuration. Thus, $x \in S$ if and only if (G_x, s, t) is a yes-instance of st-CONN. $\qquad\qquad\square$

Reflection. We believe that the proof of Theorem 5.11 (see also Exercise 5.21) justifies saying that st-CONN captures the essence of non-deterministic space-bounded computations. Note that this (intuitive and informal) statement goes beyond saying that st-CONN is $\mathcal{NL}$-complete under log-space reductions.

We note the discrepancy between the space-complexity of undirected connectivity (see Theorem 5.6 and Exercise 5.15) and directed connectivity (see Theorem 5.11 and Exercise 5.23). In this context it is worthwhile to note that determining the existence of relatively short paths (rather than arbitrary paths) in undirected (or directed) graphs is also $\mathcal{NL}$-complete under log-space reductions; see Exercise 5.24.

On the search version of stCONN. We mention that the search problem corresponding to st-CONN is log-space reducible to $\mathcal{NL}$ (by a Cook-reduction); see Exercise 5.20. Also note that accepting computations of any log-space non-deterministic machine can be found by finding directed paths in directed graphs; indeed, this is a simple demonstration of the thesis that st-CONN captures non-deterministic log-space computations.

5.3.2.2. Relating NSPACE to DSPACE

Recall that in the context of time complexity, the only known conversion of non-deterministic computation to deterministic computation comes at the cost of an

---

[22]Thus, the actual input x only affects the set of edges of G_x (whereas the set of vertices is only affected by $|x|$). A related construction is obtained by incorporating in the configuration also the (single) bit of x that resides in the machine's location on the input. In the latter case, x itself affects V_x (but not E_x, except for $E_x \subseteq V_x \times V_x$).

exponential blowup in the complexity. In contrast, space complexity allows such a conversion at the cost of a polynomial blowup in the complexity.

Theorem 5.12 (Non-deterministic versus deterministic space): *For any space-constructible $s : \mathbb{N} \to \mathbb{N}$ that is at least logarithmic, it holds that* $\text{NSPACE}(s) \subseteq \text{DSPACE}(O(s^2))$.

In particular, non-deterministic polynomial space is contained in deterministic polynomial space (and non-deterministic poly-logarithmic space is contained in deterministic poly-logarithmic space).

Proof Sketch: We focus on the special case of $\mathcal{NL}$ and the argument extends easily to the general case. Alternatively, the general statement can be derived from the special case by using a suitable upward-translation lemma (see, e.g., [123, Sec. 12.5]). The special case boils down to presenting an algorithm for deciding directed connectivity that has log-square space complexity.

The basic idea is that checking whether or not there is a path of length at most 2ℓ from u to v in G reduces (in log-space) to checking whether there is an intermediate vertex w such that there is a path of length at most ℓ from u to w and a path of length at most ℓ from w to v. That is, let $\phi_G(u, v, \ell) \stackrel{\text{def}}{=} 1$ if there is a path of length at most ℓ from u to v in G, and $\phi_G(u, v, \ell) \stackrel{\text{def}}{=} 0$ otherwise. Then $\phi_G(u, v, 2\ell)$ can be computed by scanning all vertices w in G, and checking for each w whether both $\phi_G(u, w, \ell) = 1$ and $\phi_G(w, v, \ell) = 1$ hold.[23] Hence, we can compute $\phi_G(u, v, 2\ell)$ by a log-space algorithm that makes oracle calls to $\phi_G(\cdot, \cdot, \ell)$, which in turn can be computed recursively in the same manner. Note that the original computational problem (i.e., st-CONN) can be cast as *computing $\phi_G(s, t, |V|)$* (or $\phi_G(s, t, 2^{\lceil \log_2 |V| \rceil})$) *for a given directed graph* $G = (V, E)$ *and a given pair of vertices* (s, t). Thus, the foregoing recursive procedure yields the theorem's claim, provided that we use adequate composition results. We take a technically different approach by directly analyzing the recursive procedure at hand.

Recall that given a directed graph $G = (V, E)$ and a pair of vertices (s, t), we should merely compute $\phi_G(s, t, 2^{\lceil \log_2 |V| \rceil})$. This is done by invoking a recursive procedure that computes $\phi_G(u, v, 2\ell)$ by scanning all vertices in G, and computing for each vertex w the values of $\phi_G(u, w, \ell)$ and $\phi_G(w, v, \ell)$. The punch line is that all these computations may reuse the same space, while we need only store one additional bit representing the results of all prior computations. We return the value 1 if and only if for some w it holds that $\phi_G(u, w, \ell) = \phi_G(w, v, \ell) = 1$ (see Figure 5.2). Needless to say, $\phi_G(u, v, 1)$ can be decided easily in logarithmic space.

We consider an implementation of the foregoing procedure (of Figure 5.2) in which each level of the recursion uses a designated portion of the entire storage for maintaining the local variables (i.e., w and σ). The amount of space taken by each level of the recursion is essentially $\log_2 |V|$ (for storing the current value of w), and the number of levels is $\log_2 |V|$. We stress that when computing $\phi_G(u, v, 2\ell)$, we make many recursive calls, but all these calls reuse the same work space (i.e., the portion that is designated to that level). That is, when we compute $\phi_G(u, w, \ell)$ we

---

[23]Similarly, $\phi_G(u, v, 2\ell + 1)$ can be computed by scanning all vertices w in G, and checking for each w whether both $\phi_G(u, w, \ell + 1) = 1$ and $\phi_G(w, v, \ell) = 1$ hold.

Recursive computation of $\phi_G(u, v, 2\ell)$, for $\ell \geq 1$.

For $w = 1, \ldots, |V|$ do begin   (*storing the vertex name*)
    Compute $\sigma \leftarrow \phi_G(u, w, \ell)$ (*by a recursive call*)
    Compute $\sigma \leftarrow \sigma \wedge \phi_G(w, v, \ell)$ (*by a second recursive call*)
    If $\sigma = 1$ then `return 1`.   (*success: an intermediate vertex was found*)
End   (*of scan*).
`return 0`.   (*reached only if the scan was completed without success*).

Figure 5.2: The recursive procedure in $\mathcal{NL} \subseteq \text{DSPACE}(O(\log^2))$.

reuse the space that was used for computing $\phi_G(u, w', \ell)$ for the previous w', and we reuse the same space when we compute $\phi_G(w, v, \ell)$. Thus, the space complexity of our algorithm is merely the sum of the amount of space used by all recursion levels. It follows that `st-CONN` has log-square (deterministic) space complexity, and the same follows for all of $\mathcal{NL}$ (either by noting that `st-CONN` actually represents any $\mathcal{NL}$ computation or by using the log-space reductions of $\mathcal{NL}$ to `st-CONN`). $\quad\square$

Digest. The proof of Theorem 5.12 relies on two main observations. The first observation is that a conjunction (resp., disjunction) of two Boolean conditions can be verified using space $s + O(1)$, where s is the space complexity of verifying a single condition. This follows by applying naive composition (i.e., Lemma 5.1). Actually, the second observation is merely a generalization of the first observation: It asserts that an existential claim (resp., a universally quantified claim) can be verified by scanning all possible values in the relevant domain (and testing the claim for each value), which in terms of space complexity has an additive cost that is logarithmic in the size of the domain.

The proof of Theorem 5.12 is facilitated by the fact that we may consider a concrete and simple computational problem such as `st-CONN`. Nevertheless, the same ideas can be applied directly to $\mathcal{NL}$ (or any NSPACE class).

Placing NL in NC2. The simple formulation of `st-CONN` facilitates placing $\mathcal{NL}$ in complexity classes such as $\mathcal{NC}^2$ (i.e., decidability by uniform families of circuits of log-square depth and bounded fan-in). All that is needed is observing that `st-CONN` can be solved by raising the adequate matrix (i.e., the adjacency matrix of the graph augmented with 1-entries on the diagonal) to the adequate power (i.e., its dimension). Squaring a matrix can be done by a uniform family circuits of logarithmic depth and bounded fan-in (i.e., in NC1), and by repeated squaring the nth power of an n-by-n matrix can be computed by a uniform family of bounded fan-in circuits of polynomial size and depth $O(\log^2 n)$; thus, `st-CONN` $\in \mathcal{NC}^2$. Indeed, $\mathcal{NL} \subseteq \mathcal{NC}^2$ follows by noting that `st-CONN` actually represents any $\mathcal{NL}$ computation (or by noting that any log-space reduction can be computed by a uniform family of logarithmic depth and bounded fan-in circuits).

5.3.2.3. Complementation or NL = coNL
Recall that (reasonable) non-deterministic time-complexity classes are not known to be closed under complementation. Furthermore, it is widely believed that $\mathcal{NP} \neq \text{co}\mathcal{NP}$. In contrast, (reasonable) non-deterministic space-complexity classes

are closed under complementation, as captured by the result $\mathcal{NL} = \mathrm{co}\mathcal{NL}$, where $\mathrm{co}\mathcal{NL} \stackrel{\text{def}}{=} \{\{0, 1\}^* \setminus S : S \in \mathcal{NL}\}$.

Before proving that $\mathcal{NL} = \mathrm{co}\mathcal{NL}$, we note that proving this result is equivalent to presenting a log-space Karp-reduction of st-CONN to its complement (or, equivalently, a reduction in the opposite direction; see Exercise 5.26). Our proof utilizes a different perspective on the NL-vs-coNL question, by rephrasing this question as referring to the relation between $\mathcal{NL}$ and $\mathcal{NL} \cap \mathrm{co}\mathcal{NL}$ (see Exercise 2.37), and by offering an "operational interpretation" of the class $\mathcal{NL} \cap \mathrm{co}\mathcal{NL}$.

Recall that a set S is in $\mathcal{NL}$ if there exists a non-deterministic log-space machine M that accepts S, and that the acceptance condition of non-deterministic machines is asymmetric in nature. That is, $x \in S$ implies the *existence* of an accepting computation of M on input x, whereas $x \notin S$ implies that *all* computations of M on input x are non-accepting. Thus, the existence of an accepting computation of M on input x is an absolute indication for $x \in S$, but the existence of a rejecting computation of M on input x is not an absolute indication for $x \notin S$. In contrast, for $S \in \mathcal{NL} \cap \mathrm{co}\mathcal{NL}$, there exist absolute indications both for $x \in S$ and for $x \notin S$ (or, equivalently for $x \in \overline{S} \stackrel{\text{def}}{=} \{0, 1\}^* \setminus S$), where each of the two types of indication is provided by a different non-deterministic machine (i.e., either the one accepting S or the one accepting $\overline{S}$). Combining both machines, we obtain a single non-deterministic machine that, for every input, sometimes outputs the correct answer and always outputs either the correct answer or a special ("don't know") symbol. This yields the following definition, which refers to Boolean functions as a special case.

Definition 5.13 (non-deterministic computation of functions): *We say that a* non-deterministic machine M computes the function $f : \{0, 1\}^* \to \{0, 1\}^*$ *if for every* $x \in \{0, 1\}^*$ *the following two conditions hold.*

1. *Every computation of M on input x yields an output in $\{f(x), \bot\}$, where $\bot \notin \{0, 1\}^*$ is a special symbol* (indicating "don't know").
2. *There exists a computation of M on input x that yields the output $f(x)$.*

Note that $S \in \mathcal{NL} \cap \mathrm{co}\mathcal{NL}$ if and only if there exists a non-deterministic log-space machine that computes the characteristic function of S (see Exercise 5.25). Recall that the characteristic function of S, denoted χ_S, is the Boolean function satisfying $\chi_S(x) = 1$ if $x \in S$ and $\chi_S(x) = 0$ otherwise. It follows that $\mathcal{NL} = \mathrm{co}\mathcal{NL}$ if and only if for every $S \in \mathcal{NL}$ there exists a non-deterministic log-space machine that computes χ_S.

Theorem 5.14 ($\mathcal{NL} = \mathrm{co}\mathcal{NL}$): *For every $S \in \mathcal{NL}$ there exists a non-deterministic log-space machine that computes χ_S.*

As in the case of Theorem 5.12, the result extends to any space-constructible $s : \mathbb{N} \to \mathbb{N}$ that is at least logarithmic; that is, for such s and every $S \in \mathrm{NSPACE}(s)$, it holds that $\overline{S} \in \mathrm{NSPACE}(O(s))$. This extension can be proved either by generalizing the following proof or by using an adequate upward-translation lemma.

Proof Sketch: As in the proof of Theorem 5.12, it suffices to present a non-deterministic log-space machine that computes the characteristic function of st-CONN, denoted χ (i.e., $\chi(G, s, t) = 1$ if there is a directed path from s to t in G and $\chi(G, s, t) = 0$ otherwise).

We first show that the computation of χ is log-space reducible to determining the number of vertices that are reachable (via a directed path) from a given vertex in a given graph. On input (G, s, t), the reduction computes the number of vertices that are reachable from s in the graph G and compares this number to the number of vertices reachable from s in the graph G' obtained by omitting t from G. Clearly, these two numbers are different if and only if vertex t is reachable from vertex v (in the graph G). An alternative reduction that uses a single query is presented in Exercise 5.28. Combining either of these reductions with a non-deterministic log-space machine that computes the number of reachable vertices, we obtain a non-deterministic log-space machine that computes χ. This can be shown by relying either on the non-adaptivity of these reductions or on the fact that the solutions for the target problem have logarithmic length; see Exercise 5.29. Thus, we focus on providing a non-deterministic log-space machine for computing the number of vertices that are reachable from a given vertex in a given graph.

Fixing an n-vertex graph $G = (V, E)$ and a vertex v, we consider the set of vertices that are reachable from v by a path of length at most i. We denote this set by R_i, and observe that $R_0 = \{v\}$ and that for every $i = 1, 2, \ldots,$ it holds that

$$R_i = R_{i-1} \cup \{u : \exists w \in R_{i-1} \text{ s.t. } (w, u) \in E\} \qquad (5.1)$$

Our aim is to (non-deterministically) compute $|R_n|$ in log-space. This will be done in n iterations such that at the ith iteration we compute $|R_i|$. When computing $|R_i|$ we rely on the fact that $|R_{i-1}|$ is known to us, which means that we shall store $|R_{i-1}|$ in memory. We stress that we discard $|R_{i-1}|$ from memory as soon as we complete the computation of $|R_i|$, which we store instead. Thus, at each iteration i, our record of past iterations only contains $|R_{i-1}|$.

Computing $|R_i|$. Given $|R_{i-1}|$, we non-deterministically compute $|R_i|$ by making a guess (for $|R_i|$), denoted g, and verifying its correctness as follows:

1. We verify that $|R_i| \geq g$ in a straightforward manner. That is, scanning V in some canonical order, we verify for g vertices that they are each in R_i. That is, during the scan, we select non-deterministically g vertices, and for each selected vertex w we verify that w is reachable from v by a path of length at most i, where this verification is performed by just guessing and verifying an adequate path (see Exercise 5.19).

   We use $\log_2 n$ bits to store the number of vertices that were already verified to be in R_i, another $\log_2 n$ bits to store the currently scanned vertex (i.e., w), and another $O(\log n)$ bits for implementing the verification of the existence of a path of length at most i from v to w.

2. The verification of the condition $|R_i| \leq g$ (equivalently, $|V \setminus R_i| \geq n - g$) is the interesting part of the procedure. Indeed, as we saw, demonstrating membership in R_i is easy, but here we wish to demonstrate non-membership in R_i. We do so by relying on the fact that we know $|R_{i-1}|$, which allows for a non-deterministic enumeration of R_{i-1} itself, which in turn allows for proofs of non-membership in R_i (via the use of Eq. (5.1)). Details follows (and an even more structured description is provided in Figure 5.3).

   Scanning V (again), we verify for $n - g$ (guessed) vertices that they are *not* in R_i (i.e., are *not* reachable from v by paths of length at most i). By Eq. (5.1), verifying

Given $|R_{i-1}|$ and a guess g, the claim $g \geq |R_i|$ is verified as follows.

Set $c \leftarrow 0$.   (*initializing the main counter*)
For $u = 1, \ldots, n$ do begin   (*the main scan*)
   Guess whether or not $u \in R_i$.
   For a negative guess (i.e., $u \notin R_i$), do begin
   (*Verify that $u \notin R_i$ via Eq. (5.1).*)
      Set $c' \leftarrow 0$.   (*initializing a secondary counter*)
      For $w = 1, \ldots, n$ do begin   (*the secondary scan*)
        Guess whether or not $w \in R_{i-1}$.
        For a positive guess (i.e., $w \in R_{i-1}$), do begin
          Verify that $w \in R_{i-1}$ (as in Step 1).
          Verify that $u \neq w$ and $(w, u) \notin E$.
          If some verification failed
          then halt with output $\perp$ otherwise increment c'.
        End (*of handling a positive guess for $w \in R_{i-1}$*).
      End (*of secondary scan*).   (*c' vertices in R_{i-1} were checked*)
      If $c' < |R_{i-1}|$ then halt with output $\perp$.
      Otherwise ($c' = |R_{i-1}|$), increment c. (*u verified to be outside of R_i*)
   End (*of handling a negative guess for $u \notin R_i$*).
End (*of main scan*).   (*c vertices were shown outside of R_i*)
If $c < n - g$ then halt with output $\perp$.
Otherwise $g \geq |R_i|$ is verified (since $n - |R_i| \geq c \geq n - g$).

Figure 5.3: The main step in proving $\mathcal{NL} = \mathrm{co}\mathcal{NL}$.

that $u \notin R_i$ amounts to proving that for every $w \in R_{i-1}$, it holds that $u \neq w$ and $(w, u) \notin E$. As hinted, the knowledge of $|R_{i-1}|$ allows for the enumeration of R_{i-1}, and thus we merely check the aforementioned condition on each vertex in R_{i-1}. Thus, verifying that $u \notin R_i$ is done as follows.

(a) We scan V guessing $|R_{i-1}|$ vertices that are in R_{i-1}, and verify each such guess in the straightforward manner (i.e., as in Step 1).[24]

(b) For each $w \in R_{i-1}$ that was guessed and verified in Step 2a, we verify that both $u \neq w$ and $(w, u) \notin E$.

By Eq. (5.1), if u passes the foregoing verification then indeed $u \notin R_i$.

We use $\log_2 n$ bits to store the number of vertices that were already verified to be in $V \setminus R_i$, another $\log_2 n$ bits to store the current vertex u, another $\log_2 n$ bits to count the number of vertices that are currently verified to be in R_{i-1}, another $\log_2 n$ bits to store such a vertex w, and another $O(\log n)$ bits for verifying that $w \in R_{i-1}$ (as in Step 1).

If any of the foregoing verifications fails, then the procedure halts outputting the "don't know" symbol $\perp$. Otherwise, it outputs g.

Clearly, the foregoing non-deterministic procedure uses a logarithmic amount of space. It can be verified that, when given the correct value of $|R_{i-1}|$, this procedure non-deterministically computes the value of $|R_i|$. That is, if all verifications are

---

[24]Note that implicit in Step 2a is a non-deterministic procedure that computes the mapping $(G, v, i, |R_{i-1}|) \rightarrow R_{i-1}$, where R_{i-1} denotes the set of vertices that are reachable in G by a path of length at most i from v.

satisfied then it must hold that $g = |R_i|$, and if $g = |R_i|$ then there exist adequate non-deterministic choices that satisfy all verifications.

Recall that R_n is computed iteratively, starting with $|R_0| = 1$ and computing $|R_i|$ based on $|R_{i-1}|$. Each iteration $i = 1, \ldots, n$ is non-deterministic, and is either completed with the correct value of $|R_i|$ (at which point $|R_{i-1}|$ is discarded) or halts in failure (in which case we halt the entire process and output $\bot$). This yields a non-deterministic log-space machine for computing $|R_n|$, and the theorem follows. $\qquad\qquad\square$

Digest. Step 2 is the heart of the proof (of Theorem 5.14). In this step a non-deterministic procedure is used to verify non-membership in an NL-type set. Indeed, verifying membership in NL-type sets is the archetypical task of non-deterministic procedures (i.e., they are defined so as to fit these tasks), and thus Step 1 is straightforward. In contrast, non-deterministic verification of non-membership is not a common phenomenon, and thus Step 2 is not straightforward at all. Nevertheless, in the current context (of Step 2), the verification of non-membership is performed by an iterative (non-deterministic) process that consumes an admissible amount of resources (i.e., a logarithmic amount of space).

5.3.3. A Retrospective Discussion

The current section may be viewed as a study of the "power of non-determinism in computation" (which is a somewhat contradictory term). Recall that we view non-deterministic processes as fictitious abstractions aimed at capturing fundamental phenomena such as the verification of proofs (cf. Section 2.1.5). Since these fictitious abstractions are fundamental in the context of time complexity, we may hope to gain some understanding by a comparative study, specifically, a study of non-determinism in the context of space complexity. Furthermore, we may discover that non-deterministic space-bounded machines give rise to interesting computational phenomena.

The aforementioned hopes seem to come true in the current section. For example, the fact that $\mathcal{NL} = \mathrm{co}\mathcal{NL}$, while the common conjecture is that $\mathcal{NP} \neq \mathrm{co}\mathcal{NP}$, indicates that the latter conjecture is *less generic than sometimes stated*. It is not that an existential quantifier cannot be "feasibly replaced" by a universal quantifier, but it is rather the case that the feasibility of such a replacement depends very much on the specific notion of feasibility used. Turning to the other type of benefits, we learned that st-CONN can be Karp-reduced in log-space to st-unCONN (i.e., the set of graphs in which there is no directed path between the two designated vertices; see Exercise 5.26).

Still, one may ask what does the class $\mathcal{NL}$ actually represent (beyond st-CONN, which seems actually more than merely a complete problem for this class; see §5.3.2.1). Turning back to Section 5.3.1, we recall that the class NSPACE$_{\text{off-line}}$ captures the straightforward notion of space-bounded verification. In this model (called the off-line model), the alleged proof is written on a special device (similarly to the assertion being established by it), and this device is being read freely. In contrast, underlying the alternative class NSPACE$_{\text{on-line}}$ is a notion of proofs that are verified by reading them sequentially (rather than scanning them back and forth). In this case, if the verification procedure may need to reexamine the currently read part of the proof (in the future), then it must store the relevant part (and be charged for this storage). Thus, the on-line model underlying NSPACE$_{\text{on-line}}$ refers to the standard process of reading proofs in a sequential manner and taking notes for future verification, rather than repeatedly scanning the proof back and forth. The on-line model reflects the true space complexity of taking such notes and hence of sequential verification of proofs. Indeed (as stated in Section 5.3.1), our feeling is that the off-line model allows for an unfair accounting of temporary space as well as for unintendedly long proofs.

5.4. PSPACE and Games

As stated in Section 5.2, we rarely encounter computational problems that require less than logarithmic space. On the other hand, we will rarely treat computational problems that require more than polynomial space. The class of decision problems that are solvable in polynomial space is denoted $\mathcal{PSPACE} \overset{\text{def}}{=} \cup_c \text{DSPACE}(p_c)$, where $p_c(n) = n^c$.

To get a sense of the power of $\mathcal{PSPACE}$, we observe that $\mathcal{PH} \subseteq \mathcal{PSPACE}$; for example, a polynomial-space algorithm can easily verify the quantified condition underlying Definition 3.8. In fact, such an algorithm can handle an unbounded number of alternating quantifiers (see the following Theorem 5.15). On the other hand, by Theorem 5.3, $\mathcal{PSPACE} \subseteq \mathcal{EXP}$, where $\mathcal{EXP} = \cup_c \text{DTIME}(2^{p_c})$ for $p_c(n) = n^c$.

The class $\mathcal{PSPACE}$ can be interpreted as capturing the complexity of determining the winner in certain *efficient two-party games*; specifically, the very games considered in Section 3.2.1 (modulo footnote 5 there). Recall that we refer to two-party games that satisfy the following three conditions:

1. The parties alternate in taking moves that effect the game's (global) position, where each move has a description length that is bounded by a polynomial in the length of the *initial* position.
2. The current position is updated based on the previous position and the current party's move. This updating can be performed in time that is polynomial in the length of the *initial* position. (Equivalently, we may require a polynomial-time updating procedure and postulate that the length of the current position be bounded by a polynomial in the length of the *initial* position.)
3. The winner in each position can be determined in polynomial time.

Recall that, for every fixed k, we showed (in Section 3.2.1) a correspondence between Σ_k and the problem of determining the existence of a k-move winning strategy (for the first party) in games of the foregoing type. The same correspondence exists between $\mathcal{PSPACE}$ and the problem of determining the existence of a winning strategy with polynomially many moves (in games of the foregoing type). That is, on the one hand, the set of initial positions x for which the first party has a poly(x|)-move winning strategy with respect to the foregoing game is in $\mathcal{PSPACE}$. On the other hand, by the following Theorem 5.15, every set in $\mathcal{PSPACE}$ can be viewed as the set of initial positions (in a suitable game) for which the first party has a winning strategy consisting of a polynomial number of moves. Actually, the correspondence is between determining the existence of such winning strategies and deciding the satisfiability of quantified Boolean formulae (QBF); see Exercise 5.30.

QBF and PSPACE. A quantified Boolean formula is a Boolean formula (as in SAT) augmented with quantifiers that refer to each variable appearing in the formula. (Note that, unlike in Exercise 3.7, we make no restrictions regarding the number of alternations between existential and universal quantifiers. For further discussion, see

Appendix G.2.) As noted before, deciding the satisfiability of quantified Boolean formulae (QBF) in in $\mathcal{PSPACE}$. We next show that every problem in $\mathcal{PSPACE}$ is Karp-reducible to QBF.

Theorem 5.15: QBF *is complete for $\mathcal{PSPACE}$ under polynomial-time many-to-one reductions.*

Proof: As noted before, QBF is solvable by a polynomial-space algorithm that just evaluates the quantified formula. Specifically, consider a recursive procedure that eliminates a Boolean quantifier by evaluating the value of the two residual formulae, and note that the space used in the first (recursive) evaluation can be reused in the second evaluation. (Alternatively, consider a DFS-type procedure as in Section 5.1.4.) Note that the space used is linear in the depth of the recursion, which in turn is linear in the length of the input formula.

We now turn to show that any set $S \in \mathcal{PSPACE}$ is many-to-one reducible to QBF. The proof is similar to the proof of Theorem 5.12 (which establishes $\mathcal{NL} \subseteq$ DSPACE($\log^2$)), except that here we work with an implicit graph (see Exercise 5.21, rather than with an explicitly given graph). Specifically, we refer to the directed graph of instantaneous configurations (of the algorithm A deciding membership in S), where here we use a different notion of a configuration that *includes also the entire input*. That is, in the rest of this proof, *a configuration consists of the contents of all storage devices of the algorithm* (including the input device) as well as the location of the algorithm on each device. Thus, on input x (to the reduction), we shall consider the directed graph $G = G_{x,A} = (V_x, E_A)$, where V_x represents all possible configurations with input x and E_A represents the transition function of algorithm A (i.e., the effect of a single computation step of A).

As in the proof of Theorem 5.12, for a graph G, we defined $\phi_G(u, v, \ell) = 1$ if there is a path of length at most ℓ from u to v in G (and $\phi_G(u, v, \ell) = 0$ otherwise). We need to determine $\phi_G(s, t, 2^m)$ for s that encodes the initial configuration of $A(x)$ and t that encodes the canonical accepting configuration, where G depends on the algorithm A and $m = \text{poly}(|x|)$ is such that $A(x)$ uses at most m space and runs for at most 2^m steps. By the specific definition of a configuration (which contains all relevant information including the input x), the value of $\phi_G(u, v, 1)$ can be determined easily based solely on the fixed algorithm A (i.e., either $u = v$ or v is a configuration following u). Recall that $\phi_G(u, v, 2\ell) = 1$ if and only if there exists a configuration w such that both $\phi_G(u, w, \ell) = 1$ and $\phi_G(w, v, \ell) = 1$ hold. Thus, we obtain the recursion

$$\phi_G(u, v, 2\ell) = \exists w \in \{0, 1\}^m \; \phi_G(u, w, \ell) \wedge \phi_G(w, v, \ell), \qquad (5.2)$$

where the bottom of the recursion (i.e., $\phi_G(u, v, 1)$) is a simple propositional formula (see the foregoing comment). The problem with Eq. (5.2) is that the expression for $\phi_G(\cdot, \cdot, 2\ell)$ involves two occurrences of $\phi_G(\cdot, \cdot, \ell)$, which doubles the length of the recursively constructed formula (yielding an exponential blowup).

Our aim is to express $\phi_G(\cdot, \cdot, 2\ell)$ *while using $\phi_G(\cdot, \cdot, \ell)$ only once*. This extra restriction, which prevents an exponential blowup, corresponds to the *reusing of space* in the two evaluations of $\phi_G(\cdot, \cdot, \ell)$ that take place in the computation of $\phi_G(u, v, 2\ell)$. The main idea is replacing the condition $\phi_G(u, w, \ell) \wedge \phi_G(w, v, \ell)$ by the condition "$\forall (u'v') \in \{(u, w), (w, v)\} \; \phi_G(u', v', \ell)$" (where we quantify over a two-element set that is not the Boolean set $\{0, 1\}$). Next, we reformulate the non-standard quantifier (which ranges over a specific pair of strings) by using additional quantifiers as well as some simple Boolean conditions. That is, the non-standard quantifier $\forall (u'v') \in \{(u, w), (w, v)\}$ is replaced by the standard quantifiers $\forall \sigma \in \{0, 1\} \exists u', v' \in \{0, 1\}^m$ and the auxiliary condition

$$[(\sigma = 0) \Rightarrow (u' = u \wedge v' = w)] \wedge [(\sigma = 1) \Rightarrow (u' = w \wedge v' = v)]. \quad (5.3)$$

Thus, $\phi_G(u, v, 2\ell)$ holds if and only if there exist w such that for every σ there exists (u', v') such that both Eq. (5.3) and $\phi_G(u', v', \ell)$ hold. Note that the length of this expression for $\phi_G(\cdot, \cdot, 2\ell)$ equals the length of $\phi_G(\cdot, \cdot, \ell)$ plus an additive overhead term of $O(m)$. Thus, using a recursive construction, the length of the formula grows only linearly in the number of recursion steps.

The reduction itself maps an instance x (of S) to the quantified Boolean formula $\Phi(s_x, t, 2^m)$, where s_x denotes the initial configuration of $A(x)$, (t and $m = \text{poly}(|x|)$ are as in the foregoing discussion), and Φ is recursively defined as follows

$$\Phi(u, v, 2\ell) \overset{\text{def}}{=} \begin{array}{l} \exists w \in \{0, 1\}^m \ \forall \sigma \in \{0, 1\} \exists u', v' \in \{0, 1\}^m \\ [(\sigma = 0) \Rightarrow (u' = u \wedge v' = w)] \\ \wedge [(\sigma = 1) \Rightarrow (u' = w \wedge v' = v)] \\ \wedge \Phi(u', v', \ell) \end{array} \quad (5.4)$$

with $\Phi(u, v, 1) = 1$ if and only if either $u = v$ or there is an edge from u to v. Note that $\Phi(u, v, 1)$ is a (fixed) *propositional formula* with Boolean variables representing the bits of the variables u and v such that $\Phi(u, v, 1)$ is satisfied if and only if either $u = v$ or v is a configuration that follows the configuration u in a computation of A. On the other hand, note that $\Phi(s_x, t, 2^m)$ is a *quantified formula* in which s_x, t and m are fixed and the quantified variables are not shown in the notation.

We stress that the mapping of x to $\Phi(s_x, t, 2^m)$ can be computed in polynomial time. Firstly, note that the propositional formula $\Phi(u, v, 1)$, having Boolean variables representing the bits of u and v, expresses extremely simple conditions and can certainly be constructed in polynomial time (i.e., polynomial in the number of Boolean variables, which in turn equals $2m$). Next note that, given $\Phi(u, v, \ell)$, which (for $\ell > 1$) contains quantified variables that are not shown in the notation, we can construct $\Phi(u, v, 2\ell)$ by merely replacing variables names and adding quantifiers and Boolean conditions as in the recursive definition of Eq. (5.4). This is certainly doable in polynomial time. Lastly, note that the construction of $\Phi(s_x, t, 2^m)$ depends mainly on the length of x, where x itself only affects s_x (and does so in a trivial manner). Recalling that $m = \text{poly}(|x|)$, it follows that everything is computable in time polynomial in $|x|$. Thus, given x, the formula $\Phi(s_x, t, 2^m)$ can be constructed in polynomial time.

Finally, note that $x \in S$ if and only if the formula $\Phi(s_x, t, 2^m)$ is satisfiable. The theorem follows. ∎

Other $\mathcal{PSPACE}$-complete problems. As stated in the beginning of this section, there is a close relationship between $\mathcal{PSPACE}$ and determining winning strategies in various games. This relationship was established by considering the generic game that corresponds to the satisfiability of general QBF (see Exercise 5.30). The connection between $\mathcal{PSPACE}$

and determining winning strategies in games is closer than indicated by this generic game: Determining winning strategies in several (generalizations of) natural games is also $\mathcal{PSPACE}$-complete (see [208, Sec. 8.3]). This further justifies the title of the current section.

Chapter Notes

The material presented in the current chapter is based on a mix of "classical" results (proven in the 1970s if not earlier) and "modern" results (proven in the late 1980s and even later). We wish to emphasize the time gap between the formulation of some questions and their resolution. Details follow.

We first mention the "classical" results. These include the $\mathcal{NL}$-completeness of st-CONN, the emulation of non-deterministic space-bounded machines by deterministic space-bounded machines (i.e., Theorem 5.12 due to Savitch [197]), the $\mathcal{PSPACE}$-completeness of QBF, and the connections between circuit depth and space complexity (see Section 5.1.4 and Exercise 5.12 due to Borodin [48]).

Before turning to the "modern" results, we mention that some researchers tend to be discouraged by the impression that "decades of research have failed to answer any of the famous open problems of Complexity Theory." In our opinion this impression is fundamentally mistaken. Specifically, in addition to the fact that substantial progress toward the understanding of many fundamental issues has been achieved, these researchers tend to forget that some famous open problems were actually resolved. Two such examples were presented in this chapter.

The question of whether $\mathcal{NL} = \text{co}\mathcal{NL}$ was a famous open problem for almost two decades. Furthermore, this question is related to an even older open problem dating to the early days of research in the area of formal languages (i.e., to the 1950s).[25] This open problem was resolved in 1988 by Immerman [125] and Szelepcsenyi [219], who (independently) proved Theorem 5.14 (i.e., $\mathcal{NL} = \text{co}\mathcal{NL}$).

For more than two decades, undirected connectivity (UCONN) was one of the most appealing examples of the computational power of randomness. Recall that the classical linear-time (deterministic) algorithms (e.g., BFS and DFS) require an extensive use of temporary storage (i.e., linear in the size of the graph). On the other hand, it was known (since 1979, see §6.1.5.2) that, with high probability, a random walk of polynomial length visits all vertices (in the corresponding connected component). Thus, the resulting randomized algorithm for UCONN uses a minimal amount of temporary storage (i.e., logarithmic in the size of the graph). In the early 1990s, this algorithm (as well as the entire class $\mathcal{BPL}$ (see Definition 6.11)) was derandomized in polynomial time and poly-logarithmic space (see Theorem 8.23), but despite more than a decade of research attempts, a significant gap remained between the space complexity of randomized and deterministic polynomial-time algorithms for this natural and ubiquitous problem. This gap was closed by Reingold [190], who established Theorem 5.6 in 2004.[26] Our presentation (in Section 5.2.4) follows Reingold's ideas, but the specific formulation in §5.2.4.2 does not appear in [190].

---

[25]Specifically, the class of sets recognized by linear-space non-deterministic machines equals the class of context-sensitive languages (see, e.g., [123, Sec. 9.3]), and thus Theorem 5.14 resolves the question of whether the latter class is closed under complementation.

[26]We mention that an almost-logarithmic space algorithm was discovered independently and concurrently by Trifonov [224], using a very different approach.

Exercises

Exercise 5.1 (scanning the input-tape beyond the input): Let A be an arbitrary algorithm of space complexity s. Show that there exists a functionally equivalent algorithm A' that has space complexity $s'(n) = O(s(n) + \log n)$ and does not scan the input-tape beyond the boundaries of the input.

> **Guideline:** Prove that on input x, algorithm A does not scan the input-tape beyond distance $2^{O(s(|x|))}$ from the input.
>
> (Extra hint: Consider instantaneous configurations of $A(x)$ that refer to the case that A reads a generic location on the input-tape that is not part of the input.)

Exercise 5.2 (rewriting on the write-only output-tape): Let A be an arbitrary algorithm of space complexity s. Show that there exists a functionally equivalent algorithm A' that never rewrites on (the same location of) its output device and has space complexity s' such that $s'(n) = s(n) + O(\log \ell(n))$, where $\ell(n) = \max_{x \in \{0,1\}^n} |A(x)|$.

> **Guideline:** Algorithm A' proceeds in iterations, where in the ith iteration it outputs the ith bit of $A(x)$ by emulating the computation of A on input x. The ith emulation of A avoids printing $A(x)$, but rather keeps a record of the ith location of $A(x)$'s output-tape (and terminates by outputting the final value of this bit). Indeed, this emulation requires maintaining the current value of i as well as the current location of the emulated machine (i.e., A) on its output-tape.

Exercise 5.3 (on the power of double-logarithmic space): For any $k \in \mathbb{N}$, let w_k denote the concatenation of all k-bit long strings (in lexicographic order) separated by $*$'s (i.e., $w_k = 0^{k-2}00 * 0^{k-2}01 * 0^{k-2}10 * 0^{k-2}11 * \cdots * 1^k$). Show that the set $S \overset{\text{def}}{=} \{w_k : k \in \mathbb{N}\} \subset \{0, 1, *\}$ is not regular and yet is decidable in double-logarithmic space.

> **Guideline:** The non-regularity of S can be shown using standard techniques. Toward developing an algorithm, note that $|w_k| > 2^k$, and thus $O(\log k) = O(\log \log |w_k|)$. Membership of x in S is determined by iteratively checking whether $x = w_i$, for $i = 1, 2, \ldots$, while stopping when detecting an obvious case (i.e., either verifying that $x = w_i$ or detecting evidence that $x \neq w_k$ for every $k \geq i$). By taking advantage of the $*$'s (in w_i), the ith iteration can be implemented in space $O(\log i)$. Furthermore, on input $x \notin S$, we halt and reject after at most $\log |x|$ iterations. Actually, it is slightly simpler to handle the related set $\{w_1 * *w_2 * * \cdots * *w_k : k \in \mathbb{N}\}$; moreover, in this case the $*$'s can be omitted from the w_i's (as well as from between them).

Exercise 5.4 (on the weakness of less than double logarithmic space): Prove that for $\ell(n) = \log \log n$, it holds that $\text{DSPACE}(o(\ell)) = \text{DSPACE}(O(1))$.

> **Guideline:** Let s denote the machine's (binary) space complexity. Show that if s is unbounded then it must hold that $s(n) = \Omega(\log \log n)$ infinitely often. Specifically, for every integer m, consider a shortest string x such that on input x the machine uses space at least m. Consider, for each location on the input, the sequence of the residual configurations of the machine (i.e., the contents of its temporary storage)[27] such that the ith element in the sequence represents the residual configuration of the machine at the ith time that the machine crosses (or rather passes through) this input location.

---

[27]Note that, unlike in the proof of Theorem 5.3, the machine's location on the input is not part of the notion of a configuration used here. On the other hand, although not stated explicitly, the configuration also encodes the machine's location on the storage tape.

For starters, note that the length of this "crossing sequence" is upper-bounded by the number of possible residual configurations, which is at most $t \stackrel{\text{def}}{=} 2^{s(|x|)} \cdot s(|x|)$. Thus, the number of such crossing sequences is upper-bounded by t^t. Now, if $t^t < |x|/2$ then there exist three input locations that have the same crossing sequence, and two of them hold the same bit value. Contracting the string at these two locations, we get a shorter input on which the machine behaves in exactly the same manner, contradicting the hypothesis that x is the shortest input on which the machine uses space at least m. We conclude that $t^t \geq |x|/2$ must hold, and $s(|x|) = \Omega(\log \log |x|)$ holds for infinitely many x's.

Exercise 5.5 (space complexity and halting): In continuation of Theorem 5.3, prove that for every algorithm A of (binary) space complexity s there exists an algorithm A' of space complexity $s'(n) = O(s(n) + \log n)$ that halts on every input such that for every x on which A halts it holds that $A'(x) = A(x)$.

> **Guideline:** On input x, algorithm A' emulates the execution of $A(x)$ for at most $t(|x|) + 1$ steps, where $t(n) = n \cdot 2^{s(n) + \log_2 s(n)}$.

Exercise 5.6 (some log-space algorithms): Present log-space algorithms for the following computational problems.

1. Addition and multiplication of a given pair of integers.

> **Guideline:** Relying on Lemma 5.2, first transform the input to a more convenient format, then perform the operation, and finally transform the result to the adequate format. For example, when adding $x = \sum_{i=0}^{n-1} x_i 2^i$ and $y = \sum_{i=0}^{n-1} y_i 2^i$, a convenient format is $((x_0, y_0), \ldots, (x_{n-1}, y_{n-1}))$.

2. Deciding whether two given strings are identical.
3. Finding occurrences of a given pattern $p \in \{0, 1\}^*$ in a given string $s \in \{0, 1\}^*$.
4. Transforming the adjacency matrix representation of a graph to its incidence list representation, and vice versa.
5. Deciding whether the input graph is acyclic (i.e., has no simple cycles).

> **Guideline:** Consider a scanning of the graph that proceeds as follows. Upon entering a vertex v via the ith edge incident at it, we exit this vertex using its $i + 1^{\text{st}}$ edge if v has degree at least $i + 1$ and exit via the first edge otherwise. Note that when started at any vertex of any tree, this scanning performs a DFS. On the other hand, for every cyclic graph there exists a vertex v and an edge e incident to v such that if this scanning is started by traversing the edge e from v then it returns to v via an edge different from e.

6. Deciding whether the input graph is a tree.

> **Guideline:** Use the fact that a graph $G = (V, E)$ is a tree if and only if it is acyclic and $|E| = |V| - 1$.

Exercise 5.7 (another composition result): In continuation of the discussion in §5.1.3.3, prove that *if Π can be solved in space s_1 when given an (ℓ, ℓ')-restricted oracle access to Π' and Π' is solvable is space s_2, then Π is solvable in space s such that $s(n) = 2s_1(n) + s_2(\ell(n)) + 2\ell'(n) + \delta(n)$, where $\delta(n) = O(\log(\ell(n) + \ell'(n) + s_1(n) + s_2(\ell(n))))$). In particular, if s_1, s_2 and ℓ' are at most logarithmic, then $s(n) = O(\log n)$,* because (by Exercise 5.10) in this case ℓ is at most polynomial.

Guideline: View the oracle-aided computation of Π as consisting of iterations such that in the ith iteration the ith query (denoted q_i) is determined based on the initial input (denoted x), the $i-1^{\text{st}}$ oracle answer (denoted a_{i-1}), and the contents of the work-tape at the time that the $i-1^{\text{st}}$ answer was given (denoted w_{i-1}). Note that the mapping $(x, a_{i-1}, w_{i-1}) \to (q_i, w_i)$ can be computed using $s_1(|x|) + \delta(|x|)$ bits of temporary storage, because the oracle machine effects this mapping (when x, a_{i-1} and w_{i-1} reside on different devices). Composing each iteration with the computation of Π' (using a variant of Lemma 5.2), we conclude that the mapping $(x, a_{i-1}, w_{i-1}) \to (a_i, w_i)$ can be computed (without storing the intermediate q_i) in space $s_1(n) + s_2(\ell(n)) + O(\log(\ell(n) + s_1(n) + s_2(\ell(n))))$. Thus, we can emulate the entire computation using space $s(n)$, where the extra space of $s_1(n) + 2\ell'(n)$ bits is used for storing the work-tape of the oracle machine and the $i-1^{\text{st}}$ and i^{th} oracle answers.

Exercise 5.8 (non-adaptive reductions): In continuation of the discussion in §5.1.3.3, we define non-adaptive space-bounded reductions as follows. First, for any problem Π', we define the ("direct product") problem $\overline{\Pi}'$ such that the instances of $\overline{\Pi}'$ are sequences of instances of Π'. The sequence $\overline{y} = (y_1, \ldots, y_t)$ is a valid solution (with respect to the problem $\overline{\Pi}'$) to the instance $\overline{x} = (x_1, \ldots, x_t)$ if and only if for every $i \in [t]$ it holds that y_i is a valid solution to x_i (with respect to the problem Π'). Now, a non-adaptive reduction of Π to Π' is defined as a single-query reduction of Π to $\overline{\Pi}'$.

1. Note that this definition allows the oracle machine to freely scan the sequence of answers (i.e., it can move freely between the blocks that correspond to different answers). Still, prove that this does not add much power to the machine (in comparison to a machine that reads the oracle-answer device in a "semi-unidirectional" manner (i.e., it never reads bits of some answer after reading any bit of any later answer)). That is, prove that a general non-adaptive reduction of space complexity s can be emulated by a non-adaptive reduction of space complexity $O(s)$ that when obtaining the oracle answer $(y_1, \ldots, y_t)$ may read bits of y_i only before reading any bit of $y_{i+1}, \ldots, y_t$.

   Guideline: Replace the query sequence $\overline{x} = (x_1, \ldots, x_t)$ by the query sequence $(\overline{x}, \overline{x}, \ldots, \overline{x})$ where the number of repetitions is $2^{O(s)}$.

2. Prove that if Π is reducible to Π' via a non-adaptive reduction of space complexity s_1 that makes queries of length at most ℓ and Π' is solvable in space s_2, then Π is solvable in space s such that $s(n) = O(s_1(n) + s_2(\ell(n)))$. As a warm-up, consider first the case of a general single-query reduction (of Π to Π').

   Guideline: The composed computation, on input x, can be written as $E(x, \overline{A}(G(x)))$, where G represents the query generation phase, $\overline{A}$ represents the application of the Π'-solver to each string in the sequence of queries, and E represents the evaluation phase. Analyze the space complexity of this computation by using (variants of) Lemma 5.2.

Exercise 5.9: Referring to the discussion in §5.1.3.3, prove that, for any s, any problem having space complexity s can be solved by a *constant-space* $(2s, 2s)$-restricted reduction to a problem that is solvable in *constant space*.

   Guideline: The reduction is to the "next configuration function" associated with the said algorithm (of space complexity s), where here the configuration contains also the single bit of the input that the machine currently examines (i.e., the value of the bit at the machine's location on the input device). To facilitate the computation of this function, choose a suitable representation of such configurations. Note that the bulk of the operation of the oracle machine consists of iteratively copying (with minor modification) the contents of the oracle-answer tape to the oracle-query tape.

Exercise 5.10: In continuation of §5.1.3.3, we say that a reduction is $\cdot(\cdot, \ell')$-restricted if there exists some function ℓ such that the reduction is (ℓ, ℓ')-restricted; that is, in this definition only the length of the oracle answers is restricted. Prove that any reduction of space complexity s that is $(\cdot, \ell')$-restricted is (ℓ, ℓ')-restricted for $\ell(n) = 2^{O(s(n)+\ell'(n)+\log n)}$. Actually, prove that this reduction has time complexity ℓ.

> **Guideline:** Consider an adequate notion of instantaneous configuration; specifically, such a configuration consists of the contents of both the work-tape and the oracle-answer tape as well as the machine's location on these tapes (and on the input tape).

Exercise 5.11 (transitivity of log-space reductions): Prove that log-space Karp-reductions are transitive. Define log-space Levin-reductions and prove that they are transitive.

> **Guideline:** Use Lemma 5.2, noting that such reductions are merely log-space computable functions.

Exercise 5.12 (log-space uniform $\mathcal{NC}^1$ is in $\mathcal{L}$): Suppose that a problem Π is solvable by a family of log-space uniform circuits of bounded fan-in and depth d such that $d(n) \geq \log n$. Prove that Π is solvable by an algorithm having space complexity $O(d)$.

> **Guideline:** Combine the algorithm outlined in Section 5.1.4 with the definition of log-space uniformity (using Lemma 5.2).

Exercise 5.13 (UCONN in constant degree graphs of logarithmic diameter): Present a log-space algorithm for deciding the following promise problem, which is parameterized by constants c and d. The input graph satisfies the promise if each vertex has degree at most d and every pair of vertices that reside in the same connected component is connected by a path of length at most $c \log_2 n$, where n denotes the number of vertices in the input graph. The task is to decide whether the input graph is connected.

> **Guideline:** For every pair of vertices in the graph, we check whether these vertices are connected in the graph. (Alternatively, we may just check whether each vertex is connected to the first vertex.) Relying on the promise, it suffices to inspect all paths of length at most $\ell \overset{\text{def}}{=} c \log_2 n$, and these paths can be enumerated using $\ell \cdot \lceil \log_2 d \rceil$ bits of storage.

Exercise 5.14 (warm-up toward §5.2.4.2): In continuation of §5.2.4.1, present a log-space transformation of G_i to G_{i+1}.

> **Guideline:** Given the graph G_i as input, we may construct G_{i+1} by first constructing $G' = G_i^c$ and then constructing $G' \textcircled{z} G$. To construct G', we scan all vertices of G_i (holding the current vertex in temporary storage), and, for each such vertex, construct its "distance c neighborhood" in G' (by using $O(c)$ space for enumerating all possible "distance c neighbors"). Similarly, we can construct the vertex neighborhoods in $G' \textcircled{z} G$ (by storing the current vertex name and using a constant amount of space for indicating incident edges in G).

Exercise 5.15 (st-UCONN): In continuation of Section 5.2.4, prove that the following computational problem is in $\mathcal{L}$: Given an undirected graph $G = (V, E)$ and two designated vertices, s and t, determine whether there is a path from s to t in G.

> **Guideline:** Note that the transformation described in Section 5.2.4 can be easily extended such that it maps vertices in G_0 to vertices in $G_{O(\log |V|)}$ while preserving the connectivity relation (i.e., u and v are connected in G_0 if and only if their images under the map are connected in $G_{O(\log |V|)}$).

Exercise 5.16 (bipartiteness): Prove that the problem of determining whether or not the input graph is bipartite (i.e., 2-colorable) is computationally equivalent under log-space reductions to st-UCONN (as defined in Exercise 5.15).

> **Guideline:** Both reductions use the mapping of a graph $G = (V, E)$ to a bipartite graph $G' = (V', E')$ such that $V' = \{v^{(1)}, v^{(2)} : v \in V\}$ and $E' = \{\{u^{(1)}, v^{(2)}\}, \{u^{(2)}, v^{(1)}\} : \{u, v\} \in E\}$. When reducing to st-UCONN note that a vertex v resides on an odd cycle in G if and only if $v^{(1)}$ and $v^{(2)}$ are connected in G'. When reducing from st-UCONN note that s and t are connected in G by a path of even (resp., odd) length if and only if the graph G' ceases to be bipartite when augmented with the edge $\{s^{(1)}, t^{(1)}\}$ (resp., with the edges $\{s^{(1)}, x\}$ and $\{x, t^{(2)}\}$, where $x \notin V'$ is an auxiliary vertex).

Exercise 5.17 (finding paths in undirected graphs): In continuation of Exercise 5.15, present a log-space algorithm that given an undirected graph $G = (V, E)$ and two designated vertices, s and t, finds a path from s to t in G (in case such a path exists).

> **Guideline:** In continuation of Exercise 5.15, we may find and (implicitly) store a logarithmically long path in $G_{O(\log |V|)}$ that connects a representative of s and a representative of t. Focusing on the task of finding a path in G_0 that corresponds to an edge in $G_{O(\log |V|)}$, we note that such a path can be found by using the reduction underlying the combination of Claim 5.9 and Lemma 5.10. (An alternative description appears in [190].)

Exercise 5.18 (relating the two models of NSPACE): Referring to the definitions in Section 5.3.1, prove that for every function s such that $\log s$ is space-constructible and at least logarithmic, it holds that $\text{NSPACE}_{\text{on-line}}(s) = \text{NSPACE}_{\text{off-line}}(\Theta(\log s))$. Note that $\text{NSPACE}_{\text{on-line}}(s) \subseteq \text{NSPACE}_{\text{off-line}}(O(\log s))$ holds also for s that is at least logarithmic.

> **Guideline (for $\text{NSPACE}_{\text{on-line}}(s) \subseteq \text{NSPACE}_{\text{off-line}}(O(\log s))$):** Use the non-deterministic input of the off-line machine for encoding an accepting computation of the on-line machine; that is, this input should contain a sequence of consecutive configurations leading from the initial configuration to an accepting configuration, where each configuration contains the contents of the work-tape as well as the machine's state and its locations on the work tape and on the input-tape. The emulating off-line machine (which verifies the correctness of the sequence of configurations recorded on its non-deterministic input tape) needs only store its *location within the current pair of consecutive configurations* that it examines, which requires space logarithmic in the length of a single configuration (which in turn equals $s(n) + \log_2 s(n) + \log_2 n + O(1)$). (Note that this verification relies on a two-directional access to the non-deterministic input.)

> **Guideline (for $\text{NSPACE}_{\text{off-line}}(s') \subseteq \text{NSPACE}_{\text{on-line}}(\exp(s'))$):** Here we refer to the notion of a crossing sequence. Specifically, for each location on the off-line non-deterministic input, consider the sequence of the residual configurations of the machine, where such a residual configuration consists of the bit residing in this

non-deterministic tape location, the contents of the machine's temporary storage, and the machine's locations on the input and storage tapes (but not its location on the non-deterministic tape). Show that the length of such a crossing sequence is exponential in the space complexity of the off-line machine, and that the time complexity of the off-line machine is at most double-exponential in its space complexity (see Exercise 5.4). The on-line machine merely generates a sequence of crossing sequences ("on the fly") and checks that each consecutive pair of crossing sequences is consistent. This requires holding two crossing sequences in storage, which require space linear in the length of such sequences (which, in turn, is exponential in the space complexity of the off-line machine).

Exercise 5.19 (st-CONN and variants of it are in NL): Prove that the following computational problem is in $\mathcal{NL}$. The instances have the form (G, v, w, ℓ), where $G = (V, E)$ is a directed graph, $v, w \in V$, and ℓ is an integer, and the question is whether G contains a path of length at most ℓ from v to w.

> **Guideline:** Consider a non-deterministic machine that generates and verifiers an adequate path on the fly. That is, starting at $v_0 = v$, the machine proceeds in iterations, such that in the ith iteration it non-deterministically generates v_i, verifies that $(v_{i-1}, v_i) \in E$, and checks whether $i \leq \ell$ and $v_i = w$. Note that this machine need only store the last two vertices on the path (i.e., v_{i-1} and v_i) as well as the number of edges traversed so far (i.e., i). (Actually, using a careful implementation, it suffices to store only one of these two vertices (as well as the current i).)

Exercise 5.20 (finding directed paths in directed graphs): Present a log-space oracle machine that finds (shortest) directed paths in directed graphs by using an oracle to $\mathcal{NL}$. Conclude that $\mathcal{NL} = \mathcal{L}$ if and only if such paths can be found by a (standard) log-space algorithm.

> **Guideline:** Use a reduction to the decision problem presented in Exercise 5.19, and derive a standard algorithm by using the composition result of Exercise 5.7.

Exercise 5.21 (NSPACE and directed connectivity): Our aim is to establish a relation between general non-deterministic space-bounded computation and directed connectivity in "strongly constructible" graphs that have size exponential in the space bound. Let s be space-constructible and at least logarithmic. For every $S \in \text{NSPACE}(s)$, present a linear-time oracle machine (somewhat as in §5.2.4.2) that given oracle access to x provides oracle access to a directed graph G_x of size $\exp(s(|x|))$ such that $x \in S$ if and only if there is a directed path between the first and last vertices of G_x. That is, on input a pair (u, v) and oracle access to x, the oracle machine decides whether or not (u, v) is a directed edge in G_x.

> **Guideline:** Follow the proof of Theorem 5.11.

Exercise 5.22 (an alternative presentation of the proof of Theorem 5.12): We refer to directed graphs in which each vertex has a self-loop.

1. Viewing the adjacency matrices of directed graphs as oracles (cf. Exercise 5.21), present a linear-space oracle machine that determines whether a given pair of vertices is connected by a directed path of length two in the input graph. Note that this oracle machine computes the adjacency relation of the square of the graph represented in the oracle.

2. Using naive composition (as in Lemma 5.1), present a quadratic-space oracle machine that determines whether a given pair of vertices is connected by a directed path in the graph represented in the oracle.

Note that the machine in item 2 implies that st-CONN can be decided in log-square space. In particular, justify the self-loop assumption made up front.

Exercise 5.23 (deciding strong connectivity): A directed graph is called strongly connected if there exists a directed path between every ordered pair of vertices in the graph (or, equivalently, a directed cycle passing through every two vertices). Prove that the problem of deciding whether a directed graph is strongly connected is $\mathcal{NL}$-complete under (many-to-one) log-space reductions.

> **Guideline (for $\mathcal{NL}$-hardness):** Reduce from st-CONN. Note that, for any graph $G = (V, E)$, it holds that (G, s, t) is a yes-instance of st-CONN if and only if the graph $G' = (V, E \cup \{(v, s) : v \in V\} \cup \{(t, v) : v \in V\})$ is strongly connected.

Exercise 5.24 (determining distances in undirected graphs): Prove that the following computational problem is $\mathcal{NL}$-complete under (many-to-one) log-space reductions: Given an undirected graph $G = (V, E)$, two designated vertices, s and t, and an integer K, determine whether there is a path of length at most (resp., exactly) K from s to t in G.

> **Guideline (for $\mathcal{NL}$-hardness):** Reduce from st-CONN. Specifically, given a directed graph $G = (V, E)$ and vertices s, t, consider a ("layered") graph $G' = (V', E')$ such that $V' = \cup_{i=0}^{|V|-1}\{\langle i, v\rangle : v \in V\}$ and $E' = \cup_{i=0}^{|V|-2}\{\{\langle i, u\rangle, \langle i+1, v\rangle\} : (u, v) \in E \vee u = v\}$. Note that there exists a directed path from s to t in G if and only if there exists a path of length at most (resp., exactly) $|V| - 1$ between $\langle 0, s\rangle$ and $\langle |V| - 1, t\rangle$ in G'.

> **Guideline (for the exact version being in $\mathcal{NL}$):** Use $\mathcal{NL} = \text{co}\mathcal{NL}$.

Exercise 5.25 (an operational interpretation of $\mathcal{NL} \cap \text{co}\mathcal{NL}, \mathcal{NP} \cap \text{co}\mathcal{NP}$, etc.): Referring to Definition 5.13, prove that $S \in \mathcal{NL} \cap \text{co}\mathcal{NL}$ if and only if there exists a non-deterministic log-space machine that computes χ_S, where $\chi_S(x) = 1$ if $x \in S$ and $\chi_S(x) = 0$ otherwise. State and prove an analogous result for $\mathcal{NP} \cap \text{co}\mathcal{NP}$.

> **Guideline:** A non-deterministic machine computing any function f yields, for each value v, a non-deterministic machine of similar complexity that accept $\{x : f(x) = v\}$.
>
> (Extra hint: Invoke the machine M that computes f and accept if and only if M outputs v.)
>
> On the other hand, for any function f of finite range, combining non-deterministic machines that accept the various sets $S_v \stackrel{\text{def}}{=} \{x : f(x) = v\}$, we obtain a non-deterministic machine of similar complexity that computes f.
>
> (Extra hint: On input x, the combined machine invokes each of the aforementioned machines on input x and outputs the value v if and only if the machine accepting S_v has accepted. In the case that none of the machines accepts, the combined machine outputs $\perp$.)

Exercise 5.26 (a graph algorithmic interpretation of $\mathcal{NL} = \text{co}\mathcal{NL}$): Show that there exists a log-space computable function f such that for every (G, s, t) it holds that (G, s, t) is a yes-instance of st-CONN if and only if $(G', s', t') = f(G, s, t)$ is a no-instance of st-CONN.

Exercise 5.27: Referring to Definition 5.13, prove that there exists a non-deterministic log-space machine that computes the distance between two given vertices in a given undirected graph.

> **Guideline:** Relate this computational problem to the (exact version of the) decision problem considered in Exercise 5.24.

Exercise 5.28: As an alternative to the two-query reduction presented in the proof of Theorem 5.14, show that (computing the characteristic function of) st-CONN is log-space reducible via a single query to the problem of determining the number of vertices that are reachable from a given vertex in a given graph.

> (Hint: On input (G, s, t), where $G = ([N], E)$, consider the number of vertices reachable from s in the graph $G' = ([2N], E \cup \{(t, N + i) : i = 1, \ldots, N\})$.)

Exercise 5.29 (reductions and non-deterministic computations): Suppose that computing f is log-space reducible to computing some function g and that it is either the case that the reduction is non-adaptive or that for every x it holds that $|g(x)| = O(\log |x|)$. Referring to non-deterministic computations as in Definition 5.13, prove that if there exists a non-deterministic log-space machine that computes g then there exists a non-deterministic log-space machine that computes f.

> **Guideline:** The point is adapting a composition result that refers to deterministic algorithms (for computing g) into one that applies to non-deterministic computations. Specifically, in the first case we adapt the result of Exercise 5.8, whereas in the second case we adapt the result Exercise 5.7. The idea is running the same procedure as in the deterministic case, and handling the possible failure of the non-deterministic machine that computes g in the natural manner; that is, if any such computation returns the value $\perp$ then we just halt outputting $\perp$, and otherwise we proceed as in the deterministic case (using the non-$\perp$ values obtained).

Exercise 5.30 (the QBF game): Consider the following two-party game that is initiated with a quantified Boolean formula. The game features an existential player (which tries to prove that the formula is valid) versus a universal player (which tries to invalidate it). The game consists of the parties scanning the formula from left to right such that when a quantifier is encountered, the corresponding party takes a move that consists of instantiating the corresponding Boolean variable. At the final position, when all variables were instantiated, the existential party is declared the winner if and only if the corresponding Boolean expression evaluates to true.

1. Show that, modulo some technical conventions, the foregoing QBF game fits the framework of efficient two-party games (described at the beginning of Section 5.4).
2. Prove that any efficient two-party game can be cast as a QBF game.

> **Guideline:** For part 1 define the universal player as winning in any non-final position (i.e., a position in which not all variables are instantiated). For part 2, see footnote 6 in Chapter 3.

CHAPTER SIX

Randomness and Counting

I owe this almost atrocious variety to an institution which other republics do not know or which operates in them in an imperfect and secret manner: the lottery.

Jorge Luis Borges, "The Lottery in Babylon"

So far, our approach to computing devices was somewhat conservative: We thought of them as executing a deterministic rule. A more liberal and quite realistic approach, which is pursued in this chapter, considers computing devices that use a probabilistic rule. This relaxation has an immediate impact on the notion of efficient computation, which is consequently associated with *probabilistic* polynomial-time computations rather than with deterministic (polynomial-time) ones. We stress that the association of efficient computation with probabilistic polynomial-time computation makes sense provided that the failure probability of the latter is negligible (which means that it may be safely ignored).

The quantitative nature of the failure probability of probabilistic algorithms provides one connection between probabilistic algorithms and counting problems. The latter are indeed a new type of computational problems, and our focus is on counting efficiently recognizable objects (e.g., NP-witnesses for a given instance of set in $\mathcal{NP}$). Randomized procedures turn out to play an important role in the study of such counting problems.

Summary: Focusing on probabilistic polynomial-time algorithms, we consider various types of probabilistic failure of such algorithms (e.g., actual error versus failure to produce output). This leads to the formulation of complexity classes such as $\mathcal{BPP}$, $\mathcal{RP}$, and $\mathcal{ZPP}$. The results presented include the existence of (non-uniform) families of polynomial-size circuits that emulate probabilistic polynomial-time algorithms (i.e., $\mathcal{BPP} \subset \mathcal{P}/\text{poly}$) and the fact that $\mathcal{BPP}$ resides in the (second level of the) Polynomial-time Hierarchy (i.e., $\mathcal{BPP} \subseteq \Sigma_2$).

We then turn to counting problems: specifically, counting the number of solutions for an instance of a search problem in $\mathcal{PC}$ (or, equivalently, counting the number of NP-witnesses for an instance of a decision problem in $\mathcal{NP}$). We distinguish between exact counting and approximate counting (in the sense of relative approximation). In particular, while any problem in $\mathcal{PH}$ is reducible to the exact counting class $\#\mathcal{P}$, approximate counting (for $\#\mathcal{P}$) is (probabilistically) reducible to $\mathcal{NP}$.

In general, counting problems exhibit a "richer structure" than the corresponding search (and decision) problems, even when considering only natural problems. For example, some counting problems are hard in the exact version (e.g., are #$\mathcal{P}$-complete) but easy to approximate, while others are NP-hard to approximate. In some cases #$\mathcal{P}$-completeness is due to the very same reduction that establishes the $\mathcal{NP}$-completeness of the corresponding decision problem, whereas in other cases new reductions are required (often because the corresponding decision problem is not $\mathcal{NP}$-complete but is rather in $\mathcal{P}$).

We also consider two other types of computational problems that are related to approximate counting. The first type refers to promise problems, called unique solution problems, in which the solver is guaranteed that the instance has at most one solution. Many NP-complete problems are randomly reducible to the corresponding unique solution problems. Lastly, we consider the problem of generating almost uniformly distributed solutions, and show that in many cases this problem is computationally equivalent to approximately counting the number of solutions.

Prerequisites. We assume basic familiarity with elementary probability theory (see Appendix D.1). In Section 6.2 we will rely extensively on formulations presented in Section 2.1 (i.e., the "NP search problem" class $\mathcal{PC}$ as well as the sets $R(x) \stackrel{\text{def}}{=} \{y : (x, y) \in R\}$, and $S_R \stackrel{\text{def}}{=} \{x : R(x) \neq \emptyset\}$ defined for every $R \in \mathcal{PC}$). In Sections 6.2.2–6.2.4 we shall extensively use various hashing functions and their properties, as presented in Appendix D.2.

6.1. Probabilistic Polynomial Time

Considering algorithms that utilize random choices, we extend our notion of *efficient algorithms* from *deterministic* polynomial-time algorithms to *probabilistic* polynomial-time algorithms. Two conflicting questions that arise are whether it is reasonable to allow randomized computational steps and whether adding such steps buys us anything.

We first note that random events are an important part of our modeling of the world. We stress that this does not necessarily mean that we assert that the world *per se* includes genuine random choices, but rather that it is beneficial to model the world as including random choices (i.e., some phenomena appear to us as if they are random in some sense). Furthermore, it seems feasible to generate random-looking events (e.g., the outcome of a toss coin).[1] Thus, postulating that seemingly random choices can be generated by a computer is quite natural (and is in fact common practice). At the very least, this postulate yields an intuitive model of computation and the study of such a model is of natural concern.

This leads to the question of whether augmenting the computational model with the ability to make random choices buys us anything. Although randomization is known to

---

[1]Different perspectives on the question of the feasibility of randomized computation are offered in Chapter 8 and Appendix D.4. The pivot of Chapter 8 is the distinction between being actually random and looking random (to computationally restricted observers). In contrast, Appendix D.4 refers to various notions of randomness and to the feasibility of transforming weak forms of randomness into almost perfect forms.

be essential in several computational settings (e.g., cryptography (cf. Appendix C) and sampling (cf. Appendix D.3)), the question is whether randomization is useful in the context of solving decision (and search) problems. This is indeed a very good question, which is further discussed in §6.1.2.1. In fact, one of the main goals of the current section is putting this question forward. To demonstrate the potential benefit of randomized algorithms, we provide a few examples (cf. §6.1.2.2, §6.1.3.1, and §6.1.5.2).

6.1.1. Basic Modeling Issues

Rigorous models of probabilistic (or randomized) algorithms are defined by natural extensions of the basic machine model. We will exemplify this approach by describing the model of probabilistic Turing machines, but we stress that (again) the specific choice of the model is immaterial (as long as it is "reasonable"). A probabilistic Turing machine is defined exactly as a non-deterministic machine (see the first item of Definition 2.7), *but the definition of its computation is fundamentally different*. Specifically, whereas Definition 2.7 refers to the question of whether or not there exists a computation of the machine that (started on a specific input) reaches a certain configuration, in the case of probabilistic Turing machines we refer to *the probability that this event occurs, when at each step a choice is selected uniformly among the relevant possible choices available at this step*. That is, if the transition function of the machine maps the current state-symbol pair to several possible triples, then in the corresponding probabilistic computation one of these triples is selected at random (with equal probability) and the next configuration is determined accordingly. These random choices may be viewed as the internal coin tosses of the machine. (Indeed, as in the case of non-deterministic machines, we may assume without loss of generality that the transition function of the machine maps each state-symbol pair to *exactly* two possible triples; see Exercise 2.4.)

We stress the fundamental difference between the fictitious model of a non-deterministic machine and the realistic model of a probabilistic machine. In the case of a non-deterministic machine we consider the *existence* of an adequate sequence of choices (leading to a desired outcome), and ignore the question of how these choices are actually made. In fact, the selection of such a sequence of choices is merely a mental experiment. In contrast, in the case of a probabilistic machine, at each step a real random choice is actually made (uniformly among a set of predetermined possibilities), and we consider the *probability* of reaching a desired outcome.

In view of the foregoing, we consider the output distribution of such a probabilistic machine on fixed inputs; that is, for a probabilistic machine M and string $x \in \{0, 1\}^*$, we denote by $M(x)$ the output distribution of M when invoked on input x, where the probability is taken uniformly over the machine's internal coin tosses. Needless to say, we will consider the probability that $M(x)$ is a "correct" answer; that is, in the case of a search problem (resp., decision problem) we will be interested in the probability that $M(x)$ is a valid solution for the instance x (resp., represents the correct decision regarding x).

The foregoing description views the internal coin tosses of the machine as taking place on the fly; that is, these coin tosses are performed *on-line* by the machine itself. An alternative model is one in which the sequence of coin tosses is provided by an external device, on a special "random input" tape. In such a case, we view these coin tosses as performed *off-line*. Specifically, we denote by $M'(x, r)$ the (uniquely defined) output of the residual deterministic machine M', when given the (primary) input x and random input r. Indeed, M' is a deterministic machine that takes two inputs (the first representing the actual input and the second representing the "random input"), but we consider the random variable $M(x) \stackrel{\text{def}}{=} M'(x, U_{\ell(|x|)})$, where $\ell(|x|)$ denotes the number of coin tosses "expected" by $M'(x, \cdot)$.

These two perspectives on probabilistic algorithms are closely related: Clearly, the aforementioned residual deterministic machine M' yields a randomized machine M that on input x selects at random a string r of adequate length, and invokes $M'(x, r)$. On the other hand, the computation of any randomized machine M is captured by the residual machine M' that emulates the actions of $M(x)$ based on an auxiliary input r (obtained by M' and representing a possible outcome of the internal coin tosses of M). (Indeed, there is no harm in supplying more coin tosses than are actually used by M, and so the length of the aforementioned auxiliary input may be set to equal the time complexity of M.) For sake of clarity and future reference, we summarize the foregoing discussion in the following definition.

Definition 6.1 (on-line and off-line formulations of probabilistic polynomial time):

- *We say that M is an* on-line probabilistic polynomial-time machine *if there exists a polynomial p such that when invoked on any input $x \in \{0, 1\}^*$, machine M always halts within at most $p(|x|)$ steps* (regardless of the outcome of its internal coin tosses). *In such a case $M(x)$ is a random variable.*
- *We say that M' is an* off-line probabilistic polynomial-time machine *if there exists a polynomial p such that, for every $x \in \{0, 1\}^*$ and $r \in \{0, 1\}^{p(|x|)}$, when invoked on the* primary input x *and the* random-input *sequence r, machine M' halts within at most $p(|x|)$ steps. In such a case, we will consider the random variable $M'(x, U_{p(|x|)})$, where U_m denotes a random variable uniformly distributed over $\{0, 1\}^m$.*

Clearly, in the context of time complexity, the on-line and off-line formulations are equivalent (i.e., given an on-line probabilistic polynomial-time machine we can derive a functionally equivalent off-line (probabilistic polynomial-time) machine, and vice versa). Thus, in the sequel, we will freely use whichever is more convenient.

We stress that the output of a randomized algorithm is no longer a function of its input, but is rather a random variable that depends on the input. Thus, the formulations of solving search and decision problems (see Definitions 1.1 and 1.2, respectively) will be extended to account for the new situation. One major aspect of this extension is that the output may assume values that are not necessarily correct. Needless to say, we would like the output to be correct with very high probability (but not necessarily with probability 1).

Failure probability. Indeed, a major aspect of randomized algorithms (probabilistic machines) is that they may fail (see Exercise 6.1). That is, with some specified ("failure") probability, these algorithms may fail to produce the desired output. We discuss two aspects of this failure: its *type* and its *magnitude*.

1. The type of failure is a qualitative notion. One aspect of this type is whether, in case of failure, the algorithm produces a wrong answer or merely an indication that it failed to find a correct answer. Another aspect is whether failure may occur on all instances or merely on certain types of instances. Let us clarify these aspects by considering three natural types of failure, giving rise to three different types of algorithms.

(a) The most liberal notion of failure is the one of two-sided error. This term originates from the setting of decision problems, where it means that (in case of failure) the algorithm may err in both directions (i.e., it may rule that a yes-instance is a no-instance, and vice versa). In the case of search problems two-sided error means that, when failing, the algorithm may output a wrong answer on any input. That is, the algorithm may falsely rule that the input has no solution and it may also output a wrong solution (both in case the input has a solution and in case it has no solution).

(b) An intermediate notion of failure is the one of one-sided error. Again, the term originates from the setting of decision problems, where it means that the algorithm may err only in one direction (i.e., either on yes-instances or on no-instances). Indeed, there are two natural cases depending on whether the algorithm errs on yes-instances but not on no-instances, or the other way around. Analogous cases occur also in the setting of search problems. In one case the algorithm never outputs a wrong solution but may falsely rule that the input has no solution. In the other case the indication that an input has no solution is never wrong, but the algorithm may output a wrong solution.

(c) The most conservative notion of failure is the one of zero-sided error. In this case, the algorithm's failure amounts to indicating its failure to find an answer (by outputting a special don't know symbol). We stress that in this case the algorithm *never provides a wrong answer.*

Indeed, the foregoing discussion ignores the probability of failure, which is the subject of the next item.

2. The magnitude of failure is a quantitative notion. It refers to the probability that the algorithm fails, where the type of failure is fixed (e.g., as in the foregoing discussion).

When actually using a randomized algorithm we typically wish its failure probability to be negligible, which intuitively means that the failure event is so rare that it can be ignored in practice. Formally, we say that a quantity is negligible if, as a function of the relevant parameter (e.g., the input length), this quantity vanishes faster than the reciprocal of any positive polynomial.

For ease of presentation, we sometimes consider alternative upper bounds on the probability of failure. These bounds are selected in a way that allows (and in fact facilitates) "error reduction" (i.e., converting a probabilistic polynomial-time algorithm that satisfies such an upper bound into one in which the failure probability is negligible). For example, in the case of two-sided error we need to be able to distinguish the correct answer from wrong answers by sampling, and in the other types of failure "hitting" a correct answer suffices.

In the following three sections (i.e., Sections 6.1.2–6.1.4), we will discuss complexity classes corresponding to the aforementioned three *types* of failure. For the sake of simplicity, the failure probability itself will be set to a constant that allows error reduction.

Randomized reductions. Before turning to the more detailed discussion, we mention that randomized reductions play an important role in Complexity Theory. Such reductions can be defined analogously to the standard Cook-reductions (resp., Karp-reductions), and again a discussion of the type and magnitude of the failure probability is in place. For clarity, we spell out the two-sided error versions.

- In analogy to Definition 2.9, we say that a problem Π is probabilistic polynomial-time reducible to a problem Π' if there exists a probabilistic polynomial-time oracle machine M such that, for every function f that solves Π' and for every x, with probability at least $1 - \mu(|x|)$, the output $M^f(x)$ is a correct solution to the instance x, where μ is a negligible function.
- In analogy to Definition 2.11, we say that a decision problem S is reducible to a decision problem S' via a randomized Karp-reduction if there exists a probabilistic polynomial-time algorithm A such that, for every x, it holds that $\Pr[\chi_{S'}(A(x)) = \chi_S(x)] \geq 1 - \mu(|x|)$, where χ_S (resp., $\chi_{S'}$) is the characteristic function of S (resp., S') and μ is a negligible function.

These reductions preserve efficient solvability and are transitive: See Exercise 6.2.

6.1.2. Two-Sided Error: The Complexity Class BPP

In this section we consider the most liberal notion of probabilistic polynomial-time algorithms that is still meaningful. We allow the algorithm to err on each input, but require the error probability to be *negligible*. The latter requirement guarantees the usefulness of such algorithms, because in reality we may ignore the negligible error probability.

Before focusing on the decision problem setting, let us say a few words on the search problem setting (see §1.2.2.1). Following the previous paragraph, we say that a probabilistic (polynomial-time) algorithm A solves the search problem of the relation R if for every $x \in S_R$ (i.e., $R(x) \overset{\text{def}}{=} \{y : (x, y) \in R\} \neq \emptyset$) it holds that $\Pr[A(x) \in R(x)] > 1 - \mu(|x|)$ and for every $x \notin S_R$ it holds that $\Pr[A(x) = \perp] > 1 - \mu(|x|)$, where μ is a negligible function. Note that we did not require that, when invoked on input x that has a solution (i.e., $R(x) \neq \emptyset$), the algorithm always outputs the same solution. Indeed, a stronger requirement is that for every such x there exists $y \in R(x)$ such that $\Pr[A(x) = y] > 1 - \mu(|x|)$. The latter version and quantitative relaxations of it allow for error reduction (see Exercise 6.3).

Turning to decision problems, we consider probabilistic polynomial-time algorithms that err with negligible probability. That is, we say that a probabilistic (polynomial-time) algorithm A decides membership in S if for every x it holds that $\Pr[A(x) = \chi_S(x)] > 1 - \mu(|x|)$, where χ_S is the characteristic function of S (i.e., $\chi_S(x) = 1$ if $x \in S$ and $\chi_S(x) = 0$ otherwise) and μ is a negligible function. The class of decision problems that are solvable by probabilistic polynomial-time algorithms is denoted $\mathcal{BPP}$, standing for Bounded-error Probabilistic Polynomial time. Actually, the standard definition refers to machines that err with probability at most $1/3$.

Definition 6.2 (the class $\mathcal{BPP}$): *A decision problem S is in $\mathcal{BPP}$ if there exists a probabilistic polynomial-time algorithm A such that for every $x \in S$ it holds that $\Pr[A(x) = 1] \geq 2/3$ and for every $x \notin S$ it holds that $\Pr[A(x) = 0] \geq 2/3$.*

The choice of the constant $2/3$ is immaterial, and any other constant greater than $1/2$ will do (and yields the very same class). Similarly, the complementary constant $1/3$ can be replaced by various negligible functions (while preserving the class). Both facts are special cases of the robustness of the class, discussed next, which is established using the process of error reduction.

Error reduction (or confidence amplification). For $\varepsilon : \mathbb{N} \to (0, 0.5)$, let $\mathcal{BPP}_\varepsilon$ denote the class of decision problems that can be solved in probabilistic polynomial time with error probability upper-bounded by ε; that is, $S \in \mathcal{BPP}_\varepsilon$ if there exists a probabilistic polynomial-time algorithm A such that for every x it holds that $\Pr[A(x) \neq \chi_S(x)] \leq \varepsilon(|x|)$. By definition, $\mathcal{BPP} = \mathcal{BPP}_{1/3}$. However, a wide range of other classes also equal $\mathcal{BPP}$. In particular, we mention two extreme cases:

1. For every positive polynomial p and $\varepsilon(n) = (1/2) - (1/p(n))$, the class $\mathcal{BPP}_\varepsilon$ equals $\mathcal{BPP}$. That is, any error that is ("noticeably") bounded away from $1/2$ (i.e., error $(1/2) - (1/\mathrm{poly}(n))$) can be reduced to an error of $1/3$.
2. For every positive polynomial p and $\varepsilon(n) = 2^{-p(n)}$, the class $\mathcal{BPP}_\varepsilon$ equals $\mathcal{BPP}$. That is, an error of $1/3$ can be further reduced to an exponentially vanishing error.

Both facts are proved by invoking the weaker algorithm (i.e., the one having a larger error probability bound) for an adequate number of times, and ruling by majority. We stress that invoking a randomized machine several times means that the random choices made in the various invocations are independent of one another. The success probability of such a process is analyzed by applying an adequate Law of Large Numbers (see Exercise 6.4).

6.1.2.1. On the Power of Randomization

Let us turn back to the natural question raised at the beginning of Section 6.1; that is, *was anything gained by extending the definition of efficient computation to include also probabilistic polynomial-time ones.*

This phrasing seems too generic. We certainly gained the ability to toss coins (and generate various distributions). More concretely, randomized algorithms are essential in many settings (see, e.g., Chapter 9, Section 10.1.2, Appendix C, and Appendix D.3) and seem essential in others (see, e.g., Sections 6.2.2–6.2.4). What we mean to ask here is *whether allowing randomization increases the power of polynomial-time algorithms also in the restricted context of solving decision and search problems.*

The question is whether $\mathcal{BPP}$ extends beyond $\mathcal{P}$ (where clearly $\mathcal{P} \subseteq \mathcal{BPP}$). It is commonly conjectured that the answer is negative. Specifically, under some reasonable assumptions, it holds that $\mathcal{BPP} = \mathcal{P}$ (see Part 1 of Theorem 8.19). We note, however, that a polynomial slow down occurs in the proof of the latter result; that is, randomized algorithms that run in time $t(\cdot)$ are emulated by deterministic algorithms that run in time $\mathrm{poly}(t(\cdot))$. This slow down seems inherent to the aforementioned approach (see §8.3.3.2). Furthermore, for some concrete problems (most notably primality testing (cf. §6.1.2.2)), the known probabilistic polynomial-time algorithm is significantly faster (and conceptually simpler) than the known deterministic polynomial-time algorithm. Thus, we believe that even in the context of decision problems, the notion of probabilistic polynomial-time algorithms is advantageous.

We note that the fundamental nature of $\mathcal{BPP}$ will remain intact even in the (rather unlikely) case that it turns out that randomization offers no computational advantage (i.e., even if every problem that can be decided in probabilistic polynomial time can be decided by a deterministic algorithm of essentially the same complexity). Such a result would address a fundamental question regarding the power of randomness.[2] We now turn

---

[2] By analogy, establishing that $\mathcal{IP} = \mathcal{PSPACE}$ (cf. Theorem 9.4) does not diminish the importance of any of these classes, because each class models something fundamentally different.

from the foregoing philosophical (and partially hypothetical) discussion to a concrete discussion of what is known about $\mathcal{BPP}$.

BPP is in the Polynomial-time Hierarchy. While it may be that $\mathcal{BPP} = \mathcal{P}$, it is not known whether or not $\mathcal{BPP}$ is contained in $\mathcal{NP}$. The source of trouble is the two-sided error probability of $\mathcal{BPP}$, which is incompatible with the absolute rejection of no-instances required in the definition of $\mathcal{NP}$ (see Exercise 6.8). In view of this ignorance, it is interesting to note that $\mathcal{BPP}$ resides in the second level of the Polynomial-time Hierarchy (i.e., $\mathcal{BPP} \subseteq \Sigma_2$). This is a corollary of Theorem 6.9.

Trivial derandomization. A straightforward way of eliminating randomness from an algorithm is trying all possible outcomes of its internal coin tosses, collecting the relevant statistics, and deciding accordingly. This yields $\mathcal{BPP} \subseteq \mathcal{PSPACE} \subseteq \mathcal{EXP}$, which is considered the trivial derandomization of $\mathcal{BPP}$. In Section 8.3 we will consider various non-trivial derandomizations of $\mathcal{BPP}$, which are known under various intractability assumptions. The interested reader, who may be puzzled by the connection between derandomization and computational difficulty, is referred to Chapter 8.

Non-uniform derandomization. In many settings (and specifically in the context of solving search and decision problems), the power of randomization is superseded by the power of non-uniform advice. Intuitively, the non-uniform advice may specify a sequence of coin tosses that is good for all (primary) inputs of a specific length. In the context of solving search and decision problems, such an advice must be good for *each* of these inputs,[3] and thus its existence is guaranteed only if the error probability is low enough (so as to support a union bound). The latter condition can be guaranteed by error reduction, and thus we get the following result.

Theorem 6.3: $\mathcal{BPP}$ is (strictly) *contained in* $\mathcal{P}$/poly.

Proof: Recall that $\mathcal{P}$/poly contains undecidable problems (Theorem 3.7), which are certainly not in $\mathcal{BPP}$. Thus, we focus on showing that $\mathcal{BPP} \subseteq \mathcal{P}$/poly. By the discussion regarding error reduction, for every $S \in \mathcal{BPP}$ there exists a (deterministic) polynomial-time algorithm A and a polynomial p such that for every x it holds that $\Pr[A(x, U_{p(|x|)}) \neq \chi_S(x)] < 2^{-|x|}$. Using a union bound, it follows that $\Pr_{r \in \{0,1\}^{p(n)}}[\exists x \in \{0, 1\}^n \text{ s.t. } A(x, r) \neq \chi_S(x)] < 1$. Thus, for every $n \in \mathbb{N}$, there exists a string $r_n \in \{0, 1\}^{p(n)}$ such that for every $x \in \{0, 1\}^n$ it holds that $A(x, r_n) = \chi_S(x)$. Using such a sequence of r_n's as advice, we obtain the desired non-uniform machine (establishing $S \in \mathcal{P}$/poly). ∎

Digest. The proof of Theorem 6.3 combines error reduction with a simple application of the Probabilistic Method (cf. [11]), where the latter refers to proving the existence of an object by analyzing the probability that a random object is adequate. In this case, we sought a non-uniform advice, and proved it existence by analyzing the probability that a random advice is good. The latter event was analyzed by identifying the space of possible advice with the set of possible sequences of internal coin tosses of a randomized algorithm.

---

[3]In other contexts (see, e.g., Chapters 7 and 8), it suffices to have an advice that is good on the average, where the average is taken over all relevant (primary) inputs.

6.1.2.2. A Probabilistic Polynomial-Time Primality Test

> **Teaching note:** Although primality has been recently shown to be in $\mathcal{P}$, we believe that the following example provides a nice illustration to the power of randomized algorithms.

We present a simple probabilistic polynomial-time algorithm for deciding whether or not a given number is a prime. The only number-theoretic facts that we use are

Fact 1: For every prime $p > 2$, each quadratic residue mod p has exactly two square roots mod p (and they sum up to p).[4]

Fact 2: For every (odd and non-integer-power) composite number N, each quadratic residue mod N has at least four square roots mod N.

Our algorithm uses as a black-box an algorithm, denoted sqrt, that given a prime p and a quadratic residue mod p, denoted s, returns the smallest among the two modular square roots of s. There is no guarantee as to what the output is in the case that the input is not of the aforementioned form (and in particular in the case that p is not a prime). Thus, we actually present a probabilistic polynomial-time reduction of testing primality to extracting square roots modulo a prime (which is a search problem with a promise; see Section 2.4.1).

Construction 6.4 (the reduction): *On input a natural number $N > 2$ do*

1. *If N is either even or an integer power[5] then* reject.
2. *Uniformly select $r \in \{1, \ldots, N - 1\}$, and set $s \leftarrow r^2$ mod N.*
3. *Let $r' \leftarrow$ sqrt(s, N). If $r' \equiv \pm r$ (mod N) then* accept *else* reject.

Indeed, in the case that N is composite, the reduction invokes sqrt on an illegitimate input (i.e., it makes a query that violates the promise of the problem at the target of the reduction). In such a case, there is no guarantee as to what sqrt answers, but actually a bluntly wrong answer only plays in our favor. In general, we will show that if N is composite, then the reduction rejects with probability at least $1/2$, regardless of how sqrt answers. We mention that there exists a probabilistic polynomial-time algorithm for implementing sqrt (see Exercise 6.16).

> **Proposition 6.5:** *Construction 6.4 constitutes a probabilistic polynomial-time reduction of testing primality to extracting square roots module a prime. Furthermore, if the input is a prime then the reduction always accepts, and otherwise it rejects with probability at least $1/2$.*

We stress that Proposition 6.5 refers to the reduction itself; that is, sqrt is viewed as a ("perfect") oracle that, for every prime P and quadratic residue s (mod P), returns $r < s/2$ such that $r^2 \equiv s$ (mod P). Combining Proposition 6.5 with a probabilistic

---

[4]That is, for every $r \in \{1, \ldots, p - 1\}$, the equation $x^2 \equiv r^2$ (mod p) has two solutions modulo p (i.e., r and $p - r$).

[5]This can be checked by scanning all possible powers $e \in \{2, \ldots, \log_2 N\}$, and (approximately) solving the equation $x^e = N$ for each value of e (i.e., finding the smallest integer i such that $i^e \geq N$). Such a solution can be found by binary search.

polynomial-time algorithm that computes $\mathtt{sqrt}$ with negligible error probability, we obtain that testing primality is in $\mathcal{BPP}$.

> **Proof:** By Fact 1, on input a prime number N, Construction 6.4 always accepts (because in this case, for every $r \in \{1, \ldots, N-1\}$, it holds that $\mathtt{sqrt}(r^2 \bmod N, N) \in \{r, N-r\}$). On the other hand, suppose that N is an odd composite that is not an integer power. Then, by Fact 2, each quadratic residue s has at least four square roots, and each of these square roots is equally likely to be chosen at Step 2 (in other words, s yields no information regarding which of its modular square roots was selected in Step 2). Thus, for every such s, the probability that either $\mathtt{sqrt}(s, N)$ or $N - \mathtt{sqrt}(s, N)$ equal the root chosen in Step 2 is at most $2/4$. It follows that, on input a composite number, the reduction rejects with probability at least $1/2$. ∎

Reflection. Construction 6.4 illustrates an interesting aspect of randomized algorithms (or rather reductions), that is, their ability to take advantage of information that is unknown to the invoked subroutine. Specifically, Construction 6.4 generates a problem instance (N, s), which hides crucial information (regarding how s was generated). Any subroutine that answers correctly in the case that N is prime provides probabilistic evidence that N is a prime, where the probability space refers to the missing information (regarding how s was generated in the case that N is composite).

Comment. Testing primality is actually in $\mathcal{P}$. However, the deterministic algorithm demonstrating this fact is more complex than Construction 6.4 (and its analysis is even more complicated).

6.1.3. One-Sided Error: The Complexity Classes RP and coRP

In this section we consider notions of probabilistic polynomial-time algorithms having one-sided error. The notion of one-sided error refers to a natural partition of the set of instances, that is, yes-instances versus no-instances in the case of decision problems, and instances having solution versus instances having no solution in the case of search problems. We focus on decision problems, and comment that an analogous treatment can be provided for search problems (see Exercise 6.3).

> **Definition 6.6** (the class $\mathcal{RP}$):[6] *A decision problem S is in $\mathcal{RP}$ if there exists a probabilistic polynomial-time algorithm A such that for every $x \in S$ it holds that $\Pr[A(x)=1] \geq 1/2$ and for every $x \notin S$ it holds that $\Pr[A(x)=0] = 1$.*

The choice of the constant $1/2$ is immaterial, and any other constant greater than zero will do (and yields the very same class). Similarly, this constant can be replaced by $1 - \mu(|x|)$ for various negligible functions μ (while preserving the class). Both facts are special cases of the robustness of the class (see Exercise 6.5).

Observe that $\mathcal{RP} \subseteq \mathcal{NP}$ (see Exercise 6.8) and that $\mathcal{RP} \subseteq \mathcal{BPP}$ (by the aforementioned error reduction). Defining $\text{co}\mathcal{RP} = \{\{0,1\}^* \setminus S : S \in \mathcal{RP}\}$, note that $\text{co}\mathcal{RP}$

---

[6]The initials RP stands for Random Polynomial time, which fails to convey the restricted type of error allowed in this class. The only nice feature of this notation is that it is reminiscent of NP, thus reflecting the fact that $\mathcal{RP}$ is a randomized polynomial-time class that is contained in $\mathcal{NP}$.

corresponds to the opposite direction of one-sided error probability. That is, *a decision problem S is in coRP if there exists a probabilistic polynomial-time algorithm A such that for every $x \in S$ it holds that $\Pr[A(x)=1] = 1$ and for every $x \notin S$ it holds that $\Pr[A(x)=0] \geq 1/2$.*

6.1.3.1. Testing Polynomial Identity

An appealing example of a one-sided error randomized algorithm refers to the problem of determining whether two polynomials are identical. For simplicity, we assume that we are given an oracle for the evaluation of each of the two polynomials. An alternative presentation that refers to polynomials that are represented by arithmetic circuits (cf. Appendix B.3) yields a standard decision problem in coRP (see Exercise 6.17). Either way, we refer to multivariate polynomials and to the question of whether they are identical over any field (or, equivalently, whether they are identical over a sufficiently large finite field). Note that it suffices to consider finite fields that are larger than the degree of the two polynomials.

> **Construction 6.7** (Polynomial-Identity Test): *Let n be an integer and F be a finite field. Given black-box access to $p, q : F^n \to F$, uniformly select $r_1, \ldots, r_n \in F$, and accept if and only if $p(r_1, \ldots, r_n) = q(r_1, \ldots, r_n)$.*

Clearly, if $p \equiv q$ then Construction 6.7 always accepts. The following lemma implies that if p and q are different polynomials, each of total degree at most d over the finite field F, then Construction 6.7 accepts with probability at most $d/|F|$.

> **Lemma 6.8:** *Let $p : F^n \to F$ be a non-zero polynomial of total degree d over the finite field F. Then*
>
> $$\Pr_{r_1, \ldots, r_n \in F}[p(r_1, \ldots, r_n) = 0] \leq \frac{d}{|F|}.$$

Proof: The lemma is proven by induction on n. The base case of $n = 1$ follows immediately by the Fundamental Theorem of Algebra (i.e., any non-zero univariate polynomial of degree d has at most d distinct roots). In the induction step, we write p as a polynomial in its first variable with coefficients that are polynomials in the other variables. That is,

$$p(x_1, x_2, \ldots, x_n) = \sum_{i=0}^{d} p_i(x_2, \ldots, x_n) \cdot x_1^i$$

where p_i is a polynomial of total degree at most $d - i$. Let i be the largest integer for which p_i is not identically zero. Dismissing the case $i = 0$ and using the induction hypothesis, we have

$$\Pr_{r_1, r_2, \ldots, r_n}[p(r_1, r_2, \ldots, r_n) = 0]$$
$$\leq \Pr_{r_2, \ldots, r_n}[p_i(r_2, \ldots, r_n) = 0]$$
$$\quad + \Pr_{r_1, r_2, \ldots, r_n}[p(r_1, r_2, \ldots, r_n) = 0 \mid p_i(r_2, \ldots, r_n) \neq 0]$$
$$\leq \frac{d - i}{|F|} + \frac{i}{|F|}$$

where the second term is bounded by fixing any sequence $r_2, \ldots, r_n$ for which $p_i(r_2, \ldots, r_n) \neq 0$ and considering the univariate polynomial $p'(x) \stackrel{\text{def}}{=} p(x, r_2, \ldots, r_n)$ (which by hypothesis is a non-zero polynomial of degree i). ∎

Reflection. Lemma 6.8 may be viewed as asserting that for every non-zero polynomial of degree d over F at least a $1 - (d/|\text{F}|)$ fraction of its domain does not evaluate to zero. Thus, if $d \ll |\text{F}|$ then most of the evaluation points constitute a witness for the fact that the polynomial is non-zero. We know of no efficient deterministic algorithm that, given a representation of the polynomial via an arithmetic circuit, finds such a witness. Indeed, Construction 6.7 attempts to find a witness by merely selecting it at random.

6.1.3.2. Relating BPP to RP

A natural question regarding probabilistic polynomial-time algorithms refers to the relation between two-sided and one-sided error probability. For example, *is $\mathcal{BPP}$ contained in $\mathcal{RP}$?* Loosely speaking, we show that $\mathcal{BPP}$ is reducible to $\text{co}\mathcal{RP}$ by *one-sided error* randomized Karp-reductions, where the actual statement refers to the promise problem versions of both classes (briefly defined in the following paragraph). Note that $\mathcal{BPP}$ is trivially reducible to $\text{co}\mathcal{RP}$ by *two-sided error* randomized Karp-reductions, whereas a deterministic Karp-reduction of $\mathcal{BPP}$ to $\text{co}\mathcal{RP}$ would imply $\mathcal{BPP} = \text{co}\mathcal{RP} = \mathcal{RP}$ (see Exercise 6.9).

First, we refer the reader to the general discussion of promise problems in Section 2.4.1. Analogously to Definition 2.31, we say that the promise problem $\Pi = (S_{\text{yes}}, S_{\text{no}})$ is in (the promise problem extension of) $\mathcal{BPP}$ *if there exists a probabilistic polynomial-time algorithm A such that for every $x \in S_{\text{yes}}$ it holds that $\Pr[A(x) = 1] \geq 2/3$ and for every $x \in S_{\text{no}}$ it holds that $\Pr[A(x) = 0] \geq 2/3$.* Similarly, Π is in $\text{co}\mathcal{RP}$ if for every $x \in S_{\text{yes}}$ it holds that $\Pr[A(x) = 1] = 1$ and for every $x \in S_{\text{no}}$ it holds that $\Pr[A(x) = 0] \geq 1/2$. Probabilistic reductions among promise problems are defined by adapting the conventions of Section 2.4.1; specifically, queries that violate the promise at the target of the reduction may be answered arbitrarily.

Theorem 6.9: *Any problem in $\mathcal{BPP}$ is reducible by a one-sided error randomized Karp-reduction to $\text{co}\mathcal{RP}$, where $\text{co}\mathcal{RP}$ (and possibly also $\mathcal{BPP}$) denotes the corresponding class of promise problems. Specifically, the reduction always maps a* no-*instance to a* no-*instance.*

It follows that $\mathcal{BPP}$ is reducible by a one-sided error randomized Cook-reduction to $\mathcal{RP}$. Thus, using the conventions of Section 3.2.2 and referring to classes of promise problems, we may write $\mathcal{BPP} \subseteq \mathcal{RP}^{\mathcal{RP}}$. In fact, since $\mathcal{RP}^{\mathcal{RP}} \subseteq \mathcal{BPP}^{\mathcal{BPP}} = \mathcal{BPP}$, we have $\mathcal{BPP} = \mathcal{RP}^{\mathcal{RP}}$. Theorem 6.9 may be paraphrased as saying that the combination of the one-sided error probability of the reduction and the one-sided error probability of $\text{co}\mathcal{RP}$ can account for the two-sided error probability of $\mathcal{BPP}$. We warn that this statement is not a triviality like $1 + 1 = 2$, and in particular we do not know whether it holds for classes of standard decision problems (rather than for the classes of promise problems considered in Theorem 6.9).

Proof: Recall that we can easily reduce the error probability of BPP-algorithms, and derive probabilistic polynomial-time algorithms of exponentially vanishing error probability. But this does not eliminate the error altogether (not even on "one side"). In general, there seems to be no hope of eliminating the error, unless we (either do something earthshaking or) *change the setting as done when allowing a one-sided error randomized reduction to a problem in* $\text{co}\mathcal{RP}$. The latter setting can be viewed as a two-move randomized game (i.e., a random move by the reduction followed by a random move by the decision procedure of $\text{co}\mathcal{RP}$), and it enables the application of different quantifiers to the two moves (i.e., allowing error in one direction in the first quantifier and error in the other direction in the second quantifier). In the next paragraph, which is inessential to the actual proof, we illustrate the potential power of this setting.

Teaching note: The following illustration represents an alternative way of proving Theorem 6.9. This way seems conceptually simpler but it requires a starting point (or rather an assumption) that is much harder to establish, where both comparisons are with respect to the actual proof of Theorem 6.9 (which follows the illustration).

An illustration. Suppose that for some set $S \in \mathcal{BPP}$ there exists a polynomial p' and an off-line BPP-algorithm A' such that for every x it holds that $\Pr_{r \in \{0,1\}^{2p'(|x|)}}[A'(x,r) \neq \chi_S(x)] < 2^{-(p'(|x|)+1)}$; that is, the algorithm uses $2p'(|x|)$ bits of randomness and has error probability smaller than $2^{-p'(|x|)}/2$. Note that such an algorithm cannot be obtained by standard error reduction (see Exercise 6.10). Anyhow, such a small error probability allows a partition of the string r such that one part accounts for the entire error probability on yes-instances while the other part accounts for the error probability on no-instances. Specifically, for every $x \in S$, it holds that $\Pr_{r' \in \{0,1\}^{p'(|x|)}}[(\forall r'' \in \{0,1\}^{p'(|x|)}) \, A'(x,r'r'')=1] > 1/2$, whereas for every $x \notin S$ and every $r' \in \{0,1\}^{p'(|x|)}$ it holds that $\Pr_{r'' \in \{0,1\}^{p'(|x|)}}[A'(x,r'r'')=1] < 1/2$. Thus, the error on yes-instances is "pushed" to the selection of r', whereas the error on no-instances is pushed to the selection of r''. This yields a one-sided error randomized Karp-reduction that maps x to (x,r'), where r' is uniformly selected in $\{0,1\}^{p'(|x|)}$, such that deciding S is reduced to the coRP problem (regarding pairs (x,r')) that is decided by the (on-line) randomized algorithm A'' defined by $A''(x,r') \stackrel{\text{def}}{=} A'(x,r'U_{p'(|x|)})$. For details, see Exercise 6.11. The actual proof, which avoids the aforementioned hypothesis, follows.

The actual starting point. Consider any BPP-problem with a characteristic function χ (which, in case of a promise problem, is a partial function, defined only over the promise). By standard error reduction, there exists a probabilistic polynomial-time algorithm A such that for every x on which χ is defined it holds that $\Pr[A(x) \neq \chi(x)] < \mu(|x|)$, where μ is a negligible function. Looking at the corresponding residual (off-line) algorithm A' and denoting by p the polynomial that bounds the running time of A, we have

$$\Pr_{r \in \{0,1\}^{p(|x|)}}[A'(x,r) \neq \chi(x)] < \mu(|x|) < \frac{1}{2p(|x|)} \tag{6.1}$$

for all sufficiently long x's on which χ is defined. We show a randomized one-sided error Karp-reduction of χ to a promise problem in $\text{co}\mathcal{RP}$.

> **Teaching note:** Some readers may prefer skipping the following two paragraphs and proceeding directly to the formal description of the randomized mapping (which follows). To such readers, we recommend returning to the two skipped paragraphs after reading the formal analysis.

The main idea. As in the illustrating paragraph, the basic idea is "pushing" the error probability on yes-instances (of χ) to the reduction, while pushing the error probability on no-instances to the coRP-problem. Focusing on the case that $\chi(x) = 1$, this is achieved by augmenting the input x with a random sequence of "modifiers" that act on the random-input of algorithm A' such that for a good choice of modifiers it holds that for every $r \in \{0, 1\}^{p(|x|)}$ there exists a modifier in this sequence that when applied to r yields r' that satisfies $A'(x, r') = 1$. Indeed, not all sequences of modifiers are good, but a random sequence will be good with high probability and bad sequences will be accounted for in the error probability of the reduction. On the other hand, using only modifiers that are permutations guarantees that the error probability on no-instances only increase by a factor that equals the number of modifiers that we use, and this error probability will be accounted for by the error probability of the coRP-problem. Details follow.

The aforementioned modifiers are implemented by shifts (of the set of all strings by fixed offsets). Thus, we augment the input x with a random sequence of shifts, denoted $s_1, \ldots, s_m \in \{0, 1\}^{p(|x|)}$, such that for a good choice of $(s_1, \ldots, s_m)$ it holds that for every $r \in \{0, 1\}^{p(|x|)}$ there exists an $i \in [m]$ such that $A'(x, r \oplus s_i) = 1$. We will show that, for any yes-instance x and a suitable choice of m, with very high probability, a random sequence of shifts is good. Thus, for $A''(\langle x, s_1, \ldots, s_m \rangle, r) \overset{\text{def}}{=} \vee_{i=1}^{m} A'(x, r \oplus s_i)$, it holds that, with very high probability over the choice of $s_1, \ldots, s_m$, a yes-instance x is mapped to an augmented input $\langle x, s_1, \ldots, s_m \rangle$ that is accepted by A'' with probability 1. On the other hand, the acceptance probability of augmented no-instances (for any choice of shifts) only increases by a factor of m. In further detailing the foregoing idea, we start by explicitly stating the simple randomized mapping (to be used as a randomized Karp-reduction), and next define the target promise problem.

The randomized mapping. On input $x \in \{0, 1\}^n$, we set $m = p(|x|)$, uniformly select $s_1, \ldots, s_m \in \{0, 1\}^m$, and output the pair $(x, \bar{s})$, where $\bar{s} = (s_1, \ldots, s_m)$. Note that this mapping, denoted M, is easily computable by a probabilistic polynomial-time algorithm.

The promise problem. We define the following promise problem, denoted $\Pi = (\Pi_{\text{yes}}, \Pi_{\text{no}})$, having instances of the form $(x, \bar{s})$ such that $|\bar{s}| = p(|x|)^2$.

- The yes-instances are pairs $(x, \bar{s})$, where $\bar{s} = (s_1, \ldots, s_m)$ and $m = p(|x|)$, such that for every $r \in \{0, 1\}^m$ there exists an i satisfying $A'(x, r \oplus s_i) = 1$.
- The no-instances are pairs $(x, \bar{s})$, where again $\bar{s} = (s_1, \ldots, s_m)$ and $m = p(|x|)$, such that for at least half of the possible $r \in \{0, 1\}^m$, for every i it holds that $A'(x, r \oplus s_i) = 0$.

To see that Π is indeed a co$\mathcal{RP}$ promise problem, we consider the following randomized algorithm. On input $(x, (s_1, \ldots, s_m))$, where $m = p(|x|) = |s_1| = \cdots = |s_m|$, the algorithm uniformly selects $r \in \{0, 1\}^m$, and accepts if and only if $A'(x, r \oplus s_i) = 1$ for some $i \in \{1, \dots, m\}$. Indeed, yes-instances of Π are accepted with probability 1, whereas no-instances of Π are rejected with probability at least $1/2$.

Analyzing the reduction: We claim that the randomized mapping M reduces χ to Π with one-sided error. Specifically, we will prove two claims.

Claim 1: If x is a yes-instance (i.e., $\chi(x) = 1$) then $\Pr[M(x) \in \Pi_{\text{yes}}] > 1/2$.

Claim 2: If x is a no-instance (i.e., $\chi(x) = 0$) then $\Pr[M(x) \in \Pi_{\text{no}}] = 1$.

We start with Claim 2, which is easier to establish. Recall that $M(x) = (x, (s_1, \dots, s_m))$, where $s_1, \dots, s_m$ are uniformly and independently distributed in $\{0, 1\}^m$. We note that (by Eq. (6.1) and $\chi(x) = 0$), for every possible choice of $s_1, \dots, s_m \in \{0, 1\}^m$ and every $i \in \{1, \dots, m\}$, the fraction of r's that satisfy $A'(x, r \oplus s_i) = 1$ is at most $\frac{1}{2m}$. Thus, for every possible choice of $s_1, \dots, s_m \in \{0, 1\}^m$, for at most half of the possible $r \in \{0, 1\}^m$ there exists an i such that $A'(x, r \oplus s_i) = 1$ holds. Hence, the reduction M *always* maps the no-instance x (i.e., $\chi(x) = 0$) to a no-instance of Π (i.e., an element of Π_{no}).

Turning to Claim 1 (which refers to $\chi(x) = 1$), we will show shortly that in this case, with very high probability, the reduction M maps x to a yes-instance of Π. We upper-bound the probability that the reduction fails (in case $\chi(x) = 1$) as follows:

$$\Pr[M(x) \notin \Pi_{\text{yes}}] = \Pr_{s_1, \dots, s_m}[\exists r \in \{0, 1\}^m \text{ s.t. } (\forall i) \; A'(x, r \oplus s_i) = 0]$$

$$\leq \sum_{r \in \{0,1\}^m} \Pr_{s_1, \dots, s_m}[(\forall i) \; A'(x, r \oplus s_i) = 0]$$

$$= \sum_{r \in \{0,1\}^m} \prod_{i=1}^m \Pr_{s_i}[A'(x, r \oplus s_i) = 0]$$

$$< 2^m \cdot \left(\frac{1}{2m}\right)^m$$

where the last inequality is due to Eq. (6.1). It follows that if $\chi(x) = 1$ then $\Pr[M(x) \in \Pi_{\text{yes}}] \gg 1/2$.

Combining both claims, it follows that the randomized mapping M reduces χ to Π, with one-sided error on yes-instances. Recalling that $\Pi \in \text{co}\mathcal{RP}$, the theorem follows. $\blacksquare$

BPP is in PH. The traditional presentation of the ideas underlying the proof of Theorem 6.9 uses them for showing that $\mathcal{BPP}$ *is in the Polynomial-time Hierarchy* (where both classes refer to standard decision problems). Specifically, to prove that $\mathcal{BPP} \subseteq \Sigma_2$ (see Definition 3.8), define the polynomial-time computable predicate $\varphi(x, \bar{s}, r) \overset{\text{def}}{=} \bigvee_{i=1}^m (A'(x, s_i \oplus r) = 1)$, and observe that

$$\chi(x) = 1 \Rightarrow \exists \bar{s} \, \forall r \; \varphi(x, \bar{s}, r) \tag{6.2}$$

$$\chi(x) = 0 \Rightarrow \forall \bar{s} \, \exists r \; \neg\varphi(x, \bar{s}, r) \tag{6.3}$$

(where Eq. (6.3) is equivalent to $\neg \exists \bar{s} \, \forall r \; \varphi(x, \bar{s}, r)$). Note that Claim 1 (in the proof of Theorem 6.9) establishes that *most* sequences $\bar{s}$ satisfy $\forall r \; \varphi(x, \bar{s}, r)$, whereas Eq. (6.2) only requires the existence of *at least one* such $\bar{s}$. Similarly, Claim 2 establishes that for every $\bar{s}$ *most* choices of r violate $\varphi(x, \bar{s}, r)$, whereas Eq. (6.3) only requires that for every $\bar{s}$ there exists *at least one* such r. We comment that the same proof idea yields a variety of similar statements (e.g., $\mathcal{BPP} \subseteq \mathcal{MA}$, where $\mathcal{MA}$ is a randomized version of $\mathcal{NP}$ defined in Section 9.1).[7]

6.1.4. Zero-Sided Error: The Complexity Class ZPP

We now consider probabilistic polynomial-time algorithms that never err, but may fail to provide an answer. Focusing on decision problems, the corresponding class is denoted $\mathcal{ZPP}$ (standing for Zero-error Probabilistic Polynomial time). The standard definition of $\mathcal{ZPP}$ is in terms of machines that output $\bot$ (indicating failure) with probability at most $1/2$. That is, $S \in \mathcal{ZPP}$ *if there exists a probabilistic polynomial-time algorithm A such that for every $x \in \{0, 1\}^*$ it holds that* $\Pr[A(x) \in \{\chi_S(x), \bot\}] = 1$ *and* $\Pr[A(x) = \chi_S(x)] \geq 1/2$, *where* $\chi_S(x) = 1$ *if $x \in S$ and $\chi_S(x) = 0$ otherwise.* Again, the choice of the constant (i.e., $1/2$) is immaterial, and "error reduction" can be performed showing that algorithms that yield a meaningful answer with noticeable probability can be amplified to algorithms that fail with negligible probability (see Exercise 6.6).

Theorem 6.10: $\mathcal{ZPP} = \mathcal{RP} \cap \text{co}\mathcal{RP}$.

Proof Sketch: The fact that $\mathcal{ZPP} \subseteq \mathcal{RP}$ (as well as $\mathcal{ZPP} \subseteq \text{co}\mathcal{RP}$) follows by a trivial transformation of the ZPP-algorithm, that is, replacing the failure indicator $\bot$ by a "no" verdict (resp., "yes" verdict). Note that the choice of what to say in case the ZPP-algorithm fails is determined by the type of error that we are allowed.

In order to prove that $\mathcal{RP} \cap \text{co}\mathcal{RP} \subseteq \mathcal{ZPP}$ we combine the two algorithms guaranteed for a set in $\mathcal{RP} \cap \text{co}\mathcal{RP}$. The point is that we can trust the RP-algorithm (resp., coNP-algorithm) in the case that it says "yes" (resp., "no"), but not in the case that it says "no" (resp., "yes"). Thus, we invoke both algorithms, and output a definite answer only if we obtain an answer that we can trust (which happens with high probability). Otherwise, we output $\bot$. $\qquad\qquad\Box$

Expected polynomial time. In some sources $\mathcal{ZPP}$ is defined in terms of randomized algorithms that run in expected polynomial time and always output the correct answer. This definition is equivalent to the one we used (see Exercise 6.7).

6.1.5. Randomized Log-Space

In this section we discuss probabilistic polynomial-time algorithms that are further restricted such that they are allowed to use only a logarithmic amount of space.

Prerequisites. Technically speaking, the current section is self-contained. Nevertheless, the interested reader may obtain a wider perspective on space complexity from Chapter 5.

---

[7]Specifically, the class $\mathcal{MA}$ is defined by allowing the verification algorithm V in Definition 2.5 to be probabilistic and err on no-instances; that is, for every $x \in S$ there exists $y \in \{0, 1\}^{\text{poly}(|x|)}$ such that $\Pr[V(x, y) = 1] = 1$, whereas for every $x \notin S$ and every y it holds that $\Pr[V(x, y) = 0] \geq 1/2$. We note that $\mathcal{MA}$ can be viewed as a hybrid of the two aforementioned pairs of conditions; specifically, each problem in $\mathcal{MA}$ satisfies the conjunction of Eq. (6.2) and Claim 2. Other randomized versions of $\mathcal{NP}$ (i.e., variants of $\mathcal{MA}$) are considered in Exercise 6.12.

6.1.5.1. Definitional Issues

When defining space-bounded randomized algorithms, we face a problem analogous to the one discussed in the context of non-deterministic space-bounded computation (see Section 5.3). Specifically, the on-line and the off-line versions (formulated in Definition 6.1) are no longer equivalent, unless we restrict the "off-line machine" to access its random-input tape in a uni-directional manner. The issue is that, in the context of space-bounded computation (and unlike in the case that we only care about time bounds), the outcome of the internal coin tosses (in the on-line model) cannot be recorded for free. Bearing in mind that, *in the current context*, we wish to model real algorithms (rather than present a fictitious model that captures a fundamental phenomenon as in Section 5.3), it is clear that *using the on-line version is the natural choice*.

An additional issue that arises is the need to explicitly bound the running time of space-bounded randomized algorithms. Recall that, without loss of generality, the number of steps taken by a space-bounded non-deterministic machine is at most exponential in its space complexity, because the shortest path between two configurations in the (directed) graph of possible configurations is upper-bounded by its size (which in turn is exponential in the space bound). This reasoning fails in the case of randomized algorithms, because the shortest path between two configurations does not bound the expected number of random steps required for going from the first configuration to the second one. In fact, as we shall shortly see, failing to upper-bound the running time of log-space randomized algorithms seems to allow them too much power; that is, such (unrestricted) log-space randomized algorithms can emulate non-deterministic log-space computations (in exponential time). The emulation consists of repeatedly invoking the NL-machine, while using random choices in the role of the non-deterministic moves. If the input is a yes-instance then, in each attempt, with probability at least 2^{-t}, we "hit" an accepting t-step (non-deterministic) computation, where t is polynomial in the input length. Thus, the randomized machine accepts such a yes-instance after an expected number of 2^t trials. To allow for the rejection of no-instances (rather than looping infinitely in vain), we wish to implement a counter that counts till 2^t (or so) and reject the input if 2^t trials were made and have all failed (to hit an accepting computation of the NL-machine). We need to implement such a counter within space $O(\log t)$ rather than t (which is easy). In fact, it suffices to have a "randomized counter" that, with high probability, counts to approximately 2^t. The implementation of such a counter is left to Exercise 6.18, and using it we may obtain a randomized algorithm that halts with high probability (on every input), always rejects a no-instance, and accepts each yes-instance with probability at least $1/2$.

In light of the foregoing discussion, when defining randomized log-space algorithms we explicitly require that the algorithms halt in polynomial time. Modulo this convention, the relation between classes $\mathcal{RL}$ (resp., $\mathcal{BPL}$) and $\mathcal{NL}$ is analogous to the relation between $\mathcal{RP}$ (resp., $\mathcal{BPP}$) and $\mathcal{NP}$. Specifically, the probabilistic acceptance condition of $\mathcal{RL}$ (resp., $\mathcal{BPL}$) is as in the case of $\mathcal{RP}$ (resp., $\mathcal{BPP}$).

Definition 6.11 (the classes $\mathcal{RL}$ and $\mathcal{BPL}$): *We say that a randomized log-space algorithm is* admissible *if it always halts in a polynomial number of steps.*

- *A decision problem S is in $\mathcal{RL}$ if there exists an admissible* (on-line) *randomized log-space algorithm A such that for every $x \in S$ it holds that $\Pr[A(x) = 1] \geq 1/2$ and for every $x \notin S$ it holds that $\Pr[A(x) = 0] = 1$.*

- *A decision problem S is in $\mathcal{BPL}$ if there exists an admissible* (on-line) *randomized log-space algorithm A such that for every $x \in S$ it holds that $\Pr[A(x) = 1] \geq 2/3$ and for every $x \notin S$ it holds that $\Pr[A(x) = 0] \geq 2/3$.*

Clearly, $\mathcal{RL} \subseteq \mathcal{NL} \subseteq \mathcal{P}$ and $\mathcal{BPL} \subseteq \mathcal{P}$. Note that the classes $\mathcal{RL}$ and $\mathcal{BPL}$ remain unchanged even if we allow the algorithms to run for *expected* polynomial time and have non-halting computations. Such algorithms can be easily transformed into admissible algorithms by truncating long computations, while using a (standard) counter (which can be implemented in logarithmic space). Also note that error reduction is applicable in the current setting (while essentially preserving both the time and space bounds).

6.1.5.2. The Accidental Tourist Sees It All

An appealing example of a randomized log-space algorithm is presented next. It refers to the problem of deciding undirected connectivity, and demonstrates that this problem is in $\mathcal{RL}$. (Recall that in Section 5.2.4 we proved that this problem is actually in $\mathcal{L}$, but the algorithm and its analysis were more complicated.) In contrast, recall that directed connectivity is complete for $\mathcal{NL}$ (under log-space reductions).

For the sake of simplicity, we consider the following computational problem: *Given an undirected graph G and a pair of vertices (s, t), determine whether or not s and t are connected in G*. Note that deciding undirected connectivity (of a given undirected graph) is log-space reducible to the foregoing problem (e.g., just check the connectivity of all pairs of vertices).

Construction 6.12: *On input (G, s, t), the randomized algorithm starts a* poly$(|G|)$-*long random walk at vertex s, and accepts the triple if and only if the walk passed through the vertex t. By a random walk we mean that at each step the algorithm selects uniformly one of the neighbors of the current vertex and moves to it.*

Observe that the algorithm can be implemented in logarithmic space (because we only need to store the current vertex as well as the number of steps taken so far). Obviously, if s and t are not connected in G then the algorithm always rejects (G, s, t). Proposition 6.13 implies that if s and t are connected (in G) then the algorithm accepts with probability at least $1/2$. It follows that undirected connectivity is in $\mathcal{RL}$.

Proposition 6.13: *With probability at least $1/2$, a random walk of length $O(|V| \cdot |E|)$ starting at any vertex of the graph $G = (V, E)$ passes through all the vertices that reside in the same connected component as the start vertex.*

Thus, such a random walk may be used to explore the relevant connected component (in any graph). Following this walk one is likely to see all that there is to see in that component.

Proof Sketch: We will actually show that if G is connected then, with probability at least $1/2$, a random walk starting at s visits all the vertices of G. For any pair of vertices (u, v), let $X_{u,v}$ be a random variable representing the number of steps taken in a random walk starting at u until v is *first encountered*. The reader may verify that for every edge $\{u, v\} \in E$ it holds that $E[X_{u,v}] \leq 2|E|$; see Exercise 6.19. Next, we let cover(G) denote the expected number of steps in a random walk starting at s and ending when the last of the vertices of V is encountered. Our goal is to upper-bound cover(G). Toward this end, we consider an arbitrary directed cyclic-tour C that visits all vertices in G, and note that

$$\text{cover}(G) \leq \sum_{(u,v)\in C} \mathrm{E}[X_{u,v}] \leq |C| \cdot 2|E|.$$

In particular, selecting C as a traversal of some spanning tree of G, we conclude that cover(G) $< 4 \cdot |V| \cdot |E|$. Thus, with probability at least $1/2$, a random walk of length $8 \cdot |V| \cdot |E|$ starting at s visits all vertices of G. □

6.2. Counting

We now turn to a new type of computational problems, which vastly generalize decision problems of the NP-type. We refer to counting problems, and more specifically to counting objects that can be efficiently recognized. The search and decision versions of NP provide suitable definitions of efficiently recognized objects, which in turn yield corresponding counting problems:

1. For each search problem having efficiently checkable solutions (i.e., a relation $R \subseteq \{0,1\}^* \times \{0,1\}^*$ in $\mathcal{PC}$ (see Definition 2.3)), we consider the problem of counting the number of solutions for a given instance. That is, on input x, we are required to output $|\{y : (x,y)\in R\}|$.
2. For each decision problem S in $\mathcal{NP}$, and each corresponding verification procedure V (as in Definition 2.5), we consider the problem of counting the number of NP-witnesses for a given instance. That is, on input x, we are required to output $|\{y : V(x,y)=1\}|$.

We shall consider these types of counting problems as well as relaxations (of these counting problems) that refer to approximating the said quantities (see Sections 6.2.1 and 6.2.2, respectively). Other related topics include "problems with unique solutions" (see Section 6.2.3) and "uniform generation of solutions" (see Section 6.2.4). Interestingly, randomized procedures will play an important role in many of the results regarding the aforementioned types of problems.

6.2.1. Exact Counting

In continuation of the foregoing discussion, we define the class of problems concerned with counting efficiently recognized objects. (Recall that $\mathcal{PC}$ denotes the class of search problems having polynomially long solutions that are efficiently checkable; see Definition 2.3.)

Definition 6.14 (counting efficiently recognized objects – #$\mathcal{P}$): *The class #$\mathcal{P}$ consists of all functions that count solutions to a search problem in $\mathcal{PC}$. That is, $f : \{0,1\}^* \to \mathbb{N}$ is in #$\mathcal{P}$ if there exists $R \in \mathcal{PC}$ such that, for every x, it holds that $f(x) = |R(x)|$, where $R(x) = \{y : (x,y)\in R\}$. In this case we say that f is the* counting problem associated *with R, and denote the latter by #R (i.e., #$R = f$).*

Every decision problem in $\mathcal{NP}$ is Cook-reducible to #$\mathcal{P}$, because every such problem can be cast as deciding membership in $S_R = \{x : |R(x)| > 0\}$ for some $R \in \mathcal{PC}$ (see

Section 2.1.2). It also holds that $\mathcal{BPP}$ is Cook-reducible to $\#\mathcal{P}$ (see Exercise 6.20). The class $\#\mathcal{P}$ is sometimes defined in terms of decision problems, as is implicit in the following proposition.

Proposition 6.15 (a decisional version of $\#\mathcal{P}$): *For any $f \in \#\mathcal{P}$, deciding member-ship in $S_f \stackrel{\text{def}}{=} \{(x, N) : f(x) \geq N\}$ is computationally equivalent to computing f.*

Actually, the claim holds for any function $f : \{0, 1\}^* \to \mathbb{N}$ for which there exists a polynomial p such that for every $x \in \{0, 1\}^*$ it holds that $f(x) \leq 2^{p(|x|)}$.

Proof: Since the relation R vouching for $f \in \#\mathcal{P}$ (i.e., $f(x) = |R(x)|$) is polyno-mially bounded, there exists a polynomial p such that for every x it holds that $f(x) \leq 2^{p(|x|)}$. Deciding membership in S_f is easily reduced to computing f (i.e., we accept the input (x, N) if and only if $f(x) \geq N$). Computing f is reducible to deciding S_f by using a binary search (see Exercise 2.9). This relies on the fact that, on input x and oracle access to S_f, we can determine whether or not $f(x) \geq N$ by making the query (x, N). Note that we know a priori that $f(x) \in [0, 2^{p(|x|)}]$. ∎

The counting class $\#\mathcal{P}$ is also related to the problem of enumerating all possible solutions to a given instance (see Exercise 6.21).

6.2.1.1. On the Power of $\#\mathcal{P}$

As indicated, $\mathcal{NP} \cup \mathcal{BPP}$ is (easily) reducible to $\#\mathcal{P}$. Furthermore, as stated in The-orem 6.16, the entire Polynomial-time Hierarchy (as defined in Section 3.2) is Cook-reducible to $\#\mathcal{P}$ (i.e., $\mathcal{PH} \subseteq \mathcal{P}^{\#\mathcal{P}}$). On the other hand, any problem in $\#\mathcal{P}$ is solvable in polynomial space, and so $\mathcal{P}^{\#\mathcal{P}} \subseteq \mathcal{PSPACE}$.

Theorem 6.16: *Every set in $\mathcal{PH}$ is Cook-reducible to $\#\mathcal{P}$.*

We do not present a proof of Theorem 6.16 here, because the known proofs are rather technical. Furthermore, one main idea underlying these proofs appears in a more clear form in the proof of Theorem 6.29. Nevertheless, in Appendix F.1 we present a proof of a related result, which implies that $\mathcal{PH}$ is reducible to $\#\mathcal{P}$ via *randomized* Karp-reductions.

6.2.1.2. Completeness in $\#\mathcal{P}$

The definition of $\#\mathcal{P}$-completeness is analogous to the definition of $\mathcal{NP}$-completeness. That is, *a counting problem f is $\#\mathcal{P}$-complete if $f \in \#\mathcal{P}$ and every problem in $\#\mathcal{P}$ is Cook-reducible to f.*

We claim that the counting problems associated with the NP-complete problems pre-sented in Section 2.3.3 are all $\#\mathcal{P}$-complete. We warn that this fact is not due to the mere NP-completeness of these problems, but rather to an additional property of the reductions establishing their NP-completeness. Specifically, the Karp-reductions that were used (or variants of them) have the extra property of preserving the number of NP-witnesses (as captured by the following definition).

Definition 6.17 (parsimonious reductions): *Let $R, R' \in \mathcal{PC}$ and let g be a Karp-reduction of $S_R = \{x : R(x) \neq \emptyset\}$ to $S_{R'} = \{x : R'(x) \neq \emptyset\}$, where $R(x) = \{y : (x, y) \in R\}$ and $R'(x) = \{y : (x, y) \in R'\}$. We say that g is* parsimonious *(with* respect to R and R') *if for every x it holds that $|R(x)| = |R'(g(x))|$. In such a case we say that g is a* parsimonious reduction *of R to R'.*

We stress that the condition of being parsimonious refers to the two underlying relations R and R' (and not merely to the sets S_R and $S_{R'}$). The requirement that g is a Karp-reduction is partially redundant, because if g is polynomial-time computable and for every x it holds that $|R(x)| = |R'(g(x))|$, then g constitutes a Karp-reduction of S_R to $S_{R'}$. Specifically, $|R(x)| = |R'(g(x))|$ implies that $|R(x)| > 0$ (i.e., $x \in S_R$) if and only if $|R'(g(x))| > 0$ (i.e., $g(x) \in S_{R'}$). The reader may easily verify that the Karp-reduction underlying the proof of Theorem 2.19 as well as many of the reductions used in Section 2.3.3 are parsimonious (see Exercise 2.29).

Theorem 6.18: *Let $R \in \mathcal{PC}$ and suppose that every search problem in $\mathcal{PC}$ is parsimoniously reducible to R. Then the counting problem associated with R is #$\mathcal{P}$-complete.*

Proof: Clearly, the counting problem associated with R, denoted #R, is in #$\mathcal{P}$. To show that every $f' \in$ #$\mathcal{P}$ is reducible to f, we consider the relation $R' \in \mathcal{PC}$ that is counted by f'; that is, #$R' = f'$. Then, by the hypothesis, there exists a parsimonious reduction g of R' to R. This reduction also reduces #R' to #R; specifically, #$R'(x) =$ #$R(g(x))$ for every x. ∎

Corollaries. As an immediate corollary of Theorem 6.18, we get that counting the number of satisfying assignments to a given CNF formula is #$\mathcal{P}$-complete (because R_{SAT} is $\mathcal{PC}$-complete via parsimonious reductions). Similar statements hold for all the other NP-complete problems mentioned in Section 2.3.3 and in fact for all NP-complete problems listed in [85]. These corollaries follow from the fact that all known reductions among natural NP-complete problems are either parsimonious or can be easily modified to be so.

We conclude that many counting problems associated with NP-complete search problems are #$\mathcal{P}$-complete. It turns out that also counting problems associated with efficiently solvable search problems may be #$\mathcal{P}$-complete.

Theorem 6.19: *There exist #$\mathcal{P}$-complete counting problems that are associated with efficiently solvable search problems. That is, there exists $R \in \mathcal{PF}$ (see Definition 2.2) such that #R is #$\mathcal{P}$-complete.*

Theorem 6.19 can be established by presenting artificial #$\mathcal{P}$-complete problems (see Exercise 6.22). The following proof uses a natural counting problem.

Proof: Consider the relation R_{dnf} consisting of pairs (ϕ, τ) such that ϕ is a DNF formula and τ is an assignment satisfying it. Note that the search problem of R_{dnf} is easy to solve (e.g., by picking an arbitrary truth assignment that satisfies the first term in the input formula). To see that #R_{dnf} is #$\mathcal{P}$-complete consider the following reduction from #R_{SAT} (which is #$\mathcal{P}$-complete by Theorem 6.18). Given a CNF formula ϕ, transform $\neg\phi$ into a DNF formula ϕ' by applying de-Morgan's

Law, query $\#R_{\mathrm{dnf}}$ on ϕ', and return $2^n - \#R_{\mathrm{dnf}}(\phi')$, where n denotes the number of variables in ϕ (resp., ϕ'). ∎

Reflections. We note that Theorem 6.19 is not established by a parsimonious reduction. This fact should not come as a surprise because a parsimonious reduction of $\#R'$ to $\#R$ implies that $S_{R'} = \{x : \exists y \text{ s.t. } (x, y) \in R'\}$ is reducible to $S_R = \{x : \exists y \text{ s.t. } (x, y) \in R\}$, where in our case $S_{R'}$ is NP-complete while $S_R \in \mathcal{P}$ (since $R \in \mathcal{PF}$). Nevertheless, the proof of Theorem 6.19 is related to the hardness of some underlying decision problem (i.e., the problem of deciding whether a given DNF formula is a tautology (i.e., whether $\#R_{\mathrm{dnf}}(\phi') = 2^n)$). But does there exist a $\#\mathcal{P}$-complete problem that is "not based on some underlying NP-complete decision problem"? Amazingly enough, the answer is positive.

Theorem 6.20: *Counting the number of perfect matchings in a bipartite graph is* $\#\mathcal{P}$-*complete.*[8]

Equivalently (see Exercise 6.23), the problem of computing the permanent of matrices with 0/1-entries is $\#\mathcal{P}$-complete. Recall that the permanent of an n-by-n matrix $M = (m_{i,j})$, denoted $\mathrm{perm}(M)$, equals the sum over all permutations π of $[n]$ of the products $\prod_{i=1}^{n} m_{i,\pi(i)}$. Theorem 6.20 is proven by composing the following two (many-to-one) reductions (asserted in Propositions 6.21 and 6.22, respectively) and using the fact that $\#R_{\mathrm{3SAT}}$ is $\#\mathcal{P}$-complete (see Theorem 6.18 and Exercise 2.29). Needless to say, the resulting reduction is not parsimonious.

Proposition 6.21: *The counting problem of* 3SAT *(i.e.,* $\#R_{\mathrm{3SAT}}$*) is reducible to computing the permanent of integer matrices. Furthermore, there exists an even integer* $c > 0$ *and a finite set of integers* I *such that, on input a 3CNF formula* ϕ*, the reduction produces an integer matrix* M_ϕ *with entries in* I *such that* $\mathrm{perm}(M_\phi) = c^m \cdot \#R_{\mathrm{3SAT}}(\phi)$ *where* m *denotes the number of clauses in* ϕ.

The original proof of Proposition 6.21 uses $c = 2^{10}$ and $I = \{-1, 0, 1, 2, 3\}$. It can be shown (see Exercise 6.24 (which relies on Theorem 6.29)) that, for every integer $n > 1$ that is relatively prime to c, computing the permanent modulo n is NP-hard (under randomized reductions). Thus, using the case of $c = 2^{10}$, this means that computing the permanent modulo n is NP-hard for any odd $n > 1$. In contrast, computing the permanent modulo 2 (which is equivalent to computing the determinant modulo 2) is easy (i.e., can be done in polynomial time and even in $\mathcal{NC}$). Thus, assuming $\mathcal{NP} \not\subseteq \mathcal{BPP}$, Proposition 6.21 cannot hold for an odd c (because by Exercise 6.24 it would follow that computing the permanent modulo 2 is NP-hard). We also note that, assuming $\mathcal{P} \neq \mathcal{NP}$, Proposition 6.21 cannot possibly hold for a set I containing only non-negative integers (see Exercise 6.25).

Proposition 6.22: *Computing the permanent of integer matrices is reducible to computing the permanent of 0/1-matrices. Furthermore, the reduction maps any integer matrix* A *into a 0/1-matrix* A'' *such that the permanent of* A *can be easily computed from* A *and the permanent of* A''.

---

[8]See Appendix G.1 for basic terminology regarding graphs.

Teaching note: We do not recommend presenting the proofs of Propositions 6.21 and 6.22 in class. The high-level structure of the proof of Proposition 6.21 has the flavor of some sophisticated reductions among NP-problems, but the crucial point is the existence of adequate gadgets. We do not know of a high-level argument establishing the existence of such gadgets nor of any intuition as to why such gadgets exist.[9] Instead, the existence of such gadgets is proved by a design that is both highly non-trivial and *ad hoc* in nature. Thus, the proof of Proposition 6.21 boils down to a complicated design problem that is solved in a way that has little pedagogical value. In contrast, the proof of Proposition 6.22 uses two simple ideas that can be useful in other settings. With suitable hints, this proof can be used as a good exercise.

Proof of Proposition 6.21: We will use the correspondence between the permanent of a matrix A and the sum of the weights of the cycle covers of the weighted directed graph represented by the matrix A. A cycle cover of a graph is a collection of simple[10] *vertex-disjoint* directed cycles that covers all the graph's vertices, and its weight is the product of the weights of the corresponding edges. The SWCC of a weighted directed graph is the sum of the weights of all its cycle covers.

Given a 3CNF formula ϕ, we construct a directed weighted graph G_ϕ such that the SWCC of G_ϕ equals equals $c^m \cdot \#R_{3SAT}(\phi)$, where c is a universal constant and m denotes the number of clauses in ϕ. We may assume, without loss of generality, that each clause of ϕ has exactly three literals (which are not necessarily distinct).

We start with a high-level description (of the construction) that refers to (clause) gadgets, each containing some internal vertices and internal (weighted) edges, which are *unspecified at this point*. In addition, each gadget has three pairs of designated vertices, one pair per each literal appearing in the clause, where one vertex in the pair is designated as an entry vertex and the other as an exit vertex. The graph G_ϕ consists of m such gadgets, one per each clause (of ϕ), and n auxiliary vertices, one per each variable (of ϕ), as well as some *additional directed edges*, each having weight 1. Specifically, for each variable, we introduce two tracks, one per each of the possible literals of this variable. The track associated with a literal consists of directed edges (each having weight 1) that form a simple "cycle" passing through the corresponding (auxiliary) vertex as well as through the designated vertices that correspond to the occurrences of this literal in the various clauses. Specifically, for each such occurrence, the track enters the corresponding clause gadget at the entry vertex corresponding to this literal and exits at the corresponding exit vertex. (If a literal does not appear in ϕ then the corresponding track is a self-loop on the corresponding variable.) See Figure 6.1 showing the two tracks of a variable x that occurs positively in three clauses and negatively in one clause. The entry vertices (resp., exit vertices) are drawn on the top (resp., bottom) part of each gadget.

For the purpose of stating the desired properties of the clause gadget, we augment the gadget by nine external edges (of weight 1), one per each pair of (not necessarily matching) entry and exit vertices such that the edge goes from the exit vertex to the entry vertex (see Figure 6.2). (We stress that this is an auxiliary construction that differs from and yet is related to the use of gadgets in the foregoing construction of G_ϕ.) The three edges that link the designated pairs of vertices that correspond to the

---

[9]Indeed, the conjecture that such gadgets exist can only be attributed to ingenuity.

[10]Here, a simple cycle is a strongly connected directed graph in which each vertex has a single incoming (resp., outgoing) edge. In particular, self-loops are allowed.

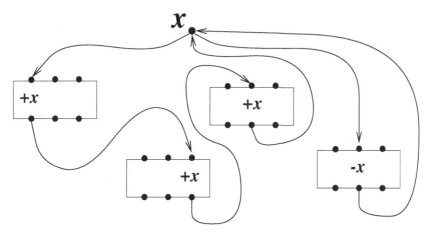

Figure 6.1: Tracks connecting clause gadgets in the reduction to cycle cover.

three literals are called nice. We say that a collection of edges C (e.g., a collection of cycles in the augmented gadget) uses the external edges S if the intersection of C with the set of the (nine) external edges equals S. We postulate the following three properties of the clause gadget.

1. The sum of the weights of all cycle covers (of the gadget) that do not use any external edge (i.e., use the empty set of external edges) equals zero.
2. Let $V(S)$ denote the set of vertices incident to S, and say that S is nice if it is non-empty and the vertices in $V(S)$ can be perfectly matched using nice edges.[11] Then, there exists a constant c (indeed the one postulated in the proposition's claim) such that, for any nice set S, the sum of the weights of all cycle covers that use the external edges S equals c.

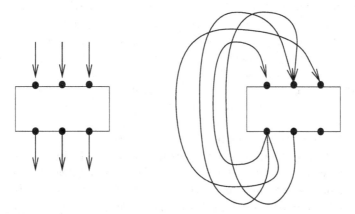

Figure 6.2: External edges for the analysis of the effect of a clause gadget. On the left is a gadget with the track edges adjacent to it (as in the real construction). On the right is a gadget and four out of the nine external edges (two of which are nice) used in the analysis.

---

[11]Clearly, any non-empty set of nice edges is a nice set. Thus, a singleton set is nice if and only if the corresponding edge is nice. On the other hand, any set S of three (vertex-disjoint) external edges is nice, because $V(S)$ has a perfect matching using all three nice edges. Thus, the notion of nice sets is "non-trivial" only for sets of two edges. Such a set S is nice if and only if $V(S)$ consists of two pairs of corresponding designated vertices.

The gadget uses eight vertices, where the first six are the designated (entry and exit) vertices. The entry vertex (resp., exit vertex) associated with the ith literal is numbered i (resp., $i + 3$). The corresponding adjacency matrix follows.

$$
\begin{pmatrix}
1 & 0 & 0 & 2 & 0 & 0 & 0 & 0 \\
0 & 1 & 0 & 0 & 3 & 0 & 0 & 0 \\
0 & 0 & 0 & 0 & 0 & 1 & 0 & 0 \\
0 & 0 & -1 & 1 & -1 & 0 & 1 & 1 \\
0 & 0 & -1 & -1 & 2 & 0 & 1 & 1 \\
0 & 0 & 0 & -1 & -1 & 0 & 1 & 1 \\
0 & 0 & 1 & 1 & 1 & 0 & 2 & -1 \\
0 & 0 & 1 & 1 & 1 & 0 & 0 & 1
\end{pmatrix}
$$

Note that the edge $3 \to 6$ can be contracted, but the resulting 7-vertex graph will not be consistent with our (inessentially stringent) definition of a gadget by which the six designated vertices should be distinct.

Figure 6.3: A Deus ex Machina clause gadget for the reduction to cycle cover.

3. For any non-nice set $S \neq \emptyset$ of external edges, the sum of the weights of all cycle covers that use the external edges S equals zero.

Note that the foregoing three cases exhaust all the possible ones. Also note that the set of external edges used by a cycle cover (of the augmented gadget) must be a matching (i.e., these edges must be vertex disjoint).

Intuitively, there is a correspondence between nice sets of external edges (of an augmented gadget) and the pairs of edges on tracks that pass through the (unaugmented) gadget. Indeed, we now turn back to G_ϕ, which uses unaugmented gadgets. Using the foregoing properties of the (augmented) gadgets, it can be shown that each satisfying assignment of ϕ contributes exactly c^m to the SWCC of G_ϕ (see Exercise 6.26). It follows that the SWCC of G_ϕ equals $c^m \cdot \#R_{3\text{SAT}}(\phi)$.

Having established the validity of the abstract reduction, we turn to the implementation of the clause gadget. The first implementation is a *Deus ex Machina*, with a corresponding adjacency matrix depicted in Figure 6.3. Its validity (for the value $c = 12$) can be verified by computing the permanent of the corresponding sub-matrices (see analogous analysis in Exercise 6.28).

A more structured implementation of the clause gadget is depicted in Figure 6.4, which refers to a (hexagon) box to be implemented later. The box contains several vertices and weighted edges, but only two of these vertices, called terminals, are connected to the outside (and are shown in Figure 6.4). The clause gadget consists of five copies of this box, where three copies are designated for the three literals of the clause (and are marked LB1, LB2, and LB3), as well as additional vertices and edges shown in Figure 6.4. In particular, the clause gadget contains the six aforementioned designated vertices (i.e., a pair of entry and exit vertices per each literal), two additional vertices (shown at the two extremes of the figure), and some edges (all having weight 1). Each designated vertex has a self-loop, and is incident to a single additional edge that is outgoing (resp., incoming) in case the vertex is an entry vertex (resp., exit vertex) of the gadget. The two terminals of each box that is associated with some literal are connected to the corresponding pair of designated

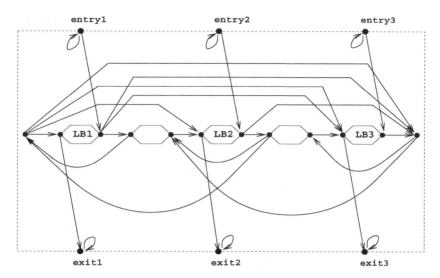

Figure 6.4: A structured clause gadget for the reduction to cycle cover.

vertices (e.g., the outgoing edge of entry1 is incident at the right terminal of the box LB1). Note that the five boxes reside on a directed path (going from left to right), and the only edges going in the opposite direction are those drawn below this path.

In continuation of the foregoing, we wish to state the desired properties of the box. Again, we do so by considering the augmentation of the box by external edges (of weight 1) incident at the specified vertices. In this case (see Figure 6.5), we have a pair of anti-parallel edges connecting the two terminals of the box as well as two self-loops (one on each terminal). We postulate the following three properties of the box.

1. The sum of the weights of all cycle covers (of the box) that do not use any external edge equals zero.
2. There exists a constant b (in our case $b = 4$) such that, for each of the two anti-parallel edges, the sum of the weights of all cycle covers that use this edge equals b.
3. For any (non-empty) set S of the self-loops, the sum of the weights of all cycle covers (of the box) that use S equals zero.

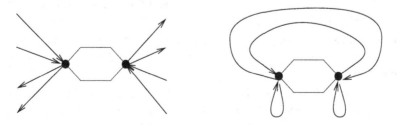

Figure 6.5: External edges for the analysis of the effect of a box. On the left is a box with potential edges adjacent to it (as in the gadget construction). On the right is a box and the four external edges used in the analysis.

—— **209** ——

Note that the foregoing three cases exhaust all the possible ones. It can be shown that the conditions regarding the box imply that the construction presented in Figure 6.4 satisfies the conditions that were postulated for the clause gadget (see Exercise 6.27). Specifically, we have $c = b^5$. As for box itself, a smaller *Deus ex Machina* is provided by the following 4-by-4 adjacency matrix

$$
\begin{pmatrix}
0 & 1 & -1 & -1 \\
1 & -1 & 1 & 1 \\
0 & 1 & 1 & 2 \\
0 & 1 & 3 & 0
\end{pmatrix}
\tag{6.4}
$$

where the two terminals correspond to the first and the fourth vertices. Its validity (for the value $b = 4$) can be verified by computing the permanent of the corresponding sub-matrices (see Exercise 6.28). ∎

Proof of Proposition 6.22: The proof proceeds in two steps. In the first step we show that computing the permanent of *integer matrices* is reducible to computing the permanent of *non-negative matrices*. This reduction proceeds as follows. For an n-by-n integer matrix $A = (a_{i,j})_{i,j\in[n]}$, let $\|A\|_\infty = \max_{i,j}(|a_{i,j}|)$ and $Q_A = 2(n!) \cdot \|A\|_\infty^n + 1$. We note that, given A, the value Q_A can be computed in polynomial time, and in particular $\log_2 Q_A < n^2 \log \|A\|_\infty$. Given the matrix A, the reduction constructs the non-negative matrix $A' = (a_{i,j} \bmod Q_A)_{i,j\in[n]}$ (i.e., the entries of A' are in $\{0, 1, \ldots, Q_A - 1\}$), queries the oracle for the permanent of A', and outputs $v \stackrel{\text{def}}{=} \operatorname{perm}(A') \bmod Q_A$ if $v < Q_A/2$ and $-(Q_A - v)$ otherwise. The key observation is that

$$\operatorname{perm}(A) \equiv \operatorname{perm}(A') \pmod{Q_A}, \text{ while } |\operatorname{perm}(A)| \le (n!) \cdot \|A\|_\infty^n < Q_A/2.$$

Thus, $\operatorname{perm}(A') \bmod Q_A$ (which is in $\{0, 1, \ldots, Q_A - 1\}$) determines $\operatorname{perm}(A)$. We note that $\operatorname{perm}(A')$ is likely to be much larger than $Q_A > |\operatorname{perm}(A)|$; it is merely that $\operatorname{perm}(A')$ and $\operatorname{perm}(A)$ are equivalent modulo Q_A.

In the second step we show that computing the permanent of non-negative matrices is reducible to computing the permanent of $0/1$-matrices. In this reduction, we view the computation of the permanent as the computation of the sum of the weights of all the cycle covers (SWCC) of the corresponding weighted directed graph (see proof of Proposition 6.21). Thus, we reduce the computation of the SWCC of directed graphs *with non-negative weights* to the computation of the SWCC of *unweighted directed graphs with no parallel edges* (which correspond to $0/1$-matrices). The reduction is via local replacements that preserve the value of the SWCC. These local replacements combine the following two local replacements (which preserve the SWCC):

1. Replacing an edge of weight $w = \prod_{i=1}^{t} w_i$ by a path of length t (i.e., $t - 1$ internal nodes) with the corresponding weights $w_1, \ldots, w_t$, and self-loops (with weight 1) on all internal nodes.

   Note that a cycle cover that uses the original edge corresponds to a cycle cover that uses the entire path, whereas a cycle cover that does not use the original edge corresponds to a cycle cover that uses all the self-loops.

2. Replacing an edge of weight $w = \sum_{i=1}^{t} w_i$ by t parallel 2-edge paths such that the first edge on the ith path has weight w_i, the second edge has weight 1, and the

intermediate node has a self-loop (with weight 1). (Paths of length two are used because parallel edges are not allowed.)

Note that a cycle cover that uses the original edge corresponds to a collection of cycle covers that use one out of the t paths (and the self-loops of all other intermediate nodes), whereas a cycle cover that does not use the original edge corresponds to a cycle cover that uses all the self-loops.

In particular, we may write each positive edge weight w, having binary expansion $\sigma_{|w|-1} \cdots \sigma_0$, as $\sum_{i:\sigma_i=1}(1+1)^i$, and apply the adequate replacements (i.e., first apply the additive replacement to the outer sum (over $\{i : \sigma_i = 1\}$), next apply the product replacement to each power 2^i, and finally apply the additive replacement to each $1 + 1$). Applying this process to the matrix A' obtained in the first step, we *efficiently* obtain a matrix A'' with 0/1-entries such that $\mathtt{perm}(A') = \mathtt{perm}(A'')$. (In particular, the dimension of A'' is polynomial in the length of the binary representation of A', which in turn is polynomial in the length of the binary representation of A.) Combining the two reductions (steps), the proposition follows. ∎

6.2.2. Approximate Counting

Having seen that exact counting (for relations in $\mathcal{PC}$) seems even harder than solving the corresponding search problems, we turn to relaxations of the counting problem. Before focusing on relative approximation, we briefly consider approximation with (large) additive deviation.

Let us consider the counting problem associated with an arbitrary $R \in \mathcal{PC}$. Without loss of generality, we assume that all solutions to n-bit instances have the same length $\ell(n)$, where indeed ℓ is a polynomial. We first note that, while it may be hard to compute $\#R$, given x it is easy to approximate $\#R(x)$ up to an additive error of $0.01 \cdot 2^{\ell(|x|)}$ (by randomly sampling potential solutions for x). Indeed, such an approximation is very rough, but it is not trivial (and in fact we do not know how to obtain it deterministically). In general, we can efficiently produce at random an estimate of $\#R(x)$ that, with high probability, deviates from the correct value by at most an additive term that is related to the absolute upper bound on the number of solutions (i.e., $2^{\ell(|x|)}$).

Proposition 6.23 (approximation with large additive deviation): *Let $R \in \mathcal{PC}$ and ℓ be a polynomial such that $R \subseteq \cup_{n \in \mathbb{N}}\{0, 1\}^n \times \{0, 1\}^{\ell(n)}$. Then, for every polynomial p, there exists a probabilistic polynomial-time algorithm A such that for every $x \in \{0, 1\}^*$ and $\delta \in (0, 1)$ it holds that*

$$\mathsf{Pr}[|A(x, \delta) - \#R(x)| > (1/p(|x|)) \cdot 2^{\ell(|x|)}] < \delta. \tag{6.5}$$

As usual, δ is presented to A in binary, and hence the running time of $A(x, \delta)$ is upper-bounded by $\mathrm{poly}(|x| \cdot \log(1/\delta))$.

Proof Sketch: On input x and δ, algorithm A sets $t = \Theta(p(|x|)^2 \cdot \log(1/\delta))$, selects uniformly $y_1, \ldots, y_t$ and outputs $2^{\ell(|x|)} \cdot |\{i : (x, y_i) \in R\}|/t$. □

Discussion. Proposition 6.23 is meaningful in the case that $\#R(x) > (1/p(|x|)) \cdot 2^{\ell(|x|)}$ holds for some x's. But otherwise, a trivial approximation (i.e., outputting the constant value zero) meets the bound of Eq. (6.5). In contrast to this notion of *additive approximation*, a *relative factor approximation* is typically more meaningful. Specifically, we will be interested in approximating $\#R(x)$ up to a constant factor (or some other reasonable factor). In §6.2.2.1, we consider a natural $\#\mathcal{P}$-complete problem for which such a relative approximation can be obtained in probabilistic polynomial time. We do not expect this to happen for every counting problem in $\#\mathcal{P}$, because a relative approximation allows for distinguishing instances having no solution from instances that do have solutions (i.e., deciding membership in S_R is reducible to a relative approximation of $\#R$). Thus, relative approximation for all $\#\mathcal{P}$ is at least as hard as deciding all problems in $\mathcal{NP}$. However, in §6.2.2.2 we show that the former is not harder than the latter; that is, relative approximation for any problem in $\#\mathcal{P}$ can be obtained by a randomized Cook-reduction to $\mathcal{NP}$. Before turning to these results, let us state the underlying definition (and actually strengthen it by requiring approximation to within a factor of $1 \pm \varepsilon$, for $\varepsilon \in (0, 1)$).[12]

Definition 6.24 (approximation with relative deviation): *Let* $f : \{0, 1\}^* \to \mathbb{N}$ *and* $\varepsilon, \delta : \mathbb{N} \to [0, 1]$. *A randomized process* Π *is called an* (ε, δ)-approximator *of* f *if for every* x *it holds that*

$$\Pr\left[|\Pi(x) - f(x)| > \varepsilon(|x|) \cdot f(x)\right] < \delta(|x|). \tag{6.6}$$

We say that f *is efficiently* $(1 - \varepsilon)$-approximable *(or just* $(1 - \varepsilon)$-approximable*) if there exists a probabilistic polynomial-time algorithm* A *that constitutes an* $(\varepsilon, 1/3)$-approximator *of* f.

The error probability of the latter algorithm A (which has error probability $1/3$) can be reduced to δ by $O(\log(1/\delta))$ repetitions (see Exercise 6.29). Typically, the running time of A will be polynomial in $1/\varepsilon$, and ε is called the deviation parameter.

We comment that the computational problem undelying Definition 6.24 is the search problem of $(1 - \varepsilon)$-approximating a function f (i.e., solving the search problem $R_{f,\varepsilon} \stackrel{\text{def}}{=} \{(x, v) : |v - f(x)| \le \varepsilon(|x|) \cdot f(x)\}$). Typically (see Exercise 6.30 for details), this search problem is computationally equivalent to the promise ("gap") problem of distinguishing elements of the set $\{(x, v) : v < (1 - \varepsilon(|x|)) \cdot f(x)\}$ and elements of the set $\{(x, v) : v > (1 + \varepsilon(|x|)) \cdot f(x)\}$.

6.2.2.1. Relative Approximation for $\#R_{\mathrm{dnf}}$

In this subsection we present a natural $\#\mathcal{P}$-complete problem for which constant factor approximation can be found in probabilistic polynomial time. Stronger results regarding unnatural $\#\mathcal{P}$-complete problems appear in Exercise 6.31.

Consider the relation R_{dnf} consisting of pairs (ϕ, τ) such that ϕ is a DNF formula and τ is an assignment satisfying it. Recall that the search problem of R_{dnf} is easy to solve and that the proof of Theorem 6.19 establishes that $\#R_{\mathrm{dnf}}$ is $\#\mathcal{P}$-complete (via a non-parsimonious

---

[12]We refrain from formally defining an F-factor approximation, for an arbitrary F, although we shall refer to this notion in several informal discussions. There are several ways of defining the aforementioned term (and they are all equivalent when applied to our informal discussions). For example, an F-factor approximation of $\#R$ may mean that, with high probability, the output $A(x)$ satisfies $\#R(x)/F(|x|) \le A(x) \le F(|x|) \cdot \#R(x)$. Alternatively, we may require that $\#R(x) \le A(x) \le F(|x|) \cdot \#R(x)$ (or, alternatively, that $\#R(x)/F(|x|) \le A(x) \le \#R(x)$).

reduction). Still, as we shall see, there exists a probabilistic polynomial-time algorithm that provides a constant factor approximation of $\#R_{\mathrm{dnf}}$. We warn that the fact that $\#R_{\mathrm{dnf}}$ is $\#\mathcal{P}$-complete *via a non-parsimonious reduction* means that the constant factor approximation for $\#R_{\mathrm{dnf}}$ does not seem to imply a similar approximation for all problems in $\#\mathcal{P}$. In fact, we should not expect each problem in $\#\mathcal{P}$ to have a (probabilistic) polynomial-time constant-factor approximation algorithm because this would imply $\mathcal{NP} \subseteq \mathcal{BPP}$ (since a constant factor approximation allows for distinguishing the case in which the instance has no solution from the case in which the instance has a solution).

The approximation algorithm for $\#R_{\mathrm{dnf}}$ is obtained by a deterministic reduction of the task of $(\varepsilon, 1/3)$-approximating $\#R_{\mathrm{dnf}}$ to an (additive deviation) approximation of the type provided in Proposition 6.23. Consider a DNF formula $\phi = \bigvee_{i=1}^{m} C_i$, where each $C_i : \{0,1\}^n \to \{0,1\}$ is a conjunction. Our task is to approximate the number of assignments that satisfy at least one of the conjunctions. Actually, we will deal with the more general problem in which we are (implicitly) given m subsets $S_1, \ldots, S_m \subseteq \{0,1\}^n$ and wish to approximate $|\bigcup_i S_i|$. In our case, each S_i is the set of assignments that satisfy the conjunction C_i. In general, we make two computational assumptions regarding these sets (while letting "efficient" mean *implementable in time polynomial in $n \cdot m$*):

1. Given $i \in [m]$, one can efficiently determine $|S_i|$.
2. Given $i \in [m]$ and $J \subseteq [m]$, one can efficiently approximate $\mathrm{Pr}_{s \in S_i}[s \in \bigcup_{j \in J} S_j]$ up to an *additive deviation of* $1/\mathrm{poly}(n+m)$.

These assumptions are satisfied in our setting (where $S_i = C_i^{-1}(1)$; see Exercise 6.32). Now, the key observation toward approximating $|\bigcup_{i=1}^{m} S_i|$ is that

$$\left| \bigcup_{i=1}^{m} S_i \right| = \sum_{i=1}^{m} \left| S_i \setminus \bigcup_{j<i} S_j \right| = \sum_{i=1}^{m} \mathrm{Pr}_{s \in S_i} \left[s \notin \bigcup_{j<i} S_j \right] \cdot |S_i| \tag{6.7}$$

and that the probabilities in Eq. (6.7) can be approximated by the second assumption. This leads to the following algorithm, where ε denotes the desired deviation parameter (i.e., we wish to obtain $(1 \pm \varepsilon) \cdot |\bigcup_{i=1}^{m} S_i|$).

Construction 6.25: *Let $\varepsilon' = \varepsilon/m$. For $i = 1$ to m do*

1. *Using the first assumption, compute $|S_i|$.*
2. *Using the second assumption, obtain an approximation $\tilde{p}_i = p_i \pm \varepsilon'$, where $p_i \stackrel{\mathrm{def}}{=} \mathrm{Pr}_{s \in S_i}[s \notin \bigcup_{j<i} S_j]$. Set $a_i \stackrel{\mathrm{def}}{=} \tilde{p}_i \cdot |S_i|$.*

Output the sum of the a_i's.

Let $N_i = p_i \cdot |S_i|$, and note that by Eq. (6.7) it holds that $|\bigcup_i S_i| = \sum_i N_i$. We are interested in the quality of the approximation to $\sum_i N_i$ provided by $\sum_i a_i$. Using $a_i = (p_i \pm \varepsilon') \cdot |S_i| = N_i \pm \varepsilon' \cdot |S_i|$ (for each i), we have $\sum_i a_i = \sum_i N_i \pm \varepsilon' \cdot \sum_i |S_i|$. Using $\sum_i |S_i| \le m \cdot |\bigcup_i S_i| = m \cdot \sum_i N_i$ (and $\varepsilon = m\varepsilon'$), we get $\sum_i a_i = (1 \pm \varepsilon) \cdot \sum_i N_i$. Thus, we obtain the following result (see Exercise 6.32).

Proposition 6.26: *For every positive polynomial p, the counting problem of R_{dnf} is efficiently $(1 - (1/p))$-approximable.*

Using the reduction presented in the proof of Theorem 6.19, we conclude that the number of *un*satisfying assignments to a given CNF formula is efficiently $(1 - (1/p))$-approximable. We warn, however, that the number of satisfying assignments to such a formula is *not* efficiently approximable. This concurs with the general phenomenon by which *relative approximation may be possible for one quantity, but not for the complementary quantity*. Needless to say, such a phenomenon does not occur in the context of additive-deviation approximation.

6.2.2.2. Relative Approximation for #$\mathcal{P}$

Recall that we cannot expect to efficiently approximate every #$\mathcal{P}$ problem, where throughout the rest of this section "approximation" is used as a shorthand for "relative approximation" (as in Definition 6.24). Specifically, efficiently approximating #R yields an efficient algorithm for deciding membership in $S_R = \{x : R(x) \neq \emptyset\}$. Thus, at best we can hope that approximating #R is not harder than deciding S_R (i.e., that approximating #R is reducible in polynomial time to S_R). This is indeed the case for every NP-complete problem (i.e., if S_R is NP-complete). More generally, we show that approximating any problem in #$\mathcal{P}$ is reducible in probabilistic polynomial time to $\mathcal{NP}$.

> **Theorem 6.27:** *For every $R \in \mathcal{PC}$ and every positive polynomial p, there exists a probabilistic polynomial-time oracle machine that when given oracle access to $\mathcal{NP}$ constitutes a $(1/p, \mu)$-approximator of #R, where μ is a negligible function (e.g., $\mu(n) = 2^{-n}$).*

Recall that it suffices to provide a $(1/p, \delta)$-approximator of #R, for any constant $\delta < 0.5$, because error reduction is applicable in this context (see Exercise 6.29). Furthermore, it suffices to provide a $(1/2, \delta)$-approximator for every problem in #$\mathcal{P}$ (see Exercise 6.33).

> **Teaching note:** The following proof relies on the notion of hashing functions, presented in Appendix D.2. Specifically, we shall assume familiarity with the basic definition (see Appendix D.2.1), at least one construction (see Appendix D.2.2), and Lemma D.4 (of Appendix D.2.3). The more advanced material of Appendix D.2.3 (which follows Lemma D.4) will not be used in the current section (but part of it will be used in §6.2.4.2).

Proof: Given x, we show how to approximate $|R(x)|$ to within some constant factor. The desired $(1 - (1/p))$-approximation can be obtained as in Exercise 6.33. We may also assume that $R(x) \neq \emptyset$, by starting with the query "is x in S_R" and halting (with output 0) if the answer is negative. Without loss of generality, we assume that $R(x) \subseteq \{0, 1\}^{\ell}$, where $\ell = \text{poly}(|x|)$. We focus on finding some $i \in \{1, \ldots, \ell\}$ such that $2^{i-4} \leq |R(x)| \leq 2^{i+4}$.

We proceed in iterations. For $i = 1, \ldots, \ell + 1$, we find out whether or not $|R(x)| < 2^i$. If the answer is positive then we halt with output 2^i, and otherwise we proceed to the next iteration. (Indeed, if we were able to obtain correct answers to all these queries then the output 2^i would satisfy $2^{i-1} \leq |R(x)| < 2^i$.)

Needless to say, the key issue is how to check whether $|R(x)| < 2^i$. The main idea is to use a "random sieve" on the set $R(x)$ such that each element passes the sieve with probability 2^{-i}. Thus, we expect $|R(x)|/2^i$ elements of $R(x)$ to pass the sieve. Assuming that the number of elements in $R(x)$ that pass the random sieve is indeed

$\lfloor |R(x)|/2^i \rfloor$, it holds that $|R(x)| \geq 2^i$ *if and only if some element of* $R(x)$ *passes the sieve.* Assuming that the sieve can be implemented efficiently, the question of whether or not some element in $R(x)$ passed the sieve is of an "NP-type" (and thus can be referred to our NP-oracle). Combining both assumptions, we may implement the foregoing process by proceeding to the next iteration as long as some element of $R(x)$ passes the sieve. Furthermore, this implementation will provide a reasonably good approximation even if the number of elements in $R(x)$ that pass the random sieve is only approximately equal to $|R(x)|/2^i$. In fact, the level of approximation that this implementation provides is closely related to the level of approximation that is provided by the random sieve. Details follow.

Implementing a random sieve. The random sieve is implemented by using a family of hashing functions (see Appendix D.2). Specifically, in the ith iteration we use a family H_ℓ^i such that each $h \in H_\ell^i$ has a poly(ℓ)-bit long description and maps ℓ-bit long strings to i-bit long strings. Furthermore, the family is accompanied with an efficient evaluation algorithm (i.e., mapping adequate pairs (h, x) to $h(x)$) and satisfies (for every $S \subseteq \{0, 1\}^\ell$)

$$\Pr_{h \in H_\ell^i}[|\{y \in S : h(y) = 0^i\}| \notin (1 - \varepsilon, 1 + \varepsilon) \cdot 2^{-i}|S|] < \frac{2^i}{\varepsilon^2 |S|} \qquad (6.8)$$

(see Lemma D.4). *The random sieve will let y pass if and only if $h(y) = 0^i$.* Indeed, this random sieve is not as perfect as we assumed in the foregoing discussion, but Eq. (6.8) suggests that in some sense this sieve is good enough. In particular, Eq. (6.8) implies that if $i \leq \log_2 |S| - O(1)$ then some string in S is likely to pass the sieve, whereas if $i \geq \log_2 |S| + O(1)$ then no string in S is likely to pass the sieve.

Implementing the queries. Recall that for some x, i and $h \in H_\ell^i$, we need to determine whether $\{y \in R(x) : h(y) = 0^i\} = \emptyset$. This type of question can be cast as membership in the set

$$S_{R,H} \stackrel{\text{def}}{=} \{(x, i, h) : \exists y \text{ s.t. } (x, y) \in R \wedge h(y) = 0^i\}. \qquad (6.9)$$

Using the hypotheses that $R \in \mathcal{PC}$ and that the family of hashing functions has an efficient evaluation algorithm, it follows that $S_{R,H}$ is in $\mathcal{NP}$.

The actual procedure. On input $x \in S_R$ and oracle access to $S_{R,H}$, we proceed in iterations, starting with $i = 1$ and halting at $i = \ell$ (if not before), where ℓ denotes the length of the potential solutions for x. In the ith iteration (where $i < \ell$), we uniformly select $h \in H_\ell^i$ and query the oracle on whether or not $(x, i, h) \in S_{R,H}$. If the answer is negative then we halt with output 2^i, and otherwise we proceed to the next iteration (using $i \leftarrow i + 1$). Needless to say, if we reach the last iteration (i.e., $i = \ell$) then we just halt with output 2^ℓ.

Indeed, we have ignored the case that $x \notin S_R$, which can be easily handled by a minor modification of the foregoing procedure. Specifically, on input x, we first query S_R on x and halt with output 0 if the answer is negative. Otherwise we proceed as in the foregoing procedure.

The analysis. We upper-bound separately the probability that the procedure outputs a value that is too small and the probability that it outputs a value that is too big. In light of the foregoing discussion, we may assume that $|R(x)| > 0$, and let $i_x = \lfloor \log_2 |R(x)| \rfloor \geq 0$. Intuitively, at any iteration $i < i_x$, we expect (at least) 2^{i_x-i} elements of $R(x)$ to pass the sieve and thus we are unlikely to halt before iteration $i_x - O(1)$. Similarly, we are unlikely to reach iteration $i_x + O(1)$ because at this stage we expect no elements of $R(x)$ to pass the sieve (since the actual expectation is $2^{-O(1)}$). A more rigorous analysis (of both cases) follows.

1. The probability that the procedure *halts in a specific iteration* $i < i_x$ equals $\Pr_{h \in H_\ell^i}[|\{y \in R(x) : h(y) = 0^i\}| = 0]$, which in turn is upper-bounded by $2^i/|R(x)|$ (using Eq. (6.8) with $\varepsilon = 1$).[13] Thus, the probability that the procedure halts *before* iteration $i_x - 3$ is upper-bounded by $\sum_{i=0}^{i_x-4} 2^i/|R(x)|$, which in turn is less than $1/8$ (because $i_x \leq \log_2 |R(x)|$). It follows that, with probability at least $7/8$, the output is at least $2^{i_x-3} > |R(x)|/16$ (because $i_x > (\log_2 |R(x)|) - 1$).

2. The probability that the procedure *does not halt in iteration* $i > i_x$ equals $\Pr_{h \in H_\ell^i}[|\{y \in R(x) : h(y) = 0^i\}| \geq 1]$, which in turn is upper-bounded by $\alpha/(\alpha - 1)^2$, where $\alpha = 2^i/|R(x)| > 1$ (using Eq. (6.8) with $\varepsilon = \alpha - 1$).[14] Thus, the probability that the procedure does not halt by iteration $i_x + 4$ is upper-bounded by $8/49 < 1/6$ (because $i_x > (\log_2 |R(x)|) - 1$). Thus, with probability at least $5/6$, the output is at most $2^{i_x+4} \leq 16 \cdot |R(x)|$ (because $i_x \leq \log_2 |R(x)|$).

Thus, with probability at least $(7/8) - (1/6) > 2/3$, the foregoing procedure outputs a value v such that $v/16 \leq |R(x)| < 16v$. Reducing the deviation by using the ideas presented in Exercise 6.33 (and reducing the error probability as in Exercise 6.29), the theorem follows. ∎

Digest. The key observation underlying the proof of Theorem 6.27 is that, while (even with the help of an NP-oracle) we cannot directly test whether the number of solutions is greater than a given number, we can test (with the help of an NP-oracle) whether the number of solutions that "survive a random sieve" is greater than zero. Since the number of solutions that survive a random sieve reflects the total number of solutions (normalized by the sieve's density), this offers a way of approximating the total number of solutions.

We mention that one can also test whether the number of solutions that "survive a random sieve" is greater than a small number, where small means polynomial in the length of the input (see Exercise 6.35). Specifically, the complexity of this test is linear in the size of the threshold, and not in the length of its binary description. Indeed, in many settings it is more advantageous to use a threshold that is polynomial in some efficiency parameter (rather than using the threshold zero); examples appear in §6.2.4.2 and in [106].

---

[13]Note that 0 does not reside in the open interval $(0, 2\rho)$, where $\rho = |R(x)|/2^i > 0$.

[14]Here we use the fact that $1 \notin (2\alpha^{-1} - 1, 1)$. A better bound can be obtained by using the hypothesis that, for every y, when h is uniformly selected in H_ℓ^i, the value of $h(y)$ is uniformly distributed in $\{0, 1\}^i$. In this case, $\Pr_{h \in H_\ell^i}[|\{y \in R(x) : h(y) = 0^i\}| \geq 1]$ is upper-bounded by $\mathsf{E}_{h \in H_\ell^i}[|\{y \in R(x) : h(y) = 0^i\}|] = |R(x)|/2^i$.

6.2.3. Searching for Unique Solutions

A natural computational problem (regarding search problems), which arises when discussing the number of solutions, is the problem of distinguishing instances having a single solution from instances having no solution (or finding the unique solution whenever such exists). We mention that instances having a single solution facilitate numerous arguments (see, for example, Exercise 6.24 and §10.2.2.1). Formally, searching for and deciding the existence of unique solutions are defined within the framework of promise problems (see Section 2.4.1).

Definition 6.28 (search and decision problems for unique solution instances): *The set of instances having unique solutions* with respect to the binary relation R is *defined as* $\mathrm{US}_R \overset{\text{def}}{=} \{x : |R(x)| = 1\}$, *where* $R(x) \overset{\text{def}}{=} \{y : (x, y) \in R\}$. *As usual, we denote* $S_R = \{x : |R(x)| \geq 1\}$, *and* $\overline{S}_R \overset{\text{def}}{=} \{0, 1\}^* \setminus S_R = \{x : |R(x)| = 0\}$.

- *The problem of* finding unique solutions for R is *defined as the* search problem R with promise $\mathrm{US}_R \cup \overline{S}_R$ (see Definition 2.29).

  In continuation of Definition 2.30, candid searching for unique solutions for R is *defined as the* search problem R with promise US_R.

- *The problem of* deciding unique solutions for R is *defined as the* promise problem $(\mathrm{US}_R, \overline{S}_R)$ (see Definition 2.31).

Interestingly, in many natural cases, the promise does not make any of these problems any easier than the original problem. That is, for all known NP-complete problems, the original problem is reducible in probabilistic polynomial time to the corresponding unique instances problem.

Theorem 6.29: *Let $R \in \mathcal{PC}$ and suppose that every search problem in $\mathcal{PC}$ is parsimoniously reducible to R. Then solving the search problem of R (resp., deciding membership in S_R) is reducible in probabilistic polynomial time to finding unique solutions for R (resp., to the promise problem $(\mathrm{US}_R, \overline{S}_R)$). Furthermore, there exists a probabilistic polynomial-time computable mapping M such that for every $x \in \overline{S}_R$ it holds that $\Pr[M(x) \in \overline{S}_R] = 1$, whereas for every $x \in S_R$ it holds that $\Pr[M(x) \in \mathrm{US}_R] \geq 1/\mathrm{poly}(|x|)$.*

We highlight the fact that the hypothesis asserts that R is $\mathcal{PC}$-complete *via parsimonious reductions*; this hypothesis is crucial to Theorem 6.29 (see Exercise 6.36). The large (but bounded-away from 1) error probability of the randomized Karp-reduction M can be reduced by repetitions, yielding a randomized Cook-reduction with exponentially vanishing error probability. Note that the resulting reduction may make many queries that violate the promise, and still yield the correct answer (with high probability) by relying on queries that satisfy the promise. (Specifically, in the case of search problems, we avoid wrong solutions by checking each solution obtained, while in the case of decision problems we rely on the fact that for every $x \in \overline{S}_R$ it always holds that $M(x) \in \overline{S}_R$.)

Proof: We focus on establishing the furthermore clause (and the main claim follows). The proof uses many of the ideas of the proof of Theorem 6.27, and we refer to the latter for motivation. We shall again make essential use of hashing functions, and rely on the material presented in Appendix D.2.1–D.2.2.

As in the proof of Theorem 6.27, the idea is to apply a "random sieve" on $R(x)$, this time with the hope that a single element survives. Specifically, if we let each element pass the sieve with probability approximately $1/|R(x)|$ then with constant probability a single element survives. In such a case, we shall obtain an instance with a unique solution (i.e., an instance of $S_{R,H}$ having a single NP-witness), which will (essentially) fulfill our quest. Sieving will be performed by a random function selected in an adequate hashing family (see Appendix D.2). A couple of questions arise:

1. *How do we get an approximation to $|R(x)|$?* Note that we need such an approximation in order to determine the adequate hashing family. Note that invoking Theorem 6.27 will not do, because the said oracle machine uses an oracle to $\mathcal{NP}$ (which puts us back to square one, let alone that the said reduction makes many queries).[15] Instead, we just select $m \in \{0, \ldots, \text{poly}(|x|)\}$ uniformly and note that (if $|R(x)| > 0$ then) $\Pr[m = \lceil \log_2 |R(x)| \rceil] = 1/\text{poly}(|x|)$. Next, we randomly map x to (x, m, h), where h is uniformly selected in an adequate hashing family.

2. *How does the question of whether a single element of $R(x)$ pass the random sieve translate to an instance of the unique-solution problem for R?* Recall that in the proof of Theorem 6.27 the non-emptiness of the set of elements of $R(x)$ that pass the sieve (defined by h) was determined by checking membership (of (x, m, h)) in $S_{R,H} \in \mathcal{NP}$ (defined in Eq. (6.9)). Furthermore, the number of NP-witnesses for $(x, m, h) \in S_{R,H}$ equals the number of elements of $R(x)$ that pass the sieve. Thus, a single element of $R(x)$ passes the sieve (defined by h) if and only if $(x, m, h) \in S_{R,H}$ has a single NP-witness. Using the parsimonious reduction of $S_{R,H}$ to S_R (which is guaranteed by the theorem's hypothesis), we obtained the desired instance.

Note that in case $R(x) = \emptyset$ the aforementioned mapping always generates a no-instance (of $S_{R,H}$ and thus of S_R). Details follow.

Implementation (i.e., the mapping M). As in the proof of Theorem 6.27, we assume, without loss of generality, that $R(x) \subseteq \{0, 1\}^{\ell}$, where $\ell = \text{poly}(|x|)$. We start by uniformly selecting $m \in \{1, \ldots, \ell+1\}$ and $h \in H_{\ell}^{m}$, where H_{ℓ}^{m} is a family of efficiently computable and pairwise-independent hashing functions (see Definition D.1) mapping ℓ-bit long strings to m-bit long strings. Thus, we obtain an instance (x, m, h) of $S_{R,H} \in \mathcal{NP}$ such that the set of valid solutions for (x, m, h) equals $\{y \in R(x) : h(y) = 0^m\}$. Using the parsimonious reduction g of the NP-witness relation of $S_{R,H}$ to R (i.e., the NP-witness relation of S_R), we map (x, m, h) to $g(x, m, h)$, and it holds that $|\{y \in R(x) : h(y) = 0^m\}|$ equals $|R(g(x, m, h))|$. To summarize, on input x the randomized mapping M outputs the instance $M(x) \overset{\text{def}}{=} g(x, m, h)$, where $m \in \{1, \ldots, \ell+1\}$ and $h \in H_{\ell}^{m}$ are uniformly selected.

The analysis. Note that for any $x \in \overline{S}_R$ it holds that $\Pr[M(x) \in \overline{S}_R] = 1$. Assuming that $x \in S_R$, with probability exactly $1/(\ell+1)$ it holds that $m = m_x$, where $m_x \overset{\text{def}}{=} \lceil \log_2 |R(x)| \rceil + 1$. Focusing on the case that $m = m_x$, for a uniformly selected

---

$h \in H_\ell^m$, we shall lower-bound the probability that the set $R_h(x) \overset{\text{def}}{=} \{y \in R(x) : h(y) = 0^m\}$ is a singleton. First, using the Inclusion-Exclusion Principle, we lower-bound $\mathrm{Pr}_{h \in H_\ell^{m_x}}[|R_h(x)| > 0]$ by

$$\sum_{y \in R(x)} \mathrm{Pr}_{h \in H_\ell^{m_x}}[h(y) = 0^{m_x}] - \sum_{y_1 < y_2 \in R(x)} \mathrm{Pr}_{h \in H_\ell^{m_x}}[h(y_1) = h(y_2) = 0^{m_x}].$$

Next, we upper-bound $\mathrm{Pr}_{h \in H_\ell^{m_x}}[|R_h(x)| > 1]$ by

$$\sum_{y_1 < y_2 \in R(x)} \mathrm{Pr}_{h \in H_\ell^{m_x}}[h(y_1) = h(y_2) = 0^{m_x}].$$

Combining these two bounds, we get

$$\mathrm{Pr}_{h \in H_\ell^{m_x}}[|R_h(x)| = 1]$$

$$= \mathrm{Pr}_{h \in H_\ell^{m_x}}[|R_h(x)| > 0] - \mathrm{Pr}_{h \in H_\ell^{m_x}}[|R_h(x)| > 1]$$

$$\geq \sum_{y \in R(x)} \mathrm{Pr}_{h \in H_\ell^{m_x}}[h(y) = 0^{m_x}] - 2 \cdot \sum_{y_1 < y_2 \in R(x)} \mathrm{Pr}_{h \in H_\ell^{m_x}}[h(y_1) = h(y_2) = 0^{m_x}]$$

$$= |R(x)| \cdot 2^{-m_x} - 2 \cdot \binom{|R(x)|}{2} \cdot 2^{-2m_x}$$

where the last equality is due to the pairwise independence property. Using $2^{m_x-2} < |R(x)| \leq 2^{m_x-1}$, it follows that

$$\mathrm{Pr}_{h \in H_\ell^{m_x}}[|R_h(x)| = 1] \geq \min_{1/4 < \rho \leq 1/2}\{\rho - \rho^2\} > \frac{1}{8}.$$

Thus, $\mathrm{Pr}[M(x) \in \mathrm{US}_R] \geq 1/(8(\ell + 1))$, and the theorem follows. ∎

Comment. Theorem 6.29 is sometimes stated as referring to the unique solution problem of SAT. In this case and when using a specific family of pairwise independent hashing functions, the use of the parsimonious reduction can be avoided. For details see Exercise 6.38.

Digest. The proof of Theorem 6.29 combines two reduction steps, which refer to the NP-witness relation of $S_{R,H}$, herein denoted R'. The main step is a many-to-one randomized reduction of the search problem of R (resp., of S_R) to the problem of finding unique solutions for R' (resp., to $(\mathrm{US}_{R'}, \overline{S}_{R'})$). The second step is a deterministic many-to-one reduction of the latter problem to the problem of finding unique solutions for R. Indeed, the proof of Theorem 6.29 focuses on the first step, while the second step is provided by the parsimonious reduction of R' to R (which is guaranteed by the hypothesis). As stated in the previous comment, in the case of SAT there is a direct way of performing the second step.

An alternative proof of Theorem 6.29. Note that the analysis of the (approximate counting) procedure that is presented in the proof of Theorem 6.27 implies that, for every $x \in S_R$, there exists an integer $i \in [\ell]$ such that, with constant probability (over the choice of $h \in H_\ell^i$), the set $\{y \in R(x) : h(x) = 0^i\}$ is non-empty and has constant size (i.e., it contains at most 100 elements). Thus, the randomized mapping $x \mapsto (x, i, h)$, where $i \in [\ell]$ and $h \in H_\ell^i$ are selected uniformly, yields a reduction of S_R to $S_{R,H}$ such that any yes-instance is mapped with noticeable probability to a yes-instance that has few (i.e., at most 100) solutions. Using an additional randomized reduction (e.g., as in Construction 6.32), one may reduce such instances (which have few solutions) to instances that have a unique solution. (For details, see Exercise 6.39.)

6.2.4. Uniform Generation of Solutions

Recall that approximately counting the number of solutions for a relation R is a straining of the decision problem S_R (which asks for distinguishing the case that some solutions exist from the case that no solutions exist). We now turn to a new type of computational problems, which may be viewed as a straining of search problems. We refer to the task of generating a uniformly distributed solution for a given instance, rather than merely finding an adequate solution. Nevertheless, as we shall see, for many natural problems (and all NP-complete ones) generating a uniformly distributed solution is randomly reducible to finding a solution.

Needless to say, by definition, algorithms solving this ("uniform generation") task must be randomized. Focusing on relations in $\mathcal{PC}$ we consider two versions of the problem, which differ by the level of approximation provided for the desired (uniform) distribution.[16]

Definition 6.30 (uniform generation): *Let $R \in \mathcal{PC}$ and $S_R = \{x : |R(x)| \geq 1\}$, and let Π be a probabilistic process.*

1. *We say that Π solves the uniform generation problem of R if, on input $x \in S_R$, the process Π outputs either an element of $R(x)$ or a special symbol, denoted $\bot$, such that $\Pr[\Pi(x) \in R(x)] \geq 1/2$ and for every $y \in R(x)$ it holds that $\Pr[\Pi(x) = y \mid \Pi(x) \in R(x)] = 1/|R(x)|$.*
2. *For $\varepsilon : \mathbb{N} \to [0, 1]$, we say that Π solves the $(1 - \varepsilon)$-approximate uniform generation problem of R if, on input $x \in S_R$, the distribution $\Pi(x)$ is $\varepsilon(|x|)$-close[17] to the uniform distribution on $R(x)$.*

In both cases, without loss of generality, we may require that if $x \notin S_R$ then $\Pr[\Pi(x) = \bot] = 1$. More generally, we may require that Π never outputs a string not in $R(x)$.

Note that the error probability of uniform generation (as in Item 1) can be made exponentially vanishing (in $|x|$) by employing error reduction. In contrast, we are not aware of any general way of reducing the deviation of an approximate uniform generation procedure (as in Item 2).[18]

In §6.2.4.1 we show that, for many search problems, approximate uniform generation is computationally equivalent to approximate counting. In §6.2.4.2 we present a direct

---

[16]Note that a probabilistic algorithm running in strict polynomial time is not able to output a perfectly uniform distribution on sets of certain sizes. Specifically, referring to the standard model that allows only for uniformly selected binary values, such algorithms cannot output a perfectly uniform distribution on sets having cardinality that is not a power of two.

[17]See Appendix D.1.1.

[18]We note that in some cases, the deviation of an approximate uniform generation procedure can be reduced. See discussion following Theorem 6.31.

approach for solving the uniform generation problem of any search problem in $\mathcal{PC}$ by using an oracle to $\mathcal{NP}$. Thus, the uniform generation problem of any NP-complete problem is randomly reducible to the problem itself (either in its search or decision version).

6.2.4.1. Relation to Approximate Counting

We show that, for many natural search problems in $\mathcal{PC}$, the approximate counting problem associated with R is computationally equivalent to approximate uniform generation with respect to R. Specifically, we refer to search problems $R \in \mathcal{PC}$ such that $R'(x; y') \overset{\text{def}}{=} \{y'' : (x, y'y'') \in R\}$ is *strongly parsimoniously reducible to R*, where a strongly parsimonious reduction of R' to R is a parsimonious reduction g that is coupled with an efficiently computable 1-1 mapping of pairs $(g(x), y) \in R$ to pairs $(x, h(x, y)) \in R'$ (i.e., h is efficiently computable and $h(x, \cdot)$ is a 1-1 mapping of $R(g(x))$ to $R'(x)$). For technical reasons, we also assume that $|g(x)| \geq |x|$ for every x.[19] Note that, for many natural search problems R, the corresponding R' is strongly parsimoniously reducible to R, where the additional technical condition may be enforced by adequate padding (cf. Exercise 2.30). This holds, in particular, for the search problems of SAT and Perfect Matching (see, e.g., Exercise 6.40). We stress that *the following result holds also for problems that are not NP-complete* (and, in fact, is more interesting for such problems).

Recalling that both types of approximation problems are parameterized by the level of precision, we obtain the following quantitative form of the aforementioned equivalence.

Theorem 6.31: *Let $R \in \mathcal{PC}$ and let ℓ be a polynomial such that for every $(x, y) \in R$ it holds that $|y| \leq \ell(|x|)$. Suppose that R' is strongly parsimoniously reducible to R, where $R'(x; y') \overset{\text{def}}{=} \{y'' : (x, y'y'') \in R\}$.*

1. From approximate counting to approximate uniform generation: *Let $\varepsilon(n) = 1/5\ell(n)$ and let $\mu : \mathbb{N} \to (0, 1)$ be a function satisfying $\mu(n) \geq \exp(-\text{poly}(n))$. Then, $(1 - \mu)$-approximate uniform generation for R is reducible in probabilistic polynomial time to a $(1 - \varepsilon)$-approximating $\#R$.*
2. From approximate uniform generation to approximate counting: *For every non-increasing and noticeable $\varepsilon : \mathbb{N} \to (0, 1)$ (i.e., $\varepsilon(n) \geq 1/\text{poly}(n)$ for every n), the problem of $(1 - \varepsilon)$-approximating $\#R$ is reducible in probabilistic polynomial time to a $(1 - \varepsilon')$-approximate uniform generation problem of R, where $\varepsilon'(n) = \varepsilon(n)/7\ell(n)$.*

In fact, Part 1 also holds in case R' is just parsimoniously reducible to R.

Note that the quality of the approximate uniform generation asserted in Part 1 (i.e., μ) is independent of the quality of the approximate counting procedure (i.e., ε) to which the former is reduced, provided that the approximate counter performs better than some threshold. On the other hand, the quality of the approximate counting asserted in Part 2 (i.e., ε) does depend on the quality of the approximate uniform generation (i.e., ε'), but cannot reach beyond a certain bound (i.e., noticeable relative deviation). Recall that for problems that are NP-complete under parsimonious reductions the quality of approximate counting procedures can be improved (see Exercise 6.34). However, *Theorem 6.31 is most*

---

[19]This technical condition allows us to replace deviation bounds expressed in terms of $|g(x)|$ by bounds expressed in terms of $|x|$, while relying on the fact that $\varepsilon(|g(x)|) \leq \varepsilon(|x|)$ holds for any non-increasing $\varepsilon : \mathbb{N} \to (0, 1)$.

useful when applied to problems that are not NP-complete,[20] because for problems that are NP-complete both approximate counting and uniform generation are randomly reducible to the corresponding search problem (see Exercise 6.42).

Proof: Throughout the proof, we assume for simplicity (and in fact without loss of generality) that $R(x) \neq \emptyset$ and $R(x) \subseteq \{0, 1\}^{\ell(|x|)}$.

Toward Part 1, let us first reduce the uniform generation problem of R to $\#R$ (rather than to approximating $\#R$). On input $x \in S_R$, we shall generate a uniformly distributed $y \in R(x)$ by randomly generating its bits one after the other. We proceed in iterations, entering the ith iteration with an $(i - 1)$-bit long string y' such that $R'(x; y') \stackrel{\text{def}}{=} \{y'' : (x, y'y'') \in R\}$ is not empty. With probability $|R'(x; y'1)|/|R'(x; y')|$ we set the ith bit to equal 1, and otherwise we set it to equal 0. We obtain both $|R'(x; y'1)|$ and $|R'(x; y')|$ by using a parsimonious reduction g of $R' = \{((x; y'), y'') : (x, y'y'') \in R\} \in \mathcal{PC}$ to R. That is, we obtain $|R'(x; y')|$ by querying for the value of $|R(g(x; y'))|$. Ignoring integrality issues, all this works perfectly (i.e., we generate an $\ell(n)$-bit string uniformly distributed in $R(x)$) as long as we have oracle access to $\#R$. Since we only have oracle access to an approximation of $\#R$, a careful implementation of the foregoing idea is in place.

Let us denote the approximation oracle by A. Firstly, by adequate error reduction, we may assume that, for every z, it holds that $\Pr[A(z) \in (1 \pm \varepsilon(n)) \cdot \#R(z)] > 1 - \mu'(|z|)$, where $\mu'(n) = \mu(n)/\ell(n)$. In the rest of the analysis we ignore the probability that the estimate of $\#R(z)$ provided by the randomized oracle A (on query z) deviates from the aforementioned interval. (We note that these rare events are the only source of the possible deviation of the output distribution from the uniform distribution on $R(x)$.)[21] Next, let us assume for a moment that A is *deterministic* and that for every x and y' it holds that

$$A(g(x; y'0)) + A(g(x; y'1)) \leq A(g(x; y')). \tag{6.10}$$

We also assume that the approximation is correct at the "trivial level" (where one may just check whether or not (x, y) is in R); that is, for every $y \in \{0, 1\}^{\ell(|x|)}$, it holds that

$$A(g(x; y)) = 1 \text{ if } (x, y) \in R \text{ and } A(g(x; y)) = 0 \text{ otherwise.} \tag{6.11}$$

We modify the ith iteration of the foregoing procedure such that, when entering with the $(i - 1)$-bit long prefix y', we set the ith bit to $\sigma \in \{0, 1\}$ with probability $A(g(x; y'\sigma))/A(g(x; y'))$ and halt (with output $\perp$) with the residual probability (i.e., $1 - (A(g(x; y'0))/A(g(x; y'))) - (A(g(x; y'1))/A(g(x; y')))$). Indeed, Eq. (6.10) guarantees that the latter instruction is sound, since the two main probabilities sum up to at most 1. If we completed the last (i.e., $\ell(|x|)^{\text{th}}$) iteration, then we output the $\ell(|x|)$-bit long string that was generated. Thus, as long as Eq. (6.10) holds (but regardless of other aspects of the quality of the approximation), every

---

[20] In fact, many approximate counting algorithms rely explicitly or implicitly on Theorem 6.31 (see, e.g., [168, Sec. 11.3.1] and [131]).

[21] Note that the (negligible) effect of these rare events may not be easy to correct. For starters, we do not necessarily get an indication when these rare events occur. Furthermore, these rare events may occur with different probability in the different invocations of algorithm A (i.e., on different queries).

$y = \sigma_1 \cdots \sigma_{\ell(|x|)} \in R(x)$ is output with probability

$$\frac{A(g(x; \sigma_1))}{A(g(x; \lambda))} \cdot \frac{A(g(x; \sigma_1 \sigma_2))}{A(g(x; \sigma_1))} \cdots \frac{A(g(x; \sigma_1 \sigma_2 \cdots \sigma_{\ell(|x|)}))}{A(g(x; \sigma_1 \sigma_2 \cdots \sigma_{\ell(|x|)-1}))} \tag{6.12}$$

which, by Eq. (6.11), equals $1/A(g(x; \lambda))$. Thus, the procedure outputs each element of $R(x)$ with equal probability, and never outputs a non-$\perp$ value that is outside $R(x)$. It follows that the quality of approximation only affects the probability that the procedure outputs a non-$\perp$ value (which in turn equals $|R(x)|/A(g(x; \lambda))$). The key point is that, as long as Eq. (6.11) holds, the specific approximate values obtained by the procedure are immaterial – with the exception of $A(g(x; \lambda))$, all these values "cancel out."

We now turn to enforcing Eq. (6.10) and Eq. (6.11). We may enforce Eq. (6.11) by performing the straightforward check (of whether or not $(x, y) \in R$) rather than invoking $A(g(x, y))$.[22] As for Eq. (6.10), we enforce it artificially by using $A'(x, y') \stackrel{\text{def}}{=} (1 + \varepsilon(|x|))^{3(\ell(|x|) - |y'|)} \cdot A(g(x; y'))$ instead of $A(g(x; y'))$. Recalling that $A(g(x; y')) = (1 \pm \varepsilon(|x|)) \cdot |R'(x; y')|$, we have

$$A'(x, y') > (1 + \varepsilon(|x|))^{3(\ell(|x|) - |y'|)} \cdot (1 - \varepsilon(|x|)) \cdot |R'(x; y')|$$

$$A'(x, y'\sigma) < (1 + \varepsilon(|x|))^{3(\ell(|x|) - |y'| - 1)} \cdot (1 + \varepsilon(|x|)) \cdot |R'(x; y'\sigma)|$$

and the claim (that Eq. (6.10) holds) follows by using $(1 - \varepsilon(|x|)) \cdot (1 + \varepsilon(|x|))^3 > (1 + \varepsilon(|x|))$. Note that the foregoing modification only affects the probability of outputting a non-$\perp$ value; this good event now occurs with probability $|R'(x; \lambda)|/A'(x, \lambda)$, which is lower-bounded by $(1 + \varepsilon(|x|))^{-(3\ell(|x|)+1)} > 1/2$, where the inequality is due to the setting of ε (i.e., $\varepsilon(n) = 1/5\ell(n)$). Finally, we refer to our assumption that A is deterministic. This assumption was only used in order to identify the value of $A(g(x, y'))$ obtained and used in the $(|y'| - 1)^{\text{st}}$ iteration with the value of $A(g(x, y'))$ obtained and used in the $|y'|^{\text{th}}$ iteration. The same effect can be obtained by just reusing the former value (in the $|y'|^{\text{th}}$ iteration) rather than reinvoking A in order to obtain it. Part 1 follows.

Toward Part 2, let use first reduce the task of approximating $\#R$ to the task of (exact) uniform generation for R. On input $x \in S_R$, the reduction uses the tree of possible prefixes of elements of $R(x)$ in a somewhat different manner. Again, we proceed in iterations, entering the ith iteration with an $(i - 1)$-bit long string y' such that $R'(x; y') \stackrel{\text{def}}{=} \{y'' : (x, y'y'') \in R\}$ is not empty. At the ith iteration we estimate the bigger among the two fractions $|R'(x; y'0)|/|R'(x; y')|$ and $|R'(x; y'1)|/|R'(x; y')|$, by uniformly sampling the uniform distribution over $R'(x; y')$. That is, taking $\text{poly}(|x|/\varepsilon'(|x|))$ uniformly distributed samples in $R'(x; y')$, we obtain with overwhelmingly high probability an approximation of these fractions up to an additive deviation of at most $\varepsilon'(|x|)$. This means that we obtain a relative approximation up to a factor of $1 \pm 3\varepsilon'(|x|)$ for the fraction (or fractions) that is (resp., are) bigger than $1/3$. Indeed, we may not be able to obtain such a good relative approximation of the other fraction (in the case that the other fraction is very small), but this does not matter. It also does not matter that we cannot tell which is the bigger fraction among the two; it only matter that we use an approximation that indicates a quantity that is,

---

[22] Alternatively, we note that since A is a $(1 - \varepsilon)$-approximator for $\varepsilon < 1$ it must hold that $\#R'(z) = 0$ implies $A(z) = 0$. Also, since $\varepsilon < 1/3$, if $\#R'(z) = 1$ then $A(z) \in (2/3, 4/3)$, which may be rounded to 1.

say, bigger than $1/3$. We proceed to the next iteration by augmenting y' using the bit that corresponds to such a quantity. Specifically, suppose that we obtained the approximations $a_0(y') \approx |R'(x; y'0)|/|R'(x; y')|$ and $a_1(y') \approx |R'(x; y'1)|/|R'(x; y')|$. Then we extend y' by the bit 1 if $a_1(y') > a_0(y')$ and extend y' by the bit 0 otherwise. Finally, when we reach $y = \sigma_1 \cdots \sigma_{\ell(|x|)}$ such that $(x, y) \in R$, we output

$$a_{\sigma_1}(\lambda)^{-1} \cdot a_{\sigma_2}(\sigma_1)^{-1} \cdots a_{\sigma_{\ell(|x|)}}(\sigma_1\sigma_2 \cdots \sigma_{\ell(|x|)-1})^{-1} \tag{6.13}$$

where for each i it holds that $a_{\sigma_i}(\sigma_1\sigma_2 \cdots \sigma_{i-1})$ is $(1 \pm 3\varepsilon'(|x|)) \cdot \frac{|R'(x;\sigma_1\sigma_2\cdots\sigma_i)|}{|R'(x;\sigma_1\sigma_2\cdots\sigma_{i-1})|}$.

As in Part 1, actions regarding R' (in this case uniform generation in R') are conducted via the parsimonious reduction g to R. That is, whenever we need to sample uniformly in the set $R'(x; y')$, we sample the set $R(g(x; y'))$ and recover the corresponding element of $R'(x; y')$ by using the mapping guaranteed by the hypothesis that g is strongly parsimonious. Finally, note that so far we assumed a uniform generation procedure for R, but using an $(1 - \varepsilon')$-approximate uniform generation merely means that all our approximations deviate by another additive term of ε'. Thus, with overwhelmingly high probability, for each i it holds that $a_{\sigma_i}(\sigma_1\sigma_2 \cdots \sigma_{i-1})$ is $(1 \pm 6\varepsilon'(|x|)) \cdot |R'(x; \sigma_1\sigma_2 \cdots \sigma_i)|/|R'(x; \sigma_1\sigma_2 \cdots \sigma_{i-1})|$. It follows that, on input x, when using an oracle that provides a $(1 - \varepsilon')$-approximate uniform generation for R, with overwhelmingly high probability, the output (as defined in Eq. (6.13)) is in

$$\prod_{i=1}^{\ell(|x|)} \left((1 \pm 6\varepsilon'(|x|))^{-1} \cdot \frac{|R'(x; \sigma_1 \cdots \sigma_{i-1})|}{|R'(x; \sigma_1 \cdots \sigma_i)|} \right) \tag{6.14}$$

where the error probability is due to the unlikely case that in one of the iterations our approximation deviates from the correct value by more than an additive deviation term of $2\varepsilon'(n)$. Noting that Eq. (6.14) equals $(1 \pm 6\varepsilon'(|x|))^{-\ell(|x|)} \cdot |R(x)|$ and using $(1 \pm 6\varepsilon'(|x|))^{-\ell(|x|)} \subset (1 \pm \varepsilon(|x|))$ (which holds for $\varepsilon' = \varepsilon/7\ell$), Part 2 follows. ∎

6.2.4.2. A Direct Procedure for Uniform Generation

We conclude the current chapter by presenting a direct procedure for solving the uniform generation problem of any $R \in \mathcal{PC}$. This procedure uses an oracle to $\mathcal{NP}$ (or to S_R itself in case it is NP-complete), which is unavoidable because solving the uniform generation problem of R implies solving the corresponding search problem (which in turn implies deciding membership in S_R). One advantage of this procedure, over the reduction presented in §6.2.4.1, is that it solves the uniform generation problem rather than the *approximate* uniform generation problem.

We are going to use hashing again, but this time we use a family of hashing functions having a stronger "uniformity property" (see Appendix D.2.3). Specifically, we will use a family of ℓ-wise independent hashing functions mapping ℓ-bit strings to m-bit strings, where ℓ bounds the length of solutions in R, and rely on the fact that such a family satisfies Lemma D.6. Intuitively, such functions partition $\{0, 1\}^\ell$ into 2^m cells and Lemma D.6 asserts that these partitions "uniformly shatter" all sufficiently large sets. That is, for every set $S \subseteq \{0, 1\}^\ell$ of size $\Omega(\ell \cdot 2^m)$, the partition induced by almost every function in this family is such that each cell contains approximately $|S|/2^m$ elements of S. In particular, if $|S| = \Theta(\ell \cdot 2^m)$ then each cell contains $\Theta(\ell)$ elements of S. We denote this family of functions by H_ℓ^m, and rely on the fact that its elements have succinct and effective representation (as defined in Appendix D.2.1).

Loosely speaking, the following procedure (for uniform generation) first selects a random hashing function and tests whether it "uniformly shatters" the target set $S = R(x)$. If this condition holds then the procedure selects a cell at random and retrieves all the elements of S residing in the chosen cell. Finally, the procedure either outputs one of the retrieved elements or halts with no output, where each retrieved element is output with a fixed probability p (which is independent of the actual number of elements of S that reside in the chosen cell). This guarantees that each element $e \in S$ is output with the same probability (i.e., $2^{-m} \cdot p$), regardless of the number of elements of S that reside with e in the same cell.

In the following construction, we assume that on input x we also obtain a good approximation to the size of $R(x)$. This assumption can be enforced by using an approximate counting procedure as a preprocessing stage. Alternatively, the ideas presented in the following construction yield such an approximate counting procedure.

Construction 6.32 (uniform generation): *On input x and $m'_x \in \{m_x, m_x + 1\}$, where $m_x \overset{\text{def}}{=} \lfloor \log_2 |R(x)| \rfloor$ and $R(x) \subseteq \{0, 1\}^\ell$, the oracle machine proceeds as follows.*

1. Selecting a partition that "uniformly shatters" $R(x)$. *The machine sets $m = \max(0, m'_x - \log_2 40\ell)$ and selects uniformly $h \in H_\ell^m$. Such a function defines a partition of $\{0, 1\}^\ell$ into 2^m cells,[23] and the hope is that each cell contains approximately the same number of elements of $R(x)$. Next, the machine checks that this is indeed the case or rather than no cell contains more than 120ℓ elements of $R(x)$ (i.e., more than twice the expected number). This is done by checking whether or not $(x, h, 1^{120\ell+1})$ is in the set $S_{R,H}^{(1)}$ defined as follows*

   $$S_{R,H}^{(1)} \overset{\text{def}}{=} \{(x', h', 1^t) : \exists v \text{ s.t. } |\{y : (x', y) \in R \wedge h'(y) = v\}| \geq t\} \quad (6.15)$$

   $$= \{(x', h', 1^t) : \exists v, y_1, \dots, y_t \text{ s.t. } \psi^{(1)}(x', h', v, y_1, \dots, y_t)\},$$

   where $\psi^{(1)}(x', h', v, y_1, \dots, y_t)$ holds if and only if $y_1 < y_2 \cdots < y_t$ and for every $j \in [t]$ it holds that $(x', y_j) \in R \wedge h'(y_j) = v$. Note that $S_{R,H}^{(1)} \in \mathcal{NP}$.

   If the answer is positive (i.e., there exists a cell that contains more than 120ℓ elements of $R(x)$) then the machine halts with output $\perp$. Otherwise, the machine continues with this choice of h. In this case, no cell contains more than 120ℓ elements of $R(x)$ (i.e., for every $v \in \{0, 1\}^m$, it holds that $|\{y : (x, y) \in R \wedge h(y) = v\}| \leq 120\ell$). We stress that this is an absolute guarantee that follows from $(x, h, 1^{120\ell+1}) \notin S_{R,H}^{(1)}$.

2. Selecting a cell and determining the number of elements of $R(x)$ that are contained in it. *The machine selects uniformly $v \in \{0, 1\}^m$ and determines $s_v \overset{\text{def}}{=} |\{y : (x, y) \in R \wedge h(y) = v\}|$ by making queries to the following NP-set*

   $$S_{R,H}^{(2)} \overset{\text{def}}{=} \{(x', h', v', 1^t) : \exists y_1, \dots, y_t \text{ s.t. } \psi^{(1)}(x', h', v', y_1, \dots, y_t)\}. \quad (6.16)$$

   Specifically, for $i = 1, \dots, 120\ell$, it checks whether $(x, h, v, 1^i)$ is in $S_{R,H}^{(2)}$, and sets s_v to be the largest value of i for which the answer is positive.

---

[23]For sake of uniformity, we also allow the case of $m = 0$, which is rather artificial. In this case all hashing functions in H_ℓ^0 map $\{0, 1\}^\ell$ to the empty string, which is viewed as 0^0, and thus define a trivial partition of $\{0, 1\}^\ell$ (i.e., into a single cell).

3. Obtaining all the elements of $R(x)$ that are contained in the selected cell, and outputting one of them at random. *Using s_v, the procedure reconstructs the set $S_v \overset{\text{def}}{=} \{y : (x, y) \in R \wedge h(y) = v\}$, by making queries to the following NP-set*

$$S_{R,H}^{(3)} \overset{\text{def}}{=} \{(x', h', v', 1^t, j) : \exists y_1, \ldots, y_t \text{ s.t. } \psi^{(3)}(x', h', v', y_1, \ldots, y_t, j)\},$$
(6.17)

where $\psi^{(3)}(x', h', v', y_1, \ldots, y_t, j)$ holds if and only if $\psi^{(1)}(x', h', v', y_1, \ldots, y_t)$ holds and the jth bit of $y_1 \cdots y_t$ equals 1. Specifically, for $j_1 = 1, \ldots, s_v$ and $j_2 = 1, \ldots, \ell$, we make the query $(x, h, v, 1^{s_v}, (j_1 - 1) \cdot \ell + j_2)$ in order to determine the j_2^{th} bit of y_{j_1}. Finally, having recovered S_v, the procedure outputs each $y \in S_v$ with probability $1/120\ell$, and outputs $\perp$ otherwise (i.e., with probability $1 - (s_v/120\ell)$).

Recall that for $|R(x)| = \Omega(\ell)$ and $m = m'_x - \log_2 40\ell$, Lemma D.6 implies that, with overwhelmingly high probability (over the choice of $h \in H_\ell^m$), each set $\{y : (x, y) \in R \wedge h(y) = v\}$ has cardinality $(1 \pm 0.5)|R(x)|/2^m$. Thus, ignoring the case of $|R(x)| = O(\ell)$, Step 1 can be easily adapted to yield an approximate counting procedure for #R; see Exercise 6.41, which also handles the case of $|R(x)| = O(\ell)$ by using ideas as in Step 2. However, our aim is to establish the following result.

Proposition 6.33: *Construction 6.32 solves the uniform generation problem of R.*

Proof: Intuitively, by Lemma D.6 (and the setting of m), with overwhelmingly high probability, a uniformly selected $h \in H_\ell^m$ partitions $R(x)$ into 2^m cells, each containing at most 120ℓ elements. Following is the tedious proof of this fact. Since $m = \max(0, m'_x - \log_2 40\ell)$, we may focus on the case that $m'_x > \log_2 40\ell$ (as in the other case $|R(x)| \leq 2^{m'_x+1} \leq 80\ell$). In this case, by Lemma D.6 (using $\varepsilon = 0.5$ and $m = m'_x - \log_2 40\ell \leq \log_2 |R(x)| - \log_2 20\ell$ (which implies $m \leq \log_2 |R(x)| - \log_2(5\ell/\varepsilon^2))$), with overwhelmingly high probability, each set $\{y : (x, y) \in R \wedge h(y) = v\}$ has cardinality $(1 \pm 0.5)|R(x)|/2^m$. Using $m'_x > (\log_2 |R(x)|) - 1$ (and $m = m'_x - \log_2 40\ell$), it follows that $|R(x)|/2^m < 80\ell$ and hence each cell contains at most 120ℓ elements of $R(x)$. We also note that, using $m'_x \leq (\log_2 |R(x)|) + 1$, it follows that $|R(x)|/2^m \geq 20\ell$ and hence each cell contains at least 10ℓ elements of $R(x)$.

The key observation, stated in Step 1, is that if the procedure does not halt in Step 1 then it is indeed the case that h induces a partition in which each cell contains at most 120ℓ elements of $R(x)$. The fact that these cells may contain a different number of elements is immaterial, because each element is output with the same probability (i.e., $1/120\ell$). What matters is that the average number of elements in the various cells is sufficiently large, because this average number determines the probability that the procedure outputs an element of $R(x)$ (rather than $\perp$). Specifically, conditioned on not halting in Step 1, the probability that Step 3 outputs some element of $R(x)$ equals the average number of elements per cell (i.e., $|R(x)|/2^m$) divided by 120ℓ. Recalling that for $m > 0$ (resp., $m = 0$) it holds that $|R(x)|/2^m \geq 20\ell$ (resp., $|R(x)| \geq 1$), we conclude that in this case some element of $R(x)$ is output with probability at least $1/6$ (resp., $|R(x)|/120\ell$). Recalling that Step 1 halts with negligible probability, it follows that the procedure outputs some element of $R(x)$ with probability at least $0.99 \cdot \min((|R(x)|/120\ell), (1/6))$. ∎

Comments. We can easily improve the performance of Construction 6.32 by dealing separately with the case $m = 0$. In such a case, Step 3 can be simplified and improved by uniformly selecting and outputting an element of S_λ (which equals $R(x)$). Under this modification, the procedure outputs some element of $R(x)$ with probability at least $1/6$. In any case, recall that the probability that a uniform generation procedure outputs $\perp$ can be deceased by repeated invocations.

Digest. Construction 6.32 is the culmination of the "hashing paradigm" that is aimed at allowing various manipulations of arbitrary sets. In particular, as seen in Construction 6.32, hashing can be used in order to partition a large set into an adequate number of small subsets that are of approximately the same size. We stress that hashing is performed by randomly selecting a function in an adequate family. Indeed, the use of randomization for such purposes (i.e., allowing manipulation of large sets) seems indispensable.

Chapter Notes

One key aspect of randomized procedures is their success probability, which is obviously a quantitative notion. This aspect provides a clear connection between probabilistic polynomial-time algorithms considered in Section 6.1 and the counting problems considered in Section 6.2 (see also Exercise 6.20). More appealing connections between randomized procedures and counting problems (e.g., the application of randomization in approximate counting) are presented in Section 6.2. These connections justify the presentation of these two topics in the same chapter.

Randomized Algorithms

Making people take an unconventional step requires compelling reasons, and indeed the study of randomized algorithms was motivated by a few compelling examples. Ironically, the appeal of the two most famous examples (discussed next) has been somewhat diminished due to subsequent findings, but the fundamental questions that emerged remain fascinating regardless of the status of these two examples. These questions refer to the power of randomization in various computational settings, and in particular in the context of decision and search problems. We shall return to these questions after briefly reviewing the story of the aforementioned examples.

The first example: primality testing. For more than two decades, primality testing was the archetypical example of the usefulness of randomization in the context of efficient algorithms. The celebrated algorithms of Solovay and Strassen [211] and of Rabin [184], proposed in the late 1970s, established that deciding primality is in $co\mathcal{RP}$ (i.e., these tests always correctly recognize prime numbers, but they may err on composite inputs). (The approach of Construction 6.4, which only establishes that deciding primality is in $\mathcal{BPP}$, is commonly attributed to M. Blum.) In the late 1980s, Adleman and Huang [2] proved that deciding primality is in $\mathcal{RP}$ (and thus in $\mathcal{ZPP}$). In the early 2000s, Agrawal, Kayal, and Saxena [3] showed that deciding primality is actually in $\mathcal{P}$. One should note, however, that strong evidence of the fact that deciding primality is in $\mathcal{P}$ was actually available from the start: We refer to Miller's deterministic algorithm [166], which relies on the Extended Riemann Hypothesis.

The second example: undirected connectivity. Another celebrated example of the power of randomization, specifically in the context of log-space computations, was provided by testing undirected connectivity. The random-walk algorithm presented in Construction 6.12 is due to Aleliunas, Karp, Lipton, Lovász, and Rackoff [5]. Recall that a deterministic log-space algorithm was found twenty-five years later (see Section 5.2.4 or [190]).

Another famous example: polynomial identity testing. A third famous example, which dates back to about the same period, is the polynomial identity tester of [65, 199, 243]. This tester, presented in §6.1.3.1, has found many applications in Complexity Theory (some are implicit in subsequent chapters). Needless to say, in the abstract setting of Construction 6.7, randomization is indispensable. Interestingly, the computational version mentioned in Exercise 6.17 has so far resisted de-randomization attempts (cf. [134]).

Other randomized algorithms. In addition to the three foregoing examples, several other appealing randomized algorithms are known. Confining ourselves to the context of search and decision problems, we mention the algorithms for finding perfect matchings and minimum cuts in graphs (see, e.g., [90, Apdx. B.1] or [168, Sec. 12.4 and Sec. 10.2]), and note the prominent role of randomization in computational number theory (see, e.g., [24] or [168, Chap. 14]). We mention that randomized algorithms are more abundant in the context of approximation problems, and, in particular, for approximate counting problems (cf., e.g., [168, Chap. 11]). For a general textbook on randomized algorithms, we refer the interested reader to [168].

While it can be shown that randomization is essential in several important computational settings (cf., e.g., Chapter 9, Section 10.1.2, Appendix C, and Appendix D.3), a fundamental question is whether randomization is essential in the context of search and decision problems. The prevailing conjecture is that randomization is of *limited help* in the context of time-bounded and space-bounded algorithms. For example, it is conjectured that $\mathcal{BPP} = \mathcal{P}$ and $\mathcal{BPL} = \mathcal{L}$. Note that such conjectures do not rule out the possibility that randomization is also helpful in these contexts; they merely says that this help is limited. For example, it may be the case that any quadratic-time randomized algorithm can be emulated by a cubic-time deterministic algorithm, but not by a quadratic-time deterministic algorithm.

On the study of $\mathcal{BPP}$. The conjecture $\mathcal{BPP} = \mathcal{P}$ is referred to as a full derandomization of $\mathcal{BPP}$, and can be shown to hold under some reasonable intractability assumptions. This result (and related ones) will be presented in Section 8.3. In the current chapter, we only presented unconditional results regarding $\mathcal{BPP}$ like $\mathcal{BPP} \subset \mathcal{P}/\text{poly}$ and $\mathcal{BPP} \subseteq \mathcal{PH}$. Our presentation of Theorem 6.9 follows the proof idea of Lautemann [150]. A different proof technique, which yields a weaker result but found more applications (see, e.g., Theorems 6.27 and F.2), was presented (independently) by Sipser [207].

On the role of promise problems. In addition to their use in the formulation of Theorem 6.9, promise problems allow for establishing complete problems and hierarchy theorems for randomized computation (see Exercises 6.14 and 6.15, respectively). We mention that such results are not known for the corresponding classes of standard decision problems. The technical difficulty is that we do not know how to enumerate and/or recognize probabilistic machines that utilize a non-trivial probabilistic decision rule.

On the feasibility of randomized computation. Different perspectives on this question are offered by Chapter 8 and Appendix D.4. Specifically, as advocated in Chapter 8, generating uniformly distributed bit sequences is not really necessary for implementing randomized algorithms; it suffices to generate sequences that look (to their user) as if they are uniformly distributed. In many cases this leads to reducing the number of coin tosses in such implementations, and at times even to a full (efficient) derandomization (see Sections 8.3 and 8.4). A less radical approach is presented in Appendix D.4, which deals with the task of extracting almost uniformly distributed bit sequences from sources of weak randomness. Needless to say, these two approaches are complementary and can be combined.

Counting Problems

The counting class $\#\mathcal{P}$ was introduced by Valiant [230], who proved that computing the permanent of 0/1-matrices is $\#\mathcal{P}$-complete (i.e., Theorem 6.20). Interestingly, like in the case of Cook's introduction of NP-completeness [58], Valiant's motivation was determining the complexity of a specific problem (i.e., the permanent).

Our presentation of Theorem 6.20 is based both on Valiant's paper [230] and on subsequent studies (most notably [31]). Specifically, the high-level structure of the reduction presented in Proposition 6.21 as well as the "structured" design of the clause gadget is taken from [230], whereas the Deus Ex Machina gadget presented in Figure 6.3 is based on [31]. The proof of Proposition 6.22 is also based on [31] (with some variants). Turning back to the design of clause gadgets, we regret not being able to cite and/or use a systematic study of this design problem.

As noted in the main text, we decided not to present a proof of Toda's Theorem [220], which asserts that every set in $\mathcal{PH}$ is Cook-reducible to $\#\mathcal{P}$ (i.e., Theorem 6.16). Appendix F.1 contains a proof of a related result, which implies that $\mathcal{PH}$ is reducible to $\#\mathcal{P}$ via probabilistic polynomial-time reductions. Alternative proofs can be found in [136, 212, 220].

Approximate counting and related problems. The approximation procedure for $\#\mathcal{P}$ is due to Stockmeyer [214], following an idea of Sipser [207]. Our exposition, however, follows further developments in the area. The randomized reduction of $\mathcal{NP}$ to problems of unique solutions was discovered by Valiant and Vazirani [233]. Again, our exposition is a bit different.

The connection between approximate counting and uniform generation (presented in §6.2.4.1) was discovered by Jerrum, Valiant, and Vazirani [132], and turned out to be very useful in the design of algorithms (e.g., in the "Markov Chain approach" (see [168, Sec. 11.3.1])). The direct procedure for uniform generation (presented in §6.2.4.2) is taken from [28].

In continuation of §6.2.2.1, which is based on [140], we refer the interested reader to [131], which presents a probabilistic polynomial-time algorithm for approximating the permanent of non-negative matrices. This fascinating algorithm is based on the fact that knowing (approximately) certain parameters of a non-negative matrix M allows for approximating the same parameters for a matrix M', provided that M and M' are sufficiently similar. Specifically, M and M' may differ only on a single entry, and the ratio of the corresponding values must be sufficiently close to one. Needless to say, the actual observation (is not generic but rather) refers to specific parameters of the matrix, which include its permanent. Thus, given a matrix M for which we need to approximate the permanent, we consider a sequence of matrices $M_0, \ldots, M_t \approx M$ such that M_0 is the all 1's matrix (for which it is easy to evaluate the said parameters), and each M_{i+1} is obtained from M_i by reducing some adequate entry by a factor sufficiently close to one. This process of (polynomially many) gradual changes allows for transforming the dummy matrix M_0 into a matrix M_t that is very close to M (and hence has a permanent that is very close to the permanent of M). Thus, approximately obtaining the parameters of M_t allows for approximating the permanent of M.

Finally, we mention that Section 10.1.1 provides a treatment of a different type of approximation problems. Specifically, when given an instance x (for a search problem R), rather than seeking an approximation of the number of solutions (i.e., $\#R(x)$), one seeks an approximation of the value of the best solution (i.e., best $y \in R(x)$), where the value of a solution is defined by an auxiliary function.

Exercises

Exercise 6.1: Show that if a search (resp., decision) problem can be solved by a probabilistic polynomial-time algorithm having zero failure probability, then the problem can be solve by a deterministic polynomial-time algorithm.

(Hint: Replace the internal coin tosses by a fixed outcome that is easy to generate deterministically (e.g., the all-zero sequence).)

Exercise 6.2 (randomized reductions): In continuation of the definitions presented in Section 6.1.1, prove the following:

1. If a problem Π is probabilistic polynomial-time reducible to a problem that is solvable in probabilistic polynomial time then Π is solvable in probabilistic polynomial time, where by solving we mean solving correctly except with negligible probability.

   Warning: Recall that in the case that Π' is a search problem, we required that on input x the solver provides a correct solution with probability at least $1 - \mu(|x|)$, but we did not require that it always returns the same solution.

   (Hint: without loss of generality, the reduction does not make the same query twice.)

2. Prove that probabilistic polynomial-time reductions are transitive.

3. Prove that randomized Karp-reductions are transitive and that they yield a special case of probabilistic polynomial-time reductions.

   Define one-sided error and zero-sided error randomized (Karp- and Cook-) reductions, and consider the foregoing items when applied to them. Note that the implications for the case of one-sided error are somewhat subtle.

Exercise 6.3 (on the definition of probabilistically solving a search problem): In continuation of the discussion at the beginning of Section 6.1.2, suppose that for some probabilistic polynomial-time algorithm A and a positive polynomial p the following holds: For every $x \in S_R \overset{\text{def}}{=} \{z : R(z) \neq \emptyset\}$ there exists $y \in R(x)$ such that $\Pr[A(x) = y] > 0.5 + (1/p(|x|))$, whereas for every $x \notin S_R$ it holds that $\Pr[A(x) = \bot] > 0.5 + (1/p(|x|))$.

1. Show that there exists a probabilistic polynomial-time algorithm that solves the search problem of R with negligible error probability.

   (Hint: See Exercise 6.4 for a related procedure.)

2. Reflect on the need to require that one (correct) solution occurs with probability greater than $0.5 + (1/p(|x|))$. Specifically, what can we do if it is only guaranteed that for every $x \in S_R$ it holds that $\Pr[A(x) \in R(x)] > 0.5 + (1/p(|x|))$ (and for every $x \notin S_R$ it holds that $\Pr[A(x) = \perp] > 0.5 + (1/p(|x|)))$?

Note that R is not necessarily in $\mathcal{PC}$. Indeed, in the case that $R \in \mathcal{PC}$ we can eliminate the error probability for every $x \notin S_R$, and perform error reduction for $x \in S_R$ as in the case of $\mathcal{RP}$.

Exercise 6.4 (error reduction for $\mathcal{BPP}$): For $\varepsilon : \mathbb{N} \to [0, 1]$, let $\mathcal{BPP}_\varepsilon$ denote the class of decision problems that can be solved in probabilistic polynomial time with error probability upper-bounded by ε. Prove the following two claims:

1. For every positive polynomial p and $\varepsilon(n) = (1/2) - (1/p(n))$, the class $\mathcal{BPP}_\varepsilon$ equals $\mathcal{BPP}$.
2. For every positive polynomial p and $\varepsilon(n) = 2^{-p(n)}$, the class $\mathcal{BPP}$ equals $\mathcal{BPP}_\varepsilon$.

Formulate a corresponding version for the setting of search problems. Specifically, for every input that has a solution, consider the probability that a specific solution is output.

> **Guideline:** Given an algorithm A for the syntactically weaker class, consider an algorithm A' that on input x invokes A on x for $t(|x|)$ times, and rules by majority. For Part 1 set $t(n) = O(p(n)^2)$ and apply Chebyshev's Inequality. For Part 2 set $t(n) = O(p(n))$ and apply the Chernoff Bound.

Exercise 6.5 (error reduction for $\mathcal{RP}$): For $\rho : \mathbb{N} \to [0, 1]$, we define the class of decision problem $\mathcal{RP}_\rho$ such that it contains S if there exists a probabilistic polynomial-time algorithm A such that for every $x \in S$ it holds that $\Pr[A(x) = 1] \geq \rho(|x|)$ and for every $x \notin S$ it holds that $\Pr[A(x) = 0] = 1$. Prove the following two claims:

1. For every positive polynomial p, the class $\mathcal{RP}_{1/p}$ equals $\mathcal{RP}$.
2. For every positive polynomial p, the class $\mathcal{RP}$ equals $\mathcal{RP}_\rho$, where $\rho(n) = 1 - 2^{-p(n)}$.

> (Hint: The one-sided error allows for using an "or-rule" (rather than a "majority-rule") for the decision.)

Exercise 6.6 (error reduction for $\mathcal{ZPP}$): For $\rho : \mathbb{N} \to [0, 1]$, we define the class of decision problem $\mathcal{ZPP}_\rho$ such that it contains S if there exists a probabilistic polynomial-time algorithm A such that for every x it holds that $\Pr[A(x) = \chi_S(x)] \geq \rho(|x|)$ and $\Pr[A(x) \in \{\chi_S(x), \perp\}] = 1$, where $\chi_S(x) = 1$ if $x \in S$ and $\chi_S(x) = 0$ otherwise. Prove the following two claims:

1. For every positive polynomial p, the class $\mathcal{ZPP}_{1/p}$ equals $\mathcal{ZPP}$.
2. For every positive polynomial p, the class $\mathcal{ZPP}$ equals $\mathcal{ZPP}_\rho$, where $\rho(n) = 1 - 2^{-p(n)}$.

Exercise 6.7 (an alternative definition of $\mathcal{ZPP}$): We say that the decision problem S is solvable in expected probabilistic polynomial time if there exists a randomized algorithm A and a polynomial p such that for every $x \in \{0, 1\}^*$ it holds that $\Pr[A(x) = \chi_S(x)] = 1$ and the expected number of steps taken by $A(x)$ is at most $p(|x|)$. Prove that $S \in \mathcal{ZPP}$ if and only if S is solvable in expected probabilistic polynomial time.

Guideline: Repeatedly invoking a ZPP algorithm until it yields an output other than $\perp$ yields an expected probabilistic polynomial-time solver. On the other hand, truncating runs of an expected probabilistic polynomial-time algorithm once they exceed twice the expected number of steps (and outputting $\perp$ on such runs), we obtain a ZPP-algorithm.

Exercise 6.8: Prove that for every $S \in \mathcal{NP}$ there exists a probabilistic polynomial-time algorithm A such that for every $x \in S$ it holds that $\Pr[A(x) = 1] > 0$ and for every $x \notin S$ it holds that $\Pr[A(x) = 0] = 1$. That is, A has error probability at most $1 - \exp(-\text{poly}(|x|))$ on yes-instances but never errs on no-instances. Thus, $\mathcal{NP}$ may be fictitiously viewed as having a huge one-sided error probability.

Exercise 6.9: Let $\mathcal{BPP}$ and $\text{co}\mathcal{RP}$ be classes of promise problems (as in Theorem 6.9).

1. Prove that every problem in $\mathcal{BPP}$ is reducible to the set $\{1\} \in \mathcal{P}$ by a *two-sided error* randomized Karp-reduction.
2. Prove that if a set S is Karp-reducible to $\mathcal{RP}$ (resp., $\text{co}\mathcal{RP}$) via a deterministic reduction then $S \in \mathcal{RP}$ (resp., $S \in \text{co}\mathcal{RP}$).

Exercise 6.10 (randomness-efficient error reductions): Note that standard error reduction (as in Exercise 6.4) yields error probability δ at the cost of increasing the randomness complexity by a *factor* of $O(\log(1/\delta))$. Using the randomness-efficient error reductions outlined in §D.4.1.3, show that error probability δ can be obtained at the cost of increasing the randomness complexity from r to $O(r) + 1.5 \log_2(1/\delta)$. Note that this allows for satisfying the hypothesis made in the illustrative paragraph of the proof of Theorem 6.9.

Exercise 6.11: In continuation of the illustrative paragraph in the proof of Theorem 6.9, consider the promise problem $\Pi' = (\Pi'_{\text{yes}}, \Pi'_{\text{no}})$ such that $\Pi'_{\text{yes}} = \{(x, r') : |r'| = p'(|x|) \wedge (\forall r'' \in \{0, 1\}^{|r'|}) A'(x, r'r'') = 1\}$ and $\Pi'_{\text{no}} = \{(x, r') : x \notin S\}$. Recall that for every x it holds that $\Pr_{r \in \{0,1\}^{2p'(|x|)}}[A'(x, r) \neq \chi_S(x)] < 2^{-(p'(|x|)+1)}$.

1. Show that mapping x to (x, r'), where r' is uniformly distributed in $\{0, 1\}^{p'(|x|)}$, constitutes a one-sided error randomized Karp-reduction of S to Π'.
2. Show that Π' is in the promise problem class $\text{co}\mathcal{RP}$.

Exercise 6.12 (randomized versions of $\mathcal{NP}$): In continuation of footnote 7, consider the following two variants of $\mathcal{MA}$ (which we consider the main randomized version of $\mathcal{NP}$).

1. $S \in \mathcal{MA}^{(1)}$ if there exists a probabilistic polynomial-time algorithm V such that for every $x \in S$ there exists $y \in \{0, 1\}^{\text{poly}(|x|)}$ such that $\Pr[V(x, y) = 1] \geq 1/2$, whereas for every $x \notin S$ and every y it holds that $\Pr[V(x, y) = 0] = 1$.
2. $S \in \mathcal{MA}^{(2)}$ if there exists a probabilistic polynomial-time algorithm V such that for every $x \in S$ there exists $y \in \{0, 1\}^{\text{poly}(|x|)}$ such that $\Pr[V(x, y) = 1] \geq 2/3$, whereas for every $x \notin S$ and every y it holds that $\Pr[V(x, y) = 0] \geq 2/3$.

Prove that $\mathcal{MA}^{(1)} = \mathcal{NP}$ whereas $\mathcal{MA}^{(2)} = \mathcal{MA}$.

Guideline: For the first part, note that a sequence of internal coin tosses that makes V accept (x, y) can be incorporated into y itself (yielding a standard NP-witness). For the second part, apply the ideas underlying the proof of Theorem 6.9, and note that an adequate sequence of shifts (to be used by the verifier) can be incorporated in the single message sent by the prover.

Exercise 6.13 ($\mathcal{BPP} \subseteq \mathcal{ZPP}^{\mathcal{NP}}$): In continuation of the proof of Theorem 6.9, present a zero-error randomized reduction of $\mathcal{BPP}$ to $\mathcal{NP}$, where all classes are the standard classes of decision problems.

> **Guideline:** On input x, the ZPP-machine uniformly selects $\bar{s} = (s_1, \ldots, s_m)$, and for each $\sigma \in \{0, 1\}$ makes the query $(x, \sigma, \bar{s})$, which is answered positively by the (coNP) oracle if for every r it holds that $\vee_i(A(x, r \oplus s_i) = \sigma)$. The machine outputs σ if and only if the query $(x, \sigma, \bar{s})$ was answered positively, and outputs $\perp$ otherwise (i.e., both queries were answered negatively).

Exercise 6.14 (completeness for promise problem versions of $\mathcal{BPP}$): Referring to the promise problem version of $\mathcal{BPP}$, present a promise problem that is complete for this class under (deterministic log-space) Karp-reductions.

> **Guideline:** The promise problem consists of yes-instances that are Boolean circuits that accept at least a 2/3 fraction of their possible inputs and no-instances that are Boolean circuits that reject at least a 2/3 fraction of their possible inputs. The reduction is essentially the one provided in the proof of Theorem 2.21, and the promise is used in an essential way in order to provide a BPP-algorithm.

Exercise 6.15 (hierarchy theorems for promise problem versions of BPTIME): Fixing a model of computation, let BPTIME(t) denote the class of promise problems that are solvable by a randomized algorithm of time complexity t that has a two-sided error probability at most 1/3. (The standard definition refers only to decision problems.) Formulate and prove results analogous to Theorem 4.3 and Corollary 4.4.

> **Guideline (by Dieter van Melkebeek):** Apply the "delayed diagonalization" method used to prove Theorem 4.6 rather than the simple diagonalization used in Theorem 4.3. Analogously to the proof of Theorem 4.6, for every $\sigma \in \{0, 1\}$, define $A_M(x) = \sigma$ if $\Pr[M'(x) = \sigma] \geq 2/3$ and define $A_M(x) = \perp$ otherwise (i.e., if $1/3 < \Pr[M'(x) = 1] < 2/3$), where $M'(x)$ denotes the computation of $M(x)$ truncated after $t_1(|x|)$ steps. For $x \in [\alpha_M, \beta_M - 1]$, define $f(x) = A_M(x + 1)$, where $f(x) = \perp$ means that x violates the promise. Define $f(\beta_M) = 1$ if $A_M(\alpha_M) = 0$ and $f(\beta_M) = 0$ otherwise (i.e., if $A_M(\alpha_M) \in \{1, \perp\}$). Note that $f(x)$ is computable in randomized time $\widetilde{O}(t_1(|x| + 1))$ by emulating a single computation of $M'(x)$ if $x \in [\alpha_M, \beta_M - 1]$ and emulating all computations of $M'(\alpha_M)$ if $x = \beta_M$. Prove that the promise problem f cannot be solved in randomized time t_1, by noting that β_M satisfies the promise and that for every $x \in [\alpha_M + 1, \beta_M]$ that satisfies the promise (i.e., $f(x) \in \{0, 1\}$) it holds that if $A_M(x) = f(x)$ then $f(x - 1) = A_M(x) \in \{0, 1\}$.

Exercise 6.16 (extracting square roots modulo a prime): Using the following guidelines, present a probabilistic polynomial-time algorithm that, on input a prime P and a quadratic residue $s \pmod{P}$, returns r such that $r^2 \equiv s \pmod{P}$.

1. Prove that if $P \equiv 3 \pmod 4$ then $s^{(P+1)/4} \bmod P$ is a square root of the quadratic residue $s \pmod{P}$.
2. Note that the procedure suggested in Item 1 relies on the ability to find an *odd* integer e such that $s^e \equiv 1 \pmod{P}$. Indeed, once such an e is found, we may output $s^{(e+1)/2} \bmod P$. (In Item 1, we used $e = (P - 1)/2$, which is odd since $P \equiv 3 \pmod 4$.)

> Show that it suffices to find an *odd* integer e together with a residue t and an *even* integer e' such that $s^e t^{e'} \equiv 1 \pmod{P}$, because $s \equiv s^{e+1} t^{e'} \equiv (s^{(e+1)/2} t^{e'/2})^2$.

3. Given a prime $P \equiv 1 \pmod 4$, a quadratic residue s, and any quadratic non-residue t (i.e., residue t such that $t^{(P-1)/2} \equiv -1 \pmod P$), show that e and e' as in Item 2 can be efficiently found.[24]

4. Prove that, for a prime P, with probability $1/2$ a uniformly chosen $t \in \{1, \ldots, P\}$ satisfies $t^{(P-1)/2} \equiv -1 \pmod P$.

Note that randomization is used only in the last item, which in turn is used only for $P \equiv 1 \pmod 4$.

Exercise 6.17: Referring to the definition of arithmetic circuits (cf. Appendix B.3), show that the following decision problem is in co$\mathcal{RP}$: *Given a pair of circuits (C_1, C_2) of depth d over a field that has more than 2^{d+1} elements, determine whether the circuits compute the same polynomial.*

> **Guideline:** Note that each of these circuits computes a polynomial of degree at most 2^d.

Exercise 6.18 (small-space randomized step-counter): As defined in Exercise 4.7, a step-counter is an algorithm that halts after issuing a number of "signals" as specified in its input, where these signals are defined as entering (and leaving) a designated state (of the algorithm). Recall that a step-counter may be run in parallel to another procedure in order to suspend the execution after a predetermined number of steps (of the other procedure) have elapsed. Note that there exists a simple deterministic machine that, on input n, halts after issuing n signals while using $O(1) + \log_2 n$ space (and $\tilde{O}(n)$ time). The goal of this exercise is presenting a (randomized) step-counter that allows for many more signals while using the same amount of space. Specifically, present a (randomized) algorithm that, on input n, uses $O(1) + \log_2 n$ space (and $\tilde{O}(2^n)$ time) and halts after issuing an expected number of 2^n signals. Furthermore, prove that, with probability at least $1 - 2^{-k+1}$, this step-counter halts after issuing a number of signals that is between 2^{n-k} and 2^{n+k}.

> **Guideline:** Repeat the following experiment till reaching success. Each trial consists of uniformly selecting n bits (i.e., tossing n unbiased coins), and is deemed successful if all bits turn out to equal the value 1 (i.e., all outcomes equal HEAD). Note that such a trial can be implemented by using space $O(1) + \log_2 n$ (mainly for implementing a standard counter for determining the number of bits). Thus, each trial is successful with probability 2^{-n}, and the expected number of trials is 2^n.

Exercise 6.19 (analysis of random walks on arbitrary undirected graphs): In order to complete the proof of Proposition 6.13, prove that if $\{u, v\}$ is an edge of the graph $G = (V, E)$ then $E[X_{u,v}] \leq 2|E|$. Recall that, for a fixed graph, $X_{u,v}$ is a random variable representing the number of steps taken in a random walk that starts at the vertex u until the vertex v is first encountered.

> **Guideline:** Let $Z_{u,v}(n)$ be a random variable counting the number of *minimal* paths from u to v that appear along a random walk of length n, where the walk starts at the

---

[24] Write $(P-1)/2 = (2j_0 + 1) \cdot 2^{i_0}$, and note that $s^{(2j_0+1) \cdot 2^{i_0}} \equiv 1 \pmod P$, which may be written as $s^{(2j_0+1) \cdot 2^{i_0}} t^{(2j_0+1) \cdot 2^{i_0+1}} \equiv 1 \pmod P$. Given that for some $i' > i > 0$ and j' it holds that $s^{(2j_0+1) \cdot 2^i} t^{(2j'+1) \cdot 2^{i'}} \equiv 1 \pmod P$, show how to find $i'' > i - 1$ and j'' such that $s^{(2j_0+1) \cdot 2^{i-1}} t^{(2j''+1) \cdot 2^{i''}} \equiv 1 \pmod P$. (Extra hint: $s^{(2j_0+1) \cdot 2^{i-1}} t^{(2j'+1) \cdot 2^{i'-1}} \equiv \pm 1 \pmod P$ and $t^{(2j_0+1) \cdot 2^{i_0}} \equiv -1 \pmod P$.) Applying this reasoning for i_0 times, we get what we need.

stationary vertex distribution (which is well defined assuming the graph is not bipartite, which in turn may be enforced by adding a self-loop). On one hand, $E[X_{u,v} + X_{v,u}] = \lim_{n \to \infty}(n/E[Z_{u,v}(n)])$, due to the memoryless property of the walk. On the other hand, letting $\chi_{v,u}(i) \overset{\text{def}}{=} 1$ if the edge $\{u, v\}$ was traversed from v to u in the ith step of such a random walk and $\chi_{v,u}(i) \overset{\text{def}}{=} 0$ otherwise, we have $\sum_{i=1}^{n} \chi_{v,u}(i) \leq Z_{u,v}(n) + 1$ and $E[\chi_{v,u}(i)] = 1/2|E|$ (because, in each step, each directed edge appears on the walk with equal probability). It follows that $E[X_{u,v}] < 2|E|$.

Exercise 6.20 (the class $\mathcal{PP} \supseteq \mathcal{BPP}$ and its relation to #$\mathcal{P}$): In contrast to $\mathcal{BPP}$, which refers to useful probabilistic polynomial-time algorithms, the class $\mathcal{PP}$ does not capture such algorithms but is rather closely related to #$\mathcal{P}$. A decision problem S is in $\mathcal{PP}$ if there exists a probabilistic polynomial-time algorithm A such that, for every x, it holds that $x \in S$ if and only if $\Pr[A(x) = 1] > 1/2$. Note that $\mathcal{BPP} \subseteq \mathcal{PP}$. Prove that $\mathcal{PP}$ is Cook-reducible to #$\mathcal{P}$ and vice versa.

> **Guideline:** For $S \in \mathcal{PP}$ (by virtue of the algorithm A), consider the relation R such that $(x, r) \in R$ if and only if A accepts the input x when using the random-input $r \in \{0, 1\}^{p(|x|)}$, where p is a suitable polynomial. Thus, $x \in S$ if and only if $|R(x)| > 2^{p(|x|)-1}$, which in turn can de determined by querying the counting function of R. To reduce $f \in$ #$\mathcal{P}$ to $\mathcal{PP}$, consider the relation $R \in \mathcal{PC}$ that is counted by f (i.e., $f(x) = |R(x)|$) and the decision problem S_f as defined in Proposition 6.15. Let p be the polynomial specifying the length of solutions for R (i.e., $(x, y) \in R$ implies $|y| = p(|x|)$), and consider the following algorithm A': On input (x, N), with probability $1/2$, algorithm A' uniformly selects $y \in \{0, 1\}^{p(|x|)}$ and accepts if and only if $(x, y) \in R$, and otherwise (i.e., with the remaining probability of $1/2$) algorithm A' accepts with probability exactly $\frac{2^{p(|x|)} - N + 0.5}{2^{p(|x|)}}$. Prove that $(x, N) \in S_f$ if and only if $\Pr[A'(x) = 1] > 1/2$.

Exercise 6.21 (enumeration problems): For any binary relation R, define the enumeration problem of R as a function $f_R : \{0, 1\}^* \times \mathbb{N} \to \{0, 1\}^* \cup \{\bot\}$ such that $f_R(x, i)$ equals the ith element in $|R(x)|$ if $|R(x)| \geq i$ and $f_R(x, i) = \bot$ otherwise. The above definition refers to the standard lexicographic order on strings, but any other efficient order of strings will do.[25]

1. Prove that, for any polynomially bounded R, computing #R is reducible to computing f_R.
2. Prove that, for any $R \in \mathcal{PC}$, computing f_R is reducible to some problem in #$\mathcal{P}$.

> **Guideline:** Consider the binary relation $R' = \{(\langle x, b \rangle, y) : (x, y) \in R \wedge y \leq b\}$, and show that f_R is reducible to #R'.
>
> (Extra hint: Note that $f_R(x, i) = y$ if and only if $|R'(\langle x, y \rangle)| = i$ and for every $y' < y$ it holds that $|R'(\langle x, y' \rangle)| < i$.)

Exercise 6.22 (artificial #$\mathcal{P}$-complete problems): Show that there exists a relation $R \in \mathcal{PC}$ such that #R is #$\mathcal{P}$-complete and $S_R = \{0, 1\}^*$. Furthermore, prove that for every $R' \in \mathcal{PC}$ there exists $R \in \mathcal{PF} \cap \mathcal{PC}$ such that for every x it holds that #$R(x) = $#$R'(x) + 1$. Note that Theorem 6.19 follows by starting with any relation $R' \in \mathcal{PC}$ such that #R' is #$\mathcal{P}$-complete.

---

[25] An order of strings is a 1-1 and onto mapping μ from the natural numbers to the set of all strings. Such order is called efficient if both μ and its inverse are efficiently computable. The standard lexicographic order satisfies $\mu(i) = y$ if the string $1y$ is the (compact) binary expansion of the integer i; that is $\mu(1) = \lambda$, $\mu(2) = 0$, $\mu(3) = 1$, $\mu(4) = 00$, etc.

Exercise 6.23 (computing the permanent of integer matrices): Prove that computing the permanent of matrices with 0/1-entries is computationally equivalent to computing the number of perfect matchings in bipartite graphs.

> **Guideline:** Given a bipartite graph $G = ((X, Y), E)$, consider the matrix M representing the edges between X and Y (i.e., the (i, j)-entry in M is 1 if the ith vertex of X is connected to the jth entry of Y), and note that only perfect matchings in G contribute to the permanent of M.

Exercise 6.24 (computing the permanent modulo 3): Combining Proposition 6.21 and Theorem 6.29, prove that for every fixed $n > 1$ that does not divide any power of c, computing the permanent modulo n is NP-hard under randomized reductions. Since Proposition 6.21 holds for $c = 2^{10}$, hardness holds for every integer $n > 1$ that is not a power of 2. (We mention that, on the other hand, for any fixed $n = 2^e$, the permanent modulo n can be computed in polynomial time [230, Thm. 3].)

> **Guideline:** Apply the reduction of Proposition 6.21 to the promise problem of deciding whether a 3CNF formula has a unique satisfiable assignment or is unsatisfiable. Note that for any m it holds that $c^m \not\equiv 0 \pmod{n}$.

Exercise 6.25 (negative values in Proposition 6.21): Assuming $\mathcal{P} \neq \mathcal{NP}$, prove that Proposition 6.21 cannot hold for a set I containing only non-negative integers. Note that the claim holds even if the set I is not finite (and even if I is the set of all non-negative integers).

> **Guideline:** A reduction as in Proposition 6.21 yields a Karp-reduction of 3SAT to deciding whether the permanent of a matrix with entries in I is non-zero. Note that the permanent of a *non-negative* matrix is non-zero if and only if the corresponding bipartite graph has a perfect matching.

Exercise 6.26 (high-level analysis of the permanent reduction): Establish the correctness of the high-level reduction presented in the proof of Proposition 6.21. That is, show that if the clause gadget satisfies the three conditions postulated in the said proof, then each satisfying assignment of ϕ contributes exactly c^m to the SWCC of G_ϕ whereas unsatisfying assignments have no contribution.

> **Guideline:** Cluster the cycle covers of G_ϕ according to the set of track edges that they use (i.e., the edges of the cycle cover that belong to the various tracks). (Note the correspondence between these edges and the external edges used in the definition of the gadget's properties.) Using the postulated conditions (regarding the clause gadget) prove that, for each such set T of track edges, if the sum of the weights of all cycle covers that use the track edges T is non-zero then the following hold:
>
> 1. The intersection of T with the set of track edges incident at each specific clause gadget is non-empty. Furthermore, if this set contains an incoming edge (resp., outgoing edge) of some entry vertex (resp., exit vertex) then it also contains an outgoing edge (resp., incoming edge) of the corresponding exit vertex (resp., entry vertex).
> 2. If T contains an edge that belongs to some track then it contains all edges of this track. It follows that, for each variable x, the set T contains the edges of a single track associated with x.

3. The tracks "picked" by T correspond to a single truth assignment to the variables of ϕ, and this assignment satisfies ϕ (because, for each clause, T contains an external edge that corresponds to a literal that satisfies this clause).

Note that different sets of the aforementioned type yield different satisfying assignments, and that each satisfying assignment is obtained from some set of the aforementioned type.

Exercise 6.27 (analysis of the implementation of the clause gadget): Establish the correctness of the implementation of the clause gadget presented in the proof of Proposition 6.21. That is, show that if the box satisfies the three conditions postulated in the said proof, then the clause gadget of Figure 6.4 satisfies the conditions postulated for it.

Guideline: Cluster the cycle covers of a gadget according to the set of non-box edges that they use, where non-box edges are the edges shown in Figure 6.4. Using the postulated conditions (regarding the box) prove that, for each set S of non-box edges, if the sum of the weights of all cycle covers that use the non-box edges S is non-zero then the following hold:

1. The intersection of S with the set of edges incident at each box must contain two (non-self-loop) edges, one incident at each of the box's terminals. Needless to say, one edge is incoming and the other outgoing. Referring to the six edges that connects one of the six designated vertices (of the gadget) with the corresponding box terminals as connectives, note that if S contains a connective incident at the terminal of some box then it must also contain the connective incident at the other terminal. In such a case, we say that this box is picked by S.

2. Each of the three (literal-designated) boxes that is not picked by S is "traversed" from left to right (i.e., the cycle cover contains an incoming edge of the left terminal and an outgoing edge of the right terminal). Thus, the set S must contain a connective, because otherwise no directed cycle may cover the leftmost vertex shown in Figure 6.4. That is, S must pick some box.

3. The set S is fully determined by the non-empty set of boxes that it picks.

The postulated properties of the clause gadget follow, with $c = b^5$.

Exercise 6.28 (analysis of the design of a box for the clause gadget): Prove that the 4-by-4 matrix presented in Eq. (6.4) satisfies the properties postulated for the "box" used in the second part of the proof of Proposition 6.21. In particular:

1. Show a correspondence between the conditions required of the box and conditions regarding the value of the permanent of certain sub-matrices of the adjacency matrix of the graph.

(Hint: For example, show that the first condition corresponds to requiring that the value of the permanent of the entire matrix equals zero. The second condition refers to sub-matrices obtained by omitting either the first row and fourth column or the fourth row and first column.)

2. Verify that the matrix in Eq. (6.4) satisfies the aforementioned conditions (regarding the value of the permanent of certain sub-matrices).

Prove that no 3-by-3 matrix (and thus also no 2-by-2 matrix) can satisfy the aforementioned conditions.

Exercise 6.29 (error reduction for approximate counting): Show that the error probability δ in Definition 6.24 can be reduced from $1/3$ (or even $(1/2) + (1/\mathrm{poly}(|x|))$) to $\exp(-\mathrm{poly}(|x|))$.

> **Guideline:** Invoke the weaker procedure for an adequate number of times and take the *median* value among the values obtained in these invocations.

Exercise 6.30 (approximation and gap problems): Let $f : \{0, 1\}^* \to \mathbb{N}$ be a polynomially bounded function (i.e., $|f(x)| = \mathrm{poly}(|x|)$) and $\varepsilon : \mathbb{N} \to [0, 1]$ be a noticeable function that is polynomial-time computable. Prove that the search problem associated with the relation $R_{f,\varepsilon} \stackrel{\text{def}}{=} \{(x, v) : |v - f(x)| \le \varepsilon(|x|) \cdot f(x)\}$ is computationally equivalent to the promise ("gap") problem of distinguishing elements of the set $\{(x, v) : v < (1 - \varepsilon(|x|)) \cdot f(x)\}$ and elements of the set $\{(x, v) : v > (1 + \varepsilon(|x|)) \cdot f(x)\}$.

Exercise 6.31 (strong approximation for some #$\mathcal{P}$-complete problems): Show that there exists #$\mathcal{P}$-complete problems (albeit unnatural ones) for which an $(\varepsilon, 0)$-approximation can be found by a (deterministic) polynomial-time algorithm. Furthermore, the running time depends polynomially on $1/\varepsilon$.

> **Guideline:** Combine any #$\mathcal{P}$-complete problem referring to some $R_1 \in \mathcal{PC}$ with a trivial counting problem (e.g., the counting problem associated with the trivial relation $R_2 = \cup_{n \in \mathbb{N}}\{(x, y) : x, y \in \{0, 1\}^n\}$). Show that, without loss of generality, it holds that $\#R_1(x) \le 2^{|x|/2}$. Prove that the counting problem of $R = \{(x, 1y) : (x, y) \in R_1\} \cup \{(x, 0y) : (x, y) \in R_2\}$ is #$\mathcal{P}$-complete (by reducing from $\#R_1$). Present a deterministic algorithm that, on input x and $\varepsilon > 0$, outputs an $(\varepsilon, 0)$-approximation of $\#R(x)$ in time $\mathrm{poly}(|x|/\varepsilon)$.
>
> (Extra hint: distinguish between $\varepsilon \ge 2^{-|x|/2}$ and $\varepsilon < 2^{-|x|/2}$.)

Exercise 6.32 (relative approximation for DNF satisfaction): Referring to the text of §6.2.2.1, prove the following claims.

1. Both assumptions regarding the general setting hold in case $S_i = C_i^{-1}(1)$, where $C_i^{-1}(1)$ denotes the set of truth assignments that satisfy the conjunction C_i.

   > **Guideline:** In establishing the second assumption note that it reduces to the conjunction of the following two assumptions:
   >
   > (a) Given i, one can efficiently generate a uniformly distributed element of S_i. Actually, generating a distribution that is almost uniform over S_i suffices.
   > (b) Given i and x, one can efficiently determine whether $x \in S_i$.

2. Prove Proposition 6.26, relating to details such as the error probability in an implementation of Construction 6.25.
3. Note that Construction 6.25 does not require exact computation of $|S_i|$. Analyze the output distribution in the case that we can only approximate $|S_i|$ up to a factor of $1 \pm \varepsilon'$.

Exercise 6.33 (reducing the relative deviation in approximate counting): Prove that, for any $R \in \mathcal{PC}$ and every polynomial p and constant $\delta < 0.5$, there exists $R' \in \mathcal{PC}$ such that $(1/p, \delta)$-approximation for $\#R$ is reducible to $(1/2, \delta)$-approximation for $\#R'$. Furthermore, for any $F(n) = \exp(\mathrm{poly}(n))$, prove that there exists $R'' \in \mathcal{PC}$ such that $(1/p, \delta)$-approximation for $\#R$ is reducible to approximating $\#R''$ to within a factor of F with error probability δ.

Guideline (for the main part): For $t(n) = \Theta(p(n))$, define R' such that $(y_1, \ldots, y_{t(|x|)}) \in R'(x)$ if and only if $(\forall i)\ y_i \in R(x)$. Note that $|R(x)| = |R'(x)|^{1/t(|x|)}$, and thus if $a = (1 \pm (1/2)) \cdot |R'(x)|$ then $a^{1/t(|x|)} = (1 \pm (1/2))^{1/t(|x|)} \cdot |R(x)|$.

Exercise 6.34 (deviation reduction in approximate counting, cont.): In continuation of Exercise 6.33, prove that if R is NP-complete via parsimonious reductions then, for every positive polynomial p and constant $\delta < 0.5$, the problem of $(1/p, \delta)$-approximation for $\#R$ is reducible to $(1/2, \delta)$-approximation for $\#R$.

(Hint: Compose the reduction (to the problem of $(1/2, \delta)$-approximation for $\#R'$) provided in Exercise 6.33 with the parsimonious reduction of $\#R'$ to $\#R$.)

Prove that, for every function F' such that $F'(n) = \exp(n^{o(1)})$, we can also reduce the aforementioned problems to the problem of approximating $\#R$ to within a factor of F' with error probability δ.

Guideline: Using R'' as in Exercise 6.33, we encounter a technical difficulty. The issue is that the composition of the ("amplifying") reduction of $\#R$ to $\#R''$ with the parsimonious reduction of $\#R''$ to $\#R$ may increase the length of the instance. Indeed, the length of the new instance is polynomial in the length of the original instance, but this polynomial may depend on R'', which in turn depends on F'. Thus, we cannot use $F'(n) = \exp(n^{1/O(1)})$ but $F'(n) = \exp(n^{o(1)})$ is fine.

Exercise 6.35: Referring to the procedure in the proof Theorem 6.27, show how to use an NP-oracle in order to determine whether the number of solutions that "pass a random sieve" is greater than t. You are allowed queries of length polynomial in the length of x, h and in the size of t.

Guideline: Consider the set $S'_{R,H} \overset{\text{def}}{=} \{(x, i, h, 1^t) : \exists y_1, \ldots, y_t \text{ s.t. } \psi'(x, h, y_1, \ldots, y_t)\}$, where $\psi'(x, h, y_1, \ldots, y_t)$ holds if and only if the y_j are different and for every j it holds that $(x, y_j) \in R \wedge h(y_j) = 0^i$.

Exercise 6.36 (parsimonious reductions and Theorem 6.29): Demonstrate the importance of parsimonious reductions in Theorem 6.29 by proving that there exists a search problem $R \in \mathcal{PC}$ such that every problem in $\mathcal{PC}$ is reducible to R (by a non-parsimonious reduction) and still the the promise problem $(\text{US}_R, \overline{S}_R)$ is decidable in polynomial time.

Guideline: Consider the following artificial witness relation R for SAT in which $(\phi, \sigma\tau) \in R$ if $\sigma \in \{0, 1\}$ and τ satisfies ϕ. Note that the standard witness relation of SAT is reducible to R, but this reduction is not parsimonious. Also note that $\text{US}_R = \emptyset$ and thus $(\text{US}_R, \overline{S}_R)$ is trivial.

Exercise 6.37: In continuation of Exercise 6.36, prove that there exists a search problem $R \in \mathcal{PC}$ such that $\#R$ is $\#\mathcal{P}$-complete and still the promise problem $(\text{US}_R, \overline{S}_R)$ is decidable in polynomial time. Provide one proof for the case that R is $\mathcal{PC}$-complete and another proof for $R \in \mathcal{PF}$.

Guideline: For the first case, the relation R suggested in the guideline to Exercise 6.36 will do. For the second case, rely on Theorem 6.20 and on the fact that it is easy to decide $(\text{US}_R, \overline{S}_R)$ when R is the corresponding perfect matching relation (by computing the determinant).

Exercise 6.38: Prove that SAT is randomly reducible to deciding unique solutions for SAT, *without using the fact that* SAT *is NP-complete via parsimonious reductions.*

Guideline: Follow the proof of Theorem 6.29, while using the family of pairwise independent hashing functions provided in Construction D.3. Note that, in this case, the condition $(\tau \in R_{SAT}(\phi)) \land (h(\tau) = 0^i)$ can be directly encoded as a CNF formula. That is, consider the formula ϕ_h such that $\phi_h(z) \overset{\text{def}}{=} \phi(z) \land (h(z) = 0^i)$, and note that $h(z) = 0^i$ can be written as the conjunction of i conditions, where each condition is a CNF that is logically equivalent to the parity of some of the bits of z (where the identity of these bits is determined by h).

Exercise 6.39 (search problems with few solutions): For any $R \in \mathcal{PC}$ and any polynomial p, consider the promise problem $(\text{FewS}_{R,p}, \overline{S}_R)$, where $\text{FewS}_{R,p} \overset{\text{def}}{=} \{x : |R(x)| \leq p(|x|)\}$.

1. Show that, for every $R \in \mathcal{PC}$, the (approximate counting) procedure that is presented in the proof of Theorem 6.27 implies a randomized reduction of S_R to $(\text{FewS}_{R',100}, \overline{S}_{R'})$, where $R'(x, i, h) = \{y \in R(x) : h(x) = 0^i\}$.
2. For any $R' \in \mathcal{PC}$ and any polynomial p', present a randomized reduction of $(\text{FewS}_{R',p'}, \overline{S}_{R'})$ to $(\text{US}_{R''}, \overline{S}_{R''})$, where $R''(x', m) = \{y_1 < y_2 < \cdots < y_m : (\forall j) y_j \in R'(x')\}$.

Guideline: Map x' to (x', m), where m is uniformly selected in $[p'(|x'|)]$.

Exercise 6.40: Show that the search problem associated with Perfect Matching satisfies the hypothesis of Theorem 6.31.

Guideline: For a given graph $G = (V, E)$, encode each matching as an $|E|$-bit long string such that the ith is set to 1 if and only if the ith edge is in the matching.

Exercise 6.41 (an alternative procedure for approximate counting): Adapt Step 1 of Construction 6.32 so as to obtain an approximate counting procedure for $\#R$.

Guideline: For $m = 0, 1, \ldots \ell$, the procedure invokes Step 1 of Construction 6.32 until a negative answer is obtained, and outputs $120\ell \cdot 2^m$ for the current value of m. For $|R(x)| > 80\ell$, this yields a constant factor approximation of $|R(x)|$. In fact, we can obtain a better estimate by making additional queries at iteration m (i.e., queries of the form $(x, h, 1^i)$ for $i = 10\ell, \ldots, 120\ell$). The case $|R(x)| \leq 80\ell$ can be treated by using Step 2 of Construction 6.32, in which case we obtain an exact count.

Exercise 6.42: Let R be an arbitrary $\mathcal{PC}$-complete search problem. Show that approximate counting and uniform generation for R can be randomly reduced to deciding membership in S_R, where by approximate counting we mean a $(1 - (1/p))$-approximation for any polynomial p.

Guideline: Note that Construction 6.32 yields such procedures (see also Exercise 6.41), except that they make oracle calls to some other set in $\mathcal{NP}$. Using the NP-completeness of S_R, we are done.

Exercise 6.43: Present a probabilistic polynomial-time algorithm that solves the uniform generation problem of R_{dnf}, where $(\phi, \tau) \in R_{\text{dnf}}$ if ϕ is a DNF formula and τ is an assignment satisfying it.

Guideline: Consider the set $\{(i, e) : i \in [m] \land e \in S_i\}$, where the S_i's are as in §6.2.2.1.

CHAPTER SEVEN

The Bright Side of Hardness

So saying she donned her beautiful, glittering golden–Ambrosial sandals, which carry her flying like the wind over the vast land and sea; she grasped the redoubtable bronze-shod spear, so stout and sturdy and strong, wherewith she quells the ranks of heroes who have displeased her, the [bright-eyed] daughter of her mighty father.

Homer, *Odyssey*, 1:96–101

The existence of natural computational problems that are (or seem to be) infeasible to solve is usually perceived as bad news, because it means that we cannot do things we wish to do. But this bad news has a positive side, because hard problems can be "put to work" to our benefit, most notably in cryptography.

It seems that utilizing hard problems requires the ability to efficiently generate hard instances, which is not guaranteed by the notion of worst-case hardness. In other words, we refer to the gap between "occasional" hardness (e.g., worst-case hardness or mild average-case hardness) and "typical" hardness (with respect to some tractable distribution). Much of the current chapter is devoted to bridging this gap, which is known by the term *hardness amplification*. The actual applications of typical hardness are presented in Chapter 8 and Appendix C.

Summary: We consider two conjectures that are related to $\mathcal{P} \neq \mathcal{NP}$. The first conjecture is that there are problems that are solvable in exponential time (i.e., in $\mathcal{E}$) but are not solvable by (non-uniform) families of small (say, polynomial-size) circuits. We show that this worst-case conjecture can be transformed into an average-case hardness result; specifically, we obtain predicates that are strongly "inapproximable" by small circuits. Such predicates are used toward derandomizing $\mathcal{BPP}$ in a non-trivial manner (see Section 8.3).

The second conjecture is that there are problems in NP (i.e., search problems in $\mathcal{PC}$) for which it is easy to generate (solved) instances that are typically hard to solve (for a party that did not generate these instances). This conjecture is captured in the formulation of *one-way functions*, which are functions that are easy to evaluate but hard to invert (in an average-case sense). We show that functions that are hard to invert in a relatively mild average-case sense yield functions that are hard to invert in a strong average-case sense, and that the latter yield predicates that are very hard to approximate (called *hard-core predicates*). Such predicates are useful for the construction of general-purpose pseudorandom generators (see Section 8.2) as well as for a host of cryptographic applications (see Appendix C).

In the rest of this chapter, the actual order of presentation of the two aforementioned conjectures and their consequences is reversed: We start (in Section 7.1) with the study of one-way functions, and only later (in Section 7.2) turn to the study of problems in $\mathcal{E}$ that are hard for small circuits.

Teaching note: We list several reasons for preferring the aforementioned order of presentation. First, we mention the great conceptual appeal of one-way functions and the fact that they have very practical applications. Second, hardness amplification in the context of one-way functions is technically simpler than the amplification of hardness in the context of $\mathcal{E}$. (In fact, Section 7.2 is the most technical text in this book.) Third, some of the techniques that are shared by both treatments seem easier to understand first in the context of one-way functions. Last, the current order facilitates the possibility of teaching hardness amplification only in one incarnation, where the context of one-way functions is recommended as the incarnation of choice (for the aforementioned reasons).

If you wish to teach hardness amplification and pseudorandomness in the two aforementioned incarnations, then we suggest following the order of the current text. That is, first teach hardness amplification in its two incarnations, and only next teach pseudorandomness in the corresponding incarnations.

Prerequisites. We assume a basic familiarity with elementary probability theory (see Appendix D.1) and randomized algorithms (see Section 6.1). In particular, standard conventions regarding random variables (presented in Appendix D.1.1) and various "laws of large numbers" (presented in Appendix D.1.2) will be extensively used.

7.1. One-Way Functions

Loosely speaking, one-way functions are functions that are easy to evaluate but hard (on the average) to invert. Thus, in assuming that one-way functions exist, we are postulating the existence of *efficient processes* (i.e., the computation of the function in the forward direction) *that are hard to reverse*. Analogous phenomena in daily life are known to us in abundance (e.g., the lighting of a match). Thus, the assumption that one-way functions exist is a complexity theoretic analogue of our daily experience.

One-way functions can also be thought of as efficient ways for generating "puzzles" that are infeasible to solve; that is, the puzzle is a random image of the function and a solution is a corresponding preimage. Furthermore, the person generating the puzzle knows a solution to it and can efficiently verify the validity of (possibly other) solutions to the puzzle. In fact, as explained in Section 7.1.1, every mechanism for generating such puzzles can be converted to a one-way function.

The reader may note that when presented in terms of generating hard puzzles, one-way functions have a clear cryptographic flavor. Indeed, one-way functions are central to cryptography, but we shall not explore this aspect here (and rather refer the reader to Appendix C). Similarly, one-way functions are closely related to (general-purpose) pseudorandom generators, but this connection will be explored in Section 8.2. Instead, in the current section, we will focus on one-way functions *per se*.

Teaching note: While we recommend including a basic treatment of pseudorandomness within a course on Complexity Theory, we do not recommend doing so with respect to cryptography. The reason is that cryptography is far more complex than pseudorandomness (e.g., compare the definition of secure encryption to the definition of pseudorandom generators). The extra complexity is due to conceptual richness, which is something good, except that some of these conceptual issues are central to cryptography but not to Complexity Theory. Thus, teaching cryptography in the context of a course on Complexity Theory is likely to either overload the course with material that is not central to Complexity Theory or cause a superficial and misleading treatment of cryptography. We are not sure as to which of these two possibilities is worse. Still, for the benefit of the interested reader, we have included an overview of the foundations of cryptography as an appendix to the main text (see Appendix C).

7.1.1. Generating Hard Instances and One-Way Functions

Let us start by examining the prophecy, made in the preface to this chapter, by which intractable problems can be used to our benefit. The basic idea is that intractable problems offer a way of generating an obstacle that stands in the way of our opponents and thus protects our interests. These opponents may be either real (e.g., in the context of cryptography) or imaginary (e.g., in the context of derandomization), but in both cases we wish to prevent them from seeing something or doing something. Hard obstacles seem useful toward this goal.

Let us assume that $\mathcal{P} \neq \mathcal{NP}$ or even that $\mathcal{NP}$ is not contained in $\mathcal{BPP}$. Can we use this assumption to our benefit? Not really: The $\mathcal{NP} \not\subseteq \mathcal{BPP}$ assumption refers to the worst-case complexity of problems, while benefiting from hard problems seems to require the ability to generate hard instances. In particular, the generated instances should be typically hard and not merely occasionally hard; that is, we seek average-case hardness and not merely worst-case hardness.

Taking a short digression, we mention that in Section 7.2 we shall see that worst-case hardness (of $\mathcal{NP}$ or even $\mathcal{E}$) can be transformed into average-case hardness of $\mathcal{E}$. Such a transformation is not known for $\mathcal{NP}$ itself, and in some applications (e.g., in cryptography) we do need the hard-on-the-average problem to be in $\mathcal{NP}$. In this case, we currently need to assume that, for some problem in $\mathcal{NP}$, it is the case that hard instances are easy to generate (and not merely exist). That is, we assume that $\mathcal{NP}$ is "hard on the average" *with respect to a distribution that is efficiently samplable*. This assumption will be further discussed in Section 10.2.

However, for the aforementioned applications (e.g., in cryptography) this assumption does not seem to suffice either: We know how to utilize such "hard on the average" problems *only when we can efficiently generate hard instances coupled with adequate solutions.*[1] That is, we assume that, for some search problem in $\mathcal{PC}$ (resp., decision problem in $\mathcal{NP}$), we can efficiently generate instance-solution pairs (resp., yes-instances coupled with corresponding NP-witnesses) such that the instance is hard to solve (resp.,

---

[1] We wish to stress the difference between the two gaps discussed here. Our feeling is that the non-usefulness of worst-case hardness (*per se*) is far more intuitive than the non-usefulness of average-case hardness that does not correspond to an efficient generation of "solved" instances.

hard to verify as belonging to the set). Needless to say, the hardness assumption refers to a person who does not get the solution (resp., witness). Thus, we can efficiently generate hard "puzzles" coupled with solutions, and so we may present to others hard puzzles for which we know a solution.

Let us formulate the foregoing discussion. Referring to Definition 2.3, we consider a relation R in $\mathcal{PC}$ (i.e., R is polynomially bounded and membership in R can be determined in polynomial time), and assume that there exists a probabilistic polynomial-time algorithm G that satisfies the following two conditions:

1. On input 1^n, algorithm G always generates a pair in R such that the first element has length n. That is, $\Pr[G(1^n) \in R \cap (\{0, 1\}^n \times \{0, 1\}^*)] = 1$.
2. It is typically infeasible to find solutions to instances that are generated by G; that is, when only given the first element of $G(1^n)$, it is infeasible to find an adequate solution. Formally, denoting the first element of $G(1^n)$ by $G_1(1^n)$, for every probabilistic polynomial-time (solver) algorithm S, it holds that $\Pr[(G_1(1^n), S(G_1(1^n))) \in R] = \mu(n)$, where μ vanishes faster than any polynomial fraction (i.e., for every positive polynomial p and all sufficiently large n it is the case that $\mu(n) < 1/p(n)$).

We call G a generator of solved intractable instances for R. We will show that such a generator exists if and only if one-way functions exist, where one-way functions are functions that are easy to evaluate but hard (on the average) to invert. That is, a function $f : \{0, 1\}^* \to \{0, 1\}^*$ is called one-way if there is an efficient algorithm that on input x outputs $f(x)$, whereas any feasible algorithm that tries to find a preimage of $f(x)$ under f may succeed only with negligible probability (where the probability is taken uniformly over the choices of x and the algorithm's coin tosses). Associating feasible computations with probabilistic polynomial-time algorithms and negligible functions with functions that vanish faster than any polynomial fraction, we obtain the following definition.

Definition 7.1 (one-way functions): *A function $f : \{0, 1\}^* \to \{0, 1\}^*$ is called one-way if the following two conditions hold:*

1. Easy to evaluate: *There exists a polynomial-time algorithm A such that $A(x) = f(x)$ for every $x \in \{0, 1\}^*$.*
2. Hard to invert: *For every probabilistic polynomial-time algorithm A', every polynomial p, and all sufficiently large n,*

$$\Pr_{x \in \{0, 1\}^n}[A'(f(x), 1^n) \in f^{-1}(f(x))] < \frac{1}{p(n)} \qquad (7.1)$$

where the probability is taken uniformly over all the possible choices of $x \in \{0, 1\}^n$ and all the possible outcomes of the internal coin tosses of algorithm A'.

Algorithm A' is given the auxiliary input 1^n so as to allow it to run in time polynomial in the length of x, which is important in case f drastically shrinks its input (e.g., $|f(x)| = O(\log |x|)$). Typically (and, in fact, without loss of generality, see Exercise 7.1), f is length preserving, in which case the auxiliary input 1^n is redundant. Note that A' is not required to output a specific preimage of $f(x)$; any preimage (i.e., element in the set $f^{-1}(f(x))$) will do. (Indeed, in case f is 1-1, the string x is the only preimage of $f(x)$ under f; but in general there may be other preimages.) It is required that algorithm A' fails (to find a preimage) with overwhelming probability, when the probability is also taken over the input distribution. That is, f is "typically" hard to invert, not merely hard to invert in some ("rare") cases.

Proposition 7.2: *The following two conditions are equivalent:*

1. *There exists a generator of solved intractable instances for some $R \in \mathcal{NP}$.*
2. *There exist one-way functions.*

Proof Sketch: Suppose that G is such a generator of solved intractable instances for some $R \in \mathcal{NP}$, and suppose that on input 1^n it tosses $\ell(n)$ coins. For simplicity, we assume that $\ell(n) = n$, and consider the function $g(r) = G_1(1^{|r|}, r)$, where $G(1^n, r)$ denotes the output of G on input 1^n when using coins r (and G_1 is as in the foregoing discussion). Then g must be one-way, because an algorithm that inverts g on input $x = g(r)$ obtains r' such that $G_1(1^n, r') = x$ and $G(1^n, r')$ must be in R (which means that the second element of $G(1^n, r')$ is a solution to x). In case $\ell(n) \neq n$ (and assuming without loss of generality that $\ell(n) \geq n$), we define $g(r) = G_1(1^n, s)$ where n is the largest integer such that $\ell(n) \leq |r|$ and s is the $\ell(n)$-bit long prefix of r.

Suppose, on the other hand, that f is a one-way function (and that f is length preserving). Consider $G(1^n)$ that uniformly selects $r \in \{0, 1\}^n$ and outputs $(f(r), r)$, and let $R \stackrel{\text{def}}{=} \{(f(x), x) : x \in \{0, 1\}^*\}$. Then R is in $\mathcal{PC}$ and G is a generator of solved intractable instances for R, because any solver of R (on instances generated by G) is effectively inverting f on $f(U_n)$. $\qquad\square$

Comments. Several candidates for one-way functions and variation on the basic definition appear in Appendix C.2.1. Here, for the sake of future discussions, we define a stronger version of one-way functions, which refers to the infeasibility of inverting the function by non-uniform circuits of polynomial size. We seize the opportunity and use an alternative technical formulation, which is based on the probabilistic conventions in Appendix D.1.1.[2]

Definition 7.3 (one-way functions, non-uniformly hard): *A one-way function f: $\{0, 1\}^* \to \{0, 1\}^*$ is said to be non-uniformly hard to invert if for every family of polynomial-size circuits $\{C_n\}$, every polynomial p, and all sufficiently large n,*

$$\Pr[C_n(f(U_n), 1^n) \in f^{-1}(f(U_n))] < \frac{1}{p(n)}$$

We note that if a function is infeasible to invert by polynomial-size circuits then it is hard to invert by probabilistic polynomial-time algorithms; that is, non-uniformity (more than) compensates for lack of randomness. See Exercise 7.2.

7.1.2. Amplification of Weak One-Way Functions

In the foregoing discussion we have interpreted "hardness on the average" in a very strong sense. Specifically, we required that any feasible algorithm fails to solve the problem

---

[2]Specifically, letting U_n denote a random variable uniformly distributed in $\{0, 1\}^n$, we may write Eq. (7.1) as $\Pr[A'(f(U_n), 1^n) \in f^{-1}(f(U_n))] < 1/p(n)$, recalling that both occurrences of U_n refer to the same sample.

(e.g., invert the one-way function) *almost always* (i.e., *except with negligible probability*). This interpretation is indeed the one that is suitable for various applications. Still, a weaker interpretation of hardness on the average, which is also appealing, only requires that any feasible algorithm fails to solve the problem *often enough* (i.e., *with noticeable probability*). The main thrust of the current section is showing that the mild form of hardness on the average can be transformed into the strong form discussed in Section 7.1.1. Let us first define the mild form of hardness on the average, using the framework of one-way functions. Specifically, we define weak one-way functions.

Definition 7.4 (weak one-way functions): *A function* $f : \{0, 1\}^* \to \{0, 1\}^*$ *is called* weakly one-way *if the following two conditions hold:*

1. Easy to evaluate: *As in Definition 7.1.*
2. Weakly hard to invert: *There exist a positive polynomial p such that for every probabilistic polynomial-time algorithm A' and all sufficiently large n,*

$$\Pr_{x \in \{0,1\}^n}[A'(f(x), 1^n) \notin f^{-1}(f(x))] > \frac{1}{p(n)} \qquad (7.2)$$

where the probability is taken uniformly over all the possible choices of $x \in \{0, 1\}^n$ and all the possible outcomes of the internal coin tosses of algorithm A'. In such a case, we say that f is $1/p$-one-way.

Here we require that algorithm A' fails (to find an f-preimage for a random f-image) with noticeable probability, rather than with overwhelmingly high probability (as in Definition 7.1). For clarity, we will occasionally refer to one-way functions as in Definition 7.1 by the term strong one-way functions.

We note that, assuming that one-way functions exist at all, there exist weak one-way functions that are not strongly one-way (see Exercise 7.3). Still, any weak one-way function can be transformed into a strong one-way function. This is indeed the main result of the current section.

Theorem 7.5 (amplification of one-way functions): *The existence of weak one-way functions implies the existence of strong one-way functions.*

Proof Sketch: The construction itself is straightforward. We just parse the argument to the new function into sufficiently many blocks, and apply the weak one-way function on the individual blocks. That is, suppose that f is $1/p$-one-way, for some polynomial p, and consider the following function

$$F(x_1, \ldots, x_t) = (f(x_1), \ldots, f(x_t)) \qquad (7.3)$$

$$\text{where } t \overset{\text{def}}{=} n \cdot p(n) \text{ and } x_1, \ldots, x_t \in \{0, 1\}^n.$$

(Indeed F should be extended to strings of length outside $\{n^2 \cdot p(n) : n \in \mathbb{N}\}$ and this extension must be hard to invert on all preimage lengths.)[3]

We warn that the hardness of inverting the resulting function F is not established by mere "combinatorics" (i.e., considering, for any $S \subset \{0, 1\}^n$, the relative volume

---

[3] One simple extension is defining $F(x)$ to equal $(f(x_1), \ldots, f(x_{n \cdot p(n)}))$, where n is the largest integer satisfying $n^2 p(n) \leq |x|$ and x_i is the ith consecutive n-bit long string in x (i.e., $x = x_1 \cdots x_{n \cdot p(n)} x'$, where $x_1, \ldots, x_{n \cdot p(n)} \in \{0, 1\}^n$).

of S^t in $(\{0, 1\}^n)^t$, where S represents the set of f-preimages that are mapped by f to an image that is "easy to invert"). Specifically, one may *not* assume that the potential inverting algorithm works independently on each block. Indeed, this assumption seems reasonable, but we do not know if nothing is lost by this restriction. (In fact, proving that nothing is lost by this restriction is a formidable research project.) In general, we should not make assumptions regarding the class of all efficient algorithms (as underlying the definition of one-way functions), unless we can actually prove that nothing is lost by such assumptions.

The hardness of inverting the resulting function F is proved via a so-called reducibility argument (which is used to prove all conditional results in the area). By a reducibility argument we actually mean a reduction, but one that is analyzed with respect to average-case complexity. Specifically, we show that any algorithm that inverts the resulting function F with non-negligible success probability can be used to construct an algorithm that inverts the original function f with success probability that violates the hypothesis (regarding f). In other words, we reduce the task of "strongly inverting" f (i.e., violating its weak one-wayness) to the task of "weakly inverting" F (i.e., violating its strong one-wayness). In particular, on input $y = f(x)$, the reduction invokes the F-inverter (polynomially) many times, each time feeding it with a sequence of random f-images that contains y at a random location. (Indeed, such a sequence corresponds to a random image of F.) Details follow.

Suppose toward the contradiction that F is not strongly one-way; that is, there exists a probabilistic polynomial-time algorithm B' and a polynomial $q(\cdot)$ so that for infinitely many m's

$$\Pr[B'(F(U_m)) \in F^{-1}(F(U_m))] > \frac{1}{q(m)} \qquad (7.4)$$

Focusing on such a generic m and assuming (see footnote 3) that $m = n^2 p(n)$, we present the following probabilistic polynomial-time algorithm, A', for inverting f. On input y and 1^n (where supposedly $y = f(x)$ for some $x \in \{0, 1\}^n$), algorithm A' proceeds by applying the following probabilistic procedure, denoted I, on input y for $t'(n)$ times, where $t'(\cdot)$ is a polynomial that depends on the polynomials p and q (specifically, we set $t'(n) \overset{\text{def}}{=} 2n^2 \cdot p(n) \cdot q(n^2 p(n))$).

Procedure I (on input y and 1^n):
For $i = 1$ to $t(n) \overset{\text{def}}{=} n \cdot p(n)$ do begin
(1) Select uniformly and independently a sequence of strings $x_1, \ldots, x_{t(n)} \in \{0, 1\}^n$.
(2) Compute $(z_1, \ldots, z_{t(n)}) \leftarrow B'(f(x_1), \ldots, f(x_{i-1}), y, f(x_{i+1}), \ldots, f(x_{t(n)}))$.

(Note that y is placed in the ith position instead of $f(x_i)$.)
(3) If $f(z_i) = y$ then halt and output z_i.

(This is considered a *success*.)
end

Using Eq. (7.4), we now present a lower bound on the success probability of algorithm A', deriving a contradiction to the theorem's hypothesis. To this end we define a set, denoted S_n, that contains all n-bit strings on which the procedure I succeeds with probability greater than $n/t'(n)$. (The probability is taken only over the coin tosses of procedure I). Namely,

$$S_n \stackrel{\text{def}}{=} \left\{ x \in \{0, 1\}^n : \Pr[I(f(x)) \in f^{-1}(f(x))] > \frac{n}{t'(n)} \right\}$$

In the next two claims we shall show that S_n contains all but at most a $1/2p(n)$ fraction of the strings of length n, and that for each string $x \in S_n$ algorithm A' inverts f on $f(x)$ with probability exponentially close to 1. It will follow that A' inverts f on $f(U_n)$ with probability greater than $1 - (1/p(n))$, in contradiction to the theorem's hypothesis.

Claim 7.5.1: For every $x \in S_n$

$$\Pr[A'(f(x)) \in f^{-1}(f(x))] > 1 - 2^{-n}$$

This claim follows directly from the definitions of S_n and A'.

Claim 7.5.2:

$$|S_n| > \left(1 - \frac{1}{2p(n)}\right) \cdot 2^n$$

The rest of the proof is devoted to establishing this claim, and indeed combining Claims 7.5.1 and 7.5.2, the theorem follows.

The key observation is that, for every $i \in [t(n)]$ and every $x_i \in \{0, 1\}^n \setminus S_n$, it holds that

$$\Pr\left[B'(F(U_{n^2 p(n)})) \in F^{-1}(F(U_{n^2 p(n)})) \big| U_n^{(i)} = x_i \right]$$
$$\leq \Pr[I(f(x_i)) \in f^{-1}(f(x_i))] \leq \frac{n}{t'(n)}$$

where $U_n^{(1)}, \ldots, U_n^{(n \cdot p(n))}$ denote the n-bit long blocks in the random variable $U_{n^2 p(n)}$. It follows that

$$\xi \stackrel{\text{def}}{=} \Pr\left[B'(F(U_{n^2 p(n)})) \in F^{-1}(F(U_{n^2 p(n)})) \wedge \left(\exists i \text{ s.t. } U_n^{(i)} \in \{0, 1\}^n \setminus S_n \right) \right]$$

$$\leq \sum_{i=1}^{t(n)} \Pr\left[B'(F(U_{n^2 p(n)})) \in F^{-1}(F(U_{n^2 p(n)})) \wedge U_n^{(i)} \in \{0, 1\}^n \setminus S_n \right]$$

$$\leq t(n) \cdot \frac{n}{t'(n)} = \frac{1}{2q(n^2 p(n))}$$

where the equality is due to $t'(n) = 2n^2 \cdot p(n) \cdot q(n^2 p(n))$ and $t(n) = n \cdot p(n)$. On the other hand, using Eq. (7.4), we have

$$\xi \geq \Pr\left[B'(F(U_{n^2 p(n)})) \in F^{-1}(F(U_{n^2 p(n)})) \right] - \Pr\left[(\forall i) \, U_n^{(i)} \in S_n \right]$$

$$\geq \frac{1}{q(n^2 p(n))} - \Pr[U_n \in S_n]^{t(n)} .$$

Using $t(n) = n \cdot p(n)$, we get $\Pr[U_n \in S_n] > (1/2q(n^2 p(n)))^{1/(n \cdot p(n))}$, which implies $\Pr[U_n \in S_n] > 1 - (1/2p(n))$ for sufficiently large n. Claim 7.5.2 follows, and so does the theorem. $\square$

Digest. Let us recall the structure of the proof of Theorem 7.5. Given a weak one-way function f, we first constructed a polynomial-time computable function F with the intention of later proving that F is strongly one-way. To prove that F is strongly one-way, we used a *reducibility argument*. The argument transforms efficient algorithms that supposedly contradict the strong one-wayness of F into efficient algorithms that contradict the hypothesis that f is weakly one-way. Hence, F must be strongly one-way. We stress that our algorithmic transformation, which is in fact a randomized Cook-reduction, makes no implicit or explicit assumptions about the structure of the prospective algorithms for inverting F. Such assumptions (e.g., the "natural" assumption that the inverter of F works independently on each block) cannot be justified (at least not at our current state of understanding of the nature of efficient computations).

We use the term a *reducibility argument*, rather than just saying a reduction, so as to emphasize that we do *not* refer here to standard (worst-case complexity) reductions. Let us clarify the distinction: In both cases we refer to *reducing* the task of solving one problem to the task of solving another problem; that is, we use a procedure solving the second task in order to construct a procedure that solves the first task. However, in standard reductions one assumes that the second task has a perfect procedure solving it on all instances (i.e., on the worst case), and constructs such a procedure for the first task. Thus, the reduction may invoke the given procedure (for the second task) on very "non-typical" instances. This cannot be allowed in our reducibility arguments. Here, we are given a procedure that solves the second task *with certain probability with respect to a certain distribution*. Thus, in employing a reducibility argument, we cannot invoke this procedure on any instance. Instead, we must consider the probability distribution, on instances of the second task, induced by our reduction. In our case (as in many cases) the latter distribution equals the distribution to which the hypothesis (regarding solvability of the second task) refers, but in general these distributions need only be "sufficiently close" in an adequate sense (which depends on the analysis). In any case, a careful consideration of the distribution induced by the reducibility argument is due. (Indeed, the same issue arises in the context of reductions among "distributional problems" considered in Section 10.2.)

An information-theoretic analogue. Theorem 7.5 (or rather its proof) has a natural information-theoretic (or "probabilistic") analogue that refers to the amplification of the success probability by repeated experiments: If some event occurs with probability p in a single experiment, then the event will occur with very high probability (i.e., $1 - e^{-n}$) when the experiment is repeated n/p times. The analogy is to evaluating the function F at a random-input, where each block of this input may be viewed as an attempt to hit the noticeable "hard region" of f. The reader is probably convinced at this stage that the proof of Theorem 7.5 is much more complex than the proof of the information-theoretic analogue. In the information-theoretic context the repeated experiments are independent by definition, whereas in the computational context no such independence can be guaranteed. (Indeed, the independence assumption corresponds to the naive argument discussed at the beginning of the proof of Theorem 7.5.) Another indication of the difference between the two settings follows. In the information-theoretic setting, the probability that the event did not occur in any of the repeated trials decreases exponentially with the number of repetitions. In contrast, in the computational setting we can only reach an unspecified negligible bound on the inverting probabilities of polynomial-time algorithms. Furthermore, for all we know, it may be the case that F can be efficiently inverted on $F(U_{n^2 p(n)})$ with success

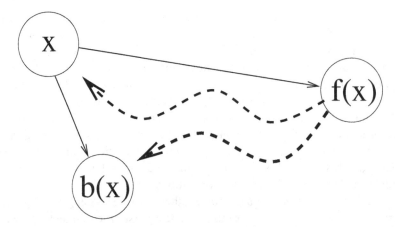

Figure 7.1: The hard-core of a one-way function. The solid arrows depict easily computable transformation while the dashed arrows depict infeasible transformations.

probability that is sub-exponentially decreasing (e.g., with probability $2^{-(\log_2 n)^3}$), whereas the analogous information-theoretic bound is exponentially decreasing (i.e., e^{-n}).

7.1.3. Hard-Core Predicates

One-way functions *per se* suffice for one central application: the construction of secure signature schemes (see Appendix C.6). For other applications, one relies not merely on the infeasibility of fully recovering the preimage of a one-way function, but rather on the infeasibility of meaningfully guessing bits in the preimage. The latter notion is captured by the definition of a hard-core predicate.

Recall that saying that a function f is one-way means that given a typical y (in the range of f) it is infeasible to find a preimage of y under f. This does not mean that it is infeasible to find partial information about the preimage(s) of y under f. Specifically, it may be easy to retrieve half of the bits of the preimage (e.g., given a one-way function f consider the function f' defined by $f'(x, r) \stackrel{\text{def}}{=} (f(x), r)$, for every $|x| = |r|$). We note that hiding partial information (about the function's preimage) plays an important role in more advanced constructs (e.g., pseudorandom generators and secure encryption). With this motivation in mind, we will show that essentially any one-way function hides specific partial information about its preimage, where this partial information is easy to compute from the preimage itself. This partial information can be considered as a "hard-core" of the difficulty of inverting f. Loosely speaking, a *polynomial-time computable* (Boolean) predicate b is called a hard-core of a function f if no feasible algorithm, given $f(x)$, can guess $b(x)$ with success probability that is non-negligibly better than one half.

> **Definition 7.6** (hard-core predicates): *A polynomial-time computable predicate b : $\{0, 1\}^* \to \{0, 1\}$ is called a* hard-core *of a function f if for every probabilistic polynomial-time algorithm A', every positive polynomial $p(\cdot)$, and all sufficiently large n's*
>
> $$\Pr\left[A'(f(x)) = b(x)\right] < \frac{1}{2} + \frac{1}{p(n)}$$
>
> *where the probability is taken uniformly over all the possible choices of $x \in \{0, 1\}^n$ and all the possible outcomes of the internal coin tosses of algorithm A'.*

Note that for every $b : \{0, 1\}^* \to \{0, 1\}$ and $f : \{0, 1\}^* \to \{0, 1\}^*$, there exist obvious algorithms that guess $b(x)$ from $f(x)$ with success probability at least one half (e.g., the algorithm that, obliviously of its input, outputs a uniformly chosen bit). Also, if b is a hard-core predicate (of any function) then it follows that b is almost unbiased (i.e., for a uniformly chosen x, the difference $|\Pr[b(x)=0] - \Pr[b(x)=1]|$ must be a negligible function in n).

Since b itself is polynomial-time computable, the failure of efficient algorithms to approximate $b(x)$ from $f(x)$ (with success probability that is non-negligibly higher than one half) must be due either to an information loss of f (i.e., f not being one-to-one) or to the difficulty of inverting f. For example, for $\sigma \in \{0, 1\}$ and $x' \in \{0, 1\}^*$, the predicate $b(\sigma x') = \sigma$ is a hard-core of the function $f(\sigma x') \overset{\text{def}}{=} 0x'$. Hence, in this case the fact that b is a hard-core of the function f is due to the fact that f loses information (specifically, the first bit: σ). On the other hand, in the case that f loses no information (i.e., f is one-to-one) a hard-core for f may exist only if f is hard to invert. In general, the interesting case is when being a hard-core is a computational phenomenon rather than an information-theoretic one (which is due to "information loss" of f). It turns out that any one-way function has a modified version that possesses a hard-core predicate.

Theorem 7.7 (a generic hard-core predicate): *For any one-way function f, the inner-product mod 2 of x and r, denoted $b(x,r)$, is a hard-core of $f'(x,r) = (f(x), r)$.*

In other words, Theorem 7.7 asserts that, given $f(x)$ and a random subset $S \subseteq [|x|]$, it is infeasible to guess $\oplus_{i \in S} x_i$ significantly better than with probability $1/2$, where $x = x_1 \cdots x_n$ is uniformly distributed in $\{0, 1\}^n$.

Proof Sketch: The proof is by a so-called reducibility argument (see Section 7.1.2). Specifically, we reduce the task of inverting f to the task of predicting the hard-core of f', while making sure that the reduction (when applied to input distributed as in the inverting task) generates a distribution as in the definition of the predicting task. Thus, a contradiction to the claim that b is a hard-core of f' yields a contradiction to the hypothesis that f is hard to invert. We stress that this argument is far more complex than analyzing the corresponding "probabilistic" situation (i.e., the distribution of $(r, b(X, r))$, where $r \in \{0, 1\}^n$ is uniformly distributed and X is a random variable with super-logarithmic min-entropy (which represents the "effective" knowledge of x, when given $f(x)$)).[4]

Our starting point is a probabilistic polynomial-time algorithm B that satisfies, for some polynomial p and infinitely many n's, $\Pr[B(f(X_n), U_n) = b(X_n, U_n)] > (1/2) + (1/p(n))$, where X_n and U_n are uniformly and independently distributed over $\{0, 1\}^n$. Using a simple averaging argument, we focus on a $\varepsilon \overset{\text{def}}{=} 1/2p(n)$ fraction of the x's for which $\Pr[B(f(x), U_n) = b(x, U_n)] > (1/2) + \varepsilon$ holds. We will show how to use B in order to invert f, on input $f(x)$, provided that x is in this good set (which has density ε).

As a warm-up, suppose for a moment that, for the aforementioned x's, algorithm B succeeds with probability p such that $p > \frac{3}{4} + 1/\text{poly}(|x|)$ rather than $p > \frac{1}{2} + 1/\text{poly}(|x|)$. In this case, retrieving x from $f(x)$ is quite easy: To retrieve the ith bit of

---

[4]The min-entropy of X is defined as $\min_v \{\log_2(1/\Pr[X = v])\}$; that is, if X has min-entropy m then $\max_v\{\Pr[X = v]\} = 2^{-m}$. The Leftover Hashing Lemma (see Appendix D.2) implies that, in this case, $\Pr[b(X, U_n) = 1|U_n] = \frac{1}{2} \pm 2^{-\Omega(m)}$, where U_n denotes the uniform distribution over $\{0, 1\}^n$.

x, denoted x_i, we randomly select $r \in \{0, 1\}^{|x|}$, and obtain $B(f(x), r)$ and $B(f(x), r \oplus e^i)$, where $e^i = 0^{i-1}10^{|x|-i}$ and $v \oplus u$ denotes the addition mod 2 of the binary vectors v and u. A key observation underlying the foregoing scheme as well as the rest of the proof is that $b(x, r \oplus s) = b(x, r) \oplus b(x, s)$, which can be readily verified by writing $b(x, y) = \sum_{i=1}^{n} x_i y_i$ mod 2 and noting that addition modulo 2 of bits corresponds to their XOR. Now, note that if both $B(f(x), r) = b(x, r)$ and $B(f(x), r \oplus e^i) = b(x, r \oplus e^i)$ hold, then $B(f(x), r) \oplus B(f(x), r \oplus e^i)$ equals $b(x, r) \oplus b(x, r \oplus e^i) = b(x, e^i) = x_i$. The probability that both $B(f(x), r) = b(x, r)$ and $B(f(x), r \oplus e^i) = b(x, r \oplus e^i)$ hold, for a random r, is at least $1 - 2 \cdot (1 - p) > \frac{1}{2} + \frac{1}{\text{poly}(|x|)}$. Hence, repeating the foregoing procedure sufficiently many times (using independent random choices of such r's) and ruling by majority, we retrieve x_i with very high probability. Similarly, we can retrieve all the bits of x, and hence invert f on $f(x)$. However, the entire analysis was conducted under (the unjustifiable) assumption that $p > \frac{3}{4} + \frac{1}{\text{poly}(|x|)}$, whereas we only know that $p > \frac{1}{2} + \varepsilon$ for $\varepsilon = 1/\text{poly}(|x|)$.

The problem with the foregoing procedure is that it doubles the original error probability of algorithm B on inputs of the form $(f(x), \cdot)$. Under the unrealistic (foregoing) assumption that B's average error on such inputs is non-negligibly smaller than $\frac{1}{4}$, the "error-doubling" phenomenon raises no problems. However, in general (and even in the special case where B's error is exactly $\frac{1}{4}$) the foregoing procedure is unlikely to invert f. Note that the *average* error probability of B (for a fixed $f(x)$, when the average is taken over a random r) cannot be decreased by repeating B several times (e.g., for every x, it may be that B always answers correctly on three-quarters of the pairs $(f(x), r)$, and always errs on the remaining quarter). What is required is an *alternative way of using* the algorithm B, a way that does not double the original error probability of B.

The key idea is generating the r's in a way that allows for applying algorithm B only once per each r (and i), instead of twice. Specifically, we will invoke B on $(f(x), r \oplus e^i)$ in order to obtain a "guess" for $b(x, r \oplus e^i)$, and obtain $b(x, r)$ in a different way (which does not involve using B). The good news is that the error probability is no longer doubled, since we only use B to get a "guess" of $b(x, r \oplus e^i)$. The bad news is that we still need to know $b(x, r)$, and it is not clear how we can know $b(x, r)$ without applying B. The answer is that we can guess $b(x, r)$ by ourselves. This is fine if we only need to guess $b(x, r)$ for one r (or logarithmically in $|x|$ many r's), but the problem is that we need to know (and hence guess) the value of $b(x, r)$ for polynomially many r's. The obvious way of guessing these $b(x, r)$'s yields an exponentially small success probability. Instead, we generate these polynomially many r's such that, on the one hand, they are "sufficiently random" whereas, on the other hand, we can guess all the $b(x, r)$'s with noticeable success probability.[5] Specifically, generating the r's in a specific *pairwise independent* manner will satisfy both these (conflicting) requirements. We stress that in case we are successful (in our guesses for all the $b(x, r)$'s), we can retrieve x with high probability. Hence, we retrieve x with noticeable probability.

A word about the way in which the pairwise independent r's are generated (and the corresponding $b(x, r)$'s are guessed) is indeed in place. To generate

---

[5]Alternatively, we can try all polynomially many possible guesses. In such a case, we shall output a list of candidates that, with high probability, contains x. (See Exercise 7.6.)

$m = \text{poly}(|x|)$ many r's, we uniformly (and independently) select $\ell \stackrel{\text{def}}{=} \log_2(m+1)$ strings in $\{0, 1\}^{|x|}$. Let us denote these strings by $s^1, \ldots, s^\ell$. We then guess $b(x, s^1)$ through $b(x, s^\ell)$. Let us denote these guesses, which are uniformly (and independently) chosen in $\{0, 1\}$, by σ^1 through σ^ℓ. Hence, the probability that all our guesses for the $b(x, s^i)$'s are correct is $2^{-\ell} = \frac{1}{\text{poly}(|x|)}$. The different r's correspond to the different *non-empty* subsets of $\{1, 2, \ldots, \ell\}$. Specifically, for every such subset J, we let $r^J \stackrel{\text{def}}{=} \oplus_{j \in J} s^j$. The reader can easily verify that the r^J's are pairwise independent and each is uniformly distributed in $\{0, 1\}^{|x|}$; see Exercise 7.5. The key observation is that $b(x, r^J) = b(x, \oplus_{j \in J} s^j) = \oplus_{j \in J} b(x, s^j)$. Hence, our guess for $b(x, r^J)$ is $\oplus_{j \in J} \sigma^j$, and with noticeable probability all our guesses are correct. Wrapping up everything, we obtain the following procedure, where $\varepsilon = 1/\text{poly}(n)$ represents a lower bound on the advantage of B in guessing $b(x, \cdot)$ for an ε fraction of the x's (i.e., for these good x's it holds that $\Pr[B(f(x), U_n) = b(x, U_n)] > \frac{1}{2} + \varepsilon$).

Inverting procedure (on input $y = f(x)$ and parameters n and ε):
Set $\ell = \log_2(n/\varepsilon^2) + O(1)$.

(1) Select uniformly and independently $s^1, \ldots, s^\ell \in \{0, 1\}^n$.

  Select uniformly and independently $\sigma^1, \ldots, \sigma^\ell \in \{0, 1\}$.

(2) For every non-empty $J \subseteq [\ell]$, compute $r^J = \oplus_{j \in J} s^j$ and $\rho^J = \oplus_{j \in J} \sigma^j$.

(3) For $i = 1, \ldots, n$ determine the bit z_i according to the majority vote of the $(2^\ell - 1)$-long sequence of bits $(\rho^J \oplus B(f(x), r^J \oplus e^i))_{\emptyset \neq J \subseteq [\ell]}$.

(4) Output $z_1 \cdots z_n$.

Note that the "voting scheme" employed in Step 3 uses pairwise independent samples (i.e., the r^J's), but works essentially as well as it would have worked with independent samples (i.e., the independent r's).[6] That is, for every i and J, it holds that $\Pr_{s^1, \ldots, s^\ell}[B(f(x), r^J \oplus e^i) = b(x, r^J \oplus e^i)] > (1/2) + \varepsilon$, where $r^J = \oplus_{j \in J} s^j$, and (for every fixed i) the events corresponding to different J's are pairwise independent. It follows that *if for every $j \in [\ell]$ it holds that $\sigma^j = b(x, s^j)$*, then for every i and J we have

$$\Pr_{s^1, \ldots, s^\ell}[\rho^J \oplus B(f(x), r^J \oplus e^i) = b(x, e^i)] \tag{7.5}$$

$$= \Pr_{s^1, \ldots, s^\ell}[B(f(x), r^J \oplus e^i) = b(x, r^J \oplus e^i)] > \frac{1}{2} + \varepsilon$$

where the equality is due to $\rho^J = \oplus_{j \in J} \sigma^j = b(x, r^J) = b(x, r^J \oplus e^i) \oplus b(x, e^i)$. Note that Eq. (7.5) refers to the correctness of a single vote for $b(x, e^i)$. Using $m = 2^\ell - 1 = O(n/\varepsilon^2)$ and noting that these (Boolean) votes are pairwise independent, we infer that the probability that the majority of these votes is wrong is upper-bounded by $1/2n$. Using a union bound on all i's, we infer that with probability at least $1/2$, all majority votes are correct and thus x is retrieved correctly. Recall

---

[6] Our focus here is on the accuracy of the approximation obtained by the sample, and not so much on the error probability. We wish to approximate $\Pr[b(x, r) \oplus B(f(x), r \oplus e^i) = 1]$ up to an additive term of ε, because such an approximation allows for correctly determining $b(x, e^i)$. A pairwise independent sample of $O(t/\varepsilon^2)$ points allows for an approximation of a value in $[0, 1]$ up to an additive term of ε with error probability $1/t$, whereas a totally random sample of the same size yields error probability $\exp(-t)$. Since we can afford setting $t = \text{poly}(n)$ and having error probability $1/2n$, the difference in the error probability between the two approximation schemes is not important here. For a wider perspective, see Appendix D.1.2 and D.3.

---

that the foregoing is conditioned on $\sigma^j = b(x, s^j)$ for every $j \in [\ell]$, which in turn holds with probability $2^{-\ell} = (m+1)^{-1} = \Omega(\varepsilon^2/n) = 1/\text{poly}(n)$. Thus, x is retrieved correctly with probability $1/\text{poly}(n)$, and the theorem follows. $\square$

Digest. Looking at the proof of Theorem 7.7, we note that it actually refers to an arbitrary black-box $B_x(\cdot)$ that approximates $b(x, \cdot)$; specifically, in the case of Theorem 7.7 we used $B_x(r) \stackrel{\text{def}}{=} B(f(x), r)$. In particular, the proof does not use the fact that we can verify the correctness of the preimage recovered by the described process. Thus, the proof actually establishes *the existence of a* $\text{poly}(n/\varepsilon)$-*time oracle machine that, for every* $x \in \{0, 1\}^n$, *given oracle access to any* $B_x : \{0, 1\}^n \to \{0, 1\}$ *satisfying*

$$\Pr_{r\in\{0,1\}^n}[B_x(r) = b(x, r)] \geq \frac{1}{2} + \varepsilon \tag{7.6}$$

outputs x with probability at least $\text{poly}(\varepsilon/n)$. Specifically, x is output with probability at least $p \stackrel{\text{def}}{=} \Omega(\varepsilon^2/n)$. Noting that x is merely a string for which Eq. (7.6) holds, it follows that the number of strings that satisfy Eq. (7.6) is at most $1/p$. Furthermore, by iterating the foregoing procedure for $\widetilde{O}(1/p)$ times we can obtain all these strings (see Exercise 7.7).

Theorem 7.8 (Theorem 7.7, revisited): *There exists a probabilistic oracle machine that, given parameters n, ε and oracle access to any function $B : \{0, 1\}^n \to \{0, 1\}$, halts after $\text{poly}(n/\varepsilon)$ steps and with probability at least $1/2$ outputs a list of all strings $x \in \{0, 1\}^n$ that satisfy*

$$\Pr_{r\in\{0,1\}^n}[B(r) = b(x, r)] \geq \frac{1}{2} + \varepsilon, \tag{7.7}$$

where $b(x, r)$ denotes the inner-product mod 2 of x and r.

This machine can be modified such that, with high probability, its output list does not include any string x such that $\Pr_{r\in\{0,1\}^n}[B(r) = b(x, r)] < \frac{1}{2} + \frac{\varepsilon}{2}$.

Theorem 7.8 means that if given some information about x it is hard to recover x, then given the same information and a random r it is hard to predict $b(x, r)$. This assertion is proved by the counter-positive (see Exercise 7.14).[7] Indeed, the foregoing statement is in the spirit of Theorem 7.7 itself, except that it refers to any "information about x" (rather than to the value $f(x)$). To demonstrate the point, let us rephrase the foregoing statement as follows: *For every randomized process Π, if given s it is hard to obtain $\Pi(s)$ then given s and a uniformly distributed $r \in \{0, 1\}^{|\Pi(s)|}$ it is hard to predict $b(\Pi(s), r)$.*[8]

A coding theory perspective. Theorem 7.8 can be viewed as a "list decoding" procedure for the Hadamard code, where the Hadamard encoding of a string $x \in \{0, 1\}^n$ is the 2^n-bit long string containing $b(x, r)$ for every $r \in \{0, 1\}^n$. Specifically, the function $B : \{0, 1\}^n \to \{0, 1\}$ is viewed as a string of length 2^n, and each $x \in \{0, 1\}^n$ that satisfies Eq. (7.7) corresponds to a codeword (i.e., the Hadamard encoding of x) that is at distance at most $(0.5 - \varepsilon) \cdot 2^n$ from B. Theorem 7.8 asserts that the list of all such x's can be (probabilistic) recovered in $\text{poly}(n/\varepsilon)$-time, when given direct access to the bits of B (and in particular without reading all of B). This yields a very strong list-decoding result for the Hadamard code, where in list decoding the task is recovering all strings that have an

---

[7]The information available about x is represented in Exercise 7.14 by X_n, while x itself is represented by $h(X_n)$.

[8]Indeed, s is distributed arbitrarily (as X_n in Exercise 7.14). Note that Theorem 7.7 is obtained as a special case by letting $\Pi(s)$ be uniformly distributed in $f^{-1}(s)$.

encoding that is within a specified distance from the given string, in contrast to *standard decoding* in which the task is recovering the unique information that is encoded in the codeword that is closest to the given string. We mention that list decoding is applicable and valuable in the case that the specified distance does not allow for unique decoding (i.e., the specified distance is greater than half the distance of the code). (Note that a very fast unique-decoding procedure for the Hadamard code is implicit in the warm-up discussion at the beginning of the proof of Theorem 7.7.)

Applications of hard-core predicates. Turning back to hard-core predicates, we mention that they play a central role in the construction of general-purpose pseudorandom generators (see Section 8.2), commitment schemes and zero-knowledge proofs (see Sections 9.2.2 and C.4.3), and encryption schemes (see Appendix C.5).

7.1.4. Reflections on Hardness Amplification

Let us take notice that something truly amazing happens in Theorems 7.5 and 7.7. We are not talking merely of using an assumption to derive some conclusion; this is common practice in mathematics and science (and was indeed done several times in previous chapters, starting with Theorem 2.28). The thing that is special about Theorems 7.5 and 7.7 (and we shall see more of this in Section 7.2 as well as in Sections 8.2 and 8.3) is that a relatively mild intractability assumption is shown to imply a stronger intractability result.

This strengthening of an intractability phenomenon (aka hardness amplification) takes place while we admit that we do not understand the intractability phenomenon (because we do not understand the nature of efficient computation). Nevertheless, hardness amplification is enabled by the use of the counter-positive, which in this case is called a reducibility argument. At this point things look less miraculous: A reducibility argument calls for the design of a procedure (i.e., a reduction) and a probabilistic analysis of its behavior. The design and analysis of such procedures may not be easy, but it is certainly within the standard expertise of computer science. The fact that hardness amplification is achieved via this counter-positive is best represented in the statement of Theorem 7.8.

7.2. Hard Problems in E

As in Section 7.1, we start with the assumption $\mathcal{P} \neq \mathcal{NP}$ and seek to use it to our benefit. Again, we shall actually use a seemingly stronger assumption; here, the strengthening is in requiring *worst-case* hardness with respect to *non-uniform* models of computation (rather than average-case hardness with respect to the standard uniform model). Specifically, we shall assume that $\mathcal{NP}$ cannot be solved by (non-uniform) families of polynomial-size circuits; that is, $\mathcal{NP}$ is not contained in $\mathcal{P}/\text{poly}$ (even not infinitely often).

Our goal is to transform this worst-case assumption into an average-case condition, which is useful for our applications. Since the transformation will not yield a problem in $\mathcal{NP}$ but rather one in $\mathcal{E}$, we might as well take the seemingly weaker assumption by which $\mathcal{E}$ is not contained in $\mathcal{P}/\text{poly}$ (see Exercise 7.9). That is, our starting point is actually that *there exists an exponential-time solvable decision problem such that any family of polynomial-size circuits fails to solve it correctly on all but finitely many input lengths.*[9]

---

[9]Note that our starting point is actually stronger than assuming the existence of a function f in $\mathcal{E} \setminus \mathcal{P}/\text{poly}$. Such an assumption would mean that any family of polynomial-size circuits fails to compute f correctly on infinitely many input lengths, whereas our starting point postulates failures on all but finitely many lengths.

A different perspective on our assumption is provided by the fact that $\mathcal{E}$ contains problems that cannot be solved in polynomial time (cf.. Section 4.2.1). The current assumption goes beyond this fact by postulating the failure of non-uniform polynomial-time machines rather than the failure of (uniform) polynomial-time machines.

Recall that our goal is to obtain a predicate (i.e., a decision problem) that is computable in exponential time but is inapproximable by polynomial-size circuits. For the sake of later developments, we formulate a general notion of inapproximability.

Definition 7.9 (inapproximability, a general formulation): *We say that $f : \{0, 1\}^* \to \{0, 1\}$ is (S, ρ)-inapproximable if for every family of S-size circuits $\{C_n\}_{n \in \mathbb{N}}$ and all sufficiently large n it holds that*

$$\Pr[C_n(U_n) \neq f(U_n)] \geq \frac{\rho(n)}{2} \tag{7.8}$$

We say that f is T-inapproximable if it is $(T, 1 - (1/T))$-inapproximable.

We chose the specific form of Eq. (7.8) such that the "level of inapproximability" represented by the parameter ρ will range in $(0, 1)$ and increase with the value of ρ. Specifically, (almost-everywhere) *worst-case* hardness for circuits of size S is represented by (S, ρ)-inapproximability with $\rho(n) = 2^{-n+1}$ (i.e., in this case $\Pr[C(U_n) \neq f(U_n)] \geq 2^{-n}$ for every circuit C_n of size $S(n)$). On the other hand, no predicate can be (S, ρ)-inapproximable for $\rho(n) = 1 - 2^{-n}$ even with $S(n) = O(n)$ (i.e., $\Pr[C(U_n) = f(U_n)] \geq 0.5 + 2^{-n-1}$ holds for some linear-size circuit; see Exercise 7.10).

We note that Eq. (7.8) can be interpreted as an upper bound on the *correlation* of each adequate circuit with f (i.e., Eq. (7.8) is equivalent to $\mathsf{E}[\chi(C(U_n), f(U_n))] \leq 1 - \rho(n)$, where $\chi(\sigma, \tau) = 1$ if $\sigma = \tau$ and $\chi(\sigma, \tau) = -1$ otherwise).[10] Thus, T-inapproximability means that no family of size T circuits can correlate f better than $1/T$.

We note that the existence of a non-uniformly hard one-way function (as in Definition 7.3) implies the existence of an exponential-time computable predicate that is T-inapproximable for every polynomial T. (For details see Exercise 7.24.) However, our goal in this section is to establish this conclusion under a seemingly weaker assumption.

On almost-everywhere hardness. We highlight the fact that both our assumptions and conclusions refer to *almost-everywhere* hardness. For example, our starting point is not merely that $\mathcal{E}$ is not contained in $\mathcal{P}/\text{poly}$ (or in other circuit-size classes to be discussed), but rather that this is the case almost everywhere. Note that by saying that f has circuit complexity exceeding S, we merely mean that *there are infinitely many n's* such that no circuit of size $S(n)$ can compute f correctly on all inputs of length n. In contrast, by saying that f has circuit complexity exceeding S almost everywhere, we mean that *for all but finite many n's* no circuit of size $S(n)$ can compute f correctly on all inputs of length n. (Indeed, it is not known whether an "infinitely often" type of hardness implies a corresponding "almost-everywhere" hardness.)

---

[10]Indeed, $\mathsf{E}[\chi(X, Y)] = \Pr[X = Y] - \Pr[X \neq Y] = 1 - 2\Pr[X \neq Y]$.

The class $\mathcal{E}$. Recall that $\mathcal{E}$ denotes the class of exponential-time solvable decision problems (equivalently, exponential-time computable Boolean predicates); that is, $\mathcal{E} = \cup_{\varepsilon} \mathrm{DTIME}(t_{\varepsilon})$, where $t_{\varepsilon}(n) \stackrel{\text{def}}{=} 2^{\varepsilon n}$.

The rest of this section. We start (in Section 7.2.1) with a treatment of assumptions and hardness amplification regarding polynomial-size circuits, which suffice for non-trivial derandomization of $\mathcal{BPP}$. We then turn (in Section 7.2.2) to assumptions and hardness amplification regarding exponential-size circuits, which yield a "full" derandomization of $\mathcal{BPP}$ (i.e., $\mathcal{BPP} = \mathcal{P}$). In fact, both sections contain material that is applicable to various other circuit-size bounds, but the motivational focus is as stated.

> **Teaching note:** Section 7.2.2 is advanced material, which is best left for independent reading. Furthermore, for one of the central results (i.e., Lemma 7.23) only an outline is provided and the interested reader is referred to the original paper [128].

7.2.1. Amplification with Respect to Polynomial-Size Circuits

Our goal here is to prove the following result.

> **Theorem 7.10:** *Suppose that for every polynomial p there exists a problem in $\mathcal{E}$ having circuit complexity that is almost-everywhere greater than p. Then there exist polynomial-inapproximable Boolean functions in $\mathcal{E}$; that is, for every polynomial p there exists a p-inapproximable Boolean function in $\mathcal{E}$.*

Theorem 7.10 is used toward deriving a meaningful derandomization of $\mathcal{BPP}$ under the aforementioned assumption (see Part 2 of Theorem 8.19). We present two proofs of Theorem 7.10. The first proof proceeds in two steps:

1. Starting from the worst-case hypothesis, we first establish some mild level of average-case hardness (i.e., a mild level of inapproximability). Specifically, we show that for every polynomial p there exists a problem in $\mathcal{E}$ that is (p, ε)-inapproximable for $\varepsilon(n) = 1/n^3$.
2. Using the foregoing mild level of inapproximability, we obtain the desired strong level of inapproximability (i.e., p'-inapproximability for every polynomial p'). Specifically, for every two polynomials p_1 and p_2, we prove that *if the function f is $(p_1, 1/p_2)$-inapproximable, then the function $F(x_1, \ldots, x_{t(n)}) = \oplus_{i=1}^{t(n)} f(x_i)$, where $t(n) = n \cdot p_2(n)$ and $x_1, \ldots, x_{t(n)} \in \{0, 1\}^n$, is p'-inapproximable for $p'(t(n) \cdot n) = p_1(n)^{\Omega(1)}/\mathrm{poly}(t(n))$.* This claim is known as Yao's XOR Lemma and its proof is far more complex than the proof of its information-theoretic analogue (discussed at the beginning of §7.2.1.2).

The second proof of Theorem 7.10 consists of showing that the construction employed in the first step, when composed with Theorem 7.8, actually yields the desired end result. This proof will uncover a connection between hardness amplification and coding theory. Our presentation will thus proceed in three corresponding steps (presented in §7.2.1.1–7.2.1.3, and schematically depicted in Figure 7.2).

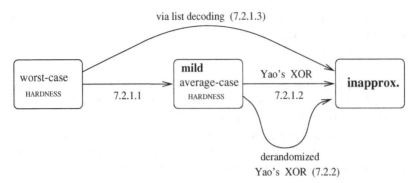

Figure 7.2: Proofs of hardness amplification: Organization.

7.2.1.1. From Worst-Case Hardness to Mild Average-Case Hardness

The transformation of worst-case hardness into average-case hardness (even in a mild sense) is indeed remarkable. Note that worst-case hardness may be due to a relatively small number of instances, whereas even mild forms of average-case hardness refer to a very large number of possible instances.[11] In other words, we should transform hardness that may occur on a negligible fraction of the instances into hardness that occurs on a noticeable fraction of the instances. Intuitively, we should "spread" the hardness of few instances (of the original problem) over all (or most) instances (of the transformed problem). The counter-positive view is that computing the value of typical instances of the transformed problem should enable solving the original problem on every instance.

The aforementioned transformation is based on the *self-correction paradigm*, to be reviewed first. The paradigm refers to functions g that can be evaluated at any desired point by using the value of g at a few random points, where each of these points is uniformly distributed in the function's domain (but indeed the points are not independently distributed). The key observation is that if $g(x)$ can be reconstructed based on the value of g at t such random points, then such a reconstruction can tolerate a $1/3t$ fraction of errors (regarding the values of g). Thus, if we can correctly obtain the value of g on all but at most a $1/3t$ fraction of its domain, then we can probabilistically recover the correct value of g at any point with very high probability. It follows that if no probabilistic polynomial-time algorithm can correctly compute g *in the worst-case sense*, then every probabilistic polynomial-time algorithm must fail to correctly compute g *on more than a $1/3t$ fraction of its domain*.

The archetypical example of a self-correctable function is any m-variate polynomial of individual degree d over a finite field F such that $|F| > dm + 1$. The value of such a polynomial at any desired point x can be recovered based on the values of $dm + 1$ points (other than x) that reside on a random line that passes through x. Note that each of these points is uniformly distributed in F^m, which is the function's domain. (For details, see Exercise 7.11.)

Recall that we are given an arbitrary function $f \in \mathcal{E}$ that is hard to compute in the worst case. Needless to say, this function is not necessarily self-correctable (based on relatively

---

[11]Indeed, worst-case hardness with respect to polynomial-size circuits cannot be due to a polynomial number of instances, because a polynomial number of instances can be hard-wired into such circuits. Still, for all we know, worst-case hardness may be due to a small super-polynomial number of instances (e.g., $n^{\log_2 n}$ instances). In contrast, even mild forms of average-case hardness must be due to an exponential number of instances (i.e., $2^n/\text{poly}(n)$ instances).

few points), but it can be extended into such a function. Specifically, we extend $f : [N] \rightarrow \{0, 1\}$ (viewed as $f : [N^{1/m}]^m \rightarrow \{0, 1\}$) to an m-variate polynomial of individual degree d over a finite field F such that $|F| > dm + 1$ and $(d + 1)^m = N$. Intuitively, in terms of worst-case complexity, the extended function is at least as hard as f, which means that it is hard (in the worst case). The point is that the extended function is self-correctable and thus its worst-case hardness implies that it must be at least mildly hard in the average-case. Details follow.

Construction 7.11 (multivariate extension):[12] *For any function $f_n : \{0, 1\}^n \rightarrow \{0, 1\}$, a finite field F, a set $H \subset F$, and an integer m such that $|H|^m = 2^n$ and $|F| > (|H| - 1)m + 1$, we consider the function $\hat{f}_n : F^m \rightarrow F$ defined as the m-variate polynomial of individual degree $|H| - 1$ that extends $f_n : H^m \rightarrow \{0, 1\}$. That is, we identify $\{0, 1\}^n$ with H^m, and define $\hat{f}_n$ as the unique m-variate polynomial of individual degree $|H| - 1$ that satisfies $\hat{f}_n(x) = f_n(x)$ for every $x \in H^m$, where we view $\{0, 1\}$ as a subset of F.*

Note that $\hat{f}_n$ can be evaluated at any desired point, by evaluating f_n on its entire domain, and determining the unique m-variate polynomial of individual degree $|H| - 1$ that agrees with f_n on H^m (see Exercise 7.12). Thus, for $f : \{0, 1\}^* \rightarrow \{0, 1\}$ in $\mathcal{E}$, the corresponding $\hat{f}$ (defined by separately extending the restriction of f to each input length) is also in $\mathcal{E}$. For the sake of preserving various complexity measures, we wish to have $|F^m| = \text{poly}(2^n)$, which leads to setting $m = n/\log_2 n$ (yielding $|H| = n$ and $|F| = \text{poly}(n)$). In particular, in this case $\hat{f}_n$ is defined over strings of length $O(n)$. The mild average-case hardness of $\hat{f}$ follows by the foregoing discussion. In fact, we state and prove a more general result.

Theorem 7.12: *Suppose that there exists a Boolean function f in $\mathcal{E}$ having circuit complexity that is almost-everywhere greater than S. Then, there exists an exponential-time computable function $\hat{f} : \{0, 1\}^* \rightarrow \{0, 1\}^*$ such that $|\hat{f}(x)| \leq |x|$ and for every family of circuit $\{C'_{n'}\}_{n' \in \mathbb{N}}$ of size $S'(n') = S(n'/O(1))/\text{poly}(n')$ it holds that $\Pr[C'_{n'}(U_{n'}) \neq \hat{f}(U_{n'})] > (1/n')^2$. Furthermore, $\hat{f}$ does not depend on S.*

Theorem 7.12 seems to complete the first step of the proof of Theorem 7.10, except that we desire a Boolean function rather than a function that merely does not stretch its input. The extra step of obtaining a Boolean function that is $(\text{poly}(n), n^{-3})$-inapproximable is taken in Exercise 7.13.[13] Essentially, if $\hat{f}$ is hard to compute on a noticeable fraction of its inputs then the Boolean predicate that on input (x, i) returns the ith bit of $\hat{f}(x)$ must be mildly inapproximable.

Proof Sketch: Given f as in the hypothesis and for every $n \in \mathbb{N}$, we consider the restriction of f to $\{0, 1\}^n$, denoted f_n, and apply Construction 7.11 to it, while using $m = n/\log n$, $|H| = n$ and $n^2 < |F| = \text{poly}(n)$. Recall that the resulting function $\hat{f}_n$ maps strings of length $n' = \log_2 |F^m| = O(n)$ to strings of length

---

[12] The algebraic fact underlying this construction is that for any function $f : H^m \rightarrow F$ there exists a unique m-variate polynomial $\hat{f} : F^m \rightarrow F$ of individual degree $|H| - 1$ such that for every $x \in H^m$ it holds that $\hat{f}(x) = f(x)$. This polynomial is called a multivariate polynomial extension of f, and it can be found in $\text{poly}(|H|^m \log |F|)$-time. For details, see Exercise 7.12.

[13] A quantitatively stronger bound can be obtained by noting that the proof of Theorem 7.12 actually establishes an error lower bound of $\Omega((\log n')/(n')^2)$ and that $|\hat{f}(x)| = O(\log |x|)$.

$\log_2 |F| = O(\log n)$. Following the foregoing discussion, we shall show that circuits that approximate $\hat{f}_n$ too well yield circuits that compute f_n correctly on each input. Using the hypothesis regarding the size of the latter, we shall derive a lower bound on the size of the former. The actual (reducibility) argument proceeds as follows. We fix an arbitrary circuit $C'_{n'}$ that satisfies

$$\Pr[C'_{n'}(U_{n'}) = \hat{f}_n(U_{n'})] \geq 1 - (1/n')^2 > 1 - (1/3t), \qquad (7.9)$$

where $t \overset{\text{def}}{=} (|H| - 1)m + 1 = o(n^2)$ exceeds the total degree of $\hat{f}_n$. Using the self-correction feature of $\hat{f}_n$, we observe that by making t oracle calls to $C'_{n'}$ we can probabilistically recover the value of ($\hat{f}_n$ and thus of) f_n on each input, with probability at least $2/3$. Using error reduction and (non-uniform) derandomization as in the proof of Theorem 6.3,[14] we obtain a circuit of size $n^3 \cdot |C'_{n'}|$ that computes f_n. By the hypothesis $n^3 \cdot |C'_{n'}| > S(n)$, and so $|C'_{n'}| > S(n'/O(1))/\text{poly}(n')$. Recalling that $C'_{n'}$ is an arbitrary circuit that satisfies Eq. (7.9), the theorem follows. $\qquad \square$

Digest. The proof of Theorem 7.12 is actually a worst-case to average-case reduction. That is, the proof consists of a self-correction procedure that allows for the evaluation of f at any desired n-bit long point, using oracle calls to any circuit that computes $\hat{f}$ correctly on a $1 - (1/n')^2$ fraction of the n'-bit long inputs. We recall that if $f \in \mathcal{E}$ then $\hat{f} \in \mathcal{E}$, but we do not know how to preserve the complexity of f in case it is in $\mathcal{NP}$. (Various indications to the difficulty of a worst-case to average-case reduction for $\mathcal{NP}$ are known; see, e.g., [43].)

We mention that the ideas underlying the proof of Theorem 7.12 have been applied in a large variety of settings. For example, we shall see applications of the self-correction paradigm in §9.3.2.1 and in §9.3.2.2. Furthermore, in §9.3.2.2 we shall reencounter the very same multivariate extension used in the proof of Theorem 7.12.

7.2.1.2. Yao's XOR Lemma

Having obtained a mildly inapproximable predicate, we wish to obtain a strongly inapproximable one. The information-theoretic context provides an appealing suggestion: Suppose that X is a Boolean random variable (representing the mild inapproximability of the aforementioned predicate) that equals 1 with probability ε. Then XORing the outcome of n/ε independent samples of X yields a bit that equals 1 with probability $0.5 \pm \exp(-\Omega(n))$. It is tempting to think that the same should happen in the computational setting. That is, if f is hard to approximate correctly with probability exceeding $1 - \varepsilon$ then XORing the output of f on n/ε non-overlapping parts of the input should yield a predicate that is hard to approximate correctly with probability that is non-negligibly higher than $1/2$. The latter assertion turns out to be correct, but (even more than in Section 7.1.2) the proof of the computational phenomenon is considerably more complex than the analysis of the information-theoretic analogue.

Theorem 7.13 (Yao's XOR Lemma): *There exists a universal constant $c > 0$ such that the following holds. If, for some polynomials p_1 and p_2, the Boolean function f is*

---

[14]First, we apply the foregoing probabilistic procedure $O(n)$ times and take a majority vote. This yields a probabilistic procedure that, on input $x \in \{0, 1\}^n$, invokes $C'_{n'}$ for $o(n^3)$ times and computes $f_n(x)$ correctly with probability greater than $1 - 2^{-n}$. Finally, we just fix a sequence of random choices that is good for all 2^n possible inputs, and obtain a circuit of size $n^3 \cdot |C'_{n'}|$ that computes f_n correctly on every n-bit input.

$(p_1, 1/p_2)$-*inapproximable, then the function* $F(x_1, \ldots, x_{t(n)}) = \oplus_{i=1}^{t(n)} f(x_i)$, *where* $t(n) = n \cdot p_2(n)$ *and* $x_1, \ldots, x_{t(n)} \in \{0, 1\}^n$, *is* p'-*inapproximable for* $p'(t(n) \cdot n) = p_1(n)^c / t(n)^{1/c}$. *Furthermore, the claim also holds if the polynomials* p_1 *and* p_2 *are replaced by any integer functions.*

Combining Theorem 7.12 (and Exercise 7.13), and Theorem 7.13, we obtain a proof of Theorem 7.10. (Recall that an alternative proof is presented in §7.2.1.3.)

We note that proving Theorem 7.13 seems more difficult than proving Theorem 7.5 (i.e., the amplification of one-way functions), due to two issues. Firstly, unlike in Theorem 7.5, the computational problems are not in $\mathcal{PC}$ and thus we cannot efficiently recognize correct solutions to them. Secondly, unlike in Theorem 7.5, solutions to instances of the transformed problem do not correspond to the concatenation of solutions for the original instances, but are rather a function of the latter that loses almost all the information about the latter. The proof of Theorem 7.13 presented next deals with each of these two difficulties separately.

Several different proofs of Theorem 7.13 are known. As just stated, the proof that we present is conceptually appealing because it deals separately with two unrelated difficulties. Furthermore, this proof benefits most from the material already presented in Section 7.1. The proof proceeds in two steps:

1. First we prove that the corresponding "direct product" function $P(x_1, \ldots, x_{t(n)}) = (f(x_1), \ldots, f(x_{t(n)}))$ is difficult to compute in a strong average-case sense.
2. Next we establish the desired result by an application of Theorem 7.8.

Thus, given Theorem 7.8, our main focus is on the first step, which is of independent interest (and is thus generalized from Boolean functions to arbitrary ones).

Theorem 7.14 (the Direct Product Lemma): *Let* p_1 *and* p_2 *be two polynomials, and suppose that* $f : \{0, 1\}^* \to \{0, 1\}^*$ *is such that for every family of* p_1-*size circuits,* $\{C_n\}_{n \in \mathbb{N}}$, *and all sufficiently large* $n \in \mathbb{N}$, *it holds that* $\Pr[C_n(U_n) \neq f(U_n)] > 1/p_2(n)$. *Let* $P(x_1, \ldots, x_{t(n)}) = (f(x_1), \ldots, f(x_{t(n)}))$, *where* $x_1, \ldots, x_{t(n)} \in \{0, 1\}^n$ *and* $t(n) = n \cdot p_2(n)$. *Then, for any* $\varepsilon' : \mathbb{N} \to (0, 1]$, *setting* p' *such that* $p'(t(n) \cdot n) = p_1(n)/\text{poly}(t(n)/\varepsilon'(t(n) \cdot n))$, *it holds that every family of* p'-*size circuits,* $\{C'_m\}_{m \in \mathbb{N}}$, *satisfies* $\Pr[C'_m(U_m) = P(U_m)] < \varepsilon'(m)$. *Furthermore, the claim also holds if the polynomials* p_1 *and* p_2 *are replaced by any integer functions.*

In particular, for an adequate constant $c > 0$, selecting $\varepsilon'(t(n) \cdot n) = p_1(n)^{-c}$, we obtain $p'(t(n) \cdot n) = p_1(n)^c / t(n)^{1/c}$, and so $\varepsilon'(m) \leq 1/p'(m)$.

Deriving Theorem 7.13 from Theorem 7.14. Theorem 7.13 follows from Theorem 7.14 by considering the function $P'(x_1, \ldots, x_{t(n)}, r) = b(f(x_1) \cdots f(x_{t(n)}), r)$, where f is a Boolean function, $r \in \{0, 1\}^{t(n)}$, and $b(y, r)$ is the inner-product modulo 2 of the $t(n)$-bit long strings y and r. Note that, for the corresponding P, we have $P'(x_1, \ldots, x_{t(n)}, r) \equiv b(P(x_1, \ldots, x_{t(n)}), r)$, whereas $F(x_1, \ldots, x_{t(n)}) = P'(x_1, \ldots, x_{t(n)}, 1^{t(n)})$. Intuitively, the inapproximability of P' should follow from the strong average-case hardness of P (via Theorem 7.8), whereas it should be possible to reduce the approximation of P' to the approximation of F (and thus derive the desired inapproximability of F). Indeed, this intuition does not fail, but detailing the argument seems a bit cumbersome (and so we only provide the clues here). Assuming that f is $(p_1, 1/p_2)$-inapproximable, we first apply Theorem 7.14 (with $\varepsilon'(t(n) \cdot n) = p_1(n)^{-c}$) and then apply Theorem 7.8 (see Exercise 7.14), inferring that P' is p'-inapproximable for $p'(t(n) \cdot n) = p_1(n)^{\Omega(1)}/\text{poly}(t(n))$. The less obvious part of the argument is reducing the approximation of P' to the approximation of F. The key observation is that

$$P'(x_1, \dots, x_{t(n)}, r) = F(z_1, \dots, z_{t(n)}) \oplus \bigoplus_{i:r_i=0} f(z_i) \qquad (7.10)$$

where $z_i = x_i$ if $r_i = 1$ and is an arbitrary n-bit long string otherwise. Now, if somebody provides us with samples of the distribution $(U_n, f(U_n))$, then we can use these samples in the role of the pairs $(z_i, f(z_i))$ for the indices i that satisfy $r_i = 0$. Considering a best choice of such samples (i.e., one for which we obtain the best approximation of P'), we obtain a circuit that approximates P' (by using a circuit that approximates F and the said choices of samples). (The details are left for Exercise 7.17.) Theorem 7.13 follows.

Proving Theorem 7.14. Note that Theorem 7.14 is closely related to Theorem 7.5; see Exercise 7.20 for details. This suggests employing an analogous proof strategy, that is, converting circuits that violate the theorem's conclusion into circuits that violate the theorem's hypothesis. We note, however, that things were much simpler in the context of Theorem 7.5: There we could (efficiently) check whether or not a value contained in the output of the circuit that solves the direct-product problem constitutes a correct answer for the corresponding instance of the basic problem. Lacking such an ability in the current context, we shall have to use such values more carefully. Loosely speaking, we shall take a weighted majority vote among various answers, where the weights reflect our confidence in the correctness of the various answers.

We establish Theorem 7.14 by applying the following lemma that provides quantitative bounds on the feasibility of computing the direct product of two functions. In this lemma, $\{Y_m\}_{m \in \mathbb{N}}$ and $\{Z_m\}_{m \in \mathbb{N}}$ are independent probability ensembles such that $Y_m, Z_m \in \{0, 1\}^m$, and $X_n = (Y_{\ell(n)}, Z_{n-\ell(n)})$ for some function $\ell : \mathbb{N} \to \mathbb{N}$. The lemma refers to the success probability of computing the direct product function $F : \{0, 1\}^* \to \{0, 1\}^*$ defined by $F(yz) = (F_1(y), F_2(z))$, where $|y| = \ell(|yz|)$, when given bounds on the success probability of computing F_1 and F_2 (separately). Needless to say, these probability bounds refer to circuits of certain sizes. (The slackness parameter ε represents a deviation from an idealized result in which the probability of correctly computing F is upper-bounded by the product of the probabilities of correctly computing F_1 and F_2, where tightening this slackness (i.e., decreasing ε) comes at the cost of decreasing the size of the circuit for which the success probability bound holds.) We stress that *the lemma is not symmetric with respect to the two functions: It guarantees a stronger* (and in fact lossless) *preservation of circuit sizes for one of the functions* (which is arbitrarily chosen to be F_1).

Lemma 7.15 (Direct Product, a quantitative two-argument version): *For $\{Y_m\}$, $\{Z_m\}$, F_1, F_2, ℓ, $\{X_n\}$ and F as in the foregoing, let $\rho_1(\cdot)$ be an upper bound on the success probability of $s_1(\cdot)$-size circuits in computing F_1 over $\{Y_m\}$. That is, for every such circuit family $\{C_m\}$*

$$\Pr[C_m(Y_m) = F_1(Y_m)] \le \rho_1(m).$$

Likewise, suppose that $\rho_2(\cdot)$ is an upper bound on the probability that $s_2(\cdot)$-size circuits compute F_2 over $\{Z_m\}$. Then, for every function $\varepsilon:\mathbb{N}\to\mathbb{R}$, the function ρ defined as

$$\rho(n) \stackrel{\text{def}}{=} \rho_1(\ell(n)) \cdot \rho_2(n - \ell(n)) + \varepsilon(n)$$

is an upper bound on the probability that families of $s(\cdot)$-size circuits correctly compute F over $\{X_n\}$, where

$$s(n) \stackrel{\text{def}}{=} \min\left\{ s_1(\ell(n)), \frac{s_2(n - \ell(n))}{\text{poly}(n/\varepsilon(n))} \right\}.$$

Theorem 7.14 is derived from Lemma 7.15 by using a *careful induction*, which capitalizes on the highly quantitative form of Lemma 7.15 and in particular on the fact that no loss is incurred for one of the two functions that are used. We first detail this argument, and next establish Lemma 7.15 itself.

Deriving Theorem 7.14 from Lemma 7.15. We write $P(x_1, x_2, \ldots, x_{t(n)})$ as $P^{(t(n))}(x_1, x_2, \ldots, x_{t(n)})$, where $P^{(i)}(x_1, \ldots, x_i) = (f(x_1), \ldots, f(x_i))$ and $P^{(i)}(x_1, \ldots, x_i) \equiv (P^{(i-1)}(x_1, \ldots, x_{i-1}), f(x_i))$. For any function ε, *we shall prove by induction on i that circuits of size $s(n) = p_1(n)/\text{poly}(t(n)/\varepsilon(n))$ cannot compute $P^{(i)}(U_{i\cdot n})$ with success probability greater than* $(1 - (1/p_2(n)))^i + (i - 1) \cdot \varepsilon(n)$, where p_1 and p_2 are as in Theorem 7.14. Thus, no $s(n)$-size circuit can compute $P^{(t(n))}(U_{t(n)\cdot n})$ with success probability greater than $(1 - (1/p_2(n)))^{t(n)} + (t(n) - 1) \cdot \varepsilon(n) = \exp(-n) + (t(n) - 1) \cdot \varepsilon(n)$. Recalling that this is established for any function ε, Theorem 7.14 follows (by using $\varepsilon(n) = \varepsilon'(t(n) \cdot n)/t(n)$, and observing that the setting $s(n) = p'(t(n) \cdot n)$ satisfies $s(n) = p_1(n)/\text{poly}(t(n)/\varepsilon(n))$).

Turning to the induction itself, we first note that its basis (i.e., $i = 1$) is guaranteed by the theorem's hypothesis (i.e., the hypothesis of Theorem 7.14 regarding f). The induction step (i.e., from i to $i + 1$) will be proved by using Lemma 7.15 with $F_1 = P^{(i)}$ and $F_2 = f$, along with the parameter setting $\rho_1^{(i)}(i \cdot n) = (1 - (1/p_2(n)))^i + (i - 1) \cdot \varepsilon(n)$, $s_1^{(i)}(i \cdot n) = s(n)$, $\rho_2^{(i)}(n) = 1 - (1/p_2(n))$ and $s_2^{(i)}(n) = \text{poly}(n/\varepsilon(n)) \cdot s(n) = p_1(n)$. Details follow.

Note that the induction hypothesis (regarding $P^{(i)}$) implies that F_1 satisfies the hypothesis of Lemma 7.15 (wrt size $s_1^{(i)}$ and success rate $\rho_1^{(i)}$), whereas the theorem's hypothesis regarding f implies that F_2 satisfies the hypothesis of Lemma 7.15 (wrt size $s_2^{(i)}$ and success rate $\rho_2^{(i)}$). Thus, $F = P^{(i+1)}$ satisfies the lemma's conclusion with respect to circuits of size $\min(s_1^{(i)}(i \cdot n), s_2^{(i)}(n)/\text{poly}(n/\varepsilon(n))) = s(n)$ and success rate $\rho_1^{(i)}(i \cdot n) \cdot \rho_2^{(i)}(n) + \varepsilon(n)$ which is upper-bounded by $(1 - (1/p_2(n)))^{i+1} + i \cdot \varepsilon(n)$. This completes the induction step.

We stress the fact that we used induction for a non-constant number of steps, and that this was enabled by the highly quantitative form of the inductive claim and the small loss incurred by the inductive step. Specifically, the size bound did not decrease during the induction (although we could afford a small additive loss in each step, but not a constant factor loss).[15] Likewise, the success rate suffered an additive increase of $\varepsilon(n)$ in each

[15]Note that if we had $s(n) = \min\{s_1(\ell(n)), s_2(n - \ell(n))\}/2$ (in Lemma 7.15) then the foregoing argument would yield that $P^{(i+1)}$ is hard for circuits of size $s_1^{(i+1)}$ such that $s_1^{(i+1)}((i + 1) \cdot n) = \min\{s_1^{(i)}(i \cdot n), s_2(n)\}/2$, which would yield a meaningless result for $P = P^{(t(n))}$ (since $s_1^{(t(n))}(t(n) \cdot n) = \min\{p_1(n), p_2(n)\}/2^{t(n)}$, where $t(n) \gg n$ and $p_i(n) < 2^n$).

step, which was accommodated by the inductive claim. Thus, *assuming the correctness of Lemma 7.15, we have established Theorem 7.14.* $\qquad\square$

Proof of Lemma 7.15: Proceeding (as usual) by the contra-positive, we consider a family of $s(\cdot)$-size circuits $\{C_n\}_{n\in\mathbb{N}}$ that violates the lemma's conclusion; that is, $\Pr[C_n(X_n) = F(X_n)] > \rho(n)$. We will show how to use such circuits in order to obtain either circuits that violate the lemma's hypothesis regarding F_1 or circuits that violate the lemma's hypothesis regarding F_2. Toward this end, it is instructive to write the success probability of C_n in a conditional form, while denoting the ith output of $C_n(x)$ by $C_n(x)_i$ (i.e., $C_n(x) = (C_n(x)_1, C_n(x)_2)$):

$$\Pr[C_n(Y_{\ell(n)}, Z_{n-\ell(n)}) = F(Y_{\ell(n)}, Z_{n-\ell(n)})]$$
$$= \Pr[C_n(Y_{\ell(n)}, Z_{n-\ell(n)})_1 = F_1(Y_{\ell(n)})]$$
$$\cdot \Pr[C_n(Y_{\ell(n)}, Z_{n-\ell(n)})_2 = F_2(Z_{n-\ell(n)}) \mid C_n(Y_{\ell(n)}, Z_{n-\ell(n)})_1 = F_1(Y_{\ell(n)})].$$

The basic idea is that if the first factor is greater than $\rho_1(\ell(n))$ then we immediately derive a circuit (i.e., $C_n'(y) = C_n(y, Z_{n-\ell(n)})_1$) contradicting the lemma's hypothesis regarding F_1, whereas if the second factor is significantly greater than $\rho_2(n - \ell(n))$ then we can obtain a circuit contradicting the lemma's hypothesis regarding F_2. The treatment of the latter case is indeed not obvious. The idea is that a sufficiently large sample of $(Y_{\ell(n)}, F_1(Y_{\ell(n)}))$, which may be hard-wired into the circuit, allows for using the conditional probability space (in such a circuit) toward an attempt to approximate F_2. That is, on input z, we select uniformly a string y satisfying $C_n(y, z)_1 = F_1(y)$ (from the aforementioned sample), and output $C_n(y, z)_2$. For a fixed z, sampling of the conditional space (i.e., y's satisfying $C_n(y, z)_1 = F_1(y)$) is possible provided that $\Pr[C_n(Y_{\ell(n)}, z)_1 = F_1(Y_{\ell(n)})]$ holds with noticeable probability. The last caveat motivates a separate treatment of z's having a noticeable value of $\Pr[C_n(Y_{\ell(n)}, z)_1 = F_1(Y_{\ell(n)})]$ and of the rest of z's (which are essentially ignored). Details follow.

Let us first simplify the notations by fixing a generic n and using the abbreviations $C = C_n, \varepsilon = \varepsilon(n), \ell = \ell(n), Y = Y_\ell$, and $Z = Y_{n-\ell}$. We call z good if $\Pr[C(Y, z)_1 = F_1(Y)] \geq \varepsilon/2$ and let G be the set of good z's. Next, rather than considering the event $C(Y, Z) = F(Y, Z)$, we consider the combined event $C(Y, Z) = F(Y, Z) \wedge Z \in G$, which occurs with almost the same probability (up to an additive error term of $\varepsilon/2$). This is the case because, for any $z \notin G$, it holds that

$$\Pr[C(Y, z) = F(Y, z)] \leq \Pr[C(Y, z)_1 = F_1(Y)] < \varepsilon/2$$

and thus z's that are not good do not contribute much to $\Pr[C(Y, Z) = F(Y, Z)]$; that is, $\Pr[C(Y, Z) = F(Y, Z) \wedge Z \in G]$ is lower-bounded by $\Pr[C(Y, Z) = F(Y, Z)] - \varepsilon/2$. Using $\Pr[C(Y, z) = F(Y, z)] > \rho(n) = \rho_1(\ell) \cdot \rho_2(n - \ell) + \varepsilon$, we have

$$\Pr[C(Y, Z) = F(Y, Z) \wedge Z \in G] > \rho_1(\ell) \cdot \rho_2(n - \ell) + \frac{\varepsilon}{2}. \qquad (7.11)$$

We proceed according to the foregoing outline, first showing that if $\Pr[C(Y, Z)_1 = F_1(Y)] > \rho_1(\ell)$ then we immediately derive circuits violating the hypothesis concerning F_1. Actually, we prove something stronger (which we will need for the other case).

Claim 7.15.1: For every z, it holds that $\Pr[C(Y, z)_1 = F_1(Y)] \leq \rho_1(\ell)$.

Proof: Otherwise, using any $z \in \{0, 1\}^{n-\ell}$ that satisfies $\Pr[C(Y, z)_1 = F_1(Y)] > \rho_1(\ell)$, we obtain a circuit $C'(y) \stackrel{\text{def}}{=} C(y, z)_1$ that contradicts the lemma's hypothesis concerning F_1. $\qquad\square$

Using Claim 7.15.1, we show how to obtain a circuit that violates the lemma's hypothesis concerning F_2, and in doing so we complete the proof of the lemma.

Claim 7.15.2: There exists a circuit C'' of size $s_2(n - \ell)$ such that

$$\Pr[C''(Z) = F_2(Z)] \geq \frac{\Pr[C(Y, Z) = F(Y, Z) \wedge Z \in G]}{\rho_1(\ell)} - \frac{\varepsilon}{2}$$

$$> \rho_2(n - \ell)$$

Proof: The second inequality is due to Eq. (7.11), and thus we focus on establishing the first inequality. We construct the circuit C'' as suggested in the foregoing outline. Specifically, we take a $\text{poly}(n/\varepsilon)$-large sample, denoted S, from the distribution $(Y, F_1(Y))$ and let $C''(z) \stackrel{\text{def}}{=} C(y, z)_2$, where (y, v) is uniformly selected among the elements of S for which $C(y, z)_1 = v$ holds. Details follow.

Let m be a sufficiently large number that is upper-bounded by a polynomial in n/ε, and consider a random sequence of m pairs, generated by taking m independent samples from the distribution $(Y, F_1(Y))$. We stress that we do not assume here that such a sample, denoted S, can be produced by an efficient (uniform) algorithm (but, jumping ahead, we remark that such a sequence can be fixed non-uniformly). For each $z \in G \subseteq \{0, 1\}^{n-\ell}$, we denote by S_z the set of pairs $(y, v) \in S$ for which $C(y, z)_1 = v$. Note that S_z is a random sample of the residual probability space defined by $(Y, F_1(Y))$ conditioned on $C(Y, z)_1 = F_1(Y)$. Also, with overwhelmingly high probability, $|S_z| = \Omega(n/\varepsilon^2)$, because $z \in G$ implies $\Pr[C(Y, z)_1 = F_1(Y)] \geq \varepsilon/2$ and $m = \Omega(n/\varepsilon^3)$.[16] Thus, for each $z \in G$, with overwhelming probability (taken over the choices of S), the sample S_z provides a good approximation of the conditional probability space.[17] In particular, with probability greater than $1 - 2^{-n}$, it holds that

$$\frac{|\{(y, v) \in S_z : C(y, z)_2 = F_2(z)\}|}{|S_z|} \geq \Pr[C(Y, z)_2 = F_2(z) \mid C(Y, z)_1 = F_1(Y)] - \frac{\varepsilon}{2}.$$

$$(7.12)$$

Thus, with positive probability, Eq. (7.12) holds for all $z \in G \subseteq \{0, 1\}^{n-\ell}$. The circuit C'' computing F_2 is now defined as follows. The circuit will contain a set $S = \{(y_i, v_i) : i = 1, \ldots, m\}$ (i.e., S is "hard-wired" into the circuit C'') such that the following two conditions hold:

1. For every $i \in [m]$ it holds that $v_i = F_1(y_i)$.
2. For each good z the set $S_z = \{(y, v) \in S : C(y, z)_1 = v\}$ satisfies Eq. (7.12).

(In particular, S_z is not empty for any good z.)

---

[16] Note that the expected size of S_z is $m \cdot \varepsilon/2 = \Omega(n/\varepsilon^2)$. Using the Chernoff Bound, we get $\Pr_S[|S_z| < m\varepsilon/4] = \exp(-\Omega(n/\varepsilon^2)) < 2^{-n}$.

[17] For $T_z = \{y : C(y, z)_1 = F_1(y)\}$, we are interested in a sample S' of T_z such that $|\{y \in S' : C(y, z)_2 = F_2(z)\}|/|S'|$ approximates $\Pr[C(Y, z)_2 = F_2(z) \mid Y \in T_z]$ up to an additive term of $\varepsilon/2$. Using the Chernoff Bound again, we note that a random $S' \subset T_z$ of size $\Omega(n/\varepsilon^2)$ provides such an approximation with probability greater than $1 - 2^{-n}$.

On input z, the circuit C'' first determines the set S_z, by running C for m times and checking, for each $i = 1, \ldots, m$, whether or not $C(y_i, z) = v_i$. In case S_z is empty, the circuit returns an arbitrary value. Otherwise, the circuit selects uniformly a pair $(y, v) \in S_z$ and outputs $C(y, z)_2$. (The latter random choice can be eliminated by an averaging argument; see Exercise 7.16.) Using the definition of C'' and Eq. (7.12), we have:

$$\Pr[C''(Z) = F_2(Z)] \geq \sum_{z \in G} \Pr[Z = z] \cdot \Pr[C''(z) = F_2(z)]$$

$$= \sum_{z \in G} \Pr[Z = z] \cdot \frac{|\{(y, v) \in S_z : C(y, z)_2 = F_2(z)\}|}{|S_z|}$$

$$\geq \sum_{z \in G} \Pr[Z = z] \cdot \left(\Pr[C(Y, z)_2 = F_2(z) \mid C(Y, z)_1 = F_1(Y)] - \frac{\varepsilon}{2} \right)$$

$$= \sum_{z \in G} \Pr[Z = z] \cdot \left(\frac{\Pr[C(Y, z)_2 = F_2(z) \wedge C(Y, z)_1 = F_1(Y)]}{\Pr[C(Y, z)_1 = F_1(Y)]} - \frac{\varepsilon}{2} \right)$$

Next, using Claim 7.15.1, we have:

$$\Pr[C''(Z) = F_2(Z)] \geq \left(\sum_{z \in G} \Pr[Z = z] \cdot \frac{\Pr[C(Y, z) = F(Y, z)]}{\rho_1(\ell)} \right) - \frac{\varepsilon}{2}$$

$$= \frac{\Pr[C(Y, Z) = F(Y, Z) \wedge Z \in G]}{\rho_1(\ell)} - \frac{\varepsilon}{2}$$

Finally, using Eq. (7.11), the claim follows. $\qquad \square$

This completes the proof of the lemma. $\qquad \blacksquare$

Comments. Firstly, we wish to call attention to the care with which an inductive argument needs to be carried out in the computational setting, especially when a non-constant number of inductive steps is concerned. Indeed, our inductive proof of Theorem 7.14 involves invoking a quantitative lemma (i.e., Lemma 7.15) that allows for keeping track of the relevant quantities (e.g., success probability and circuit size) throughout the induction process. Secondly, we mention that Lemma 7.15 (as well as Theorem 7.14) has a uniform complexity version that assumes that one can efficiently sample the distribution $(Y_{\ell(n)}, F_1(Y_{\ell(n)}))$ (resp., $(U_n, f(U_n))$). For details see [102]. Indeed, a good lesson from the proof of Lemma 7.15 is that non-uniform circuits can "effectively sample" any distribution. Lastly, we mention that Theorem 7.5 (the amplification of one-way functions) and Theorem 7.13 (Yao's XOR Lemma) also have (tight) quantitative versions (see, e.g., [91, Sec. 2.3.2] and [102, Sec. 3], respectively).

7.2.1.3. List Decoding and Hardness Amplification

Recall that Theorem 7.10 was proved in §7.2.1.1–7.2.1.2, by first constructing a mildly inapproximable predicate via Construction 7.11, and then amplifying its hardness via Yao's XOR Lemma. In this subsection we show that the construction used in the first step (i.e., Construction 7.11) actually yields a strongly inapproximable predicate. Thus, we provide an alternative proof of Theorem 7.10. Specifically, we show that a strongly inapproximable predicate (as asserted in Theorem 7.10) can be obtained by combining Construction 7.11

(with a suitable choice of parameters) and the inner-product construction (of Theorem 7.8). The main ingredient of this argument is captured by the following result.

> **Proposition 7.16:** *Suppose that there exists a Boolean function f in $\mathcal{E}$ having circuit complexity that is almost-everywhere greater than S, and let $\varepsilon : \mathbb{N} \to [0, 1]$ satisfying $\varepsilon(n) > 2^{-n}$. Let f_n be the restriction of f to $\{0, 1\}^n$, and let $\hat{f}_n$ be the function obtained from f_n when applying Construction 7.11[18] with $|H| = n/\varepsilon(n)$ and $|F| = |H|^3$. Then, the function $\hat{f} : \{0, 1\}^* \to \{0, 1\}^*$, defined by $\hat{f}(x) = \hat{f}_{|x|/3}(x)$, is computable in exponential time and for every family of circuit $\{C'_{n'}\}_{n' \in \mathbb{N}}$ of size $S'(n') = \text{poly}(\varepsilon(n'/3)/n') \cdot S(n'/3)$ it holds that $\Pr[C'_{n'}(U_{n'}) = \hat{f}(U_{n'})] < \varepsilon'(n') \stackrel{\text{def}}{=} \varepsilon(n'/3)$.*

Before turning to the proof of Proposition 7.16, let us describe how it yields an alternative proof of Theorem 7.10. Firstly, for some $\gamma > 0$, Proposition 7.16 yields an exponential-time computable function $\hat{f}$ such that $|\hat{f}(x)| \leq |x|$ and for every family of circuit $\{C'_{n'}\}_{n' \in \mathbb{N}}$ of size $S'(n') = S(n'/3)^{\gamma}/\text{poly}(n')$ it holds that $\Pr[C'_{n'}(U_{n'}) = \hat{f}(U_{n'})] < 1/S'(n')$. Combining this with Theorem 7.8 (cf. Exercise 7.14), we infer that $P(x, r) = b(\hat{f}(x), r)$, where $|r| = |\hat{f}(x)| \leq |x|$, is S''-inapproximable for $S''(n'') = S'(n''/2)^{\Omega(1)}/\text{poly}(n'')$. In particular, for every polynomial p, we obtain a p-inapproximable predicate in $\mathcal{E}$ by applying the foregoing with $S(n) = \text{poly}(n, p(n))$. Thus, Theorem 7.10 follows.

Teaching note: The following material is very advanced and is best left for independent reading. Furthermore, its understanding requires being comfortable with basic notions of error-correcting codes (as presented in Appendix E.1.1).

Proposition 7.16 is proved by observing that the transformation of f_n to $\hat{f}_n$ constitutes a "strong" code and that any such code provides a worst-case to (strongly) average-case reduction. For starters, we note that the mapping $f_n \mapsto \hat{f}_n$ is closely related to the Reed-Muller code (see §E.1.2.4), whereas we already saw a connection between "hardness amplification" and coding theory (see discussion at the end of Section 7.1.3). In the current context (of reducing the worst-case computation of f_n to an average-case computation of $\hat{f}_n$), we seek a relatively small circuit that computes f_n (correctly on each input) when given oracle access to any function f' that agrees with $\hat{f}_n$ on a sufficiently large fraction of the domain. Actually, we may relax the requirement by (switching the order of quantifiers and) allowing the small (oracle-aided) circuit to depend on f' (as well as on f_n), because f' represents some small circuit that violates the average-case complexity requirement with respect to $\hat{f}_n$ (and so the combined circuit will violate the worst-case hypothesis regarding f_n). Furthermore, wanting $f_n \in \mathcal{E}$ to imply $\hat{f}_n \in \mathcal{E}$, we wish the mapping $f_n \mapsto \hat{f}_n$ to be computable in time $2^{O(n)} = \text{poly}(|f_n|)$. These considerations lead to the following definition of a class of codes, which contain the encoding that underlies the foregoing mapping $f_n \mapsto \hat{f}_n$.

---

[18]Recall that in Construction 7.11 we have $|H|^m = 2^n$, which may yield a non-integer m if we insist on $|H| = n/\varepsilon(n)$. This problem was avoided in the proof of Theorem 7.12 (where $|H| = n$ was used), but is more acute in the current context because of ε (e.g., we may have $\varepsilon(n) = 2^{-2n/7}$). Thus, we should either relax the requirement $|H|^m = 2^n$ (e.g., allow $2^n \leq |H|^m < 2^{2n}$) or relax the requirement $|H| = n/\varepsilon(n)$. However, for the sake of simplicity, we ignore this issue in the presentation.

Definition 7.17 (efficient codes supporting implicit decoding): *For fixed functions* $q, \ell : \mathbb{N} \to \mathbb{N}$ *and* $\alpha : \mathbb{N} \to (0, 1]$, *the mapping* $\Gamma : \{0, 1\}^* \to \{0, 1\}^*$ *is said to be* efficient and supports implicit decoding *with parameters* q, ℓ, α *if it satisfies the following two conditions:*

1. Encoding (or efficiency): *The mapping* Γ *is polynomial-time computable.*

   It is instructive to view Γ *as mapping N-bit long strings to sequences of length* $\ell(N)$ *over* $[q(N)]$, *and to view each* (codeword) $\Gamma(x) \in [q(|x|)]^{\ell(|x|)}$ *as a mapping from* $[\ell(|x|)]$ *to* $[q(|x|)]$.

2. Decoding (in implicit form): *There exists a polynomial p such that the following holds. For every* $w : [\ell(N)] \to [q(N)]$ *and every* $x \in \{0, 1\}^N$ *such that* $\Gamma(x)$ *is* $(1 - \alpha(N))$-*close to w, there exists an oracle-aided[19] circuit C of size* $p((\log N)/\alpha(N))$ *such that, for every* $i \in [N]$, *it holds that $C^w(i)$ equals the ith bit of x.*

The encoding condition implies that ℓ is polynomially bounded. The decoding condition refers to any Γ-codeword that agrees with the oracle $w : [\ell(N)] \to [q(N)]$ on an $\alpha(N)$ fraction of the $\ell(N)$ coordinates, *where $\alpha(N)$ may be very small*. We highlight the non-triviality of the decoding condition: There are N bits of information in x, while the circuit C may "encode" only $p((\log N)/\alpha(N))$ bits of information about x. Thus, x is (implicitly) recovered by C based mainly on a highly corrupted version of $\Gamma(x)$. Furthermore, each desired bit of x is recovered (by C) by making at most $p((\log N)/\alpha(N))$ queries to this corrupted version of $\Gamma(x)$. We mention that the foregoing decoding condition is related to list decoding (as defined in Appendix E.1.1).[20]

Let us now relate the transformation of f_n to $\hat{f}_n$, which underlies Proposition 7.16, to Definition 7.17. We view f_n as a binary string of length $N = 2^n$ (representing the truth table of $f_n : H^m \to \{0, 1\}$) and analogously view $\hat{f}_n : F^m \to F$ as an element of $F^{|F|^m} = F^{N^3}$ (or as a mapping from $[N^3]$ to $[|F|]$).[21] Recall that the transformation of f_n to $\hat{f}_n$ is efficient. We mention that *this transformation also supports implicit decoding with parameters* q, ℓ, α such that $\ell(N) = N^3$, $\alpha(N) = \varepsilon(n)$, and $q(N) = (n/\varepsilon(n))^3$, where $N = 2^n$. The latter fact is highly non-trivial, but establishing it is beyond the scope of the current text (and the interested reader is referred to [218]).

We mention that the transformation of f_n to $\hat{f}_n$ enjoys additional features, which are not required in Definition 7.17 and will not be used in the current context. For example, there are at most $O(1/\alpha(2^n)^2)$ codewords (i.e., $\hat{f}_n$'s) that are $(1 - \alpha(2^n))$-close to any fixed $w : [\ell(2^n)] \to [q(2^n)]$, and the corresponding oracle-aided circuits can

---

[19] Oracle-aided circuits are defined analogously to oracle Turing machines. Alternatively, we may consider here oracle machines that take advice such that both the advice length and the machine's running time are upper-bounded by $p((\log N)/\alpha(N))$. The relevant oracles may be viewed either as blocks of binary strings that encode sequences over $[q(N)]$ or as sequences over $[q(N)]$. Indeed, in the latter case we consider non-binary oracles, which return elements in $[q(N)]$.

[20] Recall that, on input $w \in [q(N)]^{\ell(N)}$, a list-decoding algorithm for $\Gamma : \{0, 1\}^N \to [q(N)]^{\ell(N)}$ is required to output the list L_w containing *every* string $x \in \{0, 1\}^N$ such that $\Gamma(x)$ agrees with w on $\alpha(N)$ fraction of the locations. Turning to the foregoing decoding condition (of Definition 7.17), note that it requires outputting (bits of) one *specific* string $x \in L_w$. This can be obtained by hard-wiring (in the list-decoding circuit) the *index* of x in L_w, while taking advantage of the fact that the circuit may depend on x and w. Note, however, that the circuit obtained in this way may not satisfy the stringent decoding condition of Definition 7.17, which requires a circuit of $p((\log N)/\alpha(N))$-size. On the other hand, the decoding condition does not refer to the complexity of obtaining the aforementioned oracle-aided circuits (and, in particular, may not yield a list-decoding algorithm).

[21] Recall that $N = 2^n = |H|^m$ and $|F| = |H|^3$. Hence, $|F|^m = N^3$.

---

be constructed in probabilistic $p(n/\alpha(2^n))$-time.[22] These results are termed "list decoding with implicit representations" (and we refer the interested reader again to [218]).

Our focus is on showing that efficient codes that supports implicit decoding suffice for worst-case to (strongly) average-case reductions. We state and prove a general result, noting that in the special case of Proposition 7.16 $g_n = \hat{f}_n$ (and $\ell(2^n) = 2^{3n}$).

Theorem 7.18: *Suppose that there exists a Boolean function f in $\mathcal{E}$ having circuit complexity that is almost-everywhere greater than S, and let $\varepsilon : \mathbb{N} \to (0, 1]$. Consider a polynomial $\ell : \mathbb{N} \to \mathbb{N}$ such that $n \mapsto \log_2 \ell(2^n)$ is a 1-1 map of the integers, and let $m(n) = \log_2 \ell(2^n)$; e.g., if $\ell(N) = N^3$ then $m(n) = 3n$. Suppose that the mapping $\Gamma : \{0, 1\}^* \to \{0, 1\}^*$ is efficient and supports implicit decoding with parameters q, ℓ, α such that $\alpha(N) = \varepsilon(\lfloor \log_2 N \rfloor)$. Define $g_n : [\ell(2^n)] \to [q(2^n)]$ such that $g_n(i)$ equals the ith element of $\Gamma(\langle f_n \rangle) \in [q(2^n)]^{\ell(2^n)}$, where $\langle f_n \rangle$ denotes the 2^n-bit long description of the truth table of f_n. Then, the function $g : \{0, 1\}^* \to \{0, 1\}^*$, defined by $g(z) = g_{m^{-1}(|z|)}(z)$, is computable in exponential time and for every family of circuit $\{C'_{n'}\}_{n' \in \mathbb{N}}$ of size $S'(n') = \text{poly}(\varepsilon(m^{-1}(n'))/n') \cdot S(m^{-1}(n'))$ it holds that $\Pr[C'_{n'}(U_{n'}) = g(U_{n'})] < \varepsilon'(n') \overset{\text{def}}{=} \varepsilon(m^{-1}(n'))$.*

Proof Sketch: First note that we can generate the truth table of f_n in exponential time, and by the encoding condition of Γ it follows that g_n can be evaluated in exponential time. The average-case hardness of g is established via a reducibility argument as follows. We consider a circuit $C' = C'_{n'}$ of size S' such that $\Pr[C'_{n'}(U_{n'}) = g(U_{n'})] < \varepsilon'(n')$, let $n = m^{-1}(n')$, and recall that $\varepsilon'(n') = \varepsilon(n) = \alpha(2^n)$. Then, $C' : \{0, 1\}^{n'} \to \{0, 1\}$ (viewed as a function) is $(1 - \alpha(2^n))$-close to the function g_n, which in turn equals $\Gamma(\langle f_n \rangle)$. The decoding condition of Γ asserts that we can recover each bit of $\langle f_n \rangle$ (i.e., evaluate f_n) by an oracle-aided circuit D of size $p(n/\alpha(2^n))$ that uses (the function) C' as an oracle. Combining (the circuit C') with the oracle-aided circuit D, we obtain a (standard) circuit of size $p(n/\alpha(2^n)) \cdot S'(n') < S(n)$ that computes f_n. The theorem follows (i.e., the violation of the conclusion regarding g implies the violation of the hypothesis regarding f). $\square$

Advanced comment. For simplicity, we formulated Definition 7.17 in a crude manner that suffices for proving Proposition 7.16, where $q(N) = ((\log_2 N)/\alpha(N))^3$. The issue is the existence of codes that satisfy Definition 7.17: In general, such codes may exist only when using a more careful formulation of the decoding condition that refers to codewords that are $(1 - ((1/q(N)) + \alpha(N)))$-close to the oracle $w : [\ell(N)] \to [q(N)]$ rather than being $(1 - \alpha(N))$-close to it.[23] Needless to say, the difference is insignificant in the case that

---

[22]The construction may yield also oracle-aided circuits that compute the decoding of codewords that are almost $(1 - \alpha(2^n))$-close to w. That is, there exists a probabilistic $p(n/\alpha(2^n))$-time algorithm that outputs a list of circuits that, with high probability, contains an oracle-aided circuit for the decoding of each codeword that is $(1 - \alpha(2^n))$-close to w. Furthermore, with high probability, the list contains only circuits that decode codewords that are $(1 - \alpha(2^n)/2)$-close to w.

[23]Note that this is the "right" formulation, because in the case that $\alpha(N) < 1/q(N)$ it seems impossible to satisfy the decoding condition (as stated in Definition 7.17). Specifically, a random $\ell(N)$-sequence over $[q(N)]$ is expected to be $(1 - (1/q(N)))$-close to any fixed codeword, and with overwhelmingly high probability it will be $(1 - ((1 - o(1))/q(N)))$-close to almost all the codewords, provided $\ell(N) \gg q(N)^2$. But in case $N > \text{poly}(q(N))$,

---

269

$\alpha(N) \gg 1/q(N)$ (as in Proposition 7.16), but it is significant in case we care about binary codes (i.e., $q(N) = 2$, or codes over other small alphabets). We mention that Theorem 7.18 can be adapted to this context (of $q(N) = 2$), and directly yields strongly inapproximable predicates. For details, see Exercise 7.21.

7.2.2. Amplification with Respect to Exponential-Size Circuits

For the purpose of stronger derandomization of $\mathcal{BPP}$, we start with a stronger assumption regarding the worst-case circuit complexity of $\mathcal{E}$ and turn it to a stronger inapproximability result.

> **Theorem 7.19:** *Suppose that there exists a Boolean function f in $\mathcal{E}$ having almost-everywhere exponential circuit complexity; that is, there exists a constant $b > 0$ such that, for all but finitely many n's, any circuit that correctly computes f on $\{0, 1\}^n$ has size at least $2^{b \cdot n}$. Then, for some constant $c > 0$ and $T(n) \overset{\text{def}}{=} 2^{c \cdot n}$, there exists a T-inapproximable Boolean function in $\mathcal{E}$.*

Theorem 7.19 can be used for deriving a full derandomization of $\mathcal{BPP}$ (i.e., $\mathcal{BPP} = \mathcal{P}$) under the aforementioned assumption (see Part 1 of Theorem 8.19).

Theorem 7.19 follows as a special case of Proposition 7.16 (combined with Theorem 7.8; see Exercise 7.22). An alternative proof, which uses different ideas that are of independent interest, will be briefly reviewed next. The starting point of the latter proof is a mildly inapproximable predicate, as provided by Theorem 7.12. However, here we cannot afford to apply Yao's XOR Lemma (i.e., Theorem 7.13), because the latter relates the size of circuits that *strongly* fail to approximate a predicate defined over poly(n)-bit long strings to the size of circuits that fail to *mildly* approximate a predicate defined over n-bit long strings. That is, Yao's XOR Lemma asserts that if $f : \{0, 1\}^n \to \{0, 1\}$ is mildly inapproximable by S_f-size circuits then $F : \{0, 1\}^{\text{poly}(n)} \to \{0, 1\}$ is strongly inapproximable by S_F-size circuits, where $S_F(\text{poly}(n))$ is polynomially related to $S_f(n)$. In particular, $S_F(\text{poly}(n)) < S_f(n)$ seems inherent in this reasoning. For the case of polynomial lower bounds, this is good enough (i.e., if S_f can be an arbitrarily large polynomial then so can S_F), but for $S_f(n) = \exp(\Omega(n))$ we cannot obtain $S_F(m) = \exp(\Omega(m))$ (but rather only obtain $S_F(m) = \exp(m^{\Omega(1)})$).

The source of trouble is that amplification of inapproximability was achieved by taking a polynomial number of independent instances. Indeed, we cannot hope to amplify hardness without applying f on many instances, but these instances need not be independent. Thus, the idea is to define $F(r) = \oplus_{i=1}^{\text{poly}(n)} f(x_i)$, where $x_1, \ldots, x_{\text{poly}(n)} \in \{0, 1\}^n$ are generated from r and still $|r| = O(n)$. That is, we seek a "derandomized" version of Yao's XOR Lemma. In other words, we seek a "pseudorandom generator" of a type appropriate for expanding r to dependent x_i's such that the XOR of the $f(x_i)$'s is as inapproximable as it would have been for independent x_i's.[24]

---

we cannot hope to recover almost all N-bit long strings based on poly($q(N) \log N$) bits of advice (per each of them).

[24]Indeed, this falls within the general paradigm discussed in Section 8.1. Furthermore, this suggestion provides another perspective on the connection between randomness and computational difficulty, which is the focus of much discussion in Chapter 8 (see, e.g., §8.2.7.2).

Teaching note: In continuation of footnote 24, we note that there is a strong connection between the rest of this section and Chapter 8. On top of the aforementioned conceptual aspect, we will use technical tools from Chapter 8 toward establishing the derandomized version of the XOR Lemma. These tools include pairwise independence generators (see Section 8.5.1), random walks on expanders (see Section 8.5.3), and the Nisan-Wigderson Construction (Construction 8.17). Indeed, recall that Section 7.2.2 is advanced material, which is best left for independent reading.

The pivot of the proof is the notion of a hard region of a Boolean function. Loosely speaking, S is a hard region of a Boolean function f if f is *strongly inapproximable on a random input in S*; that is, for every (relatively) small circuit C_n, it holds that $\Pr[C_n(U_n) = f(U_n)|U_n \in S] \approx 1/2$. By definition, $\{0, 1\}^*$ is a hard region of any *strongly* inapproximable predicate. As we shall see, any *mildly* inapproximable predicate has a hard region of density related to its inapproximability parameter. Loosely speaking, hardness amplification will proceed via methods for generating related instances that hit the hard region with sufficiently high probability. But, first let us study the notion of a hard region.

7.2.2.1. Hard Regions

We actually generalize the notion of hard regions to arbitrary distributions. The important special case of uniform distributions (on n-bit long strings) is obtained from Definition 7.20 by letting X_n equal U_n (i.e., the uniform distribution over $\{0, 1\}^n$). In general, we only assume that $X_n \in \{0, 1\}^n$.

Definition 7.20 (hard region relative to arbitrary distribution): *Let $f : \{0, 1\}^* \to \{0, 1\}$ be a Boolean predicate, $\{X_n\}_{n \in \mathbb{N}}$ be a probability ensemble, $s : \mathbb{N} \to \mathbb{N}$ and $\varepsilon : \mathbb{N} \to [0, 1]$.*

- *We say that a set S is a* hard region *of f* relative to $\{X_n\}_{n \in \mathbb{N}}$ with respect to $s(\cdot)$-size circuits and advantage $\varepsilon(\cdot)$ if for every n and every circuit C_n of size at most $s(n)$, it holds that*

$$\Pr[C_n(X_n) = f(X_n)|X_n \in S] \le \frac{1}{2} + \varepsilon(n).$$

- *We say that f has a* hard region of density $\rho(\cdot)$ *relative to $\{X_n\}_{n \in \mathbb{N}}$ (with respect to $s(\cdot)$-size circuits and advantage $\varepsilon(\cdot)$) if there exists a set S that is a hard region of f relative to $\{X_n\}_{n \in \mathbb{N}}$ (with respect to the foregoing parameters) such that $\Pr[X_n \in S_n] \ge \rho(n)$.*

Note that a Boolean function f is $(s, 1 - 2\varepsilon)$-inapproximable if and only if $\{0, 1\}^*$ is a hard region of f relative to $\{U_n\}_{n \in \mathbb{N}}$ with respect to $s(\cdot)$-size circuits and advantage $\varepsilon(\cdot)$. Thus, *strongly* inapproximable predicates (e.g., S-inapproximable predicates for superpolynomial S) have a hard region of density 1 (with respect to a negligible advantage).[25] But this trivial observation does not provide hard regions (with respect to a small (i.e., close to zero) advantage) for *mildly* inapproximable predicates. Providing such hard regions is the contents of the following theorem.

---

[25]Likewise, *mildly* inapproximable predicates have a hard region of density 1 with respect to an advantage that is noticeably smaller than $1/2$.

Theorem 7.21 (hard regions for mildly inapproximable predicates): *Let* $f:$ $\{0, 1\}^* \to \{0, 1\}$ *be a Boolean predicate,* $\{X_n\}_{n\in\mathbb{N}}$ *be a probability ensemble,* $s: \mathbb{N} \to \mathbb{N}$, *and* $\rho: \mathbb{N} \to [0, 1]$ *such that* $\rho(n) > 1/\text{poly}(n)$. *Suppose that, for every circuit* C_n *of size at most* $s(n)$, *it holds that* $\Pr[C_n(X_n) = f(X_n)] \leq 1 - \rho(n)$. *Then, for every* $\varepsilon: \mathbb{N} \to (0, 1]$, *the function* f *has a hard region of density* $\rho'(\cdot)$ *relative to* $\{X_n\}_{n\in\mathbb{N}}$ *with respect to* $s'(\cdot)$*-size circuits and advantage* $\varepsilon(\cdot)$, *where* $\rho'(n) \overset{\text{def}}{=} (1 - o(1)) \cdot \rho(n)$ *and* $s'(n) \overset{\text{def}}{=} s(n)/\text{poly}(n/\varepsilon(n))$.

In particular, if f is $(s, 2\rho)$-inapproximable then f has a hard region of density $\rho'(\cdot) \approx \rho(\cdot)$ relative to the uniform distribution (with respect to $s'(\cdot)$-size circuits and advantage $\varepsilon(\cdot)$).

Proof Sketch:[26] The proof proceeds by first establishing that $\{X_n\}$ is "related" to (or rather "dominates") an ensemble $\{Y_n\}$ such that f is strongly inapproximable on $\{Y_n\}$, and next showing that this implies the claimed hard region. Indeed, this notion of "related ensembles" plays a central role in the proof.

For $\rho: \mathbb{N} \to [0, 1]$, we say that $\{X_n\}$ ρ-dominates $\{Y_n\}$ if for every x it holds that $\Pr[X_n = x] \geq \rho(n) \cdot \Pr[Y_n = x]$. In this case we also say that $\{Y_n\}$ is ρ-dominated by $\{X_n\}$. We say that $\{Y_n\}$ is critically ρ-dominated by $\{X_n\}$ if for every x either $\Pr[Y_n = x] = (1/\rho(n)) \cdot \Pr[X_n = x]$ or $\Pr[Y_n = x] = 0$.[27]

The notions of domination and critical domination play a central role in the proof, which consists of two parts. In the first part (Claim 7.21.1), we prove that, for $\{X_n\}$ and ρ as in the theorem's hypothesis, there exists an ensemble $\{Y_n\}$ that is ρ-dominated by $\{X_n\}$ such that f is strongly inapproximable on $\{Y_n\}$. In the second part (Claim 7.21.2), we prove that the existence of such a dominated ensemble implies the existence of an ensemble $\{Z_n\}$ that is *critically* ρ'-dominated by $\{X_n\}$ such that f is strongly inapproximable on $\{Z_n\}$. Finally, we note that such a critically dominated ensemble yields a hard region of f relative to $\{X_n\}$, and the theorem follows.

Claim 7.21.1: Under the hypothesis of the theorem it holds that there exists a probability ensemble $\{Y_n\}$ that is ρ-dominated by $\{X_n\}$ such that, for every $s'(n)$-size circuit C_n, it holds that

$$\Pr[C_n(Y_n) = f(Y_n)] \leq \frac{1}{2} + \frac{\varepsilon(n)}{2}. \tag{7.13}$$

Proof: We start by assuming, toward the contradiction, that for every distribution Y_n that is ρ-dominated by X_n there exists a $s'(n)$-size circuit C_n such that $\Pr[C_n(Y_n) = f(Y_n)] > 0.5 + \varepsilon'(n)$, where $\varepsilon'(n) = \varepsilon(n)/2$. One key observation is that there is a correspondence between the set of all distributions that are each ρ-dominated by X_n and the set of all the convex combination of critically ρ-dominated (by X_n) distributions; that is, each ρ-dominated distribution is a convex combination of critically ρ-dominated distributions and vice versa (cf., a special case in §D.4.1.1). Thus, considering an enumeration $Y_n^{(1)}, \ldots, Y_n^{(t)}$ of the critically ρ-dominated (by X_n) distributions, we conclude that for every distribution π on $[t]$ there exists a

---

[26]See details in [102, Apdx. A].

[27]Actually, we should allow one point of exception, that is, relax the requirement by saying that for at most one string $x \in \{0, 1\}^n$ it holds that $0 < \Pr[Y_n = x] < \Pr[X_n = x]/\rho(n)$. This point has little effect on the proof, and is ignored in our presentation.

$s'(n)$-size circuit C_n such that

$$\sum_{i=1}^{t} \pi(i) \cdot \Pr\left[C_n\left(Y_n^{(i)}\right) = f\left(Y_n^{(i)}\right)\right] > 0.5 + \varepsilon'(n). \tag{7.14}$$

Now, consider a finite game between two players, where the first player selects a critically ρ-dominated (by X_n) distribution, and the second player selects a $s'(n)$-size circuit and obtains a payoff as determined by the corresponding success probability; that is, if the first player selects the ith critically dominated distribution and the second player selects the circuit C then the payoff equals $\Pr[C(Y_n^{(i)}) = f(Y_n^{(i)})]$. Eq. (7.14) may be interpreted as saying that for any randomized strategy for the first player there exists a deterministic strategy for the second player yielding average payoff greater than $0.5 + \varepsilon'(n)$. The Min-Max Principle (cf. von Neumann [235]) asserts that in such a case there exists a randomized strategy for the second player that yields average payoff greater than $0.5 + \varepsilon'(n)$ no matter what strategy is employed by the first player. This means that there exists a distribution, denoted D_n, on $s'(n)$-size circuits such that for every i it holds that

$$\Pr\left[D_n\left(Y_n^{(i)}\right) = f\left(Y_n^{(i)}\right)\right] > 0.5 + \varepsilon'(n), \tag{7.15}$$

where the probability refers both to the choice of the circuit D_n and to the random variable Y_n. Let $B_n = \{x : \Pr[D_n(x) = f(x)] \leq 0.5 + \varepsilon'(n)\}$. Then, $\Pr[X_n \in B_n] < \rho(n)$, because otherwise we reach a contradiction to Eq. (7.15) by defining Y_n such that $\Pr[Y_n = x] = \Pr[X_n = x]/\Pr[X_n \in B_n]$ if $x \in B_n$ and $\Pr[Y_n = x] = 0$ otherwise.[28] By employing standard amplification to D_n, we obtain a distribution D_n' over $\text{poly}(n/\varepsilon'(n)) \cdot s'(n)$-size circuits such that for every $x \in \{0,1\}^n \setminus B_n$ it holds that $\Pr[D_n'(x) = f(x)] > 1 - 2^{-n}$. It follows that there exists a $s(n)$-sized circuit C_n such that $C_n(x) = f(x)$ for every $x \in \{0,1\}^n \setminus B_n$, which implies that $\Pr[C_n(X_n) = f(X_n)] \geq \Pr[X_n \in \{0,1\}^n \setminus B_n] > 1 - \rho(n)$, in contradiction to the theorem's hypothesis. The claim follows. $\qquad\square$

We next show that the conclusion of Claim 7.21.1 (which was stated for ensembles that are ρ-dominated by $\{X_n\}$) essentially holds also when allowing only critically ρ-dominated (by $\{X_n\}$) ensembles. The following precise statement involves some loss in the domination parameter ρ (as well as in the advantage ε).

Claim 7.21.2: If there exists a probability ensemble $\{Y_n\}$ that is ρ-dominated by $\{X_n\}$ such that for every $s'(n)$-size circuit C_n it holds that $\Pr[C_n(Y_n) = f(Y_n)] \leq 0.5 + (\varepsilon(n)/2)$, then there exists a probability ensemble $\{Z_n\}$ that is critically ρ'-dominated by $\{X_n\}$ such that for every $s'(n)$-size circuit C_n it holds that $\Pr[C_n(Z_n) = f(Z_n)] \leq 0.5 + \varepsilon(n)$.

In other words, Claim 7.21.2 asserts that the function f has a hard region of density $\rho'(\cdot)$ relative to $\{X_n\}$ with respect to $s'(\cdot)$-size circuits and advantage $\varepsilon(\cdot)$, thus establishing the theorem. The proof of Claim 7.21.2 uses the Probabilistic Method (cf. [11]). Specifically, we select a set S_n at random by including each n-bit long string x with probability

$$p(x) \stackrel{\text{def}}{=} \frac{\rho(n) \cdot \Pr[Y_n = x]}{\Pr[X_n = x]} \leq 1 \tag{7.16}$$

[28]Note that Y_n is ρ-dominated by X_n, whereas by the hypothesis $\Pr[D_n(Y_n) = f(Y_n)] \leq 0.5 + \varepsilon'(n)$. Using the fact that any ρ-dominated distribution is a convex combination of critically ρ-dominated distributions, it follows that $\Pr[D_n(Y_n^{(i)}) = f(Y_n^{(i)})] \leq 0.5 + \varepsilon'(n)$ holds for some critically ρ-dominated $Y_n^{(i)}$.

independently of the choice of all other strings. It can be shown that, with high probability over the choice of S_n, it holds that $\Pr[X_n \in S_n] \approx \rho(n)$ and that $\Pr[C_n(X_n) = f(X_n)|X_n \in S_n] < 0.5 + \varepsilon(n)$ for every circuit C_n of size $s'(n)$. The latter assertion is proved by a union bound on all relevant circuits, while showing that for each such circuit C_n, with probability $1 - \exp(-s'(n)^2)$ over the choice of S_n, it holds that $|\Pr[C_n(X_n) = f(X_n)|X_n \in S_n] - \Pr[C_n(Y_n) = f(Y_n)]| < \varepsilon(n)/2$. For details, see [102, Apdx. A]. (This completes the proof of the theorem.) $\qquad\square$

7.2.2.2. Hardness Amplification via Hard Regions

Before showing how to use the notion of a hard region in order to prove a derandomized version of Yao's XOR Lemma, we show how to use it in order to prove the original version of Yao's XOR Lemma (i.e., Theorem 7.13).

An alternative proof of Yao's XOR Lemma. Let f, p_1, and p_2 be as in Theorem 7.13. Then, by Theorem 7.21, for $\rho'(n) = 1/3p_2(n)$ and $s'(n) = p_1(n)^{\Omega(1)}/\text{poly}(n)$, the function f has a hard region S of density ρ' (relative to $\{U_n\}$) with respect to $s'(\cdot)$-size circuits and advantage $1/s'(\cdot)$. Thus, for $t(n) = n \cdot p_2(n)$ and F as in Theorem 7.13, with probability at least $1 - (1 - \rho'(n))^{t(n)} = 1 - \exp(-\Omega(n))$, one of the $t(n)$ random (n-bit long) blocks of F resides in S (i.e., the hard region of f). Intuitively, this suffices for establishing the strong inapproximability of F. Indeed, suppose toward the contradiction that a small (i.e., $p'(t(n) \cdot n)$-size) circuit C_n can approximate F (over $U_{t(n)\cdot n}$) with advantage $\varepsilon(n) + \exp(-\Omega(n))$, where $\varepsilon(n) > 1/s'(n)$. Then, the $\varepsilon(n)$ term must be due to $t(n) \cdot n$-bit long inputs that contain a block in S. Using an averaging argument, we can first fix the index of this block and then the contents of the other blocks, and infer the following: For some $i \in [t(n)]$ and $x_1, \ldots, x_{t(n)} \in \{0, 1\}^n$ it holds that

$$\Pr[C_n(x', U_n, x'') = F(x', U_n, x'') \mid U_n \in S] \geq \frac{1}{2} + \varepsilon(n)$$

where $x' = (x_1, \ldots, x_{i-1}) \in \{0, 1\}^{(i-1)\cdot n}$ and $x'' = (x_{i+1}, \ldots, x_{t(n)}) \in \{0, 1\}^{(t(n)-i)\cdot n}$. Hard-wiring $i \in [t(n)]$, $x' = (x_1, \ldots, x_{i-1})$ and $x'' = (x_{i+1}, \ldots, x_{t(n)})$ as well as $\sigma \overset{\text{def}}{=} \oplus_{j \neq i} f(x_j)$ in C_n, we obtain a contradiction to the (established) fact that S is a hard region of f (by using the circuit $C'_n(z) = C_n(x', z, x'') \oplus \sigma$). Thus, Theorem 7.13 follows (for any $p'(t(n) \cdot n) \leq s'(n) - 1$).

Derandomized versions of Yao's XOR Lemma. We first show how to use the notion of a hard region in order to amplify very mild inapproximability to a constant level of inapproximability. Recall that our goal is to obtain such an amplification while applying the given function on many (related) instances, where each instance has length that is linearly related to the length of the input of the resulting function. Indeed, these related instances are produced by applying an adequate "pseudorandom generator" (see Chapter 8). The following amplification utilizes a pairwise independence generator (see Section 8.5.1), denoted G, that stretches $2n$-bit long seeds to sequences of n strings, each of length n.

Lemma 7.22 (derandomized XOR Lemma up to constant inapproximability): *Suppose that $f : \{0, 1\}^* \to \{0, 1\}$ is (T, ρ)-inapproximable, for $\rho(n) > 1/\text{poly}(n)$, and assume for simplicity that $\rho(n) \leq 1/n$. Let b denote the inner-product mod 2 predicate, and G be the aforementioned pairwise independence generator. Then $F_1(s, r) = b(f(x_1) \cdots f(x_n), r)$, where $|r| = n = |s|/2$ and $(x_1, \ldots, x_n) =$*

$G(s)$, is (T', ρ')-inapproximable for $T'(n') = T(n'/3)/\text{poly}(n')$ and $\rho'(n') = \Omega(n' \cdot \rho(n'/3))$.

Needless to say, if $f \in \mathcal{E}$ then $F_1 \in \mathcal{E}$. By applying Lemma 7.22 for a constant number of times, we may transform a $(T, 1/\text{poly})$-inapproximable predicate into a $(T'', \Omega(1))$-inapproximable one, where $T''(n'') = T(n''/O(1))/\text{poly}(n'')$.

Proof Sketch: As in the foregoing proof (of the original version of Yao's XOR Lemma), we first apply Theorem 7.21. This time we set the parameters so as to infer that, for $\alpha(n) = \rho(n)/3$ and $t'(n) = T(n)/\text{poly}(n)$, the function f has a hard region S of density α (relative to $\{U_n\}$) with respect to $t'(\cdot)$-size circuits and *advantage 0.01*. Next, as in §7.2.1.2, we shall consider the corresponding (derandomized) direct product problem; that is, the function $P_1(s) = (f(x_1), \ldots, f(x_n))$, where $|s| = 2n$ and $(x_1, \ldots, x_n) = G(s)$. We will first show that P_1 is hard to compute on an $\Omega(n \cdot \alpha(n))$ fraction of the domain, and the quantified inapproximality of F_1 will follow.

One key observation is that, by Exercise 7.23, with probability at least $\beta(n) \overset{\text{def}}{=} n \cdot \alpha(n)/2$, at least one of the n strings output by $G(U_{2n})$ resides in S. Intuitively, we expect every $t'(n)$-sized circuit to fail in computing $P_1(U_{2n})$ with probability at least $0.49\beta(n)$, because with probability $\beta(n)$ the sequence $G(U_{2n})$ contains an element in the hard region of f (and in this case the value can be guessed correctly with probability at most 0.51). The actual proof relies on a reducibility argument, which is less straightforward than the argument used in the non-derandomized case.

For technical reasons,[29] we use the condition $\alpha(n) < 1/2n$ (which is guaranteed by the hypothesis that $\rho(n) \leq 1/n$ and our setting of $\alpha(n) = \rho(n)/3$). In this case Exercise 7.23 implies that, with probability at least $\beta(n) \overset{\text{def}}{=} 0.75 \cdot n \cdot \alpha(n)$, at least one of the n strings output by $G(U_{2n})$ resides in S. We shall show that every $(t'(n) - \text{poly}(n))$-sized circuit fails in computing P_1 with probability at least $\gamma(n) = 0.3\beta(n)$. As usual, the claim is proved by a reducibility argument. Let $G(s)_i$ denote the ith string in the sequence $G(s)$ (i.e., $G(s) = (G(s)_1, \ldots, G(s)_n)$), and note that given i and x we can efficiently sample $G_i^{-1}(x) \overset{\text{def}}{=} \{s \in \{0, 1\}^{2n} : G(s)_i = x\}$. Given a circuit C_n that computes $P_1(U_{2n})$ correctly with probability $1 - \gamma(n)$, we consider the circuit C_n' that, on input x, uniformly selects $i \in [n]$ and $s \in G_i^{-1}(x)$, and outputs the ith bit in $C_n(s)$. Then, by the construction (of C_n') and the hypothesis regarding C_n, it holds that

$$\Pr[C_n'(U_n) = f(U_n) | U_n \in S] \geq \sum_{i=1}^{n} \frac{1}{n} \cdot \Pr[C_n(U_{2n}) = P_1(U_{2n}) | G(U_{2n})_i \in S]$$

$$\geq \frac{\Pr[C_n(U_{2n}) = P_1(U_{2n}) \wedge \exists i \ G_i(U_{2n})_i \in S]}{n \cdot \max_i \{\Pr[G(U_{2n})_i \in S]\}}$$

$$\geq \frac{(1 - \gamma(n)) - (1 - \beta(n))}{n \cdot \alpha(n)}$$

$$= \frac{0.7\beta(n)}{n \cdot \alpha(n)} > 0.52 \, .$$

---

[29]The following argument will rely on the fact that $\beta(n) - \gamma(n) > 0.51n \cdot \alpha(n)$, where $\gamma(n) = \Omega(\beta(n))$.

This contradicts the fact that S is a hard region of f with respect to $t'(\cdot)$-size circuits and advantage 0.01. Thus, we have established that every $(t'(n) - \mathrm{poly}(n))$-sized circuit fails in computing P_1 with probability at least $\gamma(n) = 0.3\beta(n)$.

Having established the hardness of P_1, we now infer the mild inapproximability of F_1, where $F_1(s, r) = b(P_1(s), r)$. It suffices to employ the simple (warm-up) case discussed at the beginning of the proof of Theorem 7.7 (where the predictor errs with probability less than $1/4$, rather than the full-fledged result that refers to a prediction error that is only smaller than $1/2$). Denoting by $\eta_C(s) = \Pr_{r \in \{0,1\}^n}[C(s, r) \neq b(P_1(s), r)]$ the prediction error of the circuit C, we recall that if $\eta_C(s) \leq 0.24$ then C can be used to recover $P_1(s)$. Thus, for circuits C of size $T'(3n) = t'(n)/\mathrm{poly}(n)$ it must hold that $\Pr_s[\eta_C(s) > 0.24] \geq \gamma(n)$. It follows that $\mathsf{E}_s[\eta_C(s)] > 0.24\gamma(n)$, which means that every $T'(3n)$-sized circuits fails to compute $(s, r) \mapsto b(P_1(s), r)$ with probability at least $\delta(|s| + |r|) \overset{\text{def}}{=} 0.24 \cdot \gamma(|r|)$. This means that F_1 is $(T', 2\delta)$-inapproximable, and the lemma follows (when noting that $\delta(n') = \Omega(n' \cdot \alpha(n'/3))$). $\qquad\square$

The next lemma offers an amplification of constant inapproximability to strong inapproximability. Indeed, combining Theorem 7.12 with Lemmas 7.22 and 7.23 yields Theorem 7.19 (as a special case).

Lemma 7.23 (derandomized XOR Lemma starting with constant inapproximability): *Suppose that $f : \{0, 1\}^* \to \{0, 1\}$ is (T, ρ)-inapproximable, for some constant ρ, and let b denote the inner-product mod 2 predicate. Then there exists an exponential-time computable function G such that $F_2(s, r) = b(f(x_1) \cdots f(x_n), r)$, where $(x_1, \ldots, x_n) = G(s)$ and $n = \Omega(|s|) = |r| = |x_1| = \cdots = |x_n|$, is T'-inapproximable for $T'(n') = T(n'/O(1))^{\Omega(1)}/\mathrm{poly}(n')$.*

Again, if $f \in \mathcal{E}$ then $F_2 \in \mathcal{E}$.

Proof Outline:[30]   As in the proof of Lemma 7.22, we start by establishing a hard region of density $\rho/3$ for f (this time with respect to circuits of size $T(n)^{\Omega(1)}/\mathrm{poly}(n)$ and advantage $T(n)^{-\Omega(1)}$), and focus on the analysis of the (derandomized) direct product problem corresponding to computing the function $P_2(s) = (f(x_1), \ldots, f(x_n))$, where $|s| = O(n)$ and $(x_1, \ldots, x_n) = G(s)$. The "generator" G is defined such that $G(s's'') = G_1(s') \oplus G_2(s'')$, where $|s'| = |s''|$, $|G_1(s')| = |G_2(s'')|$, and the following conditions hold:

1. G_1 is the Expander Random Walk Generator discussed in Section 8.5.3. It can be shown that $G_1(U_{O(n)})$ outputs a sequence of n strings such that for any set S of density ρ, with probability $1 - \exp(-\Omega(\rho n))$, at least $\Omega(\rho n)$ of the strings hit S. Note that this property is inherited by G, provided $|G_1(s')| = |G_2(s'')|$ for any $|s'| = |s''|$. It follows that, with probability $1 - \exp(-\Omega(\rho n))$, a constant fraction of the x_i's in the definition of P_2 hit the hard region of f.

   It is tempting to say that small circuits cannot compute P_2 better than with probability $\exp(-\Omega(\rho n))$, but this is clear only in the case that the x_i's that hit the hard region are distributed independently (and uniformly) in it, which is hardly the case here. Indeed, G_2 is used to handle this problem.

---

[30] For details, see [128].

2. G_2 is the "set projection" system underlying Construction 8.17; specifically, $G_2(s) = (s_{S_1}, \ldots, s_{S_n})$, where each S_i is an n-subset of $[|s|]$ and the S_i's have pairwise intersections of size at most $n/O(1)$.[31] An analysis as in the proof of Theorem 8.18 can be employed for showing that the dependency among the x_i's does not help for computing a particular $f(x_i)$ when given x_i as well as all the other $f(x_j)$'s. (Note that this property of G_2 is inherited by G.)

The actual analysis of the construction (via a guessing game presented in [128, Sec. 3]), links the success probability of computing P_2 to the advantage of guessing f on its hard region. The interested reader is referred to [128]. $\qquad\square$

Digest. Both Lemmas 7.22 and 7.23 are proved by first establishing corresponding derandomized versions of the "direct product" lemma (Theorem 7.14); in fact, the core of these proofs is proving adequate derandomized "direct product" lemmas. We call the reader's attention to the seemingly crucial role of this step (especially in the proof of Lemma 7.23): We cannot treat the values $f(x_1), \ldots f(x_n)$ as if they were independent (at least not for the generator G as postulated in these lemmas), and so we seek to avoid analyzing the probability of correctly computing the XOR of *all these values*. In contrast, we have established that it is very hard to correctly compute all n values, and thus *XORing a random subset of these values* yields a strongly inapproximable predicate. (Note that the argument used in Exercise 7.17 fails here, because the x_i's are not independent, which is the reason that we XOR a random subset of these values rather than all of them.)

Chapter Notes

The notion of a one-way function was suggested by Diffie and Hellman [66]. The notion of weak one-way functions as well as the amplification of one-way functions (i.e., Theorem 7.5) were suggested by Yao [239]. A proof of Theorem 7.5 has first appeared in [87].

The concept of hard-core predicates was suggested by Blum and Micali [41]. They also proved that a particular predicate constitutes a hard-core for the "DLP function" (i.e., exponentiation in a finite field), provided that the latter function is one-way. The generic hard-core predicate (of Theorem 7.7) was suggested by Levin, and proven as such by Goldreich and Levin [99]. The proof presented here was suggested by Rackoff. We comment that the original proof has its own merits (cf., e.g., [105]).

The construction of canonical derandomizers (see Section 8.3) and, specifically, the Nisan-Wigderson framework (i.e., Construction 8.17) has been the driving force behind the study of inapproximable predicates in $\mathcal{E}$. Theorem 7.10 is due to [22], whereas Theorem 7.19 is due to [128]. Both results rely heavily on variants of Yao's XOR Lemma, to be reviewed next.

Like several other fundamental insights[32] attributed to Yao's paper [239], Yao's XOR Lemma (i.e., Theorem 7.13) is not even stated in [239] but is rather due to Yao's oral presentations of his work. The first published proof of Yao's XOR Lemma was given by Levin (see [102, Sec. 3]). The proof presented in §7.2.1.2 is due to Goldreich, Nisan, and

---

[31]Recall that s_S denotes the projection of s on coordinates $S \subseteq [|s|]$; that is, for $s = \sigma_1 \cdots \sigma_k$ and $S = \{i_j : j = 1, \ldots, n\}$, we have $s_S = \sigma_{i_1} \cdots \sigma_{i_n}$.

[32]Most notably, the equivalence of pseudorandomness and unpredictability (see Section 8.2.5).

Wigderson [102, Sec. 5]. For a recent (but brief) review of other proofs of Yao's XOR Lemma (as well as variants of it), the interested reader is referred to [223].

The notion of a hard region and its applications to proving the original version of Yao's XOR Lemma are due to Impagliazzo [126] (see also [102, Sec. 4]). The first derandomization of Yao's XOR Lemma (i.e., Lemma 7.22) also originates in [126], while the second derandomization (i.e., Lemma 7.23) as well as Theorem 7.19 are due to Impagliazzo and Wigderson [128].

The worst-case to average-case reduction (i.e., §7.2.1.1, yielding Theorem 7.12) is due to [22]. This reduction follows the self-correction paradigm of Blum, Luby, and Rubinfeld [40], which was first employed in the context of a (strict)[33] worst-case to average-case reduction by Lipton [157].[34]

The connection between list decoding and hardness amplification (i.e., §7.2.1.3), yielding alternative proofs of Theorems 7.10 and 7.19, is due to Sudan, Trevisan, and Vadhan [218].

Hardness amplification for $\mathcal{NP}$ has been the subject of recent attention: An amplification of mild inapproximability to strong inapproximability is provided in [121], and an indication of the impossibility of a worst-case to average-case reductions (at least non-adaptive ones) is provided in [43].

Exercises

Exercise 7.1: Prove that if one way-functions exist then there exist one-way functions that are length preserving (i.e., $|f(x)| = |x|$ for every $x \in \{0, 1\}^n$).

> **Guideline:** Clearly, for some polynomial p, it holds that $|f(x)| < p(|x|)$ for all x. Assume, without loss of generality, that $n \mapsto p(n)$ is 1-1 and increasing, and let $p^{-1}(m) = n$ if $p(n) \leq m < p(n+1)$. Define $f'(z) = f(x)01^{|z|-|f(x)|-1}$, where x is the $p^{-1}(|z|)$-bit long prefix of z.

Exercise 7.2: Prove that if a function f is hard to invert in the sense of Definition 7.3 then it is hard to invert in the sense of Definition 7.1.

> **Guideline:** Consider a sequence of internal coin tosses that maximizes the probability in Eq. (7.1).

Exercise 7.3: Assuming the existence of one-way functions, prove that there exists a weak one-way function that is not strongly one-way.

---

[33] Earlier uses of the self-correction paradigm referred to "two argument problems" and consisted of fixing one argument and randomizing the other (see, e.g., [108]); consider, for example, the decision problem in which given (N, r) the task is to determine whether $x^2 \equiv r \pmod{N}$ has an integer solution, and the randomized process mapping (N, r) to (N, r'), where $r' = r \cdot \omega^2 \bmod N$ and ω is uniformly distributed in $[N]$. Loosely speaking, such a process yields a reduction from worst-case complexity to "mixed worst/average-case" complexity (or from "mixed average/worst-case" to pure average-case).

[34] An earlier use of the self-correction paradigm for a strict worst-case to average-case reduction appears in [19], but it refers to very low complexity classes. Specifically, this reduction refers to the parity function and is computable in $\mathcal{AC}^0$ (implying that parity cannot be approximated in $\mathcal{AC}^0$, since it cannot be computed in that class (see [83, 240, 115])). The reduction (randomly) maps $x \in \{0, 1\}^n$, viewed as a sequence $(x_1, x_2, x_3, \ldots, x_n)$, to the sequence $x' = (x_1 \oplus r_1, r_1 \oplus x_2 \oplus r_2, r_2 \oplus x_3 \oplus r_3, \ldots, r_{n-1} \oplus x_n \oplus r_n)$, where $r_1, \ldots, r_n \in \{0, 1\}$ are uniformly and independently distributed. Note that x' is uniformly distributed in $\{0, 1\}^n$ and that $\mathrm{parity}(x) = \mathrm{parity}(x') \oplus r_n$.

Exercise 7.4 (a universal one-way function (by L. Levin)): Using the notion of a universal machine, present a polynomial-time computable function that is hard to invert (in the sense of Definition 7.1) if and only if there exist one-way functions.

> **Guideline:** Consider the function F that parses its input into a pair (M, x) and emulates $|x|^3$ steps of M on input x. Note that if there exists a one-way function that can be evaluated in cubic time then F is a weak one-way function. Using padding, prove that there exists a one-way function that can be evaluated in cubic time if and only if there exist one-way functions.

Exercise 7.5: For $\ell > 1$, prove that the following $2^\ell - 1$ samples are pairwise independent and uniformly distributed in $\{0, 1\}^n$. The samples are generated by uniformly and independently selecting ℓ strings in $\{0, 1\}^n$. Denoting these strings by $s^1, \ldots, s^\ell$, we generate $2^\ell - 1$ samples corresponding to the different *non-empty* subsets of $\{1, 2, \ldots, \ell\}$ such that for subset J we let $r^J \stackrel{\text{def}}{=} \oplus_{j \in J} s^j$.

> **Guideline:** For $J \neq J'$, it holds that $r^J \oplus r^{J'} = \oplus_{j \in K} s^j$, where K denotes the symmetric difference of J and J'. See related material in Section 8.5.1.

Exercise 7.6 (a variant on the proof of Theorem 7.7): Provide a detailed presentation of the alternative procedure outlined in footnote 5. That is, prove that for every $x \in \{0, 1\}^n$, given oracle access to any $B_x : \{0, 1\}^n \to \{0, 1\}$ that satisfies Eq. (7.6), this procedure makes poly(n/ε) steps and outputs a list of strings that, with probability at least $1/2$, contains x.

Exercise 7.7 (proving Theorem 7.8): Recall that the proof of Theorem 7.7 establishes the existence of a poly(n/ε)-time oracle machine M such that, for every $B : \{0, 1\}^n \to \{0, 1\}$ and every $x \in \{0, 1\}^n$ that satisfy $\Pr_r[B(r) = b(x, r)] \geq \frac{1}{2} + \varepsilon$, it holds that $\Pr[M^B(n, \varepsilon) = x] = \Omega(\varepsilon^2/n)$. Show that this implies Theorem 7.8. (Indeed, an alternative proof can be derived by adapting Exercise 7.6.)

> **Guideline:** Apply a "coupon collector" argument.

Exercise 7.8: A polynomial-time computable predicate $b : \{0, 1\}^* \to \{0, 1\}$ is called a universal hard-core predicate if for every one-way function f, the predicate b is a hard-core of f. Note that the predicate presented in Theorem 7.7 is "almost universal" (i.e., for every one-way function f, that predicate is a hard-core of $f'(x, r) = (f(x), r)$, where $|x| = |r|$). Prove that there exists no universal hard-core predicate.

> **Guideline:** Let b be a candidate universal hard-core predicate, and let f be an arbitrary one-way function. Then consider the function $f'(x) = (f(x), b(x))$.

Exercise 7.9: Prove that if $\mathcal{NP}$ is not contained in $\mathcal{P}$/poly then neither is $\mathcal{E}$. Furthermore, for every $S : \mathbb{N} \to \mathbb{N}$, if some problem in $\mathcal{NP}$ does not have circuits of size S then for some constant $\varepsilon > 0$ there exists a problem in $\mathcal{E}$ that does not have circuits of size S', where $S'(n) = S(n^\varepsilon)$. Repeat the exercise for the "almost-everywhere" case.

> **Guideline:** Although $\mathcal{NP}$ is not known to be in $\mathcal{E}$, it is the case that SAT is in $\mathcal{E}$, which implies that $\mathcal{NP}$ is reducible to a problem in $\mathcal{E}$. For the "almost-everywhere" case, address the fact that the said reduction may not preserve the length of the input.

Exercise 7.10: For every function $f : \{0, 1\}^n \to \{0, 1\}$, present a linear-size circuit C_n such that $\Pr[C(U_n) = f(U_n)] \geq 0.5 + 2^{-n}$. Furthermore, for every $t \leq 2^{n-1}$, present a circuit C_n of size $O(t \cdot n)$ such that $\Pr[C(U_n) = f(U_n)] \geq 0.5 + t \cdot 2^{-n}$. Warning: You may not assume that $\Pr[f(U_n) = 1] = 0.5$.

Exercise 7.11 (self-correction of low-degree polynomials): Let d, m be integers, and F be a finite field of cardinality greater than $t \overset{\text{def}}{=} dm + 1$. Let $p : F^m \to F$ be a polynomial of individual degree d, and $\alpha_1, \ldots, \alpha_t$ be t distinct non-zero elements of F.

1. Show that, for every $x, y \in F^m$, the value of $p(x)$ can be efficiently computed from the values of $p(x + \alpha_1 y), \ldots, p(x + \alpha_t y)$, where x and y are viewed as m-ary vectors over F.

2. Show that, for every $x \in F^m$ and $\alpha \in F \setminus \{0\}$, if we uniformly select $r \in F^m$ then the point $x + \alpha r$ is uniformly distributed in F^m.

Conclude that $p(x)$ can be recovered based on t random points, where each point is uniformly distributed in F^m.

Exercise 7.12 (low degree extension): Prove that for any $H \subset F$ and every function $f : H^m \to F$ there exists an m-variate polynomial $\hat{f} : F^m \to F$ of individual degree $|H| - 1$ such that for every $x \in H^m$ it holds that $\hat{f}(x) = f(x)$.

> **Guideline:** Define $\hat{f}(x) = \sum_{a \in H^m} \delta_a(x) \cdot f(a)$, where δ_a is an m-variate of individual degree $|H| - 1$ such that $\delta_a(a) = 1$ whereas $\delta_a(x) = 0$ for every $x \in H^m \setminus \{a\}$. Specifically, $\delta_{a_1,\ldots,a_m}(x_1,\ldots,x_m) = \prod_{i=1}^m \prod_{b \in H \setminus \{a_i\}} ((x_i - b)/(a_i - b))$.

Exercise 7.13: Suppose that $\hat{f}$ and S' are as in the conclusion of Theorem 7.12. Prove that there exists a Boolean function g in $\mathcal{E}$ that is (S'', ε)-inapproximable for $S''(n' + O(\log n')) = S'(n')/n'$ and $\varepsilon(m) = 1/m^3$.

> **Guideline:** Consider the function g defined such that $g(x, i)$ equals the ith bit of $\hat{f}(x)$.

Exercise 7.14 (a generic application of Theorem 7.8): For any $\ell : \mathbb{N} \to \mathbb{N}$, let $h : \{0, 1\}^* \to \{0, 1\}^*$ be an arbitrary function (or even a randomized mapping) such that $|h(x)| = \ell(|x|)$ for every $x \in \{0, 1\}^*$, and $\{X_n\}_{n \in \mathbb{N}}$ be a probability ensemble. Suppose that, for some $s : \mathbb{N} \to \mathbb{N}$ and $\varepsilon : \mathbb{N} \to (0, 1]$, for every family of s-size circuits $\{C_n\}_{n \in \mathbb{N}}$ and all sufficiently large n it holds that $\Pr[C_n(X_n) = h(X_n)] \leq \varepsilon(n)$. Suppose that $s' : \mathbb{N} \to \mathbb{N}$ and $\varepsilon' : \mathbb{N} \to (0, 1]$ satisfy $s'(n + \ell(n)) \leq s(n)/\text{poly}(n/\varepsilon'(n + \ell(n)))$ and $\varepsilon'(n + \ell(n)) = \Omega(n) \cdot \varepsilon(n)^{\Omega(1)}$. Show that Theorem 7.8 implies that for every family of s'-size circuits $\{C'_{n'}\}_{n' \in \mathbb{N}}$ and all sufficiently large $n' = n + \ell(n)$ it holds that

$$\Pr[C'_{n+\ell(n)}(X_n, U_{\ell(n)}) = b(h(X_n), U_{\ell(n)})] \leq \frac{1}{2} + \varepsilon'(n + \ell(n)),$$

where $b(y, r)$ denotes the inner-product mod 2 of y and r. Note that if X_n is uniform over $\{0, 1\}^n$ then the predicate $h'(x, r) = b(h(x), r)$, where $|r| = |h(x)|$, is $(s', 1 - 2\varepsilon')$-inapproximable. Conclude that, in this case, if $\varepsilon(n) = 1/s(n)$ and $s'(n + \ell(n)) = s(n)^{\Omega(1)}/\text{poly}(n)$, then h' is s'-inapproximable.

Exercise 7.15 (reversing Exercise 7.14 (by Viola and Wigderson)): Let $\ell : \mathbb{N} \to \mathbb{N}$, $h : \{0, 1\}^* \to \{0, 1\}^*$, $\{X_n\}_{n \in \mathbb{N}}$, and b be as in Exercise 7.14. Let $H(x, r) = b(h(x), r)$ and recall that in Exercise 7.14 we reduced guessing h to approximating H. Present a reduction in the opposite direction. That is, show that if H is $(s, 1 - \varepsilon)$-inapproximable (over $\{X_n\}_{n \in \mathbb{N}}$) then every s'-size circuit succeeds in computing h (over $\{X_n\}_{n \in \mathbb{N}}$) with probability at most ε, where $s'(n) = s(n) - O(\ell(n))$.

Guideline: As usual, start by assuming the existence of a s'-size circuit that computes h with success probability exceeding ε. Consider two correlated random variables X and Y, each distributed over $\{0,1\}^{\ell(n)}$, where X represents the value of $h(U_n)$ and Y represents the circuit's guess for this value. Prove that, for a uniformly distributed $r \in \{0,1\}^{\ell(n)}$, it holds that $\Pr[b(X,r) = b(Y,r)] = (1 + p)/2$, where $p \stackrel{\text{def}}{=} \Pr[X = Y]$.

Exercise 7.16 (derandomization via averaging arguments): Let $C : \{0,1\}^n \times \{0,1\}^m \to \{0,1\}^\ell$ be a circuit, which may represent a "probabilistic circuit" that processes the first input using a sequence of choices that are given as a second input. Let X and Z be two independent random variables distributed over $\{0,1\}^n$ and $\{0,1\}^m$, respectively, and let χ be a Boolean predicate (which may represent a success event regarding the behavior of C). Prove that there exists a string $z \in \{0,1\}^m$ such that for $C_z(x) \stackrel{\text{def}}{=} C(x,z)$ it holds that $\Pr[\chi(X, C_z(X)) = 1] \geq \Pr[\chi(X, C(X,Z)) = 1]$.

Exercise 7.17 (reducing "selective XOR" to "standard XOR"): Let f be a Boolean function, and $b(y,r)$ denote the inner-product modulo 2 of the equal-length strings y and r. Suppose that $F'(x_1, \ldots, x_{t(n)}, r) \stackrel{\text{def}}{=} b(f(x_1) \cdots f(x_{t(n)}), r)$, where $x_1, \ldots, x_{t(n)} \in \{0,1\}^n$ and $r \in \{0,1\}^{t(n)}$, is T'-inapproximable. Assuming that $n \mapsto t(n) \cdot n$ is 1-1, prove that $F(x) \stackrel{\text{def}}{=} F'(x, 1^{t'(|x|)})$, where $t'(t(n) \cdot n) = t(n)$, is T-inapproximable for $T(m) = T'(m + t'(m)) - O(m)$.

> **Guideline:** Reduce the approximation of F' to the approximation of F. An important observation is that for any $x = (x_1, \ldots, x_{t(n)})$, $x' = (x'_1, \ldots, x'_{t(n)})$, and $r = r_1 \cdots r_{t(n)}$ such that $x'_i = x_i$ if $r_i = 1$, it holds that $F'(x,r) = F(x') \oplus \oplus_{i : r_i = 0} f(x'_i)$. This suggests a non-uniform reduction of F' to F, which uses "adequate" $z_1, \ldots, z_{t(n)} \in \{0,1\}^n$ as well as the corresponding values $f(z_i)$'s as advice. On input $x_1, \ldots, x_{t(n)}, r_1 \cdots r_{t(n)}$, the reduction sets $x'_i = x_i$ if $r_i = 1$ and $x'_i = z_i$ otherwise, makes the query $x' = (x'_1, \ldots, x'_{t(n)})$ to F, and returns $F(x') \oplus_{i : r_i = 0} f(z_i)$. Analyze this reduction in the case that $z_1, \ldots, z_{t(n)} \in \{0,1\}^n$ are uniformly distributed, and infer that they can be set to some fixed values (see Exercise 7.16).[35]

Exercise 7.18 (reducing "standard XOR" to "selective XOR"): In continuation of Exercise 7.17, show a reduction in the opposite direction. That is, for F and F' as in Exercise 7.17, show that if F is T-inapproximable then F' is T'-inapproximable, where $T'(m + t'(m)) = \min(T(m) - O(m), \exp(t'(m)/O(1)))^{1/3}$.

> **Guideline:** Reduce the approximation of F to the approximation of F', using the fact that for any $x = (x_1, \ldots, x_{t(n)})$ and $r = r_1 \cdots r_{t(n)}$ it holds that $\oplus_{i \in S_r} f(x_i) = F'(x,r)$, where $S_r = \{i \in [t(n)] : r_i = 1\}$. Note that, with probability $1 - \exp(-\Omega(t(n)))$, the set S_r contains at least $t(n)/3$ indices. Thus, the XOR of $t(n)/3$ values of f can be reduced to the selective XOR of $t(n)$ such values (by using some of the ideas used in Exercise 7.17 for handling the case that $|S_r| > t(n)/3$). The XOR of $t(n)$ values can be obtained by three XORs (of $t(n)/3$ values each), at the cost of decreasing the advantage by raising it to a power of three.

Exercise 7.19 (reducing "selective XOR" to direct product): Recall that, in §7.2.1.2, the approximation of the "selective XOR" predicate P' was reduced to the guessing

---

[35]That is, assume first that the reduction is given $t(n)$ samples of the distribution $(U_n, f(U_n))$, and analyze its success probability on a uniformly distributed input $(x, r) = (x_1, \ldots, x_{t(n)}, r_1 \cdots r_{t(n)})$. Next, apply Exercise 7.16 when X represents the distribution of the actual input (x, r), and Z represents the distribution of the auxiliary sequence of samples.

of the value of the direct product function P. Present a reduction in the opposite direction. That is, for P and P' as in §7.2.1.2, show that if P' is T'-inapproximable then every T-size circuit succeeds in computing P with probability at most $1/T$, where $T = \Omega(T')$.

Guideline: Use Exercise 7.15.

Exercise 7.20 (Theorem 7.14 versus Theorem 7.5): Consider a generalization of Theorem 7.14 in which f and P are functions from strings to sets of strings such that $P(x_1, \ldots, x_t) = f(x_1) \times \cdots \times f(x_t)$.

1. Prove that if for every family of p_1-size circuits, $\{C_n\}_{n \in \mathbb{N}}$, and all sufficiently large $n \in \mathbb{N}$, it holds that $\Pr[C_n(U_n) \notin f(U_n)] > 1/p_2(n)$ then for every family of p'-size circuits, $\{C'_m\}_{m \in \mathbb{N}}$, it holds that $\Pr[C'_m(U_m) \in P(U_m)] < \varepsilon'(m)$, where ε' and p' are as in Theorem 7.14. Further generalize the claim by replacing $\{U_n\}_{n \in \mathbb{N}}$ with an arbitrary distribution ensemble $\{X_n\}_{n \in \mathbb{N}}$, and replacing U_m by a $t(n)$-fold Cartesian product of X_n (where $m = t(n) \cdot n$).
2. Show that the foregoing generalizes both Theorem 7.14 and a non-uniform complexity version of Theorem 7.5.

Exercise 7.21 (refinement of the main theme of §7.2.1.3): Consider the following modification of Definition 7.17, in which the decoding condition refers to an agreement threshold of $(1/q(N)) + \alpha(N)$ rather than to a threshold of $\alpha(N)$. The modified definition reads as follows (where p is a fixed polynomial): *For every $w : [\ell(N)] \to [q(N)]$ and $x \in \{0, 1\}^N$ such that $\Gamma(x)$ is $(1 - ((1/q(N)) + \alpha(N)))$-close to w, there exists an oracle-aided circuit C of size $p((\log N)/\alpha(N))$ such that $C^w(i)$ yields the ith bit of x for every $i \in [N]$.*

1. Formulate and prove a version of Theorem 7.18 that refers to the modified definition (rather than to the original one).

   Guideline: The modified version should refer to computing $g(U_{m(n)})$ with success probability greater than $(1/q(n)) + \varepsilon(n)$ (rather than greater than $\varepsilon(n)$).

2. Prove that, when applied to binary codes (i.e., $q \equiv 2$), the version in Item 1 yields S''-inapproximable predicates, for $S''(n') = S(m^{-1}(n'))^{\Omega(1)}/\text{poly}(n')$.

3. Prove that the Hadamard code allows implicit decoding under the modified definition (but not according to the original one).[36]

   Guideline: This is the actual contents of Theorem 7.8.

Show that if $\Gamma : \{0, 1\}^N \to [q(N)]^{\ell(N)}$ is a (non-binary) code that allows implicit decoding then encoding its symbols by the Hadamard code yields a binary code $(\{0, 1\}^N \to \{0, 1\}^{\ell(N) \cdot 2^{\lceil \log_2 q(N) \rceil}})$ that allows implicit decoding. Note that efficient encoding is preserved only if $q(N) \leq \text{poly}(N)$.

Exercise 7.22 (using Proposition 7.16 to prove Theorem 7.19): Prove Theorem 7.19 by combining Proposition 7.16 and Theorem 7.8.

   Guideline: Note that, for some $\gamma > 0$, Proposition 7.16 yields an exponential-time computable function $\hat{f}$ such that $|\hat{f}(x)| \leq |x|$ and for every family of circuit $\{C'_{n'}\}_{n' \in \mathbb{N}}$

---

[36]Needless to say, the Hadamard code is not efficient (for the trivial reason that its codewords have exponential length).

of size $S'(n') = S(n'/3)^{\gamma}/\text{poly}(n')$ it holds that $\Pr[C'_{n'}(U_{n'}) = \hat{f}(U_{n'})] < 1/S'(n')$. Combining this with Theorem 7.8, infer that $P(x, r) = b(\hat{f}(x), r)$, where $|r| = |\hat{f}(x)| \le |x|$, is S''-inapproximable for $S''(n'') = S(n''/2)^{\Omega(1)}/\text{poly}(n'')$. Note that if $S(n) = 2^{\Omega(n)}$ then $S''(n'') = 2^{\Omega(n'')}$.

Exercise 7.23: Let G be a pairwise independent generator (i.e., as in Lemma 7.22), $S \subset \{0, 1\}^n$ and $\alpha \overset{\text{def}}{=} |S|/2^n$. Prove that, with probability at least $\min(n \cdot \alpha, 1)/2$, at least one of the n strings output by $G(U_{2n})$ resides in S. Furthermore, if $\alpha \le 1/2n$ then this probability is at least $0.75 \cdot n \cdot \alpha$.

> **Guideline:** Using the pairwise independence property and employing the Inclusion-Exclusion formula, we lower-bound the aforementioned probability by $n \cdot \alpha - \binom{n}{2} \cdot \alpha^2$. If $\alpha \le 1/n$ then the claim follows; otherwise we employ the same reasoning to the first $1/\alpha$ elements in the output of $G(U_{2n})$.

Exercise 7.24 (one-way functions versus inapproximable predicates): Prove that the existence of a non-uniformly hard one-way function (as in Definition 7.3) implies the existence of an exponential-time computable predicate that is T-inapproximable (as per Definition 7.9), for every polynomial T.

> **Guideline:** Suppose first that the one-way function f is length preserving and 1-1. Consider the hard-core predicate b guaranteed by Theorem 7.7 for $g(x, r) = (f(x), r)$, define the Boolean function h such that $h(z) = b(g^{-1}(z))$, and show that h is T-inapproximable for every polynomial T. For the general case a different approach seems needed. Specifically, given a (length-preserving) one-way function f, consider the Boolean function h defined as $h(z, i, \sigma) = 1$ if and only if the ith bit of the lexicographically first element in $f^{-1}(z) = \{x : f(x) = z\}$ equals σ. (In particular, if $f^{-1}(z) = \emptyset$ then $h(z, i, \sigma) = 0$ for every i and σ.)[37] Note that h is computable in exponential time, but is not (worst-case) computable by polynomial-size circuits. Applying Theorem 7.10, we are done.

---

[37] Thus, h may be easy to compute in the average-case sense (e.g., if $f(x) = 0^{|x|}f'(x)$ for some one-way function f').

CHAPTER EIGHT

Pseudorandom Generators

> *Indistinguishable things are identical.*[1]
>
> G. W. Leibniz (1646–1714)

A fresh view at the *question of randomness* has been taken by Complexity Theory: It has been postulated that a distribution is random (or rather pseudorandom) if it cannot be told apart from the uniform distribution by any efficient procedure. Thus, (pseudo)randomness is not an inherent property of an object, but is rather subjective to the observer.

At the extreme, this approach says that the question of whether the world is deterministic or allows for some free choice (which may be viewed as sources of randomness) is irrelevant. *What matters is how the world looks to us and to various computationally bounded devices.* That is, if some phenomenon looks random, then we may just treat it as if it were random. Likewise, if we can generate sequences that cannot be told apart from the uniform distribution by any efficient procedure, then we can use these sequences in any efficient randomized application instead of the ideal coin tosses that are postulated in the design of this application.

The pivot of the foregoing approach is the notion of *computational indistinguishability*, which refers to pairs of distributions that cannot be told apart by efficient procedures. The most fundamental incarnation of this notion associates efficient procedures with polynomial-time algorithms, but other incarnations that restrict attention to other classes of distinguishing procedures also lead to important insights. Likewise, the *effective generation* of pseudorandom objects, which is of major concern, is actually a general paradigm with numerous useful incarnations (which differ in the Computational Complexity limitations imposed on the generation process).

Summary: Pseudorandom generators are efficient deterministic procedures that stretch short random seeds into longer pseudorandom sequences. Thus, a generic formulation of pseudorandom generators consists of specifying three fundamental aspects – the *stretch measure* of the generators; the class of distinguishers that the generators are supposed to fool (i.e., the algorithms with respect to which the *computational indistinguishability* requirement should hold); and the resources that the generators are allowed to use (i.e., their own *computational complexity*).

---

[1]This is Leibniz's *Principle of Identity of Indiscernibles*. Leibniz admits that counterexamples to this principle are conceivable but will not occur in real life because God is much too benevolent. We thus believe that he would have agreed to the theme of this chapter, which asserts that *indistinguishable things should be considered as if they were identical.*

The archetypical case of pseudorandom generators refers to efficient generators that fool any feasible procedure; that is, the potential distinguisher is any probabilistic polynomial-time algorithm, which may be more complex than the generator itself (which, in turn, has time complexity bounded by a fixed polynomial). These generators are called general-purpose, because their output can be safely used in any efficient application. Such (general-purpose) pseudorandom generators exist if and only if one-way functions exist.

In contrast to such (general-purpose) pseudorandom generators, for the purpose of derandomization a relaxed definition of pseudorandom generators suffices. In particular, for such a purpose, one may use pseudorandom generators that are somewhat more complex than the potential distinguisher (which represents a randomized algorithm to be derandomized). Following this approach, adequate pseudorandom generators yield a full derandomization of $\mathcal{BPP}$ (i.e., $\mathcal{BPP} = \mathcal{P}$), and such generators can be constructed based on the assumption that some problems in $\mathcal{E}$ have no sub-exponential-size circuits.

It is also beneficial to consider pseudorandom generators that fool space-bounded distinguishers and generators that exhibit some limited random behavior (e.g., outputting a pairwise independent or a small-bias sequence). Such (special-purpose) pseudorandom generators can be constructed without relying on any computational complexity assumption.

Introduction

The "question of randomness" has been puzzling thinkers for ages. Aspects of this question range from philosophical doubts regarding the existence of randomness (in the world) and reflections on the meaning of randomness (in our thinking) to technical questions regarding the measuring of randomness. Among many other things, the second half of the twentieth century has witnessed the development of three theories of randomness, which address different aspects of the foregoing question.

The first theory (cf., [63]), initiated by Shannon [204], views randomness as representing *lack of information*, which in turn is modeled by a probability distribution on the possible values of the missing data. Indeed, Shannon's Information Theory is rooted in probability theory. Information Theory is focused at distributions that are not perfectly random (i.e., encode information in a redundant manner), and characterizes perfect randomness as the extreme case in which the *information contents* is maximized (i.e., in this case there is no redundancy at all). Thus, perfect randomness is associated with a unique distribution – the uniform one. In particular, by definition, one cannot (deterministically) generate such perfect random strings from shorter random seeds.

The second theory (cf., [153, 156]), initiated by Solomonoff [210], Kolmogorov [147], and Chaitin [51], views randomness as representing lack of structure, which in turn is reflected in the length of the most succinct and effective description of the object. The notion of a succinct and *effective description* refers to a process that transforms the succinct description to an explicit one. Indeed, this theory of randomness is rooted in computability theory and specifically in the notion of a universal language (equiv., universal machine or computing device; see §1.2.3.4). It measures the randomness (or complexity) of objects in terms of the shortest program (for a fixed universal machine) that generates the object.[2] Like Shannon's theory, Kolmogorov Complexity is quantitative and perfect random objects appear as an extreme case. However, following Kolmogorov's approach one may say that a single object, rather than a distribution over objects, is perfectly random. Still, by definition, one cannot (deterministically) generate strings of high Kolmogorov Complexity from short random seeds.

The third theory, which is the focus of the current chapter, views randomness as an effect on an observer and thus as being relative to the *observer's abilities* (of analysis). The observer's abilities are captured by its computational abilities (i.e., the complexity of the processes that the observer may apply), and hence, this theory of randomness is rooted in Complexity Theory. This theory of randomness is explicitly aimed at providing a notion of randomness that, unlike the previous two notions, allows for an efficient (and deterministic) generation of random strings from shorter random seeds. The heart of this theory is the suggestion to view objects as equal if they cannot be told apart by any efficient procedure. Consequently, a distribution that cannot be efficiently distinguished from the uniform distribution will be considered random (or rather called pseudorandom). Thus, randomness is not an "inherent" property of objects (or distributions), but is rather relative to an observer (and its computational abilities). To illustrate this approach, let us consider the following mental experiment.

> *Alice and Bob play "head or tail" in one of the following four ways. In each of them, Alice flips an unbiased coin and Bob is asked to guess its* outcome before *the coin hits the floor. The alternative ways differ by the knowledge Bob has before making his guess.*

> *In the first alternative, Bob has to announce his guess before Alice flips the coin. Clearly, in this case Bob wins with probability* $1/2$.

> *In the second alternative, Bob has to announce his guess while the coin is spinning in the air. Although the outcome is* determined in principle *by the motion of the coin, Bob does not have accurate information on the motion. Thus we believe that, also in this case, Bob wins with probability* $1/2$.

> *The third alternative is similar to the second, except that Bob has at his disposal sophisticated equipment capable of providing accurate in-*formation *on the coin's motion as well as on the environment affecting the outcome. However, Bob cannot process this information in time to improve his guess.*

> *In the fourth alternative, Bob's recording equipment is directly connected to a* powerful computer *programmed to solve the motion equations and output a prediction. It is conceivable that in such a case, Bob can improve substantially his guess of the outcome of the coin.*

We conclude that the randomness of an event is relative to the information and computing resources at our disposal. At the extreme, even events that are fully determined by public information may be perceived as random events by an observer that lacks the relevant information and/or the ability to process it. Our focus will be on the lack of sufficient processing power, and not on the lack of sufficient information. The lack of sufficient

---

[2] We mention that Kolmogorov's approach is inherently intractable (i.e., Kolmogorov Complexity is uncomputable).

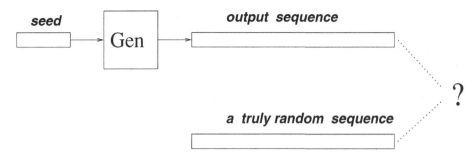

Figure 8.1: Pseudorandom generators – an illustration.

processing power may be due either to the formidable amount of computation required (for analyzing the event in question) or to the fact that the observer happens to be very limited.

A natural notion of pseudorandomness arises – a distribution is *pseudorandom* if no efficient procedure can distinguish it from the uniform distribution, where efficient procedures are associated with (probabilistic) polynomial-time algorithms. This specific notion of pseudorandomness is indeed the most fundamental one, and much of this chapter is focused on it. Weaker notions of pseudorandomness arise as well – they refer to indistinguishability by weaker procedures such as space-bounded algorithms, constant-depth circuits, and so on. Stretching this approach even further, one may consider algorithms that are designed on purpose so as not to distinguish even weaker forms of "pseudorandom" sequences from random ones (where such algorithms arise naturally when trying to convert some natural randomized algorithms into deterministic ones; see Section 8.5).

The foregoing discussion has focused on one aspect of the pseudorandomness question – the resources or type of the observer (or potential distinguisher). Another important aspect is whether such pseudorandom sequences can be generated from much shorter ones, and at what cost (or complexity). A natural approach requires the generation process to be efficient, and furthermore to be fixed before the specific observer is determined. Coupled with the aforementioned strong notion of pseudorandomness, this yields the archetypical notion of pseudorandom generators – those operating in (fixed) polynomial time and producing sequences that are indistinguishable from uniform ones by *any* polynomial-time observer. In particular, this means that the distinguisher is allowed more resources than the generator. Such (general-purpose) pseudorandom generators (discussed in Section 8.2) allow for decreasing the randomness complexity of *any efficient application*, and are thus of great relevance to randomized algorithms and cryptography. The term *general-purpose* is meant to emphasize the fact that the same generator is good for all efficient applications, including those that consume more resources than the generator itself.

Although general-purpose pseudorandom generators are very appealing, there are important reasons for also considering the opposite relation between the complexities of the generation and distinguishing tasks; that is, allowing the pseudorandom generator to use more resources (e.g., time or space) than the observer it tries to fool. This alternative is natural in the context of derandomization (i.e., converting randomized algorithms to deterministic ones), where the crucial step is replacing the random input of an algorithm by a pseudorandom input, which in turn can be generated based on a much shorter random seed. In particular, when derandomizing a probabilistic polynomial-time algorithm, the observer (to be fooled by the generator) is a fixed algorithm. In this case, employing a more complex generator merely means that the complexity of the derived deterministic algorithm is dominated by the complexity of the generator (rather than by the complexity of the original randomized algorithm). Needless to say, allowing the generator to use more resources than the observer that it tries to fool makes the task of designing pseudorandom generators potentially easier, and enables derandomization results that are not known when using general-purpose pseudorandom generators. The usefulness of this approach is demonstrated in Sections 8.3 through 8.5.

We note that the goal of all types of pseudorandom generators is to allow the generation of "sufficiently random" sequences based on much shorter random seeds. Thus, pseudorandom generators offer significant saving in the randomness complexity of various applications (and in some cases eliminating randomness altogether). Saving on randomness is valuable because many applications are severely limited in their ability to generate or obtain truly random bits. Furthermore, typically, generating truly random bits is significantly more expensive than standard computation steps. Thus, randomness is a computational resource that should be considered on top of time complexity (analogously to the consideration of space complexity).

Organization. In Section 8.1 we present the general paradigm underlying the various notions of pseudorandom generators. The archetypical case of general-purpose pseudorandom generators is presented in Section 8.2. We then turn to alternative notions of pseudorandom generators: Generators that suffice for the derandomization of complexity classes such as $\mathcal{BPP}$ are discussed in Section 8.3; pseudorandom generators in the domain of space-bounded computations are discussed in Section 8.4; and special-purpose generators are discussed in Section 8.5.

Teaching note: If you can afford teaching only one of the alternative notions of pseudorandom generators, then we suggest teaching the notion of general-purpose pseudorandom generators (presented in Section 8.2). This notion is more relevant to computer science at large and the technical material is relatively simpler. The chapter is organized to facilitate this option.

Prerequisites. We assume a basic familiarity with elementary probability theory (see Appendix D.1) and randomized algorithms (see Section 6.1). In particular, standard conventions regarding random variables (presented in Appendix D.1.1) will be extensively used. We shall also apply a couple of results from Chapter 7, but these applications will be self-contained.

8.1. The General Paradigm

Teaching note: We advocate a unified view of various notions of pseudorandom generators. That is, we view these notions as incarnations of a general abstract paradigm, to be presented in this section. A teacher who wishes to focus on one of these incarnations may still use this section as a general motivation toward the specific definitions used later. On the other hand, some students may prefer reading this section after studying one of the specific incarnations.

A generic formulation of pseudorandom generators consists of specifying three fundamental aspects – the *stretch measure* of the generators; the class of distinguishers that the generators are supposed to fool (i.e., the algorithms with respect to which the *computational indistinguishability* requirement should hold); and the resources that the generators are allowed to use (i.e., their own *computational complexity*). Let us elaborate.

Stretch function. A necessary requirement of any notion of a pseudorandom generator is that the generator is a *deterministic algorithm* that stretches short strings, called seeds, into longer output sequences.[3] Specifically, this algorithm stretches k-bit long seeds into $\ell(k)$-bit long outputs, where $\ell(k) > k$. The function $\ell : \mathbb{N} \to \mathbb{N}$ is called the stretch measure (or stretch function) of the generator. In some settings the specific stretch measure is immaterial (e.g., see Section 8.2.4).

Computational Indistinguishability. A necessary requirement of any notion of a pseudorandom generator is that the generator "fools" some non-trivial algorithms. That is, it is required that any algorithm taken from a predetermined class of interest cannot distinguish the output produced by the generator (when the generator is fed with a uniformly chosen seed) from a uniformly chosen sequence. Thus, we consider a class $\mathcal{D}$ of distinguishers (e.g., probabilistic polynomial-time algorithms) and a class $\mathcal{F}$ of (threshold) functions (e.g., reciprocals of positive polynomials), and require that the generator G satisfies the following: For any $D \in \mathcal{D}$, any $f \in \mathcal{F}$, and for all sufficiently large k's it holds that

$$| \Pr[D(G(U_k)) = 1] - \Pr[D(U_{\ell(k)}) = 1]| < f(k), \tag{8.1}$$

where U_n denotes the uniform distribution over $\{0, 1\}^n$, and the probability is taken over U_k (resp., $U_{\ell(k)}$) as well as over the coin tosses of algorithm D in case it is probabilistic. The reader may think of such a distinguisher, D, as of an observer that tries to tell whether the "tested string" is a random output of the generator (i.e., distributed as $G(U_k)$) or is a truly random string (i.e., distributed as $U_{\ell(k)}$). The condition in Eq. (8.1) requires that D cannot make a meaningful decision; that is, ignoring a negligible difference (represented by $f(k)$), D's verdict is the same in both cases.[4] The archetypical choice is that $\mathcal{D}$ is the set of all probabilistic polynomial-time algorithms, and $\mathcal{F}$ is the set of all functions that are the reciprocal of some positive polynomial.

Complexity of Generation. The archetypical choice is that the generator has to work in polynomial time (in length of its input – the seed). Other choices will be discussed as well. We note that placing no computational requirements on the generator (or, alternatively, putting very mild requirements such as upper-bounding the running time by a double-exponential function), yields "generators" that can fool any sub-exponential-size circuit family (see Exercise 8.1).

---

[3]Indeed, the seed represents the randomness that is used in the generation of the output sequences; that is, the randomized generation process is decoupled into a deterministic algorithm and a random seed. This decoupling facilitates the study of such processes.

[4]The class of threshold functions $\mathcal{F}$ should be viewed as determining the class of noticeable probabilities (as a function of k). Thus, we require certain functions (i.e., those presented at the l.h.s of Eq. (8.1)) to be smaller than any noticeable function *on all but finitely many integers*. We call the former functions negligible. Note that a function may be neither noticeable nor negligible (e.g., it may be smaller than any noticeable function on infinitely many values and yet larger than some noticeable function on infinitely many other values).

Notational conventions. We will consistently use k for denoting the length of the seed of a pseudorandom generator, and $\ell(k)$ for denoting the length of the corresponding output. In some cases, this makes our presentation a little more cumbersome (since a more natural presentation may specify some other parameters and let the seed-length be a function of the latter). However, our choice has the advantage of focusing attention on the fundamental parameter of the pseudorandom generation process – the length of the random seed. We note that whenever a pseudorandom generator is used to "derandomize" an algorithm, n will denote the length of the input to this algorithm, and k will be selected as a function of n.

Some instantiations of the general paradigm. Two important instantiations of the notion of pseudorandom generators relate to polynomial-time distinguishers.

1. General-purpose pseudorandom generators correspond to the case that the generator itself runs in polynomial time and needs to withstand *any probabilistic polynomial-time distinguisher*, including distinguishers that run for more time than the generator. Thus, the same generator may be used safely in any efficient application. (This notion is treated in Section 8.2.)
2. In contrast, pseudorandom generators intended for derandomization may run more time than the distinguisher, which is viewed as a fixed circuit having size that is upper-bounded by a fixed polynomial. (This notion is treated in Section 8.3.)

In addition, the general paradigm may be instantiated by focusing on the space complexity of the potential distinguishers (and the generator), rather than on their time complexity. Furthermore, one may also consider distinguishers that merely reflect probabilistic properties such as pairwise independence, small-bias, and hitting frequency.

8.2. General-Purpose Pseudorandom Generators

Randomness is playing an increasingly important role in computation: It is frequently used in the design of sequential, parallel, and distributed algorithms, and it is of course central to cryptography. Whereas it is convenient to design such algorithms making free use of randomness, it is also desirable to minimize the usage of randomness in real implementations. Thus, general-purpose pseudorandom generators (as defined next) are a key ingredient in an "algorithmic toolbox" – they provide an automatic compiler of programs written with free usage of randomness into programs that make an economical use of randomness.

Organization of this section. Since this is a relatively long section, a short road map seems in place. In Section 8.2.1 we provide the basic definition of general-purpose pseudorandom generators, and in Section 8.2.2 we describe their archetypical application (which was eluded to in the former paragraph). In Section 8.2.3 we provide a wider perspective on the notion of computational indistinguishability that underlies the basic definition, and in Section 8.2.4 we justify the little concern (shown in Section 8.2.1) regarding the specific stretch function. In Section 8.2.5 we address the existence of general-purpose pseudorandom generators. In Section 8.2.6 we motivate and discuss a non-uniform version of computational indistinguishability. We conclude in Section 8.2.7 by reviewing other variants and reflecting on various conceptual aspects of the notions discussed in this section.

8.2.1. The Basic Definition

Loosely speaking, general-purpose pseudorandom generators are efficient deterministic programs that expand short, randomly selected seeds into longer pseudorandom bit sequences, where the latter are defined as computationally indistinguishable from truly random sequences by *any* efficient algorithm. Identifying efficiency with polynomial-time operation, this means that the generator (being a fixed algorithm) works within *some fixed* polynomial time, whereas the distinguisher may be *any* algorithm that runs in polynomial time. Thus, the distinguisher is potentially more complex than the generator; for example, the distinguisher *may* run in time that is cubic in the running time of the generator. Furthermore, to facilitate the development of this theory, we allow the distinguisher to be probabilistic (whereas the generator remains deterministic as stated previously). We require that such distinguishers cannot tell the output of the generator from a truly random string of similar length, or rather that the difference that such distinguishers may detect (or "sense") is negligible. Here, a negligible function is a function that vanishes faster than the reciprocal of any positive polynomial.[5]

Definition 8.1 (general-purpose pseudorandom generator)**:** *A deterministic polynomial-time algorithm G is called a* pseudorandom generator *if there exists a stretch function, $\ell : \mathbb{N} \to \mathbb{N}$ (satisfying $\ell(k) > k$ for all k), such that for any probabilistic polynomial-time algorithm D, for any positive polynomial p, and for all sufficiently large k's it holds that*

$$| \Pr[D(G(U_k)) = 1] - \Pr[D(U_{\ell(k)}) = 1] | < \frac{1}{p(k)} \qquad (8.2)$$

where U_n denotes the uniform distribution over $\{0, 1\}^n$ and the probability is taken over U_k (resp., $U_{\ell(k)}$) as well as over the internal coin tosses of D.

Thus, Definition 8.1 is derived from the generic framework (presented in Section 8.1) by taking the class of distinguishers to be the set of all probabilistic polynomial-time algorithms, and taking the class of (noticeable) threshold functions to be the set of all functions that are the reciprocals of some positive polynomial.[6] Indeed, the principles underlying Definition 8.1 were discussed in Section 8.1 (and will be further discussed in Section 8.2.3).

We note that Definition 8.1 does not make any requirement regarding the stretch function $\ell : \mathbb{N} \to \mathbb{N}$, except for the generic requirement that $\ell(k) > k$ for all k. Needless to say, the larger ℓ is, the more useful the pseudorandom generator is. Of course, ℓ is upper-bounded by the running time of the generator (and hence by a polynomial). In Section 8.2.4 we show that any pseudorandom generator (even one having minimal stretch $\ell(k) = k + 1$) can be used for constructing a pseudorandom generator having any desired (polynomial) stretch function. But before doing so, we rigorously discuss the "saving in

---

[5]Definition 8.1 requires that the functions representing the distinguishing gap of certain algorithms should be smaller than the reciprocal of any positive polynomial for all but finitely many k's. The former functions are called *negligible* (cf. footnote 4, when identifying noticeable functions with the reciprocals of any positive polynomial). The notion of negligible probability is robust in the sense that any event that occurs with negligible probability will also occur with negligible probability when the experiment is repeated a "feasible" (i.e., polynomial) number of times.

[6]The latter choice is naturally coupled with the association of efficient computation with polynomial-time algorithms: An event that occurs with noticeable probability occurs almost always when the experiment is repeated a "feasible" (i.e., polynomial) number of times.

randomness" offered by pseudorandom generators, and provide a wider perspective on the notion of computational indistinguishability that underlies Definition 8.1.

8.2.2. The Archetypical Application

We note that "pseudo-random number generators" appeared with the first computers, and have been used ever since for generating random choices (or samples) for various applications. However, typical implementations use generators that are not pseudorandom according to Definition 8.1. Instead, at best, these generators are shown to pass *some* ad hoc statistical test (cf. [146]). We warn that the fact that a "pseudo-random number generator" passes some statistical tests does not mean that it will pass a new test and that it will be good for a future (untested) application. Needless to say, the approach of subjecting the generator to some ad hoc tests fails to provide general results of the form "for *all* practical purposes using the output of the generator is as good as using truly unbiased coin tosses." In contrast, the approach encompassed in Definition 8.1 aims at such generality, and in fact is tailored to obtain it: The notion of computational indistinguishability, which underlines Definition 8.1, covers all possible efficient applications and guarantees that for all of them pseudorandom sequences are as good as truly random ones. Indeed, any efficient randomized algorithm maintains its performance when its internal coin tosses are substituted by a sequence generated by a pseudorandom generator. This substitution is spelled out next.

Construction 8.2 (typical application of pseudorandom generators): *Let G be a pseudorandom generator with stretch function $\ell : \mathbb{N} \to \mathbb{N}$. Let A be a probabilistic polynomial-time algorithm, and $\rho : \mathbb{N} \to \mathbb{N}$ denote its randomness complexity. Denote by $A(x, r)$ the output of A on input x and coin tosses sequence $r \in \{0, 1\}^{\rho(|x|)}$. Consider the following randomized algorithm, denoted A_G:*

> *On input x, set $k = k(|x|)$ to be the smallest integer such that $\ell(k) \geq \rho(|x|)$, uniformly select $s \in \{0, 1\}^k$, and output $A(x, r)$, where r is the $\rho(|x|)$-bit long prefix of $G(s)$.*

That is, $A_G(x, s) = A(x, G'(s))$, for $|s| = k(|x|) = \arg\min_i \{\ell(i) \geq \rho(|x|)\}$, where $G'(s)$ is the $\rho(|x|)$-bit long prefix of $G(s)$.

Thus, using A_G instead of A, the randomness complexity is reduced from ρ to $\ell^{-1} \circ \rho$, while (as we show next) it is infeasible to find inputs (i.e., x's) on which the *noticeable behavior* of A_G is different from the one of A. For example, if $\ell(k) = k^2$, then the randomness complexity is reduced from ρ to $\sqrt{\rho}$. We stress that the pseudorandom generator G is *universal*; that is, it can be applied to reduce the randomness complexity of *any* probabilistic polynomial-time algorithm A.

Proposition 8.3: *Let A, ρ and G be as in Construction 8.2, and suppose that $\rho : \mathbb{N} \to \mathbb{N}$ is 1-1. Then, for every pair of probabilistic polynomial-time algorithms, a finder F and a tester T, every positive polynomial p and all sufficiently long n's*

$$\sum_{x \in \{0,1\}^n} \Pr[F(1^n) = x] \cdot |\Delta_{A,T}(x)| < \frac{1}{p(n)} \qquad (8.3)$$

where $\Delta_{A,T}(x) \overset{\text{def}}{=} \Pr[T(x, A(x, U_{\rho(|x|)})) = 1] - \Pr[T(x, A_G(x, U_{k(|x|)})) = 1]$, and the probabilities are taken over the U_m's as well as over the internal coin tosses of the algorithms F and T.

Algorithm F represents a potential attempt to find an input x on which the output of A_G is distinguishable from the output of A. This "attempt" may be benign as in the case that a user employs algorithm A_G on inputs that are generated by some probabilistic polynomial-time application. However, the attempt may also be adversarial as in the case that a user employs algorithm A_G on inputs that are provided by a potentially malicious party. The potential tester, denoted T, represents the potential use of the output of algorithm A_G, and captures the requirement that this output be as good as a corresponding output produced by A. Thus, T is given x as well as the corresponding output produced either by $A_G(x) \overset{\text{def}}{=} A(x, U_{k(|x|)})$ or by $A(x) = A(x, U_{\rho(|x|)})$, and it is required that T cannot tell the difference. In the case that A is a probabilistic polynomial-time *decision procedure*, this means that it is infeasible to find an x on which A_G decides incorrectly (i.e., differently than A). In the case that A is a *search procedure for some NP-relation*, it is infeasible to find an x on which A_G outputs a wrong solution. For details, see Exercise 8.2.

Proof: The proposition is proven by showing that any triple (A, F, T) violating the claim can be converted into an algorithm D that distinguishes the output of G from the uniform distribution, in contradiction to the hypothesis. The key observation is that for every $x \in \{0, 1\}^n$ it holds that

$$\Delta_{A,T}(x) = \Pr[T(x, A(x, U_{\rho(n)})) = 1] - \Pr[T(x, A(x, G'(U_{k(n)}))) = 1], \quad (8.4)$$

where $G'(s)$ is the $\rho(n)$-bit long prefix of $G(s)$. Thus, a method for finding a string x such that $|\Delta_{A,T}(x)|$ is large yields a way of distinguishing $U_{\ell(k(n))}$ from $G(U_{k(n)})$; that is, given a sample $r \in \{0, 1\}^{\ell(k(n))}$ and using such a string $x \in \{0, 1\}^n$, the distinguisher outputs $T(x, A(x, r'))$, where r' is the $\rho(n)$-bit long prefix of r. Indeed, we shall show that the violation of Eq. (8.3), which refers to $E_{x \leftarrow F(1^n)}[|\Delta_{A,T}(x)|]$, yields a violation of the hypothesis that G is a pseudorandom generator (by finding an adequate string x and using it). This intuitive argument requires a slightly careful implementation, which is provided next.

As a warm-up, consider the following algorithm D. On input r (taken from either $U_{\ell(k(n))}$ or $G(U_{k(n)})$), algorithm D first obtains $x \leftarrow F(1^n)$, where n can be obtained easily from $|r|$ (because ρ is 1-1 and $1^n \mapsto \rho(n)$ is computable via A). Next, D obtains $y = A(x, r')$, where r' is the $\rho(|x|)$-bit long prefix of r. Finally D outputs $T(x, y)$. Note that D is implementable in probabilistic polynomial time, and that

$$D(U_{\ell(k(n))}) \equiv T(X_n, A(X_n, U_{\rho(n)})), \quad \text{where } X_n \overset{\text{def}}{=} F(1^n)$$

$$D(G(U_{k(n)})) \equiv T(X_n, A(X_n, G'(U_{k(n)}))), \quad \text{where } X_n \overset{\text{def}}{=} F(1^n).$$

Using Eq. (8.4), it follows that $\Pr[D(U_{\ell(k(n))}) = 1] - \Pr[D(G(U_{k(n)})) = 1]$ equals $E[\Delta_{A,T}(F(1^n))]$, which implies that $E[\Delta_{A,T}(F(1^n))]$ must be negligible (because otherwise we derive a contradiction to the hypothesis that G is a pseudorandom generator). This yields a weaker version of the proposition asserting that $E[\Delta_{A,T}(F(1^n))]$ is negligible (rather than that $E[|\Delta_{A,T}(F(1^n))|]$ is negligible).

In order to prove that $E[|\Delta_{A,T}(F(1^n))|]$ (rather than $E[\Delta_{A,T}(F(1^n))]$) is negligible, we need to modify D a little. Note that the source of trouble is that $\Delta_{A,T}(\cdot)$ may be positive on some x's and negative on others, and thus it may be the case that $E[\Delta_{A,T}(F(1^n))]$ is small (due to cancelations) even if $E[|\Delta_{A,T}(F(1^n))|]$ is large. This difficulty can be overcome by determining the sign of $\Delta_{A,T}(\cdot)$ on $x = F(1^n)$ and changing the outcome of D accordingly; that is, the modified D will output $T(x, A(x, r'))$ if $\Delta_{A,T}(x) > 0$ and $1 - T(x, A(x, r'))$ otherwise. Thus, in each case, the contribution of x to the distinguishing gap of the modified D will be $|\Delta_{A,T}(x)|$. We further note that if $|\Delta_{A,T}(x)|$ is small then it does not matter much whether we act as in the case of $\Delta_{A,T}(x) > 0$ or in the case of $\Delta_{A,T}(x) \leq 0$. Thus, it suffices to correctly determine the sign of $\Delta_{A,T}(x)$ in the case that $|\Delta_{A,T}(x)|$ is large, which is certainly a feasible (approximation) task. Details follow.

We start by assuming, toward the contradiction, that $E[|\Delta_{A,T}(F(1^n))|] > \varepsilon(n)$ for some non-negligible function ε. On input r (taken from either $U_{\ell(k(n))}$ or $G(U_{k(n)})$), the modified algorithm D first obtains $x \leftarrow F(1^n)$, just as the basic version. Next, using a sample of size $\text{poly}(n/\varepsilon(n))$, it approximates $p_U(x) \overset{\text{def}}{=} \Pr[T(x, A(x, U_{\rho(n)})) = 1]$ and $p_G(x) \overset{\text{def}}{=} \Pr[T(x, A(x, G'(U_{k(n)}))) = 1]$ such that each probability is approximated to within a deviation of $\varepsilon(n)/8$ with negligible error probability (say, $\exp(-n)$). (Note that, so far, the actions of D only depend on the length of its input r, which determines n.)[7] If these approximations indicate that $p_U(x) \geq p_G(x)$ (equiv., that $\Delta_{A,T}(x) \geq 0$) then D outputs $T(x, A(x, r'))$ else it outputs $1 - T(x, A(x, r'))$, where r' is the $\rho(|x|)$-bit long prefix of r and we assume without loss of generality that the output of T is in $\{0, 1\}$.

The analysis of the modified distinguisher D is based on the fact that *if the approximations yield a correct decision regarding the relation between $p_U(x)$ and $p_G(x)$, then the contribution of x to the distinguishing gap of D is $|p_U(x) - p_G(x)|$.*[8] We also note that if $|p_U(x) - p_G(x)| > \varepsilon(n)/4$, then with overwhelmingly high probability (i.e., $1 - \exp(-n)$), the approximation of $p_U(x) - p_G(x)$ maintains the sign of $p_U(x) - p_G(x)$ (because each of the two quantities is approximated to within an additive error of $\varepsilon(n)/8$). Finally, we note that if $|p_U(x) - p_G(x)| \leq \varepsilon(n)/4$ then we may often err regarding the sign of $p_U(x) - p_G(x)$, but the damage caused (to the distinguishing gap of D) by this error is at most $2|p_U(x) - p_G(x)| \leq \varepsilon(n)/2$. Combining all these observations, we get

$$\Pr[D(U_{\ell(k(n))}) = 1 | F(1^n) = x] - \Pr[D(G(U_{k(n)})) = 1 | F(1^n) = x]$$

$$\geq |p_U(x) - p_G(x)| - \eta(x), \qquad (8.5)$$

where $\eta(x) = \varepsilon(n)/2$ if $|p_U(x) - p_G(x)| \leq \varepsilon(n)/4$ and $\eta(x) = \exp(-n)$ otherwise. (Indeed, $\eta(x)$ represents the expected damage due to an error in determining the sign of $p_U(x) - p_G(x)$, where $\varepsilon(n)/2$ upper-bounds the damage caused (by a wrong decision) in the case that $|p_U(x) - p_G(x)| \leq \varepsilon(n)/4$ and $\exp(-n)$ upper-bounds the probability of a wrong decision in the case that $|p_U(x) - p_G(x)| > \varepsilon(n)/4$.) Thus,

---

[7]Specifically, the approximation to $p_U(x)$ (resp., $p_G(x)$) is obtained by generating a sample of $U_{\rho(n)}$ (resp., $G'(U_{k(n)})$) and invoking the algorithms A and T; that is, given a sample $r_1, \ldots, r_t$ of $U_{\rho(n)}$ (resp., $G'(U_{k(n)})$), where $t = O(n/\varepsilon(n)^2)$, we approximate $p_U(x)$ (resp., $p_G(x)$) by $|\{i \in [t] : T(x, A(x, r_i)) = 1\}|/t$.

[8]Indeed, if $p_U(x) \geq p_G(x)$ then the contribution is $p_U(x) - p_G(x) = |p_U(x) - p_G(x)|$, whereas if $p_U(x) < p_G(x)$ then the contribution is $(1 - p_U(x)) - (1 - p_G(x)) = -(p_U(x) - p_G(x))$, which also equals $|p_U(x) - p_G(x)|$.

$\Pr[D(U_{\ell(k(n))}) = 1] - \Pr[D(G(U_{k(n)})) = 1]$ is lower-bounded by the expectation of Eq. (8.5), which equals $\mathsf{E}[|\Delta_{A,T}(F(1^n))|] - \mathsf{E}[\eta(F(1^n))]$. Combining the hypothesis that $\mathsf{E}[|\Delta_{A,T}(F(1^n))|] > \varepsilon(n)$ and the fact that $\max_{x \in \{0,1\}^n}\{\eta(x)\} \leq \varepsilon(n)/2$, we infer that $\Pr[D(U_{\ell(k(n))}) = 1] - \Pr[D(G(U_{k(n)})) = 1] > \varepsilon(n)/2$. Recalling that D runs in time poly($n/\varepsilon(n)$), this contradicts the pseudorandomness of G. The proposition follows. ∎

Conclusion. Although the foregoing refers to standard probabilistic polynomial-time algorithms, a similar construction and analysis applies to any efficient randomized process (i.e., any efficient multi-party computation). Any such process preserves its behavior when replacing its perfect source of randomness (postulated in its analysis) by a pseudorandom sequence (which may be used in the implementation). Thus, given a pseudorandom generator with a large stretch function, *one can considerably reduce the randomness complexity of any efficient application.*

8.2.3. Computational Indistinguishability

In this section we spell out (and study) the definition of computational indistinguishability that underlies Definition 8.1.

8.2.3.1. The General Formulation

The (general formulation of the) definition of computational indistinguishability refers to *arbitrary* probability ensembles. Here, a probability ensemble is an infinite sequence of random variables $\{Z_n\}_{n \in \mathbb{N}}$ such that each Z_n ranges over strings of length that is polynomially related to n (i.e., there exists a polynomial p such that for every n it holds that $|Z_n| \leq p(n)$ and $p(|Z_n|) \geq n$). We say that $\{X_n\}_{n \in \mathbb{N}}$ and $\{Y_n\}_{n \in \mathbb{N}}$ are computationally indistinguishable if for every feasible algorithm A the difference $d_A(n) \stackrel{\text{def}}{=} |\Pr[A(X_n) = 1] - \Pr[A(Y_n) = 1]|$ is a negligible function in n. That is:

Definition 8.4 (computational indistinguishability): *The probability ensembles $\{X_n\}_{n \in \mathbb{N}}$ and $\{Y_n\}_{n \in \mathbb{N}}$ are* computationally indistinguishable *if for every probabilistic polynomial-time algorithm D, every positive polynomial p, and all sufficiently large n,*

$$|\Pr[D(X_n) = 1] - \Pr[D(Y_n) = 1]| < \frac{1}{p(n)} \tag{8.6}$$

where the probabilities are taken over the relevant distribution (i.e., either X_n or Y_n) and over the internal coin tosses of algorithm D. The l.h.s. of Eq. (8.6), when viewed as a function of n, is often called the distinguishing gap *of D, where $\{X_n\}_{n \in \mathbb{N}}$ and $\{Y_n\}_{n \in \mathbb{N}}$ are understood from the context.*

We can think of D as representing somebody who wishes to distinguish two distributions (based on a given sample drawn from one of the distributions), and think of the output "1" as representing D's verdict that the sample was drawn according to the first distribution. Saying that the two distributions are computationally indistinguishable means that if D is a feasible procedure then its verdict is not really meaningful (because the verdict is almost as often 1 when the sample is drawn from the first distribution as when the sample is drawn from the second distribution). We comment that the absolute value in Eq. (8.6) can be omitted without affecting the definition (see Exercise 8.3), and we will often do so without warning.

In Definition 8.1, we required that the probability ensembles $\{G(U_k)\}_{k\in\mathbb{N}}$ and $\{U_{\ell(k)}\}_{k\in\mathbb{N}}$ be computationally indistinguishable. Indeed, an important special case of Definition 8.4 is when one ensemble is uniform, and in such a case we call the other ensemble pseudo-random.

8.2.3.2. Relation to Statistical Closeness

Two probability ensembles, $\{X_n\}_{n\in\mathbb{N}}$ and $\{Y_n\}_{n\in\mathbb{N}}$, are said to be statistically close (or statistically indistinguishable) if for every positive polynomial p and all sufficient large n the variation distance between X_n and Y_n (i.e., $\frac{1}{2}\sum_z |\Pr[X_n = z] - \Pr[Y_n = z]|$) is bounded above by $1/p(n)$. Clearly, any two probability ensembles that are statistically close are computationally indistinguishable. Needless to say, this is a trivial case of computational indistinguishability, which is due to information-theoretic reasons. In contrast, we shall be interested in *non-trivial cases* (of computational indistinguishability), which correspond to probability ensembles that are statistically far apart.

Indeed, as noted in Section 8.1, there exist probability ensembles that are statistically far apart and yet are computationally indistinguishable (see Exercise 8.1). However, at least one of the probability ensembles in Exercise 8.1 is *not* polynomial-time constructible.[9] We shall be much more interested in non-trivial cases of computational indistinguishability in which both ensembles are polynomial-time constructible. An important example is provided by the definition of pseudorandom generators (see Exercise 8.7). As we shall see (in Theorem 8.11), the existence of one-way functions implies the existence of pseudorandom generators, which in turn implies the existence of *polynomial-time constructible* probability ensembles that are statistically far apart and yet are computationally indistinguishable. We mention that this sufficient condition is also necessary (see Exercise 8.9).

8.2.3.3. Indistinguishability by Multiple Samples

The definition of computational indistinguishability (i.e., Definition 8.4) refers to distinguishers that obtain a single sample from one of the two relevant probability ensembles (i.e., $\{X_n\}_{n\in\mathbb{N}}$ and $\{Y_n\}_{n\in\mathbb{N}}$). A very natural generalization of Definition 8.4 refers to distinguishers that obtain several independent samples from such an ensemble.

> **Definition 8.5** (indistinguishability by multiple samples): *Let $s:\mathbb{N}\to\mathbb{N}$ be polynomially bounded. Two probability ensembles, $\{X_n\}_{n\in\mathbb{N}}$ and $\{Y_n\}_{n\in\mathbb{N}}$, are computationally indistinguishable by $s(\cdot)$ samples if for every probabilistic polynomial-time algorithm D, every positive polynomial $p(\cdot)$, and all sufficiently large n's*
>
> $$\left| \Pr\left[D\left(X_n^{(1)}, \ldots, X_n^{(s(n))}\right) = 1\right] - \Pr\left[D\left(Y_n^{(1)}, \ldots, Y_n^{(s(n))}\right) = 1\right] \right| < \frac{1}{p(n)}$$
>
> *where $X_n^{(1)}$ through $X_n^{(s(n))}$ and $Y_n^{(1)}$ through $Y_n^{(s(n))}$ are independent random variables such that each $X_n^{(i)}$ is identical to X_n and each $Y_n^{(i)}$ is identical to Y_n.*

[9]We say that $\{Z_n\}_{n\in\mathbb{N}}$ is polynomial-time constructible if there exists a polynomial-time algorithm S such that $S(1^n)$ and Z_n are identically distributed.

It turns out that in the most interesting cases, computational indistinguishability by a single sample implies computational indistinguishability by any polynomial number of samples. One such case is the case of polynomial-time constructible ensembles. We say that the ensemble $\{Z_n\}_{n\in\mathbb{N}}$ is polynomial-time constructible if there exists a polynomial-time algorithm S such that $S(1^n)$ and Z_n are identically distributed.

Proposition 8.6: *Suppose that* $X \stackrel{\text{def}}{=} \{X_n\}_{n\in\mathbb{N}}$ *and* $Y \stackrel{\text{def}}{=} \{Y_n\}_{n\in\mathbb{N}}$ *are both polynomial-time constructible, and s be a polynomial. Then, X and Y are computationally indistinguishable by a single sample if and only if they are computationally indistinguishable by $s(\cdot)$ samples.*

Clearly, for every polynomial s, computational indistinguishability by $s(\cdot)$ samples implies computational indistinguishability by a single sample (see Exercise 8.5). We now prove that, for efficiently constructible ensembles, indistinguishability by a single sample implies indistinguishability by multiple samples.[10] The proof provides a simple demonstration of a central proof technique, known as the *hybrid technique*.

Proof Sketch:[11] Again, the proof uses the counter-positive, which in such settings is called a reducibility argument (see Section 7.1.2 onward). Specifically, we show that the existence of an efficient algorithm that distinguishes the ensembles X and Y using several samples implies the existence of an efficient algorithm that distinguishes the ensembles X and Y using a single sample. The implication is proven using the following argument, which will be later called a "hybrid argument".

To prove that a sequence of $s(n)$ samples drawn independently from X_n is indistinguishable from a sequence of $s(n)$ samples drawn independently from Y_n, we consider *hybrid* sequences such that the ith hybrid consists of i samples of X_n followed by $s(n) - i$ samples of Y_n. The "homogeneous" sequences (which we wish to prove to be computational indistinguishable) are the extreme hybrids (i.e., the first and last hybrids). The key observation is that distinguishing the extreme hybrids (toward the contradiction hypothesis) implies distinguishing neighboring hybrids, which in turn yields a procedure for distinguishing single samples of the two original distributions (contradicting the hypothesis that these two distributions are indistinguishable by a single sample). Details follow.

Suppose, toward the contradiction, that D distinguishes $s(n)$ samples of X_n from $s(n)$ samples of Y_n, with a distinguishing gap of $\delta(n)$. Denoting the ith hybrid by H_n^i (i.e., $H_n^i = (X_n^{(1)}, \ldots, X_n^{(i)}, Y_n^{(i+1)}, \ldots, Y_n^{(s(n))}))$, this means that D distinguishes the extreme hybrids (i.e., H_n^0 and $H_n^{s(n)}$) with gap $\delta(n)$. It follows that D distinguishes a random pair of neighboring hybrids (i.e., D distinguishes H_n^i from H_n^{i+1}, for a randomly selected i) with gap at least $\delta(n)/s(n)$: the reason being that

$$\mathsf{E}_{i\in\{0,\ldots,s(n)-1\}}\left[\Pr[D(H_n^i) = 1] - \Pr[D(H_n^{i+1}) = 1]\right]$$

$$= \frac{1}{s(n)} \cdot \sum_{i=0}^{s(n)-1} \left(\Pr[D(H_n^i) = 1] - \Pr[D(H_n^{i+1}) = 1]\right) \qquad (8.7)$$

$$= \frac{1}{s(n)} \cdot \left(\Pr[D(H_n^0) = 1] - \Pr[D(H_n^{s(n)}) = 1]\right) = \frac{\delta(n)}{s(n)}.$$

---

[10]The requirement that both ensembles are polynomial-time constructible is essential; see Exercise 8.10.

[11]For more details see [91, Sec. 3.2.3].

The key step in the argument is transforming the distinguishability of neighboring hybrids into distinguishability of single samples of the original ensembles (thus deriving a contradiction). Indeed, using D, we obtain a distinguisher D' of single samples: Given a single sample, algorithm D' selects $i \in \{0, \ldots, s(n) - 1\}$ at random, generates i samples from the first distribution and $s(n) - i - 1$ samples from the second distribution, invokes D with the $s(n)$-samples sequence obtained when placing the input sample in location $i + 1$, and answers whatever D does. That is, on input z and when selecting the index i, algorithm D' invokes D on a sample from the distribution $(X_n^{(1)}, \ldots, X_n^{(i)}, z, Y_n^{(i+2)}, \ldots, Y_n^{(s(n))})$. Thus, the construction of D' relies on the hypothesis that both probability ensembles are polynomial-time constructible. The analysis of D' is based on the following two facts:

1. When invoked on an input that is distributed according to X_n and selecting the index $i \in \{0, \ldots, s(n) - 1\}$, algorithm D' behaves like $D(H_n^{i+1})$, because $(X_n^{(1)}, \ldots, X_n^{(i)}, X_n, Y_n^{(i+2)}, \ldots, Y_n^{(s(n))}) \equiv H_n^{i+1}$.
2. When invoked on an input that is distributed according to Y_n and selecting the index $i \in \{0, \ldots, s(n) - 1\}$, algorithm D' behaves like $D(H_n^i)$, because $(X_n^{(1)}, \ldots, X_n^{(i)}, Y_n, Y_n^{(i+2)}, \ldots, Y_n^{(s(n))}) \equiv H_n^i$.

Thus, the distinguishing gap of D' (between Y_n and X_n) is captured by Eq. (8.7), and the claim follows (because assuming toward the contradiction that the proposition's conclusion does not hold leads to a contradiction of the proposition's hypothesis). $\qquad\square$

The hybrid technique – a digest. The hybrid technique constitutes a special type of a "reducibility argument" in which the computational indistinguishability of *complex* ensembles is proved using the computational indistinguishability of *basic* ensembles. The actual reduction is in the other direction: Efficiently distinguishing the basic ensembles is reduced to efficiently distinguishing the complex ensembles, and *hybrid* distributions are used in the reduction in an essential way. The following three properties of the construction of the hybrids play an important role in the argument:

1. *The complex ensembles collide with the extreme hybrids.* This property is essential because our aim is proving something that relates to the complex ensembles (i.e., their indistinguishability), while the argument itself refers to the extreme hybrids.

   In the proof of Proposition 8.6 the extreme hybrids (i.e., $H_n^{s(n)}$ and H_n^0) collide with the complex ensembles that represent $s(n)$-ary sequences of samples of one of the basic ensembles.

2. *The basic ensembles are efficiently mapped to neighboring hybrids.* This property is essential because our starting hypothesis relates to the basic ensembles (i.e., their indistinguishability), while the argument itself refers directly to the neighboring hybrids. Thus, we need to translate our knowledge (i.e., computational indistinguishability) of the basic ensembles to knowledge (i.e., computational indistinguishability) of any pair of neighboring hybrids. Typically, this is done by efficiently transforming strings in the range of a basic distribution into strings in the range of a hybrid such that the transformation maps the first basic distribution to one hybrid and the second basic distribution to the neighboring hybrid.

In the proof of Proposition 8.6 the basic ensembles (i.e., X_n and Y_n) were efficiently transformed into neighboring hybrids (i.e., H_n^{i+1} and H_n^i, respectively). Recall that, in this case, the efficiency of this transformation relied on the hypothesis that both the basic ensembles are polynomial-time constructible.

3. *The number of hybrids is small* (i.e., polynomial). This property is essential in order to deduce the computational indistinguishability of extreme hybrids from the computational indistinguishability of each pair of neighboring hybrids. Typically, the "distinguishability gap" established in the argument loses a factor that is proportional to the number of hybrids. This is due to the fact that the gap between the extreme hybrids is upper-bounded by the sum of the gaps between neighboring hybrids.

   In the proof of Proposition 8.6 the number of hybrids equals $s(n)$ and the aforementioned loss is reflected in Eq. (8.7).

We remark that in the course of a hybrid argument, a distinguishing algorithm referring to the complex ensembles is being analyzed and even invoked on arbitrary hybrids. The reader may be annoyed by the fact that the algorithm "was not designed to work on such hybrids" (but rather only on the extreme hybrids). However, *an algorithm is an algorithm*: Once it exists we can invoke it on inputs of our choice, and analyze its performance on arbitrary input distributions.

8.2.4. Amplifying the Stretch Function

Recall that the definition of pseudorandom generators (i.e., Definition 8.1) makes a minimal requirement regarding their stretch; that is, it is only required that the length of the output of such generators be longer than their input. Needless to say, we seek pseudorandom generators with a much more significant stretch, firstly because the stretch determines the saving in randomness obtained via Construction 8.2. It turns out (see Construction 8.7) that pseudorandom generators of any stretch function (and in particular of minimal stretch $\ell_1(k) \stackrel{\text{def}}{=} k + 1$) can be easily converted into pseudorandom generators of any desired (polynomially bounded) stretch function, ℓ. (On the other hand, since pseudorandom generators are required (in Definition 8.1) to run in polynomial time, their stretch must be polynomially bounded.)

Construction 8.7: *Let G_1 be a pseudorandom generator with stretch function $\ell_1(k) = k + 1$, and ℓ be any polynomially bounded stretch function that is polynomial-time computable. Let*

$$G(s) \stackrel{\text{def}}{=} \sigma_1 \sigma_2 \cdots \sigma_{\ell(|s|)} \tag{8.8}$$

where $x_0 = s$ and $x_i \sigma_i = G_1(x_{i-1})$, for $i = 1, \ldots, \ell(|s|)$. (That is, σ_i is the last bit of $G_1(x_{i-1})$ and x_i is the $|s|$-bit long prefix of $G_1(x_{i-1})$.)

Needless to say, G is polynomial-time computable and has stretch ℓ. An alternative construction is considered in Exercise 8.11.

Proposition 8.8: *Let G_1 and G be as in Construction 8.7. Then G constitutes a pseudorandom generator.*

Proof Sketch:[12] The proposition is proven using the *hybrid technique*, presented and discussed in Section 8.2.3. Here (for $i = 0, \ldots, \ell(k)$), we consider the hybrid

---

[12] For more details, see [91, Sec. 3.3.3].

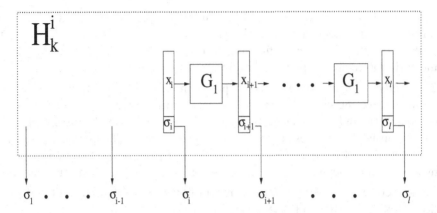

Figure 8.2: Analysis of stretch amplification – the ith hybrid.

distributions H_k^i, depicted in Figure 8.2 and defined by

$$H_k^i \stackrel{\text{def}}{=} U_i^{(1)} \cdot g_{\ell(k)-i}\big(U_k^{(2)}\big),$$

where $\cdot$ denotes the concatenation of strings, $g_j(x)$ denotes the j-bit long prefix of $G(x)$, and $U_i^{(1)}$ and $U_k^{(2)}$ are independent uniform distributions (over $\{0, 1\}^i$ and $\{0, 1\}^k$, respectively). The extreme hybrids (i.e., H_k^0 and H_k^k) correspond to $G(U_k)$ and $U_{\ell(k)}$, whereas distinguishability of neighboring hybrids can be worked into distinguishability of $G_1(U_k)$ and U_{k+1}. Details follow.

We shall focus on proving the indistinguishability of neighboring hybrids.[13] Suppose, toward the contradiction, that algorithm D distinguishes H_k^i from H_k^{i+1}. We first take a closer look at these hybrids. Note that, for $j \geq 1$, it holds that $g_j(s) \equiv (\sigma, g_{j-1}(x))$, where $x\sigma = G_1(s)$. Denoting the first $|x| - 1$ bits of x by $F(x)$ and the last bit of x by $L(x)$, we may write $g_j(s) \equiv (L(G_1(s)), g_{j-1}(F(G_1(s))))$ and $(U_1^{(1)}, U_k^{(2)}) \equiv (L(U_{k+1}), F(U_{k+1}))$. It follows that

$$H_k^i = U_i^{(1)} \cdot g_{\ell(k)-i}\big(U_k^{(2)}\big)$$

$$\equiv \big(U_i^{(1)}, L\big(G_1\big(U_k^{(2)}\big)\big), g_{(\ell(k)-i)-1}\big(F\big(G_1\big(U_k^{(2)}\big)\big)\big)\big)$$

$$H_k^{i+1} = U_{i+1}^{(1')} \cdot g_{\ell(k)-i-1}\big(U_k^{(2)}\big)$$

$$\equiv \big(U_i^{(1)}, L\big(U_{k+1}^{(2')}\big), g_{(\ell(k)-i)-1}\big(F(U_{k+1}^{(2')})\big)\big).$$

Now, combining the generation of $U_i^{(1)}$ and the evaluation of $g_{\ell(k)-i-1}$ with the distinguisher D, we distinguish the distribution $(F(G_1(U_k^{(2)})), L(G_1(U_k^{(2)}))) \equiv G_1(U_k)$ from the distribution $(F(U_{k+1}^{(2')}), L(U_{k+1}^{(2')})) \equiv U_{k+1}$, in contradiction to the pseudorandomness of G_1. Specifically, on input $x \in \{0, 1\}^{k+1}$, we uniformly select $r \in \{0, 1\}^i$ and output $D(r \cdot L(x) \cdot g_{\ell(k)-i-1}(F(x)))$. The analysis of the resulting distinguisher is based on the following two facts:

---

[13] As usual (when the hybrid technique is used), the distinguishability of the extreme hybrids (which collide with $G(U_k)$ and $U_{\ell(k)}$, respectively) implies the distinguishability of a random pair of neighboring hybrids. Thus, the following analysis will be applied to a random i (in $\{0, \ldots, k-1\}$), and the full analysis will refer to an expression analogous to Eq. (8.7).

1. When given an input that is distributed according to $G_1(U_k)$, we invoke algorithm D on input $(U_i', L(G_1(U_k)), g_{\ell(k)-i-1}(F(G_1(U_k)))) \equiv H_k^i$.
2. When given an input that is distributed according to U_{k+1}, we invoke algorithm D on input $(U_i', L(U_{k+1}), g_{\ell(k)-i-1}(F(U_{k+1}))) \equiv H_k^{i+1}$.

Thus, the probability that we output 1 on input $G_1(U_k)$ (resp., U_{k+1}) equals $\Pr[D(H_k^i) = 1]$ (resp., $\Pr[D(H_k^{i+1}) = 1]$). Hence, the distinguishability of neighboring hybrids implies the distinguishability of $G_1(U_k)$ and U_{k+1}. $\quad\blacksquare$

Conclusion. In view of the foregoing, when talking about the mere existence of pseudorandom generators, in the sense of Definition 8.1, we may ignore the specific stretch function.

8.2.5. Constructions

The constructions surveyed in this section "transform" computational difficulty, in the form of one-way functions, into generators of pseudorandomness. Recall that a *polynomial-time computable function* is called one-way if any efficient algorithm can invert it only with negligible success probability (see Definition 7.1 and Section 7.1 for further discussion). We will actually use hard-core predicates of such functions, and refer the reader to their treatment in Section 7.1.3. Loosely speaking, a *polynomial-time computable* predicate b is called a hard-core of a function f if any efficient algorithm, given $f(x)$, can guess $b(x)$ with success probability that is only negligibly higher than half. Recall that (by Theorem 7.7), for any one-way function f, the inner-product mod 2 of x and r is a hard-core of $f'(x, r) = (f(x), r)$.

8.2.5.1. A Simple Construction

Intuitively, the definition of a hard-core predicate implies a potentially interesting case of computational indistinguishability. Specifically, as will be shown implicitly in Proposition 8.9 and explicitly in Exercise 8.8, if b is a hard-core of the function f, then the ensemble $\{f(U_n) \cdot b(U_n)\}_{n \in \mathbb{N}}$ is computationally indistinguishable from the ensemble $\{f(U_n) \cdot U_1'\}_{n \in \mathbb{N}}$. Furthermore, if f is 1-1 then the foregoing ensembles are statistically far apart, and thus constitute a non-trivial case of computational indistinguishability. If f is also polynomial-time computable and length-preserving, then this yields a construction of a pseudorandom generator.

Proposition 8.9 (A simple construction of pseudorandom generators): *Let b be a hard-core predicate of a polynomial-time computable 1-1 and length-preserving function f. Then, $G(s) \stackrel{\text{def}}{=} f(s) \cdot b(s)$ is a pseudorandom generator.*

Proof Sketch:[14] Considering a uniformly distributed $s \in \{0, 1\}^n$, we first note that the n-bit long prefix of $G(s)$ is uniformly distributed in $\{0, 1\}^n$, because f induces a permutation on the set $\{0, 1\}^n$. Hence, the proof boils down to showing that distinguishing $f(s) \cdot b(s)$ from $f(s) \cdot \sigma$, where σ is a random bit, yields contradiction to the hypothesis that b is a hard-core of f (i.e., that $b(s)$ is *unpredictable* from $f(s)$). Intuitively, the reason is that such a hypothetical distinguisher also distinguishes

---

[14]For more details, see [91, Sec. 3.3.4].

$f(s) \cdot b(s)$ from $f(s) \cdot \overline{b(s)}$, where $\overline{\sigma} = 1 - \sigma$, whereas distinguishing $f(s) \cdot b(s)$ from $f(s) \cdot \overline{b(s)}$ yields an algorithm for predicting $b(s)$ based on $f(s)$. Details follow. We start with any potential distinguisher D, and let

$$\delta(k) \stackrel{\text{def}}{=} \Pr[D(G(U_k)) = 1] - \Pr[D(U_{k+1}) = 1].$$

We may assume, without loss of generality, that $\delta(k)$ is non-negative (for infinitely many k's). Observing that $G(U_k) = f(U_k) \cdot b(U_k)$ and that U_{k+1} is distributed identically to a random variable that equals $f(U_k)b(U_k)$ with probability $1/2$ and $f(U_k)\overline{b(U_k)}$ otherwise, we have

$$\Pr[D(f(U_k)b(U_k)) = 1] - \Pr[D(f(U_k)\overline{b(U_k)}) = 1] = 2\delta(k).$$

The key observation is that D effectively distinguishes (with gap $2\delta(k)$) the case that the last bit is $b(U_k)$ from the case that the last bit is $\overline{b(U_k)}$. This distinguishing ability can be transformed to predicting the value of $b(U_k)$, when given the value $f(U_k)$. Indeed, consider an algorithm A that, on input y, uniformly selects $\sigma \in \{0, 1\}$, invokes $D(y\sigma)$, and outputs σ if $D(y\sigma) = 1$ and $\overline{\sigma}$ otherwise. Then

$$\Pr[A(f(U_k)) = b(U_k)]$$
$$= \Pr[D(f(U_k) \cdot \sigma) = 1 \wedge \sigma = b(U_k)] + \Pr[D(f(U_k) \cdot \sigma) = 0 \wedge \sigma = \overline{b(U_k)}]$$
$$= \frac{1}{2} \cdot \left(\Pr[D(f(U_k) \cdot b(U_k)) = 1] + \left(1 - \Pr[D(f(U_k) \cdot \overline{b(U_k)}) = 1] \right) \right)$$

which equals $(1 + 2\delta(k))/2$. This contradicts the hypothesis that b is a hard-core of f, and the proposition follows. $\qquad\square$

Combining Theorem 7.7, Proposition 8.9, and Construction 8.7, we obtain the following corollary.

Theorem 8.10 (A sufficient condition for the existence of pseudorandom generators): *If there exists 1-1 and length-preserving one-way function then, for every polynomially bounded stretch function ℓ, there exists a pseudorandom generator of stretch ℓ.*

Digest. The main part of the proof of Proposition 8.9 is showing that the (next bit) unpredictability of $G(U_k)$ implies the pseudorandomness of $G(U_k)$. The fact that (next bit) unpredictability and pseudorandomness are equivalent, in general, is proven explicitly in the alternative proof of Theorem 8.10 provided next.

8.2.5.2. An Alternative Presentation

Let us take a closer look at the pseudorandom generators obtained by combining Construction 8.7 and Proposition 8.9. For a stretch function $\ell : \mathbb{N} \to \mathbb{N}$, a 1-1 one-way function f with a hard-core b, we obtain

$$G(s) \stackrel{\text{def}}{=} \sigma_1 \sigma_2 \cdots \sigma_{\ell(|s|)}, \tag{8.9}$$

where $x_0 = s$ and $x_i \sigma_i = f(x_{i-1})b(x_{i-1})$ for $i = 1, \ldots, \ell(|s|)$. Denoting by $f^i(x)$ the value of f iterated i times on x (i.e., $f^i(x) = f^{i-1}(f(x))$ and $f^0(x) = x$), we rewrite Eq. (8.9) as follows

$$G(s) \stackrel{\text{def}}{=} b(s) \cdot b(f(s)) \cdots b(f^{\ell(|s|)-1}(s)). \tag{8.10}$$

The pseudorandomness of G is established in two steps, using the notion of (next bit) unpredictability. An ensemble $\{Z_k\}_{k\in\mathbb{N}}$ is called unpredictable if any probabilistic polynomial-time machine obtaining a (random)[15] prefix of Z_k fails to predict the next bit of Z_k with probability non-negligibly higher than $1/2$. Specifically, we establish the following two results.

1. A **general result** asserting that *an ensemble is pseudorandom if and only if it is unpredictable*. Recall that an ensemble is pseudorandom if it is computationally indistinguishable from a uniform distribution (over bit strings of adequate length).

   Clearly, pseudorandomness implies polynomial-time unpredictability, but here we actually need the other direction, which is less obvious. Still, using a hybrid argument, one can show that (next-bit) unpredictability implies indistinguishability from the uniform ensemble. For details, see Exercise 8.12.

2. A **specific result** asserting that the ensemble $\{G(U_k)\}_{k\in\mathbb{N}}$ is unpredictable *from right to left*. Equivalently, $G'(U_n)$ is polynomial-time unpredictable (from left to right (as usual)), where $G'(s) = b(f^{\ell(|s|)-1}(s))\cdots b(f(s))\cdot b(s)$ is the reverse of $G(s)$.

   Using the fact that f induces a permutation over $\{0,1\}^n$, observe that the $(j+1)$-bit long prefix of $G'(U_k)$ is distributed identically to $b(f^j(U_k))\cdots b(f(U_k))\cdot b(U_k)$. Thus, an algorithm that predicts the $j+1^{\text{st}}$ bit of $G'(U_n)$ based on the j-bit long prefix of $G'(U_n)$ yields an algorithm that guesses $b(U_n)$ based on $f(U_n)$. For details, see Exercise 8.14.

Needless to say, G is a pseudorandom generator if and only if G' is a pseudorandom generator (see Exercise 8.13). We mention that Eq. (8.10) is often referred to as the Blum-Micali Construction.[16]

8.2.5.3. A General Condition for the Existence of Pseudorandom Generators

Recall that given any one-way 1-1 length-preserving function, we can easily construct a pseudorandom generator. Actually, the 1-1 (and length-preserving) requirement may be dropped, but the currently known construction – for the general case – is quite complex.

Theorem 8.11 (On the existence of pseudorandom generators): *Pseudorandom generators exist if and only if one-way functions exist.*

To show that the existence of pseudorandom generators implies the existence of one-way functions, consider a pseudorandom generator G with stretch function $\ell(k) = 2k$. For $x, y \in \{0,1\}^k$, define $f(x,y) \stackrel{\text{def}}{=} G(x)$, and so f is polynomial-time computable (and length-preserving). It must be that f is one-way, or else one can distinguish $G(U_k)$ from U_{2k} by trying to invert and checking the result: Inverting f on the distribution $f(U_{2k})$ corresponds to operating on the distribution $G(U_k)$, whereas the probability that U_{2k} has inverse under f is negligible.

The interesting direction of the proof of Theorem 8.11 is the construction of pseudorandom generators based on any one-way function. Since the known proof is quite complex,

---

[15]For simplicity, we define unpredictability as referring to prefixes of a random length (distributed uniformly in $\{0,\ldots,|Z_k|-1\}$). A more general definition allows the predictor to determine the length of the prefix that it reads on the fly. This seemingly stronger notion of unpredictability is actually equivalent to the one we use, because both notions are equivalent to pseudorandomness.

[16]Given the popularity of the term, we deviate from our convention of not specifying credits in the main text. Indeed, this construction originates in [41].

we only provide a very rough overview of some of the ideas involved. We mention that these ideas make extensive use of adequate hashing functions (e.g., pairwise independent hashing functions; see Appendix D.2).

We first note that, in general (when f may not be 1-1), the ensemble $f(U_k)$ may not be pseudorandom, and so Construction 8.9 (i.e., $G(s) = f(s)b(s)$, where b is a hard-core of f) cannot be used *directly*. One idea underlying the known construction is hashing $f(U_k)$ to an almost uniform string of length related to its entropy, using adequate hashing functions.[17] But "hashing $f(U_k)$ down to length comparable to the entropy" means shrinking the length of the output to, say, $k' < k$. This foils the entire point of stretching the k-bit seed. Thus, a second idea underlying the construction is compensating for the loss of $k - k'$ bits by extracting these many bits from the seed U_k itself. This is done by hashing U_k, and the point is that the $(k - k')$-bit long hash value does not make the inverting task any easier. Implementing these ideas turns out to be more difficult than it seems, and indeed an alternative construction would be most appreciated.

8.2.6. Non-uniformly Strong Pseudorandom Generators

Recall that we said that truly random sequences can be replaced by pseudorandom sequences without affecting any efficient computation that uses these sequences. The specific formulation of this assertion, presented in Proposition 8.3, refers to randomized algorithms that take a "primary input" and use a secondary "random-input" in their computation. Proposition 8.3 asserts that it is infeasible to find a primary input for which the replacement of a truly random secondary input by a pseudorandom one affects the final output of the algorithm in a noticeable way. This, however, does not mean that such primary inputs do not exist (but rather that they are hard to find). Consequently, Proposition 8.3 falls short of yielding a (worst-case)[18] "derandomization" of a complexity class such as $\mathcal{BPP}$. To obtain such results, we need a stronger notion of pseudorandom generators, presented next. Specifically, we need pseudorandom generators that can fool all polynomial-size circuits (cf. §1.2.4.1), and not merely all probabilistic polynomial-time algorithms.[19]

Definition 8.12 (strong pseudorandom generator – fooling circuits): *A deterministic polynomial-time algorithm G is called a* non-uniformly strong pseudorandom generator *if there exists a* stretch function, $\ell : \mathbb{N} \to \mathbb{N}$, *such that for any family* $\{C_k\}_{k \in \mathbb{N}}$

---

[17]This is done after guaranteeing that the logarithm of the probability mass of a value of $f(U_k)$ is typically close to the entropy of $f(U_k)$. Specifically, given an arbitrary one-way function f', one first constructs f by taking a "direct product" of sufficiently many copies of f'. For example, for $x_1, \ldots, x_{k^{2/3}} \in \{0, 1\}^{k^{1/3}}$, we let $f(x_1, \ldots, x_{k^{2/3}}) \stackrel{\text{def}}{=} f'(x_1), \ldots, f'(x_{k^{2/3}})$.

[18]Indeed, Proposition 8.3 yields an *average-case derandomization of* $\mathcal{BPP}$. In particular, for every polynomial-time constructible ensemble $\{X_n\}_{n \in \mathbb{N}}$, every Boolean function $f \in \mathcal{BPP}$, and every $\varepsilon > 0$, there exists a randomized algorithm A' of randomness complexity $r_\varepsilon(n) = n^\varepsilon$ such that the probability that $A'(X_n) \neq f(X_n)$ is negligible. A corresponding deterministic $(\exp(r_\varepsilon)$-time) algorithm A'' can be obtained, as in the proof of Theorem 8.13, and again the probability that $A''(X_n) \neq f(X_n)$ is negligible, where here the probability is taken only over the distribution of the primary input (represented by X_n). In contrast, worst-case derandomization, as captured by the assertion $\mathcal{BPP} \subseteq \text{DTIME}(2^{r_\varepsilon})$, requires that the probability that $A''(X_n) \neq f(X_n)$ is zero.

[19]Needless to say, strong pseudorandom generators in the sense of Definition 8.12 satisfy the basic definition of a pseudorandom generator (i.e., Definition 8.1); see Exercise 8.15. We comment that the underlying notion of computational indistinguishability (by circuits) is strictly stronger than Definition 8.4, and that it is invariant under multiple samples (regardless of the constructibility of the underlying ensembles); for details, see Exercise 8.16.

of polynomial-size circuits, for any positive polynomial p, and for all sufficiently large k's

$$| \Pr[C_k(G(U_k)) = 1] - \Pr[C_k(U_{\ell(k)}) = 1] | < \frac{1}{p(k)}$$

An alternative formulation is obtained by referring to polynomial-time machines that take advice (Section 3.1.2). Using such pseudorandom generators, we can "derandomize" $\mathcal{BPP}$.

Theorem 8.13 (derandomization of $\mathcal{BPP}$): *If there exists non-uniformly strong pseudorandom generators then $\mathcal{BPP}$ is contained in $\cap_{\varepsilon>0} \mathrm{DTIME}(t_\varepsilon)$, where $t_\varepsilon(n) \stackrel{\text{def}}{=} 2^{n^\varepsilon}$.*

Proof Sketch: For any $S \in \mathcal{BPP}$ and any $\varepsilon > 0$, we let A denote the decision procedure for S and G denote a non-uniformly strong pseudorandom generator stretching n^ε-bit long seeds into poly(n)-long sequences (to be used by A as secondary input when processing a primary input of length n). Combining A and G, we obtain an algorithm $A' = A_G$ (as in Construction 8.2). We claim that *A and A' may significantly differ in their* (expected probabilistic) *decision on at most finitely many inputs*, because otherwise we can use these inputs (together with A) to derive a (non-uniform) family of polynomial-size circuits that distinguishes $G(U_{n^\varepsilon})$ and $U_{\mathrm{poly}(n)}$, contradicting the the hypothesis regarding G. Specifically, an input x on which A and A' differ significantly yields a circuit C_x that distinguishes $G(U_{|x|^\varepsilon})$ and $U_{\mathrm{poly}(|x|)}$, by letting $C_x(r) = A(x, r)$.[20] Incorporating the finitely many "bad" inputs into A', we derive a probabilistic polynomial-time algorithm that decides S while using randomness complexity n^ε.

Finally, emulating A' on each of the 2^{n^ε} possible random sequences (i.e., seeds to G) and ruling by majority, we obtain a deterministic algorithm A'' as required. That is, let $A'(x, r)$ denote the output of algorithm A' on input x when using coins $r \in \{0, 1\}^{n^\varepsilon}$. Then $A''(x)$ invokes $A'(x, r)$ on every $r \in \{0, 1\}^{n^\varepsilon}$, and outputs 1 if and only if the majority of these 2^{n^ε} invocations have returned 1. □

We comment that stronger results regarding derandomization of $\mathcal{BPP}$ are presented in Section 8.3.

On constructing non-uniformly strong pseudorandom generators. Non-uniformly strong pseudorandom generators (as in Definition 8.12) can be constructed using any one-way function that is hard to invert by any non-uniform family of polynomial-size circuits (as in Definition 7.3), rather than by probabilistic polynomial-time machines. In fact, the construction in this case is simpler than the one employed in the uniform case (i.e., the construction underlying the proof of Theorem 8.11).

8.2.7. Stronger Notions and Conceptual Reflections

We first mention two stronger variants on the definition of pseudorandom generators, and conclude this section by highlighting various conceptual issues.

---

[20]Indeed, in terms of the proof of Proposition 8.3, the finder F consists of a non-uniform family of polynomial-size circuits that print the "problematic" primary inputs that are hard-wired in them, and the corresponding distinguisher D is thus also non-uniform.

8.2.7.1. Stronger (Uniform-Complexity) Notions

The following two notions represent a strengthening of the standard definition of pseudo-random generators (as presented in Definition 8.1). Non-uniform versions of these notions (strengthening Definition 8.12) are also of interest.

Fooling stronger distinguishers. One strengthening of Definition 8.1 amounts to explicitly quantifying the resources (and success gaps) of distinguishers. We choose to bound these quantities as a function of the length of the seed (i.e., k), rather than as a function of the length of the string that is being examined (i.e., $\ell(k)$). For a class of time bounds $\mathcal{T}$ (e.g., $\mathcal{T} = \{t(k) \stackrel{\text{def}}{=} 2^{c\sqrt{k}}\}_{c \in \mathbb{N}}$) and a class of noticeable functions (e.g., $\mathcal{F} = \{f(k) \stackrel{\text{def}}{=} 1/t(k) : t \in \mathcal{T}\}$), we say that a pseudorandom generator, G, is $(\mathcal{T}, \mathcal{F})$-strong if for any probabilistic algorithm D having running time bounded by a function in $\mathcal{T}$ (applied to k)[21] for any function f in $\mathcal{F}$, and for all sufficiently large k's, it holds that

$$|\Pr[D(G(U_k)) = 1] - \Pr[D(U_{\ell(k)}) = 1]| < f(k).$$

An analogous strengthening may be applied to the definition of one-way functions. Doing so reveals the weakness of the known construction that underlies the proof of Theorem 8.11: It only implies that for some $\varepsilon > 0$ ($\varepsilon = 1/8$ will do), for any $\mathcal{T}$ and $\mathcal{F}$, the existence of "$(\mathcal{T}, \mathcal{F})$-strong one-way functions" implies the existence of $(\mathcal{T}', \mathcal{F}')$-strong pseudorandom generators, where $\mathcal{T}' = \{t'(k) \stackrel{\text{def}}{=} t(k^\varepsilon)/\text{poly}(k) : t \in \mathcal{T}\}$ and $\mathcal{F}' = \{f'(k) \stackrel{\text{def}}{=} \text{poly}(k) \cdot f(k^\varepsilon) : f \in \mathcal{F}\}$. What we *would like* to have is an analogous result with $\mathcal{T}' = \{t'(k) \stackrel{\text{def}}{=} t(\Omega(k))/\text{poly}(k) : t \in \mathcal{T}\}$ and $\mathcal{F}' = \{f'(k) \stackrel{\text{def}}{=} \text{poly}(k) \cdot f(\Omega(k)) : f \in \mathcal{F}\}$.

Pseudorandom Functions. Recall that pseudorandom generators allow for efficiently generating long pseudorandom sequences from short random seeds. Pseudorandom functions (defined in Appendix C.3.3) are even more powerful: They allow *efficient direct access* to a huge pseudorandom sequence, which is not even feasible to scan bit by bit. Specifically, based on a (random) k-bit long seed, they allow direct access to a sequence of length 2^k. Put in other words, pseudorandom functions are deterministic polynomial-time algorithms that map a k-bit long seed s and a k-bit long argument x to a value $f_s(x)$ such that, for a uniformly distributed $s \in \{0, 1\}^k$, the function f_s looks random to any poly(k)-time observer that may query f_s at arguments of its choice. Thus, pseudorandom functions can replace truly random functions in any efficient application (e.g., most notably in cryptography). We mention that pseudorandom functions can be constructed from any pseudorandom generator (see Theorem C.8), and that they have found many applications in cryptography (see Appendices C.3.3, C.5.2, and C.6.2). Pseudorandom functions were also used to derive negative results in computational learning theory [232] and in the study of circuit complexity (cf. Natural Proofs [189]).

8.2.7.2. Conceptual Reflections

We highlight several conceptual aspects of the foregoing computational approach to randomness. Some of these aspects are common to other instantiations of the general paradigm (esp., the one presented in Section 8.3).

---

[21]That is, when examining a sequence of length $\ell(k)$, algorithm D makes at most $t(k)$ steps, where $t \in \mathcal{T}$.

Behavioristic versus ontological. The behavioristic nature of the computational approach to randomness is best demonstrated by confronting this approach with the Kolmogorov-Chaitin approach to randomness. Loosely speaking, a string is *Kolmogorov-random* if its length equals the length of the shortest program producing it. This shortest program may be considered the "true explanation" to the phenomenon described by the string. A Kolmogorov-random string is thus a string that does not have a substantially simpler (i.e., shorter) explanation than itself. Considering the simplest explanation of a phenomenon may be viewed as an ontological approach. In contrast, considering the effect of phenomena on certain devices (or observations), as underlying the definition of pseudorandomness, is a behavioristic approach. Furthermore, there exist probability distributions that are not uniform (and are not even statistically close to a uniform distribution) and nevertheless are indistinguishable from a uniform distribution (by any efficient device). Thus, *distributions that are ontologically very different are considered equivalent by the behavioristic point of view taken in the definition of computational indistinguishability.*

A relativistic view of randomness. We have defined pseudorandomness in terms of its observer. Specifically, we have considered the class of efficient (i.e., polynomial-time) observers and defined as pseudorandom objects that look random to any observer in that class. In subsequent sections, we shall consider restricted classes of such observers (e.g., space-bounded polynomial-time observers and even very restricted observers that merely apply specific tests such as linear tests or hitting tests). Each such class of observers gives rise to a different notion of pseudorandomness. Furthermore, the general paradigm (of pseudorandomness) explicitly aims at *distributions that are not uniform and yet are considered as such from the point of view of certain observers.* Thus, our entire approach to pseudorandomness is relativistic and subjective (i.e., depending on the abilities of the observer).

Randomness and Computational Difficulty. Pseudorandomness and computational difficulty play dual roles: The general paradigm of pseudorandomness relies on the fact that *placing computational restrictions on the observer gives rise to distributions that are not uniform and still cannot be distinguished from uniform distributions.* Thus, the pivot of the entire approach is the computational difficulty of distinguishing pseudorandom distributions from truly random ones. Furthermore, many of the constructions of pseudorandom generators rely either on conjectures or on facts regarding computational difficulty (i.e., that certain computations are hard for certain classes). For example, one-way functions were used to construct general-purpose pseudorandom generators (i.e., those working in polynomial time and fooling all polynomial-time observers). Analogously, as we shall see in §8.3.3.1, the fact that parity function is hard for polynomial-size constant-depth circuits can be used to generate (highly non-uniform) sequences that fool such circuits.

Randomness and Predictability. The connection between pseudorandomness and unpredictability (by efficient procedures) plays an important role in the analysis of several constructions (cf. Sections 8.2.5 and 8.3.2). We wish to highlight the intuitive appeal of this connection.

8.3. Derandomization of Time-Complexity Classes

Let us take a second look at the process of derandomization that underlies the proof of Theorem 8.13. First, a pseudorandom generator was used to shrink the randomness complexity of a BPP-algorithm, and then derandomization was achieved by scanning all possible seeds to this generator. A key observation regarding this process is that there is no point in insisting that the pseudorandom generator runs in time that is polynomial in its seed length. Instead, it suffices to require that the generator run in time that is exponential in its seed length, because we are incurring such an overhead anyhow due to the scanning of all possible seeds. Furthermore, in this context, the running time of the generator may be larger than the running time of the algorithm, which means that the generator need only fool distinguishers that take fewer steps than the generator. These considerations motivate the following definition of canonical derandomizers.

8.3.1. Defining Canonical Derandomizers

Recall that in order to "derandomize" a probabilistic polynomial-time algorithm A, we first obtain a functionally equivalent algorithm A_G (as in Construction 8.2) that has (significantly) smaller randomness complexity. Algorithm A_G has to maintain A's input-output behavior on all (but finitely many) inputs. Thus, the set of the relevant distinguishers (considered in the proof of Theorem 8.13) is the set of all possible circuits obtained from A by hard-wiring any of the possible inputs. Such a circuit, denoted C_x, emulates the execution of algorithm A on input x, when using the circuit's input as the algorithm's internal coin tosses (i.e., $C_x(r) = A(x, r)$). Furthermore, the size of C_x is quadratic in the running time of A on input x, and the length of the input to C_x equals the running time of A (on input x).[22] Thus, the size of C_x is quadratic in the length of its own input, and the pseudorandom generator in use (i.e., G) needs to fool each such circuit. Recalling that we may allow the generator to run in exponential time (i.e., time that is exponential in the length of its own input (i.e., the seed)),[23] we arrive at the following definition.

Definition 8.14 (pseudorandom generator for derandomizing BPTIME($\cdot$)):[24] *Let* $\ell :$ $\mathbb{N} \to \mathbb{N}$ *be a monotonically increasing function. A* canonical derandomizer of stretch ℓ *is a deterministic algorithm G that satisfies the following two conditions.*

1. *On input a k-bit long seed, G makes at most $\mathrm{poly}(2^k \cdot \ell(k))$ steps and outputs a string of length $\ell(k)$.*
2. *For every circuit D_k of size $\ell(k)^2$ it holds that*

$$| \Pr[D_k(G(U_k)) = 1] - \Pr[D_k(U_{\ell(k)}) = 1] | < \frac{1}{6} . \qquad (8.11)$$

---

[22]Indeed, we assume that algorithm A is represented as a Turing machine and refer to the standard emulation of Turing machines by circuits (as underlying the proof of Theorem 2.21). Thus, the aforementioned circuit C_x has size that is at most quadratic in the running time of A on input x, which in turn means that C_x has size that is at most quadratic in the length of its own input. (In fact, the circuit size can be made almost linear in the running time of A, by using a better emulation [180].) We note that many sources use the fictitious convention by which the circuit size equals the length of its input; this fictitious convention can be justified by considering a (suitably) padded input.

[23]Actually, in Definition 8.14 we allow the generator to run in time $\mathrm{poly}(2^k \ell(k))$, rather than in time $\mathrm{poly}(2^k)$. This is done in order not to trivially rule out generators of super-exponential stretch (i.e., $\ell(k) = 2^{\omega(k)}$). However (see Exercise 8.18), the condition in Eq. (8.11) does not allow for super-exponential stretch (or even for $\ell(k) = \omega(2^k)$). Thus, in retrospect, the two formulations are equivalent (because $\mathrm{poly}(2^k \ell(k)) = \mathrm{poly}(2^k)$ for $\ell(k) = 2^{O(k)}$).

[24]Fixing a model of computation, we denote by BPTIME(t) the class of decision problems that are solvable by a randomized algorithm of time complexity t that has two-sided error $1/3$. Using $1/6$ as the "threshold distinguishing gap" (in Eq. (8.11)) guarantees that if $\Pr[D_k(U_{\ell(k)}) = 1] \geq 2/3$ (resp., $\Pr[D_k(U_{\ell(k)}) = 1] \leq 1/3$) then $\Pr[D_k(G(U_k)) = 1] > 1/2$ (resp., $\Pr[D_k(G(U_k)) = 1] < 1/2$). As we shall see, this suffices for a derandomization of BPTIME(t) in time T, where $T(n) = \mathrm{poly}(2^{\ell^{-1}(t(n))} \cdot t(n))$ (and we use a seed of length $k = \ell^{-1}(t(n))$).

The circuit D_k represents a potential distinguisher, which is given an $\ell(k)$-bit long string (sampled either from $G(U_k)$ or from $U_{\ell(k)}$). When seeking to derandomize an algorithm A of time complexity t, the aforementioned $\ell(k)$-bit long string represents a possible sequence of coin tosses of A, when invoked on a generic (primary) input of length $n = t^{-1}(\ell(k))$. Thus, for any $x \in \{0, 1\}^n$, considering the circuit $D_k(r) = A(x, r)$, where $|r| = t(n) = \ell(k)$, we note that Eq. (8.11) implies that $A_G(x) = A(x, G(U_k))$ *maintains the majority vote of* $A(x) = A(x, U_{\ell(k)})$. On the other hand, the time complexity of G implies that the straightforward deterministic emulation of $A_G(x)$ takes time $2^k \cdot (\text{poly}(2^k \cdot \ell(k)) + t(n))$, which is upper-bounded by $\text{poly}(2^k \cdot \ell(k)) = \text{poly}(2^{\ell^{-1}(t(n))} \cdot t(n))$. This yields the following (conditional) derandomization result.

Proposition 8.15: *Let* $\ell, t : \mathbb{N} \to \mathbb{N}$ *be monotonically increasing functions and let* $\ell^{-1}(t(n))$ *denote the smallest integer* k *such that* $\ell(k) \geq t(n)$. *If there exists a canonical derandomizer of stretch* ℓ *then, for every time-constructible* $t : \mathbb{N} \to \mathbb{N}$, *it holds that* $\text{BPTIME}(t) \subseteq \text{DTIME}(T)$, *where* $T(n) = \text{poly}(2^{\ell^{-1}(t(n))} \cdot t(n))$.

Proof Sketch: Just mimic the proof of Theorem 8.13, which in turn uses Construction 8.2. (Recall that given any randomized algorithm A and generator G, Construction 8.2 yields an algorithm A_G of randomness complexity $\ell^{-1} \circ t$ and time complexity $\text{poly}(2^{\ell^{-1} \circ t}) + t$.)[25] Observe that the complexity of the resulting deterministic procedure is dominated by the $2^k = 2^{\ell^{-1}(t(|x|))}$ invocations of $A_G(x, s) = A(x, G(s))$, where $s \in \{0, 1\}^k$, and each of these invocations takes time $\text{poly}(2^{\ell^{-1}(t(|x|))}) + t(|x|)$. Thus, on input an n-bit long string, the deterministic procedure runs in time $\text{poly}(2^{\ell^{-1}(t(n))} \cdot t(n))$. The correctness of this procedure (which takes a majority vote among the 2^k invocations of A_G) follows by combining Eq. (8.11) with the hypothesis that $\Pr[A(x)=1]$ is bounded-away from $1/2$. Specifically, using the hypothesis $|\Pr[A(x)=1] - (1/2)| \geq 1/6$, it follows that the majority vote of $(A_G(x, s))_{s \in \{0,1\}^k}$ equals 1 (equiv., $\Pr[A(x, G(U_k))=1] > 1/2$) if and only if $\Pr[A(x)=1] > 1/2$ (equiv., $\Pr[A(x, U_{\ell(k)})=1] > 1/2$). Indeed, the implication is due to Eq. (8.11), when applied to the circuit $C_x(r) = A(x, r)$ (which has size at most $|r|^2$). $\qquad \square$

The goal. In light of Proposition 8.15, we seek canonical derandomizers with stretch that is as large as possible. The stretch cannot be super-exponential (i.e., it must hold that $\ell(k) = O(2^k)$), because there exists a circuit of size $O(2^k \cdot \ell(k))$ that violates Eq. (8.11) (see Exercise 8.18), whereas for $\ell(k) = \omega(2^k)$ it holds that $O(2^k \cdot \ell(k)) < \ell(k)^2$. Thus, our goal is to construct a canonical derandomizer with stretch $\ell(k) = 2^{\Omega(k)}$. Such a canonical derandomizer will allow for a "full derandomization of $\mathcal{BPP}$":

Theorem 8.16: *If there exists a canonical derandomizer of stretch* $\ell(k) = 2^{\Omega(k)}$, *then* $\mathcal{BPP} = \mathcal{P}$.

Proof: Using Proposition 8.15, we get $\text{BPTIME}(t) \subseteq \text{DTIME}(T)$, where $T(n) = \text{poly}(2^{\ell^{-1}(t(n))} \cdot t(n)) = \text{poly}(t(n))$. $\qquad \blacksquare$

---

[25]Actually, given any randomized algorithm A and generator G, Construction 8.2 yields an algorithm A_G that is defined such that $A_G(x, s) = A(x, G'(s))$, where $|s| = \ell^{-1}(t(|x|))$ and $G'(s)$ denotes the $t(|x|)$-bit long prefix of $G(s)$. For simplicity, we shall assume here that $\ell(|s|) = t(|x|)$, and thus use G rather than G'. Note that given n we can find $k = \ell^{-1}(t(n))$ by invoking $G(1^i)$ for $i = 1, \ldots, k$ (using the fact that $\ell : \mathbb{N} \to \mathbb{N}$ is monotonically increasing). Also note that $\ell(k) = O(2^k)$ must hold (see footnote 23), and thus we may replace $\text{poly}(2^k \cdot \ell(k))$ by $\text{poly}(2^k)$.

Reflections. Recall that a canonical derandomizer G was defined in a way that allows it to have time complexity t_G that is larger than the size of the circuits that it fools (i.e., $t_G(k) > \ell(k)^2$ is allowed). Furthermore, $t_G(k) > 2^k$ was also allowed. Thus, if indeed $t_G(k) = 2^{\Omega(k)}$ (as is the case in Section 8.3.2), then $G(U_k)$ *can be distinguished from* $U_{\ell(k)}$ *in time* $2^k \cdot t_G(k) = \text{poly}(t_G(k))$ by trying all possible seeds.[26] We stress that the latter distinguisher is a uniform algorithm (and it works by invoking G on all possible seeds). In contrast, for a general-purpose pseudorandom generator G (as discussed in Section 8.2), it holds that $t_G(k) = \text{poly}(k)$, while *for every polynomial p it holds that $G(U_k)$ is indistinguishable from $U_{\ell(k)}$ in time $p(t_G(k))$.*

8.3.2. Constructing Canonical Derandomizers

The fact that canonical derandomizers are allowed to be more complex than the corresponding distinguisher makes *some* of the techniques of Section 8.2 inapplicable in the current context. For example, the stretch function cannot be amplified as in Section 8.2.4 (see Exercise 8.17). On the other hand, the techniques developed in the current section are inapplicable to Section 8.2. For example, the pseudorandomness of some canonical derandomizers (i.e., the generators of Construction 8.17) holds even when the potential distinguisher is given the seed itself. This amazing phenomenon capitalizes on the fact that the distinguisher's time complexity does not allow for running the generator on the given seed.

8.3.2.1. The Construction and Its Consequences

As in Section 8.2.5, the construction presented next transforms computational difficulty into pseudorandomness, except that here, both computational difficulty and pseudorandomness are of a somewhat different form than in Section 8.2.5. Specifically, here we use Boolean predicates that are computable in exponential time but are T-inapproximable for some exponential function T (see Definition 7.9 recapitulated next). That is, we assume *the existence of a Boolean predicate and constants $c, \varepsilon > 0$ such that for all but finitely many m, the* (residual) *predicate $f : \{0, 1\}^m \to \{0, 1\}$ is computable in time* 2^{cm}, *but for any circuit C of size $2^{\varepsilon m}$ it holds that* $\Pr[C(U_m) = f(U_m)] < \frac{1}{2} + 2^{-\varepsilon m}$. (Needless to say, $\varepsilon < c$.) Recall that such predicates exist under the assumption that $\mathcal{E}$ has (almost-everywhere) exponential circuit complexity (see Theorem 7.19). With these preliminaries, we turn to the construction of canonical derandomizers with exponential stretch.

Construction 8.17 (The Nisan-Wigderson Construction):[27] *Let $f : \{0, 1\}^m \to \{0, 1\}$ and $S_1, \ldots, S_\ell$ be a sequence of m-subsets of $\{1, \ldots, k\}$. Then, for $s \in \{0, 1\}^k$, we let*

$$G(s) \stackrel{\text{def}}{=} f(s_{S_1}) \cdots f(s_{S_\ell}) \tag{8.12}$$

where s_S denotes the projection of s on the bit locations in $S \subseteq \{1, \ldots, |s|\}$; that is, for $s = \sigma_1 \cdots \sigma_k$ and $S = \{i_1, \ldots, i_m\}$, we have $s_S = \sigma_{i_1} \cdots \sigma_{i_m}$.

---

[26]We note that this distinguisher does not contradict the hypothesis that G is a canonical derandomizer, because $t_G(k) > \ell(k)$ definitely holds whereas $\ell(k) \le 2^k$ typically holds (and so $2^k \cdot t_G(k) > \ell(k)^2$).

[27]Given the popularity of the term, we deviate from our convention of not specifying credits in the main text. This construction originates in [173, 176].

Letting k vary and $\ell, m : \mathbb{N} \to \mathbb{N}$ be functions of k, we wish G to be a canonical derandomizer and $\ell(k) = 2^{\Omega(k)}$. One (obvious) necessary condition for this to happen is that the sets must be distinct, and hence $m(k) = \Omega(k)$; consequently, f must be computable in exponential time. Furthermore, the sequence of sets $S_1, \dots, S_{\ell(k)}$ must be constructible in poly(2^k) time. Intuitively, the function f should be strongly inapproximable (i.e., T-inapproximable for some exponential function T), and furthermore it seems desirable to use a set system with small pairwise intersections (because this restricts the overlap among the various inputs to which f is applied). Interestingly, these conditions are essentially sufficient.

Theorem 8.18 (analysis of Construction 8.17): *Let $\alpha, \beta, \gamma, \varepsilon > 0$ be constants satisfying $\varepsilon > (2\alpha/\beta) + \gamma$, and consider the functions $\ell, m, T : \mathbb{N} \to \mathbb{N}$ such that $\ell(k) = 2^{\alpha k}$, $m(k) = \beta k$, and $T(n) = 2^{\varepsilon n}$. Suppose that the following two conditions hold:*

1. *There exists an exponential-time computable function $f : \{0, 1\}^* \to \{0, 1\}$ that is T-inapproximable.* (See Definition 7.9.)
2. *There exists an exponential-time computable function $S : \mathbb{N} \times \mathbb{N} \to 2^{\mathbb{N}}$ such that*
   (a) *For every k and $i \in [\ell(k)]$, it holds that $S(k, i) \subseteq [k]$ and $|S(k, i)| = m(k)$.*
   (b) *For every k and $i \neq j$, it holds that $|S(k, i) \cap S(k, j)| \leq \gamma \cdot m(k)$.*

Then G as defined in Construction 8.17, with $S_i = S(k, i)$, constitutes a canonical derandomizer with stretch ℓ.

Before proving Theorem 8.18 we note that, for any $\gamma > 0$, a function S as in Condition 2 does exist with some $m(k) = \Omega(k)$ and $\ell(k) = 2^{\Omega(k)}$; see Exercise 8.19. Combining such a function S with Theorems 7.19 and 8.18, we obtain a canonical derandomizer with exponential stretch based on the assumption that $\mathcal{E}$ has (almost-everywhere) exponential circuit complexity.[28] Combining this with Theorem 8.16, we get the first part of the following theorem.

Theorem 8.19 (de-randomization of BPP, revisited):

1. *Suppose that $\mathcal{E}$ contains a decision problem that has almost-everywhere exponential circuit complexity (i.e., there exists a constant $\varepsilon_0 > 0$ such that, for all but finitely many m's, any circuit that correctly decides this problem on $\{0, 1\}^m$ has size at least $2^{\varepsilon_0 m}$). Then, $\mathcal{BPP} = \mathcal{P}$.*
2. *Suppose that, for every polynomial p, the class $\mathcal{E}$ contains a decision problem that has circuit complexity that is almost-everywhere greater than p. Then $\mathcal{BPP}$ is contained in $\cap_{\varepsilon > 0} \mathrm{DTIME}(t_\varepsilon)$, where $t_\varepsilon(n) \overset{\text{def}}{=} 2^{n^\varepsilon}$.*

Part 2 is proved (in Exercise 8.23) by using a generalization of Theorem 8.18, which in turn is provided in Exercise 8.22. We note that Part 2 of Theorem 8.19 supersedes Theorem 8.13 (see Exercise 7.24). As in the case of general-purpose pseudorandom

---

[28] Specifically, starting with a function having circuit complexity at least $\exp(\varepsilon_0 m)$, we apply Theorem 7.19 and obtain a T-inapproximable predicate for $T(m) = 2^{\varepsilon m}$, where the constant $\varepsilon \in (0, \varepsilon_0)$ depends on the constant ε_0. Next, we set $\gamma = \varepsilon/2$ and invoke Exercise 8.19, which determines $\alpha, \beta > 0$ such that $\ell(k) = 2^{\alpha k}$ and $m(k) = \beta k$. Note that (by possibly decreasing α) we get $(2\alpha/\beta) + \gamma < \varepsilon$.

generators, the hardness hypothesis made in each part of Theorem 8.19 is necessary for the existence of a corresponding canonical derandomizer (see Exercise 8.24).

The two parts of Theorem 8.19 exhibit two extreme cases: Part 1 (often referred to as the "high end") assumes an extremely strong circuit lower bound and yields "full derandomization" (i.e., $\mathcal{BPP} = \mathcal{P}$), whereas Part 2 (often referred to as the "low end") assumes an extremely weak circuit lower bound and yields weak but meaningful derandomization. Intermediate results (relying on intermediate lower-bound assumptions) can be obtained analogously to Exercise 8.23, but tight trade-offs are obtained differently (cf., [226]).

8.3.2.2. Analyzing the Construction (i.e., Proof of Theorem 8.18)

Using the time-complexity upper bounds on f and S, it follows that G can be computed in exponential time. Thus, our focus is on showing that $\{G(U_k)\}$ cannot be distinguished from $\{U_{\ell(k)}\}$ by circuits of size $\ell(k)^2$, specifically, that G satisfies Eq. (8.11). In fact, we will prove that this holds for $G'(s) = s \cdot G(s)$; that is, G fools such circuits even if they are given the seed as auxiliary input. (Indeed, these circuits are smaller than the running time of G, and so they cannot just evaluate G on the given seed.)

We start by presenting the intuition underlying the proof. As a warm-up, suppose that the sets (i.e., $S(k, i)$'s) used in the construction are disjoint. In such a case (which is indeed impossible because $k < \ell(k) \cdot m(k)$), the pseudorandomness of $G(U_k)$ would follow easily from the inapproximability of f, because in this case G consists of applying f to non-overlapping parts of the seed (see Exercise 8.21). In the actual construction being analyzed here, the sets (i.e., $S(k, i)$'s) are not disjoint but have relatively small pairwise intersection, which means that G applies f on parts of the seed that have relatively small overlap. Intuitively, such small overlaps guarantee that the values of f on the corresponding inputs are "computationally independent" (i.e., having the value of f at some inputs $x_1, \ldots, x_i$ does not help in approximating the value of f at another input x_{i+1}). This intuition will be backed up by showing that, when fixing all bits that do not appear in the target input (i.e., in x_{i+1}), the former values (i.e., $f(x_1), \ldots, f(x_i)$) can be computed at a relatively small computational cost. Thus, the values $f(x_1), \ldots, f(x_i)$ do not (significantly) facilitate the task of approximating $f(x_{i+1})$. With the foregoing intuition in mind, we now turn to the actual proof.

As usual, the actual proof employs a reducibility argument; that is, assuming toward the contradiction that G' does not fool some circuit of size $\ell(k)^2$, we derive a contradiction to the hypothesis that the predicate f is T-inapproximable. The argument utilizes the relation between pseudorandomness and unpredictability (cf. Section 8.2.5). Specifically, as detailed in Exercise 8.20, *any circuit that distinguishes $G'(U_k)$ from $U_{\ell(k)+k}$ with gap $1/6$ yields a next-bit predictor of similar size that succeeds in predicting the next bit with probability at least $\frac{1}{2} + \frac{1}{6\ell'(k)} > \frac{1}{2} + \frac{1}{7\ell(k)}$,* where the factor of $\ell'(k) = \ell(k) + k < (1 + o(1)) \cdot \ell(k)$ is introduced by the hybrid technique (cf. Eq. (8.7)). Furthermore, given the non-uniform setting of the current proof, we may fix a bit location $i + 1$ for prediction, rather than analyzing the prediction at a random bit location. Indeed, $i \geq k$ must hold, because the first k bits of $G'(U_k)$ are uniformly distributed. In the rest of the proof, we transform the foregoing predictor into a circuit that approximates f better than allowed by the hypothesis (regarding the inapproximability of f).

Assuming that a small circuit C' can predict the $i + 1^{\text{st}}$ bit of $G'(U_k)$, when given the previous i bits, we construct a small circuit C for approximating $f(U_{m(k)})$ on input $U_{m(k)}$. The point is that the $i + 1^{\text{st}}$ bit of $G'(s)$ equals $f(s_{S(k,j+1)})$, where $j = i - k \geq 0$, and so C' approximates $f(s_{S(k,j+1)})$ based on s, $f(s_{S(k,1)}), \ldots, f(s_{S(k,j)})$, where $s \in \{0, 1\}^k$ is uniformly distributed. Note that this is the type of thing that we are after, except that the circuit we seek may only get $s_{S(k,j+1)}$ as input.

The first observation is that C' maintains its advantage when we fix the best choice for the bits of s that are not at bit locations $S_{j+1} = S(k, j + 1)$ (i.e., the bits $s_{[k] \setminus S_{j+1}}$). That is, by an averaging argument, it holds that

$$\max_{s' \in \{0,1\}^{k-m(k)}} \{\Pr_{s \in \{0,1\}^k}[C'(s, f(s_{S_1}), \ldots, f(s_{S_j})) = f(s_{S_{j+1}}) \mid s_{[k] \setminus S_{j+1}} = s']\}$$

$$\geq p' \overset{\text{def}}{=} \Pr_{s \in \{0,1\}^k}[C'(s, f(s_{S_1}), \ldots, f(s_{S_j})) = f(s_{S_{j+1}})].$$

Recall that by the hypothesis $p' > \frac{1}{2} + \frac{1}{7\ell(k)}$. Hard-wiring the fixed string s' into C', and letting $\pi(x)$ denote the (unique) string s satisfying $s_{S_{j+1}} = x$ and $s_{[k] \setminus S_{j+1}} = s'$, we obtain a circuit C'' that satisfies

$$\Pr_{x \in \{0,1\}^{m(k)}}[C''(x, f(\pi(x)_{S_1}), \ldots, f(\pi(x)_{S_j})) = f(x)] \geq p'.$$

The circuit C'' is almost what we seek. The only problem is that C'' gets as input not only x but also $f(\pi(x)_{S_1}), \ldots, f(\pi(x)_{S_j})$, whereas we seek an approximator of $f(x)$ that only gets x.

The key observation is that each of the "missing" values $f(\pi(x)_{S_1}), \ldots, f(\pi(x)_{S_j})$ depend only on a relatively small number of the bits of x. This fact is due to the hypothesis that $|S_t \cap S_{j+1}| \leq \gamma \cdot m(k)$ for $t = 1, \ldots, j$, which means that $\pi(x)_{S_t}$ is an $m(k)$-bit long string in which $m_t \overset{\text{def}}{=} |S_t \cap S_{j+1}|$ bits are projected from x and the rest are projected from the *fixed* string s'. Thus, given x, the value $f(\pi(x)_{S_t})$ can be computed by a (trivial) circuit of size $\widetilde{O}(2^{m_t})$, that is, by a circuit implementing a look-up table on m_t bits. Using all these circuits (together with C''), we will obtain the desired approximator of f. Details follow.

We obtain the desired circuit, denoted C, that T-approximates f as follows. The circuit C depends on the index j and the string s' that are fixed as in the foregoing analysis. Recall that C incorporates ($\widetilde{O}(2^{\gamma \cdot |x|})$-size) circuits for computing $x \mapsto f(\pi(x)_{S_t})$, for $t = 1, \ldots, j$. On input $x \in \{0,1\}^{m(k)}$, the circuit C computes the values $f(\pi(x)_{S_1}), \ldots, f(\pi(x)_{S_j})$, invokes C'' on input x and these values, and outputs the answer as a guess for $f(x)$. That is,

$$C(x) = C''(x, f(\pi(x)_{S_1}), \ldots, f(\pi(x)_{S_j})) = C'(\pi(x), f(\pi(x)_{S_1}), \ldots, f(\pi(x)_{S_j})).$$

By the foregoing analysis, $\Pr_x[C(x) = f(x)] \geq p' > \frac{1}{2} + \frac{1}{7\ell(k)}$, which is lower-bounded by $\frac{1}{2} + \frac{1}{T(m(k))}$, because $T(m(k)) = 2^{\varepsilon m(k)} = 2^{\varepsilon \beta k} \gg 2^{2\alpha k} \gg 7\ell(k)$, where the first inequality is due to $\varepsilon > 2\alpha/\beta$ and the second inequality is due to $\ell(k) = 2^{\alpha k}$. The size of C is upper-bounded by $\ell(k)^2 + \ell(k) \cdot \widetilde{O}(2^{\gamma \cdot m(k)}) \ll \widetilde{O}(\ell(k)^2 \cdot 2^{\gamma \cdot m(k)}) = \widetilde{O}(2^{2\alpha \cdot (m(k)/\beta) + \gamma \cdot m(k)}) \ll T(m(k))$, where the last inequality is due to $T(m(k)) = 2^{\varepsilon m(k)} \gg \widetilde{O}(2^{(2\alpha/\beta) \cdot m(k) + \gamma \cdot m(k)})$ (which in turn uses $\varepsilon > (2\alpha/\beta) + \gamma$). Thus, we derived a contradiction to the hypothesis that f is T-inapproximable. This completes the proof of Theorem 8.18.

8.3.3. Technical Variations and Conceptual Reflections

We start this section by discussing a general framework that emerges from Construction 8.17, and end this section with a conceptual discussion regarding derandomization.

8.3.3.1. Construction 8.17 as a General Framework

The Nisan–Wigderson Construction (i.e., Construction 8.17) is actually a general framework that can be instantiated in various ways. Some of these instantiations, which are based on an abstraction of the construction as well as of its analysis, are briefly reviewed next,

We first note that the generator described in Construction 8.17 consists of a generic algorithmic scheme that can be instantiated with any predicate f. Furthermore, this algorithmic scheme, denoted G, is actually an *oracle machine* that makes (non-adaptive) queries to the function f, and thus the combination may be written as G^f. Likewise, the proof of pseudorandomness of G^f (i.e., the bulk of the proof of Theorem 8.18) is actually a general scheme that, for every f, yields a (non-uniform) oracle-aided circuit C that approximates f by using an oracle call to any distinguisher for G^f (i.e., C uses the distinguisher as a black-box). The circuit C does depends on f (but in a restricted way). Specifically, C contains look-up tables for computing functions obtained from f by fixing some of the input bits (i.e., look-up tables for the functions $f(\pi(\cdot)_{S_i})$'s). The foregoing abstractions facilitate the presentation of the following instantiations of the general framework underlying Construction 8.17.

Derandomization of constant-depth circuits. In this case we instantiate Construction 8.17 using the `parity` function in the role of the inapproximable predicate f, noting that `parity` is indeed inapproximable by "small" constant-depth circuits. With an adequate setting of parameters we obtain pseudorandom generators with stretch $\ell(k) = \exp(k^{1/O(1)})$ that fool "small" constant-depth circuits (see [173]). The analysis of this construction proceeds very much like the proof of Theorem 8.18. One important observation is that incorporating the (straightforward) circuits that compute $f(\pi(x)_{S_i})$ into the distinguishing circuit only increases its depth by two levels. Specifically, the circuit C uses depth-two circuits that compute the values $f(\pi(x)_{S_i})$'s, and then obtains a prediction of $f(x)$ by using these values in its (single) invocation of the (given) distinguisher.

The resulting pseudorandom generator, which uses a seed of polylogarithmic length (equiv., $\ell(k) = \exp(k^{1/O(1)})$), can be used for derandomizing $\mathcal{R}\mathcal{A}\mathcal{C}^0$ (i.e., random $\mathcal{A}\mathcal{C}^0$), analogously to Theorem 8.16. Thus, we can *deterministically* approximate, in quasi-polynomial time and up to an additive error, the fraction of inputs that satisfy a given (constant-depth) circuit. Specifically, for any constant d, given a depth-d circuit C, we can deterministically approximate the fraction of the inputs that satisfy C (i.e., cause C to evaluate to 1) to within any *additive constant error*[29] in time $\exp((\log|C|)^{O(d)})$. Providing a deterministic polynomial-time approximation, even in the case $d = 2$ (i.e., CNF/DNF formulae) is an open problem.

Derandomization of probabilistic proof systems. A different (and more surprising) instantiation of Construction 8.17 utilizes predicates that are inapproximable by small *circuits having oracle access to* $\mathcal{N}\mathcal{P}$. The result is a pseudorandom generator robust against two-move public-coin interactive proofs (which are as powerful as constant-round interactive proofs (see §9.1.4.1)). The key observation is that the analysis of

---

[29] We mention that in the special case of approximating the number of satisfying assignments of a DNF formula, *relative error* approximations can be obtained by employing a deterministic reduction to the case of additive constant error (see §6.2.2.1). Thus, using a pseudorandom generator that fools DNF formulae, we can deterministically obtain a relative (rather than additive) error approximation to the number of satisfying assignments in a given DNF formula.

Construction 8.17 provides a black-box procedure for approximating the underlying predicate when given oracle access to a distinguisher (and this procedure is valid also in case the distinguisher is a non-deterministic machine). Thus, under suitably strong (and yet plausible) assumptions, constant-round interactive proofs collapse to $\mathcal{NP}$. We note that a stronger result, which deviates from the foregoing framework, has been subsequently obtained (cf. [167]).

Construction of randomness extractors. An even more radical instantiation of Construction 8.17 was used to obtain explicit constructions of randomness extractors (see Appendix D.4). In this case, the predicate f is viewed as (an error correcting encoding of) a somewhat random function, and the construction makes sense because it refers to f in a black-box manner. In the analysis we rely on the fact that f can be approximated by combining relatively little information (regarding f) with (black-box access to) a distinguisher for G^f. For further details, see §D.4.2.2.

8.3.3.2. Reflections Regarding Derandomization

Part 1 of Theorem 8.19 is often summarized by saying that (under some reasonable assumptions) *randomness is useless*. We believe that this interpretation is wrong even within the restricted context of traditional complexity classes, and is bluntly wrong if taken outside of the latter context. Let us elaborate.

Taking a closer look at the proof of Theorem 8.16 (which underlies Theorem 8.19), we note that a randomized algorithm A of time complexity t is emulated by a deterministic algorithm A' of time complexity $t' = \text{poly}(t)$. Further noting that $A' = A_G$ invokes A (as well as the canonical derandomizer G) for $\Omega(t)$ times (because $\ell(k) = O(2^k)$ implies $2^k = \Omega(t)$), we infer that $t' = \Omega(t^2)$ must hold. Thus, derandomization via (Part 1 of) Theorem 8.19 is not really for free.

More importantly, we note that derandomization is not possible in various distributed settings, when both parties may protect their conflicting interests by employing randomization. Notable examples include most cryptographic primitives (e.g., encryption) as well as most types of probabilistic proof systems (e.g., PCP). For further discussion, see Chapter 9 and Appendix C. Additional settings where randomness makes a difference (either between impossibility and possibility or between formidable and affordable cost) include distributed computing (see [17]), communication complexity (see [148]), parallel architectures (see [151]), sampling (see Appendix D.3), and property testing (see Section 10.1.2).

8.4. Space-Bounded Distinguishers

In the previous two sections we have considered generators that output sequences that look random to any efficient procedures, where the latter were modeled by time-bounded computations. Specifically, in Section 8.2 we considered indistinguishability by polynomial-time procedures. A finer classification of time-bounded procedures is obtained by considering their *space complexity*, that is, restricting the space complexity of time-bounded computations. This restriction, which is the focus of Chapter 5, leads to the notion of pseudorandom generators that fool space-bounded distinguishers. Interestingly, in contrast to the notions of pseudorandom generators that were considered in Sections 8.2 and 8.3, the existence of pseudorandom generators that fool space-bounded distinguishers can be established without relying on computational assumptions.

Prerequisites. Technically speaking, the current section is self-contained, but various definitional choices are justified by reference to §6.1.5.1. Thus, we recommend Section 6.1.5 as general background for the current section.

8.4.1. Definitional Issues

Our main motivation for considering space-bounded distinguishers is to develop a notion of pseudorandomness that is adeqaute for space-bounded randomized algorithms. That is, such algorithms should essentially maintain their behavior when their source of internal coin tosses is replaced by a source of pseudorandom bits (which may be generated based on a much shorter random seed). We thus start by recalling and reviewing the natural notion of space-bounded randomized algorithms. Unfortunately, natural notions of space-bounded computations are quite subtle, especially when non-determinism or randomization is concerned (see Sections 5.3 and 6.1.5, respectively). Two major definitional issues regarding randomized space-bounded computations are the need for imposing explicit *time bounds* and the type of *access to the random-tape*.

1. Time bounds: The question is whether or not the space-bounded machines are restricted to time complexity that is at most exponential in their space complexity.[30] Recall that such an upper bound follows automatically in the deterministic case (Theorem 5.3), and can be assumed without loss of generality in the non-deterministic case (see Section 5.3.2), *but it does not necessarily hold in the randomized case* (see §6.1.5.1). Furthermore, failing to restrict the time complexity of randomized space-bounded machines makes them unnatural and unintentionally too strong (see §6.1.5.1 again).

    As in Section 6.1.5, seeking a natural model of randomized space-bounded algorithms, we postulate that their time complexity must be at most exponential in their space complexity.

2. Access to the random-tape: Recall that randomized algorithms may be modeled as machines that are provided with the necessary randomness via a special random-tape. The question is whether the space-bounded machine has uni-directional or bi-directional (i.e., unrestricted) access to its random-tape. (Allowing bi-directional access means that the randomness is recorded "for free," that is, without being accounted for in the space bound (see discussions in Sections 5.3 and 6.1.5).)

    Recall that uni-directional access to the random-tape corresponds to the natural model of an on-line randomized machine, which determines its moves based on its internal coin tosses (and thus cannot store its past coin tosses "for free"). Thus, as in Section 6.1.5, we consider uni-directional access.[31]

Hence, we focus on randomized space-bounded computations that have time complexity that is at most exponential in their space complexity and access their random-tape in a uni-directional manner.

---

[30]Alternatively, one can ask whether these machines must always halt or only halt with probability approaching 1. It can be shown that the only way to ensure "absolute halting" is to have time complexity that is at most exponential in the space complexity. (In the current discussion as well as throughout this section, we assume that the space complexity is at least logarithmic.)

[31]We note that the fact that we restrict our attention to uni-directional access is instrumental in obtaining space-robust generators without making intractability assumptions. Analogous generators for bi-directional space-bounded computations would imply hardness results of a breakthrough nature in the area.

—— **316** ——

When seeking a notion of pseudornadomness that is adequate for the foregoing notion of randomized space-bounded computations, we note that the corresponding distinguisher is obtained by fixing the main input of the computation and *viewing the contents of the random-tape of the computation as the only input of the distinguisher*. Thus, in accordance with the foregoing notion of randomized space-bounded computation, *we consider space-bounded distinguishers that have a uni-directional access to the input sequence that they examine*. Let us consider the type of algorithms that arise.

We consider *space-bounded algorithms that have a uni-directional access to their input*. At each step, based on the contents of its temporary storage, such an algorithm may either read the next input bit or stay at the current location on the input, where in either case the algorithm may modify its temporary storage. To simplify our analysis of such algorithms, we consider a corresponding *non-uniform model* in which, at each step, the algorithm reads the next input bit and updates its temporary storage according to an arbitrary function applied to the previous contents of that storage (and to the new bit). Note that we have strengthened the model by allowing arbitrary (updating) functions, which can be implemented by (non-uniform) circuits having size that is exponential in the space bound, rather than using (updating) functions that can be (uniformly) computed in time that is exponential in the space bound. This strengthening is motivated by the fact that the known constructions of pseudorandom generators remain valid also when the space-bounded distinguishers are non-uniform and by the fact that non-uniform distinguishers arise anyhow in derandomization.

The computation of the foregoing non-uniform space-bounded algorithms (or automata)[32] can be represented by directed layered graphs, where the vertices in each layer correspond to possible contents of the temporary storage and the transition between neighboring layers corresponds to a step of the computation. Foreseeing the application of this model for the description of potential distinguishers, we parameterize these layered graphs based on the index, denoted k, of the relevant ensembles (e.g., $\{G(U_k)\}_{k\in\mathbb{N}}$ and $\{U_{\ell(k)}\}_{k\in\mathbb{N}}$). That is, we present both the input length, denoted $\ell = \ell(k)$, and the space bound, denoted $s(k)$, as functions of the parameter k. Thus, we define a non-uniform automaton of space $s : \mathbb{N} \to \mathbb{N}$ as a family, $\{D_k\}_{k\in\mathbb{N}}$, of directed layered graphs with labeled edges such that the following conditions hold:

- The digraph D_k consists of $\ell(k) + 1$ layers, each containing at most $2^{s(k)}$ vertices. The first layer contains a single vertex, which is the digraph's (single) source (i.e., a vertex with no incoming edges), and the last layer contains all the digraph's sinks (i.e., vertices with no outgoing edges).
- The only directed edges in D_k are between adjacent layers, going from layer i to layer $i + 1$, for $i \leq \ell(k)$. These edges are labeled such that each (non-sink) vertex of D_k has two (possibly parallel) outgoing directed edges, one labeled 0 and the other labeled 1.

The result of the computation of such an automaton, on an input of adequate length (i.e., length ℓ where D_k has $\ell + 1$ layers), is defined as the vertex (in last layer) reached when

---

[32] We use the term automaton (rather than algorithm or machine) in order to remind the reader that this computing device reads its input in a uni-directional manner. Alternative terms that may be used are "real-time" or "on-line" machines. We prefer not using the term "on-line" machine in order to keep a clear distinction from randomized (on-line) algorithms that have free access to their input (and on-line access to a source of randomness). Indeed, the automata consider here arise from the latter algorithms by fixing their primary input and considering the random source as their (only) input. We also note that the automata considered here are a special case of Ordered Binary Decision Diagrams (OBDDs; see [237]).

following the sequence of edges that are labeled by the corresponding bits of the input. That is, on input $x = x_1 \cdots x_\ell$, in the ith step (for $i = 1, \dots, \ell$) we move from the current vertex (which resides in the ith layer) to one of its neighbors (which resides in the $i + 1^{\text{st}}$ layer) by following the outgoing edge labeled x_i. Using a fixed partition of the vertices of the last layer, this defines a natural notion of a decision (by D_k); that is, we write $D_k(x) = 1$ if on input x the automaton D_k reached a vertex that belongs to the first part of the aforementioned partition.

Definition 8.20 (Indistinguishability by space-bounded automata):

- *For a non-uniform automaton, $\{D_k\}_{k \in \mathbb{N}}$, and two probability ensembles, $\{X_k\}_{k \in \mathbb{N}}$ and $\{Y_k\}_{k \in \mathbb{N}}$, the function $d : \mathbb{N} \to [0, 1]$ defined as*

$$d(k) \stackrel{\text{def}}{=} |\Pr[D_k(X_k) = 1] - \Pr[D_k(Y_k) = 1]|$$

  is called the distinguishability-gap *of $\{D_k\}$ between the two ensembles.*
- *Let $s : \mathbb{N} \to \mathbb{N}$ and $\varepsilon : \mathbb{N} \to [0, 1]$. A probability ensemble, $\{X_k\}_{k \in \mathbb{N}}$, is called (s, ε)-pseudorandom if for any non-uniform automaton of space $s(\cdot)$, the distinguishability-gap of the automaton between $\{X_k\}_{k \in \mathbb{N}}$ and the corresponding uniform ensemble (i.e., $\{U_{|X_k|}\}_{k \in \mathbb{N}}$) is at most $\varepsilon(\cdot)$.*
- *A deterministic algorithm G of stretch function ℓ is called an (s, ε)-pseudorandom generator if the ensemble $\{G(U_k)\}_{k \in \mathbb{N}}$ is (s, ε)-pseudorandom. That is, every non-uniform automaton of space $s(\cdot)$ has a distinguishing-gap of at most $\varepsilon(\cdot)$ between $\{G(U_k)\}_{k \in \mathbb{N}}$ and $\{U_{\ell(k)}\}_{k \in \mathbb{N}}$.*

Thus, when using a random seed of length k, an (s, ε)-pseudorandom generator outputs a sequence of length $\ell(k)$ that looks random to observers having space $s(k)$. Note that $s(k) \leq k$ is a necessary condition for the existence of $(s, 0.5)$-pseudorandom generators, because a non-uniform automaton of space $s(k) > k$ can recognize the image of a generator (which contains at most 2^k strings of length $\ell(k) > k$). More generally, there is a trade-off between $s(k) - k$ and the stretch of (s, ε)-pseudorandom generators; for details, see Exercises 8.25 and 8.26.

Note. Recall that we stated the space bound of the potential distinguisher (as well as the stretch function) in terms of the seed length, denoted k, of the generator. In contrast, other sources present a parameterization in terms of the space bound of the potential distinguisher, denoted m. The translation is obtained by using $m = s(k)$, and we shall provide it following the main statements of Theorems 8.21 and 8.22.

8.4.2. Two Constructions

In contrast to the case of pseudorandom generators that fool time-bounded distinguishers, pseudorandom generators that fool space-bounded distinguishers can be constructed without relying on any computational assumption. The following two theorems exhibit two rather extreme cases of a general trade-off between the space bound of the potential distinguisher and the stretch function of the generator.[33] We stress that both theorems fall

---

[33]These two results have been "interpolated" in [12]: There exists a parameterized family of "space fooling" pseudorandom generators that includes both results as extreme special cases.

short of providing parameters as in Exercise 8.26, but they refer to relatively efficient constructions. We start with an attempt to maximize the stretch.

Theorem 8.21 (stretch exponential in the space bound for $s(k) = \sqrt{k}$): *For every space-constructible function $s : \mathbb{N} \to \mathbb{N}$, there exists an $(s, 2^{-s})$-pseudorandom generator of stretch function $\ell(k) = \min(2^{k/O(s(k))}, 2^{s(k)})$. Furthermore, the generator works in space that is linear in the length of the seed, and in time that is linear in the stretch function.*

In other words, for every $t \leq m$, we have a generator that takes a random seed of length $k = O(t \cdot m)$ and produces a sequence of length 2^t that looks random to any (non-uniform) automaton of space m (up to a distinguishability-gap of 2^{-m}). In particular, using a random seed of length $k = O(m^2)$, one can produce a sequence of length 2^m that looks random to any (non-uniform) automaton of space m. Thus, *one may replace random sequences used by any space-bounded computation, by sequences that are efficiently generated from random seeds of length quadratic in the space bound.* The common instantiation of the latter assertion is for log-space algorithms. In §8.4.2.2, we apply Theorem 8.21 (and its underlying ideas) for the derandomization of space-complexity classes such as $\mathcal{BPL}$ (i.e., the log-space analogue of $\mathcal{BPP}$). Theorem 8.21 itself is proved in §8.4.2.1.

We now turn to the case where one wishes to maximize the space bound of potential distinguishers. We warn that Theorem 8.22 only guarantees a sub-exponential distinguishability gap (rather than the exponential distinguishability gap guaranteed in Theorem 8.21). This warning is voiced because failing to recall this limitation has led to errors in the past.

Theorem 8.22 (polynomial stretch and linear space bound): *For any polynomial p and for some $s(k) = k/O(1)$, there exists an $(s, 2^{-\sqrt{s}})$-pseudorandom generator of stretch function p. Furthermore, the generator works in linear space and polynomial time (both stated in terms of the length of the seed).*

In other words, we have a generator that takes a random seed of length $k = O(m)$ and produces a sequence of length $\mathrm{poly}(m)$ that looks random to any (non-uniform) automaton of space m. Thus, one may *convert any randomized computation utilizing polynomial time and linear space into a functionally equivalent randomized computation of similar time and space complexities that uses only a linear number of coin tosses.*

8.4.2.1. Sketches of the Proofs of Theorems 8.21 and 8.22

In both cases, we start the proof by considering a generic space-bounded distinguisher and show that the input distribution that this distinguisher examines can be modified (from the uniform distribution into a pseudorandom one) without having the distinguisher notice the difference. This modification (or rather a sequence of modifications) yields a construction of a pseudorandom generator, which is only spelled out at the end of the argument.

Sketch of the proof of Theorem 8.21.[34] The main technical tool used in this proof is the "mixing property" of pairwise independent hash functions (see Appendix D.2). A family of functions H_n, which maps $\{0, 1\}^n$ to itself, is called mixing if for every

---

[34] A detailed proof appears in [174].

pair of subsets $A, B \subseteq \{0, 1\}^n$ for all but very few (i.e., $\exp(-\Omega(n))$ fraction) of the functions $h \in H_n$, it holds that

$$\Pr[U_n \in A \wedge h(U_n) \in B] \approx \frac{|A|}{2^n} \cdot \frac{|B|}{2^n} \qquad (8.13)$$

where the approximation is up to an additive term of $\exp(-\Omega(n))$. (See the generalization of Lemma D.4, which implies that $\exp(-\Omega(n))$ can be set to $2^{-n/3}$.)

We may assume, without loss of generality, that $s(k) = \Omega(\sqrt{k})$, and thus $\ell(k) \leq 2^{s(k)}$ holds. For any $s(k)$-space distinguisher D_k as in Definition 8.20, we consider an auxiliary "distinguisher" D'_k that is obtained by "contracting" every block of $n \stackrel{\text{def}}{=} \Theta(s(k))$ consecutive layers in D_k, yielding a directed layered graph with $\ell' \stackrel{\text{def}}{=} \ell(k)/n < 2^{s(k)}$ layers (and $2^{s(k)}$ vertices in each layer). Specifically,

- each vertex in D'_k has 2^n (possibly parallel) directed edges going to various vertices of the next level; and
- each such edge is labeled by an n-bit long string such that the directed edge (u, v) labeled $\sigma_1 \sigma_2 \cdots \sigma_n$ in D'_k replaces the n-edge directed path between u and v in D_k that consists of edges labeled $\sigma_1, \sigma_2, \ldots, \sigma_n$.

The graph D'_k simulates D_k in the obvious manner; that is, the computation of D'_k on an input of length $\ell(k) = \ell' \cdot n$ is defined by breaking the input into consecutive substrings of length n and following the path of edges that are labeled by the corresponding n-bit long substrings.

The key observation is that D'_k cannot distinguish between a random $\ell' \cdot n$-bit long input (i.e., $U_{\ell' \cdot n} \equiv U_n^{(1)} U_n^{(2)} \cdots U_n^{(\ell')}$) and a "pseudorandom" input of the form $U_n^{(1)} h(U_n^{(1)}) U_n^{(2)} h(U_n^{(2)}) \cdots U_n^{(\ell'/2)} h(U_n^{(\ell'/2)})$, where $h \in H_n$ is a (suitably fixed) hash function. To prove this claim, we consider an arbitrary pair of neighboring vertices, u and v (in layers i and $i + 1$, respectively), and denote by $L_{u,v} \subseteq \{0, 1\}^n$ the set of the labels of the edges going from u to v. Similarly, for a vertex w at layer $i + 2$, we let $L'_{v,w}$ denote the set of the labels of the edges going from v to w. By Eq. (8.13), for all but very few of the functions $h \in H_n$, it holds that

$$\Pr[U_n \in L_{u,v} \wedge h(U_n) \in L'_{v,w}] \approx \Pr[U_n \in L_{u,v}] \cdot \Pr[U_n \in L'_{v,w}], \qquad (8.14)$$

where "very few" and $\approx$ are as in Eq. (8.13). Thus, for all but $\exp(-\Omega(n))$ fraction of the choices of $h \in H_n$, *replacing the coins in the second transition* (i.e., the transition from layer $i + 1$ to layer $i + 2$) *with the value of h applied to the outcomes of the coins used in the first transition* (i.e., the transition from layer i to $i + 1$), *approximately maintains the probability that D'_k moves from u to w via v*. Using a union bound (on all triples (u, v, w) as in the foregoing), we note that, for all but $2^{3s(k)} \cdot \ell' \cdot \exp(-\Omega(n))$ fraction of the choices of $h \in H_n$, the foregoing replacement approximately maintains the probability that D'_k moves through any specific two-edge path of D'_k.

Using $\ell' < 2^{s(k)}$ and a suitable choice of $n = \Theta(s(k))$, it holds that $2^{3s(k)} \cdot \ell' \cdot \exp(-\Omega(n)) < \exp(-\Omega(n))$, and thus all but a "few" functions $h \in H_n$ are good for approximating all these transition probabilities. (We stress that the same h can be used in all these approximations.) Thus, *at the cost of extra $|h|$ random bits, we can reduce the number of true random coins used in transitions on D'_k by a factor of two, without significantly affecting the final decision of D'_k* (where again we use the fact that $\ell' \cdot \exp(-\Omega(n)) < \exp(-\Omega(n))$, which implies that the approximation errors do

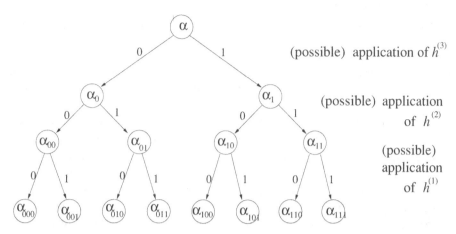

Figure 8.3: The first generator that "fools" space-bounded automata (for $i = 3$). The output of the generator (on seed $\alpha, h^{(1)}, \ldots, h^{(t)}$) consists of the concatenation of the strings denoted $\alpha_{0^t}, \ldots, \alpha_{1^t}$, appearing in the leaves of the tree. For every $x \in \{0, 1\}^*$ it holds that $\alpha_{x0} = \alpha_x$ and $\alpha_{x1} = h^{(t-|x|)}(\alpha_x)$. In particular, for $t = 3$, we have $\alpha_{011} = h^{(1)}(\alpha_{01})$, which equals $h^{(1)}(h^{(2)}(\alpha_0)) = h^{(1)}(h^{(2)}(\alpha))$, where $\alpha = \alpha_\lambda$.

not accumulate to too much). In other words, at the cost of extra $|h|$ random bits, we can effectively contract the distinguisher to half its length while approximately maintaining the probability that the distinguisher accepts a random input. That is, fixing a good h (i.e., one that provides a good approximation to the transition probability over all $2^{3s(k)} \cdot \ell'$ two-edge paths), we can replace the two-edge paths in D_k' by edges in a new distinguisher D_k'' (which depends on h) such that an edge (u, w) labeled $r \in \{0, 1\}^n$ appears in D_k'' if and only if, for some v, the path (u, v, w) appears in D_k' with the first edge (i.e., (u, v)) labeled r and the second edge (i.e., (v, w)) labeled $h(r)$. Needless to say, the crucial point is that $\Pr[D_k''(U_{(\ell'/2)\cdot n}) = 1]$ approximates $\Pr[D_k'(U_{\ell'\cdot n}) = 1]$.

The foregoing process can be applied to D_k'' resulting in a distinguisher D_k''' of half the length, and so on. Each time we contract the current distinguisher by a factor of two, and do so by randomly selecting (and fixing) a new hash function. Thus, repeating the process for a logarithmic (in the depth of D_k') number of times, we obtain a distinguisher that only examines n bits, at which point we stop. In total, we have used $t \stackrel{\text{def}}{=} \log_2(\ell'/n) < \log_2 \ell(k)$ random hash functions, denoted $h^{(1)}, \ldots, h^{(t)}$. This means that we can generate a (pseudorandom) sequence that fools the original D_k by using a seed of length $n + t \cdot \log_2 |H_n|$ (see Figure 8.3 and Exercise 8.28). Using $n = \Theta(s(k))$ and an adequate family H_n (e.g., Construction D.3), we obtain the desired $(s, 2^{-s})$-pseudorandom generator, which indeed uses a seed of length $O(s(k) \cdot \log_2 \ell(k)) = k$. □

Rough sketch of the proof of Theorem 8.22.[35] The main technical tool used in this proof is a suitable randomness extractor (as defined in §D.4.1.1), which is indeed a much more powerful tool than hashing functions. The basic idea is that when the distinguisher D_k is at some "distant" layer, say at layer $t = \Omega(s(k))$, it typically "knows" little about the random choices that led it there. That is, D_k has only $s(k)$ bits of memory, which leaves out $t - s(k)$ bits of "uncertainty" (or randomness)

---

[35] A detailed proof appears in [177].

regarding the previous moves. Thus, much of the randomness that led D_k to its current state may be "reused" (or "recycled"). To reuse these bits we need to extract *almost* uniform distribution on strings of sufficient length out of the aforementioned distribution over $\{0, 1\}^t$ that has entropy[36] at least $t - s(k)$. Furthermore, such an extraction requires some additional truly random bits, yet relatively few such bits. In particular, using $k' = \Omega(\log t)$ bits toward this end, the extracted bits are $\exp(-\Omega(k'))$ away from uniform.

The gain from the aforementioned recycling is significant if recycling is repeated sufficiently many times. Toward this end, we break the k-bit long seed into two parts, denoted $r' \in \{0, 1\}^{k/2}$ and $(r_1, \ldots, r_{3\sqrt{k}})$, where $|r_i| = \sqrt{k}/6$, and set $n = k/3$. Intuitively, r' will be used for determining the first n steps, and it will be reused (or recycled) together with r_i for determining the steps $i \cdot n + 1$ through $(i + 1) \cdot n$. Looking at layer $i \cdot n$, we consider the information regarding r' that is "known" to D_k (when reaching a specific vertex at layer $i \cdot n$). Typically, the conditional distribution of r', given that we reached a specific vertex at layer $i \cdot n$, has (min-)entropy greater than $0.99 \cdot ((k/2) - s(k))$. Using r_i (as a seed of an extractor applied to r'), we can extract $0.9 \cdot ((k/2) - s(k) - o(k)) > k/3 = n$ bits that are almost-random (i.e., $2^{-\Omega(\sqrt{k})}$-close to U_n) with respect to D_k, and use these bits for determining the next n steps. Hence, using k random bits, we produce a sequence of length $(1 + 3\sqrt{k}) \cdot n > k^{3/2}$ that fools automata of space bound, say, $s(k) = k/10$. Specifically, using an extractor of the form $\text{Ext} : \{0, 1\}^{\sqrt{k}/6} \times \{0, 1\}^{k/2} \to \{0, 1\}^{k/3}$, we map the seed $(r', r_1, \ldots, r_{3\sqrt{k}})$ to the output sequence $(r', \text{Ext}(r_1, r'), \ldots, \text{Ext}(r_{3\sqrt{k}}, r'))$. Thus, *we obtain an $(s, 2^{-\Omega(\sqrt{s})})$-pseudorandom generator of stretch function $\ell(k) = k^{3/2}$.*

In order to obtain an arbitrary polynomial stretch rather than a specific polynomial stretch (i.e., $\ell(k) = k^{3/2}$), we repeatedly apply an adequate composition, to be outlined next. Suppose that G_1 is an (s_1, ε_1)-pseudorandom generator of stretch function ℓ_1, and similarly for G_2 with respect to (s_1, ε_1) and ℓ_2. Then, we consider the following construction of a generator G:

1. On input $s \in \{0, 1\}^k$, compute $G_1(s)$, and parse it into consecutive blocks, each of length $k' = s_1(k)/2$, denoted $r_1, \ldots, r_t$, where $t = \ell_1(k)/k'$.
2. Compute and output the $t \cdot \ell_2(k')$-bit long sequence $G_2(r_1) \cdots G_2(r_t)$.

Note that $|G(s)| = \ell_1(k) \cdot \ell_2(k')/k'$, where $k' = s_1(k)/2$ and $k = |s|$. For $s_1(k) = \Theta(k)$, we have $|G(s)| = \ell_1(k) \cdot \ell_2(\Omega(k))/O(k)$, which for polynomials ℓ_1 and ℓ_2 yields $|G(s)| = \ell_1(|s|) \cdot \ell_2(|s|)/O(|s|)$. We claim that G *is an (s, ε)-pseudorandom generator, for $s(k) = \min(s_1(k)/2, s_2(\Omega(s_1(k))))$ and $\varepsilon(k) = \varepsilon_1(k) + \ell_1(k) \cdot \varepsilon_2(\Omega(s_1(k)))$.* The proof uses a hybrid argument, which refers to the natural distributions $G(U_k)$ and $U_{t \cdot \ell_2(k')} \equiv U_{\ell_2(k')}^{(1)} \cdots U_{\ell_2(k')}^{(t)}$ as well as to the intermediate hybrid distribution $I_k \stackrel{\text{def}}{=} G_2(U_{k'}^{(1)}) \cdots G_2(U_{k'}^{(t)})$. The fact that I_k and $U_{t \cdot \ell_2(k')}$ are $(s_2(k'), t \cdot \varepsilon_2(k'))$-indistinguishable (i.e., indistinguishable by automata of space $s_2(k')$ with respect to distinguishability-gap $t \cdot \varepsilon_1(k')$) follows by a general result regarding "indistinguishability by multiple samples" (see Exercise 8.27). It remains to show that I_k is indistinguishable from $G(U_k)$ by automata of space $s_1(k)/2$ with

---

[36]Actually, a stronger technical condition needs and can be imposed on the latter distribution. Specifically, with overwhelmingly high probability, at layer t, automaton D_k is at a vertex that can be reached in more than $2^{0.99 \cdot (t - s(k))}$ different ways. In this case, the distribution representing a random walk that reaches this vertex has min-entropy greater than $0.99 \cdot (t - s(k))$. The reader is referred to §D.4.1.1 for definitions of min-entropy and extractors.

respect to distinguishability-gap $\varepsilon_1(k)$. This can be proved by converting a potential distinguisher (of I_k and $G(U_k)$) into a distinguisher of $U_{\ell_1(k)} \equiv U_{t \cdot k'}$ and $G_1(U_k)$, where the new distinguisher parses the $\ell_1(k)$-bit long input into t blocks (each of length k'), invokes G_2 on the corresponding k'-bit long blocks, and feeds the resulting sequence of $\ell_1(k')$-bit long blocks to the original distinguisher.[37] $\qquad \square$

8.4.2.2. Derandomization of Space-Complexity Classes

As a direct application of Theorem 8.21, we obtain that $\mathcal{BPL} \subseteq \text{DSPACE}(\log^2)$, where $\mathcal{BPL}$ denotes the log-space analogue of $\mathcal{BPP}$ (see Definition 6.11). (Recall that $\mathcal{NL} \subseteq \text{DSPACE}(\log^2)$, but it is not known whether or not $\mathcal{BPL} \subseteq \mathcal{NL}$.)[38] A strongerd erandomization result can be obtained by a finer analysis of the proof of Theorem 8.21.

Theorem 8.23: $\mathcal{BPL} \subseteq \mathcal{SC}$, where $\mathcal{SC}$ denotes the class of decision problems that can be solved by a deterministic algorithm that runs in polynomial time and polylogarithmic space.

Thus, $\mathcal{BPL}$ (and in particular $\mathcal{RL} \subseteq \mathcal{BPL}$) is placed in a class not known to contain $\mathcal{NL}$. Another such result was subsequently obtained in [196]: Randomized log-space can be simulated in deterministic space $o(\log^2)$, specifically, in space $\log^{3/2}$. We mention that the archetypical problem of $\mathcal{RL}$ has been recently proved to be in $\mathcal{L}$ (see Section 5.2).

Sketch of the proof of Theorem 8.23.[39] We are going to use the generator construction provided in the proof of Theorem 8.21, but show that the main part of the seed (i.e., the sequence of hash functions) can be fixed (depending on the distinguisher at hand). Furthermore, this fixing can be performed in poly-logarithmic space and polynomial time. Specifically, wishing to derandomize a specific log-space computation (which refers to a specific input), we first obtain the corresponding distinguisher, denoted D_k', that represents this computation (as a function of the outcomes of the internal coin tosses of the log-space algorithm). The key observation is that the question of whether or not a specific hash function $h \in H_n$ is good for a specific D_k' can be determined in space that is linear in $n = |h|/2$ and logarithmic in the size of D_k'. Indeed, the time complexity of this decision procedure is exponential in its space complexity. It follows that we can find a good $h \in H_n$, for a given D_k', within these complexities (by scanning through all possible $h \in H_n$). Once a good h is found, we can also construct the corresponding graph D_k'' (in which edges represent two-edge paths in D_k'), again within the same complexity. Actually, it will be more instructive to note that we can determine a step (i.e., an edge-traversal) in D_k'' by making two steps (edge-traversals) in D_k'. This will allow for fixing a hash function for D_k'', and so on. Details follow.

The main claim is that the entire process of finding a sequence of $t \overset{\text{def}}{=} \log_2 \ell'(k)$ good hash functions can be performed in space $t \cdot O(n + \log |D_k|) = O(n + \log |D_k|)^2$ and time $\text{poly}(2^n \cdot |D_k|)$; that is, the time complexity is

---

[37]The new distinguisher maintains the state of the original distinguisher, while reading k'-bit long blocks of its own input (into its own state). Once a block $s' \in \{0, 1\}^{k'}$ is read, the new distinguisher updates the state of the original distinguisher by a transition that corresponds to the effect of the input-block $G_2(s')$ on the original distinguisher. Thus, a distinguisher of space $s_1(k)/2$ is converted into a distinguisher of space $(s_1(k)/2) + k' = s_1(k)$.

[38]Indeed, the log-space analogue of $\mathcal{RP}$, denoted $\mathcal{RL}$, is contained in $\mathcal{NL} \subseteq \text{DSPACE}(\log^2)$, and thus the fact that Theorem 8.21 implies $\mathcal{RL} \subseteq \text{DSPACE}(\log^2)$ is of no interest.

[39]A detailed proof appears in [175].

---

sub-exponential in the space complexity (i.e., the time complexity is significantly smaller than the generic bound of $\exp(O(n + \log|D_k|)^2))$. Starting with $D_k^{(1)} = D_k'$, we find a good (for $D_k^{(1)}$) hashing function $h^{(1)} \in H_n$, which defines $D_k^{(2)} = D_k''$. Having found (and stored) $h^{(1)}, \ldots, h^{(i)} \in H_n$, which determine $D_k^{(i+1)}$, we find a good hashing function $h^{(i+1)} \in H_n$ for $D_k^{(i+1)}$ by emulating pairs of edge-traversals on $D_k^{(i+1)}$. Indeed, a key point is that we do *not* construct the sequence of graphs $D_k^{(2)}, \ldots, D_k^{(i+1)}$, but rather emulate an edge-traversal in $D_k^{(i+1)}$ by making 2^i edge-traversals in D_k', using $h^{(1)}, \ldots, h^{(i)}$: The (edge-traversal) move $\alpha \in \{0, 1\}^n$ starting at vertex v of $D_k^{(i+1)}$ translates to a sequence of 2^i moves starting at vertex v of D_k', where the moves are determined by the 2^i-long sequence (of n-bit strings)

$$\overline{h}^{(0^i)}(\alpha), \overline{h}^{(0^{i-2}01)}(\alpha), \overline{h}^{(0^{i-2}10)}(\alpha), \overline{h}^{(0^{i-2}11)}(\alpha), \ldots, \overline{h}^{(1^i)}(\alpha),$$

where $\overline{h}^{(\sigma_i \cdots \sigma_1)}$ is the function obtained by the composition of a subsequence of the functions $h^{(i)}, \ldots, h^{(1)}$ determined by $\sigma_i \cdots \sigma_1$. Specifically, $\overline{h}^{(\sigma_i \cdots \sigma_1)}$ equals $h^{(i_{t'})} \circ \cdots \circ h^{(i_2)} \circ h^{(i_1)}$, where $i_1 < i_2 < \cdots < i_{t'}$ and $\{i_j : j = 1, \ldots, t'\} = \{j : \sigma_j = 1\}$.

Recall that the ability to perform edge-traversals on $D_k^{(i+1)}$ allows for determining whether a specific function $h \in H_n$ is good for $D_k^{(i+1)}$. This is done by considering all the relevant triples (u, v, w) in $D_k^{(i+1)}$, computing for each such (u, v, w) the three quantities (i.e., probabilities) appearing in Eq. (8.14), and deciding accordingly. Trying all possible $h \in H_n$, we find a function (to be denoted $h^{(i+1)}$) that is good for $D_k^{(i+1)}$. This is done while using an additional storage of $s' = O(n + \log|D_k'|)$ (on top of the storage used to record $h^{(1)}, \ldots, h^{(i)}$), and in time that is exponential in s'. Thus, given D_k', *we find a good sequence of hash functions, $h^{(1)}, \ldots, h^{(t)}$, in time exponential in s' and while using space $s' + t \cdot \log_2 |H_n| = O(t \cdot s')$.* Such a sequence of functions allows us to emulate edge-traversals on $D_k^{(t+1)}$, which in turn allows for (deterministically) approximating the probability that D_k' accepts a random input (i.e., the probability that, starting at the single source vertex of the first layer, automaton D_k' reaches some accepting vertex at the last layer). This approximation is obtained by computing the corresponding probability in $D_k^{(t+1)}$ by traversing all 2^n edges.

To summarize, given D_k', we can (deterministically) approximate the probability that D_k' accepts a random input in $O(t \cdot s')$-space and $\exp(O(s' + n))$-time, where $s' = O(n + \log|D_k'|)$ and $t < \log_2 |D_k'|$. For $n = \Theta(\log|D_k'|)$, this means $O(\log|D_k'|)^2$-space and $\text{poly}(|D_k'|)$-time. We comment that the approximation can be made accurate up to an additive term of $1/\text{poly}(|D_k'|)$, but an additive term of $1/6$ suffices here.

We conclude the proof by recalling the connection between such an approximation and the derandomization of $\mathcal{BPL}$ (indeed, note the analogy to the proof of Theorem 8.13). The computation of a log-space probabilistic machine M on input x can be represented by a directed layer graph $G_{M,x}$ of size $\text{poly}(|x|)$. Specifically, the vertices of each layer represent possible configurations of the computation of $M(x)$, and the edges between the ith layer and the $i + 1^{\text{st}}$ layer represent the ith move of such a computation, which depends on the ith bit of the random-tape of M (or, equivalently, on the ith internal coin toss of M).[40] Thus, the probability that M accepts x equals the probability that a random walk starting at the single vertex of the first layer of $G_{M,x}$ reaches some vertex in the last layer that represents an accepting configuration. Setting $k = \Theta(\log|x|)$ and $n = \Theta(k)$, the graph $G_{M,x}$ coincides with the graph D_k referred to at the beginning of the proof of Theorem 8.21, and D_k' is obtained from D_k by an "n-layer contraction" (see ibid.). Furthermore, D_k and D_k' can be constructed (from x) in logarithmic space (and by using the emulative composition of Lemma 5.2 we may just proceed as if D_k' is given as input). Combining this with the foregoing analysis, we conclude that the probability that M accepts x can be deterministically approximated in $O(\log|x|)^2$-space and $\text{poly}(|x|)$-time. The theorem follows. $\qquad\square$

8.5. Special-Purpose Generators

The pseudorandom generators considered so far were aimed at decreasing the amount of randomness utilized by any algorithm of certain time and/or space complexity (or even fully derandomizing the corresponding complexity class). For example, we considered the derandomization of classes such as $\mathcal{BPP}$ and $\mathcal{BPL}$. In the current section our goal is less ambitious. We only seek to derandomize (or decrease the randomness of) specific algorithms, or rather classes of algorithms that use their random bits in certain (restricted) ways. For example, the algorithm's correctness may only require that its sequence of coin tosses (or "blocks" in such a sequence) are pairwise-independent. Indeed, the restrictions that we shall consider here have a concrete and "structural" form, rather than the abstract complexity-theoretic forms considered in previous sections.

The aforementioned restrictions induce corresponding classes of very restricted distinguishers, which in particular are much weaker than the classes of distinguishers considered in previous sections. These very restricted types of distinguishers induce correspondingly weak types of pseudorandom generators (which produce sequences that fool these distinguishers). Still, such generators have many applications in Complexity Theory (and in the design of algorithms, as hinted in the foregoing paragraph). (These applications will only be mentioned briefly.)

We start with the simplest of these generators: the pairwise-independence generator, and its generalization to t-wise independence for any $t \geq 2$. Such generators *perfectly* fool any distinguisher that only observe t locations in the output sequence. This leads naturally to almost pairwise (or t-wise) independence generators, which also fool such distinguishers (albeit non-perfectly). The latter generators are implied by a stronger class of generators, which is of independent interest: the small-bias generators. Small-bias generators fool any linear test (i.e., any distinguisher that merely considers the XOR of some fixed locations in the input sequence). We then turn to the Expander Random Walk Generator: This generator produces a sequence of strings that hit any dense subset of strings with probability that is close to the hitting probability of a truly random sequence. Related notions such as samplers, dispersers, and extractors are treated in Appendix D.

---

[40]Note that $G_{M,x}$ is a "layered version" of the graph that was considered (and denoted G_x) in the proof of Theorem 5.11. Furthermore, while in the proof of Theorem 5.11 we cared about the existence of certain paths, here we care about their quantity (or rather the probability of traversing one of them).

> **Teaching note:** Unlike the constructions presented in previous sections, the constructions presented in this section do not utilize any insight into the nature of (time- or space-bounded) computation. Instead, they are based on various purely mathematical facts, and their analysis is deferred to exercises.

Comment regarding our parameterization. To maintain consistency with prior sections, we continue to present the generators in terms of the seed-length, denoted k. Since this is not the common presentation for most results presented in the sequel, we provide (in footnotes) the common presentation in which the seed-length is determined as a function of other parameters.

8.5.1. Pairwise Independence Generators

Pairwise (resp., t-wise) independence generators fool tests that inspect only two (resp., t) elements in the output sequence of the generator. Such local tests are indeed very restricted, yet they arise naturally in many settings. For example, such a test corresponds to a probabilistic analysis (of a procedure) that only relies on the pairwise independence of certain choices made by the procedure. We also mention that, in some natural range of parameters, pairwise independent sampling is as good as sampling by totally independent sample points; see Appendices D.1.2 and D.3.

A t-wise independence generator of block-length $b : \mathbb{N} \to \mathbb{N}$ (and stretch function ℓ) is a relatively efficient deterministic algorithm (e.g., one that works in time polynomial in the output length) that expands a k-bit long random seed into a sequence of $\ell(k)/b(k)$ blocks, each of length $b(k)$, such that any t blocks are uniformly and independently distributed in $\{0, 1\}^{t \cdot b(k)}$. That is, denoting the ith block of the generator's output (on seed s) by $G(s)_i$, we require that for every $i_1 < i_2 < \cdots < i_t$ (in $[\ell(k)/b(k)]$) it holds that

$$G(U_k)_{i_1}, G(U_k)_{i_2}, \ldots, G(U_k)_{i_t} \equiv U_{t \cdot b(k)}. \tag{8.15}$$

We note that this condition holds even if the inspected t blocks are selected adaptively (see Exercise 8.29). In case $t = 2$, we call the generator pairwise independent.

8.5.1.1. Constructions

In the first construction, we refer to $\mathrm{GF}(2^{b(k)})$, the finite field of $2^{b(k)}$ elements, and associate its elements with $\{0, 1\}^{b(k)}$.

> **Proposition 8.24** (*t-wise independence generator*): [41] *Let t be a fixed integer and $b, \ell, \ell' : \mathbb{N} \to \mathbb{N}$ such that $b(k) = k/t$, $\ell'(k) = \ell(k)/b(k) > t$ and $\ell'(k) \le 2^{b(k)}$. Let $\alpha_1, \ldots, \alpha_{\ell'(k)}$ be fixed distinct elements of the field $\mathrm{GF}(2^{b(k)})$. For $s_0, s_1, \ldots, s_{t-1} \in \{0, 1\}^{b(k)}$, let*
>
> $$G(s_0, s_1, \ldots, s_{t-1}) \overset{\text{def}}{=} \left(\sum_{j=0}^{t-1} s_j \alpha_1^j, \ \sum_{j=0}^{t-1} s_j \alpha_2^j, \ldots, \sum_{j=0}^{t-1} s_j \alpha_{\ell'(k)}^j \right) \tag{8.16}$$
>
> *where the arithmetic is that of $\mathrm{GF}(2^{b(k)})$. Then, G is a t-wise independence generator of block-length b and stretch ℓ.*

---

[41] In the common presentation of this t-wise independence generator, the length of the seed is determined as a function of the desired block-length and stretch. That is, given the parameters b and $\ell' \le 2^b$, the seed-length is set to $t \cdot b$.

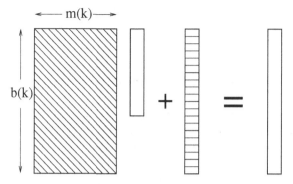

Figure 8.4: An affine transformation affected by a Toeplitz matrix.

That is, given a seed that consists of t elements of $GF(2^{b(k)})$, the generator outputs a sequence of $\ell'(k)$ such elements. The proof of Proposition 8.24 is left as an exercise (see Exercise 8.30). It is based on the observation that, for any fixed $v_0, v_1, \ldots, v_{t-1}$, the condition $\{G(s_0, s_1, \ldots, s_{t-1})_{i_j} = v_j\}_{j=1}^t$ constitutes a system of t linear equations over $GF(2^{b(k)})$ (in the variables $s_0, s_1, \ldots, s_{t-1}$) such that the equations are linearly independent. (Thus, linear independence of certain expressions yields statistical independence of the corresponding random variables.)

A somewhat tedious comment. We warn that Eq. (8.16) does not provide a fully explicit construction (of a generator). What is missing is an explicit representation of $GF(2^{b(k)})$, which requires an irreducible polynomial of degree $b(k)$ over $GF(2)$. For specific values of $b(k)$, a good representation does exist: for example, for $d \stackrel{\text{def}}{=} b(k) = 2 \cdot 3^e$ (with e being an integer), the polynomial $x^d + x^{d/2} + 1$ is irreducible over $GF(2)$. For further detail, see Appendix G.3.

We note that a construction analogous to Eq. (8.16) works for every finite field (e.g., a finite field of any prime cardinality), but the problem of providing an explicit representation of such a field remains non-trivial also in other cases (e.g., consider the problem of finding a prime number of size approximately $2^{b(k)}$). The latter fact is the main motivation for considering the following alternative construction for the case of $t = 2$.

The following construction uses (random) affine transformations (as possible seeds). In fact, better performance (i.e., shorter seed-length) is obtained by using affine transformations affected by Toeplitz matrices. A Toeplitz matrix is a matrix with all diagonals being homogeneous (see Figure 8.4); that is, $T = (t_{i,j})$ is a Toeplitz matrix if $t_{i,j} = t_{i+1,j+1}$ for all i, j. Note that a Toeplitz matrix is determined by its first row and first column (i.e., the values of $t_{1,j}$'s and $t_{i,1}$'s).

Proposition 8.25 (alternative pairwise independence generator; see Figure 8.4): [42]
Let $b, \ell, \ell', m : \mathbb{N} \to \mathbb{N}$ such that $\ell'(k) = \ell(k)/b(k)$ and $m(k) = \lceil \log_2 \ell'(k) \rceil = k - 2b(k) + 1$. Associate $\{0, 1\}^n$ with the n-dimensional vector space over $GF(2)$, and let $v_1, \ldots, v_{\ell'(k)}$ be fixed distinct vectors in the $m(k)$-dimensional vector space over

---

[42]In the common presentation of this pairwise independence generator, the length of the seed is determined as a function of the desired block-length and stretch. That is, given the parameters b and ℓ', the seed-length is set to $2b + \lceil \log_2 \ell' \rceil - 1$.

GF(2). *For $s \in \{0, 1\}^{b(k)+m(k)-1}$ and $r \in \{0, 1\}^{b(k)}$, let*

$$G(s, r) \overset{\text{def}}{=} (T_s v_1 + r, \; T_s v_2 + r, \; \ldots, \; T_s v_{\ell'(k)} + r) \tag{8.17}$$

where T_s is an $b(k)$-by-$m(k)$ Toeplitz matrix specified by the string s. Then G is a pairwise independence generator of block-length b and stretch ℓ.

That is, given a seed that represents an affine transformation defined by an $b(k)$-by-$m(k)$ Toeplitz matrix and a $b(k)$-dimensional vector, the generator outputs a sequence of $\ell'(k) \leq 2^{m(k)}$ strings, each of length $b(k)$. Note that $k = 2b(k) + m(k) - 1$, and that the stretching property requires $\ell'(k) > k/b(k)$. The proof of Proposition 8.25 is left as an exercise (see Exercise 8.31). This proof is also based on the observation that linear independence of certain expressions yields statistical independence of the corresponding random variables: Here $\{G(s, r)_{i_j} = v_j\}_{j=1}^{2}$ is a system of $2b(k)$ linear equations over GF(2) (in Boolean variables representing the bits of s and r) such that the equations are linearly independent. We mention that a construction analogous to Eq. (8.17) works for every finite field.

A stronger notion of efficient generation. Ignoring the issue of finding a representation for a large finite field, both the foregoing constructions are efficient in the sense that the generator's output can be produced in time that is polynomial in its length. Actually, the aforementioned constructions satisfy a stronger notion of efficient generation, which is useful in several applications. Specifically, there exists a polynomial-time algorithm that given a seed, $s \in \{0, 1\}^k$, and a block location $i \in [\ell'(k)]$ (in binary), outputs the ith block of the corresponding output (i.e., the ith block of $G(s)$). Note that, in the case of the first construction (captured by Eq. (8.16)), this stronger notion depends on the ability to find a representation of GF($2^{b(k)}$) in poly(k)-time.[43] Recall that this is possible in the case that $b(k)$ is of the form $2 \cdot 3^e$.

8.5.1.2. Applications (a Brief Review)

Pairwise independence generators do suffice for a variety of applications (cf., [238, 161]). Many of these applications are based on the fact that "Laws of Large Numbers" hold for sequences of trials that are pairwise independent (rather than totally independent). This fact is captured in Chebyshev's Inequality (see, e.g., §D.1.2.2), and is the basis of the (rather generic) application to sampling discussed in Appendix D.3. As a concrete example, we mention the derandomization of a fast parallel algorithm for the Maximal Independent Set problem (as presented in [168, Sec. 12.3]).[44] In general, whenever the analysis of a randomized algorithm only relies on the hypothesis that some objects are distributed in a pairwise independent manner, we may replace its random choices by a sequence of choices that is generated by a pairwise independence generator. Thus, pairwise independence generators suffice for fooling distinguishers that are derived from some natural and interesting randomized algorithms.

Referring to Eq. (8.16), we remark that, for any constant $t \geq 2$, the cost of derandomization (i.e., going over all 2^k possible seeds) is exponential in the block-length

---

[43] For the basic notion of efficiency, it suffices to find a representation of GF($2^{b(k)}$) in poly($\ell(k)$)-time, which can be done by an exhaustive search in the case that $b(k) = O(\log \ell(k))$.

[44] The core of this algorithm is picking each vertex with probability that is inversely proportional to the vertex's degree. The analysis only requires that these choices be pairwise independent. Furthermore, these choices can be (approximately) implemented by uniformly selecting values in a sufficiently large set.

(because $b(k) = k/t$). On the other hand, the number of blocks is at most exponential in the block-length (because $\ell'(k) \le 2^{b(k)}$), and so if a larger number of blocks is needed, then we can artificially increase the block-length in order to accommodate this (i.e., set $b(k) = \log_2 \ell'(k)$). Thus, the cost of derandomization is polynomial in $\max(\ell'(k), 2^{b'(k)})$, where $\ell'(k)$ denotes the desired number of blocks and $b'(k)$ the desired block-length. (In other words, $\ell'(k)$ denotes the desired number of random choices, and $2^{b'(k)}$ represents the size of the domain of each of these choices.) It follows that *whenever the analysis of a randomized algorithm can be based on a constant amount of independence* between feasibly many random choices, each taken within a domain of feasible size, *then a feasible derandomization is possible.*

8.5.2. Small-Bias Generators

As stated in §8.5.1.2, $O(1)$-wise independence generators allow for the efficient derandomization of any efficient randomized algorithm the analysis of which is only based on a *constant amount of independence* between the bits of its random-tape. This restriction is due to the fact that t-wise independence generators of stretch ℓ require a seed of length $\Omega(t \cdot \log \ell)$. Trying to go beyond constant independence in such derandomizations (while using seeds of length that is logarithmic in the length of the pseudorandom sequence) was the original motivation of the notion of small-bias generators. Specifically, as we shall see in §8.5.2.2, small-bias generators yield meaningful approximations of t-wise independence sequences (based on logarithmic-length seeds).

While the aforementioned type of derandomizations remains an important application of small-bias generators, the latter are of independent interest and have found numerous other applications. In particular, small-bias generators fool "global tests" that examine the entire output sequence and not merely a fixed number of positions in it (as in the case of limited independence generators). Specifically, a small-bias generator produces a sequence of bits that fools any linear test (i.e., a test that computes a fixed linear combination of the bits).

For $\varepsilon : \mathbb{N} \to [0, 1]$, an ε-bias generator with stretch function ℓ is a relatively efficient deterministic algorithm (e.g., working in $\text{poly}(\ell(k))$ time) that expands a k-bit long random seed into a sequence of $\ell(k)$ bits such that, for any fixed non-empty set $S \subseteq \{1, \ldots, \ell(k)\}$, the bias of the output sequence over S is at most $\varepsilon(k)$. The bias of a sequence of n (possibly dependent) Boolean random variables $\zeta_1, \ldots, \zeta_n \in \{0, 1\}$ over a set $S \subseteq \{1, .., n\}$ is defined as

$$2 \cdot \left| \Pr[\oplus_{i \in S} \zeta_i = 1] - \frac{1}{2} \right| = \left| \Pr[\oplus_{i \in S} \zeta_i = 1] - \Pr[\oplus_{i \in S} \zeta_i = 0] \right|. \qquad (8.18)$$

The factor of 2 was introduced so as to make these biases correspond to the Fourier coefficients of the distribution (viewed as a function from $\{0, 1\}^n$ to the reals). To see the correspondence, replace $\{0, 1\}$ by $\{\pm 1\}$, and substitute XOR by multiplication. The bias with respect to a set S is thus written as

$$\left| \Pr\left[\prod_{i \in S} \zeta_i = +1 \right] - \Pr\left[\prod_{i \in S} \zeta_i = -1 \right] \right| = \left| \mathsf{E}\left[\prod_{i \in S} \zeta_i \right] \right| \qquad (8.19)$$

which is merely the (absolute value of the) Fourier coefficient corresponding to S.

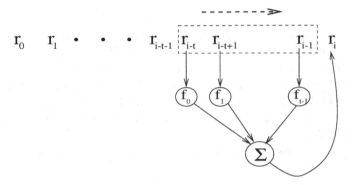

Figure 8.5: The LFSR small-bias generator (for $t = k/2$).

8.5.2.1. Constructions

Relatively efficient small-bias generators with exponential stretch and exponentially vanishing bias are known.

> **Theorem 8.26** (small-bias generators):[45] *For some universal constant $c > 0$, let $\ell : \mathbb{N} \to \mathbb{N}$ and $\varepsilon : \mathbb{N} \to [0, 1]$ such that $\ell(k) \leq \varepsilon(k) \cdot \exp(k/c)$. Then, there exists an ε-bias generator with stretch function ℓ operating in time that is polynomial in the length of its output.*

In particular, we may have $\ell(k) = \exp(k/2c)$ and $\varepsilon(k) = \exp(-k/2c)$. Three simple constructions of small-bias generators that satisfy Theorem 8.26 are known (see [10]). One of these constructions is based on Linear Feedback Shift Registers (LFSRs), where the seed of the generator is used to determine both the "feedback rule" and the "start sequence" of the LFSR. Specifically, a feedback rule of a t-long LFSR is an irreducible polynomial of degree t over GF(2), denoted $f(x) = x^t + \sum_{j=0}^{t-1} f_j x^j$ where $f_0 = 1$, and the (ℓ-bit long) sequence produced by the corresponding LFSR based on the start sequence $s_0 s_1 \cdots s_{t-1} \in \{0, 1\}^t$ is defined as $r_0 r_1 \cdots r_{\ell-1}$, where

$$r_i = \begin{cases} s_i & \text{if } i \in \{0, 1, \ldots, t-1\} \\ \sum_{j=0}^{t-1} f_j \cdot r_{i-t+j} & \text{if } i \in \{t, t+1, \ldots, \ell-1\} \end{cases} \tag{8.20}$$

(see Figure 8.5). As stated previously, in the corresponding small-bias generator the k-bit long seed is used for selecting an *almost* uniformly distributed feedback rule f (i.e., a random irreducible polynomial of degree $t = k/2$) and a uniformly distributed start sequence s (i.e., a random t-bit string).[46] The corresponding $\ell(k)$-bit long output $r = r_0 r_1 \cdots r_{\ell(k)-1}$ is computed as in Eq. (8.20).

A stronger notion of efficient generation. As in Section 8.5.1.1, we note that the aforementioned constructions satisfy a stronger notion of efficient generation, which is

---

[45] In the common presentation of this generator, the length of the seed is determined as a function of the desired bias and stretch. That is, given the parameters ε and ℓ, the seed-length is set to $c \cdot \log(\ell/\varepsilon)$. We comment that using [10] the constant c is merely 2 (i.e., $k \approx 2 \log_2(\ell/\varepsilon)$), whereas using [170] $k \approx \log_2 \ell + 4 \log_2(1/\varepsilon)$.

[46] Note that an implementation of this generator requires an algorithm for selecting an almost-random irreducible polynomial of degree $t = \Omega(k)$. A simple algorithm proceeds by enumerating all irreducible polynomials of degree t, and selecting one of them at random. This algorithm can be implemented (using t random bits) in $\exp(t)$-time, which is poly($\ell(k)$) if $\ell(k) = \exp(\Omega(k))$. A poly($t$)-time algorithm that uses $O(t)$ random bits is described in [10, Sec. 8].

---

useful in several applications. That is, there exists a polynomial-time algorithm that given a k-bit long seed and a bit location $i \in [\ell(k)]$ (in binary), outputs the ith bit of the corresponding output. Specifically, in the case of the LFSR construction, given a seed $f_0, \ldots, f_{(k/2)-1}, s_0, \ldots, s_{(k/2)-1}$ and a bit location $i \in [\ell(k)]$ (in binary), the algorithm outputs the ith bit of the corresponding output (i.e., r_i).[47]

8.5.2.2. Applications (a Brief Review)

An archetypical application of small-bias generators is their use for producing short and random "fingerprints" (or "digests") of strings such that equality/inequality among strings is (probabilistically) reflected in equality/inequality between their corresponding fingerprints. The key observation is that checking whether or not $x = y$ is probabilistically reducible to checking whether the inner product modulo 2 of x and r equals the inner product modulo 2 of y and r, *where r is produced by a small-bias generator G*. Thus, the pair (s, v), where s is a random seed to G and v equals the inner product modulo 2 of z and $G(s)$, serves as the randomized fingerprint of the string z. One advantage of this reduction is that only few bits (i.e., the seed of the generator and the result of the inner product) needs to be "communicated between x and y" in order to enable the checking (see Exercise 8.33). A related advantage is the low randomness complexity of this reduction, which uses $|s|$ rather than $|G(s)|$ random bits, where $|s|$ may be $O(\log|G(s)|)$. This low (i.e., logarithmic) randomness complexity underlies the application of small-bias generators to the construction of PCP systems (see, e.g., §9.3.2.2) and to the design of gap-amplifying reductions for problems regarding the satisfiability of systems of equations (see Section 9.3.3 and Exercise 10.6).

Small-bias generators have been used in a variety of areas (e.g., inapproximation, structural complexity, and applied cryptography; see references in [90, Sec 3.6.2]). In addition, as shown next, small-bias generators seem an important tool in the design of various types of "pseudorandom" objects.

Approximate independence generators. As hinted at the beginning of this section, small-bias is related to approximate versions of limited independence.[48] Actually, as implied by Exercise 8.34, even a restricted type of ε-bias (in which only subsets of size $t(k)$ are required to have bias upper-bounded by ε) implies that any $t(k)$ bits in the said sequence are $2^{t(k)/2} \cdot \varepsilon(k)$-close to $U_{t(k)}$, where here we refer to the variation distance (i.e., Norm-1 distance) between the two distributions. (The max-norm of the difference is bounded by $\varepsilon(k)$.)[49] Combining Theorem 8.26 and the foregoing upper bound, we obtain *generators with exponential stretch* (i.e., $\ell(k) = \exp(\Omega(k))$) that produce *sequences that are approximately $\Omega(k)$-wise independent in the sense that any $t(k) = \Omega(k)$*

---

[47]The assertion is based on the fact that

$$
\begin{pmatrix} r_{i-t+1} \\ r_{i-t+2} \\ \vdots \\ r_{i-1} \\ r_i \end{pmatrix} = \begin{pmatrix} 0 & 1 & 0 & \cdots & 0 \\ 0 & 0 & 1 & \cdots & 0 \\ \vdots & \vdots & \vdots & \cdots & \vdots \\ 0 & 0 & 0 & \cdots & 1 \\ f_0 & f_1 & f_2 & \cdots & f_{t-1} \end{pmatrix} \begin{pmatrix} r_{i-t} \\ r_{i-t+1} \\ \vdots \\ r_{i-2} \\ r_{i-1} \end{pmatrix} = \begin{pmatrix} 0 & 1 & 0 & \cdots & 0 \\ 0 & 0 & 1 & \cdots & 0 \\ \vdots & \vdots & \vdots & \cdots & \vdots \\ 0 & 0 & 0 & \cdots & 1 \\ f_0 & f_1 & f_2 & \cdots & f_{t-1} \end{pmatrix}^{i-t+1} \begin{pmatrix} s_0 \\ s_1 \\ \vdots \\ s_{t-2} \\ s_{t-1} \end{pmatrix}
$$

[48]We warn that, unlike in the case of perfect independence, here we refer only to the distribution on fixed bit locations. See Exercise 8.32 for further discussion.

[49]Both bounds are derived from the Norm-2 bound on the difference vector (i.e., the difference between the two probability vectors). For details, see Exercise 8.34.

---

bits in them are $2^{-\Omega(k)}$-*close to* $U_{t(k)}$. Furthermore, as shown in Exercise 8.40, relying on the linearity of the construction presented in Proposition 8.24, we can obtain *generators with double-exponential stretch* (i.e., $\ell(k) = \exp(2^{\Omega(k)})$) *that are approximately* $t(k)$-*independent* (in the foregoing sense). That is, we may obtain generators with stretch $\ell(k) = 2^{2^{\Omega(k)}}$ producing bit sequences in which any $t(k) = \Omega(k)$ positions have variation distance at most $\varepsilon(k) = 2^{-\Omega(k)}$ from uniform; in other words, such generators may have seed-length $k = O(t(k) + \log(1/\varepsilon(k)) + \log\log \ell(k))$. In the corresponding result for the max-norm distance, it suffices to have $k = O(\log(t(k)/\varepsilon(k)) + \log\log \ell(k))$. Thus, whenever the analysis of a randomized algorithm can be based on a logarithmic amount of (almost) independence between feasibly many binary random choices, a feasible derandomization is possible (by using an adequate generator of logarithmic seed-length).

Extensions to non-binary choices were considered in various works (see references in [90, Sec 3.6.2]). Some of these works also consider the related problem of constructing small "discrepancy sets" for geometric and combinatorial rectangles.

t-**universal set generators.** Using the aforementioned upper bound on the max-norm (of the deviation from uniform of any t locations), any ε-bias generator yields a t-*universal set generator*, provided that $\varepsilon < 2^{-t}$. The latter generator outputs sequences such that in every subsequence of length t all possible 2^t patterns occur (i.e., each for at least one possible seed). Such generators have many applications.

8.5.2.3. Generalization

In this subsection, we outline a generalization of the treatment of small-bias generators to the generation of sequences over an arbitrary finite field. Focusing on the case of a field of prime characteristic, denoted $\mathrm{GF}(p)$, we first define an adequate notion of bias. Generalizing Eq. (8.19), we define the bias of a sequence of n (possibly dependent) random variables $\zeta_1, \ldots, \zeta_n \in \mathrm{GF}(p)$ with respect to the linear combination $(c_1, \ldots, c_n) \in \mathrm{GF}(p)^n$ as $\left\| \mathsf{E}\left[\omega^{\sum_{i=1}^n c_i \zeta_i}\right] \right\|$, where ω denotes the pth (complex) root of unity (i.e., $\omega = -1$ if $p = 2$). Referring to Exercise 8.42, we note that upper bounds on the biases of $\zeta_1, \ldots, \zeta_n$ (with respect to any non-zero linear combinations) yield upper bounds on the distance of $\sum_{i=1}^n c_i \zeta_i$ from the uniform distribution over $\mathrm{GF}(p)$.

We say that $S \subseteq \mathrm{GF}(p)^n$ is an ε-bias probability space if a uniformly selected sequence in S has bias at most ε with respect to any non-zero linear combination over $\mathrm{GF}(p)$. (Whenever such a space is efficiently constructible, it yields a corresponding ε-biased generator.) We mention that the LFSR construction, outlined in §8.5.2.1 and analyzed in Exercise 8.36, generalizes to $\mathrm{GF}(p)$ and yields an ε-bias probability space of size (at most) p^{2e}, where $e = \lceil \log_p(n/\varepsilon) \rceil$. Such constructions can be used in applications that generalize those in §8.5.2.2.

8.5.3. Random Walks on Expanders

In this section we review generators that produce a sequence of values by taking a random walk on a large graph that has a small degree but an adequate "mixing" property. Such a graph is called an expander, and by taking a random walk on it we may generate a sequence of ℓ' values over its vertex set, while using a random seed of length $b + (\ell' - 1) \cdot \log_2 d$, where 2^b denotes the number of vertices in the graph and d denotes its degree. This seed-length should be compared against the $\ell' \cdot b$ random bits required for generating a sequence of ℓ' independent samples from $\{0, 1\}^b$ (or taking a random walk on a clique of size 2^b). Interestingly, as we shall see, the pseudorandom sequence (generated by the said random walk on an expander) *behaves similarly to a truly random sequence with respect to hitting any fixed subset of* $\{0, 1\}^b$. Let us start by defining this property (or rather by defining the corresponding hitting problem).

Definition 8.27 (the hitting problem): *A sequence of* (possibly dependent) *random variables, denoted* $(X_1, \ldots, X_{\ell'})$, *over* $\{0, 1\}^b$ *is* (ε, δ)-hitting *if for any* (target) *set* $T \subseteq \{0, 1\}^b$ *of cardinality at least* $\varepsilon \cdot 2^b$, *with probability at least* $1 - \delta$, *at least one of these variables hits* T; *that is,* $\Pr[\exists i \text{ s.t. } X_i \in T] \geq 1 - \delta$.

Clearly, a truly random sequence of length ℓ' over $\{0, 1\}^b$ is (ε, δ)-hitting for $\delta = (1 - \varepsilon)^{\ell'}$. The aforementioned "Expander Random Walk Generator" (to be described next) achieves similar behavior. Specifically, for arbitrary small $c > 0$ (which depends on the degree and the mixing property of the expander), the generator's output is (ε, δ)-hitting for $\delta = (1 - (1 - c) \cdot \varepsilon)^{\ell'}$. To describe this generator, we need to discuss expanders.

Expanders. By expander graphs (or expanders) of degree d and eigenvalue bound $\lambda < d$, we actually mean an infinite family of d-regular graphs, $\{G_N\}_{N \in \mathbb{S}}$ ($\mathbb{S} \subseteq \mathbb{N}$), such that G_N is a d-regular graph over N vertices and the absolute value of all eigenvalues, save the biggest one, of the adjacency matrix of G_N is upper-bounded by λ. For simplicity, we shall assume that the vertex set of G_N is $[N]$ (although in some constructions a somewhat more redundant representation is more convenient). We will refer to such a family as to a (d, λ)-expander (for $\mathbb{S}$). This technical definition is related to the aforementioned notion of "mixing" (which refers to the rate at which a random walk starting at a fixed vertex reaches uniform distribution over the graph's vertices). For further detail, see Appendix E.2.1.

We are interested in explicit constructions of such graphs, by which we mean that there exists a polynomial-time algorithm that on input N (in binary), a vertex v in G_N and an index $i \in \{1, \ldots, d\}$, returns the ith neighbor of v. (We also require that the set $\mathbb{S}$ for which G_N's exist is sufficiently "tractable" – say, that given any $n \in \mathbb{N}$ one may efficiently find an $s \in \mathbb{S}$ such that $n \leq s < 2n$.) Several explicit constructions of expanders are known (see Appendix E.2.2). Below, we rely on the fact that for every $\overline{\lambda} > 0$, there exist d and an explicit construction of a $(d, \overline{\lambda} \cdot d)$-expander over $\{2^b : b \in \mathbb{N}\}$.[50] The relevant (to us) fact about expanders is stated next.

Theorem 8.28 (Expander Random Walk Theorem): *Let* $G = (V, E)$ *be an expander graph of degree* d *and eigenvalue bound* λ. *Let* W *be a subset of* V *and* $\rho \stackrel{\text{def}}{=} |W|/|V|$, *and consider walks on* G *that start from a uniformly chosen vertex and take* $\ell' - 1$ *additional random steps, where in each such step one uniformly selects one out of the* d *edges incident at the current vertex and traverses it. Then*

---

[50]This can be obtained with $d = \text{poly}(1/\overline{\lambda})$. In fact $d = O(1/\overline{\lambda}^2)$, which is optimal, can be obtained, too, albeit with graphs of sizes that are only approximately powers of two.

the probability that such a random walk stays in W is at most

$$\rho \cdot \left(\rho + (1 - \rho) \cdot \frac{\lambda}{d} \right)^{\ell' - 1} \tag{8.21}$$

Thus, a random walk on an expander is "pseudorandom" with respect to the hitting property (i.e., when we consider hitting the set $V \setminus W$ and use $\varepsilon = 1 - \rho$); that is, a set of density ε is hit with probability $1 - \delta$, where $\delta = (1 - \varepsilon) \cdot (1 - \varepsilon + (\lambda/d) \cdot \varepsilon)^{\ell' - 1} < (1 - (1 - (\lambda/d)) \cdot \varepsilon)^{\ell'}$. A proof of Theorem 8.28 is given in [135], while a proof of an upper bound that is weaker than Eq. (8.21) is outlined in Exercise 8.43. Using Theorem 8.28 and an explicit $(2^t, \overline{\lambda} \cdot 2^t)$-expander, we obtain a generator that produces sequences that are (ε, δ)-hitting for δ that is almost optimal.

Proposition 8.29 (The Expander Random Walk Generator):[51]

- *For every constant $\overline{\lambda} > 0$, consider an explicit construction of $(2^t, \overline{\lambda} \cdot 2^t)$-expanders for $\{2^n : n \in \mathbb{N}\}$, where $t \in \mathbb{N}$ is a sufficiently large constant. For $v \in [2^n] \equiv \{0, 1\}^n$ and $i \in [2^t] \equiv \{0, 1\}^t$, denote by $\Gamma_i(v)$ the vertex of the corresponding 2^n-vertex graph that is reached from vertex v when following its ith edge.*
- *For $b, \ell' : \mathbb{N} \to \mathbb{N}$ such that $k = b(k) + (\ell'(k) - 1) \cdot t < \ell'(k) \cdot b(k)$, and for $v_0 \in \{0, 1\}^{b(k)}$ and $i_1, \ldots, i_{\ell'(k)-1} \in [2^t]$, let*

$$G(v_0, i_1, \ldots, i_{\ell'(k)-1}) \overset{\text{def}}{=} (v_0, v_1, \ldots, v_{\ell'(k)-1}), \tag{8.22}$$

where $v_j = \Gamma_{i_j}(v_{j-1})$.

Then G has stretch $\ell(k) = \ell'(k) \cdot b(k)$, and $G(U_k)$ is (ε, δ)-hitting for any $\varepsilon > 0$ and $\delta = (1 - (1 - \overline{\lambda}) \cdot \varepsilon)^{\ell'(k)}$.

The stretch of G is maximized at $b(k) \approx k/2$ (and $\ell'(k) = k/2t$), but maximizing the stretch is not necessarily the goal in all applications. In many applications, the parameters n, ε, and δ are given, and the goal is to derive a generator that produces (ε, δ)-hitting sequences over $\{0, 1\}^n$ while minimizing both the length of the sequence and the amount of randomness used by the generator (i.e., the seed length). Indeed, Proposition 8.29 suggests using sequences of length $\ell' \approx \varepsilon^{-1} \log_2(1/\delta)$ that are generated based on a random seed of length $n + O(\ell')$.

Expander Random Walk Generators have been used in a variety of areas (e.g., PCP and inapproximability (see [29, Sec. 11.1]), cryptography (see [91, Sec. 2.6]), and the design of various types of "pseudorandom" objects (see, in particular, Appendix D.3)).

Chapter Notes

Figure 8.6 depicts some of the notions of pseudorandom generators discussed in this chapter. We highlight a key distinction between the case of general-purpose pseudorandom generators (treated in Section 8.2) and the other cases (cf. Sections 8.3 and 8.4): In the former case the distinguisher is more complex than the generator, whereas in the latter cases the generator is more complex than the distinguisher. Specifically, in the

---

[51]In the common presentation of this generator, the length of the seed is determined as a function of the desired block-length and stretch. That is, given the parameters b and ℓ', the seed length is set to $b + O(\ell' - 1)$.

TYPE	distinguisher's resources	generator's resources	stretch (i.e., $\ell(k)$)	comments
gen.-purpose	$p(k)$-time, $\forall$ poly. p	poly(k)-time	poly(k)	Assumes OW
canon. derandom.	$2^{k/O(1)}$-time	$2^{O(k)}$-time	$2^{k/O(1)}$	Assumes EvEC
space-bounded robustness	$s(k)$-space, $s(k) < k$	$O(k)$-space	$2^{k/O(s(k))}$	runs in time
	$k/O(1)$-space	$O(k)$-space	poly(k)	poly$(k) \cdot \ell(k)$
t-wise independ.	inspect t positions	poly$(k) \cdot \ell(k)$-time	$2^{k/O(t)}$	(e.g., pairwise)
small-bias	linear tests	poly$(k) \cdot \ell(k)$-time	$2^{k/O(1)} \cdot \varepsilon(k)$	
expander	"hitting"	poly$(k) \cdot \ell(k)$-time	$\ell'(k) \cdot b(k)$	
random walk	$(0.5, 2^{-\ell'(k)/O(1)})$-hitting for $\{0,1\}^{b(k)}$, with $\ell'(k) = ((k - b(k))/O(1)) + 1$.			

Figure 8.6: Pseudorandom generators at a glance. By OW we denote the assumption that one-way functions exist. By EvEC we denote the assumption that the class $\mathcal{E}$ has (almost-everywhere) exponential circuit complexity.

general-purpose case the generator runs in (some *fixed*) polynomial time and needs to withstand *any* probabilistic polynomial-time distinguisher. In fact, some of the proofs presented in Section 8.2 utilize the fact that the distinguisher can invoke the generator on seeds of its choice. In contrast, the Nisan-Wigderson Generator, analyzed in Theorem 8.18 (of Section 8.3), runs more time than the distinguishers that it tries to fool, and the proof relies on this fact in an essential manner. Similarly, the space complexity of the space resilient generators presented in Section 8.4 is higher than the space bound of the distinguishers that they fool.

The general paradigm of pseudorandom generators. Our presentation, which views vastly different notions of pseudorandom generators as incarnations of a general paradigm, has emerged mostly in retrospect. We note that, while the historical study of the various notions was mostly unrelated at a technical level, the case of general-purpose pseudorandom generators served as a source of inspiration to most of the other cases. In particular, the concept of computational indistinguishability, the connection between hardness and pseudorandomness, and the equivalence between pseudorandomness and unpredictability appeared first in the context of general-purpose pseudorandom generators (and inspired the development of "generators for derandomization" and "generators for space-bounded machines"). Indeed, the study of the special-purpose generators (see Section 8.5) was unrelated to all of these.

General-purpose pseudorandom generators. The concept of *computational indistinguishability*, which underlies the entire computational approach to randomness, was suggested by Goldwasser and Micali [108] in the context of defining secure encryption schemes. Indeed, computational indistinguishability plays a key role in cryptography (see Appendix C). The general formulation of computational indistinguishability is due to Yao [239]. Using the hybrid technique of [108], Yao also observed that defining pseudorandom generators as producing sequences that are computationally indistinguishable from the corresponding uniform distribution is equivalent to defining such generators as producing unpredictable sequences. The latter definition originates in the earlier work of Blum and Micali [41].

Blum and Micali [41] pioneered the rigorous study of pseudorandom generators and, in particular, the construction of pseudorandom generators based on some simple intractability assumption. In particular, they constructed pseudorandom generators assuming the intractability of the Discrete Logarithm problem over prime fields. Their work also introduces basic paradigms that were used in all subsequent improvements (cf., e.g., [239, 118]). We refer to the transformation of computational difficulty into pseudorandomness, the use of hard-core predicates (also defined in [41]), and the iteration paradigm (cf. Eq. (8.10)).

Theorem 8.11 (by which pseudorandom generators exist if and only if one-way functions exist) is due to Håstad, Impagliazzo, Levin, and Luby [118], building on the hard-core predicate of [99] (see Theorem 7.7). Unfortunately, the current proof of Theorem 8.11 is very complicated and unfit for presentation in a book of the current nature. Presenting a simpler and tighter (cf. §8.2.7.1) proof is indeed an important research project.

Pseudorandom functions (further discussed in Appendix C.3.3) were defined and first constructed by Goldreich, Goldwasser, and Micali [95]. We also mention (and advocate) the study of a general theory of pseudorandom objects initiated in [96]. Finally, we mention that a more detailed treatment of general-purpose pseudorandom generators is provided in [91, Chap. 3].

Derandomization of time-complexity classes. As observed by Yao [239], a non-uniformly strong notion of pseudorandom generators yields improved derandomization of time-complexity classes. A key observation of Nisan [173, 176] is that whenever a pseudorandom generator is used in this way, it suffices to require that the generator run in time that is exponential in its seed-length, and so the generator may have running time greater than the distinguisher (representing the algorithm to be derandomized). This observation motivates the definition of canonical derandomizers as well as the construction of Nisan and Wigderson [173, 176], which is the basis for further improvements culminating in [128]. Part 1 of Theorem 8.19 (i.e., the "high end" derandomization of $\mathcal{BPP}$) is due to Impagliazzo and Wigderson [128], whereas Part 2 (i.e., the "low end") is from [176].

The Nisan–Wigderson Generator [176] was subsequently used in several ways transcending its original presentation. We mention its application toward fooling non-deterministic machines (and thus derandomizing constant-round interactive proof systems) and to the construction of randomness extractors [222] (see overview in §D.4.2.2).

In contrast to the aforementioned derandomization results, which place $\mathcal{BPP}$ in some worst-case deterministic complexity class based on some non-uniform (worst-case) assumption, we now mention a result that places $\mathcal{BPP}$ in an average-case deterministic complexity class (cf. Section 10.2) based on a uniform-complexity (worst-case) assumption. We refer specifically to a theorem, which is due to Impagliazzo and Wigderson [129] (but is not presented in the main text), that asserts the following: *If $\mathcal{BPP}$ is not contained in $\mathcal{EXP}$* (almost everywhere), *then $\mathcal{BPP}$ has deterministic sub-exponential-time algorithms that are correct on all typical cases* (i.e., with respect to any polynomial-time samplable distribution).

Pseudorandomness with respect to space-bounded distinguishers. As stated in the first paper on the subject of "space-resilient pseudorandom generators" [4],[52] this research direction was inspired by the derandomization result obtained via the use of general-purpose pseudorandom generators. The latter result (necessarily) depends on intractability assumptions, and so the objective was identifying natural classes of algorithms

---

[52]This paper is more frequently cited for the Expander Random Walk technique, which it has introduced.

for which derandomization is possible without relying on intractability assumptions (but rather by relying on intractability results that are known for the corresponding classes of distinguishers). This objective was achieved before for the case of constant-depth (randomized) circuits, but space-bounded (randomized) algorithms offer a more appealing class that refers to natural algorithms. Fundamentally different constructions of space-resilient pseudorandom generators were given in several works, but are superseded by the two incomparable results mentioned in Section 8.4.2: Theorem 8.21 (aka Nisan's Generator [174]) and Theorem 8.22 (aka the Nisan–Zuckerman Generator [177]). These two results have been "interpolated" in [12]. Theorem 8.23 ($\mathcal{BPL} \subseteq \mathcal{SC}$) was proved by Nisan [175].

Special-purpose generators. The various generators presented in Section 8.5 were not inspired by any of the other types of pseudorandom generator (nor even by the generic notion of pseudorandomness). Pairwise independence generators were explicitly suggested in [54] (and are implicit in [50]). The generalization to t-wise independence (for $t \geq 2$) is due to [6]. Small-bias generators were first defined and constructed by Naor and Naor [170], and three simple constructions were subsequently given in [10]. The Expander Random Walk Generator was suggested by Ajtai, Komlos, and Szemerédi [4], who discovered that random walks on expander graphs provide a good approximation to repeated independent attempts with respect to hitting any fixed subset of sufficient density (within the vertex set). The analysis of the hitting property of such walks was subsequently improved, culminating in the bound cited in Theorem 8.28, which is taken from [135, Cor. 6.1].

(The foregoing historical notes do not mention several technical contributions that played an important role in the development of the area. For further details, the reader is referred to [90, Chap. 3]. In fact, the current chapter is a revision of [90, Chap. 3], providing significantly more details for the main topics, and omitting relatively secondary material (a revision of which appears in Appendices D.3 and D.4.)

We mention that an alternative treatment of pseudorandomness, which puts more emphasis on the relation between various techniques, is provided in [229]. In particular, the latter text highlights the connections between information-theoretic and computational phenomena (e.g., randomness extractors and canonical derandomizers), while the current text tends to decouple the two (see, e.g., Section 8.3 and Appendix D.4).

Exercises

Exercise 8.1: Show that placing no computational requirements on the generator enables unconditional results regarding "generators" that fool any family of sub-exponential-size circuits. That is, making no computational assumptions, prove that there exist functions $G : \{0, 1\}^* \to \{0, 1\}^*$ such that $\{G(U_k)\}_{k \in \mathbb{N}}$ is (strongly) pseudorandom, while $|G(s)| = 2|s|$ for every $s \in \{0, 1\}^*$. Furthermore, show that G can be computed in double-exponential time.

> **Guideline:** Use the Probabilistic Method (cf. [11]). First, for any fixed circuit $C : \{0, 1\}^n \to \{0, 1\}$, upper-bound the probability that for a random set $S \subset \{0, 1\}^n$ of size $2^{n/2}$ the absolute value of $\Pr[C(U_n) = 1] - (|\{x \in S : C(x) = 1\}|/|S|)$ is larger than $2^{-n/8}$. Next, using a union bound, prove the existence of a set $S \subset \{0, 1\}^n$ of size $2^{n/2}$ such that no circuit of size $2^{n/5}$ can distinguish a uniformly distributed element of S

from a uniformly distributed element of $\{0, 1\}^n$, where distinguishing means with a probability gap of at least $2^{-n/8}$.

Exercise 8.2: Prove the following corollaries to Proposition 8.3.

1. Let A be a probabilistic polynomial-time algorithm solving a decision problem $\chi : \{0, 1\}^* \rightarrow \{0, 1\}$ (in $\mathcal{BPP}$), and let A_G be as in Construction 8.2. Prove that it is infeasible to find an x on which A_G errs with probability that is significantly higher than the error probability of A; that is, prove that on input 1^n it is infeasible to find an $x \in \{0, 1\}^n$ such that $\Pr[A_G(x) \neq \chi(x)] < \Pr[A(x) = \chi(x)] + 0.01$.

2. Let A be a probabilistic polynomial-time algorithm solving the search associated with the NP-relation R, and let A_G be as in Construction 8.2. Prove that it is infeasible to find an x on which A_G outputs a wrong solution; that is, assuming for simplicity that A has error probability $1/3$, prove that on input 1^n it is infeasible to find an $x \in \{0, 1\}^n \cap S_R$ such that $\Pr[(x, A_G(x)) \notin R] > 0.4$, where $S_R \stackrel{\text{def}}{=} \{x : \exists y \, (x, y) \in R\}$. Likewise, it is infeasible to find an $x \in \{0, 1\}^n \setminus S_R$ such that $\Pr[A_G(x) \neq \perp] > 0.4$.

Exercise 8.3: Prove that omitting the absolute value in Eq. (8.6) keeps Definition 8.4 intact.

(Hint: Consider $D'(z) \stackrel{\text{def}}{=} 1 - D(z)$.)

Exercise 8.4: Prove that computational indistinguishability is an equivalence relation (defined over pairs of probability ensembles). Specifically, prove that this relation is transitive (i.e., $X \equiv Y$ and $Y \equiv Z$ implies $X \equiv Z$).

Exercise 8.5: Prove that *if $\{X_n\}_{n \in \mathbb{N}}$ and $\{Y_n\}_{n \in \mathbb{N}}$ are computationally indistinguishable and A is a probabilistic polynomial-time algorithm, then $\{A(X_n)\}_{n \in \mathbb{N}}$ and $\{A(Y_n)\}_{n \in \mathbb{N}}$ are computationally indistinguishable.*

Guideline: If D distinguishes the latter ensembles, then D' such that $D'(z) \stackrel{\text{def}}{=} D(A(z))$ distinguishes the former.

Exercise 8.6: In contrast to Exercise 8.5, show that the conclusion may not hold in case A is not computationally bounded. That is, show that there exists computationally indistinguishable ensembles, $\{X_n\}_{n \in \mathbb{N}}$ and $\{Y_n\}_{n \in \mathbb{N}}$, and an exponential-time algorithm A such that $\{A(X_n)\}_{n \in \mathbb{N}}$ and $\{A(Y_n)\}_{n \in \mathbb{N}}$ are *not* computationally indistinguishable.

Guideline: For any pair of ensembles $\{X_n\}_{n \in \mathbb{N}}$ and $\{Y_n\}_{n \in \mathbb{N}}$, consider the Boolean function f such that $f(z) = 1$ if and only if $\Pr[X_n = z] > \Pr[Y_n = z]$. Show that $|\Pr[f(X_n) = 1] - \Pr[f(Y_n) = 1]|$ equals the statistical difference between X_n and Y_n. Consider an adequate (approximate) implementation of f (e.g., approximate $\Pr[X_n = z]$ and $\Pr[Y_n = z]$ up to $\pm 2^{-2|z|}$).

Exercise 8.7: Show that the existence of pseudorandom generators implies the existence of polynomial time constructible probability ensembles that are statistically far apart and yet are computationally indistinguishable.

Guideline: Lower-bound the statistical distance between $G(U_k)$ and $U_{\ell(k)}$, where G is a pseudorandom generator with stretch ℓ.

Exercise 8.8: Relying on Theorem 7.7, provide a self-contained proof of the fact that the existence of one-way 1-1 functions implies the existence of polynomial-time constructible probability ensembles that are statistically far apart and yet are computationally indistinguishable.

> **Guideline:** Assuming that b is a hard-core of the function f, consider the ensembles $\{f(U_n) \cdot b(U_n)\}_{n \in \mathbb{N}}$ and $\{f(U_n) \cdot U'_1\}_{n \in \mathbb{N}}$. Prove that these ensembles are computationally indistinguishable by using the main ideas of the proof of Proposition 8.9. Show that if f is 1-1 then these ensembles are statistically far apart.

Exercise 8.9 (following [88]): Prove that the sufficient condition in Exercise 8.7 is in fact necessary. Recall that $\{X_n\}_{n \in \mathbb{N}}$ and $\{Y_n\}_{n \in \mathbb{N}}$ are said to be statistically far apart if, for some positive polynomial p and all sufficiently large n, the variation distance between X_n and Y_n is greater than $1/p(n)$. Using the following three steps, prove that the existence of *polynomial-time constructible* probability ensembles that are statistically far apart and yet are computationally indistinguishable implies the existence of pseudorandom generators.

1. Show that, without loss of generality, we may assume that the variation distance between X_n and Y_n is greater than $1 - \exp(-n)$.

> **Guideline:** For X_n and Y_n as in the forgoing, consider $\overline{X}_n = (X_n^{(1)}, \ldots, X_n^{(t(n))})$ and $\overline{Y}_n = (Y_n^{(1)}, \ldots, Y_n^{(t(n))})$, where the $X_n^{(i)}$'s (resp., $Y_n^{(i)}$'s) are independent copies of X_n (resp., Y_n), and $t(n) = O(n \cdot p(n)^2)$. To lower-bound the statistical difference between $\overline{X}_n$ and $\overline{Y}_n$, consider the set $S_n \overset{\text{def}}{=} \{z : \Pr[X_n = z] > \Pr[Y_n = z]\}$ and the random variable representing the number of copies in $\overline{X}_n$ (resp., $\overline{Y}_n$) that reside in S_n.

2. Using $\{X_n\}_{n \in \mathbb{N}}$ and $\{Y_n\}_{n \in \mathbb{N}}$ as in Step 1, prove the existence of a *false entropy generator*, where a false entropy generator is a deterministic polynomial-time algorithm G such that $G(U_k)$ has entropy $e(k)$ but $\{G(U_k)\}_{k \in \mathbb{N}}$ is computationally indistinguishable from a polynomial-time constructible ensemble that has entropy greater than $e(\cdot) + (1/2)$.

> **Guideline:** Let S_0 and S_1 be sampling algorithms such that $X_n \equiv S_0(U_{\text{poly}(n)})$ and $Y_n \equiv S_1(U_{\text{poly}(n)})$. Consider the generator $G(\sigma, r) = (\sigma, S_\sigma(r))$, and the distribution Z_n that equals (U_1, X_n) with probability $1/2$ and (U_1, Y_n) otherwise. Note that in $G(U_1, U_{\text{poly}(n)})$ the first bit is almost determined by the rest, whereas in Z_n the first bit is statistically independent of the rest.

3. Using a false entropy generator, obtain one in which the excess entropy is $\sqrt{k}$, and using the latter construct a pseudorandom generator.

> **Guideline:** Use the ideas presented in §8.2.5.3 (i.e., the discussion of the interesting direction of the proof of Theorem 8.11).

Exercise 8.10 (multiple samples vs single sample, a separation): In contrast to Proposition 8.6, prove that there exist two probability ensembles that are computational indistinguishable by a single sample, but are efficiently distinguishable by two samples. Furthermore, one of these ensembles is the uniform ensemble and the other has a sparse support (i.e., only poly(n) many strings are assigned a non-zero probability weight by the second distribution). Indeed, the second ensemble is not polynomial-time constructible.

> **Guideline:** Prove that, for every function $d : \{0, 1\}^n \rightarrow [0, 1]$, there exist two strings, x_n and y_n (in $\{0, 1\}^n$), and a number $p \in [0, 1]$ such that $\Pr[d(U_n) = 1] =$

$p \cdot \Pr[d(x_n) = 1] + (1 - p) \cdot \Pr[d(y_n) = 1]$. Generalize this claim to m functions, using $m + 1$ strings and a convex combination of the corresponding probabilities.[53] Conclude that there exists a distribution Z_n with a support of size at most $m + 1$ such that for each of the first (in lexicographic order) m (randomized) algorithms A it holds that $\Pr[A(U_n) = 1] = \Pr[A(Z_n) = 1]$. Note that with probability at least $1/(m + 1)$, two independent samples of Z_n are assigned the same value, yielding a simple two-sample distinguisher of U_n from Z_n.

Exercise 8.11 (amplifying the stretch function, an alternative construction): For G_1 and ℓ as in Construction 8.7, consider $G(s) \overset{\text{def}}{=} G_1^{\ell(|s|)-|s|}(s)$, where $G_1^i(x)$ denotes G_1 iterated i times on x (i.e., $G_1^i(x) = G_1^{i-1}(G_1(x))$ and $G_1^0(x) = x$). Prove that G is a pseudorandom generator of stretch ℓ. Reflect on the advantages of Construction 8.7 over the current construction (e.g., consider generation time).

> **Guideline:** Use a hybrid argument, with the ith hybrid being $G_1^i(U_{\ell(k)-i})$, for $i = 0, \ldots, \ell(k) - k$. Note that $G_1^{i+1}(U_{\ell(k)-(i+1)}) = G_1^i(G_1(U_{\ell(k)-i-1}))$ and $G_1^i(U_{\ell(k)-i}) = G_1^i(U_{|G_1(U_{\ell(k)-i-1})|})$, and use Exercise 8.5.

Exercise 8.12 (pseudorandom versus unpredictability): Prove that a probability ensemble $\{Z_k\}_{k \in \mathbb{N}}$ is pseudorandom if and only if it is unpredictable. For simplicity, we say that $\{Z_k\}_{k \in \mathbb{N}}$ is (next-bit) unpredictable if for every probabilistic polynomial-time algorithm A it holds that $\Pr_i[A(F_i(Z_k)) = B_{i+1}(Z_k)] - (1/2)$ is negligible, where $i \in \{0, \ldots, |Z_k| - 1\}$ is uniformly distributed, and $F_i(z)$ (resp., $B_{i+1}(z)$) denotes the i-bit prefix (resp., $i + 1^{\text{st}}$ bit) of z.

> **Guideline:** Show that pseudorandomness implies polynomial-time unpredictability; that is, polynomial-time predictability violates pseudorandomness (because the uniform ensemble is unpredictable regardless of computing power). Use a hybrid argument to prove that unpredictability implies pseudorandomness. Specifically, the ith hybrid consists of the i-bit long prefix of Z_k followed by $|Z_k| - i$ uniformly distributed bits. Thus, distinguishing the extreme hybrids (which correspond to Z_k and $U_{|Z_k|}$) implies distinguishing a random pair of neighboring hybrids, which in turn implies next-bit predictability. For the last step, use an argument as in the proof of Proposition 8.9.

Exercise 8.13: Prove that a probability ensemble is unpredictable (from left to right) if and only if it is unpredictable from right to left (or in any other canonical order).

> **Guideline:** Use Exercise 8.12, and note that an ensemble is pseudorandom if and only if its reverse is pseudorandom.

Exercise 8.14: Let f be 1-1 and length-preserving, and b be a hard-core predicate of f. For any polynomial ℓ, letting $G'(s) \overset{\text{def}}{=} b(f^{\ell(|s|)-1}(s)) \cdots b(f(s)) \cdot b(s)$, prove that $\{G'(U_k)\}$ is unpredictable (in the sense of Exercise 8.12).

> **Guideline:** Suppose toward the contradiction that, for a uniformly distributed $j \in \{0, \ldots, \ell(k) - 1\}$, given the j-bit long prefix of $G'(U_k)$ an algorithm A' can predict the $j + 1^{\text{st}}$ bit of $G'(U_k)$. That is, given $b(f^{\ell(k)-1}(s)) \cdots b(f^{\ell(k)-j}(s))$, algorithm A' predicts $b(f^{\ell(k)-(j+1)}(s))$, where s is uniformly distributed in $\{0, 1\}^k$. Consider an algorithm A that given $y = f(x)$ approximates $b(x)$ by invoking A'

---

[53] That is, prove that for every m functions $d_1, \ldots, d_m : \{0, 1\}^n \to [0, 1]$ there exist $m + 1$ strings $z_n^{(1)}, \ldots, z_n^{(m+1)}$ and $m + 1$ non-negative numbers $p_1, \ldots, p_{m+1}$ that sum up to 1 such that for every $i \in [m]$ it holds that $\Pr[d_i(U_n) = 1] = \sum_j p_j \cdot \Pr[d_i(z_n^{(j)}) = 1]$.

on input $b(f^{j-1}(y))\cdots b(y)$, where j is uniformly selected in $\{0,\ldots,\ell(k)-1\}$. Analyze the success probability of A using the fact that f induces a permutation over $\{0,1\}^n$, and thus $b(f^j(U_k))\cdots b(f(U_k))\cdot b(U_k)$ is distributed identically to $b(f^{\ell(k)-1}(U_k))\cdots b(f^{\ell(k)-j}(U_k))\cdot b(f^{\ell(k)-(j+1)}(U_k))$.

Exercise 8.15: Prove that if G is a strong pseudorandom generator in the sense of Definition 8.12, then it a pseudorandom generator in the sense of Definition 8.1.

> **Guideline:** Consider a sequence of internal coin tosses that maximizes the probability in Eq. (8.2).

Exercise 8.16 (strong computational indistinguishability): Provide a definition of the notion of computational indistinguishability that underlies Definition 8.12 (i.e., indistinguishability with respect to (non-uniform) polynomial-size circuits). Prove the following two claims:

1. Computational indistinguishability with respect to (non-uniform) polynomial-size circuits is strictly stronger than Definition 8.4.
2. Computational indistinguishability with respect to (non-uniform) polynomial-size circuits is invariant under (polynomially many) multiple samples, even if the underlying ensembles are not polynomial-time constructible.

> **Guideline:** For Part 1, see the solution to Exercise 8.10. For Part 2 note that samples as generated in the proof of Proposition 8.6 can be hard-wired into the distinguishing circuit.

Exercise 8.17: Show that Construction 8.7 may fail in the context of canonical derandomizers. Specifically, prove that it fails for the canonical derandomizer G' that is presented in the proof of Theorem 8.18.

Exercise 8.18: In relation to Definition 8.14 (and assuming $\ell(k) > k$), show that there exists a circuit of size $O(2^k \cdot \ell(k))$ that violates Eq. (8.11).

> **Guideline:** The circuit may incorporate all values in the range of G and decide by comparing its input to these values.

Exercise 8.19 (constructing a set system for Theorem 8.18): For every $\gamma > 0$, show a construction of a set system S as in Condition 2 of Theorem 8.18, with $m(k) = \Omega(k)$ and $\ell(k) = 2^{\Omega(k)}$.

> **Guideline:** We assume, without loss of generality, that $\gamma < 1$, and set $m(k) = (\gamma/2)\cdot k$ and $\ell(k) = 2^{\gamma m(k)/6}$. We construct the set system $S_1,\ldots,S_{\ell(k)}$ in iterations, selecting S_i as the first $m(k)$-subset of $[k]$ that has sufficiently small intersections with each of the previous sets $S_1,\ldots,S_{i-1}$. The existence of such a set S_i can be proved using the Probabilistic Method (cf. [11]). Specifically, for a fixed $m(k)$-subset S', the probability that a random $m(k)$-subset has intersection greater than $\gamma m(k)$ with S' is smaller than $2^{-\gamma m(k)/6}$, because the expected intersection size is $(\gamma/2)\cdot m(k)$. Thus, with positive probability a random $m(k)$-subset has intersection at most $\gamma m(k)$ with each of the previous $i - 1 < \ell(k) = 2^{\gamma m(k)/6}$ subsets. Note that we construct S_i in time $\binom{k}{m(k)}\cdot (i-1)\cdot m(k) < 2^k \cdot \ell(k)\cdot k$, and thus S is computable in time $k2^k \cdot \ell(k)^2 < 2^{2k}$.

Exercise 8.20 (pseudorandom versus unpredictability, by circuits): In continuation of Exercise 8.12, show that if there exists a circuit of size s that distinguishes Z_n from U_ℓ

with gap δ, then there exists an $i < \ell = |Z_n|$ and a circuit of size $s + O(1)$ that given an i-bit long prefix of Z_n guesses the $i + 1^{\text{st}}$ bit with success probability at least $\frac{1}{2} + \frac{\delta}{\ell}$.

Guideline: Defining hybrids as in Exercise 8.12, note that, for some i, the given circuit distinguishes the ith hybrid from the $i + 1^{\text{st}}$ hybrid with gap at least δ/ℓ.

Exercise 8.21: Suppose that the sets S_i's in Construction 8.17 are disjoint and that $f : \{0, 1\}^m \to \{0, 1\}$ is T-inapproximable. Prove that for every circuit C of size $T - O(1)$ it holds that $|\Pr[C(G(U_k)) = 1] - \Pr[C(U_\ell) = 1]| < \ell/T$.

Guideline: Prove the contrapositive using Exercise 8.20. Note that the value of the $i + 1^{\text{st}}$ bit of $G(U_k)$ is statistically independent of the values of the first i bits of $G(U_k)$, and thus predicting it yields an approximator for f. Indeed, such an approximator can be obtained by fixing the the first i bits of $G(U_k)$ via an averaging argument.

Exercise 8.22 (Theorem 8.18, generalized): Let $\ell, m, m', T : \mathbb{N} \to \mathbb{N}$ satisfy $\ell(k)^2 + \widetilde{O}(\ell(k)2^{m'(k)}) < T(m(k))$. Suppose that the following two conditions hold:

1. There exists an exponential-time computable function $f : \{0, 1\}^* \to \{0, 1\}$ that is T-inapproximable.
2. There exists an exponential-time computable function $S : \mathbb{N} \times \mathbb{N} \to 2^{\mathbb{N}}$ such that for every k and $i = 1, \ldots, \ell(k)$ it holds that $S(k, i) \subseteq [k]$ and $|S(k, i)| = m(k)$, and $|S(k, i) \cap S(k, j)| \leq m'(k)$ for every k and $i \neq j$.

Prove that using G as defined in Construction 8.17, with $S_i = S(k, i)$, yields a canonical derandomizer with stretch ℓ.

Guideline: Following the proof of Theorem 8.18, just note that the circuit constructed for approximating $f(U_{m(k)})$ has size $\ell(k)^2 + \ell(k) \cdot \widetilde{O}(2^{m'(k)})$ and success probability at least $(1/2) + (1/7\ell(k))$.

Exercise 8.23 (Part 2 of Theorem 8.19): Prove that if for every polynomial T there exists a T-inapproximable predicate in $\mathcal{E}$ then $\mathcal{BPP} \subseteq \cap_{\varepsilon > 0} \text{DTIME}(t_\varepsilon)$, where $t_\varepsilon(n) \stackrel{\text{def}}{=} 2^{n^\varepsilon}$.

Guideline: Using Proposition 8.15, it suffices to present, for every polynomial p and every constant $\varepsilon > 0$, a canonical derandomizer of stretch $\ell(k) = p(k^{1/\varepsilon})$. Such a derandomizer can be presented by applying Exercise 8.22 using $m(k) = \sqrt{k}$, $m'(k) = O(\log k)$, and $T(m(k)) = \ell(k)^2 + \widetilde{O}(\ell(k)2^{m'(k)})$. Note that T is a polynomial, revisit Exercise 8.19 in order to obtain a set system as required in Exercise 8.22 (for these parameters), and use Theorem 7.10.

Exercise 8.24 (canonical derandomizers imply hard problems): Prove that the hardness hypothesis made in each part of Theorem 8.19 is essential for the existence of a corresponding canonical derandomizer. More generally, prove that the existence of a canonical derandomizer with stretch ℓ implies the existence of a predicate in $\mathcal{E}$ that is T-inapproximable for $T(n) = \ell(n)^{1/O(1)}$.

Guideline: We focus on obtaining a predicate in $\mathcal{E}$ that cannot be computed by circuits of size ℓ, and note that the claim follows by applying the techniques in §7.2.1.3. Given a canonical derandomizer $G : \{0, 1\}^k \to \{0, 1\}^{\ell(k)}$, we consider the predicate $f : \{0, 1\}^{k+1} \to \{0, 1\}$ that satisfies $f(x) = 1$ if and only if there exists $s \in \{0, 1\}^{|x|-1}$ such that x is a prefix of $G(s)$. Note that f is in $\mathcal{E}$ and that an algorithm computing f yields a distinguisher of $G(U_k)$ and $U_{\ell(k)}$.

Exercise 8.25 (limitations on the stretch of (s, ε)-pseudorandom generators): Referring to Definition 8.20, establish the following upper bounds on the stretch ℓ of (s, ε)-pseudorandom generators.

1. If $s(k) \geq 2$ and $\varepsilon(k) \leq 1/2$ then $\ell(k) < \varepsilon(k) \cdot (k + 2) \cdot 2^{k+2-s(k)}$.
2. For every $s(k) \geq 1$ and $\varepsilon(k) < 1$ it holds that $\ell(k) < 2^k$.

> **Guideline:** Part 2 follows by combining Exercises 8.37 and 8.38. For Part 1, consider toward the contradiction a generator of stretch $\ell(k) = \varepsilon(k) \cdot (k + 2) \cdot 2^{k+2-s(k)}$ and an enumeration, $\alpha^{(1)}, \dots, \alpha^{(2^k)} \in \{0, 1\}^{\ell(k)}$, of all 2^k outputs of the generator (on k-bit long seeds). Construct a non-uniform automaton of space s that accepts $x_1 \cdots x_{\ell(k)} \in \{0, 1\}^{\ell(k)}$ if for some $i \in [\ell(k)/(k + 2)]$ it holds that $x_{(i-1)\cdot(k+2)+1} \cdots x_{i\cdot(k+2)}$ equals some string in S_i, where S_i contains the projection of the strings $\alpha^{((i-1)\cdot 2^{s(k)-1}+1)}, \dots, \alpha^{(i\cdot 2^{s(k)-1})}$ on the coordinates $(i - 1) \cdot (k + 2) + 1, \dots, i \cdot (k + 2)$. Note that such an automaton accepts at least $(\ell(k)/(k + 2)) \cdot 2^{s(k)-1} = 2\varepsilon(k) \cdot 2^k$ of the possible outputs of the generator, whereas a random $(\ell(k)$-bit long$)$ string is accepted with probability at most $(\ell(k)/(k + 2)) \cdot 2^{(s(k)-1)-(k+2)} = \varepsilon(k)/2$.

Exercise 8.26 (on the existence of (s, ε)-pseudorandom generators): In contrast to Exercise 8.25, for any s and ε such that $s(k) < k - 2\log_2(k/\varepsilon(k)) - O(1)$, prove the existence of (non-efficient) (s, ε)-pseudorandom generators of stretch $\ell(k) = \Omega(\varepsilon(k)^2 \cdot 2^{k-s(k)}/s(k))$.

> **Guideline:** Use the Probabilistic Method as in Exercise 8.1. Note that non-uniform automata of space s and time ℓ can be described by strings of length $\ell \cdot 2s2^s$.

Exercise 8.27 (multiple samples and space-bounded distinguishers): Suppose that two probability ensembles, $\{X_k\}_{k\in\mathbb{N}}$ and $\{Y_k\}_{k\in\mathbb{N}}$, are (s, ε)-indistinguishable by non-uniform automata (i.e., the distinguishability-gap of any non-uniform automaton of space s is bounded by the function ε). For any function $t : \mathbb{N} \to \mathbb{N}$, prove that the ensembles $\{(X_k^{(1)}, \dots, X_k^{(t(k))})\}_{k\in\mathbb{N}}$ and $\{(Y_k^{(1)}, \dots, X_k^{(t(k))})\}_{k\in\mathbb{N}}$ are $(s, t\varepsilon)$-indistinguishable, where $X_k^{(1)}$ through $X_k^{(t(k))}$ and $Y_k^{(1)}$ through $Y_k^{(t(k))}$ are independent random variables, with each $X_k^{(i)}$ identical to X_k and each $Y_k^{(i)}$ identical to Y_k.

> **Guideline:** Use the hybrid technique. When distinguishing the ith and $(i + 1)^{\text{st}}$ hybrids, note that the first i blocks (i.e., copies of X_k) as well as the last $t(k) - (i + 1)$ blocks (i.e., copies of Y_k) can be fixed and hard-wired into the non-uniform distinguisher.

Exercise 8.28: Provide a more explicit description of the generator outlined in the proof of Theorem 8.21.

> **Guideline:** for $r \in \{0, 1\}^n$ and $h^{(1)}, \dots, h^{(t)} \in H_n$, the generator outputs a 2^t-long sequence of n-bit strings such that the ith string in this sequence equals $h'(r)$, where h' is a composition of some of the $h^{(j)}$'s.

Exercise 8.29 (adaptive t-wise independence tests): Recall that a generator $G : \{0, 1\}^k \to \{0, 1\}^{\ell(k)\cdot b(k)}$ is called t-wise independent if *for any t fixed block positions*, the distribution $G(U_k)$ restricted to these t blocks is uniform over $\{0, 1\}^{t\cdot b(k)}$. Prove that the output of a t-wise independence generator is (perfectly) indistinguishable from the uniform distribution *by any test that examines t of the blocks, even if the examined blocks are selected adaptively* (i.e., the location of the ith block to be examined is determined based on the contents of the previously inspected blocks).

Guideline: First show that, without loss of generality, it suffices to consider deterministic (adaptive) testers. Next, show that the probability that such a tester sees any fixed sequence of t values at the locations selected *adaptively* (in the generator's output) equals $2^{-t \cdot b(k)}$, where $b(k)$ is the block-length.

Exercise 8.30 (a t-wise independence generator): Prove that G as defined in Proposition 8.24 produces a t-wise independent sequence over $\mathrm{GF}(2^{b(k)})$.

Guideline: For every t fixed indices $i_1, \ldots, i_t \in [\ell'(k)]$, consider the distribution of $G(U_k)_{i_1, \ldots, i_t}$ (i.e., the projection of $G(U_k)$ on locations $i_1, \ldots, i_t$). Show that for every sequence of t possible values $v_1, \ldots, v_t \in \mathrm{GF}(2^{b(k)})$, there exists a unique seed $s \in \{0, 1\}^k$ such that $G(s)_{i_1, \ldots, i_t} = (v_1, \ldots, v_t)$.

Exercise 8.31 (pairwise independence generators): As a warm-up, consider a construction analogous to the one in Proposition 8.25, except that here the seed specifies an arbitrary affine $b(k)$-by-$m(k)$ transformation. That is, for $s \in \{0, 1\}^{b(k) \cdot m(k)}$ and $r \in \{0, 1\}^{b(k)}$, where $k = b(k) \cdot m(k) + b(k)$, let

$$G(s, r) \stackrel{\text{def}}{=} (A_s v_1 + r, \, A_s v_2 + r, \, \ldots, \, A_s v_{\ell'(k)} + r) \tag{8.23}$$

where A_s is a $b(k)$-by-$m(k)$ matrix specified by the string s. Show that G as in Eq. (8.23) is a pairwise independence generator of block-length b and stretch ℓ. (Note that a related construction appears in the proof of Theorem 7.7; see also Exercise 7.5.) Next, show that G as in Eq. (8.17) is a pairwise independence generator of block-length b and stretch ℓ.

Guideline: The following description applies to both constructions. First, note that for every fixed $i \in [\ell'(k)]$, the ith element in the sequence $G(U_k)$, denoted $G(U_k)_i$, is uniformly distributed in $\{0, 1\}^{b(k)}$. Actually, show that for every fixed $s \in \{0, 1\}^{k-b(k)}$, it holds that $G(s, U_{b(k)})_i$ is uniformly distributed in $\{0, 1\}^{b(k)}$. Next, note that it suffices to show that, for every $j \neq i$, conditioned on the value of $G(U_k)_i$, the value of $G(U_k)_j$ is uniformly distributed in $\{0, 1\}^{b(k)}$. The key technical detail is showing that, for any non-zero vector $v \in \{0, 1\}^{m(k)}$ and a uniformly selected $s \in \{0, 1\}^{k-b(k)}$, it holds that $A_s v$ (resp., $T_s v$) is uniformly distributed in $\{0, 1\}^{b(k)}$. This is easy in the case of a random $b(k)$-by-$m(k)$ matrix, and can also be proven for a random Toeplitz matrix.

Exercise 8.32 (adaptive t-wise independence tests, revisited): Note that in contrast to Exercise 8.29, with respect to *non-perfect* indistinguishability, there is a discrepancy between adaptive and non-adaptive tests that inspects t locations.

1. Present a distribution over 2^{t-1}-bit long strings in which every t fixed bit positions induce a distribution that is $t \cdot 2^{-t}$-close to uniform, but there exists a test that adaptively inspects t positions and distinguish this distribution from the uniform one with gap 1/2.

   Guideline: Modify the uniform distribution over $((t-1) + 2^{t-1})$-bit long strings such that the first $t - 1$ locations indicate a bit position (among the rest) that is set to zero.

2. On the other hand, prove that if every t fixed bit positions in a distribution X induce a distribution that is ε-close to uniform, then every test that adaptively inspects t positions can distinguish X from the uniform distribution with gap at most $2^t \cdot \varepsilon$.

   Guideline: See Exercise 8.29.

Exercise 8.33: Suppose that G is an ε-bias generator with stretch ℓ. Show that equality between the $\ell(k)$-bit strings x and y can be probabilistically checked (with error probability $(1 + \varepsilon)/2$) by comparing the inner product modulo 2 of x and $G(s)$ to the inner product modulo 2 of y and $G(s)$, where $s \in \{0, 1\}^k$ is selected uniformly. Note that this method is a randomness-efficient approximation of comparing the inner product modulo 2 of x and r to the inner product modulo 2 of y and r, where $r \in \{0, 1\}^{\ell(k)}$ is selected uniformly.

(Hint: Consider the special case in which $y = 0^{\ell(k)}$.)

Exercise 8.34 (bias versus statistical difference from uniform): Let X be a random variable assuming values in $\{0, 1\}^t$. Prove that if X has bias at most ε over any non-empty set then the statistical difference between X and U_t is at most $2^{t/2} \cdot \varepsilon$, and that for every $x \in \{0, 1\}^t$ it holds that $\Pr[X = x] = 2^{-t} \pm \varepsilon$.

Guideline: Consider the probability function $p : \{0, 1\}^t \to [0, 1]$ defined by $p(x) \stackrel{\text{def}}{=} \Pr[X = x]$, and let $\delta(x) \stackrel{\text{def}}{=} p(x) - 2^{-t}$ denote the deviation of p from the uniform probability function. Viewing the set of real functions over $\{0, 1\}^t$ as a 2^t-dimensional vector space, consider two orthonormal bases for this space. The first basis consists of the (Kroniker) functions $\{k_\alpha\}_{\alpha \in \{0,1\}^t}$ such that $k_\alpha(x) = 1$ if $x = \alpha$ and $k_\alpha(x) = 0$ otherwise. The second basis consists of the (normalized Fourier) functions $\{f_S\}_{S \subseteq [t]}$ defined by $f_S(x_1 \cdots x_t) \stackrel{\text{def}}{=} 2^{-t/2} \prod_{i \in S} (-1)^{x_i}$ (where $f_\emptyset \equiv 2^{-t/2}$).[54] Note that the bias of X over any $S \neq \emptyset$ equals $|\sum_x p(x) \cdot 2^{t/2} f_S(x)|$, which in turn equals $2^{t/2} |\sum_x \delta(x) f_S(x)|$. Thus, for every S (including the empty set), we have $|\sum_x \delta(x) f_S(x)| \leq 2^{-t/2} \varepsilon$, which means that the representation of δ in the normalized Fourier basis is by coefficients that have each an absolute value of at most $2^{-t/2} \varepsilon$. It follows that the Norm-2 of this vector of coefficients is upper-bounded by $\sqrt{2^t \cdot (2^{-t/2} \varepsilon)^2} = \varepsilon$, and the two claims follow by noting that they refer to norms of δ according to the Kroniker basis. In particular, Norm-2 is preserved under orthonormal bases, the max-norm is upper-bounded by Norm-2, and Norm-1 is upper-bounded by $\sqrt{2^t}$ times the value of the Norm-2.

Exercise 8.35 (on the existence of (non-explicit) small-bias generators): Prove that, for $k = \log_2(\ell(k)/\varepsilon(k)^2) + O(1)$, there exists a function $G : \{0, 1\}^k \to \{0, 1\}^{\ell(k)}$ such that $G(U_k)$ has bias at most $\varepsilon(k)$ over any non-empty subset of $[\ell(k)]$.

Guideline: Use the Probabilistic Method as in Exercise 8.1.

Exercise 8.36 (The LFSR small-bias generator (following [10])): Using the following guidelines (and letting $t = k/2$), analyze the construction outlined following Theorem 8.26 (and depicted in Figure 8.5):

1. Prove that r_i equals $\sum_{j=0}^{t-1} c_j^{(f,i)} \cdot s_j$, where $c_j^{(f,i)}$ is the coefficient of z^j in the (degree $t - 1$) polynomial obtained by reducing z^i modulo the polynomial $f(z)$ (i.e., $z^i \equiv \sum_{j=0}^{t-1} c_j^{(f,i)} z^j \pmod{f(z)}$).

   Guideline: Recall that $z^t \equiv \sum_{j=0}^{t-1} f_j z^j \pmod{f(z)}$, and thus for every $i \geq t$ it holds that $z^i \equiv \sum_{j=0}^{t-1} f_j z^{i-t+j} \pmod{f(z)}$. Note the correspondence to $r_i = \sum_{j=0}^{t-1} f_j \cdot r_{i-t+j}$.

---

[54]Verify that both bases are indeed orthogonal (i.e., $\sum_x k_\alpha(x) k_\beta(x) = 0$ for every $\alpha \neq \beta$ and $\sum_x f_S(x) f_T(x) = 0$ for every $S \neq T$) and normal (i.e., $\sum_x k_\alpha(x)^2 = 1$ and $\sum_x f_S(x)^2 = 1$).

2. For any non-empty $S \subseteq \{0, \ldots, \ell(k) - 1\}$, evaluate the bias of the sequence $r_0, \ldots, r_{\ell(k)-1}$ over S, where f is a random irreducible polynomial of degree t and $s = (s_0, \ldots, s_{t-1}) \in \{0, 1\}^t$ is uniformly distributed. Specifically:

   (a) For a fixed f and random $s \in \{0, 1\}^t$, prove that $\sum_{i \in S} r_i$ has non-zero bias if and only if $f(z)$ divides $\sum_{i \in S} z^i$.

   (Hint: Note that $\sum_{i \in S} r_i = \sum_{j=0}^{t-1} \sum_{i \in S} c_j^{(f,i)} s_j$, and use Item 1.)

   (b) Prove that the probability that a random irreducible polynomial of degree t divides $\sum_{i \in S} z^i$ is $\Theta(\ell(k)/2^t)$.

   (Hint: A polynomial of degree n can be divided by at most n/d different irreducible polynomials of degree d. On the other hand, the number of irreducible polynomials of degree d over GF(2) is $\Theta(2^d/d)$.)

   Conclude that for random f and s, the sequence $r_0, \ldots, r_{\ell(k)-1}$ has bias $O(\ell(k)/2^t)$.

Note that an implementation of the LFSR generator requires a mapping of random $k/2$-bit long string to *almost*-random irreducible polynomials of degree $k/2$. Such a mapping can be constructed in $\exp(k)$ time, which is $\operatorname{poly}(\ell(k))$ if $\ell(k) = \exp(\Omega(k))$. A more efficient mapping that uses an $O(k)$-bit long seek is described in [10, Sec. 8].

Exercise 8.37 (limitations on small-bias generators): Let G be an ε-bias generator with stretch ℓ, and view G as a mapping from $GF(2)^k$ to $GF(2)^{\ell(k)}$. As such, each bit in the output of G can be viewed as a polynomial[55] in the k input variables (each ranging in GF(2)). Prove that if $\varepsilon(k) < 1$ and each of these polynomials has *total degree* at most d, then $\ell(k) \leq \sum_{i=1}^d \binom{k}{i}$. Derive the following corollaries:

1. If $\varepsilon(k) < 1$ then $\ell(k) < 2^k$ (regardless of d).[56]
2. If $\varepsilon(k) < 1$ and $\ell(k) > k$ then G cannot be a linear transformation.[57]

   Guideline (for the main claim): Note that, without loss of generality, all the aforementioned polynomials have a free term equal to zero (and have individual degree at most 1 in each variable). Next, consider the vector space spanned by all d-monomials over k variables (i.e., monomial having at most d variables). Since $\varepsilon(k) < 1$, the polynomials representing the output bits of G must correspond to a sequence of independent vectors in this space.

Exercise 8.38 (a sanity check for space-bounded pseudorandomness): The following fact is suggested as a sanity check for candidate pseudorandom generators with respect to space-bounded automata. The fact (to be proven as an exercise) is that, for every $\varepsilon(\cdot)$ and $s(\cdot)$ such that $s(k) \geq 1$ for every k, if G is (s, ε)-pseudorandom (as per Definition 8.20), then G is an ε-bias generator.

Exercise 8.39: In contrast to Exercise 8.38, prove that there exist $\exp(-\Omega(n))$-bias distributions over $\{0, 1\}^n$ that are not $(2, 0.666)$-pseudorandom.

---

[55]Recall that every Boolean function over GF(p) can be expressed as a polynomial of *individual degree* at most $p - 1$.

[56]This upper bound is optimal, because (efficient) ε-bias generators of stretch $\ell(k) = \operatorname{poly}(\varepsilon(k)) \cdot 2^k$ do exist (see [170]).

[57]In contrast, bilinear ε-bias generators (i.e., with $\ell(k) > k$) do exist; for example, $G(s) = (s, b(s))$, where $b(s_1, \ldots, s_k) = \sum_{i=1}^{k/2} s_i s_{(k/2)+i} \bmod 2$, is an ε-bias generator with $\varepsilon(k) = \exp(-\Omega(k))$.
(Hint: Focusing on bias over sets that include the last output bit, prove that without loss of generality it suffices to analyze the bias of $b(U_k)$.)

Guideline: Show that the uniform distribution over the set

$$\left\{ \sigma_1 \cdots \sigma_n : \sum_{i=1}^{n} \sigma_i \equiv 0 \pmod 3 \right\}$$

has bias $\exp(-\Omega(n))$.

Exercise 8.40 (approximate t-wise independence generators (following [170])): Combining a small-bias generator as in Theorem 8.26 with the t-wise independence generator of Eq. (8.16), and relying on the linearity of the latter, construct a generator producing ℓ-bit long sequences in which any t positions are at most ε-away from uniform (in variation distance), while using a seed of length $O(t + \log(1/\varepsilon) + \log\log\ell)$. (For max-norm a seed of length $O(\log(t/\varepsilon) + \log\log\ell)$ suffices.)

> **Guideline:** First note that, for any t, ℓ' and $b \geq \log_2 \ell'$, the transformation of Eq. (8.16) can be implemented by a fixed linear (over GF(2)) transformation of a $t \cdot b$-bit seed into an ℓ-bit long sequence, where $\ell = \ell' \cdot b$. It follows that, for $b = \log_2 \ell'$, there exists a fixed GF(2)-linear transformation T of a random seed of length $t \cdot b$ into a t-wise independent bit sequence of the length ℓ (i.e., $T U_{t \cdot b}$ is t-wise independent over $\{0, 1\}^\ell$). Thus, every t rows of T are linearly independent. The key observation is that when we replace the aforementioned random seed by an ε'-bias sequence, every $i \leq t$ positions in the output sequence induce a distribution that has bias at most ε' (because these bits define a non-zero linear test on the bits of the ε'-bias sequence used as seed). Note that the length of the new seed (used to produce ε'-bias sequence of length $t \cdot b$) is $O(\log tb/\varepsilon')$. Applying Exercise 8.34, we conclude that any t positions are at most $2^{t/2} \cdot \varepsilon'$-away from uniform (in variation distance). Recall that this was obtained using a seed of length $O(\log(t/\varepsilon') + \log\log\ell)$, and the claim follows by using $\varepsilon' = 2^{-t/2} \cdot \varepsilon$.

Exercise 8.41 (small-bias generator and error-correcting codes): Show a correspondence between ε-bias generators of stretch ℓ and binary linear error-correcting codes (cf. Appendix E.1.1) mapping $\ell(k)$-bit long strings to 2^k-bit long strings such that every two codewords are at distance $(1 \pm \varepsilon(k)) \cdot 2^{k-1}$ apart.

> **Guideline:** Associate $\{0, 1\}^k$ with $[2^k]$. Then, a generator $G : [2^k] \to \{0, 1\}^{\ell(k)}$ corresponds to the code $C : \{0, 1\}^{\ell(k)} \to \{0, 1\}^{2^k}$ such that, for every $i \in [\ell(k)]$ and $j \in [2^k]$, the ith bit of $G(j)$ equals the jth bit of $C(0^{i-1}10^{\ell(k)-i})$.

Exercise 8.42 (on the bias of sequences over a finite field): For a prime p, let ζ be a random variable assigned values in GF(p) and $\delta(v) \overset{\text{def}}{=} \Pr[\zeta = v] - (1/p)$. Prove that $\max_{v \in \text{GF}(p)}\{|\delta(v)|\}$ is upper-bounded by $b \overset{\text{def}}{=} \max_{c \in \{1,\ldots,p-1\}}\{\|E[\omega^{c\zeta}]\|\}$, where ω denotes the pth (complex) root of unity, and that $\sum_{v \in \text{GF}(p)} |\delta(v)|$ is upper-bounded by $\sqrt{p} \cdot b$.

> **Guideline:** Analogously to Exercise 8.34, view probability distributions over GF(p) as p-dimensional vectors, and consider two bases for the set of complex functions over GF(p): the Kroniker basis (i.e., $k_i(x) = 1$ if $x = i$ and $k_i(x) = 0$) and the (normalized) Fourier basis (i.e., $f_i(x) = p^{-1/2} \cdot \omega^{ix}$). Note that the biases of ζ correspond to the inner products of δ with the non-constant Fourier functions, whereas the distances of ζ from the uniform distribution correspond to the inner products of δ with the Kroniker functions.

Exercise 8.43 (a version of the Expander Random Walk Theorem): Using notations as in Theorem 8.28, prove that the probability that a random walk of length ℓ' stays in W is at most $(\rho + (\lambda/d)^2)^{\ell'/2}$. In fact, prove a more general claim that refers to the probability that a random walk of length ℓ' intersects $W_0 \times W_1 \times \cdots \times W_{\ell'-1}$. The claimed upper-bound is

$$\sqrt{\rho_0} \cdot \prod_{i=1}^{\ell'-1} \sqrt{\rho_i + (\lambda/d)^2}, \tag{8.24}$$

where $\rho_i \overset{\text{def}}{=} |W_i|/|V|$.

> **Guideline:** View the random walk as the evolution of a corresponding probability vector under suitable transformations. The transformations correspond to taking a random step in the graph and to passing through a "sieve" that keeps only the entries that correspond to the current set W_i. The key observation is that the first transformation shrinks the component that is orthogonal to the uniform distribution (which is the first eigenvalue of the adjacency matrix of the expander), whereas the second transformation shrinks the component that is in the direction of the uniform distribution. For further details, see §E.2.1.3.

Exercise 8.44: Using notations as in Theorem 8.28, prove that the probability that a random walk of length ℓ' visits W more than $\alpha\ell'$ times is smaller than $\binom{\ell'}{\alpha\ell'} \cdot (\rho + (\lambda/d)^2)^{\alpha\ell'/2}$. For example, for $\alpha = 1/2$ and $\lambda/d < \sqrt{\rho}$, we get an upper bound of $(32\rho)^{\ell'/4}$. We comment that much better bounds can be obtained (cf., e.g., [120]).

> **Guideline:** Use a union bound on all possible sequences of $m = \alpha\ell'$ visits, and upper-bound the probability of visiting W in steps $j_1, \ldots, j_m$ by applying Eq. (8.24) with $W_i = W$ if $i \in \{j_1, \ldots, j_m\}$ and $W = V$ otherwise.

CHAPTER NINE

Probabilistic Proof Systems

A proof is whatever convinces me.
Shimon Even (1935–2004)

The glory attached to the creativity involved in finding proofs makes us forget that it is the less glorified process of verification that gives proofs their value. Conceptually speaking, proofs are secondary to the verification process, whereas technically speaking, proof systems are defined in terms of their verification procedures.

The notion of a verification procedure presumes the notion of computation and furthermore the notion of efficient computation. This implicit stipulation is made explicit in the definition of $\mathcal{NP}$, where efficient computation is associated with deterministic polynomial-time algorithms. However, as argued next, we can gain a lot if we are willing to take a somewhat non-traditional step and allow *probabilistic* verification procedures.

In this chapter, we shall study three types of probabilistic proof systems, called *interactive proofs*, *zero-knowledge proofs*, and *probabilistic checkable proofs*. In each of these three cases, we shall present fascinating results that cannot be obtained when considering the analogous deterministic proof systems.

Summary: The association of efficient procedures with *deterministic* polynomial-time procedures is the basis for viewing NP-proof systems as the canonical formulation of proof systems (with efficient verification procedures). Allowing *probabilistic* verification procedures and, moreover, ruling by statistical evidence gives rise to various types of probabilistic proof systems. Indeed, these probabilistic proof systems carry a probability of error (which is explicitly bounded and can be reduced by successive applications of the proof system), yet they offer various advantages over the traditional (deterministic and errorless) proof systems.

Randomized and interactive verification procedures, giving rise to *interactive proof systems*, seem much more powerful than their deterministic counterparts. In particular, such interactive proof systems exist for any set in $\mathcal{PSPACE} \supseteq \mathrm{co}\mathcal{NP}$ (e.g., for the set of unsatisfied propositional formulae), whereas it is widely believed that some sets in $\mathrm{co}\mathcal{NP}$ do *not* have NP-proof systems (i.e., $\mathcal{NP} \neq \mathrm{co}\mathcal{NP}$). We stress that a "proof" in this context is not a fixed and static object, but rather a randomized (and dynamic) process in which the verifier interacts with the prover.

Intuitively, one may think of this interaction as consisting of questions asked by the verifier, to which the prover has to reply convincingly.

Such randomized and interactive verification procedures allow for the meaningful conceptualization of *zero-knowledge proofs*, which are of great theoretical and practical interest (especially in cryptography). Loosely speaking, zero-knowledge proofs are interactive proofs that yield nothing (to the verifier) beyond the fact that the assertion is indeed valid. For example, a zero-knowledge proof that a certain propositional formula is satisfiable does not reveal a satisfying assignment to the formula nor any partial information regarding such an assignment (e.g., whether the first variable can assume the value `true`). Thus, the successful verification of a zero-knowledge proof exhibits an extreme contrast between being convinced of the validity of a statement and learning nothing else (while receiving such a convincing proof). It turns out that, under reasonable complexity assumptions (i.e., assuming the existence of one-way functions), every set in $\mathcal{NP}$ has a zero-knowledge proof system.

NP-proofs can be efficiently transformed into a (redundant) form that offers a trade-off between the number of locations (randomly) examined in the resulting proof and the confidence in its validity. In particular, it is known that any set in $\mathcal{NP}$ has an NP-proof system that supports probabilistic verification such that the error probability decreases exponentially with the number of bits read from the alleged proof. These redundant NP-proofs are called *probabilistically checkable proofs* (or PCPs). In addition to their conceptually fascinating nature, PCPs are closely related to the study of the complexity of numerous natural approximation problems.

Introduction and Preliminaries

Conceptually speaking, proofs are secondary to the verification process. Indeed, both in mathematics and in real life, proofs are meaningful only with respect to commonly agreed principles of reasoning, and the verification process amounts to checking that these principles were properly applied. Thus, these principles, which are typically taken for granted, are more fundamental than any specific proof that applies them; that is, the mere attempt to reason about anything is based on commonly agreed principles of reasoning.

The commonly agreed principles of reasoning are associated with a verification procedure that distinguishes proper applications of these principles from improper ones. A *line of reasoning* is considered valid with respect to such fixed principles (and is thus deemed a proof) if and only if it proceeds by proper applications of these principles. Thus, a line of reasoning is considered valid if and only if it is accepted by the corresponding verification procedure. This means that, technically speaking, proofs are defined in terms of a predetermined verification procedure (or are defined with respect to such a procedure). Indeed, this state of affairs is best illustrated in the formal study of proofs (i.e., *logic*), which is actually the study of formally defined proof systems: The point is that these proof systems are defined (often explicitly and sometimes only implicitly) in terms of their verification procedures.

The notion of a verification procedure presumes the notion of computation. This fact explains the historical interest of logicians in computer science (cf. [225, 55]). Furthermore, the verification of proofs is supposed to be relatively easy, and hence, a natural connection emerges between verification procedures and the notion of efficient computation. This connection was made explicit by complexity theorists, and is captured by the definition of $\mathcal{NP}$ and NP-proof systems (cf. Definition 2.5), which targets all efficient verification procedures.[1]

Recall that Definition 2.5 identifies efficient (verification) procedures with deterministic polynomial-time algorithms, and that it explicitly restricts the length of proofs to be polynomial in the length of the assertion. Thus, *verification is performed in a number of steps that is polynomial in the length of the assertion.* We comment that deterministic proof systems that allow for longer proofs (but require that verification is efficient in terms of the length of the alleged proof) can be modeled as NP-proof systems by adequate padding (of the assertion).

Indeed, NP-proofs provide the ultimate formulation of efficiently verifiable proofs (i.e., proof systems with efficient verification procedures), provided that one associates efficient procedures with *deterministic* polynomial-time algorithms. However, as we shall see, we can gain a lot if we are willing to take a somewhat non-traditional step and allow *probabilistic* (polynomial-time) algorithms and, in particular, *probabilistic* verification procedures. In particular:

- Randomized and interactive verification procedures seem much more powerful than their deterministic counterparts.
- Such interactive proof systems allow for the construction of (meaningful) zero-knowledge proofs, which are of great conceptual and practical interest.
- NP-proofs can be efficiently transformed into a (redundant) form that supports super-fast probabilistic verification via very few random probes into the alleged proof.

In all these cases, explicit bounds are imposed on the computational complexity of the verification procedure, which in turn is personified by the notion of a verifier. Furthermore, in all these proof systems, the verifier is allowed to toss coins and rule by statistical evidence. Thus, all these proof systems carry a probability of error; yet, this probability is explicitly bounded and, furthermore, can be reduced by successive application of the proof system.

One important convention. When presenting a proof system, we state all complexity bounds in terms of the length of the assertion to be proved (which is viewed as an input to the verifier). Namely, when we say "polynomial time" we mean time that is polynomial in the length of this assertion. Indeed, as will become evident, this is *the* natural choice in all the cases that we consider. Note that this convention is consistent with the foregoing discussion of NP-proof systems.[2]

---

[1]In contrast, traditional proof systems are formulated based on rules of inference that seem natural in the relevant context. The fact that these inference rules yield an efficient verification procedure is merely a consequence of the correspondence between processes that seem natural and efficient computation.

[2]Recall that Definition 2.5 refers to polynomial-time verification of alleged proofs, which in turn must have length that is bounded by a polynomial in the length of the assertion.

Notational conventions. We denote by `poly` the set of all integer functions that are upper-bounded by a polynomial, and by `log` the set of all integer functions bounded by a logarithmic function (i.e., $f \in \log$ if and only if $f(n) = O(\log n)$). All complexity measures mentioned in this chapter are assumed to be constructible in polynomial time.

Organization. In Section 9.1 we present the basic definitions and results regarding interactive proof systems. The definition of an interactive proof system is the starting point for a discussion of zero-knowledge proofs, which is provided in Section 9.2. Section 9.3, which presents the basic definitions and results regarding probabilistically checkable proofs (PCP), can be read independently of the other sections.

Prerequisites. We assume a basic familiarity with elementary probability theory (see Appendix D.1) and randomized algorithms (see Section 6.1).

9.1. Interactive Proof Systems

In light of the growing acceptability of randomized and interactive computations, it is only natural to associate the notion of efficient computation with probabilistic and interactive polynomial-time computations. This leads naturally to the notion of an interactive proof system in which the verification procedure is interactive and randomized, rather than being non-interactive and deterministic. Thus, a "proof" in this context is not a fixed and static object, but rather a randomized (dynamic) process in which the verifier interacts with the prover. Intuitively, one may think of this interaction as consisting of questions asked by the verifier, to which the prover has to reply convincingly.

The foregoing discussion, as well as the definition provided in Section 9.1.2, makes explicit reference to a prover, whereas a prover is only implicit in the traditional definitions of proof systems (e.g., NP-proof systems). Before turning to the actual definition, we highlight and further discuss this issue as well as some other conceptual issues.

9.1.1. Motivation and Perspective

We shall discuss the various interpretations given to the notion of a proof in different human contexts, and the attitudes that underlie and/or accompany these interpretations. This discussion is aimed at emphasizing that the motivation for the definition of interactive proof systems is not to replace the notion of a mathematical proof, but rather to capture other forms of proofs that are of natural interest. Specifically, we shall contrast "written proofs" with "interactive proofs," highlight the roles of the "prover" and the "verifier" in any proof, and discuss the notions of completeness and soundness that underlie any proof. (Some readers may find it useful to return to this section after reading Section 9.1.2.)

9.1.1.1. A Static Object Versus an Interactive Process

Traditionally in mathematics, a "proof" is a *fixed* sequence consisting of statements that either are self-evident or are derived from previous statements via self-evident rules. Actually, both conceptually and technically, it is more accurate to substitute for the phrase "self-evident" the phrase "commonly agreed upon" (because, at the last account, self-evidence is a matter of common agreement). In fact, in the formal study of proofs (i.e., logic), the commonly agreed upon statements are called *axioms*, whereas the commonly agreed upon rules are referred to as *derivation rules*. We highlight *a key property of mathematical proofs: These proofs are fixed (static) objects.*

In contrast, in other areas of human activity, the notion of a "proof" has a much wider interpretation. In particular, in many settings, a proof is not a fixed object but rather a process by which the validity of an assertion is established. For example, in the context of law, withstanding a cross-examination by an opponent, who may ask tough and/or tricky questions, is considered a proof of the facts claimed by the witness. Likewise, various debates that take place in daily life have an analogous potential of establishing claims and are then perceived as proofs. This perception is quite common in philosophical and political debates, and applies even in scientific debates. Needless to say, *a key property of such debates is their interactive* ("dynamic") *nature*. Interestingly, the appealing nature of such "interactive proofs" is reflected in the fact that they are mimicked (in a rigorous manner) in some mathematical *proofs by contradiction*, which emulate an imaginary debate with a potential (generic) skeptic.

Another difference between mathematical proofs and various forms of "daily proofs" is that, while the former aim at certainty, the latter are intended ("only") for establishing claims *beyond any reasonable doubt*. Arguably, an explicitly bounded error probability (as present in our definition of interactive proof systems) is an *extremely strong* form of establishing a claim beyond any reasonable doubt.

We also note that, in mathematics, proofs are often considered more important than their consequence (i.e., the theorem). In contrast, in many daily situations, proofs are considered secondary (in importance) to their consequence. These conflicting attitudes are well coupled with the difference between written proofs and "interactive" proofs: If one values the proof itself, then one may insist on having it archived, whereas if one only cares about the consequence, then the way in which it is reached is immaterial.

Interestingly, the foregoing set of daily attitudes (rather than the mathematical ones) will be adequate in the current chapter, where *proofs are viewed merely as a vehicle for the verification of the validity of claims*. (This attitude gets to an extreme in the case of zero-knowledge proofs, where we actually require that the proofs themselves be useless beyond being convincing of the validity of the claimed assertion.)

In general, we will be interested in modeling various forms of proofs that may occur in the world, focusing on proofs that can be verified by automated procedures. These verification procedures are designed to check the validity of potential proofs, and are oblivious of additional features that may appeal to humans, such as beauty, insightfulness, and so on. In the current section we will consider the most general form of proof systems that still allow efficient verification.

We note that the proof systems that we study refer to mundane theorems (e.g., asserting that a *specific* propositional formula is not satisfiable or that a party sent a message as instructed by a predetermined protocol). We stress that the (meta) theorems that we shall state regarding these proof systems will be proved in the traditional mathematical sense.

9.1.1.2. Prover and Verifier

The wide interpretation of the notion of a proof system, which includes interactive processes of verification, calls for the explicit introduction of two interactive players, called the *prover* and the *verifier*. The verifier is the party that employs the verification procedure, which underlies the definition of any proof system, while the prover is the party that tries to convince the verifier. In the context of static (or non-interactive) proofs, the prover is the transcendental entity providing the proof, and thus in this context the prover is often not mentioned at all (when discussing the verification of alleged proofs). Still, explicitly mentioning potential provers may be beneficial even when discussing such static (non-interactive) proofs.

We highlight the "distrustful attitude" toward the prover, which underlies any proof system. If the verifier trusts the prover, then no proof is needed. Hence, whenever discussing a proof system, one should envision a setting in which the verifier is not trusting the prover, and furthermore is skeptic of anything that the prover says. In such a setting the prover's goal is to convince the verifier, while the verifier should make sure that it is not fooled by the prover. (See further discussion in §9.1.1.3.) Note that the verifier is "trusted" to protect its own interests by employing the predetermined verification procedure; indeed, the asymmetry with respect to whom we trust is an artifact of our focus on the verification process (or task). In general, each party is trusted to protect its own interests (i.e., the verifier is trusted to protect its own interests), but no party is trusted to protect the interests of the other party (i.e., the prover is not trusted to protect the verifier's interest in not being fooled by the prover).

Another asymmetry between the two parties is that our discussion focuses on the complexity of the verification task and ignores (as a first approximation) the complexity of the proving task (which is only discussed in §9.1.5.1). Note that this asymmetry is reflected in the definition of NP-proof systems; that is, verification is required to be efficient, whereas for sets $\mathcal{NP} \setminus \mathcal{P}$ finding adequate proofs is infeasible. Thus, as a first approximation, we consider the question of what can be efficiently verified when interacting with an arbitrary prover (which may be infinitely powerful). Once this question is resolved, we shall also consider the complexity of the proving task (indeed, see §9.1.5.1).

9.1.1.3. Completeness and Soundness

Two fundamental properties of a proof system (i.e., of a verification procedure) are its *soundness* (or *validity*) and *completeness*. The soundness property asserts that the verification procedure cannot be "tricked" into accepting false statements. In other words, *soundness* captures the verifier's ability to protect itself from being convinced of false statements (no matter what the prover does in order to fool it). On the other hand, *completeness* captures the ability of some prover to convince the verifier of true statements (belonging to some predetermined set of true statements). Note that both properties are essential to the very notion of a proof system.

We note that not every set of true statements has a "reasonable" proof system in which each of these statements can be proved (while no false statement can be "proved"). This fundamental phenomenon is given a precise meaning in results such as *Gödel's Incompleteness Theorem* and Turing's theorem regarding the *undecidability of the Halting Problem*. In contrast, recall that $\mathcal{NP}$ was defined as the class of sets having proof systems that support efficient deterministic verification (of "written proofs"). This section is devoted to the study of a more liberal notion of efficient verification procedures (allowing both randomization and interaction).

9.1.2. Definition

Loosely speaking, an interactive proof is a "game" between a computationally bounded verifier and a computationally unbounded prover whose goal is to convince the verifier of the validity of some assertion. Specifically, the verifier employs a probabilistic polynomial-time strategy (whereas no computational restrictions apply to the prover's strategy). It is required that if the assertion holds, then the verifier always accepts (i.e., when interacting with an appropriate prover strategy). On the other hand, if the assertion is false then the verifier must reject with probability at least $\frac{1}{2}$, no matter what strategy is being employed by the prover. (The error probability can be reduced by running such a proof system several times.)

We formalize the interaction between parties by referring to the *strategies* that the parties employ.[3] A strategy for a party is a *function mapping the party's view of the inter-action so far to a description of this party's next move*; that is, such a strategy describes (or rather prescribes) the *party's next move* (i.e., its next message or its final decision) *as a function of the common input* (i.e., the aforementioned assertion), *the party's internal coin tosses, and all messages it has received so far*. Note that this formulation presumes (implicitly) that each party records the outcomes of its past coin tosses as well as all the messages it has received, and determines its moves based on these. Thus, an inter-action between two parties, employing strategies A and B, respectively, is determined by the common input, denoted x, and the randomness of both parties, denoted r_A and r_B. Assuming that A takes the first move (and B takes the last move), the correspond-ing (t-round) interaction transcript (on common input x and randomness r_A and r_B) is $\alpha_1, \beta_1, \ldots, \alpha_t, \beta_t$, where $\alpha_i = A(x, r_A, \beta_1, \ldots, \beta_{i-1})$ and $\beta_i = B(x, r_B, \alpha_1, \ldots, \alpha_i)$. The corresponding final decision of A is defined as $A(x, r_A, \beta_1, \ldots, \beta_t)$.

We say that a party employs a probabilistic polynomial-time strategy if its next move can be computed in a number of steps that is *polynomial in the length of the common input*. In particular, this means that, on input common input x, the strategy may only consider a polynomial in $|x|$ many messages, which are each of poly($|x|$) length.[4] Intuitively, if the other party exceeds an a priori (polynomial in $|x|$) bound on the total length of the messages that it is allowed to send, then the execution is suspended. Thus, referring to the aforementioned strategies, we say that A is a probabilistic polynomial-time strategy if, for every i and $r_A, \beta_1, \ldots, \beta_i$, the value of $A(x, r_A, \beta_1, \ldots, \beta_i)$ can be computed in time polynomial in $|x|$. Again, in proper use, it must hold that $|r_A|$, t and the $|\beta_i|$'s are all polynomial in $|x|$.

Definition 9.1 (interactive proof system – IP):[5] *An* interactive proof system for a set *S is a two-party game, between a* verifier *executing a* probabilistic polynomial-time strategy, *denoted V, and a* prover *that executes a* (computationally unbounded) *strategy, denoted P, satisfying the following two conditions:*

- Completeness: *For every $x \in S$, the verifier V always accepts after interacting with the prover P on common input x.*
- Soundness: *For every $x \notin S$ and every strategy P^*, the verifier V rejects with probability at least $\frac{1}{2}$ after interacting with P^* on common input x.*

We denote by $\mathcal{IP}$ the class of sets having interactive proof systems.

---

[3] An alternative formulation refers to the interactive machines that capture the behavior of each of the parties (see, e.g., [91, Sec. 4.2.1.1]). Such an interactive machine invokes the corresponding strategy, while handling the communication with the other party and keeping a record of all messages received so far.

[4] Needless to say, the number of internal coin tosses fed to a polynomial-time strategy must also be bounded by a polynomial in the length of x.

[5] We follow the convention of specifying strategies for both the verifier and the prover. An alternative presentation only specifies the verifier's strategy, while rephrasing the completeness condition as follows: *There exists a prover strategy P such that, for every $x \in S$, the verifier V always accepts after interacting with P on common input x.*

The error probability (in the soundness condition) can be reduced by successive applications of the proof system. (This is easy to see in the case of sequential repetitions, but holds also for parallel repetitions; see Exercise 9.1.) In particular, repeating the proving process for k times reduces the probability that the verifier is fooled (i.e., accepts a false assertion) to 2^{-k}, and we can afford doing so for any $k = \text{poly}(|x|)$. Variants on the basic definition are discussed in Section 9.1.4.

The role of randomness. Randomness is essential to the power of interactive proofs; that is, restricting the verifier to deterministic strategies yields a class of interactive proof systems that has no advantage over the class of NP-proof systems. The reason is that, in case the verifier is deterministic, the prover can predict the verifier's part of the interaction. Thus, the prover can just supply its own sequence of answers to the verifier's sequence of (predictable) questions, and the verifier can just check that these answers are convincing. Actually, we establish that soundness error (and not merely randomized verification) is essential to the power of interactive proof systems (i.e., their ability to reach beyond NP-proofs).

> **Proposition 9.2:** *Suppose that S has an interactive proof system (P, V) with no soundness error; that is, for every $x \notin S$ and every potential strategy P^*, the verifier V rejects with probability* one *after interacting with P^* on common input x. Then $S \in \mathcal{NP}$.*

Proof: We may assume, without loss of generality, that V is deterministic (by just fixing arbitrarily the contents of its random-tape (e.g., to the all-zero string) and noting that both (perfect) completeness and perfect (i.e., errorless) soundness still hold). Thus, the case of zero soundness error reduces to the case of deterministic verifiers.

Now, since V is deterministic, the prover can predict each message sent by V, because each such message is uniquely determined by the common input and the previous prover messages. Thus, a sequence of optimal prover's messages (i.e., a sequence of messages leading V to accept $x \in S$) can be (pre)determined (without interacting with V) *based solely on the common input x.*[6] Hence, $x \in S$ if and only if there exists a sequence of (prover's) messages that make (the deterministic) V accept x, where the question of whether a specific sequence (of prover's messages) makes V accept x depends only on the sequence and on the common input x (because V tosses no coins that may affect this decision).[7] The foregoing condition can be checked in polynomial time, and so a "passing sequence" constitutes an NP-witness for $x \in S$. It follows that $S \in \mathcal{NP}$. ∎

Reflection. The moral of the reasoning underlying the proof Proposition 9.2 is that *there is no point to interact with a party whose moves are easily predictable*, because such moves can be determined without any interaction. This moral represents the prover's point

---

[6] As usual, we do not care about the complexity of determining such a sequence, since no computational bounds are placed on the prover.

[7] Recall that in the case that V is randomized, its final decision also depends on its internal coin tosses (and not only on the common input and on the sequence of the prover's messages). In that case, the verifier's own messages may reveal information about the verifier's internal coin tosses, which in turn may help the prover to answer with convincing messages.

of view (regarding interaction with deterministic verifiers). In contrast, even an infinitely powerful party (e.g., a prover) may gain by interacting with an unpredictable party (e.g., a randomized verifier), because this interaction may provide useful information (e.g., information regarding the verifier's coin tosses, which in turn allows the prover to increase its probability of answering convincingly). Furthermore, from the verifier's point of view it is beneficial to interact with the prover, because the latter is computationally stronger (and thus its moves may not be *easily* predictable by the verifier even in the case that they are predictable in an information-theoretic sense).

9.1.3. The Power of Interactive Proofs

We have seen that randomness is essential to the power of interactive proof systems in the sense that without randomness, interactive proofs are not more powerful than NP-proofs. Indeed, the power of interactive proofs arises from the combination of randomization and interaction. We first demonstrate this point by a simple proof system for a specific coNP-set that is not known to have an NP-proof system, and next prove the celebrated result $\mathcal{IP} = \mathcal{PSPACE}$, which suggests that interactive proofs are much stronger than NP-proofs.

9.1.3.1. A Simple Example

> One day on Olympus, bright-eyed Athena claimed that nectar poured from new silver-coated jars tasted less sweet than nectar poured from older gold-decorated jars. Mighty Zeus, who was forced to introduce the new jars by the practically minded Hera, was annoyed at the claim. He ordered that Athena be served one hundred glasses of nectar, each poured at random either from an old jar or from a new one, and that she tell the source of the drink in each glass. To everybody's surprise, wise Athena correctly identified the source of each serving, to which the father of the gods responded, "My child, you are either right or extremely lucky." Since all the gods knew that being lucky was not one of the attributes of Pallas-Athena, they all concluded that the impeccable goddess was right in her claim.

The foregoing story illustrates the main idea underlying the interactive proof for Graph Non-Isomorphism, presented in Construction 9.3. Informally, this interactive proof system is designed for proving the dissimilarity of two given objects (in the foregoing story these are the two brands of Nectar, whereas in Construction 9.3 these are two non-isomorphic graphs). We note that, typically, proving similarity between objects is easy, because one can present a mapping (of one object to the other) that demonstrates this similarity. In contrast, proving dissimilarity seems harder, because in general there seems to be no succinct proof of dissimilarity (e.g., clearly, showing that a particular mapping fails does not suffice, while enumerating all possible mappings (and showing that each fails) does not yield a succinct proof). More generally, it is typically easy to prove the existence of an easily verifiable structure in a given object by merely presenting this structure, but proving the non-existence of such a structure seems hard. Formally, membership in an NP-set is proved by presenting an NP-witness, but it is not clear how to prove the non-existence of such a witness. Indeed, recall that the common belief is that $\text{co}\mathcal{NP} \neq \mathcal{NP}$.

Two graphs, $G_1 = (V_1, E_1)$ and $G_2 = (V_2, E_2)$, are called isomorphic if there exists a 1-1 and onto mapping, ϕ, from the vertex set V_1 to the vertex set V_2 such that $\{u, v\} \in E_1$ if and only if $\{\phi(v), \phi(u)\} \in E_2$. This ("edge-preserving") mapping ϕ, in case it exists, is called an *isomorphism* between the graphs. The following protocol specifies a way of proving that two graphs are not isomorphic, while it is not known whether such a statement can be proved via a non-interactive process (i.e., via an NP-proof system).

Construction 9.3 (interactive proof for Graph Non-Isomorphism):

- Common Input: *A pair of graphs, $G_1 = (V_1, E_1)$ and $G_2 = (V_2, E_2)$.*
- Verifier's first step (V1): *The verifier selects at random one of the two input graphs, and sends to the prover a random isomorphic copy of this graph. Namely, the verifier selects uniformly $\sigma \in \{1, 2\}$, and a random permutation π from the set of permutations over the vertex set V_σ. The verifier constructs a graph with vertex set V_σ and edge set*

$$E \overset{\text{def}}{=} \{\{\pi(u), \pi(v)\} : \{u, v\} \in E_\sigma\}$$

  and sends (V_σ, E) to the prover.
- Motivating Remark: *If the input graphs are non-isomorphic, as the prover claims, then the prover should be able to distinguish (not necessarily by an efficient algorithm) isomorphic copies of one graph from isomorphic copies of the other graph. However, if the input graphs are isomorphic, then a random isomorphic copy of one graph is distributed identically to a random isomorphic copy of the other graph.*
- Prover's step: *Upon receiving a graph, $G' = (V', E')$, from the verifier, the prover finds a $\tau \in \{1, 2\}$ such that the graph G' is isomorphic to the input graph G_τ. (If both $\tau = 1, 2$ satisfy the condition then τ is selected arbitrarily. In case no $\tau \in \{1, 2\}$ satisfies the condition, τ is set to 0). The prover sends τ to the verifier.*
- Verifier's second step (V2): *If the message, τ, received from the prover equals σ (chosen in Step V1) then the verifier outputs 1 (i.e., accepts the common input). Otherwise the verifier outputs 0 (i.e., rejects the common input).*

The verifier's strategy in Construction 9.3 is easily implemented in probabilistic polynomial time. We do not known of a probabilistic polynomial-time implementation of the prover's strategy, but this is not required. The motivating remark justifies the claim that Construction 9.3 constitutes an interactive proof system for the set of pairs of non-isomorphic graphs.[8] Recall that the latter is a co$\mathcal{NP}$-set (which is not known to be in $\mathcal{NP}$).

9.1.3.2. The Full Power of Interactive Proofs

The interactive proof system of Construction 9.3 refers to a specific coNP-set that is not known to be in $\mathcal{NP}$. It turns out that interactive proof systems are powerful enough to prove membership in *any* coNP-set (e.g., prove that a graph is not 3-colorable). Thus,

---

[8] In case G_1 is not isomorphic to G_2, no graph can be isomorphic to both input graphs (i.e., both to G_1 and to G_2). In this case the graph G' sent in Step (V1) uniquely determines the bit σ. On the other hand, if G_1 and G_2 are isomorphic then, for every G' sent in Step (V1), the number of isomorphisms between G_1 and G' equals the number of isomorphisms between G_2 and G'. It follows that, in this case, G' yields no information about σ (chosen by the verifier), and so no prover may convince the verifier with probability exceeding $1/2$.

assuming that $\mathcal{NP} \neq \mathrm{co}\mathcal{NP}$, this establishes that interactive proof systems are more powerful than NP-proof systems. Furthermore, the class of sets having interactive proof systems coincides with the class of sets that can be decided using a polynomial amount of work-space.

Theorem 9.4 (the IP Theorem): $\mathcal{IP} = \mathcal{PSPACE}$.

Recall that it is widely believed that $\mathcal{NP}$ is a *proper* subset of $\mathcal{PSPACE}$. Thus, under this conjecture, interactive proofs are more powerful than NP-proofs.

9.1.3.3. Sketch of the Proof of Theorem 9.4

We first show that $\mathrm{co}\mathcal{NP} \subseteq \mathcal{IP}$ by presenting an interactive proof system for the $\mathrm{co}\mathcal{NP}$-complete set of unsatisfiable CNF formulae. Next we extend this proof system to obtain one for the $\mathcal{PSPACE}$-complete set of unsatisfiable Quantified Boolean Formulae. Finally, we observe that $\mathcal{IP} \subseteq \mathcal{PSPACE}$. Indeed, proving that some $\mathrm{co}\mathcal{NP}$-complete set has an interactive proof system is the core of the proof of Theorem 9.4 (see Exercise 9.2).

We show that the set of unsatisfiable CNF formulae has an interactive proof system by using algebraic methods, which are *applied to an arithmetic generalization of the said Boolean problem* (rather than to the problem itself). That is, in order to demonstrate that this Boolean problem has an interactive proof system, we first introduce an arithmetic generalization of CNF formulae, and then construct an interactive proof system for the resulting arithmetic assertion (by capitalizing on the arithmetic formulation of the assertion). Intuitively, we present an iterative process, which involves interaction between the prover and the verifier, such that in each iteration the residual claim to be established becomes simpler (i.e., contains one variable less). This iterative process seems to be enabled by the fact that the various claims refer to the arithmetic problem rather than to the original Boolean problem. (Actually, one may say that the key point is that these claims refer to a generalized problem rather than to the original one.)

Teaching note: We devote most of the presentation to establishing that $\mathrm{co}\mathcal{NP} \subseteq \mathcal{IP}$, and recommend doing the same in class. Our presentation focuses on the main ideas, and neglects some minor implementation details (which can be found in [162, 202]).

The starting point. We prove that $\mathrm{co}\mathcal{NP} \subseteq \mathcal{IP}$ by presenting an interactive proof system for the set of unsatisfiable CNF formulae, which is $\mathrm{co}\mathcal{NP}$-complete. Thus, our starting point is a given Boolean CNF formula, which is claimed to be unsatisfiable.

Arithmetization of Boolean (CNF) formulae. Given a Boolean (CNF) formula, we replace the Boolean variables by integer variables, and replace the logical operations by corresponding arithmetic operations. In particular, the Boolean values `false` and `true` are replaced by the integer values 0 and 1 (respectively), OR-clauses are replaced by sums, and the top level conjunction is replaced by a product. This translation is depicted in Figure 9.1. Note that the Boolean formula is satisfied (resp., unsatisfied) by a specific truth assignment if and only if evaluating the resulting arithmetic expression at the corresponding 0-1 assignment yields a positive (integer) value (resp., yields the value zero). Thus, the claim that the original Boolean formula is unsatisfiable translates to the claim that the summation of the resulting arithmetic expression, over all 0-1 assignments

	BOOLEAN	ARITHMETIC
variable values	false, true	0, 1
connectives	$\neg x$, $\vee$ and $\wedge$	$1 - x$, $+$ and $\cdot$
final values	false, true	0, positive

Figure 9.1: Arithmetization of CNF formulae.

to its variables, yields the value zero. For example, the Boolean formula

$$(x_3 \vee \neg x_5 \vee x_{17}) \wedge (x_5 \vee x_9) \wedge (\neg x_3 \vee \neg x_4)$$

is replaced by the arithmetic expression

$$(x_3 + (1 - x_5) + x_{17}) \cdot (x_5 + x_9) \cdot ((1 - x_3) + (1 - x_4))$$

and the Boolean formula is unsatisfiable if and only if the sum of the corresponding arithmetic expression, taken over all choices of $x_1, x_2, \ldots, x_{17} \in \{0, 1\}$, equals 0. Thus, *proving that the original Boolean formula is unsatisfiable reduces to proving that the corresponding arithmetic summation evaluates to 0.* We highlight two additional observations regarding the resulting arithmetic expression:

1. The arithmetic expression is a low-degree polynomial over the integers; specifically, its (total) degree equals the number of clauses in the original Boolean formula.
2. For any Boolean formula, the value of the corresponding arithmetic expression (for any choice of $x_1, \ldots, x_n \in \{0, 1\}$) resides within the interval $[0, v^m]$, where v is the maximum number of variables in a clause, and m is the number of clauses. Thus, summing over all 2^n possible 0-1 assignments, where $n \leq vm$ is the number of variables, yields an integer value in $[0, 2^n v^m]$.

Moving to a finite field. In general, whenever we need to check equality between two integers in $[0, M]$, it suffices to check their equality mod q, where $q > M$. The benefit is that, if q is prime, then the arithmetic is now in a finite field (mod q), and so certain things are "nicer" (e.g., uniformly selecting a value). Thus, proving that a CNF formula is not satisfiable reduces to proving an equality of the following form

$$\sum_{x_1=0,1} \cdots \sum_{x_n=0,1} \phi(x_1, \ldots, x_n) \equiv 0 \pmod{q}, \tag{9.1}$$

where ϕ is a low-degree multivariate polynomial (and q can be represented using $O(|\phi|)$ bits). In the rest of this exposition, all arithmetic operations refer to the finite field of q elements, denoted GF(q).

Overview of the actual protocol: Stripping summations in iterations. Given a formal expression as in Eq. (9.1), we strip off summations in iterations, stripping a single summation at each iteration, and instantiate the corresponding free variable as follows. At the beginning of each iteration the prover is supposed to supply the univariate polynomial representing the residual expression as a function of the (single) currently stripped variable. (By Observation 1, this is a low-degree polynomial and so it has a short description.)[9] The verifier checks that the polynomial (say, p) is of low degree, and that it corresponds to the

---

[9] We also use Observation 2, which implies that we may use a finite field with elements having a description length that is polynomial in the length of the original Boolean formula (i.e., $\log_2 q = O(vm)$).

current value (say, v) being claimed (i.e., it verifies that $p(0) + p(1) \equiv v$). Next, the verifier randomly instantiates the currently free variable (i.e., it selects uniformly $r \in \mathrm{GF}(q)$), yielding a new value to be claimed for the resulting expression (i.e., the verifier computes $v \leftarrow p(r)$, and expects a proof that the residual expression equals v). The verifier sends the uniformly chosen instantiation (i.e., r) to the prover, and the parties proceed to the next iteration (which refers to the residual expression and to the new value v). At the end of the last iteration, the verifier has a closed form expression (i.e., an expression without formal summations), which can be easily checked against the claimed value.

A single iteration (detailed): The ith iteration is aimed at proving a claim of the form.

$$\sum_{x_i=0,1} \cdots \sum_{x_n=0,1} \phi(r_1, \ldots, r_{i-1}, x_i, x_{i+1}, \ldots, x_n) \equiv v_{i-1} \pmod{q}, \tag{9.2}$$

where $v_0 = 0$, and $r_1, \ldots, r_{i-1}$ and v_{i-1} are as determined in previous iterations. The ith iteration consists of two steps (messages): a prover step followed by a verifier step. The prover is supposed to provide the verifier with the univariate polynomial p_i that satisfies

$$p_i(z) \overset{\text{def}}{=} \sum_{x_{i+1}=0,1} \cdots \sum_{x_n=0,1} \phi(r_1, \ldots, r_{i-1}, z, x_{i+1}, \ldots, x_n) \bmod q. \tag{9.3}$$

Note that, module q, the value $p_i(0) + p_i(1)$ equals the l.h.s of Eq. (9.2). Denote by p_i' the actual polynomial sent by the prover (i.e., the honest prover sets $p_i' = p_i$). Then, the verifier first checks if $p_i'(0) + p_i'(1) \equiv v_{i-1} \pmod{q}$, and next uniformly selects $r_i \in \mathrm{GF}(q)$ and sends it to the prover. Needless to say, the verifier will reject if the first check is violated. The claim to be proved in the next iteration is

$$\sum_{x_{i+1}=0,1} \cdots \sum_{x_n=0,1} \phi(r_1, \ldots, r_{i-1}, r_i, x_{i+1}, \ldots, x_n) \equiv v_i \pmod{q}, \tag{9.4}$$

where $v_i \overset{\text{def}}{=} p_i'(r_i) \bmod q$ is computed by each party.

Completeness of the protocol. When the initial claim (i.e., Eq. (9.1)) holds, the prover can supply the correct polynomials (as determined in Eq. (9.3)), and this will lead the verifier to always accept.

Soundness of the protocol. It suffices to upper-bound the probability that, for a particular iteration, the entry claim (i.e., Eq. (9.2)) is false while the ending claim (i.e., Eq. (9.4)) is valid. Indeed, let us focus on the ith iteration, and let v_{i-1} and p_i be as in Eq. (9.2) and Eq. (9.3), respectively; that is, v_{i-1} is the (wrong) value claimed at the beginning of the ith iteration and p_i is the polynomial representing the expression obtained when stripping the current variable (as in Eq. (9.3)). Let $p_i'(\cdot)$ be any potential answer by the prover. We may assume, without loss of generality, that $p_i'(0) + p_i'(1) \equiv v_{i-1} \pmod{q}$ and that p_i' is of low-degree (since otherwise the verifier will definitely reject). Using our hypothesis (that the entry claim of Eq. (9.2) is false), we know that $p_i(0) + p_i(1) \not\equiv v_{i-1} \pmod{q}$. Thus, p_i' and p_i are different low-degree polynomials, and so they may agree on very few points (if at all). Now, if the verifier's instantiation (i.e., its choice of a random r_i) does not happen to be one of these few points (i.e., $p_i(r_i) \not\equiv p_i'(r_i) \pmod{q}$), then the ending claim (i.e., Eq. (9.4)) is false too (because the new value (i.e., v_i) is set to $p_i'(r_i) \bmod q$, while the residual expression evaluates to $p_i(r_i)$). Details are left as an exercise (see Exercise 9.3).

This establishes that the set of unsatisfiable CNF formulae has an interactive proof system. Actually, a similar proof system (which uses a related arithmetization – see

Exercise 9.5) can be used to prove that a given formula has a given number of satisfying assignments; i.e., prove membership in the ("counting") set

$$\{(\phi, k) : |\{\tau : \phi(\tau) = 1\}| = k\}.\tag{9.5}$$

Using adequate reductions, it follows that every problem in $\#\mathcal{P}$ has an interactive proof system (i.e., for every $R \in \mathcal{PC}$, the set $\{(x, k) : |\{y : (x, y) \in R\}| = k\}$ is in $\mathcal{IP}$). Proving that $\mathcal{PSPACE} \subseteq \mathcal{IP}$ requires a little more work, as outlined next.

Obtaining interactive proofs for PSPACE (the basic idea). We present an interactive proof for the set of satisfied Quantified Boolean Formulae (QBF), which is complete for $\mathcal{PSPACE}$ (see Theorem 5.15).[10] Recall that the number of quantifiers in such formulae is unbounded (e.g., it may be polynomially related to the length of the input), that there are both existential and universal quantifiers, and furthermore these quantifiers may alternate. In the arithmetization of these formulae, we replace existential quantifiers by summations and universal quantifiers by products. Two difficulties arise when considering the application of the foregoing protocol to the resulting arithmetic expression. Firstly, the (integral) value of the expression (which may involve a big number of nested formal products) is only upper-bounded by a double-exponential function (in the length of the input). Secondly, when stripping a summation (or a product), the expression may be a polynomial of high degree (due to nested formal products that may appear in the remaining expression).[11] For example, both phenomena occur in the following expression

$$\sum_{x=0,1} \prod_{y_1=0,1} \cdots \prod_{y_n=0,1} (x + y_n),$$

which equals $\sum_{x=0,1} x^{2^{n-1}} \cdot (1 + x)^{2^{n-1}}$. The first difficulty is easy to resolve by using the fact (to be established in Exercise 9.7) that if two integers in $[0, M]$ are different, then they must be different modulo most of the primes in the interval $[3, \mathrm{poly}(\log M)]$. Thus, we let the verifier selects a random prime q of length that is linear in the length of the original formula, and the two parties consider the arithmetic expression reduced modulo this q. The second difficulty is resolved by noting that $\mathcal{PSPACE}$ is actually reducible to a special form of (non-canonical) QBF in which no variable appears both to the left and to the right of more than one universal quantifier (see the proof of Theorem 5.15 or alternatively Exercise 9.6). It follows that when arithmetizing and stripping summations (or products) from the resulting arithmetic expression, the corresponding univariate polynomial is of low degree (i.e., at most twice the length of the original formula, where the factor of two is due to the single universal quantifier that has this variable quantified on its left and appearing on its right).

---

[10] Actually, the following extension of the foregoing proof system yields a proof system for the set of *unsatisfied* Quantified Boolean Formulae (which is also complete for $\mathcal{PSPACE}$). Alternatively, an interactive proof system for QBF can be obtained by extending the related proof system presented in Exercise 9.5.

[11] This high degree causes two difficulties, where only the second one is acute. The first difficulty is that the soundness of the corresponding protocol will require working in a finite field that is sufficiently larger than this high degree, but we can afford doing so (since the degree is at most exponential in the formula's length). The second (and more acute) difficulty is that the polynomial may have a large (i.e., exponential) number of non-zero coefficients and so the verifier cannot afford to read the standard representation of this polynomial (as a list of all non-zero coefficients). Indeed, other succinct and effective representations of such polynomials may exist in some cases (as in the following example), but it is unclear how to obtain such representations in general.

IP is contained in PSPACE: We shall show that, for every interactive proof system, there exists an *optimal prover strategy* that can be implemented in polynomial space, where an optimal prover strategy is one that maximizes the probability that the prescribed verifier accepts the common input. It follows that $\mathcal{IP} \subseteq \mathcal{PSPACE}$, because (for every $S \in \mathcal{IP}$) we can emulate, in polynomial space, all possible interactions of the prescribed verifier with any fixed polynomial-space prover strategy (e.g., an optimal one).

Proposition 9.5: *Let V be a probabilistic polynomial-time* (verifier) *strategy. Then, there exists a polynomial-space computable* (prover) *strategy f that, for every x, maximizes the probability that V accepts x. That is, for every P^* and every x it holds that the probability that V accepts x after interacting with P^* is upper-bounded by the probability that V accepts x after interacting with f.*

Proof Sketch: For every common input x and any possible partial transcript γ of the interaction so far, the strategy[12] f determines an optimal next-message for the prover by considering all possible coin tosses of the verifier that are consistent with (x, γ). Specifically, f is determined *recursively* such that $f(x, \gamma) = m$ if m maximizes the number of outcomes of the verifier's coin tosses that are consistent with (x, γ) and lead the verifier to accept when subsequent prover moves are determined by f (which is where recursion is used). That is, the verifier's random sequence r supports the setting $f(x, \gamma) = m$, where $\gamma = (\alpha_1, \beta_1, \ldots, \alpha_t, \beta_t)$, if the following two conditions hold:

1. r is consistent with (x, γ), which means that for every $i \in \{1, \ldots, t\}$ it holds that $\beta_i = V(x, r, \alpha_1, \ldots, \alpha_i)$.
2. r leads V to accept when the subsequent prover moves are determined by f, which means at termination (i.e., after T rounds) it holds that

$$V(x, r, \alpha_1, \ldots, \alpha_t, m, \alpha_{t+2}, \ldots, \alpha_T) = 1,$$

   where for every $i \in \{t + 1, \ldots, T - 1\}$ it holds that $\alpha_{i+1} = f(x, \gamma, m, \beta_{t+1}, \ldots, \alpha_i, \beta_i)$ and $\beta_i = V(x, r, \alpha_1, \ldots, \alpha_t, m, \alpha_{t+2}, \ldots, \alpha_i)$.

Thus, $f(x, \gamma) = m$ if m maximizes the value of $\mathsf{E}[\xi_{f,V}(x, R_\gamma, \gamma, m)]$, where R_γ is selected uniformly among the r's that are consistent with (x, γ) and $\xi_{f,V}(x, r, \gamma, m)$ indicates whether or not V accepts x in the subsequent interaction with f (which refers to randomness r and partial transcript (γ, m)). It follows that the value $f(x, \gamma)$ can be computed in polynomial space when given oracle access to $f(x, \gamma, \cdot, \cdot)$. The proposition follows by standard composition of space-bounded computations (i.e., allocating separate space to each level of the recursion, while using the same space in all recursive calls of each level). $\qquad\square$

9.1.4. Variants and Finer Structure: An Overview

In this subsection we consider several variants on the basic definition of interactive proofs as well as finer complexity measures. This is an advanced subsection, which only provides an overview of the various notions and results (as well as pointers to proofs of the latter).

---

[12]For the sake of convenience, when describing the strategy f, we refer to the entire partial transcript of the interaction with V (rather than merely to the sequence of previous messages sent by V).

9.1.4.1. Arthur-Merlin Games (Public-Coin Proof Systems)

The verifier's messages in a general interactive proof system are determined arbitrarily (but efficiently) based on the verifier's view of the interaction so far (which includes its internal coin tosses, which without loss of generality can take place at the onset of the interaction). Thus, the verifier's past coin tosses are not necessarily revealed by the messages that it sends. In contrast, in public-coin proof systems (aka Arthur-Merlin proof systems), the verifier's messages contain the outcome of any coin that it tosses *at the current round*. Thus, these messages reveal the randomness used toward generating them (i.e., this randomness becomes public). Actually, without loss of generality, the verifier's messages can be identical to the outcome of the coins tossed at the current round (because any other string that the verifier may compute based on these coin tosses is actually determined by them).

Note that the proof systems presented in the proof of Theorem 9.4 are of the public-coin type, whereas this is not the case for the Graph Non-Isomorphism proof system (of Construction 9.3). Thus, although not all natural proof systems are of the public-coin type, by Theorem 9.4 every set having an interactive proof system also has a public-coin interactive proof system. This means that, *in the context of interactive proof systems, asking random questions is as powerful as asking clever questions*. (A stronger statement appears at the end of §9.1.4.3.)

Indeed, public-coin proof systems are interactive proof systems of a restricted form. This restriction may make the design of such systems more difficult, but potentially facilitates their analysis (and especially when the analysis refers to a generic system). Another advantage of public-coin proof systems is that the verifier's actions (except for its final decision) are oblivious of the prover's messages. This property is used in the proof of Theorem 9.12.

9.1.4.2. Interactive Proof Systems with Two-Sided Error

In Definition 9.1 error probability is allowed in the soundness condition but not in the completeness condition. In such a case, we say that the proof system has **perfect completeness** (or one-sided error probability). A more general definition allows an error probability (upper-bounded by, say, $1/3$) in both the completeness and the soundness conditions. Note that sets having such generalized (two-sided error) interactive proofs are also in $\mathcal{PSPACE}$, and thus (by Theorem 9.4) allowing two-sided error does not increase the power of interactive proofs. See further discussion at the end of §9.1.4.3.

9.1.4.3. A Hierarchy of Interactive Proof Systems

Definition 9.1 only refers to the *total* computation time of the verifier, and thus allows an arbitrary (polynomial) number of messages to be exchanged. A finer definition refers to the number of messages being exchanged (also called the number of rounds).[13]

Definition 9.6 (The round complexity of interactive proof):

- *For an integer function m, the complexity class $\mathcal{IP}(m)$ consists of sets having an interactive proof system in which, on common input x, at most $m(|x|)$ messages are exchanged between the parties.*[14]

---

[13]An even finer structure emerges when considering also the total length of the messages sent by the prover (see [106]).

[14]We count the total number of messages exchanged regardless of the direction of communication.

- *For a set of integer functions, M, we let $\mathcal{IP}(M) \overset{\text{def}}{=} \bigcup_{m \in M} \mathcal{IP}(m)$. Thus, $\mathcal{IP} = \mathcal{IP}(\text{poly})$.*

For example, interactive proof systems in which the verifier sends a single message that is answered by a single message of the prover corresponds to $\mathcal{IP}(2)$. Clearly, $\mathcal{NP} \subseteq \mathcal{IP}(1)$, yet the inclusion may be strict because in $\mathcal{IP}(1)$ the verifier may toss coins after receiving the prover's single message. (Also note that $\mathcal{IP}(0) = \text{co}\mathcal{RP}$.)

Definition 9.6 gives rise to a natural hierarchy of interactive proof systems, where different "levels" of this hierarchy correspond to different "growth rates" of the round complexity of these systems. The following results are known regarding this hierarchy.

- A linear speed-up (see Appendix F.2 (or [23] and [111])): For every integer function, f, such that $f(n) \geq 2$ for all n, the class $\mathcal{IP}(O(f(\cdot)))$ collapses to the class $\mathcal{IP}(f(\cdot))$. In particular, $\mathcal{IP}(O(1))$ collapses to $\mathcal{IP}(2)$.
- The class $\mathcal{IP}(2)$ contains sets that are not known to be in $\mathcal{NP}$; e.g., Graph Non-Isomorphism (see Construction 9.3). However, under plausible intractability assumptions, $\mathcal{IP}(2) = \mathcal{NP}$ (see [167]).
- If $\text{co}\mathcal{NP} \subseteq \mathcal{IP}(2)$ then the Polynomial-time Hierarchy collapses (see [45]).

It is conjectured that $\text{co}\mathcal{NP}$ is *not* contained in $\mathcal{IP}(2)$, and consequently that interactive proofs with an unbounded number of message exchanges are more powerful than interactive proofs in which only a bounded (i.e., constant) number of messages are exchanged.[15]

The class $\mathcal{IP}(1)$, also denoted $\mathcal{MA}$, seems to be *the* "real" randomized (and yet non-interactive) version of $\mathcal{NP}$: Here, the prover supplies a candidate (polynomial-size) "proof", and the verifier assesses its validity probabilistically (rather than deterministically).

The IP-hierarchy (i.e., $\mathcal{IP}(\cdot)$) equals an analogous hierarchy, denoted $\mathcal{AM}(\cdot)$, that refers to public-coin (aka Arthur-Merlin) interactive proofs. That is, for every integer function f, it holds that $\mathcal{AM}(f) = \mathcal{IP}(f)$. For $f \geq 2$, it is also the case that $\mathcal{AM}(f) = \mathcal{AM}(O(f))$; actually, the aforementioned linear speed-up for $\mathcal{IP}(\cdot)$ is established by combining the following two results:

1. Emulating $\mathcal{IP}(\cdot)$ by $\mathcal{AM}(\cdot)$ (see Appendix F.2.1 or [111]): $\mathcal{IP}(f) \subseteq \mathcal{AM}(f + 3)$.
2. Linear speed-up for $\mathcal{AM}(\cdot)$ (see Appendix F.2.2 or [23]): $\mathcal{AM}(2f) \subseteq \mathcal{AM}(f + 1)$.

In particular, $\mathcal{IP}(O(1)) = \mathcal{AM}(2)$, even if $\mathcal{AM}(2)$ is restricted such that the verifier tosses no coins after receiving the prover's message. (Note that $\mathcal{IP}(1) = \mathcal{AM}(1)$ and $\mathcal{IP}(0) = \mathcal{AM}(0)$ are trivial.) We comment that it is common to shorthand $\mathcal{AM}(2)$ by $\mathcal{AM}$, which is indeed inconsistent with the convention of using $\mathcal{IP}$ as shorthand of $\mathcal{IP}(\text{poly})$.

The fact that $\mathcal{IP}(O(f)) = \mathcal{IP}(f)$ is proved by establishing an analogous result for $\mathcal{AM}(\cdot)$ demonstrates the advantage of the public-coin setting for the study of interactive proofs. A similar phenomenon occurs when establishing that the IP-hierarchy equals an analogous two-sided error hierarchy (see Exercise 9.8).

---

[15]Note that the linear speed-up cannot be applied for an unbounded number of times, because each application may increase (e.g., square) the time complexity of verification.

9.1.4.4. Something Completely Different

We stress that although we have relaxed the requirements from the verification procedure (by allowing it to interact with the prover, toss coins, and risk some (bounded) error probability), we did not restrict the soundness of its verdict by assumptions concerning the potential prover(s). This should be contrasted with other notions of proof systems, such as computationally sound ones (see §9.1.5.2), in which the soundness of the verifier's verdict depends on assumptions concerning the potential prover(s).

9.1.5. On Computationally Bounded Provers: An Overview

Recall that our definition of interactive proofs (i.e., Definition 9.1) makes no reference to the computational abilities of the potential prover. This fact has two conflicting consequences:

1. The completeness condition does not provide any upper bound on the complexity of the corresponding proving strategy (which convinces the verifier to accept valid assertions).
2. The soundness condition guarantees that, regardless of the computational effort spent by a cheating prover, the verifier cannot be fooled into accepting invalid assertions (with probability exceeding the soundness error).

Note that providing an upper bound on the complexity of the (prescribed) prover strategy P of a specific interactive proof system (P, V) only strengthens the claim that (P, V) is a proof system for the corresponding set (of valid assertions). We stress that the prescribed prover strategy is referred to only in the completeness condition (and is irrelevant to the soundness condition). On the other hand, relaxing the definition of interactive proofs such that soundness holds only for a specific class of cheating prover strategies (rather than for all cheating prover strategies) weakens the corresponding claim. In this advanced section we consider both possibilities.

> **Teaching note:** Indeed, this is an advanced subsection, which is best left for independent reading. It merely provides an overview of the various notions, and the reader is directed to the chapter's notes for further detail (i.e., pointers to the relevant literature).

9.1.5.1. How Powerful Should the Prover Be?

Suppose that a set S is in $\mathcal{IP}$. This means that there exists a verifier V that can be convinced to accept any input in S but cannot be fooled into accepting any input not in S (except with small probability). One may ask how powerful a prover should be such that it can convince the verifier V to accept any input in S. Note that Proposition 9.5 asserts that an optimal prover strategy (for convincing any fixed verifier V) can be implemented in polynomial space, and that we cannot expect any better for a generic set in $\mathcal{PSPACE} = \mathcal{IP}$ (because the emulation of the interaction of V with any optimal prover strategy yields a decision procedure for the set). Still, we may seek better upper bounds on the complexity of some prover strategy that convinces a *specific* verifier, which in turn corresponds to a specific set S. More interestingly, considering all possible verifiers that give rise to interactive proof systems for S, we wish to upper-bound the computational power that suffices for convincing any of these verifiers (to accept any input in S).

We stress that, unlike the case of computationally sound proof systems (see §9.1.5.2), we do not restrict the power of the prover in the soundness condition, but rather consider the minimum complexity of provers meeting the completeness condition. Specifically, we are interested in *relatively efficient* provers that meet the completeness condition. The term "relatively efficient prover" has been given three different interpretations, which are briefly surveyed next.

1. A prover is considered *relatively efficient* if, when given an auxiliary input (in addition to the common input in S), it works in (probabilistic) polynomial time. Specifically, in case $S \in \mathcal{NP}$, the auxiliary input may be an NP-proof that the common input is in the set. Still, even in this case the interactive proof need not consist of the prover sending the auxiliary input to the verifier; for example, an alternative procedure may allow the prover to be zero-knowledge (see Construction 9.10).

    This interpretation is adequate and in fact crucial for applications in which such an auxiliary input is available to the otherwise polynomial-time parties. Typically, such auxiliary input is available in cryptographic applications in which parties wish to prove in (zero-knowledge) that they have correctly conducted some computation. In these cases, the NP-proof is just the transcript of the computation by which the claimed result has been generated, and thus the auxiliary input is available to the party that plays the role of the prover.

2. A prover is considered *relatively efficient* if it can be implemented by a probabilistic polynomial-time oracle machine with oracle access to the set S itself. Note that the prover in Construction 9.3 has this property (and see also Exercise 9.10).

    This interpretation generalizes the notion of self-reducibility of NP-proof systems. Recall that by self-reducibility of an NP-set (or rather of the corresponding NP-proof system) we mean that the search problem of finding an NP-witness is polynomial-time reducible to deciding membership in the set (cf. Definition 2.14). Here we require that implementing the prover strategy (in the relevant interactive proof) be polynomial-time reducible to deciding membership in the set.

3. A prover is considered *relatively efficient* if it can be implemented by a probabilistic machine that runs in time that is polynomial in the deterministic complexity of the set. This interpretation relates the time complexity of convincing a "lazy person" (i.e., a verifier) to the time complexity of determining the truth (i.e., deciding membership in the set).

    Hence, in contrast to the first interpretation, which is adequate in settings where assertions are generated along with their NP-proofs, the current interpretation is adequate in settings in which the prover is given only the assertion and has to find a proof to it by itself (before trying to convince a lazy verifier of its validity).

9.1.5.2. Computational Soundness

Relaxing the soundness condition such that it only refers to relatively efficient ways of trying to fool the verifier (rather than to all possible ways) yields a fundamentally different notion of a proof system. The verifier's verdict in such a system is not absolutely sound, but is rather sound *provided that the potential cheating prover does not exceed the presumed complexity limits*. As in §9.1.5.1, the notion of "relative efficiency" can be given different interpretations, the most popular one being that the cheating prover strategy can be implemented by a (non-uniform) family of polynomial-size circuits. The latter interpretation coincides with the first interpretation used in §9.1.5.1 (i.e., a probabilistic polynomial-time strategy that is given an auxiliary input (of polynomial length)). Specifically, in this case, the soundness condition is replaced by the following computational soundness condition that asserts that it is infeasible to fool the verifier into accepting false statements. Formally:

> For every prover strategy that is implementable by a family of polynomial-size circuits $\{C_n\}$, and every sufficiently long $x \in \{0, 1\}^* \setminus S$, the probability that V accepts x when interacting with $C_{|x|}$ is less than $1/2$.

As in the case of standard soundness, the computational-soundness error can be reduced by repetitions. We warn, however, that unlike in the case of standard soundness (where both sequential and parallel repetitions will do), the computational-soundness error cannot *always* be reduced by parallel repetitions.

It is common and natural to consider proof systems in which the prover strategies considered both in the completeness and soundness conditions satisfy the same notion of relative efficiency. Protocols that satisfy these conditions with respect to the foregoing interpretation are called arguments. We mention that argument systems may be more efficient (e.g., in terms of their communication complexity) than interactive proof systems.

9.2. Zero-Knowledge Proof Systems

Standard mathematical proofs are believed to yield (extra) knowledge and not merely establish the validity of the assertion being proved; that is, it is commonly believed that (good) proofs provide a deeper understanding of the theorem being proved. At the technical level, an NP-proof of membership in some set $S \in \mathcal{NP} \setminus \mathcal{P}$ yields something (i.e., the NP-proof itself) that is hard to compute (even when assuming that the input is in S). For example, a 3-coloring of a graph constitutes an NP-proof that the graph is 3-colorable, but it yields information (i.e., the coloring) that seems infeasible to compute (when given an arbitrary 3-colorable graph).

A natural question that arises is whether or not proving an assertion always requires giving away some extra knowledge. The setting of interactive proof systems enables a negative answer to this fundamental question: In contrast to NP-proofs, which seem to yield a lot of knowledge, zero-knowledge (interactive) proofs yield no knowledge at all; that is, *zero-knowledge proofs are both convincing and yet yield nothing beyond the validity of the assertion being proved*. For example, a zero-knowledge proof of 3-colorability does not yield any information about the graph (e.g., partial information about a 3-coloring) that is infeasible to compute from the graph itself. Thus, zero-knowledge proofs exhibit an extreme contrast between being convincing (of the validity of an assertion) and teaching anything on top of the validity of the assertion.

Needless to say, the notion of zero-knowledge proofs is fascinating (e.g., since it differentiates proof-verification from learning). Still, the reader may wonder whether such a phenomenon is desirable, because in many settings we do care to learn as much as possible (rather than learn as little as possible). However, in other settings (most notably in cryptography), we may actually wish to limit the gain that other parties may obtained from a proof (and, in particular, limit this gain to the minimal level of being convinced of the validity of the assertion). Indeed, the applicability of zero-knowledge proofs in the domain of cryptography is vast; they are typically used as a tool for forcing (potentially malicious) parties to behave according to a predetermined protocol (without having them reveal their own private inputs). The interested reader is referred to discussions in

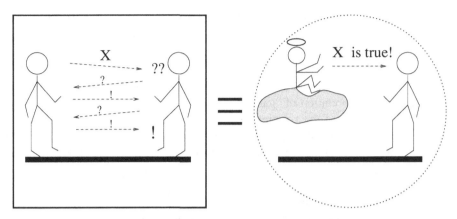

Figure 9.2: Zero-knowledge proofs – an illustration.

§C.4.3.2 and §C.7.3.2 in Appendix C (and to detailed treatments in [91, 92]). We also mention that, in addition to their direct applicability in cryptography, zero-knowledge proofs serve as a good benchmark for the study of various questions regarding cryptographic protocols.

> **Teaching note:** We believe that the treatment of zero-knowledge proofs provided in this section suffices for the purpose of a course in Complexity Theory. For an extensive treatment of zero-knowledge proofs, the interested reader is referred to [91, Chap. 4].

9.2.1. Definitional Issues

Loosely speaking, zero-knowledge proofs are proofs that yield nothing beyond the validity of the assertion; that is, a verifier obtaining such a proof only gains conviction of the validity of the assertion. This is formulated by saying that anything that can be feasibly obtained from a zero-knowledge proof is also feasibly computable from the (valid) assertion itself. The latter formulation follows the simulation paradigm, which is discussed next.

9.2.1.1. A Wider Perspective: The Simulation Paradigm

In defining zero-knowledge proofs, we view the verifier as a potential adversary that tries to gain knowledge from the (prescribed) prover.[16] We wish to state that no (feasible) adversary strategy for the verifier can gain anything from the prover (beyond conviction in the validity of the assertion). The question addressed here is how to formulate the "no gain" requirement.

Let us consider the desired formulation from a wide perspective. A key question regarding the modeling of security concerns is how to express the intuitive requirement that an adversary "gains nothing substantial" by deviating from the prescribed behavior of an honest user. The answer is that *the adversary* gains nothing *if whatever it can obtain by unrestricted adversarial behavior can be obtained within essentially the same computational effort by a benign* (or prescribed) *behavior.* The definition of the "benign behavior" captures what we want to achieve in terms of security, and is specific to the

---

[16]Recall that when defining a proof system (e.g., an interactive proof system), we view the prover as a potential adversary that tries to fool the (prescribed) verifier (into accepting invalid assertions).

security concern to be addressed. For example, in the context of zero-knowledge, *a benign behavior is any computation that is based* (only) *on the assertion itself* (while assuming that the latter is valid). Thus, a zero-knowledge proof is an interactive proof in which no feasible adversarial verifier strategy can obtain from the interaction more than a "benign party" (which believes the assertion) can obtain from the assertion itself.

The foregoing interpretation of "gaining nothing" means that any feasible adversarial behavior can be "simulated" by a benign behavior (and thus there is no gain in the former). This line of reasoning is called the simulation paradigm, and is pivotal to many definitions in cryptography (e.g., it underlies the definitions of the security of encryption schemes and cryptographic protocols); for further details, see Appendix C.

9.2.1.2. The Basic Definitions

We turn back to the concrete task of defining zero-knowledge. Firstly, we comment that zero-knowledge is a property of some prover strategies; actually, more generally, zero-knowledge is a property of some strategies. Fixing any strategy (e.g., a prescribed prover), we consider what can be gained (i.e., computed) by an *arbitrary feasible adversary* (e.g., a verifier) *that interacts with the aforementioned fixed strategy* on a common input taken from a predetermined set (in our case the set of valid assertions). This gain is compared against what can be computed by an *arbitrary feasible algorithm* (called a simulator) that is only given the input itself. The fixed strategy is zero-knowledge if the "computational power" of these two (fundamentally different settings) is essentially equivalent. Details follow.

The formulation of the zero-knowledge condition refers to two types of probability ensembles, where each ensemble associates a single probability distribution with each relevant input (e.g., a valid assertion). Specifically, in the case of interactive proofs, the first ensemble represents the output distribution of the verifier after interacting with the specified prover strategy P (on some common input), where the verifier is employing an arbitrary efficient strategy (not necessarily the specified one). The second ensemble represents the output distribution of some probabilistic polynomial-time algorithm (which is only given the corresponding input (and does not interact with anyone)). The basic paradigm of zero-knowledge asserts that for every ensemble of the first type there exist a "similar" ensemble of the second type. The specific variants differ by the interpretation given to the notion of *similarity*. The most strict interpretation, leading to perfect zero-knowledge, is that similarity means equality.

Definition 9.7 (perfect zero-knowledge, oversimplified):[17] *A prover strategy, P, is said to be* perfect zero-knowledge *over a set S if for every probabilistic polynomial-time verifier strategy, V^*, there exists a probabilistic polynomial-time algorithm, A^*, such that*

$$(P, V^*)(x) \equiv A^*(x), \quad \text{for every } x \in S$$

where $(P, V^*)(x)$ is a random variable representing the output of verifier V^* after interacting with the prover P on common input x, and $A^*(x)$ is a random variable representing the output of algorithm A^* on input x.

---

[17]In the actual definition, one relaxes the requirement in one of the following two ways. The first alternative is allowing A^* to run for *expected* (rather than strict) polynomial time. The second alternative consists of allowing A^* to have no output with probability at most $1/2$ and considering the value of its output conditioned on it having output at all. The latter alternative implies the former, but the converse is not known to hold.

We comment that any set in $co\mathcal{RP}$ has a perfect zero-knowledge proof system in which the prover keeps silent and the verifier decides by itself. The same holds for $\mathcal{BPP}$ provided that we relax the definition of an interactive proof system to allow two-sided error. Needless to say, our focus is on non-trivial proof systems, that is, proof systems for sets outside of $\mathcal{BPP}$.

A somewhat more relaxed interpretation (of the notion of similarity), leading to almost-perfect zero-knowledge (aka statistical zero-knowledge), is that similarity means statistical closeness (i.e., negligible difference between the ensembles). The most liberal interpretation, leading to the standard usage of the term zero-knowledge (and sometimes referred to as computational zero-knowledge), is that similarity means computational indistinguishability (i.e., failure of any efficient procedure to tell the two ensembles apart). Combining the foregoing discussion with the relevant definition of computational indistinguishability (i.e., Definition C.5 in Appendix C.3), we obtain the following definition.

Definition 9.8 (zero-knowledge, somewhat simplified): *A prover strategy, P, is said to be* zero-knowledge *over a set S if for every probabilistic polynomial-time verifier strategy, V^*, there exists a probabilistic polynomial-time simulator, A^*, such that for every probabilistic polynomial-time distinguisher, D, it holds that*

$$d(n) \stackrel{\text{def}}{=} \max_{x \in S \cap \{0,1\}^n} \{|\Pr[D(x, (P, V^*)(x)) = 1] - \Pr[D(x, A^*(x)) = 1]|\}$$

is a negligible function.[18] *We denote by $\mathcal{ZK}$ the class of sets having zero-knowledge interactive proof systems.*

Definition 9.8 is a simplified version of the actual definition, which is presented in Appendix C.4.2. Specifically, in order to guarantee that zero-knowledge is preserved under sequential composition, it is necessary to slightly augment the definition (by providing V^* and A^* with the same value of an arbitrary (poly($|x|$)-bit long) auxiliary input). Other definitional issues and related notions are briefly discussed in Appendix C.4.4.

On the role of randomness and interaction. It can be shown that only sets in $\mathcal{BPP}$ have zero-knowledge proofs in which the verifier is deterministic (see Exercise 9.13). The same holds for deterministic provers, provided that we consider "auxiliary-input" zero-knowledge (as in Definition C.9). It can also be shown that only sets in $\mathcal{BPP}$ have zero-knowledge proofs in which a single message is sent (see Exercise 9.14). Thus, both randomness and interaction are essential to the non-triviality of zero-knowledge proof systems. (For further details, see [91, Sec. 4.5.1].)

Advanced comment: Knowledge Complexity. Zero-knowledge is the lowest level of a knowledge-complexity hierarchy, which quantifies the "knowledge revealed in an interaction." Specifically, the knowledge complexity of an interactive proof system may be defined as the minimum number of oracle queries required in order to efficiently simulate an interaction with the prover. (See [90, Sec. 2.3.1] for references.)

---

[18]That is, d vanishes faster that the reciprocal of any positive polynomial (i.e., for every positive polynomial p and for sufficiently large n, it holds that $d(n) < 1/p(n)$). Needless to say, $d(n) \stackrel{\text{def}}{=} 0$ if $S \cap \{0,1\}^n = \emptyset$.

9.2.2. The Power of Zero-Knowledge

When faced with a definition as complex (and seemingly self-contradictory) as that of zero-knowledge, one should indeed wonder whether the definition can be met (in a non-trivial manner).[19] It turns out that the existence of non-trivial zero-knowledge proofs is related to the existence of intractable problems in $\mathcal{NP}$. In particular, we will show that if one-way functions exist, then every NP-set has a zero-knowledge proof system. (For the converse, see [91, Sec. 4.5.2] or [228].) But first, we demonstrate the non-triviality of zero-knowledge by presenting a simple (perfect) zero-knowledge proof system for a specific NP-set that is not known to be in $\mathcal{BPP}$. In this case we make no intractability assumptions (yet, the result is significant only if $\mathcal{NP}$ is not contained in $\mathcal{BPP}$).

9.2.2.1. A Simple Example

> *A story not found in the Odyssey refers to the not-so-famous labyrinth of the island of Aeaea. The sorceress Circe, daughter of Helius, challenged godlike Odysseus to traverse the labyrinth from its north gate to its south gate. Canny Odysseus doubted whether such a path existed at all and asked beautiful Circe for a proof, to which she replied that showing him a path would trivialize for him the challenge of traversing the labyrinth. "Not necessarily," clever Odysseus replied. "You can use your magic to transport me to a random place in the labyrinth, and then guide me by a random walk to a gate of my choice. If we repeat this enough times then I'll be convinced that there is a labyrinth-path between the two gates, while you will not reveal to me such a path." "Indeed," wise Circe thought to herself, "showing this mortal a random path from a random location in the labyrinth to the gate he chooses will not teach him more than his taking a random walk from that gate."*

The foregoing story illustrates the main idea underlying the zero-knowledge proof for Graph Isomorphism presented next. Recall that the set of pairs of isomorphic graphs is not known to be in $\mathcal{BPP}$, and thus the straightforward NP-proof system (in which the prover just supplies the isomorphism) may not be zero-knowledge. Furthermore, assuming that Graph Isomorphism is not in $\mathcal{BPP}$, this set has no zero-knowledge NP-proof system. Still, as we shall shortly see, this set does have a zero-knowledge interactive proof system.

Construction 9.9 (zero-knowledge proof for Graph Isomorphism):

- Common Input: *A pair of graphs, $G_1 = (V_1, E_1)$ and $G_2 = (V_2, E_2)$.*

  If the input graphs are indeed isomorphic, then we let ϕ denote an arbitrary isomorphism between them; that is, ϕ is a 1-1 and onto mapping of the vertex set V_1 to the vertex set V_2 such that $\{u, v\} \in E_1$ if and only if $\{\phi(v), \phi(u)\} \in E_2$.

- Prover's first Step (P1): *The prover selects a random isomorphic copy of G_2, and sends it to the verifier. Namely, the prover selects at random, with uniform probability distribution, a permutation π from the set of permutations over the vertex set V_2, and constructs a graph with vertex set V_2 and edge set*

$$E \stackrel{\text{def}}{=} \{\{\pi(u), \pi(v)\} : \{u, v\} \in E_2\}.$$

---

[19] Recall that any set in $\mathcal{BPP}$ has a trivial zero-knowledge (two-sided error) proof system in which the verifier just determines membership by itself. Thus, the issue is the existence of zero-knowledge proofs for sets outside $\mathcal{BPP}$.

The prover sends (V_2, E) *to the verifier.*

- Motivating Remark: *If the input graphs are isomorphic, as the prover claims, then the graph sent in Step P1 is isomorphic to both input graphs. However, if the input graphs are* not *isomorphic then no graph can be isomorphic to both of them.*

- Verifier's first Step (V1): *Upon receiving a graph, $G' = (V', E')$, from the prover, the verifier asks the prover to show an isomorphism between G' and one of the input graphs, chosen at random by the verifier. Namely, the verifier uniformly selects $\sigma \in \{1, 2\}$, and sends it to the prover (who is supposed to answer with an isomorphism between G_σ and G').*

- Prover's second Step (P2): *If the message, σ, received from the verifier equals 2 then the prover sends π to the verifier. Otherwise (i.e., $\sigma \neq 2$), the prover sends $\pi \circ \phi$ (i.e., the composition of π on ϕ, defined as $\pi \circ \phi(v) \stackrel{\text{def}}{=} \pi(\phi(v))$) to the verifier.*

  (Indeed, the prover treats any $\sigma \neq 2$ as $\sigma = 1$. Thus, in the analysis we shall assume, without loss of generality, that $\sigma \in \{1, 2\}$ always holds.)

- Verifier's second Step (V2): *If the message, denoted ψ, received from the prover is an isomorphism between G_σ and G' then the verifier outputs 1, otherwise it outputs 0.*

The verifier strategy in Construction 9.9 is easily implemented in probabilistic polynomial time. If the prover is given an isomorphism between the input graphs as auxiliary input, then also the prover's program can be implemented in probabilistic polynomial time. The motivating remark justifies the claim that Construction 9.9 constitutes an interactive proof system for the set of pairs of isomorphic graphs. Thus, we focus on establishing the zero-knowledge property.

We consider first the special case in which the verifier actually follows the prescribed strategy (and selects σ at random, and in particular obliviously of the graph G' it receives). The view of this verifier can be easily simulated by selecting σ and ψ at random, constructing G' as a random isomorphic copy of G_σ (via the isomorphism ψ), and outputting the triple (G', σ, ψ). Indeed (even in this case), the simulator behaves differently from the prescribed prover (which selects G' as a random isomorphic copy of G_2, via the isomorphism π), but its output distribution is identical to the verifier's view in the real interaction. However, the foregoing description assumes that the verifier follows the prescribed strategy, while in general the verifier may (adversarially) select σ depending on the graph G'. Thus, a slightly more complicated simulation (described next) is required.

A general clarification may be in place. Recall that we wish to simulate the interaction of an arbitrary verifier strategy with the prescribed prover. Thus, this simulator must depend on the corresponding verifier strategy, and indeed we shall describe the simulator while referring to such a generic verifier strategy. Formally, this means that the simulator's program incorporates the program of the corresponding verifier strategy. Actually, the following simulator uses the generic verifier strategy as a subroutine.

Turning back to the specific protocol of Construction 9.9, the basic idea is that the simulator tries to guess σ and completes a simulation if its guess turns out to be correct. Specifically, the simulator selects $\tau \in \{1, 2\}$ uniformly (hoping that the verifier will later select $\sigma = \tau$), and constructs G' by randomly permuting G_τ (and thus being able to present an isomorphism between G_τ and G'). Recall that the simulator is analyzed only on yes-instances (i.e., the input graphs G_1 and G_2 are isomorphic). The point is that if G_1 and G_2 are isomorphic, then the graph G' does not yield any information regarding the simulator's guess (i.e., τ).[20] Thus, the value σ selected by the adversarial verifier may depend on G' but not on τ, which implies that $\Pr[\sigma = \tau] = 1/2$. In other words, the simulator's guess (i.e., τ) is correct (i.e., equals σ) with probability $1/2$. Now, if the guess is correct then the simulator can produce an output that has the correct distribution, and otherwise the entire process is repeated.

Digest: A few useful conventions. We highlight three conventions that were either used (implicitly) in the foregoing analysis or can be used to simplify the description of (this and/or) other zero-knowledge simulators.

1. Without loss of generality, we may assume that the cheating verifier strategy is implemented by a *deterministic* polynomial-size circuit (or, equivalently, by a deterministic polynomial-time algorithm with an auxiliary input).[21]

   This is justified by fixing any outcome of the verifier's coins, and observing that our ("uniform") simulation of the various (residual) deterministic strategies yields a simulation of the original probabilistic strategy. Indeed, this justification relies on the fact that the simulation refers to verifiers with arbitrary auxiliary inputs (of polynomial length).

2. Without loss of generality, it suffices to consider cheating verifiers that (only) output their view of the interaction (i.e., the common input, their internal coin tosses, and the messages that they have received). In other words, it suffices to simulate the view that cheating verifiers have of the real interaction.

   This is justified by noting that the final output of any verifier can be obtained from its view of the interaction, where the complexity of the transformation is upper-bounded by the complexity of the verifier's strategy.

3. Without loss of generality, it suffices to construct a "weak simulator" that produces output with some noticeable[22] probability such that whenever an output is produced it is distributed "correctly" (i.e., similarly to the distribution occuring in real interactions with the prescribed prover).

   This is justified by repeatedly invoking such a weak simulator (polynomially) many times and using the first output produced by any of these invocations. Note that by using an adequate number of invocations, we fail to produce an output with negligible probability. Furthermore, note that a simulator that fails to produce output with negligible probability can be converted to a simulator that always produces an output, while incurring a negligible statistic deviation in the output distribution.

9.2.2.2. The Full Power of Zero-Knowledge Proofs

The zero-knowledge proof system presented in Construction 9.9 refers to one specific NP-set that is not known to be in $\mathcal{BPP}$. It turns out that, under reasonable assumptions,

---

[20] Indeed, this observation is identical to the observation made in the analysis of the soundness of Construction 9.3.

[21] This observation is not crucial, but it does simplify the analysis (by eliminating the need to specify a sequence of coin tosses in each invocation of the verifier's strategy).

[22] Recall that a probability is called noticeable if it is greater than the reciprocal of some positive polynomial (in the relevant parameter).

zero-knowledge can be used to prove membership in *any* NP-set. Intuitively, it suffices to establish this fact for a single NP-complete set, and thus we focus on presenting a zero-knowledge proof system for the set of 3-colorable graphs.

It is easy to prove that a given graph G is 3-colorable by just presenting a 3-coloring of G (and the same holds for membership in any set in $\mathcal{NP}$), but this NP-proof is not a zero-knowledge proof (unless $\mathcal{NP} \subseteq \mathcal{BPP}$). In fact, assuming $\mathcal{NP} \not\subseteq \mathcal{BPP}$, graph 3-colorability has no zero-knowledge NP-proof system. Still, as we shall shortly see, graph 3-colorability does have a zero-knowledge interactive proof system. This proof system will be described while referring to "boxes" in which information can be hidden and later revealed. Such boxes can be implemented using one-way functions (see, e.g., Theorem 9.11).

Construction 9.10 (Zero-knowledge proof of 3-colorability, abstract description):
The description refers to abstract non-transparent boxes that can be perfectly locked and unlocked such that these boxes perfectly hide their contents while being locked.

- Common Input: *A simple graph $G = (V, E)$.*
- Prover's first step: *Let ψ be a 3-coloring of G. The prover selects a random permutation, π, over $\{1, 2, 3\}$, and sets $\phi(v) \stackrel{\text{def}}{=} \pi(\psi(v))$, for each $v \in V$. Hence, the prover forms a random relabeling of the 3-coloring ψ. The prover sends to the verifier a sequence of $|V|$ locked and non-transparent boxes such that the vth box contains the value $\phi(v)$.*
- Verifier's first step: *The verifier uniformly selects an edge $\{u, v\} \in E$, and sends it to the prover.*
- Motivating Remark: *The boxes are supposed to contain a 3-coloring of the graph, and the verifier asks to inspect the colors of vertices u and v. Indeed, for the zero-knowledge condition, it is crucial that the prover only responds to pairs that correspond to edges of the graph.*
- Prover's second step: *Upon receiving an edge $\{u, v\} \in E$, the prover sends to the verifier the keys to boxes u and v.*

  For simplicity of the analysis, if the verifier sends $\{u, v\} \notin E$ then the prover behaves as if it has received a fixed (or random) edge in E, rather than suspending the interaction, which would have been the natural thing to do.

- Verifier's second step: *The verifier unlocks and opens boxes u and v, and accepts if and only if they contain two different elements in $\{1, 2, 3\}$.*

The verifier strategy in Construction 9.10 is easily implemented in probabilistic polynomial time. The same holds with respect to the prover's strategy, provided that it is given a 3-coloring of G as auxiliary input. Clearly, if the input graph is 3-colorable then the verifier accepts with probability 1 when interacting with the prescribed prover. On the other hand, if the input graph is not 3-colorable, then any contents put in the boxes must be invalid with respect to at least one edge, and consequently the verifier will reject with probability at least $\frac{1}{|E|}$. Hence, the foregoing protocol exhibits a non-negligible gap in the accepting probabilities between the case of 3-colorable graphs and the case of non-3-colorable graphs. To increase the gap, the protocol may be repeated sufficiently many times (of course, using independent coin tosses in each repetition).

So far we showed that Construction 9.10 constitutes (a weak form of) an interactive proof system for Graph 3-Colorability. The point, however, is that the prescribed prover strategy is zero-knowledge. This is easy to see in the abstract setting of Construction 9.10, because all that the verifier sees in the real interaction is a sequence of boxes and a random pair of *different* colors (which is easy to simulate). Indeed, the simulation of the real interaction proceeds by presenting a sequence of boxes and providing a random pair of different colors as the contents of the two boxes indicated by the verifier. Note that the foregoing argument relies on the fact that the boxes (indicated by the verifier) correspond to vertices that are connected by an edge in the graph.

This simple demonstration of the zero-knowledge property is not possible in the digital implementation (discussed next), because in that case the boxes are not totally unaffected by their contents (but are rather affected, yet in an indistinguishable manner). Thus, the verifier's selection of the inspected edge may depend on the "outside appearance" of the various boxes, which in turn may depend (in an indistinguishable manner) on the contents of these boxes. Consequently, we cannot determine the boxes' contents after a pair of boxes are selected, and so the simple foregoing simulation is inapplicable. Instead, we simulate the interaction as follows.

1. We first guess (at random) which pair of boxes (corresponding to an edge) the verifier would ask to open, and place a random pair of distinct colors in these boxes (and garbage in the rest).[23] Then, we hand all boxes to the verifier, which asks us to open a pair of boxes (corresponding to an edge).

2. If the verifier asks for the pair that we chose (i.e., our guess is successful), then we can complete the simulation by opening these boxes. Otherwise, we try again (i.e., repeat Step 1 with a new random guess and random colors). The key observation is that if the boxes hide the contents in the sense that the boxes' contents are indistinguishable based on their outside appearance, then our guess will succeed with probability approximately $1/|E|$. Furthermore, in this case, the simulated execution will be indistinguishable from the real interaction.

Thus, it suffices to use boxes that hide their contents almost perfectly (rather than being perfectly opaque). Such boxes can be implemented digitally.

Teaching note: Indeed, we recommend presenting and analyzing in class only the foregoing abstract protocol. It suffices to briefly comment about the digital implementation, rather than presenting a formal proof of Theorem 9.11 (which can be found in [100] (or [91, Sec. 4.4])).

Digital implementation (overview). We implement the abstract boxes (referred to in Construction 9.10) by using adequately defined commitment schemes.

Loosely speaking, such a scheme is a two-phase game between a sender and a receiver such that after the first phase the sender is "committed" to a value and yet, at this stage, it is infeasible for the receiver to find out the committed value (i.e., the commitment is "hiding"). The committed value will be revealed to the receiver in the second phase, and it is guaranteed that the sender cannot reveal a value other than the one committed (i.e., the commitment is "binding"). Such commitment schemes can be implemented assuming the existence of one-way functions (as in Definition 7.3); see §C.4.3.1 in Appendix C.

---

[23] An alternative (and more efficient) simulation consists of putting random independent colors in the various boxes, hoping that the verifier asks for an edge that is properly colored. The latter event occurs with probability (approximately) $2/3$, provided that the boxes hide their contents (almost) perfectly.

Zero-knowledge proofs for other NP-sets. Using the fact that 3-colorability is NP-complete, one can derive (from Construction 9.10) zero-knowledge proof systems for any NP-set.[24] Furthermore, NP-witnesses can be efficiently transformed into polynomial-size circuits that implement the corresponding (prescribed zero-knowledge) prover strategies.

Theorem 9.11 (the ZK Theorem): *Assuming the existence of* (non-uniformly hard) *one-way functions, it holds that* $\mathcal{NP} \subseteq \mathcal{ZK}$. *Furthermore, every* $S \in \mathcal{NP}$ *has a* (computational) *zero-knowledge interactive proof system in which the prescribed prover strategy can be implemented in probabilistic polynomial time, provided that it is given as auxiliary-input an NP-witness for membership of the common input in* S.

The hypothesis of Theorem 9.11 (i.e., the existence of one-way functions) seems unavoidable, because the existence of zero-knowledge proofs for "hard on the average" problems implies the existence of one-way functions (and, likewise, the existence of zero-knowledge proofs for sets outside $\mathcal{BPP}$ implies the existence of "auxiliary-input one-way functions").

Theorem 9.11 has a dramatic effect on the design of cryptographic protocols (see Appendix C). In a different vein we mention that, under the same assumption, any interactive proof can be transformed into a zero-knowledge one. (This transformation, however, does not necessarily preserve the complexity of the prover.)

Theorem 9.12 (the ultimate ZK Theorem): *Assuming the existence of* (non-uniformly hard) *one-way functions, it holds that* $\mathcal{IP} = \mathcal{ZK}$.

Loosely speaking, Theorem 9.12 can be proved by recalling that $\mathcal{IP} = \mathcal{AM}(\texttt{poly})$ and modifying any public-coin protocol as follows: The modified prover sends commitments to its messages rather than the messages themselves, and once the original interaction is completed it proves (in zero-knowledge) that the corresponding transcript would have been accepted by the original verifier. Indeed, the latter assertion is of the "NP type," and thus the zero-knowledge proof system guaranteed in Theorem 9.11 can be invoked for proving it.

Reflection. The proof of Theorem 9.11 uses the fact that 3-colorability is NP-complete in order to obtain a zero-knowledge proof for any set in $\mathcal{NP}$ by using such a protocol for 3-colorability (i.e., Construction 9.10). Thus, an NP-completeness result is used here in a "positive" way, that is, in order to construct something rather than in order to derive a ("negative") hardness result (cf., Section 2.2.4).[25]

Perfect and Statistical Zero-Knowledge. The foregoing results, which refer to computational zero-knowledge proof systems, should be contrasted with the known results

---

[24]Actually, we should either rely on the fact that the standard Karp-reductions are invertible in polynomial time or on the fact that the 3-colorability protocol is actually zero-knowledge with respect to auxiliary inputs (as in Definition C.9).

[25]Historically, the proof of Theorem 9.11 was probably the first positive application of NP-completeness. Subsequent positive uses of completeness results have appeared in the context of interactive proofs (see the proof of Theorem 9.4), probabilistically checkable proofs (see the proof of Theorem 9.16), and the study of statistical zero-knowledge (cf. [227]).

regarding the complexity of statistical zero-knowledge proof systems: Statistical zero-knowledge proof systems exist only for sets in $\mathcal{IP}(2) \cap \text{co}\mathcal{IP}(2)$, and thus are unlikely to exist for all NP-sets. On the other hand, the class Statistical Zero-Knowledge is known to contain some seemingly hard problems, and turns out to have interesting complexity-theoretic properties (e.g., being closed under complementation, and having very natural complete problems). The interested reader is referred to [227].

9.2.3. Proofs of Knowledge – A Parenthetical Subsection

> **Teaching note:** Technically speaking, this topic belongs to Section 9.1, but its more interesting demonstrations refer to zero-knowledge proofs of knowledge – hence its current positioning.

Loosely speaking, "proofs of knowledge" are interactive proofs in which the prover asserts "knowledge" of some object (e.g., a 3-coloring of a graph), and not merely its existence (e.g., the existence of a 3-coloring of the graph, which in turn is equivalent to the assertion that the graph is 3-colorable). Note that the entity asserting knowledge is actually the prover's strategy, which is an automated computing device, hereafter referred to as a machine. This raises the question of what we mean by saying that a *machine knows something*.

9.2.3.1. Abstract Reflections
Any standard dictionary suggests several meanings for the verb to know, but these are typically phrased with reference to the notion of *awareness*, a notion that is certainly inapplicable in the context of machines. Instead, we should look for a *behavioristic* interpretation of the verb to know. Indeed, it is reasonable to link knowledge with the ability to do something (e.g., the ability to write down whatever one knows). Hence, we may say that a machine knows a string α if it *can* output the string α. But this seems as total non-sense, too: A machine has a well defined output – either the output equals α or it does not, so what can be meant by saying that *a machine can do something*?

Interestingly, a sound interpretation of the latter phrase does exist. Loosely speaking, by saying that *a machine can do something* we mean that the machine can be *easily modified* such that it (or rather its modified version) does whatever is claimed. More precisely, this means that there exists an *efficient* machine that, using the original machine as a black-box (or given its code as an input), outputs whatever is claimed.

Technically speaking, using a machine as a black-box seems more appealing when the said machine is interactive (i.e., implements an interactive strategy). Indeed, this will be our focus here. Furthermore, conceptually speaking, whatever a machine knows (or does not know) is its own business, whereas what can be of interest and reference *to the outside* is whatever can be deduced about the knowledge of a machine by interacting with it. Hence, we are interested in proofs of knowledge (rather than in mere knowledge).

9.2.3.2. A Concrete Treatment
For sake of simplicity let us consider a concrete question: *How can a machine prove that it knows a 3-coloring of a graph?* An obvious way is just sending the 3-coloring to

the verifier. Yet, we claim that applying the protocol in Construction 9.10 (i.e., the zero-knowledge proof system for 3-Colorability) is an alternative way of proving knowledge of a 3-coloring of the graph.

The definition of a *verifier of knowledge of 3-coloring* refers to any possible prover strategy and links the ability to "extract" a 3-coloring (of a given graph) from such a prover to the probability that this prover convinces the verifier. That is, the definition postulates the existence of an efficient universal way of "extracting" a 3-coloring of a given graph by using any prover strategy that convinces this verifier to accept this graph with probability 1 (or, more generally, with some noticeable probability). On the other hand, we should not expect this extractor to obtain much from prover strategies that fail to convince the verifier (or, more generally, convince it with negligible probability). A robust definition should allow a smooth transition between these two extremes (and in particular between provers that convince the verifier with noticeable probability and those that convince it with negligible probability). Such a definition should also support the intuition by which the following strategy of Alice is zero-knowledge: *Alice sends Bob a 3-coloring of a given graph provided that Bob has successfully convinced her that he knows this coloring.*[26] We stress that the zero-knowledge property of Alice's strategy should hold regardless of the proof-of-knowledge system used for proving Bob's knowledge of a 3-coloring.

Loosely speaking, we say that a strategy, V, constitutes a verifier for knowledge of 3-coloring if, for any prover strategy P, the complexity of extracting a 3-coloring of G when using P as a "black-box"[27] is inversely proportional to the probability that V is convinced by P (to accept the graph G). Namely, the extraction of the 3-coloring is done by an oracle machine, called an **extractor**, that is given access to the strategy P (i.e., the function specifying the message that P sends in response to any sequence of messages it may receive). We require that the (*expected*) *running time of the extractor, on input G and oracle access to P, be inversely related* (by a factor polynomial in $|G|$) *to the probability that P convinces V to accept G.* In particular, if P always convinces V to accept G, then the extractor runs in expected polynomial time. The same holds in case P convinces V to accept with noticeable probability. On the other hand, if P never convinces V to accept, then nothing is required of the extractor. We stress that the latter special cases do not suffice for a satisfactory definition; see discussion in [91, Sec. 4.7.1].

Proofs of knowledge, and in particular zero-knowledge proofs of knowledge, have many applications to the design of cryptographic schemes and cryptographic protocols (see, e.g., [91, 92]). These are enabled by the following general result.

Theorem 9.13 (Theorem 9.11, revisited): *Assuming the existence of* (non-uniformly hard) *one-way functions, any NP-relation has a zero-knowledge proof of knowledge* (of corresponding NP-witnesses). *Furthermore, the prescribed prover strategy can be implemented in probabilistic polynomial time, provided it is given such an NP-witness.*

---

[26] For simplicity, the reader may consider graphs that have a unique 3-coloring (up to a relabeling). In general, we refer here to instances that have unique solutions (cf. Section 6.2.3), which arise naturally in some (cryptographic) applications.

[27] Indeed, one may consider also non-black-box extractors.

proof (oracle)

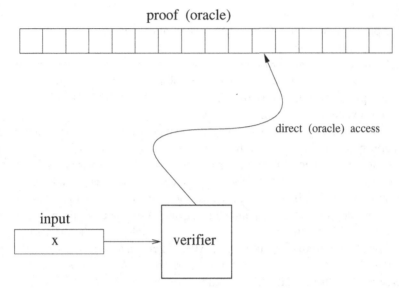

direct (oracle) access

input

x

verifier

Figure 9.3: The PCP model – an illustration.

9.3. Probabilistically Checkable Proof Systems

Teaching note: A probabilistically checkable proof (PCP) system may be viewed as a restricted type of interactive proof system in which the prover is memoryless and responds to each verifier message as if it were the first such message. This perspective creates a tighter link with previous sections, but is somewhat contrived. Indeed, such a memoryless prover may be viewed as a static object that the verifier may query at locations of its choice. But then it is more appealing to present the model using the (more traditional) terminology of oracle machines, rather than using (and degenerating) the terminology of interactive machines (or strategies).

Probabilistically checkable proof systems can be viewed as standard (deterministic) proof systems that are augmented with a probabilistic procedure capable of evaluating the validity of the assertion by examining few locations in the alleged proof. Actually, we focus on the latter probabilistic procedure, which in turn implies the existence of a deterministic verification procedure (obtained by going over all possible random choices of the probabilistic procedure and making the adequate examinations).

Modeling such probabilistic verification procedures, which may examine few locations in the alleged proof, requires providing these procedures with direct access to the individual bits of the alleged proof (so that they need not scan the proof bit by bit). Thus, the alleged proof is a string, as in the case of a traditional proof system, but the (probabilistic) verification procedure is given direct access to individual bits of this string (see Figure 9.3).

We are interested in *probabilistic verification procedures that access only few locations in the proof, and yet are able to make a meaningful probabilistic verdict regarding the validity of the alleged proof.* Specifically, the verification procedure should accept any valid proof (with probability 1), but reject with probability at least $1/2$ any alleged proof for a false assertion. Such probabilistic verification procedures are called probabilistically checkable proof (PCP) systems.

The fact that one can (meaningfully) evaluate the correctness of proofs by examining few locations in them is indeed amazing and somewhat counter-intuitive. Needless to say, such proofs must be written in a somewhat non-standard format, because standard proofs cannot be verified without reading them in full (since a flaw may be due to a single improper inference). In contrast, proofs for a PCP system tend to be very redundant; they consist of superfluously many pieces of information (about the claimed assertion), but their correctness can be (meaningfully) evaluated by *checking the consistency of a randomly chosen collection of few related pieces*. We stress that by a "meaningful evaluation" we mean rejecting alleged proofs of false assertions with constant probability (rather than with probability that is inversely proportional to the length of the alleged proof).

The main complexity measure associated with PCPs is indeed their query complexity. Another complexity measure of natural concern is the length of the proofs being employed, which in turn is related to the randomness complexity of the system. The randomness complexity of PCPs plays a key role in numerous applications (e.g., in composing PCP systems as well as when applying PCP systems to derive inapproximability results), and thus we specify this parameter rather than the proof length.

Teaching note: Indeed, PCP systems are most famous for their role in deriving numerous inapproximability results (see Section 9.3.3), but our view is that the latter is merely one extremely important application of the fundamental notion of a PCP system. Our presentation is organized accordingly.

9.3.1. Definition

Loosely speaking, a probabilistically checkable proof system consists of a probabilistic polynomial-time verifier having access to an oracle that represents an alleged proof (in redundant form). Typically, the verifier accesses only few of the oracle bits, and these bit positions are determined by the outcome of the verifier's coin tosses. As in the case of interactive proof systems, it is required that if the assertion holds then the verifier always accepts (i.e., when given access to an adequate oracle); whereas, if the assertion is false then the verifier must reject with probability at least $\frac{1}{2}$, no matter which oracle is used. The basic definition of the PCP setting is given in Part 1 of the following definition. Yet, the complexity measures introduced in Part 2 are of key importance for the subsequent discussions.

Definition 9.14 (probabilistically checkable proofs – PCP)**:**

1. *A* probabilistically checkable proof system (PCP) for a set S *is a probabilistic polynomial-time oracle machine, called* verifier *and denoted V, that satisfies the following two conditions:*
    *   Completeness: *For every $x \in S$ there exists an oracle π_x such that, on input x and access to oracle π_x, machine V always accepts x.*
    *   Soundness: *For every $x \notin S$ and every oracle π, on input x and access to oracle π, machine V rejects x with probability at least $\frac{1}{2}$.*
2. *We say that a probabilistically checkable proof system has* query complexity *$q : \mathbb{N} \to \mathbb{N}$ if, on any input of length n, the verifier makes at most $q(n)$ oracle*

---

queries.[28] *Similarly, the* randomness complexity $r : \mathbb{N} \to \mathbb{N}$ *upper-bounds the number of coin tosses performed by the verifier on a generic n-bit long input. For integer functions r and q, we denote by* $\mathcal{PCP}(r, q)$ *the class of sets having probabilistically checkable proof systems of randomness complexity r and query complexity q. For sets of integer functions, R and Q,*

$$\mathcal{PCP}(R, Q) \stackrel{\text{def}}{=} \bigcup_{r \in R, q \in Q} \mathcal{PCP}(r, q).$$

The error probability (in the soundness condition) of PCP systems can be reduced by successive applications of the proof system. In particular, repeating the process for k times reduces the probability that the verifier is fooled by a false assertion to 2^{-k}, whereas all complexities increase by at most a factor of k. Thus, PCP systems of non-trivial query complexity (cf. Section 9.3.2) provide a trade-off between the number of locations examined in the proof and the confidence in the validity of the assertion.

We note that the oracle π_x referred to in the completeness condition of a PCP system constitutes a proof in the standard mathematical sense. Indeed any PCP system yields a standard proof system (with respect to a verification procedure that scans all possible outcomes of V's internal coin tosses and emulates all the corresponding checks). Furthermore, the oracles in PCP systems of logarithmic randomness complexity constitute NP-proofs (see Exercise 9.15). However, the oracles of a PCP system have the *extra remarkable property* of enabling a lazy verifier to toss coins, take its chances, and "assess" the validity of the proof without reading all of it (but rather by reading a tiny portion of it). Potentially, this allows the verifier to examine very few bits of an NP-proof and even utilize very long proofs (i.e., of super-polynomial length).

Adaptive versus non-adaptive verifiers. Definition 9.14 allows the verifier to be adaptive; that is, the verifier may determine its queries based on the answers it has received to previous queries (in addition to their dependence on the input and on the verifier's internal coin tosses). In contrast, non-adaptive verifiers determine all their queries based solely on their input and internal coin tosses. Note that q adaptive (binary) queries can be emulated by $\sum_{i=1}^{q} 2^{i-1} < 2^q$ non-adaptive (binary) queries. We comment that most constructions of PCP systems use non-adaptive verifiers, and in fact in many sources PCP systems are defined as non-adaptive.

Randomness versus proof length. Fixing a verifier V, we say that location i (in the oracle) is relevant to input x if there exists a computation of V on input x in which location i is queried (i.e., there exists ω and π such that, on input x, randomness ω, and access to the oracle π, the verifier queries location i). The effective proof length of V is the smallest function $\ell : \mathbb{N} \to \mathbb{N}$ such that for every input x there are at most $\ell(|x|)$ locations (in the oracle) that are relevant to x. We claim that the effective proof length of any PCP system is closely related to its randomness (and query) complexity. On the one hand, *if the PCP system has randomness complexity r and query complexity q, then its effective proof length is upper-bounded by* 2^{r+q}, whereas a bound of $2^r \cdot q$ holds for non-adaptive systems (see Exercise 9.15). Thus, *PCP systems of logarithmic randomness complexity have effective proof length that is polynomial*, and hence yield NP-proof systems. On the other hand, in some sense, the randomness complexity of a PCP system can be

---

[28]As usual in Complexity Theory, the oracle answers are binary values (i.e., either 0 or 1).

upper-bounded by the logarithm of the (effective) length of the proofs employed (provided we allow non-uniform verifiers; see Exercise 9.16).

On the role of randomness. The PCP Theorem (i.e., $\mathcal{NP} \subseteq \mathcal{PCP}(\log, O(1))$) asserts that a meaningful probabilistic evaluation of proofs is possible based on a constant number of examined bits. We note that, unless $\mathcal{P} = \mathcal{NP}$, such a phenomenon is impossible when requiring the verifier to be deterministic. Firstly, note that $\mathcal{PCP}(0, O(1)) = \mathcal{P}$ holds (as a special case of $\mathcal{PCP}(r, q) \subseteq \text{DTIME}(2^{2^r q + r} \cdot \text{poly})$; see Exercise 9.17). Secondly, as shown in Exercise 9.19, $\mathcal{P} \neq \mathcal{NP}$ implies that $\mathcal{NP}$ is not contained in $\mathcal{PCP}(o(\log), o(\log))$. Lastly, assuming that not all NP-sets have NP-proof systems that employ proofs of length ℓ (e.g., $\ell(n) = n$), it follows that if $2^{r(n)} q(n) < \ell(n)$ then $\mathcal{PCP}(r, q)$ does not contain $\mathcal{NP}$ (see Exercise 9.17 again).

9.3.2. The Power of Probabilistically Checkable Proofs

The celebrated PCP Theorem asserts that $\mathcal{NP} = \mathcal{PCP}(\log, O(1))$, and this result is indeed the focus of the current section. But before getting to it we make several simple observations regarding the PCP hierarchy.

We first note that $\mathcal{PCP}(\text{poly}, 0)$ equals $\text{co}\mathcal{RP}$, whereas $\mathcal{PCP}(0, \text{poly})$ equals $\mathcal{NP}$. It is easy to prove an upper bound on the non-deterministic time complexity of sets in the PCP hierarchy (see Exercise 9.17):

Proposition 9.15 (upper bounds on the power of PCPs): *For every polynomially bounded integer function r, it holds that $\mathcal{PCP}(r, \text{poly}) \subseteq \text{NTIME}(2^r \cdot \text{poly})$. In particular, $\mathcal{PCP}(\log, \text{poly}) \subseteq \mathcal{NP}$.*

The focus on PCP systems of logarithmic randomness complexity reflects an interest in PCP systems that utilize proof oracles of polynomial length (see discussion in Section 9.3.1). We stress that such PCP systems (i.e., $\mathcal{PCP}(\log, q)$) are NP-proof systems with a (potentially amazing) extra property: The validity of the assertion can be "probabilistically evaluated" by examining a (small) portion (i.e., $q(n)$ bits) of the proof. Thus, for any fixed polynomially bounded function q, a result of the form

$$\mathcal{NP} \subseteq \mathcal{PCP}(\log, q) \tag{9.6}$$

is interesting (because it applies also to NP-sets having witnesses of length exceeding q). Needless to say, the smaller q – the better. The PCP Theorem asserts the amazing fact by which q can be made a constant.

Theorem 9.16 (the PCP Theorem): $\mathcal{NP} \subseteq \mathcal{PCP}(\log, O(1))$.

Thus, probabilistically checkable proofs in which the verifier tosses only logarithmically many coins and makes only a constant number of queries exist for every set in $\mathcal{NP}$. This constant is essentially three (see §9.3.4.1). Before reviewing the proof of Theorem 9.16, we make a couple of comments.

Efficient transformation of NP-witnesses to PCP oracles. The proof of Theorem 9.16 is constructive in the sense that it allows for efficiently transforming any NP-witness (for an instance of a set in $\mathcal{NP}$) into an oracle that makes the PCP verifier accept (with probability 1). That is, *for every* (NP-witness relation) $R \in \mathcal{PC}$ *there exists a PCP verifier V as in Theorem 9.16 and a polynomial-time computable function π such that for every $(x, y) \in R$ the verifier V always accepts the input x when given oracle access to the proof $\pi(x, y)$* (i.e., $\Pr[V^{\pi(x,y)}(x) = 1] = 1$). Recalling that the latter oracles are themselves NP-proofs, it follows that NP-proofs can be transformed into NP-proofs that offer a trade-off between the portion of the proof being read and the confidence it offers. Specifically, for every $\varepsilon > 0$, if one is willing to tolerate an error probability of ε then it suffices to examine $O(\log(1/\varepsilon))$ bits of the (transformed) NP-proof. Indeed (as discussed in Section 9.3.1), these bit locations need to be selected at random.

The foregoing strengthening of Theorem 9.16 offers a wider range of applications than Theorem 9.16 itself. Indeed, Theorem 9.16 itself suffices for "negative" applications such as establishing the infeasibility of certain approximation problems (see Section 9.3.3). But for "positive" applications (see §9.3.4.2), typically some user (or a real entity) will be required to actually construct the PCP-oracle, and in such cases the strengthening of Theorem 9.16 will be useful.

A characterization of NP. Combining Theorem 9.16 with Proposition 9.15 we obtain the following characterization of $\mathcal{NP}$.

Corollary 9.17 (the PCP characterization of NP): $\mathcal{NP} = \mathcal{PCP}(\log, O(1))$.

Road map for the proof of the PCP Theorem. Theorem 9.16 is a culmination of a sequence of remarkable works, each establishing meaningful and increasingly stronger versions of Eq. (9.6). A presentation of the full proof of Theorem 9.16 is beyond the scope of the current work (and is, in our opinion, unsuitable for a basic course in Complexity Theory). Instead, we present an overview of the original proof (see §9.3.2.2) as well as of an alternative proof (see §9.3.2.3), which was found more than a decade later. We will start, however, by presenting a weaker result that is used in both proofs of Theorem 9.16 and is also of independent interest. This weaker result (see §9.3.2.1) asserts that *every NP-set has a PCP system with constant query complexity* (albeit with polynomial randomness complexity); that is, $\mathcal{NP} \subseteq \mathcal{PCP}(\text{poly}, O(1))$.

Teaching note: In our opinion, presenting in class any part of the proof of the PCP Theorem should be given low priority. In particular, presenting the connections between PCP and the complexity of approximation should be given a higher priority. As for relative priorities among the following three subsections, we strongly recommend giving §9.3.2.1 the highest priority, because it offers a direct demonstration of the power of PCPs. As for the two alternative proofs of the PCP Theorem itself, our recommendation depends on the intended goal. On the one hand, for the purpose of merely giving a taste of the ideas involved in the proof, we prefer an overview of the original proof (provided in §9.3.2.2). On the other hand, for the purpose of actually providing a full proof, we definitely prefer the new proof (which is only outlined in §9.3.2.3).

9.3.2.1. Proving That $\mathcal{NP} \subseteq \mathcal{PCP}(\text{poly}, O(1))$

The fact that every NP-set has a PCP system with constant query complexity (regardless of its randomness complexity) already testifies to the power of PCP systems. It asserts that *probabilistic verification of proofs is possible by inspecting very few locations in a* (potentially huge) *proof.* Indeed, the PCP systems presented next utilize exponentially long proofs, but they do so while inspecting these proofs at a constant number of (randomly selected) locations.

We start with a brief overview of the construction. We first note that it suffices to construct a PCP for proving the satisfiability of a given system of quadratic equations over GF(2), because this problem is NP-complete (see Exercise 2.25).[29] For an input consisting of a system of quadratic equations with n variables, the oracle (of this PCP) is supposed to provide the evaluation of all quadratic expressions (in these n variables) at some fixed assignment to these variables. This assignment is supposed to satisfy the system of quadratic equations that is given as input. We distinguish two tables in the oracle: the first table corresponding to all 2^n linear expressions and the second table to all 2^{n^2} quadratic expressions. Each table is tested for self-consistency (via a "linearity test"), and the two tables are tested to be consistent with each other (via a "matrix-equality" test, which utilizes "self-correction"). Finally, we test that the assignment encoded in these tables satisfies the quadratic system that is given as input. This is done by taking a random linear combination of the quadratic equations that appear in the quadratic system, and obtaining the value assigned to the corresponding quadratic expression by the aforementioned tables (again, via self-correction). The key point is that each of the foregoing tests utilizes a constant number of Boolean queries, and has time (and randomness) complexity that is polynomial in the size of the input. Details follow.

> **Teaching note:** The following text refers to notions such as the Hadamard encoding, testing, and self-correction, which appear in other parts of this work (see, e.g., §E.1.2.2 in Appendix E, Section 10.1.2. and §7.2.1.1, respectively). While a wider perspective (provided in the aforementioned parts) is always useful, the current text is self-contained.

The starting point. We construct a PCP system for the set of satisfiable quadratic equations over GF(2). The input is a sequence of such equations over the variables $x_1, \ldots, x_n$, and the proof oracle consists of two parts (or tables), which are supposed to provide information regarding some satisfying assignment $\tau = \tau_1 \cdots \tau_n$ (also viewed as an n-ary vector over GF(2)). The first part, denoted T_1, is supposed to provide a Hadamard encoding of the said satisfying assignment; that is, for every $\alpha \in$ GF(2)^n this table is supposed to provide the inner product mod 2 of the n-ary vectors α and τ (i.e., $T_1(\alpha)$ is supposed to equal $\sum_{i=1}^{n} \alpha_i \tau_i$). The second part, denoted T_2, is supposed to provide all linear combinations of the values of the $\tau_i \tau_j$'s; that is, for every $\beta \in$ GF(2)$^{n^2}$ (viewed as an n-by-n matrix over GF(2)), the value of $T_2(\beta)$ is supposed to equal $\sum_{i,j} \beta_{i,j} \tau_i \tau_j$. (Indeed, T_1 is contained in T_2, because $\sigma^2 = \sigma$ for any $\sigma \in$ GF(2).) The PCP verifier will use the two tables for checking that the input (i.e., a sequence of quadratic equations) is satisfied by the assignment that is encoded in the two tables. Needless to say, these tables may not be a valid encoding of any n-ary vector (let alone one that satisfies the input), and so the verifier also needs to check that the encoding is (close to being) valid. We will focus on this task first.

Testing the Hadamard code. Note that T_1 is supposed to encode a linear function; that is, there must exist some $\tau = \tau_1 \cdots \tau_n \in$ GF(2)^n such that $T_1(\alpha) = \sum_{i=1}^{n} \tau_i \alpha_i$ holds for

---

[29]Here and elsewhere, we denote by GF(2) the 2-element field.

every $\alpha = \alpha_1 \cdots \alpha_n \in GF(2)^n$. This can be tested by selecting uniformly $\alpha', \alpha'' \in GF(2)^n$ and checking whether $T_1(\alpha') + T_1(\alpha'') = T_1(\alpha' + \alpha'')$, where $\alpha' + \alpha''$ denotes addition of vectors over $GF(2)$. The analysis of this natural tester turns out to be quite complex. Nevertheless, it is indeed the case that any table that is 0.02-far from being linear is rejected with probability at least 0.01 (see Exercise 9.20), where T is ε-far from being linear if T disagrees with any linear function f on more than an ε fraction of the domain (i.e., $\Pr_r[T(r) \neq f(r)] > \varepsilon$).

By repeating the linearity test for a constant number of times, we may reject each table that is 0.02-far from being a codeword of the Hadamard code with probability at least 0.99. Thus, using a constant number of queries, the verifier rejects any T_1 that is 0.02-far from being a Hadamard encoding of any $\tau \in GF(2)^n$, and likewise rejects any T_2 that is 0.02-far from being a Hadamard encoding of any $\tau' \in GF(2)^{n^2}$. We may thus assume that T_1 (resp., T_2) is 0.02-close to the Hadamard encoding of some τ (resp., τ').[30] (Needless to say, this does *not* mean that τ' equals the outer product of τ with itself (i.e., $\tau'_{i,j}$ does not necessarily equal $\tau_i \tau_j$).)

In the rest of the analysis, we fix $\tau \in GF(2)^n$ and $\tau' \in GF(2)^{n^2}$, and denote the Hadamard encoding of τ (resp., τ') by $f_\tau : GF(2)^n \to GF(2)$ (resp., $f_{\tau'} : GF(2)^{n^2} \to GF(2)$). Recall that T_1 (resp., T_2) is 0.02-close to f_τ (resp., $f_{\tau'}$).

Self-correction of the Hadamard code. Suppose that T is ε-close to a linear function $f : GF(2)^m \to GF(2)$ (i.e., $\Pr_r[T(r) \neq f(r)] \leq \varepsilon$). Then, we can recover the value of f at any desired point x, by making two (random) queries to T. Specifically, for a uniformly selected $r \in GF(2)^m$, we use the value $T(x + r) - T(r)$. Note that the probability that we recover the correct value is at least $1 - 2\varepsilon$, because $\Pr_r[T(x + r) - T(r) = f(x + r) - f(r)] \geq 1 - 2\varepsilon$ and $f(x + r) - f(r) = f(x)$ by linearity of f. (Needless to say, for $\varepsilon < 1/4$, the function T cannot be ε-close to two different linear functions.)[31] Thus, assuming that T_1 is 0.02-close to f_τ (resp., T_2 is 0.02-close to $f_{\tau'}$), we may correctly recover (i.e., with error probability 0.04) the value of f_τ (resp., $f_{\tau'}$) at any desired point by making 2 queries to T_1 (resp., T_2). This process is called self-correction (cf., e.g., §7.2.1.1).

Checking consistency of f_τ and $f_{\tau'}$. Suppose that we are given access to $f_\tau : GF(2)^n \to GF(2)$ and $f_{\tau'} : GF(2)^{n^2} \to GF(2)$, where $f_\tau(\alpha) = \sum_i \tau_i \alpha_i$ and $f_{\tau'}(\alpha') = \sum_{i,j} \tau'_{i,j} \alpha'_{i,j}$, and that we wish to verify that $\tau'_{i,j} = \tau_i \tau_j$ for every $i, j \in \{1, \ldots, n\}$. In other words, we are given a (somewhat weird) encoding of two matrices, $A = (\tau_i \tau_j)_{i,j}$ and $A' = (\tau'_{i,j})_{i,j}$, and we wish to check whether or not these matrices are identical. It can be shown (see Exercise 9.22) that if $A \neq A'$ then $\Pr_{r,s}[r^\top A s \neq r^\top A's] \geq 1/4$, where r and s are uniformly distributed n-ary vectors. Note that, in our case (where $A = (\tau_i \tau_j)_{i,j}$ and $A' = (\tau'_{i,j})_{i,j}$), it holds that $r^\top A s = \sum_j (\sum_i r_i \tau_i \tau_j) s_j = f_\tau(r) f_\tau(s)$ (see Figure 9.4) and $r^\top A' s = \sum_j (\sum_i r_i \tau'_{i,j}) s_j = f_{\tau'}(rs^\top)$, where $rs^\top$ is the outer-product of s and r. Thus, (for $(\tau_i \tau_j)_{i,j} \neq (\tau'_{i,j})_{i,j}$) we have $\Pr_{r,s}[f_\tau(r) f_\tau(s) \neq f_{\tau'}(rs^\top)] \geq 1/4$.

Recall, however, that we do not have direct access to the functions f_τ and $f_{\tau'}$, but rather to tables (i.e., T_1 and T_2) that are 0.02-close to these functions. Still, using

---

[30]Note that τ (resp., τ') is uniquely determined by T_1 (resp., T_2), because every two different linear functions $GF(2)^m \to GF(2)$ agree on exactly half of the domain (i.e., the Hadamard code has relative distance 1/2).

[31]Indeed, this fact follows from the self-correction argument, but a simpler proof merely refers to the fact that the Hadamard code has relative distance 1/2.

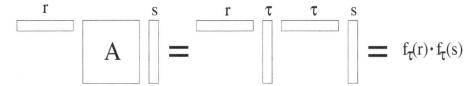

Figure 9.4: Detail for testing consistency of linear and quadratic forms.

self-correction, we can obtain the values of f_τ and $f_{\tau'}$ at any desired point, with very high probability. Actually, when implementing the foregoing consistency test it suffices to use self-correction only for $f_{\tau'}$, because we use the values of f_τ at two independently and uniformly distributed points in $GF(2)^n$ (i.e., r and s), whereas the value $f_{\tau'}$ is required at $rs^\top$, which is not uniformly distributed in $GF(2)^{n^2}$. Thus, we test the consistency of f_τ and $f_{\tau'}$ by selecting uniformly $r, s \in GF(2)^n$ and $R \in GF(2)^{n^2}$, and checking that $T_1(r)T_1(s) = T_2(rs^\top + R) - T_2(R)$.

By repeating the aforementioned (self-corrected) consistency test for a constant number of times, we may reject an inconsistent pair of tables with probability at least 0.99. Thus, in the rest of the analysis, we may assume that $(\tau_i \tau_j)_{i,j} = (\tau'_{i,j})_{i,j}$.

Checking that τ satisfies the quadratic system. Suppose that we are given access to f_τ and $f_{\tau'}$ as in the foregoing (where, in particular, $\tau' = \tau\tau^\top$). A key observation is that if τ does not satisfy a system of (quadratic) equations then, with probability $1/2$, it does not satisfy a random linear combination of these equations. Thus, in order to check whether τ satisfies the quadratic system (which is given as input), we create a single quadratic equation by taking such a random linear combination, and check whether this quadratic equation is satisfied by τ. The punch line is that *testing whether τ satisfies the quadratic equation $Q(x) = \sigma$ amounts to testing whether $f_{\tau'}(Q) = \sigma$.* Again, the actual checking is implemented by using self-correction (of the table T_2).

This completes the description of the verifier. Note that this verifier performs a constant number of codeword tests for the Hadamard code, and a constant number of consistency and satisfiability tests, where each of the latter involves self-correction of the Hadamard code. Each of the individual tests utilizes a constant number of queries (ranging between two and four) and uses randomness that is quadratic in the number of variables (and linear in the number of equations in the input). Thus, the query complexity is a constant and the randomness complexity is at most quadratic in the length of the input (quadratic system). Clearly, if the input quadratic system is satisfiable (by some τ), then the verifier accepts the corresponding tables T_1 and T_2 (i.e., $T_1 = f_\tau$ and $T_2 = f_{\tau\tau^\top}$) with probability 1. On the other hand, if the input quadratic system is unsatisfiable, then any pair of tables (T_1, T_2) will be rejected with constant probability (by one of the foregoing tests). It follows that $\mathcal{NP} \subseteq \mathcal{PCP}(q, O(1))$, where q is a quadratic polynomial.

Reflection. Indeed, the actual test of the satisfiability of the quadratic system that is given as input is facilitated by the fact that a satisfying assignment is encoded (in the oracle) in a very redundant manner, which fits the final test of satisfiability. But then the burden of testing moves to checking that this encoding is indeed valid. In fact, most of the tests performed by the foregoing verifier are aimed at verifying the validity of the encoding. Such a test of validity (of encoding) may be viewed as a test of consistency between the various parts of the encoding. All these themes are present also in more advanced constructions of PCP systems.

9.3.2.2. Overview of the First Proof of the PCP Theorem

The original proof of the PCP Theorem (Theorem 9.16) consists of three main conceptual steps, *which we briefly sketch first and further discuss later.*

Step 1: Constructing a (non-adaptive) PCP system for $\mathcal{NP}$ having *logarithmic randomness and poly-logarithmic query complexity*; that is, this PCP has the desired randomness complexity and a very low (but non-constant) query complexity. Furthermore, this proof system has additional properties that enable proof composition as in the following Step 3.

Step 2: Constructing a PCP system for $\mathcal{NP}$ having *polynomial randomness and constant query complexity*; that is, this PCP has the desired (constant) query complexity but its randomness complexity is prohibitingly high. (Indeed, we showed such a construction in §9.3.2.1.) Furthermore, this proof system too has additional properties enabling proof composition as in Step 3.

Step 3: The proof composition paradigm:[32] In general, this paradigm allows for composing two proof systems such that the "inner" verifier is used for probabilistically verifying the acceptance criteria of the "outer" verifier. That is, the combined verifier selects coins for the "outer" verifier, determines the corresponding locations that the "outer" verifier wishes to inspect (in the proof), and verifies that the "outer" verifier would have accepted the values that reside in these locations. The latter verification is performed by invoking the "inner" verifier, *without reading the values residing in all the aforementioned locations.* Indeed, the aim is to conduct this ("composed") verification while using significantly fewer queries than the query complexity of the "outer" proof system. In particular, the inner verifier cannot afford to read its input, which makes the composition more subtle than the term suggests.

Loosely speaking, the *outer* verifier should be robust in the sense that its soundness condition guarantees that, with high probability, the oracle answers are "far" from satisfying the residual decision predicate (rather than merely not satisfying it). (Furthermore, the latter predicate, which is well defined by the non-adaptive nature of the outer verifier, must have a circuit of size bounded by a polynomial in the number of queries.) The *inner* verifier is given oracle access to its input and is charged for each query made to it, but is only required to reject (with high probability) inputs that are far from being valid (and, as usual, to accept inputs that are valid). That is, the inner verifier is actually a verifier of proximity.

Composing two such PCPs yields a new PCP for $\mathcal{NP}$, where the new proof oracle consists of the proof oracle of the "outer" system and a sequence of proof oracles for the "inner" system (one "inner" proof per each possible random-tape of the "outer" verifier). The resulting verifier selects coins for the outer-verifier and uses the corresponding "inner" proof in order to verify that the outer-verifier would have accepted under this choice of coins. Note that such a choice of coins determines locations in the "outer" proof that the outer-verifier would have inspected, and the combined verifier provides the inner-verifier with oracle access to these locations (which the inner-verifier considers as its input) as well as with oracle access to the

---

[32]Our presentation of the composition paradigm follows [35], rather than the original presentation of [16, 15].

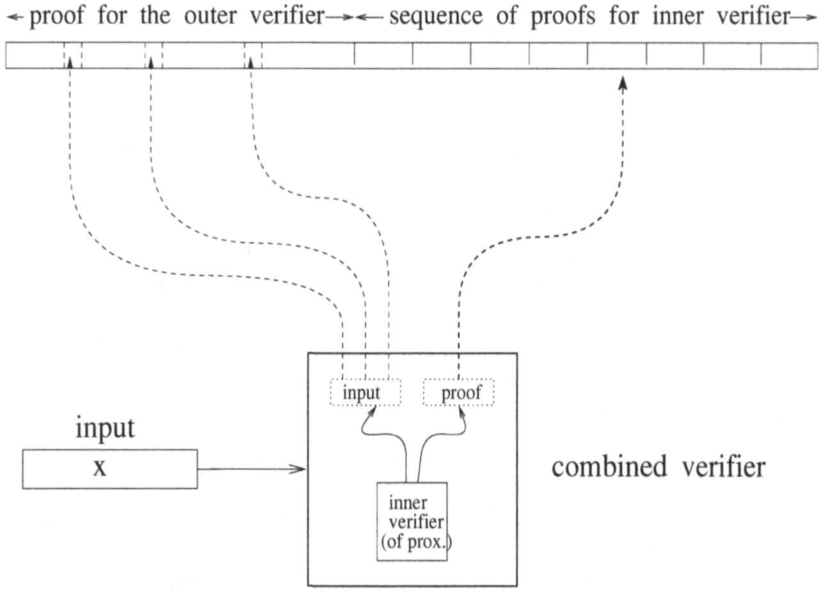

Figure 9.5: Composition of PCP system – an illustration. The dashed arrows indicate pointers from the (virtual) input and proof oracles of the inner-verifier to the actual proof of the composed verifier. These pointers (as well as the residual predicate) are determined by an invocation of the outer-verifier.

corresponding "inner" proof (which the inner-verifier considers as its proof-oracle). See Figure 9.5 (and further details that follow the current sketch).

Note that composing an outer-verifier of randomness complexity r' and query complexity q' with an inner-verifier of randomness complexity r'' and query complexity q'' yields a PCP of randomness complexity $r(n) = r'(n) + r''(q'(n))$ and query complexity $q(n) = q''(q'(n))$, because $q'(n)$ represents the length of the input (oracle) that is accessed by the inner-verifier. Recall that the outer-verifier is non-adaptive, and thus if the inner-verifier is non-adaptive (resp., robust) then so is the verifier resulting from the composition, which is important in case we wish to compose the latter verifier with another inner-verifier.

In particular, the proof system of Step 1 is composed with itself [using $r'(n) = r''(n) = O(\log n)$ and $q'(n) = q''(n) = \text{poly}(\log n)$] yielding a PCP system (for $\mathcal{NP}$) of randomness complexity $r(n) = r'(n) + r''(q'(n)) = O(\log n)$ and query complexity $q(n) = q''(q'(n)) = \text{poly}(\log \log n)$. Composing the latter system (used as an "outer" system) with the PCP system of Step 2, yields a PCP system (for $\mathcal{NP}$) of randomness complexity $r(n) + \text{poly}(q(n)) = O(\log n)$ and query complexity $O(1)$, thus establishing the PCP Theorem.

A more detailed overview – the plan. The foregoing description uses two (non-trivial) PCP systems and refers to additional properties such as robustness and verification of proximity. A PCP system of polynomial randomness complexity and constant query complexity (as postulated in Step 2) was already presented in §9.3.2.1. We thus start by discussing the notions of verifying proximity and being robust, while demonstrating their applicability to the said PCP. Next, we detail the composition of an "outer" robust PCP with an "inner" PCP of proximity. Finally, we outline the other PCP system that is used (i.e., the one postulated in Step 1).

PCPs of Proximity. Recall that a standard PCP verifier gets an explicit input and is given oracle access to an alleged proof (for membership of the input in a predetermined set). In contrast, a PCP of proximity verifier is given (direct) *access to two oracles, one representing an input and the other being an alleged proof, and its queries to both oracles are counted in its query complexity*. Typically, the query complexity of this verifier is lower than the length of the input-oracle, and hence this verifier cannot afford reading the entire input and cannot be expected to make absolute statements about it. Indeed, instead of deciding whether or not the input is in a predetermined set, the verifier is only required to distinguish the case that the input is in the set from the case that the input is *far* from the set (where far means being at *relative* Hamming distance at least 0.01 (or any other small constant)).

For example, consider a variant of the system of §9.3.2.1 in which the quadratic system is fixed[33] and the verifier needs to determine whether the assignment appearing in the input-oracle satisfies the said system or is far from any assignment that satisfies it. We use a proof-oracle as in §9.3.2.1, and a PCP verifier of proximity that proceeds as in §9.3.2.1, and in addition perform a proximity test to verify that the input-oracle is close to the assignment encoded in the proof-oracle. Specifically, the verifier reads a uniformly selected bit of the input-oracle and compares this value to the self-corrected value obtained from the proof-oracle (i.e., for a uniformly selected $i \in \{1, \ldots, n\}$, we compare the ith bit of the input-oracle to the self-correction of the value $T_1(0^{i-1}10^{n-i})$, obtained from the proof oracle).

Robust PCPs. Composing an "outer" PCP verifier with an "inner" PCP verifier of proximity makes sense provided that the *outer* verifier rejects in a "robust" manner. Hence, the soundness condition of a robust verifier requires that (with probability at least $1/2$) the oracle answers are *far* from any sequence that is acceptable by the residual predicate (rather than merely that the answers are rejected by this predicate). That is, for every no-instance x and every alleged proof $\pi = \pi_1 \pi_2 \cdots \pi_\ell \in \{0, 1\}^\ell$, it is required that, with probability at least $1/2$ over the verifier's choice of coins $\omega \in \{0, 1\}^r$, it holds that $\pi_{i_{\omega,1}} \pi_{i_{\omega,2}} \cdots \pi_{i_{\omega,q}}$ is far from any assignment that satisfies P_ω, where $i_{\omega,j}$ is the jth query made (non-adaptively) on coins ω, and P_ω is the residual predicate that determines which sequences of answers are accepted in this case. Indeed, if the outer verifier is robust, then it suffices to distinguish answers that are valid from answers that are far from being valid.

For example, if robustness is defined as referring to *relative constant distance* (which is indeed the case), then the PCP of §9.3.2.1 (as well as any PCP of constant query complexity) is trivially robust. However, we will not care about the robustness of this PCP, because we only use this PCP as an inner verifier in proof composition. In contrast, we will care about the robustness of PCPs that are used as outer verifiers (e.g., the PCP postulated in Step 1 and outlined shortly).

A closer look at proof composition. Following the foregoing sketch, we further detail the proof composition operation that is employed in the current subsection (i.e., §9.3.2.2).

---

[33] Indeed, in our applications the quadratic system will be "known" to the ("inner") verifier, because it is determined by the ("outer") verifier.

We start by detailing the two PCPs being composed. Let V_1 be a *robust* verifier of randomness complexity r_1 and query complexity q_1, and suppose that its residual decision on input x and random tape $\omega \in \{0, 1\}^{r_1(|x|)}$ can be described by a poly($q_1(|x|)$)-size circuit, denoted C_ω. That is, on input x, access to an oracle $\pi = \pi_1 \pi_2 \cdots \pi_\ell$, and random-tape $\omega \in \{0, 1\}^{r_1(|x|)}$, the verifier V_1 accepts if and only if $C_\omega(\pi_{i_{\omega,1}} \pi_{i_{\omega,2}} \cdots \pi_{i_{\omega,q_1(|x|)}}) = 1$, where $i_{\omega,j}$ is the jth query made (non-adaptively) on input x and random-tape ω. Note that membership in $C_\omega^{-1}(1)$ can be determined in time poly($|C_\omega^{-1}|$) = poly($q_1(|x|)$). Let V_2 be a verifier *of proximity* for membership in $C_\omega^{-1}(1)$, and suppose that its proximity parameter equals (or is smaller than) the robustness parameter of V_1. Actually, the verifier V_2 should either depend on the circuit C_ω or get the description of C_ω as auxiliary input.[34] Turning to the combined verifier resulting from the composition, we first postulate that, on input x, this verifier utilizes proofs of the form $(\pi, (\pi^{(\omega)})_{\omega \in \{0,1\}^{r_1(|x|)}})$, where π is a proof for V_1 (regarding the input x) and $\pi^{(\omega)}$ is a proof for V_2 (regarding membership of the string $\pi_{i_{\omega,1}} \pi_{i_{\omega,2}} \cdots \pi_{i_{\omega,q_1(|x|)}}$ in the set $C_\omega^{-1}(1)$). The combined verifier uniformly selects a random-tape $\omega \in \{0, 1\}^{r_1(|x|)}$ (for V_1), determines the locations $i_{\omega,1}, i_{\omega,2}, \ldots, i_{\omega,q_1(|x|)}$ (which V_1 would query on input x and random-tape ω), and invokes V_2 while providing it with access to the input-oracle $\pi_{i_{\omega,1}} \pi_{i_{\omega,2}} \cdots \pi_{i_{\omega,q_1(|x|)}}$ and the proof-oracle $\pi^{(\omega)}$. That is, if V_2 queries the jth bit of its input (resp., its proof) then the combined verifier queries the $i_{\omega,j}^{\text{th}}$ bit of π (resp., the jth bit of $\pi^{(\omega)}$) and provides V_2 with the bit retrieved.

Clearly, if x is a yes-instance, then using the adequate proofs π and $(\pi^{(\omega)})_{\omega \in \{0,1\}^{r_1(|x|)}}$ makes the combined verifier accept with probability 1. On the other hand, if x is a no-instance, then V_1 will "robustly reject" any π with probability at least $1/2$ (i.e., with probability at least $1/2$ over the choice of $\omega \in \{0, 1\}^{r_1(|x|)}$, it holds that $\pi_{i_{\omega,1}} \pi_{i_{\omega,2}} \cdots \pi_{i_{\omega,q_1(|x|)}}$ is far from any string in the set $C_\omega^{-1}(1)$). Now, if V_1 "robustly rejects" π when using the random-tape $\omega \in \{0, 1\}^{r_1(|x|)}$, then (for any $\pi^{(\omega)}$) the corresponding executions of V_2 will reject with probability at least $1/2$. It follows that, for any choice of its proof oracle (i.e., any π and $(\pi^{(\omega)})_{\omega \in \{0,1\}^{r_1(|x|)}}$), the combined verifier rejects each no-instance with probability at least $1/4$. Needless to say, the rejection probability can be increased by sequential repetitions.

> **Teaching note:** Unfortunately, the construction of a PCP of logarithmic randomness and poly-logarithmic query complexity for NP involves many technical details. Furthermore, obtaining a robust version of this PCP is beyond the scope of the current text. Thus, the following description should be viewed as merely providing a flavor of the underlying ideas.

PCP of logarithmic randomness and poly-logarithmic query complexity for NP. We focus on showing that $NP \subseteq \mathcal{PCP}(f, f)$, for $f(n) = \text{poly}(\log n)$, and the claimed result will follow by a relatively minor modification (discussed afterward). The proof system

---

[34]In the former case, V_2 is a circuit (with oracle access to its input and proof oracles), which incorporates the circuit C_ω. In the latter case, the formulation of PCP of proximity should be extended so as to account for inputs that are given in two parts such that the first part (e.g., C_ω) is given explicitly (as an ordinary input) and the second part (e.g., the input to C_ω) is given implicitly via oracle access. Either way, it is essential that the size of C_ω is polynomial in the length of its own input (i.e., $|C_\omega| = \text{poly}(q_1(|x|))$). In fact, an asymptotic treatment is facilitated by using the latter formulation (of two-part inputs). In this case, V_2 is actually an (extended) PCP of proximity for statements in $\mathcal{P} \subseteq \mathcal{NP}$, where the valid statements have the form (C, α) such that $C(\alpha) = 1$ (where C is presented as explicit input and α is presented as implicit input).

underlying $NP \subseteq \mathcal{PCP}(f, f)$ is based on an arithmetization of 3CNF formulae, which is different from the one used in §9.1.3.2 (for constructing an interactive proof system for $co\mathcal{NP}$). We start by describing this arithmetization, and later outline the PCP system that is based on it.

In the current arithmetization, the names of the variables (resp., clauses) of a 3CNF formula ϕ are represented by binary strings of logarithmic (in $|\phi|$) length, and a *generic* variable (resp., clause) of ϕ is represented by a logarithmic number of *new variables*, which are assigned values in a finite field F $\supset \{0, 1\}$. Indeed, throughout the rest of the description, we refer to the arithmetic operations of this finite field F (which will have cardinality poly($|\phi|$)). The (structure of the) 3CNF formula $\phi(x_1, \ldots, x_n)$ is represented by a Boolean function $C_\phi : \{0, 1\}^{O(\log n)} \to \{0, 1\}$ such that $C_\phi(\alpha, \beta_1, \beta_2, \beta_3) = 1$ if and only if, for $i = 1, 2, 3$, the ith literal in the αth clause of ϕ has index $\beta_i = (\gamma_i, \sigma_i)$, which is viewed as a variable name augmented by its sign. Thus, for every $\alpha \in \{0, 1\}^{\log |\phi|}$ there is a unique $(\beta_1, \beta_2, \beta_3) \in \{0, 1\}^{3 \log 2n}$ such that $C_\phi(\alpha, \beta_1, \beta_2, \beta_3) = 1$ holds. Next, we consider a multi-linear extension of C_ϕ over F, denoted Φ; that is, Φ is the (unique) multi-linear polynomial that agrees with C_ϕ on $\{0, 1\}^{O(\log n)} \subset F^{O(\log n)}$.

Turning to the PCP, we first note that the verifier can reduce the original 3SAT-instance ϕ to the aforementioned arithmetic instance Φ; that is, on input a 3CNF formula ϕ, the verifier first constructs C_ϕ and Φ (as in Exercise 7.12). Part of the proof oracle for this verifier is viewed as function $A : F^{\log n} \to F$, which is supposed to be a multi-linear extension of a truth assignment that satisfies ϕ (i.e., for every $\gamma \in \{0, 1\}^{\log n} \equiv [n]$, the value $A(\gamma)$ is supposed to be the value of the γth variable in such an assignment). Thus, we wish to check whether, for every $\alpha \in \{0, 1\}^{\log |\phi|}$, it holds that

$$\sum_{\beta_1 \beta_2 \beta_3 \in \{0,1\}^{3 \log 2n}} \Phi(\alpha, \beta_1, \beta_2, \beta_3) \cdot \prod_{i=1}^{3} (1 - A'(\beta_i)) = 0 \qquad (9.7)$$

where $A'(\beta)$ is the value of the βth literal under the (variable) assignment A; that is, for $\beta = (\gamma, \sigma)$, where $\gamma \in \{0, 1\}^{\log n}$ is a variable name and $\sigma \in \{0, 1\}$ indicates the literal's type (i.e., whether the variable is negated), it holds that $A'(\beta) = (1 - \sigma) \cdot A(\gamma) + \sigma \cdot (1 - A(\gamma))$. Thus, Eq. (9.7) holds if and only if the αth clause is satisfied by the assignment induced by A (because $A'(\beta) = 1$ must hold for at least one of the three literals β that appear in this clause).[35]

As in §9.3.2.1, we cannot afford to verify all $|\phi|$ instances of Eq. (9.7). Furthermore, unlike in §9.3.2.1, we cannot afford to take a random linear combination of these $|\phi|$ instances either (because this requires too much randomness). Fortunately, taking a "pseudorandom" linear combination of these equations is good enough. Specifically, using an adequate (efficiently constructible) small-bias probability space (cf. §8.5.2.3) will do. Denoting such a space (of size poly($|\phi| \cdot |F|$)) and bias at most $1/6$ by $S \subset F^{|\phi|}$, we may select uniformly $(s_1, \ldots, s_{|\phi|}) \in S$ and check whether

$$\sum_{\alpha \beta_1 \beta_2 \beta_3 \in \{0,1\}^{\ell}} s_\alpha \cdot \Phi(\alpha, \beta_1, \beta_2, \beta_3) \cdot \prod_{i=1}^{3} (1 - A'(\beta_i)) = 0 \qquad (9.8)$$

where $\ell \stackrel{\text{def}}{=} \log |\phi| + 3 \log 2n$. The small-bias property guarantees that if A fails to satisfy any of the equations of type Eq. (9.7) then, with probability at least $1/3$ (taken over

---

[35]Note that, for this α there exists a unique triple $(\beta_1, \beta_2, \beta_3) \in \{0, 1\}^{3 \log 2n}$ such that $\Phi(\alpha, \beta_1, \beta_2, \beta_3) \neq 0$. This triple $(\beta_1, \beta_2, \beta_3)$ encodes the literals appearing in the αth clause, and this clause is satisfied by A if and only if $\exists i \in [3]$ s.t. $A'(\beta_i) = 1$.

the choice of $(s_1, \ldots, s_{|\phi|}) \in S$), it is the case that A fails to satisfy Eq. (9.8). Since $|S| = \text{poly}(|\phi| \cdot |F|)$ rather that $|S| = 2^{|\phi|}$, we can select a sample in S using $O(\log |\phi|)$ coin tosses. Thus, we have reduced the original problem to checking whether, for a random $(s_1, \ldots, s_{|\phi|}) \in S$, Eq. (9.8) holds.

Assuming (for a moment) that A is a low-degree polynomial, we can probabilistically verify Eq. (9.8) by applying a "summation test" (as in the interactive proof for co$\mathcal{NP}$); that is, we refer to stripping the ℓ binary summations in iterations, where in each iteration the verifier obtains a corresponding univariate polynomial and instantiates it at a random point. Indeed, the verifier obtains the relevant univariate polynomials by making adequate queries (which specify the entire sequence of choices made so far in the summation test).[36] Note that after stripping the ℓ summations, the verifier ends up with an expression that contains three unknown values of A', which it may obtain by making corresponding queries to A. The summation test involves tossing $\ell \cdot \log |F|$ coins and making $(\ell + 3) \cdot O(\log |F|)$ Boolean queries (which correspond to ℓ queries that are each answered by a univariate polynomial of constant degree (over F), and three queries to A (each answered by an element of F)). Soundness of the summation test follows by setting $|F| \gg O(\ell)$, where $\ell = O(\log |\phi|)$.

Recall, however, that we may not assume that A is a multivariate polynomial of low degree. Instead, we must check that A is indeed a multivariate polynomial of low degree (or rather that it is close to such a polynomial), and use self-correction for retrieving the values of A (which are needed for the foregoing summation test). Fortunately, a "low-degree test"[37] of complexities similar to those of the summation test does exist (and self-correction is also possible within these complexities). Thus, using a finite field F of $\text{poly}(\log(n))$ elements, the foregoing yields $\mathcal{NP} \subseteq \mathcal{PCP}(f, f)$ for $f(n) \overset{\text{def}}{=} O(\log(n) \cdot \log \log(n))$.

To obtain the desired PCP system of logarithmic randomness complexity, we represent the names of the original variables and clauses by $\frac{O(\log n)}{\log \log n}$-long sequences over $\{1, \ldots, \log n\}$, rather than by logarithmically long binary sequences. This requires using low-degree polynomial extensions (i.e., polynomial of degree $(\log n) - 1$), rather than multi-linear extensions. We can still use a finite field of $\text{poly}(\log(n))$ elements, and so we need only $\frac{O(\log n)}{\log \log n} \cdot O(\log \log n)$ random bits for the summation and low-degree tests. However, the number of queries (needed for obtaining the answers in these tests) grows, because now the polynomials that are involved have individual degree $(\log n) - 1$ rather than constant individual degree. This merely means that the query complexity increases by a factor of $\frac{\log n}{\log \log n}$ (since the individual degree increases by a factor of $\log n$ but the number of variables decreases by a factor of $\log \log n$). Thus, we obtain $\mathcal{NP} \subseteq \mathcal{PCP}(\log, q)$ for $q(n) \overset{\text{def}}{=} O(\log^2 n)$.

Warning: Robustness and PCP of proximity. Recall that, in order to use the latter PCP system in composition, we need to guarantee that it (or a version of it) is robust as well as to present a version that is a PCP of proximity. The latter version is relatively easy to obtain (using ideas as applied to the PCP of §9.3.2.1), whereas obtaining robustness is too complex to be described here. We comment that one way of obtaining a robust PCP

---

[36]The query will also contain a sequence $(s_1, \ldots, s_{|\phi|}) \in S$, selected at random (by the verifier) and fixed for the rest of the process.

[37]By a low-degree test, we mean an oracle machine that accepts any low-degree polynomial (over F) with probability 1, and rejects (with probability at least $1/2$) any function that is far from all low-degree polynomials. An appropriate test is presented in [195] (see also Exercise 9.23).

system is by a generic application of a (randomness-efficient) "parallelization" of PCP systems (cf. [15]), which in turn depends heavily on highly efficient low-degree tests. An alternative approach (cf. [35]) capitalizes on the specific structure of the summation test (as well as on the evident robustness of a simple low-degree test).

Reflection. The PCP Theorem asserts a PCP system that obtains simultaneously the minimal possible randomness and query complexity (up to a multiplicative factor, assuming that $\mathcal{P} \neq \mathcal{NP}$). The foregoing construction obtains this remarkable result by combining two different PCPs: The first PCP obtains logarithmic randomness but uses poly-logarithmically many queries, whereas the second PCP uses a constant number of queries but has polynomial randomness complexity. We stress that *each of these two PCP systems is highly non-trivial and very interesting by itself.* We also highlight the fact that these PCPs are combined using a very simple composition method (which refers to auxiliary properties such as robustness and proximity testing).[38]

9.3.2.3. Overview of the Second Proof of the PCP Theorem

The original proof of the PCP Theorem focuses on the construction of two PCP systems that are highly non-trivial and interesting by themselves, and combines them in a natural manner. Loosely speaking, this combination (via proof composition) *preserves* the good features of each of the two systems; that is, it yields a PCP system that inherits the (logarithmic) randomness complexity of one system and the (constant) query complexity of the other. In contrast, the following alternative proof is focused at the "amplification" of (the quality of) PCP systems, via a gradual process of logarithmically many steps. We start with a trivial "PCP" system that has the desired complexities but rejects false assertions with probability inversely proportional to their length, and in each step we *double the rejection probability while essentially maintaining the initial complexities.* That is, in each step, the constant query complexity of the verifier is preserved, and its randomness complexity is increased only by a constant term. Thus, the process gradually transforms an extremely weak PCP system into a remarkably strong PCP system (i.e., a PCP as postulated in the PCP Theorem).

In order to describe the aforementioned process we need to *redefine PCP systems so as to allow arbitrary soundness error.* In fact, for technical reasons, it is more convenient to describe the process as an iterated reduction of a "constraint satisfaction" problem to itself. Specifically, we refer to systems of 2-variable constraints, which are readily represented by (labeled) graphs such that the vertices correspond to (non-Boolean) variables and the edges are associated with constraints.

Definition 9.18 (CSP with 2-variable constraints): *For a fixed finite set Σ, an instance of* CSP *consists of a graph $G = (V, E)$ (which may have parallel edges and self-loops) and a sequence of 2-variable constraints $\Phi = (\phi_e)_{e \in E}$ associated with the edges, where each constraint has the form $\phi_e : \Sigma^2 \to \{0, 1\}$. The value of an assignment $\alpha : V \to \Sigma$ is the number of constraints satisfied by α; that is, the value of α is $|\{(u, v) \in E : \phi_{(u,v)}(\alpha(u), \alpha(v)) = 1\}|$. We denote by* $\text{vlt}(G, \Phi)$ *(standing for*

---

[38]**Advanced comment:** We comment that the composition of PCP systems that lack these extra properties is possible, but is far more cumbersome and complex. In some sense, this alternative composition involves transforming the given PCP systems to ones having properties related to robustness and proximity testing.

violation) *the fraction of* unsatisfied *constraints under the best possible assignment; that is,*

$$\mathtt{vlt}(G, \Phi) = \min_{\alpha:V\to\Sigma} \left\{ \frac{|\{(u, v) \in E : \phi_{(u,v)}(\alpha(u), \alpha(v)) = 0\}|}{|E|} \right\} \qquad (9.9)$$

For various functions $\tau : \mathbb{N} \to (0, 1]$, *we will consider the promise problem* $\mathtt{gapCSP}_\tau^\Sigma$, *having instances as in the foregoing, such that the* yes-*instances, are fully satisfiable instances (i.e.,* $\mathtt{vlt} = 0$*) and the* no-*instances are pairs* (G, Φ) *for which* $\mathtt{vlt}(G, \Phi) \geq \tau(|G|)$ *holds, where* $|G|$ *denotes the number of edges in G.*

Note that 3SAT is reducible to $\mathtt{gapCSP}_{\tau_0}^{\{1,\dots,7\}}$ for $\tau_0(m) = 1/m$; see Exercise 9.24. Our goal is to reduce 3SAT (or rather $\mathtt{gapCSP}_{\tau_0}^{\{1,\dots,7\}}$) to $\mathtt{gapCSP}_c^\Sigma$, for some fixed finite Σ and constant $c > 0$. The PCP Theorem will follow by showing a simple PCP system for $\mathtt{gapCSP}_c^\Sigma$; see Exercise 9.26. (The relationship between constraint satisfaction problems and the PCP Theorem is further discussed in Section 9.3.3.) The desired reduction of $\mathtt{gapCSP}_{\tau_0}^\Sigma$ to $\mathtt{gapCSP}_{\Omega(1)}^\Sigma$ is obtained by iteratively applying the following reduction logarithmically many times.

Lemma 9.19 (amplifying reduction of gapCSP to itself): *For some finite Σ and constant $c > 0$, there exists a polynomial-time computable function f such that, for every instance (G, Φ) of $\mathtt{gapCSP}^\Sigma$, it holds that $(G', \Phi') = f(G, \Phi)$ is an instance of $\mathtt{gapCSP}^\Sigma$ and the two instances are related as follows:*

1. *If* $\mathtt{vlt}(G, \Phi) = 0$ *then* $\mathtt{vlt}(G', \Phi') = 0$.
2. $\mathtt{vlt}(G', \Phi') \geq \min(2 \cdot \mathtt{vlt}(G, \Phi), c)$.
3. $|G'| = O(|G|)$.

That is, satisfiable instances are mapped to satisfiable instances, whereas instances that violate a ν fraction of the constraints are mapped to instances that violate at least a $\min(2\nu, c)$ fraction of the constraints. Furthermore, the mapping increases the number of edges (in the instance) by at most a constant factor. We stress that both Φ and Φ' consist of Boolean constraints defined over Σ^2. Thus, by iteratively applying Lemma 9.19 for a logarithmic number of times, we reduce $\mathtt{gapCSP}_{\tau_0}^\Sigma$ to $\mathtt{gapCSP}_{\Omega(1)}^\Sigma$ and 3SAT $\in$ $\mathcal{PCP}(\log, O(1))$ follows (as detailed in Exercise 9.24 and 9.26).

Proof Outline:[39] Before turning to the proof, let us highlight the difficulty that it needs to address. Specifically, the lemma asserts a "violation amplifying effect" (i.e., Items 1 and 2), while maintaining the alphabet Σ and allowing only a moderate increase in the size of the graph (i.e., Item 3). Waiving the latter requirements allows a relatively simple proof that mimics (an augmented version of)[40] the "parallel repetition" of the corresponding PCP. Thus, the challenge is significantly decreasing the "size blowup" that arises from parallel repetition and maintaining a fixed alphabet. The first goal (i.e., Item 3) calls for a suitable derandomization, and indeed we shall use the Expander Random Walk Generator (of Section 8.5.3).

---

[39] For details, see [67].

[40] **Advanced comment:** The augmentation is used to avoid using the Parallel Repetition Theorem of [185]. In the augmented version, with constant probability (say half), a consistency check takes place between tuples that contain copies of the same variable (or query).

Those who read §9.3.2.2 may guess that the second goal (i.e., fixed alphabet) can be handled using the proof composition paradigm. (The rest of the overview is intended to be understood also by those who did not read Section 8.5.3 and §9.3.2.2.)

The lemma is proved by presenting a three-step reduction. The first step is a preprocessing step that makes the underlying graph suitable for further analysis (e.g., the resulting graph will be an expander). The value of vlt may decrease during this step by a constant factor. The heart of the reduction is the second step in which we increase vlt by any desired constant factor. This is done by a construction that corresponds to taking a random walk of constant length on the current graph. The latter step also increases the alphabet Σ, and thus a post-processing step is employed to regain the original alphabet (by using any inner PCP systems, e.g., the one presented in §9.3.2.1). Details follow.

We first stress that the aforementioned Σ and c, as well as the auxiliary parameters d and t (to be introduced in the following two paragraphs), are fixed constants that will be determined such that various conditions (which arise in the course of our argument) are satisfied. Specifically, t will be the last parameter to be determined (and it will be made greater than a constant that is determined by all the other parameters).

We start with the preprocessing step. Our aim in this step is to reduce the input (G, Φ) of gapCSP$^\Sigma$ to an instance (G_1, Φ_1) such that G_1 is a d-regular expander graph.[41] Furthermore, each vertex in G_1 will have at least $d/2$ self-loops, the number of edges will be preserved up to a constant factor (i.e., $|G_1| = O(|G|)$), and vlt$(G_1, \Phi_1) = \Theta($vlt$(G, \Phi))$. This step is quite simple: Essentially, the original vertices are replaced by expanders of size proportional to their degree, and a big (dummy) expander is superimposed on the resulting graph (see Exercise 9.27).

The main step is aimed at increasing the fraction of violated constraints by a sufficiently large constant factor. The intuition underlying this step is that the probability that a random (t-edge long) walk on the expander G_1 intersects a fixed set of edges is closely related to the probability that a random sample of (t) edges intersects this set. Thus, we may expect such walks to hit a violated edge with probability that is min$(\Theta(t \cdot \nu), c)$, where ν is the fraction of violated edges. Indeed, the current step consists of reducing the instance (G_1, Φ_1) of gapCSP$^\Sigma$ to an instance (G_2, Φ_2) of gapCSP$^{\Sigma'}$ such that $\Sigma' = \Sigma^{d^t}$ and the following holds:

1. The vertex set of G_2 is identical to the vertex set of G_1, and each t-edge long path in G_1 is replaced by a corresponding edge in G_2, which is thus a d^t-regular graph.

2. The constraints in Φ_2 refer to each element of Σ' as a Σ-labeling of the ("distance $\leq t$") neighborhood of a vertex (see Figure 9.6), and mandates that the two corresponding labelings (of the endpoints of the G_2-edge) are consistent as well as satisfy Φ_1. That is, the following two types of conditions are enforced by the constraints of Φ_2:

[41]A d-regular graph is a graph in which each vertex is incident to exactly d edges. Loosely speaking, an expander graph has the property that each moderately balanced cut (i.e., partition of its vertex set) has relatively many edges crossing it. An equivalent definition, also used in the actual analysis, is that, except for the largest eigenvalue (which equals d), all the eigenvalues of the corresponding adjacency matrix have absolute value that is bounded away from d. For further details, see §E.2.1.1 in Appendix E.

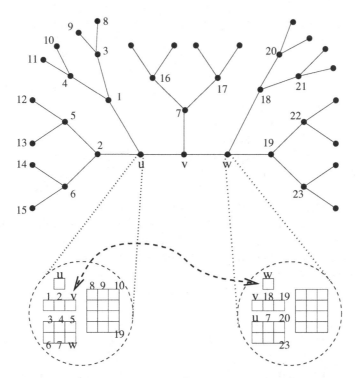

Figure 9.6: The amplifying reduction. The alphabet Σ' as a labeling of the distance $t = 3$ neighborhoods, when repetitions are omitted. In this case $d = 6$ but the self-loops are not shown (and so the "effective" degree is three). The two-sided arrow indicates one of the edges in G_1 that will contribute to the edge constraint between u and w in (G_2, Φ_2).

(consistency): If vertices u and w are connected in G_1 by a path of length at most t and vertex v resides on this path, then the Φ_2-constraint associated with the G_2-edge between u and w mandates the equality of the entries corresponding to vertex v in the Σ'-labeling of vertices u and w.

(satisfying Φ_1): If the G_1-edge (v, v') is on a path of length at most t starting at u, then the Φ_2-constraint associated with the G_2-edge that corresponds to this path enforces the Φ_1-constraint that is associated with (v, v').

Clearly, $|G_2| = d^{t-1} \cdot |G_1| = O(|G_1|)$, because d is a constant and t will be set to a constant. (Indeed, the relatively moderate increase in the size of the graph corresponds to the low randomness complexity of selecting a random walk of length t in G_1.)

Turning to the analysis of this step, we note that $\mathtt{vlt}(G_1, \Phi_1) = 0$ implies $\mathtt{vlt}(G_2, \Phi_2) = 0$. The interesting fact is that the fraction of violated constraints increases by a factor of $\Omega(\sqrt{t})$; that is, $\mathtt{vlt}(G_2, \Phi_2) \geq \min(\Omega(\sqrt{t} \cdot \mathtt{vlt}(G_1, \Phi_1)), c)$. Here, we merely provide a rough intuition and refer the interested reader to [67]. We may focus on any Σ'-labeling to the vertices of G_2 that is consistent with some Σ-labeling of G_1, because relatively few inconsistencies (among the Σ-values assigned to a vertex by the Σ'-labeling of other vertices) can be ignored, while relatively many such inconsistencies yield violation of the "equality constraints" of many edges in G_2. Intuitively, relying on the hypothesis that G_1 is an expander, it follows that the set of violated edge-constraints (of Φ_1) with respect to the aforementioned

Σ-labeling causes many more edge-constraints of Φ_2 to be violated (because each edge-constraint of Φ_1 is enforced by many edge-constraints of Φ_2). The point is that *any set F of edges of G_1 is likely to appear on a* $\min(\Omega(t) \cdot |F|/|G_1|, \Omega(1))$ *fraction of the edges of G_2* (i.e., t-paths of G_1). (Note that the claim would have been obvious if G_1 were a complete graph, but it also holds for an expander.)[42]

The factor of $\Omega(\sqrt{t})$ gained in the second step makes up for the constant factor lost in the first step (as well as the constant factor to be lost in the last step). Furthermore, for a suitable choice of the constant t, the aforementioned gain yields an overall constant factor amplification (of vlt). However, so far we obtained an instance of gapCSP$^{\Sigma'}$ rather than an instance of gapCSP$^{\Sigma}$, where $\Sigma' = \Sigma^{d'}$. The purpose of the last step is to reduce the latter instance to an instance of gapCSP$^{\Sigma}$. This is done by viewing the instance of gapCSP$^{\Sigma'}$ as a PCP-system[43] (analogously to Exercise 9.26), and composing it with an inner-verifier using the proof composition paradigm outlined in §9.3.2.2. We stress that the inner-verifier used here need only handle instances of constant size (i.e., having description length $O(d^t \log |\Sigma|)$), and so the verifier presented in §9.3.2.1 will do. The resulting PCP-system uses randomness $r \overset{\text{def}}{=} \log_2 |G_2| + O(d^t \log |\Sigma|)^2$ and a constant number of binary queries, and has rejection probability $\Omega(\text{vlt}(G_2, \Phi_2))$, which is independent of the choice of the constant t. As in Exercise 9.24, for $\Sigma = \{0, 1\}^{O(1)}$, we can easily obtain an instance of gapCSP$^{\Sigma}$ that has a $\Omega(\text{vlt}(G_2, \Phi_2))$ fraction of violated constraints. Furthermore, the size of the resulting instance (which is used as the output (G', Φ') of the three-step reduction) is $O(2^r) = O(|G_2|)$, where the equality uses the fact that d and t are constants. Recalling that $\text{vlt}(G_2, \Phi_2) \geq \min(\Omega(\sqrt{t} \cdot \text{vlt}(G_1, \Phi_1)), c)$ and $\text{vlt}(G_1, \Phi_1) = \Omega(\text{vlt}(G, \Phi))$, this completes the (outline of the) proof of the entire lemma. $\square$

Reflection. In contrast to the proof presented in §9.3.2.2, which combines two remarkable constructs by using a simple composition method, the current proof of the PCP Theorem is based on developing a powerful "combining method" that improves the quality of the main system to which it is applied. This new method, captured by the Amplification Lemma (Lemma 9.19), does not merely obtain the best of the combined systems, but rather obtains a better system than the one given. However, the quality amplification offered by Lemma 9.19 is rather moderate, and thus many applications are required in order to derive the desired result. Taking the opposite perspective, one may say that remarkable results are obtained by a gradual process of many moderate amplification steps.

9.3.3. PCP and Approximation

The characterization of $\mathcal{NP}$ in terms of probabilistically checkable proofs plays a central role in the study of the complexity of natural approximation problems (cf. Section 10.1.1). To demonstrate this relationship, we first note that any PCP system V gives rise to an approximation problem that consists of estimating the maximum acceptance probability for a given input; that is, on input x, the task is approximating the probability that

---

[42] We mention that, due to a technical difficulty, it is easier to establish the claimed bound of $\Omega(\sqrt{t} \cdot \text{vlt}(G_1, \Phi_1))$ than $\Omega(t \cdot \text{vlt}(G_1, \Phi_1))$.

[43] The PCP-system referred to here has arbitrary soundness error (i.e., it rejects the instance (G_2, Φ_2) with probability $\text{vlt}(G_2, \Phi_2) \in [0, 1]$).

V accepts x when given oracle access to the best possible π (i.e., we wish to approximate $\max_\pi \{\Pr[V^\pi(x)=1]\}$). Thus, *if $S \in \mathcal{PCP}(r, q)$ then deciding membership in S is reducible to approximating the maximum among $\exp(2^{r+q})$ quantities* (corresponding to all effective oracles), where each quantity can be evaluated in time $2^r \cdot \text{poly}$. For (the validity of) this reduction, *an approximation up to a constant factor* (of 2) *will do.*

Note that the foregoing approximation problem is parameterized by a PCP verifier V, and its instances are given their value with respect to this verifier (i.e., the instance x has value $\max_\pi \{\Pr[V^\pi(x)=1]\}$). This per se does not yield a "natural" approximation problem. In order to link PCP-systems with natural approximation problems, we take a closer look at the approximation problem associated with $\mathcal{PCP}(r, q)$.

For simplicity, we focus on the case of non-adaptive PCP-systems (i.e., all the queries are determined beforehand based on the input and the internal coin tosses of the verifier). Fixing an input x for such a system, we consider the $2^{r(|x|)}$ Boolean formulae that represent the decision of the verifier on each of the possible outcomes of its coin tosses after inspecting the corresponding bits in the proof oracle. That is, each of these $2^{r(|x|)}$ formulae depends on $q(|x|)$ Boolean variables that represent the values of the corresponding bits in the proof oracle. Thus, if x is a yes-instance then there exists a truth assignment (to these variables) that satisfies all $2^{r(|x|)}$ formulae, whereas if x is a no-instance then there exists no truth assignment that satisfies more than $2^{r(|x|)-1}$ formulae. Furthermore, in the case that $r(n) = O(\log n)$, given x, we can construct the corresponding sequence of formulae in polynomial time. Hence, the PCP Theorem (i.e., Theorem 9.16) yields *NP-hardness results regarding the approximation of the number of simultaneously satisfiable Boolean formulae of constant size.* This motivates the following definition.

Definition 9.20 (gap problems for SAT and generalized SAT): *For constants $q \in \mathbb{N}$ and $\varepsilon > 0$, the promise problem $\text{gapGSAT}^q_\varepsilon$ refers to instances that are each a sequence of q-variable Boolean formulae (i.e., each formula depends on at most q variables). The yes-instances are sequences that are simultaneously satisfiable, whereas the no-instances are sequences for which no Boolean assignment satisfies more than a $1 - \varepsilon$ fraction of the formulae in the sequence. The promise problem $\text{gapSAT}^q_\varepsilon$ is defined analogously, except that in this case each instance is a sequence of disjunctive clauses (i.e., each formula in each sequence consists of a single disjunctive clause).*

Indeed, each instance of $\text{gapSAT}^q_\varepsilon$ is naturally viewed as q-CNF formulae, and we consider an assignment that satisfies as many clauses (of the input CNF) as possible. As hinted, $\mathcal{NP} \subseteq \mathcal{PCP}(\log, O(1))$ implies that $\text{gapGSAT}^{O(1)}_{1/2}$ is NP-complete, which in turn implies that for some constant $\varepsilon > 0$ the problem $\text{gapSAT}^3_\varepsilon$ is NP-complete. The converses hold, too. All these claims are stated and proved next.

Theorem 9.21 (equivalent formulations of the PCP Theorem): *The following three conditions are equivalent:*

1. The PCP Theorem: *There exists a constant q such that $\mathcal{NP} \subseteq \mathcal{PCP}(\log, q)$.*
2. *There exists a constant q such that $\text{gapGSAT}^q_{1/2}$ is $\mathcal{NP}$-hard.*
3. *There exists a constant $\varepsilon > 0$ such that $\text{gapSAT}^3_\varepsilon$ is $\mathcal{NP}$-hard.*

The point of Theorem 9.21 is not its mere validity (which follows from the validity of each of the three items), but rather the fact that its proof is quite simple. Note that Items 2 and 3 make no reference to PCP. Thus, their (easy-to-establish) equivalence to Item 1 manifests that the hardness of approximating natural optimization problems lies at the heart of the PCP Theorem. In general, probabilistically checkable proof systems for $\mathcal{NP}$ yield strong inapproximability results for various classical optimization problems (cf. Exercise 9.18 and Section 10.1.1).

Proof: We first show that the PCP Theorem implies the NP-hardness of gapGSAT. We may assume, without loss of generality, that, for some constant q and every $S \in \mathcal{NP}$, it holds that $S \in \mathcal{PCP}(O(\log), q)$ via a non-adaptive verifier (because q adaptive queries can be emulated by 2^q non-adaptive queries). We reduce S to gapGSAT as follows. On input x, we scan all $2^{O(\log|x|)}$ possible sequence of outcomes of the verifier's coin tosses, and for each such sequence of outcomes we determine the queries made by the verifier as well as the residual decision predicate (where this predicate determines which sequences of answers lead this verifier to accept). That is, for each random outcome $\omega \in \{0, 1\}^{O(\log|x|)}$, we consider the residual predicate, determined by x and ω, that specifies which q-bit long sequence of oracle answers makes the verifier accept x on coins ω. Indeed, this predicate depends only on q variables (which represent the values of the q corresponding oracle answers). Thus, we map x to a sequence of poly($|x|$) formulae, each depending on q variables, obtaining an instance of gapGSAT^q. This mapping can be computed in polynomial time, and indeed $x \in S$ (resp., $x \notin S$) is mapped to a yes-instance (resp., no-instance) of gapGSAT$^q_{1/2}$.

Item 2 implies Item 3 by a standard reduction of GSAT to 3SAT. Specifically, gapGSAT$^q_{1/2}$ reduces to gapSAT$^q_{2^{-(q+1)}}$, which in turn reduces to gapSAT$^3_\varepsilon$ for $\varepsilon = 2^{-(q+1)}/(q-2)$. Note that Item 3 implies Item 2 (e.g., given an instance of gapSAT$^3_\varepsilon$, consider all possible conjunctions of $1/\varepsilon$ disjunctive clauses in the given instance).

We complete the proof by showing that Item 3 implies Item 1. (The same argument shows that Item 2 implies Item 1.) This is done by showing that gapSAT$^3_\varepsilon$ is in $\mathcal{PCP}(\varepsilon^{-1}\log, 3\varepsilon^{-1})$, and using the reduction of $\mathcal{NP}$ to gapSAT$^3_\varepsilon$ to derive a corresponding PCP for each set in $\mathcal{NP}$. In fact, we show that gapGSAT$^q_\varepsilon$ is in $\mathcal{PCP}(\varepsilon^{-1}\log, \varepsilon^{-1}q)$, and do so by presenting a very natural PCP-system. In this PCP-system the proof oracle is supposed to be a satisfying assignment, and the verifier selects at random one of the (q-variable) formulae in the input sequence, and checks whether it is satisfied by the (assignment given by the) oracle. This amounts to tossing logarithmically many coins and making q queries. This verifier always accepts yes-instances (when given access to an adequate oracle), whereas each no-instance is rejected with probability at least ε (no matter which oracle is used). To amplify the rejection probability (to the desired threshold of $1/2$), we invoke the foregoing verifier ε^{-1} times (and note that $(1 - \varepsilon)^{1/\varepsilon} < 1/2$). ∎

Gap amplifying reductions – a reflection. Item 2 (resp., Item 3) of Theorem 9.21 implies that GSAT (resp., 3SAT) can be reduce to gapGSAT$_{1/2}$ (resp., to gapSAT$^3_\varepsilon$). This means that there exist "gap amplifying" reductions of problems like 3SAT to themselves, where these reductions map yes-instances to yes-instances (as usual), while mapping no-instances to no-instances that are "far" from being yes-instances. That is, no-instances are mapped to no-instances of a special type such that a "gap" is created between the yes-instances and no-instances at the image of the reduction. For example, in the case of 3SAT, unsatisfiable formulae are mapped to formulae that are not merely unsatisfiable but rather have no assignment that satisfies more than a $1 - \varepsilon$ fraction of the clauses. Thus, PCP constructions are essentially "gap amplifying" reductions.

9.3.4. More on PCP Itself: An Overview

We start by discussing variants of the PCP Characterization of NP, and next turn to PCPs having expressing power beyond NP. Needless to say, the latter systems have super-logarithmic randomness complexity.

9.3.4.1. More on the PCP Characterization of NP

Interestingly, the two complexity measures in the PCP characterization of $\mathcal{NP}$ can be traded off such that at the extremes we get $\mathcal{NP} = \mathcal{PCP}(\log, O(1))$ and $\mathcal{NP} = \mathcal{PCP}(0, \text{poly})$, respectively.

> **Proposition 9.22:** *For every $S \in \mathcal{NP}$, there exists a logarithmic function ℓ (i.e., $\ell \in \log$) such that, for every integer function k that satisfies $0 \leq k(n) \leq \ell(n)$, it holds that $S \in \mathcal{PCP}(\ell - k, O(2^k))$. (Recall that $\mathcal{PCP}(\log, \text{poly}) \subseteq \mathcal{NP}$.)*

> **Proof Sketch:** By Theorem 9.16, we have $S \in \mathcal{PCP}(\ell, O(1))$. To show that $S \in \mathcal{PCP}(\ell - k, O(2^k))$, we consider an emulation of the corresponding verifier in which we try all possibilities for the $k(n)$-bit long prefix of its random-tape. $\quad\square$

Following the establishment of Theorem 9.16, numerous variants of the PCP characterization of NP were explored. These variants refer to a finer analysis of various parameters of probabilistically checkable proof systems (for sets in $\mathcal{NP}$). Following is a brief summary of some of these studies.[44]

The length of PCPs. Recall that the effective length of the oracle in any $\mathcal{PCP}(\log, \log)$ system is polynomial (in the length of the input). Furthermore, in the PCP-systems underlying the proof of Theorem 9.16, the queries refer only to a polynomially long prefix of the oracle, and so the actual length of these PCPs for $\mathcal{NP}$ is polynomial. Remarkably, *the length of PCPs for $\mathcal{NP}$ can be made nearly linear* (in the combined length of the input and the standard NP-witness), *while maintaining constant query complexity, where by nearly linear we mean linear up to a poly-logarithmic factor.* (For details see [36, 67].) This means that a *relatively modest amount of redundancy* in the proof oracle suffices for supporting probabilistic verification via a constant number of probes.

The number of queries in PCPs. Theorem 9.16 asserts that a constant number of queries suffice for PCPs with logarithmic randomness and soundness error of $1/2$ (for NP). It is currently known that this constant is at most *five*, whereas with *three* queries one may get arbitrarily close to a soundness error of $1/2$. The obvious trade-off between the number of queries and the soundness error gives rise to the robust notion of amortized query complexity, defined as the ratio between the number of queries and (minus) the logarithm

---

[44]With the exception of works that appeared after [90], we provide no references for the results quoted here. We refer the interested reader to [90, Sec. 2.4.4].

(to based 2) of the soundness error. *For every $\varepsilon > 0$, any set in $\mathcal{NP}$ has a PCP-system with logarithmic randomness and amortized query complexity $1 + \varepsilon$* (cf. [119]), whereas only sets in $\mathcal{P}$ have PCPs of logarithmic randomness and amortized query complexity less than 1.

Free-bit complexity. The original motivation for the notion of free bits came from the PCP–to–MaxClique connection (see Exercise 9.18 and [29, Sec. 8]), but we believe that this notion is of independent interest. Intuitively, this notion distinguishes between queries for which the acceptable answer is determined by previously obtained answers (i.e., the verifier compares the answer to a value determined by the previous answers) and queries for which the verifier only records the answer for future usage. The latter queries are called free (because any answer to them is "acceptable"). For example, in the linearity test (see §9.3.2.1) the first two queries are free and the third is not (i.e., the test accepts if and only if $f(x) + f(y) = f(x + y)$). The amortized free-bit complexity is defined analogously to the amortized query complexity. Interestingly, *$\mathcal{NP}$ has PCPs with logarithmic randomness and amortized free-bit complexity less than any positive constant.*

Adaptive versus non-adaptive verifiers. Recall that a PCP verifier is called non-adaptive if its queries are determined solely based on its input and the outcome of its coin tosses. (A general verifier, called adaptive, may determine its queries also based on previously received oracle answers.) Recall that the PCP characterization of NP (i.e., Theorem 9.16) is established using a non-adaptive verifier; however, it turns out that *adaptive verifiers are more powerful than non-adaptive ones in terms of quantitative results*: Specifically, for PCP verifiers making *three* queries and having logarithmic randomness complexity, adaptive queries provide for soundness error at most 0.51 (actually $0.5 + \varepsilon$ for any $\varepsilon > 0$) for any set in $\mathcal{NP}$, whereas *non-adaptive* queries provide soundness error $5/8$ (or less) only for sets in $\mathcal{P}$.

Non-binary queries. Our definition of PCP allows only binary queries. Certainly, non-binary queries can be emulated by binary queries, but the converse does not necessarily hold.[45] For this reason, "parallel repetition" is highly non-trivial in the PCP setting. Still, a Parallel Repetition Theorem that refers to independent invocations of the same PCP is known, but it is not applicable for obtaining soundness error smaller than a constant (while preserving logarithmic randomness). Nevertheless, using adequate "consistency tests" one may construct PCP-systems for $\mathcal{NP}$ using logarithmic randomness, a constant number of (non-binary) queries, and *soundness error exponential in the length of the answers*. (Currently, this is known only for sub-logarithmic answer lengths.)

9.3.4.2. Stronger Forms of PCP-Systems for NP
Although the PCP Theorem is famous mainly for its negative applications to the study of natural approximation problems (see Section 9.3.3 and §10.1.1.2), its potential for direct

---

[45]**Advanced comment:** The source of trouble is the adversarial settings (implicit in the soundness condition), which means that when several binary queries are packed into one non-binary query, the adversary need not respect the packing (i.e., it may answer inconsistently on the same binary query depending on the other queries packed with it). This trouble becomes acute in the case of PCPs, because they do not correspond to a full information game. Indeed, in contrast, parallel repetition is easy to analyze in the case of interactive proof systems, because they can be modeled as full information games: This is obvious in the case of public-coin systems, but also holds for general interactive proof systems (see Exercise 9.1).

positive applications is fascinating. Indeed, the vision of speeding up the verification of mundane proofs is exciting, where these proofs may refer to mundane assertions such as the correctness of a specific computation. Enabling such a speed-up requires a strengthening of the PCP Theorem such that it mandates efficient verification time rather than "merely" low query complexity of the verification task. Such a strengthening is possible.

Theorem 9.23 (Theorem 9.16 – strengthened): *Every set S in $\mathcal{NP}$ has a PCP-system V of logarithmic randomness complexity, constant query complexity, and quadratic time complexity. Furthermore, NP-witnesses for membership in S can be transformed in polynomial time to corresponding proof-oracles for V.*

The "furthermore" part was already stated in Section 9.3.2 (as a strengthening of Theorem 9.16). Thus, the novelty in Theorem 9.23 is that it provides quadratic verification time, rather than polynomial verification time (where the polynomial may depend arbitrarily on the set S). Theorem 9.23 is proved by noting that the CNF formulae that is obtained by reducing S to 3SAT are highly uniform, and thus the verifier V that is outlined in §9.3.2.2 can be implemented in quadratic time. Indeed, the most time-consuming operation required of V is evaluating the low-degree extension Φ (of C_ϕ), which corresponds to the input formula ϕ, at a few points. In the context of §9.3.2.2, evaluating Φ in exponential time suffices (since this means time that is polynomial in $|\phi|$). Theorem 9.23 follows by showing that a variant of Φ can be evaluated in polynomial time (since this means time that is poly-logarithmic in $|\phi|$); for details, see Exercise 9.30.

PCPs of Proximity. Clearly, we cannot expect a PCP-system (or any standard proof system for that matter) to have sub-linear verification time (since linear time is required for merely reading the input). Nevertheless, we may consider a relaxation of the verification task (regarding proofs of membership in a set S). In this relaxation the verifier is only required to reject any input that is "far" from S (regardless of the alleged proof), and, as usual, accept any input that is in S (when accompanied by an adequate proof). Specifically, in order to allow sub-linear time verification, we provide the verifier V with direct access to the bits of the input (which is viewed as an oracle) as well as with direct access to the usual (PCP) proof-oracle, and require that the following two conditions hold (with respect to some constant $\varepsilon > 0$):

Completeness: For every $x \in S$ there exists a string π_x such that, when given access to the oracles x and π_x, machine V always accepts.

Soundness with respect to proximity ε: For every string x that is ε-far from S (i.e., for every $x' \in \{0, 1\}^{|x|} \cap S$ it holds that x and x' differ on at least $\varepsilon|x|$ bits) and every string π, when given access to the oracles x and π, machine V rejects with probability at least $\frac{1}{2}$.

Machine V is called a PCP of proximity, and its queries to both oracles are counted in its query complexity. (Indeed, a PCP of proximity was used in §9.3.2.2, and the notion is analogous to a relaxation of decision problems that is reviewed in Section 10.1.2.)

We mention that *every set in $\mathcal{NP}$ has PCPs of proximity of logarithmic randomness complexity, constant query complexity, and poly-logarithmic time complexity.* This follows by using ideas as underlying the proof of Theorem 9.23 (see also Exercise 9.30).

9.3.4.3. PCP with Super-logarithmic Randomness

Our focus so far was on the important case where the verifier tosses logarithmically many coins, and hence the "effective proof length" is polynomial. Here we mention that the PCP Theorem (or rather Theorem 9.23) scales up.[46]

> **Theorem 9.24** (Theorem 9.16 – generalized): *Let $t(\cdot)$ be an integer function such that $n < t(n) < 2^{\text{poly}(n)}$. Then,* NTIME$(t) \subseteq \mathcal{PCP}(O(\log t), O(1))$.

Recall that $\mathcal{PCP}(r, q) \subseteq$ NTIME(t), for $t(n) = \text{poly}(n) \cdot 2^{r(n)}$. Thus, the NTIME Hierarchy implies a hierarchy of $\mathcal{PCP}(\cdot, O(1))$ classes, for randomness complexity ranging between logarithmic and polynomial functions.

Chapter Notes

(The following historical notes are quite long and still they fail to properly discuss several important technical contributions that played an important role in the development of the area. For further details, the reader is referred to [90, Sec. 2.6.2].)

Motivated by the desire to formulate the most general type of "proofs" that may be used within cryptographic protocols, Goldwasser, Micali, and Rackoff [109] introduced the notion of an *interactive proof system*. Although the main thrust of their work was the introduction of a special type of interactive proofs (i.e., ones that are *zero-knowledge*), the possibility that interactive proof systems may be more powerful than NP-proof systems was pointed out in [109]. Independently of [109], Babai [18] suggested a different formulation of interactive proofs, which he called *Arthur-Merlin Games*. Syntactically, Arthur-Merlin Games are a restricted form of interactive proof systems, yet it was subsequently shown that these restricted systems are as powerful as the general ones (cf., [111]). The speed-up result (i.e., $\mathcal{AM}(2f) \subseteq \mathcal{AM}(f)$) is due to [23] (improving over [18]).

The first evidence of the power of interactive proofs was given by Goldreich, Micali, and Wigderson [100], who presented an interactive proof system for Graph Non-Isomorphism (Construction 9.3). More importantly, they demonstrated the *generality and wide applicability of zero-knowledge proofs*: Assuming the existence of one-way functions, they showed how to construct zero-knowledge interactive proofs for any set in $\mathcal{NP}$ (Theorem 9.11). This result has had a dramatic impact on the design of cryptographic protocols (cf. [101]). For further discussion of zero-knowledge and its applications to cryptography, see Appendix C. Theorem 9.12 (i.e., $\mathcal{ZK} = \mathcal{IP}$) is due to [32, 130].

Probabilistically checkable proof (PCP) systems are related to *multi-prover interactive proof systems*, a generalization of interactive proofs that was suggested by Ben-Or, Goldwasser, Kilian, and Wigderson [33]. Again, the main motivation came from the zero-knowledge perspective, specifically, presenting multi-prover zero-knowledge proofs for $\mathcal{NP}$ without relying on intractability assumptions. Yet, the complexity-theoretic prospects of the new class, denoted $\mathcal{MIP}$, have not been ignored.

The amazing power of interactive proof systems was demonstrated by using algebraic methods. The basic technique was introduced by Lund, Fortnow, Karloff, and Nisan [162], who applied it to show that the Polynomial-time Hierarchy (and actually $\mathcal{P}^{\#P}$) is in $\mathcal{IP}$. Subsequently, Shamir [202] used the technique to show that $\mathcal{IP} = \mathcal{PSPACE}$, and Babai,

---

[46]Note that the sketched proof of Theorem 9.23 yields verification time that is quadratic in the length of the input and poly-logarithmic in the length of the NP-witness.

Fortnow, and Lund [21] used it to show that $\mathcal{MIP} = \mathcal{NEXP}$. (Our entire proof of Theorem 9.4 follows [202].)

The aforementioned multi-prover proof system of Babai, Fortnow, and Lund [21] (hereafter referred to as the BFL proof system) has been the starting point for fundamental developments regarding $\mathcal{NP}$. The first development was the discovery that the BFL proof system can be "scaled down" from $\mathcal{NEXP}$ to $\mathcal{NP}$. This important discovery was made independently by two sets of authors: Babai, Fortnow, Levin, and Szegedy [20] and Feige, Goldwasser, Lovász, and Safra [73]. However, the manner in which the BFL proof is scaled down is different in the two papers, and so are the consequences of the scaling down.

Babai et al. [20] start by considering (only) inputs encoded using a special error-correcting code. The encoding of strings, relative to this error-correcting code, can be computed in polynomial time. They presented an almost-linear time algorithm that transforms NP-witnesses (to inputs in a set $S \in \mathcal{NP}$) into *transparent proofs* that can be verified (as vouching for the correctness of the encoded assertion) in (probabilistic) *poly-logarithmic time* (by a random-access machine). Babai et al. [20] stress the practical aspects of transparent proofs, specifically, for rapidly checking transcripts of long computations.

In contrast, in the proof system of Feige et al. [73, 74] the verifier stays polynomial time and only two more refined complexity measures (i.e., the randomness and query complexities) are reduced to poly-logarithmic. This eliminates the need to assume that the input is in a special error-correcting form, and yields a refined (quantitative) version of the notion of probabilistically checkable proof systems (introduced in [80]), where the refinement is obtained by specifying the randomness and query complexities (see Definition 9.14). Hence, whereas the BFL proof system [21] can be reinterpreted as establishing $\mathcal{NEXP} = \mathcal{PCP}(\text{poly}, \text{poly})$, the work of Feige et al. [74] establishes $\mathcal{NP} \subseteq \mathcal{PCP}(f, f)$, where $f(n) = O(\log n \cdot \log\log n)$. (In retrospect, we note that the work of Babai et al. [20] implies that $\mathcal{NP} \subseteq \mathcal{PCP}(\text{log}, \text{polylog})$.)

Interest in the new complexity class became immense since Feige et al. [73, 74] demonstrated its relevance to proving the intractability of approximating some natural combinatorial problems (specifically, for MaxClique). When using the PCP-to–MaxClique connection established by Feige et al., the randomness and query complexities of the verifier (in a PCP-system for an NP-complete set) relate to the strength of the negative results obtained for the approximation problems. This fact provided a very strong motivation for trying to reduce these complexities and obtain a tight characterization of $\mathcal{NP}$ in terms of $\mathcal{PCP}(\cdot, \cdot)$. The obvious challenge was showing that $\mathcal{NP}$ equals $\mathcal{PCP}(\text{log}, \text{log})$. This challenge was met by Arora and Safra [16]. Actually, they showed that $\mathcal{NP} = \mathcal{PCP}(\text{log}, q)$, where $q(n) = o(\log n)$.

Hence, a new challenge arose, namely, further reducing the query complexity – in particular, to a constant – while maintaining the logarithmic randomness complexity. Again, additional motivation for this challenge came from the relevance of such a result to the study of natural approximation problems. The new challenge was met by Arora, Lund, Motwani, Sudan and Szegedy [15], and is captured by the PCP Characterization Theorem, which asserts that $\mathcal{NP} = \mathcal{PCP}(\text{log}, O(1))$.

Indeed the PCP Characterization Theorem is a culmination of a sequence of impressive works [162, 21, 20, 74, 16, 15]. These works are rich in innovative ideas (e.g., various arithmetizations of SAT as well as various forms of proof composition) and employ numerous techniques (e.g., low-degree tests, self-correction, and pseudorandomness).

Our overview of the original proof of the PCP Theorem (in §9.3.2.1–9.3.2.2) is based on [15, 16].[47] The alternative proof outlined in §9.3.2.3 is due to Dinur [67].

We mention some of the ideas and techniques involved in deriving even stronger variants of the PCP Theorem (which are surveyed in §9.3.4.1). These include the Parallel Repetition Theorem [185], the use of the Long-Code [29], and the application of Fourier analysis in this setting [116, 117]. We also highlight the notions of PCPs of proximity and robustness (see [35, 68]).

Computationally Sound Proof Systems. Argument systems were defined by Brassard, Chaum, and Crépeau [49], with the motivation of providing *perfect* zero-knowledge arguments (rather than zero-knowledge *proofs*) for $\mathcal{NP}$. A few years later, Kilian [145] demonstrated their significance beyond the domain of zero-knowledge by showing that, under some reasonable intractability assumptions, every set in $\mathcal{NP}$ has a computationally sound proof in which the randomness and communication complexities are poly-logarithmic.[48] Interestingly, these argument systems rely on the fact that $\mathcal{NP} \subseteq \mathcal{PCP}(f, f)$, for $f(n) = \text{poly}(\log n)$. We mention that Micali [165] suggested a different type of computationally sound proof systems (which he called CS-proofs).

Final comment. The current chapter is a revision of [90, Chap. 2]. In particular, more details are provided here for the main topics, whereas numerous secondary topics discussed in [90, Chap. 2] are not mentioned here (or are only briefly mentioned here). We note that a few of the research directions that were mentioned in [90, Sec. 2.4.4] have received considerable attention in the period that elapsed, and improved results are currently known. In particular, the interested reader is referred to [35, 36, 67] for a study of the length of PCPs, and to [119] for a study of their amortized query complexity. Likewise, a few open problems mentioned in [90, Sec. 2.6.3] have been resolved; specifically, the interested reader is referred to [25, 172] for breakthrough results regarding zero-knowledge.

Exercises

Exercise 9.1 (parallel error reduction for interactive proof systems): By t parallel repetitions of the proof system (P, V) we mean an interaction in which t copies of the basic system are executed in parallel such that, at the ith move, the relevant party performs the ith move for each of these t copies. Needless to say, an honest party (i.e., the verifier) will act in each copy independently of the other copies, but a dishonest prover may determine its action in each copy based on the execution of all copies. Nevertheless, prove that the error probability (in the soundness condition) decreases exponentially with the number of parallel repetitions (of the proof system).

> **Guideline:** As a warm-up, consider the special case of public-coin interactive proof systems. Next, generalize the analysis to arbitrary interactive proof systems, by considering (as a mental experiment) a "powerful verifier" that emulates the original verifier while behaving as in the public-coin model. (A direct proof appears in [90, Apdx. C.1].)

Exercise 9.2: Prove that if S is Karp-reducible to a set in $\mathcal{IP}$, then $S \in \mathcal{IP}$. Prove that if S is Cook-reducible to a set S' such that both S' and $\{0, 1\}^* \setminus S'$ are in $\mathcal{IP}$, then $S \in \mathcal{IP}$.

---

[47] Our presentation also benefits from the notions of PCPs of proximity and robustness, put forward in [35, 68].
[48] We comment that interactive proofs are unlikely to have such low complexities; see [106].

Exercise 9.3: Complete the details of the proof that $co\mathcal{NP} \subseteq \mathcal{IP}$ (i.e., the first part of the proof of Theorem 9.4). In particular, suppose that the protocol for unsatisfiability is applied to a CNF formula with n variables and m clauses. Then, what is the length of the messages sent by the two parties? What is the soundness error?

Exercise 9.4: Present an interactive proof system for unsatisfiability such that on input a CNF formula having n variables the parties exchange $n/O(\log n)$ messages.

> **Guideline:** Modify the (first part of the) proof of Theorem 9.4, by stripping $O(\log n)$ summations in each round.

Exercise 9.5 (an interactive proof system for $\#\mathcal{P}$): Using the main part of the proof of Theorem 9.4, present a proof system for the counting set of Eq. (9.5).

> **Guideline:** Use a slightly different arithmetization of CNF formulae. Specifically, instead of replacing the clause $x \vee \neg y \vee z$ by the term $(x + (1 - y) + z)$, replace it by the term $(1 - ((1 - x) \cdot y \cdot (1 - z)))$. The point is that this arithmetization maps Boolean assignments that satisfy the CNF formula to 0-1 assignments that when substituted in the corresponding arithmetic expression yield the value 1 (rather than yielding a somewhat arbitrary positive integer).

Exercise 9.6: Show that QBF can be reduced to a special form of (non-canonical)[49] QBF in which no variable appears both to the left and to the right of more than one universal quantifier.

> **Guideline:** Consider a process (which proceeds from left to right) of "refreshing" variables after each universal quantifier. Let $\phi(x_1, \ldots, x_s, y, x_{s+1}, \ldots, x_{s+t})$ be a quantifier-free Boolean formula and let $Q_{s+1}, \ldots, Q_{s+t}$ be an arbitrary sequence of quantifiers. Then, we replace the quantified (sub-)formula
>
> $$\forall y \, Q_{s+1}x_{s+1} \cdots Q_{s+t}x_{s+t} \, \phi(x_1, \ldots, x_s, y, x_{s+1}, \ldots, x_{s+t})$$
>
> by the (sub-)formula
>
> $$\forall y \exists x_1' \cdots \exists x_s' [(\wedge_{i=1}^{s}(x_i' = x_i))$$
> $$\wedge Q_{s+1}x_{s+1} \cdots Q_{s+t}x_{s+t} \, \phi(x_1', \ldots, x_s', y, x_{s+1}, \ldots, x_{s+t})].$$
>
> Note that the variables $x_1, \ldots, x_s$ do not appear to the right of the quantifier Q_{s+1} in the replaced formula, and that the length of the replaced formula grows by an additive term of $O(s)$. This process of refreshing variables is applied from left to right on the entire sequence of universal quantifiers (except the inner one, for which this refreshing is useless).[50]

---

[49] See Appendix G.2.

[50] For example,

$$\exists z_1 \forall z_2 \exists z_3 \forall z_4 \exists z_5 \forall z_6 \, \phi(z_1, z_2, z_3, z_4, z_5, z_6)$$

is first replaced by

$$\exists z_1 \forall z_2 \exists z_1' [(z_1' = z_1) \wedge \exists z_3 \forall z_4 \exists z_5 \forall z_6 \, \phi(z_1', z_2, z_3, z_4, z_5, z_6)]$$

and next (written as $\exists z_1 \forall z_2' \exists z_1' [(z_1' = z_1) \wedge \exists z_3' \forall z_4' \exists z_5' \forall z_6' \, \phi(z_1', z_2', z_3', z_4', z_5', z_6')])$ is replaced by

$$\exists z_1 \forall z_2' \exists z_1' [(z_1' = z_1) \wedge \exists z_3' \forall z_4' \exists z_1'' \exists z_2'' \exists z_3''$$
$$[(\wedge_{i=1}^{3}(z_i'' = z_i')) \wedge \exists z_5' \forall z_6' \phi(z_1'', z_2'', z_3'', z_4', z_5', z_6')]].$$

407

Exercise 9.7: Prove that if two integers in $[0, M]$ are different then they must be different modulo most of the primes in the interval $[3, L]$, where $L = \text{poly}(\log M)$. Prove the same for the interval $[L, 2L]$.

> **Guideline:** Let $a \neq b \in [0, M]$ and suppose that $P_1, \ldots, P_t$ is an enumeration of all the primes that satisfy $a \equiv b \pmod{P_i}$. Using the Chinese Reminder Theorem, prove that $Q \stackrel{\text{def}}{=} \prod_{i=1}^{t} P_i \leq M$ (because otherwise $a = b$ follows by combining $a \equiv b \pmod{Q}$ with the hypothesis $a, b \in [0, M]$). It follows that $t < \log_2 M$. Using a lower bound on the density of prime numbers, the claim follows.

Exercise 9.8 (on interactive proofs with two-sided error (following [82])): Let $\mathcal{IP}'(f)$ denote the class of sets having a two-sided error interactive proof system in which a total of $f(|x|)$ messages are exchanged on common input x. Specifically, suppose that a suitable prover may cause every yes-instance to be accepted with probability at least $2/3$ (rather than 1), while no cheating prover can cause a no-instance to be accepted with probability greater than $1/3$ (rather than $1/2$). Similarly, let $\mathcal{AM}'$ denote the public-coin version of $\mathcal{IP}'$.

1. Establish $\mathcal{IP}'(f) \subseteq \mathcal{AM}'(f + 3)$ by noting that the proof of Theorem F.2, which establishes $\mathcal{IP}(f) \subseteq \mathcal{AM}(f + 3)$, extends to the two-sided error setting.
2. Prove that $\mathcal{AM}'(f) \subseteq \mathcal{AM}(f + 1)$ by extending the ideas underlying the proof of Theorem 6.9, which actually establishes that $\mathcal{BPP} \subseteq \mathcal{AM}(1)$ (where $\mathcal{BPP} = \mathcal{AM}'(0)$).

Using the Round Speed-up Theorem (i.e., Theorem F.3), conclude that, for every function $f : \mathbb{N} \to \mathbb{N} \setminus \{1\}$, it holds that $\mathcal{IP}'(f) = \mathcal{AM}(f) = \mathcal{IP}(f)$.

> **Guideline (for Part 2):** Fixing an optimal prover strategy for the given two-sided error public-coin interactive proof, consider the set of verifier coins that make the verifier accept any fixed yes-instance, and apply the ideas underlying the transformation of $\mathcal{BPP}$ to $\mathcal{MA} = \mathcal{AM}(1)$. For further details, see [82].

Exercise 9.9: In continuation of Exercise 9.8, show that $\mathcal{IP}'(f) = \mathcal{IP}(f)$ for every function $f : \mathbb{N} \to \mathbb{N}$ (including $f \equiv 1$).

> **Guideline:** Focus on establishing $\mathcal{IP}'(1) = \mathcal{IP}(1)$, which is identical to Part 2 of Exercise 6.12. Note that the relevant classes defined in Exercise 6.12 coincide with $\mathcal{IP}(1)$ and $\mathcal{IP}'(1)$; that is, $\mathcal{MA} = \mathcal{IP}(1)$ and $\mathcal{MA}^{(2)} = \mathcal{IP}'(1)$.

Exercise 9.10: Prove that every $\mathcal{PSPACE}$-complete set S has an interactive proof system in which the designated prover can be implemented by a probabilistic polynomial-time oracle machine that is given oracle access to S.

> **Guideline:** Use Theorem 9.4 and Proposition 9.5.

Exercise 9.11 (checkers (following [39])): A probabilistic polynomial-time oracle machine C is called a checker for the decision problem Π if the following two conditions hold:

1. For every x it holds that $\Pr[C^{\Pi}(x) = 1] = 1$, where (as usual) $C^f(x)$ denotes the output of A on input x when given oracle access to f.

Thus, in the resulting formula, no variable appears both to the left and to the right of more than a single universal quantifier.

2. For every $f : \{0, 1\}^* \to \{0, 1\}$ and every x such that $f(x) \neq \Pi(x)$ it holds that $\Pr[C^f(x) = 1] \leq 1/2$.

Note that nothing is required in the case that $f(x) = \Pi(x)$ but $f \neq \Pi$. Prove that *if both $S_1 = \{x : \Pi(x) = 1\}$ and $S_0 = \{x : \Pi(x) = 0\}$ have interactive proof systems in which the designated prover can be implemented by a probabilistic polynomial-time oracle machine that is given oracle access to Π, then Π has a checker.* Using Exercise 9.10, conclude that any $\mathcal{PSPACE}$-complete problem has a checker.

> **Guideline:** On input x and oracle access to f, the checker first obtains $\sigma \stackrel{\text{def}}{=} f(x)$. The claim $\Pi(x) = \sigma$ is then checked by combining the verifier of S_σ with the probabilistic polynomial-time oracle machine that describes the designated prover, while referring its queries to the oracle f.

Exercise 9.12 (weakly optimal deciders for checkable problems (following [133])): Prove that if a decision problem Π has a checker (as defined in Exercise 9.11) then there exists a probabilistic algorithm A that satisfies the following two conditions:

1. A solves the decision problem Π (i.e., for every x it holds that $\Pr[A(x) = \Pi(x)] \geq 2/3$).
2. For every probabilistic algorithm A' that solves the decision problem Π, there exists a polynomial p such that for every x it holds that $t_A(x) = p(|x|) \cdot \max_{|x'| \leq p(|x|)} \{t_{A'}(x')\}$, where $t_A(z)$ (resp., $t_{A'}(z)$) denotes the number of steps taken by A (resp., A') on input z.

Note that, compared to Theorem 2.33, the claim of optimality is weaker, but on the other hand it applies to decision problems (rather than to candid search problems).

> **Guideline:** Use the ideas of the proof of Theorem 2.33, noting that the correctness of the answers provided by the various candidate algorithms can be verified by using the checker. That is, A invokes copies of the checker, while using different candidate algorithms as oracles in the various copies.

Exercise 9.13 (on the role of soundness error in zero-knowledge proofs): Prove that if S has a zero-knowledge interactive proof system with perfect soundness (i.e., the soundness error equals zero) then $S \in \mathcal{BPP}$.

> **Guideline:** Let M be an arbitrary algorithm that simulates the view of the (honest) verifier. Consider the algorithm that, on input x, accepts x if and only if $M(x)$ represents a valid view of the verifier in an accepting interaction (i.e., an interaction that leads the verifier to accept the common input x). Use the simulation condition to analyze the case $x \in S$, and the perfect soundness hypothesis to analyze the case $x \notin S$.

Exercise 9.14 (on the role of interaction in zero-knowledge proofs): Prove that if S has a zero-knowledge interactive proof system with a uni-directional communication then $S \in \mathcal{BPP}$.

> **Guideline:** Let M be an arbitrary algorithm that simulates the view of the (honest) verifier, and let $M'(x)$ denote the part of this view that consists of the prover message. Consider the algorithm that, on input x, obtains $m \leftarrow M'(x)$, and emulates the verifier's decision on input x and message m. Note that this algorithm ignores the part of $M(x)$ that represents the verifier's internal coin tosses, and uses fresh verifier's coins when deciding on (x, m).

Exercise 9.15 (on the effective length of PCP oracles): Suppose that V is a PCP verifier of query complexity q and randomness complexity r. Show that for every fixed x, the number of possible locations in the proof oracle that are examined by V on input x (when considering all possible internal coin tosses of V and all possible answers it may receive) is upper bounded by $2^{q(|x|)+r(|x|)}$. Show that if V is non-adaptive then the upper bound can be improved to $2^{r(|x|)} \cdot q(|x|)$.

> **Guideline:** In the non-adaptive case, all q queries are determined by V's internal coin tosses.

Exercise 9.16 (on the effective randomness of PCPs): Suppose that a set S has a PCP of query complexity q that utilizes proof oracles of length ℓ. Show that, for every constant $\varepsilon > 0$, the set S has a "non-uniform" PCP of query complexity q, soundness error $0.5 + \varepsilon$, and randomness complexity r such that $r(n) = \log_2(\ell(n) + n) + O(1)$. By a "non-uniform PCP" we mean one in which the verifier is a probabilistic polynomial-time oracle machine that is given direct access to the bits of a non-uniform $poly(\ell(n) + n)$-bit long advice.

> **Guideline:** Consider a PCP verifier V as in the hypothesis, and denote its randomness complexity by r_V. We construct a non-uniform verifier V' that, on input of length n, obtains as advice a set $R_n \subseteq \{0, 1\}^{r_V(n)}$ of cardinality $O((\ell(n) + n)/\varepsilon^2)$, and emulates V on a uniformly selected element of R_n. Show that for a random R_n of the said size, the verifier V' satisfies the claims of the exercise.
>
> (Extra hint: Fixing any input $x \notin S$ and any oracle $\pi \in \{0, 1\}^{\ell(|x|)}$, upper-bound the probability that a random set R_n (of the said size) is bad, where R_n is bad if V accepts x with probability $0.5 + \varepsilon$ when selecting its coins in R_n and using the oracle π.)

Exercise 9.17 (on the complexity of sets having certain PCPs): Suppose that a set S has a PCP of query complexity q and randomness complexity r. Show that S can be decided by a non-deterministic machine[51] that, on input of length n, makes at most $2^{r(n)} \cdot q(n)$ truly non-deterministic steps (i.e., choosing between different alternatives) and halts within a total number of $2^{r(n)} \cdot poly(n)$ steps. Conclude that $S \in \text{NTIME}(2^r \cdot poly) \cap \text{DTIME}(2^{2^r q+r} \cdot poly)$.

> **Guideline:** For each input $x \in S$ and each possible value $\omega \in \{0, 1\}^{r(|x|)}$ of the verifier's random-tape, we consider a sequence of $q(|x|)$ bit values that represent a sequence of oracle answers that make the verifier accept. Indeed, for fixed x and $\omega \in \{0, 1\}^{r(|x|)}$, each setting of the $q(|x|)$ oracle answers determines the computation of the corresponding verifier (including the queries it makes).

Exercise 9.18 (The FGLSS-reduction [74]): For any $S \in \mathcal{PCP}(r, q)$, consider the following mapping of instances for S to instances of the Independent Set problem. The instance x is mapped to a graph $G_x = (V_x, E_x)$, where $V_x \subseteq \{0, 1\}^{r(|x|)+q(|x|)}$ consists of pairs (ω, α) such that the PCP verifier *accepts* the input x, when using coins $\omega \in \{0, 1\}^{r(|x|)}$ and receiving the answers $\alpha = \alpha_1 \cdots \alpha_{q(|x|)}$ (to the oracle queries determined by x, r and the previous answers). Note that V_x contains only *accepting* "views" of the verifier. The set E_x consists of edges that connect vertices that represents mutually *inconsistent* views of the said verifier; that is, the vertex $v = (\omega, \alpha_1 \cdots \alpha_{q(|x|)})$ is connected to the vertex $v' = (\omega', \alpha'_1 \cdots \alpha'_{q(|x|)})$ if there exists i and i' such that $\alpha_i \neq \alpha'_{i'}$

---

[51] See §4.2.1.3 for definition of non-deterministic machines.

and $q_i^x(v) = q_{i'}^x(v')$, where $q_i^x(v)$ (resp., $q_{i'}^x(v')$) denotes the i-th (resp., i'-th) query of the verifier on input x, when using coins ω (resp., ω') and receiving the answers $\alpha_1 \cdots \alpha_{i-1}$ (resp., $\alpha_1' \cdots \alpha_{i'-1}'$). In particular, for every $\omega \in \{0, 1\}^{r(|x|)}$ and $\alpha \neq \alpha'$, if $(\omega, \alpha), (\omega, \alpha') \in V_x$, then $\{(\omega, \alpha), (\omega, \alpha')\} \in E_x$.

1. Prove that the mapping $x \mapsto G_x$ can be computed in time that is polynomial in $2^{r(|x|)+q(|x|)} \cdot |x|$.

   (Note that the number of vertices in G_x is upper-bounded by $2^{r(|x|)+f(|x|)}$, where $f \leq q$ is the free-bit complexity of the PCP verifier.)

2. Prove that, for every x, the size of the maximum independent set in G_x is at most $2^{r(|x|)}$.

3. Prove that if $x \in S$ then G_x has an independent set of size $2^{r(|x|)}$.

4. Prove that if $x \notin S$ then the size of the maximum independent set in G_x is at most $2^{r(|x|)-1}$.

In general, denoting the PCP verifier by V, prove that the size of the maximum independent set in G_x is exactly $2^{r(|x|)} \cdot \max_\pi \{\Pr[V^\pi(x) = 1]\}$. (Note the similarity to the proof of Proposition 2.26.)

Show that the PCP Theorem implies that *the size of the maximum independent set (resp., clique) in a graph* is *NP-hard to approximate to within any constant factor.*

> **Guideline:** Note that an independent set in G_x corresponds to a set of coins R and a partial oracle π' such that V accepts x when using coins in R and accessing any oracle that is consistent with π'. The FGLSS-reduction creates a gap of a factor of 2 between yes- and no-instances of S (having a standard PCP). Larger factors can be obtained by considering a PCP that results from repeating the original PCP for a constant number of times. The result for Clique follows by considering the complement graph.

Exercise 9.19: Using the ideas of Exercise 9.18, prove that, for any $t(n) = o(\log n)$, if $\mathcal{NP} \subseteq \mathcal{PCP}(t, t)$ then $\mathcal{P} = \mathcal{NP}$.

> **Guideline:** We only use the fact that the FGLSS-reduction maps instances of $S \in \mathcal{PCP}(t, t)$ to instances of the Clique problem (and ignore the fact that we actually get a stronger reduction to a "gap-Clique" problem). The key observation is that, when applied to n-bit long instances of a problem in $\mathcal{PCP}(t, t)$, the FGLSS-reduction runs in polynomial time and produces instances of size $2^{2t(n)} \ll n$. Thus, the hypothesis $\mathcal{NP} \subseteq \mathcal{PCP}(t, t)$ implies that the FGLSS-reduction maps instances of the Clique problem to shorter instances of the same problem. Hence, iteratively applying the FGLSS-reduction, we can reduce instances of Clique to instances of constant size. This yields a reduction of Clique to a finite set, and $\mathcal{NP} = \mathcal{P}$ follows (by the $\mathcal{NP}$-completeness of Clique).

Exercise 9.20 (a simple but partial analysis of the BLR Linearity Test): For Abelian groups G and H, consider functions from G to H. For such a (generic) function f, consider the linearity (or rather homomorphism) test that selects uniformly $r, s \in G$ and checks that $f(r) + f(s) = f(r + s)$. Let $\delta(f)$ denote the distance of f from the set of homomorphisms (of G to H); that is, $\delta(f)$ is the minimum taken over all homomorphisms $h : G \to H$ of $\Pr_{x \in G}[f(x) \neq h(x)]$. Using the following guidelines, prove that the probability that the test rejects f, denoted $\varepsilon(f)$, is at least $3\delta(f) - 6\delta(f)^2$.

1. Suppose that h is the homomorphism closest to f (i.e., $\delta(f) = \Pr_{x \in G}[f(x) \neq h(x)]$). Prove that $\varepsilon(f) = \Pr_{x,y \in G}[f(x) + f(y) \neq f(x + y)]$ is lower-bounded by $3 \cdot \Pr_{x,y}[f(x) \neq h(x) \wedge f(y) = h(y) \wedge f(x + y) = h(x + y)]$.

   (Hint: Consider three out of four *disjoint* cases (regarding $f(x) \overset{?}{=} h(x)$, $f(y) \overset{?}{=} h(y)$, and $f(x + y) \overset{?}{=} h(x + y)$) that are possible when $f(x) + f(y) \neq f(x + y)$, where these three cases refer to the disagreement of h and f on exactly one out of the three relevant points.)

2. Prove that $\Pr_{x,y}[f(x) \neq h(x) \wedge f(y) = h(y) \wedge f(x + y) = h(x + y)] \geq \delta(f) - 2\delta(f)^2$

   (Hint: Lower-bound the said probability by $\Pr_{x,y}[f(x) \neq h(x)] - (\Pr_{x,y}[f(x) \neq h(x) \wedge f(y) \neq h(y)] + \Pr_{x,y}[f(x) \neq h(x) \wedge f(x + y) \neq h(x + y)])$.)

Note that the lower bound $\varepsilon(f) \geq 3\delta(f) - 6\delta(f)^2$ increases with $\delta(f)$ only in the case that $\delta(f) \leq 1/4$. Furthermore, the lower bound is useless in the case that $\delta(f) \geq 1/2$. Thus, an alternative lower bound is needed in case $\delta(f)$ approaches $1/2$ (or is larger than it); see Exercise 9.21.

Exercise 9.21 (a better analysis of the BLR Linearity Test (cf. [40])): In continuation of Exercise 9.20, use the following guidelines in order to prove that $\varepsilon(f) \geq \min(1/6, \delta(f)/2)$. Specifically, focusing on the case that $\varepsilon(f) < 1/6$, show that f is $2\varepsilon(f)$-close to some homomorphism (and thus $\varepsilon(f) \geq \delta(f)/2$).

1. Define the vote of y regarding the value of f at x as $\phi_y(x) \overset{\text{def}}{=} f(x + y) - f(y)$, and define $\phi(x)$ as the corresponding plurality vote (i.e., $\phi(x) \overset{\text{def}}{=} \text{argmax}_{v \in H}\{|\{y \in G : \phi_y(x) = v\}|\}$).
   Prove that, for every $x \in G$, it holds that $\Pr_y[\phi_y(x) = \phi(x)] \geq 1 - 2\varepsilon(f)$.

   Extra Guideline: Fixing x, call a pair (y_1, y_2) good if $f(y_1) + f(y_2 - y_1) = f(y_2)$ and $f(x + y_1) + f(y_2 - y_1) = f(x + y_2)$. Prove that, for any x, a random pair (y_1, y_2) is good with probability at least $1 - 2\varepsilon(f)$. On the other hand, for a good (y_1, y_2), it holds that $\phi_{y_1}(x) = \phi_{y_2}(x)$. Show that the graph in which *edges* correspond to good pairs must have a connected component of size at least $(1 - 2\varepsilon(f)) \cdot |G|$. Note that $\phi_y(x)$ is identical for all vertices y in this connected component, which in turn contains a majority of all y's in G.

2. Prove that ϕ is a homomorphism; that is, prove that, for every $x, y \in G$, it holds that $\phi(x) + \phi(y) = \phi(x + y)$.

   Extra Guideline: Prove that $\phi(x) + \phi(y) = \phi(x + y)$ holds by considering the somewhat fictitious expression $p_{x,y} \overset{\text{def}}{=} \Pr_{r \in G}[\phi(x) + \phi(y) \neq \phi(x + y)]$, and showing that $p_{x,y} < 1$ (and hence $\phi(x) + \phi(y) \neq \phi(x + y)$ is false). Prove that $p_{x,y} < 1$, by showing that

$$p_{x,y} \leq \Pr_r \left[\begin{array}{l} \phi(x) \neq f(x + r) - f(r) \\ \vee\ \phi(y) \neq f(r) - f(r - y) \\ \vee\ \phi(x + y) \neq f(x + r) - f(r - y) \end{array} \right] \tag{9.10}$$

   and using Item 1 (and some variable substitutions) for upper-bounding by $2\varepsilon(f) < 1/3$ the probability of each of the three events in Eq. (9.10).

3. Prove that f is $2\varepsilon(f)$-close to ϕ.

   Extra Guideline: Denoting $B = \{x \in G : \Pr_{y \in G}[f(x) \neq \phi_y(x)] \geq 1/2\}$, prove that $\varepsilon(f) \geq (1/2) \cdot (|B|/|G|)$. Note that if $x \in G \setminus B$ then $f(x) = \phi(x)$.

We comment that better bounds on the behavior of $\varepsilon(f)$ as a function of $\delta(f)$ are known.

Exercise 9.22 (testing matrix identity): Let M be a non-zero m-by-n matrix over GF(p). Prove that $\Pr_{r,s}[r^\top Ms \neq 0] \geq (1 - p^{-1})^2$, where r (resp., s) is a random m-ary (resp., n-ary) vector.

> **Guideline:** Prove that if $v \neq 0^n$ then $\Pr_s[v^\top s = 0] = p^{-1}$, and that if M has rank k then $\Pr_r[r^\top M = 0^n] = p^{-k}$.

Exercise 9.23 (low-degree tests (following [195])): For a field of prime cardinality F and integers m and $d < |F| - 1$, we consider the set, denoted $P_{m,d}$, of all m-variate polynomials of *total degree* at most d over F. We consider the low-degree test that, when given oracle access to any function $f : F^m \to F$, selects uniformly $\overline{x}, \overline{y} \in F^m$, queries f at the points $(\overline{x} + i \cdot \overline{y})_{i=0,\ldots,d+1}$, and accepts if and only if $\sum_{i=0}^{d+1} \alpha_i f(\overline{x} + i \cdot \overline{y}) = 0$, where $\alpha_i = (-1)^{i+1} \cdot \binom{d+1}{i}$. It is well known (cf. [195]) that $f \in P_{m,d}$ if and only if for every $\overline{x}, \overline{y} \in F^m$ it holds that $\sum_{i=0}^{d+1} \alpha_i f(\overline{x} + i \cdot \overline{y}) = 0$.

1. Following the outline of Exercise 9.20, prove that the test rejects f with probability at least $(d + 2) \cdot \delta(f) - (d + 2)(d + 1) \cdot \delta(f)^2$, where $\delta(f) = \min_{g \in P_{m,d}} \{\Pr_{\overline{x} \in F^m}[f(\overline{x}) \neq g(\overline{x})]\}$.

2. Following the outline of Exercise 9.21, prove that $\varepsilon(f) \geq \min((d + 2)^{-2}, \delta(f))/2$, where $\varepsilon(f)$ denotes the probability that the test rejects f. That is, prove that if $\varepsilon(f) < (d + 2)^{-2}/2$ then f is $2\varepsilon(f)$-close to some function in $P_{m,d}$.

> **Guideline:** Define $\phi_y(x) \stackrel{\text{def}}{=} \sum_{i=1}^{d+1} \alpha_i f(\overline{x} + i \cdot \overline{y})$, and note that $\varepsilon(f) = \Pr_{\overline{x},\overline{y} \in F^m}[f(\overline{x}) \neq \phi_{\overline{y}}(\overline{x})]$. Part 1 follows by lower-bounding the probability that, for random $\overline{x}, \overline{y} \in F^m$, there exists a unique $i \in \{0, 1, \ldots, d + 1\}$ such that $f(\overline{x} + i \cdot \overline{y}) \neq g(\overline{x} + i \cdot \overline{y})$, where $g \in P_{m,d}$ is the low-degree polynomial closest to f. Part 2 follows by defining $\phi(\overline{x}) = \text{argmax}_{v \in F}\{|\{\overline{y} \in F^m : \phi_{\overline{y}}(\overline{x}) = v\}|\}$, and proceeding analogously to the three steps in the proof of Exercise 9.21. For example, analogously to the first step, prove that for every $\overline{x} \in F^m$ it holds that $\Pr_{\overline{y} \in F^m}[\phi(\overline{x}) = \phi_{\overline{y}}(\overline{x})] \geq 1 - 2(d + 1) \cdot \varepsilon(f)$.
>
> (Extra hint: Prove that $\Pr_{\overline{y}_1,\overline{y}_2 \in F^m}[\phi_{\overline{y}_1}(\overline{x}) = \phi_{\overline{y}_2}(\overline{x})] \geq 1 - 2(d + 1) \cdot \varepsilon(f).)^{52}$

Exercise 9.24 (3SAT and CSP with two variables): Show that 3SAT is reducible to $\text{gapCSP}_\tau^{\{1,\ldots,7\}}$ for $\tau(m) = 1/m$, where gapCSP is as in Definition 9.18. Furthermore, show that the size of the resulting gapCSP instance is linear in the length of the input formula.

> **Guideline:** Given an instance ψ of 3SAT, consider the graph in which vertices correspond to clauses of ψ, edges correspond to pairs of clauses that share a variable, and the constraints represent the natural consistency condition regarding partial assignments that satisfy the clauses. See a related construction in Exercise 9.18.

Exercise 9.25 (CSP with two Boolean variables): In contrast to Exercise 9.24, prove that for every positive function $\tau : \mathbb{N} \to (0, 1]$ the problem $\text{gapCSP}_\tau^{\{0,1\}}$ is solvable in polynomial time.

---

[52]In the following probabilistic statements, we shall refer to uniformly distributed $\overline{y}_1, \overline{y}_2 \in F^m$. Note that $\phi_{\overline{y}_1}(\overline{x}) = \sum_{i_1=1}^{d+1} \alpha_{i_1} f(\overline{x} + i_1 \cdot \overline{y}_1)$ which with probability at least $1 - (d - 1) \cdot \varepsilon(f)$ equals $\sum_{i_1=1}^{d+1} \alpha_{i_1} \phi_{\overline{y}_2}(\overline{x} + i_1 \cdot \overline{y}_1)$. The latter expression equals $\sum_{i_1=1}^{d+1} \sum_{i_2=1}^{d+1} \alpha_{i_1} \alpha_{i_2} f(\overline{x} + i_1 \cdot \overline{y}_1 + i_2 \cdot \overline{y}_2) = \sum_{i_2=1}^{d+1} \alpha_{i_2} \phi_{\overline{y}_1}(\overline{x} + i_2 \cdot \overline{y}_2)$, which with probability at least $1 - (d - 1) \cdot \varepsilon(f)$ equals $\sum_{i_2=1}^{d+1} \alpha_{i_2} f(\overline{x} + i_2 \cdot \overline{y}_2) = \phi_{\overline{y}_2}(\overline{x})$.

Guideline: Reduce $\text{gapCSP}_\tau^{\{0,1\}}$ to 2SAT.

Exercise 9.26: Show that, for any fixed finite Σ and constant $c > 0$, the problem gapCSP_c^Σ is in $\mathcal{PCP}(\log, O(1))$.

> **Guideline:** Consider an oracle that, for some satisfying assignment for the CSP-instance (G, Φ), provides a trivial encoding of the assignment; that is, for a satisfying assignment $\alpha : V \to \Sigma$, the oracle responds to the query (v, i) with the ith bit in the binary representation of $\alpha(v)$. Consider a verifier that uniformly selects an edge (u, v) of G and checks the constraint $\phi_{(u,v)}$ when applied to the values $\alpha(u)$ and $\alpha(v)$ obtained from the oracle. This verifier makes $\log_2 |\Sigma|$ queries and reject each no-instance with probability at least c.

Exercise 9.27: For any constant Σ and $d \geq 14$, show that gapCSP^Σ can be reduced to itself such that the instance at the target of the reduction is a d-regular expander, and the fraction of violated constraints is preserved up to a constant factor. That is, the instance (G, Φ) is reduced to (G_1, Φ_1) such that G_1 is a d-regular expander graph and $\text{vlt}(G_1, \Phi_1) = \Theta(\text{vlt}(G, \Phi))$. Furthermore, make sure that $|G_1| = O(|G|)$ and that each vertex in G_1 has at least $d/2$ self-loops.

> **Guideline:** First, replace each vertex of degree $d' > 3$ by a 3-regular expander of size d', and connect each of the original d' edges to a different vertex of this expander, thus obtaining a graph of maximum degree 4. Maintain the constraints associated with the original edges, and associate the equality constraint (i.e., $\phi(\sigma, \tau) = 1$ if and only if $\sigma = \tau$) to each new edge (residing in any of the added expanders). Next, augment the resulting N_1-vertex graph by the edges of a 3-regular expander of size N_1 (while associating with these edges the trivially satisfied constraint; i.e., $\phi(\sigma, \tau) = 1$ for all $\sigma, \tau \in \Sigma$). Finally, add at least $d/2$ self-loops to each vertex (using again trivially satisfied constraints), so as to obtain a d-regular graph. Prove that this sequence of modifications may only decrease the fraction of violated constraints, and that the decrease is only by a constant factor. The latter assertion relies on the equality constraints associated with the small expanders used in the first step.

Exercise 9.28 (free-bit complexity zero): Note that only sets in $\text{co}\mathcal{RP}$ have PCPs of *query* complexity zero. Furthermore, Exercise 9.17 implies that only sets in $\mathcal{P}$ have PCP-systems of logarithmic randomness and *query* complexity zero.

1. Show that only sets in $\mathcal{P}$ have PCP-systems of logarithmic randomness and *free-bit* complexity zero.

   (Hint: Consider an application of the FGLSS-reduction to a set having a PCP of free-bit complexity zero.)

2. In contrast, show that Graph Non-Isomorphism has a PCP-system of *free-bit* complexity zero (and linear randomness complexity).

Exercise 9.29 (free-bit complexity one): In continuation of Exercise 9.28, prove that only sets in $\mathcal{P}$ have PCP-systems of logarithmic randomness and free-bit complexity one.

> **Guideline:** Consider an application of the FGLSS-reduction to a set having a PCP of free-bit complexity one and randomness complexity r. Note that the question of whether the resulting graph has an independent set of size 2^r can be expressed as a 2CNF formula of size $\text{poly}(2^r)$, and see Exercise 2.22.

Exercise 9.30 (proving theorem 9.23): Using the following guidelines, provide a proof of Theorem 9.23. Let $S \in \mathcal{NP}$ and consider the 3CNF formulae that are obtained by the standard reduction of S to 3SAT (i.e., the one provided by the proofs of Theorems 2.21 and 2.22). Decouple the resulting 3CNF formulae into pairs of formulae (ψ_x, ϕ) such that ψ_x represents the "hard-wiring" of the input x and ϕ represents the computation itself. Referring to the mapping of 3CNF formulae to low-degree extensions presented in §9.3.2.2, show that the low-degree extension Φ that corresponds to ϕ can be evaluated in polynomial time (i.e., polynomial in the length of the input to Φ, which is $O(\log |\phi|)$). Conclude that the low-degree extension that corresponds to $\psi_x \wedge \phi$ can be evaluated in time $|x|^2$. Alternatively, note that it suffices to show that the assignment-oracle A (considered in §9.3.2.2) satisfies Φ and is consistent with x (and is a low-degree polynomial).

> **Guideline:** Note that the circuit constructed in the proof of Theorem 2.21 is highly uniform. In particular, the relation between wires and gates in this circuit can be represented by constant-depth circuits of unbounded fan-in and polynomial size (i.e., size that is polynomial in the length of the indices of wires and gates).

CHAPTER TEN

Relaxing the Requirements

The philosophers have only interpreted the world, in various ways; the point is to change it.

Karl Marx, "Theses on Feuerbach"

In light of the apparent infeasibility of solving numerous useful computational problems, it is natural to ask whether these problems can be relaxed such that the relaxation is both useful and allows for feasible solving procedures. We stress two aspects about the foregoing question: On the one hand, the relaxation should be sufficiently good for the intended applications; but, on the other hand, it should be significantly different from the original formulation of the problem so as to escape the infeasibility of the latter. We note that whether a relaxation is adequate for an intended application depends on the application, and thus much of the material in this chapter is less robust (or generic) than the treatment of the non-relaxed computational problems.

Summary: We consider two types of relaxations. The first type of relaxation refers to the computational problems themselves; that is, for each problem instance we *extend the set of admissible solutions*. In the context of search problems this means settling for solutions that have a value that is "sufficiently close" to the value of the optimal solution (with respect to some value function). Needless to say, the specific meaning of "sufficiently close" is part of the definition of the relaxed problem. In the context of decision problems this means that for some instances both answers are considered valid; specifically, we shall consider promise problems in which the no-instances are "far" from the yes-instances in some adequate sense (which is part of the definition of the relaxed problem).

The second type of relaxation deviates from the requirement that the solver provides an adequate answer on each valid instance. Instead, the behavior of the solver is analyzed with respect to a predetermined input distribution (or a class of such distributions), and bad behavior may occur with negligible probability where the probability is taken over this input distribution. That is, we replace worst-case analysis by *average-case* (or rather *typical-case*) *analysis*. Needless to say, a major component in this approach is limiting the class of distributions in a way that, on the one hand, allows for various types of natural distributions and, on the other hand, prevents the collapse of the corresponding notion of average-case hardness to the standard notion of worst-case hardness.

Organization. The first type of relaxation is treated in Section 10.1, where we consider approximations of search (or rather optimization) problems as well as approximate decision problems (aka property testing); see Section 10.1.1 and Section 10.1.2, respectively. The second type of relaxation, known as average/typicalcase-complexity, is treated in Section 10.2. The treatment of these two types is quite different. Section 10.1 provides a short and high-level introduction to various research areas, focusing on the main notions and illustrating them by reviewing some results (while providing no proofs). In contrast, Section 10.2 provides a basic treatment of a theory (of average/typical-case complexity), focusing on some basic results and providing a rather detailed exposition of the corresponding proofs.

10.1. Approximation

The notion of approximation is a very natural one, and has also arisen in other disciplines. Approximation is most commonly used in references to quantities (e.g., "the length of one meter is approximately forty inches"), but it is also used when referring to qualities (e.g., "an approximately correct account of a historical event"). In the context of computation, the notion of approximation modifies computational tasks such as search and decision problems. (In fact, we have already encountered it as a modifier of counting problems; see Section 6.2.2.)

Two major questions regarding approximation are (1) what constitutes a "good" approximation, and (2) whether it can be found more easily than finding an exact solution. The answer to the first question seems intimately related to the specific computational task at hand and to its role in the wider context (i.e., the higher level application): A good approximation is one that suffices for the intended application. Indeed, the importance of certain approximation problems is much more subjective than the importance of the corresponding optimization problems. This fact seems to stand in the way of attempts at providing a *comprehensive* theory of *natural* approximation problems (e.g., general classes of natural approximation problems that are shown to be computationally equivalent).

Turning to the second question, we note that in numerous cases natural approximation problems seem to be significantly easier than the corresponding original ("exact") problems. On the other hand, in numerous other cases, natural approximation problems are computationally equivalent to the original problems. We shall exemplify both cases by reviewing some specific results, but will not provide a *general systematic classification* (because such a classification is not known).[1]

We shall distinguish between approximation problems that are of a "search type" and problems that have a clear "decisional" flavor. In the first case we shall refer to a function that assigns values to possible solutions (of a search problem); whereas in the second case we shall refer to the distance between instances (of a decision problem).[2] We note that

---

[1] In contrast, systematic classifications of restricted classes of approximation problems are known. For example, see [56] for a classification of (approximate versions of) Constraint Satisfaction Problems.

[2] In some sense, this distinction is analogous to the distinction between the two aforementioned uses of the word *approximation*.

sometimes the same computational problem may be cast in both ways, but for most natural approximation problems one of the two frameworks is more appealing than the other. The common theme underlying both frameworks is that in each of them we extend the set of admissible solutions. In the case of search problems, we augment the set of optimal solutions by allowing also almost-optimal solutions. In the case of decision problems, we extend the set of solutions by allowing an arbitrary answer (solution) to some instances, which may be viewed as a promise problem that disallows these instances. In this case we focus on promise problems in which the yes- and no-instances are far apart (and the instances that violate the promise are closed to yes-instances).

Teaching note: Most of the results presented in this section refer to specific computational problems and (with one exception) are presented without a proof. In view of the complexity of the corresponding proofs and the merely illustrative role of these results in the context of Complexity Theory, we recommend doing the same in class.

10.1.1. Search or Optimization

As noted in Section 2.2.2, many search problems involve a set of potential solutions (per each problem instance) such that different solutions are assigned different "values" (resp., "costs") by some "value" (resp., "cost") function. In such a case, one is interested in finding a solution of maximum value (resp., minimum cost). A corresponding approximation problem may refer to finding a solution of approximately maximum value (resp., approximately minimum cost), where the specification of the desired level of approximation is part of the problem's definition. Let us elaborate.

For concreteness, we focus on the case of a value that we wish to maximize. For greater expressibility (or, actually, for greater flexibility), we allow the value of the solution to depend also on the instance itself.[3] Thus, for a (polynomially bounded) binary relation R and a *value function* $f : \{0, 1\}^* \times \{0, 1\}^* \to \mathbb{R}$, we consider the problem of finding solutions (with respect to R) that maximize the value of f. That is, given x (such that $R(x) \neq \emptyset$), the task is finding $y \in R(x)$ such that $f(x, y) = v_x$, where v_x is the maximum value of $f(x, y')$ over all $y' \in R(x)$. Typically, R is in $\mathcal{PC}$ and f is polynomial-time computable. Indeed, without loss of generality, we may assume that for every x it holds that $R(x) = \{0, 1\}^{\ell(|x|)}$ for some polynomial ℓ (see Exercise 2.8).[4] Thus, the optimization problem is recast as the following search problem: *Given x, find y such that $f(x, y) = v_x$, where $v_x = \max_{y' \in \{0,1\}^{\ell(|x|)}} \{f(x, y')\}$.*

We shall focus on *relative* approximation problems, where for some gap function $g : \{0, 1\}^* \to \{r \in \mathbb{R} : r \geq 1\}$ the (maximization) task is finding y such that $f(x, y) \geq v_x/g(x)$. Indeed, in some cases the approximation factor is stated as a function of the length of the input (i.e., $g(x) = g'(|x|)$ for some $g' : \mathbb{N} \to \{r \in \mathbb{R} : r \geq 1\}$), but often the approximation

---

[3]This convention is only a matter of convenience: Without loss of generality, we can express the same optimization problem using a value function that only depends on the solution by augmenting each solution with the corresponding instance (i.e., a solution y to an instance x can be encoded as a pair (x, y), and the resulting set of valid solutions for x will consist of pairs of the form $(x, \cdot)$). Hence, the foregoing convention merely allows for avoiding this cumbersome encoding of solutions.

[4]However, in this case (and in contrast to footnote 3), the value function f must depend both on the instance and on the solution (i.e., $f(x, y)$ may not be oblivious of x).

factor is stated in terms of some more refined parameter of the input (e.g., as a function of the number of vertices in a graph). Typically, g is polynomial-time computable.

Definition 10.1 (g-factor approximation): *Let* $f : \{0, 1\}^* \times \{0, 1\}^* \to \mathbb{R}$, $\ell : \mathbb{N} \to \mathbb{N}$, *and* $g : \{0, 1\}^* \to \{r \in \mathbb{R} : r \geq 1\}$.

Maximization version: *The g-factor approximation of maximizing f (wrt ℓ) is the search problem R such that $R(x) = \{y \in \{0, 1\}^{\ell(|x|)} : f(x, y) \geq v_x/g(x)\}$, where* $v_x = \max_{y' \in \{0,1\}^{\ell(|x|)}} \{f(x, y')\}$.

Minimization version: *The g-factor approximation of minimizing f (wrt ℓ) is the search problem R such that $R(x) = \{y \in \{0, 1\}^{\ell(|x|)} : f(x, y) \leq g(x) \cdot c_x\}$, where* $c_x = \min_{y' \in \{0,1\}^{\ell(|x|)}} \{f(x, y')\}$.

We note that for numerous NP-complete optimization problems, polynomial-time algorithms provide meaningful approximations. A few examples will be mentioned in §10.1.1.1. In contrast, for numerous other NP-complete optimization problems, natural approximation problems are computationally equivalent to the corresponding optimization problem. A few examples will be mentioned in §10.1.1.2, where we also introduce the notion of a *gap problem*, which is a promise problem (of the decision type) intended to capture the difficulty of the (approximate) search problem.

10.1.1.1. A Few Positive Examples

Let us start with a trivial example. Considering a problem such as finding the maximum clique in a graph, we note that finding a linear factor approximation is trivial (i.e., given a graph $G = (V, E)$, we may output any vertex in V as a $|V|$-factor approximation of the maximum clique in G). A famous non-trivial example is presented next.

Proposition 10.2 (factor two approximation to `minimum Vertex Cover`): *There exists a polynomial-time approximation algorithm that given a graph $G = (V, E)$ outputs a vertex cover that is at most twice as large as the minimum vertex cover of G.*

We warn that an approximation algorithm for `minimum Vertex Cover` does not yield such an algorithm for the complementary search problem (of `maximum Independent Set`). This phenomenon stands in contrast to the case of optimization, where an optimal solution for one search problem (e.g., `minimum Vertex Cover`) yields an optimal solution for the complementary search problem (`maximum Independent Set`).

Proof Sketch: The main observation is a connection between the set of maximal matchings and the set of vertex covers in a graph. Let M be any *maximal* matching in the graph $G = (V, E)$; that is, $M \subseteq E$ is a matching but augmenting it by any single edge yields a set that is not a matching. Then, on the one hand, the set of all vertices participating in M is a vertex cover of G, and, on the other hand, each vertex cover of G must contain at least one vertex of each edge of M. Thus, we can find the desired vertex cover by finding a maximal matching, which in turn can be found by a greedy algorithm. □

Another example. An instance of the traveling salesman problem (TSP) consists of a symmetric matrix of distances between pairs of points, and the task is finding a shortest tour that passes through all points. In general, no reasonable approximation is feasible for this problem (see Exercise 10.1), but here we consider two special cases in which the distances satisfy some natural constraints (and pretty good approximations are feasible).

Theorem 10.3 (approximations to special cases of TSP): *Polynomial-time algorithms exist for the following two computational problems.*

1. *Providing a 1.5-factor approximation for the special case of TSP in which the distances satisfy the triangle inequality.*
2. *For every $\varepsilon > 1$, providing a $(1 + \varepsilon)$-factor approximation for the special case of Euclidean TSP (i.e., for some constant k (e.g., $k = 2$), the points reside in a k-dimensional Euclidean space, and the distances refer to the standard Euclidean norm).*

A weaker version of Part 1 is given in Exercise 10.2. A detailed survey of Part 2 is provided in [13]. We note the difference exemplified by the two items of Theorem 10.3: Whereas Part 1 provides a polynomial-time approximation for a specific constant factor, Part 2 provides such an algorithm for any constant factor. Such a result is called a *polynomial-time approximation scheme* (abbreviated PTAS).

10.1.1.2. A Few Negative Examples

Let us start again with a trivial example. Considering a problem such as finding the maximum clique in a graph, we note that given a graph $G = (V, E)$ finding a $(1 + |V|^{-1})$-factor approximation of the maximum clique in G is as hard as finding a maximum clique in G. Indeed, this "result" is not really meaningful. In contrast, building on the PCP Theorem (Theorem 9.16), one may prove that finding a $|V|^{1-o(1)}$-factor approximation of the maximum clique in a general graph $G = (V, E)$ is as hard as finding a maximum clique in a general graph. This follows from the fact that the approximation problem is NP-hard (cf. Theorem 10.5).

The statement of such inapproximability results is made stronger by referring to a promise problem that consists of distinguishing instances of sufficiently far-apart values. Such promise problems are called gap problems, and are typically stated with respect to two bounding functions $g_1, g_2 : \{0, 1\}^* \to \mathbb{R}$ (which replace the gap function g of Definition 10.1). Typically, g_1 and g_2 are polynomial-time computable.

Definition 10.4 (gap problem for approximation of f): *Let f be as in Definition 10.1 and $g_1, g_2 : \{0, 1\}^* \to \mathbb{R}$.*

Maximization version: *For $g_1 \geq g_2$, the gap_{g_1,g_2} problem of maximizing f consists of distinguishing between $\{x : v_x \geq g_1(x)\}$ and $\{x : v_x < g_2(x)\}$, where $v_x = \max_{y \in \{0,1\}^{\ell(|x|)}} \{f(x, y)\}$.*

Minimization version: *For $g_1 \leq g_2$, the gap_{g_1,g_2} problem of minimizing f consists of distinguishing between $\{x : c_x \leq g_1(x)\}$ and $\{x : c_x > g_2(x)\}$, where $c_x = \min_{y \in \{0,1\}^{\ell(|x|)}} \{f(x, y)\}$.*

For example, the gap_{g_1,g_2} problem of maximizing the size of a clique in a graph consists of distinguishing between graphs G that have a clique of size $g_1(G)$ and graphs

G that have no clique of size $g_2(G)$. In this case, we typically let $g_i(G)$ be a function of the number of vertices in $G=(V, E)$; that is, $g_i(G) = g'_i(|V|)$. Indeed, letting $\omega(G)$ denote the size of the largest clique in the graph G, we let $\texttt{gapClique}_{L,s}$ denote the gap problem of distinguishing between $\{G=(V, E) : \omega(G) \geq L(|V|)\}$ and $\{G=(V, E) : \omega(G) < s(|V|)\}$, where $L \geq s$. Using this terminology, we restate (and strengthen) the aforementioned $|V|^{1-o(1)}$-factor inapproximability result of the maximum clique problem.

Theorem 10.5: *For some* $L(N) = N^{1-o(1)}$ *and* $s(N) = N^{o(1)}$*, it holds that* $\texttt{gapClique}_{L,s}$ *is NP-hard.*

The proof of Theorem 10.5 is based on a major refinement of Theorem 9.16 that refers to a PCP-system of amortized free-bit complexity that tends to zero (cf. §9.3.4.1). A weaker result, which follows from Theorem 9.16 itself, is presented in Exercise 10.3.

As we shall show next, results of the type of Theorem 10.5 imply the hardness of a corresponding approximation problem; that is, the hardness of deciding a gap problem implies the hardness of a search problem that refers to an analogous factor of approximation.

Proposition 10.6: *Let* f, g_1, g_2 *be as in Definition 10.4 and suppose that these functions are polynomial-time computable. Then the* gap_{g_1,g_2} *problem of maximizing* f *(resp., minimizing* f*) is reducible to the* g_1/g_2*-factor (resp.,* g_2/g_1*-factor) approximation of maximizing* f *(resp., minimizing* f*).*

Note that a reduction in the opposite direction does not necessarily exist (even in the case that the underlying optimization problem is self-reducible in some natural sense). Indeed, this is another difference between the current context (of approximation) and the context of optimization problems, where the search problem is reducible to a related decision problem.

Proof Sketch: We focus on the maximization version. On input x, we solve the gap_{g_1,g_2} problem, by making the query x, obtaining the answer y, and ruling that x has value at least $g_1(x)$ if and only if $f(x, y) \geq g_2(x)$. Recall that we need to analyze this reduction only on inputs that satisfy the promise. Thus, if $v_x \geq g_1(x)$ then the oracle must return a solution y that satisfies $f(x, y) \geq v_x/(g_1(x)/g_2(x))$, which implies that $f(x, y) \geq g_2(x)$. On the other hand, if $v_x < g_2(x)$ then $f(x, y) \leq v_x < g_2(x)$ holds for any possible solution y. $\qquad\square$

Additional examples. Let us consider $\texttt{gapVC}_{s,L}$, the gap_{g_s,g_L} problem of minimizing the vertex cover of a graph, where s and L are constants and $g_s(G) = s \cdot |V|$ (resp., $g_L(G) = L \cdot |V|$) for any graph $G=(V, E)$. Then, Proposition 10.2 implies (via Proposition 10.6) that, for every constant s, the problem $\texttt{gapVC}_{s,2s}$ is solvable in polynomial time. In contrast, sufficiently narrowing the gap between the two thresholds yields an inapproximability result. In particular:

Theorem 10.7: *For some constants* $s > 0$ *and* $L < 1$ *such that* $L > \frac{4}{3} \cdot s$ *(e.g.,* $s = 0.62$ *and* $L = 0.84$*), the problem* $\texttt{gapVC}_{s,L}$ *is NP-hard.*

The proof of Theorem 10.7 is based on a complicated refinement of Theorem 9.16. Again, a weaker result follows from Theorem 9.16 itself (see Exercise 10.4).

As noted, refinements of the PCP Theorem (Theorem 9.16) play a key role in establishing inapproximability results such as Theorems 10.5 and 10.7. In that respect, it is
adequate to recall that Theorem 9.21 establishes the equivalence of the PCP Theorem
itself and the NP-hardness of a gap problem concerning the maximization of the number
of clauses that are satisfied in a given 3-CNF formula. Specifically, $\text{gapSAT}^3_\varepsilon$ was defined
(in Definition 9.20) as the gap problem consisting of distinguishing between satisfiable
3-CNF formulae and 3-CNF formulae for which each truth assignment violates at least an
ε fraction of the clauses. Although Theorem 9.21 does not specify the quantitative relation
that underlies its qualitative assertion, when (refined and) combined with the best-known
PCP construction, it does yield the best-possible bound.

Theorem 10.8: *For every $v < 1/8$, the problem gapSAT^3_v is NP-hard.*

On the other hand, $\text{gapSAT}^3_{1/8}$ is solvable in polynomial time.

Sharp thresholds. The aforementioned opposite results (regarding gapSAT^3_v) exemplify
a sharp threshold on the (factor of) approximation that can be obtained by an efficient
algorithm. Another appealing example refers to the following maximization problem in
which the instances are systems of linear equations over GF(2) and the task is finding
an assignment that satisfies as many equations as possible. Note that by merely selecting
an assignment at random, we expect to satisfy half of the equations. Also note that
it is easy to determine whether there exists an assignment that satisfies all equations.
Let $\text{gapLin}_{L,s}$ denote the problem of distinguishing between systems in which one can
satisfy at least an L fraction of the equations and systems in which one cannot satisfy
an s fraction (or more) of the equations. Then, as just noted, $\text{gapLin}_{L,0.5}$ is trivial
(for every $L \geq 0.5$) and $\text{gapLin}_{1,s}$ is feasible (for every $s < 1$). In contrast, moving
both thresholds (slightly) away from the corresponding extremes yields an NP-hard gap
problem:

Theorem 10.9: *For every constant $\varepsilon > 0$, the problem $\text{gapLin}_{1-\varepsilon,0.5+\varepsilon}$ is NP-hard.*

The proof of Theorem 10.9 is based on a major refinement of Theorem 9.16. In fact,
the corresponding PCP-system (for NP) is merely a reformulation of Theorem 10.9: The
verifier makes three queries and tests a linear condition regarding the answers, while
using a logarithmic number of coin tosses. This verifier accepts any yes-instance with
probability at least $1 - \varepsilon$ (when given oracle access to a suitable proof), and rejects any
no-instance with probability at least $0.5 - \varepsilon$ (regardless of the oracle being accessed). A
weaker result, which follows from Theorem 9.16 itself, is presented in Exercise 10.5.

Gap location. Theorems 10.8 and 10.9 illustrate two opposite situations with respect to
the "location" of the "gap" for which the corresponding promise problem is hard. Recall
that both gapSAT and gapLin are formulated with respect to two thresholds, where each
threshold bounds the fraction of "local" conditions (i.e., clauses or equations) that are
satisfiable in the case of yes- and no-instances, respectively. In the case of gapSAT, the
high threshold (referring to yes-instances) was set to 1, and thus only the low threshold
(referring to no-instances) remained a free parameter. Nevertheless, a hardness result was
established for gapSAT, and furthermore this was achieved for an optimal value of the

low threshold (cf. the foregoing discussion of sharp thresholds). In contrast, in the case of gapLin, setting the high threshold to 1 makes the gap problem efficiently solvable. Thus, the hardness of gapLin was established at a different location of the high threshold. Specifically, hardness (for an optimal value of the ratio of thresholds) was established when setting the high threshold to $1 - \varepsilon$, for any $\varepsilon > 0$.

A final comment. All the aforementioned inapproximability results refer to approximation (resp., gap) problems that are relaxations of optimization problems in NP (i.e., the optimization problem is computationally equivalent to a decision problem in $\mathcal{NP}$; see Section 2.2.2). In these cases, the NP-hardness of the approximation (resp., gap) problem implies that the corresponding optimization problem is reducible to the approximation (resp., gap) problem. In other words, in these cases nothing is gained by relaxing the original optimization problem, because the relaxed version remains just as hard.

10.1.2. Decision or Property Testing

A natural notion of relaxation for decision problems arises when considering the distance between instances, where a natural notion of distance is the Hamming distance (i.e., the fraction of bits on which two strings disagree). Loosely speaking, this relaxation (called *property testing*) refers to distinguishing inputs that reside in a predetermined set S from inputs that are "relatively far" from any input that resides in the set. Two natural types of promise problems emerge (with respect to any predetermined set S (and the Hamming distance between strings)):

1. *Relaxed decision wrt a fixed relative distance*: Fixing a distance parameter δ, we consider the problem of distinguishing inputs in S from inputs in $\Gamma_\delta(S)$, where

$$\Gamma_\delta(S) \overset{\text{def}}{=} \{x : \forall z \in S \cap \{0, 1\}^{|x|} \ \Delta(x, z) > \delta \cdot |x|\} \tag{10.1}$$

and $\Delta(x_1 \cdots x_m, z_1 \cdots z_m) = |\{i : x_i \neq z_i\}|$ denotes the number of bits on which $x = x_1 \cdots x_m$ and $z = z_1 \cdots z_m$ disagree. Thus, here we consider a promise problem that is a restriction (or a special case) of the problem of deciding membership in S.

2. *Relaxed decision wrt a variable distance*: Here the instances are pairs (x, δ), where x is as in Type 1 and $\delta \in [0, 1]$ is a (relative) distance parameter. The yes-instances are pairs (x, δ) such that $x \in S$, whereas (x, δ) is a no-instance if $x \in \Gamma_\delta(S)$.

We shall focus on Type 1 formulation, which seems to capture the essential question of whether or not these relaxations lower the complexity of the original decision problem. The study of Type 2 formulation refers to a relatively secondary question, which assumes a positive answer to the first question; that is, assuming that the relaxed form is easier than the original form, we ask how the complexity of the problem is affected by making the distance parameter smaller (which means making the relaxed problem "tighter" and ultimately equivalent to the original problem).

We note that for numerous NP-complete problems there exist natural (Type 1) relaxations that are solvable in polynomial time. Actually, these algorithms run in *sub-linear* time (specifically, in poly-logarithmic time), when given direct access to the input. A few examples will be presented in §10.1.2.2 (but, as indicated in §10.1.2.2, this is not a generic phenomenon). Before turning to these examples, we discuss several important definitional issues.

10.1.2.1. Definitional Issues
Property testing is concerned not only with solving relaxed versions of NP-hard problems but also with solving these problems (as well as problems in $\mathcal{P}$) in *sub-linear time*. Needless to say, such results assume a model of computation in which algorithms have direct access to bits in the (representation of the) input (see Definition 10.10).

> **Definition 10.10** (a direct access model – conventions): *An algorithm with* direct access to its input *is given its* main input *on a special input device that is accessed as an oracle (see §1.2.3.6). In addition, the algorithm is given the length of the input and possibly other parameters on a* secondary input device. *The complexity of such an algorithm is stated in terms of the length of its main input.*

Indeed, the description in §5.2.4.2 refers to such a model, but there the main input is viewed as an oracle and the secondary input is viewed as the input. In the current model, poly-logarithmic time means time that is poly-logarithmic in the length of the main input, which means time that is polynomial in the length of the binary representation of the length of the main input. Thus, poly-logarithmic time yields a robust notion of extremely efficient computations. As we shall see, such computations suffice for solving various (property testing) problems.

> **Definition 10.11** (property testing for S): *For any fixed $\delta > 0$, the promise problem of distinguishing S from $\Gamma_\delta(S)$ is called* property testing for S (with respect to δ).

Recall that we say that a randomized algorithm solves a promise problem if it accepts every yes-instance (resp., rejects every no-instance) with probability at least $2/3$. Thus, a (randomized) property testing for S accepts every input in S (resp., rejects every input in $\Gamma_\delta(S)$) with probability at least $2/3$.

The question of representation. The specific representation of the input is of major concern in the current context. This is due to (1) the *effect of the representation on the distance measure* and to (2) the *dependence of direct access machines on the specific representation of the input*. Let us elaborate on both aspects.

1. Recall that we defined the distance between objects in terms of the Hamming distance between their representations. Clearly, in such a case, the choice of representation is crucial and different representations may yield different distance measures. Furthermore, in this case, the distance between objects is not preserved under various (natural) representations that are considered "equivalent" in standard studies of Computational Complexity. For example, in previous parts of this book, when referring to computational problems concerning graphs, we did not care whether the graph was represented by its adjacency matrix or by its incidence-list. In contrast, these two representations induce very different distance measures and correspondingly different property testing problems (see §10.1.2.2). Likewise, the use of padding (and other trivial syntactic conventions) becomes problematic (e.g., when using a significant amount of padding, all objects are deemed close to one another (and property testing for any set becomes trivial)).

2. Since our focus is on sub-linear time algorithms, we may not afford transforming the input from one natural format to another. Thus, representations that are considered

equivalent with respect to polynomial-time algorithms, may not be equivalent with respect to sub-linear time algorithms that have a direct access to the representation of the object. For example, adjacency queries and incidence queries cannot emulate one another in small time (i.e., in time that is sub-linear in the number of vertices).

Both aspects are further clarified by the examples provided in §10.1.2.2.

The essential role of the promise. Recall that, for a fixed constant $\delta > 0$, we consider the promise problem of distinguishing S from $\Gamma_\delta(S)$. The promise means that all instances that are neither in S nor far from S (i.e., not in $\Gamma_\delta(S)$) are ignored, which is essential for sub-linear algorithms for natural problems. This makes the property testing task potentially easier than the corresponding standard decision task (cf. §10.1.2.2). To demonstrate the point, consider the set S consisting of strings that have a majority of 1's. Then, deciding membership in S requires linear time, because random n-bit long strings with $\lfloor n/2 \rfloor$ ones cannot be distinguished from random n-bit long strings with $\lfloor n/2 \rfloor + 1$ ones by probing a sub-linear number of locations (even if randomization and error probability are allowed – see Exercise 10.8). On the other hand, the fraction of 1's in the input can be approximated by a randomized poly-logarithmic time algorithm (which yields a property tester for S; see Exercise 10.9). Thus, for some sets, deciding membership requires linear time, while property testing can be done in poly-logarithmic time.

The essential role of randomization. Referring to the foregoing example, we note that randomization is essential for any sub-linear time algorithm that distinguishes this set S from, say, $\Gamma_{0.1}(S)$. Specifically, a sub-linear time deterministic algorithm cannot distinguish 1^n from any input that has 1's in each position probed by that algorithm on input 1^n. In general, on input x, a (sub-linear time) deterministic algorithm always reads the same bits of x and thus cannot distinguish x from any z that agrees with x on these bit locations.

Note that, in both cases, we are able to prove lower bounds on the time complexity of algorithms. This success is due to the fact that these lower bounds are actually information theoretic in nature; that is, these lower bounds actually refer to the number of queries performed by these algorithms.

10.1.2.2. Two Models for Testing Graph Properties

In this subsection we consider the complexity of property testing for sets of graphs that are *closed under graph isomorphism*; such sets are called graph properties. In view of the importance of representation in the context of property testing, we explicitly consider two standard representations of graphs (cf. Appendix G.1), which indeed yield two different models of testing graph properties.

1. The adjacency matrix representation. Here a graph $G = ([N], E)$ is represented (in a somewhat redundant form) by an N-by-N Boolean matrix $M_G = (m_{i,j})_{i,j \in [N]}$ such that $m_{i,j} = 1$ if and only if $\{i, j\} \in E$.
2. Bounded incidence-lists representation. For a fixed parameter d, a graph $G = ([N], E)$ of degree at most d is represented (in a somewhat redundant form) by a mapping $\mu_G : [N] \times [d] \to [N] \cup \{\bot\}$ such that $\mu_G(u, i) = v$ if v is the ith neighbor of u and $\mu_G(u, i) = \bot$ if v has fewer than i neighbors.

We stress that the aforementioned representations determine both the notion of distance between graphs and the type of queries performed by the algorithm. As we shall see, the difference between these two representations yields a big difference in the complexity of corresponding property testing problems.

Theorem 10.12 (property testing in the adjacency matrix representation): *For any fixed $\delta > 0$ and each of the following sets, there exists a poly-logarithmic time randomized algorithm that solves the corresponding property testing problem* (with respect to δ).

- *For every fixed $k \geq 2$, the set of k-colorable graphs.*
- *For every fixed $\rho > 0$, the set of graphs having a clique* (resp., independent set) *of density ρ.*
- *For every fixed $\rho > 0$, the set of N-vertex graphs having a cut[5] with at least $\rho \cdot N^2$ edges.*
- *For every fixed $\rho > 0$, the set of N-vertex graphs having a bisection[5] with at most $\rho \cdot N^2$ edges.*

In contrast, for some $\delta > 0$, there exists a graph property in $\mathcal{NP}$ for which property testing (with respect to δ) *requires linear time.*

The testing algorithms (asserted in Theorem 10.12) use a constant number of queries, where this constant is polynomial in the constant $1/\delta$. In contrast, exact decision procedures for the corresponding sets require a linear number of queries. The running time of the aforementioned algorithms hides a constant that is exponential in their query complexity (except for the case of 2-colorability where the hidden constant is polynomial in $1/\delta$). Note that such dependencies seem essential, since setting $\delta = 1/N^2$ regains the original (non-relaxed) decision problems (which, with the exception of 2-colorability, are all NP-complete). Turning to the lower bound (asserted in Theorem 10.12), we mention that the graph property for which this bound is proved is not a natural one. As in §10.1.2.1, the lower bound on the time complexity follows from a lower bound on the query complexity.

Theorem 10.12 exhibits a dichotomy between graph properties for which property testing is possible by a constant number of queries and graph properties for which property testing requires a linear number of queries. A combinatorial characterization of the graph properties for which property testing is possible (in the adjacency matrix representation) when using a constant number of queries is known.[6] We note that the constant in this characterization may depend arbitrarily on δ (and indeed, in some cases, it is a function growing faster than a tower of $1/\delta$ exponents). For example, property testing for the set of *triangle-free* graphs is possible by using a number of queries that depends only on δ, but it is known that this number must grow faster than any polynomial in $1/\delta$.

Turning back to Theorem 10.12, we note that the results regarding property testing for the sets corresponding to max-cut and min-bisection yield approximation algorithms

---

[5]A cut in a graph $G = ([N], E)$ is a partition (S_1, S_2) of the set of vertices (i.e., $S_1 \cup S_2 = [N]$ and $S_1 \cap S_2 = \emptyset$), and the edges of the cut are the edges with exactly one end-point in S_1. A bisection is a cut of the graph to two parts of equal cardinality.

[6]Describing this fascinating result of Alon et al. [9], which refers to the notion of regular partitions (introduced by Szemerédi), is beyond the scope of the current text.

with an additive error term (of δN^2). For dense graphs (i.e., N-vertex graphs having $\Omega(N^2)$ edges), this yields a constant factor approximation for the standard approximation problem (as in Definition 10.1). That is, for every constant $c > 1$, we obtain a *c-factor approximation* of the problem of maximizing the size of a cut (resp., minimizing the size of a bisection) *in dense graphs*. On the other hand, the result regarding clique yields a so-called dual-approximation for maximum clique; that is, we approximate the minimum number of missing edges in the densest induced subgraph of a given size.

Indeed, Theorem 10.12 is meaningful only for dense graphs. This holds, in general, for any graph property in the adjacency matrix representation.[7] Also note that property testing is trivial, under the adjacency matrix representation, for any graph property S satisfying $\Gamma_{o(1)}(S) = \emptyset$ (e.g., the set of connected graphs, the set of Hamiltonian graphs, etc).

We now turn to the bounded incidence-lists representation, which is relevant only for bounded degree graphs. The problems of max-cut, min-bisection, and clique (as in Theorem 10.12) are trivial under this representation, but graph connectivity becomes non-trivial, and the complexity of property testing for the set of bipartite graphs changes dramatically.

Theorem 10.13 (property testing in the bounded incidence-lists representation):
The following assertions refer to the representation of graphs by incidence-lists of length d.

- *For any fixed d and $\delta > 0$, there exists a poly-logarithmic time randomized algorithm that solves the property testing problem for the set of connected graphs of degree at most d.*
- *For any fixed d and $\delta > 0$, there exists a sub-linear time randomized algorithm that solves the property testing problem for the set of bipartite graphs of degree at most d. Specifically, on input an N-vertex graph, the algorithm runs for $\widetilde{O}(\sqrt{N})$ time.*
- *For any fixed $d \geq 3$ and some $\delta > 0$, property testing for the set of N-vertex (3-regular) bipartite graphs requires $\Omega(\sqrt{N})$ queries.*
- *For some fixed d and $\delta > 0$, property testing for the set of N-vertex 3-colorable graphs of degree at most d requires $\Omega(N)$ queries.*

The running time of the algorithms (asserted in Theorem 10.13) hides a constant that is polynomial in $1/\delta$. Providing a characterization of graph properties according to the complexity of the corresponding tester (in the bounded incidence-lists representation) is an interesting open problem.

Decoupling the distance from the representation. So far, we have confined our attention to the Hamming distance between the representations of graphs. This made the choice of representation even more important than usual (i.e., more crucial than is common in Complexity Theory). In contrast, it is natural to consider a notion of distance between graphs that is independent of their representation. For example, the distance between

---

[7]In this model, as shown next, property testing of non-dense graphs is trivial. Specifically, fixing the distance parameter δ, we call an N-vertex graph non-dense if it has less than $(\delta/2) \cdot \binom{N}{2}$ edges. The point is that, for non-dense graphs, the property testing problem for any set S is trivial, because we may just accept any non-dense (N-vertex) graph if and only if S contains some non-dense (N-vertex) graph. Clearly, the decision is correct in the case that S does not contain non-dense graphs. However, the decision is also admissible in the case that S does contain some non-dense graph, because in this case every non-dense graph is "δ-close" to S (i.e., it is not in $\Gamma_\delta(S)$).

$G_1 = (V_1, E_1)$ and $G_2 = (V_2, E_2)$ can be defined as the minimum of the size of symmetric difference between E_1 and the set of edges in a graph that is isomorphic to G_2. The corresponding relative distance may be defined as the distance divided by $|E_1| + |E_2|$ (or by $\max(|E_1|, |E_2|)$).

10.1.2.3. Beyond Graph Properties

Property testing has been applied to a variety of computational problems beyond the domain of graph theory. In fact, computational problems such as these first emerged in the algebraic domain, where the instances (to be viewed as inputs to the testing algorithm) are functions and the relevant properties are sets of algebraic functions. The archetypical example is the set of low-degree polynomials, that is, m-variate polynomials of total (or individual) degree d over some finite field $GF(q)$, where m, d, and q are parameters that may depend on the length of the input (or satisfy some relationships; e.g., $q = d^3 = m^6$). Note that, in this case, the input is the ("full" or "explicit") description of an m-variate function over $GF(q)$, which means that it has length $q^m \cdot \log_2 q$. Viewing the problem instance as a function suggests a natural measure of distance (i.e., the fraction of arguments on which the functions disagree) as well as a natural way of accessing the instance (i.e., querying the function for the value of selected arguments).

Note that we have referred to these computational problems, under a different terminology, in §9.3.2.2 and in §9.3.2.1. In particular, in §9.3.2.1 we refereed to the special case of linear Boolean functions (i.e., individual degree 1 and $q = 2$), whereas in §9.3.2.2 we used the setting $q = \text{poly}(d)$ and $m = d/\log d$ (where d is a bound on the total degree).

Other domains of computational problems in which property testing was studied include geometry (e.g., clustering problems), formal languages (e.g., testing membership in regular sets), coding theory (cf. Appendix E.1.3), probability theory (e.g., testing equality of distributions), and combinatorics (e.g., monotone and junta functions). As discussed at the end of §10.1.2.2, it is often natural to decouple the distance measure from the representation of the objects (i.e., the way of accessing the problem instance). This is done by introducing a representation-independent notion of distance between instances, which should be natural in the context of the problem at hand.

10.2. Average-Case Complexity

> **Teaching note:** We view average-case complexity as referring to the performance on "average" (or rather typical) instances, and not as the average performance on random instances. This choice is justified in §10.2.1.1. Thus, it may be more justified to refer to the following theory by the name typical-case complexity. Still, the name average-case complexity was retained for historical reasons.

Our approach so far (including in Section 10.1) is termed worst-case complexity, because it refers to the performance of potential algorithms on each legitimate instance (and hence to the performance on the worst-possible instance). That is, computational problems were defined as referring to a set of instances, and performance guarantees were required to hold for each instance in this set. In contrast, average-case complexity allows for ignoring a negligible measure of the possible instances, where *the identity of the ignored instances is determined by the analysis of potential solvers and not by the problem's statement.*

A few comments are in place. Firstly, as just hinted, the standard statement of the worst-case complexity of a computational problem (especially one having a promise) may also ignore some instances (i.e., those considered inadmissible or violating the promise), but these instances are determined by the problem's statement. In contrast, the inputs ignored in average-case complexity are not inadmissible in any inherent sense (and are certainly not identified as such by the problem's statement). It is just that they are viewed as exceptional when claiming that a specific algorithm solves the problem; that is, these exceptional instances are determined by the analysis of that algorithm. Needless to say, these exceptional instances ought to be rare (i.e., occur with negligible probability).

The last sentence raises a couple of issues. Most importantly, a distribution on the set of admissible instances has to be specified. In fact, we shall consider a new type of computational problems, each consisting of a standard computational problem coupled with a probability distribution on instances. Consequently, the question of which distributions should be considered in a theory of average-case complexity arises. This question and numerous other definitional issues will be addressed in §10.2.1.1.

Before proceeding, let us spell out the rather straightforward motivation for the study of the average-case complexity of computational problems: It is that, in real-life applications, one may be perfectly happy with an algorithm that solves the problem fast on almost all instances that arise in the relevant application. That is, one may be willing to tolerate error provided that it occurs with negligible probability, where the probability is taken over the distribution of instances encountered in the application. The study of average-case complexity is aimed at exploring the possible benefit of such a relaxation, distinguishing cases in which a benefit exists from cases in which it does not exist. A key aspect in such a study is a good modeling of the type of distributions (of instances) that are encountered in natural algorithmic applications.

Let us consider the foregoing motivation from a slightly different perspective: The conjecture that $\mathcal{P} \neq \mathcal{NP}$ (or rather $\mathcal{NP} \not\subseteq \mathcal{BPP}$) only asserts that intractability is a feature of some instances of some problems in $\mathcal{NP}$. These intractable instances may be very rare and pathological. The theory of average-case complexity addresses the question of whether intractability can also be a feature of "typical" instances (i.e., whether intractable instances may occur with noticeable probability with respect to some simple distributions). Needless to say, the meaningfulness of the latter question depends on restricting the class of distributions such that only simple (rather than pathological) distributions are allowed. We shall consider two such classes of distributions (see §10.2.1.1 and §10.2.2.2, respectively) and show that if intractability occurs with respect to the wider class, then it occurs also with respect to the more restricted class (see Theorem 10.26).

An average-case version of the $\mathcal{P} \neq \mathcal{NP}$ question. Indeed, a fundamental question that arises is *whether every natural computational problem can be solved efficiently when restricting attention to typical instances.* The conjecture that underlies this section is that, for a well-motivated choice of definitions, the answer is negative; that is, our conjecture is that the "distributional version" of NP is not contained in the average-case (or typical-case) version of P. This means that some NP problems are not merely hard in the worst case, but are rather "typically hard" (i.e., hard on typical instances drawn from some simple distribution). This suggests that *hard instances may occur in natural algorithmic* *applications* (and not only in cryptographic (or other "adversarial") applications that are designed on purpose to produce hard instances).[8]

The foregoing conjecture motivates the development of an average-case analogue of NP-completeness, which will be presented in this section. Indeed, the entire section may be viewed as an average-case analogue of Chapter 2. In particular, this (average-case) theory identifies distributional problems that are "typically hard" provided that distributional problems that are "typically hard" exist at all. If one believes the foregoing conjecture then, for such complete (distributional) problems, one should not seek algorithms that solve these problems efficiently on typical instances.

Organization. A major part of our exposition is devoted to the definitional issues that arise when developing a general theory of average-case complexity. These issues are discussed in §10.2.1.1. In §10.2.1.2 we prove the existence of distributional problems that are "NP-complete" in the corresponding average-case complexity sense. Furthermore, we show how to obtain such a distributional version for any natural NP-complete decision problem. In §10.2.1.3 we extend the treatment to randomized algorithms. Additional ramifications are presented in Section 10.2.2.

10.2.1. The Basic Theory

In this section we provide a basic treatment of the theory of average-case complexity, while postponing important ramifications to Section 10.2.2. The basic treatment consists of the preferred definitional choices for the main concepts as well as the identification of complete problems for a natural class of average-case computational problems.

10.2.1.1. Definitional Issues

The theory of average-case complexity is more subtle than may appear at first thought. In addition to the generic conceptual difficulty involved in defining relaxations, difficulties arise from the "interface" between standard probabilistic analysis and the conventions of Complexity Theory. This is most striking in the definition of the class of feasible average-case computations. Referring to the theory of worst-case complexity as a guideline, we shall address the following aspects of the analogous theory of average-case complexity.

1. *Setting the general framework.* We shall consider distributional problems, which are standard computational problems (see Section 1.2.2) coupled with distributions on the relevant instances.
2. *Identifying the class of feasible* (distributional) *problems.* Seeking an average-case analogue of classes such as $\mathcal{P}$, we shall reject the first definition that comes to mind (i.e., the naive notion of "average polynomial time"), briefly discuss several related alternatives, and adopt one of them for the main treatment.

---

[8] We highlight two differences between the current context (of natural algorithmic applications) and the context of cryptography. Firstly, in the current context and when referring to problems that are typically hard, the simplicity of the underlying input distribution is of great concern: The simpler this distribution, the more appealing the hardness assertion becomes. This concern is irrelevant in the context of cryptography. On the other hand (see discussion at the beginning of Section 7.1.1 and/or at end of §10.2.2.2), cryptographic applications require the ability to efficiently generate hard instances *together with corresponding solutions*.

3. *Identifying the class of interesting* (distributional) *problems.* Seeking an average-case analogue of the class $\mathcal{NP}$, we shall avoid both the extreme of allowing arbitrary distributions (which collapses average-case hardness to worst-case hardness) and the opposite extreme of confining the treatment to a single distribution such as the uniform distribution.

4. *Developing an adequate notion of reduction among* (distributional) *problems.* As in the theory of worst-case complexity, this notion should preserve feasible solvability (in the current distributional context).

We now turn to the actual treatment of each of the aforementioned aspects.

Step 1: Defining distributional problems. Focusing on decision problems, we define distributional problems as pairs consisting of a decision problem and a probability ensemble.[9] For simplicity, here a probability ensemble $\{X_n\}_{n\in\mathbb{N}}$ is a sequence of random variables such that X_n ranges over $\{0, 1\}^n$. Thus, $(S, \{X_n\}_{n\in\mathbb{N}})$ is the distributional problem consisting of the problem of deciding membership in the set S with respect to the probability ensemble $\{X_n\}_{n\in\mathbb{N}}$. (The treatment of search problems is similar; see §10.2.2.1.) We denote the uniform probability ensemble by $U = \{U_n\}_{n\in\mathbb{N}}$; that is, U_n is uniform over $\{0, 1\}^n$.

Step 2: Identifying the class of feasible problems. The first idea that comes to mind is defining the problem $(S, \{X_n\}_{n\in\mathbb{N}})$ as feasible (on the average) if there exists an algorithm A that solves S such that the *average running time* of A on X_n is bounded by a polynomial in n (i.e., there exists a polynomial p such that $\mathsf{E}[t_A(X_n)] \leq p(n)$, where $t_A(x)$ denotes the running time of A on input x). The problem with this definition is that it very sensitive to the model of computation and is not closed under algorithmic composition. Both deficiencies are a consequence of the fact that t_A may be polynomial on the average with respect to $\{X_n\}_{n\in\mathbb{N}}$ but t_A^2 may fail to be so (e.g., consider $t_A(x'x'') = 2^{|x'|}$ if $x' = x''$ and $t_A(x'x'') = |x'x''|^2$ otherwise, coupled with the uniform distribution over $\{0, 1\}^n$). We conclude that the *average running time* of algorithms is not a robust notion. We also doubt the soundness of the appeal of this notion, and view the *typical running time* of algorithms (as defined next) as a more natural notion. Thus, we shall consider an algorithm as feasible if its running time is typically polynomial.[10]

We say that A is typically polynomial time on $X = \{X_n\}_{n\in\mathbb{N}}$ if there exists a polynomial p such that the probability that A runs more that $p(n)$ steps on X_n is *negligible* (i.e., for every polynomial q and all sufficiently large n it holds that $\Pr[t_A(X_n) > p(n)] < 1/q(n)$). The question is what is required in the "untypical" cases, and two possible definitions follow.

1. The simpler option is saying that $(S, \{X_n\}_{n\in\mathbb{N}})$ is (typically) feasible if there exists an algorithm A that solves S such that A is typically polynomial-time on $X = \{X_n\}_{n\in\mathbb{N}}$.

---

[9]We mention that even this choice is not evident. Specifically, Levin [154] (see discussion in [89]) advocates the use of a single probability distribution defined over the set of all strings. His argument is that this makes the theory less representation-dependent. At the time we were convinced of his argument (see [89]), but currently we feel that the representation-dependent effects discussed in [89] are legitimate. Furthermore, the alternative formulation of [154, 89] comes across as unnatural and tends to confuse some readers.

[10]An alternative choice, taken by Levin [154] (see discussion in [89]), is considering as feasible (wrt $X = \{X_n\}_{n\in\mathbb{N}}$) any algorithm that runs in time that is polynomial in a function that is linear on the average (wrt X); that is, requiring that there exists a polynomial p and a function $\ell : \{0, 1\}^* \to \mathbb{N}$ such that $t(x) \leq p(\ell(x))$ for every x and $\mathsf{E}[\ell(X_n)] = O(n)$. This definition is robust (i.e., it does not suffer from the aforementioned deficiencies) and is arguably as "natural" as the naive definition (i.e., $\mathsf{E}[t_A(X_n)] \leq \mathrm{poly}(n)$).

This effectively requires A to *correctly solve S on each instance*, which is more than was required in the motivational discussion. (Indeed, if the underlying motivation is ignoring rare cases, then we should ignore them altogether rather than ignoring them in a partial manner (i.e., only ignore their affect on the running time).)

2. The alternative, which fits the motivational discussion, is saying that (S, X) is (typically) feasible if there exists an algorithm A such that A typically solves S on X in polynomial time; that is, there exists a polynomial p such that *the probability that on input X_n algorithm A either errs or runs more that $p(n)$ steps is negligible*. This formulation totally ignores the untypical instances. Indeed, in this case we may assume, without loss of generality, that A always runs in polynomial time (see Exercise 10.11), but we shall not do so here (in order to facilitate viewing the first option as a special case of the current option).

We stress that both alternatives actually define *typical* feasibility and not *average-case* feasibility. To illustrate the difference between the two options, consider the distributional problem of deciding whether a uniformly selected (n-vertex) graph is 3-colorable. Intuitively, this problem is "typically trivial" (with respect to the uniform distribution),[11] because the algorithm may always say no and be wrong with exponentially vanishing probability. Indeed, this trivial algorithm is admissible by the second approach, but not by the first approach. In light of the foregoing discussions, we adopt the second approach.

Definition 10.14 (the class tpc$\mathcal{P}$): *We say that A typically solves $(S, \{X_n\}_{n\in\mathbb{N}})$ in polynomial time if there exists a polynomial p such that the probability that on input X_n algorithm A either errs or runs more that $p(n)$ steps is negligible.[12] We denote by tpc$\mathcal{P}$ the class of distributional problems that are typically solvable in polynomial time.*

Clearly, for every $S \in \mathcal{P}$ and every probability ensemble X, it holds that $(S, X) \in$ tpc$\mathcal{P}$. However, tpc$\mathcal{P}$ also contains distributional problems (S, X) with $S \notin \mathcal{P}$ (see Exercises 10.12 and 10.13). The big question, which underlies the theory of average-case complexity, is whether all *natural distributional versions* of $\mathcal{NP}$ are in tpc$\mathcal{P}$. Thus, we turn to identify such versions.

Step 3: Identifying the class of interesting problems. Seeking to identify reasonable distributional versions of $\mathcal{NP}$, we note that two extreme choices should be avoided. On the one hand, we must limit the class of admissible distributions so as to prevent the collapse of average-case hardness to worst-case hardness (by a selection of a pathological distribution that resides on the "worst case" instances). On the other hand, we should allow for various types of natural distributions rather than confining attention merely to the uniform distribution.[13] Recall that our aim is addressing all possible input distributions

---

[11] In contrast, testing whether a given graph is 3-colorable seems "typically hard" for other distributions (see either Theorem 10.19 or Exercise 10.27). Needless to say, in the latter distributions both yes-instances and no-instances appear with noticeable probability.

[12] Recall that a function $\mu : \mathbb{N} \to \mathbb{N}$ is negligible if for every positive polynomial q and all sufficiently large n it holds that $\mu(n) < 1/q(n)$. We say that A errs on x if $A(x)$ differs from the indicator value of the predicate $x \in S$.

[13] Confining attention to the uniform distribution seems misguided by the naive belief according to which this distribution is the *only* one relevant to applications. In contrast, we believe that, for most natural applications, the uniform distribution over instances is not relevant at all.

that may occur in applications, and thus there is no justification for confining attention to the uniform distribution. Still, arguably, the distributions occuring in applications are "relatively simple," and so we seek to identify a class of simple distributions. One such notion (of simple distributions) underlies the following definition, while a more liberal notion will be presented in §10.2.2.2.

Definition 10.15 (the class dist$\mathcal{NP}$): *We say that a probability ensemble $X = \{X_n\}_{n\in\mathbb{N}}$ is* simple *if there exists a polynomial-time algorithm that, on any input $x \in \{0, 1\}^*$, outputs $\Pr[X_{|x|} \leq x]$, where the inequality refers to the standard lexicographic order of strings. We denote by* dist$\mathcal{NP}$ *the class of distributional problems consisting of decision problems in $\mathcal{NP}$ coupled with simple probability ensembles.*

Note that the uniform probability ensemble is simple, but so are many other "simple" probability ensembles. Actually, it makes sense to relax the definition such that the algorithm is only required to output an approximation of $\Pr[X_{|x|} \leq x]$, say, to within a factor of $1 \pm 2^{-2|x|}$. We note that Definition 10.15 interprets simplicity in computational terms, specifically, as the feasibility of answering very basic questions regarding the probability distribution (i.e., determining the probability mass assigned to a single (n-bit long) string and even to an interval of such strings). This simplicity condition is closely related to being polynomial-time samplable via a *monotone* mapping (see Exercise 10.14).

Teaching note: The following two paragraphs attempt to address some doubts regarding Definition 10.15. One may postpone such discussions to a later stage.

We admit that the identification of simple distributions as the class of interesting distribution is significantly more questionable than any other identification advocated in this book. Nevertheless, we believe that we were fully justified in rejecting both the aforementioned extremes (i.e., of either allowing all distributions or allowing only the uniform distribution). Yet, the reader may wonder whether or not we have struck the right balance between "generality" and "simplicity" (in the intuitive sense). One specific concern is that we might have restricted the class of distributions too much. We briefly address this concern next.

A more intuitive and very robust class of distributions, which seems to contain all distributions that may occur in applications, is the class of polynomial-time samplable probability ensembles (treated in §10.2.2.2). Fortunately, the combination of the results presented in §10.2.1.2 and §10.2.2.2 seems to retrospectively endorse the choice underlying Definition 10.15. Specifically, we note that enlarging the class of distributions weakens the *conjecture* that the corresponding class of distributional NP problems contains infeasible problems. On the other hand, the *conclusion* that a specific distributional problem is not feasible becomes more appealing when the problem belongs to a smaller class that corresponds to a restricted definition of admissible distributions. Now, the combined results of §10.2.1.2 and §10.2.2.2 assert that a conjecture that refers to the larger class of polynomial-time samplable ensembles implies a conclusion that refers to a (very) simple probability ensemble (which resides in the smaller class). Thus, the current setting in which both the conjecture and the conclusion refer to simple probability ensembles may be viewed as just an intermediate step.

Indeed, the big question in the current context is whether dist$\mathcal{NP}$ is contained in tpc$\mathcal{P}$. A positive answer (especially if extended to samplable ensembles) would deem the P-vs-NP Question to be of little practical significant. However, our daily experience as well as much research effort indicate that some NP problems are not merely hard in the worst case, but rather "typically hard." This leads to the *conjecture that* dist$\mathcal{NP}$ *is not contained in* tpc$\mathcal{P}$.

Needless to say, the latter conjecture implies $\mathcal{P} \neq \mathcal{NP}$, and thus we should not expect to see a proof of it. In particular, we should not expect to see a proof that some specific problem in dist$\mathcal{NP}$ is not in tpc$\mathcal{P}$. What we may hope to see is "dist$\mathcal{NP}$-complete" problems; that is, problems in dist$\mathcal{NP}$ that are not in tpc$\mathcal{P}$ unless the entire class dist$\mathcal{NP}$ is contained in tpc$\mathcal{P}$. An adequate notion of a reduction is used toward formulating this possibility.

Step 4: Defining reductions among (distributional) problems. Intuitively, such reductions must preserve average-case feasibility. Thus, in addition to the standard conditions (i.e., that the reduction be efficiently computable and yield a correct result), we require that the reduction "respects" the probability distribution of the corresponding distributional problems. Specifically, the reduction should not map very likely instances of the first ("starting") problem to rare instances of the second ("target") problem. Otherwise, having a typically polynomial-time algorithm for the second distributional problem does not necessarily yield such an algorithm for the first distributional problem. Following is the adequate analogue of a Cook-reduction (i.e., general polynomial-time reduction), where the analogue of a Karp-reduction (many-to-one reduction) can be easily derived as a special case.

Teaching note: One may prefer presenting in class only the special case of many-to-one reductions, which suffices for Theorem 10.17. See footnote 15.

Definition 10.16 (reductions among distributional problems): *We say that the oracle machine M* reduces *the distributional problem (S, X) to the distributional problem (T, Y) if the following three conditions hold.*

1. Efficiency: *The machine M runs in polynomial time.*[14]
2. Validity: *For every $x \in \{0, 1\}^*$, it holds that $M^T(x) = 1$ if an only if $x \in S$, where $M^T(x)$ denotes the output of the oracle machine M on input x and access to an oracle for T.*
3. Domination:[15] *The probability that, on input X_n and oracle access to T, machine M makes the query y is upper-bounded by* $\text{poly}(|y|) \cdot \Pr[Y_{|y|} = y]$. *That is, there exists a polynomial p such that, for every $y \in \{0, 1\}^*$ and every $n \in \mathbb{N}$, it holds*

---

[14]In fact, one may relax the requirement and only require that M is typically polynomial time with respect to X. The validity condition may also be relaxed similarly.

[15]Let us spell out the meaning of Eq. (10.2) in the special case of many-to-one reductions (i.e., $M^T(x) = 1$ if and only if $f(x) \in T$, where f is a polynomial-time computable function): In this case $\Pr[Q(X_n) \ni y]$ is replaced by $\Pr[f(X_n) = y]$. That is, Eq. (10.2) simplifies to $\Pr[f(X_n) = y] \leq p(|y|) \cdot \Pr[Y_{|y|} = y]$. Indeed, this condition holds vacuously for any y that is not in the image of f.

that

$$\Pr[Q(X_n) \ni y] \leq p(|y|) \cdot \Pr[Y_{|y|} = y], \qquad (10.2)$$

where $Q(x)$ denotes the set of queries made by M on input x and oracle access to T.

In addition, we require that the reduction does not make too short queries; that is, there exists a polynomial p' such that if $y \in Q(x)$ then $p'(|y|) \geq |x|$.

The l.h.s. of Eq. (10.2) refers to the probability that, on input distributed as X_n, the reduction makes the query y. This probability is required not to exceed the probability that y occurs in the distribution $Y_{|y|}$ by more than a polynomial factor in $|y|$. In this case we say that the l.h.s. of Eq. (10.2) is dominated by $\Pr[Y_{|y|} = y]$.

Indeed, the domination condition is the only aspect of Definition 10.16 that extends beyond the worst-case treatment of reductions and refers to the distributional setting. The domination condition does not insist that the distribution induced by $Q(X)$ equals Y, but rather allows some slackness that, in turn, is bounded so as to guarantee preservation of typical feasibility (see Exercise 10.15).[16]

We note that the reducibility arguments extensively used in Chapters 7 and 8 (see discussion in Section 7.1.2) are actually reductions in the spirit of Definition 10.16 (except that they refer to different types of computational tasks).

10.2.1.2. Complete Problems

Recall that our conjecture is that dist$\mathcal{NP}$ is not contained in tpc$\mathcal{P}$, which in turn strengthens the conjecture $\mathcal{P} \neq \mathcal{NP}$ (making infeasibility a typical phenomenon rather than a worst-case one). Having no hope of proving that dist$\mathcal{NP}$ is not contained in tpc$\mathcal{P}$, we turn to the study of complete problems with respect to that conjecture. Specifically, we say that a distributional problem (S, X) is dist$\mathcal{NP}$-complete if $(S, X) \in$ dist$\mathcal{NP}$ and every $(S', X') \in$ dist$\mathcal{NP}$ is reducible to (S, X) (under Definition 10.16).

Recall that it is quite easy to prove the mere existence of NP-complete problems and that many natural problems are NP-complete. In contrast, in the current context, establishing completeness results is quite hard. This should not be surprising in light of the restricted type of reductions allowed in the current context. The restriction (captured by the domination condition) requires that "typical" instances of one problem should not be mapped to "untypical" instances of the other problem. However, it is fair to say that standard Karp-reductions (used in establishing NP-completeness results) map "typical" instances of one problem to somewhat "bizarre" instances of the second problem. Thus, the current subsection may be viewed as a study of reductions that do not commit this sin.[17]

---

[16]We stress that the notion of domination is incomparable to the notion of statistical (resp., computational) indistinguishability. On the one hand, domination is a local requirement (i.e., it compares the two distribution on a point-by-point basis), whereas indistinguishability is a global requirement (which allows rare exceptions). On the other hand, domination does not require approximately equal values, but rather a ratio that is bounded in one direction. Indeed, domination is not symmetric. We comment that a more relaxed notion of domination that allows rare violations (as in footnote 14) suffices for the preservation of typical feasibility.

[17]The latter assertion is somewhat controversial. While it seems totally justified with respect to the proof of Theorem 10.17, opinions regarding the proof of Theorem 10.19 may differ.

Theorem 10.17 (dist$\mathcal{NP}$-completeness): dist$\mathcal{NP}$ *contains a distributional problem* (T, Y) *such that each distributional problem in* dist$\mathcal{NP}$ *is reducible* (per Definition 10.16) *to* (T, Y). *Furthermore, the reductions are via many-to-one mappings.*

Proof: We start by introducing such a (distributional) problem, which is a natural distributional version of the decision problem S_u (used in the proof of Theorem 2.19). Recall that S_u contains the instance $\langle M, x, 1^t \rangle$ if there exists $y \in \cup_{i \leq t} \{0, 1\}^i$ such that machine M accepts the input pair (x, y) within t steps. We couple S_u with the "quasi-uniform" probability ensemble U' that assigns to the instance $\langle M, x, 1^t \rangle$ a probability mass proportional to $2^{-(|M|+|x|)}$. Specifically, for every $\langle M, x, 1^t \rangle$ it holds that

$$\Pr[U'_n = \langle M, x, 1^t \rangle] = \frac{2^{-(|M|+|x|)}}{\binom{n}{2}} \tag{10.3}$$

where $n \stackrel{\text{def}}{=} |\langle M, x, 1^t \rangle| \stackrel{\text{def}}{=} |M| + |x| + t$. Note that, under a suitable natural encoding, the ensemble U' is indeed simple.[18]

The reader can easily verify that the generic reduction used when reducing any set in $\mathcal{NP}$ to S_u (see the proof of Theorem 2.19), fails to reduce dist$\mathcal{NP}$ to (S_u, U'). Specifically, in some cases (see next paragraph), these reductions do not satisfy the domination condition. Indeed, the difficulty is that we have to reduce all dist$\mathcal{NP}$ problems (i.e., pairs consisting of decision problems and simple distributions) to one single distributional problem (i.e., (S_u, U')). In contrast, considering the distributions induced by the aforementioned reductions, we end up with many distributional versions of S_u, and furthermore the corresponding distributions are very different (and are not necessarily dominated by a single distribution).

Let us take a closer look at the aforementioned generic reduction (of S to S_u), when applied to an arbitrary $(S, X) \in$ dist$\mathcal{NP}$. This reduction maps an instance x to a triple $(M_S, x, 1^{p_S(|x|)})$, where M_S is a machine verifying membership in S (while using adequate NP-witnesses) and p_S is an adequate polynomial. The problem is that x may have relatively large probability mass (i.e., it may be that $\Pr[X_{|x|} = x] \gg 2^{-|x|}$) while $(M_S, x, 1^{p_S(|x|)})$ has "uniform" probability mass (i.e., $\langle M_S, x, 1^{p_S(|x|)} \rangle$ has probability mass smaller than $2^{-|x|}$ in U'). This violates the domination condition (see Exercise 10.18), and thus an alternative reduction is required.

The key to the alternative reduction is an (efficiently computable) encoding of strings taken from an arbitrary *simple* distribution by strings that have a similar probability mass under the uniform distribution. This means that the encoding should shrink strings that have relatively large probability mass under the original distribution. Specifically, this encoding will map x (taken from the ensemble $\{X_n\}_{n \in \mathbb{N}}$) to a codeword x' of length that is upper-bounded by the logarithm of $1/\Pr[X_{|x|} = x]$, ensuring that $\Pr[X_{|x|} = x] = O(2^{-|x'|})$. Accordingly, the reduction will map x to a triple $(M_{S,X}, x', 1^{p'(|x|)})$, where $|x'| < O(1) + \log_2(1/\Pr[X_{|x|} = x])$ and $M_{S,X}$ is an

---

[18] For example, we may encode $\langle M, x, 1^t \rangle$, where $M = \sigma_1 \cdots \sigma_k \in \{0, 1\}^k$ and $x = \tau_1 \cdots \tau_\ell \in \{0, 1\}^\ell$, by the string $\sigma_1 \sigma_1 \cdots \sigma_k \sigma_k 01 \tau_1 \tau_1 \cdots \tau_\ell \tau_\ell 01^t$. Then $\binom{n}{2} \cdot \Pr[U'_n \leq \langle M, x, 1^t \rangle]$ equals $(i_{|M|, |x|, t} - 1) + 2^{-|M|} \cdot |\{M' \in \{0, 1\}^{|M|} : M' < M\}| + 2^{-(|M|+|x|)} \cdot |\{x' \in \{0, 1\}^{|x|} : x' \leq x\}|$, where $i_{k, \ell, t}$ is the ranking of $\{k, k + \ell\}$ among all 2-subsets of $[k + \ell + t]$.

algorithm that (given x' and x) first verifies that x' is a proper encoding of x and next applies the standard verification (i.e., M_S) of the problem S. Such a reduction will be shown to satisfy all three conditions (i.e., efficiency, validity, and domination). Thus, instead of forcing the structure of the original distribution X on the target distribution U', the reduction will incorporate the structure of X in the reduced instance. A key ingredient in making this possible is the fact that X is simple (as per Definition 10.15).

With the foregoing motivation in mind, we now turn to the actual proof, that is, proving that any $(S, X) \in \text{dist}\mathcal{NP}$ is reducible to (S_u, U'). The following technical lemma is the basis of the reduction. In this lemma as well as in the sequel, it will be convenient to consider the (accumulative) distribution function of the probability ensemble X. That is, we consider $\mu(x) \overset{\text{def}}{=} \Pr[X_{|x|} \leq x]$, and note that $\mu : \{0, 1\}^* \to [0, 1]$ is polynomial-time computable (because X satisfies Definition 10.15).

Coding Lemma.[19] Let $\mu : \{0, 1\}^* \to [0, 1]$ be a polynomial-time computable function that is monotonically non-decreasing over $\{0, 1\}^n$ for every n (i.e., $\mu(x') \leq \mu(x'')$ for any $x' < x'' \in \{0, 1\}^{|x'|}$). For $x \in \{0, 1\}^n \setminus \{0^n\}$, let $x - 1$ denote the string preceding x in the lexicographic order of n-bit long strings. Then there exists an encoding function C_μ that satisfies the following three conditions.

1. **Compression:** For every x it holds that $|C_\mu(x)| \leq 1 + \min\{|x|, \log_2(1/\mu'(x))\}$, where $\mu'(x) \overset{\text{def}}{=} \mu(x) - \mu(x - 1)$ if $x \notin \{0\}^*$ and $\mu'(0^n) \overset{\text{def}}{=} \mu(0^n)$ otherwise.
2. **Efficient Encoding:** The function C_μ is computable in polynomial time.
3. **Unique Decoding:** For every $n \in \mathbb{N}$, when restricted to $\{0, 1\}^n$, the function C_μ is one-to-one (i.e., if $C_\mu(x) = C_\mu(x')$ and $|x| = |x'|$ then $x = x'$).

Proof. The function C_μ is defined as follows. If $\mu'(x) \leq 2^{-|x|}$ then $C_\mu(x) = 0x$ (i.e., in this case x serves as its own encoding). Otherwise (i.e., $\mu'(x) > 2^{-|x|}$) then $C_\mu(x) = 1z$, where z is chosen such that $|z| \leq \log_2(1/\mu'(x))$ and the mapping of n-bit strings to their encoding is one-to-one. Loosely speaking, z is selected to equal the shortest binary expansion of a number in the interval $(\mu(x) - \mu'(x), \mu(x)]$. Bearing in mind that this interval has length $\mu'(x)$ and that the different intervals are disjoint, we obtain the desired encoding. Details follows.

We focus on the case that $\mu'(x) > 2^{-|x|}$, and detail the way that z is selected (for the encoding $C_\mu(x) = 1z$). If $x > 0^{|x|}$ and $\mu(x) < 1$, then we let z be the longest common prefix of the binary expansions of $\mu(x - 1)$ and $\mu(x)$; for example, if $\mu(1010) = 0.10010$ and $\mu(1011) = 0.10101111$ then $C_\mu(1011) = 1z$ with $z = 10$. Thus, in this case $0.z1$ is in the interval $(\mu(x - 1), \mu(x)]$ (i.e., $\mu(x - 1) < 0.z1 \leq \mu(x)$). For $x = 0^{|x|}$, we let z be the longest common prefix of the binary expansions of 0 and $\mu(x)$ and again $0.z1$ is in the relevant interval (i.e., $(0, \mu(x)]$). Finally, for x such that $\mu(x) = 1$ and $\mu(x - 1) < 1$, we let z be the longest common prefix of the binary expansions of $\mu(x - 1)$ and $1 - 2^{-|x|-1}$, and again $0.z1$ is in $(\mu(x - 1), \mu(x)]$ (because $\mu'(x) > 2^{-|x|}$ and $\mu(x - 1) < \mu(x) = 1$ imply that $\mu(x - 1) < 1 - 2^{-|x|} < \mu(x)$). Note that if $\mu(x) = \mu(x - 1) = 1$ then $\mu'(x) = 0 < 2^{-|x|}$.

---

[19] The lemma actually refers to $\{0, 1\}^n$, for any fixed value of n, but the efficiency condition is stated more easily when allowing n to vary (and using the standard asymptotic analysis of algorithms). Actually, the lemma is somewhat easier to state and establish for polynomial-time computable functions that are monotonically non-decreasing over $\{0, 1\}^*$ (rather than over $\{0, 1\}^n$). See further discussion in Exercise 10.19.

We now verify that the foregoing C_μ satisfies the conditions of the lemma. We start with the compression condition. Clearly, if $\mu'(x) \leq 2^{-|x|}$ then $|C_\mu(x)| = 1 + |x| \leq 1 + \log_2(1/\mu'(x))$. On the other hand, suppose that $\mu'(x) > 2^{-|x|}$ and let us focus on the sub-case that $x > 0^{|x|}$ and $\mu(x) < 1$. Let $z = z_1 \cdots z_\ell$ be the longest common prefix of the binary expansions of $\mu(x - 1)$ and $\mu(x)$. Then, $\mu(x - 1) = 0.z0u$ and $\mu(x) = 0.z1v$, where $u, v \in \{0, 1\}^*$. We infer that

$$\mu'(x) = \mu(x) - \mu(x - 1) \leq \left(\sum_{i=1}^{\ell} 2^{-i} z_i + \overset{\text{poly}(|x|)}{\underset{i=\ell+1}{\sum}} 2^{-i} \right) - \sum_{i=1}^{\ell} 2^{-i} z_i < 2^{-|z|},$$

and $|z| < \log_2(1/\mu'(x)) \leq |x|$ follows. Thus, $|C_\mu(x)| \leq 1 + \min(|x|, \log_2(1/\mu'(x)))$ holds in both cases. Clearly, C_μ can be computed in polynomial time by computing $\mu(x - 1)$ and $\mu(x)$. Finally, note that C_μ satisfies the unique decoding condition, by separately considering the two aforementioned cases (i.e., $C_\mu(x) = 0x$ and $C_\mu(x) = 1z$). Specifically, in the second case (i.e., $C_\mu(x) = 1z$), use the fact that $\mu(x - 1) < 0.z1 \leq \mu(x)$. $\quad\square$

In order to obtain an encoding that is one-to-one when applied to strings of different lengths, we augment C_μ in the obvious manner; that is, we consider $C'_\mu(x) \overset{\text{def}}{=} (|x|, C_\mu(x))$, which may be implemented as $C'_\mu(x) = \sigma_1\sigma_1 \cdots \sigma_\ell\sigma_\ell 01 C_\mu(x)$ where $\sigma_1 \cdots \sigma_\ell$ is the binary expansion of $|x|$. Note that $|C'_\mu(x)| = O(\log |x|) + |C_\mu(x)|$ and that C'_μ is one-to-one (over $\{0, 1\}^*$).

The machine associated with (S, X). Let μ be the accumulative probability function associated with the probability ensemble X, and M_S be the polynomial-time machine that verifies membership in S while using adequate NP-witnesses (i.e., $x \in S$ if and only if there exists $y \in \{0, 1\}^{\text{poly}(|x|)}$ such that $M(x, y) = 1$). Using the encoding function C'_μ, we introduce an algorithm $M_{S,\mu}$ with the intention of reducing the distributional problem (S, X) to (S_u, U') such that all instances (of S) are mapped to triples in which the first element equals $M_{S,\mu}$. Machine $M_{S,\mu}$ is given an alleged encoding (under C'_μ) of an instance to S along with an alleged proof that the corresponding instance is in S, and verifies these claims in the obvious manner. That is, on input x' and $\langle x, y \rangle$, machine $M_{S,\mu}$ first verifies that $x' = C'_\mu(x)$, and next verifiers that $x \in S$ by running $M_S(x, y)$. Thus, $M_{S,\mu}$ verifies membership in the set $S' = \{C'_\mu(x) : x \in S\}$, while using proofs of the form $\langle x, y \rangle$ such that $M_S(x, y) = 1$ (for the instance $C'_\mu(x)$).[20]

The reduction. We map an instance x (of S) to the triple $(M_{S,\mu}, C'_\mu(x), 1^{p(|x|)})$, where $p(n) \overset{\text{def}}{=} p_S(n) + p_C(n)$ such that p_S is a polynomial representing the running time of M_S and p_C is a polynomial representing the running time of the encoding algorithm.

Analyzing the reduction. Our goal is proving that *the foregoing mapping constitutes a reduction of (S, X) to (S_u, U').* We verify the corresponding three requirements (of Definition 10.16).

---

[20] Note that $|y| = \text{poly}(|x|)$, but $|x| = \text{poly}(|C'_\mu(x)|)$ does not necessarily hold (and so S' is not necessarily in $\mathcal{NP}$). As we shall see, the latter point is immaterial.

1. Using the fact that C'_μ is polynomial-time computable (and noting that p is a polynomial), it follows that the foregoing mapping can be computed in polynomial time.
2. Recall that, on input $(x', \langle x, y \rangle)$, machine $M_{S,\mu}$ accepts if and only if $x' = C'_\mu(x)$ and M_S accepts (x, y) within $p_S(|x|)$ steps. Using the fact that $C'_\mu(x)$ uniquely determines x, it follows that $x \in S$ if and only if $C'_\mu(x) \in S'$, which in turn holds if and only if there exists a string y such that $M_{S,\mu}$ accepts $(C'_\mu(x), \langle x, y \rangle)$ in at most $p(|x|)$ steps. Thus, $x \in S$ if and only if $(M_{S,\mu}, C'_\mu(x), 1^{p(|x|)}) \in S_{\mathrm{u}}$, and the validity condition follows.
3. In order to verify the domination condition, we first note that the foregoing mapping is one-to-one (because the transformation $x \to C'_\mu(x)$ is one-to-one). Next, we note that it suffices to consider instances of S_{u} that have a preimage under the foregoing mapping (since instances with no preimage trivially satisfy the domination condition). Each of these instances (i.e., each image of this mapping) is a triple with the first element equal to $M_{S,\mu}$ and the second element being an encoding under C'_μ. By the definition of U', for every such image $\langle M_{S,\mu}, C'_\mu(x), 1^{p(|x|)} \rangle \in \{0, 1\}^n$, it holds that

$$\Pr[U'_n = \langle M_{S,\mu}, C'_\mu(x), 1^{p(|x|)} \rangle] = \binom{n}{2}^{-1} \cdot 2^{-(|M_{S,\mu}| + |C'_\mu(x)|)}$$

$$> c \cdot n^{-2} \cdot 2^{-(|C_\mu(x)| + O(\log|x|))},$$

where $c = 2^{-|M_{S,\mu}| - 1}$ is a constant depending only on S and μ (i.e., on the distributional problem (S, X)). Thus, for some positive polynomial q, we have

$$\Pr[U'_n = \langle M_{S,\mu}, C'_\mu(x), 1^{p(|x|)} \rangle] > 2^{-|C_\mu(x)|}/q(n). \qquad (10.4)$$

By virtue of the compression condition (of the Coding Lemma), we have $2^{-|C_\mu(x)|} \geq 2^{-1 - \min(|x|, \log_2(1/\mu'(x)))}$. It follows that

$$2^{-|C_\mu(x)|} \geq \Pr[X_{|x|} = x]/2. \qquad (10.5)$$

Recalling that x is the only preimage that is mapped to $\langle M_{S,\mu}, C'_\mu(x), 1^{p(|x|)} \rangle$ and combining Eq. (10.4) and (10.5), we establish the domination condition.

The theorem follows. ∎

Reflections. The proof of Theorem 10.17 highlights the fact that the reduction used in the proof of Theorem 2.19 does not introduce much structure in the reduced instances (i.e., does not reduce the original problem to a "highly structured special case" of the target problem). Put in other words, unlike more advanced worst-case reductions, this reduction does not map "random" (i.e., uniformly distributed) instances to highly structured instances (which occur with negligible probability under the uniform distribution). Thus, the reduction used in the proof of Theorem 2.19 suffices for reducing any distributional problem in dist$\mathcal{NP}$ to a distributional problem consisting of S_{u} coupled with *some* simple probability ensemble (see Exercise 10.20).[21]

---

[21] Note that this cannot be said of most known Karp-reductions, which do map random instances to highly structured ones. Furthermore, the same (structure-creating property) holds for the reductions obtained by Exercise 2.31.

However, Theorem 10.17 states more than the latter assertion. That is, it states that any distributional problem in $\text{dist}\mathcal{NP}$ is reducible to the *same* distributional version of S_u. Indeed, the effort involved in proving Theorem 10.17 was due to the need for mapping instances taken from any simple probability ensemble (which may not be the uniform ensemble) to instances distributed in a manner that is dominated by a single probability ensemble (i.e., the quasi-uniform ensemble U').

Once we have established the existence of one $\text{dist}\mathcal{NP}$-complete problem, we may establish the $\text{dist}\mathcal{NP}$-completeness of other problems (in $\text{dist}\mathcal{NP}$) by reducing some $\text{dist}\mathcal{NP}$-complete problem to them (and relying on the transitivity of reductions (see Exercise 10.17)). Thus, the difficulties encountered in the proof of Theorem 10.17 are no longer relevant. Unfortunately, a seemingly more severe difficulty arises: Almost all known reductions in the theory of NP-completeness work by introducing much structure in the reduced instances (i.e., they actually reduce to highly structured special cases). Furthermore, this structure is too complex in the sense that the distribution of reduced instances does not seem simple (in the sense of Definition 10.15). Actually, as demonstrated next, the problem is not the existence of a structure in the reduced instances but rather the complexity of this structure. In particular, if the aforementioned reduction is "monotone" and "length-regular" then the distribution of the reduced instances is simple enough (i.e., is simple in the sense of Definition 10.15):

Proposition 10.18 (sufficient condition for $\text{dist}\mathcal{NP}$-completeness): *Suppose that f is a Karp-reduction of the set S to the set T such that, for every $x', x'' \in \{0, 1\}^*$, the following two conditions hold:*

1. *(f is monotone): If $x' < x''$ then $f(x') < f(x'')$, where the inequalities refer to the standard lexicographic order of strings.[22]*
2. *(f is length-regular): $|x'| = |x''|$ if and only if $|f(x')| = |f(x'')|$.*

Then if there exists an ensemble X such that (S, X) is $\text{dist}\mathcal{NP}$-complete then there exists an ensemble Y such that (T, Y) is $\text{dist}\mathcal{NP}$-complete.

Proof Sketch: Note that the monotonicity of f implies that f is one-to-one and that for every x it holds that $f(x) \geq x$. Furthermore, as shown next, f is polynomial-time invertible. Intuitively, the fact that f is both monotone and polynomial-time computable implies that a preimage can be found by a binary search. Specifically, given $y = f(x)$, we search for x by iteratively halving the interval of potential solutions, which is initialized to $[0, y]$ (since $x \leq f(x)$). Note that if this search is invoked on a string y that is not in the image of f, then it terminates while detecting this fact.

Relying on the fact that f is one-to-one (and length-regular), we define the probability ensemble $Y = \{Y_n\}_{n \in \mathbb{N}}$ such that for every x it holds that $\Pr[Y_{|f(x)|} = f(x)] = \Pr[X_{|x|} = x]$. Specifically, letting $\ell(m) = |f(1^m)|$ and noting that ℓ is

---

[22] In particular, if $|z'| < |z''|$ then $z' < z''$. Recall that for $|z'| = |z''|$ it holds that $z' < z''$ if and only if there exists $w, u', u'' \in \{0, 1\}^*$ such that $z' = w0u'$ and $z'' = w1u''$.

one-to-one and monotonically non-decreasing, we define

$$
\Pr[Y_{|y|} = y] = \begin{cases} \Pr[X_{|x|} = x] & \text{if } x = f^{-1}(y) \\ 0 & \text{if } \exists m \text{ s.t. } y \in \{0, 1\}^{\ell(m)} \setminus \{f(x) : x \in \{0, 1\}^m\} \\ 2^{-|y|} & \text{otherwise (i.e., if } |y| \notin \{\ell(m) : m \in \mathbb{N}\}).^{23} \end{cases}
$$

Clearly, (S, X) is reducible to (T, Y) (via the Karp-reduction f, which, due to our construction of Y, also satisfies the domination condition). Thus, using the hypothesis that dist$\mathcal{NP}$ is reducible to (S, X) and the transitivity of reductions (see Exercise 10.17), it follows that every problem in dist$\mathcal{NP}$ is reducible to (T, Y). The key observation, to be established next, is that Y is a simple probability ensemble, and it follows that (T, Y) is in dist$\mathcal{NP}$.

Loosely speaking, the simplicity of Y follows by combining the simplicity of X and the properties of f (i.e., the fact that f is monotone, length-regular, and polynomial-time invertible). The monotonicity and length-regularity of f implies that $\Pr[Y_{|f(x)|} \leq f(x)] = \Pr[X_{|x|} \leq x]$. More generally, for any $y \in \{0, 1\}^{\ell(m)}$, it holds that $\Pr[Y_{\ell(m)} \leq y] = \Pr[X_m \leq x]$, where x is the lexicographicly largest string such that $f(x) \leq y$ (and, indeed, if $|x| < m$ then $\Pr[Y_{\ell(m)} \leq y] = \Pr[X_m \leq x] = 0$).[24] Note that this x can be found in polynomial time by the inverting algorithm sketched in the first paragraph of the proof. Thus, we may compute $\Pr[Y_{|y|} \leq y]$ by finding the adequate x and computing $\Pr[X_{|x|} \leq x]$. Using the hypothesis that X is simple, it follows that Y is simple (and the proposition follows). $\qquad\square$

On the existence of adequate Karp-reductions. Proposition 10.18 implies that a sufficient condition for the dist$\mathcal{NP}$-completeness of a distributional version of an (NP-complete) set T is the existence of an adequate Karp-reduction from the set S_u to the set T; that is, this Karp-reduction should be monotone and length-regular. While the length-regularity condition seems easy to impose (by using adequate padding), the monotonicity condition seems more problematic. Fortunately, it turns out that the monotonicity condition can also be imposed by using adequate padding (or rather an adequate "marking" – see Exercises 2.30 and 10.21). We highlight the fact that the existence of an adequate padding (or "marking") is a property of the set T itself. In Exercise 10.21 we review a method for modifying any Karp-reduction to a "monotonically markable" set T into a Karp-reduction (to T) that is monotone and length-regular. In Exercise 10.23 we provide evidence for the thesis that all natural NP-complete sets are monotonically markable. Combining all these facts, we conclude that *any natural NP-complete decision problem can be coupled with a simple probability ensemble such that the resulting distributional problem is* dist$\mathcal{NP}$-*complete*. As a concrete illustration of this thesis, we state the corresponding (formal) result for the twenty-one NP-complete problems treated in Karp's paper on NP-completeness [138].

Theorem 10.19 (a modest version of a general thesis): *For each of the twenty-one NP-complete problems treated in [138] there exists a simple probability ensemble such that the combined distributional problem is* dist$\mathcal{NP}$-*complete.*

---

[23]Having Y_n be uniform in this case is a rather arbitrary choice, which is merely aimed at guaranteeing a "simple" distribution on n-bit strings (also in this case).

[24]We also note that the case in which $|y|$ is not in the image of ℓ can be easily detected and taken care of accordingly.

The said list of problems includes SAT, Clique, and 3-Colorability.

10.2.1.3. Probabilistic Versions

The definitions in §10.2.1.1 can be extended so as to account also for randomized computations. For example, extending Definition 10.14, we have

> **Definition 10.20** (the class tpc$\mathcal{BPP}$): *For a probabilistic algorithm A, a Boolean function f, and a time-bound function* $t : \mathbb{N} \to \mathbb{N}$, *we say that the string x is t-bad for* A with respect to f *if with probability exceeding* $1/3$, *on input x, either* $A(x) \neq f(x)$ *or A runs more that* $t(|x|)$ *steps.* We say that A typically solves $(S, \{X_n\}_{n \in \mathbb{N}})$ in probabilistic polynomial time *if there exists a polynomial p such that the probability that* X_n *is p-bad for A with respect to the characteristic function of S is negligible.* We denote by tpc$\mathcal{BPP}$ the class of distributional problems that are typically solvable in probabilistic polynomial time.

The definition of reductions can be similarly extended. This means that in Definition 10.16, both $M^T(x)$ and $Q(x)$ (mentioned in Items 2 and 3, respectively) are random variables rather than fixed objects. Furthermore, validity is required to hold (for every input) only with probability $2/3$, where the probability space refers only to the internal coin tosses of the reduction. Randomized reductions are closed under composition and preserve typical feasibility (see Exercise 10.24).

Randomized reductions allow the presentation of a dist$\mathcal{NP}$-complete problem that refers to the (perfectly) uniform ensemble. Recall that Theorem 10.17 establishes the dist$\mathcal{NP}$-completeness of (S_u, U'), where U' is a quasi-uniform ensemble (i.e., $\Pr[U'_n = \langle M, x, 1^t \rangle] = 2^{-(|M|+|x|)}/\binom{n}{2}$, where $n = |\langle M, x, 1^t \rangle|$). We first note that (S_u, U') can be randomly reduced to (S'_u, U''), where $S'_u = \{\langle M, x, z \rangle : \langle M, x, 1^{|z|} \rangle \in S_u\}$ and $\Pr[U''_n = \langle M, x, z \rangle] = 2^{-(|M|+|x|+|z|)}/\binom{n}{2}$ for every $\langle M, x, z \rangle \in \{0, 1\}^n$. The randomized reduction consists of mapping $\langle M, x, 1^t \rangle$ to $\langle M, x, z \rangle$, where z is uniformly selected in $\{0, 1\}^t$. Recalling that $U = \{U_n\}_{n \in \mathbb{N}}$ denotes the uniform probability ensemble (i.e., U_n is uniformly distributed on strings of length n) and using a suitable encoding we get

> **Proposition 10.21:** *There exists* $S \in \mathcal{NP}$ *such that every* $(S', X') \in \text{dist}\mathcal{NP}$ *is randomly reducible to* (S, U).

> ***Proof Sketch:*** By the foregoing discussion, every $(S', X') \in \text{dist}\mathcal{NP}$ is randomly reducible to (S'_u, U''), where the reduction goes through (S_u, U'). Thus, we focus on reducing (S'_u, U'') to (S''_u, U), where $S''_u \in \mathcal{NP}$ is defined as follows. The string $\text{bin}_\ell(|u|) \cdot \text{bin}_\ell(|v|) \cdot u \cdot v \cdot w$ is in S''_u if and only if $\langle u, v, w \rangle \in S'_u$ and $\ell = \lceil \log_2 |uvw| \rceil + 1$, where $\text{bin}_\ell(i)$ denotes the ℓ-bit long binary encoding of the integer $i \in [2^{\ell-1}]$ (i.e., the encoding is padded with zeros to a total length of ℓ). The reduction maps $\langle M, x, z \rangle$ to the string $\text{bin}_\ell(|x|) \cdot \text{bin}_\ell(|M|) \cdot M \cdot x \cdot z$, where $\ell = \lceil \log_2(|M| + |x| + |z|) \rceil + 1$. Noting that this reduction satisfies all conditions of Definition 10.16, the proposition follows. $\qquad\square$

10.2.2. Ramifications

In our opinion, the most problematic aspect of the theory described in Section 10.2.1 is the choice to focus on simple probability ensembles, which in turn restricts "distributional versions of NP" to the class dist$\mathcal{NP}$ (Definition 10.15). As indicated in §10.2.1.1, this restriction raises two opposite concerns (i.e., that dist$\mathcal{NP}$ is either too wide or too narrow).[25] Here, we address the concern that the class of simple probability ensembles is too restricted, and consequently that the conjecture dist$\mathcal{NP} \not\subseteq$ tpc$\mathcal{BPP}$ is too strong (which would mean that dist$\mathcal{NP}$-completeness is a weak evidence for typical-case hardness). An appealing extension of the class of simple probability ensembles is presented in §10.2.2.2, yielding a corresponding extension of dist$\mathcal{NP}$, and it is shown that if this extension of dist$\mathcal{NP}$ is not contained in tpc$\mathcal{BPP}$ then dist$\mathcal{NP}$ itself is not contained in tpc$\mathcal{BPP}$. Consequently, dist$\mathcal{NP}$-complete problems enjoy the benefit of both being in the more restricted class (i.e., dist$\mathcal{NP}$) and being hard as long as some problem in the extended class is hard.

Another extension appears in §10.2.2.1, where we extend the treatment from decision problems to search problems. This extension is motivated by the realization that search problem are actually of greater importance to real-life applications (cf. Section 2.1.1), and hence a theory motivated by real-life applications must address such problems, as we do next.

Prerequisites. For the technical development of §10.2.2.1, we assume familiarity with the notion of a unique solution and results regarding it as presented in Section 6.2.3. For the technical development of §10.2.2.2, we assume familiarity with hashing functions as presented in Appendix D.2. In addition, the technical development of §10.2.2.2 relies on §10.2.2.1.

10.2.2.1. Search Versus Decision

Indeed, as in the case of worst-case complexity, search problems are at least as important as decision problems. Thus, an average-case treatment of search problems is indeed called for. We first present distributional versions of $\mathcal{PF}$ and $\mathcal{PC}$ (cf. Section 2.1.1), following the underlying principles of the definitions of tpc$\mathcal{P}$ and dist$\mathcal{NP}$.

> **Definition 10.22** (the classes tpc$\mathcal{PF}$ and dist$\mathcal{PC}$)**:** *As in Section 2.1.1, we consider only polynomially bounded search problems, that is, binary relations $R \subseteq \{0, 1\}^* \times \{0, 1\}^*$ such that for some polynomial q it holds that $(x, y) \in R$ implies $|y| \leq q(|x|)$. Recall that $R(x) \overset{\text{def}}{=} \{y : (x, y) \in R\}$ and $S_R \overset{\text{def}}{=} \{x : R(x) \neq \emptyset\}$.*
>
> - *A distributional search problem consists of a polynomially bounded search problem coupled with a probability ensemble.*
> - *The class tpc$\mathcal{PF}$ consists of all distributional search problems that are typically solvable in polynomial time. That is, $(R, \{X_n\}_{n \in \mathbb{N}}) \in$ tpc$\mathcal{PF}$ if there exists an algorithm A and a polynomial p such that the probability that on input X_n algorithm A either errs or runs more that $p(n)$ steps is negligible, where A errs on $x \in S_R$ if $A(x) \notin R(x)$ and errs on $x \notin S_R$ if $A(x) \neq \bot$.*
> - *A distributional search problem (R, X) is in dist$\mathcal{PC}$ if $R \in \mathcal{PC}$ and X is simple (as in Definition 10.15).*

Likewise, the class tpc$\mathcal{BPPF}$ consists of all distributional search problems that are typically solvable in *probabilistic* polynomial time (cf. Definition 10.20). The definitions of

---

[25]On the one hand, if the definition of dist$\mathcal{NP}$ were too liberal, then membership in dist$\mathcal{NP}$ would mean less than one may desire. On the other hand, if dist$\mathcal{NP}$ were too restricted, then the conjecture that dist$\mathcal{NP}$ contains hard problems would have been very questionable.

reductions among distributional problems, presented in the context of decision problems, extend to search problems.

Fortunately, as in the context of worst-case complexity, the study of distributional search problems "reduces" to the study of distributional decision problems.

Theorem 10.23 (reducing search to decision): $\text{dist}\mathcal{PC} \subseteq \text{tpc}\mathcal{BPPF}$ *if and only if* $\text{dist}\mathcal{NP} \subseteq \text{tpc}\mathcal{BPP}$. *Furthermore, every problem in* $\text{dist}\mathcal{NP}$ *is reducible to some problem in* $\text{dist}\mathcal{PC}$, *and every problem in* $\text{dist}\mathcal{PC}$ *is randomly reducible to some problem in* $\text{dist}\mathcal{NP}$.

Proof Sketch: The furthermore part is analogous to the actual contents of the proof of Theorem 2.6 (see also Step 1 in the proof of Theorem 2.16). Indeed, the reduction of $\mathcal{NP}$ to $\mathcal{PC}$ presented in the proof of Theorem 2.6 extends to the current context. Specifically, for any $S \in \mathcal{NP}$, we consider a relation $R \in \mathcal{PC}$ such that $S = \{x : R(x) \neq \emptyset\}$, and note that, for any probability ensemble X, the identity transformation reduces (S, X) to (R, X).

A difficulty arises in the opposite direction. Recall that in the proof of Theorem 2.6 we reduced the search problem of $R \in \mathcal{PC}$ to deciding membership in $S'_R \stackrel{\text{def}}{=} \{\langle x, y' \rangle : \exists y'' \text{ s.t. } (x, y'y'') \in R\} \in \mathcal{NP}$. The difficulty encountered here is that, on input x, this reduction makes queries of the form $\langle x, y' \rangle$, where y' is a prefix of some string in $R(x)$. These queries may induce a distribution that is not dominated by any simple distribution. Thus, we seek an alternative reduction.

As a warm-up, let us assume for a moment that R has unique solutions (in the sense of Definition 6.28); that is, for every x it holds that $|R(x)| \leq 1$. In this case we may easily reduce the search problem of $R \in \mathcal{PC}$ to deciding membership in $S''_R \in \mathcal{NP}$, where $\langle x, i, \sigma \rangle \in S''_R$ *if and only if $R(x)$ contains a string in which the ith bit equals σ*. Specifically, on input x, the reduction issues the queries $\langle x, i, \sigma \rangle$, where $i \in [\ell]$ (with $\ell = \text{poly}(|x|)$) and $\sigma \in \{0, 1\}$, which allows for determining the single string in the set $R(x) \subseteq \{0, 1\}^\ell$ (whenever $|R(x)| = 1$). The point is that this reduction can be used to reduce any $(R, X) \in \text{dist}\mathcal{PC}$ (having unique solutions) to $(S''_R, X'') \in \text{dist}\mathcal{NP}$, where X'' *equally distributes the probability mass of x* (under X) to all the tuples $\langle x, i, \sigma \rangle$; that is, for every $i \in [\ell]$ and $\sigma \in \{0, 1\}$, it holds that $\Pr[X''_{|\langle x, i, \sigma \rangle|} = \langle x, i, \sigma \rangle]$ equals $\Pr[X_{|x|} = x]/2\ell$.

Unfortunately, in the general case, R may not have unique solutions. Nevertheless, applying the main idea that underlies the proof of Theorem 6.29, this difficulty can be overcome. We first note that the foregoing mapping of instances of the distributional problem $(R, X) \in \text{dist}\mathcal{PC}$ to instances of $(S''_R, X'') \in \text{dist}\mathcal{NP}$ satisfies the efficiency and domination conditions even in the case that R does not have unique solutions. What may possibly fail (in the general case) is the validity condition (i.e., if $|R(x)| > 1$ then we may fail to recover any element of $R(x)$).

Recall that the main part of the proof of Theorem 6.29 is a randomized reduction that maps instances of R to triples of the form (x, m, h) such that m is uniformly distributed in $[\ell]$ and h is uniformly distributed in a family of hashing functions H_ℓ^m, where $\ell = \text{poly}(|x|)$ and H_ℓ^m is as in Appendix D.2. Furthermore, if $R(x) \neq \emptyset$ then, with probability $\Omega(1/\ell)$ over the choices of $m \in [\ell]$ and $h \in H_\ell^m$, there exists a unique $y \in R(x)$ such that $h(y) = 0^m$. Defining $R'(x, m, h) \stackrel{\text{def}}{=} \{y \in R(x) : h(y)=0^m\}$, this yields a randomized reduction of the search problem of R to the search problem of R' such that with noticeable probability[26] the reduction maps instances that have solutions to instances having a unique solution. Furthermore, this reduction can be used to reduce any $(R, X) \in \text{dist}\mathcal{PC}$ to $(R', X') \in \text{dist}\mathcal{PC}$, *where X' distributes the probability mass of x (under X) to all the triples (x, m, h) such that for every $m \in [\ell]$ and $h \in H_\ell^m$ it holds that $\Pr[X'_{|(x,m,h)|} = (x, m, h)]$ equals $\Pr[X_{|x|} = x]/(\ell \cdot |H_\ell^m|)$.* (Note that with a suitable encoding, X' is indeed simple.)

The theorem follows by combining the two aforementioned reductions. That is, we first apply the randomized reduction of (R, X) to (R', X'), and next reduce the resulting instance to an instance of the corresponding decision problem $(S_{R'}'', X'')$, where X'' is obtained by modifying X' (rather than X). The combined randomized mapping satisfies the efficiency and domination conditions, and is valid with noticeable probability. The error probability can be made negligible by straightforward amplification (see Exercise 10.24). $\qquad\square$

10.2.2.2. Simple Versus Samplable Distributions

Recall that the definition of simple probability ensembles (underlying Definition 10.15) requires that the accumulating distribution function is polynomial-time computable. Recall that $\mu : \{0, 1\}^* \to [0, 1]$ is called the accumulating distribution function of $X = \{X_n\}_{n\in\mathbb{N}}$ if for every $n \in \mathbb{N}$ and $x \in \{0, 1\}^n$ it holds that $\mu(x) \overset{\text{def}}{=} \Pr[X_n \leq x]$, where the inequality refers to the standard lexicographic order of n-bit strings.

As argued in §10.2.1.1, the requirement that the accumulating distribution function is polynomial-time computable imposes severe restrictions on the set of admissible ensembles. Furthermore, it seems that these simple ensembles are indeed "simple" in some intuitive sense, and that they represent a reasonable (alas, disputable) model of distributions that may occur in practice. Still, in light of the fear that this model is too restrictive (and consequently that dist$\mathcal{NP}$-hardness is weak evidence for typical-case hardness), we seek a maximalistic model of distributions that may occur in practice. Such a model is provided by the notion of polynomial-time samplable ensembles (underlying Definition 10.24). Our maximality thesis is based on the belief that the real world should be modeled as a *feasible* randomized process (rather than as an arbitrary process). This belief implies that all objects encountered in the world may be viewed as samples generated by a feasible randomized process.

Definition 10.24 (samplable ensembles and the class samp$\mathcal{NP}$): *We say that a probability ensemble $X = \{X_n\}_{n\in\mathbb{N}}$ is (polynomial-time) samplable if there exists a probabilistic polynomial-time algorithm A such that for every $x \in \{0, 1\}^*$ it holds that $\Pr[A(1^{|x|}) = x] = \Pr[X_{|x|} = x]$. We denote by samp$\mathcal{NP}$ the class of distributional problems consisting of decision problems in $\mathcal{NP}$ coupled with samplable probability ensembles.*

We first note that all simple probability ensembles are indeed samplable (see Exercise 10.25), and thus dist$\mathcal{NP} \subseteq$ samp$\mathcal{NP}$. On the other hand, there exist samplable probability ensembles that do not seem simple (see Exercise 10.26).

---

[26]Recall that the probability of an event is said to be noticeable (in a relevant parameter) if it is greater than the reciprocal of some positive polynomial. In the context of randomized reductions, the relevant parameter is the length of the input to the reduction.

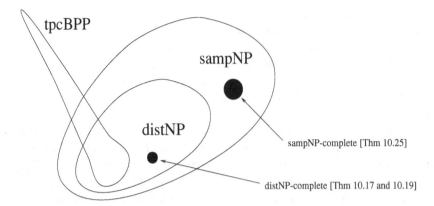

Figure 10.1: Two types of average-case completeness.

Extending the scope of distributional problems (from dist$\mathcal{NP}$ to samp$\mathcal{NP}$) facilitates the presentation of complete distributional problems. We first note that it is easy to prove that every natural NP-complete problem has a distributional version in samp$\mathcal{NP}$ that is dist$\mathcal{NP}$-hard (see Exercise 10.27). Furthermore, it is possible to prove that all natural NP-complete problem have distributional versions that are samp$\mathcal{NP}$-complete. (In both cases, "natural" means that the corresponding Karp-reductions do not shrink the input, which is a weaker condition than the one in Proposition 10.18.)

Theorem 10.25 (samp$\mathcal{NP}$-completeness): *Suppose that $S \in \mathcal{NP}$ and that every set in $\mathcal{NP}$ is reducible to S by a Karp-reduction that does not shrink the input. Then there exists a polynomial-time samplable ensemble X such that any problem in samp$\mathcal{NP}$ is reducible to (S, X)*

The proof of Theorem 10.25 is based on the observation that *there exists a polynomial-time samplable ensemble that dominates all polynomial-time samplable ensembles.* The existence of this ensemble is based on the notion of a universal (sampling) machine. For further details, see Exercise 10.28.

Theorem 10.25 establishes a rich theory of samp$\mathcal{NP}$-completeness, but does not relate this theory to the previously presented theory of dist$\mathcal{NP}$-completeness (see Figure 10.1). This is essentially done in the next theorem, which asserts that the existence of typically hard problems in samp$\mathcal{NP}$ implies their existence in dist$\mathcal{NP}$.

Theorem 10.26 (samp$\mathcal{NP}$-completeness versus dist$\mathcal{NP}$-completeness): *If samp$\mathcal{NP}$ is not contained in tpc$\mathcal{BPP}$ then dist$\mathcal{NP}$ is not contained in tpc$\mathcal{BPP}$.*

Thus, the two "typical-case complexity" versions of the P-vs-NP Question are equivalent. That is, if some "samplable distribution" versions of NP are not typically feasible then some "simple distribution" versions of NP are not typically feasible. In particular, if samp$\mathcal{NP}$-complete problems are not in tpc$\mathcal{BPP}$ then dist$\mathcal{NP}$-complete problems are not in tpc$\mathcal{BPP}$.

The foregoing assertions would all follow if samp$\mathcal{NP}$ were (randomly) reducible to dist$\mathcal{NP}$ (i.e., if every problem in samp$\mathcal{NP}$ were reducible (under a randomized version of Definition 10.16) to some problem in dist$\mathcal{NP}$); but, unfortunately, we do not know whether such reductions exist. Yet, underlying the proof of Theorem 10.26 is a more liberal notion of a reduction among distributional problems.

Proof Sketch: We shall prove that if dist$\mathcal{NP}$ is contained in tpc$\mathcal{BPP}$ then the same holds for samp$\mathcal{NP}$ (i.e., samp$\mathcal{NP}$ is contained in tpc$\mathcal{BPP}$). Relying on Theorem 10.23 and Exercise 10.29, it suffices to show that if dist$\mathcal{PC}$ is contained in tpc$\mathcal{BPPF}$ then the samplable version of dist$\mathcal{PC}$, denoted samp$\mathcal{PC}$, is contained in tpc$\mathcal{BPPF}$. This will be shown by showing that, under a relaxed notion of a randomized reduction, every problem in samp$\mathcal{PC}$ is reduced to some problem in dist$\mathcal{PC}$. Loosely speaking, this relaxed notion (of a randomized reduction) only requires that the validity and domination conditions (of Definition 10.16 (when adapted to randomized reductions)) hold with respect to a noticeable fraction of the probability space of the reduction.[27] We start by formulating this notion, when referring to distributional *search* problems.

> **Teaching note:** The following proof is quite involved and is better left for advanced reading. Its main idea is related to one of the central ideas underlying the currently known proof of Theorem 8.11. This fact, as well as numerous other applications of this idea, provide additional motivation for reading the following proof.

Definition. A relaxed reduction of the distributional problem (R, X) to the distributional problem (T, Y) is a probabilistic polynomial-time oracle machine M that satisfies the following conditions with respect to a family of sets $\{\Omega_x \subseteq \{0, 1\}^{m(|x|)} : x \in \{0, 1\}^*\}$, where $m(|x|) = \text{poly}(|x|)$ denotes an upper bound on the number of the internal coin tosses of M on input x:

Density (of Ω_x): There exists a noticeable function $\rho : \mathbb{N} \to [0, 1]$ (i.e., $\rho(n) > 1/\text{poly}(n)$) such that, for every $x \in \{0, 1\}^*$, it holds that $|\Omega_x| \geq \rho(|x|) \cdot 2^{m(|x|)}$.

Validity (with respect to Ω_x): For every $r \in \Omega_x$ the reduction yields a correct answer; that is, $M^T(x, r) \in R(x)$ if $R(x) \neq \emptyset$ and $M^T(x, r) = \bot$ otherwise, where $M^T(x, r)$ denotes the execution of M on input x, internal coins r, and oracle access to T.

Domination (with respect to Ω_x): There exists a positive polynomial p such that, for every $y \in \{0, 1\}^*$ and every $n \in \mathbb{N}$, it holds that

$$\Pr[Q'(X_n) \ni y] \leq p(|y|) \cdot \Pr[Y_{|y|} = y], \tag{10.6}$$

where $Q'(x)$ is a random variable, defined over the set Ω_x, representing the set of queries made by M on input x, coins in Ω_x, and oracle access to T. That is, $Q'(x)$ is defined by uniformly selecting $r \in \Omega_x$ and considering the set of queries made by M on input x, internal coins r, and oracle access to T. (In addition, as in Definition 10.16, we also require that the reduction does not make too short queries.)

The reader may verify that this relaxed notion of a reduction preserves typical feasibility; that is, for $R \in \mathcal{PC}$, if there exists a relaxed reduction of (R, X) to (T, Y)

---

[27]We warn that the existence of such a relaxed reduction between two specific distributional problems does not necessarily imply the existence of a corresponding (standard average-case) reduction. Specifically, although standard validity can be guaranteed (for problems in $\mathcal{PC}$) by repeated invocations of the reduction, such a process will *not* redeem the violation of the standard domination condition.

and (T, Y) is in tpc$\mathcal{BPPF}$ then (R, X) is in tpc$\mathcal{BPPF}$. The key observation is that the analysis may discard the case that, on input x, the reduction selects coins not in Ω_x. Indeed, the queries made in that case may be untypical and the answers received may be wrong, but this is immaterial. What matter is that, on input x, with noticeable probability the reduction selects coins in Ω_x, and produces "typical with respect to Y" queries (by virtue of the relaxed domination condition). Such typical queries are answered correctly by the algorithm that typically solves (T, Y), and if x has a solution then these answers yield a correct solution to x (by virtue of the relaxed validity condition). Thus, if x has a solution, then with noticeable probability the reduction outputs a correct solution. On the other hand, the reduction never outputs a wrong solution (even when using coins not in Ω_x), because incorrect solutions are detected by relying on $R \in \mathcal{PC}$.

Our goal is presenting, for every $(R, X) \in$ samp$\mathcal{PC}$, a relaxed reduction of (R, X) to a related problem $(R', X') \in$ dist$\mathcal{PC}$. (We use the standard notation $X = \{X_n\}_{n \in \mathbb{N}}$ and $X' = \{X'_n\}_{n \in \mathbb{N}}$.)

An oversimplified case. For starters, *suppose that X_n is uniformly distributed on some set $S_n \subseteq \{0, 1\}^n$ and that there is a polynomial-time computable and invertible mapping μ of S_n to $\{0, 1\}^{\ell(n)}$, where $\ell(n) = \log_2 |S_n|$.* Then, mapping x to $1^{|x| - \ell(|x|)} 0 \mu(x)$, we obtain a reduction of (R, X) to (R', X'), where X'_{n+1} is uniform over $\{1^{n - \ell(n)} 0 v : v \in \{0, 1\}^{\ell(n)}\}$ and $R'(1^{n - \ell(n)} 0 v) = R(\mu^{-1}(v))$ (or, equivalently, $R(x) = R'(1^{|x| - \ell(|x|)} 0 \mu(x))$). Note that X' is a simple ensemble and $R' \in \mathcal{PC}$; hence, $(R', X') \in$ dist$\mathcal{PC}$. Also note that the foregoing mapping is indeed a valid reduction (i.e., it satisfies the efficiency, validity, and domination conditions). Thus, (R, X) is reduced to a problem in dist$\mathcal{PC}$ (and indeed the relaxation was not used here).

A simple but more instructive case. Next, we drop the assumption that there is a polynomial-time computable and invertible mapping μ of S_n to $\{0, 1\}^{\ell(n)}$, but maintain the assumption that X_n is uniform on some set $S_n \subseteq \{0, 1\}^n$ and assume that $|S_n| = 2^{\ell(n)}$ is easily computable (from n). In this case, we may map $x \in \{0, 1\}^n$ to its image under a suitable randomly chosen hashing function h, which in particular maps n-bit strings to $\ell(n)$-bit strings. That is, we randomly map x to $(h, 1^{n - \ell(n)} 0 h(x))$, where h is uniformly selected in a set $H_n^{\ell(n)}$ of suitable hash functions (see Appendix D.2). This calls for redefining R' such that $R'(h, 1^{n - \ell(n)} 0 v)$ corresponds to the preimages of v under h that are in S_n. Assuming that h is a 1-1 mapping of S_n to $\{0, 1\}^{\ell(n)}$, we may define $R'(h, 1^{n - \ell(n)} 0 v) = R(x)$ such that x is the unique string satisfying $x \in S_n$ and $h(x) = v$, where the condition $x \in S_n$ may be *verified by providing the internal coins of the sampling procedure that generate x*. Denoting the sampling procedure of X by S, and letting $S(1^n, r)$ denote the output of S on input 1^n and internal coins r, we actually redefine R' as

$$R'(h, 1^{n - \ell(n)} 0 v) = \{\langle r, y \rangle : h(S(1^n, r)) = v \wedge y \in R(S(1^n, r))\}. \quad (10.7)$$

We note that $\langle r, y \rangle \in R'(h, 1^{|x| - \ell(|x|)} 0 h(x))$ yields a desired solution $y \in R(x)$ if $S(1^{|x|}, r) = x$, but otherwise "all bets are off" (since y will be a solution for $S(1^{|x|}, r) \neq x$). Now, although typically h will not be a 1-1 mapping of S_n to $\{0, 1\}^{\ell(n)}$, it is the case that *for each $x \in S_n$, with constant probability over the* *choice of h, it holds that h(x) has a unique preimage in S_n under h.* (See the proof of Theorem 6.29.) In this case $\langle r, y \rangle \in R'(h, 1^{|x|-\ell(|x|)}0h(x))$ implies $S(1^{|x|}, r) = x$ (which, in turn, implies $y \in R(x)$). We claim that *the randomized mapping of x to $(h, 1^{n-\ell(n)}0h(x))$, where h is uniformly selected in $H_{|x|}^{\ell(|x|)}$, yields a relaxed reduction of (R, X) to (R', X'), where $X'_{n'}$ is uniform over $H_n^{\ell(n)} \times \{1^{n-\ell(n)}0v : v \in \{0, 1\}^{\ell(n)}\}$.* Needless to say, the claim refers to the reduction that (on input x, makes the query $(h, 1^{n-\ell(n)}0h(x))$, and) returns y if the oracle answer equals $\langle r, y \rangle$ and $y \in R(x)$.

The claim is proved by considering the set Ω_x of choices of $h \in H_{|x|}^{\ell(|x|)}$ for which $x \in S_n$ is the only preimage of $h(x)$ under h that resides in S_n (i.e., $|\{x' \in S_n : h(x') = h(x)\}| = 1$). In this case (i.e., $h \in \Omega_x$) it holds that $\langle r, y \rangle \in R'(h, 1^{|x|-\ell(|x|)}0h(x))$ implies that $S(1^{|x|}, r) = x$ and $y \in R(x)$, and the (relaxed) validity condition follows. The (relaxed) domination condition follows by noting that $\Pr[X_n = x] \approx 2^{-\ell(|x|)}$, that x is mapped to $(h, 1^{|x|-\ell(|x|)}0h(x))$ with probability $1/|H_{|x|}^{\ell(|x|)}|$, and that x is the only preimage of $(h, 1^{|x|-\ell(|x|)}0h(x))$ under the mapping (among $x' \in S_n$ such that $\Omega_{x'} \ni h$).

Before going any further, let us highlight the importance of hashing X_n to $\ell(n)$-bit strings. On the one hand, this mapping is "sufficiently" one-to-one, and thus (with constant probability) the solution provided for the hashed instance (i.e., $h(x)$) yields a solution for the original instance (i.e., x). This guarantees the validity of the reduction. On the other hand, for a typical h, the mapping of X_n to $h(X_n)$ covers the relevant range almost uniformly. This guarantees that the reduction satisfies the domination condition. Note that these two phenomena impose conflicting requirements that are both met at the correct value of ℓ; that is, the one-to-one condition requires $\ell(n) \geq \log_2 |S_n|$, whereas an almost uniform cover requires $\ell(n) \leq \log_2 |S_n|$. Also note that $\ell(n) = \log_2(1/\Pr[X_n = x])$ for every x in the support of X_n; the latter quantity will be in our focus in the general case.

The general case. Finally, we get rid of the assumption that X_n is *uniformly distributed* over some subset of $\{0, 1\}^n$. All that we know is that there exists a probabilistic polynomial-time ("sampling") algorithm S such that $S(1^n)$ is distributed identically to X_n. In this (general) case, we map instances of (R, X) according to their probability mass such that x is mapped to an instance (of R') that consists of $(h, h(x))$ and additional information, where h is a random hash function mapping n-bit long strings to ℓ_x-bit long strings such that

$$\ell_x \stackrel{\text{def}}{=} \lceil \log_2(1/\Pr[X_{|x|} = x]) \rceil. \tag{10.8}$$

Since (in the general case) there may be more than 2^{ℓ_x} strings in the support of X_n, we need to augment the reduced instance in order to ensure that it is uniquely associated with x. The basic idea is augmenting the mapping of x to $(h, h(x))$ with additional information that restricts X_n to strings that occur with probability at least $2^{-\ell_x}$. Indeed, when X_n is restricted in this way, the value of $h(X_n)$ uniquely determines X_n.

Let $q(n)$ denote the randomness complexity of S and $S(1^n, r)$ denote the output of S on input 1^n and internal coin tosses $r \in \{0, 1\}^{q(n)}$. Then, we randomly map x to $(h, h(x), h', v')$, where $h : \{0, 1\}^{|x|} \to \{0, 1\}^{\ell_x}$ and $h' : \{0, 1\}^{q(|x|)} \to \{0, 1\}^{q(|x|)-\ell_x}$ are random hash functions and $v' \in \{0, 1\}^{q(|x|)-\ell_x}$ is uniformly distributed. The instance (h, v, h', v') of the redefined search problem R' has solutions that consist of pairs $\langle r, y \rangle$ such that $h(S(1^n, r)) = v \wedge h'(r) = v'$ and $y \in R(S(1^n, r))$. As we shall see, this augmentation guarantees that, with constant probability (over the choice of h, h', v'), the solutions to the reduced instance $(h, h(x), h', v')$ correspond to the solutions to the original instance x.

The foregoing description assumes that, on input x, we can efficiently determine ℓ_x, which is an assumption that cannot be justified. Instead, we select ℓ uniformly in $\{0, 1, \ldots, q(|x|)\}$, and so with noticeable probability we do select the correct value (i.e., $\Pr[\ell = \ell_x] = 1/(q(|x|) + 1) = 1/\mathrm{poly}(|x|)$). For clarity, we make n and ℓ explicit in the reduced instance. Thus, we randomly map $x \in \{0, 1\}^n$ to $(1^n, 1^\ell, h, h(x), h', v') \in \{0, 1\}^{n'}$, where $\ell \in \{0, 1, \ldots, q(n)\}, h \in H_n^\ell, h' \in H_{q(n)}^{q(n)-\ell}$, and $v' \in \{0, 1\}^{q(n)-\ell}$ are uniformly distributed in the corresponding sets.[28] This mapping will be used to reduce (R, X) to (R', X'), where R' and $X' = \{X'_{n'}\}_{n' \in \mathbb{N}}$ are redefined (yet again). Specifically, we let

$$R'(1^n, 1^\ell, h, v, h', v') = \{\langle r, y \rangle : h(S(1^n, r)) = v \wedge h'(r) = v' \wedge y \in R(S(1^n, r))\}$$

(10.9)

and $X'_{n'}$ assigns equal probability to each $X_{n', \ell}$ (for $\ell \in \{0, 1, \ldots, n\}$), where each $X_{n', \ell}$ is isomorphic to the uniform distribution over $H_n^\ell \times \{0, 1\}^\ell \times H_{q(n)}^{q(n)-\ell} \times \{0, 1\}^{q(n)-\ell}$. Note that indeed $(R', X') \in \mathrm{dist}\mathcal{PC}$.

The foregoing randomized mapping is analyzed by considering the correct choice for ℓ; that is, on input x, we focus on the choice $\ell = \ell_x$. Under this conditioning (as we shall show), *with constant probability over the choice of h, h' and v', the instance x is the only value in the support of X_n that is mapped to $(1^n, 1^{\ell_x}, h, h(x), h', v')$ and satisfies $\{r : h(S(1^n, r)) = h(x) \wedge h'(r) = v'\} \neq \emptyset$.* It follows that (for such h, h' and v') any solution $\langle r, y \rangle \in R'(1^n, 1^{\ell_x}, h, h(x), h', v')$ satisfies $S(1^n, r) = x$ and thus $y \in R(x)$, which means that the (relaxed) validity condition is satisfied. The (relaxed) domination condition is satisfied, too, because (conditioned on $\ell = \ell_x$ and for such h, h', v') the probability that X_n is mapped to $(1^n, 1^{\ell_x}, h, h(x), h', v')$ approximately equals $\Pr[X'_{n', \ell_x} = (1^n, 1^{\ell_x}, h, h(x), h', v')]$.

We now turn to analyzing the probability, over the choice of h, h' and v', that the instance x is the only value in the support of X_n that is mapped to $(1^n, 1^{\ell_x}, h, h(x), h', v')$ and satisfies $\{r : h(S(1^n, r)) = h(x) \wedge h'(r) = v'\} \neq \emptyset$. Firstly, we note that $|\{r : S(1^n, r) = x\}| \geq 2^{q(n)-\ell_x}$, and thus, with constant probability over the choice of $h' \in H_{q(n)}^{q(n)-\ell_x}$ and $v' \in \{0, 1\}^{q(n)-\ell_x}$, there exists r that satisfies $S(1^n, r) = x$ and $h'(r) = v'$. Furthermore, with constant probability over the choice of $h' \in H_{q(n)}^{q(n)-\ell_x}$ and $v' \in \{0, 1\}^{q(n)-\ell_x}$, it also holds that there are at most $O(2^{\ell_x})$ strings r such that $h'(r) = v'$. Fixing such h' and v', we let $S_{h', v'} = \{S(1^n, r) : h'(r) = v'\}$ and we note that, with constant probability over the choice of $h \in H_n^{\ell_x}$, it holds that x is the only string in $S_{h', v'}$ that is mapped to $h(x)$ under h. Thus, with constant probability over the choice of h, h' and v', the instance x is the only value in the support of X_n that is mapped to $(1^n, 1^{\ell_x},$

---

[28] As in other places, a suitable encoding will be used such that the reduction maps strings of the same length to strings of the same length (i.e., n-bit strings are mapped to n'-bit strings, for $n' = \mathrm{poly}(n)$). For example, we may encode $\langle 1^n, 1^\ell, h, h(x), h', v' \rangle$ as $1^n 01^\ell 01^{q(n)-\ell} 0 \langle h \rangle \langle h(x) \rangle \langle h' \rangle \langle v' \rangle$, where each $\langle w \rangle$ denotes an encoding of w by a string of length $(n' - (n + q(n) + 3))/4$.

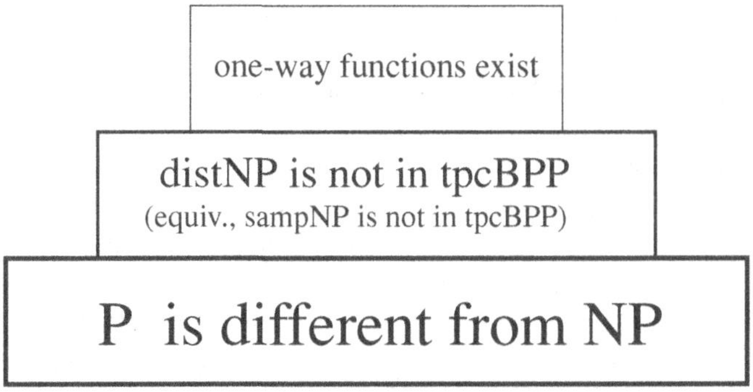

Figure 10.2: Worst-case versus average-case assumptions.

$h, h(x), h', v'$) and satisfies $\{r : h(S(1^n, r)) = h(x) \wedge h'(r) = v'\} \neq \emptyset$. The theorem follows. $\qquad\qquad\qquad\qquad\qquad\qquad\qquad\qquad\qquad\qquad\qquad\qquad\qquad\square$

Reflection. Theorem 10.26 implies that if samp$\mathcal{NP}$ is not contained in tpc$\mathcal{BPP}$ then every dist$\mathcal{NP}$-complete problem is not in tpc$\mathcal{BPP}$. This means that the hardness of some distributional problems that refer to samplable distributions implies the hardness of some distributional problems that refer to simple distributions. Furthermore, by Proposition 10.21, this implies the hardness of distributional problems that refer to the uniform distribution. Thus, hardness with respect to some distribution in an utmost wide class (which arguably captures all distributions that may occur in practice) implies hardness with respect to a single simple distribution (which arguably is the simplest one).

Relation to one-way functions. We note that the existence of one-way functions (see Section 7.1) implies the existence of problems in samp$\mathcal{PC}$ that are not in tpc$\mathcal{BPPF}$ (which in turn implies the existence of such problems in dist$\mathcal{PC}$). Specifically, for a length-preserving one-way function f, consider the distributional search problem $(R_f, \{f(U_n)\}_{n\in\mathbb{N}})$, where $R_f = \{(f(r), r) : r \in \{0, 1\}^*\}$.[29] On the other hand, it is not known whether the existence of a problem in samp$\mathcal{PC} \setminus$ tpc$\mathcal{BPPF}$ implies the existence of one-way functions. In particular, the existence of a problem (R, X) in samp$\mathcal{PC} \setminus$ tpc$\mathcal{BPPF}$ represents the feasibility of generating hard instances for the search problem R, whereas the existence of a one-way function represents the feasibility of generating instance-solution pairs such that the instances are hard to solve (see Section 7.1.1). Indeed, the gap refers to whether or not *hard instances can be efficiently generated together with corresponding solutions.* Our world view is thus depicted in Figure 10.2, where lower levels indicate seemingly weaker assumptions.

Chapter Notes

In this chapter, we presented two different approaches to the relaxation of computational problems. The first approach refers to the concept of approximation, while the second approach refers to average-case analysis. We demonstrated that various natural notions of approximation can be cast within the standard frameworks, where the framework of promise problems (presented in Section 2.4.1) is the least-standard framework we used (and it suffices for casting gap problems and property testing). In contrast, the study of

---

[29]Note that the distribution $f(U_n)$ is uniform in the special case that f is a permutation over $\{0, 1\}^n$.

average-case complexity requires the introduction of a new conceptual framework as well as addressing various definitional issues.

A natural question at this point is what we have gained by relaxing the requirements. In the context of approximation, the answer is mixed: In some natural cases we gain a lot (i.e., we obtained feasible relaxations of hard problems), while in other natural cases we gain nothing (i.e., even extreme relaxations remain as intractable as the original versions). In the context of average-case complexity, the negative side seems more prevailing (at least in the sense of being more systematic). In particular, assuming the existence of one-way functions, every natural NP-complete problem has a distributional version that is (typical-case) hard, where this version refers to a samplable ensemble (and, in fact, even to a simple ensemble). Furthermore, in this case, some problems in NP have hard distributional versions that refer to the uniform distribution.

10.2.2.3. Approximation
The following bibliographic comments are quite laconic and neglect mentioning various important works (including credits for some of the results mentioned in our text). As usual, the interested reader is referred to corresponding surveys.

Search or Optimization. The interest in approximation algorithms increased considerably following the demonstration of the NP-completeness of many natural optimization problems. But, with some exceptions (most notably [179]), the systematic study of the complexity of such problems stalled till the discovery of the "PCP connection" (see Section 9.3.3) by Feige, Goldwasser, Lovász, and Safra [73]. Indeed the relatively "tight" inapproximation results for max-Clique, max-SAT, and the maximization of linear equations, due to Håstad [116, 117], build on previous work regarding PCP and their connection to approximation (cf., e.g., [74, 16, 15, 29, 185]). Specifically, Theorem 10.5 is due to [116],[30] while Theorems 10.8 and 10.9 are due to [117]. The best-known inapproximation result for minimum Vertex Cover (see Theorem 10.7) is due to [69], but we doubt it is tight (see, e.g., [143]). Reductions among approximation problems were defined and presented in [179]; see Exercise 10.7, which presents a major technique introduced in [179]. For general texts on approximation algorithms and problems (as discussed in Section 10.1.1), the interested reader is referred to the surveys collected in [122]. A compendium of NP optimization problems is available at [64].

Recall that a different type of approximation problems, which are naturally associated with search problems, refers to approximately counting the number of solutions. These approximation problems were treated in Section 6.2.2 in a rather ad hoc manner. We note that a more systematic treatment of approximate counting problems can be obtained by using the definitional framework of Section 10.1.1 (e.g., the notions of gap problems, polynomial-time approximation schemes, etc).

Property testing. The study of property testing was initiated by Rubinfeld and Sudan [195] and reinitiated by Goldreich, Goldwasser, and Ron [97]. While the focus of [195] was on algebraic properties such as low-degree polynomials, the focus of [97] was on graph properties (and Theorem 10.12 is taken from [97]). The model of bounded-degree graphs was introduced in [103], and Theorem 10.13 combines results from [103, 104, 42]. For surveys of the area, the interested reader is referred to [77, 194].

---

[30]See also [244].

Average-case complexity

The theory of average-case complexity was initiated by Levin [154], who in particular proved Theorem 10.17. In light of the laconic nature of the original text [154], we refer the interested reader to a survey [89], which provides a more detailed exposition of the definitions suggested by Levin as well as a discussion of the considerations underlying these suggestions. (This survey [89] also provides a brief account of further developments.)

As noted in §10.2.1.1, the current text uses a variant of the original definitions. In particular, our definition of "typical-case feasibility" differs from the original definition of "average-case feasibility" in totally discarding exceptional instances and in even allowing the algorithm to fail on them (and not merely run for an excessive amount of time). The alternative definition was suggested by several researchers, and appears as a special case of the general treatment provided in [44].

Turning to §10.2.1.2, we note that while the existence of dist$\mathcal{NP}$-complete problems (cf. Theorem 10.17) was established in Levin's original paper [154], the existence of dist$\mathcal{NP}$-complete versions of all natural NP-complete decision problems (cf. Theorem 10.19) was established more than two decades later in [158].

Section 10.2.2 is based on [30, 127]. Specifically, Theorem 10.23 (or rather the reduction of search to decision) is due to [30] and so is the introduction of the class samp$\mathcal{NP}$. A version of Theorem 10.26 was proven in [127], and our proof follows their ideas, which in turn are closely related to the ideas underlying the proof of Theorem 8.11 (proved in [118]).

Recall that we know of the existence of problems in dist$\mathcal{NP}$ that are hard provided samp$\mathcal{NP}$ contains hard problems. However, these distributional problems do not seem very natural (i.e., they refer either to somewhat generic decision problems such as S_u or to somewhat contrived probability ensembles (cf. Theorem 10.19)). The presentation of dist$\mathcal{NP}$-complete problems that combine a more natural decision problem (like SAT or Clique) with a more natural probability ensemble is an open problem.

Exercises

Exercise 10.1 (general TSP): For any adequate function g, prove that the following approximation problem is NP-hard. Given a general TSP instance I, represented by a symmetric matrix of pairwise distances, the task is finding a tour of length that is at most a factor $g(I)$ of the minimum. Specifically, show that the result holds with $g(I) = \exp(|I|^{0.99})$ and for instances in which all distances are positive integers.

> **Guideline:** Use a reduction from Hamiltonian cycle problem. Specifically, reduce the instance $G = ([n], E)$ to an n-by-n distance matrix $D = (d_{i,j})_{i,j \in [n]}$ such that $d_{i,j} = \exp(\text{poly}(n))$ if $\{i, j\} \in E$ and $d_{i,j} = 1$.

Exercise 10.2 (TSP with triangle inequalities): Provide a polynomial-time 2-factor approximation for the special case of TSP in which the distances satisfy the triangle inequality.

> **Guideline:** First note that the length of any tour is lower-bounded by the weight of a minimum spanning tree in the corresponding weighted graph. Next note that such a tree yields a tour (of length twice the weight of this tree) that may visit some points several times. The triangle inequality guarantees that the tour does not become longer by "shortcuts" that eliminate multiple visits at the same point.

Exercise 10.3 (a weak version of Theorem 10.5): Using Theorem 9.16 prove that, for some constants $0 < a < b < 1$ when setting $L(N) = N^b$ and $s(N) = N^a$, it holds that $\mathrm{gapClique}_{L,s}$ is NP-hard.

> **Guideline:** Starting with Theorem 9.16, apply the Expander Random Walk Generator (of Proposition 8.29) in order to derive a PCP-system with logarithmic randomness and query complexities that accepts no-instances of length n with probability at most $1/n$. The claim follows by applying the FGLSS-reduction (of Exercise 9.18), while noting that x is reduced to a graph of size $\mathrm{poly}(|x|)$ such that the gap between yes- and no-instances is at least a factor of $|x|$.

Exercise 10.4 (a weak version of Theorem 10.7): Using Theorem 9.16 prove that, for some constants $0 < s < L < 1$, the problem $\mathrm{gapVC}_{s,L}$ is NP-hard.

> **Guideline:** Note that combining Theorem 9.16 and Exercise 9.18 implies that for some constants $b < 1$ it holds that $\mathrm{gapClique}_{L,s}$ is NP-hard, where $L(N) = b \cdot N$ and $s(N) = (b/2) \cdot N$. The claim follows using the relations between cliques, independent sets, and vertex covers.

Exercise 10.5 (a weak version of Theorem 10.9): Using Theorem 9.16 prove that, for some constants $0.5 < s < L < 1$, the problem $\mathrm{gapLin}_{L,s}$ is NP-hard.

> **Guideline:** Recall that by Theorems 9.16 and 9.21, the gap problem $\mathrm{gapSAT}_\varepsilon^3$ is NP-hard. Note that the result holds even if we restrict the instances to having exactly three (not necessarily different) literals in each clause. Applying the reduction of Exercise 2.24, note that, for any assignment τ, a clause that is satisfied by τ is mapped to seven equations of which exactly three are violated by τ, whereas a clause that is not satisfied by τ is mapped to seven equations that are all violated by τ.

Exercise 10.6 (natural inapproximability without the PCP Theorem): In contrast to the inapproximability results reviewed in §10.1.1.2, the NP-completeness of the following gap problem can be established (rather easily) without referring to the PCP Theorem. The instances of this problem are systems of quadratic equations over GF(2) (as in Exercise 2.25), yes-instances are systems that have a solution, and no-instances are systems for which any assignment violates at least one-third of the equations.

> **Guideline:** As stated in Exercise 2.25, when given such a quadratic system, it is NP-hard to determine whether or not there exists an assignment that satisfies all the equations. Using an adequate small-bias generator (cf. Section 8.5.2), present an amplifying reduction (cf. Section 9.3.3) of the foregoing problem to itself. Specifically, if the input system has m equations then we use a generator that defines a sample space of $\mathrm{poly}(m)$ many m-bit strings, and consider the corresponding linear combinations of the input equations. Note that it suffices to bound the bias of the generator by $1/6$, whereas using an ε-biased generator yields an analogous result with $1/3$ replaced by $0.5 - \varepsilon$.

Exercise 10.7 (enforcing multi-way equalities via expanders): The aim of this exercise is presenting a technique (of Papadimitriou and Yannakakis [179]) that is useful for designing reductions among approximation problems. Recalling that $\mathrm{gapSAT}_{0.1}^3$ is NP-hard, our goal is proving NP-hardness of the following gap problem, denoted $\mathrm{gapSAT}_\varepsilon^{3,c}$, which is a special case of $\mathrm{gapSAT}_\varepsilon^3$. Specifically, the instances are restricted to 3CNF formulae with each variable appearing in at most c clauses, where c (as ε) is a fixed constant. Note that the standard reduction of 3SAT to the corresponding special case (see proof of Proposition 2.23) does not preserve an approximation gap.[31] The idea is enforcing equality of the values assigned to the auxiliary variables (i.e., the copies of each original variable) by introducing equality constraints only for pairs of variables that correspond to edges of an expander graph (see Appendix E.2). For example, we enforce equality among the values of $z^{(1)}, \ldots, z^{(m)}$ by adding the clauses $z^{(i)} \vee \neg z^{(j)}$ for every $\{i, j\} \in E$, where E is the set of edges of an m-vertex expander graph. Prove that, for some constants c and $\varepsilon > 0$, the corresponding mapping reduces $\text{gapSAT}^3_{0.1}$ to $\text{gapSAT}^{3,c}_\varepsilon$.

> **Guideline:** Using d-regular expanders in the foregoing reduction, we map general 3CNF formulae to 3CNF formulae in which each variable appears in at most $2d + 1$ clauses. Note that the number of added clauses is linearly related to the number of original clauses. Clearly, if the original formula is satisfiable then so is the reduced one. On the other hand, consider an arbitrary assignment τ' to the reduced formula ϕ' (i.e., the formula obtained by mapping ϕ). For each original variable z, if τ' assigns the same value to almost all copies of z then we consider the corresponding assignment in ϕ. Otherwise, by virtue of the added clauses, τ' does not satisfy a constant fraction of the clauses containing a copy of z.

Exercise 10.8 (deciding majority requires linear time): Prove that deciding majority requires linear time even in a direct access model and when using a randomized algorithm that may err with probability at most $1/3$.

> **Guideline:** Consider the problem of distinguishing X_n from Y_n, where X_n (resp., Y_n) is uniformly distributed over the set of n-bit strings having exactly $\lfloor n/2 \rfloor$ (resp., $\lfloor n/2 \rfloor + 1$) zeros. For any fixed set $I \subset [n]$, denote the projection of X_n (resp., Y_n) on I by X'_n (resp., Y'_n). Prove that the statistical difference between X'_n and Y'_n is bounded by $O(|I|/n)$. Note that the argument needs to be extended to the case that the examined locations are selected adaptively.

Exercise 10.9 (testing majority in poly-logarithmic time): Show that testing majority (in the sense of Definition 10.11) can be done in poly-logarithmic time by probing the input at a constant number of randomly selected locations.

Exercise 10.10 (on the triviality of some testing problems): Show that the following sets are trivially testable in the adjacency matrix representation (i.e., for every $\delta > 0$ and any such set S, there exists a trivial algorithm that distinguishes S from $\Gamma_\delta(S)$).

1. The set of connected graphs.
2. The set of Hamiltonian graphs.
3. The set of Eulerian graphs.

Indeed, show that in each case $\Gamma_\delta(S) = \emptyset$.

---

[31] Recall that in this reduction, each occurrences of each Boolean variable is replaced by a new copy of this variable, and clauses are added for enforcing the assignment of the same value to all these copies. Specifically, the m occurrences of variable z are replaced by the variables $z^{(1)}, \ldots, z^{(m)}$, while adding the clauses $z^{(i)} \vee \neg z^{(i+1)}$ and $z^{(i+1)} \vee \neg z^{(i)}$ (for $i = 1, \ldots, m-1$). The problem is that almost all clauses of the reduced formula may be satisfied by an assignment in which half of the copies of each variable are assigned one value and the rest are assigned an opposite value. That is, an assignment in which $z^{(1)} = \cdots = z^{(i)} \neq z^{(i+1)} = \cdots = z^{(m)}$ violates only one of the auxiliary clauses introduced for enforcing equality among the copies of z. Using an alternative reduction that adds the clauses $z^{(i)} \vee \neg z^{(j)}$ for every $i, j \in [m]$ will not do either, because the number of added clauses may be quadratic in the number of original clauses.

Guideline (for Item 3): Note that, *in general*, the fact that the sets S' and S'' are testable within some complexity does *not* imply the same for the set $S' \cap S''$.

Exercise 10.11 (an equivalent definition of $\mathrm{tpc}\mathcal{P}$**):** Prove that $(S, X) \in \mathrm{tpc}\mathcal{P}$ if and only if there exists a polynomial-time algorithm A such that the probability that $A(X_n)$ errs (in determining membership in S) is a negligible function in n.

Exercise 10.12 ($\mathrm{tpc}\mathcal{P}$ **versus** $\mathcal{P}$ **– Part 1):** Prove that $\mathrm{tpc}\mathcal{P}$ contains a problem (S, X) such that S is not even recursive. Furthermore, use $X = U$.

Guideline: Let $S = \{0^{|x|}x : x \in S'\}$, where S' is an arbitrary (non-recursive) set.

Exercise 10.13 ($\mathrm{tpc}\mathcal{P}$ **versus** $\mathcal{P}$ **– Part 2):** Prove that there exists a distributional problem (S, X) such that $S \notin \mathcal{P}$ and yet there exists an algorithm solving S (correctly on all inputs) in time that is typically polynomial with respect to X. Furthermore, use $X = U$.

Guideline: For any time-constructible function $t : \mathbb{N} \to \mathbb{N}$ that is super-polynomial and sub-exponential, use $S = \{0^{|x|}x : x \in S'\}$ for any $S' \in \mathrm{DTIME}(t) \setminus \mathcal{P}$.

Exercise 10.14 (simple distributions and monotone sampling): We say that a probability ensemble $X = \{X_n\}_{n \in \mathbb{N}}$ is polynomial-time samplable via a monotone mapping if there exists a polynomial p and a polynomial-time computable function f such that the following two conditions hold:

1. For every n, the random variables $f(U_{p(n)})$ and X_n are identically distributed.
2. For every n and every $r' < r'' \in \{0, 1\}^{p(n)}$ it holds that $f(r') \leq f(r'')$, where the inequalities refer to the standard lexicographic order of strings.

Prove that X is simple if and only if it is polynomial-time samplable via a monotone mapping.

Guideline: Suppose that X is simple, and let p be a polynomial bounding the running time of the algorithm that on input x outputs $\Pr[X_{|x|} \leq x]$. (Thus, the binary representation of $\Pr[X_{|x|} \leq x]$ has length at most $p(|x|)$.) The desired function $f : \{0, 1\}^{p(n)} \to \{0, 1\}^n$ is obtained by defining $f(r) = x$ if the number (represented by) $0.r$ resides in the interval $[\Pr[X_n < x], \Pr[X_n \leq x])$. Note that f can be computed by binary search, using the fact that X is simple. Turning to the opposite direction, we note that any efficiently computable and monotone mapping $f : \{0, 1\}^{p(n)} \to \{0, 1\}^n$ can be efficiently inverted by a binary search. Furthermore, similar methods allow for efficiently determining the interval of $p(n)$-bit long strings that are mapped to any given n-bit long string.

Exercise 10.15 (reductions preserve typical polynomial-time solvability): Prove that if the distributional problem (S, X) is reducible to the distributional problem (S', X') and $(S', X') \in \mathrm{tpc}\mathcal{P}$, then (S, X) is in $\mathrm{tpc}\mathcal{P}$.

Guideline: Let B' denote the set of exceptional instances for the distributional problem (S', X'); that is, B' is the set of instances on which the solver in the hypothesis either errs or exceeds the typical running time. Prove that $\Pr[Q(X_n) \cap B' \neq \emptyset]$ is a negligible function (in n), using both $\Pr[y \in Q(X_n)] \leq p(|y|) \cdot \Pr[X'_{|y|} = y]$ and $|x| \leq p'(|y|)$ for every $y \in Q(x)$. Specifically, use the latter condition for inferring that $\sum_{y \in B'} \Pr[y \in Q(X_n)]$ equals $\sum_{y \in \{y' \in B' : p'(|y'|) \geq n\}} \Pr[y \in Q(X_n)]$, which is upper-bounded by $\sum_{m : p'(m) \geq n} p(m) \cdot \Pr[X'_m \in B']$ (which in turn is negligible in terms of n).

Exercise 10.16 (reductions preserve errorless solvability): In continuation of Exercise 10.15, prove that reductions preserve errorless solvability (i.e., solvability by algorithms that never err and typically run in polynomial time).

Exercise 10.17 (transitivity of reductions): Prove that reductions among distributional problems (as in Definition 10.16) are transitive.

> **Guideline:** The point is establishing the domination property of the composed reduction. The hypothesis that reductions do not make too short queries is instrumental here.

Exercise 10.18: For any $S \in \mathcal{NP}$ present a simple probability ensemble X such that the generic reduction used in the proof of Theorem 2.19, when applied to (S, X), violates the domination condition with respect to (S_u, U').

> **Guideline:** Consider $X = \{X_n\}_{n \in \mathbb{N}}$ such that X_n is uniform over $\{0^{n/2}x' : x' \in \{0, 1\}^{n/2}\}$.

Exercise 10.19 (variants of the Coding Lemma): Prove the following two variants of the Coding Lemma (which is stated in the proof of Theorem 10.17).

1. A variant that refers to any efficiently computable function $\mu : \{0, 1\}^* \to [0, 1]$ that is monotonically non-decreasing over $\{0, 1\}^*$ (i.e., $\mu(x') \le \mu(x'')$ for any $x' < x'' \in \{0, 1\}^*$). That is, unlike in the proof of Theorem 10.17, here it holds that $\mu(0^{n+1}) \ge \mu(1^n)$ for every n.
2. As in Part 1, except that in this variant the function μ is strictly increasing and the compression condition requires that $|C_\mu(x)| \le \log_2(1/\mu'(x))$ rather than $|C_\mu(x)| \le 1 + \min\{|x|, \log_2(1/\mu'(x))\}$, where $\mu'(x) \stackrel{\text{def}}{=} \mu(x) - \mu(x - 1)$.

In both cases, the proof is less cumbersome than the one presented in the main text.

Exercise 10.20: Prove that for any problem (S, X) in dist$\mathcal{NP}$ there exists a simple probability ensemble Y such that the reduction used in the proof of Theorem 2.19 suffices for reducing (S, X) to (S_u, Y).

> **Guideline:** Consider $Y = \{Y_n\}_{n \in \mathbb{N}}$ such that Y_n assigns to the instance $\langle M, x, 1^t \rangle$ a probability mass proportional to $\pi_x \stackrel{\text{def}}{=} \Pr[X_{|x|} = x]$. Specifically, for every $\langle M, x, 1^t \rangle$ it holds that $\Pr[Y_n = \langle M, x, 1^t \rangle] = 2^{-|M|} \cdot \pi_x / \binom{n}{2}$, where $n \stackrel{\text{def}}{=} |\langle M, x, 1^t \rangle| \stackrel{\text{def}}{=} |M| + |x| + t$. Alternatively, we may set $\Pr[Y_n = \langle M, x, 1^t \rangle] = \pi_x$ if $M = M_S$ and $t = p_S(|x|)$ and $\Pr[Y_n = \langle M, x, 1^t \rangle] = 0$ otherwise, where M_S and P_S are as in the proof of Theorem 2.19.

Exercise 10.21 (monotone markability and monotone reductions): In continuation of Exercise 2.30, we say that a set T is monotonically markable if there exists a polynomial-time (marking) algorithm M such that

1. For every $z, \alpha \in \{0, 1\}^*$, it holds that $M(z, \alpha) \in T$ if and only if $z \in T$.
2. Monotonicity: for every $|z'| = |z''|$ and $\alpha' < \alpha''$, it holds that $M(z', \alpha') < M(z'', \alpha'')$, where the inequalities refer to the standard lexicographic order of strings.
3. Auxiliary length requirements:
   (a) If $|z'| = |z''|$ and $|\alpha'| = |\alpha''|$, then $|M(z', \alpha')| = |M(z'', \alpha'')|$.
   (b) If $|z'| \le |z''|$ and $|\alpha'| < |\alpha''|$, then $|M(z', \alpha')| < |M(z'', \alpha'')|$.

(c) There exists a 1-1 polynomial $p : \mathbb{N} \to \mathbb{N}$ such that for every ℓ and every $z \in \cup_{i=1}^{\ell}\{0, 1\}^i$ there exists $t \in [p(\ell)]$ such that $|M(z, 1^t)| = p(\ell)$.

The first two requirements (of Condition 3) imply that $|M(z, \alpha)|$ is a function of $|z|$ and $|\alpha|$, which increases with $|\alpha|$. The third requirement implies that, for every ℓ, each string of length at most ℓ can be mapped to a string of length $p(\ell)$.

Note that Condition 1 is reproduced from Exercise 2.30, whereas Conditions 2 and 3 are new. Prove that if the set S is Karp-reducible to the set T and T is monotonically markable then S is Karp-reducible to T by a reduction that is monotone and length-regular (i.e., the reduction satisfies the conditions of Proposition 10.18).

Guideline: Given a Karp-reduction f from S to T, first obtain a length-regular reduction f' from S to T (by applying the marking algorithm to $f(x)$, while using Conditions 1 and 3c). In particular, one can guarantee that if $|x'| > |x''|$ then $|f'(x')| > |f'(x'')|$. Next, obtain a reduction f'' that is also monotone (e.g., by letting $f''(x) = M(f'(x), x)$, while using Conditions 1 and 2).[32]

Exercise 10.22 (monotone markability and markability): Prove that if a set is monotonically markable (as per Exercise 10.21) then it is markable (as per Exercise 2.30).

Guideline: Let M denote the guaranteed monotone-marking algorithm. For starters, assume that M is 1-1, and define $M'(z, \alpha) = M(z, \langle z, \alpha \rangle)$. Note that the preimage (z, α) can be found by conducting a binary search (for each of the possible values of $|z|$). In the general case, we modify the construction so as to guarantee that M' is 1-1. Specifically, let $\mathrm{idx}(n, m) = n + \sum_{i=2}^{n+m}(i - 1)$ be the index of (n, m) in an enumeration of all pairs of positive integers, and p be as in Condition 3c. Then, let $M'(z, \alpha) = M(z, C_{t(|z|, |\alpha|)}(\langle z, \alpha \rangle))$, where $t(n, m) = \omega(n + m)$ satisfies $|M(1^n, 1^{t(n,m)})| = p(\mathrm{idx}(n, m))$ and $C_t(y)$ is a monotone encoding of y using a t-bit long string.

Exercise 10.23 (some monotonically markable sets): Referring to Exercise 10.21, verify that each of the twenty-one NP-complete problems treated in Karp's first paper on NP-completeness [138] is monotonically markable. For starters, consider the sets SAT, Clique, and 3-Colorability.

Guideline: For SAT consider the following marking algorithm M. This algorithm uses two (fixed) satisfiable formulae of the same length, denoted ψ_0 and ψ_1, such that $\psi_0 < \psi_1$. For any formula ϕ and any binary string $\sigma_1 \cdots \sigma_m \in \{0, 1\}^m$, it holds that $M(\phi, \sigma_1 \cdots \sigma_m) = \psi_{\sigma_1} \wedge \cdots \wedge \psi_{\sigma_m} \wedge \phi$, where ψ_0 and ψ_1 use variables that do not appear in ϕ. Note that the multiple occurrences of ψ_σ can be easily avoided (by using "variations" of ψ_σ).

Exercise 10.24 (randomized reductions): Following the outline in §10.2.1.3, provide a definition of randomized reductions among distributional problems.

1. In analogy to Exercise 10.15, prove that randomized reductions preserve feasible solvability (i.e., typical solvability in probabilistic polynomial time). That is, if the distributional problem (S, X) is randomly reducible to the distributional problem (S', X') and $(S', X') \in \mathrm{tpc}\mathcal{BPP}$, then (S, X) is in $\mathrm{tpc}\mathcal{BPP}$.

---

[32] Actually, Condition 2 (combined with the length regularity of f') only takes care of monotonicity with respect to strings of equal length. To guarantee monotonicity with respect to strings of different length, we also use Condition 3b (and $|f'(x')| > |f'(x'')|$ for $|x'| > |x''|$).

2. In analogy to Exercise 10.16, prove that randomized reductions preserve solvability by probabilistic algorithms that err with probability at most $1/3$ on each input and typically run in polynomial time.

3. Prove that randomized reductions are transitive (cf. Exercise 10.17).

4. Show that the error probability of randomized reductions can be reduced (while preserving the domination condition).

Extend the foregoing to reductions that involve distributional *search* problems.

Exercise 10.25 (simple vs samplable ensembles – Part 1): Prove that any simple probability ensemble is polynomial-time samplable.

> **Guideline:** See Exercise 10.14.

Exercise 10.26 (simple vs samplable ensembles – Part 2): Assuming that $\#\mathcal{P}$ contains functions that are not computable in polynomial time, prove that there exists polynomial-time samplable ensembles that are not simple.

> **Guideline:** Consider any $R \in \mathcal{PC}$ and suppose that p is a polynomial such that $(x, y) \in R$ implies $|y| = p(|x|)$. Then consider the sampling algorithm A that, on input 1^n, uniformly selects $(x, y) \in \{0, 1\}^{n-1} \times \{0, 1\}^{p(n-1)}$ and outputs $x1$ if $(x, y) \in R$ and $x0$ otherwise. Note that $\#R(x) = 2^{|x|+p(|x|)} \cdot \Pr[A(1^{|x|+1})=x1]$.

Exercise 10.27 (distributional versions of NPC problems – Part 1 [30]): Prove that if S_u is Karp-reducible to S by a mapping that does not shrink the input then there exists a polynomial-time samplable ensemble X such that any problem in dist$\mathcal{NP}$ is reducible to (S, X).

> **Guideline:** Prove that the guaranteed reduction of S_u to S also reduces (S_u, U') to (S, X), for some samplable probability ensemble X. Consider first the case that the standard reduction of S_u to S is length-preserving, and prove that, when applied to a samplable probability ensemble, it induces a samplable distribution on the instances of S. (Note that U' is samplable (by Exercise 10.25).) Next, extend the treatment to the general case, where applying the standard reduction to U'_n induces a distribution on $\cup_{m=n}^{\text{poly}(n)}\{0, 1\}^m$ (rather than a distribution on $\{0, 1\}^n$).

Exercise 10.28 (distributional versions of NPC problems – Part 2 [30]): Prove Theorem 10.25 (i.e., if S_u is Karp-reducible to S by a mapping that does not shrink the input then there exists a polynomial-time samplable ensemble X such that any problem in samp$\mathcal{NP}$ is reducible to (S, X)).

> **Guideline:** We establish the claim for $S = S_u$, and the general claim follows by using the reduction of S_u to S (as in Exercise 10.27). Thus, we focus on showing that, for some (suitably chosen) samplable ensemble X, any $(S', X') \in$ samp$\mathcal{NP}$ is reducible to (S_u, X). Loosely speaking, X will be an adequate convex combination of all samplable distributions (and thus X will neither equal U' nor be simple). Specifically, $X = \{X_n\}_{n\in\mathbb{N}}$ is defined such that the sampler for X_n uniformly selects $i \in [n]$, emulates the execution of the ith algorithm (in lexicographic order) on input 1^n for n^3 steps,[33] and outputs whatever the latter has output (or 0^n in case the said algorithm has not halted

---

[33] Needless to say, the choice to consider n algorithms (in the definition of X_n) is quite arbitrary. Any other unbounded function of n that is at most a polynomial (and is computable in polynomial time) will do. (More generally, we may select the ith algorithm with p_i, as long as p_i is a noticeable function of n.) Likewise, the choice to emulate each algorithm for a cubic number of steps (rather some other fixed polynomial number of steps) is quite arbitrary.

within n^3 steps). Prove that, for any $(S'', X'') \in \text{samp}\mathcal{NP}$ such that X'' is samplable in cubic time, the standard reduction of S'' to S_u reduces (S'', X'') to (S_u, X) (as per Definition 10.15; i.e., in particular, it satisfies the domination condition).[34] Finally, using adequate padding, reduce any $(S', X') \in \text{samp}\mathcal{NP}$ to some $(S'', X'') \in \text{samp}\mathcal{NP}$ such that X'' is samplable in cubic time.

Exercise 10.29 (search vs decision in the context of samplable ensembles): Prove that every problem in $\text{samp}\mathcal{NP}$ is reducible to some problem in $\text{samp}\mathcal{PC}$, and every problem in $\text{samp}\mathcal{PC}$ is *randomly* reducible to some problem in $\text{samp}\mathcal{NP}$.

Guideline: See proof of Theorem 10.23.

---

[34]Note that applying this reduction to X'' yields an ensemble that is also samplable in cubic time. This claim uses the fact that the standard reduction runs in time that is less than cubic (and in fact almost linear) in its output, and the fact that the output is longer than the input.

Epilogue

Farewell, Hans – whether you live or end where you are! Your chances are not good. The wicked dance in which you are caught up will last a few more sinful years, and we would not wager much that you will come out whole. To be honest, we are not really bothered about leaving the question open. Adventures in the flesh and spirit, which enhanced and heightened your ordinariness, allowed you to survive in the spirit what you probably will not survive in the flesh. There were majestic moments when you saw the intimation of a dream of love rising up out of death and the carnal body. Will love someday rise up out of this worldwide festival of death, this ugly rutting fever that inflames the rainy evening sky all round?

Thomas Mann, *The Magic Mountain*, "The Thunderbolt."

We hope that this work has succeeded in conveying the fascinating flavor of the concepts, results, and open problems that dominate the field of Computational Complexity. We believe that the new century will witness even more exciting developments in this field, and urge the reader to try to contribute to them. But before bidding good-bye, we wish to express a few more thoughts.

As noted in Section 1.1.1, so far Complexity Theory has been far more successful in relating fundamental computational phenomena than in providing definite answers regarding fundamental questions. Consider, for example, the theory of NP-completeness versus the P-vs-NP Question, or the theory of pseudorandomness versus establishing the existence of one-way functions (even under $\mathcal{P} \neq \mathcal{NP}$). The failure to resolve questions of the "absolute" type is the source of common frustration, and one often wonders about the reasons for this failure.

Our feeling is that many of these failures are really due to the difficulty of the questions asked, and that one tends to underestimate their hardness because they are so appealing and natural. Indeed, the underlying sentiment is that if a question is appealing and natural, then answering it should not be hard. We doubt this sentiment. Our own feeling is that the more intuitive a question is, the harder it may be to answer. Our view is that intuitive questions arise from an encounter with the raw and chaotic reality of life, rather than from an artificial construct that is typically endowed with a rich internal structure. Indeed, natural complexity classes and natural questions regarding computation arise from looking at the reality of computation from the outside and thus lack any internal structure. Specifically, complexity classes are defined in terms of the "external behavior" of potential algorithms (i.e., the resources such algorithms require), rather than in terms of the "internal structure" (of the problem). In our opinion, this "external nature" of the definitions of complexity-theoretic questions makes them hard to resolve.

Another hard aspect regarding the "absolute" (or "lower-bound") type of questions is the fact that they call for impossibility results. That is, the natural formulation of these questions calls for proving the non-existence of something (i.e., the non-existence of efficient procedures for solving the problem in question). Needless to say, proving the non-existence of certain objects is *typically* harder than proving existence of related objects (indeed, see Section 9.1). Still, proofs of non-existence of certain objects are known in various fields and in particular in Complexity Theory, but such proofs tend to either be trivial (see, e.g., Section 4.1) or be derived by exhibiting a sophisticated process that transforms the original question into a trivial one. Indeed, the latter case is the one that underlies many of the impressive successes of circuit complexity. Thus, we are not suggesting that the "absolute" questions of Complexity Theory cannot be resolved, but are rather suggesting an intuitive explanation for the difficulties of resolving them.

The obvious fact that difficult questions can be resolved is demonstrated by several recent results, which are mentioned in this book and have "forced" us to modify earlier drafts of it. Examples include the log-space graph exploration algorithm presented in Section 5.2.4, the alternative proof of the PCP Theorem presented in §9.3.2.3, and the enrichment of average-case completeness reflected in Theorem 10.19. We also mention the results of [9, 113, 172, 242], which have significantly effected our perspective (although this is reflected less drastically in the text).

APPENDIX A

Glossary of Complexity Classes

Summary: This glossary includes self-contained definitions of most complexity classes mentioned in the book. Needless to say, the glossary offers a very minimal discussion of these classes, and the reader is referred to the main text for further discussion. The items are organized by topics rather than by alphabetic order. Specifically, the glossary is partitioned into two parts, dealing separately with complexity classes that are defined in terms of algorithms and their resources (i.e., time and space complexity of Turing machines) and complexity classes defined in terms of non-uniform circuits (and referring to their size and depth). The algorithmic classes include time complexity classes (such as $\mathcal{P}$, $\mathcal{NP}$, co$\mathcal{NP}$, $\mathcal{BPP}$, $\mathcal{RP}$, co$\mathcal{RP}$, $\mathcal{PH}$, $\mathcal{E}$, $\mathcal{EXP}$, and $\mathcal{NEXP}$) and the space complexity classes, $\mathcal{L}, \mathcal{NL}, \mathcal{RL}$, and $\mathcal{PSPACE}$. The non-uniform classes include the circuit classes $\mathcal{P}$/poly as well as $\mathcal{NC}^k$ and $\mathcal{AC}^k$.

Definitions (and basic results) regarding many other complexity classes are available at the constantly evolving *Complexity Zoo* [1].

A.1. Preliminaries

Complexity classes are sets of computational problems, where each class contains problems that can be solved with specific computational resources. To define a complexity class one specifies a model of computation, a complexity measure (like time or space), which is always measured as a function of the input length, and a bound on the complexity (of problems in the class).

We follow the tradition of focusing on decision problems, but refer to these problems using the terminology of promise problems (see Section 2.4.1). That is, we will refer to the problem of distinguishing inputs in Π_{yes} from inputs in Π_{no}, and denote the corresponding decision problem by $\Pi = (\Pi_{\text{yes}}, \Pi_{\text{no}})$. Standard decision problems are viewed as a special case in which $\Pi_{\text{yes}} \cup \Pi_{\text{no}} = \{0, 1\}^*$, and the standard formulation of complexity classes is obtained by postulating that this is the case. We refer to this case as the case of a trivial promise.

The prevailing model of computation is that of Turing machines. This model captures the notion of (uniform) algorithms (see Section 1.2.3). Another important model is the one of non-uniform circuits (see Section 1.2.4). The term *uniformity* refers to whether the algorithm is the same one for every input length or whether a different "algorithm" (or rather a "circuit") is considered for each input length.

We focus on natural complexity classes, obtained by considering natural complexity measures and bounds. Typically, these classes contain natural computational problems (which are defined in Appendix G). Furthermore, almost all of these classes can be "characterized" by natural problems, which capture every problem in the class. Such problems are called complete for the class, which means that they are in the class and every problem in the class can be "easily" reduced to them, where "easily" means that the reduction takes fewer resources than whatever seems to be required for solving each individual problem in the class. Thus, any efficient algorithm for a complete problem implies an algorithm of similar efficiency for *all* problems in the class.

Organization. The glossary is organized by topics (rather than by alphabetic order of the various items). Specifically, we partition the glossary into classes defined in terms of algorithmic resources (i.e., time and space complexity of Turing machines) and classes defined in terms of circuit (size and depth). The former (algorithm-based) classes are reviewed in Section A.2, while the latter (circuit-based) classes are reviewed in Section A.3.

A.2. Algorithm-Based Classes

The two main complexity measures considered in the context of (uniform) algorithms are the number of steps taken by the algorithm (i.e., its time complexity) and the amount of "memory" or "work space" consumed by the computation (i.e., its space complexity). We review the time complexity classes $\mathcal{P}$, $\mathcal{NP}$, co$\mathcal{NP}$, $\mathcal{BPP}$, $\mathcal{RP}$, co$\mathcal{RP}$, $\mathcal{ZPP}$, $\mathcal{PH}$, $\mathcal{E}$, $\mathcal{EXP}$, and $\mathcal{NEXP}$ as well as the space complexity classes $\mathcal{L}$, $\mathcal{NL}$, $\mathcal{RL}$, and $\mathcal{PSPACE}$.

By prepending the name of a complexity class (of decision problems) with the prefix "co" we mean the class of complement problems; that is, the problem $\Pi = (\Pi_{yes}, \Pi_{no})$ is in co$\mathcal{C}$ if and only if (Π_{no}, Π_{yes}) is in $\mathcal{C}$. Specifically, deciding membership in the set S is in the class co$\mathcal{C}$ if and only if deciding membership in the set $\{0, 1\}^* \setminus S$ is in the class $\mathcal{C}$. Thus, the definition of co$\mathcal{NP}$ and co$\mathcal{RP}$ can be easily derived from the definitions of $\mathcal{NP}$ and $\mathcal{RP}$, respectively. Complexity classes defined in terms of symmetric acceptance criteria (e.g., deterministic and two-sided error randomized classes) are trivially closed under complementation (e.g., co$\mathcal{P} = \mathcal{P}$ and co$\mathcal{BPP} = \mathcal{BPP}$) and so we do not present their "co"-classes. In other cases (most notably $\mathcal{NL}$), the closure property is highly non-trivial and we comment about it.

A.2.1. Time Complexity Classes

We start with classes that are closely related to polynomial time computations (i.e., $\mathcal{P}$, $\mathcal{NP}$, $\mathcal{BPP}$, $\mathcal{RP}$, and $\mathcal{ZPP}$), and later consider the classes $\mathcal{PH}$, $\mathcal{E}$, $\mathcal{EXP}$, and $\mathcal{NEXP}$.

A.2.1.1. Classes Closely Related to Polynomial Time
The most prominent complexity classes are $\mathcal{P}$ and $\mathcal{NP}$, which are extensively discussed in Section 2.1. We also consider classes related to randomized polynomial time, which are discussed in Section 6.1.

P and NP. The class $\mathcal{P}$ consists of all decision problem that can be solved in (deterministic) polynomial time. A decision problem $\Pi = (\Pi_{\text{yes}}, \Pi_{\text{no}})$ is in $\mathcal{NP}$ if there exists a polynomial p and a (deterministic) polynomial-time algorithm V such that the following two conditions hold:

1. For every $x \in \Pi_{\text{yes}}$ there exists $y \in \{0, 1\}^{p(|x|)}$ such that $V(x, y) = 1$.
2. For every $x \in \Pi_{\text{no}}$ and every $y \in \{0, 1\}^*$ it holds that $V(x, y) = 0$.

A string y satisfying Condition 1 is called an NP-witness (for x). Clearly, $\mathcal{P} \subseteq \mathcal{NP}$.

Reductions and NP-completeness (NPC). A problem is $\mathcal{NP}$-complete if it is in $\mathcal{NP}$ and every problem in $\mathcal{NP}$ is polynomial-time reducible to it, where polynomial-time reducibility is defined and discussed in Section 2.2. Loosely speaking, a polynomial-time reduction of problem Π to problem Π' is a polynomial-time algorithm that solves Π by making queries to a subroutine that solves problem Π', where the running time of the subroutine is not counted in the algorithm's time complexity. Typically, NP-completeness is defined while restricting the reduction to make a single query and output its answer. Such a reduction, called a Karp-reduction, is represented by a polynomial-time computable mapping that maps yes-instances of Π to yes-instances of Π' (and no-instances of Π to no-instances of Π'). Hundreds of NP-complete problems are listed in [85].

Probabilistic polynomial time (BPP, RP and ZPP). A decision problem $\Pi = (\Pi_{\text{yes}}, \Pi_{\text{no}})$ is in $\mathcal{BPP}$ if there exists a probabilistic polynomial-time algorithm A such that the following two conditions hold:

1. For every $x \in \Pi_{\text{yes}}$ it holds that $\Pr[A(x)=1] \geq 2/3$.
2. For every $x \in \Pi_{\text{no}}$ it holds that $\Pr[A(x)=0] \geq 2/3$.

That is, the algorithm has two-sided error probability (of $1/3$), which can be further reduced by repetitions. We stress that due to the two-sided error probability of $\mathcal{BPP}$, it is not known whether or not $\mathcal{BPP}$ is contained in $\mathcal{NP}$. In addition to the two-sided error class $\mathcal{BPP}$, we consider one-sided error and zero-error classes, denoted $\mathcal{RP}$ and $\mathcal{ZPP}$, respectively. A problem $\Pi = (\Pi_{\text{yes}}, \Pi_{\text{no}})$ is in $\mathcal{RP}$ if there exists a probabilistic polynomial-time algorithm A such that the following two conditions hold:

1. For every $x \in \Pi_{\text{yes}}$ it holds that $\Pr[A(x)=1] \geq 1/2$.
2. For every $x \in \Pi_{\text{no}}$ it holds that $\Pr[A(x)=0] = 1$.

Again, the error probability can be reduced by repetitions, and thus $\mathcal{RP} \subseteq \mathcal{BPP} \cap \mathcal{NP}$. A problem $\Pi = (\Pi_{\text{yes}}, \Pi_{\text{no}})$ is in $\mathcal{ZPP}$ if there exists a probabilistic polynomial-time algorithm A, which may output a special ("don't know") symbol $\bot$, such that the following two conditions hold:

1. For every $x \in \Pi_{\text{yes}}$ it holds that $\Pr[A(x) \in \{1, \bot\}] = 1$ and $\Pr[A(x)=1] \geq 1/2$.
2. For every $x \in \Pi_{\text{no}}$ it holds that $\Pr[A(x) \in \{0, \bot\}] = 1$ and $\Pr[A(x)=0] \geq 1/2$.

Note that $\mathcal{P} \subseteq \mathcal{ZPP} = \mathcal{RP} \cap \text{co}\mathcal{RP}$. When defined in terms of promise problems, all the aforementioned randomized classes have complete problems (wrt Karp-reductions), but the same is not known when considering only standard decision problems (with trivial promise).

The counting class #$\mathcal{P}$. Functions in #$\mathcal{P}$ count the number of solutions to an NP-type search problem (or, equivalently, the number of NP-witnesses for a yes-instance of a decision problem in $\mathcal{NP}$). Formally, a function f is in #$\mathcal{P}$ if there exists a polynomial p and a (deterministic) polynomial-time algorithm V such that $f(x) = |\{y \in \{0, 1\}^{p(|x|)} : V(x, y) = 1\}|$. Indeed, p and V are as in the definition of $\mathcal{NP}$, and it follows that deciding membership in the set $\{x : f(x) \geq 1\}$ is in $\mathcal{NP}$. Clearly, #$\mathcal{P}$ problems are solvable in polynomial space. Surprisingly, the permanent of positive integer matrices is #$\mathcal{P}$-complete (i.e., it is in #$\mathcal{P}$ and any function in #$\mathcal{P}$ is polynomial-time reducible to it).

Interactive proofs. A decision problem $\Pi = (\Pi_{\text{yes}}, \Pi_{\text{no}})$ has an interactive proof system if there exists a polynomial-time strategy V such that the following two conditions hold:

1. For every $x \in \Pi_{\text{yes}}$ there exists a prover strategy P such that the verifier V always accepts after interacting with the prover P on common input x.
2. For every $x \notin \Pi_{\text{no}}$ and every strategy P^*, the verifier V rejects with probability at least $\frac{1}{2}$ after interacting with P^* on common input x.

The corresponding class is denoted $\mathcal{IP}$, and turns out to equal $\mathcal{PSPACE}$. (For further details see Section 9.1.)

A.2.1.2. Other Time Complexity Classes

The classes $\mathcal{E}$ and $\mathcal{EXP}$ correspond to problems that can be solved (by a deterministic algorithm) in time $2^{O(n)}$ and $2^{\text{poly}(n)}$, respectively, for n-bit long inputs. Clearly, $\mathcal{NP} \subseteq \mathcal{EXP}$. We also mention $\mathcal{NEXP}$, the class of problems that can be solved by a non-deterministic machine in $2^{\text{poly}(n)}$ steps.[1]

In general, one may define a complexity class for every time bound and every type of machine (i.e., deterministic, probabilistic, and non-deterministic), but polynomial and exponential bounds seem most natural and very robust. Another robust type of time bounds that is sometimes used is quasi-polynomial time (i.e., $\widetilde{\mathcal{P}}$ denotes the class of problems solvable by deterministic machines of time complexity $\exp(\text{poly}(\log n))$).

The Polynomial-time Hierarchy, $\mathcal{PH}$. For any natural number k, the kth level of the Polynomial-time Hierarchy consists of problems $\Pi = (\Pi_{\text{yes}}, \Pi_{\text{no}})$ such that there exists a polynomial p and a polynomial-time algorithm V that satisfies the following two requirements:

1. For every $x \in \Pi_{\text{yes}}$ there exists $y_1 \in \{0, 1\}^{p(|x|)}$ such that for every $y_2 \in \{0, 1\}^{p(|x|)}$ there exists $y_3 \in \{0, 1\}^{p(|x|)}$ such that for every $y_4 \in \{0, 1\}^{p(|x|)} \ldots$ it holds that $V(x, y_1, y_2, y_3, y_4, \ldots, y_k) = 1$. That is, the condition regarding x consists of k alternating quantifiers.
2. For every $x \in \Pi_{\text{no}}$ the foregoing (k-alternating) condition does not hold. That is, for every $y_1 \in \{0, 1\}^{p(|x|)}$ there exists $y_2 \in \{0, 1\}^{p(|x|)}$ such that for every $y_3 \in \{0, 1\}^{p(|x|)}$ there exists $y_4 \in \{0, 1\}^{p(|x|)} \ldots$ it holds that $V(x, y_1, y_2, y_3, y_4, \ldots, y_k) = 0$.

---

[1] Alternatively, analogously to the definition of $\mathcal{NP}$, a problem $\Pi = (\Pi_{\text{yes}}, \Pi_{\text{no}})$ is in $\mathcal{NEXP}$ if there exists a polynomial p and a polynomial-time algorithm V such that the following two conditions hold:

1. For every $x \in \Pi_{\text{yes}}$ there exists $y \in \{0, 1\}^{2^{p(|x|)}}$ such that $V(x, y) = 1$.
2. For every $x \in \Pi_{\text{no}}$ and every $y \in \{0, 1\}^*$ it holds that $V(x, y) = 0$.

Such a problem Π is said to be in Σ_k (and $\Pi_k \stackrel{\text{def}}{=} \text{co}\Sigma_k$). Indeed, $\mathcal{NP} = \Sigma_1$ corresponds to the special case where $k = 1$. Interestingly, $\mathcal{PH}$ is polynomial-time reducible to $\#\mathcal{P}$.

A.2.2. Space Complexity Classes

When defining space complexity classes, one counts *only* the space consumed by the actual computation, and *not* the space occupied by the input and output. This is formalized by postulating that the input is read from a read-only device (resp., the output is written on a write-only device). Four important classes of decision problems are defined next.

- The class $\mathcal{L}$ consists of problems solvable in logarithmic space. That is, a problem Π is in $\mathcal{L}$ if there exists a standard (i.e., deterministic) algorithm of logarithmic space complexity for solving Π. This class contains some simple computational problems (e.g., matrix multiplication), and arguably captures the most space-efficient computations. Interestingly, $\mathcal{L}$ contains the problem of deciding connectivity of (undirected) graphs.
- Classes of problems solvable by randomized algorithms of logarithmic space complexity include $\mathcal{RL}$ and $\mathcal{BPL}$, which are defined analogously to $\mathcal{RP}$ and $\mathcal{BPP}$. That is, $\mathcal{RL}$ corresponds to algorithms with one-sided error probability, whereas $\mathcal{BPL}$ allows two-sided error.
- The class $\mathcal{NL}$ is the non-deterministic analogue of $\mathcal{L}$, and is traditionally defined in terms of non-deterministic machines of logarithmic space complexity.[2] The class $\mathcal{NL}$ contains the problem of deciding whether there exists a directed path between two given vertexes in a given directed graph. In fact, the latter problem is complete for the class (under logarithmic-space reductions). Interestingly, $\text{co}\mathcal{NL}$ equals $\mathcal{NL}$.
- The class $\mathcal{PSPACE}$ consists of problems solvable in polynomial space. This class contains very difficult problems, including the computation of winning strategies for any "efficient 2-party games" (see Section 5.4).

Clearly, $\mathcal{L} \subseteq \mathcal{RL} \subseteq \mathcal{NL} \subseteq \mathcal{P}$ and $\mathcal{NP} \subseteq \mathcal{PSPACE} \subseteq \mathcal{EXP}$.

A.3. Circuit-Based Classes

We refer the reader to Section 1.2.4 for a definition of Boolean circuits as computing devices. The two main complexity measures considered in the context of (non-uniform) circuits are the number of gates (or wires) in the circuit (i.e., the circuit's size) and the length of the longest directed path from an input to an output (i.e., the circuit's depth).

Throughout this section, when we talk of circuits, we actually refer to families of circuits containing a circuit for each instance length, where the n-bit long instances of the computational problem are handled by the nth circuit in the family. Similarly, when we talk of the size and depth of a circuit, we actually mean the (dependence on n of the) size and depth of the nth circuit in the family.

General polynomial-size circuits (P/poly). The main motivation for the introduction of complexity classes based on (non-uniform) circuits is the development of lower bounds. For example, the class of problems solvable by polynomial-size circuits, denoted $\mathcal{P}$/poly, is a (strict)[3] superset of $\mathcal{P}$. Thus, showing that $\mathcal{NP}$ is not contained in $\mathcal{P}$/poly would

---

[2] See further discussion of this definition in Section 5.3.

[3] In particular, $\mathcal{P}$/poly contains some decision problems that are not solvable by any uniform algorithm.

imply $\mathcal{P} \neq \mathcal{NP}$. For further discussion, see Appendix B.2. An alternative definition of $\mathcal{P}/\text{poly}$ in terms of "machines that take advice" is provided in Section 3.1.2. We mention that if $\mathcal{NP} \subset \mathcal{P}/\text{poly}$ then $\mathcal{PH} = \Sigma_2$.

The subclasses AC0 and TC0. The class $\mathcal{AC}^0$, discussed in Appendix B.2.3, consists of problems solvable by constant-depth polynomial-size circuits of *unbounded fan-in*. The analogue class that allows also (unbounded fan-in) majority-gates (or, equivalently, threshold-gates) is denoted $\mathcal{TC}^0$.

The subclasses AC and NC. Turning back to the standard basis (of $\neg$, $\vee$ and $\wedge$ gates), for any non-negative integer k, we denote by $\mathcal{NC}^k$ (resp., $\mathcal{AC}^k$) the class of problems solvable by polynomial-size circuits of *bounded fan-in* (resp., unbounded fan-in) having depth $O(\log^k n)$, where n is the input length. Clearly, $\mathcal{NC}^k \subseteq \mathcal{AC}^k \subseteq \mathcal{NC}^{k+1}$. A class commonly referred to is $\mathcal{NC} \stackrel{\text{def}}{=} \cup_{k \in \mathbb{N}} \mathcal{NC}^k$.

We mention that the class $\mathcal{NC}^2 \supseteq \mathcal{NL}$ is the habitat of most natural computational problems of linear algebra: solving a linear system of equations as well as computing the rank, inverse, and determinant of a matrix. The class $\mathcal{NC}^1$ contains all symmetric functions, regular languages as well as word problems for finite groups and monoids. The class $\mathcal{AC}^0$ contains all properties (of finite objects) that are expressible by first-order logic.

Uniformity. The foregoing classes make no reference to the complexity of constructing the adequate circuits, and it is plausible that there is no effective way of constructing these circuits (e.g., as in the case of circuits that trivially solve undecidable problems regarding unary instances). A minimal notion of constructibility of such (polynomial-size) circuits is the existence of a polynomial-time algorithm that given 1^n produces the nth relevant circuit (i.e., the circuit that solves the problem on instances of length n). Such a notion of constructibility means that the family of circuits is "uniform" in some sense (rather than consisting of circuits that have no relation between one another). Stronger notions of uniformity (e.g., log-space constructibility) are more adequate for subclasses such as AC and NC. We mention that log-space uniform NC circuits correspond to parallel algorithms that use polynomially many processors and run in poly-logarithmic time.

On the Quest for Lower Bounds

> *Alas, Philosophy, Medicine, Law, and unfortunately also Theology, have*
> *I studied in detail, and still remained a fool, not a bit wiser than before.*
> *Magister and even Doctor am I called, and for a decade am I sick and*
> *tired of pulling my pupils by the nose and understanding that we can*
> *know nothing.*[1]
>
> J. W. Goethe, Faust, lines 354–64

Summary: This appendix briefly surveys some attempts at proving lower bounds on the complexity of natural computational problems. In the first part, devoted to circuit complexity, we describe lower bounds on the *size* of (restricted) circuits that solve natural computational problems. This can be viewed as a program whose long-term goal is proving that $\mathcal{P} \neq \mathcal{NP}$. In the second part, devoted to proof complexity, we describe lower bounds on the length of (restricted) propositional proofs of natural tautologies. This can be viewed as a program whose long-term goal is proving that $\mathcal{NP} \neq \mathrm{co}\mathcal{NP}$.

We comment that while the activity in these areas is aimed toward developing proof techniques that may be applied to the resolution of the "big problems" (such as P versus NP), the current achievements (though very impressive) seem very far from reaching this goal. Current crown-jewel achievements in these areas take the form of tight (or strong) lower bounds on the complexity of computing (resp., proving) "relatively simple" functions (resp., claims) in *restricted* models of computation (resp., proof systems).

B.1. Preliminaries

Circuit complexity refers to a non-uniform model of computation (see Section 1.2.4), focusing on the size of such circuits, while ignoring the complexity of constructing adequate circuits. Similarly, proof complexity refers to proofs of tautologies, focusing on the length of such proofs, while ignoring the complexity of generating such proofs.

Both circuits and proofs are finite objects that are defined on top of the notion of a *directed acyclic graph* (dag), reviewed in Appendix G.1. In such a dag, vertices with no incoming edges are called inputs, vertices with no outgoing edges are called outputs,

---

[1]This quotation reflects a common sentiment, not shared by the author of the current book.

and the remaining vertices are called internal vertices. The size of a dag is defined as the number of its edges. We will be mostly interested in dags of "bounded fan-in" (i.e., for each vertex, the number of *incoming* edges is at most two).

In order to convert a dag into a computational device (resp., a proof), each internal vertex is labeled by a rule, which transforms values assigned to its predecessors to values at that vertex. Combined with any possible assignment of values to the inputs, these fixed rules induce an assignment of values to all the vertices of the dag (by a process that starts at the inputs, and assigns a value to each vertex based on the values of its predecessors (and according to the corresponding rule)).

- In the case of computation devices, the internal vertices are labeled by (binary or unary) functions over some fixed domain (e.g., a finite or infinite field). These functions are called gates, and the labeled dag is called a circuit. Such a circuit (with n inputs and m outputs) computes a finite function over the corresponding domain (mapping sequences of length n to sequences of length m).
- In the case of proofs, the internal vertices are labeled by sound deduction (or inference) rules of some fixed proof system. Any assignment of axioms (of the said system) to the inputs of this labeled dag yields a sequence of tautologies (at all vertices). Typically the dag is assumed to have a single output vertex, and the corresponding sequence of tautologies is viewed as a proof of the tautology assigned to the output.

We note that both models partially adhere to the paradigm of simplicity that underlies the definitions of (uniform) computational models (as discussed in Section 1.2.3): The aforementioned rules are simple by definition – they are applied to at most two values. However, unlike in the case of (uniform) computational models, the current models do not mandate a "uniform" consideration of all possible "inputs" (but rather allow a separate consideration of each finite "input" length). For example, each circuit can compute only a finite function, that is, a function defined over a fixed number of values (i.e., fixed input length). Likewise, a dag that corresponds to a proof system yields only proofs of tautologies that refer to a fixed number of axioms.[2]

Focusing on circuits, we note that in order to allow the computation of functions that are defined for all input lengths, one must consider infinite sequences of dags, one for each length. This yields a model of computation in which each "machine" has an infinite description (when referring to all input lengths). Indeed, this significantly extends the power of the computation model beyond that of the notion of *algorithm* (discussed in Section 1.2.3). However, since we are interested in lower bounds here, this extension is certainly legitimate and hopefully fruitful: For example, one may hope that the finiteness of the individual circuits will facilitate the application of combinatorial techniques toward the analysis of the model's power and limitations. Furthermore, as we shall see, these models open the door to the introduction (and study) of meaningful restricted classes of computations.

Organization. The rest of this appendix is partitioned into three parts. In Section B.2 we consider Boolean circuits, which are the archetypical model of non-uniform computing devices. In Section B.3 we generalize the treatment by considering arithmetic circuits,

---

[2]N.B., we refer to a fixed number of axioms, and not merely to a fixed number of axiom forms. Recall that an axiom form like $\phi \vee \neg\phi$ yields an infinite number of axioms, each obtained by replacing the generic formula (or symbol) ϕ with a fixed propositional formula.

which may be defined for every algebraic structure (where Boolean circuits are viewed as a special case referring to the two-element field, GF(2)). Lastly, in Section B.4 we consider proof complexity.

B.2. Boolean Circuit Complexity

In Boolean circuits the values assigned to all inputs as well as the values induced (by the computation) at all intermediate vertices and outputs are bits. The set of allowed gates is taken to be any *complete basis* (i.e., one that allows for computing *all* Boolean functions). The most popular choice of a complete basis is the set $\{\wedge, \vee, \neg\}$ corresponding to (two-bit) conjunction, (two-bit) disjunction, and negation (of a single bit), respectively. (The specific choice of a complete basis hardly affects the study of circuit complexity.)

For a finite Boolean function f, we denote by $S(f)$ the size of the smallest Boolean circuit computing f. We will be interested in sequences of functions $\{f_n\}$, where f_n is a function on n input bits, and will study their size complexity (i.e., $S(f_n)$) asymptotically (as a function of n). With some abuse of notation, for $f(x) \stackrel{\text{def}}{=} f_{|x|}(x)$, we let $S(f)$ denote the integer function that assigns to n the value $S(f_n)$. Thus, we refer to the following definition.

Definition B.25 (circuit complexity): *Let $f : \{0, 1\}^* \to \{0, 1\}^*$ and $\{f_n\}$ be such that $f(x) = f_{|x|}(x)$ for every x. The* **complexity** *of f (resp., $\{f_n\}$), denoted $S(f)$ (resp., denoted $n \mapsto S(f_n)$), is a function of n that represents the size of the smallest Boolean circuit computing f_n.*

We stress that different circuits (e.g., having a different number of inputs) are used for different f_n's. Still, there may be a simple description of this sequence of circuits, say, an algorithm that on input n produces a circuit computing f_n. In case such an algorithm exists and works in time polynomial in the size of its output, we say that the corresponding sequence of circuits is uniform. Note that if f has a uniform sequence of polynomial-size circuits then $f \in \mathcal{P}$. On the other hand, any $f \in \mathcal{P}$ has (a uniform sequence of) polynomial-size circuits. Consequently, a super-polynomial-size lower bound on any function in $\mathcal{NP}$ would imply that $\mathcal{P} \neq \mathcal{NP}$.

Definition B.25 makes no reference to the uniformity condition (and indeed the sequence of smallest circuits computing $\{f_n\}$ may be "highly non-uniform"). Actually, non-uniformity makes the circuit model stronger than Turing machines (or, equivalently, stronger than the model of uniform circuits): *There exist functions f that cannot be computed by Turing machines* (regardless of their running time), *but do have linear-size circuits.*[3] This raises the possibility that proving circuit lower bounds is even harder than resolving the P versus NP Question.

The common belief is that the extra power provided by non-uniformity is irrelevant to the P versus. NP Question; in particular, it is conjectured that NP-complete sets do not have polynomial-size circuits. This conjecture is supported by the fact that its failure will yield an unexpected collapse in the world of uniform computational complexity (see Section 3.2). Furthermore, the hope is that abstracting away the (supposedly irrelevant) uniformity condition will allow for combinatorial techniques to analyze the power and limitations of polynomial-size circuits (wrt NP-sets). This hope has materialized in the

---

[3]See either Theorem 1.13 or Theorem 3.7.

study of restricted classes of circuits (see Sections B.2.2 and B.2.3). Indeed, another advantage of the circuit model is that it offers a framework for describing naturally restricted models of computation.

We also mention that Boolean circuits are a natural computational model, corresponding to "hardware complexity" (which was indeed the original motivation for their introduction by Shannon [203]), and so their study is of independent interest. Moreover, some of the techniques for analyzing Boolean functions found applications elsewhere (e.g., in computational learning theory, combinatorics, and game theory).

B.2.1. Basic Results and Questions

We have already mentioned several basic facts about Boolean circuits. Another basic fact is that *most Boolean functions require exponential-size circuits*, which is due to the gap between the number of functions and the number of small circuits.

Thus, hard functions (i.e., functions that require large circuits and thus have no efficient algorithms) do exist, to say the least. However, the aforementioned hardness result is proved via a counting argument, which provides no way of pointing to any specific hard function. The situation is even worse: *Super-linear* circuit-size lower bounds are not known for any *explicit* function f, even when explicitness is defined in a very mild sense that only requires $f \in \mathcal{EXP}$.[4] One major open problem of circuit complexity is establishing such lower bounds.

Open Problem B.2: *Find an explicit function* $f : \{0, 1\}^* \rightarrow \{0, 1\}$ *(or even* $f : \{0, 1\}^* \rightarrow \{0, 1\}^*$ *such that* $|f(x)| = O(|x|)$*) for which* $\mathcal{S}(f)$ *is not* $O(n)$.

A particularly basic special case of this open problem is the question of *whether addition is easier to perform than multiplication*. Let $\text{ADD}_n : \{0, 1\}^n \times \{0, 1\}^n \rightarrow \{0, 1\}^{n+1}$ and $\text{MULT}_n : \{0, 1\}^n \times \{0, 1\}^n \rightarrow \{0, 1\}^{2n}$, denote the addition and multiplication functions, respectively, applied to a pair of integers (presented in binary). For addition we have an optimal upper bound; that is, $\mathcal{S}(\text{ADD}_n) = O(n)$. For multiplication, the standard (elementary school) quadratic-time algorithm can be greatly improved (via Discrete Fourier Transforms) to almost-linear time, yielding $\mathcal{S}(\text{MULT}_n) = \widetilde{O}(n)$. Now, the question is *whether or not there exist linear-size circuits for multiplication* (i.e., is $\mathcal{S}(\text{MULT}_n) = O(n)$).

Unable to report on any super-linear lower bound (for an explicit function), we turn to restricted types of Boolean circuits. There have been some remarkable successes in developing techniques for proving strong lower bounds for natural restricted classes of circuits. We describe the most important ones, and refer the reader to [46, 236] for further detail.

Recall that general Boolean circuits can compute every function. In contrast, restricted types of circuits (e.g., monotone circuits) may only be able to compute a subclass of all functions (e.g., monotone functions), and in such a case we shall seek lower bounds on the size of such restricted circuits that compute a function in the corresponding subclass. Such a restriction is appealing provided that the corresponding class of functions and the computations represented by the restricted circuits are natural (from a conceptual or practical viewpoint). The models discussed next satisfy this condition.

---

[4]Indeed, a more natural (and still mild) notion of explicitness requires that $f \in \mathcal{E}$. This notion implies that the function's description (restricted to n-bit long inputs) can be constructed in time that is polynomial in the length of the description.

B.2.2. Monotone Circuits

One very natural restriction on circuits arises by forbidding negation (in the set of gates), namely, allowing only $\wedge$ and $\vee$ gates. The resulting circuits are called monotone, and they can compute a function $f : \{0, 1\}^n \to \{0, 1\}$ if and only if f is monotone with respect to the standard partial order on n-bit strings (i.e., $x \preceq y$ if and only if for every bit position i we have $x_i \leq y_i$). An extremely natural question in this context is *whether or not non-monotone operations* (in the circuit) *help in computing monotone functions.*

Before turning to this question, we note that most monotone functions require exponential-size circuits (let alone monotone ones).[5] Still, proving a super-polynomial lower bound on the monotone circuit complexity of an explicit monotone function was open for several decades, till the invention of the so-called *approximation method* (by Razborov [187]).

Let $\mathtt{CLIQUE}_n$ be the function that, given a graph on n vertices (by its adjacency matrix), outputs 1 if and only if the graph contains a complete subgraph of size (say) $\sqrt{n}$. This function is clearly monotone, and $\mathtt{CLIQUE} = \{\mathtt{CLIQUE}_n\}$ is known to be NP-complete.

Theorem B.3 ([187], improved in [7]): *There are no polynomial-size monotone circuits for* $\mathtt{CLIQUE}$.

We note that the lower bounds are sub-exponential in the number of vertices (i.e., $\mathcal{S}(\mathtt{CLIQUE}_n) = \exp(\Omega(n^{1/8}))$), and that similar lower bounds are known for functions in $\mathcal{P}$. Thus, *there exists an exponential separation between monotone circuit complexity and non-monotone circuit complexity*, where this separation refers (of course) to the computation of monotone functions.

B.2.3. Bounded-Depth Circuits

The next restriction refers to the structure of the circuit (or rather to its underling graph): *We allow all gates, but limit the depth of the circuit.* The depth of a dag is simply the length of the longest directed path in it. So in a sense, depth captures the *parallel time* to compute the function: If a circuit has depth d, then the function can be evaluated by enough processors in d phases (where in each phase many gates are evaluated in parallel). Indeed, parallel time is a natural and important computational resource, referring to the following basic question: *Can one speed up computation by using several computers in parallel?* Determining which computational tasks can be "parallelized" when many processors are available and which are "inherently sequential" is clearly a fundamental question.

We will restrict d to be a constant, which still is interesting not only as a measure of parallel time but also due to the relation of this model to expressibility in first-order logic as well as to the *Polynomial-time Hierarchy* (defined in Section 3.2). In the current setting (of constant-depth circuits), we allow *unbounded fan-in* (i.e., $\wedge$-gates and $\vee$-gates taking any number of incoming edges), as otherwise each output bit can depend only on a constant number of input bits.

---

[5] A key observation is that it suffices to consider the set of n-bit monotone functions that evaluate to 1 (resp., to 0) on each string $x = x_1 \cdots x_n$ satisfying $\sum_{i=1}^{n} x_i > \lfloor n/2 \rfloor$ (resp., $\sum_{i=1}^{n} x_i < \lfloor n/2 \rfloor$). Note that each such function is specified by $\binom{n}{\lfloor n/2 \rfloor}$ bits.

Let PAR (for parity) denote the sum modulo two of the input bits, and MAJ (for majority) be 1 if and only if there are more 1's than 0's among the input bits. The invention of the *random restriction method* (by Furst, Saxe, and Sipser [83]) led to the following basic result.

Theorem B.4 ([83], improved in [240, 115]): *For all constant d, the functions* PAR *and* MAJ *have no polynomial-size circuit of depth d.*

The aforementioned improvement (of Håstad [115], following Yao [240]), gives a relatively tight lower bound of $\exp(\Omega(n^{1/(d-1)}))$ on the size of n-input PAR circuits of depth d.

Interestingly, MAJ remains hard (for constant-depth polynomial-size circuits) even if the circuits are also allowed (unbounded fan-in) PAR-gates (this result is based on yet another proof technique: *approximation by polynomials* [209, 188]). However, the "converse" does not hold (i.e., constant-depth polynomial-size circuits with MAJ-gates can compute PAR), and in general the class of constant-depth polynomial-size circuits with MAJ-gates (denoted $\mathcal{TC}^0$) seems quite powerful. In particular, nobody has managed to *prove that there are functions in $\mathcal{NP}$ that cannot be computed by such circuits*, even if their depth is restricted to 3.

B.2.4. Formula Size

The final restriction is again structural – we require the underlying dag to be a tree (i.e., a dag in which each vertex has at most one *outgoing* edge). Intuitively, this forbids the computation from reusing a previously computed intermediate value (and if this value is needed again then it has to be recomputed). Thus, the resulting Boolean circuits are simply Boolean formulae. (Indeed, we are back to the basic model allowing negation ($\neg$), and $\wedge$, $\vee$ gates *of fan-in 2*.)

Formulae are natural not only for their prevalent mathematical use but also because their size can be related to the depth of general circuits and to the *memory* requirements of Turing machines (i.e., their space complexity). One of the oldest results on circuit complexity is that PAR and MAJ have non-trivial lower bounds in this model. The proof follows a simple combinatorial (or information-theoretic) argument.

Theorem B.5 ([144]): *Boolean formulae for n-bit* PAR *and* MAJ *require* $\Omega(n^2)$ *size.*

This should be contrasted with the linear-size circuits that exist for both functions.[6] Encouraged by Theorem B.5, one may hope to see super-polynomial lower bounds on the formula size of explicit functions. This is indeed a famous open problem.

Open Problem B.6: *Find an explicit Boolean function f that requires super-polynomial-size formulae.*

An equivalent formulation of this open problem calls for proving a super-logarithmic lower bound on the depth of formulae (or circuits) computing f.

---

[6]We comment that $S(\text{PAR}) = O(n)$ is trivial, but $S(\text{MAJ}) = O(n)$ is not.

One appealing method for addressing such challenges is the *communication complexity method* (of Karchmer and Wigderson [137]). This method asserts that the depth of a formula for a Boolean function f equals the communication complexity in the following two-party game, G_f. In the game, the first party is given $x \in f^{-1}(1) \cap \{0, 1\}^n$, the second party is given $y \in f^{-1}(0) \cap \{0, 1\}^n$, and their goal is to find a bit location on which x and y disagree (i.e., i such that $x_i \neq y_i$, which clearly exists). To that end, the parties exchange messages, according to a predetermined protocol, and the question is what is the communication complexity (in terms of total number of bits exchanged on the worst-case input pair) of the best such protocol. We stress that no computational restrictions are placed on the parties in the game/protocol.

Note that proving a super-logarithmic lower bound on the communication complexity of the game G_f will establish a super-logarithmic lower bound on the depth of formulae (or circuits) computing f (and thus a super-polynomial lower bound on the size of formulae computing f). We stress the fact that a lower bound of a purely information-theoretic nature implies a computational lower bound!

We mention that the communication complexity method has a *monotone version* such that the depth of *monotone* circuits is related to the communication complexity of protocols that are required to find an i such that $x_i > y_i$ (rather than any i such that $x_i \neq y_i$).[7] In fact, the monotone version is better known than the general one, due to its success in leading to linear lower bounds on the monotone depth of natural problems such as perfect matching (established by Raz and Wigderson [186]).

B.3. Arithmetic Circuits

We now leave the Boolean rind, and discuss circuits over general fields. Fixing any field F, the gates of the dag will now be the standard $+$ and $\times$ operations of the field, yielding a so-called arithmetic circuit. The inputs of the dag will be assigned elements of the field F, and these values induce an assignment of values (in F) to all other vertices. Thus, an arithmetic circuit with n inputs and m outputs computes a polynomial map $p : F^n \to F^m$, and every such polynomial map is computed by some circuit (modulo the convention of allowing some inputs to be set to some constants, most importantly the constant -1).[8]

Arithmetic circuits provide a natural description of methods for computing polynomial maps, and consequently their size is a natural measure of the complexity of such maps. We denote by $\mathcal{S}_F(p)$ the size of a smallest circuit computing the polynomial map p (and when no subscript is specified, we mean that $F = \mathcal{Q}$ (the field of rational numbers)). As usual, we shall be interested in sequences of functions, one per each input size, and will study the corresponding circuit size asymptotically.

We note that, for any *fixed* finite field, arithmetic circuits can simulate Boolean circuits (on Boolean inputs) with only constant factor loss in size. Thus, the study of arithmetic circuits focuses more on infinite fields, where lower bounds may be easier to obtain.

As in the Boolean case, the existence of hard functions is easy to establish (via dimension considerations, rather than counting argument), and we will be interested in *explicit* (families of) polynomials. Roughly speaking, a polynomial is called explicit if there exists

---

[7]Note that since f is monotone, $f(x) = 1$ and $f(y) = 0$ implies the existence of an i such that $x_i = 1$ and $y_i = 0$.

[8]This allows the emulation of adding a constant, multiplication by a constant, and subtraction. We mention that, for the purpose of computing polynomials (over infinite fields), division can be efficiently emulated by the other operations.

an efficient algorithm that, when given a degree sequence (which specifies a monomial), outputs the (finite description of the) corresponding coefficient.

An important parameter, which is absent in the Boolean model, is the *degree* of the polynomial(s) computed. It is obvious, for example, that a degree d polynomial (even in one variable, i.e., $n = 1$) requires size at least $\log d$. We briefly consider the univariate case (where d is the only measure of "problem size"), which already contains striking and important open problems. Then we move to the general multivariate case, in which (as usual) the number of variables (i.e., n) will be the main parameter (and we shall assume that $d \leq n$). We refer the reader to [86, 215] for further detail.

B.3.1. Univariate Polynomials

How tight is the $\log d$ lower bounds for the size of an arithmetic circuit computing a degree d polynomial? A simple dimension argument shows that for most degree d polynomials p, it holds that $\mathcal{S}(p) = \Omega(d)$. However, we know of no explicit one:

Open Problem B.7: *Find an explicit polynomial p of degree d, such that $\mathcal{S}(p)$ is not $O(\log d)$.*

To illustrate this open problem, we consider the following two concrete polynomials $p_d(x) = x^d$ and $q_d(x) = (x + 1)(x + 2) \cdots (x + d)$. Clearly, $\mathcal{S}(p_d) \leq 2 \log d$ (via repeated squaring), and so the trivial lower bound is essentially tight. On the other hand, it is a major open problem to determine $\mathcal{S}(q_d)$, and the common conjecture is that $\mathcal{S}(q_d)$ is not polynomial in $\log d$. To realize the importance of this conjecture, we state the following proposition:

Proposition B.8: *If $\mathcal{S}(q_d) = \text{poly}(\log d)$, then the integer factorization problem can be solved by polynomial-size circuits.*

Recall that it is widely believed that the integer factorization problem is intractable (and, in particular, does not have polynomial-size circuits).

Proof Sketch: Proposition B.8 follows by observing that $q_d(t) = ((t + d)!)/(t!)$ and that a small circuit for computing q_d yields an efficient way of obtaining the value $((t + d)!)/(t!) \bmod N$ (by emulating the computation of the former circuit modulo N). Observing that $(\sum_{i=1}^{\ell} K_i)! = \prod_{i=1}^{\ell} q_{K_i}(\sum_{j=i+1}^{\ell} K_j)$, it follows that the value of $(K!) \bmod N$ can be obtained by using circuits for the polynomials $\langle q_{2^i} : i = 1, .., \lfloor \log_2 K \rfloor \rangle$. Next, observe that $(K!) \bmod N$ and N are relatively prime if and only if all prime factors of N are bigger than K. Thus, given a composite N (and circuits for $\langle q_{2^i} : i = 1, \ldots, \lfloor \log_2 N \rfloor \rangle$), we can find a factor of N by performing a binary search for a suitable K. $\qquad\square$

B.3.2. Multivariate Polynomials

We are now back to polynomials with n variables. To make n our only "problem size" parameter, it is convenient to restrict ourselves to polynomials whose total degree is at most n.

Once again, almost every polynomial p in n variables requires size $\mathcal{S}(p) \geq \exp(\Omega(n))$, and we seek explicit polynomial (families) that are hard. Unlike in the Boolean world, here there are slightly non-trivial lower bounds (via elementary tools from algebraic geometry).

Theorem B.9 ([26]): $\mathcal{S}(x_1^n + x_2^n + \cdots + x_n^n) = \Omega(n \log n)$.

The same techniques extend to proving a similar lower bound for other natural polynomials such as the symmetric polynomials and the determinant. Establishing a stronger lower bound for any explicit polynomial is a major open problem. Another open problem is obtaining a super-linear lower bound for a polynomial map of constant (even 1) total degree. Outstanding candidates for the latter open problem are the *linear* maps computing the Discrete Fourier Transform over the complex numbers, or the Walsh Transform over the rationals (for both $O(n \log n)$-time algorithms are known, but no super-linear lower bounds are known).

We now focus on specific polynomials of central importance. The most natural and well-studied candidate for the last open problem is the matrix multiplication function MM: Let A and B be two $m \times m$ matrices over F, and define $\text{MM}_n(A, B)$ to be the sequence of $n = m^2$ values of the entries of the matrix $A \times B$. Thus, MM_n is a sequence of n explicit bilinear forms over the $2n$ input variables (which represent the entries of both matrices). It is known that $\mathcal{S}_{\text{GF}(2)}(\text{MM}_n) \geq 3n$ (cf. [206]). On the other hand, the obvious algorithm that takes $O(m^3) = O(n^{3/2})$ steps can be improved.

Theorem B.10 ([62]): *For every field F, it holds that $\mathcal{S}_F(\text{MM}_n) = o(n^{1.19})$.*

So what is the complexity of MM (even if one counts only multiplication gates)? Is it linear or almost-linear or is it the case that $\mathcal{S}(\text{MM}) > n^\alpha$ for some $\alpha > 1$? This is indeed a famous open problem.

We next consider the determinant and permanent polynomials (DET and PER, resp.) over the $n = m^2$ variables representing an $m \times m$ matrix. While DET plays a major role in classical mathematics, PER is somewhat esoteric in that context (though it appears in statistical mechanics and quantum mechanics). In the context of Complexity Theory, both polynomials are of great importance because they capture natural complexity classes. The function DET has relatively low complexity (e.g., it is related to the class of polynomials having polynomial-sized arithmetic formulae), whereas PER seems to have high complexity (e.g., it is complete for the class of all "p-definable" polynomials (cf. [231]) and is complete for the counting class #$\mathcal{P}$ (see §6.2.1)). Thus, it is conjectured that PER is *not* polynomial-time reducible to DET. One restricted type of reduction that makes sense in this algebraic context is a reduction by projection.

Definition B.11 (projections): *Let $p_n : F^n \to F^\ell$ and $q_N : F^N \to F^\ell$ be polynomial maps and $x_1, \ldots, x_n$ be variables over F. We say that there is a* projection from p_n to q_N *over F, if there exists a function $\pi : [N] \to \{x_1, \ldots, x_n\} \cup F$ such that $p_n(x_1, \ldots, x_n) \equiv q_N(\pi(1), \ldots, \pi(N))$.*

Clearly, if there is a projection from p_n to q_N then $\mathcal{S}_F(p_n) \leq \mathcal{S}_F(q_N)$. Let DET_m and PER_m denote the functions DET and PER restricted to m-by-m matrices. It is known that there is a projection from PER_m to DET_{3^m}, but to yield a polynomial-time reduction one would need a projection of PER_m to $\text{DET}_{\text{poly}(m)}$. Needless to say, it is conjectured that no such projection exists.

B.4. Proof Complexity

It is common practice to classify proofs according to the level of their difficulty, but can this appealing classification be put on sound grounds? This is essentially the task undertaken by proof complexity. It seeks to classify theorems according to the difficulty of proving them, much like circuit complexity seeks to classify functions according to the difficulty of computing them. Furthermore, just like in circuit complexity, we shall also refer to a few (restricted) models, called *proof systems*, which represent various methods of reasoning. Thus, the difficulty of proving various theorems will be measured with respect to various proof systems.

We will consider only propositional proof systems, and so the theorems (in these systems) will be propositional *tautologies*. Each of these systems will be *complete* and *sound*; that is, each tautology and only a tautology will have a proof relative to these systems. The formal definition of a proof system spells out what we take for granted: the efficiency of the verification procedure. In the following definition, the efficiency of the verification procedure refers to its running time measured in terms of the *total length of the alleged theorem and proof*.[9]

Definition B.12 ([61]): *A* (propositional) proof system *is a polynomial-time Turing machine M such that a formula T is a tautology if and only if there exists a string π, called a* proof*, such that $M(\pi, T) = 1$.*

In agreement with standard formalisms, the proof is viewed as coming before the theorem. Definition B.12 guarantees the completeness and soundness of the proof system as well as verification efficiency (relative to the total length of the alleged proof–theorem pair). Note that Definition B.12 allows proofs of arbitrary length, suggesting that the length of the proof π is a measure of the *complexity* of the tautology T with respect to the proof system M.

For each tautology T, let $\mathcal{L}_M(T)$ denote the length of the shortest proof of T in M (i.e., the length of the shortest string π such that M accepts (π, T)). That is, $\mathcal{L}_M$ captures the *proof complexity* of various tautologies with respect to the proof system M. Abusing notation, we let $\mathcal{L}_M(n)$ denote the maximum $\mathcal{L}_M(T)$ over all tautologies T of length n. (By definition, for every proof system M, the value $\mathcal{L}_M(n)$ is well defined and so $\mathcal{L}_M$ is a total function over the natural numbers.) The following simple theorem provides a basic connection between proof complexity (with respect to any propositional proof system) and computational complexity (i.e., the NP-vs-coNP Question).

Theorem B.13 ([61]): *There exists a propositional proof system M such that the function $\mathcal{L}_M$ is upper-bounded by a polynomial if and only if $\mathcal{NP} = \text{co}\mathcal{NP}$.*

---

[9]Indeed, this convention differs from the convention emplyed in Chapter 9, where the complexity of verification (i.e., verifier's running time) was measured as a function of the *length of the alleged theorem*. Both approaches were mentioned in Section 2.1, where the two approaches coincide, because in Section 2.1 we mandated proofs of length polynomial in the alleged theorem.

In particular, a propositional proof system M such that $\mathcal{L}_M$ is upper-bounded by a polynomial coincides with an NP-proof system (as in Definition 2.5) for the set of propositional tautologies, which is a co$\mathcal{NP}$-complete set.

The long-term goal of proof complexity is establishing super-polynomial lower bounds on the length of proofs in any propositional proof system (and thus establishing $\mathcal{NP} \neq \text{co}\mathcal{NP}$). It is natural to start this formidable project by first considering simple (and thus weaker) proof systems, and then moving on to more and more complex ones. Moreover, various natural proof systems, capturing basic (restricted) types and "primitives" of reasoning as well as natural tautologies, suggest themselves as objects for this study. In the rest of this section we focus on such restricted proof systems.

Different branches of mathematics such as logic, algebra, and geometry give rise to different proof systems, often implicitly. A typical system would have a set of axioms and a set of deduction rules. A proof (in this system) would proceed to derive the desired tautology in a sequence of steps, each producing a formula (often called a line of the proof), which is either an axiom or follows from previous formulae via one of the deduction rules. Regarding these proof systems, we make two observations. First, proofs in these systems can be easily verified by an algorithm, and thus they fit the general framework of Definition B.12. Second, these proof systems perfectly fit the model of a dag with internal vertices labeled by deduction rules (as in Section B.1): When assigning axioms to the inputs, the application of the deduction rules at the internal vertices yields a proof of the tautology assigned to each output.[10]

For various proof systems Π, we turn to study the proof length $\mathcal{L}_\Pi(T)$ of tautologies T in proof system Π. The first observation, revealing a major difference between proof complexity and circuit complexity, is that the trivial counting argument *fails*. The reason is that, while the number of functions on n bits is 2^{2^n}, there are at most 2^n tautologies of this length. Thus, in proof complexity, even the *existence* of a hard tautology, not necessarily an explicit one, would be of interest (and, in particular, if established for all propositional proof systems, then it would yield $\mathcal{NP} \neq \text{co}\mathcal{NP}$). (Note that here we refer to hard instances of a problem and not to hard problems.) Anyhow, as we shall see, most known proof-length lower bounds (with respect to restricted proof systems) apply to very natural (let alone explicit) tautologies.

An important convention. There is an equivalent and somewhat more convenient view of (simple) proof systems, namely, as (simple) refutation systems. First, recalling that 3SAT is NP-complete, note that the negation of any (propositional) tautology can be written as a conjunction of clauses, where each clause is a disjunction of only 3 literals (variables or their negation). Now, if we take these clauses as axioms and derive (using the rules of the system) an obvious contradiction (e.g., the negation of an axiom, or better yet the empty clause), then we have proved the tautology (since we have proved that its negation yields a contradiction). Proof complexity often takes the refutation viewpoint, and often exchanges "tautology" with its negation ("contradiction").

Organization. The rest of this section is divided into three parts, referring to logical, algebraic, and geometric proof systems. We will briefly describe important representative

---

[10]General proof systems as in Definition B.12 can also be adapted to this formalism, by considering a deduction rule that corresponds to a single step of the machine M. However, the deduction rules considered here are even simpler, and more importantly they are more natural.

and basic results in each of these domains, and refer the reader to [27] for further detail (and, in particular, to adequate references).

B.4.1. Logical Proof Systems

The proof systems in this section will all have lines that are Boolean formulae, and the differences will be in the structural limits imposed on these formulae. The most basic proof system, called a Frege system, puts no restriction on the formulae manipulated by the proof. It has one derivation rule, called the cut rule: $A \vee C, B \vee \neg C \vdash A \vee B$ (for any propositional formulae A, B and C). Adding any other sound rule, like *modus ponens*, has little effect on the length of proofs in this system.

Frege systems are basic in the sense that (in several variants) they are the most common systems in logic. Indeed, polynomial-length proofs in Frege systems naturally correspond to "polynomial-time reasoning" about feasible objects. The major open problem in proof complexity is finding any tautology (i.e., a family of tautologies) that has no polynomial-long proof in the Frege system.

Since lower bounds for Frege systems seem intractable at the moment, we turn to subsystems of Frege, which are interesting and natural. The most widely studied system (of refutation) is Resolution, whose importance stems from its use by most propositional (as well as first-order) automated theorem provers. The formulae allowed as lines in Resolution are clauses (disjunctions), and so the *cut rule* simplifies to the resolution rule: $A \vee x, B \vee \neg x \vdash A \vee B$, for any clauses A, B and variable x.

The gap between the power of general Frege systems and Resolution is reflected by the existence of tautologies that are easy for Frege and hard for Resolution. A specific example is provided by the pigeonhole principle, denoted PHP_n^m, which is a propositional tautology that expresses the fact that there is no one-to-one mapping of m pigeons to $n < m$ holes.

Theorem B.14: $\mathcal{L}_{\text{Frege}}(\text{PHP}_n^{n+1}) = n^{O(1)}$ *but* $\mathcal{L}_{\text{Resolution}}(\text{PHP}_n^{n+1}) = 2^{\Omega(n)}$

B.4.2. Algebraic Proof Systems

Just as a natural contradiction in the Boolean setting is an unsatisfiable collection of clauses, a natural contradiction in the algebraic setting is a system of polynomials without a common root. Moreover, CNF formulae can be easily converted to a system of polynomials, one per clause, over any field. One often adds the polynomials $x_i^2 - x_i$ which ensure Boolean values.

A natural proof system (related to Hilbert's Nullstellensatz, and to computations of Grobner bases in symbolic algebra programs) is Polynomial Calculus, abbreviated PC. The lines in this system are polynomials (represented explicitly by all coefficients), and it has two deduction rules: For any two polynomials g, h, the rule $g, h \vdash g + h$, and for any polynomial g and variable x_i, the rule $g, x_i \vdash x_i g$. Strong length lower bounds (obtained from degree lower bounds) are known for this system. For example, encoding the pigeonhole principle PHP_n^m as a contradicting set of constant degree polynomials, we have the following lower bound.

Theorem B.15: *For every n and every $m > n$, it holds that $\mathcal{L}_{\text{PC}}(\text{PHP}_n^m) \geq 2^{n/2}$, over every field.*

B.4.3. Geometric Proof Systems

Yet another natural way to represent contradictions is by a set of regions in space that have empty intersection. Again, we care mainly about discrete (say, Boolean) domains, and a wide source of interesting contradictions are integer programs arising from Combinatorial Optimization. Here, the constraints are (affine) linear inequalities with integer coefficients (so the regions are subsets of the Boolean cube carved out by half-spaces). The most basic system is called Cutting Planes (CP), and its lines are linear inequalities with integer coefficients. The deduction rules of PC are (the obvious) addition of inequalities, and the (less obvious) division of the coefficients by a constant (and rounding, taking advantage of the integrality of the solution space).

While PHP_n^m is "easy" in this system, *exponential lower bounds are known for other tautologies*. We mention that they are obtained from the *monotone circuit* lower bounds of Section B.2.2.

APPENDIX C

On the Foundations of Modern Cryptography

It is possible to build a cabin with no foundations, but not a lasting building.

Eng. Isidor Goldreich (1906–95)

Summary: Cryptography is concerned with the construction of computing systems that withstand any abuse: Such a system is constructed so as to maintain a desired functionality, even under malicious attempts aimed at making it deviate from this functionality.

This appendix is aimed at presenting the foundations of cryptography, which are the paradigms, approaches, and techniques used to conceptualize, define, and provide solutions to natural security concerns. It presents some of these conceptual tools as well as some of the fundamental results obtained using them. The emphasis is on the clarification of fundamental concepts, and on demonstrating the feasibility of solving several central cryptographic problems. The presentation assumes basic knowledge of algorithms, probability theory, and complexity theory, but nothing beyond this.

The appendix augments the treatment of one-way functions, pseudorandom generators, and zero-knowledge proofs, given in Sections 7.1, 8.2, and 9.2, respectively.[1] Using these basic primitives, the appendix provides a treatment of basic cryptographic applications such as encryption, signatures, and general cryptographic protocols.

C.1. Introduction and Preliminaries

The rigorous treatment and vast expansion of cryptography is one of the major achievements of theoretical computer science. In particular, classical notions such as secure encryption and unforgeable signatures were placed on sound grounds, and new (unexpected) directions and connections were uncovered. Furthermore, this development was coupled with the introduction of novel concepts such as computational indistinguishability, pseudorandomness, and zero-knowledge interactive proofs, which are of independent interest (see Sections 7.1, 8.2, and 9.2, respectively). Indeed, modern cryptography is

---

[1] These augmentations are important for cryptography, but are not central to Complexity Theory and thus were omitted from the main text.

strongly coupled with Complexity Theory (in contrast to "classical" cryptography, which is strongly related to information theory).

C.1.1. The Underlying Principles

Modern cryptography is concerned with the construction of information systems that are robust against malicious attempts aimed at causing these systems to violate their prescribed functionality. The prescribed functionality may be the secret and authenticated communication of information over an insecure channel, the holding of incoercible and secret electronic voting, or conducting any "fault-resilient" multi-party computation. Indeed, the scope of modern cryptography is very broad, and it stands in contrast to "classical" cryptography (which has focused on the single problem of enabling secret communication over insecure channels).

C.1.1.1. Coping with Adversaries

Needless to say, the design of cryptographic systems is a very difficult task. One cannot rely on intuitions regarding the "typical" state of the environment in which the system operates. For sure, the adversary attacking the system will try to manipulate the environment into "untypical" states. Nor can one be content with counter-measures designed to withstand specific attacks, since the adversary (which acts after the design of the system is completed) will try to attack the schemes in ways that are different from the ones the designer had envisioned. Although the validity of the foregoing assertions seems self-evident, still some people hope that in practice ignoring these tautologies will not result in actual damage. Experience shows that these hopes rarely come true; cryptographic schemes based on make-believe are broken, typically sooner than later.

In view of the foregoing, it makes little sense to make assumptions regarding the specific *strategy* that the adversary may use. The only assumptions that can be justified refer to the computational *abilities* of the adversary. Furthermore, the design of cryptographic systems has to be based on *firm foundations*, whereas ad hoc approaches and heuristics are a very dangerous way to go.

The foundations of cryptography are the paradigms, approaches, and techniques used to conceptualize, define, and provide solutions to natural "security concerns." Solving a cryptographic problem (or addressing a security concern) is a two-stage process consisting of a *definitional stage* and a *constructive stage*. First, in the definitional stage, the functionality underlying the natural concern is to be identified, and an adequate cryptographic problem is to be defined. Trying to list all undesired situations is infeasible and prone to error. Instead, one should define the functionality in terms of operation in an imaginary ideal model, and require a candidate solution to emulate this operation in the real, clearly defined model (which specifies the adversary's abilities). Once the definitional stage is completed, one proceeds to construct a system that satisfies the definition. Such a construction may use some simpler tools, and in such a case its security is proved relying on the features of these tools.

Example. Starting with the wish to ensure secret (resp., reliable) communication over insecure channels, the definitional stage leads to the formulation of the notion of secure encryption schemes (resp., signature schemes). Next, such schemes are constructed by using simpler primitives such as one-way functions, and the security of the construction is proved via a "reducibility argument" (which demonstrates how inverting the

---

483

one-way function "reduces" to violating the claimed security of the construction; cf., Section 7.1.2).

C.1.1.2. The Use of Computational Assumptions

As in the case of the foregoing example, most of the tools and applications of cryptography exist only if some sort of computational hardness exists. Specifically, these tools and applications require (either explicitly or implicitly) the ability to generate instances of hard problems. Such ability is captured in the definition of one-way functions. Thus, one-way functions are the very minimum needed for doing most natural tasks of cryptography. (It turns out, as we shall see, that this necessary condition is "essentially" sufficient; that is, the existence of one-way functions (or augmentations and extensions of this assumption) suffices for doing most of cryptography.)

Our current state of understanding of efficient computation does not allow us to prove that one-way functions exist. In particular, as discussed in Sections 7.1.1 and C.2, proving that one-way functions exist seems even harder than proving that $\mathcal{P} \neq \mathcal{NP}$. Hence, we have no choice (at this stage of history) but to assume that one-way functions exist. As justification of this assumption, we can only offer the combined beliefs of hundreds (or thousands) of researchers. Furthermore, these beliefs concern a simply stated assumption, and their validity follows from several widely believed conjectures that are central to various fields (e.g., the conjectured that intractability of integer factorization is central to computational number theory).

Since we need assumptions anyhow, "why not just assume whatever we want" (i.e., the existence of a solution to some natural cryptographic problem)? Well, firstly, we need to know what we want; that is, we must first clarify what *exactly* we want, which means going through the typically complex definitional stage. But once this stage is completed and a definition is obtained, can we just assume the existence of a system satisfying this definition? Not really: The mere existence of a definition does not imply that it can be satisfied by any system.

The way to demonstrate that a cryptographic definition is viable (and that the corresponding intuitive security concern can be satisfied) is to prove that it can be satisfied based on a *better understood* assumption (i.e., one that is more common and widely believed). For example, looking at the definition of zero-knowledge proofs, it is not a priori clear that such proofs exist at all (in a non-trivial sense). The non-triviality of the notion was first demonstrated by presenting a zero-knowledge proof system for statements, regarding Quadratic Residuosity, which are believed to be hard to verify (without extra information). Furthermore, contrary to prior beliefs, it was later shown that the existence of one-way functions implies that any NP-statement can be proved in zero-knowledge. Thus, facts that were not known at all to hold (and were even believed to be false) have been shown to hold by "reduction" to widely believed assumptions (without which most of cryptography collapses anyhow).

In summary: *not all assumptions are equal*. Thus, "reducing" a complex, new and doubtful assumption to a widely believed and simple (or even merely simpler) assumption is of great value. Furthermore, "reducing" the solution of a new task to the assumed security of a well-known primitive typically means providing a construction that, using the known primitive, solves the new task. This means that we do not only gain confidence about the solvability of the new task but also obtain a solution based on a primitive that, being well known, typically has several candidate implementations.

C.1.2. The Computational Model

Cryptography, as surveyed here, is concerned with the construction of *efficient* schemes for which it is *infeasible* to violate the security feature. Thus, we need a notion of efficient computations as well as a notion of infeasible ones. The computations of the legitimate users of the scheme ought be efficient, whereas violating the security features (by an adversary) ought to be infeasible. We stress that we do not identify feasible computations with efficient ones, but rather view the former notion as potentially more liberal. Let us elaborate.

C.1.2.1. Efficient Computations and Infeasible ones

Efficient computations are commonly modeled by computations that are polynomial time in the security parameter. The polynomial that bounds the running time of the legitimate user's strategy is *fixed and typically explicit* (and *small*). Indeed, our aim is to have a notion of efficiency that is as strict as possible (or, equivalently, develop strategies that are as efficient as possible). Here (i.e., when referring to the complexity of the legitimate users) we are in the same situation as in any algorithmic setting. Things are different when referring to our assumptions regarding the computational resources of the adversary, where we refer to the notion of feasible, which we wish to be as wide as possible. A common approach is to postulate that feasible computations are polynomial time, too, but here the polynomial is *not a priori specified* (and is to be thought of as arbitrarily large). In other words, the adversary is restricted to the class of polynomial-time computations and anything beyond this is considered to be infeasible.

Although many definitions explicitly refer to the convention of associating feasible computations with polynomial-time ones, this convention is *inessential* to any of the results known in the area. In all cases, a more general statement can be made by referring to a general notion of feasibility, which should be preserved under standard algorithmic composition, yielding theories that refer to adversaries of running time bounded by any specific super-polynomial function (or class of functions). Still, for the sake of concreteness and clarity, we shall use the former convention in our formal definitions (but our motivational discussions will refer to an unspecified notion of feasibility that covers at least efficient computations).

C.1.2.2. Randomized (or Probabilistic) Computations

Randomized computations play a central role in cryptography. One fundamental reason for this fact is that randomness is essential for the existence (or rather the generation) of secrets. Thus, we must allow the legitimate users to employ randomized computations, and certainly (since we consider randomization as feasible) we must consider also adversaries that employ randomized computations. This brings up the issue of success probability: Typically, we require that legitimate users succeed (in fulfilling their legitimate goals) with probability 1 (or negligibly close to this), whereas adversaries succeed (in violating the security features) with negligible probability. Thus, the notion of a negligible probability plays an important role in our exposition.

One requirement of the definition of negligible probability is to provide a robust notion of rareness: A rare event should occur rarely even if we repeat the experiment for a feasible number of times. That is, in case we consider any polynomial-time computation to be feasible, a function $\mu : \mathbb{N} \to \mathbb{N}$ is called negligible if $1 - (1 - \mu(n))^{p(n)} < 0.01$ for

---

485

every polynomial p and sufficiently big n (i.e., μ is negligible if for every positive polynomial p' the function $\mu(\cdot)$ is upper-bounded by $1/p'(\cdot)$).

We will also refer to the notion of noticeable probability. Here, the requirement is that events that occur with noticeable probability will occur almost surely (i.e., except with negligible probability) if we repeat the experiment for a polynomial number of times. Thus, a function $\nu:\mathbb{N}\to\mathbb{N}$ is called noticeable if for some positive polynomial p' the function $\nu(\cdot)$ is lower-bounded by $1/p'(\cdot)$.

C.1.3. Organization and Beyond

This appendix focuses on several archetypical cryptographic problems (e.g., encryption and signature schemes) and on several central tools (e.g., computational difficulty, pseudorandomness, and zero-knowledge proofs). For each of these problems, we start by presenting the natural concern underlying it, then define the problem, and finally demonstrate that the problem may be solved. In the latter step, our focus is on demonstrating the feasibility of solving the problem, not on providing a practical solution.

Our aim is to present the basic concepts, techniques, and results in cryptography, and our emphasis is on the clarification of fundamental concepts and the relationship among them. This is done in a way independent of the particularities of some popular number theoretic examples. These particular examples played a central role in the development of the field and still offer the most practical implementations of all cryptographic primitives, but this does not mean that the presentation has to be linked to them. On the contrary, we believe that concepts are best clarified when presented at an abstract level, decoupled from specific implementations.

Actual organization. The appendix is organized in two main parts, corresponding to the Basic Tools of Cryptography and the Basic Applications of Cryptography.

> **The basic tools:** The most basic tool is computational difficulty, which in turn is captured by the notion of one-way functions. Another notion of key importance is that of computational indistinguishability, underlying the theory of pseudorandomness as well as much of the rest of cryptography. Pseudorandom generators and functions are important tools that are frequently used. So are zero-knowledge proofs, which play a key role in the design of secure cryptographic protocols and in their study.
>
> **The basic applications:** Encryption and signature schemes are the most basic applications of Cryptography. Their main utility is in providing secret and reliable communication over insecure communication media. Loosely speaking, encryption schemes are used for ensuring the secrecy (or privacy) of the actual information being communicated, whereas signature schemes are used to ensure its reliability (or authenticity). Another basic topic is the construction of secure cryptographic protocols for the implementation of arbitrary functionalities.

The presentation of the basic tools in Sections C.2–C.4 augments (and sometimes repeats parts of) Sections 7.1, 8.2, and 9.2 (which provide a basic treatment of one-way functions, pseudorandom generators, and zero-knowledge proofs, respectively). Sections C.5–C.7 provide an overview of the basic applications; that is, encryption schemes, signature schemes, and general cryptographic protocols.

Suggestions for further reading. This appendix is a brief summary of the author's two-volume work on the subject [91, 92]. Furthermore, the first part (i.e., Basic Tools) corresponds to [91], whereas the second part (i.e., Basic Applications) corresponds to [92]. Needless to say, the interested reader is referred to these textbooks for further detail (and, in particular, for missing references).

Practice. The aim of this appendix is to introduce the reader to the *theoretical foundations* of cryptography. As argued, such foundations are necessary for a *sound* practice of cryptography. Indeed, practice requires much more than theoretical foundations, whereas the current text makes no attempt to provide anything beyond the latter. However, given a sound foundation, one can learn and evaluate various practical suggestions that appear elsewhere. On the other hand, lack of sound foundations results in an inability to critically evaluate practical suggestions, which in turn leads to unsound decisions. *Nothing could be more harmful to the design of schemes that need to withstand adversarial attacks than misconceptions about such attacks.*

C.2. Computational Difficulty

Modern Cryptography is concerned with the construction of systems that are easy to operate (properly) but hard to foil. Thus, a complexity gap (between the ease of proper usage and the difficulty of deviating from the prescribed functionality) lies at the heart of modern cryptography. However, gaps as required for modern cryptography are not known to exist; they are only widely believed to exist. Indeed, almost all of modern cryptography rises or falls with the question of whether one-way functions exist. We mention that the existence of one-way functions implies that $\mathcal{NP}$ contains search problems that are hard to solve *on the average*, which in turn implies that $\mathcal{NP}$ is not contained in $\mathcal{BPP}$ (i.e., a worst-case complexity conjecture).

Loosely speaking, one-way functions are functions that are easy to evaluate but hard (on the average) to invert. Such functions can be thought of as an efficient way of generating "puzzles" that are infeasible to solve (i.e., the puzzle is a random image of the function and a solution is a corresponding preimage). Furthermore, the person generating the puzzle knows a solution to it and can efficiently verify the validity of (possibly other) solutions to the puzzle. Thus, one-way functions have, by definition, a clear cryptographic flavor (i.e., they manifest a gap between the ease of one task and the difficulty of a related one).

C.2.1. One-Way Functions

We start by reproducing the basic definition of one-way functions as appearing in Section 7.1.1, where this definition is further discussed.

Definition C.1 (one-way functions, Definition 7.1 restated): *A function* $f:$ $\{0, 1\}^* \to \{0, 1\}^*$ *is called* one-way *if the following two conditions hold:*

1. Easy to evaluate: *There exists a polynomial-time algorithm A such that $A(x) = f(x)$ for every $x \in \{0, 1\}^*$.*

487

2. Hard to invert: *For every probabilistic polynomial-time algorithm A', every polynomial p, and all sufficiently large n,*

$$\Pr[A'(f(x), 1^n) \in f^{-1}(f(x))] < \frac{1}{p(n)}$$

where the probability is taken uniformly over $x \in \{0, 1\}^n$ and all the internal coin tosses of algorithm A'.

Some of the most popular candidates for one-way functions are based on the conjectured intractability of computational problems in number theory. One such conjecture is that it is infeasible to factor large integers. Consequently, the function that takes as input two (equal-length) primes and outputs their product is widely believed to be a one-way function. Furthermore, factoring such a composite is infeasible if and only if squaring modulo such a composite is a one-way function (see [183]). For certain composites (i.e., products of two primes that are both congruent to 3 mod 4), the latter function induces a permutation over the set of quadratic residues modulo this composite. A related permutation, which is widely believed to be one-way, is the RSA function [193]: $x \mapsto x^e \bmod N$, where $N = P \cdot Q$ is a composite as above, e is relatively prime to $(P - 1) \cdot (Q - 1)$, and $x \in \{0, \ldots, N - 1\}$. The latter examples (as well as other popular suggestions) are better captured by the following formulation of a collection of one-way functions (which is indeed related to Definition C.1):

Definition C.2 (collections of one-way functions): *A collection of functions, $\{f_i : D_i \to \{0, 1\}^*\}_{i \in \bar{I}}$, is called* one-way *if there exist three probabilistic polynomial-time algorithms, I, D and F, such that the following two conditions hold:*

1. Easy to sample and compute: *On input 1^n, the output of (the index selection) algorithm I is distributed over the set $\bar{I} \cap \{0, 1\}^n$ (i.e., is an n-bit long index of some function). On input (an index of a function) $i \in \bar{I}$, the output of (the domain sampling) algorithm D is distributed over the set D_i (i.e., over the domain of the function f_i). On input $i \in \bar{I}$ and $x \in D_i$, (the evaluation) algorithm F always outputs $f_i(x)$.*
2. Hard to invert:[2] *For every probabilistic polynomial-time algorithm, A', every positive polynomial $p(\cdot)$, and all sufficiently large n's*

$$\Pr\left[A'(i, f_i(x)) \in f_i^{-1}(f_i(x))\right] < \frac{1}{p(n)}$$

where $i \leftarrow I(1^n)$ and $x \leftarrow D(i)$.

The collection is said to be a collection of permutations *if each of the f_i's is a permutation over the corresponding D_i, and $D(i)$ is almost uniformly distributed in D_i.*

For example, in case of the RSA, one considers $f_{N,e} : D_{N,e} \to D_{N,e}$ that satisfies $f_{N,e}(x) = x^e \bmod N$, where $D_{N,e} = \{0, \ldots, N - 1\}$. Definition C.2 is also a good starting

---

[2]Note that this condition refers to the distributions $I(1^n)$ and $D(i)$, which are merely required to range over $\bar{I} \cap \{0, 1\}^n$ and D_i, respectively. (Typically, the distributions $I(1^n)$ and $D(i)$ are (almost) uniform over $\bar{I} \cap \{0, 1\}^n$ and D_i, respectively.)

point for the definition of a trapdoor permutation.[3] Loosely speaking, the latter is a collection of one-way permutations augmented with an efficient algorithm that allows for inverting the permutation when given adequate auxiliary information (called a trapdoor).

Definition C.3 (trapdoor permutations): *A collection of permutations as in Definition C.2 is called a* trapdoor permutation *if there are two auxiliary probabilistic polynomial-time algorithms I' and F^{-1} such that (1) the distribution $I'(1^n)$ ranges over pairs of strings so that the first string is distributed as in $I(1^n)$, and (2) for every (i, t) in the range of $I'(1^n)$ and every $x \in D_i$ it holds that $F^{-1}(t, f_i(x)) = x$. (That is, t is a trapdoor that allows for inverting f_i.)*

For example, in case of the RSA, the function $f_{N,e}$ can be inverted by raising the image to the power d (modulo $N = P \cdot Q$), where d is the multiplicative inverse of e modulo $(P - 1) \cdot (Q - 1)$. Indeed, in this case, the trapdoor information is (N, d).

Strong versus weak one-way functions (summary of Section 7.1.2). Recall that the foregoing definitions require that any feasible algorithm *succeeds in inverting* the function *with negligible probability*. A weaker notion only requires that any feasible algorithm *fails to invert* the function *with noticeable probability*. It turns out that the existence of such weak one-way functions implies the existence of strong one-way functions (as in Definition C.1). The construction itself is straightforward, but analyzing it transcends the analogous information-theoretic setting. Instead, the security (i.e., hardness of inverting) the resulting construction is proved via a so-called reducibility argument that transforms the violation of the conclusion (i.e., the hypothetical insecurity of the resulting construction) into a violation of the hypothesis (i.e., insecurity of the given primitive). This strategy (i.e., a "reducibility argument") is used to prove all conditional results in the area.

C.2.2. Hard-Core Predicates

Recall that saying that a function f is one-way implies that, given a typical f-image y, it is infeasible to find a preimage of y under f. This does not mean that it is infeasible to find partial information about the preimage(s) of y under f. Specifically, it may be easy to retrieve half of the bits of the preimage (e.g., given a one-way function f consider the function g defined by $g(x, r) \overset{\text{def}}{=} (f(x), r)$, for every $|x| = |r|$). As will become clear in subsequent sections, hiding partial information (about the function's preimage) plays an important role in many advanced cryptographic constructs (e.g., secure encryption). This partial information can be considered as a "hard-core" of the difficulty of inverting f. Loosely speaking, a *polynomial-time computable* (Boolean) predicate b, is called a hard-core of a function f if no feasible algorithm, given $f(x)$, can guess $b(x)$ with success probability that is non-negligibly better than one half. The actual definition is presented in Section 7.1.3 (i.e., Definition 7.6).

Note that if b is a hard-core of a 1-1 function f that is polynomial-time computable then f is a one-way function. On the other hand, recall that Theorem 7.7 asserts that *for any one-way function f, the inner-product mod 2 of x and r is a hard-core of the function f', where $f'(x, r) = (f(x), r)$.*

---

[3]Indeed, a more adequate term would be a collection of trapdoor permutations, but the shorter (and less precise) term is the commonly used one.

C.3. Pseudorandomness

In practice, "pseudorandom" sequences are often used instead of truly random sequences. The underlying belief is that if an (efficient) application performs well when using a truly random sequence, then it will perform essentially as well when using a "pseudorandom" sequence. However, this belief is not supported by ad hoc notions of "pseudorandomness" such as passing the statistical tests in [146] or having large "linear complexity" (as defined in [112]). Needless to say, using such "pseudorandom" sequences (instead of truly random sequences) in a cryptographic application is very dangerous.

In contrast, truly random sequences can be safely replaced by pseudorandom sequences provided that pseudorandom distributions are defined as being computationally indistinguishable from the uniform distribution. Such a definition makes the soundness of this replacement an easy corollary. Loosely speaking, pseudorandom generators are then defined as efficient procedures for creating long pseudorandom sequences based on few truly random bits (i.e., a short random seed). The relevance of such constructs to cryptography is in providing legitimate users that share short random seeds with a method for creating long sequences that look random to any feasible adversary (which does not know the said seed).

C.3.1. Computational Indistinguishability

A central notion in modern cryptography is that of "effective similarity" (aka computational indistinguishability; cf. [108, 239]). The underlying thesis is that we do not care whether or not objects are equal; all we care about is whether or not a difference between the objects can be observed by a feasible computation. In case the answer is negative, the two objects are equivalent as far as any practical application is concerned. Indeed, in the sequel we will often interchange such (computationally indistinguishable) objects. In this section we recall the definition of computational indistinguishability (presented in Section 8.2.3), and consider two variants.

Definition C.4 (computational indistinguishability, Definition 8.4 revised):[4] *We say that* $X = \{X_n\}_{n \in \mathbb{N}}$ *and* $Y = \{Y_n\}_{n \in \mathbb{N}}$ *are* computationally indistinguishable *if for every probabilistic polynomial-time algorithm D every polynomial p, and all sufficiently large n,*

$$|\Pr[D(1^n, X_n) = 1] - \Pr[D(1^n, Y_n) = 1]| < \frac{1}{p(n)}$$

where the probabilities are taken over the relevant distribution (i.e., either X_n or Y_n) *and over the internal coin tosses of algorithm D.*

See further discussion in Section 8.2.3. In particular, recall that for "efficiently constructible" distributions, indistinguishability by a single sample (as in Definition C.4) implies indistinguishability by multiple samples (as in Definition 8.5).

---

[4]For the sake of streamlining Definition C.4 with Definition C.5 (and unlike in Definition 8.4), here the distinguisher is explicitly given the index n of the distribution that it inspects. (In typical applications, the difference between Definitions 8.4 and C.4 is immaterial because the index n is easily determined from any sample of the corresponding distributions.)

Extension to ensembles indexed by strings. We consider a natural extension of Definition C.4 in which, rather than referring to ensembles indexed by $\mathbb{N}$, we refer to ensembles indexed by an arbitrary set $S \subseteq \{0, 1\}^*$. Typically, for an ensemble $\{Z_\alpha\}_{\alpha \in S}$, it holds that Z_α ranges over strings of length that is polynomially related to the length of α.

Definition C.5: *We say that $\{X_\alpha\}_{\alpha \in S}$ and $\{Y_\alpha\}_{\alpha \in S}$ are* computationally indistinguishable *if for every probabilistic polynomial-time algorithm D, every polynomial p, and all sufficiently long $\alpha \in S$,*

$$|\Pr[D(\alpha, X_\alpha) = 1] - \Pr[D(\alpha, Y_\alpha) = 1]| \; < \; \frac{1}{p(|\alpha|)}$$

where the probabilities are taken over the relevant distribution (i.e., either X_α or Y_α) and over the internal coin tosses of algorithm D.

Note that Definition C.4 is obtained as a special case by setting $S = \{1^n : n \in \mathbb{N}\}$.

A non-uniform version. A non-uniform definition of computational indistinguishability can be derived from Definition C.5 by artificially augmenting the indices of the distributions. That is, $\{X_\alpha\}_{\alpha \in S}$ and $\{Y_\alpha\}_{\alpha \in S}$ are computationally indistinguishable in a non-uniform sense if for every polynomial p the ensembles $\{X'_{\alpha'}\}_{\alpha' \in S'}$ and $\{Y'_{\alpha'}\}_{\alpha' \in S'}$ are computationally indistinguishable (as in Definition C.5), where $S' = \{\alpha\beta : \alpha \in S \wedge \beta \in \{0, 1\}^{p(|\alpha|)}\}$ and $X'_{\alpha\beta} = X_\alpha$ (resp., $Y'_{\alpha\beta} = Y_\alpha$) for every $\beta \in \{0, 1\}^{p(|\alpha|)}$. An equivalent (alternative) definition can be obtained by following the formulation that underlies Definition 8.12.

C.3.2. Pseudorandom Generators

Loosely speaking, a pseudorandom generator is an efficient (deterministic) algorithm that on input a short random *seed* outputs a (typically much) longer sequence that is computationally indistinguishable from a uniformly chosen sequence.

Definition C.6 (pseudorandom generator, Definition 8.1 restated): *Let $\ell : \mathbb{N} \to \mathbb{N}$ satisfy $\ell(n) > n$, for all $n \in \mathbb{N}$. A* pseudorandom generator, *with* stretch function ℓ, *is a (deterministic) polynomial-time algorithm G satisfying the following:*

1. *For every $s \in \{0, 1\}^*$, it holds that $|G(s)| = \ell(|s|)$.*
2. *$\{G(U_n)\}_{n \in \mathbb{N}}$ and $\{U_{\ell(n)}\}_{n \in \mathbb{N}}$ are computationally indistinguishable, where U_m denotes the uniform distribution over $\{0, 1\}^m$.*

Indeed, the probability ensemble $\{G(U_n)\}_{n \in \mathbb{N}}$ is called pseudorandom.

We stress that pseudorandom sequences can replace truly random sequences not only in "standard" algorithmic applications but also in cryptographic ones. That is, *any* cryptographic application that is secure when the legitimate parties use truly random sequences is also secure when the legitimate parties use pseudorandom sequences. The benefit in such a substitution (of random sequences by pseudorandom ones) is that the latter sequences can be efficiently generated using much less true randomness. Furthermore, *in an interactive setting*, it is possible to eliminate all random steps from the on-line execution of a program, by replacing them with the generation of pseudorandom bits based on a random seed selected and fixed off-line (or at setup time). This allows interactive parties to generate a long sequence of common secret bits based on a shared random seed that may have been selected at a much earlier time.

Various cryptographic applications of pseudorandom generators will be presented in the sequel, but let us first recall that *pseudorandom generators exist if and only if one-way functions exist* (see Theorem 8.11). For further treatment of pseudorandom generators, the reader is referred to Section 8.2.

C.3.3. Pseudorandom Functions

Recall that pseudorandom *generators* provide a way to efficiently generate long pseudorandom sequences from short random seeds. Pseudorandom *functions*, introduced and constructed by Goldreich, Goldwasser, and Micali [95], are even more powerful: They provide efficient direct access to the bits of a huge pseudorandom sequence (Which is not feasible to scan bit by bit). More precisely, a pseudorandom function is an efficient (deterministic) algorithm that given an n-bit *seed*, s, and an n-bit *argument*, x, returns an n-bit string, denoted $f_s(x)$, such that it is infeasible to distinguish the values of f_s, for a uniformly chosen $s \in \{0, 1\}^n$, from the values of a truly random function $F : \{0, 1\}^n \rightarrow \{0, 1\}^n$. That is, the (feasible) testing procedure is given oracle access to the function (but not its explicit description), and cannot distinguish the case in which it is given oracle access to a pseudorandom function from the case in which it is given oracle access to a truly random function.

Definition C.7 (pseudorandom functions): *A pseudorandom function (ensemble), is a collection of functions* $\{f_s : \{0, 1\}^{|s|} \rightarrow \{0, 1\}^{|s|}\}_{s \in \{0,1\}^*}$ *that satisfies the following two conditions:*

1. (efficient evaluation) *There exists an efficient* (deterministic) *algorithm that given a seed, s, and an* argument, $x \in \{0, 1\}^{|s|}$, *returns* $f_s(x)$.
2. (pseudorandomness) *For every probabilistic polynomial-time oracle machine, M, every positive polynomial p, and all sufficiently large n's*

$$\left| \Pr[M^{f_{U_n}}(1^n) = 1] - \Pr[M^{F_n}(1^n) = 1] \right| < \frac{1}{p(n)}$$

where F_n denotes a uniformly selected function mapping $\{0, 1\}^n$ to $\{0, 1\}^n$.

One key feature of the foregoing definition is that pseudorandom functions can be generated and shared by merely generating and sharing their seed; that is, a "random-looking" function $f_s : \{0, 1\}^n \rightarrow \{0, 1\}^n$, is determined by its n-bit seed s. Thus, parties wishing to share a "random-looking" function f_s (determining 2^n-many values), merely need to generate and share among themselves the n-bit seed s. (For example, one party may randomly select the seed s, and communicate it, via a secure channel, to all other parties.) Sharing a pseudorandom function allows parties to determine (by themselves and without any further communication) random-looking values depending on their current views of the environment (which need not be known a priori). To appreciate the potential of this tool, one should realize that sharing a pseudorandom function is essentially as good as being able to agree, on the fly, on the association of random values to (on-line) given values, where the latter are taken from a huge set of possible values. We stress that this agreement is achieved without communication and synchronization: Whenever some party needs to associate a random value to a given value, $v \in \{0, 1\}^n$, it will associate to v the (same) random value $r_v \in \{0, 1\}^n$ (by setting $r_v = f_s(v)$, where f_s is a pseudorandom function agreed upon beforehand). Concrete applications of (this power of) pseudorandom functions appear in Sections C.5.2 and C.6.2.

Theorem C.8 (How to construct pseudorandom functions): *Pseudorandom functions can be constructed using any pseudorandom generator.*

Proof Sketch:[5] Let G be a pseudorandom generator that stretches its seed by a factor of two (i.e., $\ell(n) = 2n$), and let $G_0(s)$ (resp., $G_1(s)$) denote the first (resp., last) $|s|$ bits in $G(s)$. Let

$$G_{\sigma_{|s|} \cdots \sigma_2 \sigma_1}(s) \stackrel{\text{def}}{=} G_{\sigma_{|s|}}(\cdots G_{\sigma_2}(G_{\sigma_1}(s)) \cdots),$$

define $f_s(x_1 x_2 \cdots x_n) \stackrel{\text{def}}{=} G_{x_n \cdots x_2 x_1}(s)$, and consider the function ensemble $\{f_s : \{0, 1\}^{|s|} \to \{0, 1\}^{|s|}\}_{s \in \{0,1\}^*}$. Pictorially, the function f_s is defined by n-step walks down a full binary tree of depth n having labels at the vertices. The root of the tree, hereafter referred to as the level 0 vertex of the tree, is labeled by the string s. If an internal vertex is labeled r then its left child is labeled $G_0(r)$ whereas its right child is labeled $G_1(r)$. The value of $f_s(x)$ is the string residing in the leaf reachable from the root by a path corresponding to the string x.

We claim that the function ensemble $\{f_s\}_{s \in \{0,1\}^*}$ is pseudorandom. The proof uses the hybrid technique (cf. Section 8.2.3): The ith hybrid, denoted H_n^i, is a function ensemble consisting of $2^{2^i \cdot n}$ functions $\{0, 1\}^n \to \{0, 1\}^n$, each determined by 2^i random n-bit strings, denoted $\bar{s} = \langle s_\beta \rangle_{\beta \in \{0,1\}^i}$. The value of such function $h_{\bar{s}}$ at $x = \alpha\beta$, where $|\beta| = i$, is defined to equal $G_\alpha(s_\beta)$. Pictorially, the function $h_{\bar{s}}$ is defined by placing the strings in $\bar{s}$ in the corresponding vertices of level i, and labeling vertices of lower levels using the very rule used in the definition of f_s. The extreme hybrids correspond to our indistinguishability claim (i.e., $H_n^0 \equiv f_{U_n}$ and H_n^n is a truly random function), and the indistinguishability of neighboring hybrids follows from our indistinguishability hypothesis (by using a reducibility argument). Specifically, we show that the ability to distinguish H_n^i from H_n^{i+1} yields an ability to distinguish multiple samples of $G(U_n)$ from multiple samples of U_{2n} (by placing, on the fly, halves of the given samples at adequate vertices of the $i + 1^{\text{st}}$ level). $\qquad\qquad\square$

Variants. Useful variants (and generalizations) of the notion of pseudorandom functions include Boolean pseudorandom functions that are defined over all strings (i.e., $f_s : \{0, 1\}^* \to \{0, 1\}$) and pseudorandom functions that are defined for other domains and ranges (i.e., $f_s : \{0, 1\}^{d(|s|)} \to \{0, 1\}^{r(|s|)}$, for arbitrary polynomially bounded functions $d, r : \mathbb{N} \to \mathbb{N}$). Various transformations between these variants are known (cf. [91, Sec. 3.6.4] and [92, Apdx. C.2]).

---

[5]See details in [91, Sec. 3.6.2].

C.4. Zero-Knowledge

Zero-knowledge proofs provide a powerful tool for the design of cryptographic protocols as well as a good bench mark for the study of various issues regarding such protocols. Loosely speaking, zero-knowledge proofs are proofs that yield nothing beyond the validity of the assertion. That is, a verifier obtaining such a proof only gains conviction in the validity of the assertion (as if it were told by a trusted party that the assertion holds). This is formulated by saying that anything that is feasibly computable from a zero-knowledge proof is also feasibly computable from the (valid) assertion itself. The latter formulation follows the simulation paradigm, which is discussed next, while reproducing part of the discussion in §9.2.1.1 and making additional comments regarding the use of this paradigm in cryptography.

C.4.1. The Simulation Paradigm

A key question regarding the modeling of security concerns is how to express the intuitive requirement that an adversary "gains nothing substantial" by deviating from the prescribed behavior of an honest user. The answer provided by the simulation paradigm is that the adversary *gains nothing* if whatever it can obtain by unrestricted adversarial behavior can also be obtained, within essentially the same computational effort, by a benign behavior. The definition of the "benign behavior" captures what we want to achieve in terms of security, and is specific to the security concern to be addressed. For example, in the context of zero-knowledge, the unrestricted adversarial behavior is captured by an arbitrary probabilistic polynomial-time verifier strategy, whereas the benign behavior is any computation that is based (only) on the assertion itself (while assuming that the latter is valid). Other examples are discussed in Sections C.5.1 and C.7.1.

The definitional approach to security represented by the simulation paradigm (and more generally the entire definitional approach surveyed in this appendix) may be considered overly cautious, because it seems to prohibit also "non-harmful" gains of some "far-fetched" adversaries.[6] We warn against this impression. Firstly, there is nothing more dangerous in cryptography than to consider "reasonable" adversaries (a notion that is almost a contradiction in terms): Typically, the adversaries will try exactly what the system designer has discarded as "far-fetched." Secondly, it seems impossible to come up with definitions of security that distinguish "breaking the system in a harmful way" from "breaking it in a non-harmful way": What is harmful is application-dependent, whereas a good definition of security ought to be application-independent (as otherwise using the cryptographic system in any new application will require a full reevaluation of its security). Furthermore, even with respect to a specific application, it is typically very hard to classify the set of "harmful breakings."

C.4.2. The Actual Definition

In §9.2.1.2 zero-knowledge was defined as a property of some prover strategies (within the context of interactive proof systems, as defined in Section 9.1.2). More generally, the term may apply to any interactive machine, regardless of its goal. A strategy A

---

[6]Indeed, according to the simulation paradigm, a system is called secure only if all possible adversaries can be adequately simulated by adequate benign behavior. Thus, this approach also considers "far-fetched" adversaries and does not disregard "non-harmful" gains that cannot be simulated.

is zero-knowledge on (inputs from) the set S if, for every feasible strategy B^*, there exists a feasible computation C^* such that the following two probability ensembles are computationally indistinguishable (according to Definition C.5):

1. $\{(A, B^*)(x)\}_{x \in S} \stackrel{\text{def}}{=}$ the output of B^* after interacting with A on common input $x \in S$; and

2. $\{C^*(x)\}_{x \in S} \stackrel{\text{def}}{=}$ the output of C^* on input $x \in S$.

Recall that the first ensemble represents an actual execution of an interactive protocol, whereas the second ensemble represents the computation of a stand-alone procedure (called the "simulator"), which does not interact with anybody.

The foregoing definition does *not* account for auxiliary information that an adversary B^* may have prior to entering the interaction. Accounting for such auxiliary information is essential for using zero-knowledge proofs as subprotocols inside larger protocols. This is taken care of by a stricter notion called auxiliary-input zero-knowledge, which was not presented in Section 9.2.

Definition C.9 (zero-knowledge, revisited): *A strategy A is* auxiliary-input zero-knowledge *on inputs from S if, for every probabilistic polynomial-time strategy B^* and every polynomial p, there exists a probabilistic polynomial-time algorithm C^* such that the following two probability ensembles are computationally indistinguishable:*

1. $\{(A, B^*(z))(x)\}_{x \in S, z \in \{0,1\}^{p(|x|)}} \stackrel{\text{def}}{=}$ *the output of B^* when having auxiliary-input z and interacting with A on common input $x \in S$; and*

2. $\{C^*(x, z)\}_{x \in S, z \in \{0,1\}^{p(|x|)}} \stackrel{\text{def}}{=}$ *the output of C^* on inputs $x \in S$ and $z \in \{0, 1\}^{p(|x|)}$.*

Almost all known zero-knowledge proofs are in fact auxiliary-input zero-knowledge. As hinted, *auxiliary-input zero-knowledge is preserved under sequential composition.* A simulator for the multiple-session protocol can be constructed by iteratively invoking the single-session simulator that refers to the residual strategy of the adversarial verifier in the given session (while feeding this simulator with the transcript of previous sessions). Indeed, the residual single-session verifier gets the transcript of the previous sessions as part of its auxiliary input (i.e., z in Definition C.9). For details, see [91, Sec. 4.3.4].

C.4.3. A General Result and a Generic Application

A question avoided so far is whether zero-knowledge proofs exist at all. Clearly, every set in $\mathcal{P}$ (or rather in $\mathcal{BPP}$) has a "trivial" zero-knowledge proof (in which the verifier determines membership by itself); however, what we seek is zero-knowledge proofs for statements that the verifier cannot decide by itself.

Assuming the existence of "commitment schemes" (cf. §C.4.3.1), which in turn exist if one-way functions exist [169, 118], *there exist* (auxiliary-input) *zero-knowledge proofs of membership in any NP-set.* These zero-knowledge proofs, abstractly depicted in Construction 9.10, have the following important property: The prescribed prover strategy is efficient, provided it is given as auxiliary-input an NP-witness to the assertion (to be proved).[7] Implementing the abstract boxes (referred to in Construction 9.10) by commitment schemes, we get

> **Theorem C.10** (on the applicability of zero-knowledge proofs (Theorem 9.11, revisited)): *If* (non-uniformly hard) *one-way functions exist then every set* $S \in \mathcal{NP}$ *has an* auxiliary-input *zero-knowledge interactive proof. Furthermore, the prescribed prover strategy can be implemented in probabilistic polynomial time, provided that it is given as auxiliary-input an NP-witness for membership of the common input in S.*

Theorem C.10 makes zero-knowledge a very powerful tool in the design of cryptographic schemes and protocols (see §C.4.3.2). We comment that the intractability assumption used in Theorem C.10 seems essential.

C.4.3.1. Commitment Schemes

Loosely speaking, commitment schemes are two-stage (two-party) protocols allowing for one party to commit itself (at the first stage) to a value while keeping the value secret. At a later (i.e., second) stage, the commitment is "opened" and it is guaranteed that the "opening" can yield only a single value, which is determined during the committing phase. Thus, the (first stage of the) commitment scheme is both *binding* and *hiding*.

A simple (uni-directional communication) commitment scheme can be constructed based on any one-way 1-1 function f (with a corresponding hard-core b). To commit to a bit σ, the sender uniformly selects $s \in \{0, 1\}^n$, and sends the pair $(f(s), b(s) \oplus \sigma)$. Note that this is both binding and hiding. An alternative construction, which can be based on any one-way function, uses a pseudorandom generator G that stretches its seed by a factor of three (cf. Theorem 8.11). A commitment is established, via two-way communication, as follows (cf. [169]): The receiver selects uniformly $r \in \{0, 1\}^{3n}$ and sends it to the sender, which selects uniformly $s \in \{0, 1\}^n$ and sends $r \oplus G(s)$ if it wishes to commit to the value one and $G(s)$ if it wishes to commit to zero. To see that this is binding, observe that there are at most 2^{2n} "bad" values r that satisfy $G(s_0) = r \oplus G(s_1)$ for some pair (s_0, s_1), and with overwhelmingly high probability the receiver will not pick one of these bad values. The hiding property follows by the pseudorandomness of G.

C.4.3.2. A Generic Application

As mentioned, Theorem C.10 makes zero-knowledge a very powerful tool in the design of cryptographic schemes and protocols. This wide applicability is due to two important aspects regarding Theorem C.10: Firstly, Theorem C.10 provides a zero-knowledge proof for every NP-set, and secondly, the prescribed prover can be implemented in probabilistic polynomial time when given an adequate NP-witness. We now turn to a typical application of zero-knowledge proofs.

In a typical cryptographic setting, a user U has a secret and is supposed to take some action based on its secret. For example, U may be instructed to send several different

---

[7]The auxiliary-input given to the prescribed prover (in order to allow for an efficient implementation of its strategy) is not to be confused with the auxiliary-input that is given to malicious verifiers (in the definition of auxiliary-input zero-knowledge). The former is typically an NP-witness for the common input, which is available to the user that invokes the prover strategy (cf. the generic application discussed in §C.4.3.2). In contrast, the auxiliary-input that is given to malicious verifiers models arbitrary partial information that may be available to the adversary.

commitments (cf. §C.4.3.1) to a single secret value of its choice. The question is how other users can verify that U indeed took the correct action (as determined by U's secret and publicly known information). Indeed, if U discloses its secret, then anybody can verify that U took the correct action. However, U does not want to reveal its secret. Using zero-knowledge proofs we can satisfy both conflicting requirements (i.e., having other users verify that U took the correct action without violating U's interest in not revealing its secret). That is, U can prove in zero-knowledge that it took the correct action. Note that U's claim to having taken the correct action is an NP-assertion (since U's legal action is determined as a polynomial-time function of its secret and the public information), and that U has an NP-witness to its validity (i.e., the secret is an NP-witness to the claim that the action fits the public information). Thus, by Theorem C.10, it is possible for U to efficiently prove the correctness of its action without yielding anything about its secret. Consequently, it is fair to ask U to prove (in zero-knowledge) that it behaves properly, and so to force U to behave properly. Indeed, "forcing proper behavior" is the canonical application of zero-knowledge proofs (see §C.7.3.2).

This paradigm (i.e., "forcing proper behavior" via zero-knowledge proofs), which in turn is based on Theorem C.10, has been utilized in numerous different settings. Indeed, this paradigm is the basis for the wide applicability of zero-knowledge protocols in cryptography.

C.4.4. Definitional Variations and Related Notions

In this section we consider numerous variants on the notion of zero-knowledge and the underlying model of interactive proofs. These include black-box simulation and other variants of zero-knowledge (cf. Section C.4.4.1), as well as notions such as proofs of knowledge, non-interactive zero-knowledge, and witness indistinguishable proofs (cf. Section C.4.4.2).

Before starting, we call the reader's attention to the notion of computational soundness and to the related notion of argument systems, discussed in §9.1.5.2. We mention that argument systems may be more efficient than interactive proofs as well as provide stronger zero-knowledge guarantees. Specifically, almost-perfect zero-knowledge arguments for $\mathcal{NP}$ can be constructed based on any one-way function [172], where almost-perfect zero-knowledge means that the simulator's output is statistically close to the verifier's view in the real interaction (see a discussion in §C.4.4.1). Note that stronger security guarantee for the prover (as provided by almost-perfect zero-knowledge) comes at the cost of weaker security guarantee for the verifier (as provided by computational soundness). The answer to the question of whether or not this trade-off is worthwhile seems to be application-dependent, and one should also take into account the availability and complexity of the corresponding protocols.

C.4.4.1. Definitional Variations
We consider several definitional issues regarding the notion of zero-knowledge (as defined in Definition C.9).

Universal and black-box simulation. One strengthening of Definition C.9 is obtained by requiring the existence of a universal simulator, denoted $\mathcal{C}$, that can simulate (the interactive gain of) any verifier strategy B^* when given the verifier's program an auxiliary-input; that is, in terms of Definition C.9, one should replace $C^*(x, z)$ by $\mathcal{C}(x, z, \langle B^* \rangle)$, where $\langle B^* \rangle$

denotes the description of the program of B^* (which may depend on x and on z). That is, we effectively restrict the simulation by requiring that it be a uniform (feasible) function of the verifier's program (rather than arbitrarily depending on it). This restriction is very natural, because it seems hard to envision an alternative way of establishing the zero-knowledge property of a given protocol. Taking another step, one may argue that since it seems infeasible to reverse-engineer programs, the simulator may just as well use the verifier strategy as an oracle (or as a "black-box"). This reasoning gave rise to the notion of black-box simulation, which was introduced and advocated in [98] and further studied in numerous works. The belief was that inherent limitations regarding black-box simulation represent inherent limitations of zero-knowledge itself. For example, it was believed that the *fact* that the parallel version of the interactive proof of Construction 9.10 cannot be simulated in a black-box manner (unless $\mathcal{NP}$ is contained in $\mathcal{BPP}$) *implies* that this version is not zero-knowledge (as per Definition C.9 itself). However, the (underlying) belief that *any* zero-knowledge protocol can be simulated in a black-box manner was later refuted by Barak [25].

Honest verifier versus general cheating verifier. Definition C.9 refers to all feasible verifier strategies, which is most natural in the cryptographic setting, because zero-knowledge is supposed to capture the robustness of the prover under *any feasible* (i.e., adversarial) attempt to gain something by interacting with it. A weaker and still interesting notion of zero-knowledge refers to what can be gained by an "honest verifier" (or rather a semi-honest verifier)[8] that interacts with the prover as directed, with the exception that it may maintain (and output) a record of the entire interaction (i.e., even if directed to erase all records of the interaction). Although such a weaker notion is not satisfactory for standard cryptographic applications, it yields a fascinating notion from a conceptual as well as a complexity-theoretic point of view. Furthermore, every proof system that is *zero-knowledge with respect to the honest-verifier* can be transformed into a *standard zero-knowledge* proof (without using intractability assumptions, and in the case of "public-coin" proofs this is done without significantly increasing the prover's computational effort; see [228]).

Statistical versus Computational Zero-Knowledge. Recall that Definition C.9 postulates that for every probability ensemble of one type (i.e., representing the verifier's output after interaction with the prover), there exists a "similar" ensemble of a second type (i.e., representing the simulator's output). One key parameter is the interpretation of "similarity." Three interpretations, yielding different notions of zero-knowledge, have been extensively considered in the literature:

1. Perfect Zero-Knowledge requires that the two probability ensembles be identically distributed.[9]
2. Statistical (or Almost-Perfect) Zero-Knowledge requires that these probability ensembles be statistically close (i.e., the variation distance between them should be negligible).

---

[8]The term "honest verifier" is more appealing when considering an alternative (equivalent) formulation of Definition C.9. In the alternative definition (see [91, Sec. 4.3.1.3]), the simulator is "only" required to generate the verifier's view of the real interaction, where the verifier's view includes its (common and auxiliary) inputs, the outcome of its coin tosses, and all messages it has received.

[9]The actual definition of Perfect Zero-Knowledge allows the simulator to fail (while outputting a special symbol) with negligible probability, and the output distribution of the simulator is conditioned on its not failing.

3. Computational (or rather general) Zero-Knowledge requires that these probability ensembles be computationally indistinguishable.

Indeed, Computational Zero-Knowledge is the most liberal notion, and is the notion considered in Definition C.9. We note that the class of problems having statistical zero-knowledge proofs contains several problems that are considered intractable. The interested reader is referred to [227].

C.4.4.2. Related Notions: POK, NIZK, and WI
We briefly discuss the notions of proofs of knowledge (POK), non-interactive zero-knowledge (NIZK), and witness indistinguishable proofs (WI).

Proofs of Knowledge. Loosely speaking, proofs of knowledge are interactive proofs in which the prover asserts "knowledge" of some object (e.g., a 3-coloring of a graph), and not merely its existence (e.g., the existence of a 3-coloring of the graph, which in turn is equivalent to the assertion that the graph is 3-colorable). See further discussion in Section 9.2.3. We mention that *proofs of knowledge*, and in particular *zero-knowledge proofs of knowledge*, have many applications to the design of cryptographic schemes and cryptographic protocols. One famous application of zero-knowledge proofs of knowledge is to the construction of identification schemes (e.g., the Fiat-Shamir scheme).

Non-Interactive Zero-Knowledge. The model of non-interactive zero-knowledge (NIZK) proof systems consists of three entities: a prover, a verifier, and a uniformly selected reference string (which can be thought of as being selected by a trusted third party). Both the verifier and prover can read the reference string (as well as the common input), and each can toss additional coins. The interaction consists of a single message sent from the prover to the verifier, who is then left with the final decision (whether or not to accept the common input). The (basic) zero-knowledge requirement refers to a simulator that outputs pairs that should be computationally indistinguishable from the distribution (of pairs consisting of a uniformly selected reference string and a random prover message) seen in the real model.[10] We mention that NIZK proof systems have numerous applications (e.g., to the construction of public-key encryption and signature schemes, where the reference string may be incorporated in the public-key), which in turn motivate various augmentations of the basic definition of NIZK (see [91, Sec. 4.10] and [92, Sec. 5.4.4.4]). Such NIZK proofs for any NP-set can be constructed based on standard intractability assumptions (e.g., intractability of factoring), but even constructing basic NIZK proof systems seems more difficult than constructing *interactive* zero-knowledge proof systems.

Witness Indistinguishability. The notion of witness indistinguishability was suggested in [76] as a meaningful relaxation of zero-knowledge. Loosely speaking, for any NP-relation R, a proof (or argument) system for the corresponding NP-set is called witness indistinguishable if no feasible verifier may distinguish the case in which the prover uses one NP-witness to x (i.e., w_1 such that $(x, w_1) \in R$) from the case in which the prover is using a different NP-witness to the same input x (i.e., w_2 such that $(x, w_2) \in R$). Clearly,

---

[10]Note that the verifier does not affect the distribution seen in the real model, and so the basic definition of zero-knowledge does not refer to it. The verifier (or rather a process of adaptively selecting assertions to be proved) is referred to in the adaptive variants of the definition.

any zero-knowledge protocol is witness indistinguishable, but the converse does not necessarily hold. Furthermore, it seems that witness indistinguishable protocols are easier to construct than zero-knowledge ones. Another advantage of witness indistinguishable protocols is that they are closed under arbitrary concurrent composition, whereas (in general) zero-knowledge protocols are not closed even under parallel composition. Witness indistinguishable protocols turned out to be an *important tool in the construction of more complex protocols*. We refer, in particular, to the technique of [75] for constructing zero-knowledge proofs (and arguments) based on witness indistinguishable proofs (resp., arguments).

C.5. Encryption Schemes

The problem of providing *secret communication over insecure media* is the traditional and most basic problem of cryptography. The setting of this problem consists of two parties communicating through a channel that is possibly tapped by an adversary. The parties wish to exchange information with each other, but keep the "wiretapper" as ignorant as possible regarding the contents of this information. The canonical solution to this problem is obtained by the use of encryption schemes. Loosely speaking, an encryption scheme is a protocol allowing these parties to communicate *secretly* with each other. Typically, the encryption scheme consists of a pair of algorithms. One algorithm, called encryption, is applied by the sender (i.e., the party sending a message), while the other algorithm, called decryption, is applied by the receiver. Hence, in order to send a message, the sender first applies the encryption algorithm to the message, and sends the result, called the ciphertext, over the channel. Upon receiving a ciphertext, the other party (i.e., the receiver) applies the decryption algorithm to it, and retrieves the original message (called the plaintext).

In order for the foregoing scheme to provide secret communication, the receiver must know something that is not known to the wiretapper. (Otherwise, the wiretapper can decrypt the ciphertext exactly as done by the receiver.) This extra knowledge may take the form of the decryption algorithm itself, or some parameters and/or auxiliary inputs used by the decryption algorithm. We call this extra knowledge the decryption-key. Note that, without loss of generality, we may assume that the decryption algorithm is known to the wiretapper, and that the decryption algorithm operates on two inputs: a ciphertext and a decryption-key. (This description implicitly presupposes the existence of an efficient algorithm for generating (random) keys.) We stress that the existence of a decryption-key, not known to the wiretapper, is merely a necessary condition for secret communication.

Evaluating the "security" of an encryption scheme is a very tricky business. A preliminary task is to understand what is "security" (i.e., to properly define what is meant by this intuitive term). Two approaches to defining security are known. The first ("classical") approach, introduced by Shannon [205], is *information-theoretic*. It is concerned with the "information" about the plaintext that is "present" in the ciphertext. Loosely speaking, if the ciphertext contains information about the plaintext, then the encryption scheme is considered insecure. It has been shown that such high (i.e., "perfect") level of security can be achieved only if the key in use is at least as long as the *total* amount of information sent via the encryption scheme [205]. This fact (i.e., that the key has to be longer than the information exchanged using it) is indeed a drastic limitation on the applicability of such (perfectly secure) encryption schemes.

The second ("modern") approach, followed in the current text, is based on *Computational Complexity*. This approach is based on the thesis that it *does not matter* whether the ciphertext contains information about the plaintext, but rather whether this information can be *efficiently extracted*. In other words, instead of asking whether it is *possible* for the wiretapper to extract specific information, we ask whether it is *feasible* for the wiretapper to extract this information. It turns out that the new (i.e., "computational complexity") approach can offer security even when the key is much shorter than the total length of the messages sent via the encryption scheme.

The Computational Complexity approach enables the introduction of concepts and primitives that cannot exist under the information-theoretic approach. A typical example is the concept of *public-key encryption schemes*, introduced by Diffie and Hellman [66] (with the most popular candidate suggested by Rivest, Shamir, and Adleman [193]). Recall that in the foregoing discussion we concentrated on the decryption algorithm and its key. It can be shown that the encryption algorithm must also get, in addition to the message, an auxiliary input that depends on the decryption-key. This auxiliary input is called the encryption-key. Traditional encryption schemes, and in particular all the encryption schemes used in the millennia until the 1980s, operate with an encryption-key that equals the decryption-key. Hence, the wiretapper in these schemes must be ignorant of the encryption-key, and consequently the *key distribution* problem arises; that is, how can two parties wishing to communicate over an insecure channel agree on a secret encryption/decryption-key. (The traditional solution is to exchange the key through an alternative channel that is secure, though much more expensive to use.) The Computational Complexity approach allows for the introduction of encryption schemes in which the encryption-key may be given to the wiretapper without compromising the security of the scheme. Clearly, the decryption-key in such schemes is different from the encryption-key, and furthermore it is infeasible to obtain the decryption-key from the encryption-key. Such encryption schemes, called public-key schemes, have the advantage of trivially resolving the key distribution problem (because the encryption-key can be publicized). That is, once some Party X generates a pair of keys and publicizes the encryption-key, any party can send encrypted messages to Party X such that Party X can retrieve the actual information (i.e., the plaintext), whereas nobody else can learn anything about the plaintext.

In contrast to public-key schemes, traditional encryption schemes in which the encryption-key equals the decryption-key are called private-key schemes, because in these schemes the encryption-key must be kept secret (rather than be public as in public-key encryption schemes). We note that a full specification of either schemes requires the specification of the way in which keys are generated, that is, a (randomized) key-generation algorithm that, given a security parameter, produces a (random) pair of corresponding encryption/decryption-keys (which are identical in case of private-key schemes).

Thus, both private-key and public-key encryption schemes consist of three efficient algorithms: a key-generation algorithm denoted G, an encryption algorithm denoted E, and a decryption algorithm denoted D. For every pair of encryption- and decryption-keys (e, d) generated by G, and for every plaintext x, it holds that $D_d(E_e(x)) = x$, where $E_e(x) \stackrel{\text{def}}{=} E(e, x)$ and $D_d(y) \stackrel{\text{def}}{=} D(d, y)$. The difference between the two types of encryption schemes is reflected in the definition of security: The security of a public-key encryption scheme should hold also when the adversary is given the encryption-key, whereas this is not required for a private-key encryption scheme. In the following definitional treatment, we focus on the public-key case (and the private-key case can be obtained by omitting the encryption-key from the sequence of inputs given to the adversary).

C.5.1. Definitions

A good disguise should not reveal the person's height.
Shafi Goldwasser and Silvio Micali, 1982

For simplicity, we first consider the encryption of a single message (which, for further simplicity, is assumed to be of length that equals the security parameter, n).[11] As implied by the foregoing discussion, a public-key encryption scheme is said to be secure if it is infeasible to gain any information about the plaintext by looking at the ciphertext (and the encryption-key). That is, whatever information about the plaintext one may compute from the ciphertext, and some a priori information, can be essentially computed as efficiently from the a priori information alone. This fundamental definition of security, called semantic security, was introduced by Goldwasser and Micali [108].

Definition C.11 (semantic security): *A public-key encryption scheme (G, E, D) is* semantically secure *if for every probabilistic polynomial-time algorithm, A, there exists a probabilistic polynomial-time algorithm B such that for every two functions $f, h : \{0, 1\}^* \to \{0, 1\}^*$ and all probability ensembles $\{X_n\}_{n \in \mathbb{N}}$ that satisfy $|h(x)| =$ $\mathrm{poly}(|x|)$ and $X_n \in \{0, 1\}^n$, it holds that*

$$\Pr[A(e, E_e(x), h(x)) = f(x)] \; < \; \Pr[B(1^n, h(x)) = f(x)] + \mu(n)$$

where the plaintext x is distributed according to X_n, the encryption-key e is distributed according to $G(1^n)$, and μ is a negligible function.

That is, it is feasible to predict $f(x)$ from $h(x)$ as successfully as it is to predict $f(x)$ from $h(x)$ and $(e, E_e(x))$, which means that nothing is gained by obtaining $(e, E_e(x))$. Note that no computational restrictions are made regarding the functions h and f. We stress that the foregoing definition (as well as the next one) refers to public-key encryption schemes, and in the case of private-key schemes algorithm A is not given the encryption-key e.

The following technical interpretation of security states that it is infeasible to distinguish the encryptions of any two plaintexts (of the same length).[12] As we shall see, this definition (also originating in [108]) is equivalent to Definition C.11.

Definition C.12 (indistinguishability of encryptions): *A public-key encryption scheme (G, E, D) has* indistinguishable encryptions *if for every probabilistic polynomial-time algorithm, A, and all sequences of triples, $(x_n, y_n, z_n)_{n \in \mathbb{N}}$, where $|x_n| = |y_n| = n$ and $|z_n| = \mathrm{poly}(n)$, it holds that*

$$|\Pr[A(e, E_e(x_n), z_n) = 1] - \Pr[A(e, E_e(y_n), z_n) = 1]| = \mu(n)$$

Again, e is distributed according to $G(1^n)$, and μ is a negligible function.

---

[11] In the case of public-key schemes, no generality is lost by these simplifying assumptions, but in the case of private-key schemes, one should consider the encryption of polynomially many messages (as we do at the end of this section).

[12] Indeed, satisfying this condition requires using a probabilistic encryption algorithm.

In particular, z_n may equal (x_n, y_n). Thus, it is infeasible to distinguish the encryptions of any two fixed messages (such as the all-zero message and the all-ones message). Thus, the following motto is adequate, too:

> *A good disguise should not allow a mother to distinguish her own children.*
>
> Shafi Goldwasser and Silvio Micali, 1982

Definition C.11 is more appealing in most settings where encryption is considered the end goal. Definition C.12 is used to establish the security of candidate encryption schemes as well as to analyze their application as modules inside larger cryptographic protocols. Thus, the equivalence of these definitions is of major importance.

Equivalence of Definitions C.11 and C.12 – proof ideas. Intuitively, indistinguishability of encryptions (i.e., of the encryptions of x_n and y_n) is a special case of semantic security; specifically, it corresponds to the case that X_n is uniform over $\{x_n, y_n\}$, the function f indicates one of the plaintexts, and h does not distinguish them (i.e., $f(w) = 1$ if and only if $w = x_n$ and $h(x_n) = h(y_n) = z_n$, where z_n is as in Definition C.12). The other direction is proved by considering the algorithm B that, on input $(1^n, v)$ where $v = h(x)$, generates $(e, d) \leftarrow G(1^n)$ and outputs $A(e, E_e(1^n), v)$, where A is as in Definition C.11. Indistinguishability of encryptions is used to prove that B performs as well as A (i.e., for every h, f and $\{X_n\}_{n \in \mathbb{N}}$, it holds that $\Pr[B(1^n, h(X_n)) = f(X_n)] = \Pr[A(e, E_e(1^n), h(X_n)) = f(X_n)]$ approximately equals $\Pr[A(e, E_e(X_n), h(X_n)) = f(X_n)]$).

Probabilistic Encryption. A secure *public-key* encryption scheme must employ a probabilistic (i.e., randomized) encryption algorithm. Otherwise, given the encryption-key as (additional) input, it is easy to distinguish the encryption of the all-zero message from the encryption of the all-ones message.[13] This explains the association of the robust definitions of security with the paradigm of *probabilistic encryption*, an association that originates in the title of the pioneering work of Goldwasser and Micali [108].

Further discussion. We stress that (the equivalent) Definitions C.11 and C.12 go way beyond saying that it is infeasible to recover the plaintext from the ciphertext. The latter statement is indeed a minimal requirement from a secure encryption scheme, but is far from being a sufficient requirement. Typically, encryption schemes are used in applications where even obtaining partial information on the plaintext may endanger the security of the application. When designing an application-independent encryption scheme, we do not know which partial information endangers the application and which does not. Furthermore, even if one wants to design an encryption scheme tailored to a specific application, it is rare (to say the least) that one has a precise characterization of all possible partial information that endangers this application. Thus, we need to require that it is infeasible to obtain any information about the plaintext from the ciphertext. Furthermore, in most applications, the plaintext may not be uniformly distributed and some a priori information regarding it may be available to the adversary. We require that the secrecy of all partial information also be preserved in such a case. That is, even in the presence of a priori information on the plaintext, it is infeasible to obtain any (new)

---

[13] The same holds for (stateless) *private-key* encryption schemes, when considering the security of encrypting several messages (rather than a single message as in the foregoing text). For example, if one uses a deterministic encryption, algorithm, then the adversary can distinguish two encryptions of the same message from the encryptions of a pair of different messages.

information about the plaintext from the ciphertext (beyond what is feasible to obtain from the a priori information on the plaintext). The definition of semantic security postulates all of this. The equivalent definition of indistinguishability of encryptions is useful in demonstrating the security of candidate constructions as well as for arguing about their effect as part of larger protocols.

Security of multiple messages. Definitions C.11 and C.12 refer to the security of an encryption scheme that is used to encrypt a single plaintext (per a generated key). Since the plaintext may be longer than the key,[14] these definitions are already non-trivial, and an encryption scheme satisfying them (even in the private-key model) implies the existence of one-way functions. Still, in many cases, it is desirable to encrypt many plaintexts using the same encryption-key. Loosely speaking, an encryption scheme is secure in the multiple-messages setting if conditions as in Definition C.11 (resp., Definition C.12) hold when polynomially many plaintexts are encrypted using the same encryption-key (cf. [92, Sec. 5.2.4]). *In the public-key model*, security in the single-message setting implies security in the multiple-messages setting. We stress that this is not necessarily true *for the private-key model*.

C.5.2. Constructions

It is common practice to use "pseudorandom generators" as a basis for private-key encryption schemes. We stress that this is a very dangerous practice when the "pseudorandom generator" is easy to predict (such as the "linear congruential generator"). However, this common practice becomes sound provided one uses pseudorandom generators (as defined in Section C.3.2). An alternative and more flexible construction follows.

Private-Key Encryption Scheme based on Pseudorandom Functions. We present a simple construction of a private-key encryption scheme that uses pseudorandom functions as defined in Section C.3.3. The key-generation algorithm consists of uniformly selecting a seed $s \in \{0, 1\}^n$ for a (pseudorandom) function, denoted f_s. To encrypt a message $x \in \{0, 1\}^n$ (using key s), the encryption algorithm uniformly selects a string $r \in \{0, 1\}^n$ and produces the ciphertext $(r, x \oplus f_s(r))$, where $\oplus$ denotes the exclusive-or of bit strings. To decrypt the ciphertext (r, y) (using key s), the decryption algorithm just computes $y \oplus f_s(r)$. The proof of security of this encryption scheme consists of two steps:

1. Proving that an idealized version of the scheme, in which one uses a uniformly selected function $F : \{0, 1\}^n \rightarrow \{0, 1\}^n$, rather than the pseudorandom function f_s, is secure.
2. Concluding that the real scheme is secure (because otherwise one could distinguish a pseudorandom function from a truly random one).

Note that we could have gotten rid of the randomization (in the encryption process) if we had allowed the encryption algorithm to be history-dependent (e.g., use a counter in the role of r). This can be done if all parties that use the same key (for encryption) coordinate their encryption actions (by maintaining a joint state (e.g., counter)). Indeed, when using

---

[14]Recall that for the sake of simplicity we have considered only messages of length n, but the general definitions refer to messages of arbitrary (polynomial in n) length. We comment that, in the general form of Definition C.11, one should provide the length of the message as an auxiliary input to both algorithms (A and B).

a private-key encryption scheme, a common situation is that the same key is only used for communication between two specific parties, which update a joint counter during their communication. Furthermore, if the encryption scheme is used for FIFO communication between the parties and both parties can reliably maintain the counter value, then there is no need (for the sender) to send the counter value. (The resulting scheme is related to "stream ciphers," which are commonly used in practice.)

We comment that the use of a counter (or any other state) in the encryption process is not reasonable in the case of public-key encryption schemes, because it is incompatible with the canonical usage of such schemes (i.e., allowing all parties to send encrypted messages to the "owner of the encryption-key" without engaging in any type of further coordination or communication). Furthermore (unlike in the case of private-key schemes), probabilistic encryption is essential for the security of public-key encryption schemes *even in the case of encrypting a single message*. Following Goldwasser and Micali [108], we now demonstrate the use of *probabilistic encryption* in the construction of public-key encryption schemes.

Public-Key Encryption Scheme based on Trapdoor Permutations. We present two constructions of public-key encryption schemes that employ a collection of trapdoor permutations, as defined in Definition C.3. Let $\{f_i : D_i \to D_i\}_i$ be such a collection, and let b be a corresponding hard-core predicate. In the first scheme, the key-generation algorithm consists of selecting a permutation f_i along with a corresponding trapdoor t, and outputting (i, t) as the key-pair. To encrypt a (*single*) bit σ (using the encryption-key i), the encryption algorithm uniformly selects $r \in D_i$, and produces the ciphertext $(f_i(r), \sigma \oplus b(r))$. To decrypt the ciphertext (y, τ) (using the decryption-key t), the decryption algorithm computes $\tau \oplus b(f_i^{-1}(y))$ (using the trapdoor t of f_i). Clearly, $(\sigma \oplus b(r)) \oplus b(f_i^{-1}(f_i(r))) = \sigma$. Indistinguishability of encryptions is implied by the hypothesis that b is a hard-core of f_i. We comment that this scheme is quite wasteful in bandwidth; nevertheless, the paradigm underlying its construction (i.e., applying the trapdoor permutation to a randomized version of the plaintext rather than to the actual plaintext) is valuable in practice.

A more efficient construction of a public-key encryption scheme, which uses the same key-generation algorithm, follows. To encrypt an ℓ-bit long string x (using the encryption-key i), the encryption algorithm uniformly selects $r \in D_i$, computes $y \leftarrow b(r) \cdot b(f_i(r)) \cdots b(f_i^{\ell-1}(r))$ and produces the ciphertext $(f_i^{\ell}(r), x \oplus y)$. To decrypt the ciphertext (u, v) (using the decryption-key t), the decryption algorithm first recovers $r = f_i^{-\ell}(u)$ (using the trapdoor t of f_i), and then obtains $v \oplus b(r) \cdot b(f_i(r)) \cdots b(f_i^{\ell-1}(r))$. Note the similarity to the Blum-Micali Construction (depicted in Eq. (8.10)), and the fact that the proof of the pseudorandomness of Eq. (8.10) can be extended to establish the computational indistinguishability of $(b(r) \cdots b(f_i^{\ell-1}(r)), f_i^{\ell}(r))$ and $(r', f_i^{\ell}(r))$, for random and independent $r \in D_i$ and $r' \in \{0, 1\}^{\ell}$. Indistinguishability of encryptions follows, and thus the second scheme is secure. We mention that, assuming the intractability of factoring integers, this scheme has a concrete implementation with efficiency comparable to that of RSA.

C.5.3. Beyond Eavesdropping Security

Our treatment so far has referred only to a "passive" attack in which the adversary merely eavesdrops the line over which ciphertexts are sent. Stronger types of attacks (i.e., "active" ones), culminating in the so-called chosen ciphertext attack, may be possible in various applications. Specifically, in some settings it is feasible for the adversary to make the sender encrypt a message of the adversary's choice, and in some settings the adversary may even make the receiver decrypt a ciphertext of the adversary's choice. This gives rise to *chosen plaintext attacks* and to *chosen ciphertext attacks*, respectively, which are not covered by the security definitions considered in Sections C.5.1 and C.5.2. Here, we briefly discuss such "active" attacks, focusing on chosen ciphertext attacks (of the strongest type, known as "a posteriori" or "CCA2").

Loosely speaking, in a chosen ciphertext attack, the adversary may obtain the decryptions of ciphertexts of its choice, and is deemed successful if it learns something regarding the plaintext that corresponds to some different ciphertext (see [92, Sec. 5.4.4]). That is, the adversary is given oracle access to the decryption function corresponding to the decryption-key in use (and, in the case of private-key schemes, it is also given oracle access to the corresponding encryption function). The adversary is allowed to query the decryption oracle on any ciphertext except for the "test ciphertext" (i.e., the very ciphertext for which it tries to learn something about the corresponding plaintext). It may also make queries that do not correspond to legitimate ciphertexts, and the answer will be accordingly (i.e., a special "failure" symbol). Furthermore, the adversary may affect the selection of the test ciphertext (by specifying a distribution from which the corresponding plaintext is to be drawn).

Private-key and public-key encryption schemes secure against chosen ciphertext attacks can be constructed under (almost) the same assumptions that suffice for the construction of the corresponding passive schemes. Specifically:

Theorem C.13: *Assuming the existence of* one-way functions, *there exist* private-key *encryption schemes that are secure against chosen ciphertext attack.*

Theorem C.14: *Assuming the existence of* enhanced[15] *trapdoor permutations, there exist* public-key *encryption schemes that are secure against chosen ciphertext attack.*

Both theorems are proved by constructing encryption schemes in which the adversary's gain from a chosen ciphertext attack is eliminated by making it infeasible (for the adversary) to obtain any useful knowledge via such an attack. In the case of private-key schemes (i.e., Theorem C.13), this is achieved by making it infeasible (for the adversary) to produce legitimate ciphertexts (other than those explicitly given to it, in response to its request to encrypt plaintexts of its choice). This, in turn, is achieved by augmenting the ciphertext with an "authentication tag" that is hard to generate without knowledge of the encryption-key; that is, we use a message-authentication scheme (as defined in Section C.6). In the case of public-key schemes (i.e., Theorem C.14), the adversary can certainly generate ciphertexts by itself, and the aim is to make it infeasible (for the adversary) to produce legitimate ciphertexts without "knowing" the corresponding plaintext. This, in turn, will be achieved by augmenting the plaintext with a non-interactive zero-knowledge "proof of knowledge" of the corresponding plaintext.

Security against chosen ciphertext attack is related to the notion of *non-malleability* of the encryption scheme. Loosely speaking, in a non-malleable encryption scheme it is

---

[15]Loosely speaking, the enhancement refers to the hardness condition of Definition C.2, and requires that it be hard to recover $f_i^{-1}(y)$ also when given the coins used to sample y (rather than merely y itself). See [92, Apdx. C.1].

infeasible for an adversary, given a ciphertext, to produce a valid ciphertext for a related plaintext (e.g., given a ciphertext of a plaintext $1x$, for an unknown x, it is infeasible to produce a ciphertext to the plaintext $0x$). For further discussion, see [92, Sec. 5.4.5].

C.6. Signatures and Message Authentication

Both signature schemes and message authentication schemes are methods for "validating" data, that is, verifying that the data were approved by a certain party (or set of parties). The difference between signature schemes and message authentication schemes is that signatures should be universally verifiable, whereas authentication tags are only required to be verifiable by parties that are also able to generate them.

Signature schemes: The need to discuss "digital signatures" (cf. [66, 182]) has arisen with the introduction of computer communication to the business environment (in which parties need to commit themselves to proposals and/or declarations that they make). Discussions of "unforgeable signatures" did take place also prior to the computer age, but the objects of discussion were handwritten signatures (and not digital ones), and the discussion was not perceived as related to cryptography. Loosely speaking, a scheme for unforgeable signatures should satisfy the following requirements:

- each user can *efficiently produce its own signature* on documents of its choice;
- every user can *efficiently verify* whether a given string is a signature of another (specific) user on a specific document; but
- *it is infeasible to produce signatures of other users* to documents they did not sign.

We note that the formulation of unforgeable digital signatures also provides a clear statement of the essential ingredients of handwritten signatures. The ingredients are each person's ability to sign for him/herself, a universally agreed-upon verification procedure, and the belief (or assertion) that it is infeasible (or at least hard) to forge signatures (i.e., produce some other person's signatures to documents that were not signed by him/her such that these "unauthentic" signatures are accepted by the verification procedure).

Message authentication schemes. Message authentication is a task related to the setting considered for encryption schemes, that is, communication over an insecure channel. This time, we consider an active adversary that is monitoring the channel and may alter the messages sent over it. The parties communicating through this insecure channel wish to authenticate the messages they send such that their counterpart can tell an original message (sent by the sender) from a modified one (i.e., modified by the adversary). Loosely speaking, a scheme for message authentication should satisfy the following requirements:

- each of the communicating parties can *efficiently produce an authentication tag* to any message of its choice;
- each of the communicating parties can *efficiently verify* whether a given string is an authentication tag of a given message; but
- *it is infeasible for an external adversary* (i.e., a party other than the communicating parties) *to produce authentication tags* to messages not sent by the communicating parties.

Note that, in contrast to the specification of signature schemes, we do not require universal verification: Only the designated receiver is required to be able to verify the authentication tags. Furthermore, we do not require that the receiver cannot produce authentication tags by itself (i.e., we only require that *external parties* can not do so). Thus, message authentication schemes cannot convince *a third party* that the sender has indeed sent the information (rather than the receiver having generated it by itself). In contrast, signatures can be used to convince third parties: In fact, a signature to a document is typically sent to a second party so that in the future this party may (by merely presenting the signed document) convince third parties that the document was indeed generated (or rather approved) by the signer.

C.6.1. Definitions

Both signature schemes and message authentication schemes consist of three efficient algorithms: key generation, signing, and verification. As in the case of encryption schemes, the key-generation algorithm, denoted G, is used to generate a pair of corresponding keys; one is used for signing (via algorithm S) and the other is used for verification (via algorithm V). That is, $S_s(\alpha)$ denotes a signature produced by algorithm S on input a signing-key s and a document α, whereas $V_v(\alpha, \beta)$ denotes the verdict of the verification algorithm V regarding the document α and the alleged signature β relative to the verification-key v. Needless to say, for any pair of keys (s, v) generated by G and for every α, it holds that $V_v(\alpha, S_s(\alpha)) = 1$.

The difference between the two types of schemes is reflected in the definition of security. In the case of *signature schemes*, the adversary is given the verification-key, whereas in the case of *message authentication schemes*, the verification-key (which may equal the signing-key) is not given to the adversary. Thus, schemes for message authentication can be viewed as a private-key version of signature schemes. This difference yields different functionalities (even more than in the case of encryption): In a typical use of a signature scheme, each user generates a pair of signing- and verification-keys, publicizes the verification-key and keeps the signing-key secret. Subsequently, each user may sign documents using its own signing-key, and these signatures are *universally verifiable* with respect to its public verification-key. In contrast, message authentication schemes are typically used to authenticate information sent among a set of *mutually trusting* parties that agree on a secret key, which is being used both to produce and to verify authentication-tags. (Indeed, it is assumed that the mutually trusting parties have generated the key together or have exchanged the key in a secure way, prior to the communication of information that needs to be authenticated.)

We focus on the definition of secure signature schemes, and consider very powerful attacks on the signature scheme as well as a very liberal notion of breaking it. Specifically, the attacker is allowed to obtain signatures to any message of its choice. One may argue that in many applications, such a general attack is not possible (because messages to be signed must have a specific format). Yet, our view is that it is impossible to define a general (i.e., application-independent) notion of admissible messages, and thus a general/robust definition of an attack seems to have to be formulated as suggested here. (Note that at worst, our approach is overly cautious.) Likewise, the adversary is said to be successful if it can produce a valid signature to *any* message for which it has not asked for a signature during its attack. Again, this means that the ability to form signatures to "nonsensical" messages is also viewed as a breaking of the scheme. Yet, again, we see no way to have a general (i.e., application-independent) notion of "meaningful" messages (such that only forging signatures to them will be considered a breaking of the scheme).

Definition C.15 (secure signature schemes – a sketch): *A chosen message attack is a process that, on input a verification-key, can obtain signatures (relative to the corresponding signing-key) to messages of its choice. Such an attack is said to succeed (in existential forgery) if it outputs a valid signature to a message for which it has not requested a signature during the attack. A signature scheme is secure (or unforgeable) if every feasible chosen message attack succeeds with at most negligible probability, where the probability is taken over the initial choice of the key-pair as well as over the adversary's actions.*

One popular suggestion is signing messages by applying the inverse of a trapdoor permutation, where the trapdoor is used as a signing-key and the permutation itself is used (in the forward direction) toward verification. We warn that, in general, this scheme does not satisfy Definition C.15 (e.g., the permutation may be a homomorphism of some group).

C.6.2. Constructions

Secure *message authentication schemes* can be constructed using pseudorandom functions (or rather the generalized notion of pseudorandom functions discussed at the end of Section C.3.3). Specifically, the key-generation algorithm consists of uniformly selecting a seed $s \in \{0, 1\}^n$ for such a function, denoted $f_s : \{0, 1\}^* \to \{0, 1\}^n$, and the (only valid) tag of message x with respect to the key s is $f_s(x)$. As in the case of our private-key encryption scheme, the proof of security of the current message authentication scheme consists of two steps:

1. Proving that an idealized version of the scheme, in which one uses a uniformly selected function $F : \{0, 1\}^* \to \{0, 1\}^n$, rather than the pseudorandom function f_s, is secure (i.e., unforgeable).
2. Concluding that the real scheme is secure (because otherwise one could distinguish a pseudorandom function from a truly random one).

Note that this message authentication scheme makes an "extensive use of pseudorandom functions" (i.e., the pseudorandom function is applied directly to the message, which may be rather long). More efficient schemes can be constructed either based on a more restricted use of a pseudorandom function or based on other cryptographic primitives.

Constructing secure *signature schemes* seems more difficult than constructing message authentication schemes. Nevertheless, secure signature schemes can be constructed based on the same assumptions.

Theorem C.16: *The following three conditions are equivalent:*

1. *One-way functions exist.*
2. *Secure signature schemes exist.*
3. *Secure message authentication schemes exist.*

We stress that, unlike in the case of public-key encryption schemes, the construction of signature schemes (which may be viewed as a public-key analogue of message authentication) does not require a trapdoor property. Three central paradigms used in the construction of secure *signature schemes* are the "refreshing" of the "effective" signing-key, the usage of an "authentication tree," and the "hashing paradigm" (all to be discussed in the sequel). In addition to being used in the proof of Theorem C.16, these three paradigms are of independent interest.

The refreshing paradigm. Introduced in [110], the *refreshing paradigm* is aimed at limiting the potential dangers of chosen message attacks. This is achieved by signing the actual document using a newly (and randomly) generated instance of the signature scheme, and authenticating (the verification-key of) this random instance with respect to the fixed and public verification-key.[16] Intuitively, the gain in terms of security is that a full-fledged chosen message attack cannot be launched on a fixed instance of the underlying signature schemes (i.e., on the fixed verification-key that was published by the user and is known to the attacker). All that an attacker may obtain (via a chosen message attack on the new scheme) is signatures, relative to the original signing-key (which is coupled with the fixed and public verification-key), to random strings (or rather random verification-keys) as well as additional signatures that are each relative to a random and independently distributed signing-key (which is coupled with a freshly generated verification-key).

Authentication trees. The security benefits of the refreshing paradigm are amplified when combining it with the use of *authentication trees*. The idea is to use the public verification-key (only) for authenticating several (e.g., two) fresh instances of the signature scheme, use each of these instances for authenticating several additional fresh instances, and so on. Thus, we obtain a tree of fresh instances of the basic signature scheme, where each internal node authenticates its children. We can now use the leaves of this tree for signing actual documents, where each leaf is used at most once. Thus, a signature to an actual document consists of

1. a signature to this document authenticated with respect to the verification-key associated with some leaf, and
2. a sequence of verification-keys associated with the nodes along the path from the root to this leaf, where each such verification-key is authenticated with respect to the verification-key of its parent.

We stress that the same signature, relative to the key of the parent node, is used for authenticating the verification-keys of all its children. Thus, each instance of the signature scheme is used for signing at most one string (i.e., a single sequence of verification-keys if the instance resides in an internal node, and an actual document if the instance resides in a leaf).[17] Hence, it suffices to use a signature scheme that is secure as long as it is applied for legitimately signing a *single* string. Such signature schemes, called

---

[16]That is, consider a basic signature scheme (G, S, V) used as follows. Suppose that the user U has generated a key-pair $(s, v) \leftarrow G(1^n)$, and has placed the verification-key v on a public-file. When a party asks U to sign some document α, the user U generates a new ("fresh") key-pair $(s', v') \leftarrow G(1^n)$, signs v' using the original signing-key s, signs α using the new signing-key s', and presents $(S_s(v'), v', S_{s'}(\alpha))$ as a signature to α. An alleged signature, (β_1, v', β_2), is verified by checking whether both $V_v(v', \beta_1) = 1$ and $V_{v'}(\alpha, \beta_2) = 1$ hold.

[17]A naive implementation of the foregoing (full-fledged) signature scheme calls for storing in (secure) memory all the instances of the basic (one-time) signature scheme that are generated throughout the entire signing process (which refers to numerous documents). However, we note that it suffices to be able to reconstruct the random coins used for generating each of these instances, and the former can be determined by a pseudorandom function (applied

one-time signature schemes, are easier to construct than standard signature schemes, especially if one only wishes to sign strings that are significantly shorter than the signing-key (resp., than the verification-key). For example, using a one-way function f, we may let the signing-key consists of a sequence of n pairs of strings, let the corresponding verification-key consist of the corresponding sequence of images of f, and sign an n-bit long message by revealing the adequate preimages. (That is, the signing-key consists of a sequence $((s_1^0, s_1^1), \ldots, (s_n^0, s_n^1)) \in \{0, 1\}^{2n^2}$, the corresponding verification-key is $((f(s_1^0), f(s_1^1)), \ldots, (f(s_n^0), f(s_n^1)))$, and the signature of the message $\sigma_1 \cdots \sigma_n$ is $(s_1^{\sigma_1}, \ldots, s_n^{\sigma_n})$.)

The hashing paradigm. Note, however, that in the foregoing authentication-tree, the instances of the signature scheme (associated with internal nodes) are used for signing a pair of verification-keys. Thus, we need a one-time signature scheme that can be used for signing messages that are longer than the verification-key. In order to bridge the gap between (one-time) signature schemes that are applicable for signing short messages and schemes that are applicable for signing long messages, we use the *hashing paradigm*. This paradigm refers to the common practice of signing documents via a two-stage process: First, the actual document is hashed to a (relatively) short string, and next, the basic signature scheme is applied to the resulting string. This practice is sound provided that the hashing function belongs to a family of *collision-resistant hashing* (aka *collision-free hashing*) functions. Loosely speaking, the collision-resistant requirement means that, given a hash function that is randomly selected in such a family, it is infeasible to find two different strings that are hashed by this function to the same value. We also refer the interested reader to a variant of the *hashing paradigm* that uses the seemingly weaker notion of a family of *universal one-way hash functions* (see [171] or [92, Sec. 6.4.3]).

C.7. General Cryptographic Protocols

The design of secure protocols that implement arbitrary desired functionalities is a major part of modern cryptography. Taking the opposite perspective, the design of any cryptographic scheme may be viewed as the design of a secure protocol for implementing a corresponding functionality. Still, we believe that it makes sense to differentiate between basic cryptographic primitives (which involve little interaction) like encryption and signature schemes, on the one hand, and general cryptographic protocols, on the other hand.

In this section, we survey *general* results concerning secure *multi*-party computations, where the *two*-party case is an important special case. In a nutshell, these results assert that one can construct protocols for securely computing *any* desirable multi-party functionality. Indeed, what is striking about these results is their generality, and we believe that the wonder is not diminished by the (various alternative) conditions under which these results hold.

A general framework for casting (m-party) cryptographic (protocol) problems consists of specifying a random process[18] that maps m inputs to m outputs. The inputs to the

---

to the name of the corresponding vertex in the tree). Indeed, the seed of this pseudorandom function will be part of the signing-key of the resulting (full-fledged) signature scheme.

[18]That is, we consider the secure evaluation of randomized functionalities, rather than "only" the secure evaluation of functions. Specifically, we consider an arbitrary (randomized) process F that on input $(x_1, \ldots, x_m)$, first selects

process are to be thought of as the local inputs of m parties, and the m outputs are their corresponding local outputs. The random process describes the desired functionality. That is, if the m parties were to trust each other (or trust some external party), then they could each send their local input to the trusted party, who would compute the outcome of the process and send to each party the corresponding output. A pivotal question in the area of cryptographic protocols is to what extent this (imaginary) trusted party can be "emulated" by the mutually distrustful parties themselves.

The results surveyed in this section describe a variety of models in which such an "emulation" is possible. The models vary by the underlying assumptions regarding the communication channels, numerous parameters governing the extent of adversarial behavior, and the desired level of emulation of the trusted party (i.e., level of "security"). Our treatment refers to the security of stand-alone executions. The preservation of security in an environment in which many executions of many protocols are attacked is beyond the scope of this section, and the interested reader is referred to [92, Sec. 7.7.2].

C.7.1. The Definitional Approach and Some Models

Before describing the aforementioned results, we further discuss the notion of "emulating a trusted party," which underlies the definitional approach to secure multi-party computation. This approach follows the simulation paradigm (cf. Section C.4.1), which deems a scheme to be secure if whatever a feasible adversary can obtain after attacking it is also feasibly attainable by a benign behavior. In the general setting of multi-party computation, we compare the effect of adversaries that participate in the execution of the actual protocol to the effect of adversaries that participate in an imaginary execution of a trivial (ideal) protocol for computing the desired functionality with the help of a trusted party. If whatever the adversaries can feasibly obtain in the real setting can also be feasibly obtained in the ideal setting, then the actual protocol "emulates the ideal setting" (i.e., "emulates a trusted party"), and thus is deemed secure. This approach can be applied in a variety of models, and is used to define the goals of security in these models.[19] We first discuss some of the parameters used in defining various models, and next demonstrate the application of the foregoing approach in two important cases. For further details, see [92, Sec. 7.2 and 7.5.1].

C.7.1.1. Some Parameters Used in Defining Security Models
The following parameters are described in terms of the actual (or real) computation. In *some cases*, the corresponding definition of security is obtained by imposing some

---

at random (depending only on $\ell \stackrel{\text{def}}{=} \sum_{i=1}^{m} |x_i|$) an m-ary function f, and then outputs the m-tuple $f(x_1, \ldots, x_m) = (f_1(x_1, \ldots, x_m), \ldots, f_m(x_1, \ldots, x_m))$. In other words, $F(x_1, \ldots, x_m) = F'(r, x_1, \ldots, x_m)$, where r is uniformly selected in $\{0, 1\}^{\ell'}$ (with $\ell' = \text{poly}(\ell)$), and F' is a function mapping $(m + 1)$-long sequences to m-long sequences.

[19]A few technical comments are in place. Firstly, we assume that the inputs of all parties are of the same length. We comment that as long as the lengths of the inputs are polynomially related, the foregoing convention can be enforced by padding. On the other hand, some length restriction is essential for the security results, because in general it is impossible to hide all information regarding the length of the inputs to a protocol. Secondly, we assume that the desired functionality is computable in probabilistic polynomial time, because we wish the secure protocol to run in probabilistic polynomial time (and a protocol cannot be more efficient than the corresponding centralized algorithm). Clearly, the results can be extended to functionalities that are computable within any given (time-constructible) time bound, using adequate padding.

restrictions or provisions on the ideal model.[20] In *all cases*, the desired notion of security is defined by requiring that for any adequate adversary in the real model, there exists a corresponding adversary in the corresponding ideal model that obtains essentially the same impact (as the real-model adversary).

The communication channels. Most works in cryptography assume that communication is *synchronous* and that point-to-point channels exist between every pair of processors (i.e., a *complete network*). It is further assumed that the adversary cannot modify (or omit or insert) messages sent over any communication channel that connects honest parties. In the *standard model*, the adversary may tap all communication channels, and thus obtain any message sent between honest parties. In an alternative model, called the private-channel model, one *postulates* that the adversary cannot obtain messages sent between any pair of honest parties. Indeed, in some cases, the private-channel model can be emulated by the standard model (e.g., by using a secure encryption scheme).

Setup assumptions. Unless stated differently, no setup assumptions are made (except for the obvious assumption that all parties have identical copies of the protocol's program).

Computational limitations. Typically, the focus is on computationally bounded adversaries (e.g., probabilistic polynomial-time adversaries). However, the private-channel model allows for the (meaningful) consideration of computationally unbounded adversaries.[21]

Restricted adversarial behavior. The parameters of the model include questions like whether the adversary is "active" or "passive" (i.e., whether a dishonest party takes active steps to disrupt the execution of the protocol or merely gathers information) and whether or not the adversary is "adaptive" (i.e., whether the set of dishonest parties is fixed before the execution starts or is adaptively chosen by an adversary during the execution).

Restricted notions of security. One important example is the willingness to tolerate "unfair" protocols in which the execution can be suspended (at any time) by a dishonest party, provided that it is detected doing so. We stress that in case the execution is suspended, the dishonest party does not obtain more information than it could have obtained when not suspending the execution. (What may happen is that the honest parties will not obtain their desired outputs, but will detect that the execution was suspended.) We stress that

---

[20]For example, in the case of two-party computation (see §C.7.1.3), secure computation is possible only if premature termination is *not* considered a breach of security. In that case, the suitable security definition is obtained (via the simulation paradigm) by allowing (an analogue of) premature termination in the ideal model.

[21]We stress that, also in the case of computationally unbounded adversaries, security should be defined by requiring that, for every real adversary, whatever the adversary can compute after participating in the execution of the actual protocol is computable *within comparable time* by an imaginary adversary participating in an imaginary execution of the trivial ideal protocol (for computing the desired functionality with the help of a trusted party). That is, although no computational restrictions are made on the real-model adversary, it is required that the ideal-model adversary that obtains the same impact does so within comparable time (i.e., within time that is polynomially related to the running time of the real-model adversary being simulated).

the motivation for this restricted model is the impossibility of obtaining general secure two-party computation in the unrestricted model.

Upper bounds on the number of dishonest parties. These are assumed in some models, when required. For example, in some models, secure multi-party computation is possible only if a majority of the parties is honest.

C.7.1.2. Example: Multi-party Protocols with Honest Majority

Here, we consider an active, non-adaptive, and computationally bounded adversary, and do not assume the existence of private channels. Our aim is to define multi-party protocols that remain secure provided that the honest parties are in the majority. (The reason for requiring an honest majority will be discussed at the end of this subsection.)

We first observe that in any multi-party protocol, each party may change its local input before even entering the execution of the protocol. However, this is also unavoidable when the parties utilize a trusted party. Consequently, such an effect of the adversary on the real execution (i.e., modification of its own input prior to entering the actual execution) is not considered a breach of security. In general, whatever cannot be avoided when the parties utilize a trusted party is not considered a breach of security. We wish secure protocols (in the real model) to suffer only from whatever is also unavoidable when the parties utilize a trusted party. Thus, the basic paradigm underlying the definitions of *secure multi-party computations* amounts to requiring that the only situations that may occur in the real execution of a secure protocol are those that can also occur in a corresponding ideal model (where the parties may employ a trusted party). In other words, the "effective malfunctioning" of parties in secure protocols is restricted to what is postulated in the corresponding ideal model.

In light of the foregoing, we start by defining an ideal model (or rather the misbehavior allowed in it). Since we are interested in executions in which the majority of parties are honest, we consider an ideal model in which any minority group (of the parties) may collude as follows:

1. First, the members of this dishonest minority share their original inputs and decide together on replaced inputs to be sent to the trusted party. (The other parties send their respective original inputs to the trusted party.)
2. Upon receiving inputs from all parties, the trusted party determines the corresponding outputs and sends them to the corresponding parties. (We stress that the information sent between the honest parties and the trusted party is not seen by the dishonest colluding minority.)
3. Upon receiving the output-message from the trusted party, each honest party outputs it locally, whereas the members of the dishonest minority share the output-messages and determine their local outputs based on all they know (i.e., their initial inputs and their received output-messages).

A *secure multi-party computation with honest majority* is required to emulate this ideal model. That is, the effect of any feasible adversary that controls a minority of the parties in a real execution of such a (real) protocol can be essentially simulated by a (different) feasible adversary that controls the corresponding parties in the ideal model.

Definition C.17 (secure protocols – a sketch): *Let f be an m-ary functionality and Π be an m-party protocol operating in the real model.*

- *For a real-model adversary A, controlling some minority of the parties* (and tapping all communication channels), *and an m-sequence* $\bar{x}$, *we denote by* REAL$_{\Pi,A}(\bar{x})$ *the sequence of m outputs resulting from the execution of* Π *on input* $\bar{x}$ *under the attack of the adversary A.*
- *For an ideal-model adversary A', controlling some minority of the parties, and an m-sequence* $\bar{x}$, *we denote by* IDEAL$_{f,A'}(\bar{x})$ *the sequence of m outputs resulting from the foregoing three-step ideal process, when applied to input* $\bar{x}$ *under the attack of the adversary A' and when the trusted party employs the functionality f.*

We say that Π securely implements f with honest majority *if for every feasible real-model adversary A, controlling some minority of the parties, there exists a feasible ideal-model adversary A', controlling the same parties, such that the probability ensembles* {REAL$_{\Pi,A}(\bar{x})$}$_{\bar{x}}$ *and* {IDEAL$_{f,A'}(\bar{x})$}$_{\bar{x}}$ *are computationally indistinguishable (as in Definition C.5).*

Thus, security means that the effect of each minority group in a real execution of a secure protocol is "essentially restricted" to replacing its own local inputs (independently of the local inputs of the majority parties) before the protocol starts, and replacing its own local outputs (depending only on its local inputs and outputs) after the protocol terminates. (We stress that in the real execution the minority parties do obtain additional pieces of information; yet in a secure protocol they gain nothing from these additional pieces of information, because they can actually reproduce those by themselves.)

The fact that Definition C.17 refers to a model without private channels is reflected in the fact that our (sketchy) definition of the real-model adversary allowed it to tap all channels, which in turn effects the set of possible ensembles {REAL$_{\Pi,A}(\bar{x})$}$_{\bar{x}}$. When defining security in the private-channel model, the real-model adversary is not allowed to tap channels between honest parties, and this again effects the possible ensembles {REAL$_{\Pi,A}(\bar{x})$}$_{\bar{x}}$. On the other hand, when defining security with respect to passive adversaries, both the scope of the real-model adversaries and the scope of the ideal-model adversaries change. In the real-model execution, all parties follow the protocol but the adversary may alter the output of the dishonest parties arbitrarily depending on their intermediate internal states during the entire execution. In the corresponding ideal-model, the adversary is not allowed to modify the *inputs* of dishonest parties (in Step 1), but is allowed to modify their outputs (in Step 3).

We comment that a definition analogous to Definition C.17 can also be presented in the case that the dishonest parties are not in the minority. In fact, such a definition seems more natural, but the problem is that such a definition cannot be satisfied. That is, most (natural) functionalities do not have protocols for computing them securely in the case that at least half of the parties are dishonest and employ an adequate adversarial strategy. This follows from an impossibility result regarding two-party computation, which essentially asserts that there is no way to prevent a party from prematurely suspending the execution. On the other hand, secure multi-party computation with a dishonest majority is possible if premature suspension of the execution is not considered a breach of security (see §C.7.1.3).

C.7.1.3. Another Example: Two-Party Protocols Allowing Abort
In light of the last paragraph, we now consider multi-party computations in which premature suspension of the execution is not considered a breach of security. For simplicity,

we focus on the special case of two-party computations. (As in §C.7.1.2, we consider a non-adaptive, active, and computationally bounded adversary.)

Intuitively, in any two-party protocol, each party may suspend the execution at any point in time, and furthermore it may do so as soon as it learns the desired output. Thus, if the output of each party depends on the inputs of both parties, then it is always possible for one of the parties to obtain the desired output while preventing the other party from fully determining its own output.[22] The same phenomenon occurs even in the case that the two parties just wish to generate a common random value. In order to account for this phenomenon, when considering active adversaries in the two-party setting, we do not consider such premature suspension of the execution a breach of security. Consequently, we consider an ideal model in which each of the two parties may "shut down" the trusted (third) party at any point in time. In particular, this may happen after the trusted party has supplied the outcome of the computation to one party but before it has supplied the outcome to the other party. Thus, an execution in the corresponding ideal model proceeds as follows:

1. Each party sends its input to the trusted party, where the dishonest party may replace its input or send no input at all (which can be treated as sending a default value).
2. Upon receiving inputs from both parties, the trusted party determines the corresponding pair of outputs, and sends the first output to the first party.
3. If the first party is dishonest, then it may instruct the trusted party to halt; otherwise it always instructs the trusted party to proceed. If instructed to proceed, the trusted party sends the second output to the second party.
4. Upon receiving the output-message from the trusted party, an honest party outputs it locally, whereas a dishonest party may determine its output based on all it knows (i.e., its initial input and its received output).

A secure two-party computation allowing abort is required to emulate this ideal model. That is, as in Definition C.17, security is defined by requiring that for every feasible real-model adversary A, there exists a feasible ideal-model adversary A', controlling the same party, such that the probability ensembles representing the corresponding (real and ideal) executions are computationally indistinguishable. This means that each party's "effective malfunctioning" in a secure protocol is restricted to supplying an initial input of its choice and aborting the computation at any point in time. (Needless to say, the choice of the initial input of each party may *not* depend on the input of the other party.)

We mention that an alternative way of dealing with the problem of premature suspension of execution (i.e., abort) is to restrict the attention to single-output functionalities, that is, functionalities in which only one party is supposed to obtain an output. The definition of secure computation of such functionalities can be made identical to Definition C.17, with the exception that no restriction is made on the set of dishonest parties (and in particular one may consider a single dishonest party in the case of two-party protocols). For further details, see [92, Sec. 7.2.3].

---

[22]In contrast, in the case of an honest majority (cf., §C.7.1.2), the honest party that fails to obtain its output is not alone. It may seek help from the other honest parties, which (being in the majority and) by joining forces can do things that dishonest minorities cannot do: See §C.7.3.2.

C.7.2. Some Known Results

We next list some of the models for which general secure multi-party computation is known to be attainable (i.e., models in which one can construct secure multi-party protocols for computing any desired functionality). We mention that the first results of this type were obtained by Goldreich, Micali, Wigderson, and Yao [100, 241, 101].

In the standard channel model. *Assuming the existence of enhanced[23] trapdoor permutations*, secure multi-party computation is possible in the following three models (cf. [100, 241, 101] and details in [92, Chap. 7]):

1. Passive adversaries, for any number of dishonest parties.
2. Active adversaries that may control only a minority of the parties.
3. Active adversaries, for any number of dishonest parties, provided that suspension of execution is not considered a violation of security (cf. §C.7.1.3).

In all these cases, the adversaries are computationally bounded and non-adaptive. On the other hand, the adversaries may tap the communication lines between honest parties (i.e., we do not assume "private channels" here). The results for active adversaries assume a broadcast channel. Indeed, the latter can be implemented (while tolerating any number of dishonest parties) using a signature scheme and assuming that each party knows (or can reliably obtain) the verification-key corresponding to each of the other parties.

In the private channels model. Making no computational assumptions and allowing computationally unbounded adversaries, but *assuming private channels*, secure multi-party computation is possible in the following two models (cf. [34, 53]):

1. Passive adversaries that may control only a minority of the parties.
2. Active adversaries that may control only less than one-third of the parties.

In both cases the adversaries may be adaptive.

C.7.3. Construction Paradigms and Two Simple Protocols

We briefly sketch a couple of paradigms used in the construction of secure multi-party protocols. We focus on the construction of secure protocols for the model of computationally bounded and non-adaptive adversaries [100, 241, 101]. These constructions proceed in two steps (see details in [92, Chap. 7]): First, a secure protocol is presented for the model of passive adversaries (for any number of dishonest parties), and next, such a protocol is "compiled" into a protocol that is secure in one of the two models of active adversaries (i.e., either in a model allowing the adversary to control only a minority of the parties or in a model in which premature suspension of the execution is not considered a violation of security). These two steps are presented in the following two corresponding subsections, in which we also present two relatively simple protocols for two specific tasks, which in turn are used extensively in the general protocols.

Recall that in the model of passive adversaries, all parties follow the prescribed protocol, but at termination, the adversary may alter the outputs of the dishonest parties depending on their intermediate internal states (during the entire execution). We refer to protocols

---

[23] See footnote 15.

that are secure in the model of passive (resp., active) adversaries by the term passively secure (resp., actively secure).

C.7.3.1. Passively Secure Computation with Shares

For the sake of simplicity, we consider here only the special case of *deterministic m-ary* functionalities (i.e., functions). We assume that the m parties hold a circuit for computing the value of the function on inputs of the adequate length, and that the circuit contains only and- and not-gates. The key idea is having each party "secretly share" its input with everybody else, and having the parties "secretly transform" shares of the input wires of the circuit into shares of the output wires of the circuit, thus obtaining shares of the outputs (which allows for the reconstruction of the actual outputs). The value of each wire in the circuit is shared such that all shares yield the value, whereas lacking even one of the shares keeps the value totally undetermined. That is, we use a simple *secret sharing scheme* such that a bit b is shared by a random sequence of m bits that sum up to b mod 2. First, each party shares each of its input-bits with all parties (by secretly sending each party a random value and setting its own share accordingly). Next, all parties jointly scan the circuit from its input wires to its output wires, processing each gate as follows:

- When encountering a gate, the parties already hold shares of the values of the wires entering the gate, and their aim is to obtain shares of the value of the wires exiting the gate.
- For a not-gate this is easy: The first party just flips the value of its share, and all other parties maintain their shares.
- Since an and-gate corresponds to multiplication modulo 2, the parties need to securely compute the following randomized functionality (where the x_i's denote shares of one entry-wire, the y_i's denote shares of the second entry-wire, the z_i's denote shares of the exit-wire, and the shares indexed by i are held by Party i):

$$((x_1, y_1), \ldots, (x_m, y_m)) \mapsto (z_1, \ldots, z_m), \text{ where} \tag{C.1}$$

$$\sum_{i=1}^{m} z_i = \left(\sum_{i=1}^{m} x_i\right) \cdot \left(\sum_{i=1}^{m} y_i\right) \tag{C.2}$$

That is, the z_i's are random subject to Eq. (C.2).

Finally, the parties send their shares of each circuit-output wire to the designated party, which reconstructs the value of the corresponding bit. Thus, the parties have propagated shares of the circuit-input wires into shares of the circuit-output wires, by repeatedly conducting a passively secure computation of the m-ary functionality of Eq. (C.1) and (C.2). That is, securely evaluating the entire (arbitrary) circuit "reduces" to securely conducting a specific (very simple) multi-party computation. But things get even simpler: The key observation is that

$$\left(\sum_{i=1}^{m} x_i\right) \cdot \left(\sum_{i=1}^{m} y_i\right) = \sum_{i=1}^{m} x_i y_i + \sum_{1 \le i < j \le m} (x_i y_j + x_j y_i). \tag{C.3}$$

Thus, the m-ary functionality of Eq. (C.1) and (C.2) can be computed as follows (where all arithmetic operations are mod 2):

1. Each Party i locally computes $z_{i,i} \overset{\text{def}}{=} x_i y_i$.

2. Next, each pair of parties (i.e., Parties i and j) securely compute random shares of $x_i y_j + y_i x_j$. That is, Parties i and j (holding (x_i, y_i) and (x_j, y_j), respectively), need to securely compute the randomized two-party functionality $((x_i, y_i), (x_j, y_j)) \mapsto (z_{i,j}, z_{j,i})$, where the z's are random subject to $z_{i,j} + z_{j,i} = x_i y_j + y_i x_j$. Equivalently, Party j uniformly selects $z_{j,i} \in \{0, 1\}$, and Parties i and j securely compute the following deterministic functionality

$$((x_i, y_i), (x_j, y_j, z_{j,i})) \mapsto (z_{j,i} + x_i y_j + y_i x_j, \lambda), \tag{C.4}$$

where λ denotes the empty string.

3. Finally, for every $i = 1, \ldots, m$, the sum $\sum_{j=1}^{m} z_{i,j}$ yields the desired share of Party i.

The foregoing construction is analogous to a construction that was outlined in [101]. A detailed description and full proofs appear in [92, Sec. 7.3.4 and 7.5.2].

The foregoing construction "reduces" the passively secure computation of any m-ary functionality to the implementation of the simple 2-ary functionality of Eq. (C.4). The latter can be implemented in a passively secure manner by using a 1-out-of-4 Oblivious Transfer. Loosely speaking, a 1-out-of-k Oblivious Transfer is a protocol enabling one party to obtain one out of k secrets held by another party, without the second party learning which secret was obtained by the first party. That is, it allows a passively secure computation of the two-party functionality

$$(i, (s_1, \ldots, s_k)) \mapsto (s_i, \lambda). \tag{C.5}$$

Note that any function $f : [k] \times \{0, 1\}^* \to \{0, 1\}^* \times \{\lambda\}$ can be computed in a passively secure manner by invoking a 1-out-of-k Oblivious Transfer on inputs i and $(f(1, y), \ldots, f(k, y))$, where i (resp., y) is the initial input of the first (resp., second) party.

A passively secure 1-out-of-k Oblivious Transfer. Using a collection of enhanced trapdoor permutations, $\{f_\alpha : D_\alpha \to D_\alpha\}_{\alpha \in \bar{I}}$ and a corresponding hard-core predicate b, we outline a passively secure implementation of the functionality of Eq. (C.5), when restricted to single-bit secrets.

Inputs: The first party, hereafter called the receiver, has input $i \in \{1, 2, \ldots, k\}$. The second party, called the sender, has input $(\sigma_1, \sigma_2, \ldots, \sigma_k) \in \{0, 1\}^k$.

Step S1: The sender selects at random a permutation f_α along with a corresponding trapdoor, denoted t, and sends the permutation f_α (i.e., its index α) to the receiver.

Step R1: The receiver uniformly and independently selects $x_1, \ldots, x_k \in D_\alpha$, sets $y_i = f_\alpha(x_i)$ and $y_j = x_j$ for every $j \neq i$, and sends $(y_1, y_2, \ldots, y_k)$ to the sender.

Thus, the receiver knows $f_\alpha^{-1}(y_i) = x_i$, but cannot predict $b(f_\alpha^{-1}(y_j))$ for any $j \neq i$. Needless to say, the last assertion presumes that the receiver follows the protocol (i.e., we only consider passive-security).

Step S2: Upon receiving $(y_1, y_2, \ldots, y_k)$, using the inverting-with-trapdoor algorithm and the trapdoor t, the sender computes $z_j = f_\alpha^{-1}(y_j)$, for every $j \in \{1, \ldots, k\}$. It sends the k-tuple $(\sigma_1 \oplus b(z_1), \sigma_2 \oplus b(z_2), \ldots, \sigma_k \oplus b(z_k))$ to the receiver.

Step R2: Upon receiving $(c_1, c_2, \ldots, c_k)$, the receiver locally outputs $c_i \oplus b(x_i)$.

We first observe that this protocol correctly computes 1-out-of-k Oblivious Transfer; that is, the receiver's local output (i.e., $c_i \oplus b(x_i)$) indeed equals $(\sigma_i \oplus b(f_\alpha^{-1}(f_\alpha(x_i)))) \oplus b(x_i) = \sigma_i$. Next, we offer some intuition as to why this protocol constitutes a passively secure implementation of 1-out-of-k Oblivious Transfer. Intuitively, the sender gets no information from the execution because, for any possible value of i, the sender sees the same distribution, specifically, a sequence of k uniformly and independently distributed elements of D_α. (Indeed, the key observation is that applying f_α to a uniformly distributed element of D_α yields a uniformly distributed element of D_α.) As for the receiver, intuitively, it gains no computational knowledge from the execution because, for $j \neq i$, the only information that the receiver has regarding σ_j is the triple $(\alpha, x_j, \sigma_j \oplus b(f_\alpha^{-1}(x_j)))$, where x_j is uniformly distributed in D_α, and from this information it is infeasible to predict σ_j better than by a random guess.[24] (See [92, Sec. 7.3.2] for a detailed proof of security.)

C.7.3.2. From passively Secure Protocols to Actively Secure Ones

We show how to transform any passively secure protocol into a corresponding actively secure protocol. The communication model in both protocols consists of a single broadcast channel. Note that the messages of the original protocol may be assumed to be sent over a broadcast channel, because the adversary may see them anyhow (by tapping the point-to-point channels), and because a broadcast channel is trivially implementable in the case of passive adversaries. As for the resulting actively secure protocol, the broadcast channel it uses can be implemented via an (authenticated) Byzantine Agreement protocol, thus providing an emulation of this model on the standard point-to-point model (in which a broadcast channel does not exist). We mention that authenticated Byzantine Agreement is typically implemented using a signature scheme (and assuming that each party knows the verification-key corresponding to each of the other parties).

Turning to the transformation itself, the main idea (mentioned in §C.4.3.2) is using zero-knowledge proofs in order to force parties to behave in a way that is consistent with the (passively secure) protocol. Actually, we need to confine each party to a unique consistent behavior (i.e., according to some fixed local input and a sequence of coin tosses), and to guarantee that a party cannot fix its input (and/or its coin tosses) in a way that depends on the inputs (and/or coin tosses) of honest parties. Thus, some preliminary steps have to be taken before the step-by-step emulation of the original protocol may start. Specifically, the compiled protocol (which, like the original protocol, is executed over a broadcast channel) proceeds as follows:

1. *Committing to the local input*: Prior to the emulation of the original protocol, each party commits to its input (using a commitment scheme as defined in §C.4.3.1). In addition, using a zero-knowledge proofs-of-knowledge (see Section 9.2.3), each party also proves that it knows its own input; that is, it proves that it can decommit to the commitment it sent. (These zero-knowledge proofs-of-knowledge prevent dishonest parties from setting their inputs in a way that depends on inputs of honest parties.)
2. *Generation of local random-tapes*: Next, all parties jointly generate a sequence of random bits for each party such that only this party knows the outcome of the random sequence generated for it, and everybody else gets a commitment to this outcome. These sequences will be used as the random-inputs (i.e., sequence of coin tosses)

---

[24]The latter intuition presumes that sampling D_α is trivial (i.e., that there is an easily computable correspondence between the coins used for sampling and the resulting sample), whereas in general the coins used for sampling may be hard to compute from the corresponding outcome. This is the reason that an enhanced hardness assumption is used in the general analysis of the foregoing protocol.

for the original protocol. Each bit in the random sequence generated for Party X is determined as the exclusive-or of the outcomes of instances of an (augmented) coin-tossing protocol (cf. [92, Sec. 7.4.3.5]) that Party X plays with each of the other parties. The latter protocol provides the other parties with a commitment to the outcome obtained by Party X.

3. *Effective prevention of premature termination*: In addition, when compiling (the passively secure protocol to an actively secure protocol) *for the model that allows the adversary to control only a minority of the parties*, each party shares its input and its random-input with all other parties using a "Verifiable Secret Sharing" (VSS) protocol (cf. [92, Sec. 7.5.5.1]). Loosely speaking, a VSS protocol allows for sharing a secret in a way that enables each participant to verify that the share it got fits the publicly posted information, which includes commitments to all shares, where a sufficient number of the latter allow for the efficient recovery of the secret. The use of VSS guarantees that if Party X prematurely suspends the execution, then the honest parties can together reconstruct all Party X's secrets and carry on the execution while playing its role. This step effectively prevents premature termination, and is not needed in a model that does not consider premature termination a breach of security.

4. *Step-by-step emulation of the original protocol*: Once all the foregoing steps are completed, the new protocol emulates the steps of the original protocol. In each step, each party augments the message determined by the original protocol with a zero-knowledge proof that asserts that the message was indeed computed correctly. Recall that the next message (as determined by the original protocol) is a function of the sender's own input, its random-input, and the messages it has received so far (where the latter are known to everybody because they were sent over a broadcast channel). Furthermore, the sender's input is determined by its commitment (as sent in Step 1), and its random-input is similarly determined (in Step 2). Thus, the next message (as determined by the original protocol) is a function of publicly known strings (i.e., the said commitments as well as the other messages sent over the broadcast channel). Moreover, the assertion that the next message was indeed computed correctly is an NP-assertion, and the sender knows a corresponding NP-witness (i.e., its own input and random-input as well as the corresponding decommitment information). Thus, the sender can prove in zero-knowledge (to each of the other parties) that the message it is sending was indeed computed according to the original protocol.

The foregoing compilation was first outlined in [100, 101]. A detailed description and full proofs appear in [92, Sec. 7.4 and 7.5].

A secure coin-tossing protocol. Using a commitment scheme, we outline a secure (ordinary, as opposed to augmented) coin-tossing protocol.

Step C1: Party 1 uniformly selects $\sigma \in \{0, 1\}$ and sends Party 2 a commitment, denoted c, to σ.

Step C2: Party 2 uniformly selects $\sigma' \in \{0, 1\}$, and sends σ' to Party 1.

Step C3: Party 1 outputs the value $\sigma \oplus \sigma'$, and sends σ along with the decommitment information, denoted d, to Party 2.

Step C4: Party 2 checks whether or not (σ, d) fits the commitment c it has obtained in Step 1. It outputs $\sigma \oplus \sigma'$ if the check is satisfied and halts with output $\perp$ otherwise, where $\perp$ indicates that Party 1 has effectively aborted the protocol prematurely.

Intuitively, Steps C1–C2 may be viewed as "tossing a coin into the well." At this point (i.e., after Step C2), the value of the coin is determined (essentially as a random value), but only one party (i.e., Party 1) "can see" (i.e., knows) this value. Clearly, if both parties are honest, then they both output the same uniformly chosen bit, recovered in Steps C3 and C4, respectively. Intuitively, each party can guarantee that the outcome is uniformly distributed, and Party 1 can cause premature termination by improper execution of Step 3. Formally, we have to show how the effect of any real-model adversary can be simulated by an adequate ideal-model adversary (which is allowed premature termination). This is done in [92, Sec. 7.4.3.1].

C.7.4. Concluding Remarks

In Sections C.7.1–C.7.2 we have mentioned numerous definitions and results regarding secure multi-party protocols, where some of these definitions are incomparable to others (i.e., they neither imply the others nor are implied by them). For example, in §C.7.1.2 and §C.7.1.3, we have presented two alternative definitions of "secure multi-party proto-cols," one requiring an honest majority and the other allowing abort. These definitions are incomparable and there is no generic reason to prefer one over the other. Actually, as mentioned in §C.7.1.2, one could formulate a natural definition that implies both definitions (i.e., waiving the bound on the number of dishonest parties in Definition C.17). Indeed, the resulting definition is free of the annoying restrictions that were introduced in each of the two aforementioned definitions; the "only" problem with the resulting definition is that it cannot be satisfied (in general). Thus, for the first time in this appendix, we have reached a situation in which a natural (and general) definition cannot be satisfied, and we are forced to choose between two weaker alternatives, where each of these alternatives carries fundamental disadvantages.

In general, Section C.7 carries a stronger flavor of compromise (i.e., recognizing inherent limitations and settling for a restricted meaningful goal) than previous sections. In contrast to the impression given in other parts of this appendix, it turns out that we cannot get all that we may want (and this is without mentioning the problems involved in preserving security under concurrent composition; cf. [92, Sec. 7.7.2]). Instead, we should study the alternatives, and go for the one that best suits our real needs.

Indeed, as stated in Section C.1, the fact that we can define a cryptographic goal does not mean that we can satisfy it as defined. In case we cannot satisfy the initial definition, we should search for relaxations that can be satisfied. These relaxations should be defined in a clear manner such that it would be obvious what they achieve (and what they fail to achieve). Doing so will allow a sound choice of the relaxation to be used in a specific application.

Probabilistic Preliminaries and Advanced Topics in Randomization

What is this? Chicken Curry and Seafood Salad?
Fine, but in the same plate? This is disgusting!
Johan Håstad at Grendel's, Cambridge (1985)

Summary: This appendix lumps together some preliminaries regarding probability theory and some advanced topics related to the role and use of randomness in computation. Needless to say, each of these topics appears in a separate section.

The probabilistic preliminaries include our conventions regarding random variables, which are used throughout the book. Also included are overviews of three useful probabilistic inequalities: Markov's Inequality, Chebyshev's Inequality, and the Chernoff Bound.

The advanced topics include hashing, sampling, and randomness extraction. For hashing, we describe constructions of pairwise (and t-wise independent) hashing functions and (a few variants of) the Leftover Hashing Lemma (used a few times in the main text). We then review the "complexity of sampling": that is, the number of samples and the randomness complexity involved in estimating the average value of an arbitrary function defined over a huge domain. Finally, we provide an overview on the question of extracting almost-perfect randomness from sources of weak (or defected) randomness.

D.1. Probabilistic Preliminaries

Probability plays a central role in Complexity Theory (see, for example, Chapters 6–10). We assume that the reader is familiar with the basic notions of probability theory. In this section, we merely present the probabilistic notations that are used throughout the book and three useful probabilistic inequalities.

D.1.1. Notational Conventions

Throughout the entire book we refer only to *discrete* probability distributions. Specifically, the underlying probability space consists of the set of all strings of a certain length ℓ, taken with uniform probability distribution. That is, the sample space is the set of all ℓ-bit long strings, and each such string is assigned probability measure $2^{-\ell}$. Traditionally, *random variables* are defined as functions from the sample space to the reals. Abusing the traditional terminology, we also use the term random variable when referring to functions mapping the sample space into the set of binary strings. We often do not specify the probability space, but rather talk directly about random variables. For example, we may say that X is a random variable assigned values in the set of all strings such that $\Pr[X = 00] = \frac{1}{4}$ and $\Pr[X = 111] = \frac{3}{4}$. (Such a random variable may be defined over the sample space $\{0, 1\}^2$, so that $X(11) = 00$ and $X(00) = X(01) = X(10) = 111$.) One important case of a random variable is the output of a randomized process (e.g., a probabilistic polynomial-time algorithm, as in Section 6.1).

All our probabilistic statements refer to random variables that are defined beforehand. Typically, we may write $\Pr[f(X) = 1]$, where X is a random variable defined beforehand (and f is a function). An important convention is that *all occurrences of the same symbol in a probabilistic statement refer to the same* (unique) *random variable*. Hence, if $B(\cdot, \cdot)$ is a Boolean expression depending on two variables, and X is a random variable, then $\Pr[B(X, X)]$ denotes the probability that $B(x, x)$ holds when x is chosen with probability $\Pr[X = x]$. For example, for every random variable X, we have $\Pr[X = X] = 1$. We stress that if we wish to discuss the probability that $B(x, y)$ holds when x and y are chosen independently with identical probability distribution, then we will define *two* independent random variables each with the same probability distribution. Hence, if X and Y are two independent random variables, then $\Pr[B(X, Y)]$ denotes the probability that $B(x, y)$ holds when the pair (x, y) is chosen with probability $\Pr[X = x] \cdot \Pr[Y = y]$. For example, for every two independent random variables, X and Y, we have $\Pr[X = Y] = 1$ only if both X and Y are trivial (i.e., assign the entire probability mass to a single string).

Throughout the entire book, U_n denotes a random variable uniformly distributed over the set of all strings of length n. Namely, $\Pr[U_n = \alpha]$ equals 2^{-n} if $\alpha \in \{0, 1\}^n$ and equals 0 otherwise. We often refer to the distribution of U_n as the uniform distribution (neglecting to qualify that it is uniform over $\{0, 1\}^n$). In addition, we occasionally use random variables (arbitrarily) distributed over $\{0, 1\}^n$ or $\{0, 1\}^{\ell(n)}$, for some function $\ell : \mathbb{N} \to \mathbb{N}$. Such random variables are typically denoted by X_n, Y_n, Z_n, and so on. We stress that in some cases X_n is distributed over $\{0, 1\}^n$, whereas in other cases it is distributed over $\{0, 1\}^{\ell(n)}$, for some function ℓ (which is typically a polynomial). We often talk about probability ensembles, which are infinite sequences of random variables $\{X_n\}_{n \in \mathbb{N}}$ such that each X_n ranges over strings of length bounded by a polynomial in n.

Statistical difference. The statistical distance (aka variation distance) between the random variables X and Y is defined as

$$\frac{1}{2} \cdot \sum_{v} |\Pr[X = v] - \Pr[Y = v]| = \max_{S}\{\Pr[X \in S] - \Pr[Y \in S]\}. \quad \text{(D.1)}$$

We say that X is δ-close (resp., δ-far) to Y if the statistical distance between them is at most (resp., at least) δ.

D.1.2. Three Inequalities

The following probabilistic inequalities are very useful. These inequalities refer to random variables that are assigned real values and provide upper bounds on the probability that the random variable deviates from its expectation.

D.1.2.1. Markov's Inequality

The most basic inequality is Markov's Inequality, which applies to any random variable with bounded maximum or minimum value. For simplicity, this inequality is stated for random variables that are lower-bounded by zero, and reads as follows: *Let X be a non-negative random variable and v be a non-negative real number. Then*

$$\Pr[X \geq v] \leq \frac{\mathsf{E}(X)}{v} \tag{D.2}$$

Equivalently, $\Pr[X \geq r \cdot \mathsf{E}(X)] \leq \frac{1}{r}$. The proof amounts to the following sequence:

$$\mathsf{E}(X) = \sum_x \Pr[X = x] \cdot x$$

$$\geq \sum_{x < v} \Pr[X = x] \cdot 0 + \sum_{x \geq v} \Pr[X = x] \cdot v$$

$$= \Pr[X \geq v] \cdot v$$

D.1.2.2. Chebyshev's Inequality

Using Markov's Inequality, one gets a potentially stronger bound on the deviation of a random variable from its expectation. This bound, called Chebyshev's Inequality, is useful when having additional information concerning the random variable (specifically, a good upper bound on its variance). For a random variable X of finite expectation, we denote by $\mathsf{Var}(X) \stackrel{\text{def}}{=} \mathsf{E}[(X - \mathsf{E}(X))^2]$ the variance of X, and observe that $\mathsf{Var}(X) = \mathsf{E}(X^2) - \mathsf{E}(X)^2$. Chebyshev's Inequality then reads as follows: *Let X be a random variable, and $\delta > 0$. Then*

$$\Pr[|X - \mathsf{E}(X)| \geq \delta] \leq \frac{\mathsf{Var}(X)}{\delta^2}. \tag{D.3}$$

Proof: We define a random variable $Y \stackrel{\text{def}}{=} (X - \mathsf{E}(X))^2$, and apply Markov's Inequality. We get

$$\Pr[|X - \mathsf{E}(X)| \geq \delta] = \Pr\left[(X - \mathsf{E}(X))^2 \geq \delta^2\right]$$

$$\leq \frac{\mathsf{E}[(X - \mathsf{E}(X))^2]}{\delta^2}$$

and the claim follows. ∎

Corollary (pairwise independent sampling): *Chebyshev's Inequality is particularly useful in the analysis of the error probability of approximation via repeated sampling. It suffices to assume that the samples are picked in a pairwise independent manner, where* $X_1, X_2, \ldots, X_n$ *are* pairwise independent *if for every $i \neq j$ and every α, β it holds that* $\Pr[X_i = \alpha \wedge X_j = \beta] = \Pr[X_i = \alpha] \cdot \Pr[X_j = \beta]$. *The corollary reads as follows:* Let $X_1, X_2, \ldots, X_n$ be pairwise independent random variables with identical expectation, denoted μ, and identical variance, denoted σ^2. Then, for every $\varepsilon > 0$, it holds that

$$\Pr\left[\left|\frac{\sum_{i=1}^n X_i}{n} - \mu\right| \geq \varepsilon\right] \leq \frac{\sigma^2}{\varepsilon^2 n}. \tag{D.4}$$

Proof: Define the random variables $\overline{X}_i \overset{\text{def}}{=} X_i - \mathsf{E}(X_i)$. Note that the $\overline{X}_i$'s are pairwise independent, and each has zero expectation. Applying Chebyshev's Inequality to the random variable $\sum_{i=1}^{n} \frac{X_i}{n}$, and using the linearity of the expectation operator, we get

$$\Pr\left[\left|\sum_{i=1}^{n} \frac{X_i}{n} - \mu\right| \geq \varepsilon\right] \leq \frac{\mathrm{Var}\left[\sum_{i=1}^{n} \frac{X_i}{n}\right]}{\varepsilon^2}$$

$$= \frac{\mathsf{E}\left[\left(\sum_{i=1}^{n} \overline{X}_i\right)^2\right]}{\varepsilon^2 \cdot n^2}$$

Now (again using the linearity of expectation)

$$\mathsf{E}\left[\left(\sum_{i=1}^{n} \overline{X}_i\right)^2\right] = \sum_{i=1}^{n} \mathsf{E}\left[\overline{X}_i^2\right] + \sum_{1 \leq i \neq j \leq n} \mathsf{E}\left[\overline{X}_i \overline{X}_j\right]$$

By the pairwise independence of the $\overline{X}_i$'s, we get $\mathsf{E}[\overline{X}_i \overline{X}_j] = \mathsf{E}[\overline{X}_i] \cdot \mathsf{E}[\overline{X}_j]$, *and using* $\mathsf{E}[\overline{X}_i] = 0$, we get

$$\mathsf{E}\left[\left(\sum_{i=1}^{n} \overline{X}_i\right)^2\right] = n \cdot \sigma^2$$

The corollary follows. ∎

D.1.2.3. Chernoff Bound

When using pairwise independent sample points, the error probability in the approximation decreases linearly with the number of sample points (see Eq. (D.4)). When using totally independent sample points, the error probability in the approximation can be shown to decrease exponentially with the number of sample points. (Recall that the random variables $X_1, X_2, \ldots, X_n$ are said to be totally independent if for every sequence $a_1, a_2, \ldots, a_n$ it holds that $\Pr[\wedge_{i=1}^{n} X_i = a_i] = \prod_{i=1}^{n} \Pr[X_i = a_i]$.) Probability bounds supporting the foregoing statement are given next. The first bound, commonly referred to as the Chernoff Bound, concerns 0-1 random variables (i.e., random variables that are assigned as values either 0 or 1), and asserts the following. *Let $p \leq \frac{1}{2}$, and $X_1, X_2, \ldots, X_n$ be independent 0-1 random variables such that $\Pr[X_i = 1] = p$, for each i. Then, for every $\varepsilon \in (0, p]$, it holds that*

$$\Pr\left[\left|\frac{\sum_{i=1}^{n} X_i}{n} - p\right| > \varepsilon\right] < 2 \cdot e^{-c \cdot \varepsilon^2 \cdot n}, \text{ where } c = \max(2, \tfrac{1}{3p}). \tag{D.5}$$

The more common formulation sets $c = 2$, but the case $c = 1/3p$ is very useful when p is small and one cares about a *multiplicative* deviation (e.g., $\varepsilon = p/2$).

Proof Sketch: We upper-bound $\Pr[\sum_{i=1}^{n} X_i - pn > \varepsilon n]$, and $\Pr[pn - \sum_{i=1}^{n} X_i > \varepsilon n]$ is bounded similarly. Letting $\overline{X}_i \overset{\text{def}}{=} X_i - \mathsf{E}(X_i)$, we apply Markov's Inequality to the random variable $e^{\lambda \sum_{i=1}^{n} \overline{X}_i}$, where $\lambda \in (0, 1]$ will be determined to optimize the expressions that we derive. Thus, $\Pr[\sum_{i=1}^{n} \overline{X}_i > \varepsilon n]$ is upper-bounded by

$$\frac{\mathsf{E}[e^{\lambda \sum_{i=1}^{n} \overline{X}_i}]}{e^{\lambda \varepsilon n}} = e^{-\lambda \varepsilon n} \cdot \prod_{i=1}^{n} \mathsf{E}[e^{\lambda \overline{X}_i}]$$

where the equality is due to the independence of the random variables. To simplify the rest of the proof, we establish a sub-optimal bound as follows. Using a Taylor expansion of e^x (e.g., $e^x < 1 + x + x^2$ for $|x| \leq 1$) and observing that $\mathsf{E}[\overline{X}_i] = 0$, we get $\mathsf{E}[e^{\lambda \overline{X}_i}] < 1 + \lambda^2 \mathsf{E}[\overline{X}_i^2]$, which equals $1 + \lambda^2 p(1 - p)$. Thus, $\Pr[\sum_{i=1}^{n} X_i - pn > \varepsilon n]$ is upper-bounded by $e^{-\lambda \varepsilon n} \cdot (1 + \lambda^2 p(1 - p))^n < \exp(-\lambda \varepsilon n + \lambda^2 p(1 - p)n)$, which is optimized at $\lambda = \varepsilon/(2p(1 - p))$ yielding $\exp(-\frac{\varepsilon^2}{4p(1-p)} \cdot n) \leq \exp(-\varepsilon^2 \cdot n)$. $\qquad\square$

The foregoing proof strategy can be applied in more general settings.[1] A more general bound, which refers to independent random variables that are each bounded but are not necessarily identical, is given next (and is commonly referred to as the Hoefding Inequality). *Let $X_1, X_2, \ldots, X_n$ be n independent random variables, each ranging in the (real) interval $[a, b]$, and let $\mu \stackrel{\text{def}}{=} \frac{1}{n} \sum_{i=1}^{n} \mathsf{E}(X_i)$ denote the average expected value of these variables. Then, for every $\varepsilon > 0$,*

$$\Pr\left[\left|\frac{\sum_{i=1}^{n} X_i}{n} - \mu\right| > \varepsilon\right] < 2 \cdot e^{-\frac{2\varepsilon^2}{(b-a)^2} \cdot n} \tag{D.6}$$

The special case (of Eq. (D.6)) that refers to identically distributed random variables is easy to derive from the foregoing Chernoff Bound (by recalling footnote 1 and using a linear mapping of the interval $[a, b]$ to the interval $[0, 1]$). This special case is useful in estimating the average value of a (bounded) function defined over a large domain, especially when the desired error probability needs to be negligible (i.e., decrease faster than any polynomial in the number of samples). Such an estimate can be obtained provided that we can sample the function's domain (and evaluate the function).

D.1.2.4. Pairwise Independent Versus Totally Independent Sampling

To demonstrate the difference between the sampling bounds provided in §D.1.2.2 and §D.1.2.3, we consider the problem of estimating the average value of a function $f : \Omega \to [0, 1]$. In general, we say that a random variable Z provides an (ε, δ)-approximation of a value v if $\Pr[|Z - v| > \varepsilon] \leq \delta$. By Eq. (D.6), the average value of f evaluated at $n = O((\varepsilon^{-2} \cdot \log(1/\delta))$ *independent* samples (selected uniformly in Ω) yields an (ε, δ)-approximation of $\mu = \sum_{x \in \Omega} f(x)/|\Omega|$. Thus, the number of sample points is polynomially related to ε^{-1} and logarithmically related to δ^{-1}. In contrast, by Eq. (D.4), an (ε, δ)-approximation by n *pairwise independent* samples calls for setting $n = O(\varepsilon^{-2} \cdot \delta^{-1})$. We stress that *in both cases the number of samples is polynomially related to the desired accuracy of the estimation* (i.e., ε). *The only advantage of totally independent samples over pairwise independent ones is in the dependency of the number of samples on the error probability* (i.e., δ).

---

[1]For example, verify that the current proof actually applies to the case that $X_i \in [0, 1]$ rather than $X_i \in \{0, 1\}$, by noting that $\text{Var}[X_i] \leq p(1 - p)$ still holds.

D.2. Hashing

Hashing is extensively used in Complexity Theory (see, e.g., §6.2.2.2, Section 6.2.3, §6.2.4.2, §8.2.5.3, and §8.4.2.1). The typical application is for mapping arbitrary (unstructured) sets "almost uniformly" to a structured set of adequate size. Specifically, hashing is used for mapping an arbitrary 2^m-subset of $\{0, 1\}^n$ to $\{0, 1\}^m$ in an "almost-uniform" manner.

For any fixed set S of cardinality 2^m, there exists a 1-1 mapping $f_S : S \to \{0, 1\}^m$, but this mapping is not necessarily efficiently computable (e.g., it may require "knowing" the entire set S). On the other hand, no single function $f : \{0, 1\}^n \to \{0, 1\}^m$ can map every 2^m-subset of $\{0, 1\}^n$ to $\{0, 1\}^m$ in a 1-1 manner (or even approximately so). Nevertheless, for every 2^m-subset $S \subset \{0, 1\}^n$, a random function $f : \{0, 1\}^n \to \{0, 1\}^m$ has the property that, with overwhelmingly high probability, f maps S to $\{0, 1\}^m$ such that no point in the range has too many f-preimages in S. The problem is that a truly random function is unlikely to have a succinct representation (let alone an efficient evaluation algorithm). We thus seek families of functions that have a "random mapping" property (as in Condition 1 of the following definition), but do have a succinct representation as well as an efficient evaluation algorithm (as in Conditions 2 and 3 of the following definition).

D.2.1. Definitions

Motivated by the foregoing discussion, we consider families of functions $\{H_n^m\}_{m<n}$ that satisfy the following conditions:

1. For every $S \subset \{0, 1\}^n$, with high probability, a function h selected uniformly in H_n^m maps S to $\{0, 1\}^m$ in an "almost-uniform" manner. For example, we may require that, for any $|S| = 2^m$ and each point y, with high probability over the choice of h, it holds that $|\{x \in S : h(x) = y\}| \le \text{poly}(n)$.
2. The functions in H_n^m have succinct representation. For example, we may require that $H_n^m \equiv \{0, 1\}^{\ell(n,m)}$, for some polynomial ℓ.
3. The functions in H_n^m can be efficiently evaluated. That is, there exists a polynomial-time algorithm that, on input a representation of a function, h (in H_n^m), and a string $x \in \{0, 1\}^n$, returns $h(x)$. In some cases we make even more stringent requirements regarding the algorithm (e.g., that it runs in linear space).

Condition 1 was left vague on purpose. At the very least, we require that the expected size of $\{x \in S : h(x) = y\}$ equals $|S|/2^m$. We shall see (in Section D.2.3) that different interpretations of Condition 1 are satisfied by different families of hashing functions. We focus on t-wise independent hashing functions, defined next.

Definition D.1 (t-wise independent hashing functions): *A family H_n^m of functions from n-bit strings to m-bit strings is called* t-wise independent *if for every t distinct domain elements $x_1, \ldots, x_t \in \{0, 1\}^n$ and every $y_1, \ldots, y_t \in \{0, 1\}^m$ it holds that*

$$\Pr_{h \in H_n^m}[\wedge_{i=1}^t h(x_i) = y_i] = 2^{-t \cdot m}$$

That is, a uniformly chosen $h \in H_n^m$ maps every t domain elements to the range in a totally uniform manner. Note that for $t \ge 2$, it follows that the probability that a random

$h \in H_n^m$ maps two distinct domain elements to the same image equals 2^{-m}. Such (families of) functions are called universal (cf. [50]), but we will focus on the stronger condition of t-wise independence.

D.2.2. Constructions

The following constructions are merely a reinterpretation of the constructions presented in §8.5.1.1. (Alternatively, one may view the constructions presented in §8.5.1.1 as a reinterpretation of the following two constructions.)

Construction D.2 (*t-wise independent hashing*): *For $t, m, n \in \mathbb{N}$ such that $m \leq n$, consider the following family of hashing functions mapping n-bit strings to m-bit strings. Each t-sequence $\bar{s} = (s_0, s_1, \ldots, s_{t-1}) \in \{0, 1\}^{t \cdot n}$ describes a function $h_{\bar{s}} : \{0, 1\}^n \to \{0, 1\}^m$ such that $h_{\bar{s}}(x)$ equals the m-bit prefix of the binary representation of $\sum_{j=0}^{t-1} s_j x^j$, where the arithmetic is that of $\mathrm{GF}(2^n)$, the finite field of 2^n elements.*

Proposition 8.24 implies that Construction D.2 constitutes a family of t-wise independent hash functions. Typically, we will use either $t = 2$ or $t = \Theta(n)$. To make the construction totally explicit, we need an explicit representation of $\mathrm{GF}(2^n)$; see comment following Proposition 8.24. An alternative construction for the case of $t = 2$ may be obtained analogously to the pairwise independent generator of Proposition 8.25. Recall that a Toeplitz matrix is a matrix with all diagonals being homogeneous; that is, $T = (t_{i,j})$ is a Toeplitz matrix if $t_{i,j} = t_{i+1,j+1}$, for all i, j.

Construction D.3 (*alternative pairwise independent hashing*): *For $m \leq n$, consider the family of hashing functions in which each pair (T, b), consisting of an n-by-m Toeplitz matrix T and an m-dimensional vector b, describes a function $h_{T,b} : \{0, 1\}^n \to \{0, 1\}^m$ such that $h_{T,b}(x) = Tx + b$.*

Proposition 8.25 implies that Construction D.3 constitutes a family of pairwise independent hash functions. Note that an n-by-m Toeplitz matrix can be specified by $n + m - 1$ bits, yielding a description length of $n + 2m - 1$ bits. An alternative construction (analogous to Eq. (8.23) and requiring $m \cdot n + m$ bits of representation) uses arbitrary n-by-m matrices rather than Toeplitz matrices.

D.2.3. The Leftover Hash Lemma

We now turn to the "almost-uniform" cover condition (i.e., Condition 1) mentioned in Section D.2.1. One concrete interpretation of this condition is given by the following lemma (and another interpretation is implied by it – see Theorem D.5).

Lemma D.4: *Let $m \leq n$ be integers, H_n^m be a family of pairwise independent hash functions, and $S \subseteq \{0, 1\}^n$. Then, for every $y \in \{0, 1\}^m$ and every $\varepsilon > 0$, for all but at most a $\frac{2^m}{\varepsilon^2 |S|}$ fraction of $h \in H_n^m$ it holds that*

$$(1 - \varepsilon) \cdot \frac{|S|}{2^m} \; < \; |\{x \in S : h(x) = y\}| \; < \; (1 + \varepsilon) \cdot \frac{|S|}{2^m}. \tag{D.7}$$

Note that by pairwise independence (or rather even by 1-wise independence), the expected size of $\{x \in S : h(x) = y\}$ is $|S|/2^m$, where the expectation is taken uniformly over all $h \in H_n^m$. The lemma upper-bounds the fraction of h's that deviate from the expected behavior (i.e., for which $|h^{-1}(y) \cap S| \neq (1 \pm \varepsilon) \cdot |S|/2^m$). Needless to say, the bound is meaningful only in case $|S| > 2^m/\varepsilon^2$. Focusing on the case that $|S| > 2^m$ and setting $\varepsilon = \sqrt[3]{2^m/|S|}$, we infer that *for all but at most a ε fraction of $h \in H_n^m$ it holds that $|\{x \in S : h(x) = y\}| = (1 \pm \varepsilon) \cdot |S|/2^m$. Thus, each range element has approximately the right number of h-preimages in the set S, under almost all $h \in H_n^m$.

Proof: Fixing an arbitrary set $S \subseteq \{0, 1\}^n$ and an arbitrary $y \in \{0, 1\}^m$, we estimate the probability that a uniformly selected $h \in H_n^m$ violates Eq. (D.7). We define random variables ζ_x, over the aforementioned probability space, such that $\zeta_x = \zeta_x(h)$ equal 1 if $h(x) = y$ and $\zeta_x = 0$ otherwise. The expected value of $\sum_{x \in S} \zeta_x$ is $\mu \stackrel{\text{def}}{=} |S| \cdot 2^{-m}$, and we are interested in the probability that this sum deviates from the expectation. Applying Chebyshev's Inequality, we get

$$\Pr\left[\left|\mu - \sum_{x \in S} \zeta_x\right| \geq \varepsilon \cdot \mu\right] < \frac{\mu}{\varepsilon^2 \mu^2}$$

because $\mathsf{Var}[\sum_{x \in S} \zeta_x] < |S| \cdot 2^{-m}$ by the pairwise independence of the ζ_x's and the fact that $\mathsf{E}[\zeta_x] = 2^{-m}$. The lemma follows. ∎

A generalization (called mixing). The proof of Lemma D.4 can be easily extended to show that *for every set $T \subset \{0, 1\}^m$ and every $\varepsilon > 0$, for all but at most a $\frac{2^m}{|T| \cdot |S| \varepsilon^2}$ fraction of $h \in H_n^m$ it holds that $|\{x \in S : h(x) \in T\}| = (1 \pm \varepsilon) \cdot |T| \cdot |S|/2^m$. (Hint: Redefine $\zeta_x = \zeta(h) = 1$ if $h(x) \in T$ and $\zeta_x = 0$ otherwise.) This assertion is meaningful provided that $|T| \cdot |S| > 2^m/\varepsilon^2$, and in the case that $m = n$ it is called a mixing property.

An extremely useful corollary. The aforementioned generalization of Lemma D.4 asserts that, for any fixed set of preimages $S \subset \{0, 1\}^n$ and any fixed sets of images $T \subset \{0, 1\}^m$, most functions in H_n^m behave well with respect to S and T (in the sense that they map approximately the adequate fraction of S (i.e., $|T|/2^m$) to T). A seemingly stronger statement, which is (non-trivially) implied by Lemma D.4 itself, reverses the order of quantification with respect to T; that is, for all adequate sets S, most functions in H_n^m map S to $\{0, 1\}^m$ in an almost-uniform manner (i.e., assign each set T approximately the adequate fraction of S, where here the approximation is up to an additive deviation). As we shall see, this is a consequence of the following theorem.

Theorem D.5 (aka Leftover Hash Lemma): *Let H_n^m and $S \subseteq \{0, 1\}^n$ be as in Lemma D.4, and define $\varepsilon = \sqrt[3]{2^m/|S|}$. Consider random variables X and H that are uniformly distributed on S and H_n^m, respectively. Then, the statistical distance between $(H, H(X))$ and (H, U_m) is at most 2ε.*

It follows that, *for X and ε as in Theorem D.5 and any $\alpha > 0$, for all but at most an α fraction of the functions $h \in H_n^m$ it holds that $h(X)$ is $(2\varepsilon/\alpha)$-close to U_m.*[2] (Using the

---

[2] This follows by defining a random variable $\zeta = \zeta(h)$ such that ζ equals the statistical distance between $h(X)$ and U_m, and applying Markov's Inequality.

terminology of the subsequent Section D.4, we may say that Theorem D.5 asserts that H_n^m yields a strong extractor (with parameters to be spelled out there).)

Proof: Let V denote the set of pairs (h, y) that violate Eq. (D.7), and $\overline{V} \stackrel{\text{def}}{=} (H_n^m \times \{0, 1\}^m) \setminus V$. Then for every $(h, y) \in \overline{V}$ it holds that

$$\Pr[(H, H(X)) = (h, y)] = \Pr[H = h] \cdot \Pr[h(X) = y]$$
$$= (1 \pm \varepsilon) \cdot \Pr[(H, U_m) = (h, y)].$$

On the other hand, by the setting of ε and Lemma D.4 (which imply that $\Pr[(H, y) \in V] \leq \varepsilon$ for every $y \in \{0, 1\}^m$), we have $\Pr[(H, U_m) \in V] \leq \varepsilon$. It follows that

$$\Pr[(H, H(X)) \in V] = 1 - \Pr[(H, H(X)) \in \overline{V}]$$
$$\leq 1 - \Pr[(H, U_m)) \in \overline{V}] + \varepsilon \ \leq \ 2\varepsilon.$$

Using all these upper bounds, we upper bounded the statistical difference between $(H, H(X))$ and (H, U_m), denoted Δ, by separating the contribution of V and $\overline{V}$. Specifically, we have

$$\Delta = \frac{1}{2} \cdot \sum_{(h,y) \in H_n^m \times \{0,1\}^m} |\Pr[(H, H(X)) = (h, y)] - \Pr[(H, U_m) = (h, y)]|$$

$$\leq \frac{\varepsilon}{2} + \frac{1}{2} \cdot \sum_{(h,y) \in V} |\Pr[(H, H(X)) = (h, y)] - \Pr[(H, U_m) = (h, y)]| \ ,$$

where the first term upper-bounds the contribution of all pairs $(h, y) \in \overline{V}$. Hence,

$$\Delta \leq \frac{\varepsilon}{2} + \frac{1}{2} \cdot \sum_{(h,y) \in V} (\Pr[(H, H(X)) = (h, y)] + \Pr[(H, U_m) = (h, y)])$$

$$\leq \frac{\varepsilon}{2} + \frac{1}{2} \cdot (2\varepsilon + \varepsilon) \,,$$

where the first inequality is trivial (i.e., $|\alpha - \beta| \leq \alpha + \beta$ for any non-negative α and β), and the second inequality uses the foregoing upper bounds (i.e., $\Pr[(H, H(X)) \in V] \leq 2\varepsilon$ and $\Pr[(H, U_m) \in V] \leq \varepsilon$). The theorem follows. ∎

An alternative proof of Theorem D.5. Define the collision probability of a random variable Z, denoted $cp(Z)$, as the probability that two independent samples of Z yield the same result. Alternatively, $cp(Z) \stackrel{\text{def}}{=} \sum_z \Pr[Z = z]^2$. Theorem D.5 follows by combining the following two facts:

1. A general fact: *If $Z \in [N]$ and $cp(Z) \leq (1 + 4\epsilon^2)/N$ then Z is ϵ-close to the uniform distribution on $[N]$.*

   We prove the contrapositive: Assuming that the statistical distance between Z and the uniform distribution on $[N]$ equals δ, we show that $cp(Z) \geq (1 + 4\delta^2)/N$. This is done by defining $L \stackrel{\text{def}}{=} \{z : \Pr[Z = z] < 1/N\}$, and lower-bounding $cp(Z)$ by using the fact that the collision probability is minimized on uniform distributions. Specifically, considering the uniform distributions on L and $[N] \setminus L$, respectively, we have

$$cp(Z) \geq |L| \cdot \left(\frac{\Pr[Z \in L]}{|L|}\right)^2 + (N - |L|) \cdot \left(\frac{\Pr[Z \in [N] \setminus L]}{N - |L|}\right)^2 \quad \text{(D.8)}$$

Using $\delta = \rho - \Pr[Z \in L]$, where $\rho = |L|/N$, the r.h.s of Eq. (D.8) equals $\frac{(\rho-\delta)^2}{\rho N} +$
$\frac{(1-(\rho-\delta))^2}{(1-\rho)N} = \left(1 + \frac{\delta^2}{(1-\rho)\rho}\right) \cdot \frac{1}{N} \geq (1 + 4\delta^2) \cdot \frac{1}{N}$.

2. *The collision probability of $(H, H(X))$ is at most $(1 + (2^m/|S|))/(|H_n^m| \cdot 2^m)$. (Furthermore, this holds even if H_n^m is only universal.)*

   The proof is by a straightforward calculation. Specifically, note that $\text{cp}(H, H(X)) = |H_n^m|^{-1} \cdot \mathsf{E}_{h \in H_n^m}[\text{cp}(h(X))]$, whereas $\mathsf{E}_{h \in H_n^m}[\text{cp}(h(X))] = |S|^{-2} \sum_{x_1, x_2 \in S}$ $\Pr[H(x_1) = H(x_2)]$. The sum equals $|S| + (|S|^2 - |S|) \cdot 2^{-m}$, and so $\text{cp}(H, H(X)) < |H_n^m|^{-1} \cdot (2^{-m} + |S|^{-1})$.

It follows that $(H, H(X))$ is $2\sqrt{2^m/|S|}$-close to (H, U_m), which is actually a stronger bound than the one asserted by Theorem D.5.

Stronger uniformity via higher independence. Recall that Lemma D.4 asserts that for each point in the range of the hash function, with high probability over the choice of the hash function, *this fixed point* has approximately the expected number of preimages in S. A stronger condition asserts that, with high probability over the choice of the hash function, *every point in its range* has approximately the expected number of preimages in S. Such a guarantee can be obtained when using n-wise independent hash functions (rather than using pairwise independent hash functions).

> **Lemma D.6:** *Let $m \leq n$ be integers, H_n^m be a family of n-wise independent hash functions, and $S \subseteq \{0, 1\}^n$. Then, for every $\varepsilon \in (0, 1)$, for all but at most a $2^m \cdot (n \cdot 2^m/\varepsilon^2|S|)^{n/2}$ fraction of the functions $h \in H_n^m$, it is the case that Eq. (D.7) holds for every $y \in \{0, 1\}^m$.*

Indeed, the lemma should be used with $2^m < \varepsilon^2|S|/4n$. In particular, using $m = \log_2 |S| - \log_2(5n/\varepsilon^2)$ guarantees that with high probability (i.e., $1 - 2^m \cdot 5^{-n/2} \geq 1 - (4/5)^{n/2}$) each range element has $(1 \pm \varepsilon) \cdot |S|/2^m$ preimages in S. Under this setting of parameters $|S|/2^m = 5n/\varepsilon^2$, which is poly($n$) whenever $\varepsilon = 1/\text{poly}(n)$. Needless to say, this guarantee is stronger than the conclusion of Theorem D.5.

Proof: The proof follows the footsteps of the proof of Lemma D.4, taking advantage of the fact that here the random variables (i.e., the ζ_x's) are n-wise independent. For $t = n/2$, this allows for using the so-called $2t^{\text{th}}$ *moment analysis*, which generalizes the second moment analysis of pairwise independent sampling (presented in §D.1.2.2). As in the proof of Lemma D.4, we fix any S and y, and define $\zeta_x = \zeta_x(h) = 1$ if and only if $h(x) = y$. Letting $\mu = \mathsf{E}[\sum_{x \in S} \zeta_x] = |S|/2^m$ and $\overline{\zeta}_x = \zeta_x - \mathsf{E}(\zeta_x)$, we start with Markov's Inequality:

$$\Pr\left[\left|\mu - \sum_{x \in S} \zeta_x\right| \geq \varepsilon \cdot \mu\right] \leq \frac{\mathsf{E}[(\sum_{x \in S} \overline{\zeta}_x)^{2t}]}{\varepsilon^{2t} \mu^{2t}}$$

$$= \frac{\sum_{x_1, \dots, x_{2t} \in S} \mathsf{E}[\prod_{i=1}^{2t} \overline{\zeta}_{x_i}]}{\varepsilon^{2t} \cdot (|S|/2^m)^{2t}} \tag{D.9}$$

Using $2t$-wise independence, we note that only the terms in Eq. (D.9) that do not vanish are those in which each variable appears with multiplicity. This mean that only terms having less than t distinct variables contribute to Eq. (D.9). Now, for every

$j \leq t$, we have less than $\binom{|S|}{j} \cdot (2t!) < (2t!/j!) \cdot |S|^j$ terms with j distinct variables, and each such term contributes less than $(2^{-m})^j$ to the sum (because for every $e > 1$ it holds that $\mathsf{E}[\overline{\zeta}^e_{x_i}] < \mathsf{E}[\zeta_{x_i}] = 2^{-m}$). Thus, Eq. (D.9) is upper-bounded by

$$\frac{2t!}{(\varepsilon|S|/2^m)^{2t}} \cdot \sum_{j=1}^{t} \frac{(|S|/2^m)^j}{j!} < 2 \cdot \frac{2t!/t!}{(\varepsilon^2|S|/2^m)^t} < \left(\frac{2t \cdot 2^m}{\varepsilon^2|S|}\right)^t$$

where the first inequality assumes $|S| > n2^m$ (which is justified by the fact that the claim holds vacuously otherwise). This upper-bounds the probability that a random $h \in H_n^m$ violates Eq. (D.7) with respect to a fixed y. Using a union bound on all $y \in \{0, 1\}^m$, the lemma follows. ∎

D.3. Sampling

In many settings, repeated sampling is used to estimate the average (or other statistics) of a huge set of values.[3] Namely, given a "value" function $v : \{0, 1\}^n \to \mathbb{R}$, one wishes to approximate $\bar{v} \overset{\text{def}}{=} \frac{1}{2^n} \sum_{x \in \{0,1\}^n} v(x)$ without having to inspect the value of v at each point of the domain. The obvious thing to do is sample the domain at random, and obtain an approximation to $\bar{v}$ by taking the average of the values of v on the sample points. It turns out that certain "pseudorandom" sequences of sample points may serve almost as well as truly random sequences of sample points, and thus the foregoing problem is indeed related to Section 8.5.

D.3.1. Formal Setting

It is essential for the range of the function v to be bounded (since otherwise no reasonable approximation is possible). For simplicity, we adopt the convention of having $[0, 1]$ be the range of v, and the problem for other (predetermined) ranges can be treated analogously. Our notion of approximation depends on two parameters: accuracy (denoted ε) and error probability (denoted δ). We wish to have an algorithm that, with probability at least $1 - \delta$, gets within ε of the correct value. This leads to the following definition.

Definition D.7 (sampler): *A* sampler *is a randomized oracle machine that on input parameters n* (length), *ε* (accuracy) *and δ* (error), *and oracle access to any function $v : \{0, 1\}^n \to [0, 1]$, outputs, with probability at least $1 - \delta$, a value that is at most ε away from $\bar{v} \overset{\text{def}}{=} \frac{1}{2^n} \sum_{x \in \{0,1\}^n} v(x)$. Namely,*

$$\Pr[|\mathrm{sampler}^v(n, \varepsilon, \delta) - \bar{v}| > \varepsilon] < \delta$$

where the probability is taken over the internal coin tosses of the sampler.
A non-adaptive sampler *is a sampler that consists of two deterministic algorithms: a* sample-generating *algorithm, G, and an* evaluation *algorithm, V. On input n, ε, δ and a random* seed *of adequate length, algorithm G generates a sequence of queries, denoted $s_1, \ldots, s_m \in \{0, 1\}^n$. Algorithm V is given the corresponding sequence of v-values (i.e., $v(s_1), \ldots, v(s_m)$) and outputs an estimate to $\bar{v}$.*

We are interested in "the complexity of sampling" quantified as a function of the parameters n, ε and δ. Specifically, we will consider three complexity measures: the sample complexity

---

[3]Indeed, this problem was already mentioned in §D.1.2.4.

(i.e., the number of oracle queries made by the sampler); the randomness complexity (i.e., the length of the random seed used by the sampler); and the computational complexity (i.e., the running time of the sampler). We say that a sampler is efficient if its running time is polynomial in the total length of its queries (i.e., polynomial in both its sample complexity and in n). We will focus on efficient samplers. Furthermore, we will be most interested in efficient samplers that have optimal (up to a constant factor) sample complexity, and will seek to minimize the randomness complexity of such samplers. Note that minimizing the randomness complexity without referring to the sample complexity makes no sense.

D.3.2. Known Results

We note that all the following positive results refer to non-adaptive samplers, whereas the lower bound also holds for general samplers. For more details on these results, see [90, Sec. 3.6.4] and the references therein.

The naive sampler. The straightforward method (aka the naive sampler) consists of *uniformly and independently* selecting sufficiently many sample points (queries), and outputting the average value of the function on these points. Using the Chernoff Bound it follows that $O(\frac{\log(1/\delta)}{\varepsilon^2})$ sample points suffice. As indicated next, the naive sampler is optimal (up to a constant factor) in its sample complexity, but is quite wasteful in randomness.

It is known that $\Omega(\frac{\log(1/\delta)}{\varepsilon^2})$ samples are needed in any sampler, and that any sampler that makes $s(n, \varepsilon, \delta)$ queries must have randomness complexity at least $n + \log_2(1/\delta) - \log_2 s(n, \varepsilon, \delta) - O(1)$. These lower bounds are tight (as demonstrated by non-explicit and inefficient samplers). The foregoing facts guide our quest for improvements, which is aimed at finding more randomness-efficient ways of *efficiently* generating sample sequences that can be used in conjunction with an appropriate evaluation algorithm V. (We stress that V need not necessarily take the average of the values of the sampled points.)

The Pairwise Independent Sampler. Using a pairwise independence generator (cf. §8.5.1.1) for generating sample points, along with the natural evaluation algorithm (which outputs the average of the values of these points), we can obtain a great saving in the randomness complexity: In particular, using a seed of length $2n$, we can generate $O(1/\delta\varepsilon^2)$ pairwise independent sample points, which (by Eq. (D.4)) suffice for getting accuracy ε with error δ. Thus, this (Pairwise Independent) sampler uses $2n$ coin tosses rather than the $\Omega((\log(1/\delta))\varepsilon^{-2} \cdot n)$ coin tosses used by the naive sampler. Furthermore, for constant $\delta > 0$, the Pairwise Independent Sampler is optimal up to a constant factor in both its sample and randomness complexities. However, for small δ (i.e., $\delta = o(1)$), this sampler is wasteful in sample complexity.

The Median-of-Averages Sampler. A new idea is required for going further, and a relevant tool – random walks on expander graphs (see Sections 8.5.3 and E.2) – is needed, too. Specifically, we combine the Pairwise Independent Sampler with the Expander Random Walk Generator (of Proposition 8.29) to obtain a new sampler. The new sampler uses a t-long random walk on an expander with vertex set $\{0, 1\}^{2n}$ for *generating a sequence of $t \stackrel{\text{def}}{=} O(\log(1/\delta))$ related seeds for t invocations of the Pairwise Independent Sampler*, where each of these invocations uses the corresponding $2n$ bits to generate a sequence of $O(1/\varepsilon^2)$ samples in $\{0, 1\}^n$. The new sampler, called the Median-of-Averages Sampler, outputs the median of the t values obtained in these t invocations of the Pairwise Independent Sampler. In analyzing this sampler, we first note that each of the foregoing t invocations returns a value that, with probability at least 0.9, is ε-close to $\bar{v}$. By Theorem 8.28 (see also Exercise 8.44), with probability at least $1 - \exp(-t) = 1 - \delta$, *most of these t invocations return an ε-close approximation. Hence, the median among these t values is an (ε, δ)-approximation to the correct value.* The resulting sampler has sample complexity $O(\frac{\log(1/\delta)}{\varepsilon^2})$ and randomness complexity $2n + O(\log(1/\delta))$, which is optimal up to a constant factor in both complexities.

Further improvements. The randomness complexity of the Median-of-Averages Sampler can be decreased from $2n + O(\log(1/\delta))$ to $n + O(\log(1/\delta\varepsilon))$, while maintaining its (optimal) sample complexity (of $O(\frac{\log(1/\delta)}{\varepsilon^2})$). This is done by replacing the Pairwise Independent Sampler with a sampler that picks a random vertex in a suitable expander, samples all its neighbors, and outputs the average value seen.

Averaging samplers. Averaging (aka "oblivious") samplers are non-adaptive samplers in which the evaluation algorithm is the natural one – that is, it merely outputs the average of the values of the sampled points. Indeed, the Pairwise Independent Sampler is an averaging sampler, whereas the Median-of-Averages Sampler is not. Interestingly, averaging samplers have applications for which ordinary non-adaptive samplers do not suffice. Averaging samplers are closely related to randomness extractors, defined and discussed in the subsequent Section D.4.

An odd perspective. Recall that a non-adaptive sampler consists of a sample generator G and an evaluator V such that for every $v : \{0, 1\}^n \to [0, 1]$ it holds that

$$\Pr_{(s_1,\dots,s_m)\leftarrow G(U_k)}[|V(v(s_1), \dots, v(s_m)) - \bar{v}| > \varepsilon] < \delta, \tag{D.10}$$

where k denotes the length of the sampler's (random) seed. Thus, we may view G as a pseudorandom generator that is subjected to a class of distinguishers that is determined by a fixed algorithm V and an arbitrary function $v : \{0, 1\}^n \to [0, 1]$. Specifically, assuming that V works well when the m samples are distributed uniformly and independently (i.e., $\Pr[|V(v(U_n^{(1)}), \dots, v(U_n^{(m)})) - \bar{v}| > \varepsilon] < \delta$), we require G to generate sequences that satisfy the corresponding condition (as stated in Eq. (D.10)). What is a bit odd about the foregoing perspective is that, except for the case of averaging samplers, the class of distinguishers considered here is affected by a component (i.e., the evaluator V) that is potentially custom-made to help the generator G fool the distinguisher.[4]

D.3.3. Hitters

Hitters may be viewed as relaxations of samplers. Specifically, considering only Boolean functions, hitters are required to generate a sample that contains a point evaluating to 1 whenever at least an ε fraction of the function values equal 1. That is, a hitter is a randomized algorithm that on input parameters n (length), ε (accuracy), and δ (error),

---

[4]Another aspect in which samplers differ from the various pseudorandom generators discussed in Chapter 8 is in the aim to minimize, rather than maximize, the number of "blocks" (denoted here by m) in the output sequence. However, also in the case of samplers, the aim is to maximize the block-length (denoted here by n).

outputs a list of n-bit strings such that, for every set $S \subseteq \{0, 1\}^n$ of density greater than ε, with probability at least $1 - \delta$, the list contains at least one element of S. Note the correspondence to the (ε, δ)-hitting problem defined in Section 8.5.3.

Needless to say, any sampler yields a hitter (with respect to essentially the same parameters n, ε and δ).[5] However, hitting is strictly easier than evaluating the density of the target set: $O(1/\varepsilon)$ (pairwise independent) random samples suffice to hit any set of density ε with constant probability, whereas $\Omega(1/\varepsilon^2)$ samples are needed for approximating the average value of a Boolean function up to accuracy ε (with constant error probability). Indeed, adequate simplifications of the samplers discussed in Appendix D.3.2 yield hitters with sample complexity proportional to $1/\varepsilon$ (rather than to $1/\varepsilon^2$).

D.4. Randomness Extractors

Extracting almost-perfect randomness from sources of weak (i.e., defected) randomness is crucial for the actual use of randomized algorithms, procedures, and protocols. The latter are analyzed assuming that they are given access to a perfect random source, while in reality one typically has access only to sources of weak (i.e., highly imperfect) randomness. This gap is bridged by using randomness extractors, which are efficient procedures that (possibly with the help of little extra randomness) convert any source of weak randomness into an almost-perfect random source. Thus, randomness extractors are devices that greatly enhance the quality of random sources. In addition, randomness extractors are related to several other fundamental problems, to be further discussed later.

One key parameter, which was avoided in the foregoing discussion, is the class of weak random sources from which we need to extract almost-perfect randomness. Needless to say, it is preferable to make as few assumptions as possible regarding the weak random source. In other words, we wish to consider a wide class of such sources, and require that the randomness extractor (often referred to as the extractor) "works well" for any source in this class. A general class of such sources is defined in §D.4.1.1, but first we wish to mention that even for very restricted classes of sources, no deterministic extractor can work.[6] To overcome this impossibility result, two approaches are used:

Seeded extractors: The first approach consists of considering randomized extractors that use a relatively small amount of randomness (in addition to the weak random source). That is, these extractors obtain two inputs: a short truly random **seed** and a relatively long sequence generated by an arbitrary source that belongs to the specified class of sources. This suggestion is motivated in two different ways:

1. The application may actually have access to an almost-perfect random source, but bits from this high-quality source are much more expensive than bits from the weak (i.e., low-quality) random source. Thus, it makes sense to obtain few high-quality

---

[5]Specifically, any sampler with respect to the parameters n, ε and δ, yields a hitter with respect to the parameters n, 2ε and δ. (The need for slackness is easily demonstrated by noting that estimating the average with accuracy $\varepsilon = 1/2$ is trivial, whereas hitting is non-trivial for any accuracy (density) $\varepsilon < 1$.) The claim is obvious for non-adaptive samplers, but actually also holds for adaptive samplers. Note that adaptivity does not provide any advantage in the context of hitters, because one may assume (without loss of generality) that all prior samples missed the target set S.

[6]For example, consider the class of sources that output n-bit strings such that no string occurs with probability greater than $2^{-(n-1)}$ (i.e., twice its probability weight under the uniform distribution).

bits from the almost-perfect source and use them to "purify" the cheap bits obtained from the weak (low-quality) source. Thus, combining many cheap (but low-quality) bits with few high-quality (but expensive) bits, we obtain many high-quality bits.

2. In some applications (e.g., when using randomized algorithms), it may be possible to invoke the application multiple times, and use the "typical" outcome of these invocations (e.g., rule by majority, in the case of a decision procedure). For such applications, we may proceed as follows: First we obtain an outcome r of the weak random source, then we invoke the application multiple times such that for every possible seed s we invoke the application feeding it with $\text{extract}(s, r)$, and finally we use the "typical" outcome of these invocations. Indeed, this is analogous to the context of derandomization (see Section 8.3), and likewise this alternative is typically not applicable to cryptographic and/or distributed settings.

Few independent sources: The second approach consists of considering deterministic extractors that obtain samples from a few (say, two) *independent* sources of weak randomness. Such extractors are applicable in any setting (including in cryptography), provided that the application has access to the required number of independent weak random sources.

In this section we focus on the first type of extractors (i.e., the *seeded extractors*). This choice is motivated both by the relatively more mature state of the research of seeded extractors and by the closer connection between seeded extractors and other topics in Complexity Theory.

D.4.1. Definitions and Various Perspectives

We first present a definition that corresponds to the foregoing motivational discussion, and later discuss its relation to other topics in complexity.

D.4.1.1. The Main Definition

A very wide class of weak random sources corresponds to sources in which no specific output is too probable. That is, the class is parameterized by a (probability) bound β and consists of all sources X such that for every x it holds that $\Pr[X = x] \leq \beta$. In such a case, we say that X has min-entropy[7] at least $\log_2(1/\beta)$. Indeed, we represent sources as random variables, and assume that they are distributed over strings of a fixed length, denoted n. An (n, k)-source is a source that is distributed over $\{0, 1\}^n$ and has min-entropy at least k.

An interesting special case of (n, k)-sources is that of sources that are uniform over some subset of 2^k strings. Such sources are called (n, k)-flat. A useful observation is that *each (n, k)-source is a convex combination of (n, k)-flat sources.*

Definition D.8 (extractor for (n, k)-sources):

1. *An algorithm* $\text{Ext}: \{0, 1\}^d \times \{0, 1\}^n \to \{0, 1\}^m$ *is called an* extractor with error ε *for the class* $\mathcal{C}$ *if for every source X in $\mathcal{C}$ it holds that $\text{Ext}(U_d, X)$ is ε-close to U_m. If $\mathcal{C}$ is the class of (n, k)-sources then Ext is called a (k, ε)-*extractor.

2. *An algorithm* Ext *is called a* strong extractor with error ε *for* $\mathcal{C}$ *if for every source X in $\mathcal{C}$ it holds that $(U_d, \text{Ext}(U_d, X))$ is ε-close to (U_d, U_m). A* strong (k, ε)-*extractor is defined analogously.*

---

[7]Recall that the entropy of a random variable X is defined as $\sum_x \Pr[X = x] \cdot \log_2(1/\Pr[X = x])$. Indeed, the min-entropy of X equals $\min_x \{\log_2(1/\Pr[X = x])\}$, and is always upper-bounded by its entropy.

Using the aforementioned "decomposition" of (n, k)-sources into (n, k)-flat sources, it follows that Ext *is a (k, ε)-extractor if and only if it is an extractor with error ε for the class of (n, k)-flat sources.* (A similar claim holds for strong extractors.) Thus, much of the technical analysis is conducted with respect to the class of (n, k)-flat sources. For example, by analyzing the case of (n, k)-flat sources it is easy to see that, for $d = \log_2(n/\varepsilon^2) + O(1)$, there exists a (k, ε)-extractor Ext : $\{0, 1\}^d \times \{0, 1\}^n \to \{0, 1\}^k$. (The proof employs the Probabilistic Method and uses a union bound on the (finite) set of all (n, k)-flat sources.)[8]

We seek, however, explicit extractors, that is, extractors that are implementable by polynomial-time algorithms. We note that the evaluation algorithm of any family of pairwise independent hash functions mapping n-bit strings to m-bit strings constitutes a (strong) (k, ε)-extractor for $\varepsilon = 2^{-\Omega(k-m)}$ (see Theorem D.5). However, these extractors necessarily use a long seed (i.e., $d \geq 2m$ must hold (and in fact $d = n + 2m - 1$ holds in Construction D.3)). In Section D.4.2 we survey constructions of efficient (k, ε)-extractors that obtain logarithmic seed-length (i.e., $d = O(\log(n/\varepsilon))$). But before doing so, we provide a few alternative perspectives on extractors.

An important note on logarithmic seed-length. The case of logarithmic seed-length (i.e., $d = O(\log(n/\varepsilon))$) is of particular importance for a variety of reasons. Firstly, when emulating a randomized algorithm using a defected random source (as in Item 2 of the motivational discussion of seeded extractors), the overhead is exponential in the length of the seed. Thus, the emulation of a generic probabilistic polynomial-time algorithm can be done in polynomial time only if the seed-length is logarithmic. Similarly, the applications discussed in §D.4.1.2 and §D.4.1.3 are feasible only if the seed-length is logarithmic. Lastly, we note that logarithmic seed-length is an absolute lower bound for (k, ε)-extractors, whenever $k < n - n^{\Omega(1)}$ (and the extractor is non-trivial (i.e., $m \geq 1$ and $\varepsilon < 1/2$)).

D.4.1.2. Extractors as Averaging Samplers

There is a close relationship between extractors and averaging samplers (which are defined toward the end of Section D.3.2). We shall first show that any averaging sampler gives rise to an extractor. Let $G : \{0, 1\}^n \to (\{0, 1\}^m)^t$ be the sample-generating algorithm of an averaging sampler having accuracy ε and error probability δ. That is, G uses n bits of randomness and generates t sample points in $\{0, 1\}^m$ such that, for every $f : \{0, 1\}^m \to [0, 1]$ with probability at least $1 - \delta$, the average of the f-values of these t pseudorandom points resides in the interval $[\overline{f} \pm \varepsilon]$, where $\overline{f} \stackrel{\text{def}}{=} \mathsf{E}[f(U_m)]$. Define Ext : $[t] \times \{0, 1\}^n \to \{0, 1\}^m$ such that Ext(i, r) is the ith sample generated by $G(r)$. We shall prove that Ext is a $(k, 2\varepsilon)$-extractor, for $k = n - \log_2(\varepsilon/\delta)$.

Suppose toward the contradiction that there exists an (n, k)-flat source X such that for some $S \subset \{0, 1\}^m$ it is the case that $\Pr[\text{Ext}(U_d, X) \in S] > \Pr[U_m \in S] + 2\varepsilon$, where

---

[8]Indeed, the key fact is that the number of (n, k)-flat sources is $N \stackrel{\text{def}}{=} \binom{2^n}{2^k}$. The probability that a random function Ext : $\{0, 1\}^d \times \{0, 1\}^n \to \{0, 1\}^k$ is not an extractor with error ε for a fixed (n, k)-flat source is upper-bounded by $p \stackrel{\text{def}}{=} 2^{2^k} \cdot \exp(-\Omega(2^{d+k}\varepsilon^2))$, because p bounds the probability that when selecting 2^{d+k} random k-bit long strings there exists a set $T \subset \{0, 1\}^k$ that is hit by more than $((|T|/2^k) + \varepsilon) \cdot 2^{d+k}$ of these strings. Note that for $d = \log_2(n/\varepsilon^2) + O(1)$ it holds that $N \cdot p \ll 1$. In fact, the same analysis applies to the extraction of $m = k + \log_2 n$ bits (rather than k bits).

$d = \log_2 t$ and $[t] \equiv \{0, 1\}^d$. Define

$$B = \{x \in \{0, 1\}^n : \Pr[\text{Ext}(U_d, x) \in S] > (|S|/2^m) + \varepsilon\}.$$

Then, $|B| > \varepsilon \cdot 2^k = \delta \cdot 2^n$. Defining $f(z) = 1$ if $z \in S$ and $f(z) = 0$ otherwise, we have $\overline{f} \stackrel{\text{def}}{=} \mathsf{E}[f(U_m)] = |S|/2^m$. But, for every $r \in B$ the f-average of the sample $G(r)$ is greater than $\overline{f} + \varepsilon$, in contradiction to the hypothesis that the sampler has error probability δ (with respect to accuracy ε).

We now turn to show that extractors give rise to averaging samplers. Let $\text{Ext} : \{0, 1\}^d \times \{0, 1\}^n \to \{0, 1\}^m$ be a (k, ε)-extractor. Consider the sample-generation algorithm $G : \{0, 1\}^n \to (\{0, 1\}^m)^{2^d}$ defined by $G(r) = (\text{Ext}(s, r))_{s \in \{0,1\}^d}$. We prove that G corresponds to an averaging sampler with accuracy ε and error probability $\delta = 2^{-(n-k-1)}$.

Suppose toward the contradiction that there exists a function $f : \{0, 1\}^m \to [0, 1]$ such that for $\delta 2^n = 2^{k+1}$ strings $r \in \{0, 1\}^n$ the average f-value of the sample $G(r)$ deviates from $\overline{f} \stackrel{\text{def}}{=} \mathsf{E}[f(U_m)]$ by more than ε. Suppose, without loss of generality, that for at least half of these r's the average is greater than $\overline{f} + \varepsilon$, and let B denote the set of these r's. Then, for X that is uniformly distributed on B and is thus an (n, k)-source, we have

$$\mathsf{E}[f(\text{Ext}(U_d, X))] > \mathsf{E}[f(U_m)] + \varepsilon,$$

which (using $|f(z)| \le 1$ for every z) contradicts the hypothesis that $\text{Ext}(U_d, X)$ is ε-close to U_m.

D.4.1.3. Extractors as Randomness-Efficient Error Reductions

As may be clear from the foregoing discussion, extractors yield randomness-efficient methods for error reduction. This is the case because *erro reduction is a special case of the sampling problem*, obtained by considering Boolean functions. Specifically, for a two-sided error decision procedure A, consider the function $f_x : \{0, 1\}^{\rho(|x|)} \to \{0, 1\}$ such that $f_x(r) = 1$ if $A(x, r) = 1$ and $f_x(r) = 0$ otherwise. Assuming that the probability that A is correct is at least $0.5 + \varepsilon$ (say $\varepsilon = 1/6$), error reduction amounts to providing a sampler with accuracy ε and any desired error probability $\delta \ll \varepsilon$ for the Boolean function f_x. Thus, by §D.4.1.2, any (k, ε)-extractor $\text{Ext} : \{0, 1\}^d \times \{0, 1\}^n \to \{0, 1\}^{\rho(|x|)}$ with $k = n - \log(1/\delta) - 1$ yields the desired error reduction, provided that 2^d is feasible (e.g., $2^d = \text{poly}(\rho(|x|))$, where $\rho(\cdot)$ represents the randomness complexity of the original algorithm A). The question of interest here is how n (which represents the randomness complexity of the corresponding sampler) grows as a function of $\rho(|x|)$ and δ.

Error reduction using the extractor $\text{Ext} : [\text{poly}(\rho(|x|))] \times \{0, 1\}^n \to \{0, 1\}^{\rho(|x|)}$

	error probability	randomness complexity
original algorithm	1/3	$\rho(|x|)$
resulting algorithm	δ (may depend on $|x|$)	n (function of $\rho(|x|)$ and δ)

Needless to say, the answer to the foregoing question depends on the quality of the extractor that we use. In particular, using Part 1 of the forthcoming Theorem D.10, we note that for every $\alpha > 1$, one can obtain $n = O(\rho(|x|)) + \alpha \log_2(1/\delta)$, for any $\delta > 2^{-\text{poly}(\rho(|x|))}$. Note that, for $\delta < 2^{-O(\rho(|x|))}$, this bound on the randomness complexity of error reduction is better than the bound of $n = \rho(|x|) + O(\log(1/\delta))$ that is provided (for the reduction of one-sided error) by the Expander Random Walk Generator (of Section 8.5.3), albeit the number of samples here is larger (i.e., $\text{poly}(\rho(|x|)/\delta)$ rather than $O(\log(1/\delta))$).

Mentioning the reduction of *one-sided* error probability brings us to a corresponding relaxation of the notion of an extractor, which is called a disperser. Loosely speaking, a (k, ε)-disperser is only required to hit (with positive probability) any set of density greater than ε in its image, rather than produce a distribution that is ε-close to uniform.

> **Definition D.9** (dispersers): *An algorithm* $\mathrm{Dsp} : \{0, 1\}^d \times \{0, 1\}^n \to \{0, 1\}^m$ *is called a* (k, ε)-disperser *if for every* (n, k)-source X *the support of* $\mathrm{Dsp}(U_d, X)$ *covers at least* $(1 - \varepsilon) \cdot 2^m$ *points. Alternatively, for every set* $S \subset \{0, 1\}^m$ *of size greater than* $\varepsilon 2^m$ *it holds that* $\Pr[\mathrm{Dsp}(U_d, X) \in S] > 0$.

Dispersers can be used for the reduction of one-sided error analogously to the use of extractors for the reduction of two-sided error. Specifically, regarding the afore-mentioned function f_x (and assuming that $\Pr[f_x(U_{\ell(|x|)}) = 1] > \varepsilon$), we may use any (k, ε)-disperser $\mathrm{Dsp} : \{0, 1\}^d \times \{0, 1\}^n \to \{0, 1\}^{\ell(|x|)}$ toward finding a point z such that $f_x(z) = 1$. Indeed, if $\Pr[f_x(U_{\ell(|x|)}) = 1] > \varepsilon$ then there are fewer than 2^k points z such that $(\forall s \in \{0, 1\}^d)\, f_x(\mathrm{Dsp}(s, z)) = 0$, and thus the one-sided error can be reduced from $1 - \varepsilon$ to $2^{-(n-k)}$ while using n random bits. (Note that dispersers are closely related to hitters (cf. Appendix D.3.3), analogously to the relation of extractors and averaging samplers.)

D.4.1.4. Other Perspectives

Extractors and dispersers have an appealing interpretation in terms of bipartite graphs. Starting with dispersers, we view any (k, ε)-disperser $\mathrm{Dsp} : \{0, 1\}^d \times \{0, 1\}^n \to \{0, 1\}^m$ as a bipartite graph $G = ((\{0, 1\}^n, \{0, 1\}^m), E)$ such that $E = \{(x, \mathrm{Dsp}(s, x)) : x \in \{0, 1\}^n, s \in \{0, 1\}^d\}$. This graph has the property that *any* subset of 2^k vertices on the left (i.e., in $\{0, 1\}^n$) has a neighborhood that contains at least a $1 - \varepsilon$ fraction of the vertices of the right, which is remarkable in the typical case where d is small (e.g., $d = O(\log n/\varepsilon)$) and $n \gg k \geq m$ whereas $m = \Omega(k)$ (or at least $m = k^{\Omega(1)}$). Further-more, if Dsp is efficiently computable, then this bipartite graph is strongly constructible in the sense that, given a vertex on the left, one can efficiently find each of its neighbors. Any (k, ε)-extractor Ext $: \{0, 1\}^d \times \{0, 1\}^n \to \{0, 1\}^m$ yields an analogous graph with an even stronger property: The neighborhood multi-set of *any* subset of 2^k vertices on the left covers the vertices on the right in an almost-uniform manner.

An odd perspective. In addition to viewing extractors as averaging samplers, which in turn may be viewed within the scope of the pseudorandomness paradigm, we mention here an even odder perspective. Specifically, randomness extractors may be viewed as randomized algorithms (distinguishers) designed on purpose so as to be fooled by any weak random source (but not by an even worse source). Specifically, for any (k, ε)-extractor Ext $: \{0, 1\}^d \times \{0, 1\}^n \to \{0, 1\}^m$, where $\varepsilon \leq 1/100$, $m = k = \omega(\log n/\varepsilon)$ and $d = O(\log n/\varepsilon)$, consider the following class of distinguishers (or tests), parameterized by subsets of $\{0, 1\}^m$ such that the test associated with $S \subset \{0, 1\}^m$, denoted T_S, satisfies $\Pr[T_S(x) = 1] = \Pr[\mathrm{Ext}(U_d, x) \in S]$; that is, on input $x \in \{0, 1\}^n$, the test T_S uniformly selects $s \in \{0, 1\}^d$, and outputs 1 if and only if $\mathrm{Ext}(s, x) \in S$. Then, as shown next, any (n, k)-source is "pseudorandom" with respect to this class of distinguishers, but sufficiently "non-(n, k)-sources" are not "pseudorandom" with respect to this class of distinguishers.

1. For every (n, k)-source X and every $S \subset \{0, 1\}^m$, the test T_S does not distinguish X from U_n (i.e., $\Pr[T_S(X)=1] = \Pr[T_S(U_n)=1] \pm 2\varepsilon$), because $\text{Ext}(U_d, X)$ is 2ε-close to $\text{Ext}(U_d, U_n)$ (since each is ε-close to U_m).

2. On the other hand, for every $(n, k - d - 4)$-flat source Y there exists a set S such that T_S distinguishes Y from U_n with gap at least 0.9 (e.g., for S that equals the support of $\text{Ext}(U_d, Y)$, it holds that $\Pr[T_S(Y)=1] = 1$ but $\Pr[T_S(U_n)=1] \leq \Pr[U_m \in S] + \varepsilon = 2^{d+(k-d-4)-m} + \varepsilon < 0.1$). Furthermore, any source that has entropy below $(k/4) - d$ will be detected as defected by this class (with probability at least $2/3$).[9]

Thus, this weird class of tests deems each (n, k)-source as "pseudorandom" while deeming sources of significantly lower entropy (e.g., entropy lower than $(k/4) - d$) as non-pseudorandom. Indeed, this perspective stretches the pseudorandomness paradigm quite far.

D.4.2. Constructions

Recall that we seek explicit constructions of extractors, that is, functions $\text{Ext} : \{0, 1\}^d \times \{0, 1\}^n \to \{0, 1\}^m$ that can be computed in polynomial time. The question, of course, is of parameters, that is, having explicit (k, ε)-extractors *with m as large as possible and d as small as possible*. We first note that, except in "pathological" cases,[10] both $m \leq k + d - (2 \log_2(1/\varepsilon) - O(1))$ and $d \geq \log_2((n - k)/\varepsilon^2) - O(1)$ must hold, regardless of the explicitness requirement. The aforementioned bounds are in fact tight; that is, there exist (non-explicit) (k, ε)-extractors with $m = k + d - 2 \log_2(1/\varepsilon) - O(1)$ and $d = \log_2((n - k)/\varepsilon^2) + O(1)$. The obvious goal is meeting these bounds via explicit constructions.

D.4.2.1. Some Known Results

Despite tremendous progress on this problem (and occasional claims regarding "optimal" explicit constructions), the ultimate goal has not been reached yet. Nevertheless, the known explicit constructions are pretty close to being optimal.

> **Theorem D.10** (explicit constructions of extractors): *Explicit (k, ε)-extractors of the form* $\text{Ext} : \{0, 1\}^d \times \{0, 1\}^n \to \{0, 1\}^m$ *exist for the following cases (i.e., settings of the parameters d and m):*
>
> 1. *For $d = O(\log n/\varepsilon)$ and $m = (1 - \alpha) \cdot (k - O(d))$, where $\alpha > 0$ is an arbitrarily small constant and provided that $\varepsilon > \exp(-k^{1-\alpha})$.*
> 2. *For $d = (1 + \alpha) \cdot \log_2 n$ and $m = k/\text{poly}(\log n)$, where $\varepsilon, \alpha > 0$ are arbitrarily small constants.*

Proofs of Part 1 and Part 2 can be found in [113] and [201], respectively. We note that, for the sake of simplicity, we did not quote the best possible bounds. Furthermore, we did not mention additional incomparable results (which are relevant for different ranges of parameters).

---

[9] For any such source Y, the distribution $Z = \text{Ext}(U_d, Y)$ has entropy at most $k/4 = m/4$, and thus is 0.7-far from U_m (and $2/3$-far from $\text{Ext}(U_d, U_n)$). The lower bound on the statistical distance between Z and U_m can be proved by the contra positive: If Z is δ-close to U_m then its entropy is at least $(1 - \delta) \cdot m - 1$ (e.g., by using Fano's inequality, see [63, Thm. 2.11.1]).

[10] That is, for $\varepsilon < 1/2$ and $m > d$.

We refrain from providing an overview of the proof of Theorem D.10, but rather review the proof of a weaker result that provides *explicit* $(n^\gamma, \text{poly}(1/n))$-*extractors for the case of* $d = O(\log n)$ *and* $m = n^{\Omega(\gamma)}$, *where* $\gamma > 0$ *is an arbitrarily small constant*. Indeed, in §D.4.2.2, we review the conceptual insight that underlies this result (as well as much of the subsequent developments in the area).

D.4.2.2. The Pseudorandomness Connection

We conclude this section with an overview of a fruitful connection between extractors and certain pseudorandom generators. The connection, discovered by Trevisan [222], is surprising in the sense that it goes in a non-standard direction: It transforms certain pseudorandom generators into extractors. As argued throughout this book (most conspicuously at the end of Section 7.1.2), computational objects are typically more complex than the corresponding information-theoretical objects. Thus, if pseudorandom generators and extractors are at all related (which was not suspected before [222]), then this relation should not be expected to help in the construction of extractors, which seem an information-theoretic object. Nevertheless, the discovery of this relation did yield a breakthrough in the study of extractors.[11]

Teaching note: The current text assumes familiarity with pseudorandom generators and in particular with the Nisan-Wigderson Generator (presented in §8.3.2.1).

But before describing the connection, let us wonder for a moment. Just looking at the syntax, we note that pseudorandom generators have a single input (i.e., the seed), while extractors have two inputs (i.e., the n-bit long source and the d-bit long seed). But taking a second look at the Nisan-Wigderson Generator (i.e., the combination of Construction 8.17 with an amplification of worst-case to average-case hardness), we note that this construction can be viewed as taking two inputs: a d-bit long seed and a "hard" predicate on d'-bit long strings (where $d' = \Omega(d)$).[12] Now, an appealing idea is to use the n-bit long source as a (truth-table) description of a (worse-case) hard predicate (which indeed means setting $n = 2^{d'}$). The key observation is that *even if the source is only weakly random, then it is likely to represent a predicate that is hard on the worst case*.

Recall that the aforementioned construction is supposed to yield a pseudorandom generator whenever it starts with a hard predicate. In the current context, where there are no computational restrictions, pseudorandomness is supposed to hold against any (computationally unbounded) distinguisher, and thus here, pseudorandomness means being statistically close to the uniform distribution (on strings of the adequate length, denoted ℓ). Intuitively, this makes sense only if the observed sequence is shorter than the amount of randomness in the source (and seed), which is indeed the case (i.e., $\ell < k + d$, where k denotes the min-entropy of the source). Hence, there is hope of obtaining a good extractor this way.

To turn the hope into a reality, we need a proof (which is sketched next). Looking again at the Nisan-Wigderson Generator, we note that the proof of indistinguishability

---

[11] We note that once the connection became better understood, influence started going in the "right" direction: from extractors to pseudorandom generators.

[12] Indeed, to fit the current context, we have modified some notations. In Construction 8.17 the length of the seed is denoted by k and the length of the input for the predicate is denoted by m.

of this generator provides a black-box procedure for computing the underlying predicate when given oracle access to any potential distinguisher. Specifically, in the proofs of Theorems 7.19 and 8.18 (which holds for any $\ell = 2^{\Omega(d')}$),[13] this black-box procedure was implemented by a *relatively small circuit* (which depends on the underlying predicate). Hence, this procedure contains relatively little information (regarding the underlying predicate), on top of the observed ℓ-bit long output of the extractor/generator. Specifically, for some fixed polynomial p, the amount of information encoded in the procedure (and thus available to it) is upper-bounded by $b \overset{\text{def}}{=} p(\ell)$, while the procedure is supposed to compute the underlying predicate correctly on each input. That is, b bits of information are supposed to fully determined the underlying predicate, which in turn is identical to the n-bit long source. However, if the source has min-entropy exceeding b, then it cannot be fully determined using only b bits of information. It follows that the foregoing construction constitutes a $(b + O(1), 1/6)$-extractor (outputting $\ell = b^{\Omega(1)}$ bits), where the constant $1/6$ is the one used in the proof of Theorem 8.18 (and the argument holds provided that $b = n^{\Omega(1)}$). Note that this extractor uses a seed of length $d = O(d') = O(\log n)$. The argument can be extended to obtain $(k, \text{poly}(1/k))$-extractors that output $k^{\Omega(1)}$ bits using a seed of length $d = O(\log n)$, provided that $k = n^{\Omega(1)}$.

We note that the foregoing description has only referred to two abstract properties of the Nisan-Wigderson Generator: (1) the fact that this generator uses any worst-case hard predicate as a black-box, and (2) the fact that its analysis uses any distinguisher as a black-box. In particular, we viewed the amplification of worst-case hardness to inapproximability (performed in Theorem 7.19) as part of the construction of the pseudorandom generator. An alternative presentation, which is more self-contained, replaces the amplification step of Theorem 7.19 with a direct argument in the current (information-theoretic) context and plugs the resulting predicate directly into Construction 8.17. The advantages of this alternative include using a simpler amplification (since amplification is simpler in the information-theoretic setting than in the computational setting), and deriving transparent construction and analysis (which mirror Construction 8.17 and Theorem 8.18, respectively).

The alternative presentation. The foregoing analysis transforms a generic distinguisher into a procedure that computes the underlying predicate correctly on each input, which fully determines this predicate. Hence, an upper bound on the information available to this procedure yields an upper bound on the number of possible outcomes of the source that are bad for the extractor. In the alternative presentation, we transform a generic distinguisher into a procedure that only approximates the underlying predicate; that is, the procedure yields a function that is relatively close to the underlying predicate. If the potential underlying predicates are far apart, then this yields the desired bound (on the number of bad source-outcomes that correspond to such predicates). Thus, the idea is to encode the n-bit long source by an error-correcting code of length $n' = \text{poly}(n)$ and relative distance $0.5 - (1/n)^2$, and use the resulting codeword as a truth table of a predicate for Construction 8.17.[14] Such codes (coupled with efficient encoding algorithms) do exist (see §E.1.2.5), and the benefit in using them is that each n'-bit long string (determined by the information available to the aforementioned approximation procedure) may be

---

[13] Recalling that $n = 2^{d'}$, the restriction $\ell = 2^{\Omega(d')}$ implies $\ell = n^{\Omega(1)}$.

[14] Indeed, the use of this error-correcting code replaces the hardness-amplification step of Theorem 7.19.

$(0.5 - (1/n))$-close to at most $O(n^2)$ codewords[15] (which correspond to potential predicates). Thus, each approximation procedure rules out at most $O(n^2)$ potential predicates (i.e., source outcomes). In summary, *the resulting extractor converts the n-bit input x into a codeword $x' \in \{0, 1\}^{n'}$, viewed as a predicate over $\{0, 1\}^{d'}$ (where $d' = \log_2 n'$), and evaluates this predicate at the ℓ projections of the d-bit long seed, where these projections (to d' bits) are determined by the corresponding set system* (i.e., the ℓ-long sequence of d'-subsets of $[d]$ that is used in Construction 8.17). The analysis mirrors the proof of Theorem 8.18, and yields a bound of $2^{O(\ell^2)} \cdot O(n^2)$ on the number of bad outcomes for the source, where $O(\ell^2)$ upper-bounds the amount of information encoded in (and available to) the approximation procedure, and $O(n^2)$ upper-bounds the number of source-outcomes that correspond to codewords that are each $(0.5 - (1/n))$-close to any fixed approximation procedure.

D.4.2.3. Recommended Reading

The interested reader is referred to a survey of Shaltiel [200]. This survey contains a comprehensive introduction to the area, including an overview of the ideas that underlie the various constructions. In particular, the survey describes the approaches used before the discovery of the pseudorandomness connection, the connection itself (and the constructions that arise from it), and the "third generation" of constructions that followed.

The aforementioned survey predates the most recent constructions (of extractors) that extract a constant fraction of the min-entropy using a logarithmically long seed (cf. Part 1 of Theorem D.10). Such constructions were first presented in [159] and improved (using different ideas) in [113]. Indeed, we refer the reader to [113], which provides a self-contained description of the best-known extractor (for almost all settings of the relevant parameters).

---

[15] See Appendix E.1.4.

Explicit Constructions

It is easier for a camel to go through the eye of a needle, than for a rich man to enter into the kingdom of God.

Matthew, 19:24.

Complexity Theory provides a clear definition of the intuitive notion of an explicit construction. Furthermore, it also suggests a hierarchy of different levels of explicitness, referring to the ease of constructing the said object.

The *basic levels of explicitness* are provided by considering the complexity of fully constructing the object (e.g., the time it takes to print the truth table of a finite function). In this context, explicitness often means outputting a full description of the object in time that is polynomial in the length of that description. *Stronger levels of explicitness* emerge when considering the complexity of answering natural queries regarding the object (e.g., the time it takes to evaluate a fixed function at a given input). In this context, (strong) explicitness often means answering such queries in polynomial time.

The aforementioned themes are demonstrated in our brief review of explicit constructions of *error-correcting codes* and *expander graphs*. These constructions are, in turn, used in various parts of the main text.

Summary: This appendix provides a brief overview of aspects of coding theory and expander graphs that are most relevant to Complexity Theory. Starting with coding theory, we review several popular constructions of error-correcting codes, culminating in the construction of a "good" binary code (i.e., a code that achieves constant relative distance and constant rate). The latter code is obtained by "concatenating" a Reed-Solomon code with a "mildly explicit" construction of a "good" binary code (which is applied to small pieces of information). We also briefly review the notions of locally testable and locally decodable codes, and present a useful "list-decoding bound" (i.e., an upper bound on the number of codewords that are close to any single sequence).

Turning to expander graphs, we review two standard definitions of expansion (representing combinatorial and algebraic perspectives), and two properties of expanders that are related to (single-step and multi-step) random walks on them. We also spell out two levels of explicitness of graphs, which correspond to the aforementioned notions of basic and strong explicitness. Finally, we review two explicit constructions of expander graphs.

E.1. Error-Correcting Codes

In this section we highlight some issues and aspects of coding theory that are most relevant to the current book. The interested reader is referred to [217] for a more comprehensive treatment of the computational aspects of coding theory. Structural aspects of coding theory, which are the traditional focus of that field, are covered in standard textbook such as [163].

E.1.1. Basic Notions

Loosely speaking, an error-correcting code is a mapping of strings to longer strings such that any two different strings are mapped to a corresponding pair of strings that are far apart (and not merely different). Specifically, $C : \{0, 1\}^k \to \{0, 1\}^n$ is a (binary) code of distance d if for every $x \neq y \in \{0, 1\}^k$ it holds that $C(x)$ and $C(y)$ differ on at least d bit positions. Indeed, *the relation between k, n and d is of major concern: Typically, the aim is to have a large distance* (i.e., large d) *without introducing too much redundancy*[1] (i.e., have n as small as possible with respect to k (and d)).

It will be useful to extend the foregoing definition to sequences over an arbitrary (finite) alphabet Σ, and to use some notations. Specifically, for $x \in \Sigma^m$, we denote the ith symbol of x by x_i (i.e., $x = x_1 \cdots x_m$), and consider codes over Σ (i.e., mappings of Σ-sequences to Σ-sequences). The mapping (code) $C : \Sigma^k \to \Sigma^n$ has distance d if for every $x \neq y \in \Sigma^k$ it holds that $|\{i : C(x)_i \neq C(y)_i\}| \geq d$. The members of $\{C(x) : x \in \Sigma^k\}$ are called codewords (and in some texts this set itself is called a code).

In general, we define a metric, called the Hamming distance, over the set of n-long sequences over Σ. The Hamming distance between y and z, where $y, z \in \Sigma^n$, is defined as the number of locations on which they disagree (i.e., $|\{i : y_i \neq z_i\}|$). The Hamming weight of such sequences is defined as the number of non-zero elements (assuming that one element of Σ is viewed as zero). Typically, Σ is associated with an additive group, and in this case the distance between y and z equals the Hamming weight of $w = y - z$, where $w_i = y_i - z_i$ (for every i).

Asymptotics. We will actually consider infinite families of codes; that is, $\{C_k : \Sigma_k^k \to \Sigma_k^{n(k)}\}_{k \in S}$, where $S \subseteq \mathbb{N}$ (and typically $S = \mathbb{N}$). (N.B., we allow Σ_k to depend on k.) We say that such a family has distance $d : \mathbb{N} \to \mathbb{N}$ if for every $k \in S$ it holds that C_k has distance $d(k)$. Needless to say, both $n = n(k)$ (called the block-length) and $d(k)$ depend on k, and *the aim is having a linear dependence* (i.e., $n(k) = O(k)$ and $d(k) = \Omega(n(k))$). In such a case, one talks of the relative rate of the code (i.e., the constant $k/n(k)$) and its relative distance (i.e., the constant $d(k)/n(k)$). In general, we will often refer to *relative distances* between sequences. For example, for $y, z \in \Sigma^n$, we say that y and z are ε-close (resp., ε-far) if $|\{i : y_i \neq z_i\}| \leq \varepsilon \cdot n$ (resp., $|\{i : y_i \neq z_i\}| \geq \varepsilon \cdot n$).

Explicitness. A mild notion of explicitness refers to constructing the list of all codewords in time that is polynomial in its length (which is exponential in k). A more standard notion of explicitness refers to generating a specific codeword (i.e., producing $C(x)$ when given x), which coincides with the encoding task mentioned next. Stronger notions

---

[1]Note that a trivial way of obtaining distance d is to duplicate each symbol d times. This ("repetition") code satisfies $n = d \cdot k$, while we shall seek $n \ll d \cdot k$. Indeed, as we shall see, one can obtain simultaneously $n = O(k)$ and $d = \Omega(k)$.

of explicitness refer to other computational problems concerning codes (e.g., various decoding tasks).

Computational problems. The most basic computational tasks associated with codes are encoding and decoding (under noise). The definition of the encoding task is straightforward (i.e., map $x \in \Sigma_k^k$ to $C_k(x)$), and an efficient algorithm is required to compute each symbol in $C_k(x)$ in poly(k, $\log |\Sigma_k|$)-time.[2] When defining the decoding task we note that "minimum distance decoding" (i.e., given $w \in \Sigma_k^{n(k)}$, find x such that $C_k(x)$ is closest to w (in Hamming distance)) is just one natural possibility. Two related variants, regarding a code of distance d, are:

Unique decoding: Given $w \in \Sigma_k^{n(k)}$ that is at Hamming distance less than $d(k)/2$ from some codeword $C_k(x)$, retrieve the corresponding decoding of $C_k(x)$ (i.e., retrieve x).

Needless to say, this task is well defined because there cannot be two different codewords that are each at Hamming distance less than $d(k)/2$ from w.

List decoding: Given $w \in \Sigma_k^{n(k)}$ and a parameter d' (which may be greater than $d(k)/2$), output a list of all codewords (or rather their decoding) that are at Hamming distance at most d' from w. (That is, the task is outputting the list of all $x \in \Sigma_k^k$ such that $C_k(x)$ is at distance at most d' from w.)

Typically, one considers the case that $d' < d(k)$. See Section E.1.4 for a discussion of upper bounds on the number of codewords that are within a certain distance from a generic sequence.

Two additional computational tasks are considered in Section E.1.3.

Linear codes. Associating Σ_k with some finite field, we call a code $C_k : \Sigma_k^k \to \Sigma_k^{n(k)}$ linear if it satisfies $C_k(x + y) = C_k(x) + C_k(y)$, where x and y (resp., $C_k(x)$ and $C_k(y)$) are viewed as k-dimensional (resp., $n(k)$-dimensional) vectors over Σ_k, and the arithmetic is of the corresponding vector space. A useful property of linear codes is that their distance equals the Hamming weight of the lightest codeword other than $C_k(0^k)$ ($= 0^{n(k)}$); that is, $\min_{x \neq y}\{|\{i : C_k(x)_i \neq C_k(y)_i\}|\}$ equals $\min_{x \neq 0^k}\{|\{i : C_k(x)_i \neq 0\}|\}$. Another useful property of linear codes is that the code is fully specified by a k-by-$n(k)$ matrix, called the generating matrix, that consists of the codewords of some fixed basis of Σ_k^k. That is, the set of all codewords is obtained by taking all $|\Sigma_k|^k$ different linear combination of the rows of the generating matrix.

E.1.2. A Few Popular Codes

Our focus will be on explicitly constructible codes; that is, (families of) codes of the form $\{C_k : \Sigma_k^k \to \Sigma_k^{n(k)}\}_{k \in S}$ that are coupled with efficient encoding and decoding algorithms. But before presenting several such codes, let us consider a non-explicit code (having "good parameters"); that is, the following result asserts the existence of certain codes without pointing to any specific code (let alone an explicit one).

---

[2]The foregoing formulation is not the one that is common in coding theory, but it is the most natural one for our applications. On the one hand, this formulation is also applicable to codes with super-polynomial block-length. On the other hand, this formulation does not support a discussion of practical algorithms that compute the codeword faster than is possible when computing each of the codeword's bits separately.

Proposition E.1 (on the distance of random linear codes): *Let* $n, d, t : \mathbb{N} \to \mathbb{N}$ *be such that, for all sufficiently large k, it holds that*

$$n(k) \geq \max \left(2d(k), \frac{k + t(k)}{1 - H_2(d(k)/n(k))} \right), \tag{E.1}$$

where $H_2(\alpha) \overset{\text{def}}{=} \alpha \log_2(1/\alpha) + (1 - \alpha) \log_2(1/(1 - \alpha))$. *Then, for all sufficiently large k, with probability greater than* $1 - 2^{-t(k)}$, *a random linear transformation of* $\{0, 1\}^k$ *to* $\{0, 1\}^{n(k)}$ *constitutes a code of distance* $d(k)$.

Indeed, for asserting that most random linear codes are good it suffices to set $t = 1$, while for merely asserting the existence of a good linear code even setting $t = 0$ will do. Also, *for every constant* $\delta \in (0, 0.5)$ *there exists a constant* $\rho > 0$ *and an infinite family of codes* $\{C_k : \{0, 1\}^k \to \{0, 1\}^{k/\rho}\}_{k \in \mathbb{N}}$ *of relative distance* δ. Specifically, the constant $\rho = (1 - H_2(\delta))$ will do.

Proof: We consider a uniformly selected k-by-$n(k)$ generating matrix over GF(2), and upper-bound the probability that it yields a linear code of distance less than $d(k)$. We use a union bound on all possible $2^k - 1$ linear combinations of the rows of the generating matrix, where for each such combination we compute the probability that it yields a codeword of Hamming weight less than $d(k)$. Observe that the result of each such linear combination is uniformly distributed over $\{0, 1\}^{n(k)}$, and thus this codeword has Hamming weight less than $d(k)$ with probability $p \overset{\text{def}}{=} \sum_{i=0}^{d(k)-1} \binom{n(k)}{i} \cdot 2^{-n(k)}$. Clearly, for $d(k) \leq n(k)/2$, it holds that $p < d(k) \cdot 2^{-(1-H_2(d(k)/n(k))) \cdot n(k)}$, but actually $p \leq 2^{-(1-H_2(d(k)/n(k))) \cdot n(k)}$ holds as well (e.g., use [11, Cor. 14.6.3]). Using $(1 - H_2(d(k)/n(k))) \cdot n(k) \geq k + t(k)$, the proposition follows. ∎

E.1.2.1. A Mildly Explicit Version of Proposition E.1

Note that Proposition E.1 yields a deterministic algorithm that finds a linear code of distance $d(k)$ by conducting an exhaustive search over all possible generating matrices; that is, a good code can be found in time $\exp(k \cdot n(k))$. The time bound can be improved to $\exp(k + n(k))$, by constructing the generating matrix in iterations such that, at each iteration, the current set of rows is augmented with a single row while maintaining the natural invariance (i.e., all non-empty linear combinations of the current rows have weight at least $d(k)$). Thus, at each iteration, we conduct an exhaustive search over all possible values of the next ($n(k)$-bit long) row, and for each such candidate value, we check whether the foregoing invariance holds (by considering all linear combinations of the previous rows and the current candidate).

Note that the proof of Proposition E.1 can be adapted to assert that, as long as we have fewer than k rows, a random choice of the next row will do with positive probability. Thus, the foregoing iterative algorithm finds a good code in time $\sum_{i=1}^{k} 2^{n(k)} \cdot 2^{i-1} \cdot \text{poly}(n(k)) = \exp(n(k) + k)$. In the case that $n(k) = O(k)$, this yields an algorithm that runs in time that is polynomial in the size of the code (i.e., the number of codewords (i.e., 2^k)). Needless to say, this mild level of explicitness is inadequate for most coding applications; however, it will be useful to us in §E.1.2.5.

E.1.2.2. The Hadamard Code

The Hadamard code is the longest (non-repetitive) *linear* code over $\{0, 1\} \equiv GF(2)$. That is, $x \in \{0, 1\}^k$ is mapped to the sequence of all $n(k) = 2^k$ possible linear combinations of its bits; that is, bit locations in the codewords are associated with k-bit strings such that location $\alpha \in \{0, 1\}^k$ in the codeword of x holds the value $\sum_{i=1}^{k} \alpha_i x_i$. It can be verified that each non-zero codeword has weight 2^{k-1}, and thus this code has relative distance $d(k)/n(k) = 1/2$ (albeit its block-length $n(k)$ is exponential in k).

Turning to the computational aspects, we note that encoding is very easy. As for decoding, the warm-up discussion at the beginning of the proof of Theorem 7.7 provides a very fast probabilistic algorithm for unique decoding, whereas Theorem 7.8 itself provides a very fast probabilistic algorithm for list decoding.

We mention that the Hadamard code has played a key role in the proof of the PCP Theorem (Theorem 9.16); see §9.3.2.1.

A propos long codes. We mention that the longest (non-repetitive) binary code (called the Long-Code and introduced in [29]) is extensively used in the design of "advanced" PCP-systems (see, e.g., [116, 117]). In this code, a k-bit long string x is mapped to the sequence of $n(k) = 2^{2^k}$ values, each corresponding to the evaluation of a different Boolean function at x; that is, bit locations in the codewords are associated with Boolean functions such that the location associated with $f : \{0, 1\}^k \to \{0, 1\}$ in the codeword of x holds the value $f(x)$.

E.1.2.3. The Reed–Solomon Code

Reed-Solomon codes can be defined for any adequate non-binary alphabet, where the alphabet is associated with a finite field of n elements, denoted $GF(n)$. For any $k < n$, the code maps univariate polynomial of degree $k - 1$ over $GF(n)$ to their evaluation at all field elements. That is, $p \in GF(n)^k$ (viewed as such a polynomial), is mapped to the sequence $(p(\alpha_1), \ldots, p(\alpha_n))$, where $\alpha_1, \ldots, \alpha_n$ is a canonical enumeration of the elements of $GF(n)$.[3] This mapping is called a Reed-Solomon code with parameters k and n, and its distance is $n - k + 1$ (because any non-zero polynomial of degree $k - 1$ evaluates to zero at less than k points). Indeed, this code is linear (over $GF(n)$), since $p(\alpha)$ is a linear combination of $p_0, \ldots, p_{k-1}$, where $p(\zeta) = \sum_{i=0}^{k-1} p_i \zeta^i$.

The Reed-Solomon code yields infinite families of codes with constant rate and constant relative distance (e.g., by taking $n(k) = 3k$ and $d(k) = 2k$), but the alphabet size grows with k (or rather with $n(k) > k$). Efficient algorithms for unique decoding and list decoding are known (see [216] and references therein). These computational tasks correspond to the extrapolation of polynomials based on a noisy version of their values at all possible evaluation points.

E.1.2.4. The Reed–Muller Code

Reed-Muller codes generalize Reed-Solomon codes by considering multivariate polynomials rather than univariate polynomials. Consecutively, the alphabet may be any finite field, and in particular the two-element field $GF(2)$. Reed-Muller codes (and variants of them) are extensively used in Complexity Theory; for example, they underlie

---

[3]Alternatively, we may map $(v_1, \ldots, v_k) \in GF(n)^k$ to $(p(\alpha_1), \ldots, p(\alpha_n))$, where p is the unique univariate polynomial of degree $k - 1$ that satisfies $p(\alpha_i) = v_i$ for $i = 1, \ldots, k$. Note that this modification amounts to a linear transformation of the generating matrix.

Construction 7.11 and the PCP constructed at the end of §9.3.2.2. The relevant property of these (non-binary) codes is that, under a suitable setting of parameters that satisfies $n(k) = \text{poly}(k)$, they allow super-fast "codeword testing" and "self-correction" (see discussion in Section E.1.3).

For any prime power q and parameters m and r, we consider the set, denoted $P_{m,r}$, of all m-variate polynomials of *total degree* at most r over $GF(q)$. Each polynomial in $P_{m,r}$ is represented by the $k = \log_q |P_{m,r}|$ coefficients of all relevant monomials, where in the case that $r < q$ it holds that $k = \binom{m+r}{m}$. We consider the code $C : GF(q)^k \to GF(q)^n$, where $n = q^m$, mapping m-variate polynomials of total degree at most r to their values at all q^m evaluation points. That is, the m-variate polynomial p of total degree at most r is mapped to the sequence of values $(p(\overline{\alpha}_1), \ldots, p(\overline{\alpha}_n))$, where $\overline{\alpha}_1, \ldots, \overline{\alpha}_n$ is a canonical enumeration of all the m-tuples of $GF(q)$. The relative distance of this code is lower-bounded by $(q - r)/q$ (cf., Lemma 6.8).

In typical applications one sets $r = \Theta(m^2 \log m)$ and $q = \text{poly}(r)$, which yields $k > m^m$ and $n = \text{poly}(r)^m = \text{poly}(m^m)$. Thus, we have $n(k) = \text{poly}(k)$ but not $n(k) = O(k)$. As we shall see in Section E.1.3, the advantage (in comparison to the Reed-Solomon code) is that codeword testing and self-correction can be performed at complexity related to $q = \text{poly}(\log n)$. Actually, most complexity applications use a variant in which only m-variate polynomials of *individual degree $r' = r/m$* are encoded. In this case, an alternative presentation (analogous to the one presented in footnote 3) is preferred: The information is viewed as a function $f : H^m \to GF(q)$, where $H \subset GF(q)$ is of size $r' + 1$, and is encoded by the evaluation at all points in $GF(q)^m$ of the (unique) m-variate polynomial of individual degree r' that extends the function f (see Construction 7.11).

E.1.2.5. Binary Codes of Constant Relative Distance and Constant Rate
Recall that we seek binary codes of constant relative distance and constant rate. Proposition E.1 asserts that such codes exist, but does not provide an explicit construction. The Hadamard code is explicit but does not have a constant rate (to say the least (since $n(k) = 2^k$)).[4] The Reed-Solomon code has constant relative distance and constant rate but uses a non-binary alphabet (which grows at least linearly with k). Thus, all codes we have reviewed so far fall short of providing an *explicit construction of binary codes of constant relative distance and constant rate*. We achieve the desired construction by using the paradigm of concatenated codes [78], which is of independent interest. (Concatenated codes may be viewed as a simple analogue of the proof composition paradigm presented in §9.3.2.2.)

Intuitively, concatenated codes are obtained by first encoding information, viewed as a sequence over a large alphabet, by some code and next encoding each resulting symbol, which is viewed as a sequence over a smaller alphabet, by a second code. Formally, consider $\Sigma_1 \equiv \Sigma_2^{k_2}$ and two codes, $C_1 : \Sigma_1^{k_1} \to \Sigma_1^{n_1}$ and $C_2 : \Sigma_2^{k_2} \to \Sigma_2^{n_2}$. Then, the concatenated code of C_1 and C_2 maps $(x_1, \ldots, x_{k_1}) \in \Sigma_1^{k_1} \equiv \Sigma_2^{k_1 k_2}$ to $(C_2(y_1), \ldots, C_2(y_{n_1}))$, where $(y_1, \ldots, y_{n_1}) = C_1(x_1, \ldots, x_{k_1})$.

Note that the resulting code $C : \Sigma_2^{k_1 k_2} \to \Sigma_2^{n_1 n_2}$ has constant rate and constant relative distance if both C_1 and C_2 have these properties. Encoding in the concatenated code is straightforward. To decode a corrupted codeword of C, we view the input as an n_1-long sequence of blocks, where each block is an n_2-long sequence over Σ_2. Applying the decoder of C_2 to each block, we obtain n_1 sequences (each of length k_2) over Σ_2, and

---

[4] Binary Reed-Muller codes also fail to simultaneously provide constant relative distance and constant rate.

interpret each such sequence as a symbol of Σ_1. Finally, we apply the decoder of C_1 to the resulting n_1-long sequence (over Σ_1), and interpret the resulting k_1-long sequence (over Σ_1) as a $k_1 k_2$-long sequence over Σ_2. The key observation is that *if $w \in \Sigma_2^{n_1 n_2}$ is $\varepsilon_1 \varepsilon_2$-close to $C(x_1, \ldots, x_{k_1}) = (C_2(y_1), \ldots, C_2(y_{n_1}))$ then at least $(1 - \varepsilon_1) \cdot n_1$ of the blocks of w are ε_2-close to the corresponding $C_2(y_i)$.*[5]

We are going to consider the concatenated code obtained by using the Reed-Solomon code $C_1 : \mathrm{GF}(n_1)^{k_1} \to \mathrm{GF}(n_1)^{n_1}$ as the large code, setting $k_2 = \log_2 n_1$, and using the mildly explicit version of Proposition E.1 (see also §E.1.2.1) $C_2 : \{0, 1\}^{k_2} \to \{0, 1\}^{n_2}$ as the small code. We use $n_1 = 3k_1$ and $n_2 = O(k_2)$, and so the concatenated code is $C : \{0, 1\}^k \to \{0, 1\}^n$, where $k = k_1 k_2$ and $n = n_1 n_2 = O(k)$. The key observation is that C_2 can be constructed in $\exp(k_2)$-time, whereas here $\exp(k_2) = \mathrm{poly}(k)$. Furthermore, both encoding and decoding with respect to C_2 can be performed in time $\exp(k_2) = \mathrm{poly}(k)$. Thus, we get

Theorem E.2 (an explicit good code): *There exist constants $\delta, \rho > 0$ and an explicit family of binary codes of rate ρ and relative distance at least δ. That is, there exists a polynomial-time* (encoding) *algorithm C such that $|C(x)| = |x|/\rho$ (for every x) and a polynomial-time* (decoding) *algorithm D such that for every y that is $\delta/2$-close to some $C(x)$ it holds that $D(y) = x$. Furthermore, C is a linear code.*

The linearity of C is justified by using a Reed-Solomon code over the extension field $F = \mathrm{GF}(2^{k_2})$, and noting that this code induces a linear transformation over $\mathrm{GF}(2)$. Specifically, the value of a polynomial p over F at a point $\alpha \in F$ can be obtained as a linear transformation of the coefficient of p, when viewed as k_2-dimensional vectors over $\mathrm{GF}(2)$.

Relative distance approaching one half. Note that starting with a Reed-Solomon code of relative distance δ_1 and a smaller code C_2 of relative distance δ_2, we obtain a concatenated code of relative distance $\delta_1 \delta_2$. Recall that, for any constant $\delta_1 < 1$, there exists a Reed-Solomon code $C_1 : \mathrm{GF}(n_1)^{k_1} \to \mathrm{GF}(n_1)^{n_1}$ of relative distance δ_1 and constant rate (i.e., $1 - \delta_1$). Thus, for any constant $\varepsilon > 0$, we may obtain an explicit code of constant rate and relative distance $(1/2) - \varepsilon$ (e.g., by using $\delta_1 = 1 - (\varepsilon/2)$ and $\delta_2 = (1 - \varepsilon)/2$). Furthermore, giving up on constant rate, we may start with a Reed-Solomon code of block-length $n_1(k_1) = \mathrm{poly}(k_1)$ and distance $n_1(k_1) - k_1$ over $[n_1(k_1)]$, and use a Hadamard code (encoding $[n_1(k_1)] \equiv \{0, 1\}^{\log_2 n_1(k_1)}$ by $\{0, 1\}^{n_1(k_1)}$) in the role of the small code C_2. This yields a (concatenated) binary code of block-length $n(k) = n_1(k)^2 = \mathrm{poly}(k)$ and distance $(n_1(k) - k) \cdot n_1(k)/2$. Thus, *the resulting explicit code has relative distance* $\frac{1}{2} - \frac{k}{2\sqrt{n(k)}} = \frac{1}{2} - o(1)$, *provided that $n(k) = \omega(k^2)$.*

E.1.3. Two Additional Computational Problems

In this section we briefly review relaxations of two traditional coding-theoretic tasks. The purpose of these relaxations is to enable the design of super-fast (randomized) algorithms that provide meaningful information. Specifically, these algorithms may run in sub-linear

---

[5] This observation offers unique decoding from a fraction of errors that is the product of the fractions (of error) associated with the two original codes. Stronger statements regarding unique decoding of the concatenated code can be made based on more refined analysis (cf. [78]).

(e.g., poly-logarithmic) time, and thus cannot possibly solve the unrelaxed version of the corresponding problem.

Local testability. This task refers to testing whether a given word is a codeword (in a predetermined code), based on (randomly) inspecting few locations in the word. Needless to say, we can only hope to make an approximately correct decision, that is, accept each codeword and reject with high probability each word that is *far* from the code. (Indeed, this task is within the framework of property testing; see Section 10.1.2.)

Local decodability. Here, the task is to recover a specified bit in the plaintext by (randomly) inspecting few locations in a mildly corrupted codeword. This task is somewhat related to the task of self-correction (i.e., recovering a specified bit in the codeword itself, by inspecting few locations in the mildly corrupted codeword).

Note that the Hadamard code is both locally testable and locally decodable as well as self-correctable (based on a constant number of queries into the word); these facts were demonstrated and extensively used in §9.3.2.1. However, the Hadamard code has an exponential block-length (i.e., $n(k) = 2^k$), and the question is whether one can achieve analogous results with respect to a shorter code (e.g., $n(k) = \text{poly}(k)$). As hinted in §E.1.2.4, the answer is positive (when we refer to performing these operations in time that is poly-logarithmic in k):

> **Theorem E.3:** *For some constant $\delta > 0$ and polynomials $n, q : \mathbb{N} \to \mathbb{N}$, there exists an explicit family of codes $\{C_k : [q(k)]^k \to [q(k)]^{n(k)}\}_{k\in\mathbb{N}}$ of relative distance δ that can be locally testable and locally decodable in $\text{poly}(\log k)$-time. That is, the following three conditions hold.*
>
> 1. Encoding: *There exists a polynomial-time algorithm that on input $x \in [q(k)]^k$ returns $C_k(x)$.*
> 2. Local Testing: *There exists a probabilistic polynomial-time oracle machine T that given k (in binary)[6] and oracle access to $w \in [q(k)]^{n(k)}$ (viewed as $w : [n(k)] \to [q(k)]$) distinguishes the case that w is a codeword from the case that w is $\delta/2$-far from any codeword. Specifically:*
>   *(a) For every $x \in [q(k)]^k$ it holds that $\Pr[T^{C_k(x)}(k)=1] = 1$.*
>   *(b) For every $w \in [q(k)]^{n(k)}$ that is $\delta/2$-far from any codeword of C_k it holds that $\Pr[T^w(k)=1] \leq 1/2$.*
>
>   *As usual, the error probability can be reduced by repetitions.*
> 3. Local Decoding: *There exists a probabilistic polynomial-time oracle machine D that given k and $i \in [k]$ (in binary) and oracle access to any $w \in [q(k)]^{n(k)}$ that is $\delta/2$-close to $C_k(x)$ returns x_i; that is, $\Pr[D^w(k, i)=x_i] \geq 2/3$.*
>
>   *Self-correction holds, too: There exists a probabilistic polynomial-time oracle machine M that given k and $i \in [n(k)]$ (in binary) and oracle access to any $w \in [q(k)]^{n(k)}$ that is $\delta/2$-close to $C_k(x)$ returns $C_k(x)_i$; that is, $\Pr[D^w(k, i)= C_k(x)_i] \geq 2/3$.*

We stress that all of these oracle machines work in time that is polynomial in the binary representation of k, which means that they run in time that is poly-logarithmic in k.

---

[6]Thus, the running time of T is $\text{poly}(|k|) = \text{poly}(\log k)$.

The code asserted in Theorem E.3 is a (small modification of a) Reed-Muller code, for $r = m^2 \log m < q(k) = \text{poly}(r)$ and $[n(k)] \equiv \text{GF}(q(k))^m$ (see §E.1.2.4).[7] The aforementioned oracle machines query the oracle $w : [n(k)] \to \text{GF}(q(k))$ at a non-constant number of locations. Specifically, self-correction for location $i \in \text{GF}(q(k))^m$ is performed by selecting a random line (over $\text{GF}(q(k))^m$) that passes through i, recovering the values assigned by w to all $q(k)$ points on this line, and performing univariate polynomial extrapolation (under mild noise). Local testability is easily reduced to self-correction, and (under the aforementioned modification) local decodability is a special case of self-correction.

Constant number of (binary) queries. The local testing and decoding algorithms asserted in Theorem E.3 make a poly-logarithmic number of queries into the oracle. Furthermore, these queries (which refer to a non-binary code) are non-binary (i.e., they are each answered by a non-binary value). In contrast, the Hadamard code has local testing and decoding algorithms that use a *constant number of binary queries*. Can this be obtained with much shorter (binary) codewords? That is, redefining local testability and decodability as requiring a *constant number of queries*, we ask whether binary codes of significantly shorter block-length can be locally testable and decodable. For local testability the answer is definitely positive: One can construct such (locally testable and binary) codes with block-length that is nearly linear (i.e., linear up to poly-logarithmic factors; see [36, 67]). For local decodability, the shortest known code has super-polynomial length (see [242]). In light of this state of affairs, we advocate natural relaxations of the local decodability task (e.g., the one studied in [35]).

The interested reader is referred to [93], which includes more details on locally testable and decodable codes as well as a wider perspective. (Note, however, that this survey was written prior to [67] and [242], which resolve two major open problems discussed in [93].)

E.1.4. A List-Decoding Bound

A necessary condition for the feasibility of the list-decoding task is that the list of codewords that are close to the given word be short. In this section we present an upper bound on the length of such lists, noting that this bound has found several applications in Complexity Theory (and specifically to studies related to the contents of this book). In contrast, we do not present far more famous bounds (which typically refer to the relation among the main parameters of codes (i.e., k, n and d)), because they seem less relevant to the contents of this book.

We start with a general statement that refers to any alphabet $\Sigma \equiv [q]$, and later specialize it to the case that $q = 2$. Especially in the general case, it is natural and convenient to consider the agreement (rather than the distance) between sequences over $[q]$. Furthermore, it is natural to focus on an agreement rate of at least $1/q$, and it is convenient to state the following result in terms of the "excessive agreement rate" (i.e., the excess beyond $1/q$).[8] Loosely speaking, the following result upper-bounds the number of codewords that have a (sufficiently) large agreement rate with any fixed sequence, where the upper bound

---

[7]The modification is analogous to the one presented in footnote 3: For a suitable choice of k points $\overline{\alpha}_1, \ldots, \overline{\alpha}_k \in \text{GF}(q(k))^m$, we map $v_1, \ldots, v_k$ to $(p(\overline{\alpha}_1), \ldots, p(\overline{\alpha}_n))$, where p is the unique m-variate polynomial of degree at most r that satisfies $p(\overline{\alpha}_i) = v_i$ for $i = 1, \ldots, k$.

[8]Indeed, we only consider codes with distance $d \leq (1 - 1/q) \cdot n$ (i.e., agreement rate of at least $1/q$) and words that are at distance at most d from the code. Note that a random sequence is expected to agree with any fixed sequence on a $1/q$ fraction of the locations.

depends only on this agreement rate and the agreement rate between codewords (as well as on the alphabet size, but not on k and n).

Lemma E.4 (Part 2 [105, Thm. 15]): *Let $C : [q]^k \to [q]^n$ be an arbitrary code of distance $d \leq n - (n/q)$, and let $\eta_c \stackrel{\text{def}}{=} (1 - (d/n)) - (1/q) \geq 0$ denote the corresponding upper bound on the excessive agreement rate between codewords. Suppose that $\eta \in (0, 1)$ satisfies*

$$\eta > \sqrt{\left(1 - \frac{1}{q}\right) \cdot \eta_c} \tag{E.2}$$

Then, for any $w \in [q]^n$, the number of codewords that agree with w on at least $((1/q) + \eta) \cdot n$ positions (i.e., are at distance at most $(1 - ((1/q) + \eta)) \cdot n$ from w) is upper-bounded by

$$\frac{(1 - (1/q))^2 - (1 - (1/q)) \cdot \eta_c}{\eta^2 - (1 - (1/q)) \cdot \eta_c} \tag{E.3}$$

In the binary case (i.e., $q = 2$), Eq. (E.2) requires $\eta > \sqrt{\eta_c/2}$ and Eq. (E.3) yields the upper bound $(1 - 2\eta_c)/(4\eta^2 - 2\eta_c)$. We highlight two specific cases:

1. At the end of §D.4.2.2, we refer to this bound (for the binary case) while setting $\eta_c = (1/k)^2$ and $\eta = 1/k$. Indeed, in this case $(1 - 2\eta_c)/(4\eta^2 - 2\eta_c) = O(k^2)$.
2. In the case of the Hadamard code, we have $\eta_c = 0$. Thus, for every $w \in \{0, 1\}^n$ and every $\eta > 0$, the number of codewords that are $(0.5 - \eta)$-close to w is at most $1/4\eta^2$.

In the general case (and specifically for $q \gg 2$) it is useful to simplify Eq. (E.2) by $\eta > \min\{\sqrt{\eta_c}, (1/q) + \sqrt{\eta_c - (1/q)}\}$ and Eq. (E.3) by $\frac{1}{\eta^2 - \eta_c}$.

E.2. Expander Graphs

In this section we review basic facts regarding expander graphs that are most relevant to the current book. For a wider perspective, the interested reader is referred to [124].

Loosely speaking, expander graphs are regular graphs of small degree that exhibit various properties of cliques.[9] In particular, we refer to properties such as the relative sizes of cuts in the graph (i.e., relative to the number of edges), and the rate at which a random walk converges to the uniform distribution (relative to the logarithm of the graph size to the base of its degree).

Some technicalities. Typical presentations of expander graphs refer to one of several variants. For example, in some sources, expanders are presented as bipartite graphs, whereas in others they are presented as ordinary graphs (and are in fact very far from being bipartite). We shall follow the latter convention. Furthermore, at times we implicitly consider an augmentation of these graphs where self-loops are added to each vertex. For simplicity, we also allow parallel edges.

We often talk of expander graphs while we actually mean an infinite collection of graphs such that each graph in this collection satisfies the same property (which is informally

[9]Another useful intuition is that expander graphs exhibit various properties of random regular graphs of the same degree.

attributed to the collection). For example, when talking of a d-regular expander (graph) we actually refer to an infinite collection of graphs such that each of these graphs is d-regular. Typically, such a collection (or family) contains a single N-vertex graph for every $N \in \mathbb{S}$, where $\mathbb{S}$ is an infinite subset of $\mathbb{N}$. Throughout this section, we denote such a collection by $\{G_N\}_{N \in \mathbb{S}}$, with the understanding that G_N is a graph with N vertices and $\mathbb{S}$ is an infinite set of natural numbers.

E.2.1. Definitions and Properties

We consider two definitions of expander graphs, two different notions of explicit constructions, and two useful properties of expanders.

E.2.1.1. Two Mathematical Definitions

We start with two different definitions of expander graphs. These definitions are qualitatively equivalent and even quantitatively related. We start with an algebraic definition, which seems technical in nature but is actually the definition typically used in complexity-theoretic applications, since it directly implies various "mixing properties" (see §E.2.1.3). We later present a very natural combinatorial definition (which is the source of the term "expander").

The algebraic definition (eigenvalue gap). Identifying graphs with their adjacency matrix, we consider the eigenvalues (and eigenvectors) of a graph (or rather of its adjacency matrix). Any d-regular graph $G = (V, E)$ has the uniform vector as an eigenvector corresponding to the eigenvalue d, and if G is connected and non-bipartite then the absolute values of all other eigenvalues are strictly smaller than d. The eigenvalue bound, denoted $\lambda(G) < d$, of such a graph G is defined as a tight upper bound on the *absolute value* of all the other eigenvalues. (In fact, in this case it holds that $\lambda(G) < d - \Omega(1/d|V|^2)$.)[10] The algebraic definition of expanders refers to an infinite family of d-regular graphs and requires the existence of a *constant* eigenvalue bound that holds for all the graphs in the family.

> **Definition E.5:** *An infinite family of d-regular graphs,* $\{G_N\}_{N \in \mathbb{S}}$*, where* $\mathbb{S} \subseteq \mathbb{N}$*, satisfies the eigenvalue bound* β *if for every* $N \in \mathbb{S}$ *it holds that* $\lambda(G_N) \leq \beta$*. In such a case, we say that* $\{G_N\}_{N \in \mathbb{S}}$ *is a family of* (d, β)*-expanders, and call* $d - \beta$ *its* eigenvalue gap.

It will often be convenient to consider relative (or normalized) versions of the foregoing quantities, obtained by division by d.

The combinatorial definition (expansion). Loosely speaking, expansion requires that any (not too big) set of vertices of the graph has a relatively large set of neighbors. Specifically, a graph $G = (V, E)$ is c-expanding if, for every set $S \subset V$ of cardinality at most $|V|/2$, it holds that

$$\Gamma_G(S) \overset{\text{def}}{=} \{v : \exists u \in S \text{ s.t. } \{u, v\} \in E\} \tag{E.4}$$

has cardinality at least $(1 + c) \cdot |S|$. Assuming the existence of self-loops on all vertices, the foregoing requirement is equivalent to requiring that $|\Gamma_G(S) \setminus S| \geq c \cdot |S|$. In this case,

---

[10] This follows from the connection to the combinatorial definition (see Theorem E.7). Specifically, the square of this graph, denoted G^2, is $|V|^{-1}$-expanding and thus it holds that $\lambda(G)^2 = \lambda(G^2) < d^2 - \Omega(|V|^{-2})$.

every connected graph $G = (V, E)$ is $(1/|V|)$-expanding.[11] The combinatorial definition of expanders refers to an infinite family of d-regular graphs and requires the existence of a *constant* expansion bound that holds for all the graphs in the family.

Definition E.6: *An infinite family of d-regular graphs, $\{G_N\}_{N \in \mathbb{S}}$ is c-expanding if for every $N \in \mathbb{S}$ it holds that G_N is c-expanding.*

The two definitions of expander graphs are related (see [11, Sec. 9.2] or [124, Sec. 4.5]). Specifically, the "expansion bound" and the "eigenvalue bound" are related as follows.

Theorem E.7: *Let G be a d-regular graph having a self-loop on each vertex.[12]*

1. *The graph G is c-expanding for $c \geq (d - \lambda(G))/2d$.*
2. *If G is c-expanding then $d - \lambda(G) \geq c^2/(4 + 2c^2)$.*

Thus, any non-zero bound on the combinatorial expansion of a family of d-regular graphs yields a non-zero bound on its eigenvalue gap, and vice versa. Note, however, that the back-and-forth translation between these measures is not tight. We note that the applications presented in the main text (see, e.g., Section 8.5.3 and §9.3.2.3) refer to the algebraic definition, and that the loss incurred in Theorem E.7 is immaterial for them.

Amplification. The "quality of expander graphs improves" by raising these graphs to any power $t > 1$ (i.e., raising their adjacency matrix to the tth power), where this operation corresponds to replacing t-paths (in the original graphs) by edges (in the resulting graphs). Specifically, when considering the algebraic definition, it holds that $\lambda(G^t) = \lambda(G)^t$, but indeed the degree also gets raised to the power t. Still, the ratio $\lambda(G^t)/d^t$ deceases with t. An analogous phenomenon also occurs under the combinatorial definition, provided that some suitable modifications are applied. For example, if for every $S \subseteq V$ it holds that $|\Gamma_G(S)| \geq \min((1 + c) \cdot |S|, |V|/2)$, then for every $S \subseteq V$ it holds that $|\Gamma_{G^t}(S)| \geq \min((1 + c)^t \cdot |S|, |V|/2)$.

The optimal eigenvalue bound. For every d-regular graph $G = (V, E)$, it holds that $\lambda(G) \geq 2\gamma_G \cdot \sqrt{d - 1}$, where $\gamma_G = 1 - O(1/\log_d |V|)$. Thus, for any infinite family of (d, λ)-expanders, it must hold that $\lambda \geq 2\sqrt{d - 1}$.

E.2.1.2. Two Levels of Explicitness

Toward discussing various notions of explicit constructions of graphs, we need to fix a representation of such graphs. Specifically, throughout this section, when referring to an infinite family of graphs $\{G_N\}_{N \in \mathbb{S}}$, we shall assume that the vertex set of G_N equals $[N]$. Indeed, at times, we shall consider vertex sets having a different structure (e.g., $[m] \times [m]$

---

[11]In contrast, a bipartite graph $G = (V, E)$ is not expanding, because it always contains a set S of size at most $|V|/2$ such that $|\Gamma_G(S)| \leq |S|$ (although it may hold that $|\Gamma_G(S) \setminus S| \geq |S|$).

[12]Recall that in such a graph $G = (V, E)$ it holds that $\Gamma_G(S) \supseteq S$ for every $S \subseteq V$, and thus $|\Gamma_G(S)| = |\Gamma_G(S) \setminus S| + |S|$. Furthermore, in such a graph all eigenvalues are greater than or equal to $-d + 1$, and thus if $d - \lambda(G) < 1$ then this is due to a positive eigenvalue of G. These facts are used for bridging the gap between Theorem E.7 and the more standard versions (see, e.g., [11, Sec. 9.2]) that refer to variants of both definitions. Specifically, [11, Sec. 9.2] refers to $\Gamma_G^+(S) = \Gamma_G(S) \setminus S$ and $\lambda_2(G)$, where $\lambda_2(G)$ is the second largest eigenvalue of G, rather than referring to $\Gamma_G(S)$ and $\lambda(G)$. Note that, in general, $\Gamma_G(S)$ may be attained by the difference between the smallest eigenvalue of G (which may be negative) and $-d$.

for some $m \in \mathbb{N}$), but in all of these cases there exists a simple isomorphism of these sets to the canonical representation (i.e., there exists an efficiently computable and invertible mapping of the vertex set of G_N to $[N]$).

Recall that a mild notion of explicit constructiveness refers to the *complexity of constructing the entire object* (i.e., the graph). Applying this notion to our setting, we say that an infinite family of graphs $\{G_N\}_{N \in \mathbb{S}}$ is explicitly constructible if there exists a *polynomial-time algorithm that, on input 1^N* (where $N \in \mathbb{S}$), *outputs the list of the edges in the N-vertex graph G_N*. That is, the entire graph is constructed in time that is polynomial in its size (i.e., in poly(N)-time).

The foregoing (mild) level of explicitness suffices when the application requires holding the entire graph and/or when the running time of the application is lower-bounded by the size of the graph. In contrast, other applications refer to a huge virtual graph (which is much bigger than their running time), and only require the computation of the neighborhood relation in such a graph. In this case, the following stronger level of explicitness is relevant.

A strongly explicit construction of an infinite family of (d-regular) graphs $\{G_N\}_{N \in \mathbb{S}}$ is a *polynomial-time algorithm that on input $N \in \mathbb{S}$* (in binary), *a vertex v in the N-vertex graph G_N* (i.e., $v \in [N]$), *and an index $i \in [d]$, returns the ith neighbor of v*. That is, the "neighbor query" is answered in time that is poly-logarithmic in the size of the graph. Needless to say, this strong level of explicitness implies the basic (mild) level.

An additional requirement, which is often forgotten but is very important, refers to the "tractability" of the set $\mathbb{S}$. Specifically, we require the existence of an *efficient algorithm that given any $n \in \mathbb{N}$ finds an $s \in \mathbb{S}$ such that $n \le s < 2n$*. Corresponding to the two foregoing levels of explicitness, "efficient" may mean either running in time poly(n) or running in time poly($\log n$). The requirement that $n \le s < 2n$ suffices in most applications, but in some cases a smaller interval (e.g., $n \le s < n + \sqrt{n}$) is required, whereas in other cases a larger interval (e.g., $n \le s < $ poly(n)) suffices.

Greater flexibility. In continuation of the foregoing paragraph, we comment that expanders can be combined in order to obtain expanders for a wider range of graph sizes. For example, given two d-regular c-expanding graphs, $G_1 = (V_1, E_1)$ and $G_2 = (V_2, E_2)$ where $|V_1| \le |V_2|$ and $c \le 1$, we can obtain a $(d + 1)$-regular $c/2$-expanding graph on $|V_1| + |V_2|$ vertices by connecting the two graphs using a perfect matching of V_1 and $|V_1|$ of the vertices of V_2 (and adding self-loops to the remaining vertices of V_2). More generally, combining the d-regular c-expanding graphs $G_1 = (V_1, E_1)$ through $G_t = (V_t, E_t)$, where $N' \overset{\text{def}}{=} \sum_{i=1}^{t-1} |V_i| \le |V_t|$, yields a $(d + 1)$-regular $c/2$-expanding graph on $\sum_{i=1}^{t} |V_i|$ vertices (by using a perfect matching of $\cup_{i=1}^{t-1} V_i$ and N' of the vertices of V_t).

E.2.1.3. Two Properties

The following two properties provide a quantitative interpretation to the statement that expanders approximate the complete graph (or behave approximately like a complete graph). When referring to (d, λ)-expanders, the deviation from the behavior of a complete graph is represented by an error term that is linear in λ/d.

The mixing lemma. Loosely speaking, the following (folklore) lemma asserts that in expander graphs (for which $\lambda \ll d$), the fraction of edges connecting two large sets of vertices approximately equals the product of the densities of these sets. This property is called *mixing*.

Lemma E.8 (Expander Mixing Lemma): *For every d-regular graph* $G = (V, E)$ *and for every two subsets* $A, B \subseteq V$ *it holds that*

$$\left| \frac{|(A \times B) \cap \vec{E}|}{|\vec{E}|} - \frac{|A|}{|V|} \cdot \frac{|B|}{|V|} \right| \leq \frac{\lambda(G)\sqrt{|A| \cdot |B|}}{d \cdot |V|} \leq \frac{\lambda(G)}{d} \tag{E.5}$$

where $\vec{E}$ *denotes the set of directed edges* (i.e., vertex pairs) *that correspond to the undirected edges of* G (i.e., $\vec{E} = \{(u, v) : \{u, v\} \in E\}$ *and* $|\vec{E}| = d|V|$).

In particular, $|(A \times A) \cap \vec{E}| = (\rho(A) \cdot d \pm \lambda(G)) \cdot |A|$, where $\rho(A) = |A|/|V|$. It follows that $|(A \times (V \setminus A)) \cap \vec{E}| = ((1 - \rho(A)) \cdot d \pm \lambda(G)) \cdot |A|$.

Proof: Let $N \stackrel{\text{def}}{=} |V|$ and $\lambda \stackrel{\text{def}}{=} \lambda(G)$. For any subset of the vertices $S \subseteq V$, we denote its density in V by $\rho(S) \stackrel{\text{def}}{=} |S|/N$. Hence, Eq. (E.5) is restated as

$$\left| \frac{|(A \times B) \cap \vec{E}|}{d \cdot N} - \rho(A) \cdot \rho(B) \right| \leq \frac{\lambda\sqrt{\rho(A) \cdot \rho(B)}}{d}.$$

We proceed by providing bounds on the value of $|(A \times B) \cap \vec{E}|$. To this end we let $\bar{a}$ denote the N-dimensional Boolean vector having 1 in the ith component if and only if $i \in A$. The vector $\bar{b}$ is defined similarly. Denoting the adjacency matrix of the graph G by $M = (m_{i,j})$, we note that $|(A \times B) \cap \vec{E}|$ equals $\bar{a}^\top M \bar{b}$ (because $(i, j) \in (A \times B) \cap \vec{E}$ if and only if it holds that $i \in A$, $j \in B$ and $m_{i,j} = 1$). We consider the *orthogonal eigenvector basis*, $\bar{e}_1, \ldots, \bar{e}_N$, where $\bar{e}_1 = (1, \ldots, 1)^\top$ and $\bar{e}_i^\top \bar{e}_i = N$ for each i, and write each vector as a linear combination of the vectors in this basis. Specifically, we denote by a_i the coefficient of $\bar{a}$ in the direction of $\bar{e}_i$; that is, $a_i = (\bar{a}^\top \bar{e}_i)/N$ and $\bar{a} = \sum_i a_i \bar{e}_i$. Note that $a_1 = (\bar{a}^\top \bar{e}_1)/N = |A|/N = \rho(A)$ and $\sum_{i=1}^N a_i^2 = (\bar{a}^\top \bar{a})/N = |A|/N = \rho(A)$. Similarly for $\bar{b}$. It now follows that

$$|(A \times B) \cap \vec{E}| = \bar{a}^\top M \sum_{i=1}^N b_i \bar{e}_i$$

$$= \sum_{i=1}^N b_i \lambda_i \cdot \bar{a}^\top \bar{e}_i$$

where λ_i denotes the ith eigenvalue of M. Note that $\lambda_1 = d$ and for every $i \geq 2$ it holds that $|\lambda_i| \leq \lambda$. Thus,

$$\frac{|(A \times B) \cap \vec{E}|}{dN} = \sum_{i=1}^N \frac{b_i \lambda_i \cdot a_i}{d}$$

$$= \rho(A)\rho(B) + \sum_{i=2}^N \frac{\lambda_i a_i b_i}{d}$$

$$\in \left[\rho(A)\rho(B) \pm \frac{\lambda}{d} \cdot \sum_{i=2}^N a_i b_i \right]$$

Using $\sum_{i=1}^N a_i^2 = \rho(A)$ and $\sum_{i=1}^N b_i^2 = \rho(B)$, and applying the Cauchy-Schwartz Inequality, we bound $\sum_{i=2}^N a_i b_i$ by $\sqrt{\rho(A)\rho(B)}$. The lemma follows. ∎

The random walk lemma. Loosely speaking, the first part of the following lemma asserts that, as far as remaining "trapped" in some subset of the vertex set is concerned, a random walk on an expander approximates a random walk on the complete graph.

Lemma E.9 (Expander Random Walk Lemma): *Let $G = ([N], E)$ be a d-regular graph, and consider walks on G that start from a uniformly chosen vertex and take $\ell - 1$ additional random steps, where in each such step we uniformly select one out of the d edges incident at the current vertex and traverse it.*

Theorem 8.28 (restated): *Let W be a subset of $[N]$ and $\rho \overset{\text{def}}{=} |W|/N$. Then the probability that such a random walk stays in W is at most*

$$\rho \cdot \left(\rho + (1 - \rho) \cdot \frac{\lambda(G)}{d} \right)^{\ell-1} \tag{E.6}$$

Exercise 8.43 (restated): *For any $W_0, \ldots, W_{\ell-1} \subseteq [N]$, the probability that a random walk of length ℓ intersects $W_0 \times W_1 \times \cdots \times W_{\ell-1}$ is at most*

$$\sqrt{\rho_0} \cdot \prod_{i=1}^{\ell-1} \sqrt{\rho_i + (\lambda/d)^2}, \tag{E.7}$$

where $\rho_i \overset{\text{def}}{=} |W_i|/N$.

The basic principle underlying Lemma E.9 was discovered by Ajtai, Komlos, and Szemerédi [4], who proved a bound as in Eq. (E.7). The better analysis yielding Theorem 8.28 is due to [135, Cor. 6.1]. A more general bound that refers to the probability of visiting W for a number of times that approximates $|W|/N$ is given in [120], which actually considers an even more general problem (i.e., obtaining Chernoff-type bounds for random variables that are generated by a walk on an expander).

Proof of Equation (E.7) The basic idea is to view events occurring during the random walk as an evolution of a corresponding probability vector under suitable transformations. The transformations correspond to taking a random step in G and to passing through a "sieve" that keeps only the entries that correspond to the current set W_i. The key observation is that the first transformation shrinks the component that is orthogonal to the uniform distribution, whereas the second transformation shrinks the component that is in the direction of the uniform distribution. Details follow.

Let A be a matrix representing the random walk on G (i.e., A is the adjacency matrix of G divided by d), and let $\hat{\lambda} \overset{\text{def}}{=} \lambda(G)/d$ (i.e., $\hat{\lambda}$ upper-bounds the absolute value of every eigenvalue of A except the first one). Note that the uniform distribution, represented by the vector $\overline{u} = (N^{-1}, \ldots, N^{-1})^\top$, is the eigenvector of A that is associated with the largest eigenvalue (which is 1). Let P_i be a 0-1 matrix that has 1-entries only on its diagonal such that entry (j, j) is set to 1 if and only if $j \in W_i$. Then, the probability that a random walk of length ℓ intersects $W_0 \times W_1 \times \cdots \times W_{\ell-1}$ is the sum of the entries of the vector

$$\overline{v} \overset{\text{def}}{=} P_{\ell-1} A \cdots P_2 A P_1 A P_0 \overline{u}. \tag{E.8}$$

We are interested in upper-bounding $\|\overline{v}\|_1$, and use $\|\overline{v}\|_1 \leq \sqrt{N} \cdot \|\overline{v}\|$, where $\|\overline{z}\|_1$ and $\|\overline{z}\|$ denote the L_1-norm and L_2-norm of $\overline{z}$, respectively (e.g., $\|\overline{u}\|_1 = 1$ and

$\|\overline{u}\| = N^{-1/2}$). The key observation is that the linear transformation $P_i A$ shrinks every vector.

Main Claim. For every $\overline{z}$, it holds that $\|P_i A\overline{z}\| \leq (\rho_i + \hat{\lambda}^2)^{1/2} \cdot \|\overline{z}\|$.

Proof. Intuitively, A shrinks the component of $\overline{z}$ that is orthogonal to $\overline{u}$, whereas P_i shrinks the component of $\overline{z}$ that is in the direction of $\overline{u}$. Specifically, we decompose $\overline{z} = \overline{z_1} + \overline{z_2}$ such that $\overline{z_1}$ is the projection of $\overline{z}$ on $\overline{u}$ and $\overline{z_2}$ is the component orthogonal to $\overline{u}$. Then, using the triangle inequality and other obvious facts (which imply $\|P_i A\overline{z_1}\| = \|P_i\overline{z_1}\|$ and $\|P_i A\overline{z_2}\| \leq \|A\overline{z_2}\|$), we have

$$\|P_i A\overline{z_1} + P_i A\overline{z_2}\| \leq \|P_i A\overline{z_1}\| + \|P_i A\overline{z_2}\|$$
$$\leq \|P_i\overline{z_1}\| + \|A\overline{z_2}\|$$
$$\leq \sqrt{\rho_i} \cdot \|\overline{z_1}\| + \hat{\lambda} \cdot \|\overline{z_2}\|$$

where the last inequality uses the fact that P_i shrinks any uniform vector by eliminating $1 - \rho_i$ of its elements, whereas A shrinks the length of any eigenvector except $\overline{u}$ by a factor of at least $\hat{\lambda}$. Using the Cauchy-Schwartz Inequality,[13] we get

$$\|P_i A\overline{z}\| \leq \sqrt{\rho_i + \hat{\lambda}^2} \cdot \sqrt{\|\overline{z_1}\|^2 + \|\overline{z_2}\|^2}$$
$$= \sqrt{\rho_i + \hat{\lambda}^2} \cdot \|\overline{z}\|$$

where the equality is due to the fact that $\overline{z_1}$ is orthogonal to $\overline{z_2}$. ☐

Recalling Eq. (E.8) and using the Main Claim (and $\|\overline{v}\|_1 \leq \sqrt{N} \cdot \|\overline{v}\|$), we get

$$\|\overline{v}\|_1 \leq \sqrt{N} \cdot \|P_{\ell-1}A \cdots P_2 A P_1 A P_0 \overline{u}\|$$
$$\leq \sqrt{N} \cdot \left(\prod_{i=1}^{\ell-1} \sqrt{\rho_i + \hat{\lambda}^2} \right) \cdot \|P_0\overline{u}\|.$$

Finally, using $\|P_0\overline{u}\| = \sqrt{\rho_0 N \cdot (1/N)^2} = \sqrt{\rho_0/N}$, we establish Eq. (E.7). ■

Rapid mixing. A property related to Lemma E.9 is that a random walk starting at any vertex converges to the uniform distribution on the expander vertices after a logarithmic number of steps. Specifically, we claim that *starting at any distribution $\overline{s}$* (including a distribution that assigns all weight to a single vertex) *after ℓ steps on a (d, λ)-expander $G = ([N], E)$, we reach a distribution that is $\sqrt{N} \cdot (\lambda/d)^{\ell}$-close to the uniform distribution over $[N]$.* Using notation as in the proof of Eq. (E.7), the claim asserts that $\|A^{\ell}\overline{s} - \overline{u}\|_1 \leq \sqrt{N} \cdot \hat{\lambda}^{\ell}$, which is meaningful only for $\ell > 0.5 \cdot \log_{1/\hat{\lambda}} N$. The claim is proved by recalling that $\|A^{\ell}\overline{s} - \overline{u}\|_1 \leq \sqrt{N} \cdot \|A^{\ell}\overline{s} - \overline{u}\|$ and using the fact that $\overline{s} - \overline{u}$ is orthogonal to $\overline{u}$ (because the former is a zero-sum vector). Thus, $\|A^{\ell}\overline{s} - \overline{u}\| = \|A^{\ell}(\overline{s} - \overline{u})\| \leq \hat{\lambda}^{\ell}\|\overline{s} - \overline{u}\|$ and using $\|\overline{s} - \overline{u}\| < 1$ the claim follows.

---

[13]That is we get $\sqrt{\rho_i}\|z_1\| + \hat{\lambda}\|z_2\| \leq \sqrt{\rho_i + \hat{\lambda}^2} \cdot \sqrt{\|z_1\|^2 + \|z_2\|^2}$, by using $\sum_{i=1}^{n} a_i \cdot b_i \leq \left(\sum_{i=1}^{n} a_i^2\right)^{1/2} \cdot \left(\sum_{i=1}^{n} b_i^2\right)^{1/2}$, with $n = 2$, $a_1 = \sqrt{\rho_i}$, $b_1 = \|z_1\|$, etc.

E.2.2. Constructions

Many explicit constructions of (d, λ)-expanders are known. The first such construction was presented in [164] (where $\lambda < d$ was not explicitly bounded), and an optimal construction (i.e., an optimal eigenvalue bound of $\lambda = 2\sqrt{d-1}$) was first provided in [160]. Most of these constructions are quite simple (see, e.g., §E.2.2.1), but their analysis is based on non-elementary results from various branches of mathematics. In contrast, the construction of Reingold, Vadhan, and Wigderson [191], presented in §E.2.2.2, is based on an iterative process, and its analysis is based on a relatively simple algebraic fact regarding the eigenvalues of matrices.

Before turning to these explicit constructions, we note that it is relatively easy to prove the existence of 3-regular expanders, by using the Probabilistic Method (cf. [11]) and referring to the combinatorial definition of expansion.[14]

E.2.2.1. The Margulis-Gabber-Galil Expander

For every natural number m, consider the graph with vertex set $\mathbb{Z}_m \times \mathbb{Z}_m$ and the edge set in which every $\langle x, y \rangle \in \mathbb{Z}_m \times \mathbb{Z}_m$ is connected to the vertices $\langle x \pm y, y \rangle$, $\langle x \pm (y + 1), y \rangle$, $\langle x, y \pm x \rangle$, and $\langle x, y \pm (x + 1) \rangle$, where the arithmetic is modulo m. This yields an extremely simple 8-regular graph with an eigenvalue bound that is a constant $\lambda < 8$ (which is independent of m). Thus, we get

Theorem E.10: *There exists a strongly explicit construction of a family of $(8, 7.9999)$-expanders for graph sizes $\{m^2 : m \in \mathbb{N}\}$. Furthermore, the neighbors of a vertex in these expanders can be computed in logarithmic space.*[15]

An appealing property of Theorem E.10 is that, for every $n \in \mathbb{N}$, it directly yields expanders with vertex set $\{0, 1\}^n$. This is obvious in case n is even, but can also be easily achieved for odd n (e.g., use two copies of the graph for $n - 1$, and connect the two copies by the obvious perfect matching).

Theorem E.10 is due to Gabber and Galil [84], building on the basic approach suggested by Margulis [164]. We mention again that the (strongly explicit) (d, λ)-expanders of [160] achieve the optimal eigenvalue bound (i.e., $\lambda = 2\sqrt{d-1}$), but there are annoying restrictions on the degree d (i.e., $d - 1$ should be a prime congruent to 1 modulo 4) and on the graph sizes for which this construction works.[16]

---

[14]This can be done by considering a 3-regular graph obtained by combining an N-cycle with a random matching of the first $N/2$ vertices and the remaining $N/2$ vertices. It is actually easier to prove the related statement that refers to the alternative definition of combinatorial expansion that refers to the relative size of $\Gamma_G^+(S) = \Gamma_G(S) \setminus S$ (rather than to the relative size of $\Gamma_G(S)$). In this case, for a sufficiently small $\varepsilon > 0$ and all sufficiently large N, a random 3-regular N-vertex graph is "ε-expanding" with overwhelmingly high probability. The proof proceeds by considering a (not necessarily simple) graph G obtained by combining three uniformly chosen perfect matchings of the elements of $[N]$. For every $S \subseteq [N]$ of size at most $N/2$ and for every set T of size $\varepsilon|S|$, we consider the probability that for a random perfect matching M it holds that $\Gamma_M^+(S) \subseteq T$. The argument is concluded by applying a union bound.

[15]In fact, for m that is a power of two (and under a suitable encoding of the vertices), the neighbors can be computed by an on-line algorithm that uses a constant amount of space. The same also holds for a variant in which each vertex $\langle x, y \rangle$ is connected to the vertices $\langle x \pm 2y, y \rangle$, $\langle x \pm (2y + 1), y \rangle$, $\langle x, y \pm 2x \rangle$, and $\langle x, y \pm (2x + 1) \rangle$. This variant yields a better (known) bound on λ, i.e., $\lambda \leq 5\sqrt{2} \approx 7.071$.

[16]The construction in [160] allows graph sizes of the form $(p^3 - p)/2$, where $p \equiv 1 \pmod{4}$ is a prime such that $d - 1$ is a quadratic residue modulo p. As stated in [8, Sec. 2], the construction can be extended to graph sizes of the form $(p^{3k} - p^{3k-2})/2$, for any $k \in \mathbb{N}$ and p as in the foregoing.

561

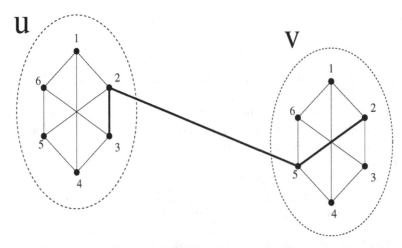

Figure E.1: Detail of the Zig-Zag product of G' and G. In this example G' is 6-regular and G is a 3-regular graph having six vertices. In the graph G' (not shown), the 2nd edge of vertex u is incident at v, as its 5th edge. The wide 3-segment line shows one of the corresponding edges of $G' \textcircled{z} G$, which connects the vertices $\langle u, 3 \rangle$ and $\langle v, 2 \rangle$.

E.2.2.2. The Iterated Zig-Zag Construction

The starting point of the following construction is a very good expander G of *constant size*, which may be found by an exhaustive search. The construction of a large expander graph proceeds in iterations, where in the ith iteration the current graph G_i and the fixed graph G are combined, resulting in a larger graph G_{i+1}. The combination step guarantees that the expansion property of G_{i+1} is at least as good as the expansion of G_i, while G_{i+1} maintains the degree of G_i and is a constant time larger than G_i. The process is initiated with $G_1 = G^2$ and terminates when we obtain a graph G_t of approximately the desired size (which requires a logarithmic number of iterations).

The Zig-Zag product. The heart of the combination step is a new type of "graph product" called the *Zig-Zag product*. This operation is applicable to any pair of graphs $G = ([D], E)$ and $G' = ([N], E')$, provided that G' (which is typically larger than G) is D-regular. For simplicity, we assume that G is d-regular (where typically $d \ll D$). The Zig-Zag product of G' and G, denoted $G' \textcircled{z} G$, is defined as a graph with vertex set $[N] \times [D]$ and an edge set that includes an edge between $\langle u, i \rangle \in [N] \times [D]$ and $\langle v, j \rangle$ if and only if $\{i, k\}, \{\ell, j\} \in E$ and the kth edge incident at u equals the ℓth edge incident at v. That is, $\langle u, i \rangle$ and $\langle v, j \rangle$ are connected in $G' \textcircled{z} G$ if there exists a "three-step sequence" consisting of a G-step from $\langle u, i \rangle$ to $\langle u, k \rangle$ (according to the edge $\{i, k\}$ of G), followed by a G'-step from $\langle u, k \rangle$ to $\langle v, \ell \rangle$ (according to the kth edge of u in G' (which is the ℓth edge of v)), and a final G-step from $\langle v, \ell \rangle$ to $\langle v, j \rangle$ (according to the edge $\{\ell, j\}$ of G). See Figure E.1 as well as further formalization (which follows).

> **Teaching note:** The following paragraph, which provides a formal description of the Zig-Zag product, can be ignored at the first reading but is useful for more advanced discussion.

It will be convenient to represent graphs like G' by their **edge-rotation function**, denoted $R' : [N] \times [D] \to [N] \times [D]$, such that $R'(u, i) = (v, j)$ if $\{u, v\}$ is the ith edge incident at u as well as the jth edge incident at v. That is, R' rotates the pair (u, i), which represents one "side" of the edge $\{u, v\}$ (i.e., the side incident at u as its ith edge), resulting in the pair (v, j), which represents the other side of the same edge (which is the jth edge incident at v). For simplicity, we assume that the (constant-size) d-regular graph $G = ([D], E)$ is edge-colorable with d colors, which in turn yields a natural edge-rotation function (i.e., $R(i, \alpha) = (j, \alpha)$ if the edge $\{i, j\}$ is colored α). We will denote by $E_\alpha(i)$ the vertex reached from $i \in [D]$ by following the edge colored α (i.e., $E_\alpha(i) = j$ if and only if $R(i, \alpha) = (j, \alpha)$). The Zig-Zag product of G' and G, denoted $G' \textcircled{z} G$, is then defined as a graph with the vertex set $[N] \times [D]$ and the edge-rotation function

$$(\langle u, i \rangle, \langle \alpha, \beta \rangle) \mapsto (\langle v, j \rangle, \langle \beta, \alpha \rangle) \quad \text{if } R'(u, E_\alpha(i)) = (v, E_\beta(j)). \tag{E.9}$$

That is, edges are labeled by pairs over $[d]$, and the $\langle \alpha, \beta \rangle^{\text{th}}$ edge out of vertex $\langle u, i \rangle \in [N] \times [D]$ is incident at the vertex $\langle v, j \rangle$ (as its $\langle \beta, \alpha \rangle^{\text{th}}$ edge) if $R(u, E_\alpha(i)) = (v, E_\beta(j))$, where indeed $E_\beta(E_\beta(j)) = j$. Intuitively, based on $\langle \alpha, \beta \rangle$, we first take a G-step from $\langle u, i \rangle$ to $\langle u, E_\alpha(i) \rangle$; then viewing $\langle u, E_\alpha(i) \rangle \equiv (u, E_\alpha(i))$ as a side of an edge of G' we rotate it (i.e., we effectively take a G'-step) reaching $(v, j') \stackrel{\text{def}}{=} R'(u, E_\alpha(i))$, and finally we take a G-step from $\langle v, j' \rangle$ to $\langle v, E_\beta(j') \rangle$.

Clearly, the graph $G' \textcircled{z} G$ is d^2-regular and has $D \cdot N$ vertices. The key fact, proved in [191] (using techniques as in §E.2.1.3), is that the relative eigenvalue bound of the Zig-Zag product is upper-bounded by the sum of the relative eigenvalue bound of the two graphs; that is, $\bar{\lambda}(G' \textcircled{z} G) \leq \bar{\lambda}(G') + \bar{\lambda}(G)$, where $\bar{\lambda}(\cdot)$ denotes the relative eigenvalue bound of the relevant graph. The (qualitative) fact that $G' \textcircled{z} G$ is an expander if both G' and G are expanders is very intuitive (e.g., consider what happens if G' or G is a clique). Things are even more intuitive if one considers the (related) replacement product of G' and G, denoted $G' \textcircled{r} G$, *where there is an edge between $\langle u, i \rangle \in [N] \times [D]$ and $\langle v, j \rangle$ if and only if either $u = v$ and $\{i, j\} \in E$ or the ith edge incident at u equals the jth edge incident at v.*

The iterated construction. The iterated expander construction uses the aforementioned Zig-Zag product as well as graph squaring. Specifically, the construction starts[17] with the d^2-regular graph $G_1 = G^2 = ([D], E^2)$, where $D = d^4$ and $\bar{\lambda}(G) < 1/4$, and proceeds in iterations such that $G_{i+1} = G_i^2 \textcircled{z} G$ for $i = 1, 2, \ldots, t - 1$, where t is logarithmic in the desired graph size. That is, in each iteration, the current graph is first squared and then composed with the fixed (d-regular D-vertex) graph G via the Zig-Zag product. This process maintains the following two invariants:

1. The graph G_i is d^2-regular and has D^i vertices.

    (The degree bound follows from the fact that a Zig-Zag product with a d-regular graph always yields a d^2-regular graph.)

2. The relative eigenvalue bound of G_i is smaller than one half (i.e., $\bar{\lambda}(G_i) < 1/2$).

    (Here, we use the fact that $\bar{\lambda}(G_{i-1}^2 \textcircled{z} G) \leq \bar{\lambda}(G_{i-1}^2) + \bar{\lambda}(G)$, which in turn equals $\bar{\lambda}(G_{i-1})^2 + \bar{\lambda}(G) < (1/2)^2 + (1/4)$. Note that graph squaring is used to reduce the relative eigenvalue of G_i before increasing it by a Zig-Zag product with G.)

In order to show that we can actually construct G_i, we show that we can compute the edge-rotation function that corresponds to its edge set. This boils down to showing that, given

---

[17]Recall that, for a sufficiently large constant d, we first find a d-regular graph $G = ([d^4], E)$ satisfying $\bar{\lambda}(G) < 1/4$, by exhaustive search.

the edge-rotation function of G_{i-1}, we can compute the edge-rotation function of G_{i-1}^2 as well as of its Zig-Zag product with G. Note that this entire computation amounts to two recursive calls to computations regarding G_{i-1} (and two computations that correspond to the constant graph G). But since the recursion depth is logarithmic in the size of the final graph (i.e., $t = \log_D |\text{vertices}(G_t)|$), the total number of recursive calls is polynomial in the size of the final graph (and thus the entire computation is polynomial in the size of the final graph). This suffices for the minimal (i.e., "mild") notion of explicitness, but not for the strong one.

The strongly explicit version. To achieve a *strongly explicit construction*, we slightly modify the iterative construction. Rather than letting $G_{i+1} = G_i^2 \textcircled{z} G$, we let $G_{i+1} = (G_i \times G_i)^2 \textcircled{z} G$, where $G' \times G'$ denotes the *tensor product of G' with itself*; that is, if $G' = (V', E')$ then $G' \times G' = (V' \times V', E'')$, where

$$E'' = \{\{\langle u_1, u_2 \rangle, \langle v_1, v_2 \rangle\} : \{u_1, v_1\}, \{u_2, v_2\} \in E'\}$$

(i.e., $\langle u_1, u_2 \rangle$ and $\langle v_1, v_2 \rangle$ are connected in $G' \times G'$ if for $i = 1, 2$ it holds that u_i is connected to v_i in G'). The corresponding edge-rotation function is

$$R''(\langle u_1, u_2 \rangle, \langle i_1, i_2 \rangle) = (\langle v_1, v_2 \rangle, \langle j_1, j_2 \rangle),$$

where $R'(u_1, i_1) = (v_1, j_1)$ and $R'(u_2, i_2) = (v_2, j_2)$. We still use $G_1 = G^2$, where (as before) G is d-regular and $\bar{\lambda}(G) < 1/4$, but here G has $D = d^8$ vertices.[18] Using the fact that the tensor product preserves the relative eigenvalue bound while squaring the degree (and the number of vertices), we note that the modified iteration $G_{i+1} = (G_i \times G_i)^2 \textcircled{z} G$ yields a d^2-regular graph with $(D^{2^i-1})^2 \cdot D = D^{2^{i+1}-1}$ vertices, and that $\bar{\lambda}(G_{i+1}) < 1/2$ (because $\bar{\lambda}((G_i \times G_i)^2 \textcircled{z} G) \leq \bar{\lambda}(G_i)^2 + \bar{\lambda}(G)$). Computing the neighbor of a vertex in G_{i+1} boils down to a constant number of such computations regarding G_i, but due to the tensor product operation, the depth of the recursion is only double-logarithmic in the size of the final graph (and hence logarithmic in the length of the description of vertices in this graph).

Digest. In the first construction, the Zig-Zag product was used both in order to increase the size of the graph and to reduce its degree. However, as indicated by the second construction (where the tensor product of graphs is the main vehicle for increasing the size of the graph), the primary effect of the Zig-Zag product is reducing the graph's degree, and the increase in the size of the graph is merely a side effect.[19] In both cases, graph squaring is used in order to compensate for the modest increase in the relative eigenvalue bound caused by the Zig-Zag product. In retrospect, the second construction is the "correct" one, because it decouples three different effects, and uses a natural operation to obtain each of them: Increasing the size of the graph is obtained by the tensor product of graphs (which in turn increases the degree), the desired degree reduction is obtained by the Zig-Zag product (which in turn slightly increases the relative eigenvalue bound), and graph squaring is used in order to reduce the relative eigenvalue bound.

[18] The reason for the change is that $(G_i \times G_i)^2$ will be d^8-regular, since G_i will be d^2-regular.

[19] We mention that this side effect may actually be undesired in some applications. For example, in Section 5.2.4 we would rather not have the graph grow in size, but we can tolerate the constant size blowup (caused by the Zig-Zag product with a constant-size graph).

Stronger bound regarding the effect of the Zig-Zag product. In the foregoing description we relied on the fact, proved in [191], that the relative eigenvalue bound of the Zig-Zag product is upper-bounded by the sum of the relative eigenvalue bounds of the two graphs (i.e., $\bar{\lambda}(G' \textcircled{z} G) \leq \bar{\lambda}(G') + \bar{\lambda}(G)$). Actually, a stronger upper bound is proved in [191]: It holds that $\bar{\lambda}(G' \textcircled{z} G) \leq f(\bar{\lambda}(G'), \bar{\lambda}(G))$, where

$$f(x, y) \stackrel{\text{def}}{=} \frac{(1 - y^2) \cdot x}{2} + \sqrt{\left(\frac{(1 - y^2) \cdot x}{2} \right)^2 + y^2} \tag{E.10}$$

Indeed, $f(x, y) \leq (1 - y^2) \cdot x + y \leq x + y$. On the other hand, for $x \leq 1$, we have $f(x, y) \leq \frac{(1-y^2) \cdot x}{2} + \frac{1+y^2}{2} = 1 - \frac{(1-y^2) \cdot (1-x)}{2}$, which implies

$$\bar{\lambda}(G' \textcircled{z} G) \leq 1 - \frac{(1 - \bar{\lambda}(G)^2) \cdot (1 - \bar{\lambda}(G'))}{2}. \tag{E.11}$$

Thus, $1 - \bar{\lambda}(G' \textcircled{z} G) \geq (1 - \bar{\lambda}(G)^2) \cdot (1 - \bar{\lambda}(G'))/2$, and it follows that the Zig-Zag product has a positive eigenvalue gap if both graphs have positive eigenvalue gaps (i.e., $\lambda(G' \textcircled{z} G) < 1$ if both $\lambda(G) < 1$ and $\lambda(G') < 1$). Furthermore, if $\bar{\lambda}(G) < 1/\sqrt{3}$ then $1 - \bar{\lambda}(G' \textcircled{z} G) > (1 - \bar{\lambda}(G'))/3$. This fact plays an important role in the proof of Theorem 5.6.

Some Omitted Proofs

A word of a Gentleman is better than a proof, but since you are not a Gentleman – please provide a proof.

Leonid A. Levin (1986)

The proofs presented in this appendix were not included in the main text for a variety of reasons (e.g., they were deemed too technical and/or out of pace for the corresponding location). On the other hand, since our presentation of them is sufficiently different from the original and/or standard presentation, we see a benefit in including them in the current book.

Summary: This appendix contains proofs of the following results:

1. $\mathcal{PH}$ is reducible to $\#\mathcal{P}$ (and in fact to $\oplus\mathcal{P}$) via randomized Karp-reductions. The proof follows the underlying ideas of Toda's original proof, but the actual presentation is quite different.
2. For any integral function f that satisfies $f(n) \in \{2, \ldots, \text{poly}(n)\}$, it holds that $\mathcal{IP}(f) \subseteq \mathcal{AM}(O(f))$ and $\mathcal{AM}(O(f)) \subseteq \mathcal{AM}(f)$. The proofs differ from the original proofs (provided in [111] and [23], respectively) only in the secondary details, but these details seem significant.

F.1. Proving That $\mathcal{PH}$ Reduces to $\#\mathcal{P}$

Recall that Theorem 6.16 asserts that $\mathcal{PH}$ is Cook-reducible to $\#\mathcal{P}$ (via deterministic reductions). Here, we prove a closely related result (also due to Toda [220]), which relaxes the requirement from the reduction (allowing it to be randomized) but uses an oracle to a seemingly weaker class. The latter class is denoted $\oplus\mathcal{P}$ and is the "modulo 2 analogue" of $\#\mathcal{P}$. Specifically, a Boolean function f is in $\oplus\mathcal{P}$ if there exists a function $g \in \#\mathcal{P}$ such that for every x it holds that $f(x) = g(x) \bmod 2$. Equivalently, f is in $\oplus\mathcal{P}$ if there exists a search problem $R \in \mathcal{PC}$ such that $f(x) = |R(x)| \bmod 2$, where $R(x) = \{y : (x, y) \in R\}$. Thus, for any $R \in \mathcal{PC}$, the set $\oplus R \stackrel{\text{def}}{=} \{x : |R(x)| \equiv 1 \pmod 2\}$ is in $\oplus\mathcal{P}$. (The $\oplus$ symbol in the notation $\oplus\mathcal{P}$ actually represents parity, which is merely addition modulo 2. Indeed, a notation such as $\#_2\mathcal{P}$ would have been more appropriate.)

Theorem F.1: *Every set in $\mathcal{PH}$ is reducible to $\oplus\mathcal{P}$ via a probabilistic polynomial-time reduction. Furthermore, the reduction is via a many-to-one randomized mapping and it fails with negligible error probability.*

The proof follows the underlying ideas of the original proof [220], but the actual presentation is quite different. Alternative proofs of Theorem F.1 can be found in [136, 212].

Teaching note: It is quite easy to prove a non-uniform analogue of Theorem F.1, which asserts that AC0 circuits can be approximated by circuits consisting of an unbounded parity of conjunctions, where each conjunction has poly-logarithmic fan-in. Turning this argument into a proof of Theorem F.1 requires a careful implementation as well as the use of transitions of the type presented in Exercise 3.8. Furthermore, such a presentation tends to obscure the conceptual steps that underlie the argument.

Proof Outline: The proof uses three main ingredients. The first ingredient is the fact that $\mathcal{NP}$ is reducible to $\oplus\mathcal{P}$ via a probabilistic Karp-reduction, and that this reduction "relativizes" (i.e., reduces $\mathcal{NP}^A$ to $\oplus\mathcal{P}^A$ for any oracle A).[1] The second ingredient is the fact that error reduction is available in the current context (of randomized reductions to $\oplus\mathcal{P}$), resulting in reductions that have exponentially vanishing error probability.[2] The third ingredient is the extension of the first ingredient to Σ_k, which relies on Proposition 3.9 as well as on the aforementioned error reduction. These ingredients correspond to the three main steps of the proof, which are outlined next:

Step 1: Present a randomized Karp-reduction of $\mathcal{NP}$ to $\oplus\mathcal{P}$.

Step 2: Decrease the error probability of the foregoing Karp-reduction such that the error probability becomes exponentially vanishing. Such a low error probability is crucial as a starting point for the next step.

Step 3: Prove that Σ_2 is randomly reducible to $\oplus\mathcal{P}$ by extending the reduction of Step 1 (while using Step 2). Intuitively, for any oracle A, the reduction of Step 1 offers a reduction of $\mathcal{NP}^A$ to $\oplus\mathcal{P}^A$, whereas a reduction of A to B having exponentially vanishing error probability allows for reducing $\oplus\mathcal{P}^A$ to $\oplus\mathcal{P}^B$ (or, similarly, reducing $\mathcal{NP}^A$ to $\mathcal{NP}^B$). Observing that $\oplus\mathcal{P}^{\oplus\mathcal{P}} = \oplus\mathcal{P}$, we obtain a randomized Karp-reduction of Σ_2 (viewed as $\mathcal{NP}^{\mathcal{NP}}$) to $\oplus\mathcal{P}$.

When completing the third step, we shall have all the ingredients needed for the general case (of randomly reducing Σ_k to $\oplus\mathcal{P}$, for any $k \geq 2$). We shall finish the proof by sketching the extension of the case of Σ_2 (treated in Step 3) to the general case of Σ_k (for any $k \geq 2$). The actual extension is quite cumbersome, but the ideas are all present in the case of Σ_2. Furthermore, we believe that the case of Σ_2 is of significant interest per se.

---

[1]Indeed, the "relativization" requirement presumes that both $\mathcal{NP}$ and $\oplus\mathcal{P}$ are each associated with a class of (standard) machines that generalizes to a class of corresponding oracle machines (see comment at Section 3.2.2). This presumption holds for both classes, by virtue of a (deterministic polynomial-time) machine that decides membership in the corresponding relation that belongs to $\mathcal{PC}$. Alternatively, one may use the fact that the aforementioned reduction is "highly structured" in the sense that for some polynomial-time computable predicate ψ this reduction maps x to $\langle x, s \rangle$ such that for every non-empty set $S_x \subseteq \{0, 1\}^{p(|x|)}$ it holds that $\Pr_s[|\{y \in S_x : \psi(x, s, y)\}| \equiv 1 \pmod 2] > 1/3$.

[2]We comment that such an error reduction is not available in the context of reductions to unique solution problems. This comment is made in view of the similarity between the reduction of $\mathcal{NP}$ to $\oplus\mathcal{P}$ and the reduction of $\mathcal{NP}$ to problems of unique solution.

> **Teaching note:** The foregoing sketch of Step 3 suggests an abstract treatment that evolves around definitions such as $\mathcal{NP}^A$ and $\oplus\mathcal{P}^B$. We prefer a concrete presentation that performs Step 3 as an extension of Step 1 (while using Step 2). This is one reason for explicitly performing Step 1 (i.e., present a randomized Karp-reduction of $\mathcal{NP}$ to $\oplus\mathcal{P}$). We note that Step 1 (i.e., a reduction of $\mathcal{NP}$ to $\oplus\mathcal{P}$) follows immediately from the NP-hardness of deciding unique solutions for some relations $R \in \mathcal{PC}$ (i.e., Theorem 6.29), because the promise problem $(\mathrm{US}_R, \overline{S}_R)$, where $\mathrm{US}_R = \{x : |R(x)| = 1\}$ and $\overline{S}_R = \{x : |R(x)| = 0\}$, is reducible to $\oplus R = \{x : |R(x)| \equiv 1 \pmod{2}\}$ by the identity mapping. However, for the sake of self-containment and conceptual rightness, we present an alternative proof.

Step 1: A direct proof for the case of $\mathcal{NP}$. As in the proof of Theorem 6.29, we start with any $R \in \mathcal{PC}$ and our goal is reducing $S_R = \{x : |R(x)| \geq 1\}$ to $\oplus\mathcal{P}$ by a randomized Karp-reduction.[3] The standard way of obtaining such a reduction (e.g., in [136, 178, 212, 220]) consists of just using the reduction (to "unique solution") that was presented in the proof of Theorem 6.29, but we believe that this way is conceptually wrong. Let us explain.

Recall that the proof of Theorem 6.29 consists of implementing a randomized sieve that has the following property. For any $x \in S_R$, with noticeable probability, a single element of $R(x)$ passes the sieve (and this event can be detected by an oracle to a unique solution problem). Indeed, an adequate oracle in $\oplus\mathcal{P}$ correctly detects the case in which a single element of $R(x)$ passes the sieve. However, by definition, this oracle correctly detects the more general case in which any odd number of elements of $R(x)$ pass the sieve. Thus, insisting on a random sieve that allows the passing of a single element of $R(x)$ seems an overkill (or at least is conceptually wrong). Instead, *we should just apply a less stringent random sieve that, with noticeable probability, allows the passing of an odd number of elements of $R(x)$*. The adequate tool for such a random sieve is a small-bias generator (see Section 8.5.2).

Indeed, we randomly reduce S_R to $\oplus\mathcal{P}$ by sieving potential solutions via a small-bias generator. Intuitively, we randomly map x to $\langle x, s \rangle$, where s is a random seed for such a generator, and y is considered a solution to the instance $\langle x, s \rangle$ if and only if $y \in R(x)$ and the yth bit of $G(s)$ equals 1. (Indeed, if $|R(x)| \geq 1$ then, with probability approximately $1/2$, the instance $\langle x, s \rangle$ has an odd number of solutions, whereas if $|R(x)| = 0$ then $\langle x, s \rangle$ has no solutions.) Specifically, we use a *strongly efficient* generator (see §8.5.2.1), denoted $G : \{0, 1\}^k \to \{0, 1\}^{\ell(k)}$, where $G(U_k)$ has bias at most $1/6$ and $\ell(k) = \exp(\Omega(k))$. That is, given a seed $s \in \{0, 1\}^k$ and index $i \in [\ell(k)]$, we can produce the ith bit of $G(s)$, denoted $G(s, i)$, in polynomial time. Assuming, without loss of generality, that $R(x) \subseteq \{0, 1\}^{p(|x|)}$ for some polynomial p, we consider the relation

$$R_2 \stackrel{\text{def}}{=} \{(\langle x, s \rangle, y) : (x, y) \in R \wedge G(s, y) = 1\} \tag{F.1}$$

where $y \in \{0, 1\}^{p(|x|)} \equiv [2^{p(|x|)}]$ and $s \in \{0, 1\}^{O(|y|)}$ such that $\ell(|s|) = 2^{|y|}$. In other words, $R_2(\langle x, s \rangle) = \{y : y \in R(x) \wedge G(s, y) = 1\}$. Then, for every $x \in S_R$, with probability at least $1/3$, a uniformly selected $s \in \{0, 1\}^{O(|y|)}$ satisfies $|R_2(\langle x, s \rangle)| \equiv 1 \pmod{2}$, whereas for every $x \notin S_R$ and every $s \in \{0, 1\}^{O(|y|)}$ it holds that $|R_2(\langle x, s \rangle)| = 0$. A key observation is that $R_2 \in \mathcal{PC}$ (and thus $\oplus R_2$ is in $\oplus\mathcal{P}$). Thus, deciding membership in S_R is randomly

---

[3]As in Theorem 6.29, if any search problem in $\mathcal{PC}$ is reducible to R via a parsimonious reduction, then we can reduce S_R to $\oplus R$. Specifically, we shall show that S_R is randomly reducible to $\oplus R_2$, for some $R_2 \in \mathcal{PC}$, and a reduction of S_R to $\oplus R$ follows (by using the parsimonious reduction of R_2 to R).

reducible to $\oplus R_2$ (by the many-to-one randomized mapping of x to $\langle x, s \rangle$, where s is uniformly selected in $\{0, 1\}^{O(p(|x|))}$). Since the foregoing holds for any $R \in \mathcal{PC}$, it follows that $\mathcal{NP}$ is reducible to $\oplus \mathcal{P}$ via randomized Karp-reductions.

Dealing with $\text{co}\mathcal{NP}$. We may Cook-reduce $\text{co}\mathcal{NP}$ to $\mathcal{NP}$ and thus prove that $\text{co}\mathcal{NP}$ is randomly reducible to $\oplus \mathcal{P}$, but we wish to highlight the fact that a randomized Karp-reduction will also do. Starting with the reduction presented for the case of sets in $\mathcal{NP}$, we note that for $S \in \text{co}\mathcal{NP}$ (i.e., $S = \{x : R(x) = \emptyset\}$) we obtain a relation R_2 such that $x \in S$ is indicated by $|R_2(\langle x, \cdot \rangle)| \equiv 0 \pmod 2$. We wish to flip the parity such that $x \in S$ will be indicated by $|R_2(\langle x, \cdot \rangle)| \equiv 1 \pmod 2$, and this can be done by augmenting the relation R_2 with a single dummy solution per each x. For example, we may redefine $R_2(\langle x, s \rangle)$ as $\{0y : y \in R_2(\langle x, s \rangle)\} \cup \{10^{p(|x|)}\}$. Indeed, *we have just demonstrated and used the fact that $\oplus \mathcal{P}$ is closed under complementation.*

We note that dealing with the cases of $\mathcal{NP}$ and $\text{co}\mathcal{NP}$ is of interest only because we reduced these classes to $\oplus \mathcal{P}$ rather than to $\#\mathcal{P}$. In contrast, even a reduction of Σ_2 to $\#\mathcal{P}$ is of interest, and thus the reduction of Σ_2 to $\oplus \mathcal{P}$ (presented in Step 3) is interesting. This reduction relies heavily on the fact that error reduction is applicable to the context of randomized Karp-reductions to $\oplus \mathcal{P}$.

Step 2: Error reduction. An important observation, toward the core of the proof, is that it is possible to drastically decrease the (one-sided) error probability in randomized Karp-reductions to $\oplus \mathcal{P}$. Specifically, let R_2 be as in Eq. (F.1) and t be any polynomial. Then, a binary relation $R_2^{(t)}$ that satisfies

$$|R_2^{(t)}(\langle x, s_1, \ldots, s_{t(|x|)} \rangle)| = 1 + \prod_{i=1}^{t(|x|)} (1 + |R_2(\langle x, s_i \rangle)|) \tag{F.2}$$

offers such an error reduction, because $|R_2^{(t)}(\langle x, s_1, \ldots, s_{t(|x|)} \rangle)|$ is odd if and only if for some $i \in [t(|x|)]$ it holds that $|R_2(\langle x, s_i \rangle)|$ is odd. Thus,

$$\Pr_{s_1, \ldots, s_{t(|x|)}}[|R_2^{(t)}(\langle x, s_1, \ldots, s_{t(|x|)} \rangle)| \equiv 0 \pmod 2]$$

$$= \Pr_s[|R_2(\langle x, s \rangle)| \equiv 0 \pmod 2]^{t(|x|)}$$

where $s, s_1, \ldots, s_{t(|x|)}$ are uniformly and independently distributed in $\{0, 1\}^{O(p(|x|))}$ (and p is such that $R(x) \subseteq \{0, 1\}^{p(|x|)}$). This means that the one-sided error probability of a randomized reduction of S_R to $\oplus R_2$ (which maps x to $\langle x, s \rangle$) can be drastically decreased by reducing S_R to $\oplus R_2^{(t)}$, where the reduction maps x to $\langle x, s_1, \ldots, s_{t(|x|)} \rangle$. Specifically, an error probability of ε (e.g., $\varepsilon = 2/3$) in the case that we desire an "odd outcome" (i.e., $x \in S_R$) is decreased to error probability ε^t, whereas the zero error probability in the case of a desired "even outcome" (i.e., $x \in \bar{S}_R$) is preserved.

A key question is whether $\oplus R_2^{(t)}$ is in $\oplus \mathcal{P}$, that is, whether $R_2^{(t)}$ (as postulated in Eq. (F.2)) can be implemented in $\mathcal{PC}$. The answer is positive, and this can be shown by using a Cartesian product construction (and adding some dummy solutions). For example, let $R_2^{(t)}(\langle x, s_1, \ldots, s_{t(|x|)} \rangle)$ consists of tuples $\langle \sigma_0, y_1, \ldots, y_{t(|x|)} \rangle$ such that either $\sigma_0 = 1$ and $y_1 = \cdots = y_{t(|x|)} = 0^{p(|x|)+1}$ or $\sigma_0 = 0$ and for every $i \in [t(|x|)]$ it holds that $y_i \in (\{0\} \times R_2(\langle x, s_i \rangle)) \cup \{10^{p(|x|)}\}$ (i.e., either $y_i = 10^{p(|x|)}$ or $y_i = 0y_i'$ and $y_i' \in R_2(\langle x, s_i \rangle)$).

We wish to stress that, when starting with R_2 as in Eq. (F.1), the foregoing process of error reduction can be used for obtaining error probability that is upper-bounded by $\exp(-q(|x|))$ for any desired polynomial q. The importance of this comment will become clear shortly.

Step 3: The case of Σ_2. With the foregoing preliminaries, we are now ready to handle the case of $S \in \Sigma_2$. By Proposition 3.9, there exists a polynomial p and a set $S' \in \Pi_1 = \text{co}\mathcal{NP}$ such that $S = \{x : \exists y \in \{0,1\}^{p(|x|)} \text{ s.t. } (x,y) \in S'\}$. Using $S' \in \text{co}\mathcal{NP}$, we apply the foregoing reduction of S' to $\oplus\mathcal{P}$ as well as an adequate error reduction that yields an upper bound of $\varepsilon \cdot 2^{-p(|x|)}$ on the error probability, where $\varepsilon \leq 1/7$ is unspecified at this point. (For the case of Σ_2 the setting $\varepsilon = 1/7$ will do, but for the dealing with Σ_k we will need a much smaller value of $\varepsilon > 0$.) Thus, for an adequate polynomial t (i.e., $t(n + p(n)) = O(p(n)\log(1/\varepsilon))$), we obtain a relation $R_2^{(t)} \in \mathcal{PC}$ such that the following holds: *For every x and $y \in \{0,1\}^{p(|x|)}$, with probability at least $1 - \varepsilon \cdot 2^{-p(|x|)}$ over the random choice of $s' \in \{0,1\}^{\text{poly}(|x|)}$, it holds that $x' \overset{\text{def}}{=} (x,y) \in S'$ if and only if $|R_2^{(t)}(\langle x', s'\rangle)|$ is odd.*[4]

Using a union bound (over all possible $y \in \{0,1\}^{p(|x|)}$), it follows that, *with probability at least $1 - \varepsilon$ over the choice of s', it holds that $x \in S$ if and only if there exists a y such that $|R_2^{(t)}(\langle\langle x,y\rangle, s'\rangle)|$ is odd.* Now, as in the treatment of $\mathcal{NP}$, we wish to reduce the latter "existential problem" to $\oplus\mathcal{P}$. That is, we wish to define a relation $R_3 \in \mathcal{PC}$ such that for a randomly selected s the value $|R_3(\langle x, s, s'\rangle)| \bmod 2$ provides an indication as to whether or not $x \in S$ (by indicating whether or not there exists a y such that $|R_2^{(t)}(\langle\langle x,y\rangle, s'\rangle)|$ is odd). Analogously to Eq. (F.1), consider the binary relation

$$I_3 \overset{\text{def}}{=} \left\{ (\langle x, s, s'\rangle, y) : \left| R_2^{(t)}(\langle\langle x, y\rangle, s'\rangle) \right| \equiv 1 (\bmod 2) \wedge G(s, y) = 1 \right\}. \tag{F.3}$$

In other words, $I_3(\langle x, s, s'\rangle) = \{y : |R_2^{(t)}(\langle\langle x,y\rangle, s'\rangle)| \equiv 1(\bmod 2) \wedge G(s,y) = 1\}$. Indeed, if $x \in S$ then, with probability at least $1 - \varepsilon$ over the random choice of s' and probability at least $1/3$ over the random choice of s, it holds that $|I_3(\langle x, s, s'\rangle)|$ is odd, whereas for every $x \notin S$ and every choice of s it holds that $\text{Pr}_{s'}[|I_3(\langle x, s, s'\rangle)| = 0] \geq 1 - \varepsilon$.[5] Note that, for $\varepsilon \leq 1/7$, it follows that for every $x \in S$ we have $\text{Pr}_{s,s'}[|I_3(\langle x, s, s'\rangle)| \equiv 1 (\bmod 2)] \geq (1 - \varepsilon)/3 \geq 2/7$, whereas for every $x \notin S$ we have $\text{Pr}_{s,s'}[|I_3(\langle x, s, s'\rangle)| \equiv 1 (\bmod 2)] \leq \varepsilon \leq 1/7$. Thus, $|I_3(\langle x, \cdot, \cdot\rangle)| \bmod 2$ provides a randomized indication to whether or not $x \in S$, but it is not clear whether I_3 is in $\mathcal{PC}$ (and in fact I_3 is likely not to be in $\mathcal{PC}$). The key observation is that there exists $R_3 \in \mathcal{PC}$ such that $\oplus R_3 = \oplus I_3$.

---

[4]Recall that $|s'| = t(|x'|) \cdot O(p'(|x'|))$, where $R'(x') \subseteq \{0,1\}^{p'(|x'|)}$ is the "witness relation" corresponding to S' (i.e., $x' \in S'$ if and only if $R'(x') = \{0,1\}^{p'(|x'|)}$). Thus, $R_2(\langle x', s'\rangle) \subseteq \{0,1\}^{p'(|x'|)+1}$ and $R_2^{(t)}(\langle x', s'\rangle)$ is a subset of $\{0,1\}^{1+t(|x'|)\cdot(p'(|x'|)+2)}$. Note that (since we started with $S' \in \text{co}\mathcal{NP}$) the error probability occurs on no-instances of S', whereas yes-instances are always accepted. However, to simplify the exposition, we allow possible errors also on yes-instances of S'. This does not matter because we will anyhow have an error probability on yes-instances of S (see footnote 5).

[5]In continuation of footnote 4, we note that actually, if $x \in S$ then there exists a y such that $(x,y) \in S'$ and consequently for every choice of s' it holds that $|R_2^{(t)}(\langle\langle x,y\rangle, s'\rangle)|$ is odd (because the reduction from $S' \in \text{co}\mathcal{NP}$ to $\oplus\mathcal{P}$ has zero error on yes-instances). Thus, for every $x \in S$ and s', with probability at least $1/3$ over the random choice of s, it holds that $|I_3(\langle x, s, s'\rangle)|$ is odd (because the reduction from $S \in \mathcal{NP}^{S'}$ to $\oplus\mathcal{P}^{S'}$ has non-zero error on yes-instances). On the other hand, if $x \notin S$ then $\text{Pr}_{s'}[(\forall y)|R_2^{(t)}(\langle\langle x,y\rangle, s'\rangle)| \equiv 0 (\bmod 2)] \geq 1 - \varepsilon$ (because for every y it holds that $(x,y) \notin S'$ and the reduction from $\text{co}\mathcal{NP}$ to $\oplus\mathcal{P}$ has non-zero error on no-instances). Thus, for every $x \notin S$ and s, it holds that $\text{Pr}_{s'}[|I_3(\langle x, s, s'\rangle)| = 0] \geq 1 - \varepsilon$ (because the reduction from $S \in \mathcal{NP}^{S'}$ to $\oplus\mathcal{P}^{S'}$ has zero error on no-instances). To sum up, the combined reduction has two-sided error, because each of the two reductions introduces an error in a different direction.

Specifically, consider

$$R_3 \stackrel{\text{def}}{=} \left\{ (\langle x, s, s' \rangle, \langle y, z \rangle) : (\langle (x, y), s' \rangle, z) \in R_2^{(t)} \wedge G(s, y) = 1 \right\}, \qquad \text{(F.4)}$$

where $\langle y, z \rangle \in \{0, 1\}^{p(|x|)} \times \{0, 1\}^{\text{poly}(|x|)}$. (That is, $\langle y, z \rangle$ is in $R_3(\langle x, s, s' \rangle)$ if $(\langle (x, y), s' \rangle, z) \in R_2^{(t)}$ and $G(s, y) = 1$.) Clearly $R_3 \in \mathcal{PC}$, and so it is left to show that $|R_3(\langle x, s, s' \rangle)| \equiv |I_3(\langle x, s, s' \rangle)| \pmod 2$. The claim follows by letting $\chi_{y,z}$ (resp., ξ_y) indicate the event $(\langle (x, y), s' \rangle, z) \in R_2^{(t)}$ (resp., the event $G(s, y) = 1$), noting that

$$|R_3(\langle x, s, s' \rangle)| \bmod 2 \equiv \oplus_{y,z}(\chi_{y,z} \wedge \xi_y)$$

$$|I_3(\langle x, s, s' \rangle)| \bmod 2 \equiv \oplus_y((\oplus_z \chi_{y,z}) \wedge \xi_y)$$

and using the equivalence of the two corresponding Boolean expressions. Thus, S is randomly Karp-reducible to $\oplus R_3 \in \oplus \mathcal{P}$ (by the many-to-one randomized mapping of x to $\langle x, s, s' \rangle$, where (s, s') is uniformly selected in $\{0, 1\}^{O(p(|x|))} \times \{0, 1\}^{\text{poly}(|x|)}$). Since this holds for any $S \in \Sigma_2$, we conclude that Σ_2 is randomly Karp-reducible to $\oplus \mathcal{P}$.

Again, error reduction may be applied to this reduction (of Σ_2 to $\oplus \mathcal{P}$) such that the resulting reduction can be used for dealing with Σ_3 (viewed as $\mathcal{NP}^{\Sigma_2}$). A technical difficulty arises since the foregoing reduction has two-sided error probability, where one type (or "side") of error is due to the error in the reduction of $S' \in \text{co}\mathcal{NP}$ to $\oplus R_2^{(t)}$ (which occurs on no-instances of S') and the second type (or "side") of error is due to the (new) reduction of S to $\oplus R_3$ (and occurs on the yes-instances of S). However, the error probability in the first reduction is (or can be made) very small and thus can be ignored when applying error reduction to the second reduction. See following comments.

The general case. First note that, as in the case of $\text{co}\mathcal{NP}$, we can obtain a similar reduction (to $\oplus \mathcal{P}$) for sets in $\Pi_2 = \text{co}\Sigma_2$. It remains to extend the treatment of Σ_2 to Σ_k, for every $k \geq 2$. Indeed, we show how to reduce Σ_k to $\oplus \mathcal{P}$ by using a reduction of Σ_{k-1} (or rather Π_{k-1}) to $\oplus \mathcal{P}$. Specifically, $S \in \Sigma_k$ is treated by considering a polynomial p and a set $S' \in \Pi_{k-1}$ such that $S = \{x : \exists y \in \{0, 1\}^{p(|x|)} \text{ s.t. } (x, y) \in S'\}$. Relying on the treatment of Π_{k-1}, we use a relation $R_k^{(t_k)}$ such that, with overwhelmingly high probability over the choice of s', the value $|R_k^{(t_k)}(\langle (x, y), s' \rangle)| \bmod 2$ indicates whether or not $(x, y) \in S'$. Using the ideas underlying the treatment of $\mathcal{NP}$ (and Σ_2) we check whether there exists $y \in \{0, 1\}^{p(|x|)}$ such that $|R_k^{(t_k)}(\langle (x, y), s' \rangle)| \equiv 1 \pmod 2$. This yields a relation R_{k+1} such that for random s, s' the value $|R_{k+1}(\langle x, s, s' \rangle)| \bmod 2$ indicates whether or not $x \in S$. Finally, we apply error reduction, while ignoring the probability that s' is bad, and obtain the desired relation $R_{k+1}^{(t_{k+1})}$.

We comment that the foregoing inductive process should be implemented with some care. Specifically, if we wish to upper-bound the error probability in the reduction (of S) to $\oplus R_{k+1}^{(t_{k+1})}$ by ε_{k+1}, then the error probability in the reduction (of S') to $\oplus R_k^{(t_k)}$ should be upper-bounded by $\varepsilon_k \leq \varepsilon_{k+1} \cdot 2^{-p(|x|)}$ (and t_k should be set accordingly). Thus, the proof that $\mathcal{PH}$ is randomly reducible to $\oplus \mathcal{P}$ actually proceeds "top down" (at least partially); that is, starting with an arbitrary $S \in \Sigma_k$, we first determine the auxiliary sets (as per Proposition 3.9) as well as the error bounds that should be proved for the reductions of these sets (which reside in lower levels of $\mathcal{PH}$), and only then we establish the existence of such reductions. Indeed, this latter (and main) step is done "bottom up" using the reduction (to $\oplus \mathcal{P}$) of the set in the ith level when reducing (to $\oplus \mathcal{P}$) the set in the $i + 1^{\text{st}}$ level.

571

F.2. Proving That $\mathcal{IP}(f) \subseteq \mathcal{AM}(O(f)) \subseteq \mathcal{AM}(f)$

Using the notations presented in §9.1.4.3, we restate two results mentioned there.

Theorem F.2 (round-efficient emulation of $\mathcal{IP}$ by $\mathcal{AM}$): *Let* $f : \mathbb{N} \to \mathbb{N}$ *be a polynomially bounded function. Then* $\mathcal{IP}(f) \subseteq \mathcal{AM}(f + 3)$.

We comment that, in light of the following linear speedup in round complexity for $\mathcal{AM}$, it suffices to establish $\mathcal{IP}(f) \subseteq \mathcal{AM}(O(f))$.

Theorem F.3 (linear speedup for $\mathcal{AM}$): *Let* $f : \mathbb{N} \to \mathbb{N}$ *be a polynomially bounded function. Then* $\mathcal{AM}(2f) \subseteq \mathcal{AM}(f + 1)$.

Combining these two theorems, we obtain a linear speedup for $\mathcal{IP}$; that is, for any polynomially bounded $f : \mathbb{N} \to (\mathbb{N}\backslash\{1\})$, it holds that $\mathcal{IP}(O(f)) \subseteq \mathcal{AM}(f) \subseteq \mathcal{IP}(f)$. In this appendix we prove both theorems.

Note: The proof of Theorem F.2 relies on the fact that, for every f, error reduction is possible for $\mathcal{IP}(f)$. Specifically, error reduction can be obtained via *parallel* repetitions (see [90, Apdx. C.1]). We mention that error reduction (in the context of $\mathcal{AM}(f)$) is also implicit in the proof of Theorem F.3 (and is explicit in the original proof of [23]).

F.2.1. Emulating General Interactive Proofs by AM-Games

In this section we prove Theorem F.2. Our proof differs from the original proof of Goldwasser and Sipser [111] only in the conceptualization and implementation of the iterative emulation process.

F.2.1.1. Overview

Our aim is to transform a general interactive proof system (P, V) into a public-coin interactive proof system for the same set. Suppose, without loss of generality, that P constitutes an optimal prover with respect to V (i.e., P maximizes the acceptance probability of V on any input). Then, for any yes-instance x, the set A_x of coin sequences that make V accept when interacting with this optimal prover contains all possible outcomes, whereas for a no-instance x (of equal length) the set A_x is significantly smaller. The basic idea is having a public-coin system in which, on common input x, the prover proves to the verifier that the said set A_x is big. Such a proof system can be constructed using ideas as in the case of approximate counting (see the proof of Theorem 6.27), while replacing the NP-oracle with a prover that is required to prove the correctness of its answers. Implementing this idea requires taking a closer look at the set of coin sequences that make V accept an input.

A very restricted case. Let us first demonstrate the implementation of the foregoing approach by considering a restricted type of a two-message interactive proof system. Recall that in a two-message interactive proof system the verifier, denoted V, sends a single message (based on the common input and its internal coin tosses) to which the prover, denoted P, responds with a single message and then V decides whether to accept or reject the input. We further restrict our attention by assuming that *each possible message of V is equally likely and that the number of possible V-messages is easy to determine* *from the input.* Thus, on input x, the verifier V tosses $\ell = \ell(|x|)$ coins and sends one out of $N = N(x)$ possible messages. Note that if x is a yes-instance then for each possible V-message there exists a P-response that is accepted by the $2^\ell/N$ corresponding coin sequences of V (i.e., the coin sequences that lead V to send this V-message). On the other hand, if x is a no-instance then, in expectation, for a uniformly selected V-message, the optimal P-response is accepted by a significantly smaller number of corresponding coin sequences. We now show how such an interactive proof system can be emulated by a *public-coin system*.

In the *public-coin system*, on input x, the prover will attempt to prove that for each possible V-message (in the original system) there exists a response (by the original prover) that is accepted by $2^\ell/N$ corresponding coin sequences of V. Recall that $N = N(x)$ and $\ell = \ell(|x|)$ are easily determined by both parties, and so if the foregoing claim holds then x must be a yes-instance. The new interaction itself proceeds as follows: First, the verifier selects uniformly a coin sequence for V, denoted r, and sends it to the prover. The coin sequence r determines a V-message, denoted α. Next, the prover sends back an adequate P-message, denoted β, and *interactively proves to the verifier* that β would have been accepted by $2^\ell/N$ possible coin sequences of V that correspond to the V-message α (i.e., β should be accepted not only by r but also by the $2^\ell/N$ coin sequences of V that correspond to the V-message α). The latter interactive proof follows the idea of the proof of Theorem 6.27: The verifier applies a random sieve that lets only a $(2^\ell/N)^{-1}$ fraction of the elements pass, and the prover shows that some adequate sequence of V-coins has passed this sieve (by merely presenting such a sequence).[6] We stress that the foregoing interaction (and in particular the random sieve) can be implemented in the public-coin model.

Waiving one restriction. Next, we waive the restriction that the number of possible V-messages is easy to determine from the input, but still assume that all possible V-messages are equally likely. In this case, the prover should provide the number N of possible V-messages and should prove that indeed there exist at least N possible V-messages (and that, as in the prior case, for each V-message there exists a P-response that is accepted by $2^\ell/N$ corresponding coin sequences of V). That is, the prover should prove that for at least N possible V-messages there exists a P-response that is accepted by $2^\ell/N$ corresponding coin sequences of V. This calls for a double (or rather nested) application of the aforementioned "lower-bound" protocol. That is, first the parties apply a random sieve to the set of possible V-messages such that only a N^{-1} fraction of these messages pass, and next the parties apply a random sieve to the set coin sequences that fit a passing V-message such that only a $(2^\ell/N)^{-1}$ fraction of these sequences pass.

The general case of $\mathcal{IP}(2)$. Treating general two-message interactive proofs requires waiving also the restriction that all possible V-messages are equally likely. In this case, the prover may cluster the V-messages into few (say, ℓ) clusters such that the messages in each cluster are sent (by V) with roughly the same probability (say, up to a factor of two). Then, focusing on the cluster having the largest probability weight, the prover can proceed as in the previous case (i.e., send i and claim that there are $2^\ell/\ell$ possible

---

[6]Indeed, the verifier can easily check whether a coin sequence r' passes the sieve as well as fits the initial message α and would have made V accept when the prover responds with β (i.e., V would have accepted the input, on coins r', when receiving the prover message β).

V-messages that are each supported by 2^i coin sequences). This has a potential of cutting the probabilistic gap between yes-instances and no-instances by a factor related to the number of clusters times the approximation level within clusters (e.g., a factor of $O(\ell)$),[7] but this loss is negligible in comparison to the initial gap (which can be obtained via error reduction).

Dealing with all levels of $\mathcal{IP}$. So far, we have only dealt with two-message systems (i.e., $\mathcal{IP}(2)$). We shall see that the general case of $\mathcal{IP}(f)$ can be dealt with by recursion (or rather by iterations), where each level of recursion (resp., each iteration) is analogous to the (general) case of $\mathcal{IP}(2)$. Recall that our treatment of the case of $\mathcal{IP}(2)$ boils down to selecting a random V-message, α, and having the prover send a P-response, β, and prove that β is acceptable by many V-coins. In other words, the prover should prove that in the conditional probability space defined by a V-message α, the original verifier V accepts with high probability. In the general case (of $\mathcal{IP}(f)$), the latter claim refers to the probability of accepting in the residual interaction, which consists of $f - 2$ messages, and thus the very same protocol can be applied iteratively (until we get to the last message, which is dealt with as in the case of $\mathcal{IP}(2)$). The only problem is that, in the residual interactions, it may not be easy for the verifier to select a random V-message (as done in the *very restricted case*). However, as already done when *waiving the first restriction*, the verifier can be assisted by the prover, while making sure that it is not being fooled by the prover. This process is made explicit in §F.2.1.2, where we define an adequate notion of a "random selection" protocol (which needs to be implemented in the public-coin model). For simplicity, we may consider the problem of uniformly selecting a sequence of coins in the corresponding (residual) probability space, because such a sequence determines the desired random V-message.

F.2.1.2. Random Selection
Various types of "random selection" protocols have appeared in the literature (see, e.g., [227, Sec. 6.4]). The common theme in these protocols is that they allow for a probabilistic polynomial-time player (called the *verifier*) to sample a set, denoted $S \subset \{0, 1\}^\ell$, while being assisted by a second player (called the *prover*) that is powerful but not trustworthy. These nicknames fit the common conventions regarding interactive proofs and are further justified by the typical applications of such protocols as subroutines within an interactive proof system (where indeed the first party is played by the higher-level verifier while the second party is played by the higher-level prover). The various types of random-selection protocols differ by what is known about the set S and what is required from the protocol.

Here, we will assume that the verifier is given a parameter N, which is supposed to equal $|S|$, and the performance guarantee of the protocol will be meaningful only for sets of size at most N. We seek a constant-round (preferably two-message) public-coin protocol (for this setting) such that the following two conditions hold, with respect to a security parameter $\varepsilon \geq 1/\text{poly}(\ell)$.

---

[7]The loss is due to the fact that the distribution of (probability) weights may not be identical on all instances. For example, in one case (e.g., of some yes-instance) all clusters may have equal weight, and thus a corresponding factor is lost, while in another case (e.g., of some no-instance) all the probability mass may be concentrated in a single cluster.

1. If both players follow the protocol and $N = |S|$ then the verifier's output is ε-close to the uniform distribution over S. Furthermore, the verifier always outputs an element of S.

2. For any set $S' \subseteq \{0, 1\}^\ell$ if the verifier follows the protocol then, no matter how the prover behaves, the verifier's output resides in S' with probability at most $\text{poly}(\ell/\varepsilon) \cdot (|S'|/N)$.

Indeed, the second property is meaningful only for sets S' having size that is (significantly) smaller than N. We shall be using such a protocol while setting ε to be a constant (say, $\varepsilon = 1/2$).

A three-message public-coin protocol that satisfies the foregoing properties can be obtained by using the ideas that underlie Construction 6.32. Specifically, we set $m = \max(0, \log_2 N - O(\log \ell/\varepsilon))$ in order to guarantee that if $|S| = N$ then, with overwhelmingly high probability, each of the 2^m cells defined by a uniformly selected hashing function contains $(1 \pm \varepsilon) \cdot |S|/2^m$ elements of S. In the protocol, *the prover arbitrarily selects a good hashing function* (i.e., one defining such a good partition of S) *and sends it to the verifier, which answers with a uniformly selected cell, to which the prover responds with a uniformly selected element of S that resides in this cell.*[8]

We stress that the foregoing protocol is indeed in the public-coin model, and comment that the fact that it uses three messages rather than two will have a minor effect on our application (see §F.2.1.3). Indeed, this protocol satisfies the two foregoing properties. In particular, the second property follows because for every possible hashing function, the fraction of cells containing an element of S' is at most $|S'|/2^m$, which is upper-bounded by $\text{poly}(\ell/\varepsilon) \cdot |S'|/N$.

F.2.1.3. The Iterated Partition Protocol

Using the random selection protocol of §F.2.1.2, we now present a public-coin emulation of an arbitrary interactive proof system, (P, V). We start with some notations.

Fixing any input x to (P, V), we denote by $t = t(|x|)$ the number of pairs of messages exchanged in the corresponding interaction, while assuming that the verifier takes the first move in (P, V).[9] We denote by $\ell = \ell(|x|)$ the number of coins tossed by V, and assume that $\ell > t$. Recall that we assume that P is an optimal prover (with respect to V), and that (without loss of generality) P is deterministic. Let us denote by $\langle P, V(r) \rangle(x)$ the full transcript of the interaction of P and V on input x, when V uses coins r; that is, $\langle P, V(r) \rangle(x) = (\alpha_1, \beta_1, \ldots, \alpha_t, \beta_t, \sigma)$ if $\sigma = V(x, r, \beta_1, \ldots, \beta_t) \in \{0, 1\}$ is V's final verdict and for every $i = 1, \ldots, t$ it holds that $\alpha_i = V(x, r, \beta_1, \ldots, \beta_{i-1})$ and $\beta_i = P(x, \alpha_1, \ldots, \alpha_i)$.

---

[8]We mention that the foregoing protocol is but one of several possible implementations of the ideas that underlie Construction 6.32. Firstly, note that an alternative implementation may designate the task of selecting a hashing function to the verifier, who may do so by selecting a function at random. Although this seems more natural, it actually offers no advantage with respect to the "soundness-like" property (i.e., the second property). Furthermore, in this case, it may happen (rarely) that the hashing function selected by the verifier is not good, and consequently the furthermore clause of the first property (i.e., requiring that the output always reside in S) is not satisfied. Secondly, recall that in the foregoing protocol the last step consists of the prover selecting a random element of S that resides in the selected (by the verifier) cell. An alternative implementation may replace this step by two steps such that first the prover sends a list of $(1 - \varepsilon) \cdot N/2^m$ elements (of S) that resides in the said cell, and then the verifier outputs a uniformly selected element of this list. This alternative yields an improvement in the "soundness-like" property (i.e., the verifier's output resides in S' with probability at most $(|S'|/N) + \varepsilon$), but requires an additional message (which we prefer to avoid, although this is not that crucial).

[9]We note if the prover takes the first move in (P, V) then its first message can be emulated with no cost (in the number of rounds).

For any partial transcript ending with a P-message, $\gamma = (\alpha_1, \beta_1, \ldots, \alpha_{i-1}, \beta_{i-1})$, we denote by $\mathrm{ACC}_x(\gamma)$ the set of coin sequences that are consistent with the partial transcript γ and lead V to accept x when interacting with P; that is, $r \in \mathrm{ACC}_x(\gamma)$ if and only if for some $\gamma' \in \{0, 1\}^{2(t-i)\cdot\mathrm{poly}(|x|)}$ it holds that $\langle P, V(r)\rangle(x) = (\alpha_1, \beta_1, \ldots, \alpha_{i-1}, \beta_{i-1}, \gamma', 1)$. The same notation is also used for a partial transcript ending with a V-message; that is, $r \in \mathrm{ACC}_x(\alpha_1, \beta_1, \ldots, \alpha_i)$ if and only if $\langle P, V(r)\rangle(x) = (\alpha_1, \beta_1, \ldots, \alpha_i, \gamma', 1)$ for some γ'.

Motivation. By suitable error reduction, we may assume that (P, V) has soundness error $\mu = \mu(|x|)$ that is smaller than $\mathrm{poly}(\ell)^{-t}$. Thus, for any yes-instance x it holds that $|\mathrm{ACC}_x(\lambda)| = 2^\ell$, whereas for any no-instance x it holds that $|\mathrm{ACC}_x(\lambda)| \leq \mu \cdot 2^\ell$. Indeed, the gap between the initial set sizes is huge, and we can maintain a gap between the sizes of the corresponding residual sets (i.e., $\mathrm{ACC}_x(\alpha_1, \beta_1, \ldots, \alpha_i)$) provided that we lose at most a factor of $\mathrm{poly}(\ell)$ per each round. The key observations is that, for any partial transcript $\gamma = (\alpha_1, \beta_1, \ldots, \alpha_{i-1}, \beta_{i-1})$, it holds that

$$|\mathrm{ACC}_x(\gamma)| = \sum_\alpha |\mathrm{ACC}_x(\gamma, \alpha)|, \tag{F.5}$$

whereas $|\mathrm{ACC}_x(\gamma, \alpha)| = \max_\beta\{|\mathrm{ACC}_x(\gamma, \alpha, \beta)|\}$. Clearly, we can prove that $|\mathrm{ACC}_x(\gamma, \alpha)|$ is big by providing an adequate β and proving that $|\mathrm{ACC}_x(\gamma, \alpha, \beta)|$ is big. Likewise, proving that $|\mathrm{ACC}_x(\gamma)|$ is big reduces to proving that the sum $\sum_\alpha |\mathrm{ACC}_x(\gamma, \alpha)|$ is big. The problem is that this sum may contain exponentially many terms, and so we cannot even afford reading the value of each of these terms.[10] As hinted in §F.2.1.1, we may cluster these terms into ℓ clusters, such that the jth cluster contains sets of cardinality approximately 2^j (i.e., α's such that $2^j \leq |\mathrm{ACC}_x(\gamma, \alpha)| < 2^{j+1}$). One of these clusters must account for a $1/2\ell$ fraction of the claimed size of $|\mathrm{ACC}_x(\gamma)|$, and so we focus on this cluster; that is, the prover we construct will identify a suitable j (i.e., such that there are at least $|\mathrm{ACC}_x(\gamma)|/2\ell$ elements in the sets of the jth cluster), and prove that there are at least $N = |\mathrm{ACC}_x(\gamma)|/(2\ell \cdot 2^{j+1})$ sets (i.e., $\mathrm{ACC}_x(\gamma, \alpha)$'s) each of size at least 2^j. Note that this establishes that $|\mathrm{ACC}_x(\gamma)|$ is bigger than $N \cdot 2^j = |\mathrm{ACC}_x(\gamma)|/O(\ell)$, which means that we have lost a factor of $O(\ell)$ of the size of $\mathrm{ACC}_x(\gamma)$. But as stated previously, we may afford such a loss.

Before we turn to the actual protocol, let us discuss the method of proving that there are at least N sets (i.e., $\mathrm{ACC}_x(\gamma, \alpha)$'s) each of size at least 2^j. This claim is proved by employing the random-selection protocol (while setting the size parameter to N) with the goal of selecting such a set (or rather its index α). If indeed N such sets exist, then the first property of the protocol guarantees that such a set is always chosen, and we will proceed to the next iteration with this set, which has size at least 2^j (and so we should be able to establish a corresponding lower bound there). Thus, entering the current iteration with a valid claim, we proceed to the next iteration with a new valid claim. On the other hand, suppose that $|\mathrm{ACC}_x(\gamma)| \ll N \cdot 2^j$. Then, the second property of the protocol implies[11] that, with probability at least $1 - (1/3t)$, the selected α is such that

---

[10] Furthermore, we cannot afford verifying more than a single claim regarding the value of one of these terms, because examining at least two values per round will yield an exponential blowup (i.e., time complexity that is exponential in the number of rounds).

[11] For a loss factor $L = \mathrm{poly}(\ell)$, consider the set $S' = \{\alpha : |\mathrm{ACC}_x(\gamma, \alpha)| \geq L \cdot |\mathrm{ACC}_x(\gamma)|/N\}$. Then $|S'| \leq N/L$, and it follows that an element in S' is selected with probability at most $\mathrm{poly}(\ell)/L$, which is upper-bounded by $1/3t$ when using a suitable choice of L.

$|\mathrm{ACC}_x(\gamma, \alpha)| < \mathrm{poly}(\ell) \cdot |\mathrm{ACC}_x(\gamma)|/N \ll 2^j$, whereas at the next iteration we will need to prove that the selected set has size at least 2^j. Thus, entering the current iteration with a false claim that is wrong by a factor $F \gg \mathrm{poly}(\ell)$, with probability at least $1 - (1/3t)$, we proceed to the next iteration with a false claim that is wrong by a factor of at least $F/\mathrm{poly}(\ell)$.

We note that, although the foregoing motivational discussion refers to proving lower bounds on various set sizes, the actual implementation refers to randomly selecting elements in such sets. If the sets are smaller than claimed, the selected elements are likely to reside outside these sets, which will be eventually detected.

Construction F.4 (the actual protocol): *On common input x, the $2t$-message interaction of P and V is "quasi-emulated" in t iterations, where $t = t(|x|)$. The ith iteration starts with a partial transcript $\gamma_{i-1} = (\alpha_1, \beta_1, \ldots, \alpha_{i-1}, \beta_{i-1})$ and a claimed bound M_{i-1}, where in the first iteration γ_0 is the empty sequence and $M_0 = 2^\ell$. The ith iteration proceeds as follows.*

1. *The prover determines an index j such that the cluster $C_j = \{\alpha : 2^j \leq |\mathrm{ACC}_x(\gamma_{i-1}, \alpha)| < 2^{j+1}\}$ has size at least $N \stackrel{\mathrm{def}}{=} M_{i-1}/(2^{j+2}\ell)$, and sends j to the verifier. Note that if $|\mathrm{ACC}_x(\gamma_{i-1})| \geq M_{i-1}$ then such a j exists.*
2. *The prover invokes the random-selection protocol with size parameter N in order to select $\alpha \in C_j$, where for simplicity we assume that $C_j \subseteq \{0, 1\}^\ell$. Recall that this public-coin protocol involves three messages with the first and last message being sent by the prover. Let us denote the outcome of this protocol by α_i.*
3. *The prover determines β_i such that $\mathrm{ACC}_x(\gamma_{i-1}, \alpha_i, \beta_i) = \mathrm{ACC}_x(\gamma_{i-1}, \alpha_i)$ and sends β_i to the verifier.*

   Toward the next iteration $M_i \leftarrow 2^j$ and $\gamma_i = (\alpha_1, \beta_1, \ldots, \alpha_i, \beta_i) \equiv (\gamma_{i-1}, \alpha_i, \beta_i)$.

After the last iteration,[12] the prover invokes the random-selection protocol with size parameter $N = M_t$ in order to select $r \in \mathrm{ACC}_x(\alpha_1, \beta_1, \ldots, \alpha_t, \beta_t)$. Upon obtaining this r, the verifier accepts if and only if $V(x, r, \beta_1, \ldots, \beta_t) = 1$ and for every $i = 1, \ldots, t$ it holds that $\alpha_i = V(x, r, \beta_1, \ldots, \beta_{i-1})$, where the α_i's and β_i's are as determined in the foregoing iterations.

Note that the three steps of each iteration involve a single message by the (public-coin) verifier, and thus the foregoing protocol can be implemented using $2t + 3$ messages.

Clearly, if x is a yes-instance then the prover can make the verifier accept with probability one (because an adequately large cluster exists at each iteration, and the random-selection protocol guarantees that the selected α_i will reside in this cluster).[13] On the other hand, if x is a no-instance then by using the low soundness error of (P, V) we can establish the soundness of Construction F.4. This is proved in the *following claim, which refers to a polynomial p that is sufficiently large.*

---

[12]Alternatively, we may modify (P, V) by adding a last V-message in which V sends its internal coin tosses (i.e., r). In this case, the additional invocation of the random-selection protocol occurs as a special case of handling the added $t + 1^{\mathrm{st}}$ iteration.

[13]Thus, at the last invocation of the random-selection protocol, the verifier always obtains $r \in \mathrm{ACC}_x(\gamma_t)$ and accepts.

Proposition F.5: *Suppose that* $|ACC_x(\lambda)| < \delta^{t+1} \cdot 2^\ell$, *where* $\delta = 1/p(\ell)$. *Then, the verifier of Construction F.4 accepts* x *with probability smaller than* $1/2$.

Proof Sketch: We first prove that, for every $i = 1, \ldots, t$, if $|ACC_x(\gamma_{i-1})| < \delta^{t+1-(i-1)} \cdot M_{i-1}$ then, with probability at least $1 - (1/3t)$, it holds that $|ACC_x(\gamma_i)| < \delta^{t+1-i} \cdot M_i$. Fixing any i, let j be the value selected by the prover in Step 1 of iteration i, and define $S' = \{\alpha : |ACC_x(\gamma_{i-1}, \alpha)| \geq \delta^{t+1-i} \cdot 2^j\}$. Then

$$|S'| \cdot \delta^{t+1-i} 2^j \leq |ACC_x(\gamma_{i-1})| < \delta^{t+1-(i-1)} \cdot M_{i-1},$$

where the second inequality represents the claim's hypothesis. Letting $N = M_{i-1}/(2^{j+2}\ell)$ (as in Step 1 of this iteration), it follows that $|S'| < 4\ell\delta \cdot N$. By the second property of the random-selection protocol (invoked in Step 2 of this iteration with size parameter N), it follows that

$$\Pr[\alpha_i \in S'] \leq \text{poly}(\ell) \cdot \frac{|S'|}{N} \leq \text{poly}(\ell) \cdot \delta,$$

which is smaller than $1/3t$ (provided that the polynomial p that determines $\delta = 1/p(\ell)$ is sufficiently large). Thus, with probability at least $1 - (1/3t)$, it holds that $|ACC_x(\gamma_{i-1}, \alpha_i)| < \delta^{t+1-i} \cdot 2^j$. The claim regarding $|ACC_x(\gamma_i)|$ follows by recalling that $M_i = 2^j$ (in Step 3) and that for every β it holds that $|ACC_x(\gamma_{i-1}, \alpha_i, \beta)| \leq |ACC_x(\gamma_{i-1}, \alpha_i)|$.

Using the hypothesis $|ACC_x(\gamma_0)| < \delta^{t+1} \cdot M_0$ and the foregoing claim, it follows that, with probability at least $2/3$, the execution of the aforementioned t iterations yields values γ_t and M_t such that $|ACC_x(\gamma_t)| < \delta \cdot M_t$. In this case, the last invocation of the random-selection protocol (invoked with size parameter M_t) produces an element of $ACC_x(\gamma_t)$ with probability at most $\text{poly}(\ell) \cdot \delta < 1/6$, and otherwise the verifier rejects (because the conditions that the verifier checks regarding the output r of the random-selection protocol are logically equivalent to $r \in ACC_x(\gamma_t)$). The proposition follows. $\square$

F.2.2. Linear Speedup for $\mathcal{AM}$

In this section we prove Theorem F.3. Our proof differs from the original proof of Babai and Moran [23] in the way that we analyze the basic switch (of MA to AM).

We adopt the standard terminology of public-coin (aka Arthur-Merlin) interactive proof systems, where the verifier is called Arthur and the prover is called Merlin. More importantly, we view the *execution* of such a proof system, on any fixed common input x, as a (full-information) game (indexed by x) between an honest Arthur and a powerful Merlin. These parties alternate in taking moves such that Arthur takes random moves and Merlin takes optimal moves with respect to a fixed (polynomial-time computable) predicate v_x that is *evaluated on the full transcript of the game's execution*. We stress that (in contrast to general interactive proof systems), each of Arthur's moves is uniformly distributed in a set of possible values that is predetermined independently of prior moves (e.g., the set $\{0, 1\}^{\ell(|x|)}$). The value of the game is defined as the expected value of an execution of the game, where the expectation is taken over Arthur's moves (and Merlin's moves are assumed to be optimal).

We shall assume, without loss of generality, that all messages of Arthur are of the same length, denoted $\ell = \ell(|x|)$. Similarly, each of Merlin's messages is of length $m = m(|x|)$.

Figure F.1: The transformation of an MA-game into an AM-game. The value of the transcript (β, α) of the original MA-game is given by $v_x(\beta, \alpha)$, whereas the value of the transcript $((\alpha^{(1)}, \ldots, \alpha^{(t)}), \beta)$ of the new AM-game is given by $\prod_{i=1}^{t} v_x(\beta, \alpha^{(i)})$.

Recall that $\mathcal{AM} = \mathcal{AM}(2)$ denotes a two-message system in which Arthur moves first and does not toss coins after receiving Merlin's answer, whereas $\mathcal{MA} = \mathcal{AM}(1)$ denotes a one-message system in which Merlin sends a single message and Arthur tosses additional coins after receiving this message. Thus, both $\mathcal{AM}$ and $\mathcal{MA}$ are viewed as two-move games, and differ in the order in which the two parties take these moves. As we shall shortly see (in §F.2.2.1), the "MA order" can be emulated by the "AM order" (i.e., $\mathcal{MA} \subseteq \mathcal{AM}$). This fact will be the basis of the "round speedup" transformation (presented in §F.2.2.2).

F.2.2.1. The Basic Switch (from MA to AM)

The basic idea is transforming an MA-game (i.e., a two-move game in which Merlin moves first and Arthur follows) into an AM-game (in which Arthur moves first and Merlin follows). In the original game (on input x), first Merlin sends a message $\beta \in \{0, 1\}^m$, then Arthur responds with a random $\alpha \in \{0, 1\}^\ell$, and Arthur's verdict (i.e., the value of this execution of the game) is given by $v_x(\beta, \alpha) \in \{0, 1\}$. In the new game (see Figure F.1), the order of these moves will be switched, but to limit Merlin's potential gain from the switch, we require it to provide a single answer that should "fit" several random messages of Arthur. That is, for a parameter t to be specified, first Arthur sends a random sequence $(\alpha^{(1)}, \ldots, \alpha^{(t)}) \in \{0, 1\}^{t \cdot \ell}$, then Merlin responds with a string $\beta \in \{0, 1\}^m$, and Arthur accepts if and only if for every $i \in \{1, \ldots t\}$ it holds that $v_x(\beta, \alpha^{(i)}) = 1$ (i.e., the value of this transcript of the new game is defined as $\prod_{i=1}^{t} v_x(\beta, \alpha^{(i)})$). Intuitively, Merlin gets the advantage of choosing its move after seeing Arthur's move(s), but Merlin's choice must fit the t choices of Arthur's move, which leaves Merlin with little gain (if t is sufficiently large).

Recall that the value, v'_x, of the transcript $(\overline{\alpha}, \beta)$ of the new game, where $\overline{\alpha} = (\alpha^{(1)}, \ldots, \alpha^{(t)})$, is defined as $\prod_{i=1}^{t} v_x(\beta, \alpha^{(i)})$. Thus, the value of the new game is defined as

$$\mathsf{E}_{\overline{\alpha}}\left[\max_{\beta}\left\{\prod_{i=1}^{t} v_x(\beta, \alpha^{(i)})\right\}\right] \tag{F.6}$$

which is upper-bounded by

$$\mathsf{E}_{\overline{\alpha}}\left[\max_{\beta}\left\{\frac{1}{t}\sum_{i=1}^{t} v_x(\beta, \alpha^{(i)})\right\}\right] \tag{F.7}$$

Note that the upper bound provided in Eq. (F.7) is tight in the case that the value of the original MA-game equals one (i.e., if x is a yes-instance), and that in this case the value of the new game is one (because in this case there exists a move β such that $v_x(\beta, \alpha) = 1$ holds for every α). However, the interesting case, where Merlin may gain something by the switch, is when the value of the original MA-game is strictly smaller than one (i.e., when x is a no-instance). The main observation is that, for a suitable choice of t, *it is highly improbable that Merlin's gain from the switch is significant.*

Recall that in the original MA-game, Merlin selects β obliviously of Arthur's choice of α, and thus Merlin's "profit" (i.e., the value of the game) is represented by $\max_\beta\{E_\alpha(v_x(\beta, \alpha))\}$. In the new AM-game, Merlin selects β based on the sequence $\bar{\alpha}$ chosen by Arthur, and we have upper-bounded its "profit" (in the new AM-game) by Eq. (F.7). Merlin's gain from the switch is thus the excess profit (of the new AM-game as compared to the original MA-game). We upper-bound the probability that *Merlin's gain from the switch exceeds a parameter*, denoted δ, as follows.

$$p_{x,\delta} \stackrel{\text{def}}{=} \Pr_{(\alpha^{(1)},\ldots,\alpha^{(t)})}\left[\max_\beta\left\{\frac{1}{t} \cdot \sum_{i=1}^{t} v_x(\beta, \alpha^{(i)})\right\} > \max_\beta\{E_\alpha(v_x(\beta, \alpha))\} + \delta\right]$$

$$\leq \Pr_{(\alpha^{(1)},\ldots,\alpha^{(t)})}\left[\exists\beta \in \{0, 1\}^m \text{ s.t. } \left|\frac{1}{t} \cdot \sum_{i=1}^{t} v_x(\beta, \alpha^{(i)}) - E_\alpha(v_x(\beta, \alpha))\right| > \delta\right]$$

$$\leq 2^m \cdot \exp(-\Omega(\delta^2 \cdot t)),$$

where the last inequality is due to combining the union bound with the Chernoff Bound. Denoting by $V_x = \max_\beta\{E_\alpha(v_x(\beta, \alpha))\}$ the value of the original game, we upper-bound Eq. (F.7) by $p_{x,\delta} + V_x + \delta$. Using $t = O((m + k)/\delta^2)$ we have $p_{x,\delta} \leq 2^{-k}$, and thus

$$V_x' \stackrel{\text{def}}{=} E_{\bar{\alpha}}\left[\max_\beta\left\{\frac{1}{t}\sum_{i=1}^{t} v_x(\beta, \alpha^{(i)})\right\}\right] \leq \max_\beta\{E_\alpha(v_x(\beta, \alpha))\} + \delta + 2^{-k}. \quad \text{(F.8)}$$

Needless to say, Eq. (F.7) is lower-bounded by V_x (since Merlin may just use the optimal move of the MA-game). In particular, using $\delta = 2^{-k} = 1/8$ and assuming that $V_x \leq 1/4$, we obtain $V_x' < 1/2$. Thus, starting from an MA proof system for some set, we obtain an AM proof system for the same set; that is, we just proved that $\mathcal{MA} \subseteq \mathcal{AM}$.

Extension. We note that the foregoing transformation as well as its analysis does not refer to the fact that $v_x(\beta, \alpha)$ is efficiently computable from (β, α). Furthermore, the analysis remains valid for arbitrary $v_x(\cdot, \cdot) \in [0, 1]$, because for any $v_1, \ldots, v_t \in [0, 1]$ it holds that $\prod_{i=1}^{t} v_i \leq (\prod_{i=1}^{t} v_i)^{1/t} \leq \sum_{i=1}^{t} v_i/t$. Thus, we may apply the foregoing transformation to any two consecutive Merlin-Arthur moves in any public-coin interactive proof, provided that all the subsequent moves are performed in t copies, where each copy corresponds to a different $\alpha^{(i)}$ used in the switch. That is, if the jth move is by Merlin, then we can switch the players in the j and $j + 1$ moves, by letting Arthur take the jth move, sending $(\alpha^{(1)}, \ldots, \alpha^{(t)})$, followed by Merlin's move, answering β. Subsequent moves will be played in t copies such that the ith copy corresponds to the moves $\alpha^{(i)}$ and β. The value of the new game may increase by at most $2^{-k} + \delta < 1/4$, and so we obtain an "equivalent" game with the two steps switched. Schematically, acting on the middle MA (indicated in bold font), we can replace $[\text{AM}]^{j_1}\text{AMA}[\text{MA}]^{j_2}$ by $[\text{AM}]^{j_1}\text{AAM}[\text{MA}]^{j_2}$, which in turn allows the collapse of two consecutive A-moves (and two consecutive M-moves if $j_2 \geq 1$). In particular (using only the case $j_1 = 0$), we get $\text{A}[\text{MA}]^{j+1} = \text{A}[\text{MA}]^j = \cdots = \text{AMA} = \text{AM}$. Thus, for any constant f, we get $\mathcal{AM}(f) = \mathcal{AM}(2)$.

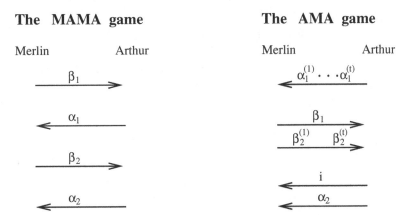

Figure F.2: The transformation of MAMA into AMA. The value of the transcript $(\beta_1, \alpha_1, \beta_2, \alpha_2)$ of the original MAMA-game is given by $v_x(\beta_1, \alpha_1, \beta_2, \alpha_2)$, whereas the value of the transcript $((\alpha_1^{(1)}, \ldots, \alpha_1^{(t)}), (\beta_1, \beta_2^{(1)}, \ldots, \beta_2^{(t)}), (i, \alpha_2))$ of the new AMA-game is given by $v_x(\beta_1, \alpha_1^{(i)}, \beta_2^{(i)}, \alpha_2)$.

We stress that the foregoing switching process can be applied only a constant number of times, because each time we apply the switch, the length of messages increases by a factor of $t = \Omega(m)$. Thus, a different approach is required to deal with a non-constant number of messages (i.e., unbounded function f).

F.2.2.2. The Augmented Switch (from $[MAMA]^j$ to $[AMA]^j A$)

Sequential applications of the "MA-to-AM switch" allows for reducing the number of rounds by any additive constant. However, each time this switch is applied, all subsequent moves are performed t times (in parallel). That is, the "MA-to-AM switch" splits the rest of the game to t independent copies, and thus this switch cannot be performed more than a constant number of times. Fortunately, Eq. (F.7) suggests a way of shrinking the game back to a single copy: Just have Arthur select $i \in [t]$ uniformly and have the parties continue with the ith copy.[14] In order to avoid introducing an Arthur-Merlin alternation, the extra move of Arthur is postponed to after the following move of Merlin (see Figure F.2). Schematically (indicating the action by bold font), we replace **MAMA** by **AM**MA**A** = **A**MA (rather than replacing **MAMA** by **A**MAMA and obtaining no reduction in the number of move alternations).

The value of the game obtained via the aforementioned augmented switch is given by Eq. (F.7), which can be written as

$$\mathsf{E}_{\alpha^{(1)},\ldots,\alpha^{(t)}}[\max_{\beta}\{\mathsf{E}_{i \in [t]}(v_x(\beta, \alpha^{(i)}))\}],$$

which in turn is upper-bounded (in Eq. (F.8)) by $\max_{\beta}\{\mathsf{E}_{\alpha}(v_x(\beta, \alpha))\} + \delta + 2^{-k}$. As in §F.2.2.1, the argument applies to any two consecutive Merlin-Arthur moves in any public-coin interactive proof. Recall that in order to avoid the introduction of an extra Arthur move, we actually postpone the last move of Arthur to after the next move of Merlin. Thus, we may apply the augmented switch to the first two moves in any block of four consecutive moves that start with a Merlin move, transforming the schematic sequence MAMA into AMMAA = AMA (see Figure F.2). The key point is that *the moves that take place after the said block* remain intact. Hence, we may apply the augmented "MA-to-AM switch" (which

---

[14]Indeed, the relaxed form of Eq. (F.7) plays a crucial role here (in contrast to Eq. (F.6)).

is actually an "MAMA-to-AMA switch") concurrently to disjoint segments of the game. Schematically, we can replace $[\text{MAMA}]^j$ by $[\text{AMA}]^j = A[\text{MA}]^j$. Note that Merlin's gain from each such switch is upper-bounded by $\delta + 2^{-k}$, but selecting $t = \widetilde{O}(f(|x|)^2 \cdot m(|x|)) = \text{poly}(|x|)$ allows for upper-bounding the total gain by a constant (using, say, $\delta = 2^{-k} = 1/8 f(|x|)$). We thus obtain $\mathcal{AM}(4f) \subseteq \mathcal{AM}(2f+1)$, and Theorem F.3 follows.

Some Computational Problems

Although we view specific (natural) computational problems as secondary to (natural) complexity classes, we do use the former for clarification and illustration of the latter. This appendix provides definitions of such computational problems, grouped according to the type of objects to which they refer (e.g., graphs, Boolean formula, etc.).

We start by addressing the central issue of the representation of the various objects that are referred to in the aforementioned computational problems. The general principle is that elements of all sets are "compactly" represented as binary strings (without much redundancy). For example, the elements of a finite set S (e.g., the set of vertices in a graph or the set of variables appearing in a Boolean formula) will be represented as binary strings of length $\log_2 |S|$.

G.1. Graphs

Graph theory has long become recognized as one of the more useful mathematical subjects for the computer science student to master. The approach which is natural in computer science is the algorithmic one; our interest is not so much in existence proofs or enumeration techniques, as it is in finding efficient algorithms for solving relevant problems, or alternatively showing evidence that no such algorithms exist. Although algorithmic graph theory was started by Euler, if not earlier, its development in the last ten years has been dramatic and revolutionary.

Shimon Even, *Graph Algorithms* [71]

A simple graph $G = (V, E)$ consists of a *finite* set of vertices V and a finite set of edges E, where each edge is an *unordered pair* of vertices; that is, $E \subseteq \{\{u, v\} : u, v \in V \wedge u \neq v\}$. This formalism does not allow self-loops and parallel edges, which are allowed in general (i.e., non-simple) graphs, where E is a multi-set that may contain (in addition to two-element subsets of V also) singletons (i.e., self-loops). The vertex u is called an end point of the edge $\{u, v\}$, and the edge $\{u, v\}$ is said to be incident at v. In such a case we say that u and v are adjacent in the graph, and that u is a neighbor of v. The degree of a vertex in G is defined as the number of edges that are incident at this vertex.

We will consider various sub-structures of graphs, the simplest one being paths. A path in a graph $G = (V, E)$ is a sequence of vertices $(v_0, \ldots, v_\ell)$ such that for every $i \in [\ell] \stackrel{\text{def}}{=} \{1, \ldots, \ell\}$ it holds that v_{i-1} and v_i are adjacent in G. Such a path is said to have length ℓ. A simple path is a path in which each vertex appears at most once, which implies that the longest possible simple path in G has length $|V| - 1$. The graph is called connected if there exists a path between each pair of vertices in it.

A cycle is a path in which the last vertex equals the first one (i.e., $v_\ell = v_0$). The cycle $(v_0, \ldots, v_\ell)$ is called simple if $\ell > 2$ and $|\{v_0, \ldots, v_\ell\}| = \ell$ (i.e., if $v_i = v_j$ then $i \equiv j$ (mod ℓ), and the cycle (u, v, u) is not considered simple). A graph is called acyclic (or a forest) if it has no simple cycles, and if it is also connected then it is called a tree. Note that $G = (V, E)$ is a tree if and only if it is connected and $|E| = |V| - 1$, and that there is a unique simple path between each pair of vertices in a tree.

A subgraph of the graph $G = (V, E)$ is any graph $G' = (V', E')$ satisfying $V' \subseteq V$ and $E' \subseteq E$. Note that a simple cycle in G is a connected subgraph of G in which each vertex has degree exactly two. An induced subgraph of the graph $G = (V, E)$ is any subgraph $G' = (V', E')$ that contains all edges of E that are contained in V'. In such a case, we say that G' is the subgraph induced by V'.

Directed graphs. We will also consider (simple) directed graphs (aka digraphs), where edges are *ordered pairs* of vertices. In this case the set of edges is a subset of $V \times V \setminus \{(v, v) : v \in V\}$, and the edges (u, v) and (v, u) are called anti-parallel. General (i.e., non-simple) directed graphs are defined analogously. The edge (u, v) is viewed as going from u to v, and thus is called an outgoing edge of u (resp., incoming edge of v). The out-degree (resp., in-degree) of a vertex is the number of its outgoing edges (resp., incoming edges). Directed paths and the related objects are defined analogously; for example, $v_0, \ldots, v_\ell$ is a directed path if for every $i \in [\ell]$ it holds that (v_{i-1}, v_i) is a directed edge (which is directed from v_{i-1} to v_i). It is common to consider also a pair of anti-parallel edges as a simple directed cycle.

A directed acyclic graph (dag) is a digraph that has no directed cycles. Every dag has at least one vertex having out-degree (resp., in-degree) zero, called a sink (resp., a source). A simple directed acyclic graph $G = (V, E)$ is called an inward (resp., outward) directed tree if $|E| = |V| - 1$ and there exists a unique vertex, called the root, having out-degree (resp., in-degree) zero. Note that each vertex in an inward (resp., outward) directed tree can reach the root (resp., is reachable from the root) by a unique directed path.[1]

Representation. Graphs are commonly represented by their adjacency matrix and/or their incidence lists. The adjacency matrix of a simple graph $G = (V, E)$ is a $|V|$-by-$|V|$ Boolean matrix in which the (i, j)-th entry equals 1 if and only if i and j are adjacent in G. The incidence list representation of G consists of $|V|$ sequences such that the ith sequence is an ordered list of the set of edges incident at vertex i.

Computational problems. Simple computational problems regarding graphs include determining whether a given graph is connected (and/or acyclic) and finding shortest paths in a given graph. Another simple problem is determining whether a given graph is bipartite, where a graph $G = (V, E)$ is bipartite (or 2-colorable) if there exists a 2-coloring of its vertices that does not assign neighboring vertices the same color. All these problems are easily solvable by BFS.

---

[1]Note that in any dag, there is a directed path from each vertex v to some sink (resp., from some source to each vertex v). In an inward (resp., outward) directed tree this sink (resp., source) must be unique. The condition $|E| = |V| - 1$ enforces the uniqueness of these paths, because (combined with the reachability condition) it implies that the underlying graph (obtained by disregarding the orientation of the edges) is a tree.

Moving to more complicated tasks that are still solvable in polynomial time, we mention the problem of finding a perfect matching (or a maximum matching) in a given graph, where a matching is a subgraph in which all vertices have degree 1, a perfect matching is a matching that contains all the graph's vertices, and a maximum matching is a matching of maximum cardinality (among all matching of the said graph).

Turning to seemingly hard problems, we mention that the problem of determining whether a given graph is 3-colorable (i.e., G3C) is NP-complete. A few additional NP-complete problems follow.

- A Hamiltonian path (resp., Hamiltonian cycle) in the graph $G = (V, E)$ is a *simple* path (resp., cycle) that passes through all the vertices of G. Such a path (resp., cycle) has length $|V| - 1$ (resp., $|V|$). The problem is to determine whether a given graph contains a Hamiltonian path (resp., cycle).

- An independent set (resp., clique) of the graph $G = (V, E)$ is a set of vertices $V' \subseteq V$ such that the subgraph induced by V' contains no edges (resp., contains all possible edges). The problem is to determine whether a given graph has an independent set (resp., a clique) of a given size.

  A vertex cover of the graph $G = (V, E)$ is a set of vertices $V' \subseteq V$ such that each edge in E has at least one end point in V'. Note that V' is a vertex cover of G if and only if $V \setminus V'$ is an independent set of V.

A natural computational problem, which is believed to be neither in $\mathcal{P}$ nor NP-complete, is the Graph Isomorphism problem. The input consists of two graphs, $G_1 = (V_1, E_1)$ and $G_2 = (V_2, E_2)$, and the question is whether there exist a 1-1 and onto mapping $\phi : V_1 \to V_2$ such that $\{u, v\}$ is in E_1 if and only if $\{\phi(u), \phi(v)\}$ is in E_2. (Such a mapping is called an isomorphism.)

G.2. Boolean Formulae

In §1.2.4.3, Boolean formulae are defined as a special case of Boolean circuits (§1.2.4.1). Here, we take the more traditional approach, and define Boolean formulae as structured sequences over an alphabet consisting of variable names and various connectives. It is most convenient to define Boolean formulae recursively as follows:

- A variable is a Boolean formula.
- If $\phi_1, \ldots, \phi_t$ are Boolean formulae and ψ is a t-ary Boolean operation then $\psi(\phi_1, \ldots, \phi_t)$ is a Boolean formula.

Typically, we consider three Boolean operations: the unary operation of negation (denoted neg or $\neg$), and the (bounded or unbounded) conjunction and disjunction (denoted $\wedge$ and $\vee$, respectively). Furthermore, the convention is to use the shorthand $\neg\phi$ for $\neg(\phi)$, and to write $(\wedge_{i=1}^{t}\phi_i)$ or $(\phi_1 \wedge \cdots \wedge \phi_t)$ instead of $\wedge(\phi_1, \ldots, \phi_t)$, and similarly for $\vee$.

Two important special cases of Boolean formulae are CNF and DNF formulae. A CNF formula is a conjunction of disjunctions of variables and/or their negation; that is, $\wedge_{i=1}^{t}\phi_i$ is a CNF if each ϕ_i has the form $(\vee_{j=1}^{t_i}\phi_{i,j})$, where each $\phi_{i,j}$ is either a variable or a negation of a variable (and is called a literal). If for every i it holds that $t_i \leq 3$ then we say that the formula is a 3CNF. Similarly, DNF formulae are defined as disjunctions of conjunctions of literals.

The value of a Boolean formula under a truth assignment to its variables is defined recursively along its structure. For example, $\wedge_{i=1}^{t}\phi_i$ has the value true under an assignment τ if and only if every ϕ_i has the value true under τ. We say that a formula ϕ is satisfiable if there exists a truth assignment τ to its variables such that the value of ϕ under τ is true.

The set of satisfiable CNF (resp., 3CNF) formulae is denoted SAT (resp., 3SAT), and the problem of deciding membership in it is NP-complete. The set of tautologies (i.e., formulae that have the value true under any assignment) is coNP-complete, even when restricted to 3DNF formulae.

Quantified Boolean formulae. In contrast to the foregoing that refers to unquantified Boolean formulae, a quantified Boolean formula is a formula augmented with quantifiers that refer to each variable appearing in it. That is, if ϕ is a formula in the Boolean variables $x_1, \ldots, x_n$ and $Q_1, \ldots, Q_n$ are Boolean quantifiers (i.e., each Q_i is either $\exists$ or $\forall$), then $Q_1 x_1 \cdots Q_n x_n \phi(x_1, \ldots, x_n)$ is a quantified Boolean formula. A k-alternating quantified Boolean formula is a quantified Boolean formula with up to k alternating sequences of existential and universal quantifiers, starting with an existential quantifier. For example, $\exists x_1 \exists x_2 \forall x_3 \phi(x_1, x_2, x_3)$ is a 2-alternating quantified Boolean formula. (We say that a quantified Boolean formula is satisfiable if it evaluates to true.)

The set of satisfiable k-alternating quantified Boolean formulae is denoted kQBF and is Σ_k-complete, whereas the set of all satisfiable quantified Boolean formulae is denoted QBF and is $\mathcal{PSPACE}$-complete.

The foregoing definition refers to the canonical form of quantified Boolean formulae, in which all the quantifiers appear at the leftmost side of the formula. A more general definition allows each variable to be quantified at an arbitrary place to the left of its leftmost occurrence in the formula (e.g., $(\forall x_1)(\exists x_2)(x_1 = x_2) \wedge (\exists x_3)(x_3 = x_1)$). Note that such generalized formulae (used in the proof of Theorems 5.15 and 9.4) can be transformed to the canonical form by "pulling" all quantifiers to the left of the formula (e.g., $\forall x_1 \exists x_2 \exists x_3 ((x_1 = x_2) \wedge (x_3 = x_1))$).

G.3. Finite Fields, Polynomials, and Vector Spaces

Various algebraic objects, computational problems, and techniques play an important role in Complexity Theory. The most dominant such objects are finite fields as well as vector spaces and polynomials over such fields.

Finite Fields. We denote by GF(q) the finite field of q elements and note that q may be either a prime or a prime power. In the first case, GF(q) is viewed as consisting of the elements $\{0, \ldots, q-1\}$ with addition and multiplication being defined modulo q. Indeed, GF(2) is an important special case. In the case that $q = p^e$, where p is a prime and $e > 1$, the standard representation of GF(p^e) refers to an irreducible polynomial of degree e over GF(p). Specifically, if f is an irreducible polynomial of degree e over GF(p), then GF(p^e) can be represented as the set of polynomials of degree at most $e - 1$ over GF(p) with addition and multiplication defined modulo the polynomial f.

We mention that finding representations of large finite fields is a non-trivial computational problem, where in both cases we seek an *efficient* algorithm that finds a representation (i.e., either a large prime or an irreducible polynomial) in time that is polynomial in the length of the representation. In the case of a field of prime cardinality, this calls for generating a prime number of adequate size, which can be done efficiently by a randomized algorithm (while a corresponding deterministic algorithm is not known). In the case of $GF(p^e)$, where p is a prime and $e > 1$, we need to find an irreducible polynomial of degree e over $GF(p)$. Again, this task is efficiently solvable by a randomized algorithm (see [24]), but a corresponding deterministic algorithm is not known for the general case (i.e., for arbitrary prime p and $e > 1$). Fortunately, for $e = 2 \cdot 3^{e'}$ (with e' being an integer), the polynomial $x^e + x^{e/2} + 1$ is irreducible over $GF(2)$, which means that finding a representation of $GF(2^e)$ is easy in this case. Thus, *there exists a strongly explicit construction of an infinite family of finite fields* (i.e., $\{GF(2^e)\}_{e \in \mathbb{L}}$, where $\mathbb{L} = \{2 \cdot 3^{e'} : \varepsilon' \in \mathbb{N}\}$).

Polynomials and Vector Spaces. The set of degree $d - 1$ polynomials over a finite field F (of cardinality at least d) forms a d-dimensional vector space over F (e.g., consider the basis $\{1, x, \ldots, x^{d-1}\}$). Indeed, the standard representation of this vector space refers to the basis $1, x, \ldots, x^{d-1}$, and (when referring to this basis) the polynomial $\sum_{i=0}^{d-1} c_i x^i$ is represented as the vector $(c_0, c_1, \ldots, c_{d-1})$. An alternative basis is obtained by considering the evaluation at d distinct points $\alpha_1, \ldots, \alpha_d \in F$; that is, the degree $d - 1$ polynomial p is represented by the sequence of values $(p(\alpha_1), \ldots, p(\alpha_d))$. Needless to say, moving between such representations (i.e., representations with respect to different bases) amounts to applying an adequate linear transformation; that is, for $p(x) = \sum_{i=0}^{d-1} c_i x^i$, we have

$$\begin{pmatrix} p(\alpha_1) \\ p(\alpha_2) \\ \vdots \\ p(\alpha_d) \end{pmatrix} = \begin{pmatrix} 1 & \alpha_1 & \cdots & \alpha_1^{d-1} \\ 1 & \alpha_2 & \cdots & \alpha_2^{d-1} \\ \vdots & \vdots & \cdots & \vdots \\ 1 & \alpha_d & \cdots & \alpha_d^{d-1} \end{pmatrix} \begin{pmatrix} c_0 \\ c_1 \\ \vdots \\ c_{d-1} \end{pmatrix} \tag{G.1}$$

where the (full rank) matrix in Eq. (G.1) is called a Vandermonde matrix. The foregoing transformation (or rather its inverse) is closely related to the task of polynomial interpolation (i.e., given the values of a degree $d - 1$ polynomial at d points, find the polynomial itself).

G.4. The Determinant and the Permanent

Recall that the permanent of an n-by-n matrix $M = (a_{i,j})$ is defined as the sum $\sum_{\pi} \prod_{i=1}^{n} a_{i,\pi(j)}$ taken over all permutations π of the set $\{1, \ldots, n\}$. This is related to the definition of the determinant in which the same sum is used except that some elements are negated; that is, the determinant of $M = (a_{i,j})$ is defined as $\sum_{\pi} (-1)^{\sigma(\pi)} \prod_{i=1}^{n} a_{i,\pi(j)}$, where $\sigma(\pi) = 1$ if π is an even permutation (i.e., can be expressed by an even number of transpositions) and $\sigma(\pi) = -1$ otherwise.

The corresponding computational problems (i.e., computing the determinant or permanent of a given matrix) seem to have vastly different complexities. The determinant can be computed in polynomial time; moreover, it can be computed in uniform $\mathcal{NC}^2$. In contrast, computing the permanent is #$\mathcal{P}$-complete, even in the special case of matrices with entries in $\{0, 1\}$ (see Theorem 6.20).

G.5. Primes and Composite Numbers

A prime is a natural number that is not divisible by any natural number other than itself and 1. A natural number that is not a prime is called composite, and its prime factorization is the set of primes that divide it; that is, if $N = \prod_{i=1}^{t} P_i^{e_i}$, where the P_i's are distinct primes (greater than 1) and $e_i \geq 1$, then $\{P_i : i = 1, \ldots, t\}$ is the prime factorization of N. (If $t = 1$ then N is a prime power.)

Two famous computational problems, identified by Gauss as fundamental ones, are testing primality (i.e., given a natural number, determine whether it is prime or composite) and factoring composite integers (i.e., given a composite number, find its prime factorization). Needless to say, in both cases, the input is presented in binary representation. Although testing primality is reducible to integer factorization, the problems seem to have different complexities: While testing primality is in $\mathcal{P}$ (see [3] (and §6.1.2.2 showing that the problem is in $\mathcal{BPP}$)), *it is conjectured that factoring composite integers is intractable.* In fact, many popular candidates for various cryptographic systems are based on this conjecture.

Extracting modular square roots. Two related computational problems are extracting (modular) square roots with respect to prime and composite moduli. Specifically, a quadratic residue modulo a prime P is an integer s such that there exists an integer r satisfying $s \equiv r^2 \pmod{P}$. The corresponding search problem (i.e., given such P and s, find r) can be solved in probabilistic polynomial time (see Exercise 6.16). The corresponding problem for composite moduli is computationally equivalent to factoring (see [183]); furthermore, extracting square roots modulo N is easily reducible to factoring N, and factoring N is randomly reducible to extracting square roots modulo N (even in a typical-case sense). We mention that even the problem of *deciding whether or not a given integer has a modular square root modulo a given composite* is conjectured to be hard (but is not known to be computationally equivalent to factoring).

Bibliography

[1] S. Aaronson. Complexity Zoo. A continueously updated Web site at `http://qwiki.caltech.edu/wiki/Complexity_Zoo/`.

[2] L. M. Adleman and M. Huang. *Primality Testing and Abelian Varieties Over Finite Fields.* Springer-Verlag Lecture Notes in Computer Science (Vol. 1512), 1992. Preliminary version in *19th STOC*, 1987.

[3] M. Agrawal, N. Kayal, and N. Saxena. PRIMES Is in P. *Annals of Mathematics*, Vol. 160 (2), pages 781–793, 2004.

[4] M. Ajtai, J. Komlos, and E. Szemerédi. Deterministic Simulation in LogSpace. In *19th ACM Symposium on the Theory of Computing*, pages 132–140, 1987.

[5] R. Aleliunas, R. M. Karp, R. J. Lipton, L. Lovász, and C. Rackoff. Random Walks, Universal Traversal Sequences, and the Complexity of Maze Problems. In *20th IEEE Symposium on Foundations of Computer Science*, pages 218–223, 1979.

[6] N. Alon, L. Babai, and A. Itai. A Fast and Simple Randomized Algorithm for the Maximal Independent Set Problem. *J. of Algorithms*, Vol. 7, pages 567–583, 1986.

[7] N. Alon and R. Boppana. The Monotone Circuit Complexity of Boolean Functions. *Combinatorica*, Vol. 7 (1), pages 1–22, 1987.

[8] N. Alon, J. Bruck, J. Naor, M. Naor, and R. Roth. Construction of Asymptotically Good, Low-Rate Error-Correcting Codes Through Pseudo-Random Graphs. *IEEE Transactions on Information Theory*, Vol. 38, pages 509–516, 1992.

[9] N. Alon, E. Fischer, I. Newman, and A. Shapira. A Combinatorial Characterization of the Testable Graph Properties: It's All About Regularity. In *38th ACM Symposium on the Theory of Computing*, pages 251–260, 2006.

[10] N. Alon, O. Goldreich, J. Håstad, and R. Peralta. Simple Constructions of Almost k-wise Independent Random Variables. *Journal of Random Structures and Algorithms*, Vol. 3 (3), pages 289–304, 1992. Preliminary version in *31st FOCS*, 1990.

[11] N. Alon and J. H. Spencer. *The Probabilistic Method.* John Wiley & Sons, 1992. Second edition 2000.

[12] R. Armoni. On the Derandomization of Space-Bounded Computations. In the proceedings of *Random98*, Springer-Verlag Lecture Notes in Computer Science (Vol. 1518), pages 49–57, 1998.

[13] S. Arora. Approximation Schemes for NP-Hard Geometric Optimization Problems: A Survey. *Math. Programming*, Vol. 97, pages 43–69, July 2003.

[14] S. Arora and B. Barak. *Complexity Theory: A Modern Approach.* Cambridge University Press, forthcoming.

[15] S. Arora, C. Lund, R. Motwani, M. Sudan, and M. Szegedy. Proof Verification and Intractability of Approximation Problems. *Journal of the ACM*, Vol. 45, pages 501–555, 1998. Preliminary version in *33rd FOCS*, 1992.

[16] S. Arora and S. Safra. Probabilistic Checkable Proofs: A New Characterization of NP. *Journal of the ACM*, Vol. 45, pages 70–122, 1998. Preliminary version in *33rd FOCS*, 1992.

[17] H. Attiya and J. Welch. *Distributed Computing: Fundamentals, Simulations and Advanced Topics*. McGraw-Hill, 1998.

[18] L. Babai. Trading Group Theory for Randomness. In *17th ACM Symposium on the Theory of Computing*, pages 421–429, 1985.

[19] L. Babai. Random Oracles Separate PSPACE from the Polynomial-Time Hierarchy. *Information Processing Letters*, Vol. 26, pages 51–53, 1987.

[20] L. Babai, L. Fortnow, L. Levin, and M. Szegedy. Checking Computations in Polylogarithmic Time. In *23rd ACM Symposium on the Theory of Computing*, pages 21–31, 1991.

[21] L. Babai, L. Fortnow, and C. Lund. Non-Deterministic Exponential Time Has Two-Prover Interactive Protocols. *Computational Complexity*, Vol. 1 (1), pages 3–40, 1991. Preliminary version in *31st FOCS*, 1990.

[22] L. Babai, L. Fortnow, N. Nisan, and A. Wigderson. BPP Has Subexponential Time Simulations Unless EXPTIME Has Publishable Proofs. *Complexity Theory*, Vol. 3, pages 307–318, 1993.

[23] L. Babai and S. Moran. Arthur-Merlin Games: A Randomized Proof System and a Hierarchy of Complexity Classes. *Journal of Computer and System Science*, Vol. 36, pages 254–276, 1988.

[24] E. Bach and J. Shallit. *Algorithmic Number Theory* (Volume I: *Efficient Algorithms*). MIT Press, 1996.

[25] B. Barak. Non-Black-Box Techniques in Crypptography. Ph.D. thesis, Weizmann Institute of Science, 2004.

[26] W. Baur and V. Strassen. The Complexity of Partial Derivatives. *Theor. Comput. Sci.* 22, pages 317–330, 1983.

[27] P. Beame and T. Pitassi. Propositional Proof Complexity: Past, Present, and Future. In *Bulletin of the European Association for Theoretical Computer Science*, Vol. 65 (June), pages 66–89, 1998.

[28] M. Bellare, O. Goldreich, and E. Petrank. Uniform Generation of NP-Witnesses Using an NP-Oracle. *Information and Computation*, Vol. 163, pages 510–526, 2000.

[29] M. Bellare, O. Goldreich, and M. Sudan. Free Bits, PCPs and Non-Approximability – Towards Tight Results. *SIAM Journal on Computing*, Vol. 27 (3), pages 804–915, 1998. Extended abstract in *36th FOCS*, 1995.

[30] S. Ben-David, B. Chor, O. Goldreich, and M. Luby. On the Theory of Average Case Complexity. *Journal of Computer and System Science*, Vol. 44 (2), pages 193–219, 1992.

[31] A. Ben-Dor and S. Halevi. In *2nd Israel Symp. on Theory of Computing and Systems*, IEEE Computer Society Press, pages 108-117, 1993.

[32] M. Ben-Or, O. Goldreich, S. Goldwasser, J. Håastad, J. Kilian, S. Micali, and P. Rogaway. Everything Provable Is Probable in Zero-Knowledge. In *Crypto88*, Springer-Verlag Lecture Notes in Computer Science (Vol. 403), pages 37–56, 1990.

[33] M. Ben-Or, S. Goldwasser, J. Kilian, and A. Wigderson. Multi-Prover Interactive Proofs: How to Remove Intractability. In *20th ACM Symposium on the Theory of Computing*, pages 113–131, 1988.

[34] M. Ben-Or, S. Goldwasser, and A. Wigderson. Completeness Theorems for Non-Cryptographic Fault-Tolerant Distributed Computation. In *20th ACM Symposium on the Theory of Computing*, pages 1–10, 1988.

[35] E. Ben-Sasson, O. Goldreich, P. Harsha, M. Sudan, and S. Vadhan. Robust PCPs of Proximity, Shorter PCPs, and Applications to Coding. *SIAM Journal on Computing*, Vol. 36 (4), pages 889–974, 2006. Extended abstract in *36th STOC*, 2004.

[36] E. Ben-Sasson and M. Sudan. Simple PCPs with Poly-log Rate and Query Complexity. In *37th ACM Symposium on the Theory of Computing*, pages 266–275, 2005.

[37] L. Berman and J. Hartmanis. On Isomorphisms and Density of NP and Other Complete Sets. *SIAM Journal on Computing*, Vol. 6 (2), 1977, pages 305–322.

[38] M. Blum. A Machine-Independent Theory of the Complexity of Recursive Functions. *Journal of the ACM*, Vol. 14 (2), pages 290–305, 1967.

[39] M. Blum and S. Kannan. Designing Programs That Check Their Work. In *21st ACM Symposium on the Theory of Computing*, pages 86–97, 1989.

[40] M. Blum, M. Luby, and R. Rubinfeld. Self-Testing/Correcting with Applications to Numerical Problems. *Journal of Computer and System Science*, Vol. 47 (3), pages 549–595, 1993.

[41] M. Blum and S. Micali. How to Generate Cryptographically Strong Sequences of Pseudo-Random Bits. *SIAM Journal on Computing*, Vol. 13, pages 850–864, 1984. Preliminary version in *23rd FOCS*, 1982.

[42] A. Bogdanov, K. Obata, and L. Trevisan. A Lower Bound for Testing 3-Colorability in Bounded-Degree Graphs. In *43rd IEEE Symposium on Foundations of Computer Science*, pages 93–102, 2002.

[43] A. Bogdanov and L. Trevisan. On Worst-Case to Average-Case Reductions for NP Problems. *SIAM Journal on Computing*, Vol. 36 (4), pages 1119–1159, 2006. Extended abstract in *44th FOCS*, 2003.

[44] A. Bogdanov and L. Trevisan. Average-Case Complexity. *Foundations and Trends in Theoretical Computer Science*, Vol. 2 (1), 2006.

[45] R. Boppana, J. Håstad, and S. Zachos. Does Co-NP Have Short Interactive Proofs? *Information Processing Letters*, Vol. 25 (May), pages 127–132, 1987.

[46] R. Boppana and M. Sipser. The Complexity of Finite Functions. In *Handbook of Theoretical Computer Science: Volume A – Algorithms and Complexity*, J. van Leeuwen (ed.), MIT Press/Elsevier, pages 757–804, 1990.

[47] A. Borodin. Computational Complexity and the Existence of Complexity Gaps. *Journal of the ACM*, Vol. 19 (1), pages 158–174, 1972.

[48] A. Borodin. On Relating Time and Space to Size and Depth. *SIAM Journal on Computing*, Vol. 6 (4), pages 733–744, 1977.

[49] G. Brassard, D. Chaum, and C. Crépeau. Minimum Disclosure Proofs of Knowledge. *Journal of Computer and System Science*, Vol. 37 (2), pages 156–189, 1988. Preliminary version by Brassard and Crépeau in *27th FOCS*, 1986.

[50] L. Carter and M. Wegman. Universal Hash Functions. *Journal of Computer and System Science*, Vol. 18, pages 143–154, 1979.

[51] G. J. Chaitin. On the Length of Programs for Computing Finite Binary Sequences. *Journal of the ACM*, Vol. 13, pages 547–570, 1966.

[52] A. K. Chandra, D. C. Kozen, and L. J. Stockmeyer. Alternation. *Journal of the ACM*, Vol. 28, pages 114–133, 1981.

[53] D. Chaum, C. Crépeau, and I. Damgård. Multi-party Unconditionally Secure Protocols. In *20th ACM Symposium on the Theory of Computing*, pages 11–19, 1988.

[54] B. Chor and O. Goldreich. On the Power of Two–Point Based Sampling. *Jour. of Complexity*, Vol. 5, pages 96–106, 1989. Preliminary version dates 1985.

[55] A. Church. An Unsolvable Problem of Elementary Number Theory. *Amer. J. of Math.*, Vol. 58, pages 345–363, 1936.

[56] N. Creignou, S. Khanna, and M. Sudan. *Complexity Classifications of Boolean Constraint Satisfaction Problems. SIAM Monographs on Discrete Mathematics and Applications*, 2001.

[57] A. Cobham. The Intristic Computational Difficulty of Functions. In *Proc. 1964 International Congress for Logic Methodology and Philosophy of Science*, pages 24–30, 1964.

[58] S. A. Cook. The Complexity of Theorem Proving Procedures. In *3rd ACM Symposium on the Theory of Computing*, pages 151–158, 1971.

[59] S. A. Cook. An Overview of Computational Complexity. Turing Award Lecture. *CACM*, Vol. 26 (6), pages 401–408, 1983.

[60] S. A. Cook. A Taxonomy of Problems with Fast Parallel Algorithms. *Information and Control*, Vol. 64, pages 2–22, 1985.

[61] S. A. Cook and R. A. Reckhow. The Relative Efficiency of Propositional Proof Systems. *J. of Symbolic Logic*, Vol. 44 (1), pages 36–50, 1979.

[62] D. Coppersmith and S. Winograd. Matrix Multiplication via Arithmetic Progressions. *Journal of Symbolic Computation*, Vol. 9, pages 251–280, 1990.

[63] T. M. Cover and G. A. Thomas. *Elements of Information Theory*. John Wiley & Sons, 1991.

[64] P. Crescenzi and V. Kann. A Compendium of NP Optimization problems. Available at `http://www.nada.kth.se/~viggo/wwwcompendium/`

[65] R. A. DeMillo and R. J. Lipton. A Probabilistic Remark on Algebraic Program Testing. *Information Processing Letters*, Vol. 7 (4), pages 193–195, 1978.

[66] W. Diffie and M. E. Hellman. New Directions in Cryptography. *IEEE Transactions on Information Theory*, IT-22 (Nov.), pages 644–654, 1976.

[67] I. Dinur. The PCP Theorem by Gap Amplification. In *38th ACM Symposium on the Theory of Computing*, pages 241–250, 2006.

[68] I. Dinur and O. Reingold. Assignment-Testers: Towards a Combinatorial Proof of the PCP-Theorem. *SIAM Journal on Computing*, Vol. 36 (4), pages 975–1024, 2006. Extended abstract in *45th FOCS*, 2004.

[69] I. Dinur and S. Safra. The Importance of Being Biased. In *34th ACM Symposium on the Theory of Computing*, pages 33–42, 2002.

[70] J. Edmonds. Paths, Trees, and Flowers. *Canad. J. Math.*, Vol. 17, pages 449–467, 1965.

[71] S. Even. *Graph Algorithms*. Computer Science Press, 1979.

[72] S. Even, A. L. Selman, and Y. Yacobi. The Complexity of Promise Problems with Applications to Public-Key Cryptography. *Information and Control*, Vol. 61, pages 159–173, 1984.

[73] U. Feige, S. Goldwasser, L. Lovász, and S. Safra. On the Complexity of Approximating the Maximum Size of a Clique. Unpublished manuscript, 1990.

[74] U. Feige, S. Goldwasser, L. Lovász, S. Safra, and M. Szegedy. Approximating Clique is Almost NP-Complete. *Journal of the ACM*, Vol. 43, pages 268–292, 1996. Preliminary version in *32nd FOCS*, 1991.

[75] U. Feige, D. Lapidot, and A. Shamir. Multiple Non-Interactive Zero-Knowledge Proofs Under General Assumptions. *SIAM Journal on Computing*, Vol. 29 (1), pages 1–28, 1999. Preliminary version in *31st FOCS*, 1990.

[76] U. Feige and A. Shamir. Witness Indistinguishability and Witness Hiding Protocols. In *22nd ACM Symposium on the Theory of Computing*, pages 416–426, 1990.

[77] E. Fischer. The Art of Uninformed Decisions: A Primer to Property Testing. *Bulletin of the European Association for Theoretical Computer Science*, Vol. 75, pages 97–126, 2001.

[78] G. D. Forney. *Concatenated Codes*. MIT Press, 1966.

[79] L. Fortnow, R. Lipton, D. van Melkebeek, and A. Viglas. Time-Space Lower Bounds for Satisfiability. *Journal of the ACM*, Vol. 52 (6), pages 835–865, 2005.

[80] L. Fortnow, J. Rompel, and M. Sipser. On the Power of Multi-Prover Interactive Protocols. In *3rd IEEE Symp. on Structure in Complexity Theory*, pages 156–161, 1988. See errata in *5th IEEE Symp. on Structure in Complexity Theory*, pages 318–319, 1990.

[81] S. Fortune. A Note on Sparse Complete Sets. *SIAM Journal on Computing*, Vol. 8, pages 431–433, 1979.

[82] M. Fürer, O. Goldreich, Y. Mansour, M. Sipser, and S. Zachos. On Completeness and Soundness in Interactive Proof Systems. *Advances in Computing Research: A Research Annual*, Vol. 5 (Randomness and Computation, S. Micali, ed.), pages 429–442, 1989.

[83] M. L. Furst, J. B. Saxe, and M. Sipser. Parity, Circuits, and the Polynomial-Time Hierarchy. *Mathematical Systems Theory*, Vol. 17 (1), pages 13–27, 1984. Preliminary version in *22nd FOCS*, 1981.

[84] O. Gabber and Z. Galil. Explicit Constructions of Linear Size Superconcentrators. *Journal of Computer and System Science*, Vol. 22, pages 407–420, 1981.

[85] M. R. Garey and D. S. Johnson. *Computers and Intractability: A Guide to the Theory of NP-Completeness*. W. H. Freeman, 1979.

[86] J. von zur Gathen. Algebraic Complexity Theory. *Ann. Rev. Comput. Sci.*, Vol. 3, pages 317–347, 1988.

[87] O. Goldreich. *Foundation of Cryptography – Class Notes*. Computer Science Dept., Technion, Israel, Spring 1989. Superseded by [91, 92].

[88] O. Goldreich. A Note on Computational Indistinguishability. *Information Processing Letters*, Vol. 34 (May), pages 277–281, 1990.

[89] O. Goldreich. Notes on Levin's Theory of Average-Case Complexity. *ECCC*, TR97-058, 1997.

[90] O. Goldreich. *Modern Cryptography, Probabilistic Proofs and Pseudorandomness*. Algorithms and Combinatorics Series (Vol. 17), Springer, 1999.

[91] O. Goldreich. *Foundation of Cryptography: Basic Tools*. Cambridge University Press, 2001.

[92] O. Goldreich. *Foundation of Cryptography: Basic Applications*. Cambridge University Press, 2004.

[93] O. Goldreich. Short Locally Testable Codes and Proofs (Survey). *ECCC*, TR05-014, 2005.

[94] O. Goldreich. On Promise Problems (a survey in memory of Shimon Even [1935-2004]). *ECCC*, TR05-018, 2005.

[95] O. Goldreich, S. Goldwasser, and S. Micali. How to Construct Random Functions. *Journal of the ACM*, Vol. 33 (4), pages 792–807, 1986.

[96] O. Goldreich, S. Goldwasser, and A. Nussboim. On the Implementation of Huge Random Objects. In *44th IEEE Symposium on Foundations of Computer Science*, pages 68–79, 2003.

[97] O. Goldreich, S. Goldwasser, and D. Ron. Property Testing and Its Connection to Learning and Approximation. *Journal of the ACM*, pages 653–750, July 1998. Extended abstract in *37th FOCS*, 1996.

[98] O. Goldreich and H. Krawczyk. On the Composition of Zero-Knowledge Proof Systems. *SIAM Journal on Computing*, Vol. 25 (1), pages 169–192, 1996. Preliminary version in *17th ICALP*, 1990.

[99] O. Goldreich and L.A. Levin. Hard-Core Predicates for Any One-Way Function. In *21st ACM Symposium on the Theory of Computing*, pages 25–32, 1989.

[100] O. Goldreich, S. Micali, and A. Wigderson. Proofs That Yield Nothing but Their Validity or All Languages in NP Have Zero-Knowledge Proof Systems. *Journal of the ACM*, Vol. 38 (3), pages 691–729, 1991. Preliminary version in *27th FOCS*, 1986.

[101] O. Goldreich, S. Micali, and A. Wigderson. How to Play Any Mental Game – A Completeness Theorem for Protocols with Honest Majority. In *19th ACM Symposium on the Theory of Computing*, pages 218–229, 1987.

[102] O. Goldreich, N. Nisan, and A. Wigderson. On Yao's XOR-Lemma. *ECCC*, TR95-050, 1995.

[103] O. Goldreich and D. Ron. Property Testing in Bounded Degree Graphs. *Algorithmica*, pages 302–343, 2002. Extended abstract in *29th STOC*, 1997.

[104] O. Goldreich and D. Ron. A Sublinear Bipartite Tester for Bounded Degree Graphs. *Combinatorica*, Vol. 19 (3), pages 335–373, 1999. Extended abstract in *30th STOC*, 1998.

[105] O. Goldreich, R. Rubinfeld, and M. Sudan. Learning Polynomials with Queries: The Highly Noisy Case. *SIAM J. Discrete Math.*, Vol. 13 (4), pages 535–570, 2000.

[106] O. Goldreich, S. Vadhan, and A. Wigderson. On Interactive Proofs with a Laconic Provers. *Computational Complexity*, Vol. 11, pages 1–53, 2002.

[107] O. Goldreich and A. Wigderson. Computational Complexity. In *The Princeton Companion to Mathematics*, forthcoming.

[108] S. Goldwasser and S. Micali. Probabilistic Encryption. *Journal of Computer and System Science*, Vol. 28 (2), pages 270–299, 1984. Preliminary version in *14th STOC*, 1982.

[109] S. Goldwasser, S. Micali, and C. Rackoff. The Knowledge Complexity of Interactive Proof Systems. *SIAM Journal on Computing*, Vol. 18, pages 186–208, 1989. Preliminary version in *17th STOC*, 1985. Earlier versions date to 1982.

[110] S. Goldwasser, S. Micali, and R. L. Rivest. A Digital Signature Scheme Secure Against Adaptive Chosen-Message Attacks. *SIAM Journal on Computing*, Vol. 17, pages 281–308, 1988.

[111] S. Goldwasser and M. Sipser. Private Coins Versus Public Coins in Interactive Proof Systems. *Advances in Computing Research: A Research Annual*, Vol. 5 (Randomness and Computation, S. Micali, ed.), pages 73–90, 1989. Extended abstract in *18th STOC*, 1986.

[112] S. W. Golomb. *Shift Register Sequences*. Holden-Day, 1967. (Aegean Park Press, revised edition, 1982.)

[113] V. Guruswami, C. Umans, and S. Vadhan. Unbalanced Expanders and Randomness Extractors from Parvaresh-Vardy Codes. In *22nd IEEE Conference on Computational Complexity*, pages 96–108, 2007.

[114] J. Hartmanis and R. E. Stearns. On the Computational Complexity of Algorithms. *Transactions of the AMS*, Vol. 117, pages 285–306, 1965.

[115] J. Håastad. Almost Optimal Lower Bounds for Small Depth Circuits. *Advances in Computing Research: A Research Annual*, Vol. 5 (Randomness and Computation, S. Micali, ed.), pages 143–170, 1989. Extended abstract in *18th STOC*, 1986.

[116] J. Håastad. Clique Is Hard to Approximate Within $n^{1-\epsilon}$. *Acta Mathematica*, Vol. 182, pages 105–142, 1999. Preliminary versions in *28th STOC* (1996) and *37th FOCS* (1996).

[117] J. Håastad. Getting Optimal In-Approximability Results. *Journal of the ACM*, Vol. 48, pages 798–859, 2001. Extended abstract in *29th STOC*, 1997.

[118] J. Håastad, R. Impagliazzo, L. A. Levin, and M. Luby. A Pseudorandom Generator from Any One-way Function. *SIAM Journal on Computing*, Vol. 28 (4), pages 1364–1396, 1999. Preliminary versions by Impagliazzo et al. in *21st STOC* (1989) and Håastad in *22nd STOC* (1990).

[119] J. Håastad and S. Khot. Query Efficient PCPs with Pefect Completeness. In *42nd IEEE Symposium on Foundations of Computer Science*, pages 610–619, 2001.

[120] A. Healy. Randomness-Efficient Sampling Within NC1. *Computational Complexity*, in press. Preliminary version in *10th RANDOM*, 2006.

[121] A. Healy, S. Vadhan, and E. Viola. Using Nondeterminism to Amplify Hardness. *SIAM Journal on Computing*, Vol. 35 (4), pages 903–931, 2006.

[122] D. Hochbaum (ed.). *Approximation Algorithms for NP-Hard Problems*. PWS Publishing, 1996.

[123] J. E. Hopcroft and J. D. Ullman. *Introduction to Automata Theory, Languages and Computation*. Addison-Wesley, 1979.

[124] S. Hoory, N. Linial, and A. Wigderson. *Expander Graphs and Their Applications. Bull. AMS*, Vol. 43 (4), pages 439–561, 2006.

[125] N. Immerman. Nondeterministic Space Is Closed Under Complementation. *SIAM Journal on Computing*, Vol. 17, pages 760–778, 1988.

[126] R. Impagliazzo. Hard-Core Distributions for Somewhat Hard Problems. In *36th IEEE Symposium on Foundations of Computer Science*, pages 538–545, 1995.

[127] R. Impagliazzo and L. A. Levin. No Better Ways to Generate Hard NP Instances Than Picking Uniformly at Random. In *31st IEEE Symposium on Foundations of Computer Science*, pages 812–821, 1990.

[128] R. Impagliazzo and A. Wigderson. P = BPP If E Requires Exponential Circuits: Derandomizing the XOR Lemma. In *29th ACM Symposium on the Theory of Computing*, pages 220–229, 1997.

[129] R. Impagliazzo and A. Wigderson. Randomness vs Time: Derandomization under a Uniform Assumption. *Journal of Computer and System Science*, Vol. 63 (4), pages 672-688, 2001.

[130] R. Impagliazzo and M. Yung. Direct Zero-Knowledge Computations. In *Crypto87*, Springer-Verlag Lecture Notes in Computer Science (Vol. 293), pages 40–51, 1987.

[131] M. Jerrum, A. Sinclair, and E. Vigoda. A Polynomial-Time Approximation Algorithm for the Permanent of a Matrix with Non-Negative Entries. *Journal of the ACM*, Vol. 51 (4), pages 671–697, 2004.

[132] M. Jerrum, L. Valiant, and V. V. Vazirani. Random Generation of Combinatorial Structures from a Uniform Distribution. *Theoretical Computer Science*, Vol. 43, pages 169–188, 1986.

[133] B. Juba and M. Sudan. Towards Universal Semantic Communication. *ECCC*, TR07-084, 2007.

[134] V. Kabanets and R. Impagliazzo. Derandomizing Polynomial Identity Tests Means Proving Circuit Lower Bounds. *Computational Complexity*, Vol. 13, pages 1-46, 2004. Preliminary version in *35th STOC*, 2003.

[135] N. Kahale. Eigenvalues and Expansion of Regular Graphs. *Journal of the ACM*, Vol. 42 (5), pages 1091–1106, 1995.

[136] R. Kannan, H. Venkateswaran, V. Vinay, and A. C. Yao. A Circuit-Based Proof of Toda's Theorem. *Information and Computation*, Vol. 104 (2), pages 271–276, 1993.

[137] M. Karchmer and A. Wigderson. Monotone Circuits for Connectivity Require Super-logarithmic Depth. *SIAM J. Discrete Math.*, Vol. 3 (2), pages 255–265, 1990. Preliminary version in *20th STOC*, 1988.

[138] R. M. Karp. Reducibility Among Combinatorial Problems. In *Complexity of Computer Computations*, R. E. Miller and J. W. Thatcher (eds.), Plenum Press, pages 85–103, 1972.

[139] R. M. Karp and R. J. Lipton. Some Connections Between Nonuniform and Uniform Complexity Classes. In *12th ACM Symposium on the Theory of Computing*, pages 302–309, 1980.

[140] R. M. Karp and M. Luby. Monte-Carlo Algorithms for Enumeration and Reliability Problems. In *24th IEEE Symposium on Foundations of Computer Science*, pages 56-64, 1983.

[141] R. M. Karp and V. Ramachandran. Parallel Algorithms for Shared-Memory Machines. In *Handbook of Theoretical Computer Science, Volume A: Algorithms and Complexity*, J. van Leeuwen (ed.), MIT Press/Elsevier, pages 869–942, 1990.

[142] M. J. Kearns and U. V. Vazirani. *An Introduction to Computational Learning Theory*. MIT Press, 1994.

[143] S. Khot and O. Regev. Vertex Cover Might Be Hard to Approximate to Within $2 - \varepsilon$. In *18th IEEE Conference on Computational Complexity*, pages 379–386, 2003.

[144] V. M. Khrapchenko. A Method of Determining Lower Bounds for the Complexity of Pi-Schemes. In *Matematicheskie Zametki*, Vol. 10 (1), pages 83–92, 1971 (in Russian). English translation in *Mathematical Notes of the Academy of Sciences of the USSR*, Vol. 10 (1), pages 474–479, 1971.

[145] J. Kilian. A Note on Efficient Zero-Knowledge Proofs and Arguments. In *24th ACM Symposium on the Theory of Computing*, pages 723–732, 1992.

[146] D. E. Knuth. *The Art of Computer Programming*, Vol. 2 (*Seminumerical Algorithms*). Addison-Wesley, 1969 (first edition) and 1981 (second edition).

[147] A. Kolmogorov. Three Approaches to the Concept of "The Amount of Information." *Probl. of Inform. Transm.*, Vol. 1 (1), 1965.

[148] E. Kushilevitz and N. Nisan. *Communication Complexity*. Cambridge University Press, 1996.

[149] R. E. Ladner. On the Structure of Polynomial Time Reducibility. *Journal of the ACM*, Vol. 22, 1975, pages 155–171.

[150] C. Lautemann. BPP and the Polynomial Hierarchy. *Information Processing Letters*, Vol. 17, pages 215–217, 1983.

[151] F.T. Leighton. *Introduction to Parallel Algorithms and Architectures: Arrays, Trees, Hypercubes*. Morgan Kaufmann Publishers, San Mateo, CA, 1992.

[152] L. A. Levin. Universal Search Problems. *Problemy Peredaci Informacii 9*, pages 115–116, 1973 (in Russian). English translation in *Problems of Information Transmission 9*, pages 265–266. A better English translation appears in [221].

[153] L. A. Levin. Randomness Conservation Inequalities: Information and Independence in Mathematical Theories. *Information and Control*, Vol. 61, pages 15–37, 1984.

[154] L. A. Levin. Average Case Complete Problems. *SIAM Journal on Computing*, Vol. 15, pages 285–286, 1986.

[155] L. A. Levin. Fundamentals of Computing. *SIGACT News*, Education Forum, special 100th issue, Vol. 27 (3), pages 89–110, 1996.

[156] M. Li and P. Vitanyi. *An Introduction to Kolmogorov Complexity and Its Applications*. Springer Verlag, August 1993.

[157] R. J. Lipton. New Directions in Testing. *Distributed Computing and Cryptography*, J. Feigenbaum and M. Merritt (eds.), DIMACS Series in Discrete Mathematics and Theoretical Computer Science, American Mathematics Society, Vol. 2, pages 191–202, 1991.

[158] N. Livne. All Natural NPC Problems Have Average-Case Complete Versions. *ECCC*, TR06-122, 2006.

[159] C.-J. Lu, O. Reingold, S. Vadhan, and A. Wigderson. Extractors: Optimal up to Constant Factors. In *35th ACM Symposium on the Theory of Computing*, pages 602–611, 2003.

[160] A. Lubotzky, R. Phillips, and P. Sarnak. Ramanujan Graphs. *Combinatorica*, Vol. 8, pages 261–277, 1988.

[161] M. Luby and A. Wigderson. Pairwise Independence and Derandomization. *Foundations and Trends in Theoretical Computer Science*, Vol. (4), 2005. Preliminary version: TR-95-035, ICSI, Berkeley, 1995.

[162] C. Lund, L. Fortnow, H. Karloff, and N. Nisan. Algebraic Methods for Interactive Proof Systems. *Journal of the ACM*, Vol. 39 (4), pages 859–868, 1992. Preliminary version in *31st FOCS*, 1990.

[163] F. MacWilliams and N. Sloane. *The Theory of Error-Correcting Codes*. North-Holland, 1981.

[164] G. A. Margulis. Explicit Construction of Concentrators. *Prob. Per. Infor.*, Vol. 9 (4), pages 71–80, 1973 (in Russian). English translation in *Problems of Infor. Trans.*, pages 325–332, 1975.

[165] S. Micali. Computationally Sound Proofs. *SIAM Journal on Computing*, Vol. 30 (4), pages 1253–1298, 2000. Preliminary version in *35th FOCS*, 1994.

[166] G. L. Miller. Riemann's Hypothesis and Tests for Primality. *Journal of Computer and System Science*, Vol. 13, pages 300–317, 1976.

[167] P. B. Miltersen and N. V. Vinodchandran. Derandomizing Arthur-Merlin Games Using Hitting Sets. *Computational Complexity*, Vol. 14 (3), pages 256–279, 2005. Preliminary version in *40th FOCS*, 1999.

[168] R. Motwani and P. Raghavan. *Randomized Algorithms*. Cambridge University Press, 1995.

[169] M. Naor. Bit Commitment Using Pseudorandom Generators. *Journal of Cryptology*, Vol. 4, pages 151–158, 1991.

[170] J. Naor and M. Naor. Small-Bias Probability Spaces: Efficient Constructions and Applications. *SIAM Journal on Computing*, Vol. 22, pages 838–856, 1993. Preliminary version in *22nd STOC*, 1990.

[171] M. Naor and M. Yung. Universal One-Way Hash Functions and Their Cryptographic Application. In *21st ACM Symposium on the Theory of Computing*, pages 33–43, 1989.

[172] M. Nguyen, S. J. Ong, and S. Vadhan. Statistical Zero-Knowledge Arguments for NP from Any One-Way Function. In *47th IEEE Symposium on Foundations of Computer Science*, pages 3-14, 2006.

[173] N. Nisan. Pseudorandom Bits for Constant Depth Circuits. *Combinatorica*, Vol. 11 (1), pages 63–70, 1991.

[174] N. Nisan. Pseudorandom Generators for Space Bounded Computation. *Combinatorica*, Vol. 12 (4), pages 449–461, 1992. Preliminary version in *22nd STOC*, 1990.

[175] N. Nisan. $\mathcal{RL} \subseteq \mathcal{SC}$. *Computational Complexity*, Vol. 4, pages 1-11, 1994. Preliminary version in *24th STOC*, 1992.

[176] N. Nisan and A. Wigderson. Hardness vs Randomness. *Journal of Computer and System Science*, Vol. 49 (2), pages 149–167, 1994. Preliminary version in *29th FOCS*, 1988.

[177] N. Nisan and D. Zuckerman. Randomness Is Linear in Space. *Journal of Computer and System Science*, Vol. 52 (1), pages 43–52, 1996. Preliminary version in *25th STOC*, 1993.

[178] C. H. Papadimitriou. *Computational Complexity*. Addison Wesley, 1994.

[179] C. H. Papadimitriou and M. Yannakakis. Optimization, Approximation, and Complexity Classes. In *20th ACM Symposium on the Theory of Computing*, pages 229–234, 1988.

[180] N. Pippenger and M. J. Fischer. Relations Among Complexity Measures. *Journal of the ACM*, Vol. 26 (2), pages 361–381, 1979.

[181] E. Post. A Variant of a Recursively Unsolvable Problem. *Bull. AMS*, Vol. 52, pages 264–268, 1946.

[182] M. O. Rabin. Digitalized Signatures. In *Foundations of Secure Computation* (R. A. DeMillo et al. eds.), Academic Press, 1977.

[183] M. O. Rabin. Digitalized Signatures and Public Key Functions as Intractable as Factoring. MIT/LCS/TR-212, 1979.

[184] M. O. Rabin. Probabilistic Algorithm for Testing Primality. *Journal of Number Theory*, Vol. 12, pages 128–138, 1980.

[185] R. Raz. A Parallel Repetition Theorem. *SIAM Journal on Computing*, Vol. 27 (3), pages 763–803, 1998. Extended abstract in *27th STOC*, 1995.

[186] R. Raz and A. Wigderson. Monotone Circuits for Matching Require Linear Depth. *Journal of the ACM*, Vol. 39 (3), pages 736–744, 1992. Preliminary version in *22nd STOC*, 1990.

[187] A. Razborov. Lower Bounds for the Monotone Complexity of some Boolean Functions. In *Doklady Akademii Nauk SSSR*, Vol. 281 (4), pages 798–801, 1985 (in Russian). English translation in *Soviet Math. Doklady*, Vol. 31, pages 354–357, 1985.

[188] A. Razborov. Lower Bounds on the Size of Bounded-Depth Networks over a Complete Basis with Logical Addition. In *Matematicheskie Zametki*, Vol. 41 (4), pages 598–607, 1987 (in Russian). English translation in *Mathematical Notes of the Academy of Sci. of the USSR*, Vol. 41 (4), pages 333–338, 1987.

[189] A. R. Razborov and S. Rudich. Natural Proofs. *Journal of Computer and System Science*, Vol. 55 (1), pages 24–35, 1997. Preliminary version in *26th STOC*, 1994.

[190] O. Reingold. Undirected ST-Connectivity in Log-Space. In *37th ACM Symposium on the Theory of Computing*, pages 376–385, 2005.

[191] O. Reingold, S. Vadhan, and A. Wigderson. Entropy Waves, the Zig-Zag Graph Product, and New Constant-Degree Expanders and Extractors. *Annals of Mathematics*, Vol. 155 (1), pages 157–187, 2001. Preliminary version in *41st FOCS*, pages 3–13, 2000.

[192] H. G. Rice. Classes of Recursively Enumerable Sets and Their Decision Problems. *Trans. AMS*, Vol. 89, pages 25–59, 1953.

[193] R. L. Rivest, A. Shamir, and L. M. Adleman. A Method for Obtaining Digital Signatures and Public Key Cryptosystems. *CACM*, Vol. 21 (Feb.), pages 120–126, 1978.

[194] D. Ron. Property Testing. In *Handbook on Randomization*, Volume 2, S. Rajasekaran, P. M. Pardalos, J. H. Reif, and J. D. P. Rolim (eds.), pages 597–649, 2001.

[195] R. Rubinfeld and M. Sudan. Robust Characterization of Polynomials with Applications to Program Testing. *SIAM Journal on Computing*, Vol. 25 (2), pages 252–271, 1996.

[196] M. Saks and S. Zhou. $\text{BP}_H\text{SPACE}(S) \subseteq \text{DSPACE}(S^{3/2})$. *Journal of Computer and System Science*, Vol. 58 (2), pages 376–403, 1999. Preliminary version in *36th FOCS*, 1995.

[197] W. J. Savitch. Relationships Between Nondeterministic and Deterministic Tape Complexities. *Journal of Computer and System Science*, Vol. 4 (2), pages 177–192, 1970.

[198] A. Selman. On the Structure of NP. *Notices Amer. Math. Soc.*, Vol. 21 (6), page 310, 1974.

[199] J. T. Schwartz. Fast Probabilistic Algorithms for Verification of Polynomial Identities. *Journal of the ACM*, Vol. 27 (4), pages 701–717, October 1980.

[200] R. Shaltiel. Recent Developments in Explicit Constructions of Extractors. In *Current Trends in Theoretical Computer Science: The Challenge of the New Century*, Vol. 1: *Algorithms and Complexity*, G. Paun, G. Rozenberg, and A. Salomaa (eds.), World Scientific, 2004. Preliminary version in *Bulletin of the EATCS 77*, pages 67–95, 2002.

[201] R. Shaltiel and C. Umans. Simple Extractors for All Min-Entropies and a New Pseudo-Random Generator. In *42nd IEEE Symposium on Foundations of Computer Science*, pages 648–657, 2001.

[202] A. Shamir. IP = PSPACE. *Journal of the ACM*, Vol. 39 (4), pages 869–877, 1992. Preliminary version in *31st FOCS*, 1990.

[203] C. E. Shannon. A Symbolic Analysis of Relay and Switching Circuits. *Trans. American Institute of Electrical Engineers*, Vol. 57, pages 713–723, 1938.

[204] C. E. Shannon. A Mathematical Theory of Communication. *Bell Sys. Tech. Jour.*, Vol. 27, pages 623–656, 1948.

[205] C. E. Shannon. Communication Theory of Secrecy Systems. *Bell Sys. Tech. Jour.*, Vol. 28, pages 656–715, 1949.

[206] A. Shpilka. Lower Bounds for Matrix Product. *SIAM Journal on Computing*, pages 1185-1200, 2003.

[207] M. Sipser. A Complexity Theoretic Approach to Randomness. In *15th ACM Symposium on the Theory of Computing*, pages 330–335, 1983.

[208] M. Sipser. *Introduction to the Theory of Computation*. PWS Publishing, 1997.

[209] R. Smolensky. Algebraic Methods in the Theory of Lower Bounds for Boolean Circuit Complexity. In *19th ACM Symposium on the Theory of Computing*, pages 77–82, 1987.

[210] R. J. Solomonoff. A Formal Theory of Inductive Inference. *Information and Control*, Vol. 7 (1), pages 1–22, 1964.

[211] R. Solovay and V. Strassen. A Fast Monte-Carlo Test for Primality. *SIAM Journal on Computing*, Vol. 6, pages 84–85, 1977. Addendum in *SIAM Journal on Computing*, Vol. 7, page 118, 1978.

[212] D. A. Spielman. *Advanced Complexity Theory*, Lectures 10 and 11. Notes (by D. Lewin and S. Vadhan), March 1997. Available from http://www.cs.yale.edu/homes/spielman/AdvComplexity/1998/ as lect10.ps and lect11.ps.

[213] L. J. Stockmeyer. The Polynomial-Time Hierarchy. *Theoretical Computer Science*, Vol. 3, pages 1–22, 1977.

[214] L. Stockmeyer. The Complexity of Approximate Counting. In *15th ACM Symposium on the Theory of Computing*, pages 118–126, 1983.

[215] V. Strassen. Algebraic Complexity Theory. In *Handbook of Theoretical Computer Science: Volume A: Algorithms and Complexity*, J. van Leeuwen (ed.), MIT Press/Elsevier, pages 633–672, 1990.

[216] M. Sudan. Decoding of Reed Solomon Codes Beyond the Error-Correction Bound. *Journal of Complexity*, Vol. 13 (1), pages 180–193, 1997.

[217] M. Sudan. Algorithmic Introduction to Coding Theory. Lecture notes, available from http://theory.csail.mit.edu/~madhu/FT01/, 2001.

[218] M. Sudan, L. Trevisan, and S. Vadhan. Pseudorandom Generators Without the XOR Lemma. *Journal of Computer and System Science*, Vol. 62 (2), pages 236–266, 2001.

[219] R. Szelepcsenyi. A Method of Forced Enumeration for Nondeterministic Automata. *Acta Informatica*, Vol. 26, pages 279–284, 1988.

[220] S. Toda. PP Is as Hard as the Polynomial-Time Hierarchy. *SIAM Journal on Computing*, Vol. 20 (5), pages 865–877, 1991.

[221] B. A. Trakhtenbrot. A Survey of Russian Approaches to *Perebor* (Brute Force Search) Algorithms. *Annals of the History of Computing*, Vol. 6 (4), pages 384–398, 1984.

[222] L. Trevisan. Extractors and Pseudorandom Generators. *Journal of the ACM*, Vol. 48 (4), pages 860–879, 2001. Preliminary version in *31st STOC*, 1999.

[223] L. Trevisan. On Uniform Amplification of Hardness in NP. In *37th ACM Symposium on the Theory of Computing*, pages 31–38, 2005.

[224] V. Trifonov. An $O(\log n \log \log n)$ Space Algorithm for Undirected st-Connectivity. In *37th ACM Symposium on the Theory of Computing*, pages 623–633, 2005.

[225] A. M. Turing. On Computable Numbers, with an Application to the Entscheidungsproblem. *Proc. Londom Mathematical Soceity*, Ser. 2, Vol. 42, pages 230–265, 1936. A Correction, *ibid.*, Vol. 43, pages 544–546.

[226] C. Umans. Pseudo-Random Generators for All Hardness. *Journal of Computer and System Science*, Vol. 67 (2), pages 419–440, 2003.

[227] S. Vadhan. A Study of Statistical Zero-Knowledge Proofs. Ph.D. thesis, MIT, 1999. Available from http://www.eecs.harvard.edu/~salil/papers/phdthesis-abs.html.

[228] S. Vadhan. An Unconditional Study of Computational Zero Knowledge. *SIAM Journal on Computing*, Vol. 36 (4), pages 1160–1214, 2006. Extended abstract in *45th FOCS*, 2004.

[229] S. Vadhan. *Lecture Notes for CS 225: Pseudorandomness*, Spring 2007. Available from http://www.eecs.harvard.edu/~salil.

[230] L. G. Valiant. The Complexity of Computing the Permanent. *Theoretical Computer Science*, Vol. 8, pages 189–201, 1979.

[231] L. G. Valiant. Completeness Classes in Algebra. In *11th ACM Symposium on the Theory of Computing*, pages 249–261, 1979.

[232] L. G. Valiant. A Theory of the Learnable. *CACM*, Vol. 27 (11), pages 1134–1142, 1984.

[233] L. G. Valiant and V. V. Vazirani. NP Is as Easy as Detecting Unique Solutions. *Theoretical Computer Science*, Vol. 47 (1), pages 85–93, 1986.

[234] J. von Neumann. First Draft of a Report on the EDVAC, 1945. Contract No. W-670-ORD-492, Moore School of Electrical Engineering, Univ. of Pennsylvania. Reprinted (in part) in *Origins of Digital Computers: Selected Papers*, Springer-Verlag, pages 383–392, 1982.

[235] J. von Neumann, Zur Theorie der Gesellschaftsspiele. *Mathematische Annalen*, 100, pages 295–320, 1928.

[236] I. Wegener. *The Complexity of Boolean Functions*. Wiley-Teubner, 1987.

[237] I. Wegener. *Branching Programs and Binary Decision Diagrams – Theory and Applications*. SIAM Monographs on Discrete Mathematics and Applications, 2000.

[238] A. Wigderson. The Amazing Power of Pairwise Independence. In *26th ACM Symposium on the Theory of Computing*, pages 645–647, 1994.

[239] A. C. Yao. Theory and Application of Trapdoor Functions. In *23rd IEEE Symposium on Foundations of Computer Science*, pages 80–91, 1982.

[240] A. C. Yao. Separating the Polynomial-Time Hierarchy by Oracles. In *26th IEEE Symposium on Foundations of Computer Science*, pages 1-10, 1985.

[241] A. C. Yao. How to Generate and Exchange Secrets. In *27th IEEE Symposium on Foundations of Computer Science*, pages 162–167, 1986.

[242] S. Yekhanin. Towards 3-Query Locally Decodable Codes of Subexponential Length. In *39th ACM Symposium on the Theory of Computing*, pages 266–274, 2007.

[243] R. E. Zippel. Probabilistic Algorithms for Sparse Polynomials. In the *Proceedings of EUROSAM '79: International Symposium on Symbolic and Algebraic Manipulation*, E. Ng (ed.). Lecture Notes in Computer Science (Vol. 72), pages 216–226, Springer, 1979.

[244] D. Zuckerman. Linear-Degree Extractors and the Inapproximability of Max-Clique and Chromatic Number. In *38th ACM Symposium on the Theory of Computing*, pages 681–690, 2006.

Index

Subject Index